WORLD PRESS
ENCYCLOPEDIA

WORLD PRESS
ENCYCLOPEDIA

Edited by
GEORGE THOMAS KURIAN

Indexed by
**Marjorie B. Bank
and James Johnson**

FACTS ON FILE, Inc.
460 Park Avenue South
New York, N.Y. 10016

WORLD PRESS ENCYCLOPEDIA

George Thomas Kurian

Published by Facts On File, Inc.
460 Park Ave. South, New York, N.Y. 10016

Library of Congress Cataloging in Publication Data

Kurian, George Thomas
  World press encyclopedia.

  Bibliography: p.
  Includes index.
  1. Liberty of the press. 2. Government and the press.
I. Title.
PN4735.K87   070   80-25120
ISBN 0-87196-392-2 Volume I   AACR1
ISBN 0-87196-497-X Volume II
ISBN 0-87196-621-2 2 Volume set

Printed in the United States of America
9 8 7 6 5 4 3 2 1

WORLD PRESS ENCYCLOPEDIA

ENCYCLOPEDIA

Volume II

THE NETHERLANDS

by Jan Wieten

BASIC DATA

Population: 14 million (1979)
Area: 41,000 sq. km. (15,826 sq. mi.)
GNP: 299 billion guilders (US $149.5 billion) (1979)
Literacy Rate: 99%
Language(s): Dutch, Frisian
Number of Dailies: 84
  Aggregate Circulation: 4,648,579
  Circulation per 1,000: 332
Number of Nondailies: 654 (including 526 "free sheets")
  Aggregate Circulation: 15,463,582 (including 14,753,182 for "free sheets")
  Circulation per 1,000: 1,112 (including 1,061 for "free sheets")

Number of Periodicals: 384
Number of Radio Stations: 10
Number of Television Stations: 2
Number of Radio Receivers: 4.360 million
  Radio Receivers per 1,000: 305
Number of Television Sets: 4.180 million
  Television Sets per 1,000: 290
Total Annual Newsprint Consumption: 350,200 metric tons
  Per Capita Newsprint Consumption: 32.9 kg. (72.4 lbs.)
Total Newspaper Ad Receipts: 1.14 billion guilders (US $570.5 million) (1979)
  As % of All Ad Expenditures: 27 (1979)

Background & General Characteristics

Although Holland is not the birthplace of the newspaper, in the early 17th century Amsterdam, its capital, became the world's first real newspaper center, with the publication of two periodicals that reported "tidings" from elsewhere in Europe.

Gradually these and other newspapers came under the control of local authorities in Amsterdam—and the other cities of the young republic—by way of a licensing system for newspaper publishers. By 1702 it was theoretically not possible to publish a new paper without permission of the local government, but in fact the liberalism of the merchants who ruled the cities, the absence of a strong central government and the competition between the main cities nourished a healthy climate for publishers. Thus the Netherlands can rightfully claim to be one of the first countries with a free and independent press.

This was due probably less to the Dutch-language newspapers of this period than to various influential journals published in Hol-

land by refugees from other parts of Europe, especially Huguenots from France, who had fled to the Netherlands' relative calm and tolerance. The Dutch authorities, though sensitive to criticism of their domestic administrative policies in the Netherlands' cities—or in the country as a whole—were less interested in the activities of newspapers mainly concerned with the affairs of other nations. Indirectly, then, they built the foundations of an independent Dutch press.

By 1798, however, things had changed. A new constitution literally—and hypocritically—sanctified press freedom while simultaneously proclaiming that any criticism of the government was "an offense against freedom of the press." Half a century had to go by before the country got back on track with the liberal constitution of 1848, which abolished censorship entirely, allowing publishers and editors free rein in airing their views.

But even under government control, the Dutch press had been taking form. The first daily newspaper appeared in 1830, with others soon surfacing in its wake. And after the 1848 constitution there was a virtual publishing boom. Between 1850 and 1866 the total number of daily and nondaily papers rose from 92 to 159, with a corresponding circulation jump—from 23,850 to 89,189. For a while readership was held back by a heavy stamp tax on the press, but less than a year after its repeal in 1869 the first cheap popular daily, *Het Nieuws van den Dag* ("News of the Day") was published. And in the ensuing years, technical innovations further paved the way for other mass-circulation newspapers.

During the second half of the 19th century the Dutch press was also shaped by—and helped to shape—the country's multiparty political system. In a sense the Netherlands were being balkanized by many factions of religious denomination, social caste and ideological outlook. This phenomenon was called "pillarization," and it did not begin to break down until the end of World War I. Even in the late 1930s pillarization could still be seen in Dutch newspapers, although by now on somewhat less rigid lines. A circulation breakdown of the daily press in 1937 shows that of 70 papers reaching half a million readers, 32 (mostly regional), were Roman Catholic, six liberal, five belonging to one of the Protestant parties, two Social Democrat, one Communist and one National Socialist, with the remaining 23 (again largely regional) independent. The leading papers were as listed in the table below:

newspapers were actually owned by that political party. This was far less so when a newspaper supported some party independently—even if regularly.

The German invasion caught neutral Holland by surprise in 1940. The army capitulated after five days of fighting, and general confusion that reigned in the country was shared by the press. A few papers soon decided to stop publishing, but a vast majority continued, some trying hard to stay free of foreign influences, many by coming to terms with the occupier through compromises, some others openly collaborating. Those that tried to stay free were swiftly abolished in a so-called press reorganization, or taken over by Nazi-appointed trustees. The decline of Holland's "legal" newspapers was compensated for by a steadily growing underground press, whose publications—printed and distributed at the cost of many lives—reached very high circulations towards the end of the war. A number of these resistance newspapers continued after the war, but most soon disappeared. Best known among the still existing newspapers of the former underground are the Protestant national daily *Trouw*; the previously independent socialist *Het Parool*; the communist daily *De Waarheid* and the socialist opinion-weekly *Vrij Nederland*. Gradually the prewar pattern was reestablished, and until the end of the 1950s remained practically unchanged.

Since then the whole "pillarization" edifice

Nationally Distributed Daily Newspapers (1937)

Newspaper	Affiliation	Circulation
Algemeen Handelsblad	Liberal	50,000
Nieuwe Rotterdamsche Courant	Liberal	35,000
Het Volk/Voorwaarts	Social-Democratic Party	119,000
De Standaard	Calvinist-Protestant Party	24,000
De Nederlander	Protestant Party	9,000
De Maasbode	Roman-Catholic	48,000
De Tijd	Roman-Catholic	6,000
De Tribune	Communist Party	15,000
Het Nationale Dagblad	National-Socialist Party	12,000
De Telegraaf	Independent	100,000
Nieuws van de Dag	Independent	250,000

Since a majority—at least in numbers though not in circulation—of the daily newspapers stood for the ideas of a specific political party or religious creed, ties between many of them were often very close, especially where the

has pretty much collapsed, a process possibly accelerated by the growing influence of television. Although TV broadcasting was organized and broadcasting time divided according to ideological and religious principles—

Political and Religious Tendency of Dutch Newspapers

Tendency	Percentage of total daily newspaper—circulation				Elections 1978	Census 1971
	1955	1964	1966	1975		
Roman Catholic	26.4	26.8	27.0	25.7	Catholic party 22.1	Catholic church 40.0
Protestant	8.7	8.2	6.6	5.2	Protestant parties 16.2	Protestant churches 36.0
Socialist	19.3	16.1	14.4	10.6	Socialist parties 33.4	
Liberal	5.1	4.6	4.3	2.3	Liberal parties 22.1	
	59.5	55.7	52.3	43.8		
Independent	40.5	44.3	47.7	56.2	other parties 6.2	no religion 23.6
	100	100	100	100	100	100

Source: Kempers and Wreten, 1976

as had been the case with radio since the 1920s—there the nonselective behavior of Dutch viewers helped bring on a nationwide confrontation of widely diverging political outlooks and regional cultures. This in turn brought a new ideological self-reliance to the press. Many newspapers identified with parties or special interest groups disappeared. Others—to broaden their bases of circulation and even existence—loosened or actually broke their ties with the groups they originally belonged to. In 1967 the largest remaining political newspaper, *Het Vrije Volk,* ended its formal association with the Labor party. The table above gives some impression of the changing face of the Dutch press. In most cases the labels show that strong affiliations in 1955 had diminished visibly 20 years later.

Local and regional daily papers have almost 60 percent of the Netherlands' total newspaper circulation; the national newspapers have about 40 percent, while four small specialized dailies (finance, economy, shipping and building) share the rest. The regional press has slowly grown in total circulation and so has the quality of its content. Except for an extra emphasis on regional and local news most regional papers are now not unlike those published nationally.

Before the war all newspapers were evening papers, although some had morning editions. Since then the pattern has changed. Regional papers are still mainly an evening

Largest Newspapers by Circulation

De Telegraaf (national)	600,790	(752,430 with its affiliated evening paper *Nieuws van de Dag* included)
Algemeen Dagblad (national)	358,328	
Volkskrant (national)	239,400	
Haagsche Courant (regional)	194,620	
Het Parool (national)	161,400	
Het Vrije Volk (regional)	160,533	
De Gelderlander (regional)	154,514	
Trouw (national)	141,300	
Nieuwsblad van het Noorden (regional)	139,587	
De Limburger (regional)	134,350	
NRC Handelsblad (national)	133,115	

press, but nationwide the morning papers have by far the largest circulations; the largest popular dailies, *De Telegraaf* and *Algemeen Dagblad,* are both morning papers. The total daily circulation shared by *De Telegraaf* (with its evening paper, *Het Nieuws van de Dag*) and *Algemeen Dagblad* rose from 19.9 to 23.9 percent between 1970 and 1980. However, the distinction between the popular press and quality or elite papers is less clear in the Netherlands than in many other countries, although the liberal *NRC-Handelsblad* comes closest to meeting those standards. A yellow press does not exist, although there was a short-lived experiment with one such tabloid newspaper (even this format made it a curiosity) during the spring of 1980. Also of high quality and influence are the *Volkskrant,* once the organ of the Roman Catholic trade union; the Protestant daily *Trouw;* and the popular *Telegraaf,* the last mainly because of its ability to help focus attention on political issues through its high circulation and willingness to make use of that readership.

Since the war the number and circulation of a group of periodicals generally referred to as "opinion weeklies" have grown. The weeklies show some resemblance to newsmagazines and sunday papers. In 1979 eight periodicals with a total circulation of 517,578 were reckoned among this category. The conservative *Elseviers Magazine,* largest of these weeklies, had a 1979 circulation of 134,650.

Most national newspapers have a rather heterogeneous audience with a slight over-representation of higher-income groups. The readership of local and regional newspapers reflects best the stratification of the population. Generally, the opinion weeklies reach the better-educated and higher-income levels.

In all provinces of the Netherlands except one—Friesland, where Frisian and Dutch are spoken together—Dutch is the official and only language used. However, nonregional ethnic minorities like the South Moluccans and people from Surinam have their own periodicals, but no daily newspapers. Since the 1960s there has been a considerable influx of migrant workers from Mediterranean countries, especially Turkey and Morocco. Their numbers were estimated in 1978 at 95,000, and 55,400 respectively. The number of South Moluccans, most of whom came from the former Dutch East Indies in the early 1950s (and most of whom are without nationality today) is estimated at between 25,000 and 30,000. About 200,000 people with Dutch passports emigrated from Surinam shortly before and since that country's independence.

All this new readership is also reflected in the hitherto normal pattern of sales in the Netherlands of foreign newspapers and periodicals.

Ecomonic Framework

More than half of the Dutch gross national product is derived from exports, the Federal Republic of Germany being the country's best customer. However, the 1980 balance of payments showed a deficit of about Fl. 4.5 billion ($500 million). Industry profits are relatively low. Labor income quotas have reached 97.5 percent—highest level in the world—leaving little room for investment. Unemployment passed the 7 percent mark in December 1980. Still, this figure does not immediately affect consumption, because of high and long-lasting unemployment benefits. The country's social security system is

---

Mean sale of best-selling foreign daily newspapers and news weeklies in 1980

Dailies		News weeklies	
Hürriyet (Turkey)	3,500	*Time* (USA)	3,250
Bild (FRG)	3,000	*Newsweek* (USA)	2,850
Tercüman (Turkey)	2,250	*Sunday Times* (UK)	2,500
Int'l Herald Tribune (USA)	2,200	*Bild am Sonntag* (FRG)	2,000
Daily Telegraph (UK)	1,150	*Observer* (UK)	1,500
Financial Times (UK)	1,050	*Sunday Telegraph* (UK)	1,450
Le Monde (France)	1,000	*Sunday Express* (UK)	1,350
Ware Tijd (Surinam)	1,000	*Sunday Mirror* (UK)	1,250
The Times (UK)	850	*News of the World* (UK)	1,000
Daily Express (UK)	850	*l'Express* (France)	1,000

Source: van Gelderen import b.v.

perhaps the most comprehensive in the world. Public expenditure, including social security payments, amounts to over 60 percent of the national income. And despite such costs, inflation has been kept relatively low: between 6.5 and 7 percent in 1980.

The real state of the economy is closely related to the revenues from the country's large natural gas reserves—Fl. 8.6 bn. ($4.3 billion) in 1980. A small part of it will be allocated to improving the position of Dutch industry, instead of being incorporated in the government's general budget.

The biggest publishing company in the Netherlands, Elsevier-NDU, has a turnover of more than Fl. 1 bn. ($500 million). Like other big publishers it has been steadily expanding abroad in recent years. As yet these publishers show no signs of having been seriously affected by the recession. And until quite recently no such influence has been noticeable in the newspaper industry. The income from advertising, presumably the first to be hit by the consequences of a sagging economy, has risen steadily in recent years. At the moment however, this growth seems to be lagging particularly in decreased earnings from retail trade advertising—attributed to the reduced purchasing power caused by the depression. On the other hand, partly because of inflation, the media have faced substantially rising costs, especially in newsprint and distribution and government tariffs.

Since the introduction of advertising on television and radio in 1967–68 the print media have had an important competitor for revenues. In the first years of its existence radio-TV advertising outlet caused considerable income losses for newspapers and other periodicals. Between 1967 and 1973, however, the print media were compensated for these losses by a refund of approximately 130 million guilders from the earnings of STER, the radio- and TV-advertising foundation. The broadcast organizations themselves are also competitors of the print media for advertising in their magazines, which have the exclusive right of publishing complete radio and TV program information.

Almost all daily newspapers are published by limited liability companies, sometimes within holding companies. In some cases a foundation, cooperative or association acts as publisher. In others the original publisher, or publisher's family, still has influence. Only a very few papers still have a close relationship to a political party, such as the

Market shares, by percentage, of the 24 independent newspaper publishing companies (1980):	
1. Holding De Telegraaf (2 national, 2 regional titles)	18.62
2. Elsevier-NDU (2 national, 5 regional titles)	15.29
3. Perscombinatie (3 national titles)	13.39
4. Audet (5 regional titles)	9.63
5. Sijthoff Pers (5 regional, 1 specialized title)	6.99
6. VNU (4 regional titles)	6.22
7. Van der Loeff (7 regional titles)	3.69
8. Damiate Holding (7 regional titles)	3.51
9. Holding Utrechts Nieuwsblad (4 regional titles)	3.20
10. Nieuwsblad van het Noorden (1 regional title)	3.00
11. Wegener's Couranten Concern (9 regional titles)	2.74
12. Leeuwarder Courant (1 regional title)	2.48
13. Verenigde Noordhollandse Dagbladen (7 regional titles)	1.97
14. Kluwer (4 regional, 1 specialized title)	1.59
15. Koninklijke Tijl (4 regional titles)	1.42
16. Provinciale Zeeuwse Courant (1 regional title)	1.31
17. De Gooi- en Eemlander (1 regional title)	1.22
18. Twentsche Courant (1 regional title)	1.15
19. Reformatorisch Dagblad (1 national title)	0.99
20. Friesch Dagblad (1 regional title)	0.56
21. Nederlands Dagblad (1 national title)	0.51
22. Het Financieele Dagblad (1 specialized title)	0.47
23. Dagblad Scheepvaart (1 specialized title)	0.05
24. De Waarheid (1 national title)	(no exact circulation data)

Source: *De Journalist,* August 21, 1980

communist daily *De Waarheid* and the *Nederlands Dagblad,* closely tied to one of the small Calvinist parties.

The 1960s and the early 1970s witnessed a wave of press concentration, caused by a variety of factors, among them economic. Wages, relatively stable in the 20 years since the war, had reached a point where they could no longer be kept in check, resulting in the so-called "wage-explosion" of 1964. In the printing trade alone, wages suddenly rose by about 17 percent. Investments in technology-developed production facilities brought on overcapacity. Earnings from advertising, especially those of the national dailies, tended to decrease, partly because of the advent of radio-TV advertising, partly owing to the ever-larger share of the advertising market secured by the growing number of free non-daily door-to-door newspapers. (Newspaper publishers have since managed to control much of this profitable market, eight big newspapers alone now holding a 55 percent share in the free-sheet circulation.) Lagging subscription rates made several upward leaps but the growth in newspaper readership continued to stagnate.

The result of all this was that quite a few newspapers were forced to liquidate, or to cooperate with other papers. Between 1968 and 1980 the number of newspaper publishing firms declined from 35 to 24, while the circulation of the three biggest publishers rose in the same period from 34.7 to 47.3 percent.

Mean circulation per publisher was 197,000 in 1980, compared to 60,000 in 1960 and 122,000 in 1970. Statistically, a newspaper publishing company today has 3.5 newspaper titles and 2.1 editorially independent newspapers; in 1970 these numbers were 2.9

and 1.5 respectively. Most newspapers that have disappeared, either by liquidation or mergers with healthier operations, were originally in the lower-circulation categories. In two-thirds of Holland's 49 more or less self-contained areas, only one local newspaper exists or it reaches such a high percentage of the population that it has virtually no competitors. Such is also the case in 14 of the 17 cities with more than 100,000 inhabitants.

Newspapers in the Netherlands generally are delivered to subscribers. Newsstand copy sale is unimportant, except for some national dailies. The popular *Telegraaf* and *Algemeen Dagblad* have the highest percentages of newsstand sales, both about 30 percent of their total circulation. The mean newsstand sale of regional newspapers is only four percent. Most newspapers have their own distributing organizations. Some very small national papers completely depend on the services of the Post Office, and other national dailies sometimes make use of postal delivery in remote areas with slight coverage. (Newspapers also enjoy reductions on normal postal rates.)

The mean price of a single copy of a Dutch newspaper today is about Fl. 0.65 ($0.30). In the 1950s a system of fixed retail prices for newspapers, set by the publishers' organization, was in force, but with the growing competition in the years that followed several publishers disassociated themselves from the agreement. Rate increases for subscriptions, loose-sale and advertisements became dependent upon the approval of the minister of economic affairs, to prevent inflationary development of prices.

In the period up to 1965 lagging subscription rates led to a growing share of earnings from advertising (65 percent) in the gross

Number of Newspapers by Circulation Category			
Circulation	Disappeared 1970–1979	Number in 1970	Number in 1979
National dailies			
< 100,000	2	8	6
100,000–250,000	1	3	4
250,000–500,000	—	2	1
> 500,000	—	1	1
Regional dailies			
< 50.000	5	20	10
50,000–100,000	1	12	11
100,000–250,000	—	4	10
250,000–500,000	—	—	1

Source: Brouwer, 1979

revenues of newspaper companies. The ensuing price rises and stagnant advertising growth almost balanced the two sources of income by 1975. Since then, however, newspaper advertising volume has rapidly grown, so that now about 60 percent of the earnings are derived from advertising—which occupies almost half of a daily's mean 28 pages.

The national paper industry supplies twenty-four percent of the needed newsprint, a drop from 35 percent in 1970. The total newsprint supply for the Dutch market amounted to 460,000 metric tons in 1979, of which 87 percent went to the dailies. The members of NDP, the newspaper publishers' organization, guaranteed to buy 117,300 metric tons of newsprint from the nation's paper industry in 1980. The mean price per ton for newsprint rose from Fl.28. ($14) in 1970 to approximately Fl.57. ($28.50) in 1979.

The ongoing concentration in the press was not the least among the reasons for the Socialist-Christian Democrat Den Uyl government to try to develop a "coherent mediapolicy." In a memorandum on mass mediapolicy it published in 1975 measures were proposed to preserve the necessary press diversity—some of these measures being aimed at equalizing unequal economic conditions in the print media. Especially because of these inequitable conditions the memorandum urged that general measures of support for the press (such as the abovementioned reduced postal rates) be replaced by a system of specific support. A measure of the Dutch government's readiness to provide more specific support had already been shown in 1974, with the establishment of the so-called Industrial Fund for the Press, giving financial assistance to publications in danger of discontinuation if credits from other sources were impossible to obtain. As proposed in the 1975 memorandum, newly established newspapers could also receive loans from the fund. By 1980 total credits granted by the fund (to two daily newspapers and other periodicals) came to Fl. 13. m.

Other proposed measures to preserve or further diversification in the press included more control of mergers, editorial statutes stipulating rights and duties of journalists, research into the feasibilities of noncommercial press operation, and a financial regulation to compensate newspapers unable to attract advertising because of low circulation, limited coverage and other handicaps. This last proposal, if implemented, would have cost about Fl.13m. in 1980, and three to four dailies would have benefited from it. However, it was rejected by the minister of culture, partly because it did not make profitable newspapers ineligible.

By 1974 already more than 40 percent of Dutch journalists had had some experience with press concentration, varying from minor forms of technical cooperation between publications to outright liquidation of the newspaper they had worked for. In many cases newsmen were confronted only at a very late stage with the results of negotiations that had been held. This among other things led to ever stronger pressure from the journalists' organization, NVJ (Nederlandse Vereniging van Journalisten) for so-called editorial statutes—whereby the rights and duties of publishers (owners, managers), editors in chief and journalists, together with the editorial identity of the newspapers would be formally established. In 1976 NVJ first reached an agreement with the publishers on a framework would serve as a model for editorial statutes to be negotiated at every single newspaper. Since the 1977 collective agreement between publishers and journalists each newspaper has been obliged to have such a statute, each of which is based in general on the largest possible independence of the editorial staff by clearly separating editorial and commercial functions and interests. The same sort of agreements have been reached with the publishers of opinion weeklies and general interest magazines.

Originally NVJ was a strictly professional organization. In conflicts over the continuation of press organs threatened in their independent existence it was often directly opposed to the organizations of technical personnel. Gradually, however, the journalist group and the trade unions came closer together, and in 1973 NVJ decided to affiliate itself to the then existing Consultation Committee of the three Dutch trade unions (Socialist, Roman-Catholic and Protestant). In 1976, after the Socialist and Roman Catholic union had decided to merge as the FNV (Federatie Nederlandse Vakbeweging: Federated Netherlands Trade Union Movement), NVJ opted for joining this body. In March 1980 NVJ supported the strike of the federation and its printers union against changes in the Wage Act that allowed government regulation of wage increases. Some newspapers were unable to come out, while others contained only news about the strike. (Similar "sympathy" actions were held at the Dutch press agency ANP and in broadcasting media.) In some cases the printers prevented editorial staffs from publishing newspapers, sometimes the publishers counteracted by preventing publication of "action papers."

Although NVJ has had a strike fund since 1958, strikes by journalists used to be a rare phenomenon, employed mainly in cases of direct danger to the existence of one's own newspaper. An estimated 75 percent of Dutch journalists are organized in NVJ.

Journalists' salaries have been regulated in annually negotiated collective agreements since 1947. According to the collective agreement of 1979, minimum salaries vary from Fl.23,560 ($11,780) to Fl.68,500 ($34,250) per year (after 10 years in the highest scale). General editors, being full-time journalists, earn at least Fl.71,375 ($35,688). Apprentices have a commencing salary of Fl.20,150 ($10,075).

Also under the terms of the collective agreement, an "editorial committee"—a body representing the journalists working for a newspaper—must be consulted (together with other groups) on the introduction of new technical equipment (such as computer-connected keyboards, whether or not combined with visual display terminals) in determining its effect on their working conditions.

Apart from the rapid introduction of electronic photocomposition in recent years, a growing number of regional newspapers has switched from hot type to offset. The first national newspapers will probably follow suit this year. The Netherlands Broadcasting Foundation (NOS) has begun an experimental "Teletekst" (Ceefax)—which is considered to be broadcasting—without participation by the newspapers.

Press Laws

Freedom of the press is guaranteed in Article 7 of the Netherlands Constitution. The phrasing of the article has remained unaltered since 1848. Another article contains provisions on freedom of information in the European Convention, ratified by the Dutch government in 1954, thus giving it the status of national law. And since March 1979 the UN Covenants on Civil and Political Rights and on Economic, Social and Cultural Rights have also been put into operation in the Netherlands.

Article 7 reads: "No one needs prior permission to publish by the printing-press thoughts or feelings, except for everyone's responsibility under the law." Legally, this article protects not only the press but all related means of public-directed expression, such as photographs, drawings and even neon-signs. The Supreme Court also has always given a broad interpretation to the word "publish." After World War II, when the law required licenses for bookseller's shops, lending libraries and the printing trade, the Supreme Court decided that no such licenses could be demanded for these businesses because of their service functions for the freedom of the press.

The responsibility under civil and criminal law for expressed "thoughts and feelings," as voiced in the phrase "except for everyone's responsibility under the law" of Article 7 of the constitution, applies to every citizen. There are no special rules for professional journalists, the profession itself is expected to establish a code or administration of disciplinary justice, if thought necessary. However, journalists are not exempt from violations under Article 7, which may be divided into three categories:

1. Offenses against the security of the state, the peace, and morals (deliberate publication of state/defense secrets, sedition, pornography).

2. Special insult (of members of the royal family, any group of the population, blasphemy).

3. Simple insult of an individual, defamation and calumny; in these cases formal complaint by the party defamed is needed to initiate criminal proceedings.

Defamation is described in Article 261 of the Penal Code as a deliberate attack on someone's honor or reputation, by imputation of a certain fact, with the apparent intention of making it public. Under Dutch criminal law, however, defamation is not actionable if the accused has acted in the public interest or in necessary defense. If the defense of "public interest" is applied, a judge may allow the defense of truth. And although proving a plea of truth in itself does not free one from liability, it may help to establish the public interest of the statements. The defense of "public interest" is accepted in most cases, except when the statement has been expressed in an unnecessarily grievous form. The maximum penalty for defamation is one year's imprisonment. If the statement is made contrary to one's better judgment, that is, with malicious intent, then the offense becomes calumny and carries a higher maximum penalty of three year's imprisonment.

The prime responsibility in such cases rests with the author of the article, although a newspaper editor may, as the person on whose instruction the story was printed, be punished as "co-offender." In that case the editor's intention to commit the crime must be shown. As a rule, publishers and printers are not prosecuted.

Criminal actions for insult or defamation are quite rare. More common are civil actions, based on Articles 1408 and 1409 ("insult") and 1401 ("unrightful act") of the Civil Code. The latter offense is more actionable than the former. As in the Penal Code, deliberate intent to defame or insult is required— and also impossible to establish provided the defense of the public interest is accepted. An action under article 1401, sometimes settled summarily, is in fact based on the general rules of civil liability. An "unrightful act," however, is any act or negligence in public media with respect to someone else's person or goods. Unintentional insult and defamation can also come under the "unrightful act" article, although proof of "a guilty act" is required. That would be the case if the untruth of a statement and the injury to the person involved were known in advance. Under the same article the defense of "acting in the public interest" is possible, though here too articles must not take an unnecessarily damaging form. Again, the author of an article is normally held to be responsible for its content, and the newspaper editor is usually seen as co-responsible. Further, the publisher may also be sued, on grounds of indirect responsibility. Penalties for "unrightful act" vary. Apart from damages to the plaintiff, a prohibition of the publication, and distribution of statements to that effect, may be issued. Rectification or reply at the expense of the defendant may also be imposed.

Journalists in the Netherlands have no statutory right to refuse to reveal their sources when testifying in court. This was recently confirmed by the Supreme Court. Thus, at least in principle, journalists unwilling to name their sources in a criminal case might be punished by conditional imprisonment. However, if the journalist has clearly acted in the public interest, then a case of "force majeure" may be claimed. Further,

any suit for defamation or similar injury in the media is usually time-devouring and chancy, because jurisprudence clearly shows that no narrow limits are put on the freedom of the press and that the public-interest plea of a journalist is accepted by the court in most cases.

There is the alternative possibility of turning to the Journalism Council (Raad voor de Journalistiek), founded in 1969 by three press organizations to pass judgment on the conduct of all journalists, whether members or not. The council consists of five members: two journalists, two nonjournalists and a chairman who is a lawyer but not a journalist. Although this body does not apply sanctions, its findings are published in De Journalist, the organ of the press groups.

A general law on the press does not exist in the Netherlands. The only statutory regulation in this area is a 1951 act dealing with the institution of the government's Press Council, whose members advise the minister of culture on all matters concerning the press. Most of the 13 to 17 members come either from journalism or publishing; three are members of Parliament, both government and Opposition. In March 1980 the Minister of Culture organized a group to prepare statutory provisions regarding the press and the Industrial Fund for the Press. The group consists of members of the Press Council, the board of the fund and some civil servants.

On May 1, 1980 a "freedom of information" act was passed in the Netherlands. Under its provisions government bodies are obliged in principle to satisfy requests for information. Government must also furnish information on its own policies and publish all recommendations of nonofficial advisory committees. (In the media field such committees include the Foundation Industrial Fund for the Press, the Press Council and the Broadcasting Council.) In certain instances information may be withheld: if its public release might endanger the security of the state, or if it is potentially damaging to relations with other countries, to the tracing and prosecution of criminals, the prevention of unfair advantages to special-interest groups, and to the protection of privacy.

Censorship

Although pre-publication censorship is excluded by Article 7 of the constitution ("no one needs prior permission"), exceptions can be made when the country is in a state of war, siege or emergency. Broadcasting, however, has observed a set of rules somewhat different from those applied to the press. Until quite recently the Broadcasting Act contained an article stating that electronic-media content was subject to *post*-broadcast control by the minister of culture. Possible penalties included—after a first reprimand—exclusion from broadcasting for a certain period, or cancellation of a station's license "if the continuation of it might endanger the security of the state, the peace, or good morals." Some reprimands were given before the government-control provision was expunged from the Broadcasting Act. In one case the sanctions had been applied unlawfully, in a manner comparable to pre-publication censorship. In 1963 the KRO network was warned in advance that broadcasting time might be withdrawn if an interview with former French Prime Minister Georges Bidault—then connected with the OAS, a terrorist group operating in Algeria against the De Gaulle government—was aired.

State-Press Relations

No information ministry exists in the Netherlands. The State Information Service is in charge of government information and communication. It comes under the Ministry of General Affairs (prime minister). The Ministry of Transport and Works is in charge of PTT affairs, but the Ministry of Culture, Recreation and Social Welfare is actually closest to the media, especially with the broadcast media. The minister of culture has, for instance, the final decision on advice from the Industrial Fund for the Press to grant a loan to a newspaper in danger of discontinuation.

The prime aim of all government press-support measures—whether general or specific—has been to enable the print media to continue to exercise their informative function and to uphold the diversity of information that is needed in a democratic society. No state control of the press seems intended by such measures. In the case of print media at least, the state is and always has been reluctant to infringe on its privileges and on the rights of its professionals. (This is substantiated by the total absence of licensing and other regulations.) Nevertheless there is a

tendency (disapproved of officially), especially in crisis situations such as hijackings where hostages have been taken, to keep journalists away from the scene, or at least to restrict their room for operating.

Suspension and confiscation of newspapers are unknown in the Netherlands.

Attitude Toward Foreign Media

In principle the same regulations that apply to the Dutch press and to the Dutch journalists are also applicable to foreign correspondents and to foreign publications. That does mean that there are no other restrictions than those laid down in the law.

The Netherlands Association of Journalists is a very critical member of the International Federation of Journalists. It has a sympathetic attitude towards the so-called Capri conferences, where representatives of both IFJ and IOJ (the International Organization of Journalists) meet. It supported the French initiative to join a European club of journalists consisting of members of both organizations. The newspaper publishers' association (NDP) is affiliated to the Fédération Internationale des Editeurs de Journaux et Publications (FIEJ), and the International Press Institute has quite a few members from the Netherlands.

The Netherlands delegation to the 20th Session of the General Conference of UNESCO in Paris in 1978 supported that body's declaration on the mass media. In explaining its vote, however, reservations were voiced concerning the concept of a new international information order. If this led to government control of editorial content, said the delegation, "we shall not be willing to go along with that." The Netherlands also supported the UNESCO compromise resolution on the final report at the Belgrade conference in 1980.

News Agencies

The one Dutch international news agency is ANP (Algemeen Nederlands Persbureau: the General Netherlands Press Bureau). It was established in 1934 as a nonprofit cooperative venture with the newspaper publishing companies as members, and replaced some smaller private agencies. ANP's principal customers are all Dutch daily newspapers, which pay for its services according to their circulation. Other subscribers include nondailies, radio and television, government offices and industry. ANP employs 150 journalists, and for domestic news also has 700 correspondents at its disposal. For news from abroad it has contacts with UPI, Reuters, Agence France-Press and Deutsche Presse Agentur, plus exchange contracts with East and West European agencies and an experimental arrangement with Inter Press Service. There are no ANP links with the government.

About 40 press bureaus and news agencies are active in the Netherlands. Some are branch offices of foreign news agencies such as AFP (France), Antara (Indonesia), Belga (Belgium), dpa (West Germany), Reuters (U.K.) and UPI (U.S.). The other agencies—commercial, church affiliated, private—have limited, mostly domestic functions. The only independently operating international news agency in the Netherlands is the Associated Press (AP).

A number of Dutch newspaper companies or groups of companies have their own combined news services. The newspapers involved are mainly regional dailies. In most cases they serve as correspondents for the entire service.

Electronic News Media

Unlike the press, the broadcasting system in the Netherlands has been organized according to the old "pillarization" principles of the 1920s, air time being divided among at least five broadcasting groups of diverse religious and political orientations. The Broadcasting Act of 1967 made the entry of new organizations possible, partly through establishment of a common Netherlands Broadcasting Foundation (NOS), partly by setting up three categories of broadcasting organizations: "A" (those with more than 400,000 subscribers, "B" (between 250,000 and 400,000) and "C" (100,000 to 250,000). Broadcasting time is divided between them at a ratio of 5:3:1. Candidate broadcasting associations having more than 400,000 members can get air time during a probation period. According to the 1967 Broadcasting Act and recent amendments to it, broadcasting associations must be nonprofit organizations whose programming contains reasonable proportions of culture, information, education and entertainment, and which is aimed at satisfying the cultural, religious or spiritual needs of the people to such a degree that the broadcasts may be considered to be in the public interest. The associations must also represent the country's various social, cultural, political and religious outlooks, and be organized in such a way that their members and contributors may influence their policies. A new broadcasting organization has to demonstrate that what it offers is sufficiently original so that its participation will enhance the diversity of national programming.

At present there are eight such broadcasting associations. (See chart below.)

Most broadcasting organizations have their own current affairs programs. TV news is provided by NOS, the overall organization; on radio ANP. However, interpretation and comment on the news are considered to be the function of the broadcasting associations.

Broadcasting is financed from license fees and advertising, in a ratio of approximately 3:1 (1976). Advertising is aired in blocks around the news broadcasts.

Broadcasting Associations			
Association	Orientation	Category	Total membership (Dec. 1977)
AVRO	Neutral	A	783,176
TROS	Independent	A	730,000
KRO	Roman-Catholic	A	598,770
VARA	Socialist	A	543,000
NCRV	Protestant	A	488,704
VOO (former pirate station)	Independent	C	220,000
VPRO	Progressive	C	194,727
EO	Fundamentalist Protestant	C	166,000

Education & Training

The first journalism school in the Netherlands was established in Utrecht in 1967. Students get three years' training in journalism and other more general subjects. The establishment of the school was a drastic departure from previous practice, and also from the idea that journalists were (and should be) trained on the job. Before the Utrecht school's foundation, there were two part-time courses for apprentice journalists at the University of Amsterdam and the Catholic University of Nijmegen. Some publishers still have their own training courses for journalists. In 1980 a new Journalism School was started at Tilburg. It has a Roman Catholic background. A Protestant journalism school will be established at Zwolle/Kampen in 1981.

A number of journalistic awards and prizes have been instituted in recent years, among them the Prize for Daily Newspaper Journalism, established by NDP, the association of newspaper publishers. NOTU, the organization of periodical publishers, has established a foundation to promote journalism in that branch of the print media; in 1980 the foundation initiated an awards program for journalism in professional magazines. Other Dutch-media awards are the Lucas-Ooms Prize for magazine journalism, the Silver Camera of the Netherlands Association of Photojournalists, and the yearly prize of the circle of theatre critics.

The principal journalist organization in the Netherlands is NVJ, the Netherlands Association of Journalists, with a current membership of more than 4,000—an estimated 75 percent of all journalists in Holland. Some members left the association in 1976—when NVJ joined the Federated Netherlands Trade Union Movement—to establish a new organization, AVJ, the General Association of Journalists. However, the split does not show in NVJ's membership, which has continually grown in recent years. Its media representation is as follows: daily newspapers, 2,050; magazines, 777; broadcasting, 322; freelance, 299; photojournalists, 113; press agencies, 107; nondaily newspapers, 66; free sheets, 102.

Summary

A favorable judgment by almost any standard might be passed on the overall situation of the press in the Netherlands. There are ten national dailies with different editorial identities to choose from. There are regional dailies of good journalistic quality in every part of the country, providing not only local but foreign and national news as well. There are eight opinion weeklies reflecting almost every shade of opinion. And there is a plethora of weekly, monthly, bimonthly and quarterly magazines, ranging from gossip to science. And most of all these are doing well.

The press has also matured. It has become less parochial since the war—although there remains a distinct aura of sectarianism in some newspapers. And the press may also have become more investigative; editors and reporters do not shrink back so often now from the role of watchdog over officialdom. The traditional interest in world affairs has not changed, but the press today gives more value for money, and more volume as well: most newspapers now have regular magazine-like sections. Newspapers and magazines are also better looking (though not always more readable) today because of new technology. Readership, too, has steadily grown—faster than the growth of the population—and yet publishers still manage to find and fill new holes in the market; the most recent being a craving for gossip magazines.

There is also a less sunny side. The remaining publishers may be rather well off at the moment, but "remaining" is the operative word. During the 1960s and early 1970s many independent newspaper companies and independent newspapers were swallowed in mergers or simply folded. Some of those that survived have felt obliged to become less distinctive—and thus less colorful—to broaden their base of subsistence. The fear of a further loss of diversity subsided when the economic recession seemed to bring an advertising boom instead of a slump. As a result, measures against further concentration virtually came to a halt. Thus the 1979 merger between the giant publishing firms of Elseviers and NDU came as a shock. Other similar mergers have followed since. In the 1960s and early 1970s it could at least be said that the poor merged with the poor, or that the wealthy swallowed the poor. But now the wealthy seem to merge with the wealthy, without any apparent necessity.

But appearances may be deceptive. As the impact of the recession makes itself felt, there is less optimism about earnings from advertising. Although still growing, the volume of some advertising categories has begun to shrink. There is also concern over influence of technological innovation. A heated debate, for example, has been going on about how to categorize new media-systems like Ceefax and Viewdata. Should they be defined as "broadcasting" or as "press"? The different answers to these questions clearly reflect the interests at stake.

Uneasiness may be more pervasive in broadcasting circles than in the press. The unique character of the Dutch broadcasting system, based as it is on associations founded by distinct groups in the population, had already been impaired since 1967 by the influx of news broadcasting organizations that recruited their following more by popular programming than by reflecting opinions. A more imminent danger seems to loom now: not the reception of foreign television by cable, but rather the possibility of commercial satellite broadcasting directed (without any controls) towards the Netherlands. This is seen as a dangerous threat to the system in two ways. First, advertisers would be attracted to the less restrictive commercial broadcaster, thus removing one of the two financial supports of Dutch TV, namely income from advertising. (The other is license fees). Second, the commercial transmitter would be able to provide more expensive—that is better and more popular—programming than the financially straitened Dutch organizations, thus taking not only money but audiences. The one constant factor in all proposed remedies is more time or better facilities for TV advertising—a possibility that creates uncertainty and anxiety in the Dutch print media.

Has the press become more or less free since the war? There is no simple answer to this question. Probably some progress has been made, albeit uneven. At first, press concentration had an adverse effect on press freedom, but journalists have managed to create editorial statutes guaranteeing some measure of independence, undisturbed by any intrusion of commercial interests. However, there are doubts as to whether the journalists' affiliation with the trade unions will have the same effect. The government policy of specific financial support for the sake of diversity may be hazardous, but has as yet shown no sign of efforts to infringe on independence. And respect for the information-seeking task of the press has certainly grown, as witnessed by the creation of more statutory guarantees and the government's own assumption of greater obligations to be informative than in the past. Still, uneasiness prevails in many circumstances where media and government meet—especially in situations of crisis, which have become more frequent with the growth of terrorist violence. In those situations the interests of both parties may conflict so sharply that no harmonious way out seems possible.

Developments in both society and mass communications have made such strides that there is no longer any sound basis for consensus on the future of the press and the future of its freedom. Some are optimistic, others less so. Both seem able to provide sound evidence for their arguments. But the common feeling is that of uncertainty.

CHRONOLOGY

1975	Government memorandum on its mass-media policy includes proposals to uphold existing press diversity, prevent further market-oriented programming in radio and TV.	Netherlands Association of Journalists (NVJ) joins Federated Netherlands Trade Union Movement (FNV). About 90 members leave NVJ to found new organization.
1976	Article in *Elseviers Magazine* hints that one MP and other prominent Dutchmen are on a list of KGB agents; when two regional dailies later reveal MP's name, he institutes proceedings against the editors of all three publications.	**1977** Supreme Court rejects claim by editor of *Elseviers Magazine* of journalistic privilege to refuse to answer questions in court. In Collective Agreement for newspapers, certain editorial statutes become obligatory—including definition of rights

and duties of owners, directors, editors in chief and journalists, as well as editorial identity of newspapers.

1978   The two editors of regional dailies fined for not naming source of their story on MP alleged to be on KGB list.

1979   Supreme Court rules fines to be legitimate means of forcing witnesses to testify.

Two of biggest Netherlands' publishing companies, Elsevier and NDU, merge.

1980   Memorandum by ministers of justice and home affairs on press-police relations disapproves of infringements on press freedom in crisis situations, noting that confiscation of films and photographs are forms of pre-publication censorship and thus strictly forbidden under Article 7 of constitution.

Act on the Publicity of Administration becomes law—obliging government to give asked- and unasked-for information, except in limited (but vaguely formulated) cases.

Changes in the Broadcasting Act give some discretionary powers to minister of culture in deciding on whether applicants for broadcasting licenses will contribute to diversity.

Regulation proposed (and rejected by the minister) for compensation of dailies in reverse proportion to their advertising revenues.

Newspaper strikes: some publications unable to come out, others print only news about the strikes themselves, sometimes under pressure from printers.

BIBLIOGRAPHY

Bardoel, J., et al. *Marges in de media.* Baarn, 1975.

Boukema, P. J. *Enkele aspecten van de vrijheid van meningsuiting in de Duitse Bondsrepubliek en in Nederland.* Amsterdam, 1966.

———. "The Limits of Freedom of Information in the Netherlands." *Netherlands Reports to the VIIIth International Congress of Comparative Law Research.* Deventer, 1970, p. 289.

Brants, K. and Kok, W. "The Netherlands: An End to Openness?" *Journal of Communication.* Summer 1978, p. 90.

Brouwer, M. "De concentratie in de dagbladpers." *Intermediair,* December 21, 1979.

Cuilenburg, J. J. van. *Lezer, krant en politiek.* Amsterdam, 1977.

Haak, K. van der, with Spicer, J. *Broadcasting in the Netherlands.* London, 1977.

Hemels, J., *De journalistieke eierdans.* Assen, 1972.

———. *Persvrijheid? Antwoord aan uilen en valken.* Amsterdam, 1975.

Hemels, J. M. H. J. "De structuur van de omroep; de structuur van de pers." In

Galjaard, J. M., ed. *Besturen in openheid.* Brussels: 1975–79.

Kempers, F. *Mediabeleid en mediaonderzoek.* Amsterdam, 1977.

Kempers, F. and Wieten, J. *Journalisten en persconcentratie.* Amsterdam, 1976.

Klaver, F. *Media in the Netherlands.* Strasbourg, 1976.

———. *Pers- en omroeprecht.* Amsterdam, 1970.

Kolhoff, W. *Pressekonzentration und Konzentrationspolitik in den Niederlanden.* West Berlin, 1979.

Kwant, R. C. *Gedrang rondom het podium.* Amsterdam, 1975.

Lensen, A. C. M. and Pijl, G. J. van der. *Rentabiliteitsonderzoek van de Nederlandse Dagbladpers.* Tilburg, 1976.

Lichtenberg, L. "Financiële overheidssteun en ontwikkelingen in de pers in Nederland." *Massacommunicatie.* 6:5–6, (1978): 175.

———. "Het persbeleid van de overheid." *Intermediair,* September 12, 1980.

Lijphart, A. *Democracy in Plural Societies: A Comparative Exploration.* New Haven, Conn., 1977.

————. "Consociational Democracy: Types of Western Democratic Systems." *World Politics.* 21: 2, p. 207.

Media en massacommunicatie in Nederland. Samengesteld door de Directie Radio, Televisie en Pers, Ministerie van Cultuur, Recreatie en Maatschappelijk Werk. Rijswijk, 1978.

Meij, J. M. de, *De vrijheid en de verantwoordelijkheid van de pers.* Utrecht, 1975.

Neerven, J. P. S. van. *Marketing in het dagbladbedrijf.* Utrecht, 1974.

Noomen, G. W. *Beweren en motiveren.* Amsterdam, 1977.

Nota over het massamedia-beleid. Uitgebracht door de Minister van Cultuur, Recreatie en Maatschappelijk Werk. 's-Gravenhage, 1975.

Oorburg, J., Boven, T. van, and Jolink, D. *His Master's Voice: Yes or No?* Groningen, 1974.

Pers-koncentratie. Sunschrift. Nijmegen, 1972.

Pijl, G. van der. *Een ontwerp compensatieregeling voor Nederlandse dagbladen.* Tilburg, 1979.

————. *Mogelijke compensatieregelingen ten behoeve van de Nederlandse Dagbladpers.* Tilburg, 1977.

Rapport van de werkgroep redactionele medezeggenschap. Amsterdam, 1974.

Rooij. M. *Het dagbladbedrijf in Nederland.* Leiden, 1956.

———. *Kranten: Dagbladpers en maatschappij.* Amsterdam, 1974.

Schneider, M. with Hemels, J. *De Nederlandse krant 1618-1978.* Baarn, 1979.

Schuijt, G. "De juridische en journalistiek-ethische bezwaren tegen stakingen van journalisten ontleed en weersproken." *Massacommunicatie* 8:5 (1980): 189.

Stoppelman, B. "The Dutch Magazine Market. A Description." *Gazette* 22: 1 (1977): 5.

Vlasblom, M. "Drukpers en vrijheid van meningsuiting." *Massacommunicatie* 6: 5-6 (1978): 154.

Vree, F. van. "De vooroorlogse pers als machtsinstrument." *Massacommunicatie* 8:5 (1980): 214.

Wieten, J. "Media Pluralism: The Policy of the Dutch Government." *Media, Culture and Society.* 1979, p. 171.

NEW ZEALAND

by Brian Priestley

BASIC DATA

Population: 3,129,000
Area: 268,276 sq. km. (99,262 sq. mi.)
GNP: NZ$18.9 billion (US$19.2 billion) (1979)
Literacy Rate: 98%
Language(s): English
Number of Dailies: 44
  Aggregate Circulation 1,009,000
  Circulation per 1,000: 310
Number of Nondailies: 10
  Aggregate Circulation: 494,000
  Circulation per 1,000: 632
Number of Periodicals: 480
Number of Radio Stations: 59

Number of Television Stations: 2
Number of Radio Receivers: 3 million
  Radio Receivers per 1,000: 878
Number of Television Receivers: 885,000
  Television Sets per 1,000: 263
Total Annual Newsprint Consumption: 86,200 metric tons
  Per Capita Newsprint Consumption: 27.8 kg. (61.16 lbs.)
Total Newspaper Ad Receipts: NZ$96.6 million (US$98 million) (1979)
  As % of All Ad Expenditures: 35.2

Background & General Characteristics

New Zealand has upwards of five dozen newspapers of one sort or another to serve a population of just over three million. From a circulation manager's point of view, the scenery gets in the way. The two islands measure a little more than 1,000 miles from north to south, and much of the countryside is mountainous and sparsely populated. Roads are often winding, an 80-kilometer-an-hour (50 m.p.h.) speed limit is strictly enforced and train services tend to be infrequent and slow. In such a setting, the small-town newspaper still holds its own.

New Zealanders tend to be literate, much traveled, well off by most people's standards and enthusiastic readers of newspapers and magazines. It is as though the country's very remoteness spurs its people on to keep in touch with what is happening in the rest of the world.

Most New Zealanders live in the North Island. The country's largest concentration of people is in the Auckland area, which has now grown to a population of more than 800,000. The capital city of Wellington (351,000) is in the south of the North Island on a great natural harbor opening out on to

Cook Strait. The main population centers of the South Island are the Christchurch area (327,000) and Dunedin (120,200). Although about one-tenth of New Zealanders think of themselves as being Maoris or Polynesians, English is the language used by newspapers and magazines.

In the late 1960s Dean Edward W. Barrett of the Columbia University Graduate School of Journalism commented that the New Zealand media were "decent, respectful, and reasonably responsible," although they often appeared to "lack thoroughness, penetration, and the ability to look beneath surface announcements."

If papers are now occasionally less decent and often a good deal less respectful, Barrett's verdict still looks reasonable today. Most New Zealand daily papers attempt to provide a balanced coverage of national, international and local news, although they face obvious difficulties. Small circulations mean small staffs. In such conditions investigative journalism can often seem an expensive luxury, although some difficult and far-ranging inquiries have recently been carried out. The state of the New Zealand media is one of freedom tempered by an often confusing legal code and an obstructive Official

Secrets Act, both of which pose obvious problems to all journalists. If New Zealanders frequently complain because their papers are not better, visiting journalists are often surprised at the standards attained by the local media.

Although the backbone of the nation's press is composed of the seven metropolitan papers, based on the four main cities, they are by no means the end of the story. Every sizable country town has its own daily paper, and weekly or fortnightly papers proliferate, often being bought at the local dairy or delivered in the mailbox as giveaways. In a country so rich in local sports teams and community institutions, the giveaways provide an essential service at the grass roots of society and their news columns are widely read.

The country's first paper—the *New Zealand Gazette and Britannia Spectator*—was published in 1840 at the beginning of the first major wave of immigration from Britain. It was not alone for long. By the 1860s newspapers were being established at the rate of nine a year, although many quickly went out of business in a society often marked by bitter parochialism and a rough-and-ready frontier temperament. These were days when editors had to fear not only bankruptcy but horsewhippings and social ostracism as well.

The circulation of news was greatly facilitated by the founding of the New Zealand Press Association in 1880, and by 1911 there were 193 publications that could be described as newspapers serving a population of 1,058,000.

Through most of its history, the New Zealand press has been in the British tradition and its standards of excellence have tended to be set by British journalism. Although bonds with Britain are now weakening, New Zealand and British journalists usually find it easy enough to work in each others' countries.

New Zealand papers do not, on the whole, take up positions on religious or ethnic matters except to preach a general tolerance. New Zealand governments tend to be interventionist, and the larger papers normally lean towards the National party, which intervenes under the banner of free enterprise, rather than the Labor party, which manages things in the name of socialism. Journalism is not hidebound or party-based, however, and editors usually attempt to give both sides a fair hearing.

The seven metropolitan papers and the leading provincial dailies are broadsheets. Apart from *The Dominion*, which is usually smaller, the number of pages in a metropolitan can vary from 24 on a Monday to 48 or more on a Saturday. *Truth* and the two Sunday papers are tabloids with an average size of roughly 48 pages. Weeklies and giveaways are frequently tabloid.

Twenty-two of the 44 dailies with ABC-audited circulations are evening newspapers. Between 1970 and 1979 the circulation of these 22 papers fell from 525,301 to 506,850, a drop of 18,451. This, however, was far exceeded by a fall of 33,804 in the circulation of the three metropolitan evenings: the *Auckland Star* lost 19,150, the *Evening Post* 8,854 and the *Christchurch Star* 5,800. Throughout the rest of the country evening newspapers generally maintained their position against the threat posed by television news bulletins, and "quality" morning papers prospered. The *New Zealand Herald* rose from 223,000 to 239,800, *The Press* from 68,500 to 76,000 and the *Otago Daily Times* from 41,000 to 44,916, while the *Timaru Herald,* the *Southland Times* and the *Daily News* all showed increases in circulation.

Sundays are normally a time for sport or other outdoor activities, which may explain why quality Sunday papers do not exist. Again, there is no tradition of Sunday deliveries and readers must buy their copies from corner shops. Whatever the reasons, Sunday papers are generally tabloid, resolutely popular and sprinkled with "girlie" pictures. The newspaper success of the 1970s was the rise of the *Sunday News,* from 90,001 in 1970 to 182,660 in 1979. Unlike some of its competitors, it has gusto.

In the same genre are Saturday sports papers, which continue to sell on Sunday. They include Auckland's *8 O'Clock,* with a circulation of about 100,000, and Christchurch's *Weekend Star,* selling about 36,000 copies.

Magazine sections are common in the larger daily papers, the most popular day for them being Saturday. Many papers carry special arts and entertainment pages on that day, and advertising supplements are frequent. Some papers are also trying to build up Wednesday as the day for midweek magazines, the theory being that people who buy for the magazine section twice a week are likely to become regular readers.

There is no foreign language press.

No consideration of the New Zealand media would be complete without mentioning the 400 or so magazines and newsletters. Foremost among these must be *The Listener,* with a circulation of more than 320,000. The country's largest-selling publication is owned by the Broadcasting Corporation of New Zealand and has a monopoly on the right to publish full details of radio and television programs more than 24 hours ahead of their screening times. However, *The Listener* is far more than a program guide; it contains some of the best New Zealand writing on current affairs and politics, and a full range of cultural criticism. *Listener* leading articles and contributors have often been strongly critical of government policy, while politicians and other newspapers have frequently criticized the monopoly over advance information.

Other influential magazines include the New Zealand *Woman's Weekly* (220,000), the *National Business Review* and a wide range of business and farming publications. New Zealand is a country where community and professional affairs are still vigorous—evident in the magazines available, from the *Pharmacy Digest* to the *New Zealand Electronics Review* and the *Taranaki Federated Farmers Journal.*

Since the number of potential readers in New Zealand is usually severely limited, press media must be attractive to a wide spectrum of people. Although evening papers tend to be rather "brighter" than mornings, most New Zealand dailies are middle-of-the-road productions, read by people from a variety of backgrounds and with varying degrees of intelligence. If New Zealand papers fall short of British standards, if they lack the authority of the expertise of *The Times* and *The Guardian,* they provide a far more comprehensive information service than the *Daily Express* or *The Sun.* Dailies often try to avoid taking sides on the issues that are splitting their communities, believing it to be their business to present both points of view. Some weeklies—like *Truth* and the *Sunday News*—are discernibly more popular and make free use of editorial opinions. In general, however, stories tend to be straightforward, factual, slightly superficial, nonpartisan pieces of news reporting.

Almost every township in New Zealand has a newspaper of one sort or another, while major cities usually possess two dailies plus a string of giveaways concentrating on the local news. Competition is the norm in the larger cities. In both Auckland and Christchurch the evening and morning papers are owned by different companies, while in Dunedin the *Otago Daily Times* was challenged briefly by *The Star* of Christchurch, which attempted to fill the vacuum caused by the death of the city's traditional evening paper. Both Wellington daily papers are owned by the same company; one of them, *The Dominion,* is among the most criticized papers in the country.

Another area of strong competition is Hawke's Bay, on the east coast of the North Island, where the continuing battle between the *Napier Daily Telegraph* and the *Hawke's Bay Herald-Tribune* reflects the rivalry of the neighboring towns of Napier and Hastings.

Since most daily circulations tend to be confined to the area in which a newspaper is printed, it is difficult to select the most influential papers. With the possible exception of *The Dominion,* all the seven daily papers in the list above carry considerable influence in the areas they serve. Thus, a government dealing with a Dunedin problem would normally be far more concerned about the opinions of the *Otago Daily Times* than those of the much larger *New Zealand Herald.*

On national matters, many people would regard the *Herald* as probably the country's most influential paper, while the *Evening Post, The Press* and *The Star* might compete for the other two places. This omits *Truth,* however, a weekly that influences by muckraking and by breaking many news stories, and *The Listener,* the country's largest-selling periodical. (The last is not shown above because of its quasi-official status.)

Economic Framework

In recent years, New Zealand has had to face a loss of traditional markets following Britain's entry into the European Economic Community—and also because of recently adopted agricultural protectionism in many other developed countries. The results of rising unemployment, an inflation rate of 16 to

Number of Newspapers by Circulation Groups (ABC audited only)	
Below 10,000	22
10,000 to 25,000	12
25,000 to 50,000	5
50,000 to 100,000	4
100,000 to 500,000	5

10 Largest Newspapers (including weeklies) by Circulation

Newspaper	Circulation	
New Zealand Herald	239,800	Conservative Auckland morning daily; arguably the country's most influential newspaper.
Sunday News	182,660	Bright and breathless Sunday tabloid.
NZ Truth	153,592	Despite campaigns, pin-ups, exposés and sex, falling sales of this weekly suggest the mixture has lost its magic.
Auckland Star	118,850	Evening paper often thought weak on news, but one of New Zealand's pioneers in investigative reporting.
Sunday Times	105,034	Slightly more "respectable" tabloid than the *Sunday News*, but many journalists would argue it lacks the *News*'s flair.
Evening Post	90,909	Wellington's main paper.
The Press	76,000	Largest paper in the South Island. This Christchurch morning may look old-fashioned, but it continues to sell well and its foreign news is excellent.
The Star	62,700	Christchurch evening, with a reputation for saying what it thinks.
The Dominion	60,174	Wellington's much-criticized morning paper, now aiming, with some success, at a more popular image.
Otago Daily Times	44,916	Rather old-fashioned morning daily, strongly identified with the readers and city of Dunedin.

18 percent and a far from buoyant economy have certainly been noticed by newspaper companies, but many nevertheless continue to do reasonably well.

Those dailies facing no local competition have generally been able to withstand the chillier economic climate, while morning newspapers in the main cities have enjoyed circulation growth and increasing advertising. The problem has been with the three main city evening papers, which all have suffered from lower circulation and static or declining advertising volume.

Publishers suggest various reasons for the evening-paper losses: (1) morning publication gives more opportunity and time for extended circulation; (2) evenings face more competition from TV and radio in news and entertainment—also in advertising to a degree; (3) increased competition for evening leisure time (TV, pub entertainment, night racing, etc.) is a curb on evening papers; (4) morning-tea breaks are now mandatory in all offices and factories, and provide a good opportunity for morning papers to be read; (5) the difficulties of distributing evening newspapers in congested city streets at peak traffic hours; (6) heavy local retail display advertising in evening newspapers makes attractive news layout more difficult than for morning papers, with their heavier and compact classifieds at the back of the paper.

About 70 percent of the 1 million papers sold in New Zealand every day are accounted for by the sales of the seven metropolitan papers. During 1979 Wilson and Horton Ltd. (publishers of the *New Zealand Herald*) lifted profits by 66.46 percent to a new record of NZ$4.6 million (US$4.14 million) tax paid, while *The Christchurch Press* increased its profit by 60.7 percent to NZ$609,420 (US$548,478). The profits of the diversified New Zealand News Ltd. group (publishers of the evening papers *The Auckland Star* and the *Christchurch Star* as well as two smaller provincial papers and a number of magazines and community papers) declined 5 percent to NZ$2.85 million (US$2,565,000). Independent Newspapers Ltd. of Wellington (publishers of *The Dominion*, the *Evening Post*, the *Sunday News*, the *Sunday Times*, *The Waikato Times* and *Truth*) enjoyed a 27-percent profit rise to NZ$1.9 million (US$1.71 million) after a particularly bad year in 1978.

When considering profits, however, it may be significant that while the three principal morning newspapers have yet to invest in new technology and a new form of printing, the main evening papers have already made the expensive change.

New Zealand daily papers lost only .56 percent of sales between 1970 and 1979, a figure that underlines the strength of newspapers in this country. And since 1970 the growth of community newspapers has greatly improved the coverage of grass-roots affairs in many areas.

So far as advertising is concerned, newspapers appear to be more than holding their own against state-owned television and radio, as well as the private radio stations (in which papers are not permitted to hold more than 30 percent of the capital). The Newspaper Publishers Association attributes much of this success to the effectiveness of the cooperative Newspaper Advertising Bureau, which has countered television and radio advertising with research and presentations to advertisers.

New Zealand newspapers are generally owned by private companies. In country areas, companies may sometimes be controlled by families or even individuals, but the "proprietor" is no longer a significant force in New Zealand journalism. Neither the government nor the political parties own newspapers or have shares in them. While the government is empowered to examine any monopolies which may be against the public interest, this power has not so far been invoked in the case of the media.

The two main owner-publisher groups are Independent Newspapers Ltd. (*The Dominion*, the *Evening Post, The Waikato Times, Truth*, the *Sunday News* and the *Sunday Times*) and New Zealand News Ltd. (*Auckland Star, The Star of Christchurch*, the *Daily News*, the *Taranaki Herald* and community newspapers in Auckland and Christchurch). But, as the *New Zealand Herald, The Press* and many others have shown, it is quite possible for a paper to prosper on its own. Competition can be lively in the main centers, but distribution problems are such that papers in country towns normally find it possible to fend off the big-city competition.

About 312,000 metric tons of newsprint are manufactured in New Zealand every year. That not used locally is exported. Newsprint is usually bought under contract, and average cost to newspapers under long term contract is currently NZ$403 (US$363) per metric ton to the nearest main port.

Since New Zealand newspapers are not, on the whole, highly partisan, there is usually not a great deal of editorial policy for lobbyists to influence.

The country has many special interest lobbies, but it would be hard to find evidence that any of them had achieved any special powers of influence over the press. In recent years, for instance, New Zealand's most persistent and hard-fought debate has been about abortion, and the pro-abortion lobby has been counterbalanced by the equally fervent Society for the Protection of the Unborn

Child. However, the two bodies have more or less canceled one another out; some editors have even been known to measure the amount of space being given to them both with a ruler.

Occasionally, however, a barefaced commercial "puff" will appear in one of the smaller papers, and the journalists' unions have sometimes complained about the lack of labeling for advertising features in some of the larger dailies. But on the whole it is understood by both sides that advertising matters are kept out of the editorial offices. Although figures vary, a typical ad ratio might be 40 percent editorial, 60 percent advertisements.

Employment in the newspaper industry is estimated at 16,850, broken down as follows: journalists, 1300; production, 2250; circulation, 11,200 (including about 10,900 children and other part-time delivery workers); maintenance, 200; management/sales, 1,900.

The major unions are:
New Zealand (except Northern) Journalists Union
Northern Journalists Union
New Zealand Printing and Related Trades Union
New Zealand Photoengravers Union
New Zealand Sales Advertising Representatives Guild
New Zealand Clerical Workers Union

The country's first major journalists' strike took place in 1976, when members of the Wellington-based New Zealand (except Northern) Journalists' Union struck for 48 hours over an arbitration award. NZPA staff walked out for 48 hours in the following year, while 1978 saw a NZJU strike over a pay claim and a strike involving all INL group publications in August, after the group had announced a 10 percent staff cut. In October the union held a 12-day strike over back pay.

Labor relations have been happier since 1978, partly because of the agreements then reached, and partly because of dissensions within the union. Some members have argued that the less militant Northern Journalists Union had achieved comparable results with far less upset.

In general, industrial relations are reasonably good within newspapers and this may be shown by the fact that the changeover to offset, Di Litho, or plastic plate printing has been going on without major upheavals. Certainly a part of the price for this has been that journalists generally do not type into computer terminals yet, but new technology is being widely installed and the transition has been relatively painless.

In mid-1980, a journalist's average pay rate was about NZ$217 (US$213) a week.

The two journalists' unions have tended to support any measures that would tend to promote press freedom and easier access to information. "Reporter Power," however, arrived late in New Zealand, and does not yet seem to have gathered significant support.

Almost all daily newspapers cost 15 cents a copy, but a rise to 20 cents is being widely forecast.

The first daily to be printed offset was the *Nelson Evening Mail,* in 1963, followed by the *Rotorua Post* and *Northern Advocate* a few years later. Today all provincial papers are printed offset, Di Litho, or by plastic plates with front-end computerized typesetting to various degrees of sophistication. By mid-1980 four of the metropolitans were equipped with advanced computerized typesetting systems, which were not being fully exploited owing to restrictions placed by journalists and printers on input. Two were printed by Di Litho and two by NAPP plastic plates. The remaining three morning metropolitans were printed by conventional stereo plates, with limited, but increasing, use of computer typesetting. Publishers claim the printed quality of New Zealand papers is "in advance of Britain and at least on a par with the USA." The country's press is up with world technology in most other aspects, except perhaps in the use of computers in advertising accounting. As yet, however, there is no satellite news transmission.

Press Laws

New Zealand has no written constitution, and there are few special privileges or guarantees for the media. The right of the journalist or the newspaper to seek information is based on the right of all individuals or businesses to do the same thing. New Zealand post offices still display the telephone numbers of government ministers, and their chief aides, so that members of the public may call them if they wish.

Any newspaper "containing public news or observations thereon which is printed for sale or distribution and is published in New Zealand periodically at intervals not exceeding forty days" must be registered under the Newspapers and Printers Act (1955). To register, the publisher must merely complete an affidavit stating the paper's name, its place of publication, and names of the publisher, printer and editor. The affidavit is lodged with the registrar of the nearest High Court. Under the same act, all books, pamphlets, magazines or periodicals must bear the printer's name and business address.

Bonds are not posted by New Zealand journalists or newspaper owners. The media are nevertheless much concerned with legal problems, not a few arising from the paucity of privileges enjoyed by the journalist.

As in England, a defamatory statement may broadly be described as anything "which may tend to lower the plaintiff in the estimation of right-thinking members of society generally," or "a publication without justification which is calculated to injure the reputation of another by exposing him to hatred, contempt and ridicule." Since it is no secure defense to argue that the defamation was accidental—or even that one had never heard of the person defamed and did not know that he or she existed—there are endless ways in which a careless or unlucky newspaper can defame someone.

The problems may be even worse than in Britain. The New Zealander lives in a smaller and less sophisticated society, and one in which it is difficult to escape one's own reputation. This may explain why New Zealanders seem even readier than the British to take action when they believe themselves to have been defamed. Since awards of NZ$15,000 (US$13,500) can be made—and legal costs must be added to the newspaper's bill—the law of defamation constitutes a major hazard.

Two frequent defenses are that the passage in question was a fair comment on a matter of public importance, or that it was justified because it was true. In either case, it is normally necessary to prove the absolute truth of any factual statements made by the media. Although a growing number of editors are prepared to dig deeper in order to support a defense of justification, many newspapers lack both the money and the staff numbers to allow them to undertake anything resembling investigative journalism.

In December 1978 a government committee on defamation recommended that the balance between reputation and freedom of speech in New Zealand required some adjustment in favor of freedom of speech. The committee suggested that the news media should enjoy qualified privilege where a publisher had acted with reasonable care, and had given the persons defamed an opportunity to explain or contradict the offending passage. The government delayed taking any action on the report.

While courts are traditionally open and fully reportable to the public, there are exceptions to the rule. It is usually illegal to publish accounts of proceedings in the Children's and Young Persons' Court, and other restrictions hedge the reporting of matrimonial cases. More difficult to forecast, for the journalist, are suppression orders made under section 46 of the Criminal Justice Act (1954). They prohibit "any report relating to any proceedings in respect of any offence, of the name of the person accused or convicted of the offence, or the name of any other person connected with the proceedings." Not only may names not be given, but it is also unlawful to publish "any name of particulars likely to lead to his identification" once the court has made a suppression order.

This can raise more problems because courts have tended to assume that some members of the public read widely and watch television. A story that would identify an individual if read in conjunction with a different story on another page in the paper—or even an item in a rival paper or on a television news bulletin—could be held to be an infringement of the act. The position is the more difficult because suppression orders can be retroactive—especially inconvenient with material that the newspaper may already have set up in type.

Although reasoned criticisms of courts and judicial decisions may be published, it is in contempt of court to publish "disrespectful" statements about a court, a judge or the judicial system. It is also in contempt to publish anything that could interfere with the course of justice once a case is due to be tried. The *sub judice* rule covers both comment and fact—printing details of the circumstances in which a crime was committed can be construed as contempt. Pictures may be in contempt, and special care has to be taken with pictures of accused people where there is the slightest possibility that a trial might involve problems of identity.

If the law on publishing *sub judice* material is stringent, in practice it is rarely invoked. In recent years newspapers have emerged unscathed after referring to a man charged with an offense as a "Mr. Big" of the drug world before his trial, or publishing pictures of accused men—which might cer-

tainly have affected police lineups. Editors who obey the law have complained that rivals who do not have escaped unpunished. The present situation is widely seen as being both confusing and unsatisfactory.

In New Zealand it is not an offense to "express in good faith and in decent language, or to attempt to establish by arguments used in good faith and conveyed in decent language, any opinion whatever on any religious subject" (Crimes Act of 1961). Should the language be calculated to provoke or outrage religious feelings, a prosecution for blasphemous libel could follow. There has only been one reported case, however, and that was in 1922.

Under section 2 of the Indecent Publications Act (1963), the word "indecent" includes "describing, depicting, expressing, or otherwise dealing with matters of sex, horror, crime, cruelty, or violence in a manner that is injurious to the public good." The act set up an Indecent Publications Tribunal of five people, who would establish whether books or sound recordings submitted to them were of an indecent nature. Since the tribunal's jurisdiction does not extend to any publication published at intervals of less than a month, most magazines and all daily or weekly papers are excluded. The courts would determine whether a newspaper was guilty of indecency, but they would have to use the same criteria as the tribunal. Among the factors that must be taken into consideration are: the dominant effect of the publication as a whole, its literacy or artistic merit, whether any person is likely to be corrupted by reading it, and whether it displays an honest purpose or contains camouflage designed to render the indecent parts acceptable.

The Official Secrets Act (1951) prohibits people who are or have been in government service from passing on information acquired as a result of that service. In his book *News Media Law in New Zealand*, Professor J.F. Burrows states, "A strong argument could be advanced that this section was only intended to apply to information which could legitimately be described in lay terms as a 'state secret.'" This has not been the view of successive governments.

Although governments have normally been reluctant to prosecute under the act, it can be a major hindrance to journalists in search of information. According to the *National Business Review,* the act was once invoked to prevent a journalist discovering the number of potted plants in offices being tended by government gardeners in Wellington. It is an offense for a journalist to incite another person to infringe on the act, or to receive information communicated in contravention of it, unless he can show that this communication was "contrary to his desire." In 1978 the government set up the Danks Committee to consider the whole business of government information and official secrets.

There is no consistent or coherent body of law protecting individual privacy as such, although the subject is touched on in many sections of the law. Privacy is very much a consideration in the law covering public nuisance, trespass and electronic eavesdropping, for instance, but often there is no clear guideline for the journalist to follow. Thus the law on recording telephone conversations is remarkably confusing, and journalists disagree about its interpretation.

Censorship

There is no censorship; the New Zealand Press Council is a voluntary body modeled on the British pattern. The council was established in 1972 "to consider and adjudicate on complaints about the conduct of the Press or the conduct of persons and organisations towards the Press." A complaint can be submitted to the council only after the editor of the newspaper concerned has been given a chance to deal with it. The council may pursue its own investigation, which will normally end with the issue of a statement to the press. It is customary for these adjudications to be published widely, and newspapers criticized by the council usually publish its findings without comment.

The council received 50 complaints in 1979. Of these, six were upheld, two partially upheld, 13 not upheld and 13 withdrawn or lapsed. Jurisdiction was declined in three cases, and four were still awaiting decision at the end of the year. A similar body, the Broadcasting Tribunal, considers complaints concerning radio and television.

New Zealand has no freedom of information acts. However, in February 1981 the Danks Committee report recommended an Official Information Act and called for a "progressive increase in the availability of information," suggesting that "the principle would be that information should be available unless there is good reason for withholding it." The report further argued that an independent Information Authority should

be set up to act as the instrument for a progressive enlargement of the area of information that is to be publicly available, and called for a repeal of the Official Secrets Act. It added: "The conclusion emerges that it is no longer acceptable to set out a sweeping rationale for the protection of official information or to expect that the public will accept in the future that certain areas of government business are inviolate simply because government says so."

The Prime Minister announced that the government would consider introducing legislation based on the report.

State-Press Relations

The government's Information and Publicity Services Division is a part of the Tourist and Publicity Department. As the government's central communications agency, it is active in most important spheres of official publicity and information work. It conveys information on policies or programs either directly to the public or through the news media. The heart of the division are the press officers, organized into operational groups, who provide public relations and publicity and information services for ministers, government departments and other official agencies.

Some government departments also look after much of their own publicity. The Ministry of Agriculture and Fisheries has an elaborate and effective information department for the dissemination of news on farming. The Department of Scientific and Industrial Research is concerned with circulating technical or research data throughout the country.

Governments and politicians are frequently criticised by all the media, including "editorial" comments in programs transmitted by the state-owned Broadcasting Corporation of New Zealand. The limits are those set by the law of defamation: while it is normally permissible to question a politician's competence, an attack upon his honesty or integrity by the media would have to be very carefully considered and backed by hard evidence. In return, individual journalists, interviewers or editors are sometimes attacked by politicians in the House of Representatives or elsewhere.

In May 1980, for instance, the prime minister, Robert Muldoon, took strong exception to a series in *The Dominion* about plans to build plants in Taranaki to convert natural gas into petrol. *The Dominion* published several "replies" from Muldoon, but excised two paragraphs from one of them, which were critical of *The Dominion* staff. Muldoon replied by banning *The Dominion* staff from his daily press conferences until the paragraphs were published. Although some parliamentary journalists threatened a boycott, editors disagreed over what to do. On the one hand, editorial independence seemed to be under threat; on the other, some editors strongly felt the *Dominion* series had been irresponsible and the prime minister's criticisms were broadly justified. *The Dominion* finally published the two paragraphs after receiving an assurance that its staff would be allowed back into the prime minister's press conferences.

In August 1980 Muldoon visited a regional Commonwealth heads of state conference at New Delhi, before beginning a tour of China. The editor of *The Listener* asked that Tom Scott, a political writer and cartoonist, be permitted to accompany the official party. Not only was permission refused, but Muldoon wrote to the Commonwealth secretariat asking that Scott should not be accredited to the conference.

Scott is a light-hearted, if erratic writer, with an eye for the ridiculous. Muldoon and some of his senior colleagues had no particular reason to love him, and in July 1979 *The Listener* paid Muldoon NZ$12,000 (US $10,800) after he had been defamed in a Scott article. In statements explaining his decision to ban Scott from the conference and the party, Muldoon claimed it was "inappropriate" for a writer of his type to report a sensitive Commonwealth conference, and that he felt incidents after a late-night party in Scott's room during a National party conference made him an unsuitable person to tour China.

In the event the Commonwealth secretariat showed no inclination to have Scott banned and the Indian government accredited him to the conference without demur. The Parliamentary Press Gallery and the Commonwealth Press Union were among the bodies joining in the protests against the prime minister. Scott did not go on the China tour, but the incident was certainly not a happy one for Muldoon. The spectacle of a prime minister apparently obsessed with the case of one basically lightweight journalist, while the country faced all sorts of deep economic and social problems, was not well received by the public, and it may be that the Scott case cost Muldoon significant votes when the National party surprisingly lost the "safe" seat of East Coast Bays in a by-election a few weeks after the affair broke.

Governments do attempt to influence the ways in which news is presented, but there is no evidence to suggest that they are particularly successful. Thus, lobby journalists attending prime ministerial press conferences are usually respectful, and their questions frequently do not probe very deeply. Once the news item or announcement has traveled outside the Parliament buildings, however, it may be subjected to a barrage of hostile criticism. Governments have been accused of trying to hide material unfavorable to them by announcing it on busy news days when, hopefully, it will be overshadowed by other items. Or, it is suggested, they spread, in advance, the idea that the news is likely to be even worse, so that reality, when it arrives, turns out to be something of a relief. Yet, it may be that if bad news sometimes fails to make an impact it is more because the media—with smaller staffs and shortages of informed specialists—have failed to push through the necessary follow-ups than because of any manipulation by the government.

New Zealand is a small country, in which almost everybody reads a newspaper and watches television news bulletins. Under such conditions, the media, politicians and public opinion are closely entwined. When drawing up his policies, the New Zealand politician considers likely media reaction and adjusts things accordingly, in the same way that a farmer views the morning weather. Indeed, the Muldoon government was at one time accused of being more concerned with headlines, in the short run, than with long-term government policies. The media and the politicians influence each other constantly.

No newspapers have been suspended in recent years, and no journalists imprisoned. Any attempt to control the media through economic sanctions or licensing would certainly arouse a massive protest. Imports of printing and newspaper equipment, and of newsprint, are exempt from import licensing. Major government advertising is normally carried out by the Information and Publicity Services Division, which is not thought of as a political body.

Attitude Toward Foreign Media

Accreditation for foreign correspondents is sometimes required for media groups accompanying VIP visitors to New Zealand. This may happen in cases where it is necessary to limit attendance at functions (say, during a Royal visit) or where security may pose problems (such as a tour by a visiting head of state). In all cases, accreditation is a simple procedure, requiring only the journalist's full name, date and country of birth, and a passport-size black and white photograph. If a visa is required for New Zealand, then the correspondent must have that visa even when accompanying a visiting head of state. Foreign correspondents resident in New Zealand may also require accreditation to some government departments, such as defense and police. All applications are considered on an individual basis.

Visitors are not permitted to take notes during debates in the House of Representatives, and accreditation to the Parliamentary Press Gallery is determined by the Speaker. Foreign correspondents are not restricted in any way so far as the material they transmit from New Zealand is concerned.

In January 1980 Dr. Sergei Zimin, correspondent of the USSR's Novosti news agency, was expelled from the country after the prime minister described him as "of no value to New Zealand." The expulsion was part of a complex quarrel, during which each country requested the removal of the other's ambassador. The decision was taken in cabinet. A foreign affairs spokesman said it was not a "journalistic" decision, but part of the New Zealand protest against the Russian invasion of Afghanistan.

As of July 1, 1980 no license is required for the importation of foreign newspapers and periodicals, but they must, of course, conform to the law on obscenity.

Under the News Media Ownership Act 1965, newspapers and broadcasting stations may not be owned by overseas companies or individuals. The act applies to "any paper containing principally or exclusively news of general public interest, or observations thereon, which is printed for sale and is published in New Zealand periodically at intervals not exceeding eight days." In companies set up to operate newspapers or broadcasting stations, 80 percent of the voting power must be in the hands of New Zealand residents, and no one domiciled outside the country should be able to control more than 15 percent of the votes. Nor can anyone domiciled outside New Zealand be empowered to require or prohibit the publication of any item or comment. Proxy votes and sales of shares are subject to inspection under the act.

The act does not apply to any newspaper in which even as much as nine-tenths of the news content is merely a copy of an overseas publication (local editions of *Time* or *Newsweek,* for example), or to papers with an average circulation of not more than 5,000, or to any paper in which news and comment is mainly "of a purely religious, scientific, technical, scholastic, commercial, business, farming, health, or sporting nature."

The New Zealand media are not normally susceptible to foreign propaganda, and obviously slanted opinions from abroad will usually be met by hostile comment, if indeed they ever see print. However, a considerable controversy was caused in July 1980 by the decision of the Board of the New Zealand Broadcasting Corporation not to show the television film "Death of a Princess." The Saudi Arabian government had threatened financial sanctions against countries showing the film. New Zealand, urgently trying to find alternative markets to offset the partial loss of traditional sales of meat and dairy produce to Britain, was using Saudi Arabian oil, and some journalists had claimed it was also raising loans in Saudi Arabia. Prime Minister Muldoon asked the corporation not to show the film. It was asserted that the board's decision not to show "Death of a Princess" was partly because overseas reactions had suggested the film's authenticity to be extremely doubtful, and partly out of a desire not to offend New Zealand's Muslim population. The decision was widely criticized.

Anyone discussing the question of foreign propaganda at length would also have to consider the matter of South African government involvement in the campaign for increased sporting ties between South Africa and New Zealand, particularly in rugby football. South African officials in New Zealand have proved themselves assiduous writers of letters to newspapers, and supporters of sporting links have found themselves being offered trips to South Africa. It might nevertheless be possible to argue that much of this effort has been counterproductive.

Although the papers may carry more international news than most of their American or British counterparts, New Zealanders often feel themselves to be a long way from many parts of the world. Several international press organizations have New Zealand members, but the Commonwealth Press Union must take pride of place. Many editors belong to the union, which makes it possible for them to take part in wide-ranging Commonwealth discussions on new techniques, ethics and such matters as the freedom of the press. For many New Zealanders the outside world consists mainly of Australia, Britain, the United States and Western Europe, with countries like Iran or Afghanistan making sudden forays into the headlines from time to time. Africa, for instance, is certainly not well reported in the country, but neither is there much evidence that New Zealanders are eager to read about African politics.

New Zealand supported the UNESCO Declaration, although its delegation commented: "We could not have accepted, and still cannot accept, that in principle, far less in practice, the State should have the capacity to direct, determine or influence in any way the activities of the media, or that the state should be able to decide what information should be published by the media or in what manner that information should be presented. Our interpretation of this declaration must take full account of these principles."

News Agencies

The New Zealand Press Association is a "co-operative, independent, non-profitmaking, news gathering organisation," which celebrated its centenary in 1980. It is at the heart of New Zealand newsgathering. Although NZPA has its own staff in Wellington, most copy is written by reporters working for the 34 subscribing newspapers that take the service. Copy from newspapers flows into the computers in the association's Wellington headquarters, where it is edited before being circulated throughout the country. It has been estimated that the network now carries something like 20 million words a year.

NZPA has staffmen in London, Washington and Australia, but most foreign news enters the country as a result of NZPA agreements with the Australian Associated Press and Reuters. NZPA now supplies world news to local radio and television news services, besides providing Reuters Economic Services, by teleprinter, to banks, stockbrokers and other commercial firms.

The NZPA service is cheap, comprehensive and reasonably efficient. Without it, many of the prosperous country-town dailies might find it hard to stay in business. If foreign news tends to be biased in favor of stories originating in Britain and the United States, no doubt that is in line with the interests of most New Zealand readers.

The system nevertheless has its defects. A mistake in an NZPA report from the provinces is likely to be published by all 34 subscribers, which can invest the association with an almost biblical authority. The domination of home news coverage by NZPA can also lead to complacency by reporters, who find they are not obliged to face direct competition from other newspapermen on important stories. Since only one association reporter may represent the nation's newspapers on quite large stories, if he or she does not ask all the necessary questions, then nobody may ask them. Often the only competitors in sight may be from radio or television, and their requirements can, of course, be rather different. But despite such flaws, the organization works with a good deal of success most of the time.

Electronic News Media

Both television channels and 50 of the country's 59 radio stations are controlled by the government-appointed Broadcasting Corporation of New Zealand. The Broadcasting Act (1976) also established the New Zealand Broadcasting Tribunal as the body with the authority to issue warrants for the operation of radio and television stations and to hear complaints about public broadcasting stations.

The corporation and the tribunal are required to report annually to the minister of broadcasting, who lays their reports before Parliament. The act also requires both bodies to "have regard to the general policy of the government in relation to broadcasting" and to comply with any directions given in writing by the minister pursuant to this policy. But the act specifically denies authorization for the minister to give directions concerning a particular program or complaint.

In practice, this means that news and comment on radio and television are free. There is no difficulty in voicing anti-government ideas or opinions, so long as these can be considered fair comment or are replied to by somebody taking an opposing point of view.

In the late 1970s, indeed, it was sometimes argued that television current-affairs commentators were criticizing the government more effectively than the official Opposition. Matters came to a head in September 1977, when a special committee was set up to inquire into a "Dateline Monday" program on the government's security service. The program was judged to have been unfair. Since then tempers have lowered on both sides, and television current-affairs programs have arguably become better balanced and more professional.

Education & Training

Entrants to journalism have usually been trained in one of three centers. The Auckland Technical Institute offers two 18-week courses in news reporting a year for 24 students a course. The Wellington Polytechnic offers a one-year course in basic journalism and publishing, for between 60 and 70 students. The University of Canterbury provides a one-year diploma course for 18 to 20 graduates. Other entrants to the profession may begin by joining a newspaper, where their training will normally be overseen by a senior member of staff serving as "office tutor" under the auspices of the New Zealand Journalists' Training Board. The Board also provides short courses for more experienced professionals. More than 700 journalists have so far taken the five-part videotape course on media law produced by staff members of the University of Canterbury and South Pacific Television.

The Qantas Press Awards cover journalism, press photography and cartoons published during each calendar year. Winners in both senior and junior divisions receive overseas trips as prizes.

Major journalistic organizations include:

The Broadcasting Corporation of New Zealand, P.O. Box 98, Wellington

New Zealand Community Newspapers Association inc., P.O. Box 183, Putaruru

Independent Broadcasters Association (New Zealand) Inc., P.O. Box 2632, Wellington

Newspaper Advertising Bureau, P.O. Box 6569, Auckland

Newspaper Publishers Association of New Zealand (Inc), P.O. Box 1066, Wellington

New Zealand Press Association Ltd., P.O. Box 1599, Wellington

Summary

While they can be accused of being superficial or over-respectful toward authority, New Zealand newspapers are generally of a far higher quality than might be expected in a country of 3 million people tucked away in a remote corner of the Pacific Ocean. Despite the challenges from television and radio, papers have usually prospered in recent years, and the growth of the community press in the last decade has done much to improve the reporting and discussion of local affairs.

In a country where so many publications exist on a shoestring, the danger of superficiality is always present. At least there is now evidence that increasing numbers of journalists in all the media are beginning to look beneath the surface, and sound investigative inquiries are being carried out.

If the New Zealand editor sometimes seems to lack the confidence of his British or American counterpart, there are good historical reasons for it. Britain's entry into the European Economic Community and virtual withdrawal from the Pacific have left New Zealand with a sense of isolation, and the nation faces the task of working out ways to cope with this new situation. For the first time the country is very much on its own, and it lacks the high-quality publications of comment and analysis that do so much to form opinion in larger countries.

At the beginning of the 1980s, journalists would strongly disagree about New Zealand's rating on the scale of press freedom. As a result of the Muldoon government, there are those who have claimed the country is teetering on the edge of becoming a fascist state, or that the liberties of the journalist are being seriously threatened by the prime minister. The evidence, nevertheless, seems to show that where journalists have stood up for themselves—with the support of their colleagues—it has been the prime minister who has lost status and prestige. Indeed it might even be argued that his constant sniping at the media has done much to encourage a new spirit of vigor and independence among journalists.

The outlook for the 1980s must depend upon the general economic climate, and the prospects are no easier to predict in New Zealand than elsewhere. The nation nevertheless has abundant natural resources, and—given reasonable leadership—the prospects may be good. New Zealand, after all, has surpluses of food, scenery, and peace and quiet—all of which should continue to command a cash value in the years ahead.

The breadth of the Pacific confers no immunity from silicon chips or any other contemporary problem, but New Zealand newspapers seem to have a secure place in the community; their equipment is, on the whole, up to date, while their modern entrants into journalism tend to be intelligent and well trained. For journalists the problems may often continue to be boredom and lack of scope in a small country rather than job insecurity or repression. Critics will no doubt continue to blame local journalists because—on most days—the papers on sale in Matamata or Hokitika hardly rival *The Washington Post* or *The Times* of London. In fact, however, New Zealand newspapers compare reasonably well with the British provincial press, and with many of the smaller American papers.

Confidence may not be the appropriate mood for the 1980s, and there must be lean years ahead for New Zealand while the country introduces new technology to make it less dependent on imported oil. Nor is it yet possible to forecast what effect computer-based information systems will have on the media as a whole. The key to the situation may be that New Zealand journalists deal with an interested and literate public that is accustomed to reading newspapers and the advertising in them—and pretty well convinced that journalism should be both responsible and free. Whatever the problems of the future, New Zealand journalists possess in their readers a priceless asset that should help to see them through.

CHRONOLOGY

1976 New Zealand's first large-scale strike by journalists: the New Zealand Journalists' Union leads a 48-hour strike over arbitration award.

1977 Committee on Defamation suggests: "The balance between reputation and freedom of speech in New Zealand requires some adjustment in favour of free speech and a free press."

1978 NZPA introduces computerized messge-switching system. In outspoken series of editorials *Christchurch Star* suggests replacement of Prime Minister Muldoon. After strong reactions from members of the public and the National party, Editor Michael Forbes resigns on July 13. Agrees to withdraw resignation after meeting of *Star* staff and board of N.Z. News Ltd. NZJU strike over a pay claim begins a bad four months of labor relations. On August 12, Independent Newspapers Ltd. announcement of a 10 percent cut in staff numbers is followed by strike involving all the group's publications. On October 9, the union begins strike over back pay. *Auckland Star* series uncovers international "Mr. Asia" drug ring.

1979 *Evening Star,* Dunedin, ceases publication after 116 years.

1980 Novosti correspondent, Dr. Sergei Zimin, expelled during dispute over Afghanistan; Prime Minister describes him as "of no value to New Zealand." Prime Minister bans members of *The Dominion* staff from his press conferences unless paper prints two paragraphs excised from one of his statements. New Zealand Broadcasting Corporation agrees not to show television film "Death of a Princess" after government pressure. *Listener* columnist and cartoonist Tom Scott banned from prime ministeral party in China. Prime Minister Muldoon unsuccessfully attempts to prevent Scott's accreditation to Commonwealth regional conference in New Delhi.

BIBLIOGRAPHY

Burrows, J.F. *News Media Law in New Zealand.* Wellington, N.Z., 1974.

Miller, F. W. G. *Ink on My Fingers.* Wellington, N.Z., 1967.

Sanders, James. *Dateline—NZPA: The New Zealand Press Association 1880-1980.* Auckland, N.Z., 1979.

Scholefield, Guy H. *Newspapers in New Zealand.* Wellington, N.Z., 1958.

The Press 1861-1961. Christchurch, N.Z., 1963.

NICARAGUA

by John Spicer Nichols

BASIC DATA

Population: 2.5 million
Area: 139,083 sq. km. (53,700 sq. mi.)
GNP: 17 billion cordobas (US$1.7 billion) (1979)
Literacy Rate: 88% (gov't. est.)
Language(s): Spanish
Number of Dailies: 3
  Aggregate Circulation: NA
  Circulation per 1,000: NA
Number of Nondailies: NA
  Aggregate Circulation: NA
  Circulation per 1,000: NA

Number of Periodicals: NA
Number of Radio Stations: 33
Number of Television Stations: 2
Number of Radio Receivers: 500,000 (est.)
  Radio Receivers per 1,000: 250 (est.)
Number of Television Sets: 125,000 (est.)
  Television Sets per 1,000: 50 (est.)
Total Annual Newsprint Consumption: NA
  Per Capita Newsprint Consumption: NA
Total Newspaper Ad Receipts: NA
  As % of All Ad Expenditures: NA

Background & General Characteristics

In July 1979 the Sandinista guerrillas took control of the Nicaraguan government, replacing one of the longest-standing and most repugnant dictatorships in Latin America and ending a bloody revolutionary war in which the national and foreign press played an unusually large role. For more than 40 years, the Somoza family had ruled Nicaragua as its private plantation by maintaining complete control of the National Guard and a monopoly on the nation's economy. But the Somozas' failure to effectively suppress the Nicaraguan opposition press—primarily the newspaper *La Prensa*—and the hostile foreign press corps was an essential ingredient in the collapse of the family dynasty.

La Prensa and its martyred editor became international symbols of resistance against the dictatorship and are the prime example of the tradition of political advocacy in Nicaraguan journalism. Like all of the country's press, *La Prensa* was founded as a political tool of powerful combatants for national power. Rather than functioning as a news medium intended to carry balanced and dispassionate reporting of national affairs, *La Prensa* was an active participant in the revolution that overthrew the Somoza government.

As Nicaragua attempts to recover from the revolutionary war that claimed nearly 50,000 lives, left countless more wounded or homeless and destroyed most of the nation's productive capacity, the national media remain instruments of the dominant political forces and continue to have symbolic importance in the highly volatile revolutionary process. Although most of the Sandinista leaders running the Nicaraguan government are Marxists, they have espoused a philosophy of political pluralism and, probably more importantly, badly need the cooperation of the non-Marxist private sector in rebuilding the war-torn economy. The Sandinistas also

---

Research for this chapter was funded in part by the College of the Liberal Arts, Pennsylvania State University (Thomas F. Magner, associate dean for Research and Graduate Studies). The author also wishes to thank Professor R. Thomas Berner, Penn State, and Charles T. Salmon, University of Minnesota. Portions of this chapter were adapted from the author's contribution to Thomas W. Walker, ed., *Nicaragua in Revolution* (New York: Praeger, 1981).

need the cooperation of the Catholic Church, the most influential institution in Nicaraguan society. Loss of church approval would seriously drain the widespread popular support that the revolutionary government has enjoyed.

The government's treatment of the media, backed by the church and the private sector, has become a key barometer of the viability of the tense political alliance. For example, a Sandinista attempt to close or seriously repress *La Prensa*, which has been embarrassingly critical of the government and stridently supportive of the private sector, certainly would signal the end of Nicaragua's political pluralism and mixed economy. Without private investment, the government would be unable to satisfy the political and economic expectations of the public, and the future course of the revolution would be in serious doubt.

Nicaragua's first newspaper, *El Telégrafo Nicaragüense*, was founded in 1835 by the president of the country, Jose Zepeda, as a political forum for his government. In the following century and a half, most newspapers were also founded to further the cause of local dictators, special interest groups or, most often, Nicaragua's two major political parties—the Liberals and Conservatives. The major figure in the history of Nicaraguan journalism, Pedro Joaquín Chamorro Cardenal, was the epitome of this tradition of political advocacy. Chamorro, the product of more than a century of highly partisan Conservative party politics, was the descendant of one of the most prominent families in Nicaragua and a long line of important public figures including four Conservative presidents. In 1930 Chamorro's father bought the newspaper *La Prensa* as a voice of the Conservative platform and opposition to the Liberal party, controlled by the Somoza family. Chamorro became editor and publisher of *La Prensa* following his father's death in 1952.

However, long before Chamorro gained a worldwide reputation as a respected opposition journalist, he established a domestic record for political militancy. On numerous occasions, beginning when he was a university student in the 1940s, Chamorro was arrested, jailed or exiled on various charges of revolutionary activity—including leading a violent political demonstration, running guns, organizing an invasion force to overthrow the government and participating in the assassination of Anastasio Somoza García, the first of the Somozas to hold the presidential office. Chamorro denied any complicity in the assassination but readily admitted the other actions.

In the mid-1960s, Chamorro retired from overt revolutionary activity to concentrate on journalistic and political opposition to the Somoza family rule. At first, the Somozas responded to the journalistic opposition with long stretches of rigid censorship of *La Prensa* and other nongovernment media, but as the years advanced, the Somoza government used more sophisticated controls such as withholding official advertising, hoarding newsprint, levying heavy taxes, cutting off official news sources and bribing reporters. However, the most effective control was ownership of the media. By the time the Somoza dynasty fell in 1979, virtually all of the Nicaraguan media were owned either by the Somoza family, its cronies, the government or the National Guard. But despite Somoza's pressure, Chamorro continued to publish *La Prensa*.

The Somozas' attempts to silence Chamorro's lonely voice of opposition brought the attention of several international and regional media watchdog and human rights organizations, especially the Inter-American Press Association. Each time the Somozas would censor or otherwise repress Chamorro's criticism, the IAPA would file a protest. When the Somozas responded to the international pressure and lifted the censorship, Chamorro, strengthened by the international support, became even more acid in his criticism of the government and, consequently provoked the Somozas to take stronger action in repressing *La Prensa*.

By the 1970s, Chamorro had become a regional *cause célèbre*, and President Anastasio Somoza Debayle, heir to the family dynasty, was trapped in a hopelessly downward spiral. Each time he punished Chamorro for his antigovernment polemics, he also boosted Chamorro's international reputation and tarnished his own. Each action or inaction by Somoza inevitably required that he would have to take harsher action against Chamorro in the future. Chamorro won several major awards for his opposition, including the prestigious Maria Moors Cabot Award from Columbia University in the United States and the IAPA's Mergenthaler Award.

The beginning of the end for the Somoza dynasty came on December 23, 1972, when an earthquake destroyed Managua, the capital city, and killed nearly 10,000 people. The Somozas and their cronies, who had not been modest in their corruption prior to the earthquake, used the rebuilding effort to expand their personal wealth and increase their control of the Nicaraguan economy. The corruption was so blatant that U.S. political columnist Jack Anderson awarded Somoza the title "The Greediest Ruler in the World," and the Nicaraguan enterpreneural class, which had traditionally supported or at least not resisted the Somoza government, joined the opposition.

Simultaneous to the urban discontent with Somoza, the rural guerrilla army, Sandinista National Liberation Front (FSLN), stepped up its battle to overthrow the government. For decades, the Somoza family had been adept at preventing a coalition between the Marxist-dominated guerrillas and the more conservative business sector, but the Somoza family greed during the reconstruction and *La Prensa*'s increasingly sympathetic coverage of the guerrilla forces paved the way to a revolutionary alliance. Chamorro, who was highly regarded among the moderate opposition, editorially endorsed the formation of a broad coalition of opposition groups to bring down Somoza.

In January 1978 Chamorro was killed by assassins believed to be sympathetic to Somoza if not actually under the direction of Somoza or his lieutenants. Although the forces of opposition were already in progress, Chamorro's assassination, magnified by his national and international popularity, created a wave of protest that sparked the Nicaraguan revolution and brought an end to the Somoza dynasty.

After the assassination, *La Prensa* went far beyond journalistic opposition. Xavier Chamorro, Pedro Joaquin's brother and *La Prensa*'s new editor, turned the newspaper's offices into the headquarters for the anti-Somoza forces of both the political left and right. A general strike that followed Chamorro's assassination was coordinated from the newspaper's offices. Much of the staff clandestinely fought with or worked for the Sandinistas while continuing their reporting duties; two were to become top Sandinista commanders, while the assassinated editor's youngest son, Carlos Fernando, eventually became editor of the Sandinista newspaper *Barricada*. Recognizing that *La Prensa* had become a dangerous opposition force, the Somoza government could no longer cater to international opinion and allow the newspaper to continue publishing. In 1978 and 1979, as the guerrillas grew stronger and Somoza's National Guard lashed back, *La Prensa*'s reporters were arrested and beaten, its offices were the target of repeated machine-gun attacks, and finally the newspaper was bombed out of production in a coordinated attack by the guard's tanks, aircraft and ground forces.

The Sandinista victory in July 1979 brought many superficial changes and several substantive changes in the Nicaraguan press, but two things have remained the same. First, members of the Chamorro family still dominate the Nicaraguan newspaper business, and second, the press continues as a highly partisan political tool. Each of the three daily newspapers published in postwar Nicaragua is directed by a Chamorro. However, family dominance does not mean family unity. Each newspaper not only has a distinct editorial policy but an entirely different relationship with the new revolutionary government.

The most substantial changes took place at *La Prensa*, which returned to publication shortly after the Sandinista victory. The newspaper had the same name, was published in the same location, was still owned by the Chamorro family, was directed by the slain editor's long-time deputy, Pablo Antonio Cuadra, and his oldest son, Pedro Joaquin Chamorro V. But it was not the same newspaper that had earned a worldwide reputation. Following a Chamorro family feud that was a microcosm of the national political debate, most of the staff and top editors and some of the family members departed for competing newspapers. The new *La Prensa* became highly critical of the revolutionary government it helped to create, and supportive of the private-business sector that was rapidly losing national political clout to the Sandinistas, its former revolutionary allies. Despite the changes, however, *La Prensa* continues to be the nation's circulation leader and an international symbol, rightly or wrongly, of Nicaraguan nationalism and press freedom.

The majority of the old *La Prensa* technical and editorial staff left to found a cooperatively owned newspaper, *El Nuevo Diario*, that editorially supported the new revolutionary government. They were led by Xavier Chamorro, who had replaced his dead brother as editor of *La Prensa*, and Daniel Aguirre Solis, *La Prensa*'s former news editor and one of the country's most distinguished journalists. The mission of the new daily, according to Xavier Chamorro, is to support the revolution from outside the government. In the summer of 1980 *El Nuevo Diario* was staff rich but money poor, and running last in the battle for circulation and national symbolism.

The nation's third daily is *Barricada*, the official voice of the FSLN. Its first issue, which appeared only a few days after the Sandinista victory, was printed at the facilities of the former Somoza newspaper *Novedades*. It was originally staffed by inexperienced journalism students from the national university and an assortment of foreign Marxists, whose own revolutions had failed elsewhere in Latin America, and who were attracted to Nicaragua. As a result, the content of *Barricada* was dogmatic, stilted, frequently inaccurate, and bore a remarkable resemblance to *Granma*, the Cuban party newspaper. For example, *Barricada* published a photograph doctored to imply that Alfonso Robelo Callejas, president of a new Opposition party, National Democratic Movement, was friendly with Somoza. (Robelo, who was active in the anti-Somoza campaign, is the chief spokesman for the private-business sector and formerly was a member of the Junta of National Reconstruction until he resigned in 1980 in protest against the revolutionary government's swing to the left.)

The top Sandinista leadership privately expressed great dissatisfaction with *Barricada* because its doctrinaire line frequently embarrassed the FSLN and limited its flexibility in making new policy. In 1980, to make *Barricada* respectable, the Sandinistas moved Chamorro's youngest son, Carlos Fernando, from his position of deputy minister of culture in the revolutionary government to the editorship of the newspaper. The quality of the staff and the editorial content subsequently improved, but the shrill criticism of *La Prensa*, Robelo and others protesting the direction of the new government continued.

All three dailies have editorial offices in Managua but are distributed nationwide. Because of the war damage, only one modern press, belonging to the defunct newspaper *Centroamericana* in the city of Leon, was in operation; for a short time during the summer of 1980 all three newspapers were printed in the same plant, *La Prensa* reaching the streets in the early morning, *El Nuevo Diario* in the late morning and *Barri-cada* in the afternoon. (Later in 1980 *Barricada* moved the expropriated Somoza presses into its own new facilities in Managua.) As a result, the dailies have an identical format—10 to 12 standard-size pages. In addition to the physical appearance, some aspects of the three newspapers' content are similar. All carry heavy doses of copy from international news agencies, at least one page of national and international sports news, and lengthy features recounting the insurrection. But in other areas of content and tone, the newspapers differ greatly. *La Prensa* most closely resembles the standard Latin American newspaper. It has the greatest diversity of hard-news content but also carries the usual fare of crime, violence, social notes and soft-news items. The focal point of *La Prensa*, of course, is its editorials, many of which are highly literate, insightful and often critical of the government. *Barricada* makes no pretense to objectivity in its news columns and carries long descriptions of the activities and speeches of the Sandinista commanders, articles supporting new government programs, and the least amount of hard news. *El Nuevo Diario*, while somewhat more restrained in its support of the government, is closer in tone and content to *Barricada* than *La Prensa*.

Several nondaily newspapers and magazines sprouted up after the insurrection. All are published by various divisions of the revolutionary government, the FSLN or political groups allied with them. The weeklies are *El Brigadista*, *Poder Sandinista*, *Desde La Calle*, and *El Trabajador*, of which most influential are *Poder Sandinista*, a FSLN publication designed to explain Nicaragua's economic problems in basic terminology to the common man, and *El Trabajador*, a newspaper for the Nicaraguan worker published by the semiofficial labor party. In addition, the Nicaraguan Communist party publishes a biweekly, *Avance*. At least two monthlies, *El Pez y La Serpiente* and *Patria Libre*, also appeared in 1980. The latter is a slick-paper magazine published by the Ministry of the Interior (Nicaraguan police force) and is filled with interviews with the Sandinista commanders, reports of their activities and articles about revolutionary heroes. All publications are in Spanish, the national language.

Nicaraguans are predominantly Spanish-speaking *mestizos* (mixed Indian and Spanish blood) living in the countryside. Despite Nicaragua's rich farmland and mineral wealth and the lack of many of the serious demographic problems that plague its neighbors (such as overpopulation or large numbers of unintegrated Indians), the majority of the population lives in severe poverty. Immediately before the revolution, almost half of the deaths in Nicaragua were those of children under five years, and life expectancy was only 50 years. Nearly three-quarters of the people lived in inadequate housing—a problem aggravated by the 1972 earthquake. Malnutrition and unemployment were widespread. The destruction from the revolutionary war has only compounded the problems. In 1977 per capita income was 9,660 córdobas ($966), although unevenly distributed. Immediately after the war, per capita income had dropped to 5,160 córdobas ($516).

Without question, the biggest single accomplishment of the Sandinista government has been to reduce illiteracy dramatically. Prior to the revolution, between 50 and 70 percent of the population could not read and write Spanish. From March through August 1980, the FSLN mobilized the entire Nicaraguan society, including all the mass media, for a literacy campaign modeled on the 1961 Cuban effort. More than 180,000 students, teachers, housewives and other volunteers (including 1,200 Cuban teachers) were recruited, trained and sent into the countryside to teach reading and writing. The campaign cost more than $20 million, mostly borrowed from abroad, and at its conclusion, the government claimed that illiteracy had been reduced to about 12 percent.

In pre-revolutionary Nicaragua, where the per capita number of newspaper copies was among the lowest in the Americas and the majority of the population was illiterate, the press played a significant role only for the privileged classes. Thus, the stereotype of a crusading newspaper editor inflaming the *masses* to revolt against an evil dictator does not represent reality. To the extent that the opposition press did affect the broader base of Nicaraguan people, it was not so much for its content, but rather as a political symbol. However, the huge increase in the number of literates is likely not only to increase newspaper readership but also to change the standards by which readers judge the press. "It's beautiful to learn how to read," a young Nicaraguan peasant told *The New York Times*. "Soon I'll be able to read *La Prensa*." For a sizable number of new literates, the content of *La Prensa* and other newspapers, in addition to their political symbolism and tradition, will become increasingly important. How that will change circulation patterns and affect the intense competition among the Managua dailies should be an important indicator of popular support for the policies of the new revolutionary government.

Economic Framework

As the result of the devastating revolutionary war and the earlier plundering of the national treasury by Somoza and his cronies, Nicaragua is virtually bankrupt. In addition to war damages in excess of 18 billion córdobas ($1.8 billion), the Sandinista government inherited a national debt of over 16 billion córdobas ($1.6 billion)—with only 30 million córdobas ($3 million) left in the Central Bank. Only foreign aid from several countries and international organizations and stern economic measures have prevented complete financial collapse.

The Sandinistas' hope for rebuilding the Nicaraguan economy and carrying out social and political reforms rests almost entirely on their ability to coexist with the private sector. Although the Sandinistas expropriated roughly 40 percent of the economy previously owned by the Somozas, the Nicaraguan private sector still controls the majority of the nation's productive capacity and, therefore, has tremendous influence over economic recovery. Without business cooperation the FSLN woud have to resort to draconian economic measures and postpone social reforms. But in order to retain this cooperation, the Sandinistas must make compromises in their basically Marxist political ideology. Serious disagreements between the two groups arose frequently in 1980, and on several occasions the highly contradictory Marxist-private enterprise alliance came close to unraveling.

One controversy revolves around the Sandinistas' establishment of the Union of Nicaraguan Journalists (UPN) as a closed-shop union. UPN was started informally in 1978 as an underground opposition group of journalists attempting to overthrow Somoza, and several of its members are now top Sandinista commanders or high government officials. All print and broadcast journalists are supposed to be members of the union in order to practice journalism in Nicaragua. To become a member of UPN, journalists must be graduates of a journalism training program at one of Nicaragua's universities. Practicing journalists without university backgrounds were grandfathered if they had five years or more of significant professional experience, no criminal record and, in the opinion of the union, had good moral character and no previous involvement with Somoza. However, most *La Prensa* editors and reporters are not UPN members.

Probably because of the union's underground activities and the special role of journalism in the revolution, UPN was appointed to hold a seat on the Council of State, the provisional legislature of the revolutionary government. Incidentally, Commander Bayardo Arce, president of the Council of State and member of the FSLN Directorate, was a reporter for *La Prensa* and an early member of the union.

Not only do Nicaraguan newspapers have great symbolic importance, but their economic status is an important manifestation of the national political debate. Advertising is probably the best example. During the summer of 1980 *La Prensa* was carrying the most advertising of the three dailies, and the majority of its ads were from private businesses. In contrast, *Barricada* had the least advertising—almost all from the government. *El Nuevo Diario* had a little of both government and private-sector advertising.

La Prensa's longer experience in the newspaper business also gives it an edge. It has a wider and more efficient distribution network, priority on production facilities, and established supply lines. Of particular importance is the supply of newsprint, a commodity so scarce in Nicaragua that it is often used as barter in the media business. During much of 1980 *La Prensa* had the only newsprint supply, and was reselling it to the other newspapers at exorbitant prices.

Circulation figures are not audited, so estimates vary widely. Nonetheless all sources, including the competing newspapers themselves, agree that *La Prensa* is leading in the fierce competition. The range in circulation estimates in 1980 was: *La Prensa*, 55,000 to 75,000; *Barricada*, 20,000 to 65,000; *El Nuevo Diario*, 20,000 to 45,000. *La Prensa* and *El Nuevo Diario* sell for 2 córdobas (20 cents) and *Barricada* for 1 córdoba (10 cents).

Press Laws & Censorship

Most of the measures that the Somoza government used to repress Chamorro and *La Prensa* were within the letter, if not the spirit, of Nicaraguan law. Prior censorship of the news media and other suspension of civil rights were legal under martial-law provisions, and most of the criminal and civil charges filed to harass Chamorro appear to have had basis in Nicaraguan pre-revolutionary law.

One of the first official acts of the revolutionary government was to abolish the Constitution and replace it with a series of provisional laws, proclamations and decrees. The Statute on Rights of Nicaraguans says, "Freedom of information is one of the fundamental principles of authentic democracy." But much as the pre-revolutionary Constitution, the new guarantee of freedom of expression is not absolute: "The exercise of these freedoms brings with it duties and responsibilities, and consequently may be subject to certain necessary formalities, conditions, and restrictions specified by law," and this is followed by a list of general equivocations.

The Junta of the Government of National Reconstruction issued in August 1979 the General Provisional Law on the Media of Communication, which elaborates the principles in the bill of rights and details the exceptions. Sections of the law prohibit media content that portrays women as sexual objects and promotes laziness, subversion, other crimes, and human degradation. Violence, pornography and advertising of tobacco and liquor in the media are also banned. In addition to listing what must not be printed or broadcast, the provisional law also states the type of content that must be disseminated, such as "...to express a legitimate preoccupation for the defense of the victories of the revolution, the process of reconstruction and the problems of the Nicaraguan people." The new press law also empowers the government to prevent the economic dominance of the media by any social or economic group, and to nationalize all media in which Somoza and his allies had invested.

In the fall of 1980 the junta issued a series of decrees that placed a "news embargo" on specific topics considered "counterrevolutionary." Specifically banned were discussion of certain military and security matters, publishing unconfirmed reports on food shortages, and other topics that would endanger the public order or economic stability. UPI reported in November 1980 that six reporters, both Nicaraguan and foreign, had been arrested and later released for alleged violations of the decrees, but this author could not independently confirm the UPI report.

"I would not call anyone who disagrees with the government's thinking counterrevolutionary," said Dr. Arturo J. Curz, moderate member of the ruling junta in an interview with *La Prensa* shortly after the decrees were issued. "That is simply the right to disagree and this must be respected TODAY, TOMORROW and ALWAYS. Adopting a different attitude would mean adopting an imperious, dictatorial and totalitarian attitude and this could never be justified." However, Dr. Curz added that the media had a responsibility not to issue "incorrect or distorted reports" that would foster panic among the public and destabilize the economy and the government.

The Sandinistas have publicly committed themselves to ending emergency rule, initiating judicial review of government action and holding elections. However, these have been slow in forthcoming, according to the private sector: the government announced in 1980 that the first national elections would be held in 1985.

State-Press Relations

The tensions between the government and the private sector, and therefore between the government and the privately owned media, have waxed and waned since the Sandinista victory. The most serious confrontation came in the spring of 1980 and, of course, involved *La Prensa*. The Chamorro family, missing its patriarch, was deeply divided over the editorial direction of the newspaper. One faction of the family, headed by Xavier Chamorro, then editor of *La Prensa*, wanted to support the government. The other faction, led by Pedro Chamorro, favored a pro-business editorial policy and criticism of the new government. The family feud simmered for months until Violeta Barios de Chamorro, the slain editor's widow and briefly a member of the ruling junta, sided with the pro-business faction and removed Xavier as editor.

When the dismissal was announced, the Sandinista-backed union responded by closing down the newspaper, and the confrontation escalated into a major national crisis that gained international attention. The organization representing the private businessmen demanded that the *La Prensa* strike should be resolved in favor of the pro-business faction of the Chamorro family as a demonstration of the Sandinistas' commitment to political and economic pluralism. After lengthy discussions on that and other matters of concern to the private sector, the Sandinista negotiators agreed to the demand, but before the government acted to resolve the strike, the factions of the Chamorro family reached their own accord, which allowed Xavier to take an estimated 25 percent of *La Prensa's* assets (and most of its staff) to start his own newspaper, *El Nuevo Diario*. *La Prensa* was also allowed to reopen, and the tensions between the competing forces eased for several months.

Despite the government's desire to control the flow of certain types of news, it has been relatively open in its treatment of reporters from all media, including *La Prensa*. Sandinista commanders and junta members frequently hold press conferences, grant interviews with domestic and foreign journalists, and appear on radio and television call-in programs to answer questions and complaints from the Nicaraguan public. The Directorate of Publication and Press of the junta and the National Secretariat of Propaganda and Political Education of the FSLN also conduct extensive information programs to enlist national and world support for the revolution.

Attitude Toward Foreign Media

The ability of the Somoza dictatorship to stay in power and dominate virtually every aspect of Nicaraguan life was predicated, in large part, on its relationship with the United States. Throughout the 20th century, the United States governed Nicaragua directly or indirectly. For most of the period between 1912 and 1933, U.S. Marines occupied the country to "maintain public order," and helped the local National Guard fight the rebels led by Augusto Sandino, from whom the present government got its name. The actual or perceived threat that the United States would intervene again to keep the Somozas in power tended to strengthen the support of the regime's allies and discourage its opposition.

In 1978 a Nicaraguan diplomat in Washington boasted that Somoza had "more friends in Congress than [President] Carter." Despite the probable exaggeration, Somoza did have strong support on Capitol Hill. Less than a year before the Sandinista victory, 78 U.S. congressmen sent a strongly worded letter to President Carter urging him to increase U.S. support for Somoza, who they described as "a long and consistent ally." Even within the Carter administration, the possibility of sending U.S. or U.S.-backed troops to intervene in Nicaragua was seriously discussed as late as 1979.

Despite Washington's apparent propensity to intervene, the growing and consistently negative coverage of the Somoza regime by U.S. and other foreign media helped to undercut U.S. support for the government. Starting as a trickle in 1975, coverage of the widespread corruption and human rights violations by the Somoza dictatorship and of rising opposition—not only from the guerrillas but also the Catholic Church and moderate businessmen—flooded North American newspapers and television screens by 1979. Without his traditional U.S. support, Somoza grew increasingly vulnerable to his domestic opposition.

Although the basic conditions that were reported had existed in Nicaragua for decades, the foreign press corps did not converge in large numbers on Nicaragua until the late 1970s. In those years a combination of events brought several foreign reporters to Nicaragua and called their attention to the deeper story that was going unreported in the major media. Foremost among these correspondents was Alan Riding, Mexico City bureau chief of The New York Times. Riding, who had covered the 1972 earthquake, returned in 1974 when the Sandinistas raided the home of a Somoza government official and took foreign and local dignitaries hostage. While covering that story, he discovered the depth of public resentment of the Somoza government and the growing sympathy for the opposition. He returned again in 1975 to write an in-depth article on human rights violations in the country, and subsequently made a point of stopping off in Nicaragua to update the situation each time he was in the region, primarily for coverage of the Panama Canal treaties. Once an acknowledged leader in U.S. journalism such as The New York Times took an interest in a story, the highly competitive foreign press corps also rushed to Nicaragua for the story. But these correspondents, unlike Riding, were not particularly familiar with the background and important issues in the Nicaraguan conflict. La Prensa Editor Chamorro, who by that time was well known in regional journalistic circles, was happy to supply the visiting correspondents with briefings. The first stop for virtually all foreign correspondents arriving in Managua was the office of La Prensa—a tradition that continued after the war.

Somoza quickly concluded that the influx of foreign correspondents in the late 1970s was a threat to the survival of his government, since news dispatches weakened U.S. support and strengthened local opposition. He responded by launching an elaborately funded public relations campaign to improve the image of his government in the United States and discredit the foreign press corps. Leading Somoza's publicity counterattack were Norman L. Wolfson, then chairman of the New York public relations firm of Norman, Lawrence, Patterson and Farrell; William C. Cramer, former U.S. congressman from Florida and Nicaraguan lobbyist in Washington; and Ian R. MacKenzie, director of the Washington-based Nicaraguan Government Information Service. The publicists arranged some favorable news and editorial treatment in conservative U.S. newspapers (even guest columns with Somoza's byline in such major dailies as The New York Times and Christian Science Monitor), appearances by Somoza on national TV interview programs, and interviews with many of the country's most respected journalists. In a related attempt to manipulate the press, Somoza covertly bought the controlling interest in Vision, a respected Latin American magazine, and other publications in the chain that owned it.

When the public relations campaign failed to stem the criticism in the foreign press, the Somoza forces resorted to intimidation and, finally, physical violence. Several correspondents were denied entry or expelled. Others were threatened or even roughed up. In the Somoza-owned domestic media, the foreign correspondents were described as communist agents, and other efforts to control outside coverage grew ugly.

In June 1979 ABC-TV correspondent Bill Stewart and his news crew were stopped at a Managua roadblock. A Nicaraguan guardsman ordered Stewart to his knees, then to lie on his belly with his hands behind his head. When Stewart obeyed, the soldier shot him in the head. The replay after replay of the videotape of Stewart's murder shocked U.S. television audiences, undercut the last vestiges of Somoza's international support—and did nothing to improve the coverage of Somoza in the foreign press. While most correspondents believe that Somoza did not directly order the killing of Stewart, they felt that Somoza's characterizations of foreign correspondents as communists created the atmosphere that led to the assassination.

The opposition forces also were not without propaganda resources. When the Sandinistas failed to win a military victory in the fall of 1978, they retrenched and designed a political strategy to overthrow Somoza. As part of the new strategy, representatives of the FSLN and other opposition groups contacted foreign correspondents, at first guardedly and later vigorously. Such respected U.S. journalists as Karen DeYoung, deputy foreign editor of the *Washington Post*, and Bob Sherman, a staffer for the Jack Anderson column, were invited to visit clandestine guerrilla camps to interview Sandinista commanders. Their reporting brought details of FSLN policies and activities to U.S. opinion makers and identified the growing Nicaraguan conflict as a major foreign policy concern.

The importance of foreign correspondents in the revolution has led the current Sandinista government to be extraordinarily cooperative with the foreign press corps covering postwar Nicaragua but, at the same time, extremely sensitive to criticism lest the world media might participate in the undoing of their government also. The Sandinistas have expressed dismay to Riding, DeYoung and other correspondents who covered the revolutionary war, about articles these reporters have written identifying problems in the new government. Yet despite the FSLN's apparent misunderstanding of the tendency of the Western press to criticize any government, regardless of who is in power, foreign correspondents generally are not restricted in their work and have easy access to revolutionary leaders in both the FSLN and the junta.

News flow into Nicaragua also is relatively unrestrained. Publications from a variety of countries and ideological perspectives are available in Managua. In addition, the domestic media subscribe to international news agencies, plus UPI, dpa and ABC News, are Reuter, and Prensa Latina. All of those agencies, plus UPI, dpa and ABC News, are represented by local stringers in Nicaragua; however, none are full-time correspondents.

News Agencies

In 1979 the revolutionary government began the Nicaraguan News Agency (ANN), which provides international service primarily through the Non-Aligned News Agencies Pool. ANN does not have a domestic service.

Electronic News Media

The first radio network in Nicaragua, Radio Nacional, was built in 1931 by the U.S. Marines occupying the country and was intended primarily for military use by the Nicaraguan National Guard. Television was founded in 1955 as a commercial enterprise of the Somoza family and its allies. The tradition of strong government control of broadcasting—established before the revolution—continues today under the Sandinista government. Prior to the revolution, 125 radio stations were in operation in Nicaragua. In 1980, 33 radio stations were on the air, about 25 of which were headquartered in Managua. The junta or the FSLN owns and operates 13 of those stations, all of which were expropriated from the Somoza family and its alleged allies. Voice of Nicaragua is the official station of the junta, Radio Sandino of the FSLN. The remaining 20 stations are privately owned but subject to considerable government pressure. All stations, including the private ones, are linked together in the Sandinista Radio Network and are strongly urged to carry programming that the government deems important, particularly speeches and news conferences of government leaders and educational material used to support the literacy program. Almost all cooperate.

Only eight of the 20 private stations carry regular news programming, and of those three routinely espouse official government policies. Five stations (Radio Mundial, Fabuloso 7, Me Preferida, Radio Exito and Radio Católica) carry news and commentaries that deviate from the government position. Radio Mundial has the largest listenership, and Radio Católica generally is considered the most influential. "Radio newspapers," news programs prepared by independent contractors who buy air time from station owners and, in turn, sell advertising to support the programs, continue to a lesser degree in postwar Nicaragua.

Nicaragua's Central American neighbors and the United States have expressed concern about the revolutionary government's propaganda activities, primarily through Radio Sandino. The FSLN's clandestine radio station during the insurrection, Radio Sandino went on the air in about June 1978 with programming that combined official communiqués, revolutionary music, instructions in making Molotov cocktails or using M-1 rifles, and exhortations like "Go out and kill as many Somozistas as you can for the glory of the revolution." There is evidence that during the insurrection some of Radio Sandino's programming was broadcast from transmitters in Cuba. Similar evidence has surfaced that clandestine radio broadcasting for the leftist guerrillas in El Salvador is being transmitted by Radio Sandino from Nicaragua.

Immediately after the Sandinista victory, all four television channels, two of which were owned outright by Somoza, were expropriated and declared "privileged media" to be used for educational, cultural and political purposes. Two channels, comprising the Sandinista Television System, have returned to the air under the centralized control of a committee composed of Sandinista commanders and the minister of culture, the celebrated poet-priest Ernesto Cardenal. Approximately 50 percent of all programming is produced in the United States, including feature films, reruns of TV serials, and a large quantity of sports. Most of the 10 percent of programming produced locally is news, public affairs, and lengthy features that recount revolutionary victories and memorialize fallen guerrillas. The only regular TV news program is "Noticiero Sandinista," which appears nightly on Channel 2. Speeches of the commanders and discussion of new government policies dominate the 40-minute newscast. The small amount of foreign news concentrates on violence in the neighboring Central American countries. Advertising from government agencies and private enterprise alike also is aired, although not during the newscast. U.S. intelligence reports indicate that a large percentage of the Cuban advisers and technicians in Nicaragua have been assigned to the television network and other communications facilities.

Education & Training

Two Nicaraguan universities, the Jesuit-run Central American University (UCA) and the National Autonomous University, grant four-year degrees in journalism. The UCA journalism school was founded in 1967 as a North American-style skills-oriented program. In 1974 it changed to a school of communication, took a more academic approach and added programs in advertising, public relations and social communication. Although the Central American University program appears to be the best in the country, it will be closed down by 1983 in an efficiency move designed by the Sandinistas. The national university will have the only journalism program, although UCA's social communication program is scheduled to be merged into it. Most of the staffers for the new Sandinista daily *Barricada* are or were journalism students at the national university. *Barricada* Editor Carlos Fernando Chamorro describes their revolutionary fervor as high but their journalistic skills as low.

Summary

The press was an essential ingredient in the Nicaraguan revolution. The opposition newspaper *La Prensa* and its martyred editor Pedro Joaquin Chamorro were political symbols around which the diverse opposition rallied to overthrow the Somoza dictatorship. In the post-insurrection period, the revolution was characterized by volatility, instability and a high level of tension between the factions that had joined to form the opposition. Reflecting these divisions, each of Nicaragua's three daily newspapers had distinct editorial policies regarding the new Sandinista government. In addition to arguing over the direction of the revolution, the newspapers engaged in stiff competition for readers, advertisers and the legacy of the pre-revolutionary *La Prensa*. Ironically, all three newspapers were headed by a member of the Chamorro family.

With all major media entrenched in political camps, the course of Nicaraguan journalism in the 1980s will depend on the distribution of political power. If the Sandinistas fulfill their promise of developing a pluralistic political and economic system, *La Prensa* and a few privately owned radio stations will survive and continue to criticize the new government. But as in many media systems, the ability to criticize the government has been circumscribed by a wide range of controls. Foremost among them in Nicaragua are economic pressures, a closed-shop journalists' union, the new press law and other extralegal constraints.

The most important change for the Nicaraguan press under the Sandinista government has been the rapid reduction of illiteracy, especially among the rural peasants. How the Nicaraguan press, which traditionally has communicated only with the nation's educated minority, deals with its new mass audience and, in turn, how the audience responds to the highly politicized press, will portend the role of journalism in revolutionary Nicaragua.

CHRONOLOGY

1975 In-depth article on human rights violations in Nicaragua by Alan Riding of *The New York Times* is first round in verbal assault by foreign press corps on repression by and corruption in Somoza government. Riding subsequently won the Maria Moors Cabot Award from Columbia University, in part for his reporting of the Nicaraguan revolution.

1978 Pedro Joaquín Chamorro, editor of *La Prensa* and internationally known opposition journalist, is killed by assassins believed under direction of or in sympathy with Somoza government; assassination sparks strikes and escalation of opposition, eventually leading to Somoza government's overthrow. Karen DeYoung of *Washington Post* and Bob Sherman of Jack Anderson's column visit clandestine guerrilla camps, report details of Sandinista activities and policies.

1979 Alfonso Rojo, Spanish journalist for *Diario 16*, arrested, jailed, later expelled from Nicaragua; government charges—and some of Rojo's fellow journalists corroborated—that he was actively assisting Sandinista guerrillas.

ABC-TV newsman Bill Stewart shot and killed by Nicaraguan guardsman; at least 20 foreign correspondents leave country in protest; frequent replay in U.S. of videotape of Stewart's execution seriously undercuts support for Somoza government.

Opposition newspaper *La Prensa* destroyed by government troops.

Somoza government collapses. Sandinista National Liberation Front takes control of government. Sandinista newspaper *Barricada* begins publication.

Revolutionary government issues bill of rights guaranteeing freedom of press, and provisional press law restricting publication of certain types of information. Press is exhorted to actively support revolution.

1980 Government closes down *El Pueblo*, small daily newspaper published by Frente Obrero, radical-left organization including disgruntled former Sandinistas, by government and jails its editors on combination of charges, including subversion and illegally storing arms.

Oscar Leonardo Montalvan, news director of Radio Mil, expelled from Union of Nicaraguan Journalists and forced off the air shortly after criticizing FSLN; Montalvan, whose newscast had Nicaragua's largest audience of nongovernment radio programs, was reportedly heading revamp of news and public affairs programming of Radio Católica, one of the country's most influential media.

La Prensa, following brief reappearance after Sandinista victory, shuts down in Sandinista-backed-union strike. Dispute exemplifies ideological split within Chamorro family and entire nation about course of revolution. Strike resolved when one of Chamorro factions and much of *La Prensa* staff get permission to start competing daily, *El Nuevo Diario*.

Revolutionary government issues a series of decrees prohibiting publication of information on security matters or news that might destabilize economy and government; *La Prensa* and representatives of private sector call decrees serious infringement on press freedom.

BIBLIOGRAPHY

Anderson, Jack. "Nicaragua Press Subject to Somoza's Wrath." *Washington Post,* November 29, 1978, p. C29.

Busey, James L. "Nicaragua and *La Prensa* After Somoza" (typewritten manuscript).

Chamorro, Pedro Joaquin. *Los Somoza: Una Estripe Sangrienta.* Buenos Aires, 1979.

DeYoung, Karen. "Politics by Media in Managua." *Washington Post*, February 9, 1978, p. A22.

———. "Top Managua Paper Assumes Watchdog Role." *Washington Post*, August 28, 1979. Copy:

Hale, Andrew. "Death in Managua." *Index on Censorship* (May–June 1978), pp. 56-57.

Harris, Robert. "Nicaragua—The Censor at Work." *Index on Censorship* (November–December 1977), pp. 23-30.

Knudson, Jerry. "The Nicaraguan Press and the Sandinista Revolution." Typewritten manuscript.

La Batalla por Nicaragua, Cuadernos de *uno más uno.* Mexico, 1980.

Ley General y Reglamento Sobre Medios de Comunicacion. La Dirreción de Divulgación y Prensa de la Junta de Gobierno de Reconstrucción Nacional. Managua, 1979.

Maslow, Jonathan Evan. "Letter from Nicaragua: The Junta and the Press—A Family Affair." *Columbia Journalism Review* (March–April 1981).

Millett, Richard. *Guardians of the Dynasty: A History of the U.S.-Created Guardia Nacional de Nicaragua and the Somoza Family.* New York, 1977.

Morris, John Ryan, et al. *Area Handbook for Nicaragua.* Washington, 1970.

Nichols, John Spicer. "News Media in the Nicaraguan Revolution." In Thomas W. Walker, ed., *Nicaragua in Revolution.* New York, 1981.

Report on the Situation of Human Rights in Nicaragua. Organization of American States, Washington, D.C., 1978.

Riding, Alan. "Newspaper Family Typifies Nicaragua's Divisions." *The New York Times*, May 24, 1980, p. 10.

———. "Nicaragua: A Delicate Balance." *The New York Times Magazine*, December 2, 1979. p. 75.

Somoza, Anastasio, as told to Jack Cox. *Nicaragua Betrayed.* Boston-Los Angeles, 1980.

Wolfson, Norman L. "Selling Somoza: The Lost Cause of a PR Man." *National Review*, July 20, 1979, pp. 907-919.

NIGERIA

by Robert L. Nwankwo and George Kurian

BASIC DATA

Population: 75.84 million (1980)
Area: 924,630 sq. km. (357,000 sq. mi.)
GNP: 31 billion naira (US$ 55.31 billion) (1979)
Literacy Rate: 25%
Language(s): English; also Hausa, Yoruba, Ibo
Number of Dailies: 21
  Aggregate Circulation: NA
  Circulation per 1,000: NA
Number of Nondailies: 17
  Aggregate Circulation: NA
  Circulation per 1,000: NA
Number of Periodicals: 44
Number of Radio Stations: 7

Number of Television Stations: 9
Number of Radio Receivers: 5.25 million (1977)
  Radio Receivers per 1,000: 71 (1977)
Number of Television Sets: 450,000 (1977)
  Television Sets per 1,000: 6 (1977)
Total Annual Newsprint Consumption: 23,700 metric tons
Per Capita Newsprint Consumption: 0.4 kg. (0.88 lb.)
Total Newspaper Ad Receipts: 13 million naira (US$ 23.7 million) (1979)
  As % of All Ad Expenditures: 28.8

Background & General Characteristics

Iwe Thorin, Nigeria's first newspaper, was in the Yoruba language, and was founded by missionaries in 1859. It soon became Africa's first bilingual paper when English was added as a second language. It sold for 30 cowrie shells—a high price for such a novelty.

Some four years later a West Indian immigrant, Robert Campbell, founded the *Anglo-African* in Lagos. It survived for three years despite a style more appropriate for Victorian Britain than tropical Africa. After *Anglo-African* folded the entire territory now known as Nigeria was without newspapers of any kind for more than a dozen years. The disappearance of the Lagos press was perhaps due to the fact that the colony was administered from Freetown in Sierra Leone and was remote from the centers of power.

By 1900, 10 newspapers had appeared in Nigeria. Virtually all were African papers owned and edited by Nigerians or by black Americans from North America or West Indians. While the newspaper lacked the technical refinement of the Western press, it gave the African nationalists their best weapon

against their white rulers. While the masses remained silent, the African journalists were the first to hold out the hope of eventual independence for the colonies. "We are not clambering for immediate independence," the *Lagos Times and Gold Coast Advertiser* said in an editorial in March 1881, "but it should always be borne in mind that the present order of things will not last forever. A time will come when the colonies on the west coast will be left to regulate their own internal and external affairs." Seventy-odd years were to elapse before this prophecy was fulfilled.

As the African press became bolder, the British authorities began to take a less than kindly look at this new phenomenon. In 1917 Governor Lord Lugard, the architect of modern colonial Nigeria, framed a law giving himself the authority to appoint a press censor, to seize printing presses, to confiscate newspapers and to impose a bond of £250 on undesirable publishers. When the Colonial Office ordered Lugard not to enforce these laws, he simply ignored the instructions. When pressed, Lugard claimed that the original instructions never reached him! The "mendacious native press," as Lugard described it, had become the political equivalent of the African drum, a unique means of communication, a sounding board for African ideas and opinions. It thrived on two things: the growing literacy, and the ambivalence of the colonial authorities, who did not know whether to encourage it or put it down.

West Africa's first successful daily was founded in Lagos in 1925 by Herbert Macaulay. Known as the *Daily News,* it was also West Africa's first political party newspaper, serving as the spokesman of Macaulay's National Democratic Party. Alarmed at the popularity of Macaulay's creation, the European traders and the more conservative Africans joined together and put up enough money to start a rival called the *Daily Times.* The founding of the *Daily Times* was a landmark in the history of African journalism. From its very first issue dated June 1, 1926 it displayed a professionalism unmatched by its contemporaries. Its headlines and news stories were unlike anything that Nigerian readers were used to until that time. Before long it had unusual features like a women's page and a sports page. Much of the *Daily Time's* success was due to the young African who served as its first editor, Ernest Ikoli, who helped it to steer a middle course between ultranationalism and ultraconservatism.

Another landmark was the appearance in 1937 of the *West African Pilot,* a daily launched in Lagos by the most dynamic nationalist of his day, Nnamdi Azikiwe. U.S.-trained Zik earned his spurs as an editor on I. T. A. Wallace-Johnson's *African Morning Post* of the Gold Coast, as Ghana was known before independence. *The Morning Post's* masthead slogan proclaimed the ideal that motivated Zik's journalistic career: "Independence in All Things and Neutral in Nothing Affecting the Destiny of Africa." Pride in Africa and things African was the theme and core of Zik's journalism. Within three years of its founding the *West African Pilot* sold 12,000 copies; the figure more than doubled in the 1940s, with a readership estimated at between 10 and 20 per copy. Zik not only brought Africa its brightest newspaper but also created West Africa's first newspaper chain—the Associated Newspapers of Nigeria, known as the Zik Group. Besides the flagship, *The Pilot,* the group comprised the *Eastern Nigerian Guardian* at Port Harcourt, the *Nigerian Spokesman* at Onitsha, the *Southern Nigerian Defender* at Warri, *The Comet* at Kano and, until it folded, *The Northern Advocate* at Jos. The Zik Group was

the frequent target of the colonial government's displeasure. *The Pilot* and *The Comet* were banned for six weeks in 1945 and when they reappeared they were denied official advertising, a form of subsidy. But Zik would always strike back with an ingenuity that was a source of despair for the authorities. When *The Pilot* was banned in Lagos, he brought the *Southern Nigerian Defender* from Warri to take its place in the capital. A Colonial Office memo summarizes the official attitude toward the Zik group: "They are like plague. They are afflicting the whole country." The Zik newspapers were hit badly by the war; the British authorities used the newsprint quotas as a curb and as a bait. Relations between the government and Zik grew worse after the war. In 1946 the government denied Zik a permit to operate a wireless station, leading him to publish a long list of acts of alleged victimization of his papers by the British. He launched an appeal for money from his readers, and donations came from all over the world. But Zik had no desire to become a martyr. Accusing the government of plotting to kill him, he went into hiding, emerging from it to lead the nation as its first president on independence.

The mid-forties witnessed a growing challenge to the hold of the Zik dailies as well as older newspapers. The government had established a press of its own with a clutch of newspapers in tribal languages and the *Nigerian Citizen* in English. The Action Group Party founded a new daily in Lagos called the *Daily Service,* which joined forces with the *Nigeria Tribune* in Ibadan to form the Amalgamated Press of Nigeria. Thus, on the eve of independence Nigeria had three large newspaper chains, two private and one official.

The Nigerian press was yet to experience its most powerful push into the postwar newspaper age. The man who was responsible for that push was a strange Irishman named Cecil King, the publisher of the prosperous *Daily Mirror* of London. His African adventure began in 1947 when at the suggestion of a British colonial officer he purchased for a modest £46,000 the Lagos *Daily Times* and its two magazines, *West Africa* and *West African Review.* King's recipe for the *Daily Times* was not different from the one that had propelled the *Daily Mirror* to its dominance on British newsstands: Give the reader what he wants. Very soon, the *Daily Times* became an African version of the *Daily Mirror*—minus the sex. Described as the most potent influence on the Nigerian press, King is best remembered for his many innovations that have outlasted his empire as well as the British Empire. He assembled the first rotary printing press in the country and set up the most modern photoengraving and typesetting plant on the west coast. He played down crime and sex because he felt that the African temperament was too volatile to be exposed to them day after day. He organized the colony's first news service covering all major regions. He attracted to the profession —and trained—some of the country's finest journalists, who later went on to top positions elsewhere. Finally, he built up one of the most efficient bus transportation systems in west Africa. Originally designed to transport his papers to the urban centers by six o'clock in the morning, the King's buses, as they were known, resembled gaudy, festooned floats carrying not only the *Daily Times* but also passengers, freight, goats and other animals. In some years, surprisingly, the buses even made a profit. Very soon the King group began to move up the coast, first to Ghana, where it established the *Daily Graphic,* and later to Sierra Leone, where it bought out the *Daily Mail.*

King's success was not lost on his rival and contemporary, Lord Roy Thomson. A man with a terrier's nose for profits, Thomson decided to make his first move into tropical Africa on the invitation of Chief Obafemi Awolowo, leader of the Action Group, which owned the *Daily Express* of Lagos. Together they formed the Amalgamated Press of Nigeria with Thomson holding 50 percent. Thomson appointed white managers but the editorial staff remained black; nevertheless, the group's papers were redolent of Fleet Street; events in Europe and America crowded out local stories. The death of Sir Winston Churchill, for example, filled three pages of the slim paper.

From the beginning Thomson was caught in the crossfire between the fiercely antagonistic tribal and political groups, one of which was led by his partner, Awolowo. Trying to get out before the situation got worse, Thomson agreed to merge with the *Morning Post,* a state-run daily founded by Nigeria's first prime minister, Abubakar Tafawa Balewa, that was losing money every year. But before the merger went through, Tafawa Balewa was ousted and assassinated in a military coup in 1966. Thomson sold off the printing press and closed the books on his costly African adventure.

Eight years later, the last British presence in the Nigerian press was removed when the London Mirror Group sold all its shares in the *Daily Times* and the *Sunday Times* of Lagos a few weeks before the Nigerian Enterprise Promotion Decree came into force requiring that all stock in Nigerian companies be owned by Nigerians themselves.

The soldiers who took over the country in 1966 found it more difficult to subdue the press, which—bred in the best traditions of British liberalism—remained restive throughout the 1970s. Most newsmen believed that the military rule was only temporary, and that once they had cleaned up the mess the soldiers would return to the barracks. Under both General Aguiyi-Ironsi and General Yakubu Gowon the press retained a large degree of freedom. It could do so because, in the words of Lateef Jakande, publisher of the *Nigerian Tribune,* "of three things: the tradition of press freedom instilled by Zik and others, the courage and professional spirit of Nigerian editors and publishers and the good sense of some of those in authority." Although the military had the power to impose censorship, no attempt was made to do so. State-press relations were not always smooth. Sometimes newsmen who had piqued the officers found themselves picked up without warning and detained for a considerable time, as happened to Chief Theo Ola, news editor of the *Daily Times.* But every time such an incident happened, the press would raise such a hue and cry that the military would become more conciliatory. But the pattern of harassment followed by a brief respite continued. The late 1970s brought a new crisis of confidence, as the *Christian Science Monitor* described it, in the relations between the military and the press. Newspapers were full of stories of corruption and bribery at the highest levels in the government, of "vast wealth hidden abroad," and of millionaires in uniform. The inspector general of police retaliated by threatening to take "drastic and unpleasant measures to curb the excess of the press." The confrontation came to a head in an incident that is regarded as a landmark in the history of the Nigerian press. On July 30, 1973 Mineri Amakiri, a reporter on the *Nigerian Observer* at Port Harcourt, was arrested on the orders of the military governor of the Rivers State for a rather innocuous report on a teachers' strike that unfortunately coincided with the governor's birthday. Amakiri was given 24 lashes across his back, had his beard and hair shaved off, was locked up for 27 hours and then was thrown out into the street. The outcry was almost universal. Amakiri filed suit against the police officer who carried out the assault and was awarded £5,375 as damages and costs. This is the only case on record of an African journalist successfully suing an official in a country ruled by the military. The military became more circumspect in dealing with errant journalists, contenting themselves by deportation and threats of prosecution. Sometimes they would come out with a tu quoque allegation, as when chief of staff Major General David Ejoor accused Nigerian journalists of being "corrupt." Occasionally the editor of a government newspaper would be dismissed for inciting the public against the junta.

Unable to control the press, the junta decided to take another tack. In 1975 it took a 60 percent shareholding in the *Daily Times,* the *Sunday Times,* and eight other magazines and newspapers. Not long after this it also acquired the New Nigerian Group. These acquisitions virtually brought the entire newspaper industry under state control with a stable of newspapers that included *Sketch, Standard, Herald* and *Observer.* There were only three independent newspapers left: the *Nigerian Tribune, West African Pilot* and *Daily Express.* Since independence the number of independent newspapers had been reduced by 70 percent.

The Nigerian press is no longer as bold and independent as it once was, but it still is the largest and the best in West Africa. The return to civilian rule in 1979 has not brought any dramatic shifts in the structure of the press. As of 1981, 21 daily newspapers were being published in the country, all but one in English. Six are published in Lagos and three in Ibadan; the other newspaper towns are Enugu, Onitsha, Kaduna, Calabar, Ilorin, Benin City, Jos, Port Harcourt, Ikeja, Owerri and Yaba. The largest circulation is enjoyed by the *Daily Times,* the old Cecil King paper; its circulation of 350,000 dwarfs that of every other paper. The runners up are the *New Nigerian* (120,000), *Nigerian Chronicle* (80,000), *Evening Times,* the evening edition of the *Daily Times* (65,000), *Nigerian Tribune* (50,000), *The Renaissance* (50,000), *Daily Sketch* (40,000) and the *West African Pilot* (26,000). Aggregate circulation is reported by UNESCO for only eight newspapers (527,000) because most of the smaller newspapers do not publish their circulation figures or do not have their circulation audited by a reliable body.

There are 11 Sunday newspapers, led by the *Sunday Times* with a circulation of over 420,000. Both the *Sunday Punch* and the *Sunday Sketch* have circulations well over 150,000 and the *Sunday Chronicle* over 90,000. The periodical press consists of 22 weeklies, 16 of them published in Lagos and three in Ibadan; 15 of these weeklies are published in English, four in Yoruba and two in Hausa. *Lagos Weekend,* published by the Daily Times Group, leads in this category with a circulation of over 250,000. Of the monthlies, the largest circulation is again reported by a Daily Times publication, *Headlines,* with a circulation of 205,000. At least four more monthlies enjoy circulations over 100,000: *Drum,* a picture monthly read all over Africa (172,000), *Flamingo* (100,000), *Spear* (150,000) and *Quest* (100,000). Eleven of the monthlies are based in Lagos and two in Ibadan; 14 are published in English. Of the nine quarterly journals, seven are published from Lagos and two from Ibadan. Seven are published in English, one in both English and French and one in Yoruba and English. The *Yoruba Challenge,* published by the Sudan Interior Mission in Lagos, has the largest circulation of any quarterly, with sales of 65,000 copies.

Most Nigerian dailies are published in tabloid format. There are only four dailies that come out in broadsheet size, the *West African Pilot* being the most notable. Each issue contains less than 20 pages on the average. The front page generally focuses on domestic news, with foreign news on page two and the following pages. Editorials sometimes appear on the front page. Regular features usually include news briefs as well as columns covering other geographical areas. The most popular features, comic strips and sports, usually appear on the last pages. During its formative years, the Nigerian press tended to be flamboyant, verging on the irresponsible. Cecil King is credited with introducing a more sober and serious type of journalism that has survived to this day.

The *Daily Times* is considered to be the most influential Nigerian newspaper. The paper has had a great impact on the course of mass communications development in Nigeria. Its influence on the character of the Nigerian public is also significant, although in the 1960s and again after its takeover by the government in 1975, its credibility was severely questioned by sections of the Nigerian public who disliked the paper's lack of clear positions on public issues and who doubted that a government-owned newspaper could truly be editorially independent, especially when professional politicians were appointed to policy-making roles.

In contrast to the effect of government takeover on the *Daily Times,* the influences and prestige of the *New Nigerian* were enhanced by the federal government's acquisition of the paper. As the voice of the NPC (Northern Peoples' Congress) government, which founded the paper in 1966, the *New Nigerian* had been influential in Nigerian politics. Notwithstanding the technical excellence of the paper and its often frank and bold editorial opinions, it had been considered a sectional paper by many Nigerians. The federal government takeover reduced this perception, although many Nigerians still think that the paper needs to convince the public that it is not an official mouthpiece of the NPN (National Party of Nigeria) and that it is not pro-northern Nigeria.

The *Nigerian Tribune,* established in 1949 and associated with the leadership of the defunct Action Group of Nigeria and with the present leaders of the UPN (Unity Party of Nigeria) has exerted considerable political impact in Nigeria. The paper has been so fearless and tenacious in its fight against social problems that it is considered by some as bordering on the irresponsible. Almost directly counter in point of view and influence to the *Tribune* is the recently founded *National Concord,* which has been linked with some powerful members of the NPN. Some Nigerians find the *Concord* to be rather selective in its objectivity and increasingly parochial and partisan in its coverage and treatment of issues. The *Daily Star* is another newspaper that wields significant influence, mainly because its perceived role as the organ of top leadership of the NPP (Nigerian Peoples' Party).

Economic Framework

Newspapers and other means of communication are an integral part of Nigeria's political life. The close and visible association between political-constitutional development and the mass media makes it difficult, if not impossible, for Nigerians to think of politics without the press or of a state apparatus without media outlets. One of the priorities for each of the new states created as a result of recent constitutional changes in Nigeria is to set up some print and broadcast systems. Thus, while the size and activity of the Nigerian press is strongly influenced by the state

of the economy, the media in Nigeria are more a political than an economic institution. This circumstance makes the life and policy of many Nigerian media organizations as fickle, fleeting and unpredictable as the direction of the nation's politics.

The Nigerian press suffers from severe economic problems, most of them common to black Africa. Printing machinery is expensive, forcing newspapers to rely on second-hand equipment. Transportation facilities are slow and unreliable in most areas outside of the main cities. Major dailies have their own distribution systems, mainly buses and trains, while smaller dailies are sold only in the place of their publication. Turnover of publications is so high that the official press directory is outdated within months. Competition is intense, making it difficult for the smaller publications to charge a price that will permit them to survive. Recent price hikes have brought the price of each major newspaper in Nigeria up to 25 kobo (50 cents), and provincial state-owned newspapers are asking for huge grants from governments in efforts to keep the price down.

The outstanding characteristic of the Nigerian press is its mixed ownership. Historically the press has its roots in private entrepreneurs and publishers, but it passed almost imperceptibly into government hands during the 1960s and 1970s until today state-owned papers account for the majority of the newspapers and the bulk of the circulation. The Daily Times group, 60 percent owned by the government, towers above all others; its circulation is larger than that of all private dailies combined; it also publishes the country's largest selling Sunday paper, weekly and monthly, as well as the most important business daily, the *Business Times,* and the best selling evening daily, *Evening Times.*

Two other major dailies are also under government ownership: *Daily Sketch* and *New Nigerian.* Four provincial governments run their own newspapers, and in each case they enjoy a virtual monopoly: *Nigerian Chronicle,* published by the Cross River State Newspaper Corporation; *Nigerian Herald,* published by the Kwara State Printing and Publishing Corporation; *Nigerian Tide,* published by the Rivers State Newspaper Corporation, and *The Statesman,* published by Imo (State) Newspapers.

The private sector is represented by three major dailies: the *West African Pilot,* the oldest of the three, which has actually declined in circulation since its heyday before independence; the *Nigerian Tribune,* affiliated with the Action Group, which has the largest circulation among the private papers; and the *Daily Express,* published by the Commercial Amalgamated Printers. *The Punch,* founded only in 1976, has managed to build up an impressive circulation of 150,000, reflecting the growth of Ikeja, the capital of Lagos State. Part of its success may also be attributable to its most distinguishing feature—the "page three girl," a young, usually European woman photographed topless. Although competition had led to the demise of several dailies, new entries have kept the total number of dailies at a stable level of between 20 and 24 for over a decade.

Controversy continues over the government's ability to tilt the balance of competition in its favor, especially considering the scarcity and the high cost of print and broadcast facilities and the federal government's control of imports and exports.

Many Nigerians contend that owning and running a newspaper should be strictly a private business and that the entry of the government into newspaper industry will not only put competitors at a gross disadvantage but also encourage sycophancy in the press. Others argue that because of the regional imbalance in the publication and distribution of Nigerian newspapers and because most nongovernment papers delight in publishing only what government fails to do, it is essential for the government in a developing country like Nigeria to own newspapers in order to ensure effective and wide publicity of government activities. These advocates of government ownership maintain that only the existence of government-owned papers guarantees that the national interest is protected in a media world dominated by giant international corporations.

Government is less of a presence in weekly and monthly publications. Here private enterprises, religious and professional organizations and educational institutions are very active. It has been strongly suggested that geographical location and circulation patterns influence the Nigerian press more critically than ownership. Similarly, advertising despite increases in its volume and alloted space—to the annoyance of many readers—does not seem to affect media content significantly, nor do special-interest lobbies appear to exert any systematic impact on editorial policies.

Economic constraints as well as constitutional provisions, such as the one prohibiting private and state government ownership of broadcast stations without presidential permission, have combined to lessen the need for any strong antitrust legislation relating to media ownership. There has, in fact, been a decrease in private newspaper chain ownership since the decline in influence of the most important chain, the Zik Group of newspapers, and since the federal government acquired majority control of the Daily Times Group.

Nigeria does not produce any newsprint. Consumption grew dramatically from 5,300 tons per annum in 1965 to 17,100 tons in 1970 and 23,700 tons in 1975 but has remained stable since then. The per capita consumption of 0.4 kg. is close to the continental average of Africa. The cost of newsprint has risen sharply in recent years—e.g., 60 percent during a six-month period in 1974.

As one of the richest markets in black Africa, Nigeria has a well-developed advertising industry. Most multinational advertising firms have offices in Lagos, which serves as the hub of the marketing network of West Africa. In 1979 advertising expenditures constituted 0.17 percent of GNP and $1.00 per capita. While these figures are not impressive, advertising expenditures grew by 97 percent between 1972 and 1974, 57 percent between 1974 and 1976 and 50 percent between 1977 and 1979. Newspapers receive the largest segment of ad expenditures: 28.8 percent as compared to 18.3 percent for its nearest competitor, radio.

The Nigerian Union of Journalists, established in 1954, was one of the earliest trade unions in the newspaper industry in Africa. Under the trade union reorganization of 1977, NUJ was recognized as one of the constituent unions of the Nigerian Labour Congress. The Nigerian Guild of Editors (NGE) looks after editorial problems and has a code of conduct for members' journalistic staffs. The Newspaper Proprietors' Association of Nigeria (NPAN) represents the interests of newspaper owners and is involved in the training of journalists and in the improvement of management operations. The Nigerian Press Organization was set up as an umbrella organization following the Press Council decree promulgated by the federal military government in 1978; it is comprised of representatives from the NUJ, the NGE and NPAN.

Journalism has enjoyed a significant boost in prestige since national independence was achieved in 1960, partly because of a rise in the average educational level of Nigerian journalists. The government's involvement in the mass media and constitutional debates over press freedom have also helped to elevate the status of journalists in the eyes of the public. In addition, some nationally known journalists have been elected to high offices, including state governorships. While many observers bemoan the lack of professional courage evidenced by certain journalists, all seem to agree that the standard of writing and the treatment of news have greatly improved.

Press Laws & Censorship

Before 1967 the constitution specified that "every person shall be entitled to freedom of expression, including freedom to hold opinions and to receive and impart ideas and information without interference." These rights were, however, subject to limitation by laws justifiable in the interests of defense, public order and safety, public morality and public health. Despite changes in the constitution, following the army takeover, the government continued to acknowledge the general principles embodied in the former constitutional provisions. The media, with their gut survival instincts, were quick to sense that the military government's tolerance had short limits. Occasionally the press would test these limits with a mixture of timidity and boldness, and if the junta did not react unfavorably would proceed to consolidate their gains. On the other hand, if the heavy arm of authority descended on them, they would scamper to the safety of more familiar grounds. It is surprising on how many occasions the press succeeded with these tactics.

The return to civilian government in 1979 and the relaxation of the military grip caused a flurry of journalistic activity. Blaring headlines returned to the front pages; investigative reporters were let loose to flex their muscles after many years of inactivity. There were undoubtedly many excesses and even President Shagari was caricatured mercilessly in independent publications. Nevertheless, there have been no indications of any desire on the part of the government to reimpose restrictions on the free flow of news and the expression of opinions in newspapers.

The principal regulatory laws of the press include the Federal Newspaper Ordinance of 1917, the Publications Ordinance of 1950, the Newspaper (Amendment) Act of 1964, the Sedition Laws of 1964, and the Nigerian Criminal Code. All newspapers are required to be registered, and signed copies of every issue must be deposited with the government. The name and the address of both the publisher and the editor must appear in every issue. In many states a monetary deposit must be made or a bond must be signed in order to obtain a license to publish. The deposit will be forfeit if the publisher should abuse any of the privileges of the press.

One of the last acts of the military government was to set up a Nigerian Press Council in 1978. A self-regulatory body, the council has wide powers, including the enforcement of a code of conduct to define the duties of journalists in "maintaining in spirit as well as in deed the unity and stability of Nigeria." The council consists of a chairman and five members representing various professional associations. The minister of information appoints the chairman and members to the council and approves the terms and conditions of employees of the council.

The decree creating the Press Council has been called a well-intentioned attempt by the government to upgrade and streamline the legal and regulatory system of press control in Nigeria. Some Nigerians, including some journalists, believe it is necessary for everybody to be reminded that the guarantee of press freedom is not a license to the press to do whatever it likes and, in any case, that it is better to have a body with recognized national accountability to oversee non-legal complaints against the press than to leave that responsibility to the whims of state and federal government functionaries. This group also claims that there have been no cases of government censorship of the press arising from the stringent and controversial 1964 Newspaper Admendment Act, which provides for a fine of about $400 or imprisonment for a term of one year for a newspaper publication that publishes any statement, rumor or report knowing or having reason to believe that such statement, rumor or report is false; that the defamation, copyright and other Nigerian laws relating to the press are quite liberal, and not unlike those in countries such as the United States and Britain; and that the Nigerian judiciary is quite independent and has been tenacious in its support of press freedom.

Proponents of drastic relaxation of press laws and a hands-off policy by the government in regard to journalistic activities point out that government is already too heavily involved in the operation of mass communications; that there are constant reports and incidents of direct interference by politicians and government officials, including state governors, in the day-to-day operation of the press; and that government enforcement of press regulations is more likely to be directed at suppressing opposition party papers than at safeguarding the public interest or curbing reckless reporting by newspapers.

On the first point, they emphasize that the government controls the entire broadcast industry, has become dominant in the print media, and inordinately influences the entire mass communication system by issuing daily news releases on government activities, organizing press conferences and briefings, and preparing and distributing publicity materials and pamphlets. Some newspapers publish upwards of 80 percent of these materials with little editing. Furthermore, it is feared that the News Agency of Nigeria, which has a vested monopoly on collecting news in Nigeria for sale to foreign news agencies, may turn out to be another arm of government control.

There have also been instances when the press or a particular newspaper was forbidden to print certain news or even to obtain such. Some state-owned papers have allegedly been prevented from reporting agitations for the creation of additional states and state visits by politicians of opposing political parties. In 1975 a *New Nigerian* reporter was barred from covering a land suit proceeding and two journalists with the now-defunct *Renaissance* were arrested in connection with the publication of a feature story referring to the "Killing of Biafra," which the editorial board of the paper later disclaimed. Two years later the press was prohibited from reporting the proceedings of a public officer's assets probe and the *Daily Times* was ordered to discontinue its coverage of the Constituent Assembly because of negative evaluation of some aspects of the proceedings on the paper's front page. Recently, the *Tribune*'s plant in Ibadan was sealed off by the Nigerian police because of unspecified suspicions following the publication of strident anti-federal government news items by the paper.

Perhaps the most drastic government action against a publication since the end of the civil war in 1970 was a two-year prohibition of circulation imposed on a popular magazine called *Newbreed*. This action was taken by the federal military government in June 1978 under the war-time Newspaper Decree 17 of 1967. It was said that the mid-June 1978 issue of the magazine, 50,000 copies of which were impounded by the government, "carried a picture of Chief Obafemi Awolowo and asks who's ganging up against Chief Awolowo" and contained another story titled "The Uses and Abuses of NSO [Nigeria Security Organization]" as well as an analysis of the possible uses of such government organizations.

State-Press Relations

One of the redeeming features of the Nigerian society is its pluralism, which has enabled it to survive the pressures of state-imposed homogeneity. Extended to the media, this pluralism has encouraged a multiplicity of voices, jealously guarded by the contending religious, ethnic and political groups as a means of preserving their separate identities. The constitution ensures that the federal government will not be able to silence diversity in the media without the cooperation of the state governments. The press laws and their administration is one of the residual subjects within the legislative competence of each state. As a result the federal information department does not play a major role in controlling the media. Press and broadcasting services owned by the government are run by statutory public corporations.

The last years of military rule were particularly severe; the junta was close to achieving total control over the press when they decided to step down. In June 1978 a two-year ban was imposed on the fortnightly newsmagazine *Newbreed* under the Newspapers (Prohibition of Circulation) Decree 17 of 1967 for allegedly exacerbating tribal and religious tensions. In late 1978 two newspaper editors were suspended for publishing stories the government viewed as inaccurate.

The euphoria is state-press relations that followed the restoration of civilian government in 1979 did not last long, as journalists began to train their guns on familiar targets. Their first target was the salaries of new government representatives. The *Daily Times* began leading the campaign but soon found itself in trouble when the government (which owns 60 percent of the paper's stock) quietly changed the management. The *Nigerian Tribune* followed by launching an attack on members of the government. These attacks prompted President Shagari to issue a mild rebuke to the press, much to the surprise of journalists who had looked upon him as a strong advocate of press freedom.

Attitude Toward Foreign Media

After the end of the civil war (which Nigeria regarded as fomented partly by the Western media) foreign correspondents had difficulty in obtaining entry visas. They had to go through the News Agency of Nigeria, and those suspected of not being sympathetic to Nigerian interests received no response to their applications. The situation changed after the installation of a civilian administration. The immigration authorities were instructed not to ban any foreign correspondents. Nigerian embassies and consulates abroad, however, still exercise prudence in granting visas. They are believed to maintain extensive dossiers on foreign journalists, especially those who have written on Nigeria. Once within the country few Western correspondents were harassed, and IPI has not reported any instances of imprisonment or expulsion of foreign correspondents in recent years.

A few Western publications were banned in the years prior to 1975, but barring such occasional incidents, Nigeria has maintained a fairly good record in its treatment of the foreign media. The major world news agencies operate in Nigeria and foreign broadcasts are received without any government interference. Similarly, imported publications, including international air editions of *Time, Newsweek, The New York Times, The Times* of London, the *International Herald Tribune,* and other international publications and periodicals, are available.

Like most African nations, Nigeria has consistently supported fellow African Amadou Mahtar M'Bow's efforts through the UNESCO to legitimize state control over the media and limit their activity to one of "constructive criticism" on the Soviet model.

News Agencies

The national news agency is the News Agency of Nigeria (NAN), founded in 1978. Despite the size of its press, Nigeria was among the last countries in Africa to set up its own news agency.

Electronic News Media

Public broadcasting is a joint responsibility of the federal and state governments. The federal agencies in this field are the Federal Radio Corporation of Nigeria, founded in 1978 to replace the Nigerian Broadcasting Corporation, and the Nigerian Television Authority, founded in 1976. Regional autonomy is strongly emphasized in the FRC's and NTA's charters. The national radio network owned by the federal government is divided into five zones: Lagos, Enugu, Ibadan, Kaduna and external. In addition, each state has a broadcasting corporation. NTV has nine stations, at Aba/Owerri, Benin City, Enugu, Ibadan, Jos, Kaduna, Kano, Lagos, Port Harcourt and Sokoto; other stations are being set up at nine additional centers. Radio is perhaps the most pervasive of all mass media while television is the least effective and the most elitist. Both radio and television are heavily subsidized by the state although they also receive revenues from advertising and license fees.

Education & Training

There was no college-level journalism training in Nigeria until the establishment of a U.S.-style department of journalism at the University of Nigeria Nsukka in the early 1960s. Since then two more universities have established departments of journalism, including the Institute of Mass Communication in Lagos. The Institute, which offers a three-year degree program and a diploma at the completion of a nine-month training course, is the regional training center for broadcasting personnel in all anglophone African countries. The Nigerian Institute of Journalism was inaugurated in 1971 as a joint venture of the Nigerian Newspaper Proprietors' Association, the Nigerian Guild of Editors, the International Press Institute and the Ford Foundation. The Institute offers a crash program for working journalists, usually lasting three months.

Summary

In vitality and dynamism the Nigerian press has declined since independence. The bulk of the daily press is in government hands, and the press as a whole has not experienced a growth proportionate to that of the economy. But compared to most other African countries the Nigerian press is still in good shape.

There are a number of hopeful signs. There is strong evidence that press freedom as a social and professional philosophy is very well entrenched in Nigeria. The tenaciousness and frankness with which journalist and other Nigerian groups condemn any attempts to interfere with press freedom and the general recognition and expectation that that kind of reaction is legally and normatively justifiable are strong indications that press freedom is an integral part of the Nigerian political culture. Furthermore government does not interfere ideologically with journalism and mass communications training programs. Nigeria has some of the finest journalists on the continent, many of them trained under Zik and Cecil King and Percy Roberts of the *Daily Times*. These are a hardy breed whom governments may be able to mute but never muzzle. The Fleet Street traditions survive, if not in Kakawa Street where the *Daily Times* lords over it contemporaries, then in many of the smaller newspapers founded before or just after independence. The oil-fueled prosperity is evident everywhere in the country and has put new life into many of the older national institutions, including the media.

Finally, the Nigerian press is highly political. It is unlikely that it will be effectively suppressed by the government as long as party politics endure in Nigeria.

CHRONOLOGY

1975   Two top journalists with *Renaissance* arrested in connection with feature on "Killing of Biafra."
New Nigerian reporter barred from taking notes in proceedings of land suit at Oguta (Anambra State) High Court.
International Press Conference held in Lagos.
Coup topples General Gowon and makes Murtala Rama Mohamed military head of state.
New Nigerian and *Gaskiya Ta Ki Kwabo* taken over by federal military government, which also acquired 60 percent equity shares of Daily Times Group.

1976   Murtala Mohamed assassinated in coup attempt; Olusegun Obasanjo becomes head of state February 15.
Federal government takes over all responsibility for television broadcasting and all television stations.
The Punch, a daily, founded.

1977   Nigerian Television Authority (NTA) created by military decree.
Daily Times barred from covering proceedings of Constituent Assembly.

1978   News Agency of Nigeria (NAN), created by federal government in 1976, begins operation.
Government passes decree setting up Nigerian Press Council.
Federal Radio Corporation replaces Nigerian Broadcasting Corporation.
Lagos gets new daily, *The Nationalist*.
Military government imposes two-year ban on fortnightly newsmagazine *Newbreed*.

1979   Code of Conduct for Nigerian Press set up by Nigerian Press Organization.
Military step down and civilian government restored. New constitution reaffirms guarantees of freedom of expression.
Management of *Daily Times* reshuffled in effort to remove executives critical of government policies.

BIBLIOGRAPHY

Aboaba, D. "The Nigerian Press Under Military Rule." Doctoral Dissertation, State University of New York at Buffalo, 1979.

Anamaleze, John, Jr. *The Nigerian Press: The People's Conscience.* New York, 1979.

Asaju, Michael. "Assessing Nigeria's Newspapers." *West Africa,* July 21, 1981, p. 1337.

Barton, Frank. *The Press of Africa: Persecution and Perseverance.* New York, 1979.

Daura, Mamman. "Editing a Government Newspaper in Nigeria." In Olav Stokke, *Reporting Africa,* New York, 1971.

Duyile, Dayo. *Media and Mass Communication in Nigeria.* Ibadan, Nigeria, 1979.

Elias, T. O., *Nigerian Press Law.* London, 1969.

Jakande, Lafeet. *The Role of the Mass Media in a Developing Country.* Ile-Ife, Nigeria, 1974.

Ladele, Olu, et al. *History of Nigerian Broadcasting Corporation.* Ibadan, Nigeria, 1979.

Nwankwo, Robert. "Political Culture or Professional Underdevelopment: Identity and Leadership in African and Afro-American Press." *Resources in Education,* March 1979.

Omu, Fred. *Press and Politics in Nigeria 1880–1937.* London, 1978.

Wilcox, Dennis. *Mass Media in Black Africa.* New York, 1975.

NORWAY

by Harold A. Fisher

BASIC DATA

Population: 4,066,134 (1979)
Area: 323,895 sq. km. (125,056 sq. mi.)
GNP: 214.38 billion krone (US$43.52 billion) (1979)
Literacy Rate: 98%
Language(s): Norwegian
Number of Dailies: 72 (1979)
   Aggregate Circulation: 1,682,900
   Circulation per 1,000: 414
Number of Nondailies: 88 (1979)
   Aggregate Circulation: 451,214
   Circulation per 1,000: 111
Number of Periodicals: 3,855 (1977)

Number of Radio Stations: NA
Number of Television Stations: NA
Number of Radio Receivers: 1,318,000 (1977)
   Radio Receivers per 1,000: 326
Number of Television Sets: 1,163,431 (1981)
   Television Sets per 1,000: 286
Total Annual Newsprint Consumption: 94,400 metric tons (1977)
Per Capita Newsprint Consumption: 23.3 kg. (51.4 lb.)
Total Newspaper Ad Receipts: 1.5 billion krone (US$304.7 million) (1979)
   As % of All Ad Expenditures: 46.5

Background & General Characteristics

Although circulations of newspapers are typically small in Norway, the industry may be characterized as an active, lively one that enjoys a large measure of constitutionally guaranteed freedom. In fact, the Norwegian press is one of the world's freest. Most of the papers represent a definite orientation toward some particular political party or political view. Most of press activity occurs in the more populous eastern regions of the country.

In 1979 Norway was the home of 160 newspapers, with a total circulation of 2,134,114. Seventy-two of the papers were dailies, with a total circulation of about 1,682,000 copies, or an average circulation of 23,360 each. Only a few of these dailies claimed high circulation. The other 88 papers, mostly nondailies that appear two or three times each week, average about 5,100 copies each and reach slightly over 451,000 readers in all. In addition, depending on which source is quoted, there are between 2,000 and 4,000 periodicals, with a circulation of well over two million.

Norway has no newspaper chains and only one private grouping. Instead, newspapers are privately owned, usually by corporations; shares are held by individuals and/or by political parties. Because circulations are low, many of the smaller and medium-sized papers have been experiencing financial difficulties.

The Norwegian newspaper audience is, in general, well educated, affluent and appreciative of the values of a free and responsible press. Illiteracy is very low, well below two percent. All children between seven and 16 must attend school, and many choose higher education as well.

Although there is a single language—Norwegian—it has two slightly different forms that are officially recognized as equal. The older form, Borkmal, is employed in about 80 percent of the nation's schools; the other 20 percent teach in the newer Neo-Norwegian form, or Nynorsk.

Most of Norway's urban population concentrations are in the south and east. The rugged western Atlantic coastal and the colder northern Arctic Circle regions are sparsely populated. Consequently, most publishing and other media activities are concentrated in the southern and eastern cities. The rugged geography of Norway splits the country into a number of well-defined regions, mostly rather isolated from each other. This results in close-knit societies in the regions and helps to explain why Norway has about 160 newspapers.

After Sweden and Great Britain, Norway has one of the world's highest readership rates, with about one daily for every three persons. The rural areas are well served both by the numerous small local dailies and by a diverse range of nondailies and periodicals.

Although many Norwegian papers employ bold headlines, numerous photographs, and techniques of strong popular and entertainment appeal, the news and commentary are generally serious and of high quality. Most provide a steady diet of serious informative features. Since the press considers education of the public a primary goal, cultural and historical articles abound. Another indicator of quality is the signed and dated chronicle ("kronikk"), which is spread across the bottom of the editorial page. The kronikk is generally a thought-provoking essay on some important intellectual or political subject. Another factor that contributes to quality is the political orientation each paper represents; editors feel they must give the best representation possible in the interests of serving their favorite party well.

Norway's press history is deep-rooted. As early as about the 14th century the clergy was circulating handwritten reports about noteworthy events. Printed newssheets appeared sporadically in the 1600s. The country's first formal paper, the *Norske Intelligenz Seddeler,* was founded in Bergen in 1763.

Since Norway was then part of the Danish monarchy, the earliest papers were strictly censored. By 1800 some papers began publicly to oppose both the Danish king and union with Denmark. Their influence helped Norway to declare independence in 1814, and the national decision to adopt a constitution similar to that of the United States. The new constitution provided the basis for the free press that Norway now enjoys, and Norwegian newspapers soon began to play important roles as sources of information and shapers of the country's public opinion.

By the 1830s local and municipal governments began to play a key role in the affairs of the nation, and a local political press arose to report and to reflect this new interest.

Norway experienced its version of the Industrial Revolution in the mid-1800s, and with it came expansion and growth of the press. A few years later political disagree-

ments between liberals and conservatives led to national political parties, and newspapers sprang up to champion them. Thus, the pattern of today's partisan journalism was firmly established.

Between the beginning of the 20th century and World War II the press enjoyed a period of rapid expansion. About 80 newspapers and numerous periodicals were founded during this period.

Then the Nazi occupation of Norway closed many papers during World War II. The German invaders jailed or executed many editors. But the Germans could not prevent the rise of some 300 underground newspapers, which, at great risk to themselves, kept Norwegians informed about the course of the war and events outside the country. The underground papers got their news from British shortwave broadcasts and published anywhere from a few hundred to 20,000 copies on mimeograph machines and secretly placed presses. They used devious means to inform the public surreptitiously about events of the war not reported or falsified by the Germans. The construction of stories and even the wording of advertisements gave clues to the real truth. These sheets served as valuable morale boosters to the freedom-loving Norwegians.

Today, newspapers and periodicals are published almost exclusively in Norwegian. A few periodicals represent the views of the official Lutheran Church or other special interests, but most are purely commercial ventures.

Newspapers, however, reflect a strong political orientation. A few papers are actually owned by political parties, such as Oslo's *Arbeiderbladet,* the Labour Party's official organ, and *Friheten,* the Communist Party's mouthpiece. But most papers, even though they would like to call themselves nonpolitical, have definite party leanings. They are, however, independent of direct party attachments.

Papers that support Labour Party views are most numerous, but most of their circulations are small. Conservative Party supporters are nearly as numerous; their ranks include Oslo's prestigious *Aftenposten.* Papers representing the Liberal Party are next in number, followed by those that back the Agrarian Party. Supporters of all other parties lag far behind these first four. However, a high percentage of the papers prefer to call themselves independent, which masks their leanings toward their favorite political party.

Most Norwegian dailies employ regular-size pages, standard formats, eight columns, with a liberal number of color pictures and some front-page advertising. Makeup is neat and orderly. In the case of *Aftenposten,* the nation's leading daily, advertising accounts for about 65 percent of the morning edition's space and about 46 percent of the evening edition. *Aftenposten* averages 44 pages for its morning editions and 16 for the evening version, but small circulation dailies are considerably thinner.

Papers are well organized, with a news and commentary section at the beginning, one on sports, another on business and financial items, and a fourth on features, political news and the like. In the past newspaper stories were written in chronological order; recently the summary lead and the most-important-news-first style of news agencies have been gaining acceptance, especially for national and international stories. Most papers are open to opinions of all kinds and carry numerous letters from readers. Although the practice is now dying, many of the papers are still agglutinated at the fold.

The leading daily, *Aftenposten,* has both an a.m. and a p.m. edition, with the former claiming the larger sales. Papers across the country are divided between morning and evening editions. In keeping with Norwegian law, no newspapers are published on Sundays. Consequently, big weekend editions are published on Saturdays.

Norway's many small local dailies are mostly printed outside the towns. For years, for example, *Lofotposten,* which has been a leader north of the Polar Circle, has been published at the Svolvaer fishing station. Since about 1977, air transportation to even remote villages has made possible same-day delivery of all Norwegian papers. Even tiny towns on the distant Russian border are reached on the day of publication. Most Norwegian papers are bought by subscription.

Norway has nearly 4,000 periodicals. However, except for a few, their circulations are low. Women's magazines are particularly popular and make up over one-fourth of the circulation. Leading women's magazines include *Alle Kvinner* (circulation 102,865 in 1979), *Mitt Liv* (46,070) and *Det Nye* (126,340). Especially popular family-type magazines include *Allers* (238,780), *Det Beste* (247,470), *Familien* (100,050), *Hjemmet* (368,250), and *Norsk Ukeblad* (310,675). There are specialist periodicals that focus on farming, trade, economics, literary matters, the arts, labor, ship-ping and on numerous other trades, professions and special interests.

A number of Norwegian cities can boast of two or more competing papers. Oslo leads with eight, followed by Bergen with five. Kristiansand, Molde and Stavanger are home base for three. Two competing papers vie in 19 cities: Alesund, Arendal, Bodo, Drammen, Floro, Gjovik, Kristiansund, Larvik, Moss, Namsos, Narvik, Sandefjord, Skien, Stjordal, Tonsberg, Tromso, Trondheim, Vadso and Voss.

Low circulation characterizes most Norwegian papers. Average circulation for all 160 newspapers, daily and those published less frequently, reaches around 13,330. Only one city, Oslo, produces papers with circulations over 100,000. There the high circulation dailies are *Aftenposten, Verdens Gang* and *Dagbladet.* Papers with 50,000–100,000 circulation come from four cities: Bergen, Oslo, Stavanger and Trondheim. There are eight dailies with circulations between 25,000 and 50,000. Thirty-two claim circulations between 10,000 and 25,000. Most of the country's remaining 25 papers have circulations below 10,000, with many selling only 2,000 to 3,000 copies daily.

In 1979 the three Oslo leaders in circulation, *Aftenposten, Verdens Gang* and *Dagbladet,* could also be considered Norway's most influential dailies, with *Aftenposten* the clear leader nationally and among high-quality elite dailies internationally.

Economic Framework

Because of her climate and geographic structure, less than three percent of Norway's land is cultivated. Many Norwegians make their living from the sea; her fishermen take about one-twentieth of the world's catch, and fish is a major export. Manufacture of aluminum, electro-technical products and engineering also contribute heavily to the nation's predominantly industrialized economy. Since the 1960s the North Sea oil industry has boomed, but exploratory investments must still be paid off. Another formerly profitable industry, ship building, has run into financial difficulties. Inflation and the increased cost of living have plagued the financial outlook.

The resultant decrease in real living standards has pushed many of the small and medium-sized papers into financial difficulty. Help for them has come from private indi-

10 Largest Newspapers by Circulation (1979)		
Newspaper	Place of Publication	Circulation
Aftenposten	Oslo	223,840 (a.m.)
		159,610 (p.m.)
Verdens Gang	Oslo	171,370
Dagbladet	Oslo	124,005
Bergens Tidende	Bergen	84,770
Addresseavisen	Trondheim	76,310
Arbeiderbladet	Oslo	60,090
Stavanger Aftenblad	Stavanger	53,780
Faedrelands- vennen	Kristiansand	38,550
Drammens Tidende og Buskeruds Blad	Drammen	34,920
Summorsposten	Alesund	33,000

viduals, political parties and other organizations. Some of the papers have economized by sharing news copy, even though they represent differing political views. But all this has not been sufficient to keep the smaller papers out of financial trouble.

So, aid for the economically struggling papers has also come from the Norwegian government. Papers first felt financial pressures in the late 1960s, when there were 156 newspapers and their continuance was deemed vital to the country's political and democratic life. Press subsidies totalling 15 million crowns (about $2.5 million) were introduced in 1969. By 1975 the subsidies had grown to 70 million crowns, half of them for government advertising.

In 1972 a Press Fund was set up to grant cheap loans to newspapers, a life-saver to the country's smaller papers that had not been able to make ends meet because of low circulation incomes. Annual subsidies have continued ever since. Much of the initiative for press support has come from the papers. Direct aid from the government has been in the form of subsidies, loans, help with distribution costs, government advertising, and training and research grants. The government has, in fact, become one of the papers' biggest advertisers and the amount spent on government advertising is roughly that given to production subsidies. The government states that all papers benefit about equally from its advertising.

Indirect aid has included preferential postal rates, exemptions from sales taxes, value-added tax (VAT) concessions, special telephone and telegraph rates, help to news agencies, and subsidies for joint distribution and production and for the political parties with which the papers are associated.

For a while there were fears the government assistance might affect the freedom of the press or that the government would show favoritism. But such fears have not been substantiated up to the present. Most of such objections came from the Conservative Party, on the grounds they would distort free competition. But these arguments softened with time. Today production subsidies go to about two-thirds of all Norwegian newspapers, while the leading newspapers in each district get the lion's share of the advertising.

The subsidies are based on the amount of newsprint used for the editorial portion of each paper. All small newspapers with a circulation of 10,000 or less receive an equitable share. Others with higher circulations can get subsidies only if they are not the leading paper in their district in advertising revenues. Papers with a circulation of over 80,000 are not eligible for production subsidies.

Both the broadcasting and the print media are vigorous and healthy in Norway. Their services are complementary. Both enjoy a strong measure of independence from government.

Norway has no major publishing chains; newspapers are primarily privately owned. Most of the larger papers are owned by corporations in which individuals and/or political parties hold shares. For example, the Norwegian Federation of Trade Unions and the Labour Party own and subsidize the Labour press. A Conservative holding company, Libertas, subsidizes a few Conservative papers; but most Conservative-leaning papers prefer financial independence. In recent years, there has been a loosening of party ties, especially on the part of papers that are politically in the center. Only a few papers are actually operated as official mouthpieces of political parties.

At present, only one private ownership group exists in which the owners are all private individuals. The Schibsted Group publishes Aftenposten and VG, with a total circulation of over 550,000. This group also provides evidence of the fact that party affiliation is less important than in the past, for Aftenposten is a Conservative paper and VG is an Independent Liberal one.

A number of Norway's papers are of high

quality. *Aftenposten* is perhaps the leading quality elite daily. In general, the press gives priority to provision of serious information and to materials that educate the public. While entertainment and human interest features are present to stimulate readership, there is a steady diet of cultural and historical features. Serious intent is the theme that runs throughout the entire press. The kronikk is a characteristic feature of many papers. Much space is devoted to literature, music, the theater and the arts. Most papers feature editorial pages.

Despite the financial stringencies faced by many papers during the 1970s, the great majority have survived. In 1970 there were 81 dailies; today there are 72.

Norway produces several times as much newsprint as she consumes. In 1977, for example, internal consumption of newsprint totaled over 94,000 metric tons while exports exceeded 340,000 metric tons. Thus the Norwegian newspaper industry has an advantage of a cheap, abundant supply of newsprint.

Press Laws

The Norwegian Constitution guarantees press freedom. Article 100 specifically states:

> There shall be liberty of the press. No person must be punished for any writing, whatever its contents may be, which he has caused to be printed or published, unless he wilfully and manifestly has either himself shown or incited others to disobedience to the laws, contempt of religion or morality or the constitutional powers, or resistance to their orders, or has advanced false and defamatory accusations against any other person. Everyone shall be free to speak his mind frankly on the administration of the State or on any other subject whatsoever.

No subset of laws exists to further restrain the press. Reporters, editors and managers are as answerable to penal and other laws as any other citizen. Thus journalists bear a heavy responsibility for what appears in their papers, especially in matters that may be libelous.

Journalists may legally conceal their sources, but in case of trials, they may be subject to imprisonment if they refuse to disclose such information. Since 1951, a law has permitted editors and publishers to refuse to tell where they received information.

Cases of editors being imprisoned for failing to reveal their sources at trials are very rare.

Censorship

The only censorship the Norwegian press has experienced occurred during the Danish monarchy in the latter part of the 18th century and during the World War II Nazi occupation. Undoubtedly those experiences have contributed to national desire to establish and protect a free, unfettered press.

State-Press Relations

Oversight of the media in Norway comes under the minister for communications. Under his ministry, the Norwegian Broadcasting Corporation controls all radio and television. The corporation has a director-general, an administrative director, a foreign relations officer, a press and information officer, a director of radio programs and a director of TV programs. Publishers of dailies and periodicals also relate to this ministry.

The press, even within the state's broadcasting monopoly, can and does criticize government. However, the emphasis on the educational role of the press is kept in balance with the adversary role it also carries. Until a few years ago representatives of the press treated government officials with considerable deference and respect. Several recent developments have altered that relationship. First, the current revolution in mass communications has often given the press informational insights even officials have lacked. Also, the introduction of the Freedom of Information Act now permits the Norwegian press unprecedented insights into administrative procedures. Finally, recent emphasis on investigative journalism has made journalists bolder and more suspicious of Norwegian governmental officials.

The Norwegian government recognizes these changes and continues to realize that knowledge of official information is necessary to the political process and that the mass media must have freedom of access to such information if democracy is to thrive. Norway allows about as free access to official documents of the government as any country in the world. The Norwegian Foreign Minister both recognized the new tensions between government and the press and reaffirmed the need for a free press in his 1979 address to the Norwegian Union of Journalists.

While the government encourages the press to keep its reports balanced and to relax its criticism of government, there is no overt official attempt to manage the news. Rather, the government appeals to the press for support, understanding and interpretation of the time-consuming processes made necessary by democratic rule. Because of the high degree of accessibility to information about matters of public interest, the press has always exercised considerable influence on governmental policies.

Although the state has had to subsidize the press since 1969, it has tried earnestly to be fair and to avoid exercising control through its benefits to the press. Neither printing equipment nor journalists are subject to licenses or to direct restrictions.

Attitude Toward Foreign Media

Foreign correspondents have free access to Norwegian affairs. However, foreign ownership of the Norwegian press is officially discouraged. Both the government and the press are in sympathy with Western press organizations on media issues discussed in UNESCO. Partly because of Norway's extended exposure to the sea and her interests in trade, the country is especially interested in international affairs. It is also desirous of a free press everywhere and protective of the rights and freedom of journalists in countries where the state controls the press.

Norwegian journalists have been very active in the International Press Institute, which seeks to protect journalists' rights and freedoms everywhere. Norway served as host to the 21st International Press Institute Assembly in Oslo.

News Agencies

Norway has two national press agencies. The A/C Norsk Telegrambrya (Norwegian News Agency or NTB) was founded in 1867 and is located in Oslo. It is owned by the press itself, with a large number of papers as shareholders. It serves as the principal feeder of information to the press and to the Norwegian Broadcasting Services. Its director is Per Monson, a former director of the International Press Institute. NTB signifies the Norwegian Telegram Bureau. When Norway was under Nazi occupation, the agency was forced to carry the German bulletins and many then said the NTB was an acronym for "Not To Believe" for obvious reasons.

The second agency is the Norsk Press Service A/C, or Norwegian Press Service. Also located in Oslo, it distributes the services of the Associated Press in Norway, which a number of papers receive.

A number of foreign news bureaus are located in Oslo: Agence France-Presse (France), Agentstvo Pechate Novosti (USSR), Associated Press (U.S.), Deutsche Presse-Agentur (West Germany) and Reuters (U.K.). The Agenzia Nationale Stampa Associata (Italy) and United Press International (U.S.) also keep correspondents in the capital.

Electronic News Media

Both radio and television are state monopolies in Norway. Income to operate the services comes from individual license fees on sets and from state subsidies. Sound broadcasting officially began in 1925 and the initial televison transmissions commenced in 1960. Coverage for radio broadcasting is 100 percent across the country and nearly so for television.

Both radio and television maintain regular news services. Even though broadcasting services are controlled by the state, broadcast journalists, like their print press counterparts, enjoy full freedom to report virtually without restrictions. The Norwegian Broadcasting Services feature numerous lively news commentaries and documentaries in addition to the regular newscasts. News programs draw heavy audiences. According to recent opinion polls, radio news bulletins are considered to be most reliable, followed by TV news and then newspapers. Perhaps the Norwegian audience balances its sources of information between electronic and printed news better than some peoples, as Norwegians remain among the world's highest subscribers to and readers of newspapers.

Education & Training

Norwegian universities have fully accredited journalism and mass media programs, and they are supplemented with a required period of practical training in the field. However, many of the present journalists got their start on the job as apprentices. Newspapers seek staff members who have the highest possible general knowledge, preferably those with college or postgraduate degrees in the arts, social sciences or hard sciences. Papers then frequently provide journalistic training during service.

Both the journalists' organizations and individual papers provide awards and special recognition to journalists who have distinguished themselves.

The Norwegian Press Association, or Presseforbundet, was founded in 1910 by Olav Thommessen, a former editor of Oslo's daily *Verdens Gang.* When the owner of *Verdens Gang* interfered in editorial matters, Thommessen quit in protest and immediately started his own new paper, *Tidens Tegn,* which soon became one of the country's leading dailies. His negative experience led Thommessen to collaborate with other journalists in the formation of Presseforbundet.

Today, Presseforbundet is comprised of three organizations. One is for working journalists and has a membership of over 2,500. Another is for editors, with a membership of more than 200. The third is for management. Presseforbundet serves as spokesman for the press in governmental and public matters. In the 1920s it set up a seven-member Press Council, composed of five representatives from the working press and two from the reading public. The council rules when one paper files with it a complaint against another paper or when the public has a grievance against a newspaper. The paper involved is expected to publish the council's findings, be they favorable or adverse. Although this is an honor system and the council has no jurisdictional authority, to date involved papers have always obeyed its decisions and published its findings in full.

Summary

The Norwegian press, long one of the world's most unfettered, has remained healthy and diverse, despite its need for government subsidies since 1969. Most papers are small; average circulation is only slightly over 13,000. Competition is particularly stiff in Oslo, where eight dailies vie for sales.

Norwegian journalism is high quality, with Oslo's *Aftenposten* one of the world's leading elite dailies.

Although the press has become increasingly adversarial in recent years, the government recognizes and even encourages this role, realizing that a free, responsible press is a necessity to the operation of a truly democratic society. The press is strong partly because it is unified by a dynamic press organization, the Presseforbundet, and served by a respected Press Council. Both handle affairs of the press in an orderly and effective manner.

Because of its diversity, its generally high quality and its high credibility, the Norwegian press appears to have a bright future. The only real possible cloud in the future of the Norwegian press is the question of economic viability and the accepted need for governmental support. Official subsidies in a variety of forms appear to be a necessity now for sustaining a diverse press; there is a danger such dependence could weaken the ability of the press to perform its adversary function. Thus far the Parliament has insisted that subsidies be made on condition that they have nothing to do with the content of papers subsidized. It seems that spirit may continue to exist.

If it does, the Norwegian press will continue to be a model free press in a free, democratic society.

CHRONOLOGY

1975	Printers boycott advertisements for travel to Spain.
1977	Air delivery of newspapers throughout Norway makes possible same-day delivery of dailies everywhere.
	Foreign minister clarifies current press and state relations, reaffirms principle of a free press.
	Annual International Press Institute Assembly held in Oslo.
1978	Some problems with security leaks in the press occur.

BIBLIOGRAPHY

"All Have Been Created Equal—On Paper, That Is...." *IPI Report*. September/October 1973, pp. 10-11.

Frost, J.M., ed. *World Radio TV Handbook, 1981*. London, 1981.

"Institute Affairs: Per Monsen, Norway." *IPI Report*, June 1975, p. 4.

Knapp, Viktor, ed. *National Reports: Norway*. Paris, 1972

Merrill, John, Bryan, Carter, and Alisky, Marvin. *The Foreign Press*. Baton Rouge, La., 1970.

Merrill, John, and Fisher, Harold. *The World's Great Dailies*. New York, 1980.

Nilson, Philos. "Norway—Government, Administration and Politics." UDA 128/79, September 1979, Oslo, Norway.

Norway Information. "Political Facts and Figures." October 1977.

Norwegian Telecommunications Administration. *Telecommunications in Norway*. Oslo, 1975.

Ostgaard, Einar. "Effects of Growing Dependence on Government Aid." *IPI Report*, April 1976, pp. 18-19.

Peaslee, Amos J. *Constitutions of Nations, Vol. III, Europe*. New York, 1980.

"Press Freedom Report: Norway." *IPI Report*, December 1975, p. 4.

Rowat, Donald C. "Security Leaks in Norway and the Public Right to Know." *Canadian Forum*, May 1978.

Royal Ministry of Foreign Affairs Press Department Reference Papers. "Norway's Constitution—A Brief History." No. 122, 1970.

Royal Norwegian Ministry of Foreign Affairs. "The Government and the Mass Media." Doc. 042/79, April 25, 1979, Oslo, Norway.

Smith, Anthony. "Who's Afraid of Handouts?" *IPI Report*, May/June 1977, pp. 21-22.

"Subsidy Principle Accepted, But...." *IPI Report*, November 1975, pp. 8-9.

Thomsen, Per. "Norway." *IPI Report*, April 1977, pp. 4-5.

PAKISTAN

by George Kurian

BASIC DATA

Population: 85,279,000 million
Area: 803,000 sq. km. (309,958 sq. mi.)
GNP: Rs 192 billion (US$19.4 billion) (1978)
Literacy Rate: 21%
Language(s): Urdu, English, Sindhi, Pushtu, Gujerati
Number of Dailies: 104
  Aggregate Circulation: 965,000
  Circulation per 1,000: 12.7
Number of Nondailies: 355
  Aggregate Circulation: NA
  Circulation per 1,000: NA
Number of Periodicals: 1,145

Number of Radio Stations: 12
Number of Television Stations: 5
Number of Radio Receivers: 1.54 million
  Radio Receivers per 1,000: 18
Number of Television Sets: 545,800
  Television Sets per 1,000: 6.4
Total Annual Newsprint Consumption: 19,000 metric tons
Per Capita Newsprint Consumption: 0.3 kg. (0.66 lb.)
Total Newspaper Ad Receipts: NA
  As % of All Ad Expenditures: NA

Background & General Characteristics

The Pakistani press is a direct descendant of the so-called Muslim or League press of pre-independence India, founded primarily to counteract the influential Hindu nationalist press and to advance the demands for a separate Muslim state in the Indian subcontinent. The Islamic press faced the dual disadvantage of competing with the much more powerful nationalist press, which was bitterly opposed to the partition of India, and catering to a less literate and less wealthy Muslim minority. Although its circulation was meager, the League press (so called because of its association with the Muslim League) was an effective medium in the consolidation of Muslim public opinion. Prominent among the Muslim newspapers of this period were *Comrade* (Calcutta/Delhi, 1911–14 and 1924–26), *Hamdard* (Delhi, 1913), *Al-Hilal* (Calcutta, 1912–16, 1927) and *Zamindar* (Lahore, 1911–16, 1920–57); all of these were edited by political figures rather than newspapermen, and thus represented a kind of personalized journalism concerned less with news than with ideology.

By 1925 the Muslim press had grown in size and circulation and comprised about 220 newspapers in nine languages including Urdu, English and Bengali. The Urdu papers numbered 120, English 18 and Bengali 14. By regions, undivided Punjab had 85, all except four in Urdu, United Provinces 44, Bombay and Sind 37 and Madras 26. Undivided Bengal had 22, of which only six were published from the Muslim areas comprising present-day Bangladesh. Very few of these papers were known, let alone read, outside of the Muslim community and only 11 had circulations sizable enough to make them financially viable: *Al-Balagh* and *Musalman* of Calcutta, *Muslim Rajput* of Amritsar, *Muslim Outlook* of Lahore, *Rahbar-i-Deccan* of Hyderabad, *Hamdam* of Lucknow, *Aligarh Gazette* of Aligarh, *Paisa Akhbar* of Lahore, *Qaumi Report* of Madras and *Al-Awam* and *Al Jamiat* of Delhi.

During the 1930s the Muslim press entered a period of consolidation and expansion under the impetus of the Islamic revival generated by Muhammad Ali Jinnah's Muslim League. Jinnah inspired the founding of the Muslim news agency known as the Oriental Press of India, and also helped to establish several dailies and weeklies in English, Urdu and Gujerati. The best known of these is *Dawn,* the official organ of the League, which became a powerful advocate of Muslim interests under the editorship, ironically enough, of a Syrian (Indian) Christian journalist, Pothan Joseph, and later of Altaf Husain. By the mid-1940s a Muslim daily or weekly existed in every province—some of them enjoying a prestige and circulation comparable to the Hindu nationalist papers. Among the most prominent of these were *Azad* of Calcutta; *The Star of India* and *Morning News*, also of Calcutta; *Manshoor* of Delhi; *Nawai-i-Waqt, The Pakistan Times* and *Eastern Times* of Lahore; *The Muslim Times, Watan, Morning Herald, The Star of Bombay* and *The Weekly Observer* of Allahabad; *New Life* of Patna, *Sind Times* of Karachi, *Khyber Mail* of Peshawar and *Assam Herald* of Shillong. The first All-India Muslim Newspapers Convention at New Delhi on the eve of independence in 1947 was attended by about 100 editors. The same convention launched an All-India Muslim Newspapers Association and an All-India Muslim Working Journalists Association.

The years immediately preceding independence were critical for the Muslim press. The state governments supporting the Indian National Congress confiscated a number of Muslim papers—*The Star, New Life* and *Zamindar* among them—while the high cost of newsprint and printing equipment led to the closure of many others. The material situation of the Muslim press was not improved by the two-way migration that accompanied independence and partition. Although Pakistan inherited Lahore, a major publishing center (Rudyard Kipling once worked there), the majority of journalists and publishers were Hindus or Sikhs, who fled to India with their presses. The Muslim presses that moved to Pakistan were too small to make up the loss. The three exceptions were *Dawn, Jang* and *Anjam,* which switched publishing from Delhi to Karachi and formed the nucleus of the Pakistani press.

Pakistani society in 1947 may be best described as both pre-industrial and pre-literate. This explains the slow growth of the Pakistani press and its anemic state during the country's infancy. It took six years for the number of dailies to reach 55, but by 1958 the figure had reached 103. There was a slump during the next three years due partly to constraints imposed by the martial-law regime but less than a year after martial law ended in 1962 the press began to pick up lost ground, and by 1970 the number of dailies had risen to 117. This period also witnessed the spectacular growth of weeklies, fortnightlies and monthlies, of which 1,145 were reported in 1970.

Papers grew not only in number but in size. Three of the largest dailies almost doubled their sizes between 1948 and 1970. The growth pattern was also reflected in daily circulation, which rose from 120,000 in 1950 to 399,250 in 1965. Most of this increase was accounted for by Urdu and Bengali dailies. *Imroz*, for example, had tripled its circulation between 1965 and 1968, while in the late 1960s *Nawa-i-Waqt* sold over 80,000 copies, *Jang* 150,000 copies and the East Bengal daily *Ittefaq* 33,000. Total daily circulation passed the million mark in 1970, but it was still a low 8.3 copies per 1,000 inhabitants, which placed it in the same class as India.

On the eve of the dismemberment of the country and the establishment of Bangladesh, dailies were published in six languages (English, Urdu, Bengali, Sindhi, Pushtu and Gujerati) and periodicals in about 10. Of the 112 dailies, 25 were in English, 64 in Urdu, 11 in Bengali, six in Sindhi, three in Pushtu and three in Gujerati. About one-third of all publications (dailies, nondailies and periodicals) were published in Urdu and about 20 percent each in English and Bengali. All the Bengali papers became part of the Bangladeshi press in 1972.

Although the territorial changes in the Indian subcontinent have been the principal determinants in the evolution of the Pakistani press, political changes have been equally far-reaching. The country has enjoyed a true democratic government for only 16 years since 1947 and has suffered more political violence than any other country in South Asia. The effect of such instability has been to restrict the size of the press, to discourage the growth of new publications and to subject existing papers to frequent closures. Newspapers, especially the smaller ones, rise and fade rapidly. During elections, many "dead" journals are reborn under various titles, only to disappear after the votes are counted.

In 1980, 104 dailies and 355 weeklies and biweeklies were published in Pakistan: seven in Bahwalpur, nine in Hyderabad, 21 in Karachi, 16 in Lahore, 13 in Lyallpur, four in Multan, 11 in Peshawar, eight in Quetta, six in Rawalpindi, four in Sargodha and five in Sukkur. Fourteen of these dailies are published in English, seven in Sindhi, five in Urdu and Pushtu, one in Gujerati, one in Sindhi and Gujerati, and the remainder in Urdu. Few newspapers publish circulation figures, but UNESCO reported a total circulation of 965,000 in 1977 (down from 1.839 million in 1965) for dailies yielding a per capita circulation of 12.7 per 1,000 inhabitants. This places Pakistan—in terms of readership—in the lowest 20 countries in the world. (No circulation figures have been collected for nondailies and periodicals.) The largest circulation is (claimed by the Urdu morning daily, *Jang*, which sells about 200,000 copies) in Karachi and 100,000 in Rawalpindi. No other paper sells over 100,000 copies; the second-ranking *Zamana* claims a circulation of 90,000, *Imroz* (Lahore and Multan) 50,000 and *Azad* 25,000. Although English-language newspapers enjoy much smaller circulation, they occupy a special position on the press scene. In addition to the *Dawn*, which is believed to reflect official policies closely, the most important English-language dailies are the *Daily News* and the *Morning News* of Karachi and the *Pakistan Times* of Lahore.

Pakistani papers are characterized by the intensity of their political affiliations. Political news and essays dominate the columns to the virtual exclusion of cultural, educational and economic subjects. Dailies average eight to 10 pages with somewhat larger Sunday editions. One page is usually devoted to editorials, features and letters to the editor. Sports and business news are relegated to the back pages. Most of the notices and advertisements are placed by the government or its many agencies.

It is significant that despite its common origin, the journalism of India and Pakistan has developed on divergent lines. Very few Pakistani publications display the maturity that characterizes the Indian press. While three Indian papers appear in *The World's Great Dailies*, none from Pakistan has made that list. Even *Dawn*, the country's most influential daily, is little known to, or read by, the outside world. The absence of an elite press is due partly to economic conditions and partly to the climate of political authoritarianism, the latter having stifled creativity and journalistic initiative for decades.

Economic Framework

During its early years, the Pakistani press was almost entirely privately owned. Although some papers were considered semi-official, the first attempt at creating a party press came in 1954 when the *Pakistan Stan-*

dard was launched by the Muslim League. From 1951 virtually every major political party commanded its own official organ, and the fortunes of parties and publications alike varied with the composition of the government in power. Following the Press and Publication Ordinance of September 1963 the government of Muhammad Ayub Khan proceeded to convert existing papers into "official" organs through the establishment of a National Press Trust, with an initial capital investment of $5.25 million (approximately 52 million rupees) financed by 24 prominent industrialists who did not participate in the trust's management. Avowedly set up to "publish newspapers with a truly national outlook and devoted to the cause of national progress and solidarity and to...develop all other forms of mass information," the trust acquired 10 dailies and one weekly—including the *Morning News* and *Pakistan Times*. The chairmen of the trust, usually nominated by the government, are retired civil servants or army generals. Because of their close association with the powers that be, trust newspapers have been described as a class of "paid pipers"; former prime minister Zulfikar Ali Bhutto called the trust the "Maria Walewska [i.e., mistress] of the Information Ministry."

Because of its small capital base and circulation revenues, even the press outside of direct government control is financially dependent on government advertising for its survival. This dependence is heightened by a severe newsprint shortage in the country, placing newspapers at the mercy of the government for newsprint allocations. Press subservience is reinforced by the sheer economics of publication.

Available financial data, however, indicate that at least the major newspapers and newspaper groups have sizable annual revenues and incomes in Pakistani terms. In the early 1970s two of the papers reported annual revenues of over 9.9 million rupees ($1 million): *Morning News* 18.8 million rupees ($1.9 million) and *Jang* 29.5 million rupees ($2.98 million) while the Progressive Papers group (comprising the *Pakistan Times* and *Imroz*) reported 28 million rupees ($2.83 million). Two others reported annual revenues over five million rupees ($500,000): *Dawn*, 6,732,000 rupees ($680,000) and *Nawa-i-Waqt*, 5,306,400 rupees ($536,000). *Dawn* was the most profitable of these enterprises, reporting an annual income of 2,910,600 rupees ($294,000).

The amount of advertising revenues has not been determined or revealed, but according to one estimate it was well above 148.5 million rupees ($15 million) in the late 1970s. Of this, government advertising accounts for over one-third. Because the Pakistani economy is largely service oriented, the majority of advertisers are small- and middle-scale service industries. The proportion of advertising to news content is generally on the scale of 1:2. *Dawn* and *Pakistan Times* lead in ad volume with 46.7 percent and 43.9 percent respectively. The percentage of government advertising to total advertising is also greater in these publications, at 39.4 percent and 65.4 percent respectively.

Newspapers have always been expensive in relation to wage levels in the country. With a threefold rise in the average price of newspapers between 1960 and 1978, even middle-class workers find it difficult to afford a regular newspaper subscription. A metropolitan daily, for example, costs about 5 percent of the average wages of a factory worker. This explains the slow rise in circulations for most dailies. Over the years, *Dawn* has remained at its 1959 circulation figure. Between 1959 and 1965 *Pakistan Times* gained only 7,450 subscribers, despite the launching of a new Rawalpindi edition. The greatest gains were reported by the mass-circulation Urdu dailies. Between 1959 and 1980, for example, *Jang* increased its circulation tenfold, from 35,377 to over 300,000. However, because of the lack of audited circulation figures (although an Audit Bureau of Circulation has been in existence since 1956), many newspapers tend to inflate their circulation data to mislead advertisers.

Except for Baluchistan, where transportation facilities are poor or nonexistent, other towns are well connected by air, rail and roads, making delivery and distribution relatively quick and inexpensive. Most metropolitan dailies have their own distribution networks.

Technological developments have affected the Pakistani press only marginally. During the early years all dailies except the *Civil and Military Gazette* were hand composed. The first rotary presses were set up by *Dawn, Pakistan Times* and the *Evening Times* around 1950, but the *Morning News* was printed on a flatbed press until 1966. Circulation gains during the 1960s and 1970s have enabled all metropolitan dailies to acquire rotary presses, but smaller regional newspapers still use letterpresses. Language news-

papers (except Gujerati) are not set in type but handwritten by *katibs* (scribes) on butter paper and then transferred to metal plates. Language papers also face another serious problem: translating wire service copy (in English) into the language of the paper, a time-consuming and expensive operation in itself.

English-language newspapers carry a good deal of syndicated material, especially on foreign affairs. Pictorial content has also improved considerably during the 1970s. During an average month *Dawn* and *Pakistan Times* carry between 160 and 210 pictures, representing 4.84 percent and 6.4 percent of their newsholes. All newspapers flaunt their religious orientation by carrying quotations from the Koran and the Hadith (the sayings of the Prophet Muhammad) below the editorial mastheads. The extreme religious sensitivity of Muslim readers has precluded any open discussion of, or comments about, religious issues. The *mullahs* (priests) exercise virtual censorial powers over all publications, and offending papers might find their offices burned down by a mob.

The principal newspaper labor union is the Pakistan Federal Union of Journalists. Before the military takeover in 1977 the union staged a number of strikes—against newspaper proprietors and government threats to close papers.

Press Laws

Pakistan is classified by Freedom House as a not-free country where the laws are designed to keep the press subservient to the interests of the state. The constitution of 1973, amended in 1979, stipulates that "every citizen shall have the right to freedom of speech and expression and there shall be freedom of the press, subject to any reasonable restrictions imposed by the law in the interest of Islam, or the integrity, security, or defense of Pakistan or any part thereof, friendly relations with foreign states, public order, decency or morality, or in relation to contempt of court, defamation or incitement to an offense." The emphasis in Pakistani press history has been on the restrictions, not on the freedom, of the press, although both have equal constitutional standing.

In addition to the restraints implicit in the language of the constitution, succeeding military and civilian governments have introduced their own decrees, regulations and laws —threatening the press from every side. These include:

• The West Pakistan Press and Publications Ordinance, the law that the military has used most extensively since it came to power. It broadens the definition of "objectionable material" so that a publisher can be penalized for practically any printed word or sketch disliked by the government. The publisher is usually required to deposit a very heavy security bond, which he cannot afford to lose. If he does not own his own press, printers may be persuaded to drop him the moment the government threatens action against his paper.

• Amended Penal Code Section 499, which provides for arrest without warrant and imprisonment up to five years and a fine, for criticism, however mild, of the president and others in power.

• Section 124-A of the Pakistan Penal Code, which deals with sedition. Sedition trials are designed to ruin publishers financially because the army-controlled judiciary is invariably expected to render the guilty verdict.

• Official Secrets Act.

• Martial Law Regulation 49, which prohibits the publications of views contrary to Islam and the ideology and integrity of Pakistan. Government actions under this regulation cannot be challenged in a civil court.

Censorship

Formal censorship was reimposed on the Pakistani press in October 1979. The blanket control replaced years of self-censorship by Pakistani journalists. *The Times* of London characterized the censorship as "more severe than anyone can remember in the 32 years of [Pakistan's] troubled existence." Even letters to the editor are censored and paragraphs cut out. Blank spaces are common occurrences in newspaper columns. Neither truth nor public interest may be used to justify publication of news items that the censors consider offensive.

Press censorship had first been imposed in Pakistan in 1971, on the outbreak of the civil war in East Pakistan. It was lifted in 1972 when Bhutto became president, although most of the formal controls and mechanisms were retained. The threat of formal reimposition remained throughout the Bhutto years. In 1973 Bhutto warned newspaper editors that "press freedom cannot [take] precedence

over survival of the nation." In the same year he threatened reprisals against the press if it "distorts the news and resorts to endless invectives and diatribes causing subversion and chaos." In 1975 all newspapers were forced to agree to operate under "press advice" given by officials over the telephone. Twice the government reimposed censorship for brief periods: in October 1975, when the press was prohibited from publishing news of the political situation in the Punjab, and in April 1977, when it was forbidden to publish reports of the opposition's campaign against Bhutto. During these periods uniformed policemen visited newspaper offices to enforce compliance.

State-Press Relations

Until 1958, when martial law was imposed for the first time, the Pakistani press enjoyed a fair measure of freedom. But since that year the press has been fighting a losing battle to maintain its rights, and with every national crisis (the civil war of 1971, the language riots of 1972, agitation against the breakaway-Muslim Ahmadi sect in 1974 and the fall of Bhutto in 1977) it has lost ground. Considering the press to be a political institution, the government has devised a number of checks to keep the media in line with official policies, and to penalize errant newspapers. To rationalize their press curbs, government leaders have characterized Pakistani papers as anti-national, irresponsible and immoral. In 1973 the central information minister said, "Newspapers...have promoted forces of disruption....Some...have maligned the head of state and sought to undermine the morale and discipline of the armed forces...headlines have been blown out of proportion...leading to a sense of despondency and despair." At the same time, government efforts to control the press were described as being designed to "promote healthy, intelligent, and patriotic journalism."

In addition to the legal controls already described, the government wields a broad array of levers to manipulate the press. Only five need be mentioned here. First, the sole authority of the government to allocate newsprint has been used to punish opposition papers and to bring them to their knees. Second, government advertising is used as a carrot to entice financially insecure papers. Under Bhutto a newspaper earned government advertising on the basis of its "constructive" policies. The list of newspapers that have failed in recent years to earn government advertising—or which have forfeited their claim to it as least temporarily—is quite long: *Dawn, Jang, Nawa-i-Waqt, Hurriyet, Jasarat, Shahbaz, Mehran, Outlook, Frontier Guardian* and *Pakistan Economist*, to name only a few. Third, the government directly controls major metropolitan dailies through the National Press Trust. Fourth, the government owns the country's major news agency, the Associated Press of Pakistan, and thus can control news at the source. Finally, the Information Department can require newspapers to display prominently government handouts, news items, speeches and statements.

Relations between the state and the press grew worse under Bhutto—as documented in the *White Paper on Misuse of Media, December 20, 1971 to July 4, 1977*, published by the Pakistan government in 1978. It described in detail how individual newspapers and journalists were manipulated to serve the purposes of Bhutto's political party. In addition to the control mechanisms noted above, Bhutto used a number of others, such as punitive tax audits, pressure on private companies to withdraw advertising from blacklisted publications, and withholding permission to import printing equipment.

The first order of business for the military regime of General Zia-ul-Haq—which ousted Bhutto—was to destroy the credibility of the previous government and acquire the patina of legitimacy for itself. Press curbs were relaxed and publications were allowed to express their opinions with relative freedom. However, none of the press laws on the statute books was cut down. Right-wing publications banned by Bhutto were allowed to reappear. Similarly, a more permissive policy was adopted in the granting of licenses to new publications, especially those favorable to the Zia regime. At the same time, the government began to move against Bhutto-owned newspapers: *Musawat, Hilal-e-Pakistan* and *Nusrat*, all published by the Bhutto Trust. (This trust was renamed the Sheikh Zayed bin Sultan Trust and its officers replaced by government nominees.) The editor of *Musawat* was arrested and the paper itself was closed with no reasons given. This led to the most serious confrontation between the regime and the press in the 1970s. A number of journalists went on a hunger strike, which was supported by the Pakistan Federal Union

of Journalists and the All-Pakistan Newspaper Employees Confederation. In a volte-face, the government permitted *Musawat* to resume publication under a new management. But in January and February 1978 skirmishes between the government and the press continued. The editor and the printer of the *Sun*, published in Karachi, were sentenced to 10 lashes and a year of hard labor for printing an abusive line about Zia. The magazine *Herald* was ordered to deposit a security of $3,000 for "publishing material designed to create public revulsion and bring the government into contempt." The reclosing of *Musawat* in April touched off daily hunger strikes by journalists that lasted for over 29 days. In May 11 newspapers were banned and required to deposit securities, 13 others were fined and two nationalized. The flogging of four newspaper employees in jail led to such an international uproar that Zia was forced to back down. The two journalist unions put forth a charter of demands that included:

• Release of all arrested journalists and press workers
• Rehiring of dismissed journalists
• Removal of ban on newspapers
• Withdrawal of notices demanding securities from publications
• Revocation of the Press and Publications Ordinance
• Disbanding of the National Press Trust
• Freedom to publish without government license
• Revision of wages

In order to press their demands the union members went on hunger strike and the government retaliated by arresting 30 journalists and their sympathizers. The strikes continued until by September 1978 over 250 people were under arrest. Early in that month Minhaj Barna, head of the journalists unions, threatened to fast until death unless the government freed all newsmen (who, he alleged, were being tortured) and reinstated the dismissed employees of the National Press Trust newspapers. The government acceded to most of these demands but then proceeded to tighten the screws on the press. To divide and weaken the journalistic community the regime encouraged the formation of rival unions, financed them and then entered into bogus negotiations with them. Censorship was imposed on eight dailies. Four weeklies were banned; another was suspended and its publishers forced to dismiss the editorial staff for publication of an article alleging graft and nepotism by Zia's family. Three publications were required to deposit securities for publishing objectionable articles. The editor and publisher of another were arrested under the Official Secrets Act for publishing excerpts from an allegedly secret memorandum by General Zia instructing the provincial military administrators to crush leftist groups. By the time the government was ready to execute Bhutto, the opposition press had been effectively silenced. Nor did the assault end after Bhutto's execution. The editors of two more publications were arrested, and the publishers of five others were served with notices to deposit securities.

Not satisfied even with these measures, the government imposed full censorship in October 1979—along with martial law. The censorship was applicable to all printed matter, including that copied by hand. Section 499 of the Penal Code was also amended to make libel a cognizable offense—even when the "libel" was actually true and in the public interest to be known—and to empower the government to arrest editors and publishers without warrant. Bhutto's newspaper *Musawat* was finally forced to close and its printing shop sealed, in defiance of a High Court order permitting its publication.

Attitude Toward Foreign Media

Along with the crackdown on the domestic press, the Zia regime began moving against foreign correspondents and the few Pakistanis working for foreign publications. According to *Asiaweek*, a list of correspondents who are personae non gratae has been drawn up by the government. One of them, Salamat Ali, Punjab-born correspondent of the Dow Jones-owned *Far East Economic Review*, was arrested in 1979 for writing an article on unrest in Baluchistan. He was accused of promoting national disunity—a crime for which the maximum punishment is death—and sentenced to one year's rigorous imprisonment. It is believed that Ali was arrested in an attempt to gauge foreign reaction to the widening offensive against the press. The response was an international uproar, and the government released Ali—but without any retraction of the charges against him.

Foreign publications have fared no better. *Newsweek* was banned in December 1979 because it published an imaginary picture of Muhammad and carried a critical report on the burning of the U.S. Embassy in the capital. Chris Sherwell, a correspondent for the London *Financial Times*, was attacked by a group of thugs while investigating reports about Pakistan's alleged attempts to build a nuclear bomb. Later, he was forced to leave the country.

Not surprisingly, Pakistan enthusiastically supports UNESCO attempts to legitimize and institutionalize state control over national media.

News Agencies

There are two major news services operating in Pakistan: the Associated Press of Pakistan (APP) and Pakistan Press International (PPI). Because foreign news services cannot operate independently, they have associated themselves with one or the other of these agencies. APP, the older of the two, was founded in 1947 and has links with Reuters, dpa, Tass and the New China News Agency, while PPI is associated with AP, AFP and some East European wire agencies. The third local agency, United Press of Pakistan (UPP), confines itself to domestic news and feature articles.

Electronic News Media

Both radio and television are state monopolies, administered through the Pakistan Broadcasting Corporation and the Pakistan Television Corporation. Radio broadcasting comprises 12 stations in Bahawalpur, Dera Ismail Khan, Gilgit, Hyderabad, Islamabad, Karachi, Lahore, Multan, Peshawar, Quetta, Rawalpindi and Skardu. Television facilities include five stations at Karachi, Lahore, Rawalpindi, Quetta and Peshawar, and seven rebroadcast stations.

Broadcasting suffered a serious loss of credibility when it failed to report the debacle in East Pakistan in 1971 and blacked out news of Bhutto's execution in 1979. In a bid to Islamicize Pakistani society the military regime has introduced a strict code of ethics for radio and TV programs. Female announcers and newscasters are required to cover their heads, and scenes showing women smoking, riding motorcycles or dancing are banned. While music is deemphasized, the airwaves are inundated with religious hymns and Koran readings.

Education & Training

Journalistic training is provided by two institutions: the University of Karachi and the University of Punjab.

Summary

Years of authoritarian rule have robbed Pakistani media of much of their political influence. An opposition press has ceased to exist or, at least, does not pose any significant threat to the present government. Because of the prevailing religious milieu, the press's social role is also muted. Economically, the print media have made little progress in the past 33 years, either in terms of attracting new readership or acquiring new printing technology. The situation is not dissimilar to that in other developing countries under military dictatorships. However, given the right political climate, the Pakistani press might have—and might yet—become a flourishing and vigorous institution.

CHRONOLOGY

1975	Censorship imposed for a brief period in the wake of disturbances in the Punjab.
	Press advisory system introduced, requiring publishers and editors to carry out "advice" given by government officials over telephone.
	Press and Periodicals Ordinance amended.
1976	A National Press Commission set up and a Code of Ethics for Journalists proposed by government and opposed by press.
1977	Temporary censorship imposed by Bhutto to black out news of opposition.
	Bhutto overthrown in army coup led by General Zia-ul-Haq. Bhutto's newspaper, *Musawat*, suspended; journalists go on hunger strike to protest paper's suspension.
1978	*Sun* suspended as press and Zia regime enter on collision course.

Over 250 arrested as journalists' strike continues.

Union leader Minhaj Barna enters on hunger strike.

Government permits *Musawat* to reopen and reinstates some dismissed journalists, but continues moves against opposition press.

1979   Along with full martial law, censorship reimposed and Penal Code amended to provide for arrest of editors and publishers without warrant.

Salamat Ali, correspondent of *Far Eastern Economic Review*, arrested and sentenced to a year of hard labor for writing article on unrest in Baluchistan, designed, in the words of government, to "foment hatred."

Musawat finally forced to close and its print shop sealed in defiance of High Court orders.

BIBLIOGRAPHY

All-Pakistan Newspaper Society. *All-Pakistan Newspaper Society, Annual Report, 1980.*

Lent, John A. *Newspapers in Asia.* Hong Kong, 1981.

Wilber, Donald. *Pakistan.* New Haven, Conn., 1964.

PANAMA

by Robert N. Pierce

BASIC DATA

Population: 1,887,000
Area: 75,650 sq. km. (29,200 sq. mi.)
GNP: 2.5 billion balboas (US$2.5 billion) (1979)
Literacy Rate: 82%
Language(s): Spanish, English
Language(s): Spanish
Number of Dailies: 6
   Aggregate Circulation: 136,000
   Circulation per 1,000: 79
Number of Nondailies: 11
   Aggregate Circulation: NA
   Circulation per 1,000: NA
Number of Periodicals: 143

Number of Radio Stations: 114
Number of Television Stations: 13
Number of Radio Receivers: 270,000
   Radio Receivers per 1,000: 157
Number of Television Sets: 186,000
   Television Sets per 1,000: 108
Total Annual Newsprint Consumption: 3,400 metric tons
Per Capita Newsprint Consumption: 1.9 kg. (4.2 lb.)
Total Newspaper Ad Receipts: 12.7 million balboas (US$12.7 million) (1976)
As % of All Ad Expenditures: NA

Background & General Characteristics

For much of the period since Columbus discovered it in 1501, Panama has existed as a nation primarily for the convenience of foreigners traveling somewhere in search of wealth. First there were the Spanish, bringing the riches of Peru for transshipment from the Pacific Ocean to the Atlantic on their way to the homeland. Then came the Americans, rushing to get to the California goldfields and, after completion of the Panama Canal in 1914, ushering the merchant ships of the world on their way to profit. In the 1970s money itself was the transient commodity as the country became a haven for tax-avoiding bankers.

All this has had its benefits, particularly from the influence of the U.S. presence in the Canal Zone, occupied from 1903 until its return to Panama in 1979 under a new treaty. The country ranks among the most advanced in Latin America on most of the usual indices—literacy above 80 percent; health care provided by more doctors per patient than in countries such as Mexico, Brazil and Chile; and a per-capita income of $1,449*, also among the best in the region.

But economic advantages are even more unevenly distributed among the people than in many Latin American countries, and the middle class so needed by mass media is much less emergent. The desperately poor are to be found at every hand, and they provide a weak market for sophisticated institutions of communication.

Because of its historic position as a client of larger powers, Panama has been able to offer its citizens little sense of national pride. But beginning in the 1960s the universally popular crusade to gain control of the canal proved to be a galvanizing force. This was accelerated in 1968 with a coup that ended the rotation of the presidency among various elite families who manipulated the political process. The next year General Omar Torrijos, commander of the National Guard, emerged in control of government and took advantage of the canal fever to gain unprecedented public support.

*The rate of exchange is 1 balboa=US$1.00.

These national tendencies have been reflected somewhat in the journalistic life of Panama. The capital city—and it alone—has always had a somewhat varied selection of the major media, first newspapers, then radio, then television. But the quality has never been distinguished, because the press has not emerged as an important separate institution as in neighboring countries. Until 1980 there were only two ownerships of daily newspapers, one the government and the other a company that had been founded in 1852 by bored American travelers between ships taking them to the California goldfields.

Whatever the causes of this deficiency, it cannot be laid entirely to the nature of the market. With high literacy and adequate income to buy newspapers, Panamanians could support media that are more ambitious. Furthermore, they are relatively easy to reach, as 51 percent live in urban areas. Language is no problem; although 14 percent of the people speak English as a first language, nearly all use Spanish easily.

Rather, the content of newspapers is not of the quality and diversity that would make a majority of consumers spend 20 or 25 cents on a copy. The layout of most papers is jumbled and badly printed, the writing is turgid and filled with rambling sentences; and the thrust of most stories is to glorify the deeds of the government or some favorite politician. Inexpensively obtained foreign news, drawn from various international agencies, is abundant in the morning newspapers, filling holes that otherwise would go for locally written material.

Television news is generally viewed as little different from that of newspapers, although its foreign coverage through agency material and satellite feed compares well with other countries'. (An English-language television channel operated by the U.S. military carries ABC News live via satellite, although the signal often fails.) Radio news programs for the most part are highly opinionated commentary, which, while offering one of the few anti-government voices, are usually so shrill and unreliable as to be disbelieved by listeners.

A sharp departure from the general pattern of journalism came in 1980 with the appearance of *La Prensa,* a morning daily. While its writing displays the same faults as the others, its editing is modern and professional. It also offers some variety in content and presents news of political dissent. Another daily, the small afternoon paper called *Ya,* also is critical of the government but has little informative content.

Domestically produced magazines provide little rivalry for other media. *Análisis* is the best regarded, dealing in political commentary. Others are *Diálogo Social,* a leftist publication; *Más,* a struggling magazine of general interest; a television guide; and *Lotería,* a monthly intellectual journal incongruously published by the national lottery system.

The history of Panamanian journalism provides a clear indicator of the trends just noted. The Panama City area was one of the earliest New World points of settlement, and for the first two centuries of Spanish colonization it ranked with Mexico City and Lima as an opulent capital. However, it did not develop the cultural glitter of the other two cities, and it was not until 1821, the year of independence from Spain, that the first printing press arrived. During the next 28 years more than 30 newspapers appeared, most of them organs of opinion on the controversial relations with the parent government in Colombia, with which Panama had been joined even before the end of the colonial period. More than once Panama severed ties with Bogotá, only to rejoin by choice or force.

In 1849 there began an episode unparalleled in Latin American press history. This was the founding of openly North American English-language newspapers, to such an extent that they played a central role in the area's journalistic life.

Three U.S. citizens had arrived by ship from the East Coast to cross the isthmus and join the California Gold Rush, and were waiting for the overcrowded and infrequent ships carrying passengers from Panama City to California. They had little to do except sit in the hotels and idly discuss the hazard of the crossing. Local U.S. nationals were planning a celebration of Washington's birthday, so the three new arrivals decided to start a weekly newspaper to mark the occasion, thereby acting (as they said in the first issue) "to relieve the tedium of our, perhaps protracted stay in this, to us strange land, surrounded by the people, institutions and language so dissimilar to our own." There was nothing in the paper to indicate any concern for the journalistic needs of the Panamanians. It covered four letter-sized pages, an eighth of the space being taken by a listing of North Americans (including the publishers) who had arrived a week before.

Within a few months the publishers had

moved on to California, but the *Panama Star,* as they named their paper, was continued haltingly by other U.S. citizens. In 1853 the *Star* added Spanish-language columns called *La Estrella,* which later developed into a separate newspaper—today the best-known daily in Panama. By the next year at least three more U.S. papers had started, and one of these, the *Herald,* was merged with the *Star.* Thus they became the *Star and Herald,* an English-language paper that still exists as the sister of *La Estrella de Panamá.* In 1882 a Panamanian family, the Duques, bought both papers, and the control continues today.

Various other dailies came and went in the succeeding century, among them the *Panama American* and *El Panamá América,* founded in 1925 by another North American as a dual-language pair of dailies. They later became property of Arnulfo Arias, a longtime political leader, together with another tabloid called *Crítica.* After the 1968 military coup that brought Torrijos to power, Arias went into exile. The government, wanting a counterweight to the dominant Duque newspapers, fostered the founding of a corporation, Editora Renovación S.A. (ERSA), which bought up the Arias papers at a fair price. ERSA has operated at a loss ever since and has shuffled its collection of papers several times—founding a morning paper, *Matutino,* and an evening one, *La República,* and discontinuing the *Panama American* pair. *La Prensa* and *Ya,* the two opposition papers, also were born in recent years.

All the papers are full-sized except *Crítica* and *Ya. La Estrella* overshadows all the others in space, as its advertising has increased healthily in recent years, and it averages 40 pages daily. *La Prensa* is making a strong bid for the same upper- and middle-class market and usually runs 24 pages. The ERSA papers and *Ya* typically run the equivalent of 20 full-sized pages or fewer. *La Estrella* has the only Sunday edition.

Weekly newspapers occasionally emerge in secondary cities, such as Colón and David, but have little importance. The U.S. military command publishes a weekly for its personnel, and the *Miami Herald* Latin American edition sells heavily among Americans working on the canal.

All the dailies fluctuate in the 15,000–22,000 circulation range except for the *Star and Herald,* with about 8,000, and *Ya* with less than 5,000. Most suffered setbacks when prices rose from 5 to 10 cents earlier in the 1970s to 20 or 25 cents before 1980.

The *Estrella-Star and Herald* combination remains the favorite news source, other than foreign publications, of the business establishment. Although its circulation has slipped slightly, its advertising keeps rising, with up to 160 pages run during the Christmas shopping season, even though it was paying $580 a ton for newsprint by 1980.

Edited in a shabby but historic building in the city's colonial section, *La Estrella* soon will move to a new building in the suburbs now occupied by the printing plant. Its composition is in cold type, printed on letterpress, but the appearance falls far short of international standards. The company does have a profitable commercial printing branch using offset, on which it puts out a sports weekly and a television guide. In 1980 it started running a weekly magazine section called *K,* produced in Miami in cooperation with newspapers in various Latin American countries.

For about four years after the 1968 coup, *La Estrella* maintained a reputation as a paper mildly in opposition to the government, often printing news displeasing to the Torrijos regime. Then the government passed down the message that the owners either had to change to a more cooperative publisher or see their papers expropriated. They chose the former, and two family members—Tomás Altamirano Duque and Carlos Ozores Typaldos—have emerged as director and subdirector, respectively. They also have served as ministers of housing and foreign affairs in recent years, and Altamirano Duque waged a gaudy and successful campaign in the pages of his newspapers to become one of the first freely elected legislators in the regime's experimental step toward democracy in 1980.

Filling somewhat the role formerly occupied by *La Estrella*—but with more vigor—is apparently the prospect for *La Prensa.* Its founding in 1979 followed a pattern totally innovative in the context of Latin American journalism. Its founders organized the project a full year before the scheduled start of publication on August 1, 1980. A rigid timetable spelled out detailed stages such as feasibility studies, selling of stock under careful controls, purchases of equipment and outfitting of a building, printing of prototype and trial-run editions, hiring of personnel and making contracts for advertising and subscriptions. The founders sought and received the support of the Inter-American Press Association, and experts from other countries helped in the planning under IAPA auspices.

The company was capitalized at $1 million, subscribed by 375 shareholders, none owning more than $7,500 in stock. Backers were mostly business and professional people, headed by a dynamic executive, Roberto Eisenmann Jr., who had spent three years in exile.

The first statement of the company's prospectus laid out the rationale for the paper: "An independent, objective and free press does not exist today in Panama." It noted that studies conducted indicated that advertisers and readers would support a paper that merited credibility. "We went ahead because the time was ripe, international pressure was building up, and the government had announced its intent to open up the political process," said Eisenmann.

La Prensa gave an indication of its intent during its first month when it began publishing information about a projected new bridge over the canal, which had been shrouded in financial mystery. Other media picked up the story, although mostly to defend the government's position.

Within a month after its start, *La Prensa* had achieved its 12-month goal of 15,000 circulation, 40 percent advertising ratio and 16-page editions. Its founders had budgeted enough to cover losses for one year. They were attempting to convert most sales to subscriptions, a more solid financial base never previously achieved by a Panamanian newspaper. "Even though profit is not our primary motivation," the prospectus said, "the newspaper will be managed with a high business sense because only with economic solvency can we guarantee its independent line."

Economic Framework

Like most countries, Panama was hit hard economically by the oil crisis beginning in 1973. However, unlike many Latin American neighbors, it did not recover in two or three years but continued to register per capita slippages in gross income. This was partly because it relies so heavily on ship traffic and so little on its own production for revenue. By the end of the 1970s there were signs that the economy was beginning to turn around, with the inflow of banking institutions, the growth of tourism spurred by its bargain buys in low-taxed imports, and the invest-

ment optimism brought on by a peaceful transition under the canal treaties. The energy handicap also moved toward partial solution with work on the Bayano River hydroelectric dam, which by 1987 is expected to provide 150 megawatts of power per day, or 85 percent of the nation's needs.

And despite economic problems, the middle class has been growing steadily—and most media have managed to survive. The ERSA newspapers do so with a government subsidy amounting to a reported $600,000–1 million a year. *La Estrella* weathered a financial crisis in the mid-1970s, when it took a $2 million loan, and was getting the lion's share of newspaper advertising by the end of the decade. The two television channels were so saturated with commercials that advertising orders were backed up for months. Most radio stations are small operations that need and get little income.

Matutino, *La República* and *Crítica* are owned by ERSA, and *La Prensa* has no owners other than holders of its public stock. Most radio stations are commercial operations except for one owned by the World Missionary Radio Fellowship. The television stations are owned by two old-line families, the Chiaris of Channel 2 and the Violetas of Channel 4. Also, the U.S. Southern Command operates a television station and a medium-wave radio station in the former Canal Zone. The Panamanian government has its own television and radio facilities.

Panama does not have a wide range of class-oriented media as in some countries. The ERSA papers tend to be more populist in appeal than the others, but the distinction is not sharp.

In comparison with the population, the media are greatly overconcentrated in Panama City, where newspaper sales range from two-thirds to three-fourths of the total, although the capital has only one-fourth of the national population. About 80 percent of the television sets are in Panama City and Colón, although an estimated 85 percent of the population are within reach of a television signal. The only exception to the media imbalance is in radio stations; of the nation's 92 medium-wave transmitters, only 27 are in the capital. Radio signals can be picked up all over the country, and it is estimated that 70 percent of the homes have receivers, although this rises to 90 percent in Panama City.

Newsprint is as well supplied to Panama as to any small country, and the abundance of shipping going through the canal helps, although the distance from producing countries adds to the shipping cost. Even though the government waives import taxes on newsprint, the price had risen to nearly $600 in 1980. The government has never used newsprint allocations as a political weapon.

The only episodes of substantial advertiser influence on the media in recent years have come through the government. Spasmodically the regime has pressured businessmen to avoid advertising in media that displease officials, and state advertising has been used the same way. Such measures were used against *La Prensa* in its earliest stages, although they were not sustained evenly. Generally *La Estrella* runs about 50 percent of its space in ads, *La Prensa* about 40 and the ERSA papers less than 25.

Unions played little part in the Panamanian press until the late 1970s, when the Syndicate of Journalists formed a united front against both the Duque papers and the ERSA group and secured a full-time minimum wage of $500 monthly. Strikes have continued to plague both companies, however.

Press Laws

Constitutional remedies to press-freedom difficulties receive little attention in Panamanian public life, as the government makes basic law practically at will through the National Legislative Council, which until 1980 was completely appointed by the president (one-third was elected that year).

For several years in the mid-1970s there were discussions between government officials and the Syndicate of Journalists about complaints from both sides. Officials felt that the media were often misleading the public about facts and intentions, particularly on economic matters. The journalists, while preferring complete freedom, at least hoped to get a set of ground rules that would let them know where they stood. They—or at least many of the working reporters—also wanted a law requiring a journalism education.

Late in 1976 General Torrijos headed a government delegation that met with syndicate members and thrashed out the complaints. Torrijos conceded that the government had been too bureaucratic about issuing information and too intent on acting rather than explaining. But he criticized the press for sensationalizing economic problems and stirring up public excitement.

Out of the meeting came a joint commission of the two sides charged with drawing up a national information policy. This led to the adoption in 1978 of three laws. These concerned general press matters, licensing of journalists, and establishment of a Technical Board of Journalism.

The general law had few provisions as compared with other such statutes in Latin America. Its only guaranty of freedom was in saying, "any newspaper can be published without necessity of prior authorization"; on the other hand, it did not, as is often done, list the ways this freedom can be abridged. The two most notable inclusions were these:

1. A prohibition of false news or documents that are supposititious, altered or incorrectly attributed to specific sources.

2. A requirement that any newspaper or broadcast news program give free space or time to "clarification or rectifications" sent in by anyone who believes himself offended by any material in the medium.

Both these provisions were types frequently enacted in Latin America in the 1970s, even in democracies, and arise from politicians' resentment toward what they see—often correctly—as abuses by vicious and careless journalists.

Another common requirement that was adopted for Panama was the requirement that owners, stockholders, and officials of mass media must be Panamanians.

Other articles required that any news medium notify the government of intent to publish and that it preserve all materials used in preparing news for 30 days. There also were prohibitions of items that invade privacy, identify minors in crimes, refer to a person's physical defect, and publicize a subscription to pay someone's fine. The latter refers to attempts by people convicted of a crime to solicit money from the public to pay their fine.

Penalties for violating any of the articles range from public condemnation and fines to closing of the news medium.

The "Law Regulating the Exercise of the Journalistic Profession," although also derived from other such measures being passed by Latin countries, was of much more significance than those in democracies because in Panama there was little to bridle the dictatorship from its abuse. Its provisions were similar to the model for such laws: those working in the news field were required to have a journalism degree from a Panamanian university or a foreign one approved by the University of Panama; among the exempt were those with five years' experience when the law took effect. Even regular opinion writers were included, although writers of occasional items or specialized columns were not. Internal organs for labor, religious and student groups also were exempt, as were news media in smaller cities that had no licensed journalists. Foreign correspondents "will be accredited as such" by the Technical Board, the law said, and they were to pay dues to the journalists' organization. Private businesses devoted even partially to journalism were required to hire licensed journalists. Final-year university students could serve internships. Penalties for violations were to be $100-$500 fines.

The law also contained some provisions enlarging the rights of journalists: They were not to be compelled to write anything against their will for publication, they could not be compelled to reveal the sources of their news, and they were guaranteed free access to both public and private news events "except in special cases," not defined in the law.

The third law set up the Technical Board, which was charged with administering the other laws and also a code of ethics that it was to draw up. Its members were to consist of a presidential appointee as chairman and representatives of four journalists' groups. The Journalists' Union had studied such legislation in other countries and suggested the main outlines of the law for Panama.

Censorship

Direct censorship has never been used in recent times in Panama, except during the first few months of the military regime, which started in October 1968. *El Mundo,* a major morning newspaper, was punished by having a censor posted in its offices, apparently because it was owned by David Samudio, an opposition politician. Within a few days Samudio closed down his paper, refusing to accept censorship. The government confiscated the issue in which Samudio announced the closure in a front-page editorial, but it circulated from hand to hand.

Nearly all Panama's newspapers and television newscasters have practiced self-censorship ever since, but some radio commentators have been notable for their unbridled criticism of the government. In 1971 the government announced the appointment of a three-man censorship board empowered to prohibit, by any means needed, material that "would be offensive to the national dignity," would propagandize "exotic theories or totalitarian systems" or would aim for "destruction of the country's democratic and republican system of government or would be contrary to public order."

The media have frequently been told what types of material they must not carry, but the board has largely been able to rely on editors to do their own inspection. At various times the government has forbidden media to report anything but its own version of economic problems, strikes, student disorders, the canal treaty negotiations of the mid-1970s and even reference to restrictions on news. Besides these topics, others have been sanctioned for television and radio, including such vague categories as "notoriously false or slanted information," even if it is attributed to others; "obscene language deemed harmful to public morality," and expressions used "to degrade, defame or dishonor an individual."

Penalties used by the government have consisted mostly of permanent or temporary closures of media, generally brief jailings, and exile, also of limited duration.

Twice, in 1974 and 1975, two brothers tried to found an opposition daily but in both cases policemen raided the offices and hauled off equipment and newsprint, forbidding the start of the paper—which was to be called *Quiubo* ("What's Up") the first time, and *La Opinión Pública* the second. The brothers, Ramón and Alfredo Jiménez, protested to the Inter-American Press Association and won its support, but the government stood firm.

It is notable that Alfredo Jiménez was one of the founding staff members of *La Prensa,* the opposition daily the government allowed to be born in 1980.

Jailings usually have resulted from spirited journalistic attacks on the Torrijos government. Such was the case in 1974 when five men, including a 75-year-old retiree, were sentenced to one to two years in prison. This came as the canal negotiations were getting serious, and Torrijos sometimes gave in to anger at the criticism from the treaty's opponents. A Panamanian executive of the Goodyear tire firm also was held for 22 days, apparently for charging communist infiltration in the government. The prisoner, Florencio Enrique Delgado, credited news of his arrest in the *Miami Herald* with bringing about his release.

The fact that the jailings occur gives some

indication of the remarkable resiliency of Panamanians in political matters. The Torrijos restrictions have never prevented criticism, only punished it occasionally. Information also spreads quickly, as happened during the most sensitive stages of the canal treaty talks, when the citizens mostly were very suspicious that their rights would be bargained away. Handbills and mimeographed sheets frequently revealed the innermost secrets of the negotiations. This dissemination takes place, however, with little help from the main-line newspapers and television stations and instead is carried out by political partisans.

State-Press Relations

Propaganda has been a prominent feature of what Torrijos tries to characterize as a revolution. Major themes have been the general's vigorous efforts to improve the lot of the poor and his defiance of the United States and the Panamanian old-line elite who despise him. The propaganda was centered around the personality of Torrijos in the early years, quoting him in epigrams such as "Better to die on one's feet than live on one's knees." When he began turning the reins of government over to civilians by inducting Aristides Royo as president in 1978, he deliberately lowered his visibility and faded from the propaganda.

Torrijos orchestrated a propaganda drive more related to U.S.-style public relations during the campaign to get the canal treaty accepted both in Panama and the United States. The Panamanians, who got a chance to vote on the treaty in a 1977 plebescite, were caught up in a flood of persuasion from the government. Despite vehement opposition from many political factions, which were allowed free expression until the last week of the campaign, the voters gave a strong endorsement to the pact.

Torrijos also turned his efforts toward the U.S. public as the crucial Senate vote on the treaty approached. He hired former publicists for Barry Goldwater and Hubert Humphrey to fashion his U.S. campaign. Agan he and the Carter Administration prevailed over strong counter-propaganda heavily financed by U.S. conservative interests.

Torrijos's most visible weapon in his quest for public support is the ERSA group of papers, property of friends of the government. In the early days of the regime the government radio, then called Radio Libertad, was a strident voice of the pro-Castro wing, largely copying Cuban propaganda. However, it later changed to Radio Nacional and became more moderate.

Attitude Toward Foreign Media

Panama has been improving as a source for foreign news media, with its convention facilities, good hotels, resort attractions, airline crossroads, banking eminence and, very importantly, the events surrounding the canal. Despite this, no major U.S. news medium keeps a full-time correspondent posted in the country. AP had a bureau during the height of the canal crisis but later closed it.

Most often the coverage is done by roving correspondents, which is easy because Panama is a convenient stopover on trips to and from South America. Since the Torrijos regime increasingly has been trying to burnish its foreign image in recent years, and as the general likes to turn his robust charm on foreigners, correspondents usually have little trouble. The only incident causing much alarm in recent years was the expulsion of Sally Chardy, a correspondent for NBC Radio who was living in Panama. She had telephoned President Royo at five a.m. to get him to comment on a report about the possible extradition of the shah of Iran from Panama, and Royo apparently said something that caused him diplomatic embarrassment. Chardy was ordered out of the country on short notice, but was allowed to return less than a month later after apologizing for the call.

The legal grounds on which Chardy was expelled were the requirement that correspondents register with the government, a rule usually ignored by visitors. However, none of the other battery of weapons against foreign exposure—censorship of cables, restrictions on import of foreign media and the like—are to be found in Panama, which generally has an air of openness similar to that of a democracy, not of a police state.

Despite the heavy U.S. influence on the 19th-century press in Panama, no foreign investment is to be found today in the mainstream media, although the U.S. military has its publications and broadcast media, and the World Missionary Radio Fellowship has one station.

The government has supported the developing-nation initiatives in UNESCO for an official international news agency, and it calls its own publicity service Panapress. However, it has not been among the leaders in the UNESCO dispute, and the matter has stirred little domestic interest.

News Agencies

No domestic news agency exists in Panama, although some media take part in ACAN, the Central American agency sponsored by the Spanish service EFE, which has a Panama office. A wide range of North American and European agencies are subscribed to by local media; Prensa Latina of Cuba and Tass of the Soviet Union also are received.

Electronic News Media

Panama is well developed in availability of broadcast signals, although their professionalism is much less distinguished. The country has 92 medium-wave radio stations and four each of short-wave and public FM stereo stations. Thus it is truly the saturation medium. The capital city alone has 27 stations. An estimated half-million radio sets are used in the country.

Radio consists of the typical Latin American pattern of music, sports and soap operas most of the day, with heavy reliance on imported materials. But from six to eight a.m. the airwaves come alive with varied, combative commentary programs, in which analysts read the day's newspapers aloud and give their opinions. The government often shuts down such programs temporarily, but no public outcry usually follows because this is considered to be inviting trouble.

The country's two commercial television stations, Channels 2 and 4, have not been known for political daring and program innovation, although they draw large audiences and are very profitable. They frequently receive foreign programs by film, tape or satellite (Panama had one of the earliest satellite ground stations). Both carry about 13 hours daily and broadcast in color; together they have eight repeaters outside the capital. Channel 11, the government station operated by the University of Panama, started in 1978 and has a small daily schedule, much of the programming being provided by donations from abroad. It leans heavily on the educational and cultural side

and is little used by the government for propaganda.

The U.S. military television (Channel 8, repeated on the Atlantic side as Channel 10), consists of the latest serials, news and sports from the networks, all without commercials, and gives U.S. servicemen and canal personnel a taste of video life back home. Although it does not try to invade the Panamanian airwaves, it is heavily used by the national population. It also has carefully avoided antagonizing the Panamanians in the canal disputes, and has received a guarantee that it will continue so long as the U.S. military presence does.

An estimated 250,000 television sets—a high figure for a small, poor country—are in use in Panama. One reason for this is the duty-free import of sets from abroad, placing them in the same price range as in the United States.

Although television causes little trouble for the government, it must meet rigid consumer-protection standards by law. Stations must send all advertisements dealing with health (food, cosmetics, medicine) to an official agency for censorship. The government also enforces rules such as those against smoking or drinking on the screen, competitive advertising and superlatives in health commercials.

Although advertisements for print media are allowed to come into the country without restriction, those used in broadcasting are required to have all the audio segment made locally. The government tried to discourage use of imported visuals by taxing them at $750 each—raised to $2,000 in 1981. This effort had already largely succeeded, mainly because replacement of film by videotape had made it feasible.

Education & Training

Although Panamanian journalistic leaders are keenly aware of international norms of completeness and impartiality in news coverage, they have shown little tendency so far to emulate those norms. There are signs of a new approach, such as the founding of the daily La Prensa, but how deeply this runs is still in question. Editors usually blame the shortage of well-trained reporters for the lag in their own country. The newspapers, lacking sufficient advertising revenue, do not pay reporters enough to get their best efforts, the typical salary being well below the $500 monthly minimum for full-time work. Thus they must work at two or three jobs, one of them usually being a government public relations position.

A new licensing law requires a university journalism degree, and there is some hope for improvement through training in the journalism programs at the University of Panama and the University of Santa María. So far, the quality of instruction has not made a good reputation, much of the emphasis being put on polemic writing.

Summary

Journalism largely reflects the two factors that make Panama run—politics and commerce. The shape of these factors, and thus of journalism, has been determined since 1968 by the peculiar mix of leftism and rightism in the Torrijos revolution, and also by the evolution of its policies, generally toward liberalization.

The tendency of the Torrijos movement has been to go back gradually to the barracks, with the traditionally turbulent political competition returning as quickly as allowed. Because of his personal popularity and the many successes of his programs, Torrijos probably will maintain the option of stepping in again—with approval from the masses—any time the political elites drive the country to the chaos that existed before 1968. The mass media can be expected to be both a cause and a victim of any such changes.

CHRONOLOGY

1968 National Guard takes over government amid electoral crisis; Gen. Omar Torrijos emerges as leader of coup in 1969.

1969 Daily newspaper, *El Mundo,* gets resident censor and owner shuts down paper in protest. Four newspapers in Arias group closed by government but reopen after installing editors acceptable to junta. Editors continue to be ousted frequently.

1970 Government-related corporations buys Arias newspapers after financial dispute among its owners.

1974 Panama Canal negotiations spawn steady stream of rumors outside the media.
Ramón Jiménez jailed just before he and brother Alfredo start new daily, *Quiubo.* They are ordered to abandon plan.
Five prominent political activists sentenced to prison for criticizing government.

1975 Officials raid printing office to prevent start of *La Opinión Pública,* another newspaper planned by Jiménez brothers,

Officials warn broadcasters they must censor themselves about canal negotiations.

1976 Goodyear tire executive jailed three weeks for criticizing government.

1977 Panamanian government enters propaganda warfare over approval of canal treaty by hiring American publicists for U.S. campaign.
Wide public debate allowed before Panamanian plebiscite, which approves treaty.

1978 In cooperation with journalists' association, government drafts law requiring university education and official certification as prerequisites for news work.

1979 Government suspends certification of radio newsman for criticism. Other reporters stage public protest; president cancels order after Supreme Court rules it void.

1980 American reporter Sally Chardy expelled from Panama. She apologizes for discourtesy and is readmitted.
New independent newspaper, *La Prensa,* founded.

BIBLIOGRAPHY

McCullough, David G. *The Path Between the Seas.* New York, 1977.

Pierce, Robert N. *Keeping the Flame.* New York, 1979.

UNESCO. *World Communications.* Paris, 1975.

United States, Panama and the Panama Canal. Council of the Americas. New York, 1976.

Weil, Thomas E. *Area Handbook for Panama.* Washington, D.C., 1972.

PAPUA NEW GUINEA

by Colleen C. Moore

BASIC DATA

Population: 3,123,000
Area: 461,693 sq. km. (178,260 sq. mi.)
GNP: 1.17 billion kinas (US$1.7 billion) (1978)
Literacy Rate: 15%
Language(s): English, Pidgin and Motu
Number of Dailies: 2
  Aggregate Circulation: 39,000
  Circulation per 1,000: 6
Number of Nondailies: 3
  Aggregate Circulation: 13,000
  Circulation per 1,000: 2
Number of Periodicals: 110

Number of Radio Stations: 22
Number of Television Stations: None
Number of Radio Receivers: 125,000
  Radio Receivers per 1,000: 43
Number of Television Sets: NA
  Television Sets per 1,000: NA
Total Annual Newsprint Consumption: 1.1 metric tons
Per Capita Newsprint Consumption: 0.4 kg. (.9 lb.)
Total Newspaper Ad Receipts: NA
  As % of All Ad Expenditures: NA

Background & General Characteristics

Papua New Guinea is a rugged island-nation of 3 million people. The nation's two daily newspapers, *The Papua New Guinea Post-Courier* and the *Nuigini News,* have a combined circulation of 39,000. Only six copies of a daily are available for every 1,000 people in Papua New Guinea, but each daily is read by about five people. At present daily newspapers are published on weekdays only.

The three weekly newspapers—*Wantok, The Times of Papua New Guinea* and the *Arawa Bulletin*—have an aggregate circulation of at least 13,000. There are only two copies of a nondaily for every 1,000 people, but a survey showed that each copy of a *Wantok* supplement was read by about 23 people.

The growth in the total number of daily and weekly newspapers has been slow. A decade passed before the number of daily newspapers increased from one in 1969 to two in 1980. Fewer nondailies exist now than in the past since some have been combined to form dailies or weeklies. *Niugini News* is a combination of three former regional newspapers. Two weeklies were joined to form *The Papua New Guinea Post-Courier.* A weekly market newssheet was merged with the weekly *Wantok.*

Newspaper circulation has grown faster than the number of newspapers published. The daily *Post-Courier*'s circulation has almost doubled, from 14,000 in 1975 to 25,000 in 1980. The weekly *Wantok*'s circulation increased from 8,000 in 1972 to 10,000 in 1980.

More than 110 periodicals are now published in Papua New Guinea. These deal with such topics as education, religion, entertainment, sociology, medicine, agriculture, anthropology and politics.

The radio audience outnumbers newspaper readership in Papua New Guinea. There are Christian and national radio networks, as well as 19 provincial stations. No television stations exist in Papua New Guinea, but the use of video is growing. A film service conducted by the government includes projectors, mobile units and a library of more than 600 educational films. Imported films are shown in 13 fixed cinemas, one drive-in and 23 mobile units. The cinemas have a total seating capacity of 7,305, with three seats for every 1,000 people. The drive-in has an annual attendance of 188,000.

From a random scanning of a few *Papua New Guinea Post-Couriers,* it appeared that half of the newspaper space was devoted to ads. *The Post-Courier* sold shares to the public in 1979, and as a result, one-third of the newspaper is owned by the community.

The Post-Courier has 20 editorial employees, of whom 87 percent are natives. Its production staff is 99 percent Papua New Guinean.

Papua New Guinea, the second largest noncontinental island in the world, is an anachronism of the 20th century. It is an independent country with a mountainous interior that shelters Stone Age men, and a tropical coastal plain settled by Jet Age Australian expatriots. Communication between these two regions is strained because of both the rugged terrain and diverse cultural backgrounds. Not only does the Jet Age populace have difficulty communicating with the native Papua New Guineans, but the natives find it hard to communicate with each other. Members of different communities are divided by the 750 distinctly different languages spoken in Papua New Guinea. The Papua New Guinea government has adopted three official languages—English, Motu and Pidgin—but natives are frequently incapable of speaking even one of them. English is spoken only by a small number of the educated urban population, and Motu and Pidgin are lingua francas, established to facilitate communication among people of many different linguistic backgrounds. But they have been opposed socially and aesthetically. Almost all of the Papua New Guineans live in thousands of rural communities.

Papua New Guinea is burdened by illiteracy. Only 28 percent of children aged five through 19 are in school, and the government can afford only one teacher for every 119 students. Few families in Papua New Guinea have any books in their homes besides the Bible and a hymn book.

Political discussion via the press has historically been influential in countries seeking their independence, but this did not occur in Papua New Guinea. The limited usefulness of printed communications in the nation-to-be can be seen in the 1964 elections. At that time the Australian government undertook a political education program, sending 500 foot patrols to 12,000 villages, where thousands of pamphlets and hundreds of tape recorders, loudspeakers, drawings, projectors, filmstrips and flipcharts were distributed or otherwise made available. Although the pamphlets were the most widespread, they

had the least impact. There was no press coverage of the election. None of the candidates accepted one newspaper's offer of free publicity, nor did they pay for any advertisements, and there was no controversial correspondence. As a result, people were taught how to vote rather than why.

The major newspapers in Papua New Guinea traditionally served the needs of expatriots and the military more than natives. During World War I, Australian troops invaded German New Guinea and retained control under a League of Nations mandate. At this time three major army newspapers existed; these English-language publications were devoted entirely to the needs of military personnel and included war news, government notices and social and recreational information. A similar periodical was published by Australian forces during World War II, to sustain the morale of servicemen in the New Guinea campaign.

Papua New Guinea only recently attained independence—in 1975—so that much of its media reflect the culture of others. Journalism in Papua New Guinea began in 1888 with a four-page hand-set weekly, *The Torres Straits Pilot and New Guinea Gazette.* Two later expatriot newspapers, started in 1917 and 1925 respectively, had white supremacist editorial tones. Both papers defended the white settler and scorned "interfering 'do-gooders'" from Australia. By the outbreak of World War II, three commercial newspapers were being published in Papua New Guinea. When they ceased publication after their presses had been destroyed by the Japanese, the expatriots produced weekly newssheets with typewriters and office duplicating machines.

The first newspaper to appear after World War II was the *South Pacific Post* at Port Moresby, in 1951. Initially the newspaper emphasized Australian and overseas news, but the staff soon discovered that its readers were more concerned with local events. In 1959 the *New Guinea Times Courier* was started in Lae. Both newspapers were tabloids, and both were owned by the same newspaper company in Australia. In 1969 the two papers were merged into *The Papua New Guinea Post-Courier,* a single national daily. *The Post-Courier* attracts an educated expatriot audience primarily, but its appeal to native Papua New Guineans has been growing steadily. Numerous letters are written to the paper by local people, and a native, Luke Sela, was appointed editor in 1976.

The *Post-Courier*'s value is limited because many rural areas are out of its reach. It is distributed to most major urban centers on the day of publication. The *Post-Courier* is published in English in Port Moresby and follows a moderate, middle-of-the-road policy.

Newspapers aimed at a native audience have been irregularly published and erratically received in Papua New Guinea. In 1962 the *South Pacific Post* established *Nu Gini Toktok,* a weekly eight-page tabloid. *Nu Gini Toktok* was published in Pidgin English and distributed free throughout Papua New Guinea. A special writing style was used to compensate for the low educational standard of the natives: every word over two syllables had to be explained. Stories and photographs for *Nu Gini Toktok* were actively solicited from the readers.

Nu Gini Toktok carried little international news except for stories about the United Nations or the South Pacific Commission, both of which have responsibilities in Papua New Guinea. The newspaper had sports stories, self-help columns on health and housing, market reports on the current prices for copra and cocoa, comic strips and a radio broadcasting column.

Although the language in *Nu Gini Toktok* was aimed at native New Guineans, the newspaper's editor and style were Australian. The stories themselves were frequently translations of articles that appeared in the English-language newspaper. The inconsistency between management and readership kept circulation at a low 4,000. *Nu Gini Toktok* was printed at a loss in the 1960s, which it tried to overcome with an advertising campaign. But the paper's efforts to promote itself failed, and *Nu Gini Toktok* went out of business in 1970.

In that same year a much more successful Pidgin newspaper, *Wantok,* was started. *Wantok* is published near Wewak by a Catholic mission, appears weekly and has a nationwide circulation of about 10,000. It covers local, national and overseas news. At the government's request, copies of *Wantok* are sent to all primary schools in the country. The reason for *Wantok*'s success is its objective: "to make available useful information to the ordinary man and woman in Papua New Guinea and to provide news behind the news." It also aims "to become a truly Papua New Guinean publication." Despite its Catholic Church sponsorship, *Wantok*'s policy is ecumenical.

Since Papua New Guinea's independence in 1975, several provinces have started their own newspapers, and *The Post-Courier* finally began receiving some competition. *Niugini News* was started in 1979. It provides national and Australian news in simple English for expatriots and Papua New Guinea natives. *Niugini News* has helped alleviate the distribution problem of the press in Papua New Guinea. It is produced in Lae but distributed nationwide, thus, like *Wantok,* satisfying the outlying areas' need for a national newspaper.

The successful Wantok Publications broadened their audience when they bought *The Times of Papua New Guinea* in 1980. *The Times* is an English weekly distributed mainly to urban centers. The *Arawa Bulletin* is another regional paper in English. It represents the trend toward provincial newspapers.

The newspaper with the largest circulation remains *The Papua New Guinea Post-Courier,* with 25,000 subscribers four days a week and 30,000 subscribers on Friday. It is a tabloid with short articles, large sensational headlines and an average length of 32 pages. Many pictures are used to compensate for the natives' illiteracy and lack of a common language. Sports are placed on the back page. Cartoons have their own page and can also be seen on the bottom of a few other pages. Movies advertised in the newspaper cover a variety of tastes: war, horror, James Bond and family pictures. Some of the topics touched by the numerous letters to the editor are modern dress, the water supply and why New Guinea tribes continue to fight. On the opposite page from the "Letters to the Editor" is an article by "Gemini," the pen name for *The Post-Courier*'s foreign correspondent. Some of Gemini's stories were on unrest in Botswana and Jamaica. *The Post-Courier* also contains numerous Australian Associated Press (AAP) stories on subjects ranging from the American president to the Middle East War.

Political papers began in Papua New Guinea with the evolution of parties. *Pangu Nius* was established in 1970 as a monthly newspaper in English and Pidgin. A year later the United Party established a newspaper in English, Pidgin and Motu. Both newspapers had difficulty obtaining advertising.

More successful than the party papers are the mission publications. Most missions produce a newsletter in simple English or a native language. Currently there are nine principal church publications, some of which are printed in three languages.

No city in Papua New Guinea has competing commercial newspapers, although there are cities with both a commercial newspaper and a religious newsletter. Two newspapers have a circulation under 10,000: *The Times of Papua New Guinea* and *Arawa Bulletin*. Two other newspapers have a circulation from 10,000 to 25,000: *Wantok* and *Niugini News*. Only *The Papua New Guinea Post-Courier*, as mentioned above, can claim a circulation of 25,000.

The Post-Courier is also the most influential newspaper because it is the most established and is in an urban location. *Niugini News* is second in influence because it reaches an audience *The Post-Courier* cannot, being distributed to outlying areas and published in simple English. The third most influential paper is *Wantok*, which reaches an audience that can read only Pidgin, and is distributed to the schools.

Printed communications in Papua New Guinea are usually run by Australian chains, religious missions, anthropological groups or the government's Office of Information. The *Herald* and *Weekly Times* of Melbourne own *The Papua New Guinea Post-Courier*. The Summer Institute of Linguistics publishes spellers, readers and primers in local languages. Often while the linguists are with a group of people, they produce a periodical and some agricultural, legal or health pamphlets. The commercial press in Papua New Guinea is directed toward popular interests, while the government press and the Summer Institute of Linguistics are directed toward education.

Each religious denomination in Papua New Guinea has its own publishing house. The Methodist mission's Trinity Press publishes a monthly religious paper, *A Nilai Ra Dovot* (The Voice of Truth). The Lutheran Kristen Press produces religious publications and fills a commercial need as well. The Catholic Wantok Publications own the most print communications. Besides *Wantok* and *The Times of Papua New Guinea* they produce *New Nation*, a children's pictorial magazine.

In Papua New Guinea there can be no decline in competition between newspapers because there is no competition. In 1978 the government established a committee to investigate an alternate national newspaper, but no report is available on this method of inspiring competition.

Economic Framework

Since most Papua New Guineans are farmers, a large audience awaits agricultural news and information. The Papua New Guinea government can afford extensive media projects, including agricultural education, because the budget is balanced and financially sound. Since the end of World War II the Department of Agriculture, Stock and Fisheries in the Australian administration has used radio, films and publications to educate the Papua New Guineans. The Public Health Department and the Special Services Division of the Department of Education have also used extensive mass communications.

Communication in Papua New Guinea is better served by radio, because radio does not face the handicaps of illiteracy or distance. More languages and more cultures can be represented on radio than in national newspapers. Among all mass media, provincial radio seems to promise the greatest benefit for Papua New Guineans, especially those in rural areas.

Press Laws

In 1979 the Papua New Guinea government established a committee to review its information services. This committee described Papua New Guinea's constitution as "providing a broad base for free flow of information between people and government. Although at present there are no laws which limit or authorize freedom of the press, certain laws do provide support for insuring circulation of news." Fundamental to the constitution are directives declaring that all citizens have a right to participate in the country's development and that this development should be achieved through native ways.

Freedom of expression, guaranteed to all people, whether citizens or noncitizens, includes holding opinions and relaying ideas and information via the press and other mass media. Access to mass media may be secured through an act of Parliament so that interested persons and groups can communicate certain ideas or refute false statements.

The right to circulate information is distinguished in Papua New Guinea from the right to obtain information. Noncitizens do not have an automatic right to the latter because the government believes that noncitizens are capable of exercising too much outside influence on national public opinion. Citizens have the right to obtain official documents except for those papers relating to such areas as national security, trade secrets, financial institutions and geophysical information.

The constitutional guarantees of press freedom have been peripherally narrowed by specific acts of Parliament. The Post and Telegraph Act restricts giving out information about letters that pass through a post office. The Protection of Private Communications Act defines when personal communications may be intercepted and what use may be made of the intercepted information. The Defamation Act protects individuals from spoken or written statements that might injure them or cause others to injure them. The Evidence Act describes the laws relating to court evidence and to the discovery of certain documents like bankers' books and business records. The Commercial Advertisement Act guards against misleading commercial advertising so that the public welfare can be protected.

The Printers and Newspapers Act covers the registration of printing and warns of nonregistering. According to this act, the printer's and publisher's names must be printed in the newspaper.

Luke Sela, present editor of *The Papua New Guinea Post-Courier,* wrote:

> Papua New Guinea certainly has a free press. We are not dictated to by the government. The government does not run a news service, and all media representatives, including Australian Associated Press (AAP) and a number of Australian radio and newspaper representatives, work independently to supply their organizations on a daily basis.

The Information Services Review Committee believes that it may be necessary to draft legislation on press freedom because of the increase in literacy and literature in Papua New Guinea. The committee also foresees the possibilities of passing legislation to protect journalists and to prevent noncitizens from monopolizing communications.

Censorship

The present Customs Act restricts the importation of goods into Papua New Guinea. Print material may not enter the country if it is blasphemous or obscene, or emphasizes matters of sex, horror, violence or crime. Print material is not allowed if it is likely to encourage depravity or if it advertises depraved literature. Films and slides can be imported into Papua New Guinea if they are not blasphemous, obscene or likely to encourage crime. The film or slide must not be offensive to the people of Papua New Guinea or a friendly nation.

If the film, slide, print material or advertising matter meets the criteria of the Customs Act, a license authorizing importation is issued. Interpretation of these criteria rests with the chief censor of the Bureau of Customs, or with the Censorship Board and the Censorship Committee. Appointments to the board and the committee are for three years. The board controls importing print material and consists of a chairman and at least four other respected members of the community. The committee controls film imports and besides the chief censor consists of seven members, two of whom are women.

However, in practice the burden of censorship has become the responsibility of the chief censor. Since 1978 the Censorship Board and the Censorship Committee have not met to perform their duties. Films have been imported on the basis of voluntary information provided by the importers, and print material has been assessed by referring to the publishers' and literature's reputation. At present video programs are being imported without control of any kind because video is not included in the legislation on film imports.

An immediate review of all existing censorship policies has been recommended by the Information Services Review Committee, as has the establishment of a communication tribunal to monitor all media activities. The committee reasoned that coordinating all censorship activities into a single, full-time body would result in more consistent standards than charging several groups with different responsibilities.

State-Press Relations

According to the Information Services Review Committee, a developing country's communications should be given top priority. In Papua New Guinea the Office of Information operates under the Prime Minister's Department but is responsible to the Minister of the Media. The Office of Information has five

730 Papua New Guinea

divisions. The Information Division provides national and provincial government news, national and overseas publicity, government public relations, and technical assistance to departments using mass media. The Government Liaison Division implements and evaluates national communication projects. The Policy Secretariat Division formulates national communication policy. There is also a Division of Management Services, Staff Development, and Training. The Production Division is the largest of the five divisions. It designs artwork for publications and has the capacity to translate materials into two native languages. The division produces films and video and publishes print materials, including a national government newspaper, *Our News*. *Our News* is published every two weeks in English, Pidgin and Motu. Although circulated nationwide at no charge, *Our News* is distributed ineffectively.

The Information Services Review Committee considers the Office of Information unable to provide its extensive range of services due to a shortage of skilled manpower, an inept administration and a lack of policy formulation. To replace the ineffective Office of Information, the committee recommends a new Department of Communication, which should fulfill indigenous communication needs and universal communication functions, such as entertaining and informing. Communication in Papua New Guinea needs to dispel the natives' fear of changing lifestyles, government and values. According to the Information Services Review Committee, communication must raise aspirations, widen horizons and contribute to liberation and nationalization; the Department of Communication should use the media to focus the public's attention on modern practices.

Government intervention with the commercial media started in 1942 when the Australian army closed one newspaper on censorship grounds. After World War II several events, such as native riots, focused attention on the need for improved communications between the government and the people. Dr. Barry Shaw, a Visiting Fellow in Papua New Guinea, described the extent of managed news:

> There is some behind-the-scenes manipulation of the press by the government from time to time, but no more than in many other western countries. By any standards, especially those of the Third World, I would describe the press in Papua New Guinea as

"free" and an important vehicle for criticism and comment, especially through the "Letter to the Editor" columns.

There will probably be more control of the media in the future. Many government leaders in Papua New Guinea are concerned that there is too much reporting of violence, crime and corruption, which they describe as "negative" issues. They have discussed tablishing a Papua New Guinea Press Council to hear complaints about inaccurate or biased reporting and to encourage higher standards and greater responsibility for professional journalists.

The Information Services Review Committee believes that reporters suffer from alienation and unprofessional reputations. Some government departments have openly communicated their hostility toward the media. To improve communications, the committee recommends that the government schedule meet-the-press sessions and establish a tribunal, which would have a small, full-time staff and be autonomous and neutral. It would monitor media activities, enforce standards, grant broadcasting licenses and adjudicate copyright infringement. As an "ombudsman," the tribunal would assist the government and private citizens in handling misunderstandings and grievances with the media.

Attitude Toward Foreign Media

A visitor traveling to Papua New Guinea for business purposes must obtain a business visa. The capital, Port Moresby, can be reached by air via Australia, Hong Kong, Manila, Japan, Indonesia and Hawaii. Once in Papua New Guinea, international telephone, telegraph, teletype and postal services are available.

Almost all of the domestic media in Papua New Guinea would have foreign ownership if not for government publications and support from international organizations. UNESCO is starting a radio program for teachers, to counteract their isolation and lack of contact with the Department of Education and Culture. In 1976 a visiting UNESCO team assessed Papua New Guinea's 15-year Broadcasting Development Plan.

Outsiders who want to read about Papua New Guinea in newspapers are faced with a scarcity of information. In *The New York*

Times, only 21 articles appeared on Papua New Guinea from 1974 through 1978. These articles, however, were written on location and were usually accompanied with a map. Other stories in different newspapers came from Reuters, UPI and AP. Most reporting covered Papua New Guinea's independence, its first elections, first stamps and first United Nations representation. Some attention was given to the primitiveness of Papua New Guinea in articles on tribal slayings and witch doctors, but independence movements proved to be the most common topic.

News Agencies

News from Papua New Guinea is frequently sensationalized. The Information Services Review Committee believes one alternative to negative news coverage is to establish a government news agency, which would produce stories beneficial to the country's development.

The New Guinea News Service is an independent newsgathering organization that exists without the political tone of a government news agency. It was established in 1969 in Port Moresby by John Ryan, a former journalist with the Australian Associated Press and the Australian Broadcasting Commission. Besides providing general news coverage for AP and for international radio and television outlets, the service is engaged in general publishing, public relations and advertising.

The Papua New Guinea Post-Courier receives its international news from Reuters, AP, UPI and the AAP.

Electronic News Media

Although gains in all communication media are important in Papua New Guinea, radio's success is the most far-reaching. Radio stations use major local dialects. Papua New Guineans have little reading material, but a sociologist who studied one native village discovered radios in half the homes.

A native missionary choir was featured when radio broadcasting was introduced to Papua New Guinea in 1934 by Australia. In 1946, when the Australian Broadcasting Commission (ABC) acquired the Port Moresby army station, ABC looked to the Australian administration to help solve cul-

tural problems. The Special Services Division of the Department of Education agreed to organize and deliver all programs for indigenous listeners. On the ABC station 40 percent of the programs were for natives, 30 percent for expatriots and the other 30 percent for both groups. News, talks, sports, information and entertainment were among the radio programs broadcast.

Even though the Department of Education was contributing to ABC programming for the indigenous population, the Papua New Guinea administration decided to begin its own broadcasting system. The Administration Broadcasting Service (ABS) began in 1961 under the Department of Information and Extension Services. Programming on an ABS station included traditional and pop music, children's shows and features on health, agriculture and business. Local government council meetings and overseas news were also broadcast.

Since ABS was an extension service of the government, radio programs were used to influence attitudes. A programming policy of the 1961 Broadcasting Services Committee was to obtain an understanding and acceptance of the government's functions. The Australian administration concentrated on using radio to reach densely populated areas or areas with special local problems.

In 1973 the dual system of ABS and ABC was merged into the Papua New Guinea Broadcasting Commission, with passage of the Broadcasting Commission Act in that year. The commission's duty is "to insure cooperation with the government in broadcasting social, political, economic, and educational programs."

The last type of programming may be the most significant. The educational extension service provided by radio is more important than class education since less than one-third of Papua New Guineans go to any sort of school at any level. Those who do attend school benefit from radio because educational broadcasting decreases isolation and upgrades educational standards. A two-hour "School of the Air" radio program assists children receiving education through correspondence schools.

To supplement radio's annual grant from the government, commercials were started in 1977. Commercials may be broadcast during 90 program-hours a week out of a possible 130 program-hours.

Concurrent with the establishment of the

Papua New Guinea Broadcasting Commission in 1973 was passage of the Radiocommunication Act, which authorizes the government to establish, license and regulate the country's electronic media. Significantly, the act includes potential TV broadcasting, but for various reasons a government policy on TV has not yet evolved. One committee has argued that the natives are too naive for television, but there is no proof of television's effects in Papua New Guinea. The Information Services Review Committee is recommending government control of television content through censorship and by assuring Papua New Guinean management of broadcasts.

Education & Training

Journalists in Papua New Guinea begin their training by taking typing, shorthand and basic reporting classes. They gain their experience through contact with other reporters. According to the Information Services Review Committee, this informal training has not produced journalists of a high professional caliber. Charges of irresponsible reporting and celebrity journalism have been heard at national and provincial levels. The committee recommended that the government train journalists as one of the functions of the proposed Department of Communication.

The Information Services Review Committee encouraged a code of ethics for national and overseas journalists. Believing that the Journalists Association of Papua New Guinea should contribute to higher standards, the committee recommended that a National Press Council be established for handling complaints on media inaccuracy and plagiarism.

Summary

Papua New Guinea gained its independence in 1975, but its communications systems are still transferring from foreign to local rule. The indigenous readership has grown over the past decade. In the 1960s the Pidgin newspaper *Nu Gini Toktok* never attracted a large readership, but the Pidgin *Wantok* proved successful in the 1970s. Even the Australian-owned newspaper, *The Papua New Guinea Post-Courier,* has a Papuan staff and editor. Unfortunately, neither the Australian nor the native administrations have provided high journalism standards, and there has been no commercial competition to serve as a stimulus. Whether or not the government chooses to follow the recommendations of its Information Services Review Committee will determine the future of communications in Papua New Guinea.

CHRONOLOGY

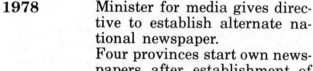

1975	Papua New Guinea gains independence from Australian trusteeship. National Broadcasting Commission drafts Broadcasting Development Plan for next 15 years. Evidence Act revises and amends laws relating to evidence, discovery of documents; Post and Telegraph Act restricts giving out information about letters that pass through post offices.
1976	Commercial Advertisement Act restricts false or misleading advertising.
	Luke Sela, a native, appointed editor of *The Papua News Guinea Post-Courier.*
1978	Minister for media gives directive to establish alternate national newspaper. Four provinces start own newspapers after establishment of provincial government.
1979	*Niugini News,* country's second national newspaper, is started. Government establishes committee to review information services in Papua New Guinea.

BIBLIOGRAPHY

Belshaw, Cyril S. *The Great Village: The Economic and Social Welfare of Hanuabada, an Urban Community in Papua.* London, 1957.

Bettison, David G., Hughes, Colin, and Van der Veur, Paul W., eds. *The Papua New Guinea Elections 1964.* Canberra, 1965.

Brennan, Paul W. *Report of the Review of Information Services in Papua New Guinea.* Port Moresby, 1979.

Essai, Brian. *Papua and New Guinea: A Contemporary Survey.* Melbourne, 1961.

Frazier, Thomas Lide. "A Study of the Development, Format, and Content of the *Nu Gini Toktok,* Neo-Melanesian Newspaper of New Guinea." M.A. thesis, Louisiana State University, 1969.

Hatanka, Sachiko. "Leadership and Socio-Economic Change in Sinasina, New Guinea Highlands." *New Guinea Research Bulletin* 45 (1972): 63.

Richstad, Jim, McMillan, Michael, and Barney, Ralph. *The Pacific Islands Press.* Honolulu, Hawaii, 1973.

Richstad, Jim, and Nnaemeka, Tony. "News from Nowhere: Sources of International News in the Pacific Islands." Paper presented at the Association for Education in Journalism Convention, Houston, 1979.

Ryan, Peter, ed. *Encyclopedia of Papua and New Guinea.* Melbourne, 1972.

Sela, Luke. Correspondence, October 1980.

Shaw, Barry, Papua New Guinea Visiting Fellow. Correspondence, September 1980.

UNESCO. *World Communications.* Great Britain, 1975.

U.S. Department of State. "Papua New Guinea." *Background Notes.* Washington, D.C., 1980.

Wilcox, Dennis L. "Radio: Its Nation-Building Role in New Guinea." *Gazette* 29 (1973).

BIBLIOGRAPHY

PERU

by George Kurian

BASIC DATA

Population: 17,388,000 (1980)
Area: 1,284,640 sq. km. (496,000 sq. mi.)
GNP: 2.484 trillion soles (US$10.3 billion) (1978)
Literacy Rate: 45–50%
Language(s): Spanish
Number of Dailies: 34
   Aggregate Circulation; 828,000
   Circulation per 1,000: 51
Number of Nondailies: 31
   Aggregate Circulation: 2,799,000
   Circulation per 1,000: 179
Number of Periodicals: 595

Number of Radio Stations: 230
Number of Television Stations: 4
Number of Radio Receivers: 2,050,000
   Radio Receivers per 1,000: 134
Number of Television Sets: 780,000
   Television Sets per 1,000: 50
Total Annual Newsprint Consumption: 28,600 metric tons
Per Capita Newsprint Consumption: 4.7 kg. (10.4 lb.)
Total Newspaper Ad Receipts: NA
   As % of All Ad Expenditures: NA

Background & General Characteristics

The Peruvian press is one of the oldest in the continent. The country's first newspaper, *El Mercurio Peruano,* was founded in 1791 by a group of liberal intellectuals who used their publication as a literary forum. *El Mercurio Peruano* set the tone for the numerous short-lived newspapers during the next half century. It was not until 1839 that the first true newspaper appeared: *El Comercio,* which is still being published today. Owned by a landowning family, *El Comercio* was the voice of the traditionally wealthy groups: the bankers, land owners and exporters. Its first issue proclaimed that the paper would be dedicated to "order, liberty and knowledge." Even though order and liberty eluded the Peruvians for most of their history, the press has remained an insuppressible source of knowledge.

Most of the newspapers that followed *El Comercio* were founded in Lima, but none of them is older than this century. (Four provincial papers, however, date from the 19th century: *El Minero* of Cerro de Pasco, *El Comercio* of Cuzco, *El Imparcial* of Huacho and *La Industria* of Trujillo.) The second oldest paper in Lima is *La Prensa,* founded in 1903. Unlike *El Comercio* it represented the newer stratum of the upper class—the merchants and the industrialists. *La Cronica* followed in 1912. It was the first evening paper in the country. The lifting of censorship during the presidency of Manuel Prado led to increased press activity during the years following World War II. One result was the founding of *Ultima Hora* in 1950 as Lima's second evening daily. The 1960s witnessed the founding of more Lima papers: three morning dailies, *Correo, Expreso* and *Ojo,* and the evening daily *Extra.* In a different category is the official state gazette, *El Peruano,* founded in 1825 and published every morning.

Peru has a strong regional press, with 25 daily newspapers being published from 12 cities: Arequipa, Cerro de Pasco, Chiclayo, Cuzco, Huacho, Huancayo, Ica, Iquitos, Pacasmayo, Piura, Puno, Tacna and Trujillo. With an aggregate circulation of around 130,000 and an average circulation of 5,000, regional papers do not enjoy the influence of the Lima dailies. Nevertheless, in the absence of a national newspaper, they dominate the local scene. Almost all of them describe themselves as independent. Sixteen are published in the morning and nine in the evening.

Although Indians constitute 46 percent of the population (or even a majority, if a proper ethnic census were to be held), Peruvian newspapers appear to be directed solely to the non-Indian, particularly white, readers. On the other hand, there are two dailies in Chinese, one in Japanese and a few non-dailies for the English and German communities in the larger towns.

Lima has a quality press comparable to the best in Latin America. The staff organization is professional. Competition is keen. Most of the larger dailies maintain circulation departments, and coupons and contests are commonly used to stimulate newspaper sales. Most newsmen work on a part-time basis and full-time employment is confined to key editorial personnel. Because of the prestige attached to newspaper writing, contributors are willing to work without pay and a byline is a magic password to fame.

The best-selling daily newspaper in 1980 was *La Cronica,* an illustrated evening paper that, like its competitor *Ultima Hora,* stresses crime, cheesecake and sports. It also has the most modern newspaper plant, a nine-floor building that also houses its radio affiliate Radio La Cronica. *Ojo* has the largest circulation of the morning dailies. In terms of national and world news coverage Peru's outstanding newspaper is *La Prensa.* It is a moderate conservative paper founded by the Pedro Beltran family and, like Beltran himself, has experienced many ups and downs.

9 Largest Dailies by Circulation		
La Cronica	Evening	230,000
Ojo	Morning	180,000
Extra	Evening	134,000
Ultima Hora	Evening	130,000
Expreso	Morning	110,000
La Prensa	Morning	98,000
El Comercio	Morning	90,000
Correo	Morning	80,000
El Peruano	Morning	75,000

Aggregate circulation of daily newspapers is reported by UNESCO at 828,000 (1977) and per capita circulation at 51 per 1,000 inhabitants. Peru ranks 50th in the world in the latter respect.

Of the 31 nondaily newspapers, the only ones of any consequence are the three Lima papers, *Peru Popular, Voz Obrera,* and *Lea.* The periodical press consists of 595 titles; the most notable are the weeklies *Vanguardia, Rochabus, Oiga* and *7-Dias* and the fortnightly *Caretas.* The English-language *Lima Times,* formerly *Peruvian Times,* concentrates on business and financial news.

Economic Framework

One of the first acts of President Fernando Belaunde on his election in 1980 was to restore freedom of the press and return Peruvian dailies, nationalized in 1974, to their former owners. This meant that *El Comercio* was returned to the Miro Quesada family, *La Prensa* to the Pedro Beltran interests, *La Cronica* to the Manuel Prado interests, and *Expreso* and *Extra* to the Manuel Ulloa interests. The Peruvian press has thus come full circle back into private hands. Although most newspaper publishing companies have a number of shareholders, they are closely identified with a prominent individual and serve the interests of a particular sector of the economy. There is virtually no group ownership, except for morning and evening papers published by the same management. Morning papers tend to exemplify serious quality journalism, while evening tabloids tend to be sensational.

Distribution is mainly on the street, through newsboys and newsstands. Lima dailies have distribution agents in the provinces, enabling provincial readers to receive morning editions on the day of publication.

The principal labor union in the newspaper industry is the Federation of Journalists of Peru, affiliated to the International Organization of Journalists. No serious strikes have been reported in recent years.

Press Laws & Censorship

With the return of civilian rule, most of the restrictive press laws introduced by presidents Velasco Alvarado and Morales Bermudez were taken off the statute book. This act, hailed by the Inter-American Press Association as "the most auspicious event for the freedom of the press in the hemisphere in the last [few] years," also restored freedom of expression, returned seven dailies to their former owners, and reinstated editors and general managers dismissed by the Velasco government.

The new law, strongly opposed by leftist groups as well as APRA, the nationalist alliance, virtually eliminated government control over all forms of media and de-established official censorship. The press is now subject only to the normal legal restraints relating to libel, sedition, etc. More importantly, it has ended the harassment of journalists and publishers, thus creating a climate in which they can exercise their functions without fear.

At the same time, the Belaunde administration has initiated a new system of licensing of journalists that has caused much concern in the press as a potentially coercive tool. A recent law authorizes the creation of an autonomous collegium that would act independently to monitor ethical, cultural and social standards in journalism. Affiliation is essential for all those who practice journalism although, at the same time, they are free to write without prior authorization. New candidates are also required to have a degree in journalism. The collegium will be funded from the proceeds of a one percent tax paid by all mass media on advertising revenues. While opposed by conservative newspapers, such as *El Comercio,* the law has the unanimous support of the major journalistic trade unions.

State-Press Relations

According to *El Comercio,* Peru is enjoying under the Belaunde government "the fullest freedom of expression." This is a remarkable turnaround for a country that throughout the 1970s had one of the worst records in this respect. It is also typical of the swift alternation between freedom and repression that the Peruvian press has experienced throughout its history. In this century it enjoyed brief respites from official control under the two presidential terms of Manuel Prado, from 1945 to 1948 and from 1956 until 1962. In the 1960s the Press Freedom Index created by the University of Missouri School of Journalism placed it sixth on the scale—above the United States—with a near perfect +2.76 (with +4 as the maximum and -4 as the lowest). Within the next decade it had slipped to the bottom half of the category. K. Q. Hill and P. A. Hurley in their 30-year survey of press freedom in Latin America ranked Peruvian press freedom as poor in the 1950s, good in the early 1960s, average by 1970 and poor again in 1975.

The Peruvian press reached its nadir under the administrations of presidents Velasco and Bermudez. In a series of decrees culminating in the "cooperativization" of the press, the government virtually destroyed every vestige of press freedom. These decrees were the Law of the Freedom of the Press of 1969, the 1970 Law of Industries and Law of the Journalist, the 1971 General Telecommunications Law and the 1974 Press Law. The 1974 Freedom of the Press Law tightened the law of criminal libel and disrespect, providing fines and/or prison terms for insulting the regime. It also required government press releases to be printed on the first page and barred both Peruvian exiles and foreign citizens from owning shares in the media.

In two documents, "Ideological Bases of the Peruvian Revolution" and the "Inca Plan," the regime spelled out the philosophical premises behind these decrees. The rhetoric sounded strangely Marxist. It contended that the "Peruvian Revolution" did not accept contradictions and that "to achieve full popular participation it must expropriate the media and hand them over to organizations that represent the majority of the population, that is, farmers, laborers, etc." The government was to determine how it should be criticized! The crowning rationale was the time-honored definition of the press as a "public service." What could be better than that such a public service should be controlled by that most public of all institutions, the government itself. Velasco went further and claimed that freedom of expression never existed in Peru and therefore hardly needed to be taken away. Freedom of the press, he said, was only freedom for the businessmen and families that owned it.

The 1974 Press Law nationalized the entire media and incorporated it as an "organized social sector." In the same year the government closed down the last remaining independent political newspaper and expropriated several others. In 1976 the government replaced the editors of five of the six major dailies and suppressed 12 political journals charged with sabotage. Six were allowed to reappear after a few months but the other six remained banned. There was a ban on publication of papers with a circulation of more than 20,000 copies. The editors and managers of all publications were appointed by the government.

The 1976 ouster of Velasco and his replacement by Gen. Morales Bermudez seemed to augur for a while a reversal of government policy toward the media. Bermudez, proclaiming the Second Phase of the Revolution, had acknowledged the need to restore freedom of expression and also the failure of his predecessor's socialization policies. But the guiding ideology of the revolution had not changed, and Bermudez shared Velasco's distrust of the press. "The press," he said, "has contributed to the apparent weakening of authority." He required newspapers not to "follow the sensationalist, alienating and venal line which has characterized their reporting...[or become] twisters of the truth, and instigators of disunity and class struggles among Peruvians." Internationally known magazines, such as *Caretas* and *Gente,* were closed by decree. The "whereases" in the decree said that "nondaily papers and sporadic periodicals [are] abusing the rights granted them by the law...engaging in campaigns designated to hinder economic recovery measures, destroying the unity of the armed forces and subverting public peace and order." Protesting this decree, novelist Vargas Llosa said, "The Government makes a mistake, for to suppress an expression of discontent is not to suppress discontent. On the contrary, it is the best way to increase it." Undeterred, the government created a high-level commission under Gen. Jose Villalobos, the national chief of information, to draft a new press law and to make the functioning of the press as an organized social sector more effective. The purchase and distribution of newsprint was placed under government control, and all new publications were required to obtain prior state permission. The weekly *El Tiempo* suspended publication as censorship was extended to magazines, although the government claimed that it was not censorship but only "revising the content of publications before they went out on the streets." *El Tiempo*'s editor, Alfonso Bella Tuesta, was in retaliation deported to Argentina. The journalist Jorge Castro de los Rios, vice president of the Peruvian Federation of Journalists, was sentenced to 16 months of probation and a fine of 20,000 soles for offending the Peruvian Air Force.

By 1978 the regime had begun to acknowledge the unwisdom of its media policies and retrace its steps. Its Third Press Law, Decree Law #22244 of 1978, desocialized the press but continued other restrictions, such as limits regarding circulation, number of shareholders, and capitalization. Also, the state did not immediately give up direct control over publications but instead appointed a board of directors made up of representatives of the government to "temporarily manage the confiscated papers." Control was also maintained through SINADI (National Information System) and the Sociedad Paramonga Limitada, which enjoyed a monopoly over newsprint import and distribution. Even harassment of journalists continued well into 1980. In that year Julio Cabrera Moreno, editor of *Equis,* a weekly newsmagazine, was charged by the Ministry of Interior after publication of a story linking the minister of the interior with smuggling rings. Augusto Zimmerman, publisher of the leftwing journal *Kausachum,* was jailed for three months for insulting national symbols.

Toward the end of his term Bermudez admitted that "the expropriation of the Lima dailies was the greatest error made by the revolutionary government." This was perhaps the most appropriate epitaph for the darkest chapter in Peruvian media history. It ended when the popularly elected Belaunde government took office in 1980.

Attitude Toward Foreign Media

Foreign media suffered as much as the domestic media in the Velasco/Bermudez years. The LATIN news agency was shut down in 1974 for alleged "persistent and insidious campaign" against the Peruvian regime abroad. Reuters correspondents were detained on several occasions; two AP reporters were expelled. Most foreign correspondents were subjected to brief detentions. The London *Financial Times* correspondent was taken to task for an adverse report on Peruvian economy. Harassment of foreign reporters ceased with the restoration of press freedom in 1980.

President Bermudez supported the 1978 UNESCO Declaration on the Media, which closely reflected his own policies. The Belaunde administration has not yet articulated its stand on the subject.

News Agencies

There is no national news agency. Newspapers depend largely on their own correspondents and on official government radio news bulletins as well as foreign bureaus, such as AP, AFP, Reuters and UPI.

Electronic News Media

Radio and television broadcasting are regulated by the General Telecommunications

Law of 1971. All broadcasting facilities are owned by the state, either by itself or in partnership with others. The Oficina Nacional de Informacion (ONI) administers the fully government-owned stations and the Empresa Nacional de Telecomunicaciones (ENTEL-PERU) for partly owned stations. Of the 230 radio stations, the most powerful are those run by the government network, Radio Nacional, comprising 13 stations. The principal commercial stations are Radio America, Radio El Sol and Radio Panamericana. Television, introduced in 1958, is concentrated in Lima; the only station outside the capital is Televisora Continental at Arequipa. Lima's six stations include two government-owned ones; Ministerio de Educacion Publica and Televisora Universidad de Lima—Canal 13. The four other commercial stations have majority government ownership. News and information make up only 5 percent of the total TV broadcasting time of 390 hours a week.

Education & Training

The first Peruvian school of journalism was established in 1945 at the Catholic University in Lima. This was followed by the University of San Marcos in 1947. Today, there are six university level schools of journalism, three at Lima, one at Cuzco, one at Piura, and one at Arequipa. There are also three journalism schools not affiliated with universities, at Lima, Trujillo, and Huancayo.

Summary

Peru's recent press history provides a case study in survival. In a bitter decade-long confrontation with an authoritarian regime, it proved its essential indestructibility. Where the press is threatened, the Peruvian experience should be an encouraging lesson.

CHRONOLOGY

1974 President Velasco Alvarado's troops seize Lima newspapers. Under Press Law all newspapers nationalized and incorporated into single "organized social sector." LATIN's Lima office closed.

1976 President Velasco ousted and replaced by General Morales Bermudez. *Caretas,* nation's most prominent magazine, forced to close. *El Tiempo* closed and its editor deported. Journalist Jorge Castro de los Rios convicted of offending Air Force. Thirteen magazines suspended.

1978 Under its Third Press Law government desocializes press while retaining full control.

1980 Julio Cabrera Moreno, editor of *Equis,* and Augusto Zimmerman publisher of *Kausachum,* penalized under press laws. In first popular elections in over a decade, Belaunde Terry elected president; Belaunde revokes military-inspired press laws and restores nation's newspapers to their former owners. Government establishes collegium to which all journalists are required to belong. IAPA hails Peru's return to community of free-press nations.

BIBLIOGRAPHY

Harding, C. "Press Experiment in Peru." *Index on Censorship,* July-August 1978.
_____. "Peru's Hot Potato." *Index on Censorship,* November 1980.
Hill, K. W., and Hurley, P.A. "Press Freedom in Latin America: A Thirty Year Survey." *Latin American Research Review,* 15:2 (1980).
Pierce, Robert N. *Keeping the Flame: Government and Media in Latin America.* New York, 1979.

PHILIPPINES

by Cynthia D. Hill

BASIC DATA

Population: 46.35 million (1978, est.)
Area: 299,681 sq. km. (115,707 sq. mi.)
GNP: 208.43 billion pesos (US$28.11 billion) (1979)
Literacy Rate: 80%
Language(s): English, Spanish, Tagalog, local dialects
Number of Dailies: 19
 Aggregate Circulation: 964,476
 Circulation per 1,000: 20
Number of Nondailies: 143 (1975)
 Aggregate Circulation: 1,028,735
 Circulation per 1,000: 130

Number of Periodicals: 101 (1979)
Number of Radio Stations: 455 (1979)
Number of Television Stations: 26 (1979)
Number of Radio Receivers: 2 million (1979)
 Radio Receivers per 1,000: 43 (1979)
Number of Television Sets: 1 million (1979)
 Television Sets per 1,000: 22 (1979)
Total Annual Newsprint Consumption: 68,700 metric tons
 Per Capita Newsprint Consumption: 1.6 kg. (3.7 lbs.)
Total Newspaper Ad Receipts: NA
 As % of All Ad Expenditures: NA

Background & General Characteristics

After more than three centuries of Spanish rule, the Philippines declared its independence on June 12, 1898. But Spain ceded the Philippines to the United States, which held the islands until July 4, 1946. The media finally obtained their freedom after World War II, and by the 1960s had evolved into one of the most vital and free national presses in Asia. During this time, other Philippines media were also demonstrating signs of growing independence. Various bills designed to protect newsmens' sources of information, to open government files to the public and to provide specific definitions of libel were passed or seriously considered in the 1960s. The media, particularly the press, did not at all times show an enlightened vision of their responsibility and tended toward exaggeration and sensationalism—although occasional efforts to police themselves were undertaken through such organizations as the Philippine Press Institute. In 1965 Ferdinand Marcos was elected president, and reelected in 1969. His second term saw increasing political dissatisfaction, culminating—on September 21, 1972—in his declaration of martial law in the Philippines. On January 17, 1981, by another Marcos proclamation, martial law came to an end.

The pre-martial law press of the Philippines was one of the freest and most militant in the world, restricted only by libel laws and certain economic problems. Journalism was a factor in the growth and development of the Philippines and exercised an important influence on the political scene. Filipino newspapers often exposed corrupt government practices, and few public figures took legal action against what they claimed were false reports, for fear of notoriety that might be associated with such action. The general attitude of most critics of the press was that an excessive press was better than a controlled one.

Before the proclamation of martial law in 1972, the press had a privileged position in the Philippines. It enjoyed the inherited free-for-all traditions introduced under American tutelage. These were later reinforced by the loose political rivalry of the postwar parties.

Within the limits of the libel laws, criticism was defended as a healthy reaction to the conservatism of the establishment. The press was outspoken in comment and convictions. Four major English dailies, with Tagalog counterparts, were reinforced by evening papers and a large number of weeklies. These were an integral part of urban and rural life. Foreign and national news came verbatim from agency reports, and while a large part of the daily news also consisted of columnists' contributions and social gossip, news was generally authenticated and editorial comment authoritative and reasonable.

During the first years of Marcos's presidency, Philippine papers paid comparatively little attention to books, art, science or foreign affairs. Instead, they concentrated on politics, crime and social doings. Most papers were family owned, and their news columns as well as editorials reflected the owners' outside interests. The largest of the Philippine newspapers was the English-language *Manila Times,* the only one whose owners had no outside holdings except for other publications and broadcasting stations. Filipino journalists began interpretive and investigative reporting in the late 1960s. Reporting crusades, reminiscent of the Pulitzer period in the United States, caused newspaper circulation in Manila to rise dramatically. Once again the *Manila Times* led other newspapers, such as the *Manila Chronicle, Manila Daily Bulletin* and the *Philippines Daily Express.* Provincial newspapers joined in the muckraking with similar effects on circulation. Editors ran numerous articles on political chicanery, gambling, prostitution and kickback rackets.

With the declaration of martial law, Marcos ordered the confiscation or closure of all media establishments, and freedom of the press disappeared. In February 1974, five months after the declaration of martial law, three national newspapers were in operation. At present there are six publication groups, the majority connected with Marcos. They are:

1. Philippine Daily Express Group, published by Juan Perez, but owned by President Marcos and partly financed from the President's contingent fund.
2. Bulletin Today Group, published and owned by Hans Menzi, a former presidential aide.
3. Evening Post-Daily Group, owned and published by Juan Tuvera, a presidential assistant, and his wife, a biographer to Imelda Marcos, the president's wife.
4. Weekly Examiner, owned and operated by Leon Ivy, appointed by President Marcos as governor of the Development Bank of the Philippines.
5. United Daily News, a Chinese-English daily owned by a special interest group.
6. Times Journal-Daily and Manila Journal-Weekly, owned by a group headed by Benjamin Romualdez, a brother of Imelda Marcos.

The national press is published in the three main languages—Tagalog, Spanish and English. As in other once-colonized countries, the correlation between political eminence and language has been marked in the Philippines. English, which followed Spanish, is still the dominant language in the Philippine press. Filipino (Tagalog), the dialect of the region around Manila, has become the official language, apparently stimulated by increasing nationalistic fervor. The three most influential newspapers, *Bulletin Today, Daily Express* and *Times Journal,* are in English. All of these are published in Manila, site of the country's media concentration. Two other cities, Cebu City and Davao City have competing papers.

At present there is a small but noticeable increase in the number of provincial newspapers in the country. This may be seen particularly in the establishment of papers in certain provinces where no publication existed before: Cagayan Valley, Bulacan, Batangas, Oriental Mindoro, Sorsogon, Masbate and Bohol. This growth, while encouraging, is offset by the consideration of those newspapers in various areas of the country that ceased publication with the declaration of martial law—leading to a situation where certain communities had no local press whatever.

Furthermore, both the local and national press no longer have their pre-martial law reach. Using as basis the entire output of all press publications in the Philippines and the number of readers and potential readers in the country, local and national papers can account for only about 10 percent of the total literate population, or just about one newspaper copy per issue for every three households in general. This is further hindered by areas in the country that have yet to be reached by any newspaper medium. In Regions X and XI for example, no provincial press can be found in the provinces of Lanao del Sur, Maranaw (created after martial law), Bukidnon, Agusan del Sur, Surigao del Norte, Surigao del Sur, Davao Oriental, Davao del Norte, South Cotabato and Sultan Kudarat. Such a situation also exists in the Luzon provinces of Ilocos Sur, Abra, Batanes, Quirino and Bataan.

Economic Framework

The Philippines is predominantly an exporting country, earning over 60 percent of its foreign exchange from coconut products, sugar, timber, copper concentrates, tropical fruit and other commodities. Manufacturing is unevenly split between buoyant, export-oriented light industry (garments and electronics, for example,) and stagnating, protected, import-substitution industries. Export performance remains subject to commodity demand cycles, but it is increasingly benefiting from the growth of a competitive manufacturing sector.

The Philippines enjoys an international-trade advantage in its cheap labor costs, which remain considerably lower than elsewhere in industrialized Asia. The government sought to hold the purchasing power of wage earners at a reasonable level by ordering an increase in the minimum wages and cost-of-living allowances in April 1979, with an additional cost-of-living allowance hike in August. At that time the minimum basic wage in metropolitan Manila was raised in August 1979 to 21.30 pesos or ($2.89) a day. However, there were wide-ranging exemptions, including export industries and plantation workers, that limited the effect of the measure. Consequently real wages for many workers declined during the year.

Nor has export health removed a serious import problem. The high cost of importing 90 percent of the country's oil has contributed to a rise in the inflation rate to 25 percent and resulted in a 13.32 billion pesos ($1.8 billion) balance-of-trade deficit. To correct such imbalances, the Marcos government is using a two-pronged strategy to finance long-range development and increase the GNP growth rate, which was six percent in 1979. One part of the strategy involves substantial international borrowing from both private sources and multinational banks to finance industrial growth. The other part will be to provide larger incentives for foreign investment in industrial projects.

Philippine media have undergone extensive self-examination and self-evaluation since the years of martial law. Today, the nation's press is economically better than at any other time in its history. In earlier years, serious economic problems existed: production costs were high, advertising was limited, various languages hampered sales, distribution and transportation presented problems and money was not available. All that has changed. Today, the giant news organizations hold the key positions in the Print Media Council, and have used them to their own economic advantage. Thus the situation for the established newspaper chains is favorable. No major newspaper has reported losses, whereas before martial law newspapers were generally unprofitable. Radio and television have made strides to rediscover the commercial possibilities of Filipino music. The cinema industry is profitable.

Before 1975 loans for the electronic media were difficult to obtain. The banks questioned such loans because broadcast permits were for six months' or one year's duration, with no certainty that the station would be on the air the following year. Radio permits are now valid for three years, and renewable for another three ad infinitum, thus enabling stations to borrow money for expansion. Moreover, every station is encouraged to improve technical facilities and equipment. This is partially possible because of a presidential decree allowing radio and television stations to import, virtually free of duty and taxes, new equipment and facilities for improving the quality of broadcasting. Any taxes that are due can be paid in air time to the government for developmental programs. The broadcasting media have also found that an increase in Filipino programming carries large economic gains. This has encouraged a profitable record industry to develop, which aids Filipino composers. Nearly all broadcasting stations have reported profits in recent years. Investors are now buying into radio stations that used to be sole proprietorships.

There are two general features which can be cited in the operations of both print and broadcast media in the Philippines today. One is that the mass media are primarily in the hands of the private sector. All major dailies and magazines in the country are owned by private corporations or individuals; in broadcasting, 205 stations are operated by the private sector as against 15 radio stations under government control. The term "industry" can be applied to both media in the sense that they operate much the same way as private corporations—the predominant goal being to increase earnings or profits.

The private character of broadcast media ownership often has adverse as well as positive consequences, notably in radio. The overconcentration of stations in urban centers is due as much to the profit motive as it is to lack of initiative to venture into areas that are equally promising but still need to be tapped. A recent Broadcast Media Council study on gross billings of radio stations in the Philippines showed that the nontraditional broadcast areas are turning up a higher percentage of advertising volume than the traditional areas. Thus, a relatively high percentage of growth over the past two years was noted in Isabela, Occidental and Oriental Mindoro, Albay, Camarines Norte, Masbate, Sorsogon, Samar, Negros Oriental and others.

The relatively low advertising expenditures on both broadcast and print media in the Philippines have been termed "detrimental" to the growth of the local advertising industry by the chairman of the Asian Federation of Advertising Associations. Comparing advertising expenditures of countries in the region covered by the Association of Southeast Asian Nations, the Philippines ranked fourth in 1977. With a population of about 44.5 million and total advertising expenditures of approximately 599.92 million pesos ($81.4 million), the Philippines had a per capita rate of only approximately 13.49 pesos ($1.83).

There are 40 advertising agencies in the Philippines that are recognized by the Philippine Media Association. These agencies receive a maximum of 15 percent commission from the various media. (This standard rate also applies to foreign agencies.) The following is a breakdown of advertising by principal media in percentages:

Print	40
Radio	25
Television	25
Other	10
	(including outdoor and cinema)

Press Laws

Press freedom exists in theory under the Philippine Constitution. It is cited in Article IV, Section 8 of the Bill of Rights, providing that "no law shall be passed abridging the freedom of speech, or of the press, or the right of the people peaceably to assemble and petition the Government for redress of grievances."

In the early 1970s press freedom began expressing itself in a strong adversary posture, arising from dissatisfaction and concern over a worsening economic crisis. Indeed, in the fall of 1970 publishers meeting in secret agreed to pursue identical editorial positions on vital political and economic issues. Pooled editorials were published on the front pages of major Manila dailies. Their position was vigorously anti-establishment. Publisher biases entered the news columns. The weeklies, remoter from current facts than their daily counterparts, tended to be even more emphatic. By 1971 the press was under considerable fire from the government, which resented its "non-objectivity." Finally, President Marcos curtailed the amount of government information reaching the mass media; sources were closed off. The press retaliated by conjuring up crisis after crisis for the front pages and the airwaves. The credibility of the press and government degenerated to a new low. Unable to stem the tide of violent anti-government demonstrations and of the general breakdown of the economy, the president resorted to the ultimate weapon under the constitution. On September 21, 1972, charging that the press had exceeded its freedom by distortions, tendentious reporting, speculation and criticism which damaged society and weakened resistance to communism, President Marcos imposed martial law.

The declaration diminished the protection that the media had enjoyed under the Philippine Constitution, which—notably in its "First Amendment" clauses—closely resembles the constitution of the United States. There are five basic points in the scope of constitutional press freedom in the Philippines:

1. Freedom of the press includes the right to freely utter and print and publish any statements without previous censorship of the government except so far as their blasphemy, obscenity or scandalous character may be a public offense, or as by their falsehood and malice they may injuriously affect the standing, reputation, or pecuniary interest of individuals.

2. Freedom of publication includes the right to criticize the general affairs of the government.

3. Freedom of speech and freedom of the press include the right to disseminate infor-

mation concerning the facts of a labor dispute.

4. Freedom of speech includes liberty of circulation.

5. Freedom of speech extends to "free trade in ideas."

Limitations on press freedom state that the privilege of free speech and press is generally limited by the police power of the state for the promotion of public safety, public morals, and national security. Thus the right to free speech may be regulated through the exercise of the police power of the state. The limitations, based on numerous U.S. cases, include:

1. Laws of exclusion from the mails of newspapers containing seditious or libelous articles.

2. Laws authorizing a committee to make a full and complete investigation with respect to violations of subversive activities.

3. Laws punishing the advocacy of the necessity and propriety of overthrowing an organized government.

4. Laws punishing the offense of sedition or of inciting sedition.

Numerous other limitations exist, most of them also in the United States: Philippine libel laws, obscenity laws, public information laws, shield laws, and other media regulations closely resemble U.S. laws. The difference results from the strict enforcement of the limitations in the Philippines following the declaration of martial law.

The 1981 lifting of martial law would seem to signal a shift to more leniency. But analysts of Filipino affairs explain that even with the new decree the president's power will remain supreme. Presidential involvement in appointment of judges and control of the village chiefs is only one reason why. Nor did the end of martial law affect Marcos's right to authorize the military to arrest suspected subversives, end strike bans on vital industries, and control licensing of mass media.

Philippine laws also affect the advertising industry, but they do not constitute restriction on advertising. Instead, they are designed to protect legitimate business and industry from unscrupulous and unfair competition.

Censorship

Marcos's control of censorship is evident not only in the organization but in the content of the media. Since martial law, the media have portrayed the goals and aspirations of the government. They also reflect positive and passive news, usually ignoring negative characteristics of the government and Philippine society. All this stems from a set of tight news-reporting guidelines issued by Marcos with the reopening of "normal" media operations. In an interview with newsmen, Marcos charged that the press, radio and television had been infiltrated by communist propagandists and had been guilty of distortions, dissident reporting against the government, wide speculation and criticism that had damaged society in the Philippines and weakened resistance to communism. Under the new regulations, news media were ordered "to print and broadcast accurate, objective, straight news reports of positive national value consistent with the efforts of the Philippine government to meet the dangers and threats that occasioned the proclamation of martial law and the efforts to achieve a New Society as set forth by the President."

Coming under the ban are materials that "tend to incite or otherwise inflame people or individuals against the government," as well as items that "dominate or jeopardize" the military or law authorities or glorify or sensationalize crime. These items include society news, political advertising and commentary of any kind, including sports and entertainment. The guidelines also state: "Informative foreign news items may be printed or broadcast by the local media but in no case must any foreign news be printed or broadcast which puts it in the same category as any of the prohibited materials enumerated above. Similarly, no news material or opinions emanating from abroad may be disseminated by any wire agency through any Philippines recipient which is of the same type as any of the prohibited materials enumerated above." The same rules apply to foreign correspondents, whether based in the Philippines or not. The guidelines also provide for censorship of all photographs and dispatches coming into the Philippines.

What appears in the media today is a constant flood of positive information on the president and his family. Although this is a major change from pre-martial law days, regulations seem to be returning slowly to that time. Society news is back and crime is on page one. The difference, however, is that it is only the news that the government wishes to be published. Opponents of Marcos are speaking out in the papers to some degree, but their stories are buried on inside pages while Marcos is always front-page copy. Primitivo Mijares, a former high official in the Marcos government, agrees with this evaluation. Testifying at hearings of the 1975 Subcommittee on International Organization in the U.S. House of Representatives, Mijares said that the media in the Philippines are exclusively for Marcos to manipulate: "The opposition are not given a chance to have their side heard or published; it is as if they never exist at all. Even the matter of peace and order is established as a fact by simply prohibiting the publication of crime stories."

Government domination of television content is extensive. Marcos controls three of the five Manila stations, Imelda Marcos, the first lady, dominates the nightly news, while daughter Imee has a weekly talk show called "Metromagazine." At any time of the day or night, all stations simultaneously will interrupt their programming for live coverage of a Ferdinand Marcos speech, press conference, hospital dedication or airport reception. Viewers cannot miss the government's message by turning off the news. Filipino producers of popular situation comedies receive monthly development communications called "devcomms," outlining the government policy (nutrition, population control, urban renewal) that will be woven into upcoming plots.

This dissemination of positive news has been an intrinsic facet of Marcos's martial law. And Marcos has made sure that the information has been available to the media. The closure of newspapers and broadcasting stations following the imposition of martial law created an information vacuum in the Philippines. This was quickly filled by the Presidential Press Office, which was renamed the Department of Public Information. This was a national news service and a bureau for broadcast. A number of regulatory committees were spawned within the department, such as the Bureau of Standards for Mass Media and the Bureau of National and Foreign Information. The department also became the major manufacturer of news, press releases, books, radio and television programs, and even an album entitled "No Shade But Light," a recording of excerpts of presidential speeches.

Today, according to Marcos, the intensity of media regulation has decreased to a self-censorship level. However, journalists are still under strong pressure. In March 1973, the government allowed the press to resume its activities under the supervision of the Mass Media Council, which was composed of

officers selected by Marcos, who personally instructed editors and reporters "to write and talk about positive things." After a high level of self-regulation finally evolved, Marcos seemingly decreed the removal of direct government supervision of the news media in May 1973, when he abolished the Mass Media Council and created the Media Advisory Council. All this meant, however, was that government supervision of the mass media was shifted from one council to another. And in October 1974, when Marcos finally abolished the Media Advisory Council and authorized the creation of self-regulatory councils for the printing and broadcast media, he retained control of licenses for the press—and still does. Moreover, press and broadcasting councils can accept or reject applications of journalists, and as these councils are formed only by members appointed by Marcos, only the semantics of the regulations have really been changed.

On January 17, 1981, when President Marcos finally ended martial law in the Philippines after eight years, he described his decision as "an encounter with destiny." The gesture seems to critics to be a largely cosmetic move designed to improve Marcos's international image, as he had used the previous several weeks to establish new legal weapons that can be used at will to stop any threat of opposition. Habeas corpus remains suspended in crimes against state security. The Public Order Act, a decree that appeared during the week previous to the lifting of martial law, gives Marcos the power to muzzle the press and hold anyone in preventive detention simply by declaring that a "grave emergency" is imminent. So it appears today that despite the country's freedom from martial law, the censorship policies of the Philippines will not substantially change. Many critics fear that what were once the instruments of martial law alone have now become a part of the regular legal system, and could be employed at any president's whim.

State-Press Relations

The disappearance of the completely free press was one of the first results of Marcos's martial law declaration. The only newspaper that was allowed to remain open was the Marcos-owned *Daily Express*. Of course this was a pro-government paper (edited by the first lady's cousin). It claimed to report "objective news," but had neither crime coverage nor political comment. The major established newspapers such as the *Manila Times, Manila Chronicle, Philippine Herald, Mabuhay* and *Manila Daily Bulletin* were closed, with the result that the circulation of the *Daily Express* reached about 400,000. In 1974 competition was introduced by allowing publication of a new newspaper, the *Times-Journal,* and the reopening of the *Manila Daily Bulletin.* The latter, which had the second largest circulation before martial law, changed its masthead to *Bulletin Today* and climbed to a circulation of over 200,000. The *Times-Journal* and the *Daily Express* became the country's second and third largest daily newspapers. The *Philippine Herald* had also received permission to resume publishing and was about to go to press when the approval was withdrawn without explanation.

Marcos arrested hundreds of journalists and people involved with the media. They were jailed without formal charges, placed in unemployment lines or denied permission to leave the country. Those newsmen detained included the publisher of the *Manila Times,* an independent English-language daily with a morning circulation of about 186,000; a columnist for the *Times* who had been one of the President's principal critics; a *Times* reporter; the editor of *Graphic,* an English-language weekly magazine; the editor of the *Manila Chronicle;* a *Chronicle* columnist; and the editor of the *Philippine Free Press.* Before censorship by martial law the *Free Press* had crusaded for political and economic reform. The most celebrated case among the journalist detentions was that of Eugenio Lopez, Jr.—imprisoned for alleged involvement in a plot to assassinate the president. At the time of his arrest—without a warrant—Lopez was publisher of the *Manila Chronicle,* the second largest daily in the country, and president of the ABS-CBN radio network. For a year prior to the declaration of martial law, he had become more critical of the authoritarian steps taken by the Marcos regime. When the *Chronicle* was closed under a censorship decree its facilities were taken over by the *Times-Journal,* owned by Governor Benjamin Romualdez, brother of Imelda Marcos. Before and after proclaiming martial law Marcos had criticized the oligarchic control of the nation's mass media by families such as Lopez's. He now explained the suspension and confiscation of these family newspapers without remuneration as a move to break up the oligarchies.

After the declaration of martial law, the broadcasting media consisted of one radio station, operated by the Philippine Broadcasting Service, and one of the country's original television stations. Today, Marcos controls one of the largest and probably one of the most influential broadcasting services in the Philippines—Kanlaon Broadcasting System (KBS). It is owned by Ambassador Roberto Benedicto, a close Marcos associate. This system absorbed the ABS-CBN stations that were expropriated from the Lopez family. Primitivo Mijares—the former high official in the Marcos government who has labeled himself as Marcos's media confidant —has said that a permit was signed enabling Benedicto, acting as Marcos's front man, to take over Lopez's multimillion dollar broadcasting complex without reimbursement.

KBS is also the dominant force in Filipino television, managing three of Manila's five stations (the only full color television channels in the Philippines). Manila's other radio and television stations are also under some form of government control, answering to various governmental agencies.

Two other electronic-media networks in the Philippines are the Intercontinental Broadcasting Corporation and the Republic Broadcasting System. Although the people of the Philippines have access to these—and to all broadcasting media—the government still exercises content control over the channels.

Attitude Toward Foreign Media

With the imposition of martial law in the Philippines, the restrictions that were placed on the domestic media also applied to the foreign media. Marcos made this clear: "the same rules apply to foreign correspondents whether based in the Philippines or not. No foreign dispatch will be filed from the Philippines which impugns, discredits, questions or criticizes any positive effort of the government, the government itself or any of its duly constituted authorities. Nor will any dispatch be filed which speaks unfairly or inaccurately of the Philippines or Filipinos...." The regulations also permitted censorship of all photographs; pictures could be taken only of "normal city life and of interviews with authorized officials and offices." Forbidden were photographs of military installations, airports and seaports and Malacanang, the presidential palace. News dispatches coming into the Philippines from abroad were censored, along with stories written by Filipinos for home consumption or by foreign correspondents to be sent to other countries. Editorials and commentary were prohibited along with gossip columns.

When martial law was declared, troops gathered at the front door of the Associated Press's Manila bureau. Within minutes, a combat-clad national policeman walked in and told Night Editor George Reyes to vacate the office. The bureau was then closed for thirty hours, and AP operated from the home of a staff member. When the staffers were allowed to return, they found that national policemen were making daily visits to the office.

Most of the censorship "guidelines" were vague, since the censors could rely on the regulation that read: "These rules may be amended or modified without prior notice." This extreme form of control lasted until November 1972, when Marcos lifted censorship on foreign news dispatches.

Even before martial law, high-handed methods were used against the press, notably when two Chinese newspapermen were deported from Manila to Taiwan. Quintin Yuyitung and his brother Rizal, editor and publisher respectively of the Chinese-language daily paper, the *Chinese Commercial News,* were delivered to authorities in Taiwan following accusations that their newspaper had printed news favorable to communism and derogatory to the Philippines government. No charges could have been brought against them in a trial before a Philippine court, so they were deported to a jurisdiction that guaranteed their neutralization as journalists. They were confined to a "house of reformatory education" for two years. Numerous other foreign newsmen were held for questioning, among them two Australian journalists who were detained for several hours in 1974. In the same year, however, the government declared that international news agencies and foreign newsmen "shall have unimpeded freedom" in working in the Philippines. This resulted from a battle Associated Press Manila Bureau Chief Arnold Zeitlin had with the government after answering a series of charges that included "unethical journalism" and "false, malicious and erroneous reporting." But in 1976 Zeitlin was refused reentry. No reason was given for the action, and officials refused Zeitlin permission to see the commissioner of immigration.

Foreign publications also had problems in the Philippines. *Far Eastern Economic Review* was banned because of a libel suit brought against the magazine by Philippine Defense Minister Juan Ponce Enrile. All copies of the publication were seized in compliance with an attachment order from a Manila court. The subject of Enrile's complaint was a reference to him which referred to "Manuel Abello, senior partner of Defense Minister Juan Ponce Enrile's law firm of Angara, Abello, Concepcion, Regala and Cruz..." In his complaint, Enrile said the statement implied that he had an interest in the law firm. He said that he had not practiced since joining the government.

The Philippines is a country that creates favorable international impressions through the staging of such expensive extravaganza as Miss Universe contests or Muhammad Ali boxing matches. It is also very sensitive about its press image. The result is that the government has begun to pay closer attention to the foreign correspondents in its midst—chastising them for screening Asian events through a Western bias; favoring those who are sympathetic to local governmental concerns, punishing those who are not. The penalties include stiffer entrance requirements, denial of access to newsworthy people and events, pre-publication censorship and expulsion from the country. The Philippines has been expelled from membership in the International Press Institute.

As already mentioned, observers have said that the removal of martial law in the Philippines was only cosmetic surgery to improve an image that had been badly tarnished in recent years. It is also considered significant that repeal came shortly two events that were to have an impact on Manila: the change of administration in Washington, D.C., and the pope's visit to the Philippines in February 1981. A source close to Marcos said, "He [Marcos] and Imelda are obsessed with the image of the Philippines in the international media. The prospects of hundreds of foreign journalists descending for the Pope's visit was one of the key factors pushing Marcos to get rid of the martial-law label." What the pope and journalists got on their tour of the Philippines was a manicured version of what had been previously planned. One stop on the pope's itinerary was a Manila slum called Tondo that had been beautified beyond recognition. But at the insistence of Mrs. Marcos, a papal visit to a leper colony was canceled.

News Agencies

The Philippines' National News Service was reconstituted after 1972 as the Philippine News Agency. It provides news of daily events to both the print and broadcast media, and sends copy abroad to the news services of Philippine embassies and consulates. The agency also provides service to foreign correspondents in the Philippines, who had been freed from censorship in 1974, and maintains correspondents in major Philippine cities as well as Jakarta and Tokyo. The government has also set up a Philippine Overseas Information and News Trust (POINT), designed to counteract anti-Marcos propaganda abroad. Foreign agencies with bureaus in Manila include AP, UPI, AFP, CNA, Antara, Reuters, and Tass.

Electronic News Media

The first television station in the Philippines opened in 1953. Television was criticized during its initial decade for poor election coverage, political use and unethical and immoral program content. Most of the problems still existed just before martial law because the Radio Control Board had not developed rules designed especially for the television medium. But these complaints against television had also been directed at the radio industry since its beginning in 1922.

Before martial law, the Philippine broadcasting media had enjoyed the same freedoms as the press. They also endured the same restrictions when martial law was declared. Perhaps they were treated even more harshly. Troops entered radio and television studios, arrested some broadcasters, sealed the studios and placed the stations themselves under military control. (At one station, Eagle Broadcasting, owned by the Iglesia Ng Kristo church, guards refused to accept the martial-law decree, opened fire and killed nine soldiers. The military returned with reinforcements, killing nearly a dozen Eagle Broadcasting guards before the decree could be served.)

Marcos set forth the regulation that radio and television shall "broadcast accurate, objective, straight news reports of the government to meet the dangers and threats that occasioned the proclamation of martial law, and the efforts to achieve a 'new society.'" Furthermore, editorials, "opinion, com-

mentary, comments or asides" were forbidden over the air. Marcos's Media Advisory Council (which replaced his Mass Media Council in 1973) also set policies, not only for the press but news and public-events broadcasting and religious programming. News reporting was to be factual, fair, and free of bias; materials tending to incite people against the government were strictly prohibited. News shows were not to sensationalize details or create panic and unnecessary alarm. Commentary and analysis had to be clearly identified, while uniform and simultaneous scheduling of news and public-affairs programs by all stations and networks was encouraged to promote and increase the audiences. In 1974, Marcos decentralized mass-media censorship, and the Bureau of Broadcasts, under the Department of Public Information, controlled Philippine electronic-media content. It was headed by a newspaper columnist, Teodoro Valencia.

Philippine developmental news and public-affairs programming—intended to keep Filipinos informed of the country's progress in economic planning and implementation—were emphasized on both radio and television. That plan has continued since the end of martial law. Among locally produced news and public-affairs television shows on the Bureau of Broadcasts channels are "Sandiwa" (public affairs), "Balita" (news in the vernacular), "Saling Pusa" (information for children), "Enterprise" (documentary) and "Paligsahan 74" (sports clinics). Other locally produced television shows stress national development and Philippine culture and history. One example is "Lagusan" (life in the city as seen by a journalist).

According to one publication, radio and television also carry numerous pro-governmental broadcasts. Regular programs are interrupted for a presidential speech or other official function. A once-weekly forum on grass-roots issues is simulcast on radio and television. In the early morning every day development topics—most frequently agriculture—are discussed on almost all stations for an hour. TV news comes on three times a day—in the late morning, early evening and late night. On many radio stations it is heard every hour.

Currently, the trend for the broadcast media seems to be the rationalization of the industry, that is, the reduction in the number of radio stations, particularly in areas where overcrowding among several stations has resulted in cutbacks in earning or income.

While pre-martial-law radio stations have been closed in the major cities or urban centers, new radio stations have been granted permits to operate in the less developed areas of the country, or where radio stations have not previously operated. South Cotabato, for example, has five radio stations operating at present where none had existed before martial law. Metropolitan Manila, a congested broadcast area with 52 radio stations and seven television stations in 1971, is now reduced to 33 radio and five TV stations. Residents in other parts of the Philippines will receive improved television broadcasts from the Manila area with the installation of a $2 million earth satellite station. Domestic Satellite Philippines (Domsat) will operate the station at Ma, a district in Davao, 620 miles south of Manila.

Education & Training

Media training is offered in institutes and schools of mass communication and journalism at the Universities of the Philippines (Quezon City), Santo Tomas (Manila) and Silliman (Negros Island); at the Philippine Press Institute and the Lyceum of the Philippines (Manila) and the Ateneo Graduate School and Siena College (Quezon City). Technical training for government telecommunications engineers is provided by the Telecommunications Training Institute at Valenzuela, Bulucan.

The newly opened Asian Institute of Journalism in Manila is attempting to bridge the gap between journalistic theory and practice. The institute is a nonprofit, non-stock graduate school of mass communication, the first of its kind in Asia. It now offers two programs on a trimester plan: a graduate course in media management and a master's degree in journalism; and will also offer short-term seminars and workshops for practicing journalists. The AIJ is envisioned as a training center for journalists oriented to what UNESCO member-countries describe as "the new international information and communication order"—with its more balanced flow of communication, effective transfer of technology and emphasis on rural development. At the AIJ graduate students will have free, round-the-clock access to the Times-Journal publications and the institute's own two dailies and four magazines. At the Editorial Clinic, the student can work on the coverage or interpretation of an issue. When he is taught the printer's craft he can work on various stages of producing the newspaper—from typesetting to pasteup. Some graduates will be development communicators, who can interpret sociopolitical environments within the Asian-Pacific context, and become a partner in the development efforts of the country. The AIJ will also train media managers.

Professional associations include a journalists' newspaper guild, a press club, an overseas press club and associations of film producers and distributors. The Publishers Association of the Philippines, Inc. has 400 members and a set of guidelines that amount to one rule: the publishers are held solely responsible for any violation of the law of the land, and for any breach of professional ethics.

Summary

Even since being repealed, Marcos's martial law has hindered the dissemination of information in the Philippines. The country's once-free press is now just the voice of the government. Journalists are still subject to arrest without warrant and to detention for an indefinite period without charge. Consequently the media have been reluctant to voice even the mildest criticism of government policies. There is nothing but praise for the Marcos family and associates. Press credibility is now so low that it is seen as a mere publicity machine totally lacking legitimacy. One foreign reporter has remarked—only partly in jest—that the only reliable domestic news is in the classified ads.

What the future holds for the Philippine media is a question that certainly needs to be examined. The history of the Philippines shows that the people have constantly fought for their freedom. It is something of which they are extremely proud. This pride will not differ in their quest to return the press to the free state it once knew. Even though many problems existed with the pre-martial law press under Marcos, these problems could have been eliminated by strengthening a regulatory commission, such as the Philippine Press Institute. The Press Council set a code of ethics for the press in the mid-1960s, but it never was enforced. And yet it could have succeeded if it had received some governmental backing.

Meanwhile the Philippines will have to rely on a growing underground press for the dissemination of news. Pointing out the failure of government programs, this illicit press calls for nationwide resistance to the authorities. The Philippines has had effective underground newspaper systems at crisis periods in the past. The underground press today is well organized. Most of its papers are produced by mimeograph and use the Filipino language. It even has its own news agency, Balita ng Malayang Pilipino (Free Philippines News Service). The underground periodicals—as well as chain letters and Xerox copies of banned materials—travel national networks, as their readers take seriously the request in the logotypes,

"pass this newsletter on to a friend after reading." The papers are distributed in markets, on campuses and even door-to-door, despite the threat of at least six months imprisonment for possession of them.

Today the media operate in an ostensibly free country since the lifting of martial law, but they still face self-censorship. Although many controls have been removed in theory, the fear of imprisonment remains. Marcos still wields great power in the industy and will continue to exercise it. The post-martial-law media in the Philippines are free, but only to a thin point.

CHRONOLOGY

1975 February: Manila newspaperman, Primitivo Mijares, who asserts that he was "chief censor" for Marcos, seeks asylum in U.S.

1976 October: Government closes two Roman Catholic radio stations in Mindanao, claiming the stations had broadcast messages to the communist-led underground. Later, two religious magazines are also closed.

November: Government denies reentry by AP Manila Bureau Chief Arnold Zeitlin. Marcos says action is taken because of alleged activities that "endanger the security of the country."

1977 June: Philippine Immigration Commissioner Edmundo M. Reyes orders expulsion of Bernard Wideman, reporter for *Washington Post* and *Far Eastern Economic Review,* accused of writing unfavorable articles about Philippine martial-law regime.

1978 April: Government investigates charges that foreign journalists in Manila interfered in balloting; it is also implied that some of the correspondents are "foreign subversive elements."

Lorenzo J. Cruz, director of Bureau of National and Foreign Information, calls in *New York Times* correspondent Fox Butterfield and *Washington Post* correspondent Joy Matthews to advise them that Marcos considers their election coverage unfair.

1978 September: Marcos orders military authorities to drop investigation of 24 priests, nuns and editorial staff on two Roman Catholic magazines, accused of inciting sedition. Presidential clemency is granted to the staff of *The Communicator* and *Signs of the Times,* in line with government policy of reconciliation and national unity.

1981 January: Martial law lifted, but tight controls on media remain.

BIBLIOGRAPHY

"Back to the Good Old Days." *Far Eastern Economic Review,* December 1978, p. 22.

Brown, Robert U. "Philippines 'Freedom.'" *Editor & Publisher,* January 25, 1979, p. 40.

Chabalier, Herve. "Manila Awaits the Pope." *World Press Review,* February 1981, p. 34.

"Controls Eased for Foreign Press in Philippines." *Editor & Publisher,* October 7, 1972, p. 4.

DeVoss, David. "Southeast Asia's Intimidated Press." *Columbia Journalism Review,* October 7, 1972, p. 14.

Estrada, Hugo S. "The Weekly Newspaper in the Philippines." *Grassroots Editor,* January 1960, p. 23.

"Expelled Correspondents." *IPI Report,* January 1974, p. 18.

George, T. J. S. "Mr. Marcos Shapes the New Society." *Far Eastern Economic Review,* October 7, 1972, p. 14.

Guillermo, Artemio R. "Decline and Fall of the Freest Press in Asia." *The Quill,* April 1975, p. 21.

Guioguio, Reynaldo V. "A Look at the Mass Media Situation in the Philippines: Implications in Education and Research." *Media Asia.* No. 2, 1980, p. 71.

International Market Information Series. *Foreign Economic Trends and Their Implications for the United States: Philippines.* Manila, 1980.

Kuhn, Delia and Ferdinand. *The Philippines Yesterday and Today.* New York, 1966.

Lent, John A., *Broadcasting in Asia and the Pacific.* Philadelphia, 1978.

———. "Jammed." *IPI Report,* September 1976, p. 6.

———. "Most Philippine Papers Stick to Government Line Under Martial Law." *IPI Report,* November 1976, p. 5.

———. "Press Freedom in Asia: The Quiet but Complete Revolution." *Gazette.* No. 1, 1978, p. 51.

———. "Underground Press Fills the Gaps in the Philippines." *IPI Report,* December 1974, p. 6.

Lightfoot, Keith. *The Philippines.* New York, 1973.

"Marcos All-Clear for Jesuit Editor." *IPI Report,* September 1978, p. 3.

"Marcos' 'Yes and Yes' Vote." *Time,* December 26, 1977, p. 26.

Merrill, John C., Bryan, Carter R., and Alisky, Marvin. *The Foreign Press.* Baton Rouge, La., 1964.

Mohs, Mayo. "An End at Last to Martial Law." *Time,* February 2, 1981, p. 72.

"News Media Blackout Ordered by Philippine President Marcos." *Editor & Publisher,* September 29, 1972, p. 11.

Paine, George. "Industrial Development May Benefit U.S. Firms." *World Trade Outlook for the Far East and South Asia,* April 1980, p. 11.

Pasricha, Josephine A. "Honing the Mediamen's Many-Sided Craft." *Manila Times Journal,* July 13, 1980, p. 4.

"Philippines Bars AP Man." *IPI Report,* December 1976, p. 9.

Polotan, Kerima. "Philippine Journalism, 1977." *Fookien Times Philippine Yearbook.* Manila, 1977, p. 344.

"Press Freedom Report—Asia." *IPI Report,* January 1975, p. 20.

Quijano, Juan. "Philippines." *IPI Report,* July 1977, p. 12.

Rosenberg, David A. *Marcos and Martial Law in the Philippines.* Ithaca, N.Y., 1979.

Rupp, Carla Marie. "Marcos Lifts Controls on Foreign Newsmen." *Editor & Publisher,* March 16, 1974, p. 12.

"Sanitary Tour." *Time,* February 16, 1981, p. 51.

"Satellite for Better Telecasts." *Television/Radio Age,* September 22, 1980, p. 27.

"Taiwan—Philippines—and an Unholy Alliance." *IPI Report,* January 1971, p. 8.

"The Review and Juan Ponce Enrile." *Far Eastern Economic Review,* November 10, 1978, p. 28.

U.S. Congress. House Committee on International Relations. *Human Rights in South Korea and the Philippines: Implications for U.S. Policy, Hearings Before a Subcommittee on International Organizations.* 94th Cong., 1st sess., 1975.

Valencia, Teodoro F. "Broadcast Media Move Ahead in '78." *Fookien Times Philippines Yearbook.* Manila, 1978.

———. "The Media Today—An Appraisal." *Fookien Times Philippines Yearbook.* Manila, 1977.

Vreeland, Nena. *Area Handbook for the Philippines.* Washington, D.C., 1976.

Willey, Fay, and Came, Barry. "The Pope's Hard Choice." *Newsweek,* February 23, 1981, p. 55.

World Communications. Paris, 1975.

Yoyitung, Quintin. "A Battle Won but a War Lost." *IPI Report,* July–August 1973, p. 3.

POLAND

by Paul Underwood

BASIC DATA

Population: 35,383,000
Area: 312,354 sq. km. (120,569 sq. mi.)
GNP: 3.09 trillion zlotys (US$ 108.3 billion)
Literacy Rate: 98%
Language (s): Polish
Number of Dailies: 44
  Aggregate Circulation: 8.331 million
  Circulation per 1,000: 240
Number of Nondailies: 38
  Aggregate Circulation: 1.971 million
  Circulation per 1,000: 57
Number of Periodicals: 2,400

Number of Radio Stations: 36
Number of Television Stations: 66
Number of Radio Receivers: 8.486 million
  Radio Receivers per 1,000: 242
Number of Television Sets: 7.474 million
  Television Sets per 1,000: 213
Total Annual Newsprint Consumption: 127,000 metric tons
  Per Capita Newsprint Consumption: 3.7 kg. (8.14 lb.)
Total Newspaper Ad Receipts: NA
  As % of All Ad Expenditures: NA

Background & General Characteristics

Poland, the largest country in Eastern Europe after the Soviet Union, lies in the geographical center of the European continent. Even though it is one of the more industrialized nations of the area, about one-quarter of its over 35 million people still work in agriculture.

As a result of World War II, Poland lost nearly half its previous territorial holdings but gained extensive lands in the north and west. The exchange made Poland one of the most ethnically homogeneous countries in Europe: 98 percent of its population is Polish.

Much of the industrialization of the country has come since the war and the imposition of Communist rule. Most industries are state owned and operate within a planned economy, although agriculture is about 85 percent private. The per capita income is in the neighborhood of $2,500 a year. About 98 percent of the population is literate and Polish-speaking. The only minorities are small groups of Ukrainians and White Russians in the eastern part of the country.

Geography constitutes no barrier to communication. Most of the country is lowland, a part of the great northern European plain. The mountains to the south, along the Czech border, reach only to about 8,000 feet and are cut by several passes.

Poland is a member of the Soviet bloc and her media are organized on the Soviet model. Nevertheless, the press is freer than many of its Eastern European counterparts and bears more resemblance to the Western European press in both makeup and content.

The printing press came early to Poland. The first went into operation in the mid-15th century, just 20 years after Gutenberg published his Bibles in Germany. This was Poland's "Golden Age," when she was one of the largest countries in Europe, a center of literature and art, with a degree of freedom unsurpassed elsewhere on the continent.

Newspapers, however, did not develop for another 200 years. The first publications were religious works, but these were soon followed by the fruits of Polish scholarship: works on geography, philology, political theory and, above all, science, for this was the age of Copernicus. Historians, taking up the work of the monkish chroniclers—who in earlier days had laboriously written out annual accounts of events—now produced classic descriptions of the country and its past, many of which became famous throughout Europe.

Krakow, Warsaw and Lublin all became important centers of printing. But printers were not free to publish what they pleased. Each had to have a royal warrant to operate and such warrants were customarily held not by the printer but by high-ranking clergy or members of the leading gentry families, under whose protection the printers worked and who, of course, dictated what could and could not be published.

Prose and verse were equally represented in 15th- and 16th-century Polish literature. And while Latin was the language of administration and science, the use of Polish developed as a result of the struggle between Catholics and Protestants over the hearts and souls of the people. When the Protestant sects began using Polish in their services, Catholics were also forced to use it in both theological controversy and in their efforts to convince the public. The origin of Polish literature coincided with the Reformation.

But the glory days passed all too soon. The opening of the 17th century brought wars with Russia and Sweden—the start of almost two centuries of struggle with those two nations, and with the Turks and the Germans as well; in the end, these conflicts were to see Poland wiped from the map.

From the very start, the troubles exposed the basic weakness of the country: the lack of unity among the great gentry families that were the real rulers. The effects of this disunity were particularly disastrous because of the so-called *liberum veto*, which required that every measure introduced into the nation's Parliament had to be approved unanimously. This was even extended later to provide that a veto automatically dissolved Parliament and cancelled any measure that had been adopted previously in the session. The result was that nothing got done.

The middle of the 17th century witnessed the appearance (in 1661) of the country's first newspaper, the weekly *Merkurjusz Polski* ("Polish Mercury") in Krakow. It did not last long, nor did any of its immediate successors. The gentry did not want the public informed about political affairs. Suppression was the certain fate of any offending publication. But the next century brought a slow but steady development of the press. In 1729, two papers, *Kurjer Warsawski* and *Kurjer Polski* of Krakow, were founded and were able to survive for some period of time, partly by foregoing political comment.

Meanwhile Poland's situation was going from bad to worse. In 1772 Russia, Prussia and Austria joined to make the first partition of the country, each taking a sizable portion of the kingdom's territory. The shock opened the eyes of at least some of the gentry to the dangers facing the country. Reforms were undertaken in various fields, climaxed in 1791 by the adoption of a new constitution that eliminated the *liberum veto* and, among other things, provided for freedom of the press. Newspapers now began to appear in various parts of the truncated country, one of which, the *Gazeta Warszawski*, succeeded in surviving until the Nazi invasion in 1939. So quick was the country's newspaper growth that some historians date the real beginning of the Polish press to the 1791 constitution.

Poland's neighbors did not want it to regain power. At the instigation of some gentry who opposed the new constitution, Russia and Prussia intervened once more in 1793, again grabbing large areas of the country and reducing Poland to a third of its original size. A revolt led by Thaddeus Kosciuszko broke out in the following year, but although the rebels won some battles, they were eventually overwhelmed. A third partition followed. It wiped Poland from the map.

Napoleon's conquests gave the Poles new hope and in 1807, after victories over the Austrians and the Prussians, he forced the reconstruction of a Polish state—now called the Duchy of Warsaw—out of provinces that had been annexed by the two defeated powers. However, Napoleon was no friend of press freedom. He permitted only one paper to publish in the duchy and that under tight French control.

The duchy did not outlast Napoleon: with his downfall it was occupied by the Russians. Still, Poland did not completely vanish as a state. Tsar Alexander I established part of the territory that had been annexed by Russia as a separate kingdom—with himself as king, of course—and granted its people a constitution that even promised freedom of the press. However, a revolution in 1830 and another in 1863 changed all that. The Russians imposed measures aimed at destroying the language and even the nationality of Poland, including suppression of all Polish newspapers. Similar steps were instituted by the Prussians with the intent of Germanizing their areas. In both sections, however, underground and exile papers circulated widely, helping to keep alive the ideal of a free and independent Poland.

Austrian rule was quite different. In the territory it had annexed, known as Galicia, Vienna at first clamped a tight censorship on the press. But eventually Galicia became reorganized as a province of the Hapsburg empire and was given a constitution that even afforded some measure of press freedom. Under this comparatively liberal regime, the area became the refuge of Polish patriots and the center of Polish national life.

No such relaxation occurred in either the German- or the Russian-ruled sections, except for a brief period in 1905 when Tsar Nicholas II was forced to lift press censorships. This lasted only about a year, however, before controls were reimposed and the clamps remained on until the end of World War I and the rebirth of an independent Poland, with Marshal Pilsudski, a hero of the struggle for freedom, as head of state.

The country had been devastated by the war and the 1920s proved to be a period of severe economic and political strain. A multitude of political parties sprang up. A new constitution guaranteed freedom of the press and newspapers also mushroomed, most of them representing political factions and dependent on those groups for economic support. Even the promise of press freedom proved illusory, for authorities held the power to censor and even confiscate papers. Political administration also was unstable, and frequently irresponsible. In the first seven years of independence, the government changed 13 times as the result of the vagaries of a feuding Parliament. Newspapers came and went as parties rose and fell. Finally, in 1923, Pilsudski publicly demonstrated his disgust by withdrawing into private life.

Three years later, however, he engineered a coup, seizing power and instituting rule by decree. News concerning public issues was restricted by threats of fines and imprisonment. Although kept rigidly in line, 165 newspapers managed to stay in business but communist and socialist publications were closed or forced underground.

With Pilsudski's death in 1935 his regime was carried on by a group of officers known as "the colonels." But some of the more authoritarian aspects were relaxed, including certain press restrictions. Censorship and confiscations of editions continued but were far less frequent and constituted less of a problem than before. By this time, the Polish press had come to resemble its counterparts in western Europe in both appearance and content, emphasizing political, cultural and economic news. The number of

papers again increased, reaching a total of 620 by 1938. Two hundred and eight of these were dailies. Most were small, with circulations of only 3,000 to 10,000, but several were sizable, their circulations going as high as 200,000.

The Nazi invasion in 1939 and the division of the country once again—by Germany and the Soviet Union—immediately brought the suppression of established newspapers. But an underground press quickly came into being. Hundreds of illegal newspapers were published and circulated throughout the country during the wartime years, despite the fact that the penalty for mere possession of one was death.

In 1944, as Russian armies drove the Germans back within their own eastern borders, old prewar Polish newspapers began to reappear, along with the underground papers, which could now publish openly. For a brief period there was relative freedom. But soon the communists, backed by the Soviet Union, took control of the country and the press. Now began a period of totalitarian rule, based on close dependence on Moscow and a Stalinist system of terror. It lasted until the mid-1950s when, following Stalin's death, a struggle for power erupted between the Stalinist and anti-Stalinist wings of the Polish Communist Party (officially known as the Polish United Workers Party).

During the accompanying political turmoil, the press enjoyed a degree of freedom previously unmatched under communism. Various publications led a drive for greater liberalization of the regime, most notably the cultural weekly *Nowa Kultura* and a small paper called *Po Prostu* ("Plain Speaking"). The latter came eventually to be regarded as a symbol of the whole struggle for Polish press freedom. Previously *Po Prostu* had been a dull and servile weekly for youth, published by the Party-controlled Union of Polish Youth. In 1955 it got a new editor and a new editorial board and immediately began raising explosive political issues. It obviously received support and encouragment from members of the most liberal-reformist wing of the Party and soon became the spokesman for young intellectuals and students.

The political struggle culminated in 1956 in the ouster of the old Stalinist party and government leadership and their replacement by a new group, headed by Wladyslaw Gomulka as the party chief. It appeared that Poland had embarked on a completely new course. But this too proved to be largely an illusion. As soon as it could, the new regime began tightening the screws again. *Po Prostu* was closed down in 1957, along with several other publications.

However, things never slipped all the way back to the grim pre-1953 conditions. A number of "small freedoms"—Western-style entertainment, cabaret satire often flavored with political accents, jazz from the West—all were tolerated and private conversations were free. Although censored and tightly controlled, the Polish press also remained relatively freer than the press in other Soviet-bloc countries. Even the Roman Catholic Church, a political as well as a religious force in the nation, was able to express its views in a variety of periodicals.

With the turn of the decade into the 1970s, economic issues sparked strikes and riots that led to Gomulka's ouster and his replacement by Edward Gierek. Again hopes were raised that controls on the press might be eased. But despite a few largely meaningless gestures in that direction, nothing really happened. The Gierek regime continued to insist on press conformity to the official version of news and to its interpretation of Marxist ideology. Party spokesmen called for a more critical press but made it clear that such criticism "must be used in accordance with party policy, bearing in mind its program and strategy of action."

With the official newspapers closed to them, dissidents turned to the weapon that had been used so often before in Poland—the underground publication. By the end of the decade, a new generation of these had flowered, being published despite continued police raids and confiscations, and at times reaching circulations as high as 30,000.

By 1980, economic difficulties had brought widespread labor unrest, which climaxed in the organization of the independent labor union movement called Solidarity. With the support of other elements of the population, Solidarity pressed for reform of the censorship system, greater public access to the press, and other steps toward true Polish independence.

About 2,400 periodical publications appear in Poland today, including some 100 weeklies and 50 newspapers that publish at least twice a week. Subscription prices are arbitrarily low; one Polish newspaper estimated a few years ago that overall sales amounted to only about 0.4 percent of the value of all merchandise sold in the country. The industry regularly employs about 7,000 journalists. Another 2,000 to 3,000 work part time or for factory house organs.

All regularly circulated dailies are printed in Polish. There is one German-language biweekly, and a variety of official publications are printed in more than 20 languages but these latter are intended for foreign audiences and have little if any internal circulation.

A variety of religious publications are available but only those put out by Polish Catholic organizations are of political significance. It should be noted that one group of such periodicals is not recognized by the church hierarchy: those published by PAX, a "progressive," that is pro-communist, but self-proclaimed Catholic movement loosely linked to the government. PAX publishes one daily paper, *Slowo Powszechne* of Warsaw, and at least 10 other periodicals.

The papers approved by the church leadership include three weeklies, the most important of which is *Tygodnik Powszechny* ("Universal Weekly"), published in Krakow under the auspices of a Catholic political organization known as Znak. It is read carefully throughout the country, being the work of highly influential Catholic laymen who, it is believed, reflect the views of the hierarchy. These views are very important in heavily Catholic Poland because the church there represents a power center rivaling the government.

Although print is a highly important aspect of the Polish media system, broadcasting, particularly TV, is more popular. It does, after all, provide some entertainment, an element lacking in most newspapers, although some do run comics, crossword puzzles and other features. Moreover, Poles generally feel that while papers have carried all the official propaganda—which, back in the "free" days of 1956, was characterized by one of the nation's leading poets as "conglomerations of liturgy and thieves' jargon"—they have kept the public basically uninformed. Many people automatically assume that the opposite of what is printed is the truth, which is often, but not always, the fact.

According to Poland's constitution, radio and television are government organs while print is public property. Private individuals and companies may not publish newspapers; this right is given only to political parties, civic organizations and institutions.

Of course, the reality is that the vast majority of periodicals are published by the Party, either directly or through its control of a large publishing group called RSW Prasa, the top officials of which are all important

Party figures. Two allied political parties that have been permitted a continued existence, on paper, at least, publish a few newspapers and journals. The PAX organization also functions as a publishing house.

One interesting recent development has been the grant to the independent Solidarity union organization—which became a nationwide phenomenon in late 1980 and early 1981—of the right to publish its own paper. The first issue appeared April 3, 1981 with a fixed circulation of 500,000.

Most Polish newspapers are deadly serious publications but a few could be characterized as "popular," particularly *Express Wieczorny,* the big Warsaw afternoon tabloid. The magazine field is somewhat different. Those aimed particularly at women, sports fans and other specific groups lean much more to the popular side.

As indicated previously, the concentration of press ownership and control is far greater than anywhere in the West, although the form is different. And the effect of this concentration is multiplied by the fact that RSW Prasa also has a monopoly of all distribution. This means that only in the underground papers or occasionally in Catholic, literary or student publications can non-Party or non-governmental voices be heard.

All newspapers and periodicals are subject to censorship, even the religious publications; only the underground papers escape. So while some differences, even some criticisms, may appear in the press from time to time, nothing that runs counter to the basic Marxist ideology or questions the supremacy of the Party may be printed.

Newspapers are published in all major Polish cities and towns but the largest concentration is in Warsaw, the capital. There are important publications based elsewhere, however, particularly in the cities of Krakow, Katowice and Lodz. Publishing itself is heavily concentrated. An organization known as RSW Prasa, created in 1947 as a "cooperation" of the Communist Party, is responsible for about 95 percent of the total daily circulation throughout the country. It also publishes—again from a circulation standpoint—more than half the nation's periodicals. It has a monopoly of all newspaper distribution in the country as well as the export and import of newspapers, periodicals and books.

Most Polish papers are broadsheet size although a few appear in tabloid format. All have relatively few pages. Even *Trybuna Ludu* ("Peoples Tribune"), the organ of the ruling party's Central Committee, customarily appears in no more than eight- to 10-page editions. There are no Sunday papers in the Western sense. Many dailies print only six days of the week, some skipping Sundays, others Mondays. A few print every day. But the papers that do appear on Sundays are virtually the same size and appearance of those published on other days of the week.

Most of the major dailies come out in the morning, although there are evening papers that, in some cases, boast impressive circulation figures. An example is *Express Wieczorny* ("Evening News") of Warsaw which, in circulation terms, is the capital's second largest newspaper, trailing only the nationally distributed *Trybuna Ludu,* which is supposed to be required reading for all Party members.

10 Largest Dailies by Circulation	
1. *Trybuna Ludu* ("People's Tribune")	970,000
2. *Express Wieczorny* ("Evening News")	500,000+
3. *Trybuna Robotnica* ("Workers Tribune")	500,000+
4. *Gromada Rolnik Polski* ("Polish Village and Farmer")	430,000
5. *Zycie Warszawy* ("Warsaw Life")	360,000
6. *Gazeta Robotnicza* ("Workers Gazette")	293,000
7. *Glos Robotniczy* ("Workers Voice")	278,000
8. *Gazeta Pomorska* ("Pomeranian Gazette")	270,000
9. *Gazeta Zachodnia* ("Western Gazette")	237,000
10. *Szandar Mlodych* ("Youth Banner")	235,000

As in all Communist-ruled countries, newspapers and other periodicals are published with geographical or special-interest group in mind: farmers, youth, the army, intellectuals, sports fans and the like. Therefore, although 11 Polish cities have more than one newspaper published in the same time slot, they are not considered competitors in the Western sense.

Despite specialization, however, critics complain that papers are too much the same. In times of political stress—however, as in 1956, 1968 and 1980-81—more significant differences are apt to surface, clearly reflecting the views of different factions or groupings within the Party leadership. This is the reason for the widespread belief among Poles that some of the official papers do not speak for the Party itself as much as they speak for specific elements within its ranks.

In terms of influence, *Trybuna Ludu*, the Party's official voice, must be given first place, but ranking the others poses problems. In fact, two weeklies, the Catholic *Tygodnik Powszechny* and Warsaw's *Polityka*, may carry more real weight than any of the other dailies, the first because of its connections with the Catholic Church, the second because of its relationship to the Party. An official newspaper—in fact, its longtime editor became a deputy premier in the government in 1980—*Polityka* was designed to appeal to the intellectual elite, non-Party as well as Communist. Much more sophisticated in approach, more open and outspoken than most of the others, it is frequently criticized by the more ideologically oriented publications. Yet, since it is widely considered the voice of what is known as the "orthodox revisionist" wing of the Party, and since it has survived barrages of criticism from *Trybuna Ludu* and other obviously powerful arbiters, Poles generally assume, probably correctly, that it has protectors in the top leadership. It is surely not without significance that in January 1981 *Polityka's* weekly press run was increased from 300,000 to 400,000 copies. Even so, it is usually sold out in a few hours.

Economic Framework

The Polish economy, like that of the Soviet Union, is centrally planned and directed. Although there has been much talk—in true Polish fashion—of economic reform and decentralization, the system remains highly centralized. The only exceptions are the nation's private farmers and a miniscule private enterprise sector. State production activities must comply with government instructions, which are multitudinous and very detailed. Such activities are not subject to the same economic necessities that impel enterprise in the West. This does not mean that economic goals are ignored but only that they are secondary to other considerations.

This is also true of the media, even though much of the print sector is not directly published by the government. All media are deemed essential to the informational and propaganda activities of the government and Party. If they turn a profit, that's good, but if they don't they will not disappear: subsidies will keep them going. The operations of the publishing giant RSW Prasa provide an illustration of the way such things work in Poland. The finances and investments of this organization actually form part of the government's budget and the state comes up with the money. In return, RSW Prasa turns over the greater part of its income to the Party.

Under this system, the ups and downs of the national economy have little direct impact on the press. The economic problems that came to a head in 1980 with food shortages, strikes and other protests may have influenced the content of newspapers and periodicals but did not affect their operations.

Poland produces about 50,000 tons of newsprint a year and the press must get along on that. Set amounts are allocated by the government to specific papers and periodicals. It is by limiting the amount of newsprint for some papers that their circulations are held down. For example, *Tygodnik Powszechny* can print only 40,000 copies a week on its allocation even though it could undoubtedly sell many more if the newsprint were made available.

Advertising, particularly display, is more evident than in any other Soviet-bloc nation except Hungary. Some Warsaw papers have reported as much as 30 percent of their total space devoted to ads. Most are small classified-style ads, but two- and three-column displays for large consumer durables like automobiles and refrigerators are not uncommon in capital-city papers like *Zycie Warszawa*.

Nevertheless, total spending nationwide on advertising is very small by Western standards: only about 15 percent of the total is spent on the media. The bulk goes for things like trade fair exhibits, posters and store displays. Advertising is carried on radio but not on TV. The average total radio-commercial time per day has been estimated at about an hour and a half, spread over five or six different time periods.

All advertising other than the small classified type is placed either by production enterprises or elements of the internal trade network—all under state control. As in other Communist-ruled countries, however welcome advertising might be to the media, it is not vital to survival nor does it have any effect on editorial policies.

The majority of Polish journalists, including virtually all who work for major publications and for broadcast, are members of the Polish Journalists Association. Most appear proud of the fact that this is not an official trade union—that is, not a part of the government's Central Council of Trade Unions—but rather what is referred to as a "creative" union. Only about half the members of the association are also members of the Communist Party, an unusually low figure for a Soviet-bloc nation. Some are members of the two allied parties, Democratic and Peasant, but the rest apparently claim no specific political affiliation. An article in a Polish newspaper in 1978 disclosed that, at that time, 28.5 percent of the association's members were women.

Journalists are customarily paid on a "string"—so much per story—in other words, on a piece-rate basis. This enables the better-known reporters to enjoy relatively high incomes while many of their juniors complain of being underpaid.

Press Laws

Article 71 of the Polish Constitution guarantees freedom of the press, along with freedom of speech, meetings and demonstrations. However, it adds that the state is to make printing materials, equipment, buildings and other essentials "available to the working people." In practice, this means that the state is the sole supplier. Furthermore, all printing equipment must be registered and nothing is supposed to be printed without approval—even movie tickets. All print operations are under the supervision of the government's Central Office for the Control of the Press, Publications and Theater.

Oddly enough, the basic press law in Poland dates back to 1938. It was promulgated during the prewar authoritarian rule of the colonels. However, that law provided for censorship and the present regime has simply amended it, usually by decree, whenever deemed necessary. This has been done particularly in the organization of the broadcasting system.

The code forbids the mass media to criticize the system of government, disclose state secrets, damage the country's international relations, induce violations of law and order or publish inaccurate information. In addition, there are laws against libel and obscenity similar to those in other European countries.

In another article, the constitution forbids the "setting up of, and participation in, associations, the aims and activities of which are directed against the political or social system or against the legal order of the Polish People's Republic"—a kind of catch-all, since the Party could decide that almost any other organization fits the proscription.

Polish courts are creatures of the Party and government and lack any real independence, although Poles generally feel they have a better chance of fair treatment from judges than citizens of some of the neighboring Eastern European countries.

Censorship

The Central Office for the Control of the Press, Publications and Theater is the censorship agency. It is specifically charged with ensuring that military, economic and other "secret" information is not divulged by the press. And it should be understood that in Poland, as in the rest of the Soviet bloc, a good deal of information considered harmless in the West comes under the heading of "secret." However, the most important aspect of the censorship lies not so much in its power to sort through the press for materials to be excluded, but rather in the regime's power to select what is made available for publication.

This was one of the reasons why the regime felt confident enough to lift direct censorship for two of Warsaw's newspapers in 1973, making the editors personally responsible instead. Since the editors were top Party people, the move appeared to be more of a gesture than a significant step.

While the essential role of the censorship office is to guard against the disclosure of secret information, it is also supposed to see that nothing critical of the Soviet Union, or anything that questions the rightness of Communist rule in Poland, is printed. Yet the restrictions go far beyond these.

Information on important internal developments, unless it would make the government and the Party look good, has been regularly blacked out. For example, when the strikes that culminated in the formation of the Solidarity union movement first began in 1980, the government tried to contain the situation by saying nothing about it. Not a word appeared in the press or was broadcast, despite the fact that the unrest involved even a big tractor factory on the outskirts of Warsaw. Of course the information spread, both by word of mouth and the underground papers. Foreign correspondents reported the developments and their reports were played back by Western radio. All Poles knew what was going on almost immediately. Still, it was nearly a month before the government permitted any reports to be published in Polish papers. Even when it finally admitted that strikes were occurring, the official propaganda apparatus continued to turn out its own contrived versions of the reality.

Poles look upon this sort of thing as an affront to their intelligence and the result has been, for the press as well as for the government, a loss of credibility that by now is virtually complete. As Karol Malcuzynski, one of the nation's best known journalists, said recently, "Even bad news is not believed."

Malcuzynski was quoted in an interview in 1980 as asserting that extensive TV coverage of floods that engulfed large areas of the country during the spring had been seen by many people as nothing but an orchestrated exaggeration designed to try to justify poor harvests. He added: "In a developed, critical and intelligent society like ours, which has access to many different sources of information, this type [the government's] of propaganda is suicidal."

The 1978 article mentioned earlier pointed up some of the problems all this causes journalists in Poland. Noting that relatively few young people were choosing to enter the field, the author suggested that one of the reasons for their reluctance was the daily exposure to the "most delicate, ticklish, sometimes drastic restrictions imposed on one's creative freedom in the name of ideological reasons."

Journalists, like actors and musicians, are dependent on society, on the public, the article noted, but added that the journalist is the least independent of these since "the press is, of all the cultural superstructure, the biggest field and the most attractive and successful propaganda instrument." Further: "The centralization of the press has reached an intensity that—let us be frank—is not propitious to a creative pursuit of journalism.... Many times a journalist must give in, adapt to various demands and censorships, must work and make creative efforts in situations and under systems imposed upon him."

A basic reform of the censorship system was one of the promises made by the government to the striking workers in the summer of 1980. However, differences between the draft law the government wanted and another prepared by nonofficial experts stalled action. Both drafts called for continuation of censorship, but the government wanted to keep control by having the censoring office placed under the jurisdiction of the Council of Ministers, while the unofficial draft called for it to be placed under parliament. The unofficial draft also would exempt certain publications not designed for general distribution and would also require that any deletions by a censor be made public. The government opposed both these provisions. On the other hand, the government's draft called for jail sentences and fines for violations of censorship rules, which the authors of the unofficial version opposed.

Both sides agreed, however, that any new censorship rules must be part of a new press code to replace the old 1938 law. There has been no indication when this new code might be forthcoming.

State-Press Relations

Censorship is not the only cross Polish journalists have to bear. They have long complained of the bureaucratic hurdles that are placed in the way of gathering information essential to adequate reporting of even routine matters.

An existing law specifies that officials have a duty to answer criticisms and questions. However, as an article in one of Warsaw's newspapers several years ago made clear, there are many ways in which this law is circumvented. "Among them is claiming official secrets," the article said, adding, "It is 'high treason,' for instance, to try to obtain any information from the principal of a primary school...one needs permission of the board of education to visit a school and talk to the children."

The article further pointed out that with few exceptions, "no ministry employe will give any information to a journalist without the permission of the department director or vice minister. No employes of a national council will give any information without the permission of the council chairman or someone 'on a higher level.'"

Various government offices have information departments to which the press has access, most notably the Foreign Ministry. However, most government statements and announcements are issued through the official news agency, Polska Agencja Prasowa, known as PAP, in much the same way that Tass functions as the official voice of the Soviet government.

While the Polish press, like its counterparts in other Soviet-bloc countries, may not criticize the basics of the Communist system, it can criticize the operations and administration of the government and the economy on lower levels, and make suggestions as to reforms or improvements. In addition, it has long seen itself as the principal mechanism in the system for relaying public opinion to the Party and government leadership.

Nevertheless, it is extremely difficult, if not downright impossible, to cite any specific case in which the press has had a direct impact on any official decision or action. However, the regime has been known to respond to pressure, either from within the Party or as a result of actions taken by large groups of citizens, as in the Solidarity union movement.

This lack of impact is hardly surprising given the fact that, to the Party and government, the press is not an independent agent but rather is *their* agent, their tool. They control it from start to finish—since they also control the allocation of funds, newsprint and equipment, as well as censorship over the final product.

Attitude Toward Foreign Media

All foreign correspondents in Poland must obtain special visas from the Press and Information Department of the Ministry of Foreign Affairs. A press card is issued, authorizing correspondents—in a personal capacity only—to operate on behalf of their organizations. The correspondent can hire local help, but in no case may this help do any actual journalistic work. The regulations state that correspondents are subject to the laws of the state.

There is no direct censorship and a correspondent may file copy freely via any existing channel. However, a story deemed unfavorable can result in a summons to the Press and Information Department, where the correspondent may undergo a lecture that could range from "it's too bad you don't know any better" to veiled and even outright threats of expulsion if a different tone is not evident in future stories.

Every correspondent is well aware that these are not idle threats. Expulsions of offending foreign newspeople have not been uncommon. However, since relatively few Western correspondents have been permanently stationed in Poland in recent years, a bigger problem is the "blacklist," containing the names of correspondents who have offended in some way on a previous trip and are barred from entering again.

As far as the availability of foreign media is concerned, Poland probably stands at the top of the list among Soviet-bloc countries. A wide range of foreign magazines and newspapers is generally available in the cities, not just for the benefit of tourists, as in some authoritarian states, but for the Polish reader as well. While none of these are imported in large numbers, copies are to be found on racks in special clubs throughout the country.

The Polish media—and the government, of course—pay particular attention to Soviet newspapers and broadcasts, and Tass is the source of a good part of the news printed in Polish papers and carried on broadcast programs. However, both the media and the government are very sensitive to news and comment in other countries, particularly when such matters concern Poland. This is due in part to natural curiosity, of course, but also to the fact that vast numbers of Poles listen to foreign news broadcasts, particularly those of the BBC, Voice of America, Radio Free Europe and various West German stations, and also read foreign publications.

The number of stories that appear in the Polish press in reaction to something appearing in such broadcasts or publications testifies to their effectiveness. Many Poles make no bones about the fact that, particularly in times of crisis, they read, listen to—and pay more heed to—foreign media than to their own.

The Polish Journalists Association is affiliated with a great many international press organizations, but its closest ties are with the International Journalists Organization, headquartered in Prague, Czechoslovakia.

News Agencies

The principal national news agency is PAP (Polska Agencja Prasowa). This is legally a government department and it serves as the voice of the state. It is also the sole official supplier of foreign news to the Polish media. It has its own correspondents both at home and abroad, with about 20 bureaus in foreign countries.

PAP subscribes to at least 32 different foreign news agencies, including not only Tass but all the major Western European and

American services, for both news and photographs. The agency's headquarters are in Warsaw, where it services the whole country by wire, broadcasting stations and publications. It is the major gatekeeper in the Polish media system.

There are also three other specialized agencies. The most familiar is the Polska Agencja Interpress, which is described as a "cooperative" agency. It has some functions similar to those of the Soviet Union's Novosti agency, in that foreign correspondents and foreign news organizations are supposed to arrange for interviews with officials, meetings, tours, TV filming and other coverage through Interpress. It is also charged with the distribution of books, periodicals and similar informational materials about Poland in foreign countries, and also some feature material for domestic publications.

Associated with Interpress is the Centralna Agencja Fotograficzna, the national photo agency. It, too, has contracts with foreign organizations, supplying them with news photos and receiving others from them for relay on to Polish publications.

The third agency, Agencja Robotnicza (Workers' Agency), is the least important, although it does issue news summaries and features to the Polish media; this material is also available, of course, to the foreign press.

The official news agencies of all the Soviet-bloc countries have bureaus in Warsaw, as do many Western agencies, including Reuters, Associated Press, United Press International and Agence France-Presse. However, these do not serve any Polish publications directly but only through PAP.

Electronic News Media

As noted previously, broadcasting in Poland is a government function. Radio dates back to 1926. However, during World War II all existing facilities were destroyed and had to be replaced after the Nazi defeat. Regular television broadcasting did not get underway until 1954 but by 1960 all the major regions of the country had their own stations.

Under various decrees and laws approved after the war—the last in 1960—all broadcasting is directed by the Committee for Radio and Television, the members of which are appointed by the government's Council of Ministers, and they are obviously the government's agents. The committee is responsible for all program and budget plans (which, however, must be approved by parliament), and for the production and transmission of all programming. However, the actual transmitting equipment and connecting land-lines are controlled by the government's Post and Telegraph Service.

License fees—paid by the owners of radios and TV sets—constitute the principal source of income for the broadcasting services, although there is some from advertising. In 1973 fees for TV amounted to the equivalent of about $125 a year per owner. Radio fees, of course, were less. Although these fees are high in relation to average income, they have never brought in enough to meet all broadcasting costs. A state subsidy makes up the shortfall.

News is an important feature of broadcasting in Poland: news and information programs account for about a quarter of total regular programming on radio and an even larger percentage on TV. Most programming is aired from the national center in Warsaw but some does originate in other cities, seven of which have their own TV centers.

Poland places great emphasis on educational broadcasting, supplying programs designed to supplement primary and secondary school classes, as well as adult education materials dealing with everything from farm practices to foreign-language training.

The regime of course keeps close watch over the material broadcast, not so much through direct intervention as by making certain of the loyalty and ideological correctness of those persons in charge of the actual operations. Still, there have been problems. The previously mentioned Karol Malcuzynski, a former member of the *Trybuna Ludu* staff and now the country's most popular TV commentator, has been dropped from the air several times, most notably when he refused to support the 1968 Soviet-led invasion of Czechoslovakia, in which Polish troops participated. Malcuzynski is a severe critic of some of the government's "informational" programming. He once described a particular radio show, which features pop music mixed with anti-Western propaganda, as an "infamous broadcast," and added: "In this manner, after returning from the lines [of would-be customers] in front of the stores, we could grieve over the problems of the English with galloping inflation, the drug problems of Scandinavia or the housing problems of

Austria. Half of Poland ridiculed [the program]. The other half was mad about it. But it was officially believed that the show was a clever strengthening of the ideological front."

Education & Training

The Institute of Journalism at the University of Warsaw offers a two-year post-graduate professional program in journalism, with courses in both newspaper work and broadcasting. A similar program is also available at the Silesian University in Katowice. Neither of these are degree-granting programs: in journalism education, the Poles follow the usual European practice of giving professional training to persons who have already earned a university diploma.

There are also a number of related courses and programs offered at various other universities, the most notable being the advanced school for film and television at the University of Lodz, which has an international reputation. To improve the skills of persons already working in the field, the Journalism Center in Warsaw, operated by the Journalists Association, offers short-term specialized training courses.

There is also a Press Research Center in Krakow.

Summary

The future of the media in Poland is very much up in the air at the moment. While it is almost certain that the basic structure and methods of operation will not change much as long as Communist rule remains, content and approach to news is a different matter; under the impact of the unrest that has gripped the country since the middle of the 1980, these have already changed somewhat, and could change more, if the regime does not succeed in clamping the lid back on things, as it did in 1956.

The extent of the change so far is probably best exemplified by the fact that on September 19, 1980, the national radio broadcast its first regular religious service since 1949—a hiatus of 31 years. Such broadcasts are now a regularly scheduled feature on the state radio network. The question now is: can the Polish people make this and other possible changes stick in the face of the inherently totalitarian spirit and drive of the ruling Party?

CHRONOLOGY

1976   Federation of Socialist Unions of Polish Youth begins publication of a new magazine, *Razem*.

1977   KOR's *Robotnik*, the first of many new underground papers, makes its appearance.

1980   Polish Radio broadcasts its first regular religious service since 1949.

1981   Trade union federation Solidarity launches its official organ. Two-thirds of Poland's 60,000 printers shut down publication of most Polish newspapers in two-day strike to protest government media campaign against Solidarity and to push trade union's demand for more access to TV and radio.

BIBLIOGRAPHY

Anon. "Your Man in Poland—the Rules He Must Obey." *IPI Report*, November–December 1973, p. 10.

Brown, J. F. *The New Eastern Europe: The Khrushchev Era and After.* New York, 1966.

Darnton, John. "Pole Scorns Censorship, and Isn't Censored." *The New York Times,* September 14, 1980, p. 3.

Dziewandwski, M. K. "Poland." In *The Communist States at the Crossroads,* Adam Bromke, ed. New York, 1965.

Editor and Publisher Yearbook. New York, 1980.

Fikus, Dariusz, and Podemski, Stanislaw. "Censorship Under Fire." *Polityka.* Warsaw, November 15, 1980, p. 3.

Hanson, Philip. *Advertising and Socialism.* White Plains, N.Y., 1974.

Heneghan, Thomas E., and Celt, Ewa. "Polityka and Polish Politics." *Radio Free Europe Background Report,* July 26, 1977.

Kozniewski, Kazimierz. "Journalists." *Polityka.* Warsaw, February 11, 1978.

Merrill, John C., Bryan, Carter, and Alisky, Marvin. *The Foreign Press.* Baton Rouge, La., 1970.

Olsen, Kenneth E. *The History Makers.* Baton Rouge, La., 1966.

Paulu, Burton. *Broadcasting in Eastern Europe.* Minneapolis, 1974.

Portal, Roger. *The Slavs.* New York, 1969.

Radio Free Europe. "The Campaign Against KSS 'KOR' Intensifies." *RFE Polish Situation Report,* December 20, 1980, p. 23.

Skrzypek, Stanislaw. "The Profession of Journalism in Poland: A Profile." *Journalism Quarterly,* Autumn 1972.

Syrop, Konrad. *Spring in October: The Polish Revolution of 1956.* New York, 1959.

UNESCO. *World Communications: A 200 Nation Survey of Press, Radio and Television.* Paris and New York, 1975.

Walendowski, Tadeusz. "The Polish Summer of 1980." *Columbia Journalism Review,* November–December 1980, p. 31.

Zimmer, Paul E., ed. *National Communism and Popular Revolt in Eastern Europe.* New York, 1956.

PORTUGAL

by Harold A. Fisher

BASIC DATA

Population: 9,819,600 (1979)
Area: 92,072 sq. km. (36,829 sq. mi.)
GNP: 100.4 billion escudos (US$2.1 billion) (1977)
Literacy Rate: 65%
Language(s): Portuguese
Number of Dailies: 28
   Aggregate Circulation: 527,000
   Circulation per 1,000: 54
Number of Nondailies: 307
   Aggregate Circulation: NA
   Circulation per 1,000: NA
Number of Periodicals: 1,000

Number of Radio Stations: 4
Number of Television Stations: 1
Number of Radio Receivers: 1.6 million
   Radio Receivers per 1,000: 164
Number of Television Sets: 1.2 million
   Television Sets per 1,000: 125
Total Annual Newsprint Consumption: 30,000 metric tons
   Per Capita Newsprint Consumption: 3.39 kg. (7.5 lb.)
Total Newspaper Ad Receipts: 428.3 million escudos (US$8.6 million) (1979)
   As % of All Ad Expenditures: 19.1 (1979)

Background & General Characteristics

Portugal's newspaper industry reflects the wear and tear of years of government control and oppression, economic privation, low circulations, a politically polarized readership and mediocre journalism.

The malaise predates abolition of press censorship in 1974, to a time when the press was owned or controlled almost entirely by a handful of financial groups and bank-owning families. To this powerful, well-heeled oligarchy newspapers were more essential as tools of influence than of profit or fact. Instead of developing skilled editorial staffs, the owners overloaded their papers with bureaucrats and unneeded administrators. At the same time, relentless state censorship discouraged objective reporting and criticism. With the exception of a few papers, the Portuguese press caved into these pressures and settled into a dull conformity with government and owner policies.

In its early days the Portuguese press enjoyed almost unlimited freedom under a monarchical, Church-oriented government. The confusion, lawlessness and disorder between 1910 and 1926 led to a military coup and the establishment of the "New State." Dr. Antonio Salazar's and Dr. Marcello Caetano's right-wing dictatorships (1932-1974), placed the press under censorship and close surveillance. They also assigned government officials to the staffs of Lisbon's leading newspapers and took over some of the dailies. The relaxation of censorship in 1974 represented a theoretical return to the earliest traditions of press freedom. This freedom remains somewhat elusive, however.

With the overthrow of Caetano's regime in 1974, the press began to show some signs of life. But as the army coup d'etat developed into a revolution, the newspaper industry became politically polarized, backing party ideologies at the expense of objectivity. Meanwhile, as the revolution brought the economy to a standstill, newspaper advertising dropped dramatically. When the government nationalized banks and insurance companies in 1975, many papers faced bankruptcy, and the government either inherited them or had to prop them up with subsidies. Labor unrest followed. Left-wing workers ousted editors and took control of the government-owned papers. Order was restored by a right-wing military crackdown late in 1975.

As the political unrest cooled, circulations continued to drop. Then a 1976 decree nationalized several newspaper publishing groups. A year later, however, the government announced it could no longer subsidize unprofitable publications and told failing newspapers that they should either adopt government guidelines to improve their financial viability or face bankruptcy.

Amid this roller-coaster environment, the Portuguese press has had little opportunity to produce high quality journalism. Rather, it has had to struggle both to claim and hold its freedoms and to overcome the economic obstacles facing Europe's poorest nation.

About one-third of Portugal's population remains rural. The urban population is concentrated in two principal cities, Lisbon (1978 population: 859,200) and Oporto (1978 population: 333,300). There exists a small economic and cultural elite—bankers, financiers, industrialists and professionals. Yet Portugal does not have a large, well-educated middle class. The media reflect this gulf between a small elite and a large agricultural and industrial working class.

Although education is now compulsory until age 14 and the nation boasts 11 universities and about 30 technical and vocational institutes, an estimated 35 percent of the adult population remains illiterate. This helps keep newspaper circulations low, with less than one paper for every 18 people. At the same time, the revolution has produced privations, while inflation, in the order of 25 percent in 1978 and 1979, has made newspapers unaffordable for Portugal's numerous poor.

Although most Portuguese dailies are conservative in policy and fairly serious in content, their makeup borders on the sensational. Compared with the serious appearance of West Germany's *Frankfurter Allegemeine* or France's *Le Monde,* Portuguese papers are gaudy. Design of pages, especially the front ones, is crowded and confused. Editors often fill front pages with rambling editorials that have little relation to the events of the day. Papers use generous amounts of color (usually red) for borders, boxes and headlines. They often underscore headlines, a technique borrowed from the French. They may also place boldface and italic type on the same page. Large photographs, drawings, cartoons, varied size headline decks, ornamental borders and circus makeup all combine to make reading a Portuguese paper something of a chore. In spite of their sensational makeup, however, Portuguese newspapers normally emphasize serious material while playing down entertainment and sensational stories.

The majority of the Portuguese dailies use standard-size pages with seven or eight columns to the page. Weekday papers seldom exceed 14 to 16 pages. Sunday editions run longer, containing 20 to 24 pages, with 12 to 14 pages devoted to advertising.

Except for a few Lisbon dailies *(A Capital, Diario de Lisboa, Diario Popular* and *Jornal Novo),* most Portuguese papers are morning publications. There are no independent Sunday newspapers; instead, such dailies as *Diario de Notícia* publish Sunday editions.

Typically, international and domestic news appear on the front page and on one or two of the inside pages. Reviews and cultural items often occupy the second page. Government, local and sports news appear on the middle and back pages, where, except for a few front page ads, most advertisements also run.

Only a few of Portugal's dailies trace their roots to the monarchy. *Diário de Noticia,* Lisbon's oldest paper, was founded in 1864. Oporto's *O Comércio do Porto* preceded *Diário* by a decade. Most papers, however, were started during the Salazar regime.

At the outset, papers tended to be owned by individuals or families. Later, they were taken over by banking and financial groups. Still later, they became state-owned. Although most newspapers and newspaper publishing groups have been nationalized since the 1974 coup, a few, such as *Diário de Lisboa,* have been handed back to private ownership.

The nation does have a single unifying language, Portuguese, and there is only one foreign language paper, an English publication. The country's predominant religion is Roman Catholicism, so that the Portuguese press reflects little ethnic or religious diversification. It does divide according to political orientation, however; *Correio da Manhã* (Lisbon) and *O Primeiro de Janeiro* (Oporto) are considered independent, while Oporto's *O Comércio do Porto* is labelled conservative. In fact, newspapers have been important tools in the political struggles between left-wing socialists and communists and right-wing conservatives during and since the revolution of the mid-1970s.

In addition to its ownership of several financially failing papers, the government publishes its own official daily gazette, Lisbon's morning *Diário de Republica.* Another special-interest daily, the *Jornal de Madeira*, with a circulation of about 8,000, is published in Madeira by the Catholic Church.

A number of special interests are represented by the nondailies and periodicals. For English-speaking Portuguese, the foreign business and diplomatic communities and Portugal's increasing tourist trade, there is the fortnightly *Anglo-Portuguese News*. *Avanta* serves as a weekly political organ of the Communist Party, as does *Luta Popular* for the Portuguese Workers' Communist Party. *Fôlha GDS* appears weekly and *Democracia 76* fortnightly as the voices of the Center Democratic Party. The Social Democratic Party publishes its paper *Povo Livre* each week, and the Socialist Party speaks each month through its 7,000-circulation monthly, *Portugal Socialista*. A fortnightly, *Jornal Portugues de Economia e Financas* keeps readers abreast of economic and financial affairs, while *O Tempo e o Modo,* a monthly, deals with political questions. Two weeklies specialize in humor and social criticism, *Gaiola Aberta* and *Os Ridiculos*. Other weeklies and periodicals specialize in sports, motoring, fashion, art or entertainment.

Most papers are published in two major cities, Lisbon and Oporto. Lisbon sees Portugal's heaviest newspaper competition with 10 dailies, several of which are among the nation's largest. Three dailies compete in Oporto, while Braga, Evora and Madeira each host two low-circulation rivals. Although papers are smaller, competition is brisk in the Azores. Here Ponta Delgada serves as the home of three small dailies and Horta and Angra do Heroísmo have two each. Because of Portugal's small size (approximately 37,000 square miles), most of the large papers circulate throughout the country as national dailies: Nevertheless, Portugal can boast of no high-circulation daily. Only five papers report circulations around 50,000: *O Diário, Diário de Notícia* and *Diário Popular* in Lisbon, and *O Comércio do Porto* and *Jornal de Notícia* in Oporto. The circulations of six dailies, five in Lisbon and one in Oporto, fall in the 25,000–50,000 copy range. All other 17 dailies circulate less than 10,000 copies. Concrete evidence of Portugal's declining circulations is reflected in Lisbon's popular paper, *Diário Popular,* which reported a circulation of 140,000 in 1970 contrasted with about 83,000 in 1979, and in *Diário de Notícia,* which dropped from Portugal's most popular paper, with 155,000 copies in 1970, to only 66,500 copies in 1979.

Other dailies have suffered similar circulation setbacks.

10 Largest Dailies by Circulation

Newspaper	Place of Publication	Circulation
Diário Popular	Lisbon	83,480
Jornal de Notícia	Oporto	79,840
Diario de Notícia	Lisbon	66,500
O Diário	Lisbon	55,310
O Comércio do Porto	Oporto	53,220
O Primeiro de Janeiro	Oporto	48,000
O Dia	Lisbon	45,100
Diário de Lisboa	Lisbon	42,300
A Capital	Lisbon	40,000
Correio de Manhã	Lisbon	40,000

The nation's 10 largest dailies by circulation appear in the accompanying table. Lisbon's *Jornal Novo* commands the 11th position with 39,000, after which reported circulations drop off sharply. In terms of popularity, Lisbon's *Diário Popular* certainly ranks high. However, in terms of lasting editorial influence and content quality, *Diário de Notícia, Diário de Lisboa, Diário da República, O Comércio do Porto* and *O Primeiro de Janeiro* must all be mentioned. All have survived Portugal's numerous political and economic crises while earning a reputation for sound journalism.

Economic Framework

Under Salazar and Caetano, Portugal was a traditionally agricultural nation. The smaller industrial sector was controlled by large financial groups. Chief exports were clothing, textiles, wood products and wine. In recent years, drought and lack of mechanization have stagnated agricultural production. The 1974 coup and the resulting revolution disrupted industrial progress. The loss of African colonies to independence has denied Portugal an important source of cheap raw materials.

World recession and high inflation have also taken their toll of the Portuguese economy. The cost of living increased over 400 percent between 1963 and 1978. Higher levels of consumption have pushed the imbalance of trade to the point where the cost of imports was more than double the price obtained from exports in 1978. The chief imports have been foodstuffs and petroleum, both commodities whose prices have become highly inflated. Two major sources of revenue, tourism and remittances from workers abroad, almost ceased during the revolution and withdrawal from Africa of the mid- to late-1970s. About two-thirds of the country's productive capacity was nationalized during the same period. Unemployment and the national budget deficit rose dramatically, and the government even had to weigh the advisability of eliminating certain development projects.

This unfavorable economic climate has influenced the media, particularly the print press, in several ways. Those problems, in turn, have reduced the variety of the press and have, in some cases, even threatened its continuing existence as an independent force. Although Portuguese newsstands continue to offer a wide choice of publications, they have been a poor indicator of the economic crisis in the newspaper industry. While government takeovers since the 1974 coup continue, circulations, never very high, keep falling. Meanwhile, the price of newspapers has increased by over 300 percent during the past few years. To further add to the woes, government subsidies to papers have not been equitable. The evening daily, *A Luta,* for example, was allowed to fold simply because a government-owned distribution company was failing to return proceeds from sales to the paper. Recently, the government has moved to restore papers to their private owners, sometimes before the latter are financially capable of resuming management. Even the papers taken over by the state have continued to suffer heavy annual losses.

Both radio and television were nationalized in 1975 and have not felt the economic pressures to the same degree as the print press. Furthermore, television has grown rapidly and is thus compounding the negative impact of the newspapers' declining circulations.

Before the revolution all the important Lisbon papers—*A Capital, Diário de Lisboa, Diário de Noticia, Diário Popular, Jornal de Comércio* and *O Século*—were owned by banking and financial groups.

With the overthrow of the Caetano regime the newspaper owner banks and financial groups were nationalized. Those actions were formalized in the government's decree law No. 639/76 passed in 1976 which nationalized four groups—Sociedade Nacional de Tipografia, Sociedade Industrial de Im-

prensa, Sociedade Gráfica de A Capital and Emprêsa Nacional de Publicidade—and set up in their place two state-owned groups— Emprêsa Pública dos Jornais Notícia e Capital (EPNC) and Emprêsa Pública doe Jornais O Século e Diário Popular (EPSP). In so doing, the government nationalized four of the country's leading papers (*Diário de Notícia, O Século, Diário Popular* and *A Capital)* and placed several other under its guardianship and subsidization program.

These moves proved expensive, however. It cost over 350 million escudos ($7 million) annually just to keep the government-owned papers alive. Now the government is turning papers back to private owners. In 1979 Lisbon's *Diário de Lisboa* and Oporto's independent *Jornal de Notícia* and conservative *O Comércio do Porto* were all handed back to their previous owners.

In recent years, Portugal has produced little newsprint, and the rising costs of importing it has added to the financial troubles of the newspaper industry. To date, the government has not established a newsprint allocation policy.

As business has recovered from the effects of the revolution, the amount of advertising in Portugal's papers has been increasing, thus providing some financial relief. But few papers can rely solely on advertising and sales revenues, given their low readerships and spiraling expenses.

A series of strikes has compounded the grim financial situation that faces the Portuguese press. In 1975, 24 journalists from *Diário de Noticia* struck in protest of their paper's pro-communist policies. Upon their dismissal, they started their own paper, the *Notícia dos 24.* The same year, the International Press Institute had to intercede in a printers–journalists dispute that had prevented the first printing of the new daily *Tempo.* Also in 1975, anti-communist workers tried to take control of *O Século,* shutting it down for a day. During 1979, journalists staged a series of partial strikes to back claims for higher pay (their average take-home pay is less than 2,000 escudos ($400) per month, among the lowest in Europe). In September 1980 television journalists struck to protest the government's policy allowing no TV election campaign coverage other than broadcasts by the political parties.

Since most of the major Lisbon and Oporto dailies enjoy national coverage, that has posed the problem of too many national dailies in a country of this size. The nation's 10 top dailies account for about 85 percent of all newspaper circulation. However, any conclusions drawn from circulation figures are suspect because of the publishers' tendency to inflate sales reports.

Press Laws

When rebel military officers took over the government in 1974, they abolished press censorship. The 1976 constitution built on that spirit by declaring that the state should uphold "the right to freedom of expression and information, and of the press; [and] the right of political parties, trade unions and professional organizations to utilize the radio and television broadcasting facilities."

The 1976 constitution guarantees the freedom of the press insofar as it affects freedom of expression and creativity by journalists and writers; the freedom of all journalists, even those who do not serve mass media belonging to the state or to political parties; the right to found dailies and other publications; the right of societies and professional organizations to have their own publications and the independence of the press.

Even before these freedoms were spelled out, however, the government had already instituted several restrictions on the media. In 1974 a committee of seven military officers was established to regulate the media until the constitution could be ratified. The media were required to publish full texts of declarations by Portugal's provisional president. However, the government did establish a joint committee of press management and journalists to draw up the new press laws.

Journalists and newspapers do not need licenses in Portugal. But the Portuguese law does forbid unreasonable or insulting attacks on the president, foreign heads of state or the commander of the military forces. The new press law, adopted in 1975, gives journalists the right to keep secret their sources of information. It also provides for the creation of a press council. Papers cannot divulge secret military information. There are also libel and defamation decrees.

Censorship

Prior to the 1974 coup, press censorship was heavy. Publishers and editors were directly responsible for everything published. Fear of punishment made them apply vigorous self-censorship. Where that did not take place, the government could—and did—activate a precensorship law. The coup abolished censorship on April 25, 1974, however, and that day the newspaper *República* announced that it was publishing without censorship for the first time. There has been no overt censorship since, but the government has been somewhat heavy-handed and sensitive about any materials that attack the president or the military.

State-Press Relations

The Portuguese minister of information is responsible for the fair administration of the provisions of the constitution regarding the press and of the press laws. He also oversees the government's media subsidies program. The combination makes him a powerful decision-maker.

Before the overthrow of the Caetano government in 1974, editors and journalists were responsible for anything appearing in print. All journalists were registered and could be struck off the register, thus losing their rights to function as journalists. They were also subject to criminal proceedings. Jailings of journalists were frequent. In 1973, for example, the secretary of the journalists' union was sentenced to a year in jail for subversion.

Since the revolution, the government has still shut down newspapers. However, much of that action must be related to the continuing struggle of the Communists against the victorious right wing. At least on the surface, papers have been closed down only because of their financial instability, but journalists have still been jailed for overtly attacking the president or the military. As recently as late 1980, a political cartoonist was forced to pay a 250,000 escudos ($5,000) fine for lampooning the president.

Although the government has interfered with the operations of the press and broadcasting in numerous ways since 1976—partly because it has been thrust in that role to prop up failing dailies—it has not tried overtly to attack the press' constitutionally guaranteed freedoms. The nation's political parties, and especially the Communist Party, have accused the government of manipulating the media through its handling of subsidies. While the minister of information did announce a major reorganization plan for the media in mid-1977, it has never been implemented. But the threat of government interference or takeover is ever-present, especially since it already owns several papers and subsidizes many others.

It has been in this matter of subsidies and financial aid that the government has exercised the greatest control over the press since the revolution. Here the government has laid itself open to criticisms that it has shown favoritism. Communist and socialist papers were allowed to collapse while state-run competitors with much larger deficits have been kept alive. Critics also charge that it has deliberately manipulated the press; that it has reduced diversity by shutting down papers and that it has left the newspaper industry dependent on its whims. As of this writing, the government continues to provide financial aid while it seeks to return as many papers as possible to private ownership.

Attitude Toward Foreign Media

Few foreign correspondents reside in Portugal, mostly because it is off the mainstream of newsmaking events. Those who do live in the country are free to report their stories without hindrance. Even during the autocratic regimes of Salazar and Caetano and during the revolution, foreign reporters were shown deference and not generally curbed. However, foreign correspondents have often found that government officials were unwilling to speak openly and in detail about controversial issues. Thus, news has often been restricted at the source.

While foreign ownership of the media is prohibited, foreign dailies and periodicals circulate freely. Those citizens who read a second language are avid consumers of foreign papers. High adult illiteracy and generally low education levels keep demand low, however.

The Portuguese press is active in international media organizations. Print journalists have participated in International Press Institute activities, and recently the IPI has made a major contribution to a journalism training program in Portugal. Portuguese radio and television cooperate with the work of the European Broadcasting Union, and the television services frequently exchange news with the Eurovision network.

News Agencies

Six news agencies, none of them large or powerful, operate in Portugal. Perhaps the best known is Agência Notíciosa Portuguesa (ANOP). Another is the Agência Universal

de Imprensa, Lda. (Unipress). The rest are specialized. Agência Europeia de Imprensa handles European news and Agência Literaria Imprensa e Promocoes focuses on literary materials.

A number of news agencies maintain bureaus in Lisbon. In 1980 Agence France-Presse (AFP), Agência EFE (Spain), Novosti (USSR), ADN (East Germany), API (Brazil), AP and UPI (U.S.), Prensa Latina (Cuba), Reuters (U.K.), and Xinhua (People's Republic of China) all had bureaus there. In addition, ANSA (Italy), CTK (Czechoslovakia), Deutsche Presse-Agentur (West Germany) and Tass (USSR) all kept correspondents in Portugal.

Electronic News Media

Both radio and television were nationalized in 1975. Radiodifusão Portuguesa, E.P. (RDP) was founded in that year after nine private stations were nationalized and merged with the existing national broadcasting company. The only radio station not included in the takeover, Radio Renasçenca, was given back to the Roman Catholic Church. The Portuguese radio network provides three home services broadcasts daily plus an international service. Radiotelevisão Portuguesa, E.P. (RTP) has studios in Lisbon, Oporto, Ponta Delgada and Funchal. It broadcasts two programs, serving 90 percent of the population on VHF and 60 percent on UHF. Both radio and television reflect governmental views in their news and informational programs. However, the broadcast journalists have considerable freedom to structure their own newscasts, and numerous items from Eurovision and syndicated television news services are used in the television newscasts. Radio news bulletins, meanwhile, are more restricted to reporting governmental news and views.

Education & Training

Portuguese journalists are poorly paid, and thus there is little monetary incentive to draw well-educated personnel into the profession. Yet the country has produced a number of outstanding journalists, many of whom learned their profession on the job. Portuguese universities do not have well-established journalism programs. Consequently, the International Press Institute has both encouraged Portuguese journalists to go to the United States to spend time training on regional papers or in university journalism programs. It has recently allocated funds and personnel to initiate a journalism training program within Portugal.

Two press associations function in the country, one for nondailies, called the Associação da Imprensa Nao-Diária, and the other for dailies, named the Associação da Imprensa Diária. The former was founded in 1920, the latter in 1976 after the new constitution took effect. Prior to that time, the government controlled the National Union of Journalists, and membership was obligatory for everyone in the journalistic profession.

Summary

While the Portuguese press was freed from over 50 years of censorship by a 1974 revolution and the 1976 constitution, it faces grave financial and political problems. High illiteracy and the attractions of television combine to keep circulations low. Despite increased advertising revenues, high costs of newsprint and of subscriptions contributes further to the problems caused by revolution, recession, inflation and other economic factors.

Portuguese newspapers remain gaudy and confused in appearance. They still represent political views and remain generally short in content and low in quality. No elite paper has yet risen from the ranks. As they are returned to private owners, dailies again face the problem of ownership by groups more interested in them for political influence and tax shelters than for quality journalism.

In addition, the press has been the focus of a continuing struggle between the ousted Communists and the right-wing now in power. That impasse continues. Finally, Portugal has yet to establish its planned training program for journalists and media specialists.

Meanwhile, radio and television journalism has been nationalized since 1975. While broadcast journalists have considerable freedom, radio has usually been content to voice government bulletins. Television journalists have demonstrated some initiative and their efforts are bolstered by quality news exchanges with Eurovision.

Thus, the outlook for Portuguese journalism in the 1980s remains clouded. It does appear that the incumbent government is seriously trying to preserve a diverse press and return it to private hands. In the past two years, the Portuguese economic and political pictures have brightened considerably. Exports have increased and foreign investors are being encouraged. But inflation and costs also continue to rise. Consequently, the press will undoubtedly have to continue its economic and political struggles. Improvement can, at best, be only gradual.

CHRONOLOGY

1974	Military coup d'etat abolishes press censorship. Poorly paid journalists strike for better wages and conditions.
1975	Government nationalizes all broadcasting except Roman Catholic Radio Renascença to ensure "ideological pluralism." Several dailies fail because of economic woes, including a favorite, *A Republica;* the specialist *Jornal do Comércio* and Portugal's oldest and most respected, *O Século.*
1976	New constitution provides for press freedom.
1977	Government increases restrictions on subsidies by enforcing guidelines for financial improvement; purpose is to encourage independent ownership.
1979	Three dailies returned to private ownership. *A Luta,* founded as a cooperative in 1975, ceases publication.
1980	International Press Institute plans journalism training program. Television journalists strike in protest of limited election campaign coverage.

BIBLIOGRAPHY

Baklanoff, Eric. *The Economic Transformation of Spain and Portugal.* New York, 1978.

"Breaking Up the Monopoly." *The Economist.* October 4, 1975, p. 53.

Collis, Peter. "Cold Wind of Reality Shakes Portuguese Press as Planned Government Scrapping of Subsidies Brings Threat of Closure to Many Newspapers." *IPI Report.* February 1977, pp. 9–11.

"Control of Portuguese Press Stiffened." *IPI Report.* May/June, 1972, p. 24.

Fisher, Harold A. "The EBU: Model for Regional Cooperation in Broadcasting." *Journalism Monographs,* no. 68 Lexington, Ky., 1980.

"A Government's First Weapon." *IPI Report.* September 1974, pp. 1,3,6,7.

"IPI 1973 Press Freedom Report." *IPI Report.* January 1974, pp. 7–11.

McShane, Denis. "The Battle for Radio Renascença." *New Statesman.* July 18, 1975, p. 74.

Merrill, John, Bryan, Carter, and Alisky Marvin. *The Foreign Press.* Baton Rouge, La., 1970.

"Portugal: Censorship Warning." *IPI Report.* February 1977, p. 2.

"Portugal Survey." *The Economist.* June 14, 1980, pp. 3–25.

"Press Freedom in Portugal: Raul Rego Interviewed." *IPI Report.* November 1975, pp. 1,4,6,7.

"Press Freedom Report, 1975: Portugal." *IPI Report.* December 1975, pp. 4–5.

"The Press Under Pressure: Portugal." *IPI Report.* June/July 1974, p. 14; April/May 1975, p. 14; June 1975, pp. 7–8; July 1975, p. 7; August 1975, p. 7; September 1975, p. 7; October 1975, p. 7; December 1975, p. 13; January 1976, p. 6; February 1976, p. 6.

Reed, David. "Putting Back the Pieces of the 'Lisbon Jigsaw'." *IPI Report.* March 1979, pp. 6–7.

"Warm Welcome for IPI in Portugal." *IPI Report.* October 1977, p. 7.

"World Press Freedom Review, 1977." *IPI Report.* January 1978, pp. 3–12.

"World Press Freedom Review, 1979: Portugal." *IPI Report.* December 1979, p. 12.

"World Press Freedom Review, 1980: Portugal." *IPI Report.* December 1980, p. 12.

RUMANIA

by Paul Underwood

BASIC DATA

Population: 22,151,000
Area: 237,503 sq. km. (91,676 sq. mi.)
GNP: 301.73 billion lei (US$67.5 billion)
Literacy Rate: 99%
Language(s): Rumanian, German, Hungarian; some Serbo-Croatian, Greek, Armenian, Yiddish
Number of Dailies: 34
   Aggregate Circulation: 3,711,000
   Circulation per 1,000: 171
Number of Nondailies: 25
   Aggregate Circulation: 735,800
   Circulation per 1,000: 34

Number of Periodicals: 553
Number of Radio Stations: 76
Number of Television Stations: 1
Number of Radio Receivers: 3,104,000
   Radio Receivers per 1,000: 145
Number of Television Sets: 2,963,000
   Television Sets per 1,000: 138
Total Annual Newsprint Consumption: 44,100 metric tons
   Per Capita Newsprint Consumption: 2.0 kg. (4.4 lb.)
Total Newspaper Ad Receipts: NA
   As % of All Ad Expenditures: NA

Background & General Characteristics

As in the other Eastern European nations, the Rumanian media structure is patterned after that of the Soviet Union and reflects the same basic philosophy. Newspapers, magazines, radio and television are tools of the government and the ruling Communist Party, assigned the task of forming "socialist consciousness" among the people.

Before World War II, Rumania was one of the most economically backward countries in Europe, even though it was well endowed with mineral, fuel and timber resources and blessed with vast expanses of fertile soil. Even today, after years of rapid industrialization and economic growth, about half the working population is still agricultural.

Although money incomes and living standards have been rising and the supply of consumer goods is much improved, Rumanians are still relatively ill-supplied. The per capita consumption of such consumer durables as automobiles, TV sets and refrigerators is still low, even in comparison with the country's Eastern European neighbors, let alone Western nations.

In the immediate post-World War II years, the regime initiated an adult education drive to eliminate illiteracy, an objective officially reached in 1956. Although some pockets remain among older persons in more remote rural areas, illiteracy is no longer the problem it once was.

About a quarter of the country is mountainous but, generally speaking, the terrain does not constitute much of a barrier to travel and communications. The population is distributed fairly evenly throughout the country, with the heaviest concentration in the area around Bucharest in the Danube valley.

Eighty-seven percent of the population is Rumanian, and Rumanian is the national language, although German and Hungarian, the languages of the two principal minority groups, enjoy official parity. Most of the members of these two minorities live in Transylvania, which before World War II, was part of Hungary.

Before the Communists took over, Rumania enjoyed an active and diversified press, but now it is little more than a propaganda tool for the state. Even so, indications are that Bucharest is not happy with its work. Recent years have witnessed repeated complaints by regime leaders about the quality and efficiency of the media, especially TV. As a result, the 1970s witnessed recurring changes in the supervisory structure, personnel and practices of print and broadcast outlets alike.

The Rumanians trace the history of their press back to 1829, when Ion Eliade-Radulescu founded *Curierul Romanescu* ("Rumanian Courier"), in Bucharest. At that time, the country was nominally part of the Ottoman Empire but was actually under Russian military control. Other newspapers and journals, generally short-lived, appeared in subsequent years, most of them revolutionary in spirit and passionate advocates of the independence and unification of the then separate Rumanian principalities of Wallachia and Moldavia.

The struggle for these goals continued for decades, encouraged by a press that was often forced to operate in exile, smuggling its publications into the country. The situation began to change for the better in 1866, when Rumania's national assembly, with the consent of the major European powers, chose Prince Charles of Hohenzollern-Sigmaringen as the country's ruler. He did much to modernize the country. Nevertheless, newspapers remained relatively few in number and almost uniformly poor, both economically and in terms of quality.

It was not until the 1870s that better papers began to appear—and not until the early 1880s, after the securing of complete independence, that the press gained real freedom. Many new papers were established, most of them partisan political publications although a few became recognized, both at home and abroad, as solid informational organs. These included *Universul,* the first Rumanian newspaper with nationwide circulation, and *Adeverul* ("Truth"), which also campaigned vigorously for various social and economic reforms.

By early in the present century, the Rumanian press included several hundred papers and periodicals and enjoyed relative prosperity. However, trouble lay just ahead. A bloody peasant revolt swept the country in 1907. Relations with neighboring countries turned sour—to some extent a result of press agitation over the conditions of millions of Rumanians living under the rule of those very neighbors. As the pre-World War I tension between the Russian and Austro-Hungarian Empires grew, the international position of Rumania—highly vulnerable to pressure from both sides—became more and more precarious. And the press, like the people generally, became increasingly divided over future courses of action. When the war finally came in 1914, Rumania remained neutral for two years but in 1916 joined the Allies. It was a disastrous move. Rumania's armies were defeated and the country occupied. Most papers—except those that had supported the Central Powers—were suppressed.

The end of the war meant freedom once again, and a vast increase in territory, but the country was economically crippled. New political parties sprang up, together with a proliferation of political organs that thrived on bitter partisanship. On the bright side, a new national constitution, promulgated in 1923, guaranteed freedom of the press and barred not only censorship but suppression of publications. The next few years saw the growth of a relatively large and diversified press, heavily political but boasting several papers that enjoyed national reputations.

However, trouble all too soon erupted again with the worldwide economic depression of the 1930s. Political crisis followed political crisis until King Carol established a personal dictatorship. A new, fascist-type constitution was promulgated, and press laws similar to those in Nazi Germany were imposed. The press was effectively muzzled.

The outbreak of World War II found Rumania once again in the middle—between the Soviet Union and the Axis powers. King Carol attempted to remain neutral but had to cede large territories to neighboring states. Eventually he was forced to abdicate in favor of a new dictatorship under Nazi control. All newspapers except those supporting Germany were suppressed and Rumania joined in Hitler's 1942 attack on the Soviet Union.

But within two years the battle tide had turned and in 1944, with Hitler's panzers in retreat and Russian armies approaching Rumanian territory, Carol's son, young King Michael, enlisted the aid of loyal politicians and generals to overthrow the dictatorship and put Rumania on the Allied side. A new government, which included Communists for the first time, restored the former democratic constitution and press freedoms. Old papers reappeared and new ones, including the Communist *Scinteia* ("Spark"), came on the market.

This reblossoming, however, was soon blasted by the Soviets, who assumed control of all communications and much of Rumania's economic life. Opposition papers were expropriated or suppressed under a regime even more drastic than that imposed by the Nazis. Michael finally abdicated under Russian pressure. A new constitution—modeled after that of the Soviet Union—was adopted, and the press was completely forced into the Soviet mold.

Most periodicals in the country are printed in Rumanian, although 17 newspapers, 11 of them dailies, are published in minority languages, including German, Hungarian and Serbian. There are also publications in Greek, Armenian and Yiddish. The most important papers are published in Bucharest, the nation's capital. However, there is a relatively well-developed regional press, with dailies in 19 of the country's administrative districts. All are published under the auspices of the Communist Party and the government. This is true as well of the minority-language publications, whose orientation and ideology must conform to Party rules.

Most papers are printed in a somewhat reduced broadsheet size, with relatively few pages. Even *Scinteia,* the principal Party organ, seldom exceeds eight pages. This has been particularly true since 1974, when the Party's Central Committee ordered reductions in the numbers of pages and copies printed. The Central Committee also cut the publication frequency of some newspapers and periodicals and simply abolished others. The order, apparently aimed at achieving a balance between the domestic production and consumption of newsprint as well as eliminating duplication, asserted that in the years immediately previous there had been an "exaggerated" increase in the number of publications as well as an "unjustified" number of pages in some papers.

Practically all the major papers in Bucharest, as well as those in the regional centers, are published Tuesday through Sunday, with no publication on Mondays. There are no special Sunday papers or sections. As is common in Communist-ruled countries, Rumania has a great many specialized publications, dealing with everything from culture to farming. Most of these are weeklies, bimonthlies or monthlies. However, two nationally circulated Bucharest dailies— *Sportul* ("The Sport") and *Scinteia Tineretului* ("Spark of Youth")—could be placed in this group. The first is published by the National Council for Training and Sport, the second by the Communist Youth Union.

Competition in the Western sense does not exist among the media. Even in Bucharest, each of the seven dailies is designed to appeal to a specific audience and is not seen as competing with the others. In the few regional centers with more than one daily, invariably one is a Rumanian-language publication and others are in minority languages. An example is the city of Timisoara, in western Rumania, where there are three dailies, one printed in Rumanian, another in Hungarian and the third in German. All three are published by the Timis County Communist Party Committee and the local Peoples' Council.

Among all Rumanian papers, only *Scinteia* claims more than a one million circulation. Two other Bucharest papers, *Sportul* and *Romania Libera* ("Free Rumania"), circulate just over 300,000 daily. Two more, *Informatia Bucharestiului* ("Bucharest Information") and *Scinteia Tineretului,* run over 200,000. Only one of the others, the Hungarian-language *Elore* ("Forward") tops 100,000. The remaining capital-city daily, the German-language *Neuer Weg* ("New Way"), claims 65,000. All the regional papers are smaller: the top three barely exceed 50,000 copies per issue, 15 fall in the 25,000-50,000 range, eight from 10,000 to 25,000 and two fewer than 10,000.

None of the regional papers circulate throughout the country, as do the Bucharest dailies. In terms of circulation, the top three regionals are *Drum Nou* ("New Road") of Brasov, *Flacara Iasului* ("Flame of Iasi") and *Drapelul Rosu* ("Red Flag") of Timisoara.

Of all the papers, by far the most influential are *Scinteia,* the chief Party organ and equivalent of Moscow's *Pravda, Romania Libera,* more or less the Rumanian version of *Izvestia,* and *Scinteia Tineretului.*

In 1976 the Party abolished the former professional Journalists' Union, replacing it with a Journalists' Council as a part of the national trade union organization. The council was assigned such responsibilities as ensuring that the "sociopolitical duties of the press as outlined by the party" were carried out, and playing an active role in training journalists. An action program published by the Party at that time emphasized that all the media had to intensify political and ideological indoctrination efforts: "The political and ideological training of journalists, as well as their general and professional knowledge, must be improved, and all journalists must be enrolled in the country's social and political activity."

Economic Framework

Since the media in Rumania, like those of other Communist-ruled countries, are tools of the regime and supported by it, they are not subject to the same economic necessities as those of capitalist nations. They receive income from both circulation and advertising, although few probably meet the costs of publication from these sources. Advertising, particularly, is not much of an influence on the balance sheet and none at all on editorial policy, not only because there is little of it but also because the Party really decides both.

Nonetheless, the Rumanian media are still affected by other economic factors, chiefly cost to consumers. Despite considerable development since World War II, Rumania is still a relatively poor country and the cost of newspapers, magazines and TV and radio sets is a burden for many citizens. Also, there are clearly limits to the regime's willingness to subsidize the media, as witnessed by the 1974 restrictions on page size, number of pages and print runs. These clearly represented a refusal on the part of the regime to sacrifice any of its scarce foreign exchange to buy additional newsprint on the world market.

However, this kind of reluctance may be more true with regard to print than broadcast. Newspapers tend to be heavily packed with official propaganda while short on entertainment—the usual Communist pattern. This may help explain why broadcasting has become the biggest and most important form of mass communication in the country. By the end of 1978 Rumanians had registered and bought licenses for over three million radios.

The reluctance of the government to reallocate foreign exchange from industrial development to the press may also help to explain the fact that Rumanian newspapers have not yet moved to install any of the new printing and editing technologies that are becoming common in the West.

Press Laws & Censorship

The Rumanian Constitution guarantees freedom of speech and the press but notes immediately that these freedoms "cannot be used for aims hostile to the socialist system and to the interests of the working people." And this, in practice, means that only the Party and government, as self-proclaimed representatives of the working people, may publish newspapers. Broadcasting, too, is a state monopoly. Newsmen must belong to the official Journalists' Council, for which they qualify by examination and Party approval.

A 1974 Press law gave to the Press and Printing Committee of the government's Council of Ministers the power to oversee all publishing authorizations, newsprint supply and allocation, the operation of all printing plants, the distribution of all publications and the issuance of journalist cards. Among other principal provisions of the law are:

Press organs are not obliged to disclose to those concerned the sources of information on the basis of which they have edited the published material; the undisclosed sources are a professional secret.

For the protection of the interests of society and individuals against the misuse of the right to freedom of expression in the Press, it is forbidden to publish and disseminate through the Press materials which:

a. are contrary to the Constitution.

b. contain attacks against the socialist social order [and] the principles of the internal and foreign policy [of the Party and government].

c. defame the Party and State leadership.

d. communicate secret information, facts or documents, which are defined as such by the law.

e. contain false or alarming information and comments, which endanger or disturb public order or constitute a danger for the security of the State.

f. call for the disrespect of the laws of the State and for the perpetration of acts which are criminal offenses.

g. disseminate fascist, obscurantist, antihumanitarian views, disseminate chauvinist propaganda, incite to racial hatred or national hatred, or to acts of violence, or offend national feelings.

h. offend against good morals or incite to the violation of the standards of ethics and of social life.

i. give information on current trials and thereby anticipate judgments which are to be made by the legal organs.

j. make untrue statements which detract from an individual's reputation or his social or professional prestige, or in which insults, libels or threats are uttered against a person.

Despite this last provision it is hard to imagine—considering that both the media and the courts are creatures of the Party and government—that any ordinary citizen could win a libel suit against a newspaper, let alone the broadcast media, which are operated directly by the state.

One final provision of the 1974 law specified that in every organ of the press responsibility for compliance with the list of restrictions lay with the editor in chief. It added: "The Committee for the Press and Printed Matter should supervise the observance of the restrictions and, if necessary" draw the attention of the editors in chief to contraventions so that they might "take the necessary measures."

This provision suggested that a priori censorship would be ended and that full responsibility for what got published would fall on the editors in chief. Indeed, the idea was repeated several times in subsequent years by President Nicolae Ceausescu, although there has been no indication that such a policy was ever actually implemented. And any notion that it might some day come into being apparently was laid to rest in December 1977, when a decree by the State Council abolished the Committee for Press and Printed Matter, which had been an arm of the government's Council of Ministers, and give its powers to the Council on Socialist Culture and Education, which is, in effect, the national Ministry of Culture. While the powers specifically transferred included the right to issue journalists' cards and to authorize publication, the main effect of the decree was to clear up the censorship question. It specified that the council "will serve as a central records office providing the editors of newspapers and periodicals, radio and TV and publishing houses with the lists prepared by ministries and other national agencies of the type of data and information which, according to the law, may not be published." The decree further stated that the council would "guide the publishing houses and exert control over their output," clearly indicating not only pre- but post-censorship powers.

In addition, the council was specifically assigned the job of distributing paper quotas to all publishing houses and of exerting "control over the way in which this paper is utilized."

The scope of the council's powers make it clear that it is a far more powerful body than its predecessor, since not only are its censorship powers spelled out more clearly but it is also "directly responsible for the import of all books, film and phonograph records" and, in addition, must approve the scheduling of any professional or amateur artistic performance anywhere in the country.

The regime decreed several other changes in the 1974 Press law. One of these gave the Council on Socialist Culture and Education the power to suspend offending publications pending final decisions by "proper bodies or courts of law." Previously, the law had said nothing about suspensions. Another revision involved the makeup of the editorial control boards of individual publications. Instead of being composed simply of the editor in chief, his deputies, the editorial secretary and other responsible officials of the enterprise, these boards were now to include representatives of other social groups, particularly Party officials.

Perhaps the most important feature of the changes, however, was the creation of a new category of journalists, "called cooperating journalists." This particular section of the 1977 law stipulated that "journalistic functions can also be performed by other working people acting as cooperating journalists who will not be members of the editorial staff" but will instead, "support the periodicals in their work." It went on to note that these people were to perform such tasks as putting out house organs in their places of employment and preparing broadcasts of their factory radio stations. They also could help distribute newspapers where they worked and "explain to the working personnel the contents of the main articles published in the national and local papers, as well as contribute reports to the national and local press on activities at their factory, farm or office."

The "cooperating journalist" is not considered a professional however. According to the text of the law, only those "who have obtained special results in their press activity" can apply to take the examination attesting to their talent and skills and thereby qualify for the status of professionals.

State-Press Relations

Quite clearly, news in Rumania is what the government says is news, and nothing else. It is all managed. As in the Soviet Union, the media may criticize factory managers, local officials and others for inefficiency or malfeasance but they dare not criticize the Party or the government, or question, in any way, the "socialist structure of society." In this connection it should be noted that there have been no publicized cases of newspaper suspensions in recent years, although as a result of the 1974 restrictions on paper usage several periodicals disappeared from circulation, either outright or as a result of having been forced to combine with other similar publications. Neither have there been any reports of newsmen jailed for press law violations, although indications are that many have lost their jobs in recent years, at least partly as a result of the reduction in the number of publications.

State and Party control over the media is complete. They provide the subsidies or other funds that keep both print and broadcast going; they allocate newsprint, control the import of equipment and license the journalists, who must belong to their union.

Attitude Toward Foreign Media

Foreign correspondents can be accredited by the Rumanian Foreign Ministry on application to its Press Department, which issues the special visas foreign newsmen are required to have to be able to report from that country. However, correspondents normally have no problems filing their copy. No prior approval is needed to transmit stories, beyond the customary ascertaining of financial responsibility. Theoretically, at any rate, foreign newsmen could be subject to provisions of the various press laws although there have been no instances of any being charged with violations. Such an action, even in cases of violations, would be unusual. The customary practice is simply to cancel the visa of a correspondent who offends in any way, in effect expelling him or her immediately.

Correspondents deemed "unfriendly" usually find it difficult if not impossible to obtain another visa. There is no way of knowing how many may have been so affected because nothing is ever made public about newsmen's visa applications, granted or not.

The media scene in Rumania could aptly be described as strictly Rumanian. There are neither foreign ownership nor interests in any of the media. It is very difficult to find foreign newspapers or magazines—regardless of origin—anywhere in the country. Import restrictions, clearly, are very tight. A great deal of foreign propaganda—from both East and West—is directed toward Rumania. It is difficult to say whether it has any direct effect on the media. Obviously, however, it would have to have some impact on the leadership before it could be reflected in the newspapers or on broadcasts.

The journalists' trade union council has affiliation with the International Organization of Journalists, which is headquartered in Prague, Czechoslovakia.

News Agencies

The Rumanian national news agency is the Agentia Romana de Presa, known as Agerpres. It was set up in 1949 as a government department but was reorganized under a 1978 State Council decree and is now referred to as a "Party and state" institution. Its executive is a "leading council," whose members are appointed by presidential decree and whose chairman is a representative of the Party's Central Committee. The membership includes representatives of the Central Committee, the State Council and the Council of Ministers, as well as representatives of certain editorial staffs and press institutions, government ministries and public organizations.

The Agerpres headquarters are in Bucharest and it has domestic bureaus in principal regional centers throughout the nation, as well as foreign bureaus in 22 countries. Agerpres also has exchange agreements with 36 other agencies, including all the major international ones, West as well as East. However, Agerpres alone supplies news to domestic media, and claims more than 4,000 subscribers. In addition to its domestic service it supplies reports of developments in Rumania in English, French, Spanish, Russian, German and Arabic. Its charges to domestic subscribers and the basis on which they are calculated apparently have never been publicized.

No Western agencies have permanent representation in Bucharest although the Soviet bloc is heavily represented, with the USSR's Tass and Novosti, East Germany's ADN, Bulgaria's BTA, Czechoslovakia's CTK, Hungary's MTI and Poland's PAP. Others with Bucharest bureaus include Yugoslavia's Tanjug and Communist China's Hsinhua.

The 1978 decree reorganizing Agerpres specified that authors of articles prepared and disseminated by the agency are responsible for "the political content and orientation of the respective article, for the objectivity of the information it contains, for reflecting the truth and for safeguarding state secrets." The decree also noted that the editorial staffs, which act as collective leadership bodies entrusted with running Agerpres, are responsible for "the political and ideological content of the material, for respecting the Press Law, the other laws of the country, and for the safeguarding of state secrets." The leading council, for its part, is to guide and exert control over the entire operation of the agency and is "responsible for providing orientation for this activity in accordance with the Party program, with the decisions taken and assignments set by the Party and state leadership."

Electronic News Media

Of all the nation's media, the two that have particularly concerned the nation's leadership over the past 10 years have been radio and TV—a fact that has resulted in recurrent criticism, personnel reshuffles and reorganizations. The latest of these overhauls came at the end of 1977. Under provisions of a decree issued in December of that year, all Rumanian broadcast operations are controlled by the National Council on Radio and TV, a body that operates under the direct supervision of the Party's Central Committee and the government's Council of Ministers.

Actual operations are under the control of the Rumanian Radio and TV Network, which is headed by a director general and an "executive bureau" composed of the director-general, his deputies, editors in chief and directors, as well as Party representatives. The bureau's function is to prepare guidelines for all broadcast operations "in conformity with party and state policy." It is also responsible for "the political and ideological content as well as for the artistic and journalistic level of the broadcasts." The 1977 law also provided for the setting up within the National Council of special commissions which, "in order to safeguard the high level of political and professional competence" would "review the most important TV and radio programs...in order to recommend the ones fit for public performance."

Party control is emphasized throughout the structure. By law, the head of the National Council must be a secretary of the Central Committee. Both the council chief and the director general are appointed by presidential decree. Members of the council, as well as the executive bureau, must include Party appointees in addition to workers' representatives.

Radio broadcasts three programs on both long and medium wave, as well as FM, from its headquarters in Bucharest. In addition, six regional stations not only serve as relay points for the national network but also originate some of their own programming, including broadcasts in Hungarian, Serbo-Croatian and German. About 80 hours of the 250 hours broadcast weekly consist of news and information programs.

The 1977 decree put particular emphasis on the service's international programming, which broadcasts about 200 hours a week in 13 languages, including English, and is beamed to Africa, the Middle East, Asia, and North and South America as well as Europe —being assigned to the task of "propagating the Party and States's international policy" abroad.

The TV service consists of two channels, which carry education as well as entertainment and news and information programming. In addition, a limited number of hours are devoted to broadcasts in the two principal minority languages, Hungarian and German.

A sizable share of the TV entertainment programming used to consist of American- and British-produced features, including such serials as "Colombo," "Mannix," "The Fugitive" and "The Sheriff in New York." In recent years, however, Ceausescu has repeatedly criticized both radio and TV for both superficiality and poor quality programs as well as for paying insufficient attention to "political-educational problems." Apparently as a result, all such foreign programs were banned last year and have remained off the air despite protests from viewers. This has been interpreted as part of a new trend in the Party's cultural policy, a trend that has taken on an increasingly outspoken anti-Western aspect, coupled with tighter regulations on the country's artists, writers, filmmakers and TV producers. The basic theme was outlined by Ceausescu in a 1980 speech in which he demanded that the nation's writers fight "the retrograde bourgeois ideology, the decadent philosophy, morals and culture of the contemporary capitalist world."

Education & Training

In keeping with the generally enhanced role of the Party in all aspects of the media, journalism education is in the hands of the Stefan Gheorghiu Academy, a Party educational institution in Bucharest that also has the responsibility of training "party and government cadres." The academy offers a full professional training program as well as short-term courses to improve the skills of journalists already working in the media in various parts of the country.

Summary

During the last 20 years, Rumania has succeeded in establishing an international stance that differs markedly from that of the Soviet Union and most of its allies in several significant aspects. There has been no such development on the domestic scene, however. Controls over almost all aspects of daily life have remained tight. Only a few tentative steps toward relaxation in cultural fields have been evident. Now, however, it appears that even these moves have been withdrawn, and that the direction of policy is toward even tighter control and absolute party dictation over all forms of communication.

CHRONOLOGY

1974 Government imposes restrictions on number and size of pages and print runs of newspapers.

    Press law assigns direction and control of press to Press and Printing Committee of Council of Ministers.

1976 Journalists' Union abolished and replaced by Journalists' Council.

1977 State Committee for Press and Printing abolished and replaced by Council on Socialist Culture and Education.

1978 National news agency, Agerpress, reorganized as Party and state institution.

BIBLIOGRAPHY

Constantinescu, Miron, Daicoviciu, Constantin, and Pascu, Stefan. *Histoire de la Roumanie.* Paris, 1970.

Directia Centrala de Statistica. *Anuaral Statistic al Republicii Socialiste Romania 1979.* Bucharest, 1979.

International Press Institute. *The Press in Authoritarian Countries.* Zurich, 1959.

Merrill, John C., Bryan, Carter R. and Alisky, Marvin. *The Foreign Press.* Baton Rouge, 1970.

Olson, Kenneth E. *The History Makers.* Baton Rouge, 1966.

Paulu, Burton. *Broadcasting in Eastern Europe.* Minneapolis, 1974.

Radio Free Europe. "Decree of Structure and Functions of Agerpress Published," *Romanian Situation Report.* January 30, 1978, p. 11.

Radio Free Europe. "New System of Censorship Adopted." *Romanian Situation Report.* July 8, 1977, p. 2.

Radio Free Europe. "The Romanian Press Celebrates Its 150th Birthday," *Romanian Situation Report.* May 18, 1979, p. 5.

Radio Free Europe. "Romanian Press Law Modified," *Romanian Situation Report.* January 30, 1978, p. 8.

Radio Free Europe. "Romanian Radio and TV Reorganized," *Romanian Situation Report.* January 19, 1978, p. 16.

Radio Free Europe. "Setup of the Council on Socialist Culture and of the National Council on Radio and Television." *Romanian Situation Report.* October 24, 1978, p. 8.

Stavrianos, L.S. *The Balkans Since 1453.* New York, 1966.

SAUDI ARABIA

by George Kurian

BASIC DATA

Population: 8,224,000 (1980)
Area: 2,331,000 sq. km. (900,000 sq. mi.)
GNP: SR 213 billion (US$62.64 billion) (1979)
Literacy Rate: 15.1%
Language (s): Arabic
Number of Dailies: 10
   Aggregate Circulation: 200,000
   Circulation per 1,000: 28
Number of Nondailies: 8
   Aggregate Circulation: 30,000
   Circulation per 1,000: 3
Number of Periodicals: 20
Number of Radio Stations: 4

Number of Television Stations: 12
Number of Radio Receivers: 275,000
   Radio Receivers per 1,000: 29
Number of Television Sets: 300,000
   Television Sets per 1,000: 32
Total Annual Newsprint Consumption: 8,000
   metric tons (1979)
   Per Capita Newsprint Consumption: 1.1 kg.
   (2.42 lb.)
Total Newspaper Ad Receipts: SR 150.6
   (US$44.3 million) (1979)
   As % of All Ad Expenditures: 72.9

Background & General Characteristics

The Saudi Arabian press is a relatively recent phenomenon; the country's first newspaper, *al Hijaz,* appeared only in 1908, published by the Ottoman authorities in Mecca. For the next 17 years the press was limited to Hijaz province, and even there all the newspapers were run by resident foreigners and were read only by the literary elite. The situation did not change materially even when the Saudi Dynasty unified the country. The Hijaz press flourished as a literary rather than a news medium. Even the official Saudi government journal, *Umm al Qura*, contained primarily literary articles; so did the two private papers, *Sawt al Hijaz* and *Madinah al Manawarah*. When World War II came, all papers except *Umm al Qura* were suspended because of financial difficulties. It was not until the late 1940s that a modern press, in the most limited sense of that term, re-appeared in the country. *Sawt al Hijaz* re-emerged as *Bilad al Sa'udiyah* in 1946, and *Madinah* resumed in 1947, both as news-oriented dailies published from Jiddah.

By the 1950s the incredible surge of wealth that flowed out of the Arabian oil wells began transforming the country, and with it the media. Wealthy families went into publishing, establishing newspapers as business or political ventures or both. By 1963 the government found it necessary to issue its first press law imposing strict guidelines for the new breed of editors and publishers. The law discouraged investigative reporting and aggressive editorial criticism. The government did not want the emerging fourth estate to get out of hand or pose a challenge to established traditional institutions. Even without these legal constraints, the Saudi press has remained a 19th-century institution and never emerged as a dynamic national force in its own right. Because barely 15 percent of the population is literate, there is no viable readership base. The owners have never invested much in production facilities. When the new Arabic daily, *al Sharq al Awsat*, was founded in 1978, its publishers set up editorial offices in London, staffed by Lebanese and Palestinian journalists in exile, printed the paper there, and had it flown to Saudi Arabia every morning.

In 1980 the Saudi press comprised 10 dailies with a circulation reported to be close to 200,000. (The actual circulation figures are not verifiable because of the absence of an audit bureau of circulation.) Seven of the papers are published in Arabic and three in English (*Arab News*, published by the Saudi Research and Marketing Company, *Saudi Gazette*, published by the Okaz Organization, and *Saudi Review*, published by a consortium of newspapers). Six of the newspapers are published from Jiddah, two from Riyadh, one from Mecca and one from Dammam. The largest circulation is claimed by *al-Madinah al-Munawara,* with sales of 60,000 copies daily, followed by *al-Yaum* (42,000), *al-Bilad* (25,000), and *Okaz* (20,000). None of the other papers sells over 10,000 copies. In per capita circulation of dailies, Saudi Arabia ranks considerably lower than Arab countries of comparable population, with 28 copies per 1,000 inhabitants.

Three of the nine major weeklies are in English; all monthlies are in Arabic. The government remains the largest periodical publisher, issuing both *Hajj*, the most widely read religious periodical, and the English-language *News from Saudi Arabia*. Aramco, the principal foreign oil concessionaire, has an extensive publication program, including the *Arabian Sun*, in English, and *Oil Caravan* and *Qafilat al Zaft*, in Arabic.

As elsewhere in the Arab world where privately owned media are permitted, newspapers function as personal vehicles of their publishers or patrons. There is no tradition of objective reporting. Editorials are generally placed on the front page, set in a different type face. Stylistic merit is considered more important than factual content, and most articles begin and end with quotations from the Koran or classical Arabic poetry. Relatively little space is devoted to advertising and the ads that do appear are drab and dreary, with no pictures.

Newspapers differ from each other only in the amount of space they give to secondary stories and nonpolitical items. If the king makes a public statement, takes a trip, or receives an important visitor, that news will be the top story in all newspapers and the text will be the same word for word. In other fields newspapers display some freedom and variety. Some emphasize Islamic items, some international news and others local and Arab news.

Economic Framework

Under state regulations, all newspapers and periodicals are published by press organizations and are administered by boards of directors with full autonomous powers. Press organizations are privately owned in the case of non-government publications but many, such as *al-Madinah al-Munawara*, are closely associated with the royal family and have princes of the royal line as directors or publishers.

All dailies are published six days a week, Saturday through Thursday (the Muslim sabbath, falling on Friday, is a holiday). The format reflects the influence of Egyptian editors during the 1950s. The average daily has only a few pages. The first page usually carries international and national news as well as the editorial; one page is usually devoted to women or other special supplements; women's supplements, such as *She* or *New Eve*, are edited by women. Cartoons are extremely popular. Although the quality of printing has improved in recent years, it is still poor compared to other Arab countries.

Trade unions are illegal in the kingdom and the last (illegal) strike was in 1956.

Newsprint, all of it imported, is freely available in the country, and there is no tendency to use newsprint supplies to control the press.

Press Laws & Censorship

Saudi Arabia's current press law, promulgated in 1963, declares that the press is private and the state has no right to interfere with it except for the sake of the general welfare. In such cases, which the law says will occur only "rarely" ("*nadiran*"), the government has the right to stop the paper from publishing. The law also gives the government influence over personnel selection. The Information Ministry can veto any candidate for the board of directors, also selects the editor-in-chief and the board chairman from among a slate of candidates nominated by the board.

Although under private ownership, printing and publishing establishments are required to be licensed by the government. The terms of the license state that each publishing organization (consisting of no less than 15 individuals of Saudi Arabian nationality) must be approved by the Ministry of Information, have a minimum of SR 100,000 in assets, and be headed by a director general. Further, the law requires that all editorial functions must be supervised by a committee formed from members of the organization. The government has the right to revoke the license of any organization without citing reasons.

State-Press Relations

The press's ownership is private, its communication functions are closely monitored by the government through the Director General of Broadcasting, Press and Publications. While there is no formal censorship, newspapers face suppression and their editors dismissal if they print anything deemed offensive by the government. In a recent vivid demonstration of state power over the media on March 16, 1980, the authorities "ordered" the dismissal of Turki Abd-Allah al-Sudari, chief editor of the pro-government and privately owned *Al-Riyadh,* and banned him from writing in the future.

These legal powers over the media are not used too often; the media are as tradition-bound as other national institutions and have no inclination to rock the boat. Further, the media are owned by the establishment with a powerful stake in the status quo. The state and the media thus have an excellent understanding of the needs and tolerances of the other. So long as the wishes of the royal family are met and the demands of the religious leaders are not ignored, the state prefers not to interfere overtly in actual media operations. When it does, it is done quietly, many times secretly, so as to cause minimum friction. Often it takes only a phone call from the minister of information to persuade an editor not to stray too far from the official line. If the phone call is ignored, the ministry may proceed to levy a fine. For example, one newspaper was fined for quoting a Syrian editorial calling for the elimination of imperialist interests in the Arab world, and another for reporting anarchist demonstrations in a foreign country. The result is that on sensitive issues newspapers tend to adopt such a similar stance that, in the words of a Saudi editor, "they might as well be official newspapers."

Attitude Toward Foreign Media

Foreign newspapers and periodicals—mostly of Egyptian origin—are freely available in the larger towns and cities, but they are subject to the same stringent regulations as domestic publications with regard to their conformity to Islamic mores and sensitivities. As a result, the vast majority of Western publications, laced with sex and alcohol ads, will not even qualify for entry into the kingdom. Leftist publications are also taboo.

Western correspondents have found Riyadh and Jiddah to be among the top "discomfort stations" in the world. Their visas as well as cables are constantly monitored for political and cultural content. Official displeasure is made known in subtle and quiet ways, although always ending in the correspondent's quick departure.

News Agencies

The collection and dissemination of news within the country is the exclusive responsibility of the Saudi News Agency (SNA), a semi-official enterprise directed by the Ministry of Information. Its English-language daily newsletter summarizes important information from Saudi newspapers and broadcasts. Foreign news agencies represented in the country include AFP, AP, MENA, Reuters and UPI. No communist news agencies are allowed to function in the country.

Electronic News Media

Radio broadcasting was introduced by the late King Saud over the disapproval of the Wahhabi ulema, Islamic theologians. In answer to their objections, he asserted that since radios were not mentioned in the Koran, it could not be assumed that Allah intended to prohibit their use. He ordered that parts of the Koran be broadcast and clinched the discussion with the argument: "Can anything be bad which transmits the word of God?" Today, radio commands the largest mass media audience in the country.

Radio broadcasting is the responsibility of the Saudi Arabian Broadcasting Service and television that of the Saudi Arabian Government Television Service. There are three medium-wave transmitters at Riyadh, Jiddha and Dhammam and four short-wave transmitters at Riyadh and Jiddah providing country-wide reception. There are 12 television stations, at Riyadh, Jiddah, Medina, Dammam, Qassim, Abha, Hail, Albaha, Sakaka, Al-Qurayat, Wadiadda-Wasir and Tabuk. Aramco operates a private radio station, Aramco Radio and a private television station, Dahran HZ-22-TV or Aramco TV.

Education & Training

There are no institutions providing journalism training within the country.

Summary

Established by the elite for the elite, the Saudi Arabian press is a minor institution with very little influence or power to change politics and society. It is so designed by the state because a stronger press could conceivably pose a threat to the country's medieval political system.

CHRONOLOGY

1978   A new Arabic daily, *al Sharq al Awsat*, founded with printing facilities in London.

1980   Turki Abd-Allah al-Sudari, editor of *Al-Riyadh*, is ordered dismissed by the government.

BIBLIOGRAPHY

Rugh, William A. *The Arab Press*. Syracuse, N.Y., 1979.

SINGAPORE

by Elliott S. Parker

BASIC DATA

Population: 2.3 million (1978, est.)
Area: 616 sq. km. (238 sq. mi.)
GNP: S$20.5 billion (US$9.5 billion) (1979)
Literacy Rate: 72%
Language(s): Malay, English,Chinese, (Mandarin, officially), Tamil
Number of Dailies: 9
  Aggregate Circulation: 553,150 (1979, est.)
  Circulation per 1,000: 241 (1979, est.)
Number of Nondailies: NA
  Aggregate Circulation: NA
  Circulation per 1,000: NA

Number of Periodicals: NA
Number of Radio Stations: 2
Number of Television Stations: NA
Number of Radio Receivers: 440,260
  Radio Receivers per 1,000: 191
Number of Television Sets: 379,706
  Television Sets per 1,000: 165
Total Annual Newsprint Consumption: NA
  Per Capita Newsprint Consumption: NA
Total Newspaper Ad Receipts: S$69.8 billion (US$32.3 million) (1978, est.)
  As % of All Ad Expenditures: 59 (1978, est.)

Background & General Characteristics

Singapore entered the 1970s with a spate of government closings of newspapers resulting in worldwide discussion. The prime minister presented the government case to the International Press Institute at the annual meeting in Helsinki in 1971.

Then, as now, the press system of the island is dominated by two competitive Chinese papers and the Straits Times Group, which publishes the two English papers.

The *Straits Times* was started in 1845. It was preceded by other, now extinct, English papers: the *Singapore Chronicle* (1824–37), *Singapore Free Press,* and the *Singapore Journal of Commerce.* The first Chinese daily was the *Lat Pau (Jia Bao)** (1881). Singapore was originally one of the Straits Settlements along with Penang and Malacca, the two latter now part of Malaysia. This relationship meant that the resident of Singapore also had access to papers published in those towns. Early residents of Singapore also had one of the first papers of satire and humor, the *Straits Produce,* founded in 1868. At the

turn of the century, Singapore started to become a center for publishing Malay-language periodicals for distribution throughout the archipelago. Many of these magazines dealt with Islam, and would become important in the rise of nationalism that culminated in independence from Britain for Singapore and Malaysia in 1957.

Singapore was founded in 1819 by Sir Stamford Raffles as a commercial center. It was under British Indian rule until 1867, when it became a crown colony administered from London. In 1965, Singapore separated from Malaysia as an independent republic.

As a nation of immigrants, most Singaporeans speak several languages. Eighty-four percent of people over 15 years old read at least one language. The four official languages are Malay, English, Chinese (Mandarin), and Tamil. About 75 percent of the population speak Chinese, fifteen percent speak Malay, and eight percent an Indian language as their mother tongue. Most Singapore Chinese actually do not speak Mandarin Chinese, but one of the mutually unintelligible dialects. Forty-two percent of the

---

*In this chapter, the transliterated, or translated, name as given on the nameplate is given first, if any. This is followed by the pinyin transliteration.

Chinese speakers speak Hokkien. More than eighty percent of Chinese speakers speak Hokkien, Teochew or Cantonese. However, to establish Mandarin as the main language of the Chinese community, the Singapore government has begun a massive campaign through all mass media to advocate and popularize the use of hanyu pinyin, a Romanized version of Mandarin. It is hoped this will facilitate communication among various dialect groups.

This emphasis on Chinese led to a new Chinese afternoon paper being started in late 1980 by the publishers of the major daily *Nanyang Siang Pau*. Only a few years previously, the consensus in Singapore and other Southeast Asian countries was that the Chinese press was in decline. The new paper, *Kuai Bao*, hopes to capitalize on steadily rising affluence and literacy in Mandarin Chinese, and the fact that almost 90 percent of the adult population read at least one paper daily, with many reading at least two.

During the first part of the 20th century, many of the revolutionary battles occurring in China were fought out in the pages of Chinese newspapers throughout the overseas Chinese communities in Southeast Asia. Each faction founded papers to promote their cause. Although now independent, one daily's nameplate bears the calligraphy of Chiang Kai-shek.

The two main Chinese dailies today are *Nanyang Siang Pau (Nan Yang Shang Bao)* and the *Sin Chew Jit Poh (Xing Zhou Ri Bao)*. *Sin Chew* has a circulation of 111,000 and 55 percent of the adult Chinese readership, while *Nanyang* has a circulation of 85,000 and 44 percent of the readership. Both papers run Sunday editions whose circulations are slightly higher. Both are morning broadsheet journals averaging about 30 pages in the daily editions. The Sunday editions have pictorial supplements. These papers are traditional and noted for their coverage of international affairs and financial matters.

The remaining two Chinese papers are growing faster than either *Nanyang Siang Pau* or the *Sin Chew Jit Poh*. The tabloid *Shin Min Daily News (Xin Ming Ri Bao)* and *Min Pao Daily (Min Bao Ri Bao)* with circulations of 81,000 and 41,000 respectively, are gaining significant proportions of readers through an emphasis on crime, violence and sex. They have nearly one-third of the Chinese readership.

While papers of other linguistic groups are read mainly within their homogeneous ethnic communities, English papers are read by people of all language groups.

English-language papers on the island are all published by the Straits Times Group. The flagship is the morning broadsheet-size *Straits Times*, with a circulation of 200,000; the afternoon paper, the *New Nation*, has a circulation of 40,000. About half of the newspaper-reading adults read one of these papers. Both the *Straits Times* and the *New Nation* have Sunday editions. A more recent arrival (1976) is the specialized *Business Times*. In 1980 a "new concept in reading" was started: the *Singapore Post*—an English-language tabloid published twice a week with local poetry, features, and news of movie personalities.

The Straits Times Group also publishes the sole Malay-language paper—*Berita Harian*, and its Sunday edition, *Berita Minggu*. The daily circulation of *Berita Harian* is 30,000, reaching slightly less than 10 percent of the reading public.

Indian readers have either the Tamil-language daily *Tamil Murasu* or *Malaysia Malayali*, the Malayalam-language paper. In 1980 another Tamil paper, *Tamil Malar*, suspended publication for financial reasons. The circulation of *Tamil Murasu* is 8,000 with 800 for *Malaysia Malayali*.

On the larger papers, the quality of journalism is quite high. With the deemphasis on the various Chinese dialects and a strong push behind Mandarin, these papers are rapidly dispensing with use of colloquial dialect expressions.

The Chinese press has been in the forefront of layout and typographical changes. In 1974, both major Chinese papers began using 2,248 simplified Chinese characters, and in 1979 both initiated a horizontal layout, reading left-to-right, and putting the front page where one would expect to find it on an English paper. In Singapore, the latter papers emulate the appearance and layout of the popular press in England.

Singapore's most influential paper remains the *Straits Times* since, as an English-language daily, it is the one read by people from all linguistic groups, although it does not carry the ethnic or cultural flavor of the vernacular papers. On the other hand, the Chinese papers do a better job of covering local news and analyzing contemporary issues.

Nanyang Siang Pau and *Sin Chew Jit Poh*, in cooperation with three local banks, have registered a company to start a morning English-language daily to compete with the *Straits Times.* Tentatively named the *Chronicle,* it is expected to begin publishing in 1981, and will enable the backers to compete for advertising revenue. It is estimated that two-thirds of the advertising revenue for newspapers is spent in English-language papers—all owned by the Straits Times Group.

Almost half of Singapore's reading public never, or rarely, reads magazines. Of the remainder who do, about half read entertainment periodicals. The two dominant magazine publishers are Times Periodicals, part of the Straits Times Group, and MPH Magazines. The main confrontation of these two publishers is in the women's field. Times Periodicals publishes *Her World* which competes with MPH's *Female.* Both have circulations around 20,000. Times Periodicals also produces, among others, *Fanfare,* directed to the younger entertainment audience, along with *Singapore Business* and *The Straits Times Annual.* MPH publications include *Living* and a Chinese-language monthly for women entitled *Petticoat.*

Economic Framework

Singapore's economy, though almost completely dependent on imported goods, continues to have a relatively low rate of inflation with increasing productivity. In 1978, the government launched a new economic policy that would put less emphasis on imported workers from nearby countries, while stressing the need for a reindustrialization plan. This was further defined in 1980 when the prime minister in his National Day speech to the nation called for a commitment to making Singapore an "information and knowledge center."

Newspaper readership has continued to grow, with 88 percent of literate adults reading a daily paper. Television viewing grew rapidly until 1977 and then leveled off, while radio listenership has remained relatively static. Cinema attendance has continued to increase slightly each year.

The Straits Times Group dominates the publishing field. Not only does it publish newspapers and a variety of monthly magazines, but it also has interests in other regional papers such as the *Borneo Bulletin, The Asia Magazine, New Straits Times* (Malaysia), the *Bangkok Post* and the *Asian Wall Street Journal.* Through the Dow Jones organization, the group also has financial links with the *Far Eastern Economic Review,* the *Business Times of Malaysia,* and the *South China Morning Post* in Hong Kong. The group has further expanded to include joint ventures from Oman to New Zealand and Australia, dealing in commercial printing, book distribution, music cassette production and real estate.

The two Chinese papers have travel agency subsidiaries, and *Sin Chew Jit Poh* began publishing a business magazine in Chinese in July 1980.

Distribution of newspapers is by small vendors operating sidewalk stalls. It is estimated that only 15 percent of the copies are home-delivered.

Most newsprint is imported from Canada, the remainder from Scandinavia and New Zealand. The 1980 price was $490 per ton.** There is no restriction on newsprint importation.

Singapore has not had a major strike or work stoppage in recent years. The Singapore National Union of Journalists is patterned after British journalists unions, but in the last several years no strikes have occurred, although industrial actions have been called for.

The total number of working journalists is estimated to be 900. A university graduate with no experience can expect to start working on one of the larger papers with a salary of about $1,000 a month, including bonuses and transportation allowance. Wages on all newspapers increased 20 percent in 1980 on the recommendation of the National Wages Council.

The daily *Straits Times, Tamil Murasu* and *Berita Harian* sell for 12 cents, the two large Chinese papers for about 20 cents; these prices reflect a 33 percent increase in 1980 and a doubling of the 1974 price.

All major papers are now printed by offset, the smaller ones still by letterpress. The Straits Times Group utilizes electronic copy for all its newspapers. On the large Chinese papers, repro proofs are pulled and page negatives shot. Chinese typewriters are used for some classified ads and non-time-sensitive features. The Chinese papers are rapidly upgrading their printing facilities to remain competitive with each other. *Nanyang Siang Pau* installed a 60,000-copy-hour press in

---

**In this chapter, all Singapore currency was converted at the rate of $US1=$S2.10.

1979 to allow them to print later, and *Sin Chew Jit Poh* has ordered a major new press line to be installed in late 1981.

Singapore is one of the major advertising centers in Asia, with over 40 agencies. Together, they handled a total billing of $87.3 million in 1979, an increase of 63% since 1977. As a share of GNP, ad expenditures have been estimated at one percent, equal to that of West Germany. Advertising expenditures in the print media alone totaled $66.5 million.

Press Laws

The primary law governing newspapers is The Newspaper and Printing Presses Act of 1974. This act requires every printing to be registered and that the owner apply for an annual license. Further, the publisher of any newspaper must be a company in which all directors are Singapore citizens, and for which two kinds of shares—management and ordinary—are issued. At least one percent of the shares must be management shares, which are equal to 200 votes in any election of directors or staff; owners of management shares require approval by the minister of culture. (An amendment to the act in 1977 made it illegal for any one shareholder to own more than three percent of the company.) Nor may a newspaper company accept any foreign funds, except for bona fide commercial purposes without the minister's approval. Every newspaper must apply for an annual permit to publish, which may require a bond; the government may withdraw the permit at any time if it is shown the newspaper is not in accord with the law. Newspapers printed in Malaysia must apply for a special permit to circulate in Singapore.

The law also provides for fines and/or imprisonment for persons printing, selling, distributing, or possessing an unlicensed paper.

Under The Essential (Control of Publications and Safeguarding of Information) Regulation, the government can decide what may be printed. In 1969, this act was used to prevent discussion in print of the government decision to abolish jury trials for capital offenses. In 1973 an editor of *Nanyang Siang Pau* was fined for publishing some letters to the editor from servicemen without the prior consent of the Ministry of Defense. In 1977 Ho Kwon Ping, Singapore correspondent of the *Far Eastern Economic Review,* was found guilty of "disseminating protected information" in an article on the manufacture and export of M-16 rifles and the purchase of secondhand boats from the United States. He was fined $3,600. But this was not the end of it. Under the Internal Security Act (ISA) a person may be detained almost indefinitely without being brought to trial. A month after being found guilty of the above charge, Ho was detained under the ISA on charges of writing "falsehoods" and "pro-communist ideas." He was released unconditionally after two months.

Concurrent with Ho's detention, another correspondent, Arun Senkuttuvan of the London *Financial Times* and *The Economist,* was also detained under the ISA. He was released after two months and deprived of his Singapore citizenship. Said Zahari, editor of the Malay-language *Utusan Melayu* in Singapore in the early 1960's, was released from detention in 1979 after being held under the ISA for nearly 16 years. No trial was held and Said refused to sign any confession. In 1974 a freelance *Newsweek* correspondent, *Newsweek's* Singapore distribution manager and the company handling the magazine's retail sales were fined for allegations against officials, and held in contempt of court, for an article written in New York based on material furnished by the Singapore correspondent.

Censorship

The task of censoring and controlling the distribution and sale of undesirable publications, films and videotapes falls to the Ministry of Culture under the Undesirable Publications Act and the Cinematograph Act, the government being "responsible in upholding the moral standards of the society and in preventing its erosion by decadence and permissive values." Violence, sex and scenes offending the racial or religious sensitivities of Singapore's multi-ethnic society are cut. "Yellow culture"—the culture of the West—advocating hippyism, drug abuse, and permissiveness, is also censored. Advertisements for proprietary medicines are screened as well. Advertising promoting smoking is banned from all media.

In 1979, 76,346 publications were submitted for examination and 391 were banned on moral grounds; at the same time 1,300 films were presented for examination and 4.5 percent banned. About one-third passed only with cuts required on moral, violent, political, or ethnic grounds. At the same time, photography books with nudes, which would have been banned a decade earlier, were passed, as were novels such as *Lady Chatterley's Lover.*

In January 1980 two Chinese papers, the *Min Pao Daily* and the *Shin Min Daily News,* were denied a publishing permit for eight days. Subsequently, the permits were renewed for three months, rather than the normal one year, after the papers pledged not to continue to play up crime, sex and violence.

State-Press Relations

No administrative rules exist to restrict officials from talking to the press and each department has a public relations officer to help the journalist gather information and to help set up interviews. Neither the social or political traditions, however, support extensive information-gathering activity.

The Information Division of the Ministry of Culture is responsible for accrediting correspondents and journalists, releasing government statements and advance copies of speeches by officials, and arranging interviews with high-ranking members of the government.

The right to criticize the government must be seen in the light of what the government, and many Singaporeans, see as the legitimate role of the press: a partner in Singapore's development. The press is seen primarily as an institution to help in the many campaigns to change Singapore: to save water, be courteous, or limit the size of families.

The government sees little need for newspapers to reflect the needs and desires of the people. Members of Parliament are expected to meet with their constituents once a week and each community center has party branches; thus it is felt that there is minimal necessity for the newspapers to investigate and criticize. In recent years, however, more criticism has been seen in print. Letters to the editor have greatly improved in quality and are softly voicing objections to lower-level government servants and the younger politicians.

Some things are still avoided by writers and editors: military secrets, personal attacks on Prime Minister Lee Kuan Yew and stories that might stir up racial or religious feelings.

The decade opened, however, with major attacks against the press. In 1966, the tabloid *Eastern Sun* started publishing in Singapore. It had financial troubles from the start and Lee Kuan Yew felt that after the split between Singapore and Malaysia, the paper's reporters were more loyal to the latter. *Eastern Sun* was finally forced to close in 1971, when it was found to have been importing newsprint from North Korea and was accused of taking a loan from communist sources in Hong Kong at low interest.

In 1971 the government moved against *Nanyang Siang Pau* under the Internal Security Act. Four senior executives, the editor in chief, chief editorial writer, general manager and a public relations officer were detained without trial. The last of the eight was released in 1973. They had been accused of glamorizing communism—even though two were bitterly anti-communist as well as members of the Kuomintang—and of stirring up racial issues.

About the same time the "*Herald* Affair" began. The *Singapore Herald* was started in 1970 with a circulation of 12,500. When it ceased publishing in 1971 its circulation was 50,000. The paper was accused of taking money from hostile forces outside the republic. The government forced the Chase Manhattan Bank in Singapore to foreclose on loans they had made to the *Herald,* and with the paper in shaky financial condition, its license to publish was revoked.

In 1976 the editor of the Malay-language *Berita Harian* and his assistant were detained under the ISA. They later "confessed" to "putting Communism in a favorable light" and implicated the managing director of the *New Straits Times* in Malaysia as the mastermind of the scheme.

Attitude Toward Foreign Media

Foreigners desiring to be accredited as correspondents in Singapore must furnish a letter from their employer and apply to the Immigration Department for an employment pass and a one-, two-, or three-year visa. In addition to the letter from the employer, the applicant must furnish either a local sponsor or a bank guarantee. The sponsor may be a local newspaper. This process may take several weeks, but it can be handled before arrival in Singapore. Applicants from communist countries are dealt with on a government-to-government basis.

After the visa is issued, the correspondent

applies to the Press Liaison Officer in the Information Division of the Ministry of Culture for accreditation. This accreditation allows the correspondent access to non-public areas and a box in the press office, where the reporter or photographer will receive government releases and announcements.

There are 650 accredited writers or photographers in Singapore. This figure does not distinguish between local and foreign correspondents, but in 1980 about 65 foreign correspondents were accredited. Most cover the region, not only Singapore. If the correspondents do not need the services of the Information Division, no accreditation is required. Several hundred correspondents, not permanently based in the country, file stories or photographs from Singapore every year.

Among the media organizations represented are: *Asahi Shimbun, Sekai Nippon, Yomiuri Shimbun, The Age* of Melbourne, *The Sydney Morning Herald, The Hindu, The Asian Wall Street Journal, Far Eastern Economic Review, Christian Science Monitor, Asiaweek, Daily Telegraph* (London), *The Observer* (London), *Stern* magazine, *The Times* (London), The Australian Broadcasting Commission, The British Broadcasting Corporation, Nippon Hoso Kyokai (NHK), SWF Broadcasting Corporation (Vienna), Visnews and the State Committee for Television and Radio of the USSR. No prior approval is required to send cables.

Correspondents are rarely denied visas. A Radio Australia correspondent whose visa to work in Indonesia was not renewed was also denied a visa for Singapore. The government apparently did not want to give sanctuary to someone who had offended one of the country's neighbors.

No foreign journalists have been jailed although several have been banned or expelled. In the aftermath of the "*Herald* Affair," several journalists were not allowed to remain. The *Herald's* expatriate foreign editor and features editor were forced to leave, and the visa for a freelance correspondent of the *New York Times* was not renewed.

Also following the *Herald* episode, foreigners may not own Singapore newspapers. Any income to a newspaper from a foreign source is required to be reported.

The Controller of Undersirable Publications examines foreign newspapers and magazines. Those advocating communism, inciting religious or social animosity or judged to be obscene are confiscated and destroyed. Publications may be banned for general use, but exempted for personal use or research.

News Agencies

Singapore has no domestic news agency. Newspapers are free to subscribe to their agency of choice. None of the international agencies furnish computer-compatible files to newspapers in Southeast Asia.

Although Singapore does not have some of the advantages of Hong Kong, more correspondents are being Singapore-based to cover the Southeast Asia region, since Singapore has good airline connections to all the Far East. Agencies represented on the island include Reuters, United Press International, Associated Press, Agence France Press, Tass, Kyodo News Service, Jiji Press, Pan-Asian Newspaper Alliance, Algemeiner Deutscher Nachrichtendienst, Deutsche Presse Agentur, Central News Agency (Taiwan) and United News of India.

Electronic News Media

In February 1980 broadcasting was changed from a division within the Ministry of Culture to a statutory body, with a governing board appointed by the Ministry of Culture. This new Singapore Broadcasting Corporation (SBC) is supported by advertising and license fees. The government may also make grants to the corporation.

In 1980 there were 440,000 licenses for radios and 380,000 for television sets. However, the number of actual television and radio sets is greater since an annual radio license is good for any number of sets at the same address and a license for television also covers radios.

The radio service operates five independent, self-contained services, each catering to a particular linguistic section of the population. Programs are broadcast in Mandarin, Chinese dialects, English, Tamil and Malay. The SBC has no world service.

SBC television operates on two channels, broadcasting in the four official languages. About 70 percent of the TV material is imported from England, Taiwan, Hong Kong, the United States and other countries. However, programs classed as "imported" may also be made locally, but not in the SBC studios.

A private, wired radio network is operated by Rediffusion Ltd. It has about 92,000 subscribers (1977). The British Broadcasting Corporation has a station on the island to relay the BBC World Service.

Generally, the same considerations that govern the content of print media are applied to the electronic media. All imported programs are previewed by a committee of censors composed of politicians, academics and members of the community. Censorship is stricter for television feature films than for cinemas: passionate kissing scenes and advertisements for ladies underclothes are not allowed to be shown on TV during the evening hours, when children might be watching.

Education & Training

At various times, education and training for journalists has been proposed for Singapore. Nanyang University once asked American professors to lecture on mass communications and propose a program, but no proposal was implemented. Shortly thereafter, Nanyang University—originally seen as a center of Chinese education in Southeast Asia when it was formed in 1956—merged with Singapore University to form the National University of Singapore, and all plans for mass-communications training were shelved.

However, the Straits Times Group has in-house courses and seminars for journalists, and the Asian Mass Communication Research and Information Centre (AMIC) was formed in 1971 to disseminate mass communication information and organize training programs. It conducts short courses and seminars in various countries throughout Asia; dealing with all media, these programs are directed to journalists, administrators or researchers.

Funded by the Friedrich-Ebert-Stiftung—a West German foundation—and the Singapore government, AMIC also publishes items of interest to mass communications experts, including a series of monographs and a bibliography series in addition to a quarterly journal, *Media Asia*.

The Singapore National Union of Journalists (SNUJ) is affiliated with the Confederation of ASEAN Journalists, composed of journalists from the ASEAN countries of Thailand, Malaysia, Singapore, Indonesia and the Philippines. In 1978 the SNUJ started a periodical called *The Journalist (Wartawan)*.

A Singapore Press Club serves a social function for domestic and foreign journalists.

Summary

As an island nation, Singapore has a narrow media base, but very high penetration. It boasts one of the highest newspaper readerships in Asia, and with increased emphasis on both Mandarin and English, circulation will increase.

Newspapers are running items that might not have appeared a few years ago, as they now hire more formally trained journalists, while at the same time, the public is becoming a more discerning consumer of media. History and culture have produced a society more concerned with the overall welfare of the community than the rights of a single individual. This type of society expects a government to exert some control on the media.

The government is allowing a wider range of articles and publications to appear as it becomes more self-confident and local and regional stability increases. With a conscious and planned program to make Singapore an information and knowledge society, the need for a variety of publications will increase. Newspapers are beginning to run more articles by specialized writers and the public is seeing a greater variety of subjects covered.

However, in its desire to build a "Rugged Society," the government will only slowly loosen controls on the media.

Growing affluence means that more households will buy several papers, while language campaigns will guarantee some increase in sales. The forecast of the death of Chinese papers over the last decade was premature. English-language papers will remain a bridge between cultures, but the Tamil and Malay journals will have to fight to keep even the relatively small position they maintain at present.

CHRONOLOGY

1974 *Newsweek* correspondent guilty of contempt of court.

Newspapers and Printing Presses Act passed.

Newspapers begin using simplified Chinese characters.

1976 *Berita Harian* editors arrested.

1977 Correspondent for *Far Eastern Economic Review* arrested.

Financial Times correspondent arrested.

Amendment to 1974 Newspaper Act passed.

1979 *Utusan Melayu* editor released after 16 years' detention.

Chinese papers begin new layout style.

1980 *Min Pao Daily* and *Shin Min Daily News* suspended.

Kuai Bao, new paper, begins publication.

BIBLIOGRAPHY

AMIC Secretariat. *Mass Communication in Singapore: An Annotated Bibliography.* Singapore, 1977.

Amnesty International. *Report of an Amnesty International Mission to Singapore, 30 November to 5 December 1978.* London, 1980.

Byrd, Cecil K. *Early Printing in the Straits Settlements 1806-1858: A Preliminary Inquiry.* Singapore, 1970.

Careem, Nicky. "Newspapers Diversify to Maintain Profits." *Insight,* August 1980, pp. 16-19.

Chen Mong Hock. *The Early Chinese Newspapers of Singapore, 1881-1912.* Singapore, 1967.

Chen, Peter S. J. "The Case for a Fourth English Language Newspaper." *The Journalist (Wartawan)* (1979), pp. 18-23.

Cho Nan Sheng, ed. *Hsing Chou 50 Nien: 1929-1979* [Fifty Years of the Sin Chew Jit Poh]. Singapore, 1979.

"English is the Language for Success in Singapore." *Media,* May 1979, pp. 31, 33.

Gale, John. "IPI in Turbulent Assembly Calls for Singapore Probe." *Editor & Publisher,* 19 June 1971, pp. 14-15, 21.

Kuo, Eddie C. Y. "Multilingualism and Mass Media Communications in Singapore." *Asian Survey,* October 1978, pp. 1067-83.

Lau Teik Soon. "Singapore and Political Stability." *Pacific Community,* January 1972, pp. 378-88.

Lee Kuan Yew. "The Mass Media and New Countries." *Asia Pacific Record,* June 1971, pp. 15-18.

Lent, John A. *Asian Mass Communication: A Comprehensive Bibliography and Supplement.* Philadelphia, 1975, 1978.

Parker, Elliott S., and Parker, Emelia M., *Asian Journalism: A Selected Bibliography of Sources on Journalism in China and Southeast Asia.* Metuchen, N.J., 1979.

Polsky, Anthony. "Lee Kuan Yew Versus the Press." *Pacific Community,* October 1971, pp. 183-203.

Roff, William R. *Bibliography of Malay and Arabic Periodicals Published in the Straits Settlements and Peninsular Malay States 1876-1941.* London, 1972.

Singapore. *The Newspaper and Printing Presses Act, 1974 (No. 12 of 1974).* Singapore, 1974.

Tay [Cheng], B. H. *Hsin-chia-p'o Hua Wen Pao Yeh Shih 1881-1972.* (History of Chinese Newspapers in Singapore, 1881-1972). Singapore, 1973.

Willer, Thomas F. "Perceptions of Women in Singapore: A Computerized Analysis of Newspaper Coverage." *Studies in Third World Societies,* December 1979, pp. 65-78.

SOUTH AFRICA

by John C. Merrill

BASIC DATA

Population: 28,096,000
Area: 1,222,480 sq. km. (488,992 sq. mi.)
GNP: R41 billion (US$50 billion) (1979)
Literacy Rate: 99% (white) 50% (black)
Language(s): Afrikaans, English, Bantu, Zulu
Number of Dailies: 23
   Aggregate Circulation: 1,728,000
   Circulation per 1,000: 66
Number of Nondailies: 7
   Aggregate Circulation: NA
   Circulation per 1,000: NA
Number of Periodicals: 200
Number of Radio Stations: 17

Number of Television Stations: 2
Number of Radio Receivers: 2.5 million
   Radio Receivers per 1,000: 89
Number of Television Sets: 1.5 million
   Television Sets per 1,000: 53
Total Annual Newsprint Consumption: 196,900 metric tons (1978)
   Per Capita Newsprint Consumption: 7.5 kg. (16.5 lb.)
Total Newspaper Ad Receipts: R121 million (US$146.4 million) (1979)
   As % of All Ad Expenditures: 28.4 (1979)

Background & General Characteristics

The first attempts at printing in South Africa were made in the late 18th century by Johann Christian Ritter, bookbinder of the Dutch East India Company who had a very simple press. When the British occupied the Cape in 1795, they brought with them the first printing press of any real size and significance. It was used to print an official weekly sheet called the *Cape Town Gazette and African Advertiser.* This paper lasted for 24 years.

What is usually considered the birth of the free press in South Africa took place in 1824 with the appearance of the *South African Commercial Advertiser,* edited by John Fairbairn and Thomas Pringle. It was a very outspoken paper for the time, and after only 18 issues it was silenced by the authorities. Although briefly reinstituted three years later, it did not last out the year. But while it lasted, it introduced the idea of free and critical journalism in South Africa.

Many newspapers and journals of widely different viewpoint and quality sprang up during the 19th century. These were mainly in Cape Town, and later, as white occupation expanded, in Natal, the Orange Free State and the Transvaal. A few of these old papers still exist—notable among them being *The Cape Times,* the oldest South African daily.

The first Dutch newspaper in the Cape was *De Verzamelaar,* a literary weekly, founded in 1826. A large number of Dutch journals were published in the Cape region during the 19th century, but most of them had very short lives. The first Afrikaans (a language similar to Dutch-German spoken by the non-British white citizens of the country) newspaper was also published at the Cape—*Die Afrikaanse Patriot,* edited by Rev. S. J. du Toit. It lasted from 1876 to 1904. The first magazine in the country was *The South African Journal,* published by Fairbairn and Pringle and begun the same year—1824—as the paper the two edited.

Early Johannesburg was the home of a number of newspapers, the first being *Digger's News* in 1886. *The Mining Argus* followed it. Then came others, most of them specializing in mining information.

After the Rebellion of 1914, when feelings were running high among the emerging Afrikaner nationalists, a Dutch-Afrikaans daily, *Die Burger,* appeared in Cape Town. It has always been a good newspaper, and even today is considered one of the best of the country's dailies and a significant one in the world context. It is the oldest of the Afrikaans dailies still publishing.

Since the 19th century press freedom has been especially important to South African journalists. It has been debated openly and often heatedly in the country. Despite the fact that various government actions in recent years have been used to control and punish the South African press, it continues to enjoy many traditional Western freedoms.

Despite these periodic government excesses and the normal economic problems faced by all press systems, the press of South Africa is healthy and vigorous. It has its problems, of course—economic and otherwise—but is generally one of substantial quality.

The main printing and publishing centers, as well as principal broadcasting outlets, are in or near Johannesburg, Cape Town and Durban. Broadcasting is highly developed and housed in modern facilities; all the main newspapers have well-equipped and modern buildings, with high-speed presses and color lithography machines.

Some 100 provincial or "platteland" papers are published in the countryside. A few are dailies and biweeklies, but most are weekly papers serving specific localities and covering local affairs. Most are bilingual and give little or no attention to political affairs of national scope. Friday is the favorite day of the week for their publication. Quality varies greatly, and many such publications are hardly more than one-person affairs. Others are part of newspaper groups and are more sophisticated. Some of these platteland papers have even formed modest groups of their own. A few of them, such as the *Paarl Post* and the *Graaff-Reinet Advertiser,* have long and colorful histories.

As in many countries the South African press comes in for much criticism of its foreign coverage. It is generally considered quite modest. The situation, however, is improving, and the serious papers of the country probably give their readers more foreign news than they want. The Argus Company, especially, has developed a strong foreign news network; this company also has done a great deal to collect and distribute much in-depth feature and interpretive material.

The Afrikaans newspapers have a modest corps of their own correspondents, but mainly rely on stringers who are growing in quality and prestige. Although there are some exceptions, layout in South African papers follows the British practice of flamboyant pages with typographical ornaments (borders around stories, etc.) and large pictures.

The English-language press has opposed the ruling National Party on many issues, particularly racial policy. The Afrikaans press has traditionally supported the National Party, to which it is bound by close political and language ties. Beginning in 1976, however, the editors of the Afrikaans papers began to speak out more critically about certain aspects of government policy. Political coverage in the so-called black press, which is white-owned, is increasing; and criticism of the government is becoming increasingly outspoken.

A majority of the leading newspapers are published by four press corporations: English papers by Argus Printing and Publishing Co. and South African Associated Newspapers, Afrikaans papers by Perskor and Nasionale Pers. The English-language papers have larger circulations than the Afrikaans-language papers because more blacks read the former and most papers aimed specifically at black readers are published in English. It should be added that far more Afrikaaners read English papers than the reverse. Although speakers of Afrikaans among the white South Africans clearly outnumber users of English, only seven dailies are published in Afrikaans, as against sixteen in English, including the four largest.

Johannesburg, the republic's largest city (some 1.5 million) and most important publishing center, has four English-language dailies and three in Afrikaans. Durban has two in English, and one in Zulu (the country's main African language). Cape Town has two in English and one in Afrikaans. Port Elizabeth has two in English, and one in Afrikaans. Pretoria, the administrative capital, has one in English and one in Afrikaans, and Bloemfontein, the chief city of the Orange Free State, also has one in each language.

About 115 nondaily, general interest newspapers appear once, twice or three times a week. The country's top circulation figure of 465,000 copies is held by a Johannesburg English-language Sunday paper *The Sunday Times.*

Twenty-three dailies, seven weeklies and 200 periodicals are published in South

South African Dailies by City and Circulation

Newspaper	Language	City	Circulation
Die Volksblad (e)	(Afrikaans)	Bloemfontein	27,000
The Friend (m)	(English)	Bloemfontein	7,000
The Argus (e)	(English)	Cape Town	100,000
Cape Times (m)	(English)	Cape Town	71,000
Die Burger (m)	(Afrikaans)	Cape Town	70,000
Daily News (e)	(English)	Durban	92,000
Ilanga (e)	(Zulu)	Durban	92,000
Natal Mercury (m)	(English)	Durban	64,000
Daily Dispatch (m)	(English)	East London	31,000
Star (e)	(English)	Johannesburg	170,000
Rand Daily Mail (m)	(English)	Johannesburg	130,000
Post (d)	(English)	Johannesburg	115,000
Die Transvaler (m)	(Afrikaans)	Johannesburg	83,000
Citizen (d)	(English)	Johannesburg	72,000
Die Vaterland (e)	(Afrikaans)	Johannesburg	65,000
Beeld (d)	(Afrikaans)	Johannesburg	64,000
Diamond Fields Advertiser (m)	(English)	Kimberley	8,000
Natal Witness (m)	(English)	Pietermaritzburg	18,000
Eastern Province Herald (d)	(English)	Port Elizabeth	28,000
Evening Post (e)	(English)	Port Elizabeth	24,000
Die Oosterlig (d)	(Afrikaans)	Port Elizabeth	11,000
Pretoria News (e)	(English)	Pretoria	28,000
Hoofstad (e)	(Afrikaans)	Pretoria	18,000

*e—evening, m—morning

Africa. The largest circulations are held by the Sunday papers of Johannesburg; the largest daily of the country, the *Star,* is also published in Johannesburg.

All major English-language newspapers are opposition-minded while all Afrikaans ones are NP-orientated. The press thus reflects more starkly than does the white electorate itself the parallel Afrikaans and British traditions in South African public life.

Afrikaans newspapers that have deviated too far from popular Afrikaner thinking, have seen a lingering death. Among the casualties have been famous old newspapers with roots in the 19th century *(Die Volkstem* in the Transvaal and *Ons Land* in the Cape). On

Major South African Weeklies by Circulation

Newspaper	City	Circulation
Sunday Times	Johannesburg	465,000
Rapport (Afrikaans)	Johannesburg	405,000
Sunday Tribune	Durban	130,000
Sunday Post	Johannesburg	125,000
Sunday Express	Johannesburg	92,000
Cape Herald	Cape Town	75,000
Post Natal	Durban	48,000

the other hand, English-language publications that have favored NP thinking, have by and large not been viable.

The Afrikaans market is being contested between the two Afrikaans publishing giants, the Cape-based Nasionale Pers and the Transvaal-based Perskor, which both also have large magazine and book-publishing interests in Afrikaans and English as well as in Bantu languages. Ironically, they own jointly, on a 50–50 basis, the sole and very successful Afrikaans Sunday newspaper, *Rapport,* with a circulation that trails closely that of the biggest English-language newspaper, the *Sunday Times,* and on one occasion exceeded it. *Rapport* is a 1971 amalgamation—after a tough circulation battle—of two Afrikaans Sundays, *Die Beeld* and *Dagbreek,* owned respectively by Nasionale Pers and Perskor.

Nasionale Pers, in the interests of its viability, then decided to invade the lucrative Transvaal market with a morning daily, *Beeld,* which began publishing in 1974 in an area where Perskor already had four newspapers: *Die Transvaler* (morning) and *Die Vaderland* (afternoon) in Johannesburg, and *Oggendblad* (morning) and *Hoofstad* (afternoon) in Pretoria.

The struggle, primarily waged between

Beeld and *Die Transvaler,* is estimated to have cost both firms unprecedented amounts already. It is revealing the true potential of Afrikaans newspaper readership in an area where Afrikaans circulations have lagged further behind English circulations for a much longer period than in the western Cape and the Orange Free State.

In the latter predominantly Afrikaans-speaking, province, *Die Volksblad* (Nasionale Pers) outstripped *The Friend* many years ago and now sells about four times as many copies. During the latter half of 1975 the Cape *Die Burger* (Nasionale Pers) drew level with its English morning rival of 60 years, *The Cape Times,* for the first time.

The combined circulations of the three Afrikaans morning newspapers in the Johannesburg-Pretoria region have attained a size similar to that of the *Rand Daily Mail,* a feat long considered beyond the reach of the Afrikaans newspaper industry.

By and large the Indian and "coloured"* communities tend to read the same publications as whites.

The *World* now banned, increased its circulation from about 77,000 in 1967 to nearly 160,000 in 1976. Its weekend companion sold more than 200,000 copies. *Llanga,* a Zulu-language biweekly in Natal, increased its circulation from 24,000 in 1967 to 82,000 in 1977. *Imvo,* a Xhosa–English-language publication based in King William's Town, has also shown a substantial increase—from 17,000 in 1967 to 57,000.

Catering especially for Cape "coloured" readers in so-called extra editions, *Rapport* and *Die Burger* have acquired an important readership in the Cape, the former claiming to have more "coloured" readers than any other publication. The "extra" circulation of the latter makes up almost 20 percent of its total sales and provides more than a third of its total readership.

These extra editions present essentially the same newspaper bought by the present general public, except that material of special group interest—mainly social and sports items—is added or substituted. The differentiation seems to be economically successful despite adverse political criticism.

Two Sunday newspapers already mentioned, dominate the South African circulation scene. The English-language *Sunday Times* and the Afrikaans-language *Rapport* between them have a circulation of about a million and an unduplicated readership of two million whites. These newspapers are read in about 75 percent of all white homes each week, as well as by a substantial proportion of blacks, Indians and "coloureds" in the main urban areas. Both tend to be popular and contain far less hard news than would be the case in many other countries. In addition to financial and business sections, general magazine sections and the main news section, both also cater to the special group interests of black and "coloured" readers.

Based on quality journalism, public service and defense of democratic principles, particularly in the face of increasing government intimidation, the *Rand Daily Mail* ranks among the leading newspapers of the free world. Operating in a racially divided society dominated by apartheid, the *Daily Mail* has, since its inception in 1902, spoken out for South Africa's black and minority populations. Of all the English-language papers it has the highest readership among South African blacks. The *Mail,* acting as the voice of liberal dissent, has consistently opposed apartheid and has won a reputation, and several awards, for excellent investigative reporting of such politically sensitive subjects as prison conditions and housing, educational and transportation arrangements affecting the nation's non-white populations.

In addition to its domestic coverage, the *Daily Mail* provides top-notch international reporting with a staff of full-time correspondents and stringers. The paper also uses wire, wirephoto and syndication services.

The high quality of the *Daily Mail* content is matched by that of its makeup, for which it has also received awards. It was the first South African newspaper to employ full-color news photography and advertising. The paper publishes in a 10-column broadsheet using a variety of horizontal and vertical patterns. Its circulation in the late 1970s was estimated at about 138,000.

South African newspapers are structured along British lines, which for historic reasons have exerted a far greater influence than either the Continental or the American press. They operate on the theory of a separation of powers between management and editorial, although the Afrikaans newspa-

---

*The term "coloured" is an official designation used to classify those of mixed race, most especially of mixtures of black, white or Indian blood.

pers, of which the oldest ones were originally established as journals of Afrikaner nationalist opinion, tend to show a closer link in political thinking between their two controlling elements than do most publications of the English-language press.

The two big Afrikaans groups both have cabinet ministers on their boards, a fact that exposes them to sporadic taunts of being a "kept" press. This unsatisfactory situation is rooted in political history and rivalry. The English-language press also knows cases where press barons with strong political views, or managements acting under political harassment have either dismissed or eased out editors who interpreted their autonomy rather too loosely.

During the last few years, with the NP's domination of Parliament appearing unassailable, Afrikaans editors in the Transvaal have become much more politically adventurous. Meanwhile some English-language editors have played a leading role in a successful Progressive Party (now Progressive Federal Party—PFP) assault against the traditional opposition leadership and policies of the United Party (UP).

The newspapers concerned reflect a frustration felt by many English-speaking, middle-class voters, among whom the cry for a "more dynamic opposition" heralded the growth of the Progressives from a one-woman party in Parliament before 1974 to a sizable band of 12 members in 1976. After the total collapse of the UP in 1977 and Sir De Villiers Graaff's resignation as opposition leader, the PFP won 17 seats in a general election in November, attaining the status of official opposition in a parliament of 165 members, of whom 13 belong to two other opposition groups and the rest to the governing party.

Despite varying opinions as to whether the final outcome will prove to be destructive or creative, this was indeed a formidable show of press power. Certainly the old opposition hegemony of the UP, closely cooperating with most English-language newspapers, was broken up completely.

Consumer magazines are an important element in the "big press" of South Africa. Many are tied to newspaper groups, cushioning the effect of ups and downs in the newspaper market itself. They are mainly glossy publications, ranging in price from 20 cents to R1,00 (U.S. 17 to 87 cents). By the middle of 1978 the apprehension felt over television's effect on advertising volume seemed amply

justified. Some papers had gone into the red as a result of revenues lost to television advertising. Fear of an extension of the present limit of five percent of viewing time and increased rates had galvanized the industry into energetic, although largely behind-the-scenes action.

At the same time television broadcasts are given extensive treatment as news by the whole of the press, and newspapers as well as magazines are competing for the favor of the viewing public by publishing program listings and background material.

Two of Perskor's consumer magazines have been converted into official television magazines by arrangement with the South African Broadcasting Corporation (SABC). Their preferential position regarding the publication of TV programs raised an outcry that has achieved some effect.

Overall, some thinning of the highly competitive and overpopulated consumer magazines market can probably be expected.

Economic Framework

In recent years the South African press has come to grips with the revolution in printing techniques that has shaken up the industry all over the world. Modern processes of photosetting, lithographic and gravure printing, and widespread use of color photography in the daily press now coexist with obsolescent letter-press printing in some fairly big urban plants and most small rural ones.

Printing, with its allied trades like bookbinding, has grown rapidly into a massive industry of about 1,000 firms employing about 30,000 people. The number of copies of newspapers printed has doubled since the mid-1950s, with a corresponding increase in the consumption of newsprint, which is wholly produced locally at an annual rate of about 180,000 tons. Financially, rapid cost inflation and recessionary tendencies in the national economy recently contributed to a rather grim outlook for some press concerns.

SAAN (South African Associated Newspapers) took the lead in converting to the "electronic journalism" of VDTs (video-display terminals) at its Johannesburg and Cape Town plants, eliminating the typesetter as well as the more recent perforator. Other newspaper companies are planning to follow suit, forseeing no serious clashes with the trade unions involved.

The last few years have seen important

takeover bids and amalgamations. The most notable success has been the acquisition of a whole range of magazines published by Republican Publications by the Afrikaans group, Perskor.

The most sensational failure was the attempt by an Afrikaner entrepreneur, Louis Luyt, in cooperation with the then leader of the opposition, Sir De Villiers Graaff, to gain control of SAAN, publishers of an important chain of dailies and Sundays that had long been sharply critical of Sir De Villiers's party and policies.

Subsequently, in September 1976, Luyt launched his own daily newspaper on the Rand, named *The Citizen*, taking a political line described as "moderate, centrist and conservative." Another newspaper in that crowded market, and one pursuing a more sympathetic course as regards government policies than the rest of the English-language press, naturally raised intense curiosity and speculation. *The Citizen* was sold by Luyt to largely undisclosed interests during the first half of 1978. Although its circulation has burgeoned its long-range viability will probably remain a matter of debate for some time.

In respect of corporate control, South African dailies and Sundays are well organized into groups that have grown mainly by way of takeovers. Newspaper groups became both functional and economic necessities as the press became big business. The pioneer in this respect (and still the pacesetter) has been the Argus Company, which dominates the English-language market in South Africa economically and, through an associate company, the Rhodesian market even more completely.

The size of the country—1,800 km separating the main centers of Cape Town and Johannesburg—still precludes national dailies. The only really national newspapers are the two Sundays, *Sunday Times* and *Rapport*, both published simultaneously in various cities, using the printing facilities of related dailies. But even the Sundays cater to regional and group interests with differentiated editions.

Mainly on account of the language situation, a system of quasimonopoly over large areas of the newspaper press exists. In general no newspaper faces direct competition in the same language at the same time and place. The exceptions are the Sunday field to a limited extent, and the Afrikaans and English morning press in the southern Transvaal.

The two directly competing English Sunday papers in Johannesburg, *Sunday Times* and *Sunday Express,* are controlled by one group, SAAN, but they also face some competition from the Argus Group's Natal-based *Sunday Tribune. Rapport* is alone in the Afrikaans field.

In the southern Transvaal the *Rand Daily Mail* competes with *The Citizen; Die Transvaler* competes with *Beeld* and to some extent with its own sister, *Oggendblad*, in Pretoria. The two Afrikaans afternoons, *Die Vaderland* (Johannesburg) and *Hoofstad* (Pretoria), belong to the same group and maintain a profitable link-up in advertising.

The major South African press groups are:
• The Argus Printing and Publishing Company: *The Star*, Johannesburg (sole English-language afternoon); *The Daily News,* Durban (sole afternoon); *The Argus,* Cape Town (sole afternoon); *Diamond Fields Advertiser,* Kimberley (sole daily); *The Friend,* Bloemfontein (sole morning); *Pretoria News* (with SAAN minority shareholding), Pretoria (sole English-language afternoon); *Sunday Tribune,* Durban; *Post* (new daily after the banning of *The World*) and *Ilanga* (bi-weekly), specifically for blacks; *The Cape Herald,* Cape Town (weekly), for "coloureds."

The Argus Group also has a minority shareholding in the SAAN Group. An attempt at a complete takeover in 1973 was thwarted by a government warning to the effect that this would be intolerably monopolistic and could precipitate legislation along British lines.

• Nasionale Pers: *Die Burger,* Cape Town (sole Afrikaans morning); *Beeld,* Johannesburg (Afrikaans morning); *Die Volksblad,* Bloemfontein (sole afternoon); *Oosterlig,* Port Elizabeth (sole Afrikaans), and a half share in *Rapport*. It also controls a family of magazines including *Huisgenoot, Sarie Marais, Fair Lady, Landbouweekblad, Bollie* and *Topsport*.

• Perskor: *Die Transvaler* (Afrikaans morning) and *Die Vaderland* (sole Afrikaans afternoon), Johannesburg; *Oggendblad* (sole Afrikaans morning) and *Hoofstad* (sole Afrikaans afternoon), Pretoria; *Tempo* (Durban) and several country papers. It has a half share in *Rapport*. Among the other papers and magazines in the Perskor fold are the weekly *Financial Gazette,* two papers for blacks—*Bona* and *Imvo*—*Rooi Rose, Darling, Farmer's Weekly, South African Garden and Home, Charmaine, Keur, Kyk, Living and*

Loving, and two radio and television magazines.

• SAAN: *Rand Daily Mail,* Johannesburg (English morning); *The Cape Times,* Cape Town (sole English morning); *Sunday Times; Sunday Express; Financial Mail* (weekly). SAAN has the controlling interest in Eastern Province Newspapers Limited, which publishes the *Eastern Province Herald* (sole morning), *Evening Post* (sole English afternoon) and *Weekend Post,* all at Port Elizabeth. It also has a one-third holding in *The Natal Mercury,* Durban (sole morning).

The distribution and sale of newspapers in a far-flung country like South Africa present special problems of organization as well as of finance. The cost of circulation forms a much more substantial part of general publication costs than in most European countries.

In the cities newspapers rely heavily on street sales and house-to-house delivery, largely by schoolboys; but cafés and general dealers' stores provide additional selling points, with postal delivery declining in importance. Distribution outside the cities is maintained by railway and special truck services, often covering hundreds of kilometers on a single run. The cost of bulk transport by air is generally prohibitive.

Much of the distribution of newspapers is undertaken by the Allied Publishing Company, owned by a consortium of some of the media owners. It commands a nation-wide distribution network and mainly distributes the English-language papers. The Afrikaans press groups, Nasionale Pers and Perskor, handle most of their distribution themselves.

The advertising industry in South Africa can hold its own with those of most free-enterprise countries. Until 1978, when TV advertising came into being, the principal channels for advertising were radio, newspapers, magazines, the cinema, posters and direct mail. Advertising expenditures have risen constantly and rapidly in South Africa: from R 140 million ($161 million) in 1970 to R 325 million ($374 million) in 1977, and to nearly R 400 million ($460 million) in 1980.

Advertising has been controlled voluntarily since 1945. Through the NPU and the Association of Accredited Practitioners in Advertising all print media have a code of control that makes it possible for undesirable or untruthful advertising to be removed quickly. The SABC has equally effective controls over the airwaves. In addition, advertisers have created the ASA (Advertising Standards Authority), comparable to the one in Britain. Through its committees, the ASA has control over all South African advertising, and usually its request to a medium that an advertisement be removed is heeded.

In South Africa there are some 50 advertising agencies, some of them partly owned by international agencies. South African agencies have available to them regular media research data, and can supply any form of market data asked of them. This market research in South Africa costs much the same as it does in any other country.

The South African market is very diverse, and this makes great demands on the agencies' creativity as advertising must fit the needs and expectations of many different groups scattered throughout the country.

A tremendous amount of advertising is concentrated in South African Sunday newspapers and other large-circulation dailies. This usually results in mammoth editions where editorial matter is forced to trickle like tiny streams through vast areas of advertising. On the average, however, the South African newspaper has to carry 50–60 percent advertising in order to be viable. (Most dailies run from 20 to 36 pages.)

As in other areas of South African life, trade unions in the industrial sector are segregated. The major journalists' union is the South African Society of Journalists, with some 600 members. There is only limited unionization in the black and "coloured" press.

Press Laws

Under the terms of the Newspaper and Imprint Registration Act (No. 63 of 1971), any person intending to print and publish a newspaper in South Africa or SWA/Namibia at intervals not exceeding one month, must apply to the Secretary for the Interior, Pretoria, for the registration of such a newspaper. A fee of R5,00 ($5.75) must accompany each application.

In addition to the usual common law checks on the press there are statutory restraints in certain prescribed fields. Thus sections 118 and 119 of the Defence Act (No. 44 of 1957) prohibit the publication of certain specified information and photographs that have a bearing on the defense of the country. Similarly section 44 of the Prisons Act (No. 8 of 1959) prohibits the publication of certain specified information regarding prisons and prisoners.

Section 6 of the Public Health Act (No. 36 of 1919) requires that all proceedings related to venereal disease before any court of law shall be in camera, and section 65 of the act prohibits the publication of advertisements for sexual stimulants or cures for venereal disease.

Section 6 of the Internal Security Act (No. 44 of 1950) (orignally enacted as the Suppression of Communism Act) prohibits, in summary, the publication of any periodical or other publication that professes, by its name or otherwise, to propagate communism, or which is published or disseminated by or under the direction of any organization that has been declared an unlawful organization under section 2 of the same act, or which serves to express views or convey information calculated to further the achievement of any of the objects of communism, or which is a continuation or substitution, whether or not under another name, of any periodical or other publication, the printing, publication or dissemination of which has been prohibited under this section of the act.

Newspapers may not quote a "listed" person without the permission of the Minister of Justice, a "listed" or "banned" person being one whose freedom of political action has been curtailed for a certain period. Several hundred people fall into this category.

In court cases dealing with sexual transgressions, publication of the names of complainants and minors is prohibited under certain laws. In some cases the magistrate or judge has the discretion to prohibit publication of the entire proceedings.

The Publications and Entertainments Act is designed to control magazines, books, films and public entertainments. Newspapers that are members of the NPU are specifically excluded from its provisions.

Prior to 1963 there was no control over the distribution of undesirable publications, but control was exercised over the importation of such material through customs and excise legislation. The Publications and Entertainments Act was adopted by Parliament in 1963 to control the distribution and exhibition of indecent, obscene or offensive publications, objects, films and public entertainments. Such publications or objects were prohibited if they were found to be undersirable by the Publications Control Board or a court of law.

This act was superseded by the Publications Act of 1974. A Directorate of Publications was established, consisting of a chairman with legal background known as the director of publications, and a deputy director with a maximum of three assistant directors, appointed by the Minister of the Interior and selected for their educational qualifications and experience.

The directorate appoints local committees to assist it. Advisory committees for "coloureds" and Indians are also provided.

An appeal against the decisions of the Directorate of Publications no longer falls to the courts. Instead, a Council of Appeal has been established consisting of at least three members under a chairman with a legal background.

The act states that no person shall produce or distribute a publication if it has been declared undesirable in a notice in the *Government Gazette*. All films must be submitted to committees of the directorate, which may prohibit such films either completely or in part. The committees are also empowered to prohibit any public entertainment or order parts of it to be cut.

The term "undesirable" is defined as follows: publications, objects, public entertainments or parts thereof that are indecent or obscene or offensive or harmful to public morals; that are blasphemous or offensive to the religious convictions of any one of the population groups; that present any section of the population in a ridiculous or contemptible manner; that are harmful to sound relations among the various population groups; and that are prejudicial to the safety of the state, the general welfare and peace and good order in the community.

In terms of the act the director of publications has the power, for instance, to grant exemptions to students to use banned publications and to film societies to screen banned films.

The penalty for a first offense is a maximum fine of R500/($575) or imprisonment for six months. The penalties for a second or subsequent offense are much heavier.

The Afrikaans- as well as the English-language press has opposed government efforts to further restrict reporting. Provisions in the 1979 Advocate General Bill that would have limited reporting of government corruption were dropped in 1980 after a strong protest from most major newspapers.

Censorship

The South African press constitutes one of the few collective mass media on the continent that can be described as "free" in the

Western sense. The simple and acid test is, of course, whether press freedom is being *openly* debated at all. In South Africa the debate is both vigorous and perennial.

It reached a dramatic climax in the early months of 1977, when the government produced a press bill that immediately had all newspapers, including those supporting the NP, up in arms. On paper the proposals hardly seemed to call for such a stormy reaction. They envisaged the establishment of a statutory press board to supplant the one created by the industry itself, a widening of the Press Code, and as an ultimate sanction, the closing down of erring newspapers after due process. The government's case boiled down to the proposition that self-discipline by the press had not worked. After a few anxious and turbulent weeks of controversy and negotiation between representatives of the press union and the govenment, the bill was withdrawn for a year on condition that the press put its house in order. In practice this amounted to a strengthening of the press code, a speeding up of press board procedures, and public representation on the board, without affecting its status as an institution of the press, and not of the state. At the same time the prime minister administratively created a one-person secretariat for handling press affairs, including public and government complaints concerning the press.

Thus was averted, on the one hand, what some saw as the thin end of the wedge of state control, and on the other, what many had come to regard as increasing and intolerable license on the part of sections of the press in matters touching the safety and very existence of this besieged social system.

In the second half of 1977 a new storm involving the press arose as a result of drastic security action at a time of high tension in some black townships. Apart from the banning of a number of "black consciousness" organizations and the "preventive detention" of certain individuals the government suppressed Johannesburg's main newspapers for blacks, *The World* and *The Weekend World,* and locked up black editor Percy Qobosa. Donald Woods, editor of East London's *Daily Dispatch* was banned (silenced), as was Dr. Beyers Naudé of the Christian Institute, whose publication *Pro Veritate,* had to cease publication. Woods later left South Africa to join overseas campaigns for an economic boycott of the country, and Qobosa was eventually released. He has since become a *journaliste celébre* among critics of South Africa's apartheid racial policies.

These events impaired South Africa's image as a society enjoying a great measure of press freedom. Nevertheless there was little overt evidence during the following months of the opposition (English-language) press losing either ideological aggressiveness or investigative vigor.

State-Press Relations

The opposition press of South Africa is vigorous—especially at times—and carries much reporting and comment critical of basic government policies, especially material regarding separate development (*apartheid*) and the condition of the various racial communities. The South African press can, and does, criticize the government and is quite lively in its general social commentary.

The South African press exercises control over itself. The NPU in 1962 established the South African Press Council in consultation with the government, and in 1963 Parliament specifically excluded newspapers published by members of the NPU from the provisions of the Publications and Entertainments Act. Practically all newspapers in the country are published by members of the NPU.

One of the Press Council's functions is to hear and decide on complaints against the press in cases where the complainants have failed to obtain redress from newspapers or where they have no remedy in a court of law.

The council consists of a retired judge assisted by other members. Its constitution has been redrafted to ensure equal representation of the press and the public. It seeks to maintain high professional standards in newspapers and to deal with infringements of the voluntary press code of the NPU. The code stresses the freedom of the press as indivisible from that of the individual. It guards against departure from facts in reporting, distortion and significant omissions. It holds that accuracy should be checked within limits of practicability, that news reports should be free of slanting, that headlines should fairly reflect content, that posters should not exaggerate and that obscene and salacious reporting and presentation should be avoided.

The Press Code was amended in 1974 to compel newspapers to act in a responsible and cautious manner in matters that may engender feelings of hostility among the various racial, ethnic, religious and cultural groups in the country. In addition, the press must execute to the letter the agreements which the NPU has made with various departments of state, e.g., the South African Police.

The Press Council may impose a fine of up to R10,000 ($11,494) on newspapers that infringe the provisions of the Press Code. Until 1974 the only penalty was a public reprimand. During the first half of 1976 two fines were imposed.

Attitude Toward Foreign Media

There is no official attitude toward foreign media in South Africa, but the visitor quickly sees that nobody is quite satisfied with the coverage of South African news. The whites are, for the most part, convinced that foreign news coverage is biased against South Africa—or at least against its government—and that most news stories appearing in the foreign press are negatively loaded in almost every respect. The complaint is often heard from both the white nonjournalist and journalist alike that foreign journalists are not really interested in getting a balanced view of events or exploring the complexities of South African affairs. Rather they see the foreign press as exploiting minor incidents and complaints regarding blacks and "coloureds" and of encouraging radical elements in the country to violence. From time to time, certain issues of magazines such as *Time,* felt by the government to be biased or unfair to South Africa, are withheld from sale or certain stories are blotted out.

It is obvious that white government officials also have little regard for the way foreign journalists treat the country. Journalists from other countries who try to cover government activities in South Africa generally complain of government sensitivity, irritability, and secrecy. Foreign embassies—with a few exceptions—acknowledge the South African government's defensiveness and criticism.

The blacks and "coloureds," on the other hand, have their own criticism of the foreign press. They feel that it is too timid in its reporting of what they see as government excesses and the immoral aspects of apartheid. They see the press—especially the European and American segments—as pulling its punches, hiding much news and trying too hard to stay on the good side of

government officials. Therefore, it is difficult in South Africa to find anyone—in any sector of the country—who has a very good feeling about the foreign press.

The South African government spends a great deal of money and energy on propaganda both internal and external. A large number of publications are issued by various government departments and the Bureau of National and International Communication. The latter publishes more than 50 magazines and newspapers for all sections of the South African population and also for readers abroad.

There are 13 publications with a total circulation of 506,000 printed in 11 different Bantu languages for the various black peoples, one for the Indian community and two for the "coloureds"—one of which appears in Windhoek for the Rehoboth community of SWA /Namibia. *Progressus* has a circulation of 75,000 and is published in English and Afrikaans. These publications are mainly for internal distribution.

South African Panorama is an attractive, glossy magazine published in South Africa in English and Afrikaans. It has a wide South African circulation. In addition, some 96,000 English copies are earmarked monthly for the English-speaking world, while a further 136,908 copies are published in French, German, Spanish and Portuguese for Europe and South America. *South African Panorama* first appeared in 1956.

South African Digest, an illustrated weekly news magazine, has a print order of 118,000 and is mainly intended for overseas consumption. It first appeared in 1954 and reflects events throughout South Africa. Its Afrikaans counterpart, *Suid-Afrikaanse Oorsig,* has a circulation of 17,000.

One of the major goals of South African media policy is to influence public opinion in the United States and to support and promote a pro-apartheid press at home and abroad. Its covert operations in pursuit of these goals came into the open following a national scandal that led to the resignation of President John Vorster in 1979. The government commission headed by Judge Rudolf Erasmus documented the use of public funds to establish a pro-South African voice in the U.S media. It said that the South African government had lent John McGoff, a U.S. publisher $11.5 million to try to buy the *Washington Star.* When he failed, McGoff purchased the *Sacramento Union.* He was given an additional $1.35 million to buy 50% of UPITN, an international television news agency linked to UPI.

News Agencies

The South African Press Association (SAPA) is the national news agency of the country and operates in a fashion similar to the Associated Press of the United States. It is owned and operated as a non-profit organization by the main newspaper groups of South Africa. It was founded by them in 1938. Succeeding the Reuter South African Press Agency which had been the main news agency in the country from the time of its founding in 1910. Today SAPA supplies domestic and foreign news to all Sunday and daily papers of the country and to the national broadcasting services.

It receives its foreign news from AP and from Reuters—with which it has exchange agreements—by radio teleprinter from New York and London. SAPA also has special services that go to certain shipping companies for use at sea. The agency also provides its internal service to Agence-France Presse for use in its world service.

The news collected by SAPA comes from member newspapers, branch offices, correspondents in the country and in SWA/Namibia, Botswana, Swaziland, Lesotho, Zimbabwe and Mozambique. SAPA's headquarters are in Johannesburg and are linked with other South African cities and with Salisbury in neighboring Zimbabwe. It maintains branch offices in Cape Town, Durban, Pretoria, Bloemfontein and Umtata, and an overseas bureau in London.

Five important foreign news agencies are represented in South Africa. Reuters (U.K.) provides a special South African news service for the republic and neighboring countries and has bureaus in at least sixteen South African cities. Agence-France Presse (France) in Johannesburg, has a radio-teletype link with Paris and sends out some 30,000 words daily in English and French in addition to its African bulletins issued biweekly in English and daily in French. Both AP and UPI (U.S.) have bureaus in Johannesburg, as does Deutsche Presse-Agentur (West Germany).

Several foreign newspapers, as well as British and American television companies, have representatives in South Africa. British dailies especially give good coverage to South Africa. Major U.S. papers—*The Washington Post, The New York Times, The Los Angeles Times* and *The Christian Science Monitor*—as well as *Time* and *Newsweek* have correspondents or reporters based in South Africa. The U.S. newsmagazines are available on local newsstands.

Electronic News Media

South African radio and television are operated by the South African Broadcasting Corporation (SABC), a public corporation and the country's only broadcasting authority. Created in 1936, it provides internal radio services in several languages as well as Afrikaans and English. FM broadcasts from SABC reach practically the entire population. The SABC has an external service—Radio South African—that beams to Africa, Europe and North American in several languages. Its broadcasts total 156 hours a week.

SABC broadcasts 20 radio program services and two television services, totalling more than 2,000 hours a week in 24 languages. The corporation's programs are transmitted out of nearly 120 FM transmitters. Presently some 98 percent of the population has access to FM radio.

Closed-circuit television installations have existed in South Africa for some time; in 1976 a new public television broadcasting service came into being in both black-and-white and color. The service is noncommercial but has made time available for advertising. SABC-TV broadcasts five hours daily from 5:30 p.m. to 10:30 p.m., with programs divided equally between English and Afrikaans. In 1980 SABC-TV was planning the early inauguration of a separate channel for blacks.

More than 50 percent of all television programs presently broadcast are South African-produced, and among the nationally produced programs are news, drama, sports, actualities and children's shows. In their purchase of programs from abroad SABC's producers also give special emphasis to these programming areas.

South Africa has the largest television audience in Africa with more than 1.5 million licensed sets, surpassing Egypt which is now in second place. An estimated 3.5 million viewers watch South African television during the daily peak period. This is a considerable increase since 1976 when some one million persons in the country watched SABC's inaugural programs.

SABC's elaborate six-story television complex at Auckland Park covers 15 acres on the southern side of Johannesburg's Broadcasting Centre. It is equipped with the most modern equipment, and with transmitters that give TV coverage to 50 percent of the population. That coverage is being constantly expanded. South African television employs more than 1,000 people in various television disciplines.

Radio in South Africa is especially well-developed. SABC controls all radio broadcasting under policies directed by a board appointed by the president of the Republic. All income is derived from license fees and from advertising revenues drawn from the corporation's commercial services.

National services—in English and Afrikaans—are on the air for 17 hours a day with news, cultural programming and entertainment. The third national program, "Radio Springbok," is commercial and broadcasts only sponsored programs, news and advertising for 18 hours daily.

For its national and commercial radio services, SABC uses 70 medium-wave transmitters, 17 FM transmitters and 12 short-wave transmitters. Radio Bantu is SABC's special service in the seven main African languages. This service is provided almost entirely by a network of 78 FM stations grouped in nine areas of the country. These seven programs jointly total nearly 600 hours a week of news, talk, religious shows, school programs, drama, sports and programs for special age groups, etc. They reach an estimated four million listeners.

External broadcasting is operated by the Voice of South Africa from shortwave transmitters at Bloemendal in the Transvaal. Programs in nine languages are beamed to 23 different areas in Africa, Europe, the Middle East, Australia and New Zealand. The SABC is served by 40 foreign correspondents. News is also supplied by seven international news agencies. The SABC gives business news special priority.

Education & Training

The philosophy of journalism education in South Africa remains that of on-the-job training, much the same as it is in Britain. However, this is slowy changing. University courses in communication and journalism have proliferated in the past decade. The University of Potchefstroom has had a degree program in communications and press since 1960, and more recently many other universities are following suit.

The University of South Africa and the Rand Afrikaans University have recently set up communications departments. In 1970, Rhodes University (Grahamstown), set up journalism (three years) and visual communications programs as well as a diploma program in photography (one year). Journalism and communications courses are also offered at the University of Orange Free State (Bloemfontein) and at the Natal and Witwatersrand technological institutes. In 1978 the University of Stellenbosch began a postgraduate honors program in journalism.

Journalism education in universities, although expanding, is still viewed with considerable suspicion by many practitioners and academics in the Republic of South Africa. The majority of South African journalists and media workers, therefore, still get their necessary training by serving as apprentices and cub reporters for varying periods.

Increasingly, however, as communications programs improve in the universities and more and more university-trained journalists and communications workers are proving capable out in the field, the reputation of university programs is improving. Some of the world's outstanding scholar-teachers in journalism and communications now teach in South African universities.

Summary

In a country as volatile as South Africa it is very difficult to say much about the long-term future. Although South Africa still certainly possesses the freest press in Africa, it has not lived down certain actions taken against the press in the 1960s and 1970s. Since then, the press has had many skirmishes with the government—especially with Prime Minister Botha.

In spite of the great potential for press control—and some notable instances of it—the press of South Africa remains vital, energetic and critical—within the context of certain important taboos—such as racial apartheid and national security.

So, while in the area of substantial discussion of controversial issues and newspaper criticism of government activities the South African press must be considered relatively free, certain racial practices, that give very little voice to non-white opinion, make the whole issue of press freedom in South Africa questionable and suspect.

The short-term future of the country's communications industry, however, looks reasonably bright. Both the printed press and broadcasting are growing rapidly. Ever increasing numbers of the country's residents are being brought into the communications network. Barring revolutionary upheaval that will end the current social system, there is little reason to believe that South Africa's current communications enterprises will not continue to prosper. However there are many pressing concerns that South Africa will have to cope with during the remainder of the century. For good or bad and these developments cannot be viewed outside the context of the vast African continent—or even outside the context of the Western "developed" nations. The future of South Africa's press will depend largely upon these developments.

CHRONOLOGY

1971   South African government approves establishment of a television service.

1976   Television service in English and Afrikaans begins.

1977   In wake of Soweto riots government suppresses Johannesburg's main newspaper for blacks—*The World* and *Weekend World*—and bans certain journalists.

1978   Television advertising introduced.

1979   Prime Minister Botha withdraws certain legislation (Advocate General Bill) that offends press, bringing more peaceful and stable times to it.

BIBLIOGRAPHY

Ainslie, Rosalynde. *The Press in Africa*. London, 1966.

Barton, Frank. *The Press in Africa: Persecution and Perseverance*. London, 1979.

Broughton, Morris. *Press and Politics of South Africa*. Cape Town, 1961

Cutten, T.E.G. *A History of the Press in South Africa*. Cape Town, 1935.

DeVilliers, Rene M. "Freedom of the Press." *South African Outlook*.

———. *The Press and the People*. Johannesburg, 1968.

Dodson, Don. *Communications and Development: African and Anglo-American Parallels*. Lexington, Ky., 1973.

Doob, Leonard. *Communication in Africa*. New Haven, Conn. 1961.

First, Ruth. *Power in Africa*. New York, 1970.

Fischer, Heinz-Dietrich. *Die grossen Zeitungen: Portraets der Weltpresse*. Munich, 1966.

Hachten, William A. *Mass Communications in Africa: An Annotated Bibliography*. Madison, Wis., 1971.

———. *Muffled Drums: The News Media in Africa*. Ames, Iowa, 1971.

Head, Sydney W. *Broadcasting in Africa*. Philadelphia, 1974.

Information Service of South Africa. *South Africa 1979. The Official Yearbook of the Republic of South Africa*. Johannesburg, 1979.

Katzen, May. *Mass Communication: Teaching and Studies at Universities: A Worldwide Survey on the Role of Universities in the Study of Mass Media*. Paris, 1975.

Merrill, John C. *The Elite Press: Great Newspapers of the World*. New York, 1968.

———, Bryan, Carter, and Alisky, Marvin. *The Foreign Press*. Baton Rouge, La., 1970.

———, and Harold A. Fisher. *The World's Great Dailies: Profiles of 50 Newspapers*. New York, 1980.

Patel, D.B. "Mass Communications and Development of Africa" in *Africa in World Affairs*. Ed. Ali Mazuri and Hasu Patel. New York, 1973.

Potter, Elaine. *The Press as Opposition: The Political Role of South African Newspapers*. London, 1975.

Rosenthal, E. *Today's News Today: Story of the Argus Company.* Johannesburg, 1956.

Rubin, Barry. "The Uncertain Future of South Africa's Press." *Washington Journalism Review.* November 1980.

St. Leger, F.Y. "The African Press in South Africa." *Communications in Africa.* 1:1 (1972).

South Africa Foundation. *The Press.* Johannesburg, 1964.

South Africa. *Commission on Inquiry into the Press: Report.* Pretoria, 1964.

South Africa, Dept. of Information. *This is South Africa.* February 1978.

SPAIN

by Henry F. Schulte

BASIC DATA

Population: 37,774,000
Area: 505,050 sq. km. (191,919 sq. mi.)
GNP: Pts 9.28 trillion (US$142.3 billion)
Literacy Rate: 97%
Language(s): Spanish (Catalan, Galician, Valencian); Basque
Number of Dailies: 143
  Aggregate Circulation: 3.3 million
  Circulation per 1,000: 128
Number of Nondailies: 24
  Aggregate Circulation: 3.63 million
  Circulation per 1,000: 28

Number of Periodicals: 5,508
Number of Radio Stations: 442
Number of Television Stations: 60
Number of Radio Receivers: 9.3 million
  Radio Receivers per 1,000: 259
Number of Television Sets: 6,640,000
  Television Sets per 1,000: 185
Total Annual Newsprint Consumption: 221 metric tons
Per Capita Newsprint Consumption: 6 kg. (13.2 lbs.)
Total Newspaper Ad Receipts: Pts 1.94 billion (US$294.5 million) (1979)
  As % of All Ad Expenditures: 23 (1979)

Background & General Characteristics

Spain is divided into 50 provinces, including the Balearic Islands and the Canary Islands. The mainland falls into half a dozen regions, with somewhat different histories and traditions and, in some cases, very distinct languages. These regions include the Basque country, centered in northern Spain and extending to the French border; Catalonia, lying to the south and east of the Basque country and, in a sense, radiating out from Barcelona; Castile, the central part of Spain where Madrid is located; Galicia, lying to the north of Portugal; and Andalusia in the south.

Madrid, the nation's media capital as well as its political capital, has a population of about 4.5 million. That is expected to reach 8 million by the end of the century if Spaniards continue a two-decades-old process of deserting the rural areas for the larger cities.

Although Spain's literacy rate is 97 percent, newspaper circulation is comparatively low. At the beginning of the 1970s, 104 copies of newspapers were printed per 1,000 population. By the end of that decade the figure had dropped to 98 per 1,000.

Unlike some mass media systems, that of Spain in 1980 must be characterized as in flux or in transition. The death in November 1975 of Francisco Franco, Spain's dictator since 1936, had a profound effect on mass communications, particularly the print media. At first somewhat gradually, then with fewer and fewer inhibitions, the press tested its right to report openly and to criticize political institutions, political processes and political figures—rights denied to it during the Franco years. However, there still exist attitudes and laws that carried over from the Franco era—and which sometimes function not only as brakes on freedom but threats to those working in the media.

At the end of the 1970s, Spain had somewhere between 117 and 123 daily newspapers (depending on the agency doing the counting and the moment when count was taken), fewer than 100 traditional weekly newspapers and 30 *Hojas del Lunes.* (The *Hoja del Lunes,* a phenomenon unique to Spain, is circulated Monday morning by local journalists' associations—*Asociaciones de la Prensa* —which have monopoly rights to the Monday newspaper business. The *Hojas'* weekly national circulation is about 700,000.)

In 1980, according to estimates made by the Association of Editors of Spanish Dailies

(*Asociación de Editores de Diarios Españoles,* or AEDE), Spain's equivalent of the American Newspaper Publishers Association, daily newspaper circulation was about 3.3 million, up from 3 million at the beginning of the decade, but down from a 1975 high of nearly 3.5 million. Weekly newspapers, including various editions of the *Hoja del Lunes,* had a circulation roughly 10 percent greater than the dailies.

The number of daily newspapers declined during the 1970s. In 1971 Spain had 135 dailies—117 of which could be described as of general interest. By 1980 that had decreased to somewhere between 117 (the figure provided by AEDE) and 123, the number listed by GM *(Guia de los Medios,* Spain's equivalent of *Standard Rate and Data).* At the beginning of the 1970s there were 4,192 non-newspaper periodicals with a total circulation of more than 34 million. By 1978 that had risen to 7,012, 884 of which periodicals were weekly.

However, the decline of newspaper circulation in the 1970s was offset by growing television and radio audiences, keeping pace with the increase in population.

According to AEDE figures, newspaper advertising revenue in Spain was about $75 million in 1978—not more than 20 percent of all advertising revenue during the year. During 1978 Spain used roughly 168,000 metric tons of newsprint. Of that, 105,000 tons were produced locally and 61,000 tons were imported, representing a decrease in the use of newsprint between 1975 and 1978 of about 10,000 metric tons, or six percent. Annual per capita consumption amounted to about nine pounds per person in 1978.

Daily newspapers are published in 60 Spanish cities, with competitive situations in 23 cities. Madrid has the largest number of dailies, 13; Barcelona second with 12. There are two Basque-language dailies, one daily published in Catalan and two printed in English. Circulation runs from a low of roughly 2,000 for Madrid's *Informe Económico, Internacional Urgente* to 186,000 for Barcelona's *La Vanguardia.* Average circulation is about 25,000.

At least eight dailies are published by organizations which claim some form of allegiance to the Catholic Church. The largest venture is the *Editorial Católica, S.A.* whose flagship newspaper is the Madrid morninger *Ya,* with a circulation of more than 124,000. Politically, Spanish newspapers range from Communist to conservative to the extreme right. The Communist party (*Partido Comunista Española* or PCE) controls at least one newspaper, Madrid's *Mundo Obrero,* and two magazines, *Triunfo* and *La Calle.* The Catholic press tends to be centrist in its politics. *ABC* of Madrid, traditionally one of the nation's more influential newspapers, is more conservative. During the Franco years and before Juan Carlos became king, *ABC* was known as the organ of monarchism. Another traditionally influential newspaper, *La Vanguardia,* is classified as independent centrist. Among the newspapers started since the end of the Franco regime, the leaders seem to be Madrid's *El País,* independent, liberal-left in its orientation, and *Diario 16,* centrist.

With varying degrees of commitment, regional newspapers support claims to autonomy, a major political issue in the Spain of the 1970s and most certainly, of the 1980s. Two such dailies are published in Basque: *Deia* of Bilbao and *Egin* of San Sebastian, both founded in 1977. By the end of 1979, *Deia* had a circulation of 50,200 and *Egin* 45,700. However, each newspaper had reduced the proportion of Basque-language content because of what a Spanish government official called "...technical problems, such as the tremendous task of translating all wire-service information..."

The government itself runs a chain of 29 newspapers left over from the Franco regime. They are the remnants of the once powerful *Prensa del Movimiento,* the voice of the *Movimiento Nacional,* the Falangist organization. The latter was dissolved in April 1977, by the government of Prime Minister Adolfo Suarez. The *Prensa del Movimiento* came under the administrative control of the Ministry of Information and Tourism, which had been founded in 1951, and, when that was decreed out of existence, under the Ministry of Culture. At this time *Prensa del Movimiento* included 35 daily newspapers, 36 radio stations, and the news agency Pyresa (an acronym for *Prensa y Radio Español*). In June 1978, the communications system that had belonged to the national syndicates—the government-sponsored labor unions of the Franco era—was also turned over to the Ministry of Culture. This included a small chain of radio stations, the Madrid daily *Pueblo* and the news agency SIS *(Servicio de Informacion Sindical).*

In July 1979 the government closed six National Movement newspapers that were not self-supporting, including the Madrid daily *Arriba* and Barcelona's *La Prensa y Solidaridad Nacional,* as well as the Pyresa agency. The newspapers and radio stations that remained were formed into the *Medios de Comunicaciones Social del Estado* (MCSE). In all, the government found itself operating MCSE, the national television system and two radio networks.

In terms of size and influence, Madrid and Barcelona dominate the nation's newspaper scene: 25 dailies, about 20 percent of the nation's total, are published in the two cities. Ten cities have more than two newspapers— Bilbao, La Coruña, Oviedo, San Sebastian, Sevilla, Valladolid and Zaragoza, all on the mainland; Palma de Mallorca in the Balearic Islands; and Las Palmas and Santa Cruz de Tenerife in the Canary Islands. An additional 11 cities have competing newspapers.

Most of Spain's newspapers have adopted tabloid formats, since they depend on newsstand sales rather than subscriptions. Not all papers officially report their circulation figures. Of those that do, 14 were in the under-10,000 circulation group; 23 in the 10,000-25,000 group; 24 in the 25,000-50,000; 12 in the 50,000-100,000; and five with circulations of more than 100,000. The largest circulation of any newspaper in Spain is that of Barcelona's *La Vanguardia,* which in 1979 sold an average of 186,000 copies daily and 254,000 copies of its Sunday edition. The country's second largest daily is *El País,* the liberal Madrid morning newspaper, which published its first issue in 1976. By mid-1980 it had a daily circulation of 183,000 and a Sunday circulation of 263,000.

Other major dailies include: *ABC* of Madrid, daily circulation 135,000; *Ya* of Madrid, 124,000; *Pueblo* of Madrid, 79,000; *La Voz de Galicia* of La Coruña, 71,000; *El Correo Español* of Bilbao, 69,500; and *El Alcazar* of Madrid, 69,000. Two of the nation's 10 largest dailies are devoted to sports: *AS,* published in Barcelona, with a daily circulation of 153,000, and *Marca,* published in Madrid, with 90,000 readers.

The three most influential newspapers are *La Vanguardia* and *ABC* of Madrid, which have traditionally been so considered, and *El País,* which in less than five years has achieved an international reputation for quality.

Spain's population is concentrated around the coast and in the province of Madrid; in fact, one-third of the nation's "inland" population lives in Madrid. Castilian Spanish is Spain's official language, according to Article 3 of the 1978 Constitution, which specifies that "the other languages of Spain shall also be official in the respective self-governing communities in accord with their statutes." Four other languages are spoken on the mainland—Basque, Catalan, Galician and Valencian. About 72.8 percent of the Spanish people consider Castilian (or Andalusian, which differs only slightly) or Valencian their first language. About 16.4 percent speak Catalan, while some 8.2 percent speak Galician and 2.3 percent speak Basque. The emergence of daily newspapers in languages other than Castilian Spanish (and, to a very limited extent, English) was a phenomenon dating from the period of press freedom that began shortly after Franco's death.

The Spanish press entered the post-Franco years with very little tradition of independence. Years of censorship of all controversial matters, and of anything that might reflect badly on Spain, had not been conducive to developing a full understanding of all the implications of press freedom. Nor had those years fostered a high level of skill in aggressive investigative reporting. Why bother if the results would not be printed? Foreign news, sports news and critical articles dealing with literary-artistic matters filled the nation's newspapers. During the Franco years, the Spanish press did develop a number of capable critics of the arts, literature and drama, as well as many fine literary stylists.

The controls of the Franco dictatorship were no departure from the mainstream of Spanish communications tradition. Since 1810, when the so-called Cortes of Cadiz passed a *Ley de Libertad de Imprenta* (Free Press Law), the nation's newspapers had swung like a pendulum between freedom and restriction. "Sometimes," wrote Spanish newsman, educator and sometime government official Juan Beneyto in 1961, "there has been free expression to the point of anarchy: at other times, previous censorship to the point of a padlock on the mouth."

Despite periodic swings towards press freedom, government controls had been the mainstream of Spanish press policy. The political, economic and social consequences of the periods of press freedom had tended to reinforce the commitment to controls. The press had been used traditionally as a political instrument, either to promote change for those desiring power or to preserve the status quo for those holding power. Spain's history suggests that the practice of journalism was often not considered a goal in itself but rather a stepping stone to other careers, frequently in government.

When Franco died such things weighed heavily on the press. It did not emerge into the new era of freedom totally professional in all its attitudes, or always fully aware of the responsibilities that accompany freedom. Rather, it began a period of occasional extremes and sometimes heated debate about the relation of a free press to government and to society. Today the press wears its freedom with more grace, but the debate has not ended.

Economic Framework

The period from 1960 on was one of immense growth for Spain. During that time, the nation changed from a predominantly agricultural to a manufacturing economy. Its growth rate was spectacular, matching that of Japan. By 1980, however, Spain was beset by problems—the same problems that afflicted many other nations of the world. Its economic growth rate had dropped. Its inflation rate was between 15 and 16 percent—high, although down from 24.5 percent in 1977. About 12 percent of the work force was unemployed. Nonetheless, there had been a radical improvement in the standard of living for most Spaniards. In the past two decades, salaries and wages in Spain have improved drastically, keeping pace with a period of sharp economic growth that lasted until 1978. This is reflected in salaries in the news business. In the early 1960s, government regulations specified that a sub-editor working on a Madrid newspaper would be paid 7,000 pesetas (about $100) per month. Today, a beginning reporter in Spain would start somewhere between $500 and $1,000 per month, depending on the periodical and its location. Salaries for newsmen with experience range up to $2,000 a month in Madrid. Weekend and overnight pay differentials are negotiated on a company-by-company basis, but the government does mandate that each employee shall receive the equivalent of three extra monthly salaries annually.

A major concern to the private sector of mass communication in Spain has been competition from the government-owned television operation, its radio stations, and the *Media de Comunicaciones Social del Estado.* Newspapers in Madrid sell for 25 pesetas (about 40 cents) per copy. Even with advertising revenue added to that income, most papers have hovered just above the break-even point at best. Some faced serious economic problems as the 1970s ended. This was largely because the government-owned television-radio operations took in about four advertising dollars for every one spent on newspaper advertising. And, as *The New York Times* reported in late 1979, the government did not seem prepared or willing to give up control of television. "Although the press is free," correspondent James M. Markham reported, "television remains firmly and lucratively under the Government's control. While its reach is tremendous, it is a center of yawn-provoking mediocrity, featherbedding and corruption. But neither the Socialists nor the Communists are eager to give television an autonomous status, such as it has in Britain, since they would like to inherit it one day."

Newspapers in Spain tend to fall into either an elite or a popular category. Low circulations and relatively low readership suggest papers that probably serve the more discerning. The new and very successful Madrid daily *El Pais* —which describes itself as "liberal, independent of the dominant political power or of any party, or any economic group"—reports that more than half its readers have university-level educations and that more than 80 percent have at least high school educations.

Roughly one-quarter of the daily newspapers in the country, the 29 newspapers of the MCSE chain, are owned and operated by the government. *Editorial Católica,* a nonpolitical operation supported by businessmen who are active in social welfare and support the Church, controls five dailies, headed by *Ya* of Madrid and the Logos new agency. *Prensa Española* owns *ABC* of Madrid, *ABC* of Sevilla and the prestigious weekly magazine, *Blanco y Negro.* The government controls the MCSE, and certainly influences the news agency EFE, which is the largest distributor of foreign news in Spain. Finally, there are the 30 *Hojas del Lunes,* controlled and published by the various independent press associations *(Asociaciones de la Prensa).*

As noted above, some political parties have their own publications. The Communist party publishes the newspaper *Mundo Obrero* and two magazines. The Socialist Workers party puts out the weekly *El Socialista.* Despite a decline in the number of newspapers during the decade beginning in 1971, only two cities, Alicante and Burgos, suffered the loss of competitive situations.

The government's participation in operating communications media is recognized by Article 20 of the 1978 Constitution. Since there is no obvious trend towards media concentrations similar to that found elsewhere, there is no antitrust legislation equal to that found in the United States.

The government not only controls the import of newsprint but the distribution of newsprint that is domestically produced. AEDE estimates 1980 consumption would be about 190,000 metric tons. Of that, roughly 110,000 metric tons was produced in Spain, the rest imported, with a vast difference in cost. Imported newsprint costs newspapers about $500 per metric ton; the domestic product $650. In order to support domestic production, the government pays newspapers a difference of 11 pesetas (about 15 cents) per kilo as a direct subsidy—amounting to more than $150 per ton. Newspaper executives claim that newspapers can purchase imported newsprint only after they have bought a "quota" of domestic newsprint.

Advertising is somewhat less important economically to Spain's newspapers than it is in the United States. *El Pais,* which, although a newcomer, is very successful financially, reported that only 40 percent of its non-subsidy income is derived from advertising: 55 percent comes from street sales and 2.5 percent from subscriptions. Little evidence exists to suggest that advertising considerations or advertisers exert undue influence on the editorial content of Spain's dailies, or that special interest groups have control over editorial policies—especially of the newspapers that call themselves "independent." Obviously, some are aligned with political parties, either because of financial backing or ideological commitment. Such commitment would be reflected in editorial policies.

About 4,300 Spanish journalists belong to professional organizations. The nation's journalists associations, open only to graduates of a school of journalism and thus eligible to be enrolled on the government's Official Registry of journalists, have about 3,500 members. The Journalists' Union, open to all working newspersons, regardless of whether they are enrolled in the official registry, had about 800 members at the end of 1979. Both the Workers' Commissions (the Communist body) and the General Workers' Union (UGT) have sections for photographers, printers and others involved in the production of the print media. There are journalists' unions in many major cities, including Madrid, as well as 49 journalists associations *(Asociaciones de la Prensa).* In addition, there is an association of newsstand operators. That group as well as the journalists' associations support their own benefit funds for their members.

Since 1975, there have been at least 10 strikes directed against independent newspapers, one against two MCSE, and one against the nation's state-run broadcasting system. Most have involved demands for improved wages or working conditions, but one, which flared up briefly in Madrid and Barcelona, was in protest over a terrorist attack on the Barcelona magazine *El Papus.* A strike, begun in July 1977 against the *Diario de Barcelona,* led to the eventual acquisition by the newspapers' employees of 48 percent of the company's stock. Early in 1980 workers struck *Informaciones,* Madrid's oldest evening newspaper, when they were not paid. According to company executives, the paper was losing about $1.4 million per year and could not pay the wages. The strike closed the newspaper from early February until July, when a group of workers put the paper back into operation with its work force reduced from 300 to 50.

Two of the many functions of the various press associations are to "defend the rights and protect the interests of the journalistic profession..." and to "watch over and actively promote the right of freedom of expression as indispensable to the exercise of the journalistic profession...." At least one newspaper, *El Pais,* has set a series of rules governing its editorial operation. These rules provide the editorial staff access to the pages of the paper if two-thirds of the newsroom employees decide that "an editorial position damages their dignity or their professional image...." The newsroom rules also specify that professional secrecy is "a right and an ethical obligation of journalists," and have further established an editorial committee that functions as a mediating body if there are problems between one or more news/editorial employees and the newspaper's management.

Most Spanish newspapers sell the bulk of their copies over the counter rather than through subscriptions. That is partly a national tradition, partly because of apartment dwelling rather than living in homes in the cities, and partly the consequence of Spain's being, until recently, a poor nation. *El Pais* probably has more or less typical circulation patterns, its newsstand sales being 22 times its subscription sales. Most Spanish newspapers sell for between 20 and 30 pesetas (28 and 42 cents) per copy. In Madrid the price is 25 pesetas for a daily newspaper—raised to that figure from 20 pesetas two years ago and up from two or three pesetas in the early 1960s.

The top 10 newspapers in the country, which circulate a total of about 1,150,000 copies daily, account for one-third of the total daily national newspaper circulation. More and more of the newspapers are moving towards the "new technology," as a means of improving quality and cutting costs. The government is fostering such modernization, having budgeted the equivalent of more than $10 million to help newspapers acquire new equipment. Madrid newspapers run the gamut of production capabilities. The new *El Pais* has one of the more modern plants in Europe. *Informaciones,* on the other hand, must modernize if it is to stay in business, a fact underlined by a financial crisis in 1980. There is a consensus among newspaper executives that many Spanish newspapers have too many employees and will have to reduce the size of their work forces. The potentially wider use of the "new technology" will help in that process.

Press Laws

Article 20 of the Spanish Constitution of 1978 provides for freedom of speech and of the press. It also spells out the rights of individuals to privacy and, in general terms, the right to be protected from libel or slander. Significantly, the constitution not only guarantees the "right to freely communicate or receive truthful information by any means of dissemination whatsoever..." but also specifies: "The exercise of these rights may not be restricted by any kind of prior censorship."

The same article specifies that the "freedoms are limited by respect for [constitutional rights], by the precepts of the laws implementing it, and especially by the right to honor, to privacy, to personal reputation and to the protection of youth and childhood."

Article 56 declares that the person of the king shall be "inviolable," and, thus, cannot be criticized by the press.

Until the passage of the 1978 constitution, the active press law in Spain had been one approved in 1966. That law had supplanted a print law of 1883 and a Spanish Civil War emergency press law decreed in 1938. The 1966 law, which moved the Spanish press towards freedom but did not establish a free press, eliminated prior censorship. However, it did specify that there were certain limits on freedom "imposed by respect for morality and the truth; submission to reigning public and constitutional order; the demands of national defense, of the security of the States and the maintenance of internal and external public peace; the reserve owning to the action of the government, of the Cortes and of the Administration; the independence of the tribunals in the application of the Laws, and the safeguarding of private affairs and honor."

The 1966 law also decreed that "the administration will be able to order immediately... the confiscation, withdrawal and destruction of any printed matter that offends that which is moral or good custom, which has an obscene or pornographic character, which tends to pervert youth or children, or lacks the respect owed to the Catholic religion or whatever other [religion] that may have proselytes in Spain." Furthermore, the administration was given the power to suspend the "distribution of any printed matter which implies an inciting to subversion or the alteration of the public order, endangers the public peace or attempts a crime against the obedience owed to the laws or the dignity of the constituted authorities."

The death of Franco and the promulgation of the 1978 constitution did not replace the 1966 document with another press law. The question arose, Was the press subject to any control at all? Elements in the government argued that previous laws had not been superseded. During the post-Franco period, labeled by some "The springtime of the Spanish press," the government turned to a 1945 Code of Military Justice, which authorized military courts to try crimes against the military and, by implication, authority in general. As of June 1980, according to the International Press Institute, more than 100 court cases were pending against 700 journalists, some in military courts. That was in spite of the fact that the constitution limited the jurisdiction of military courts to specifically military matters and that a law of 1978 ordered that offenses involving freedom of speech or of the press be brought before civilian courts or tribunals.

Meanwhile, the Spanish press was split over whether there was a need for press law to spell out in detail the rights and responsibilities of a free press. Some newsmen argued that there should be no such law, adopting what was described informally as a "First Amendment" (after the U.S. Bill of Rights) posture. Others favored passage of a press law.

A draft press law, backed by Luis María Ansón, head of the Spanish news agency EFE and president of the National Federation of Associations of the Press, contained two conditions that were especially galling to many Spanish newsmen. One condition specified that every active Spanish journalist had to be accredited by the government. Accreditation, a long-time tradition in Spain, would involve being enrolled in the Registry of Professional Journalists. The other condition specified that only graduates of a recognized school of journalism (Facultad de Ciencias de la Información, Seccion Périodismo) could be accredited. The actual press card would be issued by the Federation of Press Associations and the individual association involved.

The idea of such a press law, which many found reminiscent of the 1966 law, was attacked by journalists all over the country. In one case, 50 senior Madrid newsmen protested in writing to the nation's secretary of state for information. Similar protests occurred across the nation, from newsmen and press unions alike. The secretary of state for information, Joseph Melia, himself supported the proposal. As he told a gathering in southern Spain, it was his position that "a licensed journalist is much more responsible than one who comes into the profession to delve into politics." In addition, the law's supporters used the argument that journalism was a profession parallel to medicine or law, and therefore its practitioners had to be educated specifically for their professional roles. The law did attempt to fill in some gaps left by the constitution. The draft did provide for a guarantee "of the right to access to sources of information and of full freedom to collect data of public interest...." The 1978 Constitution had enunciated in principle the ideal of professional secrecy, suggesting that a future law should spell out such a right—and any limits attached to it. The draft did that.

In October 1980 an agreement was reached between Ansón's Federation of Press Associations and the three unions which had media-related members—the Journalists' Union, the media branch of the Communist Workers' Commissions and the media unit of the General Trades Unions. They signed an accord which provided for a "two track" entry into the profession—by working or by graduation from an accredited school. That agreement would last until a new press law could be approved, and would be administered by a special commission set up by the four signatories. The agreement went on to specify that all would try to ensure that out-of-work journalists would be given priority in hiring. Finally, the agreement reaffirmed the desirability of maintaining press freedom; of limiting investment in Spain's media to Spaniards and Spanish capital; assuring workers a voice in editorial decisions; of spelling out the right to secrecy noted in the Constitution; and of ensuring that press crimes would be tried by normal civilian courts under civil laws.

Censorship

During most of the Franco years, the Ministry of Information and Tourism was charged with the responsibility of censoring the press. The process of censorship was based on the 1938 law, which gave the government the right to regulate the size and number of periodicals; participate in the designation of the administrators of periodicals; supervise press activity and control the journalism profession; and censor all publications. Until 1962, all printed works except those of the Catholic Church were subjected to prepublication censorship by a subsection of the Information and Tourism Ministry. In the case of newspapers and magazines, the office of the Director-General of the Press was responsible for censorship. Newspapers in Madrid were required to submit their copy to the ministry before publication. In other cities, copy was submitted to the local "delegation" of the ministry. Even the foreign files of the official news agency EFE, which had a monopoly on foreign news, were submitted to the censor. That which was not approved for publication was sent to newspaper editors on an informational basis only.

In 1962 Manual Fraga Iribarne was named minister of information and tourism and began the process of dismantling censorship. His first step was to do away with prior censorship outside of Madrid and Barcelona. In 1966 the process was completed. The government approved the new press law that eliminated prior censorship and withdrew from the government the right to appoint or be consulted over the appointment of a newspaper's senior official. However, the elimination of prior censorship did not mean freedom of the press. Newspapers became responsible for self-censorship. Fraga's law left intact part of the old mechanism by providing for what was called "voluntary consultation." The 1966 law stated: "The Administration can be voluntarily consulted about the content and diffusion of all classes of printed matter, as much by its author as by those persons who are responsible for its publication and diffusion. The approval or silence of the Administration will eliminate the responsibility of the consultors to the Administration."

That law also provided for fines of between $1,500 and $15,000 and jail sentences of up to six months for violations.

Obviously the passage of that law did not open up vast vistas of freedom, although it was a relaxation, a liberalization for the Spanish press. The government continued to apply sanctions—to confiscate issues of publications, to fine and imprison newsmen and to order foreign correspondents out of the country.

Nor did the law compel government officials to provide information to newsmen. Most officials, prompted either by fear of or contempt for the press, failed to cooperate with attempts to seek information, though one of the presumed functions of the Ministry of Information and Tourism was to help the press.

Nonetheless the 1966 law did witness a drift towards more freedom. Newspapers began discussing alternatives of government that might develop after Franco's death. They covered demonstrations and strikes, which had not traditionally been reported on before. A weekly magazine in the Catalan language was launched.

Further liberalization followed Franco's death. The Ministry of Information and Tourism was transformed into a Ministry of Culture. The constitution of 1978 guaranteed the rights of a free press. However, there were problems of transition and of tradition. The press did not emerge into unrestricted freedom. There remained laws, carried over from the Franco years, that were used in attempts to control and muzzle journalists. There were those in government who remained fearful of freedom, concerned that it might degenerate into license as it had on past occasions.

In the months before Franco's death, the government had expelled at least one foreign

journalist. It had suspended the weekly news magazine *Triunfo* for four months. It had confiscated various periodicals, a process that reached a peak in October 1975, when, after the promulgation of an anti-terrorist law, issues of *Cambio 16, Doblón, Posible, Destino* and other publications were seized. It had ordered all radio stations to submit tapes of their newscasts to the Ministry of Information and Tourism. It had sentenced the editor of a daily in Seville to two years' imprisonment for reporting that mercenary forces had been landed at an American navy base at Rota in preparation for an invasion of Portugal; and arrested Barcelona newsman José María Huertas Claveria for an article in the newspaper *Tele-Exprés* entitled the "Underground Erotic Life," which was considered insulting to the armed forces. The arrest became an international incident when workers on five Barcelona dailies carried out a one-day protest strike and International Press Institute director Ernest Meyer intervened.

State-Press Relations

Franco's death brought a new freedom and sense of purpose to the Spanish press, which became more critical and more probing in its coverage of government, politics and political figures. That freedom had other dimensions. In January 1976, for example, for the first time in history magazines illustrated with photographs of nudes appeared on the nation's newsstands.

However, attempts at control had not ended. The government continued to act against publications it found offensive, to bring suits against newsmen and to confiscate controversial issues of newspapers and magazines. In mid-January a British television newsman, attempting to film a strike-bound Madrid Chrysler plant, was detained, interrogated and searched. Soon thereafter, the government confiscated an issue of the weekly *Cambio 16* for speculating about the king's plans for political liberalization. During the year, it again confiscated *Cambio 16*, plus issues of such publications as *Sábado Gráfico* and *Asturias Semanal*. It suspended the magazine *Ajoblanco* for four months, fined it 250,000 pesetas (about $3,700) and started legal proceedings against at least four publications deemed pornographic. Such government action continued through the end of the 1970s.

Writing in the *IPI Report* for July 1978, *El*

Pais Editor Juan Luis Cebrían summed up the situation: "The press laws now in force in Spain are totally contradictory to the new constitution, although the present laws are not enforced to the point that they were in previous times. But the press law, even though not used for prior censorship, is still used as a whipping post for journalists and the media." By mid-1980, nearly five years after Franco's death and more than one year after the passage of the new constitution, there seemed to be an increase in the number of cases brought against journalists, and also in the size of the penalties. In January the Supreme Court confirmed a court ruling which disqualified newsman Federico Puig Oliver from working for six years and one day because of a story written for the sports weekly *Galicia Deportiva* of Vigo.

Also in January one of Spain's outstanding younger news executives and advocates of the "First Amendment" type of freedom, found himself a victim of the press law. Miguel Aguilar Angel Tremoya, director of *Diario 16,* a Madrid morning newspaper founded in 1976, was hauled into military court and asked to name the sources for a story claiming that the government had stopped a military coup. Charges were brought against Aguilar and a military prosecutor demanded a six-month prison sentence. Germán Alvarez Blanco, editor of the weekly *Sábado Gráfico,* faced similar charges for his reportage of the same incident. And none other than *El País* Editor Cebrían was also sentenced for a press crime—disrespect toward the courts. In April 1978 Cebrían had commented editorially on a series of trials of journalists. The sentencing of journalist Mayte Mancebo, he wrote, "brings to mind the best Nazi times or the present time of Idi Amin...." Cebrían was initially sentenced by a military court to two years of "provisional liberty." Technically that meant that he could not continue in an active role as a newspaper executive, but the sentence was not carried out. In May 1980 the nation's Supreme Court sentenced him to three months in jail and a fine of $700. However, that sentence was suspended.

In June 1980, as mentioned above, the International Press Institute reported more than 100 cases pending against some 700 journalists. The Communist weekly, *La Calle,* had reported in April that 60 Spanish newsmen were in some stage of prosecution for press crimes. The confiscation of issues of periodicals continued.

In addition to the threat of legal proceedings, the state had other actual or potential sources of press control. One was a two-peseta-per-copy subsidy (3 cents) paid to almost all of the nation's daily newspapers. Based on circulation figures for the second half of 1979, that amounted to about $95,000 per day, or $22 million per year. For *La Vanguardia,* the nation's largest-circulation daily, the subsidy came to about $835,000 during the second half of 1979. For *ABC,* then the largest-circulation daily in Madrid, the subsidy for six months was more than $612,000. In 1978 the various editions of the *Hoja del Lunes* had received a total of $650,000. Further, the press was dependent on the government for the newsprint subsidy of 11 pesetas (15 cents) for each kilo of domestic newsprint a newspaper bought. That amounted to more than $20 million a year. Finally, the government had set aside about $10 million to help newspapers modernize their news and printing operations by acquiring the "new technology."

Such sums, inappropriately used or even withheld, could provide political leverage against the press.

Support offered independent non-state periodicals amounted to no more than a fraction of that provided to the government-operated media. In 1980 $222 million were budgeted for support of all the mass media. Of that, about $180 million, or 82 percent of the total, were to be used for the government-run newspapers, national television, the state radio networks and the news agency EFE.

According to provincial newsmen, the press outside the largest cities is more subject to manipulation. At an August 1980 conference considering the "Function of the Press in Social Change," Santander newsman Juan G. Bedoya reported that the proximity of regional or local newspapers to sources "of information, influence, and power" made them "more sensitive to manipulation, controls, and even the temptation to not carry out journalistic responsibilities." Bedoya, editor of Santander's *Hoja del Lunes,* added that the "percentage of powerful manipulators...whether they be judges, police, politicians, members of the military or simply citizens, is much higher in the provinces."

Attitude Toward Foreign Media

Foreign correspondents are required to register with the government, as are Spanish newsmen. They must establish that they are bona fide correspondents for legitimate periodicals or agencies, and that the bulk of their income is derived from their news work. Those who are accredited receive an official press card that carries some privileges with it. It allows foreign correspondents to maintain automobiles with non-Spanish registration and entitles them to discounts on the fares of the state-run railroads. A practice of providing gasoline at diplomatic discounts has been discontinued as has been a system of special rates in government-run hotels.

Since the end of World War II, there has been no systematic censorship of stories sent out of Spain by the 100–125 foreign correspondents usually accredited to the country. However, there are still occasions when foreign newsmen are expelled. In January 1976 Joaquin Mejia, the non-Spanish editor of the weekly *Granada Semanal,* was expelled. Shortly thereafter, Luigi Sommaruga, a correspondent for the Roman newspaper *Il Messaggero,* was ordered to leave Spain. During 1979 two foreign correspondents were expelled. One was a Chilean who had attempted to photograph Spanish deputy Gabriel Cisneros as he was being treated in an intensive care unit for wounds received moments before in a terrorist attack. Another was Jan Keulen of the Dutch newspaper *De Volkskrant.* Keulen was expelled for hinting at police involvement in a cafe bombing.

During the Franco years, there was regular censorship of foreign periodicals. Today, that is not the case. More foreign periodicals are freely imported and freely displayed on newsstands. However, foreign ownership of the Spanish media is forbidden by the provisions of the 1966 press law. And the draft press law circulating in Spain during 1980 provided that "fifty-one percent of the assets and capital of mass media concerns is necessarily to belong to individuals or organizations of Spanish nationality and residents of Spain." There is little to suggest that the Spanish media are subjected to any special foreign attempts at propaganda. Their news is brought to them, generally, by the news agency EFE, which maintains its own staff of foreign correspondents and also receives news from a number of other major international news services. Much of the programming of the state-run television services is produced outside Spain.

In the past few years, Spanish news organizations and individuals have affiliated themselves with international organiza-tions—on both sides of the Iron Curtain. One of Spain's journalist unions is associated with the International Federation of Journalists. Spanish newsmen participate in International Press Institute activities, maintaining their own national committee. Editor Cebrian of *El Pais* is a member of the IPI international executive board. Pedro Crespo de Lara, executive secretary-general of the Association of Editors of Spanish Dailies, was elected vice-president of the World Committee on Press Freedom early in 1980. The news agency EFE maintains agreements of one kind or another with 27 foreign news agencies, including seven from the communist countries of Europe. The Spanish government has not taken a strong stand on the 1978 UNESCO Declaration.

New Agencies

One news agency, EFE, is the major distributor of news in Spain. On occasion, EFE has been described as the "official news agency" and as a "semi-official news agency." Both descriptions are indicative of the traditional links between EFE and the government. Over the years, the government has exercised the prerogative of appointing EFE directors, and has helped finance EFE's operations, thus nourishing its growth over the past two decades.

EFE describes itself as the "top Spanish language wire service" and claims to be the fifth largest such operation in the world. With 2,200 employees worldwide, staffing 78 bureaus on five continents, it has 570 subscribers in Spain and 1,590 abroad. Until recently, EFE had been broken up into distinct foreign and domestic operations, a sports operation and a photo service, each using a different name. However, in 1978 all EFE operations were centralized under one name, with the exception of its special services branch, which is still called FIEL.

There 200,000 shares of EFE stock, held by 375 shareholders. The government is among those shareholders, having acquired some stock by direct purchase and other shares by indirect acquisition. Among government agencies holding stock, according to EFE publications, are the MCSE newspapers; the defunct party newspaper *Arriba;* the press and radio of the *Falange* (which no longer exists in that form); the Direction-General of the Press, a government office that has dropped that title, and the National Institute of Industry (INI). INI, labor union officials say, holds 33 percent of EFE's stock.

In 1980 EFE received $1.1 billion pesetas (more than $15.5 million) from the government. The agency's detractors refer to it as a "subsidy." EFE's president, Luis Maria Ansón, denies that, describing the money as payment for services EFE provides the Spanish government.

All Spanish newspapers receive EFE's services. For years, it was the sole channel for the distribution of foreign news in Spain, news it received from United Press International. However, that has changed. Other news agencies are providing news to the nation's media, including direct service to newspapers by international news agencies and major syndicated services.

In terms of size, however, it is almost impossible to speak of a competitor to EFE. Yet the Agencia Europa does provide domestic and foreign news to the Spanish press. Other agencies which have provided domestic news over the years include Logos, established in 1928 by an organization of publishers of Catholic newspapers, and Mencheta, owned and operated by the Peris Mencheta family. In September 1979, newspapers and businesses in northern Spain opened the agency Castilla Press.

Electronic News Media

The nation is served by four major radio networks—*Radio Nacional Española* and *Radio Cachena Española,* both supported by the government; a network supported by the Catholic Church; and a group of independents, of which *Sociedad Española de Radiodifusión* (SER) is most important.

Two major televison channels—one UHF, the other VHF—serve the nation. Both are located in Madrid and both are run by the government, a fact which draws the fire of the nation's nongovernmental media. There are four regional production centers in the country, which is dotted with repeater stations. *Televisión Española* covers 95 percent of the nation with its VHF colorcasts and 40 percent of the nation with UHF-casts, also in color. In 1975 there were 8 million radios in the country, or 220 per 1,000 population. Statistics for the same year reveal that there were 7.4 million television sets, or 204 per 1,000 population. At the beginning of the 1970s there had been 214 radios and 174 television sets per 1,000 population; by 1978,

that had increased to 228 radios and 184 television sets.

During an average week, *Radio Nacional Española* devoted 41 percent of its air time to entertainment programming, 28 percent to news and informational programming, 21 percent to programs about the arts, letters or science, 2 percent to education and 2 percent to women's, children's, religious and miscellaneous programming. An estimated 56 percent of the material broadcast was produced in Spain.

Television programming broke down to: 20.5 percent educational, 47.9 percent informational, including news and special events, and 31.6 percent entertainment. About 80 percent of the programming is imported, mainly from the United States, European Broadcasting Union member-countries and Latin America. The nation's first network, the VHF operation, reaches 98 percent of the country's population. The second network (UHF) reaches about 50 percent of the urban population.

Television in Spain is a state monopoly, and responsibility for that medium—together with the two government-owned and operated radio networks—has been shuffled from one ministry to another in recent years. *Radio-Television Española* was originally under the Ministry of Information and Tourism, and with the closing of that department moved to the Ministry of Culture. In August 1980 a royal decree shifted responsibility for RTVE once more: to the Ministry of the Presidency of the Government. The move was to be effective January 1, 1981. By coincidence, the director-general of RTVE, Fernando Arias-Salgado, was the brother of the minister of the presidency of the government, Rafael Arias-Salgado. The decree came at a time of growing complaints about the political and ideological balance of news and documentary presentations on Spanish television. In February, Alfonso Guerra, a Socialist party deputy, raised the question of news manipulation and fiscal corruption in Parliament. According to *The New York Times,* he asked the government "to demonstrate to public opinion that TV is not a den of thieves."

The following month, the Socialist party brought criminal charges against RTVE because, as Socialist deputy Pedro Bofill told *El Pais,* RTVE "is using its programs, radio as much as television, for political purposes, on the occasion of the upcoming elections in Catalonia." In May, *El País* reported that

RTVE lost 2 billion pesetas ($28 million) during 1979, despite government assistance amounting to 5,844,000,000 pesetas ($83.3 million).

Education & Training

There are three major communications schools in Spain, two of which are official: the *Facultades de Ciéncias de Información* in the Universities of Madrid and of Barcelona. The third is that of the University of Navarra in Pamplona. The unit in Madrid is probably typical. In 1980 it had roughly 7,000 students and 320 faculty members (many part time). The school is divided into three sections. One teaches journalism; another deals with film, television and radio; the third incorporates advertising and public relations.

Enrollment in journalism schools has grown greatly in recent years. As a result, the faculty of the University of Madrid imposed a limit on the admission of first-year students in the fall of 1980. Only 900 students were admitted to the school. Of that number, 650 opted to enter journalism training, 150 went into preparation for work in the electronic media or film, and 100 selected programs in either advertising or public relations.

The major Spanish journalists association is the nationwide group of Associations of the Press. There are 49 such associations, banded together into the national Federation of the Associations of the Press of Spain. The associations are more than social groups. They have as their goal the defense of the rights and interests of newsmen as well as the "promotion" of high technical and social standards within the profession. What sets the organizations apart from journalists groups elsewhere is the emphasis on raising funds to provide benefits to needy journalists and their families. The Madrid association is capitalized at 1 billion pesetas (more than $14 million) and its annual budget, according to its bylaws, is 200 million pesetas ($2.8 million). As mentioned earlier, the Monday morning newspapers *(Hojas del Lunes)* are the associations' monopoly; revenues from their circulation are also of great value. And various other fund-raising projects are listed in the associations' bylaws. Income so derived is used for a variety of benefits for associations members, including medical services, emergency loans, scholarships for the children of newsmen, and "suitable pro-

fessional activities" for retired or incapacitated members.

An estimated 3,500 journalists belong to the 49 individual associations.

Summary

Some observers of the Spanish press have described it as absolutely free, as the freest press in Europe. Those Spanish newsmen involved in legal proceedings because of "press crimes" might disagree. If freedom of the press is something guaranteed by law, by tradition, and by sociopolitical commitment, then the press in Spain is not absolutely free. There *are* restrictions on the press, both legal and psychological.

In June 1980 *El País* Editor Juan Luis Cebrián—one of Spain's most outspoken advocates of press freedom—flew to New York to receive the *World Press Review*'s designation as "International Editor of the Year." In his acceptance speech, Cebrián said that "there are difficult years ahead for freedom of the press and of speech in today's democratic Spain"; the nation, he observed, was in the midst of a "recession of freedom." Among the problems cited by Cebrián—and other Spanish newsmen—are:

The national economy. A high inflation rate, high unemployment, and a drop in the national economic growth rate have tended to alarm many people. Observers note that there are some in Spain who blame democratic institutions for economic problems.

The impact of terrorism on the nation. In early November 1980, the year's death toll from terrorist attacks stood at 106. In 1979, 99 had been murdered by terrorists. Some blame the democratic system—and indirectly, the press—for not dealing severely with acts of terrorism, but the press itself has not escaped terrorist assault. In August 1980 José Javier Uranga, director of *El Diario de Navarra,* was shot, presumably for his paper's opposition to the idea of linking Navarre's political future to that of the Basque provinces. It was presumed that the shooting, which hospitalized but did not kill Uranga, was the work of the Basque separatist organization ETA—*Euskadi ta Askatasune* (Basque Homeland and Liberty).

Even earlier, in 1978, there were at least four terrorist attacks on the Spanish media. The managing editor of *El Correo Español* of Bilbao, lost an eye in an ETA bombing, while the editor of that city's *Hoja del Lunes* was shot to death. The Basque magazine *Askatasuna* was the target of an arson attack attributed to rightist elements opposed to the ETA. A letter bomb exploded in the offices of *El País,* killing one person and injuring two others. And a year before, another bomb had exploded in the office of the Barcelona-based satirical magazine *El Papus,* killing two persons. In a mid-1978 report, The International Press Institute said that there had been more than 20 terrorist attacks on Spanish media since the death of Franco.

Further obstacles to press freedom in Spain include: the continued intervention of military courts in the cases of so-called "press crimes"; a nostalgia on the part of some Spaniards for the security and stability of the Franco years; and the continuing requirement, a carryover from the Franco era, that journalists must have official press cards and, in turn, degrees from recognized schools of journalism. And perhaps the greatest single problem is the competition from the state-operated media, especially television, for advertising income. Those media siphon off nearly four-fifths of the pesetas spent annually on advertising. In addition, they receive 82 percent of the total monies spent on media subsidies by the government. All this hurts the independent media. There is also much bitterness felt toward RTVE, which, according to its detractors, is politically partisan, an instrument of government policy and mismanaged.

The problems facing the Spanish press are not of the press itself. They are problems of an economic and political nature, as well as the natural difficulties accompanying the transition from an authoritarian to a democratic government. The Spanish press has the basis, the will and the impetus to continue exercising the rights of freedom if the system in which it must exist continues to be free.

CHRONOLOGY

1975
November   Francisco Franco, Spain's dictator since 1936, dies. King Juan Carlos I installed as head of a constitutional monarchy. Madrid Journalists' Association protests proliferation of government acts against press.

1976
April   First issue of *El País* published.

1977
April   Second article of 1966 Press Law—an article listing those institutions that press cannot criticize—abolished. (Among previously listed institutions was National Movement.)

1977
April   Social Communications Media of the state created from press of National Movement.

1978
February   Association of Editors of Daily Newspapers of Spain (AEDE) founded.

1978
December   Law passed providing for constitutional protection of individual fundamental rights, under which crimes committed in exercise of freedom of expression come under civil-court jurisdiction rather than that of military tribunals.

1978
December   Spain's new constitution, guaranteeing freedom of the press, approved.

1979
March   State credit for modernization of nation's newspapers established.

1980
April   Communist magazine, *La Calle,* reports 60 Spanish journalists under indictment for some form of "press crime."

1980
May   A General Assembly of International Press Institute resolution expresses "deep disappointment that Spain's advance toward democracy over the last few years has been retarded by the retention of practices and measures which

have seriously eroded or are likely to erode the freedom of the press." Assembly specifically attacks practice of bringing journalists to trial before military courts, continued existence of state-run newspaper chain (MCSE), and proposed law to continue practice of requiring official press credentials and specific university degree.

BIBLIOGRAPHY

Asociación de Editores de Diarios Españoles. *AEDE,* nos. 1–3, June 1979, December 1979, July 1980.

Asociación de la Prensa de Madrid. *Estatutos de la Asociación de la Prensa de Madrid,* n.d.

Boletín Oficial del Estado. *Constitucion Española.* 2d ed. Madrid, 1979.

Cebrián, Juan Luis. "Problems of the Spanish Spring." *IPI Report,* July 1978, p. 12.

EFE. *Agencia EFE, S.A.: History and Organization.* Madrid, 1980.

Estatuto de la Redacción. Madrid: *El País,* 1980.

Federación de Asociaciones de la Prensa de España. *Draft for a Bill: Information and Mass Media Act.* Unpublished. Madrid, 1979.

———. *Estatutos.* Madrid, 1979.

Gorostiaga, Eduardo. "Twenty Years of Television in Spain." *EBU Review,* vol. 28, January 1977, p. 17.

GM: Guia de los Medios, no. 60, 1980.

International Press Institute. "Pressures on the Press Mount Again in Spain." *IPI Report,* May–July 1980, p. 15.

Markham, James M. "Reform Zeal Seems to Ebb in Spain as Violence Grows." *The New York Times,* February 19, 1980, p. A4.

———. "Spain's Papers Regain Liberty but Few Bother to Read Them." *The New York Times,* November 26, 1980, p. A8.

Schulte, Henry F. *The Spanish Press, 1470–1966.* Urbana, Ill., 1968.

Una Ojeado a El País. Madrid: *El País,* 1979.

Vasquez de Prada, Rodrigo. "The Mass Media and Spain Today." *The Democratic Journalist,* April 1980, p. 9.

SRI LANKA

by George Kurian

BASIC DATA

Population: 14.72 million
Area: 65,500 sq. km. (25,283 sq. mi.)
GNP: Rs 52.66 billion (US$3.41 billion) (1979)
Literacy Rate: 82%
Language(s): Sinhala, English, Tamil
Number of Dailies: 14
  Aggregate Circulation: 612,000
  Circulation per 1,000: 49
Number of Nondailies: 196
  Aggregate Circulation: NA
  Circulation per 1,000: NA
Number of Periodicals: 465

Number of Radio Stations: 1
Number of Television Stations: 1
Number of Radio Receivers: 537,000
  Radio Receivers per 1,000: 36.5
Number of Television Sets: NA
  Television Sets per 1,000: NA
Total Annual Newsprint Consumption: 2,000
  metric tons
  Per Capita Newsprint Consumption: 0.1 kg.
  (0.22 lb.)
Total Newspaper Ad Receipts: NA
  As % of All Ad Expenditures: NA

Background & General Characteristics

The Sri Lankan press is a British creation. Until the late 19th century newspapers in the country—the island then known as Ceylon—were published in English, by Englishmen and for Englishmen. While the earliest news publication was the *Government Gazette,* launched by the British administration three months after the island was declared a crown colony in 1802, the first newspaper in the conventional sense was the *Colombo Journal,* published from 1832. When the *Journal* died within two years, its place was taken by the *Observer and Commercial Advertiser* and (12 years later) by the *Ceylon Times.* Both these papers were destined to play a key role in shaping of the Sri Lankan press; the former was acquired in 1923 by D. R. Wijewardene, a major newspaper proprietor, and the latter became the *Times of Ceylon.* By the turn of the century, Ceylonese entered newspaper publishing with *Ceylon Independent* (owned by Sir Hector Van Cuylenberg), *Standard, Ceylon Morning Leader,* and *Ceylonese.* In 1918 Wijewardene founded the country's first newspaper chain, Associated Newspapers of Ceylon, with the flagship of the company, *Ceylon Daily News.*

The Sinhala-language press had a later start. The first newspaper in Sinhala, *Lakminapahana,* was founded in 1862 as a weekly; the first daily in the language was *Dinamina,* founded by H. S. Perera in 1908 and later acquired by Wijewardene. A Tamil daily, *Thinakaran,* was added to the Wijewardene group in 1932.

By the late 1940s the island's press had become a duopoly, the lion's share of the market belonging to Associated Newspapers of Ceylon Limited (ANCL)— popularly known as Lake House, after the brooding colonial mansion where it was housed— and the *The Times of Ceylon,* which had passed into Ceylonese hands on independence in 1948. ANCL published the *Daily News, Dinamina,* and a third Sinhala daily, *Janata,* while *Times of Ceylon* published two other dailies, the *Morning Times* and the Sinhala *Lankadipa.* During the prime ministerships of W. R. D. Bandaranaike and his widow, the country's largest book publishing company, M. D. Gunasena, launched a Sinhala daily, *Dawasa,* which achieved quick success and soon surpassed the Times group with the second largest share of the daily newspaper market. In the mid-1970s Gunasena's journals, known as Independent Newspapers, enjoyed 25 percent of the market while ANCL claimed 40 percent and the Times Group 17 percent. The rest of the market was shared by two Tamil newspapers, *Virakesari* and *Eelanadu,* and three political dailies: *Aththa,* published by the pro-Moscow Communist party, *Janadina,* organ of the Trotskyite Lanka Sama Samaja party, and *Sirilaka* put out by Bandaranaike's Sri Lanka Freedom party.

In 1980 14 dailies were published in Sri Lanka; of these 12 were published in the morning and two in the afternoon. There were also 12 Sunday papers. Seven papers are published in English, 10 in Sinhala, and nine in Tamil. It is interesting to note that although Sinhalese form the overwhelming majority, Tamils are better served with newspapers and they also control five of the six major newspaper groups. All papers are published in Colombo with the exception of *Eelanadu,* which serves the heavily Tamil population of Jaffna.

ANCL publishes five dailies (two in Sinhala, two in English and one in Tamil) and three Sunday newspapers. Independent Newspapers has five dailies (two in Sinhala, two in Tamil and one in English) and three Sunday newspapers, the Times group three dailies (two in English, one in Sinhala), and the Express group two Tamil dailies. All these groups also publish specialized weeklies and periodicals dealing with culture, literature, astrology, cinema, and other features.

The average daily has between four and eight pages. Most papers carry local news almost exclusively; the Press Commission reported that only four newspapers devoted more than 4 percent of their contents to foreign news: *Times of Ceylon* 19.7 percent, *Dawasa* 15.3 percent, *Daily Mirror,* 13.5 percent, and *Observer* 13.4 percent.

According to UNESCO, aggregate circulation of dailies in the mid-1970s was around 612,000, or roughly 49 per 1,000 inhabitants, placing Sri Lanka 73rd among world nations in this respect. UNESCO also reported 196 nondailies and 465 periodicals. No circulation figures were cited for nondailies, but periodicals had an aggregate circulation of 1.45 million, or 104 per 1,000 inhabitants.

An island-wide survey conducted in the early 1970s by the Audit Bureau of Circulation reported that 58 percent of the males and 28 percent of the females claimed to read newspapers. The survey also revealed that readership of English-language dailies was confined to the upper middle classes and the elite; that borrowing newspapers was a widespread habit; that in rural areas most people read papers in cafes, libraries and community centers; and that readership of the morning papers was considerably higher than that of both evening papers and periodicals. The survey also found that only 3 percent of the men and 4 percent of the women read English publications regularly, while the relative percentages for Sinhala were 42 percent and 16 percent.

Economic Framework

The country's largest newspaper group, ANCL, ceased to be a private company in 1973 when the Bandaranaike government nationalized 75 percent of its shares, with the balance retained by the Wijewardene family. The nationalized shares are being held in trust by a public trustee until they are sold to the general public. Before the takeover, ANCL had a subscribed capital of $1 million, with four directors owning more than two-thirds of the entire issue, the balance being distributed among 38 others. The Times of Ceylon, a public company, had a share capital of approximately Rs 5. 6 million ($700,000) with 75 shareholders, of whom the Sangarapillai Trust held a controlling 40 percent. Independent Newspapers, a private company, had a capital of approximately Rs 1.4 million ($180,000) with 14 shareholders, all of whom were members of the Gunasena family. Express Newspapers, also a private company, had a capital of approximately Rs 1.4 million ($180,000) with 19 shareholders and an all-Indian board of directors. Eelanadu, another private company, had a share capital of approximately Rs 720,000 ($90,000) with 28 shareholders and also an all-Indian board of directors. Thus, the major newspapers were controlled by 178 people.

While ANCL maintained its profitability throughout the 1970s (although it lost much of its circulation immediately following the government takeover) the Times of Ceylon company repeatedly faced bankruptcy in the late 1970s, finally compelling the government to assume control under the provisions of the Business Acquisitions Act. The profitability of the other papers, most of them private companies, are not disclosed, but none of them is believed to be seriously in the red.

In the opinion of the Press Commission, "the more powerful advertisers and private capitalist interests, both foreign and local,... have a pervasive and powerful influence over newspaper organization and policies." The commission identified these interests as the Lever Brothers subsidiary of Unilever, Ceylon Tobacco, Ceylon Theaters, Grant Advertising and International Advertising Services, but did not furnish evidence of pressure from any of them. However, the commission did observe that newspapers devoted "far too much space" for advertising; the *Sunday Observer* leading with 61 percent and followed by *Daily News* with 38.5 percent, *Silumina* with 38.4 percent, *Dinamina* with 36.1 percent, *Sunday Times* with 34.4 percent, *Lankadipa* with 31.4 percent, *Observer* with 39.4 percent and *The Times of Ceylon* with 28.7 percent. The severe newsprint shortage in recent years has curtailed the number of pages and led to a loss of ad revenues.

Press Laws

The constitution guarantees freedom of speech and the press, but these safeguards have not protected the press from the slow encroachments and even the direct onslaughts of the state. Direct censorship is permitted under the anti-terrorism law and was indeed imposed in July/August 1980 during a state of emergency. In addition, parliamentary privileges can be invoked to shield parliamentary discussion or government policies from journalistic investigation. The provisions relating to the criminal law of defamation are to be found in Chapter XIX of the Penal Code; to avoid penalties under this provision a defendant has to prove that the statements made are not only true but in the public interest.

The Bandaranaike government created a seven-member Press Council as a press-monitoring agency and its powers and regulations constitute the principal legal means of controlling the press. Clause 16 of the Press Council Law makes it an offense for a newspaper to publish without official approval "any matter which purports to be the proceedings of... a meeting of cabinet ministers; any matter which purports to be the contents of... any document sent by or to any or all of the ministers... or any matter which purports to be a decision... of the cabinet." Other types of news that cannot be published without prior official approval include "any statement relating to monetary, fiscal, exchange control, or import control measures alleged to be under consideration by the gov-

ernment... or by the Central Bank, the publication of which is likely to lead to the creation of shortages or windfall profits or otherwise adversely affect the economy of Sri Lanka or any official secret within the meaning of the Official Secrets Act or any matter relating to the military, naval, air force or police establishments equipment or installation which is likely to be prejudicial to the defense and security of the country." Clause 16 also makes it an offense to publish "any proposal or other matter alleged to be under consideration by any ministry when it is false."

Under Clause 15 it is an offense to publish any profane, indecent or obscene matter, defamatory matter, or advertising matter injurious to public morality. Offenses in violation of these provisions are triable before the regular courts, not the Press Council, which has no powers except of an administrative and advisory character. Its only judicial powers are stated in Clause 9, which empowers it, on receipt of a complaint, to hold an inquiry, summon the editor and correct, censure, and order an apology. The decisions of the council are open to review by the Supreme Court. While the council is not an independent body it has the right to prescribe a code of ethics for journalists, and to undertake and promote technical and other research.

Censorship

There are no official censorship agencies although censorship may be imposed for brief periods under the Anti-Terrorism Law. Such temporary control may prohibit only specified subjects and does not involve pre-censorship. For example, in 1977, when public service strikes spread throughout the country, all references to the strikes were ordered to be deleted from all newspapers. The newspapers responded by publishing issues with blank spaces on their front pages.

State-Press Relations

For a country and a press of so small a size, Sri Lanka has had stormy state-press relations concluding, as expected, in the taming of the press and enlarged state powers over the media. The press has played a decisive role in every election since 1946. With the introduction of a parliamentary system under the Soulbury Constitution, Lake House, as ANCL was known, became a virtual king-maker. From 1947 to 1956, when the country was governed by the United National Party (UNP), Lake House was almost a member of the "inner cabinet," with access to government secrets and influencing public opinion in favor of the ruling party. When W. R. D. Bandaranaike formed the Sri Lanka Freedom Party (SLFP) in 1952 Lake House launched a media campaign against it—over the years the campaign took on the character of a crusade. Later it became a vendetta. With his Buddhist and Sinhalese supporters, Bandaranaike alleged that the media were in the hands of Christians. After the SLFP victory in the 1956 elections, Lake House became the principal bastion of the opposition, opposing Bandaranaike's socialist policies tooth and claw. The monopoly press came under parliamentary scrutiny in 1959 when a private motion was introduced to take the press from private ownership and entrust it to an "independent" corporation for "the benefit of the people."

Following Bandaranaike's assassination in the same year the rift between SLFP and Lake House widened as the latter became a prime target for the leftist propaganda. Pro-government critics argued that "if freedom of the press tends to disrupt national unity [and promotes] civil commotion and conflict between communities, it might become necessary for the state to introduce restrictions [designed to restore] order and promote unity." It was further argued that "freedom of the press has in effect become the freedom of newspaper proprietors to malign their enemies [and] promote conservative and reactionary policies."

In 1960 a Press Commission was appointed as a preliminary move toward taking over the Lake House and Times newspapers and vesting them "in statutory public corporations with unlimited share capital in which individual holdings will be restricted so as to ensure a broad-based ownership." The Press Commission report alleged that the Lake House and Times papers were "chiefly responsible for the prevailing disunity of the various racial and religious groups in the country and that the editorial staffs of those newspapers, many of whom had been educated in Roman Catholic missionary schools which conditioned them to accept the Graeco-Roman-Christian tradition as something superior readily fell into line with the wishes of the management to fight for the preservation

of the undue privileges that a certain class [i.e. Christians] had obtained from foreign rulers." Following the report, a bill was introduced in Parliament in 1964 to provide for the setting up of a Press Council and a Press Tribunal by the Judicial Service Commission "to exercise general supervision and control over newspaper business, to ensure a high standard of journalistic ethics and to present the news to the public fairly, accurately and with regard to truth." The bill was defeated when a number of SLFP members crossed the floor to vote with the opposition. There were allegations from leftist politicians that huge sums of money were spent by Lake House to persuade these members to change their votes, but no proof of bribery was ever established.

The UNP victory in the 1965 general elections brought a lull in the state-press conflict until 1970, when SLFP was returned to power with an overwhelming majority. The first order of business for the Sirimavo Bandaranaike government was to resume its efforts to humble Lake House and discredit the press. Backed by a ruling from the Constitutional Court, presided over by Justice Jaya Pathirana, a former member of SLFP, the Assembly passed the Press Council Bill, establishing a seven-member Press Council and the Associated Newspapers of Ceylon Ltd. (Special Provisions) Bill. The latter placed Lake House under a public trustee and a board of directors appointed by Justice Pathirana and reducing the shares held by the Wijewardene family to 25 percent. In upholding the legality of this bill, the Constitutional Court held that "right to property is non-existent" and that "the wide circulation of Lake House newspapers gave it an undue advantage in moulding public opinion to its own way of thinking." The court further declared that the bill was "in the interests of national economy, the development of collective forms of property, raising of the moral and cultural standards of the people [and the elimination of] economic and social privileges."

The controls placed on the press by the Bandaranaike government took a heavy toll on press credibility and economic viability, even after SLFP was overthrown. Some of the best editors and journalists either left or were dismissed and replaced by untrained political appointees. Because of poor management, circulations were halved and many previously profitable newspapers, such as *The Times of Ceylon*, were forced to fold temporarily. A group of financiers, headed by

Mrs. Bandaranaike's son, Anura, bought a controlling interest in *The Times of Ceylon* in 1975, enabling it to resume publication a year later after transfusion of money from SLFP supporters. However, it continued to suffer financial losses, forcing the government of J. R. Jayewardene—which came to power in 1977—to take it over in the interests of the employees and to satisfy creditors who were moving in to foreclose. The Independent Newspapers group, which had been forced to close in 1974, resumed publication after UNP's return to power, but its financial condition remained anemic. Higher production costs also hurt the press as papers were forced to rely on the state-run Eastern Paper Mills Corporation for their newsprint supplies. Circulations of most publications dropped sharply because of higher newsstand prices—up to 50 cents by the late 1970s. An exception was the Lake House group, which remained relatively profitable because of higher newsprint allocations and heavy government advertising support.

Although Jayewardene was swept into power on a plank that included a free and independent press, few of the controls set up by his predecessor have been dismantled. According to the *Far Eastern Economic Review*, journalists who stray too far from government guidelines are "fired unceremoniously." Opposition newspapers continue to be denied the nationalized transportation facilities for distribution of their issues.

Attitude Toward Foreign Media

Foreign media have remained relatively free of government intervention. No special visas are required for foreign correspondents; neither is prior official approval required for cables. In recent years there have been no jailings or expulsions of overseas newspeople. Import restrictions on foreign publications are based on foreign exchange availability rather than political considerations.

The Sri Lankan government supports the 1978 UNESCO Declaration and subsequent attempts to enlarge state control over the media.

News Agencies

The national news agency is the Press Trust of Ceylon, a state-owned corporation, founded in 1951 as a private company. It maintains a permanent bureau in Colombo but employs no foreign correspondents and receives foreign news through Reuters and Press Trust of India.

Foreign news bureaus in Colombo include AFP, dpa, Iraqi News Agency, Tanjug, UPI, AP and Xinhua.

Electronic News Media

Sri Lanka Broadcasting Corporation, formerly, Radio Ceylon, is a public corporation under the Ministry of Information, financed by listeners' licenses and advertising revenues. The corporation operates nine medium-wave transmitters, eight FM transmitters, and 12 short-wave transmitters. The national service has three language programs: Sinhala (74 hours weekly), Tamil (72 hours), and English (45 hours), with an alternative light program in Sinhala known as Radio Sandhaya (31 hours weekly). The commercial service consists of a domestic network on the air for 192 hours a week and an overseas service for 116 hours. Experimental television began in 1979 as a private venture and was taken over by the government later that year.

Education & Training

The only training facility for journalists on the island is the Vidyalankara Campus of the University of Sri Lanka, established in 1973.

Summary

The past two decades have been critical in the history of the Sri Lankan press, bringing to a head the inherent conflict between the state and the fourth estate. By the end of the 1970s the conflict had ended in favor of the state, with the press tamed although not muzzled. The Jayewardene government has been reluctant to dismantle the control mechanisms established so effectively by the Socialist administration of Sirimavo Bandaranaike, and the economic problems of the press have tended to reinforce its dependence on the state.

CHRONOLOGY

1975   *The Times of Ceylon* folds; Prime Minister Sirimavo Bandaranaike's son and nephew acquire controlling interest in the Times group.

1976   *The Times of Ceylon* resumes publication.

1977   Court acquits reporter charged with failing to reveal his source of information.
Independent Newspapers group, suspended in 1974, resumes publication.
Temporary censorship imposed on publication of news relating to public employees' strike.

1979   *The Times of Ceylon,* facing bankruptcy, is taken over by government in effort to avoid foreclosure.

BIBLIOGRAPHY

Lent, John A. *Newspapers in Asia.* Hong Kong, 1981.

SWEDEN

by George Kurian

BASIC DATA

Population: 8,254,000
Area: 448,070 sq. km. (173,243 sq. mi.)
GNP: 408.79 billion krone (US$98.6 billion)
Literacy Rate: 99%
Language(s): Swedish
Number of Dailies: 108
  Aggregate Circulation: 4,183,000
  Circulation per 1,000: 515
Number of Nondailies: 53
  Aggregate Circulation: 367,400
  Circulation per 1,000: 45
Number of Periodicals: 4,000
Number of Radio Stations: 3

Number of Television Stations: 1
Number of Radio Receivers: 2,984,207
  Radio Receivers per 1,000: 367
Number of Television Sets: 2,701,493
  Television Sets per 1,000: 333
Total Annual Newsprint Consumption: 263,900 metric tons
  Per Capita Newsprint Consumption: 32 kg. (70.5 lb.)
Total Newspaper Ad Receipts: 1.78 billion krone (US$433.4 million)
  As % of All Ad Expenditures: 25.9

Background & General Characteristics

Statistics show that Swedes are among the most avid newspaper readers in the world. In 1978 there were 138 newspapers, with a combined circulation of more than 4.7 million or 571 copies per 1,000 inhabitants. For a long time there has been a slow but steady increase both in total circulation and in per capita circulation. The number of newspapers, however, has declined sharply during the postwar era from 216 in 1945. Most of the closures have affected newspapers competing with others of larger circulation in the same community. As a result, an increasing number of communities have become one-newspaper towns.

The increasing concentration of newspaper ownership in fewer hands has affected even relatively large dailies such as the leading Social Democratic morning paper *Stockholms-Tidningen*, which was discontinued in 1966, and the Liberal *Goteborgs Handels-och Sjofarts-Tidning*, which ceased publication in 1973.

This trend has left Sweden with fewer and larger newspapers, and yet economic conditions have deteriorated to such a degree that the future looks very uncertain for a large number of the surviving newspapers. The implications of this development are aggravated by the political orientation of the Swedish daily press. Traditionally the newspapers have tended to sympathize with and even actively advocate political party programs and ideologies. However, the political lineup has not been representative of the political preferences of the electorate. While Social Democrats and Communists have been sharing approximately half the popular vote for decades, their share of the press amounts to only about one-sixth of the total circulation. Conversely, non-Socialist parties with a com-

Newspaper Publication by Community

Number of Newspapers in one community	Number of Publishing Communities		
	1950	1960	1970
5 or more	2	1	1
4	3	2	1
3	15	6	1
2	31	23	17
1	42	56	62

bined voter support of barely 50 percent have been supported by four newspapers out of five.

Circulation by Political Affiliation or Sympathy	
Conservative, Liberal and Center	72.9%
Independent Non-Socialist	11.0%
Social Democratic and Communist	16.1%

As the Social Democratic press is younger and less well consolidated than its competitors, it is more vulnerable to the process of concentration. Thus the political press structure in the future could be expected to be even more disproportionate than at present.

As in most other countries with free-enterprise systems, economic realities tend to reinforce the process of concentration. Only 13 newspapers are published daily, and these account for more than 50 percent of the total circulation, while the 64 provincial papers published six days a week account for 30 percent and the four evening papers account for 20 percent. There are only 19 areas in which two or more morning papers compete. However, competition in these communities is being sustained thanks only to considerable subsidies by the state. There are only two newspapers, *Expressen* and *Aftonbladet*, with nationwide distribution, and both are newsstand evening papers.

The number of newspapers in Sweden reached a peak around 1920 when approximately 240 independent papers were published, most of them in small editions of less than 1,000 copies. The 1950s was a decade of economic crisis for many newspapers, ultimately ending in the discontinuation of more than 30 percent. Most closures involved papers with editions of fewer than 5,000 copies but those with larger circulations also suffered. Seven of the papers had circulations of more than 30,000, while one, *Stockholms-Tidnigen*, had an edition of over 130,000. Since 1969 newspaper mortality has been checked; only two newspapers of high periodicity have closed. This is attributable to the program of direct press subsidies extended during the 1970s.

Along with newspaper closures there has been a related, if ironic, phenomenon: new entries, of which there have been no less than 48 since 1940. Of these only two newspapers of high periodicity have survived. Of new entries with low periodicity, 20 of 37 have survived, but many of them today are dependent on state subsidies. One new entry, *Dagens Industri*, was founded as recently as February 1976 by Sweden's largest magazine publishing firm, Ahlen and Akerlund.

The role and functions of the Swedish press cannot be understood without some reference to its history. The first publication that may be called a newspaper appeared in the mid-1600s; called *Ordinari post Tijender*, it carried news of the Thirty Years' War. It was controlled by the state, and since then news has been closely coupled with politics. Not until the next century did the press develop functions above and beyond transmitting messages from the government to the citizens. Journals of debate and comment began to appear and newspapers began to assume a critical role in the evolution of Swedish culture. The first paper to combine news, commentary, and entertainment was *Aftonbladet*, which appeared in 1830. *Aftonbladet's* publisher, Lars Johan Hierta, a liberal merchant, typified the newly emergent middle class of pre-industrial Sweden, and the success of his paper reflected the growing influence of this class. *Dagens Nyheter*, founded

Total Newspaper Circulation by Frequency of Issue and Type (000s)					
Periodicity	Metropolitan		Provincial	Total	%
	AM	PM			
7-Day	1,260.5	1,169.5	131.8	2,561.8	52.5
6-Day	–	–	1,665.3	1,665.3	34.1
5-Day	–	27.2	97.6	124.8	2.6
4-Day	–	–	56.4	56.4	1.2
3-Day	–	–	186.2	186.2	3.8
2-Day	–	44.3	31.8	76.1	1.6
1-Day	–	85.9	118.4	204.3	4.2
Total	1,260.5	1,326.9	2,287.5	4,874.9	100.0
%	25.9	27.2	46.9	100.0	

by Rudolf Wall in 1864, quickly gained a large circulation as the result of the introduction of universal elementary education in 1842 and the opening of the first main rail line in the 1860's. But its circulation was still limited to a small social group. Not until the turn of the century did the first true mass circulation newspaper appear, *Stockholms-Tidningen*, founded by Anders Jeurling. Around this time the political polarization of the press became sharper than ever before. The relationship between the dailies and the political parties was generally ideological and intellectual rather than economic or organizational, although the latter more explicit ties were not unknown.

It might have been expected that the increasing concentration of newspaper ownership in recent times would lead to a weakening of the bonds between parties and the press. But such trends are barely discernible. The Conservatives have traditionally had the support of numerous large papers. These include *Svenska Dagbladet* and *Sydsvenska Dagbladet* and regional papers, such as *Barometern*, *Smalandsposten* and *Ostgota Correspondenten*. The Liberal Party is supported by the influential *Dagens Nyheter* as well as a number of smaller papers, such as *Goteborgs-Posten*. The largest organ of the Center Party is *Skanska Dagbladet* in Malmo. Since the closure of *Stockholms-Tidningen* in 1966, the ruling Social Democratic Party has lacked a large newspaper organ. The Communist press accounts for only 0.1 percent of the total circulation with *Norrskensflamman* as its principal newspaper.

Some loosening of these historic ties between party and press has occurred. The *Dagens Nyheter*, for example, has begun to demonstrate a greater measure of independence. Similarly, *Sydsvenska Dagbladet*, the largest paper in Malmo, broke with the Conservative Party during the 1960s and declared itself independent liberal instead. There also has been a more visible effort to achieve objectivity in the news columns, although party loyalty dictates editorial page policy. On the other hand, the Center and Liberal parties have extended their ownership of regional newspapers.

The Social Democratic press is strongest in the far north but in the whole of mid-Sweden it has less that 20 percent of the circulation. Non-Socialist papers reach over 80 percent of the households in a majority of the municipalities; they have more than 60 percent coverage in 78 percent of the municipalities. This is remarkable if only because Social Democrats have consistently gained over 40 percent of the electoral votes in Sweden's post–World War II elections and have been in government almost continuously since 1932.

According to John Merrill and Harold Fisher, the most influential daily in Sweden is *Svenska Dagbladet*, which, however, ranks only fifth in circulation behind *Goteborgs-Posten* (304,600), *Dagens Nyheter* (431,000), *Aftonbladet* (449,100) and *Expressen* (544,800).

In addition to newspapers Sweden has a healthy and prosperous periodical press. According to a recent government survey, there were about 2,500 magazines and journals of some consequence; the combined annual circulation of the 1,400 periodicals for which figures are available comes to approximately 560 million.

Magazines and Journals in Sweden

Type of Periodical	% of Total Circulation	% of Total Number of Titles
Popular Press	52	7
Organizational Press	38	40
Professional Press	4	15
Cultural & Political Press	3	10
Civil Service Press	2	8
House Organs	1	15
Other	1	5

% of Net Newspaper Circulation by Political Affiliation

Year	Conservative	Independent Liberal	Center	Liberal	Social Democratic	Communist	Other
1945	23.8	–	4.8	49.5	14.6	1.6	5.7
1960	22.5	–	3.8	45.9	22.5	0.7	4.6
1970	17.8	5.4	3.0	48.4	20.9	0.1	4.3
1974	17.6	6.6	4.1	46.4	20.0	0.4	4.9

The popular press in Sweden is of roughly the same character as that in other European countries. The combined circulation is over one-half of total periodical circulation, and the average Swedish household reads a couple of weekly magazines regularly. A handful of publishers dominate the market. Circulation has been stagnant in recent years, but generally speaking, family magazines appear to be regaining some of their lost ground. Roughly half of the organizational press comprises periodicals published by religious and related organizations, while economic organizations, such as trade and commercial associations, publish some 200 titles and labor and professional associations another 100. The rest is accounted for by sports, student and other organizations. Both the organizational press and the cultural and political press receive state subsidies.

Economic Framework

The economic context, in Sweden as in most countries, is determined largely by the necessity for newspapers to focus on two markets simultaneously: consumers and advertisers. On the whole advertising is estimated to account for 60 percent of the industry's revenues, although the breakdowns for individual papers differ vastly. In comparison with other advanced countries, Swedish newspapers have small circulations. Only five newspapers are being published in editions of over 100,000 copies. The largest provincial papers have circulations of between 50,000 and 100,000 copies. High-periodicity newspapers sold by subscription have an average circulation of approximately 20,000 copies and low-periodicity papers approximately 6,000 copies. Nevertheless, Sweden has the largest per capita newspaper readership in the world—572 per 1,000, according to the *Book of World Rankings*—with a total circulation of close to 4.6 million, as compared to 2.8 million in 1945. This represents an increase of 60 percent, more than double the 30 percent increase in population during the same period. By category, morning papers have successfully held on to their circulation while evening papers, particulary the *Expressen* and *Aftonbladet*, have made sizable gains. Total circulation for the evening press is 1.2 million copies, compared to 0.3 million copies in 1945; the number of copies per 1,000 inhabitants has climbed to 164 from 48 in 1975.

Because consumption is nearing the saturation point the only means of increasing revenues is by raising the subscription price and advertising rates, and both have been done. Subscription rates have gone up by more than 40 percent. Advertising has also been subjected to major hikes, but the volume has at the same time expanded. Newspaper advertising accounts for an estimated 40 percent of total advertising expenditures. However, the rising costs of newspaper advertising space may stimulate direct mail and may undermine the competitive situation of newspapers vis-à-vis other forms of advertising.

Ownership of the Swedish press is quite diverse. It may be classified in terms of three distinct categories: (1) private, (2) foundation, and (3) organizational.

Privately owned newspapers are generally Conservative, Liberal, or independent. Foundation ownership is also more common among bourgeois papers. Most Liberal papers are owned by foundations, while newspapers owned by organizations are either Social Democratic or affiliated with the Center Party.

Ownership of the Swedish Press				
Form of Ownership	Number	%	Circulation	%
Private	65	44.2	2,881,200	59.1
Foundations	22	15.0	529,600	10.9
Organizations	57	38.8	1,369,800	28.1
Other	3	2.0	94,300	1.9

A few large newspapers, often owned by the same owner or belonging to the same chain, dominate the Swedish press. The largest of these is the Bonnier group, with *Dagens Nyheter* and *Expressen*, which together account for 21.5 percent of total newspaper circulation in Sweden. The group controls a greater circulation than all the Social Democratic papers combined. The Hjorne family owns *Goteborgs-Posten* and *Goteborgs-Tidningen*, with a combined circulation of 400, 000 copies or 8.2 percent of total newspaper circulation. The Ander family owns a chain of eight provincial newspapers. Eighteen Social Democratic newspapers make up the corporation A-pressen AB, 51 percent of which is controlled by the Social Democratic Party and 49 percent by the Confederation of Trade Unions and certain individual unions. Private owners have established different traditions with respect to control over the content of their newspapers. In many cases the owner also serves as editor. The Bonniers, on the other hand, have drawn a firm line between ownership and editorial control. No Bonnier holds an editorial position on any of the family papers.

The content and appearance of Swedish papers are the products of long tradition. The style of journalism has been influenced in the post–World War II period by both television, on the one hand, and tabloids, on the other. The newspaper content of the Swedish press was analyzed by the 1972 Parliamentary Commission on the Press, which studied seven newspapers in terms of four categories: (1) news and reportage, (2) editorial opinion and commentary, (3) other editorial copy, and (4) advertisements. The proportion of news and reportage varied from 40 percent for *Sydsvenska Dagbladet* to 13 percent for *Goteborgs-Posten*, that of editorial copy from 42 percent for *Skanska Dagbladet* to 19 percent for *Goteborgs-Posten*, and advertisements from 67 percent for *Goteborgs-Posten* to 17 percent for *Sydvenska Dagbladet*. Interestingly, the proportion of editorial commentary remained more or less the same for all papers at 1 percent. Metropolitan papers carried more national and international news—about 50 percent—while provincial papers had 80 percent of their news copy dealing with local and parochial issues. Because of the pervasive influence of television and its instant coverage of national and international news, regional newspapers no longer feel bound to report all the events of the day but feel free to concentrate on items of specifically local interest. Swedish papers also devote considerable space to political and economic news relative to general news. Politics claims between 30 and 36 percent of a typical issue of a major newspaper and between 20 and 23 percent of a smaller local newspaper. The relative ratio for economic news is between 25 and 30 percent for larger newspapers and between 22 and 23 percent for local newspapers. The proportion of general news is higher in local newspapers, with *Falu-Kuriren* devoting up to 58 percent of its space to this category.

Many Swedes read two or more newspapers. The most common pattern is one morning paper plus one evening paper. Reading an evening paper alone is quite rare. A study of reader preferences in three clearly distinct areas of news coverage reveals that interest in foreign news and local news seem to have an inverse relationship. In *Sydsvenska Dagbladet* 60 percent of the readers have an interest in foreign news as compared to 84 percent in local news, while in *Dala-Demokraten* 91 percent have an interest in local news as compared to 42 percent in foreign news. At the same time 80 percent of the adult population reported reading at least one article in a newspaper daily. However, they spend only 30 minutes reading their newspaper, as against 60 minutes listening to the radio and 75 minutes watching television. But despite the press's relative weaknesses, the Parliamentary Commission on the Press found that newspapers play a more vital role than radio or television in molding public opinion.

As in most countries three types of papers may be distinguished in relationship to the markets they serve: monopoly, competitive, and complementary. Of the first class there are some 70, of the second some 20 and of the third some 25. Practically all the monopoly papers are high-coverage papers, that is, papers with a more than 50 percent household coverage. Ten of them dominate their respective markets completely, with coverage ratios of over 80 percent. Generally speaking, they can dictate both their newsstand prices and their advertising rates. The largest newspapers in this group are the *Goteborgs-Posten, Ostgota Correspondenten, Vestmanlands Lans Tidning*, and *Upsala Nya Tidning*. The situation for competing papers is less encouraging. The number of communities that support two or more papers is down to 20 from a high of 50 in 1945. (Malmo is Sweden's only three-paper community, with *Sydsvenska Dagbladet, Arbetet*, and *Skanska Dagbladet*.) In most cases of competing newspapers, one of the papers has a low coverage while the other has high market penetration. The spread in more than half the cases exceeds 50 percent. Complementary papers are traditional newspapers in the sense that they are organs of news and opinion as well as advertising, with the same pattern of distribution as other newspapers but with lower periodicity. Many of them are suburban newspapers published in the greater Stockholm or greater Gothenberg area. They also usually form a link in some sort of newspaper chain. They derive their commercial strength from their ability to offer advertisers higher coverage or lower prices within a given portion of a larger newspaper's circulation area. Within this group are also newspapers strongly identified with a party or other organization.

Prevailing pricing policy generates a greater amount of revenue from advertisers than from readers. Consequently, advertising market conditions determine the economy of the industry and the growth potential of newspapers. A newspaper's competitive advertising strength is usually expressed as household coverage or penetration, that is, the number of issues per 100 households in a given area. The Parliamentary Commission on the Press found that there is a positive correlation between the degree of household coverage and a paper's commercial success. The Commission introduced the terms low-coverage papers, to designate newspapers with less than 50 percent household coverage in their place of issue, and high-coverage papers, to designate papers with 50 percent household coverage and more. The Commission's analysis revealed that low-coverage papers showed losses of seven percent of total sales revenue while papers with over 60 percent coverage showed seven to eight percent profits on total revenue.

In one respect, however, conditions of competition have changed during the 1970s. In response to government incentives, newspaper distribution in Sweden has been reorganized so as to equalize distribution costs for newspapers competing in one and the same place of issue. The lion's share of the Swedish press is sold by subscription. Single-copy sales amount to only between five and 10 percent of total circulation. The National Post Office carries about 20 percent of the total volume, but the rest was distributed privately until recently. Today private distribution has been totally replaced by a joint distribution. Presbyren, the Swedish Press Bureau, currently distributes about 675 million newspapers and periodicals annually, or about two million a day.

The concept is widely held in Sweden that the press is a public utility that should not be allowed to suspend service to the people. As a result, Sweden has had a unique system of industrial relations in the press whereby all disputes between newspaper publishers and journalists as well as production staff are subject to arbitration if the parties involved are unable to reach an agreement through direct negotiations. It prohibits strikes and lockouts and any other similar action likely to provoke industrial conflict. This agreement is embodied in two contracts: that between Publishers' Association and the Swedish Compositors' Union (later enlarged by unions representing lithographers, distributors and other workers) of 1937, and that between the Newspaper Employers Association and the Swedish Journalists' Union of 1969. According to these agreements, employers and employees are required to work out collective agreements failing which an impartial chairman will be entrusted with bringing about an agreement. In the last instance, the chairman shall refer an unsettled dispute to a special arbitration court consisting of three nonpartisan persons appointed jointly by the parties. Under these agreements Sweden has enjoyed uninterrupted labor peace in its newspaper establishments for more than 30 years. Above all, it has helped to characterize stoppage of newspaper publication, either by lockout or by strikes, as a violation of the concept of freedom of the press, and, in effect, a violation of the constitution.

Press Laws

Sweden seems to have been the first country in the world to establish freedom of the press. In 1766 Parliament adopted a Freedom of the Press Act as a part of the constitution. More recently similar legislation has been passed for radio and television, without yet becoming constitutional law.

After the promulgation of the first press act the last decades of the 18th century witnessed a relapse into censorship, but since the constitutional reforms of 1809, freedom of the press has prevailed. The present Freedom of the Press Act dates from 1949, with several subsequent amendments. As part of the constitution, this act is protected by special safeguards. Thus, to gain legal force, any amendment or abrogation of the act must be confirmed by two successive parliaments, with general elections taking place between the first and second readings.

In Sweden, as in some other democracies, public censorship of the press as well as other serious restrictions on publishing and distribution of printed matter are explicitly forbidden. However, the Swedish lawmakers set out to safeguard press freedom by an elaborate combination of measures unique at the time of inception and to this very day emulated only by a few other countries.

Foremost among these devices is the invention of the term "responsible publisher." Any periodical appearing four times a year or more must appoint a responsible publisher, who alone is answerable for the contents of the publication. He alone can be held accountable for any violation of the Freedom of the Press Act. The responsible publisher is appointed by the owner of the publication. He must be a Swedish citizen domiciled in Sweden (or, since 1978, an alien domiciled in Sweden) and neither a minor nor an undischarged bankrupt. Being the only person who can be taken to court for what is printed in the newspaper, the responsible publisher has the right to decide whether any given item should be published or not. In theory, it requires him to read, prior to publication, every word in the paper, but since this is obviously impracticable, he must delegate this responsibility to trusted subordinates. In certain exigencies, however, the law provides a chain of responsibility according to which the responsible publisher's responsibility may be transferred to the owner of the paper, and, if that is not possible, to the printer, and, as a last resort, to the distributor. The last link in the chain, the distributor, is often the party held responsible in cases of foreign publications imported into Sweden where the prior links are not subject to Swedish law. In the matter of damages, the court may insist on the shared responsibility of both publisher and owner.

The net effect of this provision is to exempt sources of information from criminal liability. In fact, the law explicitly prohibits the investigation or disclosure of newsmen's sources. It follows that a person who contributes to a newspaper as a reporter or informant is not only protected against legal action, but his identity becomes immaterial and thus inadmissible as a point of law. This protection is extended even to state and municipal employees, who are thus free to give information to newspapers and other media without fear of legal repercussions. The rationale for such extreme protection of media sources is that the mass media has the duty to watch over the conduct of government and society and needs the fullest possible freedom to do so. There are, of course, some exceptions to the general rule of impunity and anonymity of sources, especially where the gathering or divulging of information constitutes or involves high treason, espionage, or other related crimes. Similarly, the protection is inapplicable when an official violates his pledge of professional secrecy and in criminal cases where it may interfere with due process.

Another remarkable feature of the Freedom of the Press Act is the principle of free access to public documents, introduced as early as 1766. The principle gives all citizens (and even aliens) the right to turn to a state or municipal agency and ask to be shown any document in their files, regardless of whether or not the document concerns him personally. Officials are legally required to comply and even to supply copies of the documents requested. The right of access is monitored by the Parliamentary Ombudsman, whose prime duty is to supervise the implementation of the act.

There are numerous exceptions to the rule of access to public documents but these are clearly spelled out in the Secrecy Act (which is not part of the corpus of constitutional law and thus may be easily amended). Among categories of documents to which access may be denied are those relating to national security and foreign relations, criminal matters, private financial matters, and information concerning the integrity and safety of individuals. In most cases the maximum duration of confidentiality is specified, but restrictions may be lifted at any time before the expiration of the term of secrecy. Where requests for public documents are rejected, the applicant is entitled to a written statement quoting the legal authority for withholding the document and informing him of his right to appeal against the decision. The highest appellate authority is the Supreme Administrative Court.

Offenses punishable under Freedom of the Press Act include high treason, instigation to war, incitement to riot, conspiracy, sedition, etc., as well as threats to or contempt of minority groups on grounds of race, color, creed and ethnic origin. Pornography is no longer punishable under Swedish law. Most of the legal actions against newspapers concern libel.

In addition, the media are protected from legal harassment through special procedures and rules. Public prosecution under the Freedom of the Press Act may be initiated only by the Chancellor of Justice and not by local public prosecutors. The chancellor is obliged to obtain the consent of the Cabinet before acting in cases with political implications. The press cases are tried by jury (unless both parties agree to waive a jury trial), although the jury is an institution otherwise alien to the Swedish legal system. The jury is comprised of nine lay members, of whom six must be in agreement for a conviction.

Furthermore, the act specifies that the jury and the judge must be guided by a special bias in favor of the media, and that accusations must be tried with a view to the spirit and intent rather than the wording of documents.

Press freedoms are also guarded by a number of organizations, such as the Swedish Press Council, set up in 1916, the first of its kind in the world. It is sponsored by the Swedish Newspaper Publishers' Association, the Publicists' Club (the national press club), and the Union of Swedish Journalists. The council is composed of six members; two represent the general public, three are appointed by the sponsoring press organizations and the sixth is the chairman, who holds the casting vote. The latter has always been a member of the Supreme Court. The council does not deal with cases in which a paper has broken a press law but hears complaints from anyone who has a grievance against a newspaper. The council can compel an offending newspaper to publish a retraction and also to pay a fine not exceeding Skr 5,550. In 1969 the office of the Press Ombudsman (PO) was established to supervise the adherence to ethical standards. The PO is also entitled to act on his own initiative, or to issue ex officio criticism of the newspaper. In the case of serious grievances, he will file a complaint with the Press Council, which will then publish a statement acquitting or censuring the newspaper. In 1978, a typical year, the PO received 420 complaints, initiated another 36 and reprimanded 27 publications. The Press Council considered 101 cases, censured 56 and acquitted 45.

Swiss journalists are also guided by a voluntary code of ethics first adopted in 1923 by Publicistklubben and revised and readopted in 1974. Another instrument of self-regulation is the monthly *Gronkopings Veckoblad*, which has been blasting away at the Swedish press for more than 75 years. Many editors have had their reputations singed in its pages, which use parodies and cartoons effectively.

Censorship

There is no censorship in Sweden in any form of media, with the sole exception of the motion picture industry. Motion pictures intended for public showing are previewed by the National Board of Film Censorship, which is empowered to delete sequences or to ban the film altogether.

State-Press Relations

Swedish press policy has aroused considerable interest abroad. In Sweden, perhaps more than in any other Western country, the state has actively intervened to maintain diversity in the press. Through a program of selective as well as general subsidies to the press, government policy has managed to curb an accelerating trend toward local monopolies.

Libertarian ideology has long been the dominant influence in Swedish press policy. This ideology may best be described in terms of the following four basic principles: (1) competition of ideas, (2) democratization, (3) surveillance of authorities and (4) free right of establishment. The new constitutional statute on freedom of the press adopted in 1949 was wholly imbued with these four principles. It sought by all conceivable means to guarantee press freedoms against encroachment by the state.

Unlike many other Western democracies, Sweden has abandoned the concept of absolute freedom of the press to one of selective state economic support and intervention in order to preserve competition and variety in the press. State intervention is designed to counter market forces that favor concentration of ownership and threaten basic democratic values.

As the state became increasingly involved in the affairs of the newspaper industry, the need arose for more precise formulations of policy goals. The 1972 Parliamentary Commission on the Press was directed to formulate these goals. The commission responded by defining the proper role of mass media in a democratic society. The basis of press policy, the commission asserted, must derive from a representative democracy's needs for efficient means of communication. The commission found that the press served four functions, all vital in the proper functioning of a democratic society: (1) all-round information, (2) commentary and analysis of the news, (3) surveillance and scrutiny of those in power and (4) facilitation of communication within and between various groups in society. Based on the premise that a democratic government is only as free and as efficient as its press, it became necessary for the state to take positive action to counter market forces leading to closures and to stimulate new entries. Economic concentration inevitably led to the press becoming the organ of a select few, whether they be private individuals or organizations.

The guiding principles behind Sweden's press policy are summed up as follows:

• Competition between newspapers on regional markets should be stimulated. The presence of two or more newspapers in a place of issue is necessary to maintain the reader's freedom of choice.

• Where economic competition has left but one paper on the local market, press policy must seek to break the monopoly by stimulating the emergence of complementary papers.

• The formation of chains must be investigated. The details of press ownership must be made public knowledge and all changes in the ownership structure must be registered.

• Press policy must be designed and implemented so as to eliminate fears over the possible intervention in or influence over the content of individual newspapers.

• The rules for implementing state press policy must be unequivocal and must not be modified to suit or favor one paper over another.

• Collaboration between newspapers must be encouraged, as it offers obvious advantages in terms of utilization of resources.

• The system of rules governing the extension of state support shall be based on an analysis of market conditions and shall encourage efficient economic management of recipient firms.

• State aid to the press shall be administered by a board equipped with resources for the conduct of further analyses of the state of the industry as well as specific market situations.

The basic purpose of these principles is to ensure that the Swedish press retains its variety while guarding against the risks implied in state intervention. The editorial independence of newspapers is not jeopardized. Questions of press ethics, for example, are not the concern of the state board, but are left to the industry's own organizations. Support is extended to newspapers regardless of their politics.

• State support for the press has been both direct and indirect. Indirect support consists of:

• State contributions to opinion-generating activities on the part of the parliamentary parties, often used to finance party newspapers.

• Exemption from value-added tax on subscription and single-copy sales.

• Lower scales of tax on advertising in newspapers than in magazines—six percent instead of 10 percent—with only revenues in excess of Skr 3 million being subject to tax.

• Privileged status with respect to publication of state and local government advertising.

• Postal distribution according to a special newspaper rate. According to the National Post Office (Postverket) the distribution rebate on newspapers and periodicals yields an annual deficit of Skr 80 and 100 million.

The principles governing direct support to newspapers address themselves to two main areas: competitive relations and collaborative relations. With respect to the first, measures are taken to combat inequalities in the competitive relations between newspaper firms and strengthen the competitive status of individual firms in the long run. With respect to the second, government policy stimulates newspaper firms to collaborate in areas where they have previously engaged in competition.

In chronological order, state aid to the press has taken four forms: (1) state loans, (2) production subsidies, (3) development aid and (4) establishment aid.

State loans were introduced in 1970 to help finance modernization and rationalization. Loans are extended only to such projects as are unable to secure financing on the commercial credit market on normal terms. Projects involving collaboration with other newspaper firms are given priority. The maximum period of the loans is 20 years, and the loans are exempt from amortization during a five-year period and from interest for a maximum period of five years.

The principal instrument of government support is the program of production subsidies, introduced in 1971. These subsidies are largely restricted to low-coverage newspapers (up to 50 percent household coverage in the place of issue, with a successive reduction from 40 percent upwards). The amount of the subsidy is directly related to the volume of newsprint devoted to editorial comment—Skr 11,000 per ton of editorial copy with an additional 4 percent for newspapers in metropolitan areas. Eligible newspapers must be normally published at least once a week, sold mainly by subscription, have a circulation of at least 2,000 copies and carry less than 50 percent advertising. The highest amount granted to a metropolitan daily is currently Skr 23.4 million, and the least Skr 2.4 million; the corresponding figures for the provincial papers are Skr 6.3 million and Skr 1 million. Newspapers of low periodicity (one to three issues per week) may also receive production subsidies. Here, however, the subsidy granted for papers distributed nationally is on a different scale from that granted regional papers. To be eligible for support, the low-periodicity paper may have no greater than 30 percent coverage of its home market, with the subsidy being successively reduced from 20 percent upward. In some cases there is very little difference in the size and circulation of competing newspapers. To avoid unfairly tipping the balance in favor of the slight underdog, the rules also permit extension of production subsidies to the paper with higher coverage. However, such subsidies are exceptional and to date have been granted only to six papers. The state also provides development aid to monopoly newspapers operating in small markets, especially for the purpose of increasing their periodicity. The ceiling for this subsidy is Skr 600,000 for one- to three-day newspapers and Skr 1.2 million for four- to seven-day newspapers.

Another form of aid is support for the establishment of complementary papers. The state does not decide whether or not a paper is worth starting. That judgment is reserved to the publishers themselves. The Press Subsidies Council, however, determines whether or not the paper in question has any prospects of obtaining production subsidies in the future. To discourage purely speculative entries, support is extended in the form of interest- and amortization-free loans, which are remitted after one year if the recipient qualifies for a production subsidy. Establishment grants ranging from Skr 0.9 and Skr 1.35 million have been extended to six papers to date.

Subsidies are basically designed to stimulate competition, which is one goal of Swedish press policy. The other goal is to promote collaboration and discourage certain forms of competition. Measures promoting collaboration include: (1) joint distribution rebates, (2) coproduction subsidies, (3) subsidies toward cooperation in advertising sales and (4) subsidies for industry-wide projects. Two firms currently serve the subscribed press with rebated nationwide joint distribution services. Two additional firms offer regional services. The rebate is three ore per copy per day. While coproduction and cooperation in advertising have not produced significant changes in the market structure of the press, state measures have been most effective in promoting industry-wide projects, aimed toward rationalizing certain newspaper management functions. Newspapers purchase newsprint coopera-

tively, own their own wire service, administer single-copy distribution jointly as well as training programs, and conduct research and technical development through a central organization.

In order to ensure that the extension of incentives to collaborative projects does not infringe upon the journalistic integrity of the press, a number of conditions have been laid down. These include:

• The collaboration should be defensible on economic grounds. The initiative should reside with the papers themselves and the assistance should be extended for only a limited period of time.

• The collaboration should serve the goals of Swedish press policy. It should be extended to both recipients and nonrecipients of production and development subsidies, should be offered to locally competing newspapers only, and should in no way disadvantage weaker newspapers.

The ceiling for a coproduction subsidy is Skr 500,000 and that for an industry-wide collaborative project Skr 100,000. In the case of cooperative advertising sales, six percent of the total revenues derived from joint advertising is paid out annually for a period up to five years.

• Total direct government subsidies to the press in 1978 are listed in the accompanying table.

Total Direct Government Subsidies to Press	
	Skr million
Production Subsidies	189
Development Grants	12
Establishment Grants	4.8
Joint Distribution Rebates	64
Aid to Collaboration	7
Total	276.8

Subsidies are financed by a 10 percent tax on all advertising, except in the case of newspaper advertising, where the tax is three percent. Subsidies are administered by the Press Subsidies Board, formed in 1976. The board consists of eight members, of whom five are members of Parliament. All are appointed by the government. The board has four primary responsibilities: (1) to analyze developments in press economy, (2) to administer economic assistance and to evaluate it consequence, (3) to maintain a register of newspaper ownership and (4) to administer and maintain a newspaper loan fund. The board publishes annual reports on the economic status of the industry and state press policy.

Goverment subsidies to the press have become a vital source of income to the press as a whole, and it is doubtful if they will be ever abandoned. Roughly one of every three newspapers has received loans. More than 90 percent of the funds have been extended to individual newspaper firms. Production subsidies have been extended to 64 papers, 58 of which are secondary or low-coverage papers. By political inclination, 55 percent of the total disbursements is accounted for by Social Democratic newspapers and 25 percent by three metropolitan papers, *Svenska Dagbladet* (Conservative, Stockholm), *Skanska Dagbladet* (Center, Malmo) and *Goteborgs Handels -och Sjofarts- Tidning* (Liberal, Gothenburg). The most successful element of the subsidy program has been the joint distribution scheme, introduced in 1970. This scheme has almost entirely replaced private distribution, with over 80 percent participation by the subscribed press, as compared to 10 percent participation at the beginning of the program. During this period the National Post Office has lost about one-third of the volume of newspapers it distributed prior to 1970. In order to keep newspapers from abandoning postal distribution altogether, almost half the volume of postal deliveries has been rebated.

The main objective of state aid to the press has been to brake the prevailing tendencies toward concentration. This goal has largely been realized. Since the introduction of state aid only two recipient newspapers have been forced to reduce their periodicity and only one paper has ceased publication. The program has resulted in a radical change in the economic climate under which the Swedish press operates. Press revenues have shown a marked improvement. Production subsidies amount to 20 percent of four- to seven-day papers' and 25 percent of one- to three-day papers' annual revenues. Smaller papers have been enabled to invest in modernization and adopt stronger marketing strategies. If anything, the subsidies have given the low-coverage newspapers breathing space and some competitive edge in an industry with a high mortality rate.

As might be expected in an open society such as Sweden's, the state does not exert any influence over the press through the allocation of newsprint, labor union manipulation, import licenses for printing equipment or licensing of journalists. Advertising support is extended to all papers equally.

Attitude Toward Foreign Media

There are no special procedures for accreditation of foreign correspondents or restrictions on the flow of news into or out of Sweden.

News Agencies

The only national news agency is the Tidningarnas Telegrambyra (TT), a cooperative news agency founded in 1921, working in conjunction with Reuters, AFP, Groupe 39 agencies and dpa. It has its headquarters in Stockholm, with branches in Goteborg, Malmo, Sundsvall and Lulea and over 500 part-time correspondents throughout the country. It has three foreign bureaus in Brussels, Moscow and New York. TT's 154 subscribers (including 140 newspapers) receive a daily service of 25,000 words of national and local news and 11,000 words of foreign news in Swedish as well as a daily broadcast with five newscasts and a telephone service. TT's offices are linked with Reuters European multiplex circuit by the Scanplex data-transmission service and with domestic subscribers by a permanent teleprinter network. About 75 newspapers receive teletypesetting services.

Other smaller news agencies include the Svenska Nyhetsbyran (the Swedish Conservative Press Agency) and the Svensk-Internationella Pressbyran (SIP), the Swedish International Press Bureau.

Foreign news agencies with bureaus in Sweden include AFP, ANSA, ADN, Anatolian News Agency, AP, dpa, Hsinhua, Jewish Telegraphic Agency, Kyodo News Service, News Agency Pyresa, Novosti, Polska Agencj Prasowa, Reuters, Tass, UPI, Belga, Tanjug, and Agerpress.

There is no state intervention in news agency operations.

Electronic News Media

Broadcasting in Sweden has been the exclusive domain of the Swedish Broadcasting Corporation (Sveriges Radio AB), a joint stock company, since 1925. Television began regular operations in 1956, with a second channel introduced in 1969. SBC comprises four wholly owned and independent subsidiaries: one for nationwide radio, one for national and regional TV, one for local radio, and one for educational radio and television. The parent company is owned by three groups of shareholders: popular movements, including evangelical groups, consumer cooperatives and labor unions; newspaper and press organizations; and business organizations. Shares are distributed among the three groups in the ratio of 60:20:20. The Board of Governors consists of 15 members; the chairman and six other members are appointed by the government, five by the shareholders, two by the employees, and the 15th is the director general. The parent company is responsible for finance, coordination and long-term planning.

The state exerts control over the broadcast media in several respects. Under the Broadcast Law of 1978 freedom of expression is granted to the broadcasters without restrictions other than those that apply to all forms of the media. The law prohibits censorship or cancellation of programs prior to broadcast. Commercials are prohibited. Distribution of programs is the responsibility of the National Telecommunications Administration. In the case of radio, the Radio Council (radionamnden), whose members are appointed by the government, determines whether the programs, comply with the Broadcasting Liability Act. Finally, the Parliament determines the annual broadcasting budget and also fixes the amount of the receiver license fees.

Education & Training

Since 1960 there have been two institutes in journalism, one in Stockholm and one in

Goteborg, that train newsmen. Except for editors, editorial writers and foreign correspondents, there are very few Swedish journalists with university training. Most of them have passed the "student's examination," corresponding to about two years of college in the United States. About 95 percent of all editorial workers belong to the Union of Swedish Journalists. According to the British journalist Gerard Fay, "Swedish reporters know what news is and how to get it....[They] are not behind any in the world in getting...exclusive information and using it very often against the will of government departments and other political and commercial pressure groups."

Summary

Sweden has undoubtedly a healthy mass media system helped by high levels of literacy, a working democracy that protects freedom of expression, an advanced economy, an equitable distribution of wealth and a high degree of technological sophistication. Nevertheless, the press is faced with serious economic problems; timely intervention by the state in the early 1970s has averted for a time being the closures of a number of low-coverage papers, but the same process has made the press extremely dependent on state aid. Press subsidies now total hundreds of millions annually and have reached a point where it is inconceivable that the subsidy system could be abolished without immediately jeopardizing vast numbers of newspapers. Whether the Swedish press likes it or not, it will have to live with a system of permanent dependence on the state and the taxpayers.

CHRONOLOGY

1978	The fourth Commission on the Press is appointed. Press subsidies are increased.	ters announces final decision to set up Nordsat, a communication satellite.
1980	The Nordic Council of Minis-	

BIBLIOGRAPHY

Engwall, L. *Swedish Newspapers in the Post-War Period.* (Stockholm, 1974).

Forskning om Massmedier. SOU (Statens Offentliga Utredningar—Swedish Government Official Reports). Stockholm, 1977.

Furhoff, L. *Makten over Medierna.* Lund, 1974.

Furhoff, L., and Hederberg, H. *Dagspressen i Sverige.* Stockholm, 1969.

Gustafsson, K.E., *Foretaget och Reklamen* (Goteborg, 1970).

Hadenius, S., Seveborg, J.O., and Weibull, L. *Partipress.* Halmstad, 1970.

Hadenius, S., and Weibull, L. *Press, Radio, TV.* Stockholm, 1975.

Handlingssekretess och Tystnadsplikt—Forslag Till ny Sekretsslag: SOU Stockholm, 1977.

Kronvall, K. *Partipressen Idag.* Lund, 1971.

Pers, A. Y. *Den Svenska Pressen.* Stockholm, 1967.

Massmediegrundlag: SOU. Stockholm, 1975.

Svensk Press: Pressens Funtioner i Samhallet SOU. Stockholm, 1978.

Svensk Press: Presstodet och Tidningskonkurrensen SOU. Stockholm, 1974.

Svensk Press: Statlig Presspolitik SOU. Stockholm, 1979.

Svensk Press: Tidningar i Samverkan SOU. Stockholm, 1975.

Tollin, S. *Svensk Dagspress.* Stockholm, 1967.

Westerstahl, J. *Objektiv Nyhetsformedling.* Stockholm, 1972.

Wickstrom, B. *Tidningsforetagens Konkureensmedel.* Gothenburg, 1958.

SWITZERLAND

by Harold A. Fisher

BASIC DATA

Population: 6,297,000 (1979, est.)
Area: 41,293 sq. km. (15,943 sq. mi.)
GNP: 155.2 billion Swiss francs (US$97 billion) (1979)
Literacy Rate: 99%
Language(s): French, German, Italian
Number of Dailies: 116 (1977)
   Aggregate Circulation: 2,262,000 (1978)
   Circulation per 1,000: 333 (1978)
Number of Nondailies: 169 (1977)
   Aggregate Circulation: 6,441,439 (1978)
   Circulation per 1,000: 1,000 (1978)
Number of Periodicals: (Included under nondailies)

Number of Radio Stations: 6 (1977)
Number of Television Stations: 3 (1977)
Number of Radio Receivers: 2,172,000 (1978)
   Radio Receivers per 1,000: 333 (1978)
Number of Television Sets: 1,895,000 (1978)
   Television Sets per 1,000: 300 (1978)
Total Annual Newsprint Consumption: 152,500 metric tons (1977)
Per Capita Newsprint Consumption: 28.2 kg. (62 lb.) (1977)
Total Newspaper Ad Receipts: 1.3 billion Swiss francs (US$526 million) (1976)
   As % of All Ad Expenditures: 59

Background & General Characteristics

Switzerland has a diversified, significant and generally high-quality press. Across the past 40 years, the number of publications has decreased steadily. In 1939, when the country's population stood at about four million, there were 406 newspaper titles. By 1974, when the population had risen to over six million, the number of papers had dropped to 292. Now there are an estimated 231 dailies and nondailies, over six of which have circulations of over 100,000 and only 14 over 50,000. Today, the number of nondailies, now about 170, is divided between 152 publications that appear one to three times weekly, and of which 17 are published less frequently.

The characteristics of the Swiss reading public strongly influence the nature of the press. Several factors give print media a fragmented and diversified nature. The high literacy of the populace (over 98 percent), coupled with compulsory education to age 14 and the high per capita income of over 19,000 Swiss francs ($12,000) per annum per person in 1980 provide a well-educated, affluent readership. The presence of three official languages—German (spoken by about 65 percent of the population), French (spoken by 18 percent) and Italian (12 percent)—has divided the press into three main sectors.

The division of the Swiss Confederation into 20 cantons and six half-cantons generates strong interest in local news and further fragments the press into numerous local papers. Over half of the Swiss papers have circulations of under 5,000, with a number selling less than 1,000 copies daily. The absence of large cities (only five with populations over 100,000), the heavy rural population and the mountainous terrain further diversify the print media. As a result, the press in Switzerland is decentralized and the majority of the papers are regional or local. Even papers with high circulations, such as Zurich's *Tages-Anzeiger* and Basel's *Basler Zeitung,* are regional in their interest and outreach. Only three dailies have a truly national character—*Blick, Neue Zürcher Zeitung* and *La Suisse*—and, except for *Blick,* their circulations are mainly confined to their language area.

The history of the Swiss press reaches back into the 18th century with the founding of

Feuille d'Avis de Lausanne in 1762, 24 years after the country became independent. Switzerland has always been free, economically stable and devoid of major disruptive social and political upheavals; and such conditions have combined to give its people a traditional, conservative and high-quality press. Switzerland is the home of two of the world's most respected elite dailies, the German-language *Neue Zürcher Zeitung,* founded in 1780, and the French-language *Journal de Genève,* established in 1826. Except for the popular and sensational high-circulation *Blick,* Swiss newspapers are typically staid and serious. Many have a party-political orientation in their editorial policies.

The percentage of newspapers published in each of the three major languages corresponds quite closely with the population distribution of each lingual grouping. About 69 percent of dailies are printed in German and distributed primarily in the northern and eastern cantons; about 25 percent appear in French in the western cantons; and five percent are published and distributed in Italian cantons in the south. A tiny minority of one percent is published in Romansch in the eastern canton of Grisons. According to circulation data, the French-speaking populace reads newspapers most avidly, followed by the German-speaking and then the Italian communities.

The presence of nearly a million immigrant workers prior to 1975—about 650,000 now that restrictions on alien workers have been imposed—plus general Swiss interest in foreign news results in the importation of over 100,000 copies of French, German, Italian and Spanish newspapers each day. The cosmopolitan nature of residents in the international urban centers, plus the high numbers of foreign businessmen and tourists, also leads to some demands for English-language papers.

The political party allegiances of the Swiss newspapers have considerable bearing on their distribution. In general, the press is politically conservative and anti-socialist. It also represents the primary opposition to government. Many of the papers, small and large, have strong party allegiances; however, party ownership is less frequent than independent owners' use of their papers for party support. The Swiss are loyal subscribers to party papers, and will typically continue to subscribe to a paper even after they have abandoned its party allegiances; consequently, many Swiss take papers whose views they cannot support. This phenomenon results in uneven distribution of party publications. The Social Democrats, now in the political majority, have the fewest papers, while the Radicals, at present a minority, have by far the most dailies supporting their views. At the same time, most of the Swiss party-affiliated dailies confine their opinions to local and domestic issues, a factor which again contributes to the regional and fragmented nature of the press.

In terms of layout and content, the papers of the German-speaking sector are the most conservative. The French-speaking press has been more open to modern trends in makeup. Most of Swiss dailies are of tabloid size. The *Neue Zürcher Zeitung,* for example, measures just 19 by 13 inches. Except for *Blick,* the appearance is serious, somewhat gray, with a paucity of illustrations. Nor are Swiss papers thick or lengthy. A typical length varies from 24 to 28 pages.

Most Swiss dailies present a mixture of news, features and advertisements. Heavy emphasis is placed on material relating to the immediate locality in which the paper is published. Traditionally, comment dominates the front page and often much of the inside pages, for the Swiss press assumes the role of educator or informed advisor to the public, especially about local government and political conditions. Such commentary usually does not extend to foreign affairs.

All of the bigger cities have several dailies; some are published in the morning, others in the afternoon or evening. As in most of Europe, only a few publish on Sunday. *La Suisse,* a morning paper with a daily circulation of about 65,000, publishes 107,000 copies on Sundays. *Neue Zürcher Zeitung* also publishes seven times weekly; its Sunday edition contains a supplement called "Wochenende," which is filled with well-illustrated feature articles.

Supplements, magazine sections and special feature pages are also a regular feature of weekday papers in most of the leading cities. *Neue Zürcher Zeitung,* for example, carries a supplement each day and special features irregularly but frequently. Its regular supplements include "Literatur und Kunst" on the artistic fields, "Forschung" on scientific and medical developments, "Technik" on technological advances, "Tourismus" on travel and vacationing and "Film" and "Radio und Fernsehen" on the mass media.

The European edition of the *International Herald-Tribune* is now published in Zurich and is widely read by Switzerland's foreign business and tourist communities.

One communist daily, the *La Voix Ouvrière,* is published in Geneva. A dozen dailies represent Catholic views. The largest of this latter grouping is *La Liberté,* with a circulation of 32,000. However, most of the Catholic papers have low circulations.

At least a dozen Swiss cities have two or more competing papers. The largest cities—Geneva, Zurich and Berne—produce several dailies each. Newspapers published in the larger cities also tend to have the largest circulations. Zurich, for example, is the home of *Blick* (272,000), *Tages-Anzeiger* (260,000), *Tagblatt der Stadt Zurich* (186,000), *Neue Zürcher Zeitung* (115,000) and *Die Tat* (35,000), plus several smaller dailies. *La Suisse* (65,000), *Tribune de Genève* (71,000), *Journal de Genève* (19,000), *Le Courrier* (13,500) and *La Voix Ouvrière* (8,000) are all published in Geneva. Other cities with competing dailies include Basel, Berne, Lausanne, Lugano, Lucerne, Gall, Winterthur and Biel.

Statistics show that nearly one-half of Swiss dailies have a circulation of less than 10,000 copies per day, and about half of all dailies either show losses or about break even financially. In 1977 only 14 papers had circulations of over 50,000. Most of the rest (about 30 percent) reported daily circulations of 10,000 to 25,000.

10 Largest Dailies by Circulation	
Blick	272,000
Tages-Anzeiger Zurich	260,000
Tagblatt der Stadt Zurich	186,000
Berner Zeitung	120,000
Neue Zürcher Zeitung	115,000
Basler Zeitung	111,000
24 Heures Lausanne	101,000
Luzerner Tagblatt	83,000
Tribune de Genève	71,000
La Suisse	65,000

Perhaps Switzerland's most influential newspaper is also its best elite, high-quality daily, *Neue Zürcher Zeitung,* termed by many informed critics "the best newspaper in the world." Another quality paper, *Tages-Anzeiger Zurich,* is really a family paper, with predominantly regional circulation. A third daily considered influential out of proportion to its circulation is the high-quality *Journal de Genève.* Among Switzerland's more popular papers, *Blick* has no rival, although its influence lies in its popular appeal rather than in its journalistic content. It is not identified with any party or geographical area; rather, its readers are scattered throughout the German-speaking cantons.

Economic Framework

Three factors combine to make Switzerland one of the world's most economically secure nations. First, it serves as a leading international banking center. Second, its breathtaking scenery and world-famous hotel system make tourism an important source of revenue. Finally, it is considered one of the world's leading industrial nations; although Switzerland has no significant natural resources except water, it has produced numerous high-quality export goods, among them clocks, watches, machine tools, textiles, foodstuffs, chocolate, chemicals and pharmaceuticals. Consequently, until recently, this small landlocked nation has been able to maintain a favorable import-export trade balance. The combination of banking, tourism and industrial output has provided a rising GNP, which reached 157,890 million Swiss francs ($97,463 million) in 1978 or an average annual per capita income of about 20,000 Swiss francs ($12,345).

Switzerland's generally healthy economic climate has produced media growth and security to at least a degree. Consumers can afford multiple radio sets, at least a single television set per family and more than one daily newspaper. For the same reason, the magazine and book publishing industries also thrive. A number of illustrated magazines have circulations of well over 100,000, among them *Pro, Trente Jours, Illustrazionè Ticinese, Der Schweizerische Beobachter, Ringiers Unterhaltungsblätter* and *Das Beste,* the last the German edition of *Reader's Digest.*

One effect of a healthy economy for the media has been rising circulations. Gross daily newspaper circulation in the country has risen slowly but steadily, from 2.21 million in 1965 to over 2.2 million in 1978. The net result has been to give even the smaller papers a certain degree of financial stability amid spiraling material and production costs.

Most Swiss dailies rely for about 90 percent of their circulation income on subscriptions. The exception is *Blick,* which sells almost all its copies on the streets of Zurich and many towns and villages in the German-speaking sectors of the country.

Another source of financial security is the rising amount of advertising. Since the advent of television advertising, competition for the advertiser's trade has become increasingly competitive. However, newspaper publishers are hoping ad revenues will not fall off, since they now pay 70 to 80 percent of the costs of newspaper publishing.

Swiss advertising on radio is illegal and therefore all income to operate radio broadcasting must come from license fees. That leaves television and the newspapers to vie for advertiser support. Gross expenditures for advertising in newspapers are approximately 10 times those for television—1,288,700,000 Swiss francs ($526 million) for newspaper advertising versus 137.2 million Swiss francs ($56 million) for TV ads in 1976. Advertisers consider television the prime advertising medium; according to one study, if they had to choose only one outlet for advertising, 90 percent would elect television.

However, opportunities for newspaper advertising are considerably greater than for TV: the state-owned television has three regional lingual outlets on which advertising for each is limited to 20 minutes per day, whereas dailies total well over 100 and each offers space for national, retail and classified advertising.

Newspapers have three advertising-rate charges: Swiss, local and foreign. The local price is charged if the advertiser has an office in the same city in which the newspaper is published. Swiss prices are paid by all Swiss nationals who have their base in the country, and are usually 15 percent higher than local rates. Foreign advertisers pay 20 percent to 30 percent more than the local price. Discounts, in all cases, are made to repeat customers.

In 1978 *Blick*, the largest national newspaper, was charging approximately 2,590 Swiss francs ($4,200) for a full-page black-and-white ad and 3,395 Swiss francs ($5,500) for full-page color. Full-page costs in the largest regional daily, *Tages-Anzeiger Zurich,* were 1,420 Swiss francs ($2,300) for full-page black-and-white and about 2,800 Swiss francs ($4,500) for color.

Magazines receive about 13 percent of the gross advertising expenditures in the Swiss media.

Advertising in Switzerland is affected by the fact that the country has no national press, as such; because of the language distribution, all papers are really regional. The larger-circulation newspapers receive a disproportionate share of the advertising revenue. Consequently, they grow while the small papers, whose limited advertising profit is whittled away still further by an ever-increasing number of free advertising papers, must merge or be taken over if they are not to fail financially.

Advertisers in Swiss newspapers face certain handicaps. One of them is the prohibition of advertising for medical products, which are under the control of the Inter-Cantonal Control Council for Medicine. A further limitation is found in an early closing date for ads, usually one to three days before publication. And the manufacturer of a national product wishing to place the same advertisement in all of Switzerland's main newspapers would need to contact at least two dozen different publishing houses.

But the availability of advertising space still exceeds the demand, giving the advertiser certain choices and prerogatives. Because of this fact, advertisers can bring pressure on editorial decision-makers. In 1979 the Migros Cooperative retail grocery chain purchased Zurich's *Die Tat* to help solve its financial problems. Then the chain appointed a new editor and the staff struck in protest. Amid controversy, Migros closed down the paper. In the same year, automobile importers withheld their advertisements from Zurich's *Tages-Anzeiger* for over six months in protest against an article in the paper criticizing the auto industry lobby to import cars with substandard emission controls. The boycott was carried out despite Swiss law, which forbids "organized" avoidance of an entrepreneur to inflict punishment for such action. Another important advertiser, the Globus department store, cut its advertising budget with *Tages-Anzeiger* because of its reporting of the May 1980 youth riots.

These confrontations led to conflict within the Swiss press over whether content should be controlled by editors or by publishers under advertiser influence. In October 1980, when the editors of two Lucerne papers—*Luzerner Neueste Nachrichten* and *Thurgauer Zeitung*—were dismissed, readers marched in the streets and 13 journalists resigned after protesting that the dismissals were the last stage in campaigns by the publishers to gain control of editorial content.

Ninety percent of Swiss papers sell through subscriptions, although *Blick* relies almost entirely on street sales. But, as opposed to other sensational European papers, which sell most heavily in the cities, *Blick,* partly because it is not identified with any geographical region or party, has readers evenly distributed throughout all German-speaking cantons and sells particularly well in rural districts.

Until the end of World War II, ownership of the Swiss press was concentrated in the hands of individual proprietors; most were families who had started their papers as private business ventures. However, as already mentioned, the number of newspapers has been steadily declining in recent years. This structural change comes partly from realignments and mergers, and partly as a response to pressure for highly expensive modernization. The cost of new equipment, rising prices of newsprint and other materials and increased wage demands from compositors and printers have forced mergers as a means of financial survival.

However, nearly all of Switzerland's small-circulation papers are owned by individual families, some having been under the proprietorship of the same family since the 19th century. Owners of these small papers often rely heavily on other publishing business to maintain financial viability.

The largest chain of newspapers in Switzerland is the "Lausanne Group," Publicitas S.A., Lausanne, which operates *24 Heures, Tribune Le Matin* and *La Suisse.* Another joint ownership is Wolfrath, which combines *Feuille d'Avis de Neuchatel* and *L'Express.* Despite the growing number of chains, no individual, corporation or party exercises an ownership monopoly in any city or region.

Because most Swiss papers are local in character, distribution networks are small. The Swiss rail system provides fast, efficient delivery for national and regional papers. The regional and lingual characteristics of the press eliminate the need for facsimile transmission to branch publishing centers.

Switzerland is self-sufficient in the bulk of the newsprint its publishing industry requires. In 1970 it produced 120 million metric tons, and by 1973 production had risen to 173 million metric tons, nearly 23 million of which were being exported. Between 1970 and 1977 Swiss domestic newsprint consumption rose from just a little over 121,000 metric tons to nearly 153,000 tons. This continuing rise in newsprint production has persisted despite the steady decline in the number of newspapers during the same period, and reflects a gradual rise in total newspaper circulation.

Newspaper workers in Switzerland are represented by the Association de la Presse Suisse affiliated with the International Federation of Journalists.

As indicated earlier, about half of Swiss papers sell less than 10,000 copies and scores have circulations of only a few hundred or thousand. The top 10 dailies account for approximately 25 percent of the total circulation. Considering the inflationary rise in costs and materials, the prices of Swiss papers have remained relatively stable, although there have been some hikes in subscriptions. *Neue Zürcher Zeitung* still sells on the street for 70 rappen (about 40 cents).

Despite the fact that the Swiss press faces increasing financial difficulties, recent technical advances have made newsroom equipment innovations essential. Consequently, the changeover from lead type to photosetting is completed or in process almost everywhere and offset has generally replaced letterpress. From 70 to 80 percent of these technological innovative costs must be paid for by advertising; therefore, maintenance of advertising has become crucial for Swiss papers. Unfortunately, at the very same time, commercial advertisers have become increasingly interested in television advertising, since it gives the mass coverage that Swiss regional and local papers cannot provide.

Press Laws

Article 55 of the Swiss Federal Constitution states: "The freedom of the press shall be guaranteed." At the same time, the country has no specific press laws. Newspapers and journalists are not required to register or to procure licenses to operate. The state's powers are confined to legal penalties for abuse of press freedom. This condition leads many to consider the Swiss press the freest in the world.

However, this liberty is limited by the sanctions found in other parts of the constitution and in directives that have been placed in the nation's various legal codes and administrative and police regulations. And there are also communal and cantonal regulations.

Libel laws place some legal restrictions on the press. Swiss law punishes only malicious or fabricated slander and treats attacks on private individuals more seriously than those on public officials.

In general, the Swiss press, little interested in sensationalism, has exercised decorum and restraint in its reporting, thus avoiding strains where codes conflict.

But recently, the government and the press have clashed over the right of journalists to refuse to reveal their sources of information. Swiss law has always recognized the right to professional secrecy of doctors, lawyers and clergymen. However, journalists have not had a similar right to withhold evidence. In some specific circumstances, the court has chosen to recognize a higher interest, as, for example, the discovery of abuses of the public interest. In a case involving disclosure of secret information in 1957, an Associate Press correspondent was imprisoned and fined with the intent to force him to reveal his sources. Journalists have been fined or imprisoned several times since for disregarding judges' orders to disclose their own sources. Contention over this problem resulted in a 1968 federal law designed to provide legal protection for journalistic confidentiality except in cases involving the security of the state. But in 1979 the government decided there should be a police investigation of information leaks from the Council of State and its commissions. Documents submitted to these bodies are considered confidential. In the test case, police ordered a reporter from *Weltwoche* to tell them what he knew and to bring his notebooks for investigation. The journalist refused to share his notes or to reveal his sources of information and he was not subsequently prosecuted.

Censorship

During World War II, despite the conflict raging around her borders, Switzerland remained neutral. To maintain that neutrality, the Swiss Federal Council made it illegal for the press to insult publicly the ruler or diplomatic representatives of any foreign state. Since there were few pro-Nazi papers in the country at the time, most editors were forced by the ruling to curb their criticism of German leaders and their policies. Today, Articles 296 and 197 of the Swiss Penal Code still make insulting a foreign state, an international organization, or one of their representatives an act punishable by fine or imprisonment. The articles are no longer interpreted as rigidly as in the war, but they still apply to show Switzerland's determination to remain neutral and to maintain the good will

of other nations. No such censorship is extended to criticism of the Swiss national government or to cantonal or communal authorities.

Swiss law also protects military secrets. In 1973, three Zurich *Tages-Anzeiger* reporters were given suspended sentences for revealing classified information—the site of a military installation—in their newspaper.

State-Press Relations

With the exception of disagreement over revelation of reporter sources of information and forbidding of criticism of the representatives of foreign governments and organizations, the Swiss government allows the press to operate freely. Press criticism of government is both allowed and practiced; however, the conservative Swiss journalists have always been tactful and restrained in their reportorial conduct.

Swiss papers actively seek to influence public opinion and government policies through their editorials. About two-thirds of the dailies are, in fact, journals of opinion rather than journals of fact interested in reporting only hard news. They speak out their parties' views frankly through commentary on the front pages and on many of the inside pages. *Neue Zürcher Zeitung,* for example, unashamedly seeks to shape governmental and public opinion in accord with its own Liberal views of free order, a democratic state and an open society. The fact that Swiss officials know papers are actively seeking to impart their party ideologies has the effect of maintaining a balance of party views within government. In the case of the nation's frequent elections and referenda, the press takes on the role of informed adviser, telling readers which way to vote. Also, the system of proportional representation in Swiss elections always results in the formation of a coalition government; under these circumstances the functions of government and those in opposition are described by the press, a service that makes the print media essential to Swiss democracy.

Jailing of journalists and confiscation of newspapers is almost unheard of in Switzerland. Nor does the state seek to control the press through licensing, advertising support or manipulation of labor unions.

But the question of government subsidies for the press has been debated for the past decade. As early as 1972, the Department of

Justice charged several commissions to investigate the financial health of the press and propose any necessary measures of aid. During the recession of 1973–74 the idea of subsidies seemed appealing to many papers threatened with bankruptcy. There was agreement that subsidies would help, but the question was how. Then the Federal Council decided that while direct aid would menace press competition, long-term indirect help was needed. This was especially true of the political press, with its special role of informing the regions, cantons and communities; its participation in the political process was considered invaluable. The situation was aggravated when the German-speaking Social Democratic chain collapsed.

On May 1, 1975 the Huber Commission proposed a constitutional change, designed to provide subsidies for the press. One provision was that the federal government could regulate the media in order to assure that the balance of the press would be preserved. Differences over the meaning of the proposal arose within the Swiss press. Smaller political papers greeted the proposal enthusiastically; they believed the health of the political papers to be the most important issue facing the Swiss press. But larger papers felt the proposal would restrict initiative, bring government interference into papers' financial affairs, and create restrictions. Some even wondered how important the political press was to the country. The commission continues, as does the debate over press subsidies.

Attitude Toward Foreign Media

The Swiss government is protective of its own press in that it forbids foreign ownership of Swiss papers. Some international dailies are permitted to operate; for example, one of the *International Herald-Tribune*'s principal offices is in Zurich. Foreign correspondents of all nations with proper credentials are allowed to function freely. They are not required to secure prior approval for cablegrams or telephone messages.

Swiss press agencies interact freely with international wire, photo and visual news organizations. All the major news agencies function in the country; many have branch offices in Geneva or Zurich. For a time, Zurich was the home of the International Press Institute. And Geneva is the program center for the news and information programming operations of the European Broadcasting Union and Eurovision. There are also United Nations recording studios and press operations in Geneva.

Foreign newspapers are allowed free circulation in Switzerland. The West German press has made few inroads among Swiss readers; most of its papers go to Germans in Switzerland on business or as tourists. French and Italian papers circulate more freely in the west and south and offer competition to the Swiss French- and Italian-language presses.

With numerous foreign diplomats and business organizations headquartering in Switzerland, there is demand for a wide range of foreign newspapers. But outside dailies are regarded as sources of information rather than as opportunities for foreign propaganda. That has not always been the case. During World War I, the Germans and the French used Swiss papers as propaganda organs to represent their respective sides. By World War II, because of Swiss insistence on neutrality, only a handful of pro-Nazi papers were operating. Today, with the permissiveness of the Swiss open democratic society and its free press, such papers as the communist daily *La Voix Ouvrière* can espouse its party views openly. However, its circulation has grown little in the past decade.

News Agencies

Switzerland has only one wire news agency. In English, it is known as the Swiss News Agency, in German as the Schweizerische Despechenagentur A. G., and in French as the Agence Télégraphique Suisse S.A. Founded in 1894, it is located in Berne and serves as the national agency for Swiss political and general news under its chief editor, Hanspeter Kleiner. It is jointly owned by about 40 of Switzerland's leading newspapers, each of which furnishes news input to the service. It has links with all the major world press agencies operating in Switzerland—UPI, AP, Agence France-Presse, Tass and Deutsche Presse-Agentur.

A private news service, the Swiss Political Press Agency, extends important cultural and political coverage to the nation's numerous medium-range and small-circulation papers. The Schweizer Feuilletondienst and the Service de Press Suisse also provide the press with cultural reports and features. These smaller, private agencies reflect the federal emphasis in the 1975 Clottu Report on the importance of bringing Swiss culture closer to the general public and of awakening a greater appreciation of Swiss history and traditions.

Electronic News Media

In Switzerland radio and television are under the direction of the Swiss Broadcasting Corporation (SBC), a private company serving the public interest under a license granted by the Swiss Federal Council. For radio broadcasts, there are five medium-wave, 196 VHF and 12 short-wave transmitters. In addition, the Swiss Wire Network Service provides six program services to some 400,000 subscribers on the PTT telephone cable network. Television is aired on three channels for the entire nation by a network of 855 transmitters and signal boosters.

The SBC's charge is to support the nation's cultural, spiritual and artistic values. Its complex organizational structure is based upon three regional societies reflecting the country's three language divisions. The Radio und Fernsehgeselschaft der Deutschen und der Rätoromanischen Schweiz (RDRS) is headquartered in Basel and Zurich, with a television studio in Zurich and six other member societies with studios or production centers. The Société de Radiodiffusion et de Télévision de la Suisse Romande (SRTR) has its center in Lausanne with a television studio in Geneva and two member-societies. Lugano is the production and administrative center for the Società Cooperativa per la radiotelevisione nella Svizzero Italiana (CORSI). Recently, there have been increased efforts to coordinate programming between the three regional societies.

The only governmental control in the system comes when the Central Board of SBC meets. This top administrative body consists of representatives of the regional societies and of the Post Office and the government. The government, as the concessionary authority, elects the majority of the Central Board members, and thus becomes the main instrument of governmental control of broadcasting. The Department of Posts and Railways is charged with assuring that Central Board decisions are carried out by the director general, who is also elected by the Central Board and who assumes responsibility for organization of the program services, maintenance of program standards and the

effective management of broadcasting. There are many representatives of local interests on the Central Board—educators, businessmen, lawyers, newspaper editors and members of listener organizations—who provide a public check on governmental control of the Central Board.

Two radio programs are broadcast in each of the three main language regions. The First Programs contain a mixture of news and information, entertainment and light music. The Second Program provides more serious fare, including news commentaries and discussions.

The three television programs broadcast two news and current affairs shows twice daily. The main evening news, broadcast at eight p.m. on weeknights, is prepared by the Swiss Telegraph Agency, the country's primary news agency. Another edition of the news is broadcast late in the evening, shortly before transmissions end at 11 p.m. Many of the news items on television come from Eurovision feeds. The European Broadcasting Union's operational center for programs in Geneva brings together the choice news stories from Eurovision, Intervision and the news capitals of the world, and Swiss television benefits from the EBU network in this way.

Swiss television provides excellent coverage of the many local referenda that are so crucial to the country's community and cantonal political life. Time is reserved on Tuesday evenings for previews of forthcoming referenda; results are broadcast on the following Sundays.

Because of their geographical position, most Swiss viewers can choose from up to as many as six additional television signals coming from adjoining countries. This enables the citizenry to check the content of Swiss television news and information programs against those of their neighbor nations.

Education & Training

Some Swiss universities—such as the University of Zurich—have journalism departments or schools. However, most Swiss journalists traditionally have and still do gain their skills by working as apprentices under experienced reporters, writers and editors. A high percentage of Swiss journalists have completed postgraduate work, usually in the social sciences, law or literature. Nearly all of the foreign correspondents of *Neue Zürcher Zeitung,* for example, have doctoral degrees in history, law, economics or literature.

Journalists have formed an Association of the Swiss Press, which looks after their professional interests and publishes a regular bulletin.

Summary

The Swiss press is conservative, diverse and party oriented. Most newspapers have low circulations, usually under 10,000, and during the past decade, the smaller and middle-range circulation papers (10,000 to 25,000) have been experiencing mounting difficulty in maintaining sufficient advertising revenue to remain economically viable. Advertising resources have increasingly been drained off to television and the large newspapers.

Yet the Swiss press has a bright future. Every household still subscribes to at least one paper and it is the nature of Swiss television that it will not claim much more of the advertising revenues than it does at present. Undoubtedly, economic realities will make necessary more newspaper mergers and chains, but press ownership will remain sufficiently diversified to provide multiple party and news views.

CHRONOLOGY

1975 to Present Debate continues over press-subsidy plans to aid smaller Swiss politically oriented papers and impact government subsidization would have on constitutionally guaranteed press freedom.

1978 *Die Tat,* old established Zurich newspaper, closes down after power struggle between editors and management over election of a new editor. Case includes question of how much power advertisers should have, as Migros Cooperative had taken over the paper and changed its format to salvage it.

1979 In test case of reporter privilege to withhold sources of information, police order correspondent from *Weltwoche* to reveal sources and bring notebooks for investigation. Reporter refuses, is not prosecuted.

Swiss auto importers withhold advertising from Zurich's *Tages-Anzeiger* after paper runs nine-page article criticizing importers' lobbying efforts to import autos with substandard emission controls.

1980 Switzerland's best elite daily with high circulation, *Neue Zürcher Zeitung,* celebrates its 200th anniversary.

BIBLIOGRAPHY

"A Quick Look Around: Switzerland." *IPI Report,* September 1972, p. 6.

Baur, Arthur. "Swiss Press Bill Could Enforce Right of Reply." *IPI Report,* April 1976, p. 17.

Bollinger, Ernst. *La Presse Suisse: Structure et Diversité.* Berne, 1976.

"Car Firms Boycott Swiss Newspapers." *IPI Report,* October 1979, p. 4.

"Direct Subsidies: A Tonic for the Weak or…" *IPI Report,* October 1976, pp. 10–11.

Drack, Marcus. "The Swiss Broadcasting Corporation." *The Swiss Broadcasting Corporation Press and Documentation.* November 1971.

Durrenmatt, Peter. *Wie Frei Ist Die Presse?* Bern, 1971.

Fisher, Harold. "The EBU: Model for Regional Cooperation in Broadcasting." *Journalism Monographs,* no. 68, Lexington, Ky., 1980.

Jager, Josef. *Das Bild der Schweizer Presse.* Bern, 1967.

Matt, Alphons. "Italian-Speaking Switzerland Slants News to Interest Italy." *IPI Report,* September 1974, pp. 8–9.

Merrill, John, Bryan, Carter, and Alisky, Marvin. *The Foreign Press.* Baton Rouge, La., 1970.

Merrill, John, and Fisher, Harold. *The World's Great Dailies: Profiles of 50 Newspapers.* New York, 1980.

Sandford, John. *The Mass Media of the German-Speaking Countries.* London, 1976.

Schwabe, Erich, ed. *Switzerland: 1980.* Bern, 1980.

Staub, Hans. "Switzerland." *IPI Report,* July 1976, pp. 8–9.

"Swiss Newspaper is 200 Years Old." *IPI Report.* January–February 1980, p. 3.

Tschani, Hans. "Four-Point Probe of Measures to Aid Swiss Press." *IPI Report,* September 1974, p. 9.

TAIWAN (Republic of China)

by Elliott S. Parker

BASIC DATA

Population: 17.3 million (1980,est.)
Area: 36,169 sq. km. (13,965 sq. mi.)
GNP: NT$827.5 billion (US$24 billion)
Literacy Rate: 90%
Language(s): Mandarin Chinese
Number of Dailies: 31
   Aggregate Circulation: 3.32 million
   Circulation per 1,000: 190
Number of Nondailies: 176
   Aggregate Circulation: NA
   Circulation per 1,000: NA
Number of Periodicals: 1,800

Number of Radio Stations: 35
Number of Television Stations: 3
Number of Radio Receivers: 4.2 million
   Radio Receivers per 1,000: 243
Number of Television Sets: 2.55 million
   Television Sets per 1,000: 147
Total Annual Newsprint Consumption: 63,000 metric tons
Per Capita Newsprint Consumption: 17.6 kg. (38.7 lb.)
Total Newspaper Ad Receipts: NT$3.07 billion (US$85.2 million) (1979)
   As % of All Ad Expenditures: 40

Background & General Characteristics

The Chinese have traditionally had great respect for the printed word and are avid newspaper readers. On Taiwan this interest is supported by a literacy rate of over 90 per cent. Several mutually unintelligible Chinese dialects are spoken, such as Hakka and Amoy, but Mandarin is considered the standard. Although the speech differs, the written word is essentially universal, understood even by people who do not speak the same dialect. This, combined with rising affluence (US$1,316 per capita income in 1979), guarantees a widely read press. The population is estimated to be 17.3 million (1980). The largest city is Taipei, with a population of over 2 million. The five largest cities, Taipei, Keelung, Taichung, Tainan and Kaohsiung, contain 25 percent of the population.

Although the history of the modern Chinese press dates from the middle of the last century, the history of the press on Taiwan is relatively short.

During 50 years of Japanese occupation of the island, the Chinese language was prohibited and most papers were propaganda organs of the colonial government. After restoration of Taiwan to the Republic of China, the only newspaper was *TaiWan Hsin Shen Pao.** This previously Japanese-language newspaper had been reorganized by the Japanese from six papers around the island in 1944. The Taiwan provincial government took control of it in 1945 and renamed it the *Taiwan Hsin Shen Pao (Tai Wan Xin Sheng Bao).* The paper currently has an estimated circulation of about 300,000.

The oldest paper, *Central Daily News (Zhong Yang Ri Bao),* is also the official paper of the Kuomintang, the ruling party. It was founded in Canton in 1926 and moved to Taiwan in 1949.

The earliest papers on Taiwan, due to the shortage of newsprint and facilities, were published in the form of mimeographed sheets on foolscap.

Of the 31 daily newspapers currently in

---

*In this chapter, the common or most noted name of a newspaper is given first, followed by the newspaper's own transliteration or translation of the name (if any). The last transliteration is *pinyin* style. If no standard transliteration is used, the name is only given in *pinyin*. Chinese names of places and people follow the traditional style.

circulation, 16 are published in the capital, Taipei, five are published in the southern city of Kaohsiung and four in Taichung. Tainan, Hualien, Kinmen (Quemoy), Matzu, Chiayi and Penghu each support one paper. Ideologically there is not a great diversity of views. Papers range along a spectrum from ruling-party organ to pro-government.

The Tainan paper, *Zhong Hua Ri Bao Nan Bu Ban,* is the southern edition of the *China Daily News (Zhong Hua Ri Bao)* in Taipei. All but three of the papers are broadsheet size, about 17 by 22 inches, and average 12 pages per issue, although two, the Kaohsiung paper, *Cheng Gong Wan Bao,* and the *Zhong Guo Ri Bao* of Taichung, are single-leaf, two-page papers. Of the 31 papers, six are evening papers: the *Great China Evening News (Da Hua Wan Bao), Min Tzu Evening News (Min Zu Wan Bao), The Independence Evening News (Zi Li Wan Bao)* and the *China News (Ying Wen Zhong Guo Ri Bao),* all in Taipei; and the *Zhong Guo Wan Bao* and the *Cheng Gong Wan Bao* in Kaohsiung.

Two English-language papers, the *China Post (Ying Wen Zhong Guo You Bao)* and the *China News,* are both published in Taipei.

Most papers that are published on Sunday include a supplement. The *China Post* includes the *Asia Magazine,* a supplement distributed from Hong Kong every other week.

Circulation of all newspapers is secret, known only to the publishers and certain editors, so any circulation figures can only be an informed guess. The two largest papers are undoubtedly the *China Times (Zhong Kuo Ri Bao)* and the *United Daily News (Lian He Boa)* with circulations around 1 million. The third largest paper is the *Central Daily News* with an estimated circulation of about 400,000-500,000. These three papers account for more than 70 percent of the total circulation of the 31 papers. Of the remainder, the tabloid *Mandarin Daily News (Gwoyeu Rhybaw, Kuo Yue Ri Bao)* has one of the highest circulations, although the readership is mostly among students, since the Chinese phonetic alphabet is used at the side of the traditional Chinese characters, serving as a pronunciation guide.

The four afternoon papers in Taipei have a combined circulation of less than 100,000. The English-language *China Post* and *China News* have circulations in the 50,000-60,000 range, with the *China Post* probably leading the *China News.*

The three largest papers are also the most influential or authoritative. The *United Daily News* and *The China Times* are independent and widely read by businessmen, intellectuals and government leaders. The *Central Daily News* is considered the most authoritative paper since it reflects the thinking of the ruling party.

Of the English-language press, the *China Post* is the oldest, most influential and most widely known. For the tourist and foreign businessman, it is important for its coverage of local events. Local students buy it to increase their fluency in English.

The *United Daily News* has several sister papers. The *Economic Daily News (Jing Ji Ri Bao),* published daily except Sunday, has a circulation of about 200,000. A weekly edition is also published. A Spanish-language biweekly tabloid, *Quincenario Economico,* is also published. *Min Sheng Pao (Min Sheng Bao)* is also owned by the *United Daily News* and is looked on as a lighter newspaper, emphasizing features and less hard news. The *United Daily News* also has an economic interest in United States newspapers—*The World Journal (Shi Jie Ri Bao),* published in San Francisco and New York.

The sister paper of the *China Times* is the *Commercial Times (Gong Shang Ri Bao).*

The *United Daily News,* the *Central Daily News* and the *China Times* all have overseas editions. These are four-page condensations of the Taipei edition printed on lightweight airmail paper and popular among Chinese students overseas.

The overall quality of the larger Chinese papers is very high with excellent, although somewhat skewed, coverage of international affairs. The level of language usage of the English papers is somewhat less than that of the Chinese papers and as the circulation declines, the quality also declines. The smaller papers tend to have looser editing, somewhat fanciful writing at times and less emphasis on objectivity.

Economic Framework

With an annual growth rate of around eight percent over most of the last decade, and limitations on the number of pages, the larger newspapers are in an enviable position. Advertising space is at such a premium that even the center gutter is used for ads; potential advertisers stand in line until their turn to buy space comes up. Advertisers wield relatively little influence on papers' editorial policies. Due to the limited amount of space, newspapers are in a position to pick and choose who they will sell space to.

With few exceptions, newspapers are privately owned. However, almost all are published or edited by members of the ruling party, the Kuomintang. The *Youth Warrior Daily (Qing Nian Zhan Shi Bao)* is owned by the army, but the staff is a combination of army and civilians and is sold on the street with all the other papers.

The half-dozen largest papers are in excellent financial condition, able to afford new buildings and equipment and good salaries. Many of the remaining papers are very small with antiquated equipment and low salaries; their financial positions are precarious.

Sixty percent, or more, of the circulation of the largest papers is in the capital, Taipei. Distribution to other parts of the island is by truck—a three- to four-hour journey from Taipei in the north to Kaohsiung in the south. Some papers like the *United Daily News,* which has 22 separate editions, run one or two pages of news of particular local areas. The entire paper is still printed in Taipei. Few of the papers published outside the capital have major distribution in the capital, although the principal paper in the south, the *Taiwan Times (Tai Wan Ri Bao),* does have significant distribution in the north.

The government restricts newspapers to 12 pages. Not only does this limit the amount of foreign exchange used for newsprint importation, but it forces advertisers to use some of the smaller papers, which would otherwise probably be forced to sell out to larger papers. About one-third of the newsprint is imported, and carries an import tax of 20 percent. (Printing equipment, however, may be imported freely and used without publication licenses.) Most of the imported newsprint is used by the larger papers, which require higher-quality paper to run ROP color on web offset presses; their publishers feel that the local paper is not suitable. Locally produced newsprint, on the other hand, is subsidized by the government. Newsprint used for newspapers carries a discount of about one-third. In 1980 the average cost per ton was about US$550.*

Labor unions are not a power. Although each city with a newspaper has an association of journalists, these operate mainly as professional organizations with limited arbitration power. In the relatively few cases of labor unrest, the government labor office assists in working out mutually acceptable alternatives. Recently this has mainly affected the larger papers, which are starting to use new technology; the government helps to find other jobs or retraining programs for excess labor.

It is estimated that about 8,000 people are employed as writers, editors and photographers on newspapers. Wage scales range from $110 per month on Chinese-language evening papers for a beginning writer or editor, to more than $850 for an experienced journalist on the largest papers.

With few exceptions, reporters are free to write what they please, but due to the page limitations, there is extreme competition for space and bylines.

Daily Chinese-language papers are sold for 10 cents, an increase from seven cents in 1978. The two English-language papers sell for 17 cents.

All major papers are printed by offset. Computer technology has not yet been introduced at the writing and editing levels, due to the great number of characters required in the Chinese language. Publishers of the large, affluent papers have been quick to introduce web offset presses, not only of local manufacture, but from Japan and the United States. The two English-language papers are able to take advantage of cold-type front end systems.

Press Laws

The constitution of the Republic of China, adopted in 1946, guarantees freedom of speech and press among others. At the height of the Chinese civil war in 1948, the national assembly enacted "temporary provisions effective during the period of Communist rebellion," and a "state of siege" was declared in Taiwan when the nationalist government retreated to the island. Martial law limits the constitutional guarantees of individual rights and gives the authorities the right to control the press.

Newspapers are permitted to publish under the Publication Law, written in 1930 and revised in 1937, 1952, 1958 and 1973. The

---

*Local currency throughout the rest of this chapter has been converted to U.S. equivalents at the rate of US$1=NT$36.

Publication Law also contains sections dealing with libel, protection of publishers, suspension of publication, registration and subsidies to printers and publishers.

Under the Publication Law and martial law, the authorities have the right to limit freedom of speech and freedom of the press. The authorities conduct post-publication censorship and recall articles and publications that oppose "basic policy" or which are excessively critical.

Not only does the national government have the power to control publications, but provincial and municipal authorities may control printing, distribution or possession of printed matter. Under martial law, the military authorities also have the power of control. Trials for sedition are held in military courts.

All newspapers must be registered with the Government Information Office. The government currently limits registration to 31 papers. There have been 31 papers in existence since 1961, although the number was as high as 32 in 1953 and low as 29 in 1952. A bond is not required for registration, but paid-up capital must be at least $250,000, necessary equipment must be available and the publisher must have either practical experience or formal training in journalism. Individual journalists are not required to be licensed.

Since 1949 no newspapers have been suspended permanently, although one was suspended for one week. The same, however, is not true of magazines. New registrations for magazines were suspended in 1978 for one year. The suspension on registration was lifted at the announced time; 1979 seemed a period of liberalization on the island and many magazines critical of, or opposed to, the ruling party appeared. Accordingly the government suspended individual issues or revoked licenses of more magazines in 1979 than in the preceding 20 years. The year ended with a riot after a rally sponsored by *Formosa* magazine calling for more independence for the Taiwanese population—those people native to the island who want greater power in a government dominated by people from the mainland of China. Eight staff members of the magazine were arrested and tried in a military court for sedition and sentenced to terms of from 12 years to life.

Contrary to previous trials of this type, the proceedings were open to both foreign and local press. Local papers assigned teams of reporters to take down the testimony verbatim and devoted one to two pages to the trial every day. As a result, more people were able to hear the defendants' arguments than would have read them in the magazine itself. At that time, the circulation of *Formosa* was estimated at about 100,000.

Other magazines that have had issues banned or were suspended include *Chang Chiao, New Generation Monthly, New Horizons, Spring Wind, The Asians, The Current* and *The Eighties.*

Censorship

The agency most closely concerned with monitoring the press is the Publications Department in the Government Information Office (GIO).

When censorship occurs, it is usually after publication. Newspapers are seldom censored. The brunt of censorship has been been borne by local magazines and imported magazines and newspapers. Despite the government's moves against various magazines in 1979, magazines are for the most part freer to criticize than newspapers. It is generally agreed that certain topics are forbidden: advocating independence for Taiwan, criticizing the president or glorifying communism. However, lower officials have been—and are—regularly criticized, as have been policies, while stories regularly appear about the People's Republic of China and its leaders.

In the last few years many observers have seen an easing of censorship and growing confidence on the part of the government. At one time a publication with a picture of any communist leader from the mainland would be prohibited from entering the country. Later they were allowed in if the faces were blacked out. In 1979 an issue of *Time* magazine was allowed in even though it had a picture of Deng Xiaoping, vice-premier of the People's Republic of China, on the cover. It was not allowed on newsstands, however.

Under the Publication Law, publications may be warned, suspended, confiscated or fined if it is found that they "made false statements" in the original application for registration, if they are "published under conditions different from what were originally registered," commit or instigate others to commit "sedition or treason,... offenses against the public order... or offenses against religion and the dead or against public morals." Article 34 says publications may be subjected to "prohibitions or restrictions" if they publish "political, military or diplomatic secrets, or items considered detrimental to law and order."

Although the GIO may suspend or deregister a publication, most censorship cases in the past have been tried in military courts.

The Statute for the Punishment of Sedition defines a "rebel" as anyone who "plans to destroy the national policy, occupy the national territory, or, by illegal means to change the constitution or overthrow the government" or "makes propaganda beneficial to the rebels by written words, books or speeches." Another statute makes it a crime not to denounce a person suspected of having committed these acts.

The National Press Council of the Republic of China is "entrusted with the task of promoting self-discipline, ethical standards, freedom of press, and social responsibility" among its members, which includes newspapers, radio and television stations and news agencies.

The council also has the job of settling complaints made by individuals or organizations against biased or misleading news reports or advertisements. The council has no legal power, but if the complaints are found to be valid, "adequate redress for innocent victims would be asked of the press media involved."

By 1976 the National Press Council had received 16 complaints: three were upheld, three rejected and seven withdrawn by the complainants. The press council has also promulgated codes of ethics for journalists, radio broadcasters and television workers.

Two articles of the Publication Law specifically address the relationship between government administrators and the press. Article 26 states, "Government agencies shall facilitate newspapers or magazines in coverage of news or collection of material." For this purpose each goverment office has a permanent public relations officer. Article 28 instructs the government to take "effective measures" if the work of "...authors, editors, or printers meets with any infringement or hindrance."

State-Press Relations

The Government Information Office monitors the media. It also sets general standards for the electronic media, registers publications, supervises the accreditation of foreign correspondents and acts as a liaison between government departments and journalists and correspondents.

The GIO comes directly under the Executive Yuan, one of the five branches of government. The Executive Yuan resembles the cabinet of a Western country.

In theory, publications have the right to criticize the government; in practice there are some limitations. Although the last few years have seen much more criticism being printed both in domestic and external publications, local editors and writers observe certain understood restrictions. No criticism is seen of Chiang Ching-kuo, president of the Republic of China and son of Chiang Kai-shek, and no positive references to communism will be aired or printed. This does not preclude stories about the Chinese mainland or articles about other communist countries. Articles about leaders on the mainland, however, have the titles put in quotations, such as "Premier" Hua Guo-feng, and the administration is not called a government but the "political power."

Simplified characters and the *pinyin* system of transliteration are assumed to promote communism and are not allowed to be used in newspapers.

Another sensitive topic is the Taiwanese independence movement, which advocates independence for Taiwan, opposing both the rule of the Kuomintang on Taiwan and reunification with the People's Republic of China. This idea and its advocacy formed the basis of the "Kaohsiung Incident" of December 1979, which led to the arrest and trial of some 40 people, including editors, writers and clergymen, and the suspension of *Formosa* magazine.

Attitude Toward Foreign Media

The first step in becoming an accredited foreign correspondent on Taiwan is to apply to the nearest representative of the Taiwan government. This representative then submits the application to the Government Information Office in Taipei along with recommendations. The GIO checks the listed qualifications; it is expected that the applicant be a reporter or photographer with a recognized media organization. If the applicant is a freelancer, the application must list previous experience.

The GIO then informs the Immigration Department to issue the required visa. The first visa is good for six months. Subsequent visas will be issued for one-year periods. This visa also allows the applicant to work on Taiwan. No applicants have been refused visas.

The GIO will also issue a press card, which serves primarily as identification, allowing the holder access to non-public areas and events.

No prior approval is required to send cables from Taiwan.

Publications represented in Taipei include: *Asian Wall Street Journal, New York Times, Pacific Stars and Stripes, Newsweek, Sankei Shimbun, Korea Times, London Daily Telegraph, Tages Anzeiger, National Catholic News, The Phillipines Examiner, Time, Modern Asia, Far Eastern Economic Review,* To the Point International, National Broadcasting Company, American Broadcasting Company and the Columbia Broadcasting System.

The import of foreign publications is regulated by the Department of Publications. Publications contrary to national policy or customs or judged obscene are not permitted to circulate or enter the country. *Playboy,* for instance, is not allowed to enter. Customs officials may confiscate material at the port of entry.

In principle, foreigners may own and operate newspapers on Taiwan on a reciprocal basis: for every Chinese-owned paper allowed in the foreign owners' country, one would be allowed on Taiwan. Currently, no foreign-owned papers operate on the island.

News Agencies

The major domestic news agency is the Central News Agency (CNA) formed in Canton in 1924 and incorporated in 1973 with the leading newspapers as shareholders. It sees itself "as a bridge between the government and people."

CNA has contracts with the Associated Press, United Press International, Reuters, Agence France Presse and Deutsche Presse Agentur. It also has exchange agreements with agencies in Saudi Arabia, Japan, Colombia, Indonesia, Malaysia, Italy and Spain, among others.

All incoming material from its own overseas staff in 31 cities or from other agencies is received at the main office in Taipei, edited, and translated into Chinese for distribu-

tion to all newspapers and television stations and most radio stations on Taiwan. Papers may also subscribe directly to news agencies.

CNA has daily broadcasts to the United States in both Chinese and English. This is relayed to Chinese-language newspapers in New York and San Francisco. English-language broadcasts are relayed to other media. A telephoto service for Chinese-language papers in the United States was started in 1979.

Daily facsimile transmission to CNA bureaus in Hong Kong, Manila, Bangkok and Seoul average about 25,000 words for the local Chinese-language papers. Through the Far East News Agency, feature articles are distributed to clients in Bangkok, Manila, Singapore and Kuala Lumpur.

Domestically, CNA distributes mimeographed releases six times a day to clients in Taipei. Because most are morning papers, page facsimile is used to transmit late-breaking news beginning about 10:30 p.m.

A daily service to television and radio stations lasts from 8 a.m. to 1 p.m. and from 4 p.m. to 7:30 p.m.

Newspapers using CNA service are charged between $835 and $5,600, depending on the papers' circulation.

Although individuals cannot subscribe to the Chinese-language releases, CNA publishes the daily English-language *Express News* on a subscription basis. This mimeographed, legal-sheet-size release carries both domestic and international news and averages 25 pages. A companion publication, *Express News Financial Edition* is published six times a week, carrying worldwide market reports and economic and trade news.

CNA has a facsimile service for Chinese seamen aboard ships at sea; two pages are transmitted daily. CNA also broadcasts daily to guerrilla units on the mainland.

Although CNA overshadows all others, there are 43 smaller agencies on Taiwan. Thirty-three are based in Taipei. These smaller agencies have mainly domestic clients and specialize in such areas as military affairs, youth activities or economics. A few also serve the overseas Chinese community. Most local papers subscribe to at least two of these agencies.

Foreign agencies represented on Taiwan by bureaus or correspondents are AP, UPI, AFT, AFP, Reuters, Pan Asia Newspapers Alliance, Naigai News, East Asia News and the Hapdong News Agency.

Electronic News Media

The provisions of the Broadcasting and Television Law of 1976 set out broad guidelines. The regulatory agency is the Government Information Office, which in turn is given the power to establish new stations, control program and advertising content, grant awards and assistance for significant achievements, and penalize violations of the law. This basic law is expanded by Norms of Broadcasting and Television Programs (GIO letter, 1977); Rules Regulating Enterprises Supplying Broadcasting and Television Programs (GIO Directive, 1977); and Rules for the Control of Broadcasting and Television Personnel (GIO letter, 1977). Technical personnel and engineering standards are set by the Ministry of Communications.

Under these guidelines, educational and cultural programs (to promote "Chinese culture, develop social education and supplement school education") should occupy at least 20 percent of the time; news programs ("news reports, features, interviews, symposia, analyses, comments, live broadcasts") at least 20 percent; public service ("weather reports, time reports, emergency notices, public security") at least 10 percent; and entertainment ("singing, music, drama, movie film, novel, story, comedy, quiz, dancing, variety shows") cannot be more than 50 percent of the time.

Radio broadcasts conform to slightly different guidelines. At least 15 percent of the time is devoted to news and not more than 55 percent of the time can be entertainment. Educational and cultural and public service content remain the same.

Radio dramas are limited to two hours and "only one TV drama program in a day can last 60 minutes and others shall not last longer than 30 minutes."

The number and duration of commercials is also limited. Any half-hour program may have a total of five minutes of advertisements: at the beginning and the end and up to two insertions.

The Norms of Broadcasting cover not only the allocation of time but of quality. Programs are urged to avoid negativeness and "provide a humorous, interesting, elegant and lively plot based on the spirit of optimism...and...positiveness"; and, in a drama series, each episode should have a complete plot and "heroes may not be frequently disparaged and villains may not be too numerous."

Mandarin, as the official language, is used for the majority of programs, in addition to some use of the various dialects spoken on the island. An exception to Chinese-language broadcasts is International Community Radio Taipei (ICRT), the former American Forces Network Taiwan (AFNT), which was turned into a nonprofit station after the diplomatic break in 1979. It is supported by individual contributions, grants from corporations and a major grant from the GIO.

Education & Training

Journalism education on Taiwan closely resembles journalism education in the United States, as many administrators and professors have either studied journalism here or have worked with newspapers or news agencies with close ties to their American counterparts.

The most noted and largest journalism education program is at Chengchi University, located in the suburbs of Taipei. The university offers both undergraduate and master's degrees in journalism. On average, about 60 B.A. and eight M.A. degrees are awarded each year. The university also publishes an annual journal, *Mass Communications Research (Xin Wen Xue Yan Jiu)*, reporting the research of students and staff.

One of the oldest journalism departments is the private World College of Journalism.

Percentage Distribution of Radio Programs	
Entertainment	55%
Education	20
News	15
Public service	10

Percentage Distribution of Television Programs	
Entertainment	50%
Education	20
News	20
Public service	10
Percentage of television programs imported: 25%	

Originally a vocational school founded on the mainland, it now takes graduates of high schools or junior high schools into three-and five-year courses in journalism, printing and related fields. It graduates about 1,000 students per year.

The Political Warfare College has a department of journalism to train officers in the armed services to become information officers and journalists. About 40 graduates per year receive B.A. degrees.

The Chinese Cultural University (formerly the College of Chinese Culture) was founded in 1962 and introduced an undergraduate program in journalism the following year. This program awards about 60 B.A. degrees and 10 M.A. degrees each year.

Six students per year graduate from Fu Jen Catholic University with a B.A. degree.

National Taiwan Normal University in Taipei has a journalism section within the Department of Social Education.

Most large papers and the Central News Agency offer internships to journalism students during vacations. Once a year, newspapers give examinations for potential employees to test their knowledge of current events, Chinese, and one other language (usually English). About two percent of the applicants will find jobs on newspapers. The others will go into advertising, public relations or government service.

In addition to the Taiwan's National Press Council, major cities have journalists' associations. The most active of the city associations is the Taipei Journalist's Association, which extends membership to editorial employees and executives of both newspapers and electronic media. This group publishes the decennial *Press Milestones of the Republic of China* on National Journalists Day, September 1.

The News Editors Association was formed in 1952. It publishes the semiannual *Journalism (Pao Hsueh, Bao Xue),* the only periodical of journalism criticism, research and history on Taiwan. The contents are in Chinese.

Domestic news agencies formed the National News Agencies Association in 1963. Members are all publishers of news agencies.

The Newspaper Enterprise Association is a national organization of newspaper publishers.

The Press Institute of the Republic of China was formed in 1976. Recently the Institute of Education for Mass Communication of the Republic of China was formed.

Summary

The press of Taiwan is lively and viable. Given the high literacy and the emphasis on education and international trade, in addition to traditional respect for the printed word, the press will continue to remain a central part of the Taiwanese lifestyle.

Press and government are so closely interrelated that any major changes in the press will be dependent on government policy. There is more control on the press than in some other countries, but though potentially Draconian, the enforcement of these laws has been progressively weaker in line with the general confidence of the government.

In the late 1970s, the press began to reflect this confidence. Journalists started to feel their way while becoming more responsible, and government began to consider the media as something more than a mere nuisance at best and seditious at worst. Papers started to criticize more freely, pointing out corruption and inefficiency, and readers were more open and trusting in their letters and calls to editors.

The Kaohsiung-*Formosa* magazine incident in 1979 must be considered a critical test case in contemporary Taiwan journalism. The incident may, in the future, be seen as a watershed in the development of the press. Not only was the trial open but it was fully reported in the domestic media, and the press demonstrated itself as a mature, professional institution.

Most magazines have extremely small circulations, even the largest less than 100,000. The prestigious magazines remain the vehicle of most serious journalism and political comment.

In the 1980s, competition will determine the topography of journalism in Taiwan. Small, local papers must continue to fight to remain viable and the larger papers will be attempting to expand their circulation among the rapidly growing body of new readers outside the major towns. One way of doing this is to aim for particular target audiences with special pages. In several places, local newssheets are already in existence. These publications are for small, very specific areas, are usually published weekly—and often by journalists who could not find jobs on the establishment papers. This whole gamut of publications is indicative of the need to appeal more directly to the populace.

There will also be competition for advertisers' money as radio and television continue to bleed off some advertising dollars from the print media.

Mechanically, papers are investing in new buildings and equipment; even the smallest newspaper shows increased quality of presswork. In the next decade, printers and publishers will find practical ways to use computers for printing and in newsrooms.

The larger newspapers and serious magazines are also beginning to invest in people, by trying to find writers and editors who are also knowledgeable in particular fields. Readers should find more features and comment on things that affect them directly.

CHRONOLOGY

1976 *Taiwan Political Review* suspended and editor sentenced to 10 years.
1978 Chiang Ching-kuo elected President.
1979 United States normalizes relations with Peoples' Republic of China.
International Community Radio-Taipei takes over from

Armed Forces Network-Taiwan. Riot outside *Formosa* magazine offices in Kaohsiung.
1980 First newspaper passes 1 million circulation mark.
Defendants in "Kaohsiung Incident" tried and convicted.
The Eighties magazine suspended one year.

BIBLIOGRAPHY

Amnesty International. *Amnesty International Briefing: Taiwan (Republic of China).* London, 1980.

Clayton, Charles C. "Taiwan." In *The Asian Newspapers' Reluctant Revolution,* John A. Lent, ed. Ames, Iowa: Iowa State University Press, 1971.

Government Information Office. *The Publication Law of The Republic of China.* Taipei, 1975.

Jacobs, J. Bruce. "Taiwan's Press: Political Communications Link and Research Resource." *China Quarterly,* December 1976, pp. 778-88.

Kazer, Bill, "Taiwan's Press Votes for Freedom." *Far Eastern Economic Review,* December 22, 1978, pp. 22-23.

Lent, John A. *Asian Mass Communication: A Comprehensive Bibliography* and *Supplement.* Philadelphia, 1975, 1978.

Long, Hwa Shu, "The Modern Chinese Press on Taiwan." Master's thesis, University of Missouri, 1958.

Ma Hsin-yeh, "The Press in Free China." *Free China Review,* January 1953, pp. 9-15.

Parker, Elliott S., and Parker, Emelia M. *Asian Journalism: A Selected Bibliography of Sources on Journalism in China and Southeast Asia.* Metuchen, N.J., 1979.

Sterba, James P. "Freedom of Expression Remains a Transitory Thing in Taiwan." *The New York Times,* March 23, 1980, Section 4, p. 1.

Taibei Shi Xin Wen Ji Zhe Gong Hui. *Zhong Hua Min Guo Xin Wen Nian Jian (Press Milestones of the Republic of China)* Taipei, 1971.

Tang, Pan Pan, "China's Central News Agency: Fifty Years for Freedom, 1924-1973," Master's thesis, Southern Illinois University, 1973.

Tseng Hsu-pai, Editor, *Zhong Guo Xin Wen Shi (History of Chinese Journalism).* Taipei, 1966.

Yang Shou-jung, ed. *Mass Communication in Taiwan: An Annotated Bibliography.* Singapore, 1977.

Yu, Helen Y. Y. "Formosa's English-Language Newspaper: China Post." Master's thesis, University of Missouri, 1958.

Zhong Hua Min Guo Chu Ban Nian Jian (Publications Yearbook Republic of China). Taipei, 1980.

TANZANIA

by Dennis L. Wilcox

BASIC DATA

Population: 17.4 million
Area: 946,925 sq. km. (365,608 sq. mi.)
GNP: Sh 24.5 billion (US$ 3 billion) (est.)
Literacy Rate: 63%
Language(s): Swahili, English
Number of Dailies: 3
   Aggregate Circulation: 87,728
   Circulation per 1,000: 5
Number of Nondailies: 17
   Aggregate Circulation: 213,000 (1975)
   Circulation per 1,000: 13 (est.)

Number of Periodicals: 17
Number of Radio Stations: 1
Number of Television Stations: 1
Number of Radio Receivers: 310,000 (1977 est.)
   Radio Receivers per 1,000: 17.8
Number of Television Sets: 9,000 (1978 est.)
   Television Sets per 1,000: .5
Total Annual Newsprint Consumption: NA
   Per Capita Newsprint Consumption: NA
Total Newspaper Ad Receipts: NA
As % of All Ad Expenditures: NA

Background & General Characteristics

The Tanzanian press is dominated—through ownership and editorial control—by either the government or the ruling party, CCM (Chama cha Mapinduzi: Revolutionary party) in this nation that has become the leading model on the continent for African socialism.

As such, the press represents a direct contrast to its neighbor on the north, Kenya, where print media are almost exclusively owned and operated by private commercial interests. Just as Tanzania is the leading exponent of African socialism, Kenya is probably the showcase on the continent for Western capitalism and free enterprise. Thus, in Anglophone East Africa, two neighboring nations epitomize two totally different press systems—each reflecting the political philosophy of its nation's economic and governmental structure.

The press of Tanzania is highly centralized and considered an integral tool in the process of national development. The press is the government and ruling party's communication link to the nation's citizens. It not only tells them about development progress in their country but also exhorts them to support any number of governmental campaigns toward economic self-sufficiency. The press,

then, is not utilized as a watchdog on government but primarily as a voice of government and of the ruling party in this authoritarian one-party state.

The press, for example, has played a major role in the promotion of nationwide literacy training. As a result, the government claims that within the past decade 63 percent of the nation's youth and adults have learned to read and write—an impressive figure compared to the rest of Black Africa, especially considering that Tanzania remains one of the poorest countries in the world with an annual per capita income of $180.

The population of 17.4 million is spread across a land the size of Texas and Colorado, 90 percent of the people living in rural areas as subsistence farmers. The remaining population is urban—with Dar es Salaam, Moshi, Arusha, Dodoma and Zanzibar Town (on Zanzibar Island, 20 miles off the mainland) as the major centers. Given the vast distances in Tanzania, and the lack of good communication links, newspaper readership is concentrated in these urban areas.

For all practical purposes, Dar es Salaam, the capital, is also the hub of Tanzania's journalistic activity. All publications are headquartered there and so are the large printing companies.

A number of tribal dialects are spoken by

the nine major ethnic groups, but the lingua franca and official language of the nation is Swahili, spoken by about 90 percent of the population, with the other 10 percent speaking Sukuma. In city centers, English is also widely used in business, trade and higher education.

Tanzania's newspapers are elitist media in terms of distribution and numbers of readers. Dar es Salaam, for example, has less than five percent of Tanzania's population, but accounts for over half of the country's newspaper circulation. The content of the press is in the popular, mass-appeal vein, but the major problem, if literacy is as high as the government claims, is effective distribution networks.

The quality of Tanzania's news media has improved in the past decade; journalists are more professional and the various papers, particularly the dailies, tend to write news items objectively and factually.

News about national development programs, of course, gets major play, but excessive political rhetoric and exhortations seem to be disappearing in the press. In addition, foreign news is now reported in a straightforward manner. During the Vietnam war, for example, editors regularly used such terms as "South Vietnamese Puppet Troops" and characterized the North Vietnamese as "liberation forces." In those days, South Africa was always described as a "fascist state."

The Tanzanian press still suffers, however, from a lack of resources to adequately modernize production facilities. The daily and weekly press is still printed on vintage letterpress machinery and the linotype is still the workhorse for setting type. Large headlines must still be set by hand. Modern typefaces are non-existent. Visiting a daily newspaper plant in Tanzania is like a trip back in time to a half-century ago.

In sum, the press is a level above most of its counterparts in Black Africa, but still ranks somewhat below the press of Kenya and Nigeria in sophistication and production technology.

Tanzania's press was developed under British colonial rule, beginning in 1916 when the Allies took control of what had previously been a German colony; subsequently the country, then known as Tanganyika, became a League of Nations mandated territory administered by Great Britain. Tanganyika received its independence in 1961 and formed a union with Zanzibar in 1964—to form the country's present name, Tanzania.

Under British rule, the governor could prohibit any report or news story thought to be contrary to the public interest. News (in Swahili) was provided for most of the colonial period by the government's own public relations department, while libel and sedition laws were serious obstacles to the development of any indigenous press. Julius Nyerere, who became the nation's president after independence, was even jailed by the British for criminal libel. As editor of a political newsletter published by the Tanganyika African National Union (TANU) he wrote that several district officials were guilty of bias and discrimination.

Like other African nationalist leaders, Nyerere fully exploited the indigenous press (what there was of it) to espouse independence. When he became president he continued to perceive the press as a political instrument for mobilizing the masses. One observer has said, "If President Nyerere is officially the teacher of the nation, then the party press is the preacher." (Nyerere has always been called "Mwalimu"—the teacher —by his fellow Tanzanians.)

It was not until 1967, however, that Nyerere, speaking at Arusha, announced that Tanzania would follow the path of African socialism as a means of national development. Major businesses were nationalized. So, too, were all news media; today only several church publications are exempted from a press exclusively dominated by the ruling party (Tanzania became a formal one-party state in 1965) and the government.

As in communist nations, the relationship between the party and the government often becomes blurred. In general, however, CCM (formerly TANU) sets broad policy and the government implements it. Nyerere, who has won every election since independence by a landslide, is also CCM's head. At lower levels, voters do have a choice between several party candidates for the same office.

Given Tanzania's political structure, it is not surprising that the daily newspaper with the highest circulation (60,000) is *Uhuru* ("Freedom"), the official organ of the CCM. *Uhuru* is a 12-page tabloid published in Swahili. The Party's Sunday paper is *Mzalendo* ("The Patriot"), an eight-column broadsheet published in Swahili with a circulation of 40,000. Speaking for CCM, these two newspapers—both published in Dar es Salaam—are the most influential in Tanzania.

A second Dar es Salaam daily is the English-language *Daily News*, an eight-column broadsheet with eight pages during the week and 12 on Friday. Its antecedent was the *Tanzania Standard*, nationalized in 1970 and subsequently operating as a government newspaper with the editors appointed by President Nyerere. Its circulation is 28,000. The *Daily News* also publishes the *Sunday News*, with a circulation of 28,288. Like the weekday edition, it is an eight-column broadsheet averaging 12 pages.

The daily and Sunday *News* circulate primarily in Dar es Salaam. Their primary readership is the diplomatic community, British expatriates, tourists and governmental civil servants. Both papers carry more international news than *Uhuru* or *Mzalendo*.

A third daily, *Kipanga* (the word for a bush knife used throughout East Africa), is published in Swahili on the island of Zanzibar. It is operated and funded by the Ministry of Information. Its circulation is unavailable, but it probably doesn't go beyond the island.

Other weeklies or periodicals in Tanzania tend to represent official government publications—*Gazette of the United Republic, Government Gazette* and *Ushirika* (Cooperative Union of Tanzania)—are examples.

The only publications not under direct government or party control are two church periodicals: *Kiongozi* ("The Leader"), a fortnightly in Swahili published by the Roman Catholic Church (circulation 23,000), and *Uhuru na Amani* ("Freedom and Peace"), a Swahili publication of the Evangelical Lutheran Church (circulation 12,000). *Kiongozi* includes a large percentage of secular news and, it is said, gets high readership among the opinion leaders of the nation.

Publications by an opposition political party are nonexistent in this formal one-party state.

Economic Framework

Tanzania's economy is growing at the rate of about six percent a year, and its annual population growth is about three percent. By any standard, however, Tanzania is a poor nation requiring large amounts of foreign aid. Its major benefactors in the past have been the Soviet Union, Eastern Europe and China. The Chinese have provided technicians, and their major accomplishment was the building in 1976 of a 1,162-mile railway line from the coast to the mining centers of Zambia. But Nyerere follows a policy of nonalignment, and since both East and West see Tanzania as an ideological battleground, the country also receives aid from Great Britain, the United States and the nations of Western Europe. The United States, for example, has supplied foodstuffs in major amounts during the past several years because of a drought in much of East Africa.

Tanzania's valuable foreign exchange and resources were heavily strained in 1978–79 when a border conflict with Uganda eventually resulted in a full-scale invasion of that country and the toppling of the Idi Amin regime. In addition, Tanzania lost particularly important foreign exchange—from tourists—when it closed the border with its capitalist neighbor, Kenya, in 1977.

All this has meant that the media in Tanzania have been given low priority in terms of modernization or extensive circulation expansion. The press remains almost exclusively an urban institution, and television is still considered a luxury that the nation cannot afford to develop. The TV station in Zanzibar (Africa's first color station, opened in 1973) is an incongruous showcase for the relatively independent, but poor, Zanzibar government. On more than one occasion Nyerere has said that television

Largest Newspapers by Circulation

Name	Circulation	Frequency	Ownership
Uhuru	60,000	Daily	Ruling Party
Mzalendo	40,000	Sunday	Ruling Party
Sunday News	28,000	Sunday	Government
Daily News	27,728	Daily	Government
Kiongozi	23,000	Fortnightly	Church
Uhuru na Amani	12,000	N/A	Church

Note: The circulation of the daily *Kipanga* is not known.

will not come to the Tanzania mainland in the foreseeable future.

The government and CCM have a monopoly on the press and broadcasting in the nation. The largest-circulation daily, *Uhuru*, is the party organ. The *Daily News* is owned and operated by a government corporation, while the third daily, Zanzibar's *Kipanga*, is directly controlled by the Ministry of Information.

The *Daily News* is the result of a 1972 merger of the *Tanzania Standard* and a paper called the *Nationalist*, which, before its own nationalization by the government in 1970, had been a privately owned publication and part of the Standard Group in Nairobi, Kenya. Such ownership was not compatible with the development of the nation along socialist lines. In announcing the take-over of the *Standard*, Nyerere said that it should serve the interest of the people and support the socialist ideology as defined by the Arusha Declaration. He also wrote in an editorial, entitled "A Socialist Paper For the People," that the paper "...will strive to encourage and maintain a high standard of socialist discussions." Nyerere himself appoints the *Daily News*'s board of directors and also reserves the right to appoint the paper's editor.

In addition to the press and broadcasting, the government or the party also owns or controls practically all of Tanzania's printing presses. There are some joint ventures, but it is understood that the government will always own at least 51 percent of the stock.

Newsprint availability is a serious problem because 100 percent of the supply must be imported with valuable foreign exchange. The State Trading Corporation must approve all newsprint orders, and there rarely is enough money to purchase quantities for any newspaper to expand its size or circulation base.

Most newspaper advertising comes from government agencies and corporations. An average issue of the *Daily News*, for example, will contain about 40 percent advertising. Government advertising is a direct subsidy to the operation of the newspapers, but the newspapers probably still run at a deficit.

Press Laws

The nation's constitution includes "freedom of expression" in its preamble as one of the fundamental rights of man, but freedom of the press is not expressly guaranteed by the document.

In addition, press freedom is somewhat circumscribed to the extent that the constitution forbids criticism of the major principles and programs of the government and the party. Although criticism of poor administration—especially at lower levels—is permitted, the concept of African socialism set forth in the Arusha Declaration is not subject to debate or discussion.

A press law passed in 1968 gives the president authority to ban any newspaper, but this has now become virtually irrelevant since all publications are controlled by the government and CCM. It can still be used, however, against the several publications owned by religious groups, or even various foreign publications.

There are also laws on the books that allow the government to detain citizens, including journalists, without benefit of formal charges or trial. In fact, Amnesty International announced in 1978 that the government was detaining 26 political activists without trial or access to legal counsel. A year earlier, the international group claimed that 1,000 citizens were being detained without due process. Given the structure of the media in Tanzania, native journalists are rarely detained—they are already employees of the government and loyal to the party.

Libel and sedition laws are in force, mostly inherited from the British colonial administration. Journalists are not licensed in a formal sense, but they do undergo a political screening before they are hired. Newspapers are registered, like any other business, but they are not required to post any bond.

The nation's judicial system is based on English common law. There is a three-level court system with right of appeal to the High Court. The judiciary is empowered by the constitution to review legislation and edicts, but the independence of judges is tempered by the fact that President Nyerere can appoint and remove them almost at will. Nyerere has been in power for 20 years, and it is unlikely that a court or a judge would go directly against his wishes.

Censorship

The Ministry of Information and Broadcasting Services is directly responsible for monitoring the press, but the president's office embodies both the ruling party and governmental apparatus. Guidelines for editorial policy and treatment of the news come from this office—and are followed by the press.

Since the press is either government or party controlled, there is little need for pre-publication or post-publication censorship.

State-Press Relations

President Nyerere has compared a developing nation to a country at war—at war for its very existence. In such a situation it is only logical and natural that newspapers everywhere would accept limitations on their freedom. A specific function of state-press relations in Tanzania was also outlined in 1980 by Ndugu Benjamin Mkapa, minister of foreign affairs. Speaking in 1980 to students at the Tanzania School of Journalism, he explained that journalists should act as a bridge between the people and their government.

The 1970s were a decade of relative quiet on the press front in terms of bannings or confiscations. The last major nongovernmental press outlet was nationalized in 1970. The editor of the Roman Catholic weekly *Kiongozi* was probably one of the last journalists to be arrested and fined. In 1971 he printed a critical article saying that too many young girls were becoming pregnant while in the national service. Today such imprisonment is rare—primarily because all leading journalists and editors are members of CCM, and have "paid their dues," so to speak, to the party and government. Tanzania journalism is a closed-loop system where possible dissidents have already been weeded out.

The government and party encourage the press by (1) official advertising, (2) direct budget subsidies and (3) reduced postal rates.

Attitude Toward Foreign Media

Visas are required of all foreign visitors and, officially, foreign correspondents are processed no differently from anyone else. On an unofficial basis, however, they are scrutinized much more closely and asked more questions. If a person's passport lists "journalist" as a profession, the visa is often delayed until approval comes from Dar es Salaam. Moreover, journalists require official permission to interview ordinary citizens or do research in government archives. (If it

is any consolation, anthropologists are also subjected to the same procedures.)

In other words, foreign correspondents are treated with suspicion. There is a perception that Western journalists are in the country to defame the government or its national development program. A correspondent of Agence France Presse was briefly detained for questioning after he observed a student demonstration protesting a government policy. On another occasion, foreign journalists were banned from the country during an African heads-of-state summit meeting. Two British journalists were expelled in 1979 with no official reason given.

The procedures to admit a foreign correspondent are so precautionary that there is no real review of the cables they file. It must be remembered, however, that the government operates the telecommunications system.

There is no official import restriction on foreign publications, but the State Trading Corporation must approve any imports because of foreign-exchange problems. In theory, any objectable publication can be stopped by the Trading Corporation at this point. In general, however, foreign publications are so expensive that only the ruling elite can afford them. Consequently, their impact on the general population is not very great. In terms of movies, there is a review of foreign films for content (mostly sex and violence) before they are allowed into the country.

Given the socialist ideal, foreign ownership of media facilities is prohibited. However, foreign investment in media is not ruled out if the investor is compatible with socialist ideals, although the government must own at least 51 percent of the stock.

Citizens of Tanzania with short-wave radios can listen to Voice of America, Radio Moscow, Radio Peking, The Republic of South Africa, or the BBC. Most of these services are available in Swahili.

Tanzania strongly favors the creation of a Pan African News Agency (PANA) as an alternative to Western-dominated international news services. The government also supports the 1978 UNESCO Declaration calling for a new world information order in which developing nations have a larger role.

News Agencies

The major domestic news agency is Shihata, established in 1976 to report on national events and also disseminate world news stories within Tanzania.

At least four foreign news bureaus are regularly represented in Dar es Salaam: EFE (Spain), Novosti (USSR), Allgemeiner Deutscher Nachrichtendienst (East Germany) and Reuters (Britain). Another four agencies staff bureaus on a somewhat irregular basis: Ceskoslovenski Tiskova Kancelar (Czechoslovakia), Hsinhua (China), Prensa Latina (Cuba) and Tass (USSR).

Although newspapers may subscribe to any international news agency, the more common practice is to receive news through Shihata.

The major issue related to world-news flow is reliance on Western-oriented news agencies. Like other nonaligned nations, Tanzania believes that this constitutes a form of cultural imperialism. It is also felt that the western agencies tend to concentrate on a country's negative aspects instead of informing the world about its accomplishments.

Electronic News Media

Broadcasting in Tanzania, as in nearly all Africa, is a state-owned and -operated medium. It is administered by the Ministry of Information and Broadcasting and funded out of the national budget. Other revenue includes some commercial advertising on one program, but no license fees are charged.

Given the nation's overall economic climate, particularly its scarcity of financial resources, radio is considered far more cost effective than any other medium in terms of reaching the general population. Not only does it span the country's vast distances, but a single village loudspeaker can amplify its message to hundreds or even thousands. Indeed, most of Tanzania's national development programs (particularly literacy training and agricultural innovations) have been carried out by combining radio messages with the personal visits of party workers and agricultural extension specialists. In a developing nation with a poor road system, and where nine-tenths the population live in rural areas, radio's potential far outstrips that of the printed media.

Tanzania has five short-wave and four medium-wave transmitters. Three types of broadcast material are available: a national program in Swahili, external programming in English and a commercial program in Swahili. In terms of international propa-

ganda broadcasting, Tanzania is more active than most African states. It has broadcasts beamed to South Africa and Southwest Africa (Namibia) in Afrikaans and regional dialects. Other programs are produced for Uganda, Kenya, Mozambique, Angola, and Zimbabwe.

Radio is also used extensively in primary and secondary schools during the regular term.

Radio Zanzibar broadcasts in Swahili over three wavelengths. In addition, Zanzibar's color television station is on the air for several hours a day. The signal reaches the coastal area of Tanzania, and there has been an increase of television sets in Dar es Salaam. In general, however, the TV audience is on the island.

There are an estimated 310,000 radios and 9,000 television sets.

Broadcasting personnel are part of the nation's civil service, and many have been trained abroad. The top administrators are appointed by President Nyerere. They must have professional competence—and be members in good standing of CCM.

Education & Training

The primary mode of journalism training is through the Publicity Media Institute at the Nzegezi Social Training Center, which offers an 18-month course leading to a diploma certificate. References to a Tanzania School of Journalism also appear in the literature. In 1980, about 60 students were enrolled.

In addition, the major newspapers provide training programs. There is a Tanzania Press Club and a journalists' association based in Dar es Salaam.

Summary

The media in Tanzania are highly centralized, and controlled by the government or the ruling political party in this formalized one-party state. As such, the press is perceived as a valuable tool of the government to inform and inspire the population. It does not meet Western standards of objectivity and independence, but it does reflect the nation's political and economic philosophy.

This is not to say that the press is a passive, bland mouthpiece of government. The ruling party is broad based and there are differences of opinion when it comes to national planning or administration of specific projects. The press does engage in open discussion of issues, but always within the framework of the ruling party's interpretation of socialist principles.

The trend in Tanzania, if any, is for the status quo to continue. The press and broadcasting will remain an integral part of the government apparatus. Expansion of print circulation will be slow, due to lack of modern technology and the necessary transportation links within the country. Radio will continue to be the primary vehicle of mass communication; television will not be available for most of the 1980s.

The scarcity of resources will mean some additional consolidation of the mass media. The growth of specialized publications to serve an expanding middle class is a fleeting possibility.

Tanzania has many economic problems, and press development reflects them sharply.

CHRONOLOGY

No events of significance to press development have occurred since the early 1970s.

BIBLIOGRAPHY

Europa Yearbook. London, 1979.

Hachten, William. *Muffled Drums.* Ames, Iowa, 1971.

Stokke, Olav. *Mass Communications in Africa—Freedoms and Functions.* Uppsala, Sweden, 1971.

UNESCO. *World Communications.* New York, 1975.

U.S. Department of State. *Basic Data on Sub-Saharan Africa.* Washington, D.C., 1979.

Wilcox, Dennis L. *Mass Media in Black Africa: Philosophy and Control.* New York, 1975.

THAILAND

by John Lent

BASIC DATA

Population: 44.2 million
Area: 514,000 sq. km. (198,000 sq. mi.)
GNP: Bht 523 billion (US$26.9 billion)
Literacy Rate: 81.8% (1970)
Language(s): Thai, Chinese, English
Number of Dailies: 116
    Aggregate Circulation: 1.5–2 million
    Circulation per 1,000: 34
Number of Nondailies: 108
    Aggregate Circulation: 1 million
    Circulation per 1,000: 23
Number of Periodicals: 150

Number of Radio Stations: 222
Number of Television Stations: 8
Number of Radio Receivers: 5,361,000 (1975)
    Radio Receivers per 1,000: 140
Number of Television Sets: 761,015
    Television Sets per 1,000: 17
Total Annual Newsprint Consumption: 54,000 metric tons
Per Capita Newsprint Consumption: 1.2 kg. (2.6 lb.)
Total Newspaper Ad Receipts: Bht 279.5 million (US$13.7 million) (1979)
    As % of All Ad Expenditures: 15 (1979)

Background & General Characteristics

Two words most frequently come to mind when thinking about Thai mass media: uncertainty and color. Uncertainty surfaces nearly everywhere, even when trying to establish the number of newspapers, for in Thailand, newspaper licenses are purchased for nonpublishing newspapers, as a hedge against future government harassments. The problem is complicated by the sporadic births and deaths of newspapers (and other media) under the various military and civilian governments that have ruled Thailand since the 1932 overthrow of the absolute monarchy. Bafflement continues when attempting to count the number of radio stations, because Thai radio stations switch call letters and frequencies during the course of a broadcast day.

The second key word, "color," can be applied both to the format and content of Thai newspapers. Main dailies, for example, can be identified by trademark colors used in their logotypes and/or banners, and for years, in the wrappers that enveloped them. The content of the large newspapers has been as sensationalized as their large front-page banners and photo collages; it has included serialized versions of the sexual exploits of former prime ministers, cartoon panels vividly portraying sex themes and crime and other meant-to-be tantalizing fare. In fact, for a number of years, the phrase *journalisme à la siamoise,* not identifiable with responsible journalism, was considered appropriate for the Thai press.

Especially because of its confused character, the Thai press does not lend itself to neat, capsulized treatment. In a discussion of Thai newspapers, exceptions and contrasting figures are often included.

From the birth of Thailand's press in 1844 until the abolition of the absolute monarchy in 1932, journalism and politics were closely entwined. Dr. Dan Beach Bradley, the missionary who started the first newspaper, used it in an attempt to influence King Mongkut. Throughout the latter 19th century, royalty took an interest in journalism, publishing newspapers to disseminate the official, authoritative word.

The bloodless coup of 1932, which ended the control of the royal family, ushered in not only a number of quasi-parliamentary constitutions and dictatorial regimes but a climate of political instability that inevitably affected the press. Coups brought in protégés of those who were replaced, and old constitutions were repeated almost verbatim. John D. Mitchell wrote that the resultant press was marked by:

> (1) individual papers frequently published as outlets for particular individuals who led cliques within the complicated pattern of politics-in-government; (2) papers much more interested in sensation and entertainment than news as such; and (3) a press concentrated in Bangkok, a pattern that did not change significantly for nondaily papers until well after World War II and remained undisturbed for daily papers until the 1960s.

All of this is still important for the Thailand press; it is an axiom that press freedom fluctuates widely depending on who is in power.

Even in periods of democratic rule, the Thai press, paradoxically, has been less free than during the absolute monarchy, especially the so-called Golden Age of Thai Journalism (1910-25), when Rama VI reacted to what he considered to be unfair but also welcomed fair criticism of government. For example, from the time the People's party took over in 1932, and banned the opposition press, all newspapers have been linked to political parties.

Especially repressive during the "democratic" period was the prime ministership of Field Marshal Sarit Thanarat (1959-63), who instituted Announcement No. 17, licensing all prospective newspaper publishers. Announcement No. 17 made newspaper licenses commercially profitable products, resulting in speculation in license selling and renting to newspapers that wanted to publish, a practice common into the 1970s. Under Sarit, newspapers were punished with warnings, impounding and/or destruction. This worst of all post-1932 governments left lingering effects on the profession, as some of Thailand's best journalists were scared off, never to return to writing.

Some changes (whether positive is subject to debate) occurred under the Thanom government (1963-73), when press controls were initially much lessened. With relative freedom and the advent of better technology, the press in the early part of this regime started to act as an industrial enterprise—clamoring for circulation, and in the process becoming rather sensationalized. But the up-and-down nature of Thai-style freedom of the press was seen in the late 1960s, when severe legal restrictions accounted for correspondingly strict self-censorship. After a coup in 1971, a Thanom coalition issued Announcement No. 3, promising to abolish censorship—except for those newspapers that represented voices trying to divide the nation. Because of its fluctuating relationships with government and its new role as an industrial concern with interests to protect, the press was considered rather timid in the early 1970s, leading to its being termed "journalism of conformity." Exceptions were the *Nation,* started in 1971 as the first Thai-owned English-language daily, which claimed it would strive for objective reporting; *Prachathippatai,* taken over by a new group of journalists in 1973 and popular among politicized students; and the older *Siam Rath.* They represented a more articulate and responsible type of journalism than that practiced by *Thai Rath, Daily News, Siam* and *Ban Muang,* which played up sex, escapism and violence.

The three-year period after the October 1973 student revolution that brought down the Thanom coalition was definitely the freest, and one of the most prosperous financially, for the press. The interim government appointed by the king, and led by Professor Sanya Thammasak, was very popular with Thai journalists, for it lifted the ban on new newspapers and promulgated a constitution that guaranteed press freedom, abolished censorship and restricted ownership of newspapers to Thais. Despite his liberalism, however, Sanya did not repeal Announcement No. 17, and speculation in licenses became rampant. By December 6, 1974, 853 newspaper and periodical licenses had been issued, 177 of which were for dailies. Only 10 percent of the licenses were ever used by their applicants. Thus Sanya's year-and-a-half administration was noted for a press that was free but also very irresponsible—resorting to sensationalism, extortion, bribery and in some cases violence. But the free-wheeling nature of license issuance at least practically ended the monopoly that had existed in newspaper publishing. A new group of journalists appeared, criticizing the practices of their predecessors and aiming to promote responsible journalism in papers such as *Prachachart, Prachathippatai, Siangmai, Athipat* and *Nation.*

Thus, when Sanya left office in February 1975, the press could be characterized as a mixture of responsible and irresponsible elements. The government of M. R. Kukrit Pramoj—which succeeded, in March 1975, the very short-lived coalition led by his brother, M. R. Seni Pramoj—maintained a high level of freedom of the press. Kukrit himself was a newspaperman, who, in 1950, had been founding head of *Siam Rath,* to which he contributed popular political columns. Yet he was not very popular with the press, at least for a few months, because he said he would not tolerate irresponsible journalism. Under his administration, Announcement No. 17 stayed in effect, and a new press act was promulgated, calling for a 17-21-member committee to control the press along ethical lines.

All this ended in the bloody coup of October 1976, which reversed many of the gains of the previous three years. The constitution was suspended, and for the first time in Thai history, all newspapers were stopped, some never to reappear.

The daily press of Thailand in 1980 can be characterized as highly concentrated, relatively young and usually portrayed as frivolous and sensational. As in many states of Southeast Asia, dailies are concentrated in the capital city, Bangkok, with some less frequent and relatively insignificant papers upcountry. The result is that while Bangkok ranks as one of the most newspaper-saturated cities in the world, the nation as a whole might be considered newspaper poor.

The number of newspapers in Thailand depends to some extent on the statistical source. The 18 dailies included in the 1980–81 *Asian Press and Media Directory* have a total circulation of about 2.03 million, and are published in the Thai (10), Chinese (four) and English (four) languages. The largest dailies (all in Thai) are *Thai Rath* (700,000), started in 1958 and emphasizing sensational content; *Daily News* (400,000), founded in the late 1940s originally as *Naeo na deli niu,* which has been a leader in innovations such as the four-color wrapper and western cartoons with Thai captions; *Ban Muang* (150,000), founded in 1963, and *Dao Siam* (140,000), founded in 1974. In the intermediate circulation range are *Tawan Siam* (97,000), a Thai daily founded in 1976; *The Daily Times* (95,000), founded as a Thai daily in 1974 by the dissident staff of *Daily News; Siam Rath* (80,000), the Thai paper founded by M. R. Kukrit Pramoj in 1950; *Sing Sian Yit Pao* (80,000), leading Chinese daily started in 1950 by Aw Boon Haw of the Tiger Balm ointment fortune in Hong Kong; and *Daily Mirror* (70,000), a Thai language paper started in 1978. Other Chinese dailies have relatively small circulations: *Universal,*

50,000; *Sirinakorn* and *New Chinese,* 20,000 each. The four English-language dailies have less than 60,000 total circulation, led by the *Bangkok Post,* founded by Alexander MacDonald and sold to the Thomson Group in 1963, with 21,000; followed by *Nation Review,* with 18,000; *Bangkok World,* founded in 1957 by General Phao Sriyanond, and later sold to Thomson, with 10,000; and *Business Times,* with 8,000. The *Post* and *World* were merged into Allied Newspapers Ltd. in the late 1970s.

Statistics given in 1979 listed the total number of dailies as 116. Broken down by language, 99 were in Thai, two in Thai-English, four in English, 10 in Chinese and one in Japanese. At the same time, there were another 108 weeklies, 93 of which were in Thai, nine in Thai-English and six in English. Most Thai newspapers are meant for morning audiences. An earlier source, in 1976, claimed only 26 dailies with a total circulation of 1.6 million, and 497 nondailies, with 1 million total circulation.

Many of Thailand's newspapers are newcomers to the field; the oldest do not go back much more than 35 years. Of the 18 dailies in the directory mentioned above, the *Bangkok Post* is the oldest, dating to 1946. Five were started in the 1950s *(Bangkok World, Siam Rath, Sing Sin Yit Pao, Thai Rath* and *Universal),* two in the 1960s *(Daily News* and *Sirinakorn)* and ten in the 1970s *(Ban Muang, Bangkok Pimthai, Business Times, Daily Mirror, Dao Siam, Daily Times, Matichon, Nation Review, New Chinese* and *Tawan Siam).* The youthfulness of these newspapers is attributable to the instability caused by changes of government, especially that of October 1976.

Although charges are regularly leveled against Thailand's newspapers for being sensationalist and frivolous, the content analyses done in the 1970s only looked at these characteristics obliquely. Thammasat University researcher Somkuan Kaviya was more direct when he reported in 1978 that the more serious dailies emphasize opinion articles, social problems, news and economic and political events, while most papers (those popular with masses) stress sensationalism in the form of "pompous [sic] front pages, gossip and personalized news (more than 25 percent)." He said foreign news was not used very often, making up four or five percent of the content. From Guy B. Scandlen's 1970 analysis, which separated the urban and rural press, it is difficult to determine how sensational the press was at that time. Scandlen showed that advertising took up 22.2 percent of urban papers and 37.2 percent of rural papers; arts, culture and entertainment, 9.2 percent of urban, 12.3 of rural; and human interest, 9.0 and 8.6, respectively. Urban newspapers devoted more space to national government news than did rural papers, which focused on local government. In 1973 Scandlen said, the highest percentage of space went to advertisements (30.9 percent in urban; 31.4 in rural), followed by human interest stories (19.7 and 16.6, respectively), and government news (12.4 and 5.8). The frivolity charge has often been associated with Thai newspapers' propensity to devote much space to lottery results. Scandlen found that lotteries comprised 15 percent of the urban papers' content, with 10 percent in rural papers. Chinese dailies carried 2.5 times more advertising than either Thai or English counterparts, and English-language dailies carried more sports and disaster news than the other language presses. Chinese dailies had six times more human interest stories than English and 2.5 times more than Thai dailies. In the provinces, all papers had a high percentage of advertising space, but gave very little to science or medicine.

Credibility of the press among Thai readers apparently has increased, especially after the October 1973 student revolution. There was a time in the early 1960s when radio information was more believable than that of newspapers. Three USIS surveys during that decade confirmed this point. Scandlen and Ken Winkler reported that in the mid-1970s daily reading of newspapers generally was increasing: among highly educated people, the figure rose from 62 percent in 1964 to 73 percent in 1969; among those with little or no education from 22 to 37 percent. Daily newspaper reading is not a habit with Thais for the same reasons it is not in other developing nations: relatively low, functional literacy rates; urban bias of press content, and low purchasing power of the people. In 1971, in an effort to increase newspaper reading, especially in rural areas, the Ministry of Education developed a newspaper-reading-center scheme. The villagers built the centers, while the ministry provided the furniture and subscriptions to three newspapers, the latter chosen by the villagers. By the mid-1970s at least 1,300 villages had their own newspaper reading centers.

As the idea of up-country newspapers be-
came more persistent in the 1970s, the rural populations were served with information more relevant to their needs and wishes. It is difficult to know how many such papers exist, as the figures vary from one reporting agency to another. Provincial newspapers have been small in circulation (averaging 1,500 to 17,000), nondaily (many appearing every five to 10 days) and plagued with problems, some of which will be mentioned later. A few up-country communities and their newspapers in 1976–77 might be mentioned here. In Chiang Mai, the oldest paper was *Khon Muang,* a tabloid begun in 1952. There were others such as *Thai News* (11,000 circulation), *Thin Thai* and *Raming.* In Lampang, the Thai-language *Ekkarat* published five times monthly, and in Uttaradit, *Prachasan* appeared every five days. In Nakorn Ratchasima, *Chao'isan,* a Thai weekly, was the leading local paper of the northeast; *Chao Tai,* a Thai paper in Yala, served the same role for the south.

Economic Framework

The mid-1970s were poor years economically for the Thai press. Newsprint prices skyrocketed—as did the cost of nearly everything—and after the 1973 revolution newspapers faced the problem of increased circulation without having adequate newsprint and equipment. Specialized and up-country newspapers were more particularly affected. One paper designated for selective readers, *Sarn Siam,* lasted only five months and lost $250,000. Provincial papers definitely operated on a shoestring—some were published so irregularly that they appeared only when lottery results were issued. The newspapers in the non-Bangkok area depended on job printing for capital.

Newspapers are individually owned in Thailand, while electronic media are government operated and controlled. Except in an instance or two, ownership is not concentrated in groups or cross-channel structures, and it is in the hands of Thai nationals. A 1974 constitutional subcommittee drew up a law forbidding majority foreign ownership of any Thai media, but that constitution was scrapped with a later change of government. Today, although there are no Thai laws dealing specifically with foreign ownership of newspapers, under business legislation, foreign ownership in media cannot exceed 50 percent.

A very recent incident concerning foreign ownership (in this case, in two or more nations), and possibly concentration of media, was the exposure in November-December 1980 that at least 40 percent of the shares of the *Bangkok Post* had been sold to the *Straits Times* of Singapore. The *Post* had been the center of controversy previously, when it was purchased by the Thomson Group of England and Canada in the mid-1960s. Before Thomson sold the paper in 1979, the Thai ownership share had been raised to 51 percent. The concerns in the 1980 transaction were whether Thai stockholders had been offered the shares or told of the *Straits Times'* purchase. A senior Commerce Ministry official said at the time that ownership of newspapers was a "matter of national interest." There might have been concern also because the *Straits Times* itself is tied in with a fast-growing international media conglomerate.

The total advertising expenditure in Thailand, listed in the 1980–81 *Asian Press and Media Directory,* was $153.4 million, or $3.48 per capita. These figures become more important when compared with past years. In 1968, the total was $12.5 million; in 1972, $33.9 million; in 1976, $79.9 million, and in 1977, $99.2 million. Content analyses in the 1970s showed that advertisers apparently had found new marketing channels in newspapers, judging by the space devoted to display advertising. Again, some figures are in order: in 1976, newspapers accounted for $14.7 million of the national advertising budget, while in 1977, the amount rose to $25.5 million. Television's figures were $40.4 million in 1976, $42.0 million in 1977; radio's, $9.2 million and $12.5 million, respectively.

Although 100 firms are listed as advertising agencies, only 25 are serious operators. More than one-half of total billings go to the major agencies, such as Ted Bates, Ogilvy and Mather, Diethelm Advertising, Ling-McCann Ericson, SSC and B Lintas, C. J. L. Niramit, Dentsu, Leo Burnett, Grant and Associated Communication Corporation. These major multinational agencies, mostly United States-based, received a boost in the mid-1960s, when they bought up various small agencies.

Distribution of newspapers is through subscriptions and newsstand sales, with most Bangkok dailies having a national distribution system that can reach most parts of the country within 24 hours.

As indicated earlier, the price of dailies makes newspaper purchasing a luxury. The price of a daily (B1.50, or 7.5 cents, in the mid-1970s) can pay for a midday meal in some areas. Thus, a study carried out by Chulalongkorn University in 1972 reported that newspaper subscriptions ranked seventh among household possessions in the Bangkok-Thonburi region (25.2 percent of households surveyed were subscribers), seventh among provincial-urban households (21.7 percent subscribing) and sixth in rural areas (3.5 percent).

More recently a survey by SRG News showed that newspaper, radio and television audiences were nearly evenly matched. In 1979 the percentage of adults claiming to have read at least one daily "yesterday," was between 63 and 66 percent, a drop from the 78 percent in 1975. Corresponding figures for television were 64 percent in 1979 and 62 percent in 1975; for radio, 60 percent in both years.

In the mid-1970s it was reported that Thailand's 19 paper manufacturers produced a large quantity of printing paper but no newsprint, although the country was ideal for pulp mills, with an abundance of raw materials (such as wood, bagasse, bamboo and rice straw), water and cheap labor. The argument against local newsprint production at the time dealt with the large capital outlay necessary for a mill to compete internationally, given the limited domestic demand. Others claimed that a demand was present and that a mill would protect newspapers against severe increases in the price of newsprint. The price fluctuations were rather high in the early 1970s; in 1971 the required 50,000 tons cost B180 million ($9 million), while two years later, 55,000 tons were priced at B280 million ($14 million). The results were that in August 1973 all Chinese dailies stopped their evening editions; earlier, Thai and English dailies had raised their prices per copy. After the October 1973 revolution, many of the new licensees to operate newspapers could not bring out their first editions because of newsprint shortages. The prices increased even more drastically later in the decade. Apparently a newsprint operation was started in 1975. The company, Phoenix Pulp and Paper, was described by *Asiaweek* in late 1979 as one of the biggest industrial investments—as well as one of the slowest—in Thailand's recent years. Guaranteed by overseas loans, Phoenix produced a high-quality paper. By 1979, of the total newsprint consumption of 54,000 metric tons, 35,000 were reportedly produced in Thailand.

Most of the newsprint goes to Bangkok dailies, which used 200 tons daily in the mid-1970s. As a dramatization of how little newsprint is used by up-country papers, in the mid-1970s, all 180 provincial papers, averaging 1,500 copies a week, had a total press run of 270,000, or 70 percent of that of *Thai Rath* for one day.

Ninety percent of Thailand's printing industry also is concentrated in Bangkok. Letterpress is used by 70 percent of the nearly 2,000 registered Thai printers, who oftentimes must use worn-out typefaces. Letterpress printers buy second-hand machines from Europe, where type height is larger than in Thailand, resulting in the need for modifications. By 1980, however, all major dailies in Bangkok had converted to offset printing.

The economic picture of up-country newspapers in Thailand is very gloomy, as newspapers suffer from inadequate printing equipment, expensive newsprint, stiff competition from Bangkok dailies, nonstandardized advertising rates that are too inexpensive, lack of capital, shortages of experienced reporters and correspondents, and poor communication infrastructures—such as radio, telephone, vehicles and good roads. For example, electricity is often cut for long periods of time in some regions. Sumkuan Kaviya reported in 1971 that newspapers sell well in towns only if it is lottery day, and even then it is difficult for vendors to collect payment from patrons.

Throughout the newspaper industry, both in Bangkok and up-country, employment conditions are bad. Unlike neighboring Malaysia and Singapore, Thailand has no labor unions for newspaper personnel, resulting in low wages and poor working conditions. Because of these factors, some Thai reporters have been known to take bribes for placing or removing individuals' names in headlines.

A specific labor-management problem that existed in the early 1970s was the accusation that at the Thomson-owned *Post,* management discriminated against Thais.

Press Laws & Censorship

Over the years there have been a number of Thai press laws that journalists have considered unfair. Announcement No. 17, which licenses periodicals, has been on the books for over a generation, while other decrees are more recent. After the October 1976 coup,

Thai generals and their prime minister, Thanin Kraivichien, prescribed National Administrative Reform Council Decree 42, which allowed censorship of the press. Under Thanin's stern anti-communist rule, few publishers escaped shutdown on grounds of being national security risks. Decree 42, which remained in effect in 1980, and was being vigorously opposed by groups such as the Federation of Thai Journalists, empowers police to close any newspapers the government wishes suspended. Under Paragraph 6, it is forbidden to publish any material "which is untrue...or may create alarm, anxiety or horror among the citizens...or which instigates or stirs up unrest."

In August 1980, *Thai Rath* was a victim of Decree 42, when it was closed and its editor arrested for an exposé of the police. Whereas two or three years before, such a closure would have been an everyday fact of life, the 1980 incident caused a reaction. An investigating committee was formed, lawyers were hired and the case was taken to international bodies for support. Previously, such solidarity was unheard of because the press groups were split in their objectives, but by 1980 they were unified in the Federation of Thai Journalists. Although *Thai Rath* was on the streets a day after its closing, the fight it engendered continued. The press sought repeal of Decree 42 and asked for amendments to the Printing Act of 1941, which gives the Interior Ministry powers to grant or revoke publishing licenses.

Part of the problem also involves the 1973 decision of the Interior Ministry to designate Bangkok police and provincial governors as "press officers," with powers to close papers. The Federation of Thai Journalists wants authority over newspaper closures shifted to the courts and thinks of Prime Minister Prem Tinsulanond as a friend in this effort. When repeal of Decree 42 was broached in the past, the government said it retained the law because the press was not able to control itself, and because some of its members were influenced by advocates of undesirable ideals. The police said the law was useful, especially in cases such as that of 1979, when *Daily News,* accused of lese majesty, was closed, thus preventing mob violence. The press replied that it was practicing discipline through self-regulatory guidelines it set up in June 1979. Although the subject was discussed regularly in the mid-1970s, a press council has not become functional in Thailand.

Still other laws, and their effects on media,

can be mentioned. For example, the Thai Penal Code, Section 115, states:

Any person who uses speech, written material or any other means publicly to commit any act which is not an act within the intention of the constitution, or is not for the purpose of honestly expressing opinions or criticism
1) with intent to bring about a change in law or government through the use of force or violence
2) with intent to bring about disorder or discontentment among the people to the extent that disturbances are caused within the kingdom
3) with intent to cause violations of the law by the people is liable to imprisonment for a period not exceeding seven years.

Articles 29 and 45 of the Printing Act B.E. 2484 were used in November 1979 to close 57 dailies and to threaten 32 other papers with legal action. The closures resulted because the dailies never printed for public circulation as stipulated in Article 45; the other 32 newspapers printed weekly when they had daily permits. These articles are designed to eliminate the practice of publishers purchasing spare licenses. The five press associations reacted with a statement that without a definite government policy on the press, newspapers had to get reserve licenses in case they were closed.

Another governmental action did not bode well for a free Thai press; in October 1978 the National Legislative Assembly debated press freedom, and as a result deleted two paragraphs from the draft constitution. One paragraph dealt with prohibiting the closure of newspapers, the other with prepublication censorship.

State-Press Relations

The major governmental organization with communication functions is the Public Relations Department, under the Office of the Prime Minister. Other related agencies are the divisions of Publication, News, Public Opinion Survey, Radio Engineering, License, Home Broadcasting and Overseas Broadcasting, all of which are also under the Office of the Prime Minister. The Public Relations Department has been accused of attempting to manage the news; most of these charges relate to broadcasting.

As is not the case in other Asian countries (e.g., India, Sri Lanka), one does not hear of the Thai government exercising control through newsprint or advertising allocations, subsidies or import licenses on printing equipment. Rather, the government manipulates the press through the various abovementioned legal restraints. There have been a number of instances of arrests of journalists and suspensions of newspapers since the October 1976 coup. When the military seized control then, all newspapers for the first time in Thai history were banned and hundreds of students, politicians and journalists were arrested. Publications that were seen leaning toward communism were confiscated and burned, and after two days, all publishers and broadcasting managers were summoned to command headquarters to be told the terms under which they could resume. The newspapers were directed to apply to the junta for permission to publish, and when they began publication, they had to be censored under a seven-point code. At least five newspapers (mostly Chinese and *Nation*), considered radical, were not allowed to resume. The next government, that of Prime Minister Kriangsak Chamanand, loosened censorship temporarily.

Attitude Toward Foreign Media

The 1976–77 *Asian Press and Media Directory* reported that there were correspondents in Thailand from Japan, the United States, Australia, Malaysia, England, Taiwan, Hong Kong, Germany, Switzerland and the Soviet Union. Together they represented 35 different media agencies. Additionally, all Thai newspapers depend to varying degrees on Associated Press, United Press International, Agence France Presse and Reuters.

Attitudes toward the foreign media sway according to the government in power. After the 1976 coup, there was heavy censorship of foreign publications, such as *The New York Times, Newsweek, International Herald-Tribune, Asian Wall Street Journal, Far Eastern Economic Review* and several Kuala Lumpur and Singapore dailies. All foreign media had to be submitted to a five-man censorship committee before distribution. If any article violated the seven-point censorship code, it was cut from the issue or the entire issue was banned. In 1977 a *Far Eastern Economic Review* correspondent was expelled from Thailand, having been accused of writing that was detrimental to national security.

At the beginning of the 1980s, the government seems to have a more relaxed attitude toward foreign media and their representatives.

News Agencies

Thailand is still attempting to establish a national news agency acceptable to the media. The Thailand News Agency (TNA), started in late 1977, is criticized for not being independent, being a part of the Mass Communication Organization of Thailand, a state enterprise. Lacking adequate staff, TNA receives its budget and policy guidelines from the government. By mid-1978 the agency sent its mimeographed Thai-language report to 45 subscribers daily and was planning to work in English.

The government has been wondering whether to restructure TNA or to create a new agency. Some observers believe that power rivalries in Thailand have prevented the development of a centralized news agency in the past.

Electronic News Media

Radio was introduced to Thailand in 1930, television in 1954. Broadcasting is the domain of governmental agencies, chief of which are the military and the police, who own 90 percent of radio and two of eight television stations; and the Public Relations Department (PRD), operator of the national station, Thai National Broadcasting System, or Radio Thailand, with home, overseas and rural services. Other broadcasting companies are Thai Television Ltd., managed by PRD, whose shareholders include nine other department units; Post and Telegraph; Kasetsart and Chulalongkorn universities, Royal Household Bureau and the Ministry of Education. Financing is by government subsidies and commercial advertising, and most radio and television stations operate on a commercial basis.

Thailand has medium, short-wave and VHF-FM radio transmissions. The exact number of stations is difficult to gauge because of sporadic births and deaths of stations under military rule, and because, as mentioned earlier, some stations switch call letters and frequencies during the day, causing constant overlap. In 1979, *Communications Profiles* listed the number at 222.

Radio is the most effective way of reaching the most people; in excess of 30 million, or 75 percent of the population, can be reached by the 5,360,735 radio receivers serving 4,996,000 households. Of this total, 840,000 are in municipal areas. By regions, the Northeast has 28.1 percent of the sets; the North, 23.7 percent; Central (excluding Bangkok), 26 percent; Bangkok, 11.2 percent, and South, 11 percent. Between 1974 and 1975 the number of radio receivers increased by 4.9 percent, or 250,000.

Radio programming is primarily in Thai, with some use of regional dialects and English. From one set of statistics, Thai National Broadcasting System is on the air 166 hours weekly, 124 of which are billed as nationally produced. The breakdown is 74 hours for light entertainment; 25 for news and information; 15 for education; 15 for broadcasts for national minorities; 6.5 for broadcasts for special audiences and 3.5 for cultural programs. The overseas service is in Chinese, Malay, French, Cambodian, Laotian and English.

Government control of radio is pervasive; for example, Radio Thailand is charged with entertaining, educating, explaining government acts, countering communist propaganda and encouraging cooperation of the public in implementing government policies. All radio and television news and opinion are written and composed daily by the Public Relations Department.

Thirty transmitters are used by Thailand's eight private and public television stations to telecast to the 761,015 sets in use. In 1975 the number of television-owning households was 734,000, or 10.8 percent of the national total, with 463,000 of these in municipal areas. By regions, 49.2 percent of the receivers were in Bangkok; 29.5 percent in the Central region (excluding Bangkok); 8.5 percent Northeast; 7.6 North, and 5.3 South. Between 1974 and 1975 the number of receiving sets increased by 6.5 percent, or 47,000.

Most television stations operate between 5 a.m. and 11 p.m. on weekdays, and 10 a.m. and 11 p.m. on Saturdays and Sundays. Programming, which is in Thai, is heavily sponsored. The breakdown of one station, Thai Television Company, was: light entertainment, 29 hours; education, 11.5 hours; news and information, 10, and commercials, 5.5. In the early 1970s, over one-half of the television shows were made in Thailand by nationals; 25 percent were Western originated; 13.5 Japanese; 6.8 Chinese; 2.4 Indian, and 2.8

unknown. Guy Scandlen reported that Thai shows attracted larger audiences even when pitted against top United States programs.

In recent years, the government has stepped up its control of television programming, especially overseas news brought in by satellite. In 1979 the army's Channel 5 complained that two other channels controlled by the Prime Minister's Office used satellite-relayed foreign news not acceptable because it could harm national security. The government's Radio and Television Administration Board, chaired by a general, organized a meeting of the channels, which agreed to set up a joint committee to censor their own programs. The committee included representatives of the Supreme Command Information Center, Special Branch Police Division, Public Relations Department and the television news sections. Channels 3 and 7 were not happy with the censorship move; other channels owned by the government showed no alarm.

There are several major RTAB guidelines for screening satellite news. Under ordinary circumstances, all television stations will jointly screen the news, using their own discretion following the regulations imposed by the RTAB. When problems arise—whether a news item or television footage is against the existing regulations—the screening committee should be consulted. If, after the consultation, there remain conflicting opinions among the television stations on the news in question, the committee will intervene to make decisions with national interest taken into account. If there is an unexpected critical problem, the screening committee will join the television station in studying the problem closely and deciding on the proper practical solution. In any case, the RTAB should also be consulted.

Education & Training

Although journalism training was first offered at Chulalongkorn University 30 years ago, and while at least four other institutions (Chiang Mai University, Thammasat University, Educational Television Service and UNDP/UNICEF's Development Support Communication Service) offer training, a chief problem of the Thai press relates to lack of training and professionalization. A mid-1970s survey, carried out by Scandlen and Winkler, showed that of 95 newspeople interviewed, nine had master's degrees, 40 had bachelor's degrees, 12 had completed vocational training, 11 had finished high school, and 20 had eighth to 12th grade educations. Eighty-four of the 95 said they were trained on the job; only seven had academic journalism preparation. The newspapers complain that universities do not adequately train journalism graduates, while the universities say their mandate is to educate more broadly.

Newspapers have a code of ethics similar to that of the press in the United States, but a number of newsmen have failed to recognize it. Bribery and scandalmongering, as well as other abuses, are practiced by newspeople, some say because low wages and poor employment conditions allow nearly anyone to become a reporter.

After the first domestic journalists' association was formed in 1941, no fewer than seven others came forth to voice common interests. Among these have been the Journalist Association of Thailand, Press Association of Thailand, Provincial Journalist Association of Thailand, Reporters Association of Thailand and Thai Writers' Cooperative. For years, the Thai press was hampered by the split nature of these organizations; only Thailand sent separate delegations to the Confederation of ASEAN Journalists meetings. In June 1980 the eight Thai press organizations were grouped together in the Federation of Thai Journalists, an action which should help the Thai newspapers in their domestic struggles with government and in their representations abroad.

Summary

A number of major trends regarding the Thai press arose in the mid-1970s. Among them were the availability of more press freedom, at least temporarily; possible self-censorship through a proposed press council that did not materialize; the growth of diverse kinds of newspapers; emergence of a new group of young reporters and journalists; an awakening of public awareness to a proper role for the press; and the continued growth of the up-country press despite its many problems. Later developments, such as the establishment of a newprint-producing company, the merging of the press associations into a more solid front and the consideration of a national news agency, were encouraging signs. No doubt the 1970s represented a major metamorphosis for the press.

CHRONOLOGY

1973   Overthrow of Thanom coalition; press restrictions lifted.

1975   Newspaper publisher and columnist, M. R. Kukrit Pramoj, becomes prime minister.

1976   Military coup overthrows government, bans all newspapers and tightens press control. National Administrative Reform Council Decree 42 instituted, allowing for censorship.

1977   Controversial Thailand News

Agency formed.
Constitution revised, omits two key paragraphs on press.

1979   57 dailies closed, 32 other papers threatened under Printing Act B.E. 2484.

1980   *Thai Rath* suspended for exposés of police under Decree 42. *Bangkok Post* exposed as having sold large percentage of shares to Singapore *Straits Times*.

BIBLIOGRAPHY

"A Paper Prize." *Asiaweek,* December 7, 1979, p. 56.

Asian Press and Media Directory 1976-1977. Hong Kong, 1976.

Asian Press and Media Directory 1980-81. Hong Kong, 1980.

"A Singapore Connection." *Asiaweek,* December 5, 1980, pp. 42-43.

"Bangkok's Press Flexes a New Muscle." *Asiaweek,* October 17, 1980, p. 28.

Boonrak Boonyaketmala. "Thailand." In *Newspapers in Asia: Contemporary Problems and Trends,* John A. Lent, ed. Hong Kong, forthcoming.

Communication Profiles: Thailand. Singapore, 1979.

"Fight for Freedom." *Asian Messenger,* Autumn 1979-Spring 1980, pp. 27-28.

Kaviya, Somkuan. "Newspapers and News Agency in Thailand: A Monologue with Developed Countries." *Media Asia.* 5:3, (1978): 148-50.

———. *Directory Mass Communication Resources in Thailand.* Bangkok, 1971.

Lent, John A. "The Burnt-Out Candle: Thailand's Brief Experiment with Press Freedom 1973-1976." In *A Guide to Research*

Materials on Thailand and Laos, Robert Hearn, ed. Auburn, N.Y., 1977.

Mitchell, John D. "Thailand." In *The Asian Newspapers' Reluctant Revolution,* John A. Lent, ed. Ames, Iowa, 1971.

"News Selection." *Asian Messenger,* Autumn 1979-Spring 1980, pp. 27-28.

"No Panic Allowed." *Asian Messenger,* Autumn 1979-Spring 1980, pp. 27-28.

Scandlen, Guy B. "Thailand." In *Broadcasting in Asia and the Pacific,* John A. Lent, ed. Philadelphia and Hong Kong, 1978.

Scandlen, Guy B., and Winkler, Ken. "Thailand." In *Newspapers in Asia: Contemporary Problems and Trends,* John A. Lent, ed. Hong Kong, forthcoming.

Somchat Santisook. "Bangkok Tragedy." *Index on Censorship,* March-April 1977, pp. 19-24.

"SRG Surveys Highlight Southeast Asian Trends." *SRG News,* March 1980.

"Summary Closure of 57 Papers." *Asian Messenger,* Autumn 1979-Spring 1980, pp. 27-28.

"TV Censorship." *Asian Messenger,* Autumn 1979-Spring 1980, pp. 27-28.

TRINIDAD AND TOBAGO

by George Kurian

BASIC DATA

Population: 1,154,000 (1980)
Area: 5,128 sq. km. (1,980 sq. mi.)
GNP: TT $9.36 ($US 3.9 billion) (1979)
Literacy Rate: 95%
Language(s): English
Number of Dailies: 5
   Aggregate Circulation: 164,978
   Circulation per 1,000: 175
Number of Nondailies: 2
   Aggregate Circulation: 167,200
   Circulation per 1,000: 156
Number of Periodicals: 24
Number of Radio Stations: 2

Number of Television Stations: 2
Number of Radio Receivers: 275,000
   Radio Receivers per 1,000: 246
Number of Television Sets: 125,000
   Television Sets per 1,000: 112
Total Annual Newsprint Consumption: 6,300
   metric tons (1977)
   Per Capita Newsprint Consumption: 6.1 kg.
   (13.4 lb.)
Total Newspaper Ad Receipts: US$3.9 million
   (1979)
As % of All Ad Expenditures: 18.4

Background & General Characteristics

As a former British colony, Trinidad and Tobago inherited a press modelled on Fleet Street. It had been dominated since 1917 by the *Trinidad Guardian*, now called the *Guardian*. The *Guardian* was owned by white (or near-white) businessmen and passed into the hands of Roy (later Lord) Thomson. Throughout the turbulent 1930s and 1940s—until the rise of Eric Williams as a political figure in the 1950s— the *Guardian* was the major influence molding public opinion and defending the interests of the status quo. The *Guardian* became the favorite target of Williams. He realized that the paper stood in his way of rallying mass support behind his party, the People's National Movement, and he used every opportunity to discredit it. Even as prime minister, Williams continued to clash with the *Guardian* on almost every national and international issue, accusing the paper of ignoring his speeches, intimidating potential foreign investors, and promoting U.S. and British propaganda. He showed his disfavor openly and dramatically; he once cleaned his shoes with a copy of the newspaper and then

publicly burned it. By the mid-1970s Thomson realized that he could not continue to provoke the government, and sold two-thirds of the stock in his Trinidad Publishing Company to a local entrepreneur, Charles McEnearney. In 1976 he sold a further 10 percent to the employees. There was, however, no government interference or pressure in the transaction and the government never acquired any of the stock.

For a number of years the *Guardian*'s only competitor was an equally conservative paper called the *Trinidad Chronicle*, formerly the *Port of Spain Gazette*. The owners of the *Chronicle* were of French and Portuguese descent and exhibited a distinctly Roman Catholic bias in reporting. The *Chronicle* folded in 1959. For the next four years, Trinidad and Tobago was a one-newspaper country. No local or foreign investor had the money—much less the inclination—to attempt to establish a rival to the morning *Guardian* and its sister evening publication, the *Evening News*.

It was left to a Fleet Street group, the IPC (International Publishing Corporation), a British publishing giant founded by Lord Northcliffe, to bring variety again to

Trinidadian journalism. In 1963 the IPC founded the *Daily Mirror*, the same name as that of its successful London daily. IPC sent its experts to train local journalists to write and run the newspaper. It bought web offset presses and trained local workers to produce a quality of printing, especially in color, still unsurpassed among local dailies. The *Daily Mirror* represented the first concerted effort to introduce mass-oriented tabloid journalism that was bright and brash, colorful and provocative. With large photos and arresting layouts and headlines, and the ceaseless pursuit of human interest stories and angles, it provided an exciting alternative to the conservative *Guardian*. To its dramatic approach to news coverage it added technical competence in production. Under its editor, Patrick Chookolingo, the *Mirror* became what it promised to be: "a vigorous and outspoken newspaper...applauding with zest and criticizing freely." The circulation figures surpassed IPC's expectations: an audited net daily sale of 50,843 and a Sunday sale of 61,828. But after 33 months, in 1967, the *Mirror* closed. The reasons were never made public, but it is believed that the closure was related to the government's growing displeasure with the paper's editorial policies. In its brief lifespan, the *Mirror* gave Trinidadian journalism its finest days.

The success of the *Daily Mirror* was not lost on the local community. Within months, the displaced staff of the *Mirror* had persuaded a handful of local businessmen to start a new paper called the *Trinidad & Tobago Express*. The *Express* struggled against many odds, even surviving an advertising boycott in 1970 organized because it was considered too soft on the emerging Black Power movement. By the early 1970s it had established itself and even began giving the rival *Guardian* a run for its money.

Since the mid-1970s Trinidad and Tobago has become a thriving media market. In 1977 two new newspapers were started: the *Sun*, an evening paper published by the *Express* (as a rival to the *Evening News*, the *Guardian*'s evening edition) and the *Southern Star*, published in San Fernando by Robert Montano, a local businessman. A few others have been announced, including a daily by Motilal Moonan, a construction tycoon, and Patrick Chookolingo, former editor of the *Express* and publisher of the successful gossip weeklies, *The Bomb* and *Sunday Punch*.

In 1980 aggregate circulation of the two major newspaper groups totaled 164,978, of which the *Guardian* group claimed 58,103 and the *Express* group 75,037. These figures do not include the sales of Sunday editions, which are considerably higher: for the *Sunday Guardian* 101,496 and for the *Sunday Express* 72,461. Larger Sunday circulations are explained by the fact that many people buy just one paper for the week and read it on their day off. Because of the high rate of literacy in the islands, the per capita circulations are higher than those of the neighboring countries: 175 per 1,000 inhabitants. Sunday circulations yield much higher figures; in fact, it is believed that the *Sunday Guardian* is bought by one-tenth of the population.

All Trinidadian papers describe themselves as independent, partly because of a dislike of labels and partly because of a growing disenchantment with party politics. As in other healthy media systems, newspapers are strictly commercial institutions, rising or falling by the balance sheets. Newspaper activism, long discouraged by the late Eric Williams, has never been a prominent feature of Trinidadian journalism.

The islands also have a vigorous periodical press, but in this sector the so-called yellow weeklies have a free rein. The most popular of the weeklies are *The Bomb* and the *Sunday Punch*, both of which specialize in exposes and seamy stories. There are 12 other periodicals, including a Chinese weekly and five government publications.

Economic Framework

In the mid-seventies, following the oil boom, the fortunes of the publishing industry experienced an upswing that is still continuing. When OPEC raised its oil prices in 1973 Trinidad and Tobago became a rich country overnight, with enough wealth to sustain a diverse and financially prosperous media. According to David Renwick, a media observer, advertisers "are falling over themselves to spend money on advertisements and promotions in anything that appears in printed form." The *Express*, for example, has reported annual profit increases of over 21 percent; the Trinidad Publishing Company, the *Guardian*'s parent company, had annual profits of close to $2 million in the late 1970s.

One direction in which Trinidad and Tobago media has been developing is lending financial and technical aid to the media of less developed Caribbean nations. Since 1974, the *Express* has provided the struggling newspapers of less fortunate islands in the Caribbean with both money and personnel.

The idea grew out of Publisher Ken Gordon's conviction that "the only way to get rid of foreign domination of the press is to get local people to develop expertise." When the Barbados *Nation* ran into difficulties just a few months after its first issue in 1974, the *Express* lent support in return for equity in the paper. The same was done for the *Voice of St. Lucia, Grenada Torchlight* and *Jamaica Daily News;* in each case the *Express* obtained participation in the management with Gordon serving on all four boards. The *Express* has a 25 percent share of equity in the *Nation, Torchlight* and *Voice of St. Lucia* and a smaller one in the *Jamaica Daily News.* The *Express* does not interfere in the editorial policies of these newspapers.

Although most emerging nations are experiencing a shortage of skilled journalists and production staff, this is not the case in Trinidad and Tobago. The *Guardian*, for example, has a staff of over 500, of which until recently only one was an expatriate. Salary scales range from TT$500 ($208) to TT$2,200 ($917) a month. Working journalists and press-related workers are represented by the Bank and General Workers Union, which has launched several successful strikes against managements in recent years. In an effort to reduce labor costs, publishers are investing heavily in new printing equipment and technology. The *Guardian*, in one of its largest expansion plans ever, has sunk TT$16.8 million ($7 million) on new equipment designed to displace 100 workers. As a result of these improvements, Trinidad and Tobago has one of the most advanced newspaper production facilities in the Caribbean.

Press Laws & Censorship

Trinidad and Tobago is the only nation in the Caribbean with specific constitutional guarantees of press freedom. These guarantees were incorporated in the constitution at the instance of Eric Williams. Williams never interfered with the actual running of opposition newspapers or favored their takeover as many other Caribbean leaders did. At the same time, he used legal means to curb the natural exuberance of the Trinidadian press. Frequently he would bring libel suits against opposition newspapers, or invoke the application of certain obscure censorship laws on the statute book. After the Black Power revolt in April 1970, the Emergency Powers Regulation Act went into effect for seven months to limit publicity given to the leaders of the revolt, and the government was empowered to control and censor media content and even to ban publication. Despite the critical stance of the press, the government did not make use of these powers. In 1971 a new sedition law was enacted that some journalists found objectionable.

Beyond these sporadic instances, there has been no institutionalized state control over the Trinidadian media.

State-Press Relations

Williams ran the islands more or less as he liked for 16 years, until his death in 1981. Under his administration, the state and the press were locked in an adversary relationship that he seemed to enjoy. Despite his surface hostility, Williams never interfered with the press, and Trinidadian newsmen have said that Williams should be given "high marks for the way he tolerated even abuses of press freedom." On the other hand, Williams was not above acting spitefully against the media that attacked him. He made it his policy to ignore the press as he chose. He never held press conferences and rarely spoke to newsmen. Other ministers in the Williams cabinet gave reporters the runaround. But although it was both common and acceptable for government officials to castigate the media, little effort was made to carry out the threats. The tension between the administration and the press did contribute to a degree of self-censorship and a nagging fear of reprisals, however, which inhibited journalistic initiative.

In addition, the government periodically applied certain economic pressures to which the press was inherently susceptible. These included issuance of printing and advertising contracts and licenses. This device did not always work as well as it did in other neighboring countries, because the newspapers had other sources of revenue.

The most important document defining the official relationships between the media and the government was the Third Five-Year Plan, promulgated in 1969. The stated purpose of this plan was to develop a positive national identity. The plan laid out certain principles guiding government's policy toward the mass media: (1) no transfer of ownership could be made without government permission; (2) foreign enterprise could neither establish new facilities nor acquire existing locally owned ones; (3) ownership of electronic media should remain with the government.

Attitude Toward Foreign Media

While official policy is opposed to foreign participation in the local media, there have been no efforts to discriminate against foreign news agencies or to extend controls over transnational media. There are no import restrictions on foreign publications; special visas are not required for foreign correspondents, nor is prior approval required for cables.

In common with other developing nations, Trinidad and Tobago supports UNESCO efforts to extend and legitimize state control over the media.

News Agencies

Trinidad and Tobago does not have a national news agency but is a member of CANA (Caribbean News Agency). (See chapter on Jamaica for details of CANA.)

Newspapers as well as broadcasting stations also use Reuters, UPI, AP and ADN.

Electronic News Media

One of the goals of the Third Five-Year Plan of 1969 was to nationalize broadcasting, and this has been successfully accomplished. By purchasing Radio 610 and Trinidad & Tobago Television from Roy Thomson, the government has eliminated foreign and private influences from electronic media. According to the official guidelines, broadcasting is placed in the hands of an independent management outside of political parties. The companies are to operate on a commercial basis under a broad-based board of directors.

Radio broadcasting is the responsibility of the National Broadcasting Service (NBS), television of the Trinidad & Tobago Television Company (TTT). Both are financed through advertising revenues.

There has also been a major shift in program content. While other countries in the Caribbean depend on foreign sources for 60 to 80 percent of their programming, NBS and TTT use only half that much; further, Trinidad and Tobago is exporting its programs to its neighbors.

There are four radio transmitters and three TV transmitters in Trinidad and Tobago.

Education & Training

Journalism education and training is a new development in the Caribbean. The Institute of Mass Communication at the University of the West Indies at Mona, Jamaica, is the main training ground for journalists. There is also an Extra-Mural Studies Unit in the Caribbean islands, a part-time project begun in 1976. Both the *Guardian* and the *Express* provide intensive in-house, on-the-job training to their apprentices and workers.

Summary

While most developing nations in the Caribbean have experienced serious problems in maintaining a viable and free media system, Trinidad and Tobago has been an exception. Buoyed by oil revenues, the islands have provided a case study of a flourishing and privately owned press enjoying more freedom today than under the British or other colonial powers.

CHRONOLOGY

1977   Express Newspapers founds *The Sun*, an evening tabloid; Gerard Montano founds the *Southern Star*, a new daily from San Fernando.

BIBLIOGRAPHY

Lent, John A. *Third World Mass Media and Their Search for Modernity: The Case of the Commonwealth Caribbean, 1717-1976.* Cranbury, N.J., 1981.

"How Independent are Commonwealth Caribbean Mass Media in the Era of Independence?" *Revista/Review Interamericana,* vol. 6, no. 1, Spring 1976.

"Commonwealth Caribbean: Production and Consumption of Mass Media," *Caribbean Studies,* vol. 16, no. 2, July 1976.

TURKEY

by Christine Ogan

BASIC DATA

Population: 45,182,000 (1980)
Area: 766,640 sq. km. (295,923 sq. mi.)
GNP: 2.08 trillion lira (US$58.7 billion) (1979)
Literacy Rate: 62%
Language(s): Turkish, Kurdish
Number of Dailies: 255 (est.)
  Aggregate Circulation: 1.4 million (est.)
  Circulation per 1,000: NA
Number of Nondailies: 618
  Aggregate Circulation: NA
  Circulation per 1,000: NA
Number of Periodicals: NA
Number of Radio Stations: 29

Number of Television Stations: 7
Number of Radio Receivers: 4,228,000
  Radio Receivers per 1,000: 105
Number of Television Sets: 1,769,000
  Television Sets per 1,000: 44
Total Annual Newsprint Consumption: 112,200 metric tons
  Per Capita Newsprint Consumption: 2.7 kg. (5.9 lb.)
Total Newspaper Ad Receipts: 1.23 billion lira (US$35 million) (1979)
  As % of All Add Expenditures: 20.3 (1979)

Background & General Characteristics

The Turkish press has been described as vigorous and independent. In spite of problems arising from government censorship—at present and during previous times of political stress—the country's media have tried to serve as a check on the leadership of the Turkish Republic.

Turkey is nearly 770,000 square kilometers in area, somewhat smaller than Texas and Louisiana combined. Because part of the country—about three percent of the land and eight percent of the people—lies on the European continent, with the rest in Asia, Turkey is described as both a European and an Asian nation. Certainly it is more European than most of its Middle Eastern neighbors in social orientation, the secular nature of the government and the educational level of the populace.

Surrounded by less literate societies and by countries where the press is more controlled, Turkey stood almost unique in the Middle East of 1980, even when considering the policies and controls of the country's own National Security Council—the military junta in power.

Although literacy in Turkey is low com- pared with that of developed Western nations, considerable gains have been made in basic education since the 1950s, when only about one-third of the population could read and write. Today the literacy rate stands at over 60 percent.

This advance owes much to a language reform program—begun in 1928 under the direction of Kemal Ataturk, leader of the First Turkish Republic—which changed the alphabet from an Arabic to a Latin base, thus making spelling and reading much easier. Initially the reform did not help the press, because many readers were immediately not able to understand the new alphabet. But that has changed conspicuously over the years, with ongoing efforts to purify the Turkish language through the removal of Persian and Arabic words. Today Turkish is spoken by nearly 85 percent of the population, with Kurdish used by six to eight million people. (There are, however, no Kurdish periodicals, and Kurdish is not spoken on the government-owned radio.) Other minority groups include Arabs, located along the Syrian border, plus Greeks, Armenians and Jews, who live mainly in Istanbul, supporting their own schools and newspapers.

The people of Turkey are about 98.1 percent

Muslim, 95.5 percent of which are Sunni Muslim and 4.5 percent adhere to the Alevi, a Shiite Muslim sect. Jewish, Greek and Armenian minorities follow Jewish, Greek Orthodox and other Christian religions. The non-Muslim population totals 200,000–260,000.

Political affiliation in Turkey does not necessarily follow religious or ethnic lines. The government itself is secular (although some extremists have sought the establishment of a Muslim theocracy). Until the banning of political organizations by the military junta in September 1980, left-wing parties were often led by student and other youth groups. Through the 1970s the several left-wing groups increasingly attracted support from disgruntled members of minority ethnic and religious elements. The opposite wing attracted anti-socialist, pro-nationalist factions that oppose the granting of extensive rights to minority groups.

Before the banning, Turkey's major parties were the left-of-center Republican People's Party, or Ataturk's party, led by Bulent Ecevit until his resignation after the coup. The conservative Justice Party, under Suleyman Demirel, was RPP's strongest opponent. In the 1970s leadership seesawed between Ecevit and Demirel, but because neither could control the government without forming coalitions with one or more of the right- or left-wing extremist parties, leadership was weak under both men.

Turkey's daily press is published in the morning, for the most part, seven days a week; some print several editions during the day. There is also a handful of evening papers. Several of the larger-circulation dailies, among them *Milliyet, Hurriyet* and *Tercuman*, include an extra six to eight color pages in the Sunday editions, but magazine sections, as they are known in the United States and Britain, are not common. Most newspapers are broadsheet size, from eight to 12 pages in length. (Because newsprint is scarce, the front and back pages are often made of better-quality paper than inside pages. Publication of much of the regional press is erratic, and many of these papers are only four pages in length.

The foreign-language press is small. One English-language paper, *The Daily News*, printed in Ankara, has a circulation of 5,000. Istanbul is the home of the Armenian *Marmara*, with 1,727 readers, and a Greek paper, *Apoyevmatini*, which circulates 3,442 copies

daily. Other foreign dailies—found in the large cities of Ankara, Istanbul and Izmir—are published in German, French and English. A total of 821 foreign publications exist in the country, but most are weeklies, journals or quarterlies.

All of the big Istanbul papers are also printed in Ankara and Izmir on the same day. Five of the top-circulation dailies are also printed in Munich for the 654,000 Turkish workers living in West Germany. The other large Turkish cities have competing papers of their own, and face additional competition from the Istanbul dailies, which are circulated nationally, even to small towns. Although the papers in these small communities have low circulations and are often short-lived, 108 Turkish towns and cities publish one or more dailies. Most have been able to survive through indirect government subsidies in the form of official advertising. No daily published outside of Ankara, Istanbul or Izmir has a circulation of more than 15,000; usually the figure is below 10,000.

Turkey's largest newspapers boast readerships of 38,000 to 850,000. (Only one paper in the top 10 is actually published outside Istanbul—*Yeni Asir*, which originates in Izmir.) However, circulation figures among the "big ten" vary widely, probably due to self-report and the desire to inflate the actual number of readers. Even so, the names of the top-circulation newspapers remain the same: *Hurriyet, Saklambac, Gunaydin, Tercuman, Milliyet, Aksam, Cumhuriyet, Yeni Asir, Son Havadis* and *Dunya*. (*Aksam* is the only paper in the group on which there is considerable disagreement; reports of its circulation range from 2,000 to 95,000. Nonetheless, *Aksam* is the oldest newspaper in the country with continuous publication.)

According to a 1973 report, 86 percent of the total newspaper circulation was taken up by the five largest papers. The three top selling dailies—*Hurriyet, Gunaydin* and *Saklambac*—are owned by the Simavi family. All three are prone to yellow journalism, *Saklambac* being the worst in this respect.

It would be difficult to determine what "the" most influential Turkish papers are, especially considering the growth of splinter political parties in Turkey prior to their banning in 1980. Traditionally *Cumhuriyet* has been the most serious and influential of the dailies. Although well down the list in circulation, the moderate-left, pro-RPP paper has been called *The New York Times* of the Turkish press by at least one specialist. Founded in 1924 to support Ataturk's revolution, *Cumhuriyet* is one of Turkey's oldest newspapers—and probably the most respected. The independent *Hurriyet*, by virtue of its 600,000-plus circulation, may be the second most influential daily—even though it tends toward sensationalism and uses much color. After these two, a third choice is more difficult. Depending on political orientation, the independent *Milliyet*, a moderately left-of-center daily, the pro-JP *Tercuman* or conservative *Son Havadis* might be selected.

Economic Framework

Forty percent of Turkey's wealth is controlled by nine percent of its households, and unemployment stands at 25-30 percent. (At the time of the coup, some 40,000 workers were also on strike. Although strikes were promptly banned by the military government and workers ordered back to their jobs, industrial production was functioning at about half capacity in 1980.) Inflation was estimated at 55-65 percent late in 1980 after the military takeover. (Earlier in the year there had been reports of the figure exceeding 100 percent.) Between 1970 and 1977 real GNP growth was about seven percent per year but slowed to three percent after that time because of major imbalances in the economy. An oil debt of about $3 billion* added to the 1980 financial burden.

In the face of these economic problems, it is difficult to understand how the press functions at all. But in fact overall circulation has grown in recent years. Although the number of dailies decreased from 472 in 1961 to 255 (or 370, depending on the source of the report) in 1979, reported overall daily circulation rose during the same period—from 1,300,000 to 1,400,000. However, since the population increased about 40 percent in that time, this overall circulation growth translates to a large per capita decrease. UNESCO reported a decline of newspaper circulation from 5.1 per 100 in 1960 to 4.1 in 1969. Since television and radio receivers per capita have increased substantially in the last 20 years, more people may be substituting one news source for another. After all, the purchase of a radio or television is a one-time cost and not subject to inflationary increases after purchase. The price of a daily newspaper was about 11 cents in 1980, an increase of 1,000 percent in 10 years.

Of course the overall cost of living has risen correspondingly. Between 1970 and 1973 the consumer price index increased an average of 16 percent per year; in 1974 the increase was 24 percent; in 1975, 21 percent; in 1976, 17 percent; in 1977, 26 percent; and in 1978, 62 percent; while the 1979 figure approached 100 percent.

The inflationary trend can be attributed to many causes: increases in foreign workers' remittances, which have expanded the money supply and the banks' credit base; rises in international commodity prices—particularly of oil and petroleum products; a deteriorating balance of payments, which has prevented additional imports; and dependence on foreign short-term borrowing.

Newsprint may not be quite as serious a problem. Between 1969 and 1972 its price increased greatly—by 227 percent. And, of the 70,000 metric tons of newsprint consumed in 1974, only 11,000 tons were produced within the country. However, the situation had improved somewhat by 1977, when 79 percent of the 112,000 metric tons needed for newspapers was produced in Turkey. The remainder was imported. OECD figures show that newsprint output increased 10.1 percent in 1976-77 over 1975, was down 12.3 percent in 1977-78 and showed a positive trend of 2.4 percent again in 1979-80.

In the national press, this kind of inflation has touched off fierce competition for circulation. Newspapers run giveaway contests and lotteries for cars, appliances and apartments. A more popularly slanted editorial approach —including heavy use of color, shorter articles, longer headlines and more sensational news—has also been part of the trend to gain readership. And because of such circulation-oriented efforts, the credibility of the press has declined.

Further, in spite of tight money and high import taxes, the Turkish government also claims that most large newspapers have access to computerized typesetting and offset printing and—as mentioned above—make

---

*Local currency throughout this chapter has been converted into U.S. equivalents at the rate of 87.95 Turkish lira = $1.00.

extensive use of color. However, no details about the extent of use of the new technology are available.

Press Laws

Although the publication and distribution of Turkish newspapers and the financial resources and conditions pertaining to journalism are regulated by law, no legislation restricts the press from freedom of expression in political, economic, financial or technical areas. The 1960 constitution, promulgated in 1961, grants freedom to Turkey's press. This is the indirect result of the actions of Adnan Menderes, prime minister from 1950 until the revolution in 1960. Menderes was the leader of the then newly formed Democratic Party (DP), and he had made campaign promises to loosen government control of the press. But in 1954, as the opposition began to criticize DP policies, Menderes responded with more stringent amendments to press laws. Among other things, he denied journalists in libel cases the right to produce evidence in court against the government. Menderes also made it a crime to criticize the government or government officials; this included articles that would undermine the people's confidence in their government. Truth was not accepted as a legitimate defense for printing news of official error or corruption.

However, Article 22 of the present constitution provides that "freedom of the press and the obtaining of information can be restricted by law only in order to safeguard national security or public morality, to prevent attacks on the dignity, honor and rights of individuals; to prevent instigations to commit crimes; and to assure proper implementation of judicial functions."

This article has been used several times as a rationale for closing down publications for a period of time, jailing journalists or banning publications altogether. While the constitution states that periodicals can be closed down only by court judgment in the event of conviction for specific offences, times of political stress have brought on frequent closings of certain extremist publications. In fact, in the aftermath of the 1980 coup, the National Security Council suspended the entire constitution. It also closed down three papers—*Demokrat* and *Aydinlik* of the extreme left, and *Hergun*, a radical rightist publication. (Later, however, most of the constitution was reinstated.)

Censorship

Pre-publication censorship was common during the late 1950s. Police with court orders would remove objectionable material from the papers at press time—leaving blank columns in the published editions. This form of censorship went on in spite of a constitutional article forbidding prior restraint. When it was not totally effective, the Menderes government resorted to fining and jailing journalists; between 1954 and 1958, 1,161 newsmen were prosecuted and 288 convicted under Menderes's press law. Menderes also believed that since the opposition newspapers were working against his government, the government-operated radio system should be used to rebut statements appearing in the opposition press. Before his time, the radio had been state controlled but nonpartisan.

Menderes's actions toward the press and radio contributed to the 1960 coup—and to the present government's censorship policy. The National Union Committee (NUC) observed how it was possible under provisions of the constitution for an administration to manipulate and control the mass media for its own political purposes. Thus censorship remains—although more self-imposed than in earlier days, and following certain officially designated "guidelines." Any articles or pictures that criticize the military leaders or Kemal Ataturk are forbidden. With the banning of political parties by the military, so too was writing in support of such parties forbidden. Articles that are not objectively written, or which do not comply with statements by the National Security Council, the Aegean Force and the Martial Law Command are also out of order. More specifically forbidden is information about political-party activities and terrorist actions until authorized, so that security forces can operate without publicity. Sensational material that might excite the public is also ruled out. In a *New York Times* article, correspondent Marvine Howe said that the result of all this has been a shift toward economic and financial reporting. Since the press has only been told what not to write about, journalists have chosen to criticize the government's economic policies—for some reason a safer area.

Nonetheless newspapers have felt the sting of the "guidelines." *Cumhuriyet* was closed for 10 days in November 1980, because of an expressed "derogatory attitude" toward Ataturk and exaggerated economic reports (perhaps not so safe a subject after all) that could have led to inciting public dissatisfaction. *Cumhuriyet*'s editor, Nadir Nadi, said that the military government had the support of the paper, but that *Cumhuriyet*'s role was one of constructive criticism—a role it would continue to play.

State-Press Relations

The 1970s was a decade of problems for the Turkish press. In 1971 there were 849 prosecutions against journalists for various press-law violations, while in 1972 754 cases were pending—in addition to 220 convictions that were being appealed. Newsmen mostly chose to go to jail rather than be silenced. Following the 1973 elections, and with a new government under Prime Minister Bulent Ecevit, many of the convicted journalists were released. However, the press continued to be accused of violating laws that prohibited publishing stories on clandestine organizations and the propagation of communism.

In spite of restrictive laws and other controls, the 1960s and 1970s were years of expansion and relative freedom for the press compared to the Menderes era. One result of their earlier harassment had been a meeting, in 1960, of the Journalists Association and the Trade Union of Istanbul Journalists called a meeting of Istanbul newsmen. From this meeting emerged a code of press ethics, which established a 10-member Honor Court or press council. Although the council has been somewhat effective during times of political unrest—particularly during the periods of national violence in the 1970s—it has lacked legal power, as is true of most national press councils, and has depended on newspaper membership for support. Since some newsmen have not wanted to subject themselves to the sanctions arising from violations of the press-ethics code, they have withheld or withdrawn membership, thus weakening the power of the court.

In addition to the legal restrictions placed on the press, the government has been able to exert control through other means. Newspapers are indirectly subsidized through official advertising. Since the violent period in 1970-71, the government has placed an increasing amount of advertising in its own publication, the *Resmi Gazete* (Official Newspaper). When small independent papers are deprived of these subsidies, they have financial difficulties. The loss of official advertising may well have contributed to the reduction of the total number of Turkish dailies.

More dangerous than government control of journalists' activities in the 1970s was the political-terrorist threat. The terrorists' most prominent victim in the press was Abdi Ipekci, moderate editor of the influential daily, *Milliyet*, and a former vice-chairman of the International Press Institute. In January 1979 Ipekci was shot and killed by rightist gunmen as he drove to work. In spite of his death and those of several other right- and left-oriented journalists, the Istabul Journalist Association said that Turkish newsmen would continue to fight for press freedom. However, continued attacks and threats in 1980 forced them to call off a national press holiday.

Attitude Toward Foreign Media

Turkey has not taken a very active part in the nonaligned-nation push for a new international information order. Perhaps because of the relatively free nature of the country's own press—the national papers support correspondents and stringers in most major capitals—Turkey has been less than sympathetic to the complaints against the media by many developing countries. The severity of internal political and economic problems, plus the threat of terrorism in a country with the most political killings in the world have also prevented Turkish journalists from discerning any external threat from foreign news outlets. The sole expulsion in recent years was that of a Tass correspondent who reportedly told the German magazine *Stern* that Turkey would be turned into a socialist state. He was asked to leave for his involvement in Turkish internal affairs.

Foreign news bureaus located in Ankara include AFP, EFE, ANSA, AP, Bulgarian Telegraph Agency, Deutsche Presse-Agentur (dpa), Novinska Agencija Tanjug, Reuters, UPI, Tass and Xinhua. Several independent American and European papers also have correspondents in the country.

According to Turkish law, all foreign-language publications in Turkey must be owned by Turkish citizens.

Most major West European dailies and newsmagazines—including *Time, Newsweek* and the *International Herald Tribune*—are found on the newsstands in Istanbul, Ankara and Izmir. Outside of these major cities, there is not a large market for foreign-language publications. Communist-country publications have been more restricted in their circulation—at times banned altogether. In November 1980 the Ankara martial law command took a leftist publisher into custody for possessing outlawed Marxist books. He was later reported beaten to death by a military guard.

In the past the Turkish press has reacted negatively to anti-Turkish sentiment expressed in U.S. newspapers—especially on the 1974 Cyprus crisis and the subsequent embargo placed on arms and aid to Turkey; on the poppy-growing and opium-production problem, and also the pro-Greek and pro-Armenian articles that appeared in European and American newspapers alike. Criticism of the foreign press, however, has been more issue oriented than country oriented.

News Agencies

The main news agency in Turkey is the semi-official Anadolu Ajansi (Anatolian Agency) founded in 1920 by Ataturk. At first the function of the agency was to issue news bulletins and printed pamphlets and books both within the country and for distribution abroad. Today the agency has offices in Ankara, Istanbul, Izmir, and Adana, a permanent staff of 180 and 517 correspondents in various parts of the country. The agency supports no foreign correspondents but operates in cooperation with other foreign agencies. A daily bulletin of 25,000 to 35,000 words of national news is issued and an additional 10,000 to 15,000 words of foreign and economic news is sent to 65 newspapers and 130 other subscribers.

Turk Haberler Ajansi was begun as a cooperative in 1950. Unlike Anadolu Ajansi, this agency has permanently based foreign correspondents in the United Kingdom, the United States, France and Federal Republic of Germany, as well as correspondents throughout Turkey.

Hurriyet has its own agency in Istanbul, and there are several other small agencies. These include Akajans, ANKA, EBA, a commercial agency; IKA Haber, an economic/commercial agency that publishes bulletins in Turkish and English; and Yurt Haberler Ajansi. All of these agencies are headquartered in Ankara.

Electronic News Media

From the beginning of radio broadcasting in 1927, radio was perceived by Ataturk as a force to promote modernization and nationalism. The first radio station was owned privately, but when its license expired in 1936 the government took over control of Turkish radio by building its own station, supervised by the Bureau of the Press Directorate. With the opening of the new station in 1938, radio programming immediately began serving the goals of government, providing news of the republic and information about such government activities and interests as agricultural innovations and modern home-economics techniques.

In 1927 there were only 5,000 radio sets in Turkey, but the number had increased to 100,000 by 1942. The number of sets per 100 in 1942 was still only .41, however, and most receivers were located in the big cities of Ankara and Istanbul. However, the changes in broadcasting since 1960 have been dramatic.

Before the establishment of the Turkish Radio and Television Corporation (TRT) in 1964, the total transmission power of the 12 existing radio stations in Turkey was 525 kw, and these stations were able to reach only an estimated 42.6% of the population. But due to TRT's efforts, the Third Five-Year Plan (1973-1977) estimated that by 1977 every person in the country would be able to receive at least one national and one regional radio station. The number of licensed receivers per 100 inhabitants more than doubled from 4.9 in 1960 to 10.7 in 1976. These UNESCO figures require some interpretation. It is difficult to determine the actual number of radio receivers per 100 persons owing to avoidance of the annual license fees (taxes) on receivers paid to the Turkish government: some people simply fail to register their radios. Moreover, portable sets are not subject to the tax.

According to 1978 statistics, there were 12 regional, five provincial and two external (Voice of Turkey) stations in operation. Four additional short- and medium-wave stations were located in Ankara, Istanbul and Izmir.

The combined power of all the stations was over 3100 kw.

Programs are also broadcast externally to Turks living abroad, particularly in Germany, and in fifteen other languages besides Turkish.

Television is the fastest growing mass medium in Turkey by far. In 1960 the only available TV programming came from an experimental station operated by Istanbul Technical University on a limited schedule. Some persons in the country watched TV broadcasts from nearby foreign countries—accounting for the 1,000 receivers recorded by UNESCO in 1963.

In 1963 Turkey signed a technical-assistance agreement with West Germany, accepting equipment and technical personnel for the operation of the first station. In 1968, the first public TV station in Turkey was launched in Ankara on a three-night-a-week schedule. In 1971 links were made with Istanbul, Izmir and Eskisehir, and in 1972 with Balikesir and Edirne. By 1978 there were five daily hours of programs on weekdays, nine hours on Saturday and 14 hours on Sunday—beamed from seven transmitters to cities all over the country. These transmitters covered approximately 50 percent of the population. Data in 1976 showed 1,769,000 licensed receivers, or 4.32 sets per 100 population.

In 1975 most receivers were still located in cities and towns, with only approximately 5 percent in villages. This situation is expected to change as more transmitters are built and village TV reception improves.

Like radio, ownership of a TV set must be registered with the government and a tax paid, unless the set is classified as portable. Therefore, actual figures on ownership of TV sets are virtually impossible to determine. The Third Five-Year-Plan projections called for 82 percent coverage of the nation by 1980, making TV a vast potential tool for development.

Many TV programs are purchased from Western nations—England, France, and the United States—a large number via Eurovision, a network linkup arrangement among Western European nations for special broadcasts. Thus aspects of Western culture enter homes of many Turkish families each day. Also shown on TV are news, Turkish and Western music programs, Turkish and Western films, historical programs, some children's programming, concerts, special religious programs, sports and cultural offerings—in general a varied offering with appeal to wide interests.

Radio and TV are controlled by TRT, a state-owned autonomous organization. The Radio and Television Act of 1963 defined TRT as an "autonomous public economic establishment possessing juridical personality." Administered by a board composed of representatives from the university, the arts and government, its functions are to (1) operate broadcasting facilities and (2) provide news services and educational, instructional and cultural programs.

In 1972 the government accused TRT of encouraging "public disorder and subversion" through its broadcasts and withdrew its autonomous status. Heavy censorship of TRT news was common during periods of political crises in the 1970s. All broadcasts concerning the martial law command and descriptions of violent activities were banned at various times. More recently the government has sought to obtain political control of the organization. After the 1980 coup, the junta appointed a military officer, Major General Servet Bilgi, to run TRT.

Education & Training

Some form of mass media education is offered at eight different schools in Turkey. Four-year degree-granting programs are available at the Basin Yayin Yuksek Okulu (School for Journalism and Broadcasting) in the political science faculty of Ankara University, and the Basin, Yayin, Sinema ve Halkla Iliskiler Okulu at Ege University (Journalism, Film and Public Relations Department of the Aegean University) in Izmir.

Ankara is the home of a college-level vocational school in the Ankara Academy of Economic and Commercial Sciences (Gazetecilik Yuksek Okulu) and the Baskent Gazetecilik Ozen Yuksek Okulu.

There are three sources of journalism education in Istanbul: the Gazetecilik Enstitusu, which is part of the economics faculty at Istanbul University; the Sinema-Televizyon Enstitusu of the State Academy of Fine Arts (this school began a degree program in 1977); and the Gazetecilik ve Halkla Iliskiler Yuksek Okulu, a four-year program.

In addition, the Eskisehir Academy of Economic and Commercial Sciences has a vocational school with television emphasis, the Sinema ve Televizyon Yuksek Okulu.

UNESCO has noted that the Press Institute and TRT offer their own training courses. The first personnel trained for TRT were sent to Germany.

About 800 of Turkey's newsmen are members of the Union of Journalists, established in 1952, while some 2,000 belong to the Journalists Organization, founded in 1926, still others to the Turkish Press Institute. (Obviously there are dual and triple memberships.) Local and regional associations and unions also exist.

Summary

If the mass media in Turkey are to improve and expand over the coming years, the Turkish economy in general will have to make some rapid advances. Obviously a good press system cannot develop in a country where there is insufficient fuel to keep people warm in the winter, and an inflationary trend so extreme that many have to worry over the source of the next meal.

Any further Turkish press expansion, and particularly continuation of press freedom, is particularly dependent on the political system. If the country's leadership returns to the civilians and violence is controlled, the press may also return to a state of normality. Under the control of the military, the media will never be able to function fully as a check on government excesses or mistakes. Many journalists have suffered imprisonment and a few have died for defending press freedom in recent years. And the freedom journalists seek is not only freedom from government control but the freedom to walk the streets and go about the business of newsgathering without fear of torture or assassination by political extremists.

CHRONOLOGY

1972 Turkey's press-freedom situation reported as worst in Europe. Turkish Radio and Television Corporation loses its autonomy.... Nearly a dozen journals, mostly left-oriented publications, are shut down.... Newspapers in Istanbul suspended for a time.... Police arrest several journalists, beat up one cartoonist.... At year's end most journalists in detention are released.

1974 More imprisoned journalists granted amnesty for their offenses under the emergency command as country returns to democracy.

1975 Fourteen journalists jailed for alleged publication of state secrets during Turkey's military landing on Cyprus. Also arrested on same charges are *Yanki* publisher Mehmet Ali Kislali; director of *Hurriyet* and that paper's Ankara correspondent, and several members of left-wing weekly, *Aydinlik*. ... Director of the state broadcasting network dismissed for endangering national security.

1976 Freedom House lists Turkey as having a "free" press system.

1977 Leyla Cumbus of *Halkin Sesi* arrested and tried for libeling the Turkish armed forces.

1978 Leyla Cumbus released in May.

1979 Martial law forces ban 22 Ankara papers for "insulting state forces, inciting criminal acts and weakening morale." ...Remzi Ozgener, editor of Kurdish periodical, arrested.... Attacks on offices of *Hergun*, conservative daily supported by National Action Party, result in one death and several injuries.... *Milliyet* editor Abdi Ipekci assassinated by rightwing extremists.... Chief news editor and a columnist for *Hergun* are jailed 20 months for article criticizing coordination board established as liaison between martial law commands of 13 provinces.... Later, gunmen attack offices of the board, leaving one dead.

1980 By mid-year 2,000 persons killed in political violence include several journalists.... Recai Unal, crime reporter for leftist daily *Demokrat*, kidnapped, tortured and murdered in July.... Mete Atabek dies when caught in crossfire of two terrorist groups.... Two gunmen kill staff member of rightist daily *Ortadogu;* three terrorists murder Istanbul television producer; bomb explosion kills reporter in Trabzon.... Istanbul Journalists Association calls off traditional press holiday in July, renouncing terrorism and pledging Turkish newsmen's backing of fight for press freedom.... Following September takeover journalists charged with violating military ban on political activities.... *Cumhuriyet* closed for 10 days for "derogatory attitude."

BIBLIOGRAPHY

"A Bird's Eye View of the History of Turkish Journalism." *Turkish Digest* Vol. 6, No. 6, pp. 14-15.

Borchard, David. "Turkish Rulers Order 70 p.c. Pay Rises and Prohibit Strikes." *The Guardian,* September 15, 1980, p. 1.

Constitution of the Turkish Republic. Ankara, 1961.

Editor & Publisher International Yearbook— 1980. New York, 1980.

Emery, Walter B. *National and International Systems of Broadcasting.* East Lansing, Mich., 1969.

Europa Year Book. London, 1980.

Frey, Frederick W. *The Mass Media and Rural Development in Turkey, Report No. 3.* Cambridge, Mass., 1966.

Giritli, Ismet. *Fifty Years of Turkish Political Development: 1919-1969.* Istanbul, 1969.

Hardcastle, Bruce. "Turkey's Trials." *The New Republic,* October 11, 1980, pp. 13-15.

Howe, Marvine. "Turkish Junta Acts on Prison Torture." *The New York Times,* November 24, 1980.

_____. "Turks Winning War Against Terror, Premier Says." *The New York Times,* December 7, 1980, p. 6.

_____. "Turks Outline Path Back to Democracy." *The New York Times,* November 2, 1980.

Index on Censorship (June 1980), p. 69.

IPI Report. (May–July 1980), p. 3.

IPI Report. (May 1979), p. 16.

IPI Report. (March 1979).

IPI Report. (June 1975), p. 6.

Jenkins, Loren. "At Night, Istanbul Cowers under 'The Anarchy's Grip.'" *The Washington Post,* September 5, 1980, p. A13.

_____. "Junta Leader Outlines Reforms to Save Turkish Democracy." *The Washington Post,* September 17, 1980, p. A21.

_____. "Neo-Fascist Surrenders in Turkey." *The Washington Post,* September 15, 1980, p. 1.

Jones, J. Clement. *Mass Media Codes of Ethics and Councils.* Paris, 1980.

Karpat, Kemal H., "The Mass Media: Turkey," in Robert E. Ward and Dankwart A. Rustow, *Political Modernization in Japan and Turkey.* Princeton, N.J. 1964.

Merrill, John C. *et al. The Foreign Press.* Baton Rouge, La. 1970.

_____. "Turkey Nears the End of its Tether." *The Middle East,* August 1979, pp. 70-71.

Munir, Metin. "New Headaches for Old." *The Middle East,* April 1979, pp. 50-52.

_____. "West to Extend Turkey Lifeline." *The Middle East,* February 1979, p. 12.

1979 Division Membership Directory and International Guide. International Communication Division of Association for Education in Journalism.

Nyrop, Richard F. *Area Handbook for the Republic of Turkey.* Washington, D.C., 1973.

_____, ed. *Turkey: A Country Study.* Washington, D.C., 1980.

OECD Economic Surveys. Turkey. Paris, April 1980.

Ogan, Christine. "A Return to Aktepe: A Study of Communication and Development in a Turkish Squatter Settlement." Chapel Hill, N.C., 1976.

Onulduran, Ersin. *Political Development and Political Parties in Turkey.* Ankara, 1974.

Sahin, Haluk. "Broadcasting Autonomy in Turkey: 1961-1971." Bloomington, Ind., 1974.

Topuz, Hifzi. *100 Soruda; Turk Basin Tarihi.* Istanbul, 1973.

Turkish Information Office. *Facts About Turkey.* Ankara, 1973.

Turkish State Planning Organization. *A Summary of the Third Five Year Development Plan, 1973-77.* Ankara, 1974.

UNESCO. *World Communications*. New York, 1975.

UNESCO. *Statistics on Radio and Television 1960-76*. Paris, 1978.

UNESCO Statistical Yearbook, 1978-79. Paris, 1980.

United Nations. *Statistical Yearbook, 1962*. New York, 1963.

United Nations. *Statistical Yearbook, 1974*. New York, 1974.

Willings Press Guide 1980. West Sussex, England, 1980.

"Yillik Inflasyon." *Cumhurriyet,* November 28, 1980, p. 1.

UGANDA

by Harold A. Fisher

BASIC DATA

Population: 12,779,600 (1978)
Area: 241,139 sq. km. (93,104 sq. mi.)
GNP: NA
Literacy Rate: NA
Language(s): English (official), Luganda,
   Ki-Swahili
Number of Dailies: 1
   Aggregate Circulation: NA
   Circulation per 1,000: NA
Number of Nondailies: 1
   Aggregate Circulation: NA
   Circulation per 1,000: NA
Number of Periodicals: 7

Number of Radio Stations: 1
Number of Television Stations: 1
Number of Radio Receivers: 250,000 (1977)
   Radio Receivers per 1,000: 20 (1977)
Number of Television Sets: 81,000 (1977)
   Television Sets per 1,000: 7 (1977)
Total Annual Newsprint Consumption: 200
   metric tons
Per Capita Newsprint Consumption: 0.02 kg.
   (0.04 lb.)
Total Newspaper Ad Receipts: NA
   As % of All Ad Expenditures: NA

Background & General Characteristics

Uganda's once small but healthy, diverse and stimulating newspaper industry has been repressed and stripped of its last vestiges of freedom during the nation's past decade of revolution, dictatorships and unsuppressed violence. Whereas four lively dailies and 17 nondailies were thriving in 1970, today there exists but one weak, government-dominated daily and one small, threatened weekly. Besides government harassment, the press faces severe economic limitations brought about by the hardships of ten years of turmoil, civil war and oppressive dictatorship, which decimated the literate population and brought the economy to a virtual standstill. Even if press freedom were encouraged in Uganda today, few would possess the capital to improve the press or to invest in advertising. The same economic crisis severely limits circulation, a condition unlikely to improve rapidly.

The Idi Amin military dictatorship either eliminated or jailed most of Uganda's numerous competent national journalists and broadcasters. Subsequent regimes, except for a brief respite, have continued such discouraging tactics. As a result, many of the jour-

nalists remaining after Amin have chosen voluntary exile. The foreign press, meantime, has been and continues to be harassed.

Uganda's newspaper audience presents other overburdening problems to the struggling industry. English serves as the official language and the lingua franca of commerce and the well-educated. But it is written and spoken primarily in the urban centers, while numerous local languages and dialects are spoken by Uganda's rural people, who comprise about 83 percent of the total population. The Uganda Broadcasting Corporation has chosen to serve this diversity by broadcasting daily programs in as many as 23 languages and dialects. But the newspaper industry, because of the need for an economically viable readership, publishes only in Luganda, the most important local language, and in English. Luganda presents an additional complexity: a high percentage of the country's educated elite are the Luganda-speaking Baganda, who read both English and Luganda, and who have long been, from a political view, the nation's most controversial sector. Many were eliminated during Amin's days of power. Thus, Uganda readers today represent a small clientele in just two languages. Readers do not represent a large, wealthy group on which newspapers can build an audience and be assured of a steady income.

Because of President Amin's pressure to convert Uganda to an Islamic state, today's press readers find themselves also divided by religious interests. Christian papers were banned during the Amin regime as he paved the way for an all-Islamic state.

Even with the fine Ugandan rail and road transport system before Amin's rule, distribution of newspapers was always limited mainly to the cities and towns. Now, a decade of neglect by the Amin and subsequent governments has so deteriorated the transport system that circulation is even more confined.

War and the oppressive Amin regime have had other devastating effects upon the newspaper readership. For a time, the educated were deliberately exterminated, causing most of the remainder to flee; the business economy stopped, throwing readers out of work and robbing them of the ability to subscribe; and increased cost of living and of materials inflated newspaper production costs and paper prices beyond the reach of many. All these factors have had the net effect of reducing its audience when the press has most needed readership and support.

Prior to the reign of Idi Amin, Uganda had a lively, competitive press with good, if not the highest quality, journalistic practices. The press was frank and often controversial. Until Uganda became an independent member of the Commonwealth in 1962, the mass media were dominated by British money and British journalism. In 1902 A.M. Jeevanjee, from India, started the East African Standard Group. He brought in W. H. Tiller, a journalist from England, to produce the *African Standard,* (later it became the *East African Standard*), the *Mombasa Times* and the *Uganda Argus.* The last was founded in Kampala in 1955. Since Uganda had no news agency, the *Argus* shared wire services with the *East African Standard.* Like other European-owned newspapers that remained in Africa after independence, the *Uganda Argus* reflected a strong desire to survive under the presidencies of the Kabaka (until 1967) and of Dr. Milton Obote's first term (1967-1971). During this time, the *Argus* tried to be as neutral as possible and avoided stong editorials.

By 1970 Uganda had four thriving dailies and 17 nondaily periodicals. The *Uganda Argus,* published in English, claimed a daily circulation of over 21,000. Three other dailies were being published in Luganda: the *Taifa Empya* (circulation 12,721), which was similar in many respects to Kenya's *Daily Nation; Munno* (circulation 10,000), owned and operated by the Roman Catholic Church; and *Omukulembeze,* a Ministry of Information publication. The periodicals included three in English: *People* (a weekly), the *Nile Gazette* (published monthly by the Catholic diocese of Arua) and *A Magazine for Christian Leaders in Africa* (a monthly with a circulation of 8,500). Three periodicals of importance published in Luganda were *Kizito* (a monthly for children, selling approximately 35,000 copies), *Musizi* (circulation 10,000) and *New Day.* The last was published partly in English and partly in Luganda and was the voice of the Anglican Diocese of East Africa.

Until Amin became head of state in 1971, Uganda's press published in two languages, English and Luganda, partly because the Baganda exercised strong influences on government, business and education, especially in Kampala. Because the Roman Catholic and Anglican churches were strong and growing among the predominantly Christian Baganda, Lango and Acholi tribes, there were a number of thriving religious publications (*Munno, Nile Gazette, New Day* etc.). Dailies and periodicals generally avoided sensitive political issues. Kampala was, as it remains, the center of nearly all publishing activity.

Today, after a decade of dictatorship and civil strife, what few Christian publications remain are struggling to survive, and all other papers are dominated by government and, in general, are forced to express the official views. The lone remaining daily is the *Uganda Times,* published in English in Kampala. The remaining weekly, *Ngabo* (in Luganda), is under heavy pressure to comply with governmental dictates.

Economic Framework

A decade of upheaval and military dictatorship, coupled with drought and famine, have wreaked havoc on the national economy and have further weakened the nation's besieged media. Agriculture serves as the basis of the economy and provides a livelihood for about 83 percent of the population. For several years during the 1970s, production lagged as the civil war raged. Although the high level of world coffee prices enabled

Uganda to maintain a favorable balance of trade during part of Amin's dictatorship, output of tea, tobacco and cotton fell markedly. By the end of his rule, over half of the country's tea plantations had been abandoned. In 1975 Amin nationalized the copper mines and their production fell. Two years later he expelled all non-citizen Asians, who had been the backbone of Uganda's commerce and retail trades. By that time most other skilled foreign personnel had left or been expelled. Meanwhile President Amin spent most of the nation's foreign exchange earnings on arms and military supplies.

When the provisional government under the leadership of Dr. Yusuf Lule took over in April 1979, production of vital income-producing crops and goods had reached a virtual standstill. Uganda had incurred enormous debts. Reconstruction of the collapsed economy was hampered by the continuing occupation by Tanzanian troops, political uncertainties, shortages of essential goods, black market trading and soaring inflation. Conditions were further aggravated by drought and famine in the northern part of the country.

Uganda's economic woes during the past decade have seriously affected the media. During his rule, Amin controlled and used the media as his personal propaganda tools; the truth about Uganda's collapsing economy was never told. That reduced the credibility of the media to almost nil in the minds of most of the audience, and they turned to whatever outside sources of information they could get, particularly foreign broadcasts. Partly for economic and partly for political reasons, virtually all newspapers and non-daily periodicals disappeared.

The interim governments, from Amin's fall to the present rule of Obote, allowed a brief revival of the press, which is again threatened by the present government. However, the shattered economy has not been conducive to rapid reconstruction of the press. Newsprint and production costs have risen drastically during the decade; there are few with the capital to rebuild the newspaper and magazine industry; there are fewer potential readers with sufficient economic solvency to afford subscriptions; and there is only a weak market for retail advertising to support the media.

Prior to Amin, ownership of the press was in the hands of private individuals and church organizations, with the government competing with a paper of its own. During Amin's rule, the government took over nearly all papers. The succession of governments that followed the Amin dicatorship has continued to own and publish the lone daily, the *Uganda Times*, while private owners have published what little competition remains among the periodicals.

Until a decade ago, Uganda had a good transport system to enable wide disbursement of publications. The system has deteriorated since Amin expelled the Asians. Rail connections with neighboring Kenya have been broken for several extended periods. Most of the roads are in poor condition, hampering distribution.

Advertising in Uganda's media has always been subdued and has had little effect on editorial polices. A considerable amount of paid advertising was allowed to support news programs on Radio Uganda.

Press Laws

Initially after independence, Ugandan press laws were based on the British system the nation had inherited. Although the government controlled radio and television—the norm in most newly independent African countries—the publishers could report and write almost what they wished. During Obote's first presidency (1967–71), a new definitive constitution established a unitary republic, and Uganda became a one-party state. Although the press still had legal freedom, the government began pressuring the press to follow the party line and to contribute to nation-building. President Obote, noting that the press was failing to appreciate what his government was doing in East Africa, remarked: "The press will not be allowed to place obstacles in our path. We cannot have a government and a press enjoying the same responsibility." From that time, the press began to experience oppression from the Uganda government.

Although he did not revoke the Constitution when he came to power in 1971, General Amin did order the suspension of the legal system and concentrated all legislative power in his own hands. At first he sought the assistance of a Defense Council and a Council of Ministers he had nominated, but as time passed, he became more dictatorial. In 1973 he signed a decree authorizing his government to ban newspapers "for a certain period or indefinitely."

That was but the first step in his repression

of all independence on the part of the country's newspapers and broadcasting system. Amin's government took over the daily *Argus*, began to publish it under the title of *Voice of Uganda* and made its editors state employees. Then Amin, already head of state, leader of the government and commander-in-chief of the armed forces, appointed himself editor-in-chief of the *Voice of Uganda*, even though he could hardly write a sentence in English. He would call the newsroom, dictate a story in appalling English, then direct the editor to attribute the story either to himself or to someone he chose, such as a military spokesman or someone from a government ministry. Newspapers, radio and television were all forced to carry his lengthy speeches in full. During his 1971–79 regime, Amin was, in himself, the law of the press. He banned papers and jailed, expelled or had exterminated all journalists who displeased him.

During the brief interim governments in 1979 and 1980 of Presidents Yusuf Lule and Godfrey Binaisa, the press returned for a very short period of time to some of its earlier constitutional freedoms. Despite Uganda's serious economic problems, a number of new publications sprang up and published for a while. While Lule was in office, he appointed a journalist, Etekar Ejalu, as minister for lands and tourism.

Then anonymously published pamphlets appeared in Kampala threatening death to any journalist who continued to support President Binaisa or who failed to name Tanzanian troops guilty of nighttime looting and killings. Television journalist Bob Odongo Nayenda was shot for failing to follow the line prescribed in the pamphlets. At the same time, the government also expected the press to be a "positive ally" and to identify itself with the efforts of the ruling Uganda National Liberation Front to rebuild the country. Two journalists planning to launch a paper calling for immediate general elections of a permanent government were arrested. The newly won press freedom slipped away. And oppression of the press has worsened considerably since the general elections in December 1980 returned Dr. Milton Obote to the presidency and the Uganda Peoples' Congress to power.

State-Press Relations & Censorship

Relations with the media have always theoretically been under the direction of the minister of information. In practice, however, President Amin personally took charge of the media and, after the Military Commission overthrew President Godfrey Binaisa in May 1980, Paulo Muwanga, chairman of the Military Commission, took charge of press relations. Obote's government has again delegated relations with the media to the Ministry of Information.

Since the time of Obote's first term in office (1967–71), the government in power has dominated the national press and has used a variety of suppressive controls, among them censorship, bannings, expulsions, jailings and even "disappearance" of newsmen. The bannings and arrests of local newsmen began under Obote's first term.

But it was Amin who took full control of the media and who abused and manipulated the press more than any other Uganda leader since independence. In addition to threatening, expelling and murdering foreign journalists, Amin violated the local press in every way imaginable. In 1973 his troops closed down *The People,* a thriving weekly, because it mildly criticized the government's overbearing intolerance. The same year, Amin's forces killed Father Clement Kigundu, the editor of the Roman Catholic daily *Munno,* published in Luganda. Amin had once praised *Munno* because it "printed the truth," but later it represented to him the Christian forces in Uganda, which he was trying to destroy after his conversion to Islam. Father Kigundu was locked in his car, which was then set on fire. The newspaper died with its editor. A short while later, Amin closed down the largest circulation Luganda daily, *Taifa Empya.* By this time many well-qualified Uganda journalists had foreseen their fate and had fled the country.

One of Amin's first acts as president was to take over the *Uganda Argus,* rename it the *Voice of Uganda* and make it his personal propaganda tool. News coverage of anything but Amin's acts and words became sparse; about all the paper could do was to begin and end each issue with the words "President Amin." *Voice of Uganda* reporters and photographers had to exercise special care in demonstrating their loyalty and in trying to fit in with Amin's mercurial and unpredictable moods and acts. During the 1973 Middle East war, when Tanzania's Vice-President Aboud Jumbe visited Uganda, a *Voice of Uganda* journalist asked his opinion about the Arab-Israeli war. Amin was furious. He accused the journalist of being an imperialist and a Zionist and assigned the ruthless State Research Bureau to liquidate him. Fortunately the reporter sensed danger and fled to Kenya before he could be captured, but his family was badly beaten up by Amin's forces. Later a *Voice of Uganda* sports editor titled a story "Tanzania's Young Africans Gun Down KCC"; Amin sent troops after him for being pro-Tanzanian and anti-Uganda in his description of a Tanzanian football match win. The editor was also forced to escape to Kenya.

One journalist had to flee because his picture of the information minister taken at the close of the OAU meeting on the Pan African News Agency was not published. The truth was that the picture was out of focus and showed the minister's mouth wide open. The same minister also charged the photographer had taken a picture of President Amin with an empty plate in his hand at a luncheon after the closing of the OAU meeting. According to the minister, the picture showed Amin as a beggar asking for food!

Other journalists had to flee Uganda for similar trivial offenses. Many were less fortunate and simply disappeared from sight, particularly during the army purges of 1977 when the Anglican Archbishop of Uganda and two cabinet ministers were murdered and many Christians and other suspected of being disloyal were killed or simply disappeared. During this period, newspapers and magazines once known for their fearlessness and frankness closed down, and the *Voice of Uganda* terrorized, threatened and defamed any Ugandans Amin did not like.

With the fall of Amin's regime in 1979, several weekly party-oriented papers sprang to life, among them the *Citizen*, the organ of the opposition Democratic Party; the *Weekly Topic*, a paper of the small leftist Uganda Patriotic Movement; and the *Economy*. The defunct *Taifa Empya* was revived as a weekly Luganda tabloid. Foreign newspapers were again allowed, and Kenyan and British newspapers reappeared in the streets.

Although the interim governments encouraged more open reporting, strong pressures were brought to assure that papers allied themselves with the official views and desires. Roland Kakooza, editor of the *Economy,* and Charles Sinabulya, a reporter for *The Citizen*, were arrested when Information Minister Picho Owiny accused them of irresponsibility. The two papers were threatened with closure. After a time, both men were released.

After Amin, the *Voice of Uganda* became the *Uganda Times*. Its editor-in-chief, Ilakut Ben Bella, was detained by President Binaisa's Internal Affairs Minister Paulo Muwanga for publishing a story that three Tanzanian soldiers based in Uganda had been stoned to death for robbing villagers. Muwanga accused Ben Bella of using his position as editor to disclose unfavorable information about his country to sources abroad, and of hobnobbing with foreign journalists. As chairman of the Military Commission, Muwanga publicly attacked both native and foreign journalists. At one press conference he reportedly said, "There's plenty of room in our jails" for reporters who get out of line.

Since Obote returned to power late in 1980, his government has declared it is "not going to share power with anyone." Five newspapers, the *Citizen, Economy,* the *Weekly Topic, Afrika* and *Mulengera,* have already been banned; reporters have been admonished to "report constructively" or "a few heads will roll." Ben Bella was detained by police for several days after reporting army rampages in the remote East Madi district, and then released. Recently, the Obote government has been turning its attention to suppression of foreign journalists.

Attitude Toward Foreign Media

The foreign media have suffered much from Uganda's series of repressive governments. Expulsion of foreign journalists began under Obote's first presidency. Then the Amin regime made foreign media and correspondents the targets of bannings, deportations, detentions and murders.

In 1972 British journalist David Martin, a reporter for the BBC and *The Observer*, was told he would be arrested if he attempted to visit Uganda. Another British journalist was detained by the Ugandan army, asked numerous superfluous questions and released only after payment of 600 pounds sterling. In 1973 Philip Short, a correspondent for *The Times*, Reuters and the BBC, was expelled for sending to the United Kingdom some pictures he had obtained from the Ministry of Information. After Amin had praised Short for reporting the truth, he accused him of being an agent of imperialism and Zionism. Several Western news wire agencies were expelled. In June 1975 all British journalists in Uganda were told they were no longer welcome. Some correspondents were killed; others were deported. The only correspondents left unmolested during Amin's time were those from the USSR and from the New China News Agency. No foreign journalist was allowed into Uganda during Amin's army purges.

Foreign newspapers were banned in 1974 for "supporting imperialists, Zionists and colonialists." They included Britain's *Sunday Post* and Kenya's *Sunday Nation, Daily Nation* and the *East African Standard*. In January 1975 the Amin government announced a total ban on the sale of foreign newspapers and magazines, with a jail penalty for anyone who broke it.

After an attempted army revolt in 1978, Amin warned all Ugandans not to transmit news to "hostile" countries. A foreign journalist attempting to investigate the story was jailed at the border for several days and released only after payment of an enormous fine. American free-lance journalist Nicholas Stroh was brutally murdered at Mbarara, where he had gone to investigate an army barracks massacre by forces loyal to Amin.

Amin's worst atrocity against foreign journalists occurred during the height of the struggle between the coalition of Uganda freedom fighters and Tanzanian soldiers against his troops, shortly before he was ousted from power in April 1979. Four foreign correspondents, two Germans and two Swedes, were trying to get a story on the struggle. They were Hans Bollinger and Wolfgang Stiens of the German *Stern* magazine and Arne Lemberg and Earl Bergman, reporters for Sweden's *Expressen* and *Svenska Dagbladet* respectively. After crossing Lake Victoria in a fishing boat, the four were seized by Amin's soldiers, taken to a police station outside Kampala, and, after a cursory interrogation, murdered in cold blood. Only a few weeks earlier, Bollinger had been arrested in Kampala and had been saved from almost certain execution only by the intervention of the German ambassador.

Since Amin's downfall the rejection of foreign journalists, although milder, has continued. The were regarded as suspect under the Binaisa government. Just three days before the general elections in December 1980, two British journalists, Christabel King of the *Daily Telegraph* and Nick Worral, reporter for the BBC, *Observer* and *Daily Express*, were barred from re-entering Uganda on grounds that their reporting had been unsympathetic to Uganda. After the re-election of Obote, Kenyan newspapers have

again disappeared from the streets of Uganda. Foreign journalists have been severely criticized for reporting anti-government guerilla attacks and the subsequent wanton murder of suspected civilians. The new government has been accusing foreign correspondents of bringing insecurity to the nation by distortions suiting the whims of their foreign editors. Resident foreign journalists have been harassed and threatened, and a visiting BBC correspondent has been denied accreditation.

It appears Ugandans are again tuning in to foreign broadcasts to find out what is happening in their country, and many liken the present suppression of foreign journalists to that of Amin's regime.

Uganda has generally supported the UNESCO positions on the media, especially those calling for greater state control over the flow of news.

News Agencies

Prior to Amin's dictatorship, no national news agency existed, but the Uganda Catholic Information Service (UCI) provided a weekly news bulletin. Reuters had a correspondent in Kampala, and the Associated Press and United Press International had stringers in the capital.

Today, a national news agency, the Uganda News Agency (UNA), operates in Kampala and serves the entire country. Its correspondents report Ugandan events and developments, and it carries reports from foreign news wire agencies. Its director is Nathan Epenu and its editor-in-chief Zulu Karobane.

Novosti (USSR), and Tass (USSR) have bureaus in Kampala and the AP (U.S.) and Reuters (U.K.) are also represented there.

Electronic News Media

Radio has always been Ugandans' principal source of information. The independent government before Amin developed an excellent multilingual program schedule of news and information soon after it came to power in the 1960s. Television also had a good multilingual schedule of educational and informational programming.

Radio Uganda, with two networks, the Red and the Blue, attempts to provide reliable news and information services in as many as

23 different languages. In addition to English, French, Swahili and Arabic internal and external broadcasts, the organization has programmed in 19 Ugandan tribal languages. To provide maximum service, the organization has established a system of 11 regional transmitters, with all scheduling and programming controlled from its 13 studios in Kampala. When it has operated as envisioned, Radio Uganda has exchanged newsworthy, informational and educational programs between regions; often, all transmitters have carried information of national concern, such as talks by the president or one of the government ministers. While this system, underwritten partly by Dutch and British firms, has been expensive, it has provided some vital informational services for the entire nation.

Radio Uganda has always stressed news. Each Radio Uganda channel has carried up to five hours of news each day. But because no one language receives continuous service on any single channel, many of the broadcasts have been unintelligible to large portions of the audience. This has driven large proportions of the Uganda audience to listen to the Voice of Kenya, Radio Zaire, Radio Tanzania, Radio Burundi, the BBC and the Voice of America.

Uganda Television has also provided regular news services. Its television for schools has been particularly effective. Uganda has had a plan for regional television services similar to that of Radio Uganda, but the civil strife has halted its development.

Education & Training

Before and during the first years after independence, Uganda broadcasters received training in BBC, Thomson Television College, Deutsche Welle, Dutch and Eastern European institute programs. During the 1950s and 1960s, several UNESCO-sponsored short courses were held in Kampala. Uganda technical trainees often spent two terms at the Uganda Technical College, followed by a term of apprenticeship at Radio Uganda, but this training was only marginally adequate. A number of broadcasters and journalists had trained in American universities. Some had gone to Africa-based institutes, such as the All-African Conference of Churches Training Center and the Kenya Institute of Mass Communications in Nairobi. A number of journalists had received training while attached to the Ugandan or British newspapers.

In 1971 a Uganda School of Journalism was established at the Institute of Public Administration in Kampala. In 1973 the Centre for Continuing Education at Makerere University in Kampala had planned to construct studios for training radio and television personnel. But the conditions imposed by the Amin government halted all effective training and most seasoned journalists were killed, expelled or forced to flee the country. As a result Uganda is currently in dire need of an effective training program for its broadcasters and journalists.

Summary

The future for Uganda's media is difficult to predict. If the present restrictions on the national press and on foreign journalists continue, it would appear the media will remain weak puppets of the one-party government. Even if the media could maintain a small degree of freedom from government, the economic strength of the press seems too weak and the tiny core of remaining trained journalists too small to rebuild quickly a strong press. It seems safe to conclude therefore that, at a minimum, the struggle ahead for the Uganda press is certain to be long and arduous.

CHRONOLOGY

1977   General Amin's army carried out purges; Anglican Archbishop and two cabinet ministers murdered and many journalists jailed, murdered or disappear.

1978   American journalist murdered while reporting Mbarara barracks massacre.

1979   Four foreign journalists, two Germans and two Swedes, murdered by Amin's forces.
Several weekly newspapers revived during brief respite from goverment repression of the press.
The editor of the *Economy* and a reporter for *The Citizen*

arrested and their papers threatened with closure for "irresponsible" reporting.

1980 Two British journalists barred from entering Uganda to report the general elections.

Uganda Times editor-in-chief

detained for publishing story about the stoning of Tanzanian occupation troops by Ugandans.

1981 Five weekly newspapers banned by the Obote government.

BIBLIOGRAPHY

Africa South of the Sahara, 1979-1980. London, 1979.

"Amin Seeks Guns for Self, U.S. Education for Children," *Toledo Blade*, February 8, 1981, p. 22.

"Amin's Agents Kill Four Brave Men." *IPI Report*, April 1979, p. 3.

"A Quick Look Around: Uganda." *IPI Report*, April 1973, p. 6.

"Britons Barred from Uganda Elections." *IPI Report*, January 1981, p. 2.

"Change in East Africa." *IPI Report*, June 1979, pp. 15–16.

"Don't Force Me to Bar You." *IPI Report*, November 1979, p. 3.

"Editor Held in Uganda." *IPI Report*, May 1981, p. 4.

"Freedom Review of 1979: Uganda." *IPI Report,* December 1979, p. 6.

Hachten, William A. *Muffled Drums: The News Media in Africa.* Ames, Iowa, 1971.

Head, Sydney W. *Broadcasting in Africa.* Philadelphia, 1974.

"IPI Hits Out at Uganda Bannings." *IPI Report*, April 1981, p. 3.

Lansner, Thomas. "Africa's Most Diverse Press Suddenly Falls in Uganda." *The Press*, June-July 1981, pp. 15–16.

Merrill, John C., Bryan, Carter R., and Alisky, Marvin. *The Foreign Press.* Baton Rouge, La., 1970.

"Newsman Joins Lule's Freedom Team." *IPI Report*, June 1979, p. 3.

"Obote Regains Uganda Presidency, but Disputes, Challenges Remain." *Christian Science Monitor*, December 15, 1980, p. 12.

"Press Freedom Report: Africa: Uganda." *IPI Report*, January 1974, p. 15.

"Press Freedom Report, 1974: Uganda." *IPI Report*, January 1975, p. 15.

"Press Freedom Report, 1975: Uganda." IPI Report, December 1975, p. 14.

"Uganda." *IPI Report*, December 1980, p. 14.

"Uganda: Back to Milton Obote." *Christian Science Monitor*, December 15, 1980, p. 24.

"Uganda: Retreat from a Collision Course." *Time*, March 14, 1977, p. 24.

Uganda Ministry of Education. *Broadcast to Schools.* Kampala, 1972.

"Ugandan Editor Detained after Story of Troops in Clash." *IPI Report*, January/February 1980, p. 3.

"The World Press Freedom Review of 1978: Uganda." *IPI Report,* January 1979, p. 11.

"The World Press Score in Capsule Form: Uganda." *IPI Report*, February 1973, p. 7.

USSR

by John J. Karch

BASIC DATA

Population: 265,500,000
Area: 22,402,000 sq. km. (8.65 million sq. mi.)
GNP: 801 billion rubles (US$1.08 trillion) (1979)
Language(s): Russian, Lithuanian, Latvian, Estonian, Finnish, Karelian, Georgian, Armenian, Iranian (among over 200 languages and dialects)
Number of Dailies: 694 (1978)
  Aggregate Circulation: 103,796,000 (1978)
  Circulation per 1,000: 400 (1978)
Number of Nondailies: 7,242 (1978)
  Aggregate Circulation: 67,311,000 (1978)
  Circulation per 1,000: 300 (1978)
Number of Periodicals: 4,838 (1978)

Number of Radio Stations: over 1,000 (1980)
Number of Television Stations: 123 (1978)
Number of Radio Receivers: 115 million (est., 1980)
  Radio Receivers per 1,000: 433
Number of Television Sets: 57 million (est., 1980)
  Television Sets per 1,000: 214
Total Annual Newsprint Consumption: 1,135,300 metric tons (1977)
  Per Capita Newsprint Consumption: 4.4 kg. (9.68 lbs.) (1977)
Total Newspaper Ad Receipts: NA
  As % of All Ad Expenditures: NA

Background & General Characteristics

The Soviet Union is one of the leading countries in the world newspaper industry, with nearly 8,000 newspapers (close to 700 dailies) and a combined circulation of 470 million. Of the total newspapers, over 5,000 are in Russian, the remainder in 54 other languages of this multinational state. The press industry is a state monopoly; publications represent the Communist party, government or "public organizations." The Party exercises total control. No individuals or other groups are permitted to publish, or even to exist. The principal function of the newspaper is "educational" in disseminating information and propaganda among the masses domestically and abroad to ensure that only Marxist-Leninist ideology and current policies of the Communist party are published.

With the "communication explosion" in recent years, people's access to the mass media in the Soviet Union has changed from largely collective to mainly individual and private exposure. Soviet Russia's population, third largest in the world, was 262,436,000 according to the January 17, 1979 census, an increase of 21 million since the 1970 census. Half of the population is under 30 years of age. The July 1, 1980 estimate was 265,500,000. Some 193,200,000 (or 73.6 percent) of the people live in the western part of the country, with 69.2 million (26.4 percent) in Asia. During recent decades migration has resulted in the transformation from a predominantly rural (80 percent in 1926 and 60 percent in 1951) to an urban society. Females (141.6 million, or 53.3 percent) outnumbered males (123.9 million, or 46. 7 percent) by 17.7 million, the result of Stalin's purges and World War II losses. In 1980 cities over 100,000 population numbered 272; 45 were over 500,000 and 20 over 1,000,000. The largest cities are Moscow (8.1 million, an increase of 1 million since 1970), Leningrad (4.6 million), Kiev (2.2 million), Tashkent (1.8 million) and Baku (1.6 million). The national literacy rate is 99.8 percent—making nearly every Soviet citizen a newspaper reader.

The quality of Soviet journalism is difficult to assess because the Communist press has an entirely different function from that of the West, and reporting by journalists must be within rigidly prescribed parameters established by the ruling Communist party, which either owns or controls—through the government or "public organizations"—all media. The Party's established "Basic Principles of the Soviet Press" apply to all journalists. These are party-mindedness *(partinost),* ideological content *(ideinost),* patriotism *(otechestvennost),* truthfulness *(pravdivost),* popular character *(narodnost),* mass accessibility *(massovost),* and criticism and self-criticism *(kritika i samokritika).* Every principle intends to enhance the Party and communism. "Freedom of the Press" and "objectivity" are rejected as harmful bourgeois concepts. Editors and journalists are schooled, indoctrinated and carefully selected. Journalistic content must reflect Marxist-Leninist ideology, current Party policies, socialist realism and communist achievements and superiority. Moreover, it must wage propaganda campaigns against real or imagined enemies, domestic and foreign, punctuated by a special vocabulary, repeated ad nauseam. These strictures pertain not only to political analyses but to all reporting.

By Western standards, and occasionally acknowledged by Soviet officials as well as readers, the Soviet press is dull, repetitious and uninteresting; it is filled with propaganda clichés and written in a formalistic style. Although there has been some change the past two decades to make the press more interesting by including previously shunned human interest items and entertainment, Soviet papers still avoid the sensationalism so prevalent in many Western newspapers and magazines. Readers' letters, and replies, although of interest, are not a substitute because these too are not spontaneous but usually officially generated. Within this confining context, the Soviet press, although purposeful and tendentious, is extremely serious, stressing political, economic, educational and scientific/technological themes. Sensationalism, entertainment and yellow journalism are rejected. The *Great Soviet Encyclopedia* characterizes yellow journalism as "the most reactionary, mercenary bourgeois journalism" appearing in "the basest bourgeois publications."

However, there is a conscious effort to increase readership by adoption of modern techniques—more appealing layout, typography and illustrations. Also, some newspapers are making a conscious effort to attract youthful readers. Most progress has been made with certain evening newspapers (in the fall of 1980 *Rigas Balls* in Latvia even began a column for single people to advertise for partners) but the central organs, led by *Pravda* and *Izvestia,* are the models for other newspapers to become more interesting and readable—to the extent that this is allowed.

The Soviet press has important traditions rooted in pre-revolutionary Russia: those of the social critic, censor, educator, political activist, agitator, propagandist and organizer. Emigré revolutionary publications began in the 1850s, and the first Russian Social Democratic Labor party newspapers appeared toward the end of the 19th century. The subsequently renowned *Iskra* ("The Spark") was established by Lenin in 1900 in Geneva and smuggled into Tsarist Russia. A practical revolutionary, Lenin recognized that "ideas are weapons," and that a newspaper is "not only a collective propagandist and a collective agitator, it is also a collective organizer." Accordingly *Iskra* was designed to convey one central message—Marxism—and to amalgamate the various factions into one movement. Since Lenin's celebrated 1902 propaganda tract *Shto Delat?* ("What Is To Be Done?"), Soviet leaders have considered the press (indeed all media) as a powerful ideological weapon.

The first legal Bolshevik newspaper, *Novaya Zhizn* ("New Life"), which Lenin helped found, was published in St. Petersburg (now Leningrad) during October-December 1905. The Bolsheviks began the publication of *Pravda* ("Truth") in 1912, with Stalin as an organizer. It was intended to be a mass political newspaper. (Other parties and factions had their own newspapers, which were instruments in their internecine struggles.) *Pravda* was suppressed in 1914 but resumed publication on March 5, 1917, to be used as a weapon during the revolution. The November 10, 1917 "Decree on the Press" and "General Regulations on the Press" eliminated all opposition media and established censorship; in 1922 the censorship organization Glavlit was established. Henceforth the Soviet press was to be based on Leninist principles. For Lenin and later CP regimes the newspaper has been inseparable from the political organization, always functioning as mass propagandist. During the early post-revolutionary years the CP, led by Lenin, established an extensive network of Party, government and specialized publications at national and lower levels. *Pravda* has been the model. The leadership emphasized political-ideological education and strict Party guidance. The political importance of newspapers was illustrated during World War II. The Party mobilized its propaganda against Nazi Germany and stressed the heroism and patriotism of the Soviet military as it created a network of newspapers for the front, publishing, by 1943, some 128 dailies and 600 other newspapers.

The Soviet Union has over 200 languages and dialects. Of the 262.4 million population, Russians accounted for 137.4 million (52 percent), Ukrainians 42.3 million and Belorussians 9.5 million; all three languages are Slavic. Other Indo-European language groups are Baltic (Lithuanian and Latvian); Iranian (including Tadzhik, Kurdish, Baluchi and Pamir); Moldavian and Armenian. Turkic languages include Azerbaidzhan, Kazakh, Kirghiz, Turkmenian and Uzbek; the Finno-Ugric are Estonian, Finnish, Karelian, and Komi; Caucasian include Georgian and numerous others.

While there is no "state" language in the Soviet Union, Russian is used in international relations, and domestically it is the predominant language of communication and sine qua non for vertical bureaucratic growth. Russian is the second "native language" in the 14 non-Russian republics. For the present, "bilingualism" is the official objective, but many non-Russian critics have accused Soviet authorities of imposing "linguistic Russification" on the other nationalities.

Although the USSR's numerous non-Russian nationalities and special interest groups cannot be considered as "minorities and groups" in the American sense, their press-media needs are met—to a point. In addition to the central press—published in Moscow in Russian, and distributed throughout the Soviet Union— newspapers are published in non-Russian languages on several levels, from republic to autonomous republic and autonomous *oblast* (county) to city and below. The Republic papers are similar in makeup and content to the central papers but, in serving their readership, contain coverage of developments in their particular republics. In 1978 there were 158 republican papers with a circulation of 26,325,000, and 95 autonomous republic and *oblast* papers with a total readership of 4,219,000.

However, despite the Soviet Union's multinational, multilingual makeup, of the 7,936 newspapers published in 1978, 5,092 were in Russian, 1,304 in Ukrainian, 189 in Uzbek, 163 in Kazakh, 128 in Belorussian and 123 in Georgian, while 49 other nationalities had 103 or less with 18 having one. Clearly Russian is the dominant language. Besides the central newspapers, *(Pravda* and *Izvestia),* even some of the republic CP organs (such as *Kommunist Tadzhikistana:* "Tadzhik Communist") are in Russian.

"Russification" continues to be a concern to the many ethnic groups within the Soviet Union, as is "Sovietization" and "atheism." The slogan "national in form, socialist in content" portends an ominous future for ethnic-group viability and for distinct nationalities. From the beginning of Communist rule, the Soviet regime has tried to create an atheistic society. Accordingly, various measures are applied against religious bodies and expressions. The regime conducts antireligious propaganda, but does not permit any pro-religious publications, but despite the enormous, one-sided campaign, religion in the Soviet Union has been preserved—and closely identified with ethnicity. Most of the faithful belong to the Orthodox Church (Russians, Ukrainians, Belorussians, Moldavians and Georgians), followed by the Muslims in the Central Asiatic republics, Lutherans in Latvia and Estonia and Roman Catholics in Lithuania and western Ukraine.

Only one political party and one ideology exists in the Soviet Union. The Communist party permits no alternative to, nor competition with, Marxism-Leninism as currently interpreted by the ruling Politburo, headed by the secretary general. The Soviet state is organized and functions on the principle of "democratic centralism"; that is, once a decision is adopted by the Party, compliance is absolute and all officials and media are required to reflect approved policies in the context of Communist ideology. No minority or alternative views are permitted to be voiced or printed. A vast apparatus, including the KGB (acronym for Committee on State Security) ensures compliance.

Soviet newspapers are generally four or six pages long and contain no advertising. The regular format is 42x60 cm (16x23 in.), the tabloid-size format 30x42 cm (11.5x16 in.). *Pravda* runs six pages daily except Mondays, when it is eight. This is the standard for other central and republic newspapers in makeup and content. The weekly newspapers—such as *Literaturnaya Gazeta:* "Literary Newspaper''; and *Za Rubezhom:*

"Abroad"—have 16, 24 or more pages. The regular newspapers have eight columns, the tabloid size six. Most republic newspapers run four pages; about two-thirds are regular size, the rest tabloids, the same ratio pertaining to the newspapers in the autonomous republics. The *kray* (territory) and *oblast* (province) newspapers are four pages, about half regular and half tabloid. The *rayon* (district) newspapers are tabloids, mostly four pages, the rest two. The city newspapers are generally four-page tabloids. Various enterprises and institutions publish their own newspapers, generally of two-page tabloid size (although sometimes four pages in the larger enterprises). Papers at state and collective farms are of smaller size. On the bottom rung, the "wall newspapers" are in effect bulletin boards with reports, articles, and illustrations prepared especially to highlight holidays and special events.

Of the 694 dailies (appearing four or more times weekly), 658 are morning newspapers, 36 evening, with total respective circulations of 99,334,000 and 4,452,000.

Generally Soviet morning newspapers appear six days a week, Tuesday through Sunday, *Pravda* being the only one that appears seven days weekly. The government organ *Izvestia,* an afternoon newspaper, contains the Sunday supplement *"Nedelya"* ("Week"), which includes features and satire—largely anti-Western. But Soviet readers go without magazine, book-review or other sections.

Major cities publish evening newspapers, such as *Vechernaya Moskva* ("Evening Moscow"), which have a more appealing format and a relaxed tone, as they report a greater amount of human interest material that is played down by the dailies.

In order to propagate Marxism-Leninism and official Soviet policies and achievements, Moscow also targets numerous publications for foreign audiences. For Soviet overseas propaganda foreign nationals are employed to ensure quality translations into their languages. In 1978 22 newspapers in 11 foreign languages were published, with a total circulation of 1,177,000. By far the largest foreign-language readerships are in English (two papers, 672,000 copies) and German (three papers, 207,000 copies). Others are French (one paper, 72,000 copies), Polish (four papers, 207,000 copies), Hungarian (five papers, 64,000 copies), Arabic, Greek, Spanish, Korean, Finnish and Latin. The best known is the weekly *Moscow News,* published in four languages (English,

French, Arabic and Russian, the latter added in 1980), with a circulation of 3,230,000.

In 1978 the foreign-language periodicals numbered 101 in 21 languages with circulation totaling 45,593,000. The leading publications are *Soviet Union,* an illustrated monthly magazine; *Soviet Woman,* an illustrated 40-page monthly; *Soviet Film,* a 44-page illustrated monthly; and *Soviet Military Review,* a monthly of the *Krasnaya Zvezda* (Red Star) publishing house. The most favored foreign languages for Soviet periodicals are English (50 publications), French (45), German (34) and Spanish (33).

A sizable number of other Soviet magazines are published abroad. For example, as part of the U.S.—USSR Cultural Exchange Agreement, *Soviet Life* is printed and distributed commercially in the United States with a monthly run of 62,000, while the U.S. International Communication Agency's *Amerika* is printed in the United States with the same number of copies but distributed in the Soviet Union by Soyuzpechat. "Returns" of *Amerika* appear to be a barometer of U.S.-Soviet relations. Normally these figures run between 800 and 900 copies, but since the invasion of Afghanistan 10,000 copies of the tremendously popular U.S. magazine have been returned monthly.

Many specialized publications are also produced by various Soviet groups, including the Communist Youth League (Komsomol) with 132 newspapers and a circulation of 21,402,000—the largest; the grade-school organization called the Pioneers with 16,927,000 readers; industry and construction with seven separate publications; transport and agriculture with 43; culture, literature and art with 17; education with 16; and physical culture and sports with 15.

Despite the large number of Soviet newspapers and other periodicals, none can be called competitive in the Western sense. Generally a republic capital will have the Soviet central newspapers in addition to its own CP Central Committee and its CP government and Party organs. For example, Alma Ata, capital of Kazakhstan, has the Kazakh-language *Sotsialistik Kazakhstan,* which is the organ of the Kazakhstan CP Central Committee, the Supreme Soviet, and the Council of Ministers; and also the daily Russian-language *Kazakhstanskaya Pravda,* published by the CP, Supreme Soviet and the Council of Ministers. In addition, there are republic Komsomol dailies, the increasing number of evening papers, and specialized publications. All are officially established as organs of the CP, government, or "public organizations," and all must conform to the dictates of the ruling Communist party. This does not create a climate for circulation wars.

While the Soviet Union publishes data on total number of newspapers (7,936) and on total circulation per issue (171 million), information of the number of newspapers by circulation groups is not available. However, the major all-Union newspapers with the largest circulations are published in Moscow and distributed throughout the 15 Soviet republics. Large daily circulations are enjoyed by such major Russian and republican publications as Leningrad's *Leningradskaya Pravda* (350,000), Kiev's *Pravda Ukrainy* (440,000), Riga's *Cina* (215,000) and Vilnius's *Komjaunimo Tiesa* (Komsomol Truth) (198,000).

Of the Soviet Union's 7,936 newspapers, 30 are all-Union; 158 republic; 313 *kray, oblast* and *okrug;* 95 autonomous Republic and *oblast;* 683 city; 2,946 *rayon;* 3,076 house organs; and 635 collective farm.

10 Largest Newspapers* by Circulation	
1. *Pravda* ("Truth")	11,000,000
2. *Komsomolskaya Pravda* ("Communist Youth League Truth")	10,000,000
3. *Pioneerskaya Pravda* ("Pioneer Truth")	8,600,000
4. *Trud* ("Labor")	8,600,000
5. *Selskaya Zhizn* ("Country Life")	8,500,000
6. *Izvestia* ("News")	8,600,000
7. *Sovietskaya Rossia* ("Soviet Russia")	3,230,000
8. *Sovietskiy Sport* ("Soviet Sport")	3,500,000
9. *Literaturnaya Gazeta* ("Literary Newspaper")	2,600,000
10. *Krasnaya Zvezda* ("Red Star")	2,400,000
*Accounting for 64.6 percent of total daily circulation in the Soviet Union.	

Unquestionably the most influential newspaper is *Pravda* (Truth), organ of the Central Committee of the Communist party, and the only paper published 365 days a year. Its 11 million circulation is the largest in the world,

and its total readership is estimated at 50 million. *Pravda* authoritatively reflects Marxist-Leninist ideology, Party policies and pronouncements and important domestic and foreign news. Tass (the Soviet news agency) disseminates *Pravda's* editorials, required reading for Party members. Next in importance is *Izvestia* ("News"), organ of the Presidium of the Supreme Soviet of the USSR (Soviet Parliament), published daily except Monday, and emphasizing government relations and foreign news. Certain items are carried by both and frequently their featured articles are reprinted in lower-level newspapers. *Komsomolskaya Pravda,* organ of the Communist Youth League, is perhaps the third most influential. Its expressed goal, targeted toward the 38 million Komsomol members, is "the communist upbringing" of future Party, government and other leaders. Published twice weekly, *Komsomolskayà Pravda* serves as the example for the 131 other Komsomol newspapers and 26 periodicals.

Economic Framework

The Soviet Union has the second largest economy in the world, surpassed only by that of the United States. However, its command economy is beset by serious problems, including central planning developed by the State Planning Committee (Gosplan), bureaucratic inflexibility and poor management. Weaknesses include shortages (especially of consumer goods), transportation, agriculture, energy, housing, labor and productivity, and low-quality workmanship. Hard currency is a continual problem. Growth rates were scaled down during the 1976–80 five-year plan, and the 1981–85 plan is expected to encounter similar difficulties, including shortages and decreased growth. Lack of incentive is a major problem. Among the troubled sectors of the economy are the logging, pulp and paper industries.

Some 135 million people are employed in the national economy, but the standard of living for the preponderance of the population is low, with conveniences taken for granted in Western countries virtually unknown. According to official statistics for 1979, the average wage was 163.3 rubles ($243.73) per month; management-technical employees received 208.9 rubles ($311.79), "blue collar" workers 180.4 rubles ($269.25) and agricultural 146 rubles ($217.91). Certain sectors are paid poorly; the lowest is the cultural with an average monthly pay of only 104.7 rubles ($156.27). A minority—high CP members, top government officials (also CP members), high-ranking military officers, select intellectuals and artists—are not only highly paid but, more importantly, receive a variety of valuable perquisites. Many millions, on the other hand, lead a bare existence; especially affected are the 48 million pensioners, many of whom receive close to the 45 rubles ($67.50) minimum legal pension; the highest is only 120 rubles ($180).

Officially there is no unemployment, but there is a high redundant and underemployed labor force in menial low-paid jobs. Defense, for political and military purposes, has high priority, and the officer corps, especially the marshals and generals, are among the highest paid, with extravagant perquisites.

The depressed economy affects the media in various ways—there is a shortage of newsprint, a need for expansion and modernization of printing plants and an inability for many to purchase radios and TV receivers. The newspapers are least affected, their prices being kept low by state subsidies. Ideology and politics, not profit or readership, are key factors in establishing, amalgamating or abolishing newspapers and periodicals. However, production costs and newsprint are also factors. In 1976 the Novosti news agency was reduced substantially in staff positions and some of its operations transferred partly for economy purposes, and in the late 1970s a number of technical journals were forced to cease publication in order to conserve newsprint.

Although Soviet newspapers cannot be considered "popular" by U.S. standards, some departures from the heavy political-economic fare have been made in recent years to include limited human interest stories and illustrations in several city newspapers, such as *Vechernaya Moskva* ("Evening Moscow") and *Vecherniy Leningrad* ("Evening Leningrad"); also more interesting are sport publications like *Sovietskiy Sport* and periodicals on culture, mass media and popular science. The politically satirical *Krokodil* ("Crocodile"), the 16-page biweekly published by *Pravda,* contains not only vicious illustrations aimed at the West, especially the United States, but also colorful cartoons and articles critical of domestic bureaucracy and inefficiency.

The Soviet Union is the largest nation on earth, covering a Euro-Asian land mass of 22,402,200 sq. km. (8,649,490 sq. mi.), about two and one-half times the size of the United States, stretching 11,000 km. (6,000 mi.) from West to East (through 11 time zones), and 4,500 km. (3,000 mi.) North to South. Most of the country is above 50 degrees north latitude (Winnipeg, Canada). Obviously this geography has a marked influence on the distribution of publications. Some three-quarters of the people live in the Western, European part of the USSR, with a more highly developed transportation network and such large cities as Moscow, Leningrad and Kiev. Moscow is the political and publishing capital, with the major publishing houses of *Pravda* and *Izvestia* as well as central television and radio stations. To overcome geographical impediments, the Soviet regime has developed a decentralized printing network, republic radio centers and short-wave transmissions and, for television communication, space satellites and over 2,000 land-based relay stations.

However, with technological advances helping to shorten the vast geographical distances in the Soviet Union, the electronic media have been making great strides. Both radio and TV have expanded dramatically in recent years. This has been a blessing and a concern to Soviet leaders. On the one hand, politicization by radio can be communicated to Soviet citizens rapidly even in remote areas; on the other hand, possession of radios and TV sets dilutes the "collective" idea as it increases private listening and viewing. Moreover, short-wave radios (about two-thirds of total) can pick up foreign broadcasts, a detested reality that prompts Moscow to resort to jamming.

There is no individual, independent or private ownership of newspapers or other media in the Soviet Union; all are owned and operated by the ruling Communist party or by other Party or Party-approved "public organizations". Competition as known in the West is rejected by the Soviets as "complete subjugation of the mass circulation press to the will of the monopolies." On the contrary, constitutional and legislative provisions are cited—for example, "anti-state slander" and "agitation or propaganda"—to prevent any publication and dissemination of information not approved or controlled by the Communist party.

Distribution of newspapers and periodicals is the responsibility not of the publishers but of Soyuzpechat (acronym for Main Administration for the Distribution of Printed Matter), the state-owned network under the Ministry of Communication. The preponderance of the newspapers (about 80 percent) are purchased by subscription, and the remainder are sold at newstands or kiosks and at communication centers; newsstand sales are much higher in the larger cities, some of which also have automatic vending machines.

Subscription publications are picked up at the printing plant, sorted, wrapped, and transported by special units of the postal service system, which includes the periodical dispatch section. Dispatch units operate either at the printing plants or at the post offices. At the end of 1979 the Soviet Union had 90,000 post offices, and during that year the post offices handled some 43 billion copies of newspapers and magazines.

Soyuzpechat also conducts annual subscription campaigns. Orders are accepted throughout the year at all post offices, communication centers and distribution points, and also by a network of volunteers. For more timely deliveries of central newspapers, Moscow has been developing regional printing facilities. However, distribution in such a vast area, with severe climatic conditions and an underdeveloped transportation network, presents serious problems, including administrative inefficiency, manual handling, delays in deliveries, nondeliveries and superfluous copies of certain publications.

Distribution is most timely in the largest cities and in the western part of the country. The shortcomings tend to become worse in direct proportion to the delivery distance from Moscow.

State subsidies keep newspaper prices low by Western standards: generally two to four kopeks (about three cents to six cents). For example, the four-page *Trud* costs four kopeks (six cents), the six-page *Izvestia* and the six-page *Pravda* each three kopeks (four and a half cents) and *Pravda*'s eight-page edition four kopeks (six cents). The 24-page tabloid-size weekly *Za Rubezhom* costs 20 kopeks (about thirty cents).

Approximately 8,000 newspapers (with total circulation of 170 million copies), 5,000 magazines (with press runs of over 3 billion copies), and 85,000 books and brochures (1.8 billion copies) are published yearly. Nearly 500,000 hectares of forest are leveled annually, producing 4.5 million cubic meters of timber earmarked for paper. But despite Russia's vast areas of timberland there is a shortage of paper and of certain publications, especially books. The vice chairman of the State Committee for Publishing Houses, Printing Plants, and the Book Trade agreed that the problem cannot be solved only by the traditional forms of printing, and stated that the specialists on the committee were prepared to participate in activities connected with developing microform publications and making them widely available.

In 1978 the Communist party Central Committee, noting the scarce paper stocks, adopted a resolution for their more intelligent use, and also to improve the informational content of the magazines. The Central Committee reduced highly specialized literature by 10 percent in 1978, and made cutbacks in the size of over 300 magazines in 1979, releasing over 11,000 tons of paper for other use. In implementing the resolution, the committee provided more information per page and, with the saved paper, increased the press runs of the most popular publications—such as children's magazines. Magazine editorial-office associations are being established to coordinate planning, editing, and publishing to eliminate duplication. The establishment of an economically sound specialized magazine publishing house is seen as a "pressing problem." The Soviet goal is to create a system that will use the minimum amount of paper and still meet the nation's needs for its variety of periodicals.

Commercial advertising in either the print or electronic media has no influence on editorial policies. Promotion of Communist ideas and policies, on the other hand, is fulsome. Since the entire economy—sources, production, retailing—is state owned and operated, as are the media, advertising has been an inconsequential factor in the press industry. However, in recent years advertising has received more space to inform the population about available consumer goods. "Inform" is the operative word; it takes precedence over producing revenue.

Advertising in newspapers and magazines that carry it amounts to less than five percent of any issue. Television advertising is confined to one hour a week (7 to 8 p.m.) on Channel 2 of the Moscow Center. Radio ad announcements are heard at 6:45, 7:35, 8:35 and 11:35 a.m. and 12:15 p.m. on weekdays, 1:50 p.m. on Saturdays and 6:30 p.m. on Sundays.

Industrial relations are highly structured, in agreements signed early every year by a government enterprise administration and trade-union committee involved. The agreement obliges both parties to fulfill the production plan, improve the organization of production and labor, raise labor productivity and develop socialist competition. It also contains basic provisions on work and wages as established by law.

Although trade unions are considered to be the "embodiment of a tie between the CP and the toiling masses," strikes are prohibited. However, in the event of any strikes, slowdowns or other serious labor problems, coverage by the media would be refused and information on the incident suppressed. Should it become public, officials and the media would denounce or deny it or both. For example, U.S. press reports of strikes at two Soviet auto plants in May 1980 were repudiated by the official news agency Tass, which "regarded the inventions of these slanderers as nauseating."

Total employment in the "publishing industry" is approximately 500,000. Of the journalists some 63,000 are members of the USSR Union of Journalists. However, in addition to these professional reporters, and in accordance with the Party's policy of maintaining ties with the masses, the Soviet press utilizes "over 5 million" so-called "volunteer" worker-peasant correspondents ("*Rabselkor*"). Workers are members of trade unions, which are organized on an industrial basis. Those in some parts of the newspaper industry belong to the Communication Workers Union, Timber, Paper, and Woodworking Industry Workers Union and Cultural Workers Union. These and 27 other Communist party-controlled unions, with a membership of 127 million, are organized nationally under the Central Council of Trade Unions (AUCCTU) whose major purpose is not to campaign for workers' benefits but to assist management by exhorting workers to greater production and productivity. No "free" alternative unions are permitted. Recent efforts to establish them were thwarted.

Basic wage rates and fixed salaries are established by the Soviet government by agreement with the AUCCTU. Industrial (blue-collar) workers receive a wage determined by several factors including "skills requirement," working conditions and regional coefficients. Tables of "official salaries" are established by the Council of Min-

isters for managers and professional employees. Pay levels vary perceptibly. A typesetter may receive only about the average blue-collar wage, but a bonus for night work increases this markedly. Many "white-collar" employees receive valuable perquisites, especially those in the higher echelons. In 1980, for example, the editor in chief of *Pravda*, a member of the Central Committee, received 550 rubles ($820.90) a month, perhaps the highest. Other editors in chief of central newspapers may receive about 500 rubles ($746.27), deputy editors 400 rubles ($597.01), members of newspaper boards 300 rubles ($447.76), department heads 250 rubles ($373.13), and the average journalist 200 rubles ($298.51). Editors and journalists of local newspapers receive less than those on central organs. These are basic salaries. Many editors and journalists earn substantial extra income from their articles, other writing and bonuses; their perquisites—for some of more importance than the salary—include special housing, *dachas* (country houses), stores, clubs, honoraria and the opportunity to travel.

In return for higher pay and perquisites editors and journalists are expected—indeed required—to give total obedience to the ruling CP, of which most are members. While they are proscribed from writing critically of Marxist-Leninist ideology, Party leadership and negative aspects of Soviet society, reporters are able to pursue investigative reporting, of a sort. As such they can have a devastating effect in attacking individuals or groups for ostensible wrongdoing. Theoretically the accused has recourse under Article 7 of the Criminal Code, but in reality anyone so charged has virtually no chance against the powerful press that represents the Party, government or Party-sponsored organization. Frequently the accusation alone is synonymous with a verdict of guilty.

Some 4,000 printing enterprises are located throughout the USSR. The biggest and best houses use mostly offset and gravura printing. The largest of all, the Pravda printing house, also employs letterpress. Among its many publications are *Pravda, Komsomolskaya Pravda, Sovietskaya Rossiya, Sovietskaya Kultura,* the satirical *Krokodil* and the magazine *Kommunist.* Approximately 11 million daily copies of Pravda's newspapers comprise two-thirds of the Soviet Union's total, while the remainder are printed in 40 other cities throughout the country. Matrices are flown to 10 publishing centers, while the rest receive the material by teletype. The Izvestia Printing House publishes *Izvestia, Trud* ("Labor", organ of the trade unions) and *Moscow News* (in four languages). Matrices of *Izvestia* and *Trud* are sent by facsimile to 43 cities. The result is speedy delivery (usually the same day) of these major newspapers to all sections of the USSR, thus achieving more effective communication with citizens who, increasingly, have access to foreign broadcasters for the latest information.

Press Laws

Perhaps nothing has preoccupied Soviet leadership more than the dissemination of ideas. Lenin not only said "ideas are weapons" but "ideas become a force when they get hold of the masses." These expressions have guided Communist leaders and explain Soviet domestic and foreign communication policies, dominated totally by the Party.

As did the 1918 and 1936 documents, the 1977 Soviet Constitution provides for basic rights and freedoms. According to Article 50 "citizens of the USSR are guaranteed freedom of speech, of the press, and of assembly, meetings, street processions and demonstrations." Also, "Exercise of these political freedoms is ensured...by broad dissemination of information, and by the opportunity to use the press, television, and radio." Article 51 provides for "the right to associate in public organizations that promote their political activity and initiative and satisfaction of their various interests." Soviet spokesmen claim that political and economic shortcomings can be criticized, and that major Party and government decisions are open to discussion in the media.

A truer measure of these rights and freedoms is embodied in the constitutional provisions on "duties of the citizens of the USSR." According to Article 39, "Enjoyment by citizens of their rights and freedoms must not be to the detriment of the interests of society or the state, or infringe the rights of other citizens."

Since the Communist Party is the ultimate arbiter of these rights and duties, the constitutional provisions are thus only theoretical. Freedom-minded individuals, commonly referred to as "dissidents," have invoked constitutional provisions and Basket III of the Helsinki Agreements in pursuit of basic freedoms. Essentially, however, the Party's

monopoly role in the media effectively precludes any deviation from its policies, frequently in disregard of the constitution and the laws.

In 1917, shortly after the Bolsheviks seized power, Lenin signed the "Decree on the Press" and "General Regulations on the Press" which prohibited all competing print news-media and established censorship. As with the constitutional provisions, laws governing freedom of expression and the press follow the precedents set by Lenin, enabling the Party to maintain monopoly control of the media—which it exercises through its own organization, through an extensive government network and through dominance of public organizations.

The Criminal Code of the Russian Soviet Federated Socialist Republic (RSFSR), which took effect January 1, 1961, and similarly the codes of the other 14 Republics, essentially restrict freedom of speech and the press. Article 70 of the RSFSR Code, most frequently applied against dissidents, says: "Agitation or propaganda carried on for the purpose of subverting or weakening Soviet authority or of committing particular, especially dangerous crimes against the state, or circulating for the same purpose slanderous fabrications which defame the Soviet State and social system, or circulating or preparing or keeping for the same purpose, literature of such content, shall be punished by deprivation of freedom for a term of six months to seven years, with or without additional exile for a term of two to five years, or by exile for a term of two to five years."

Further, Article 71 forbids "propagandizing of war" and Article 72 bans "anti-Soviet organizations." Article 190-1 states: "The systematic circulation in an oral form of fabrications known to be false which defame the Soviet state and social system and, likewise, the preparation or circulation in written, printed or any form of works...shall be punished by deprivation of freedom for a term not exceeding three years, or by correctional tasks for a term not exceeding one year, or by a fine not exceeding 100 rubles."

Communist-controlled government agencies, including the judiciary, have acted against real or imagined violators of these provisions, or even in disregard of laws, as they proceed against dissenters and other "enemies of the state."

The Communist party, through its Central Committee, issues permits for publishing newspapers and magazines. Following the

October (1917) Revolution, anti-Communist newspapers were eliminated and a network of newspapers created by Communist party decrees and regulations. In addition, Party-controlled government and "public organizations" are permitted to publish newspapers. No others are allowed to exist legally. Newspapers are established or discontinued by the Party's Central Committee decrees or resolutions.

In addition to the constitutional provisions other press-related laws apply in the Soviet Union. Article 130 of the Criminal Code of the RSFSR covers "Defamation, that is, the circulating of fabrications known to be false which defame another person" and "work printed or reproduced by other means." Article 131 establishes punishment for "insult," and Article 228 for "making, circulating, or advertising pornographic writings, printed publications, pictures or any other articles of pornographic character, or trading in them or keeping them for the purpose of sale or dissemination...." "Blasphemy" had been included under Article 70 (Agitation and Propaganda) in the 1966 trial of writer Andrei Sinyavsky; the judge ruled that there was implied intent to depict Lenin negatively. State secrets, enumerated by decrees of the Council of Ministers, are chillingly well protected under Article 64 (treason), Article 65 (espionage), Article 75 (divulgence of state secrets). The last provides for deprivation of freedom (if not for treason or espionage) of from two to five years or, if serious consequences result, from five to eight years.

Under the constitution citizens are allowed to criticize the government: "Every citizen of the USSR has the right to submit proposals to state bodies and public organizations for improving their activity, and to criticize shortcomings in their work....Persecution for criticism is prohibited." And: "Citizens of the USSR have the right to lodge a complaint against the actions of officials, state bodies and public bodies." Among principles established for the press are criticism and self-criticism (kritika i samokritika), which theoretically encourage the press to include in criticism the performances of the Party and government. In early 1979 the Central Committee even created a "Department of Letters" and a "Sector for Analysis of Public Opinion, Sociological Research and Development" to gauge public opinion more effectively.

In reality, the only allowed criticism of the government bureaucracy or an economic en-terprise is that sanctioned by the Party, as in, say, published letters to the editor. Any other criticism—by dissidents, for example—is likely to be considered an anti-state activity. Information is controlled by the CP through parallel government organizations from the center down to localities. The Party utilizes the media fully in the "educational" process of the citizenry and in public discussion of economic and other shortcomings and reforms. However, the principle of "democratic centralism" applies—that is, once a decision is adopted by the Party, no criticism of that policy is allowed, only its non-performance. Marxism-Leninism and the pre-eminence of the Party and its leaders are outside the parameters of criticism.

Against dissidents, Soviet authorities frequently invoke Articles 70 and 190-1 of the Criminal Code—"anti-Soviet agitation and propaganda"—which, critics charge, are unconstitutional. Article 70 includes "slanderous fabrications which defame the Soviet State and social system" and provides for more severe penalties than the later Article 190-1.

Despite or because of the Party-government's unyielding stand on freedom of expression, the Soviet Union has spawned a nest of clandestine defiance—mainly in the form of underground literature and political propaganda that is produced on hidden typewriters or sometimes written in longhand (In the USSR this is called samizdat; self-publication.) Circulation figures, of course, are not available, but the few samizdat case histories mentioned below suggest that readership is far from negligible.

There are a number of well-known typed unofficial "journals." The Chronicle of Current Events, begun in 1968, uses the journalistic style of reporting on human rights. Poiski ("Searches"), a "fat journal" (tolsty zhurnal), reminiscent of a publication during the Tsarist period, was another attempt to type and distribute articles on public affairs. Six issues appeared in 1978 and 1979, when it was suppressed and its staff tried on charges of anti-Soviet slander; Valery Abramkin, the editor, was sentenced in 1980 to three years in prison. Metropole, a 1979 collection of uncensored anthologies, which ventured into new ideas, was "published" by 24 Soviet writers. Following an official rejection of their request to have it published, the journal was suppressed and the writers blacklisted, with some expelled from the Writers Union. The Woman and Russia (renamed Maria) was the first feminist underground magazine, writing critically of Soviet males and conditions. Initially the editors were merely harassed, but when the journal called on wives and mothers to persuade soldiers not to fight in Afghanistan, the KGB invaded the Leningrad apartment of three editors and issued an ultimatum to leave the Soviet Union or face trials; the three chose the former.

Jews in the USSR stopped publication in the summer of 1979 and a former editor and an emigration activist, Viktor Brailovsky, was arrested in November 1980 on a charge of "defaming the Soviet state and public order." *Khristianin* (Christian) press was started in 1971 by reform Baptists, who vainly submitted a written request to Prime Minister Aleksei Kosygin for legal approval. In 1974 the KGB discovered the printing press in Latvia, confiscated the equipment and arrested seven people preparing the printing of 15,000 copies of the Gospel. They were tried in March 1975 and sentenced to varying terms. However, the *Khristianin* press continued to issue reports and in 1977 and 1978 KGB repression led to more arrests and prison terms.

While some *samizdat* journals are eliminated, others are "published," including the *Chronicle of the Lithuanian Catholic Church,* the Lithuanian *Ausra* ("The Dawn"), *Vytis* ("The Knight"), *Ateitis* ("The Future") and *Pastoge* ("Shelter").

Soviet authorities are continually watchful not only for *samizdat* but for *tamizdat* ("published there"—meaning the West) and *magnitizdat* (tape recordings), which they neither control nor influence. The authorities attempt to confiscate these upon discovery, and harass and interrogate their editors, many of whom are prosecuted and imprisoned.

Censorship

Restrictions on expression and freedom of the press—indeed on all publications—are imposed by several government and Party organizations. Under the control and direction of the CP, the most important government censorship agency is the Main Administration for Safeguarding State Secrets in the Press *(Glavnoye Upravlenie po Okhrane Gosudarstvennykh Tayn v Pechati),* under the Council of Ministers. Its common name continues to be Glavlit, acronym for the first

organization, which has existed in various forms since 1922. Glavlit's responsibilities are to "exercise all aspects of politico-ideological, military and economic control over productions of the press, manuscripts, photographs, pictures, etc., intended for publication or distribution, and also over radio broadcasts, lectures and exhibitions." Similar control has been exercised over television transmissions.

Glavlit functionaries are assigned to all publishing enterprises with responsibility for pre-publication censorship. The "glavlitchik," as the censor is called, reads the copy twice before the printing and is the last official to study the final proofs; thus even the final editorial changes are screened by him. Major newspapers, such as *Literaturnaya Gazeta,* may have two glavitchiks, while local papers are likely to have only one.

For guidance Glavlit representatives have a manual (popularly known as the "Talmud") containing lists of prohibited materials that are continually updated. When the censor is satisfied with the "purity" of the issue, his Glavlit number of approval is affixed to the publication. Failure to detect the publication of a "state secret" may lead to eight years' imprisonment.

In addition, the (State) Committee for State Security, KGB *(Komitet Gosudarstvennoy Bezopasnosti),* is concerned with the prevention of undesirable information and the dissemination of misinformation. It is the principal controlling agency against Soviet dissidents and their *samizdat* materials. KGB also conducts covert information programs abroad, while the Party Central Committee's International and International Information Departments, under Politburo's direction, manage Soviet foreign propaganda operations.

Perhaps the most pervasive form of pre-publication censorship exists in the outlook created by the Party-controlled system. Throughout their entire upbringing, Soviet citizens are imbued with the idea of conformist behavior. The directors of press and publication enterprises are CP stalwarts, as are chief editors, members of the editorial boards, department heads and many of the writers and journalists. Policy guidances are established by supervisory personnel of the publications, conferences with Party officials and leads contained in Tass dispatches and *Pravda* editorials. With training and experience, professional personnel develop an acute sensitivity to the approved and forbidden—

which results in a kind of "self-censorship" mentality.

Perhaps the best way to illustrate the effect of the Soviet censorship system in practice is in the strikes in Poland and the invasion of Afghanistan.

The Polish trauma began with the July 1, 1980 Polish government increase in meat prices, which resulted in widespread strikes and received heavy media coverage within Poland and in the Western countries, including the United States. However, Soviet media hardly mentioned these developments until August 19, when Tass, Radio Moscow, and USSR TV referred to a speech by Polish Party chief Edward Gierek the previous day; on August 20 *Pravda* carried a summary of it. The reports referred to "work stoppages" rather than "strikes" and played up "anti-socialist elements." Subsequent coverage was sparse, highly selective and distorted. On August 25 Tass filed a substantial summary of Gierek's speech—quoting Gierek on the formation of the new trade union, based on free, secret and democratic elections—but *Pravda* and Radio Moscow ignored this development.

Increasingly the West became the critical target of Soviet media, which themselves grew more vitriolic in tone. On August 25 a Tass political commentator accused the United States and Western Europe of "making use of the present situation as an excuse for expanding a licentious, slanderous campaign whose goal is to blacken and discredit socialism." Two days later Tass charged the Western media with "performing an openly instigative function." When Tass reported the Polish government-union agreement on September 1 it made no mention of the independent trade unions. Instead the Soviet media zeroed in on Western "imperialist circles" and political leaders—singling out President Carter for his "notorious human rights policy"—and alleging "interference in Polish internal affairs." Also attacked was AFL-CIO President Lane Kirkland for his own "interference."

Coverage of Prime Minister Jozef Pinkowski's September 5 speech to the Polish *Sejm* (Parliament) was selective, referring only to his remarks on the role of trade unions and deleting his favorable comments about the Catholic Church. It was not until September 6 that Tass mentioned the Polish strike leader Lech Walesa by name for the first time. The word "strike" had been first used on August 31 but was hardly seen or heard in subsequent reports. Tass's spotty coverage of the mounting Polish crisis continued through autumn. Speeches by Stanislaw Kania, the new prime minister, were reported in detail, but Tass also failed to mention such items as shortages of meat supplies, strikes, Party demotions, and free election of Party authorities. However, Tass eventually included Kania's reference to the "new trade unions," the first clear, direct admission of their existence in the Soviet media. No reference to Soviet troops in Poland was made in the Soviet media until November 3, when Radio Volga mentioned that Soviet political officers visited a Polish unit.

The Soviet Union justified its December 27, 1979 invasion of Afghanistan as rendering support to revolutionary "fighters for true freedom." In February 1980 *Pravda* reported that the Soviet-backed "Revolutionary Council called on the people to create voluntary detachments for the fight against killers, saboteurs and thieves." The Soviet leaders and media had labeled Afghan resistance fighters as "counterrevolutionaries" and charged the West with "interfering in the internal affairs" of Afghanistan with weapons and propaganda. At an October 16, 1980 dinner for Afghan President Babrak Karmal, Brezhnev attacked the United States in strong language: "Feverish military preparations and unrestrained propaganda—even, it might be said, eulogizing of nuclear war—have reached an unprecedented level in the United States." These themes were carried uniformly by the Soviet media throughout the first year of the Red Army invasion and occupation of Afghanistan. The Soviet citizen would never know from information supplied by domestic media that the Soviet Army in Afghanistan totaled upwards of 100,000 troops, and that thousands had been killed in actions against Afghan tribesmen—perhaps the best guerrilla fighters in the world.

State-Press Relations

In the Soviet Union, domestic and foreign information policy and guidance are in the hands of the highest echelon of the Communist party, the Politburo. Control and supervision are exercised by two departments of the Central Committee: the International Information Department (IID) and the Propaganda Department (PD). The information programs are administered through an extensive government structure at various levels.

The IID, created in 1978, has the responsibility for Tass and Novosti, the two Soviet news-information agencies, and for *Pravda, Izvestia,* Radio Moscow and the information sections of the embassies. PD controls printing, publishing and distribution; journals, newspapers, television and radio; Party propaganda, mass agitation, and cultural and educational work.

The major publishing and printing enterprises are supervised by the Council of Ministers, through the State Committee for Publishing Houses, Printing Plants, and the Book Trade. The electronic media are administered by the State Committee for Television and Radio, also under the Council of Ministers.

Management of news is painstakingly thorough. Domestic and foreign stories are reported by Tass in accordance with strict Party requirements. Importation of foreign information is rigidly scrutinized and censored. Similarly analyses, features, cartoons, photographs and all other reportage in the newspapers and periodicals are prepared to advance Communist objectives and reflect current Party policies. Should censorship discover objectionable items in any copy, its writers and editors are promptly chastised, even subjected to punitive action. Thus, the only alternative Soviet citizens have in reporting non-censored information is through their own limited devices, including word of mouth and the *samizdat* of the human-rights activists or dissidents.

The Georgian journalist and musicologist Merab Kostava was arrested in 1977. Together with a Georgian poet and other dissidents, he was charged with "anti-Soviet agitation and propaganda" for being involved with the *samizdat* journals *The Golden Fleece* and *The Georgian Herald.*

Yevgeny Barras, a Jew and a former reporter for *Moskovskaya Pravda, Komsomolskaya Pravda* and *Sovietska Kultura,* requested permission in 1973 to emigrate with his family to Israel, an unpatriotic act. He was refused. Unable to find employment as a journalist, he was a porter in a dairy in 1977.

Vyacheslav Chornovil, a journalist, was one of a number of Ukrainian Nationalist dissidents arrested in January, 1972. Author of *The Chornovil Papers* (reports on Soviet 1964–65 trials published in Western Europe), he was tried for "fabrications" slandering the Soviet state and sentenced in 1967 to three years in labor camps, later reduced to 18 months. Upon release he worked as a railwayman and continued to write critically about abuses of Socialist legality in *samizdat* journals. In 1973 he was tried on charges of "anti-Soviet agitation and propaganda"; after 13 months of detention he was sentenced to seven years' imprisonment and five years' exile.

Others were blacklisted for allegedly contributing to *samizdat* journals. On October 1, 1980 several editors of the unofficial journal *Polski* were convicted of wrongdoing. They were Valerii Abramkin, convicted of anti-Soviet slander under Article 190-1 of the RSFSR Criminal Code and given the maximum sentence of three years' deprivation of freedom. Yurii Grimm, sentenced to three years in a labor camp for anti-Soviet slander; and Victor Sokirko, given a three-year suspended sentence after pleading guilty to a charge of anti-Soviet slander.

Viktor Railovsky, a computer expert and an editor of the *samizdat* journal *Jews in the USSR* (which ceased publication in 1979), was arrested in November 1980 on a charge of "defamation of the Soviet state and public order."

Attitude Toward Foreign Media

For a foreign reporter to become accredited, the correspondent's organization must initiate the procedure by submitting a written application to the Soviet embassy for a visa and certification as a resident correspondent in the Soviet Union. The embassy forwards the nomination to the Ministry of Foreign Affairs (Press Department: Otdel Pechati) in Moscow. After an extensive investigation, a decision is made to issue a visa entitling the correspondent and his dependents to enter the country. On arrival in Moscow, the Foreign Ministry issues a certification *(udostoverenie),* which is both a press identification and, in effect, an internal passport, renewable yearly. The visa procedure normally takes four to six weeks, sometimes longer.

In considering accreditation important factors appear to be the nominee's background, his (and his organization's) views of the Soviet Union and Communism (and for Americans, the existing East–West—especially U.S.–Soviet—political relations). In 1978 Moscow refused to accept the bureau chief of the Italian *Corriera della Sera* because of his "interest" in Soviet dissidents. However, rejections are not too frequent because a quid pro quo is usually applied.

Visa procedures for special assignments (say, two to three weeks) begin with the visa application to a Soviet embassy. The support of the application—by Soviet Radio, TV, Tass or some other Soviet organ—is required for timely approval; otherwise the waiting period may be lengthy. The Soviet Foreign Ministry presently cables or calls the embassy with its decision.

In Moscow the foreign correspondent is dependent for all services (translator, driver, maid and others) on the UPDK (Administration for Servicing the Diplomatic Corps of the Ministry of Foreign Affairs). The correspondents, especially TV reporters, face hardships and obstacles unknown in the West. Western journalists in particular are severely limited in obtaining access to high-ranking officials (despite the theoretical possibility to speak to such officials directly), sources (notably "dissidents") and long-distance travel facilities. Travel within Moscow is hampered by occasional surveillance and harassment , but out-of-capital movement is even more difficult. Travel requests must be filed 48 hours in advance, with the Foreign Ministry detailing the itinerary. TV applications can take as many as eight months for a decision, which may be negative. The degree of harassment appears to correspond to the temperature of bilateral political relations.

Prior to establishing residence in Moscow, foreign correspondents are issued single or multiple entry-exit visas for themselves and their dependents, usually for one year, renewable yearly. If a single entry visa is granted, the multiple visa can be obtained in Moscow. Issuance of visas for some correspondents has been delayed, denied, or limited to a shorter period of time. In 1979 the visa of David Satter, an American correspondent for London's *Financial Times,* who was attacked by Soviet newspapers for his reporting and alleged "hooligan" behavior, was renewed for only six weeks, a punitive measure, while his case was being considered. The United States and the USSR have a reciprocity arrangement regarding the number of accreditations; this is often applied to expulsions. Currently, the Soviet Union has more correspondents in the United States than Americans have in Moscow. However, this situation exists not because of Soviet limitations but due to practical considera-

tions by the Americans, the cost of maintaining a bureau in Moscow being the dominant factor.

Until 1961 resident correspondents were required to submit their copy to a censor at the Central Telegraph Office who had authority to approve the dispatch or delete objectionable material. Today, stories can be filed directly by telex, cable or telephone. And since the Helsinki security and cooperation conferences of 1975 and 1978, photographs, videotape and unprocessed film can also be sent by accredited foreign correspondents without censorship. However, the dispatches are suspected to be monitored by Soviet functionaries, and organizations such as AP, UPI and Reuters, which have agreements with Tass for sending photos, may occasionally be refused. Tass has refused to transmit a photo of two policemen removing a woman from outside the U.S. Embassy, and pictures showing the Soviet wife of a U.S. professor who chained herself to the embassy fence to protest Soviet refusal to allow her to emigrate to the United States. However, such material can be dispatched later from a foreign country.

In recent years there has been a shift from preventive to punitive censorship. Authorities have displayed almost paranoiac sensitivity to reporting of the Soviet scene by Western foreign correspondents. Because of its reciprocal agreements, Moscow seldom jails foreign correspondents, but its resort to harassment has often served to handcuff and almost blindfold "hostile" reporters. Harassment measures include tapped telephones, private reprimands, media attacks, official warnings, exclusion from high-level interviews, denial of travel requests, threats to local contacts, physical jostling, slashing of auto tires, legal charges, and finally expulsion. Soviet authorities are especially sensitive to foreign TV correspondents, who are no longer dependent on the state-controlled Novosti agency or the State Committee for Television and Radio Broadcasting for camera crews. Since 1978 TV networks, including NBC, CBS and ABC have been allowed for the first time to have their own camera crews with the most modern newsgathering equipment, such as electronic cameras. However, official approval for out-of-town coverage and restrictive shooting constitute prior and on-the-spot censorship to guard against alleged "anti-Soviet" transmissions.

The strongest anti-Western tactics—arrest

or expulsion from the Soviet Union, or both—are not common, but neither are they unknown.

William Cole, CBS News correspondent, was expelled in 1973 for filming interviews with Soviet dissidents Andrei Amalrik and Vladimir Bukovsky. (Both Russians were tried, convicted and imprisoned). CBS was not permitted to assign a reporter until twenty months later. The AP's George Krimsky, accused by *Literaturnaya Gazeta* of being a CIA agent, was detained briefly in 1977 while covering a dissident demonstration, then expelled on charges of currency violations and spying, which AP denied. (In retaliation, Tass correspondent Vladimir Alexeyev was expelled from Washington; the State Department voiced its regret over "a step backward from the objective of improving working conditions for journalists contained in the Helsinki Final Act and from the more fundamental interests of promoting a freer flow of information.")

On the eve of the follow-up Helsinki Conference held in Belgrade in 1979, Robert Toth of the *Los Angeles Times* was seized by Soviet security agents in Moscow for allegedly receiving "state secrets" from a scientist on parapsychology. The State Department protested his detention and interrogation, and President Carter himself expressed concern. However, Toth was seized and questioned again. The U.S. Embassy lodged three formal protests over these summary arrests and interrogations, which lasted more than 13 hours. Toth was finally permitted to leave the Soviet Union.

Moscow expelled Austrian radio/TV correspondent Edward Hutter in 1978 for alleged "offenses against Soviet law"; in the following year Robert Stengl of West German TV and his cameraman were expelled for "anti-Soviet reporting".

Some Western correspondents have gotten off more easily. In 1978 British journalist Nora Beloff was held at the Hungarian border for 24 hours for allegedly "spreading hostile propaganda." A CBS correspondent, physically assaulted by the KGB after filming a gun-battle, was forced—together with a Reuters reporter—to surrender his film. A UPI photographer was also manhandled by plainclothes police when he tried to photograph the same scene. In 1979 David Satter, an American employed by London's *Financial Times,* was first attacked in the media, then found his car and office vandalized.

Soviet authorities also attempt to restrict citizen contact with foreign press representatives, preferring instead to have the latter go through official channels. The attempted "sanitizing" includes special apartments for foreign correspondents, with guards. For their part Soviet citizens who contact Western reporters face warnings or even jail. The result has been greater isolation of Western correspondents and reticence on the part of ordinary Russians even to greet the "outsiders."

Import restrictions on foreign publications are exacting. The major responsibility for banning foreign publications considered "anti-Soviet" is discharged by the censors. Disallowed materials include those deemed anti-Communist, subversive and pornographic. The censors scrutinize minutely reading materials of foreign tourists, as well as printed and illustrated matter of U.S. and other Western participants at Soviet-sponsored exhibits.

Contrary to the Helsinki Accords on the free flow of information, the Soviet Union imposes drastic limits on sales of Western newspapers and magazines. A Soviet promise in 1976, following Helsinki, that 12 Western newspapers would be placed on sale has been kept: the Western journals found at the Intourist hotels, generally maintained for foreigners, are mostly communist organs like London's *Morning Star.* Perhaps only about 50 copies each of such papers as the *International Herald Tribune, The Times* of London and *Le Monde* of Paris are delivered through the Soviet Post Office—mainly to designated institutions and individuals. In January 1981 *The New York Times* sent 19 copies of the weekday and 27 of the Sunday editions, all by subscription.

The availability of Western newspapers increases during extraordinary events when large numbers of foreigners are present. During the 1980 Olympics Western publications were available at hotels and at the special newsstand in the Press Center; the conclusion of the Olympics was accompanied by the disappearance of the newspapers. One can spend a two- or three-year tour in Moscow without seeing a noncommunist Western newspaper for sale.

In 1972 the Soviet Union proposed that UNESCO adopt a covenant regulating the international dissemination of mass information. The rationale for the Soviet position was that the mass media, employed in the "irrevocable ideological struggle," are incompatible with detente and peaceful coexistence. Thus, Moscow favored UNESCO's 1978 Declaration on Fundamental Principles "as an important move against alleged 'information imperialism.'" The 1980 UNESCO General Conference at Belgrade adopted by consensus a resolution to postpone until its 1983 conference the nonaligned nations' restrictive proposal, supported by the Soviet Union, for a "New World Information and Communications Order."

Most Western nations and news organizations fear this would inhibit correspondents and restrict the "free flow of information" as contained in the Helsinki Final Act and as provided in Article 19 of the Universal Declaration of Human Rights. At its annual meeting following Belgrade the Inter-American Press Association resolved: "To energetically condemn the efforts of UNESCO and some nations to promote a New World Order of Information and Communication if the proposals continue to be designed to establish marked totalitarian policies which will help governments gain absolute domination and control of social communication media."

The Soviet position was fully in accordance with the principle of "irreconcilability of the ideological struggle," and with its effort to minimize and censor Western—and maximize communist—dissemination of information programs and influences in nonaligned countries.

News Agencies

The Soviet Union has two news agencies with clearly defined functions: Tass (*Telegrafnoye Agentstvo Sovietskovo Soyuza*: Telegraph Agency of the Soviet Union) and Novosti (*Agenstvo Pechati Novosti* or APN: The News Press Agency). The latter, created in 1961 by several organizations, is basically a quasi-official information agency (if any Soviet news agency can be called quasi-official) that distributes a variety of materials, especially features about the Soviet Union, to foreign countries and also disseminates information about foreign countries to domestic media. Tass, a state monopoly, is in effect the single official Soviet news agency. It consists of the central office in Moscow, a network of 72 correspondent offices and three bureaus in the RSFSR, and news agencies in the 14 other Union Republics. Tass dissemi-

nates news, features and photos to the central press, to republic, provincial and specialized enterprises and to radio and television.

Since 1971 Tass has functioned directly under the USSR Council of Ministers, with ministerial rank. However, effective control is maintained by the Central Committee of the CP. The managing board is composed of the director general, several deputies and heads of editorial departments (including foreign and domestic news services, Communist Countries, photographic service and sports desk), a central communications board concerned with technical operations, the currency financial department and other subdivisions.

Tass has some 500 correspondents and 360 photographic reporters to prepare domestic reports at the central office. It also has a network of cable teleprinters connecting Moscow with 300 cities. The news services of Tass are disseminated to 3,700 Soviet newspapers and 50 radio and 80 television stations.

According to Tass, its bureaus and correspondents in 1980 were accredited to 125 countries, and it also has agreements for news-service exchange with other world and national agencies. Tass itself provides services to more than 400 news and press agencies, information ministries, editorial boards of newspapers and journals and television and radio broadcasting companies in 93 countries. It transmits to and receives daily information from nearly 500 newspaper pages in Russian, English, French, Spanish, German and Arabic. Some 550 hours are transmitted by radio teleprinter daily over 150,000 km (93,000 mi.) of international lines. From 5 to 6.5 million photographs and over 2 million plastic plates are disseminated to Soviet and foreign subscribers annually. News agencies of the communist countries are linked with Tass's Photo International Communication Circuit, through which topical photo services are exchanged by phototelegraph. Novosti claims to have information exchanges with more than 100 international and national agencies, over 100 radio and television companies, more than 7,000 foreign newspapers and magazines published in 65 languages, and 120 publishing houses. Further Novosti claims there are correspondents in 80 countries and an annual transmission to foreign media of 60,000 articles and more than 2 million photo prints.

Tass's ministerial rank indicates the importance assigned to its information by Soviet leaders. The republic news agencies, which disseminate Tass's material and report local news, are also controlled by Tass, ensuring ideological and political conformity at all levels. A former Tass director has emphasized that information must necessarily contain the Party's interpretation: "Soviet information not only contains facts but analyzes them in a Marxist way...it serves the cause of Communism, the cause of fighting the bourgeois ideology hostile to us."

Tass correspondents claim that they attempt to file stories from their countries that are significant, interesting and of quality to be published or broadcast. However, they are mindful of official domestic constraints placed on them, as well as bilateral (such as U.S.-Soviet) and international relations—the latter focusing largely on support of the Third World.

Interpretation and censorship have caused Tass to be habitually slower with its reports than its competitors. Some news is not even reported, especially when "undesirable." Foreign news agencies, correspondents, and broadcasters have almost continually scooped Tass, even on Soviet domestic events. In addition, Tass's customers—domestic and foreign—complain about its dull, lackluster and cliché-ridden style.

Tass also distributes specially prepared confidential foreign and domestic information for targeted groups. The so-called White Tass bulletin goes to such recipients as editors and columnists for reference purposes, the "Red Tass" to high-level Party, government and media leaders. But the most information is received by the highest-level officials, including Politburo members.

Novosti claims non-government status but within the Soviet system the content of its materials must of necessity enhance Marxism-Leninism, Soviet policies and Communist achievements. Novosti disseminates news features, commentaries and photographs, largely for external use but also run domestically. It publishes books and magazines, and provides services to foreign correspondents within the USSR.

A CIA report notes that both Tass and Novosti disseminate much of their material to the foreign press without charge. Thus the volume is not an entirely valid measure of their impact.

Major foreign news agencies have bureaus in Moscow, including AP, UPI, Reuters, AFP, DPN and the communist countries. Numerous newspapers, magazines, radio and television organizations have resident correspondents. Other correspondents cover special events (such as the Olympics), or are on ad hoc assignments. The 17 U.S. bureaus in 1979 included *The New York Times, Christian Science Monitor, The Washington Post, Newsweek, Time,* ABC, CBS and NBC.

Electronic News Media

While traditionally the press has occupied the leading position in the Soviet media, radio and TV, state monopolies, have shown spectacular growth in recent years. The development has been prompted by the country's geographical expanse, technological improvements, and competition from international broadcasters.

Of necessity, Tass, the official news agency, feels compelled today to feed TV with fast-breaking news, ahead of the slower newspapers, in order to cope with possible domestic leaks, avoid being scooped by Western broadcasters and to give events the official Soviet interpretation.

As with the Soviet press, the electronic media are designed to further the official state policies. Accordingly, the Party guidelines to the print media apply to radio and TV as well: not only to function as channels of information but, more purposefully, to serve the Soviet state by inculcating and propagandizing. Journalism training and indoctrination, the levers of control, general directives and current guidances are essentially the same for Soviet radio and TV as for Soviet print media.

Censorship is to radio and TV broadcasts as it is to newspapers and magazines. Both radio and TV operate under the State Committee for Radio and Television, which is vertically organized through various administrative levels. Radio programs emanate from Central Broadcasting in Moscow, through republic and regional stations, down to the local radio-diffusion exchanges (a wired system). Television programs are transmitted by Central and relay stations and also by a satellite system. Soviet TV is connected to the East European Intervision (*Intervideniye*) System. In comformity with ideological principles and Party directives, Soviet newscasts are highly structured and predictably dull. The news is selective and not always the latest; commentaries and features always support the Party policies and reflect favorably on the Soviet and other communist societies.

Without an alternative news network, Soviet citizens often turn to external radio-TV outlets. There are numerous opportunities to listen to short-wave foreign broadcasters, despite Moscow's continued jamming of Radio Liberty (RL) and renewed jamming (during the Polish crisis) of the Voice of America, Deutsche Welle, and the BBC. The location of some Soviet listeners makes it possible for them to receive certain European domestic transmissions that are not jammed.

Listeners need not understand English to receive BBC and VOA broadcasts. BBC broadcasts in Russian 33.2 hours weekly; while VOA broadcasts in Russian 112 hours weekly, Ukrainian 28, Armenian 8¾, Georgian 8¾ and Uzbek 7. VOA also has programs in the Estonian, Latvian and Lithuanian languages (8¾ hours each weekly), and in English to Europe (63 hours weekly). RL is the most prolific broadcaster, transmitting 462 hours weekly to the Soviet Union in Russian and 14 other languages, about work events and developments within the Soviet Union itself. Others broadcasting to the Soviet Union are the People's Republic of China (154 hours weekly in Russian), Sweden, the Vatican, Israel, Canada and Luxembourg.

The impact of foreign broadcasts on the Soviet regime and the media has been substantial. It is estimated that out of 115 million radio sets (1980), 45 million are short wave, and word-of-mouth communication is enormous in this information-deprived society. Jamming has interfered with but not prevented listening; Moscow simply does not have the capability to isolate its population from the outside world and from each other. With Soviet media ignoring certain events critical of the USSR abroad or delaying the reporting of others (such as the death of Prime Minister Kosygin in December 1980 by 36 hours), the inquisitive populace is naturally turned to other sources. Foreign broadcasters, too, carry news and features of ethnic, religious, and dissident activities differently from the way official Soviet media would handle them, if at all. RL, on the other hand, not only reports dissidence but airs verbatim readings of *samizdat* material.

In 1964, to supplement jamming, Moscow established a competitive radio station ("*Mayak*"), which broadcasts continuously on current issues (through, for example, Radio Moscow's "International Observers Roundtable"), and attacks foreign broadcasters for allegedly conducting "psychological warfare," resuming the "Cold War" and "interfering in Soviet internal affairs."

Education & Training

Major Soviet universities, with departments and faculties of journalism, grant a regular degree following a five-year full-time or six-year night school and correspondence course of study. Dating from early 1950s these faculties have contributed significantly to the improved professionalism of journalism in the USSR. The largest and most prestigious faculty of journalism is at Moscow State University; others are at major Russian and republic universities, such as Leningrad, Vladivostok, Kiev and Tashkent. Moscow's Institute of International Relations has a Faculty of International Journalism. The Academy of Social Sciences, under the Central Committee of the CP, has a Chair of Journalists and a Chair of Literature, Art and Journalism. These are choice postgraduate assignments given to those destined for ranking positions. Upon completion of the five-year journalism course at Moscow State or one of the other universities, the new graduates are assigned by the Faculty of Journalism to a newspaper (the majority), or to radio or television. Some become journalists by training at the publication itself, including work with Tass.

Additional training for working journalists consists of in-service programs conducted under the auspices of the Union of Journalists, and of advanced courses prepared by the union and various university journalism faculties.

Moscow State University has a Chair of Television and Radio Broadcasting, while other journalism faculties of some other major universities (such as Kiev) have sections to prepare radio-TV specialists.

The USSR Union of Journalists (*Soyuz Zhurnalistov SSSR*), organized in 1959 and totaling 63,000 in January 1979, is open to journalists, photographers, artists and editors who have been employed in the press, radio, television, news agencies and publishing houses for at least three years, and have "displayed high professional skill." A board of directors manages the union's activities, and a secretariat directs professional and organizational matters. The union has branches at various levels, down to primary units at editorial offices. The Central House of Journalists is in Moscow.

According to its statutes, the union's duty is to "actively propagate the great thoughts of scientific communism, Soviet patriotism and socialist internationalism,...[and] to participate in an unceasing struggle for peace, democracy and progress, against hostile bourgeois ideology, colonialism and imperialism." A member of the International Union of Journalists (IOJ)—controlled by the Soviet Union, with headquarters in Prague—the union publishes the monthly magazine *Zhurnalist* ("Journalist"), the weekly *Za Rubezhom* ("Abroad") which carries reprints of foreign press articles, Sovietskoefoto ("Soviet Photo"), *Informatsionnyi Vestnik* ("Information Bulletin"), and Demokraticheskii Zhurnalist ("Democratic Journalist"), the Russian-language publication of IOJ.

Some journalists who have published books may become members of the more prestigious USSR Union of Writers (*Soyuz Pisateley SSSR*), and many Soviet writers contribute to newspapers and magazines. Their major role is ideological and political rather than creative. The Union of Writers had a membership of 8,344 in January 1979. The Moscow Branch has about 1,910 members, half of whom are also CP members. The union publishes the weekly *Literaturnaya Gazeta* ("Literary Newspaper"). Those members considered politically unreliable (concerned, say, over the fate of dissidents) are expelled from the union and thus deprived of access to publishing—leading them to despair and for some, who published abroad, forced emigration. An attempt by a number of young writers in 1980 to form an independent club ("*Belles Lettres*") to publish experimental works was rejected.

Two awards, both monetary, are made exclusively to journalists. The prestigious Vorovsky Prize (*Premiya Vorovsky*) is awarded by the USSR Union of Journalists for foreign reporting, and The Union of Journalists' Prize is given for domestic reporting.

Summary

The Soviet and Western media have nothing in common. All media are owned and controlled rigidly by the state and Communist party. Only the Party, State and approved "public organizations" are permitted to publish and broadcast. In this monopolistic system information flows from the center to the lowest level. No individuals or competing groups are allowed to function. While the constitution and legislative acts provide for "guarantees" of basic rights and freedoms, in reality the authorities have rejected all attempts by dissidents for even a modicum of freedom. Despite repressions, the courageous and enterprising dissidents have managed, by *samizdat*, to distribute copies from hand to hand and, through foreign journalists and international broadcasters, communicate with the Soviet public. While Moscow severely restricts the import of Western publications, an increasing number of Soviet citizens has access to information transmitted by Western broadcasters. Soviet restrictions on the free flow of information are clearly illustrated by its jamming of the Voice of America and other foreign broadcasters, a fact that was noted at the Madrid Conference on the Helsinki Accords in December 1980.

More than the print media, radio and TV have had substantial growth, resulting in greater access to international broadcasters while more listening and viewing now takes place in privacy than in collectives.

With the continuing increase in the population and the Party's recognition of the power of the media to communicate ideas, the Soviet regime will likely continue to control all media as rigidly as possible to prevent any opposition party, organization or medium from surfacing, and to attempt to minimize outside information influences. With international attention focused on Soviet adherence to, or violations of, the Helsinki Accords, internal dissidents can be expected to campaign, however unsuccessfully, for the regime's responsiveness to basic human rights, including alternative organizations and freedom of travel and expression. Soviet authorities can be expected to reject any attempts to create competing organs and suppress all alleged "anti-state" activities.

CHRONOLOGY

The major highlight of press history in the past five years has been the continuation of the struggle for freedom of thought, press and expression—the freedom of basic human rights, as provided for in Article 19 of Universal Declaration of Human Rights and the

Helsinki Accords. Thwarted from exercising these rights openly, human rights activists reverted to *samizdat*. A number of these have been of religious orientation. Moreover, various Helsinki "observer groups" were organized.

The major *samizdat* work has been the *Chronicle of Current Events,* founded in 1968, which continues to function despite harassment, intimidation, trials, imprisonment and banishment of its editors and contributors. The *Chronicle* and other *samizdat* documents have in effect challenged the regime's monopoly on mass information and literature.

1974	Alexander Solzhenitsyn, author, expelled for his support of the dissidents and his depiction of life under Soviet rule. In 1970 he had won a Nobel Prize in literature for the ethical force with which he pursued the indispensable traditions of Russian literature. He now lives in the United States, continuing his crusade for human rights.
1976	Andrei Amalrik, writer and human rights activist, twice exiled to Siberia, leaves Soviet Union under pressure. In November 1980 he is killed in auto accident in Spain on way to conference of dissidents in Madrid.
1977-79	CP decrees on printing and reduction of periodical publications to avoid thematic duplication, cut sizes of hundreds of journals and reallocate thousands of tons of paper for more popular publications, especially children's. Helsinki "observer groups" in Moscow,

Kiev, Vilnius, Tbilisi and Yerevan organize to report violations of Helsinki Accords, members announce their participation and sign reports, many arrested or permitted to emigrate.

1978	The three major U.S. TV networks (NBC, CBS, ABC) and others permitted to bring own camera crews to Moscow. In reorganizing its foreign propaganda mechanism, CP establishes International Information Department within Central Committee, with control over Tass, Novosti, Pravda, Izvestia Radio Moscow and Embassy Information sections, for more effective programming.
1979	CP Central Committee Decree "On Further Improvement of Ideological and Political-Educational Work" provides mass media with high-level policy on agitation and propaganda, outlines program of press action, including study of public opinion. Andrei Sakharov, Nobel Prize winner, physicist and human rights activist, is exiled to Gorki in December, following his condemnation of Soviet invasion of Afghanistan.
1980	Sakharov prohibited from communicating with foreigners, requests open court hearing. Voices inside Soviet Union and in outside world, especially Western countries—including the CPs of France, Italy, Spain —criticize his exile. In January 1980 Council of Ministers strips Sakharov of title of "Hero of Socialist Labor" and of other prizes and awards.

BIBLIOGRAPHY

Austin, Anthony, "Letter from Moscow: The Metropol Affair." *The New York Times Book Review,* March 2, 1980, p. 3.

Barghoorn, Frederick C. *Soviet Foreign Propaganda.* Princeton, N.J., 1964.

Binyon, Michael. "Paper Where Tomorrow's News Began Yesterday." *The Times,* February 22, 1980, p. 1.

Buzek, Antony. *How the Communist Press Works.* New York, 1964.

Conquest, Robert, ed. *The Politics of Ideas in the U.S.S.R.* New York, 1967.

Dewhirst, Martin, and Farrell, Robert. *The Soviet Censorship.* Metuchen, N.J., 1973.

Fromson, Murray. "Dateline Moscow: Censorship of Our TV News." *Columbia Journalism Review,* September–October 1975, p. 32.

Gorokhoff, Boris I. *Publishing in the U.S.S.R.* Bloomington, Ill., 1959.

Great Soviet Encyclopedia. Tanslation of 3d ed., vols. 1-25. New York, 1970-80.

Hannah, Gayle Durham. *Soviet Information Networks.* 1977.

Harasymiw, Bohdan, ed. *Education and the Mass Media in the Soviet Union and Eastern Europe.* New York, 1975.

Hollander, Gayle Durham. *Soviet Political Indoctrination: Developments in Mass Media and Propaganda Since Stalin.* New York, 1972.

Hopkins, Mark W. *Mass Media in the Soviet Union.* New York, 1970.

Karatnycky, Adrian. "Soviet Press: In for the Long Haul: Reporting the Line on Afghanistan." *Commonweal,* May 23, 1980, p. 294.

Katz, Zev. *The Communications System in the USSR.* Cambridge, Mass., 1977.

Kruglak, Theodore E. *The Two Faces of Tass.* Minneapolis, 1962.

Levshina, I. S. "The Educational Potential of the Mass Media." Translated from *Sovetskaya Pedagogika,* no. 2, 1975. *Soviet Education,* November 1978, p. 28.

Lisann, Maury. *Broadcasting to the Soviet Union: International Politics and Radio.* New York, 1975.

Luryi, Yuri, and Feifer, George. "The Indisputable Soviet Press." *Saturday Review,* October 28, 1978, p. 19.

Markham, James W. *Voices of the Red Giants; Communications in Russia and China.* Ames, Iowa, 1967.

Martin, L. John. *International Propaganda: Its Legal and Diplomatic Control.* Minneapolis, 1958.

Merrill, John C., Bryan, Carter, and Alisky, Marvin. *The Foreign Press: A Survey of World's Journalism.* Baton Rouge, La., 1970.

Merrill, John C., and Fisher, Harold A. *The World's Great Dailies.* New York, 1980, pp. 170-76, 242-50.

Powell, David E. *Antireligious Progaganda in the Soviet Union: A Study of Mass Persuasion.* Cambridge, Mass., 1975.

Salisbury, Harrison E. "The Russia Reagan Faces." *The New York Times Magazine,* February 1, 1981, p. 30.

"Soviets Search for the Hidden Facts." Reprinted from *Neue Zürcher Zeitung.* IPI Report, October 1980, p. 10.

Tokes, Rudolf L., ed. *Dissent in the USSR: Politics, Ideology, and People.* Baltimore, 1975.

Tolkunov, Lev. "The Responsibility of the Mass Media." *New Times,* Moscow, no. 6, February 1977, p. 13.

Tsukasov, S. "Enhancing the Effectiveness and Quality of the Soviet Press." Translated from *Kommunist,* no. 7, 1977. *Soviet Education,* November 1978, p. 53.

UNESCO. *Statistical Yearbook 1977.* Paris, 1978.

UNESCO. *World Communications: A 200-Country Survey of Press, Radio, Television and Film.* Paris, 1975.

"USSR." *Europa Yearbook 1980: A World Survey.* London, 1980, pp. 1216-1320.

Whitney, Craig R. "Soviet Reporters Investigate, Too, But Only Within Limits Set At Top." *The New York Times,* March 27, 1978, p. 1.

UNITED KINGDOM

by James W. Welke

BASIC DATA

Population: 55.9 million
Area: 244,104 sq. km. (94,214 sq. mi.)
GNP: £159,133.5 million (US$353.63 billion) (1979)
Literacy Rate: 98%
Language(s): English
Number of Dailies: 107
   Aggregate Circulation: 23,139,000
   Circulation per 1,000: 410
Number of Nondailies: 1,085
   Aggregate Circulation: 38,248,000
   Circulation per 1,000: 690
Number of Periodicals: 5,000 (including "freesheets")

Number of Radio Stations: 24
Number of Television Stations: 2
Number of Radio Receivers: 39 million
   Radio Receivers per 1,000: 700
Number of Television Sets: 18,381,161
   Television Sets per 1,000: 330
Total Annual Newsprint Consumption: 1,451 million metric tons
Per Capita Newsprint Consumption: 26 kg. (57.2 lb.)
Total Newspaper Ad Receipts: £94 billion (US$ 2.09 billion) (1979)
   As % of All Ad Expenditures: 40.7 (1979)

Background & General Characteristics

The British press is one of the most editorially vital in the world. Although the newspaper industry is beset by serious economic problems and a slow but continuous decline in circulation, Britain's per capita newspaper readership is surpassed only by that of Japan and the Soviet Union among the major countries. Political and cultural expression is unfettered and the press is often outspoken in its criticism of the government.

While many newspapers unmistakably express a certain political and editorial viewpoint or philosophy, they are almost always financially independent and rarely follow the line of any particular party. Furthermore, certain newspapers have trustee arrangements designed to protect the integrity and independence of their editorial policy against possible ownership influence.

Britain is an ideal geographic marketplace for a newspaper industry. The total area of the nation is small, and British rail system provides frequent and extensive transportation services that facilitate newspaper distribution. Literacy is very high, and virtually everyone speaks the common language, English, although Celtic languages are also spoken by some of the population in Scotland, Wales and Northern Ireland. The bulk of the population is concentrated in England: in the Midlands, south and near London.

The tradition of the British press dates back to the 17th century. Perhaps the first true newspaper was the *Oxford Gazette*, published twice weekly beginning in 1665 and retitled the *London Gazette* after 23 issues. The first British daily, the *Daily Courant*, appeared in London in 1702, and 17 years later the *Daily Post* was founded by, among others, Daniel Defoe, the author of *Robinson Crusoe* and generally considered the first great English journalist. Around this time several periodicals began publication, with such contributors as Defoe, Dean Swift, Richard Steele and Joseph Addison.

During the latter half of the 1700s additional newspapers were founded, including the *Morning Chronicle*, whose drama critic was William Hazlitt; the *Morning Post*, for which both Charles Lamb and Samuel Taylor Coleridge wrote; and the *Daily Universal Register*, which soon became *The Times* of London.

The next century brought technical innovations, the lifting of various duties on newspapers and the development of a national railway network, which enabled mass production of newspapers and distribution to a much wider audience. Meanwhile a growth in population and increasing urbanization coupled with a rise in literacy created a demand for newspapers with a mass appeal. The first morning daily aimed at a mass readership was the *Daily Mail*. Begun in 1896, it featured news briefs, human interest stories, sports items and political gossip, and within four years its circulation rose from 400,000 to one million. The publication of the *Daily Mail* started the division in the British daily press between "popular" and "quality" newspapers, which continues to this day. The populars were designed for those who wanted news of a more entertaining or sensational nature presented in a concise manner, while the qualities attracted those who desired full information on a broad range of topics. The success of the *Daily Mail* led to the founding of three other mass-circulation newspapers, two of which—the *Daily Mirror* (1903) and the *Daily Sketch* (1909)—used a tabloid format.

Newspaper readership rose considerably during the period between the two World Wars as the major popular newspapers embarked on competitive circulation drives. Following the outbreak of World War II, the public's interest in war news and restrictions on newspaper size because of newsprint rationing induced people to buy two or even three newspapers a day. The trend continued after the war with a rise in both the standard of living and the level of education. After newsprint rationing was abolished in the mid-1950s, multiple buying declined as the size of newspapers grew.

Newspaper circulation decreased from 37 million in 1970 to 33 million in 1978, but those figures mask the experiences of individual newspapers and the fact that the circulation of certain papers held steady and that of others increased.

Currently there are about 130 daily (morning and evening) and Sunday newspapers, including specialized papers, such as religious, foreign-language, sports, and business publications. That total includes 10 national (i.e., circulated throughout the nation on the day of issue) mornings, seven national Sundays and one London evening. The remainder are provincial morning, evening and Sunday papers, the bulk of which are published in the English provinces. In addition there are over 1,000 weekly newspapers produced throughout the British Isles.

Four of the morning and three of the Sunday nationals are described as quality newspapers; despite their conservative style the Sunday qualities put out color supplements that are included with the rest of the paper. There are six mornings and four Sundays in the popular category. The populars are generally tabloids and the qualities usually follow a broadsheet format, although the pattern is not rigid. The national mornings and Sundays—both popular and quality—and their circulations are listed in the accompanying table.

National Newspapers	
Newspaper (founding date)	**Circulation (average Jan.-June 1979)**
Morning Populars	
Daily Express (1900)	2,405,609
Daily Mail (1896)	1,943,793
Daily Mirror (1903)	3,623,039
Daily Star (1978)	937,866 (April-June 1979)
Morning Star (1966)	34,558
The Sun (1969)	3,793,007
Morning Qualities	
The Daily Telegraph (1855)	1,476,887
Financial Times (1888)	206,360
The Guardian (1821)	379,429
The Times (1785)*	
Sunday Populars	
News of the World (1843)	4,708,575
The Sunday People (1881)	3,930,849
Sunday Express (1918)	3,257,728
Sunday Mirror (1963)	3,888,631
Sunday Qualities	
The Observer (1791)	1,124,018
The Sunday Telegraph (1961)	1,278,894
The Sunday Times (1822)*	

*Publication of *The Times* and *The Sunday Times* was suspended for 11 months in 1978-79. In 1980 circulation of *The Times* was 285,000 and that of *The Sunday Times* was 1.4 million.

Although mainly concerned with regional and local news, the provincial dailies also cover national affairs. The total circulation of regional morning and evening newspapers is estimated at over six million. The largest selling provincial daily newspapers, which are located in the industrial midlands and north, include the *Manchester Evening News*, with a circulation of over 346,000; the *Birmingham Evening Mail*, circulation over

340,000; and the *Express and Star and Shropshire Star* (Staffordshire), circulation over 329,000. In Northern Ireland, the daily *Belfast Telegraph* leads all other papers with a circulation of 186,000. In Wales, the daily *South Wales Echo* has a circulation in excess of 110,000 and the *Western Mail*, the quality Welsh morning newspaper, has recently dropped to 75,000 from 120,000. The *Daily Record* in Scotland exceeds 730,000 daily and *The Scotsman*, the quality Scottish newspaper, has a circulation above 89,000.

Special-interest newspapers naturally have more modest circulations. They are important media, nevertheless. The daily sporting newspapers *Sporting Chronicle* and *The Sporting Life* have circulations of more than 45,000 and 83,000 respectively. Both are national morning publications. There are 31 religious weekly newspapers, including the *Christian Herald,* which has the largest circulation of the interdenominational British newspapers, the *Catholic Herald,* the *Church Times* and the *Jewish Chronicle.* Business newspapers include *Lloyd's List* and the *Journal of Commerce,* a Liverpool morning paper.

The United Kingdom has a considerable and varied immigrant population, particularly in the metropolitan centers of the midlands and the south, that includes Cypriots, Irish, Indians, Pakistanis, Poles and West Indians. These groups are served by a rapidly growing number of foreign-language newspapers, the majority of which are weeklies published in London.

An alternative press devoted mainly to radical politics, ecology, sex, religion and the occult developed rapidly in the late 1960s and early 1970s, but by 1980 well over half of the approximately 1,250 publications begun in those years had disappeared. A recent development is the expansion of some small left-wing or radical newspapers in the suburbs surrounding metropolitan and industrial areas. These local papers were created to fill the gap caused by the frequent disruptions in the availability of established newspapers, which has resulted primarily from union-management problems. Local freesheets, which depend entirely on advertising revenue, have experienced rapid growth in recent years.

The most influential newspapers in Great Britain are *The Times, The Daily Telegraph, The Guardian* and the *Financial Times* among the quality newspapers and the *Daily Mirror* and *Daily Mail* among the popular newspapers. Although its circulation is small compared with that of other national newspapers, the *Financial Times* is read in some 120 countries around the world. Both at home and abroad it is considered an authoritative source of information on political, economic, national and international affairs.

In their book *The World's Great Dailies: Profiles of Fifty Newspapers,* John C. Merrill and Harold A. Fisher rank three of Britain's four quality dailies among the world's elite newspapers: *The Times, The Guardian* and *The Daily Telegraph.* Almost two centuries old, *The Times* has always been looked on as "the Establishment paper, a daily to read to keep up with the affairs of empire," according to Merrill and Fisher. It has embodied the highest standards of newspaper journalism and earned the respect of opinion makers, financiers and statesmen in Britain and around the world. Back in the mid-19th century, when it was the world's most influential paper, *The Times* introduced the concept of an independent news journal responsible only to the people.

The Times strives to provide its readers with complete coverage of national, international and business news, which in an average issue (28–32 pages) take up respectively 14 percent, 10 percent and almost 20 percent of the paper's total content. In addition to reporting the activities of Parliament and the national government, the paper runs a number of excellent features and devotes space each day to science, the judiciary, important social events and entertainment.

As they have for years, the leader (main editorial) and op-ed pages, perhaps the paper's greatest assets, continue to provide penetrating, forceful and thought-provoking editorials and intellectual debates.

Since the days when its correspondents reported the end of the Crimean War, *The Times* has gone to great lengths to keep its readers informed about international news. Over the last two decades it has broadened and strengthened its coverage of world affairs, particularly in Western Europe.

Many improvements in *The Times,* including increased foreign coverage, sharper editorials and better-quality writing, were achieved under William Rees-Mogg, who was editor from 1967 to 1981. His accomplishments were more noteworthy considering they were made during a period of declining circulation (450,000 in the late sixties to 284,000 in 1978); financial setbacks—aggravated by circulation battles and high inflation—resulting in annual losses that in recent years have averaged about £600,000 ($1.25 million); and repeated labor-management disputes. Financial and labor problems eventually led to the sale of *The Times* and *The Sunday Times* in February 1981.

To the left of *The Times, The Guardian* is the spokesman for progressive liberal thinking and social reform. Founded in 1821 by John Edward Taylor as the *Manchester Guardian,* it rose from a regional publication to become one of the nation's leading newspapers, thanks largely to its liberal appeal, balanced reporting, high-caliber international coverage and relative financial stability. A measure of *The Guardian's* success is its circulation; more than 370,000 in the first half of 1979, about three-fourths of whom were subscribers. Furthermore its readership has been estimated at over one million. The people who read *The Guardian* are generally younger (their median age is 33, compared with 38 for *The Times* and 42 for *The Daily Telegraph*), more affluent and better educated than the average British citizen; 75 percent are white-collar workers and 30 percent are college-educated.

The Guardian's reporting covers all aspects of society. The paper's wide interests include industry, business, economics, government, art, literature, science and history. Traditionally excelling in international reporting, it has a staff of about eight full-time foreign correspondents, supplemented by stringers around the world, and uses six wire services. *The Guardian's* foreign and national correspondents have won numerous awards.

The *Guardian Weekly,* a small-format collection of the daily's best stories, enjoys a wide readership in intellectual circles and is the most widely read foreign paper in the United States; its circulation is about 40,000.

Throughout its 150-year history *The Guardian* has taken a number of unpopular stands, which at times have resulted in a loss of readership. It presented minority views on pacifism and internationalism during World War I and opposed Britain's takeover of the Suez Canal in 1956. Nevertheless, since the 1950s its circulation has risen to well over 300,000, surpassing that of *The Times. The Guardian* remains "Britain's non-conformist conscience," a role in which it takes pride.

To the right of *The Times* and at the opposite end of the spectrum from *The Guardian* is *The Daily Telegraph.* Representing the conservative (small "c") point of view, *The Telegraph* is known for its comprehensive news coverage, mixture of serious and lighter news, high-quality reporting and middle-class orientation.

From its founding in 1855 by Colonel Arthur Burroughes Sleigh, *The Telegraph* has sought to report the news just as it happens with no attempt to hide or shade the truth. The paper has spoken out on issues without regard to the prevailing sentiment among government officials or the public. One of the most striking examples was its continued warnings in the 1930s about the dangers posed by Nazi Germany and its consistent opposition to a policy of appeasement. Some newspapers at the time chose to ignore the problem and others even opposed Britain's preparations for war.

Following World War II *The Telegraph* became the first quality to sell more than one million copies per day. In the first half of 1979 its circulation was over 1.4 million, while that of *The Sunday Telegraph,* a similar publication produced by a separate staff, was over 1.2 million.

One of *The Telegraph's* foremost traditions has been its dedication to complete and accurate reporting of world affairs. In the 19th century it sent correspondents to cover such widely separated events as the Civil War in the United States and the Maori War in New Zealand. In recent years it has reported the Vietnam War, the conflict in the Middle East and India's political struggles. The paper's foreign staff includes about 15 full-time reporters and more than 100 stringers. It also employs the services of three news agencies. Complementing the foreign staff is a team of reporters who cover the workings of Parliament, the government and the various political parties as well as general news areas; crime and sex are reported but not sensationalized.

The Telegraph assigns specialist correspondents to handle a variety of fields, including science, law, medicine, agriculture, fashion, finance, travel, sports and the arts. The paper's human interests stories have been one of its strongest attractions. A careful blend of hard news and stimulating features has helped to make *The Daily Telegraph* by far the best-selling quality newspaper in Britain.

There are over 4,000 periodicals published in Britain, categorized as general, specialized, trade, technical and professional. The weekly periodicals with the highest circulation are *Radio Times* and *TV Times*, followed by several women's magazines. Among the leading journals of opinion are *The Economist,* a politically independent and highly respected publication that covers economic, political and social topics; the *New Statesman,* a review of politics, literature and the arts with an independent socialist political outlook; the *Spectator*, a similar journal reflecting an independent conservative viewpoint; and the *Tribune*, which expresses the position of the left wing of the British Labour Party. The publication of trade, technical, scientific, business and professional journals, providing in-depth coverage of hundreds of subjects, has become one of the most important facets of the British publishing industry.

Economic Framework

The overall economy of the United Kingdom has been plagued by unemployment, an inefficient industrial plant, double-digit inflation and the declining value of the pound sterling against other major currencies. With the development of the North Sea oil fields and the prospect of energy self-sufficiency, the pound sterling gained strength and stability in 1979-80, but since then it has begun to drop again.

These factors plus frequent labor disruptions have exacerbated the financial problems of newspapers. Many of the daily and Sunday national newspapers are unprofitable operations, and the Royal Commission on the Press concluded in 1977 that they were likely to remain so.

The provincial newspapers are still generally profitable because they operate in a monopolistic situation, whereas the national newspapers do not. No town in the United Kingdom, has more than one daily evening newspaper. London had two evening newspapers until October 31, 1980, when the 99-year-old *Evening News,* the nation's largest selling evening newspaper with a circulation exceeding 450,000, merged with the other London evening paper, the *Evening Standard.* The *Evening News* cited continuously rising production costs as the reason for the move. Prior to the merger the *Evening Standard* had a circulation above 370,000. With the competition from the *Evening News* eliminated, the *Evening Standard* is expected to realize a significant increase in circulation.

A competitive factor within the mass media is the growth of advertising-supported broadcasting (despite a fall in demand for commercial time at the end of 1980 because of the nation's economic plight). Broadcasting was noncommercial until 1954, when the Independent Television Authority (ITA) was established. In 1973 local commercial radio (Independent Local Radio, ILR) was added and in 1980 approval for a new commercial television channel was successfully making its way through Parliament. Competition for advertising revenue from television has primarily affected the national newspapers, but local radio draws away revenue from the provincial press. Nevertheless, the print media continue to attract the major share of total advertising expenditures.

Advertising's contribution to offsetting the cost of newspaper production is of primary importance to all sectors of the press, particularly the quality papers and the regional daily and local weekly publications. The Evening Newspaper Advertising Bureau Ltd. and the Weekly Newspaper Advertising Bureau were established to promote advertising in the regional and local press. The amount of space devoted to advertising differs considerably among the various classes of newspapers. Generally ad space ranges from 40 percent in popular national newspapers to 50 percent in local weeklies. However, wide variations exist even within a class.

There is no evidence to indicate that the relationship between advertisers and the publications they advertise in is anything but purely business or that advertising has an adverse impact on editorial policy.

Ownership of national and regional dailies is concentrated mainly in the hands of a comparatively small number of large press publishing groups, but there are also some 200 independent regional and local newspaper publishers. While ownership concentration in the national press industry has not increased significantly during the past decade, economic considerations make the impetus toward consolidation strong.

The larger chain publishers include Associated Newspapers Group Ltd., Mirror Group Newspapers Ltd., Express Newspapers and News Group Newspapers Ltd. Some newspapers, for example, *The Guardian,* the *Daily Express* and the *Evening Standard*, are operated by trusts, which provide a large measure of protection against political manipulation. In such arrangements, ownership of the enterprise is generally vested in trustees, or the enterprise is operated in accordance with a deed of trust. There are also restrictions on the transfer of shares and other provisions designed to protect the character of certain papers.

Although most enterprises are organized as limited liability companies, individual and partner ownership survives. The major national newspaper and periodical publishers have interests ranging across the whole spectrum of communications, including TV and radio program companies. However, there are legal prohibitions against the control or ownership of any program company by a single newspaper or publishing company. The Independent Broadcasting Authority (IBA) may end its contract with a company if it finds that newspaper shares in the company are contrary to the public interest.

The Independent Broadcasting Authority Act of 1973 has provisons aimed at protecting local newspapers in areas where local independent radio stations operate. Generally, local newspapers have been offered the chance to buy shares in the program company providing radio services in their area, but a local paper that has a monopoly in an area is not allowed to gain a controlling interest in a local radio station.

Experience to date seems to indicate that the free expression of opinion is not threatened by amalgamation, and that common ownership does not necessarily entail a suppression of independent editorial views. Newspapers controlled by the same undertaking often approach public questions from somewhat different standpoints and most editors enjoy a considerable degree of latitude and freedom in these matters.

The Monopolies and Mergers Act of 1965 regulates the acquisition and sale of newspaper enterprises. Mergers or acquisitions involving publications with an average circulation of 500,000 or more per day must be approved by the Monopolies and Mergers Commission after it considers the effect on the public interest. All such cases are referred to the commission except those involving papers with a daily average circulation of less than 25,000. After passage of the Monopolies and Mergers Act of 1965, *The Times* and *The Sunday Times* merger approved in 1966 and the Crusha and Son Ltd. transfer of three weekly papers to the Thomson Newspaper Ltd. chain in 1968 were the two most significant mergers. Only five other cases were considered prior to 1977. In

mid-1981 the commission approved the £5 million ($11.9 million) sale of *The Observer* to Lonrho Ltd., a British trading company owned by Roland "Tiny" Rowland, contingent upon the acceptance of certain conditions aimed at guaranteeing the editorial independence of the paper, including the appointment of six independent directors to *The Observer*'s board. A few months earlier Rupert Murdoch, the Australian press magnate, bought *The Times,* along with *The Sunday Times* and the Literary, Education and Higher Education Supplements, from the International Thomson Organisation for £11 million ($27.3 million). Although several MPs had asked that the matter be brought before the commission because Murdoch already owned two large selling British newspapers—the London *Daily Sun* and *News of the World*—the government said that since the two papers being purchased were presently unprofitable, the panel was not obliged to examine the sale. Murdoch had given assurances that the editors would control the contents of the publications.

Serious financial difficulties had prompted both sales, particularly that of *The Times* and *The Sunday Times*, which from 1967-81 had lost an estimated $169 million. The management of the Thomson Organisation had suspended publication of *The Times* and *The Sunday Times* for 11 months during 1978-79 in an effort to win union approval of changes aimed at improving efficiency. After publication was resumed, continued difficulties with some of the unions involved prevented implementation of changes that had been agreed upon, particularly the use of computerized equipment that management considered essential to its efficiency drive.

The introduction of new computerized production technology is a continuing source of union-management strife in the newspaper industry, with management claiming the technology is essential to economic survival and the unions arguing it will result in a severe loss of jobs. There is no question that one of the problems plaguing the industry is outdated production techniques and equipment and that newspapers which fail to adopt new processes to improve their productivity will continue to experience economic hardships.

Despite union opposition the national newspapers have begun to invest in computerized photocomposition through offset printing. Photocomposition can be combined with computer storage and handling of data, substituting electronic for manual methods.

Video display terminals (VDTs) and other computerized equipment are also being introduced into the editorial process. The adoption of new printing techniques has been more rapid in the provincial press, where composition represents a large proportion of operating and production costs.

Murdoch's purchase of *The Times* and *The Sunday Times* may signal some progress in the continuing battle over computerized technology and the related issue of job security. The sale was achieved after the unions representing the papers' employees accepted an agreement that provided for the elimination of over 500 positions—composing room workers, journalists and clerks—and a complete switchover of the daily *Times,* and eventually *The Sunday Times,* to cold-type printing. However, the unions agreed to such measures only when faced with the threat that both publications would shut down permanently if no accord was reached.

Newspaper industrial relations in the United Kingdom are among the worst in the world. Official strikes and unofficial job actions are frequent. In addition to the dispute over computerized production techniques and reduced manning levels, other major issues include closed shops and reporter approval of new editors, which has gained ground recently along with participation by working journalists in the management of newspapers and periodicals through special advisory committees or membership on the board of directors. For example, an agreement between the *New Statesman* and the National Union of Journalists (NUJ) stipulates that the staff will have an editor of its choice. Confrontations have erupted over the way newspaper industry labor problems are presented to the public and both production and journalist unions have become involved in this issue. Production unions have held brief work stoppages over anti-trade union cartoons and news items unfavorable to the labor movement.

Some critics have suggested that the strong union presence in both the production and editorial areas of the newspaper industry represents a new kind of threat to traditional freedom of the press. The National Union of Journalists, the largest journalist union, has a code of conduct, written in 1936, that includes general statements affirming the basic tenets of responsibility and free journalism as well as emphasizing union loyalty, and a journalist can be expelled, fined or suspended for violations of the code. There is and has been a great deal of controversy over

this issue in the United Kingdom. The seriousness of this threat to a free press is more apparent when it is viewed along with the issue of closed shops. For example, a journalist employed by a company with a closed-shop agreement could be required to resign from the Institute of Journalists and to join the National Union of Journalists. And this situation has occurred.

The Trade Union and Labour Relations (Amendment) Act 1976 provided for the development of a press charter containing guidance on practical matters relating to press freedom, especially labor-management agreements concerning closed shops. The government and publishers discussed the provisions of such a charter in 1977-78 but failed to reach an agreement. A debate was held on the issue in the House of Lords early in 1978. Parliament was to consider a code of conduct for closed shops and picketing by strikers in the fall of 1980 under the Employment Act. In any event the closed-shop dispute is likely to continue in the near future.

A further threat to a free and unfettered press is the union view of newspaper operation perhaps best summarized at a TUC Conference on Trade Unions and the Media in 1977. Essentially it was proposed that the press should have the equivalent of an "operator's license" granted on the basis of clearly defined standards of responsibility and accountability. The precedent exists in the form of the royal charter and license and agreement that authorizes the BBC and the license authorizing the Independent Broadcasting Authority.

Union-management relations in the provincial press are better, but not without problems. There was a lengthy strike of provincial journalists in 1979 and a six week printers' strike against the local press early in 1980. Walkouts of short duration have been frequent. On May 14, 1980 the Trades Union Congress (TUC) called for a "Day of Action," and union members were encouraged to stay home in protest over Conservative government policy. The nationwide response by workers in all industries was patchy, but the national newspapers were virtually closed down. The publications not affected on May 14 were affected the next day. On May 26, a holiday, few newspapers were available in London because of a deliverymen's walkout to stress their demand for more pay for holiday work.

The main trade unions are the National Union of Journalists (NUJ), representing reporters, photographers and editors; the

Institute of Journalists (IOJ), representing reporters and editors; the Guild of British Newspaper Editors, representing editors; the National Society of Operative Printers, Graphical and Media Personnel (NATSOPA), representing secretaries, editorial assistants, copy readers, assistant machine minders and assistant engineers; the National Graphical Association (NGA), representing wire room workers, keyboard operators, compositors, readers, stereotypers and machine minders; the Society of Lithographic Artists, Designers, Engravers and Process Workers (SLADE); the Society of Graphical and Allied Trades (SOGAT), representing printers and circulation staff; and the Amalgamated Union of Engineering Workers (AUEW), representing engineers. All practicing journalists are eligible for membership in either the NUJ, which has about 29,600 members, or the IOJ, which has some 2,300 members.

Unionized journalists and production staffs on the national newspapers command exceptionally high salaries. (In 1980 the average salary for a journalist in Britain was estimated at about £170 ($405) a week.) This in itself is not critical, and it can be argued that newspaper employees should receive compensation commensurate with the overall high quality of most of the Fleet Street product: the national newspaper. However when the salary levels are figured in with the cost of overstaffing created by redundancy and outmoded job protection policies and the financial impact of work stoppages, the economic situation facing newspapers (and to some extent broadcasters) becomes severe.

Another major expense for newspapers is the rising cost of newsprint, which accounts for roughly one-third of average national newspaper costs. About 75 percent of Britain's requirements are imported, mainly from Canada and Scandinavia.

Morning newspapers are normally picked up by wholesalers at the newspaper offices or, in the case of out-of-town subscriptions, are shipped by rail or, in some cases, by air to their destinations. They are then delivered to retailers. Sunday papers are normally distributed directly to retailers.

All the national daily and Sunday papers but one are printed on Fleet Street in London, although five of the dailies and four of the Sunday papers produce northern editions in Manchester, which account for about 25 percent of the total national press production. One national daily is printed in Manchester. An edition of the *Financial Times* is also printed in Frankfurt. In 1979 the national

newspapers ranged in price from seven pence (16 cents) to 20 pence (44 cents) for the dailies and 14 pence (31 cents) to 22 pence (49 cents) for the Sundays.

Press Laws

The United Kingdom is a constitutional monarchy with no written constitution. The constitution is an aggregation of legal precedent and custom; no single document exists. The British press operates within this tradition as one of the great free presses of the world. There are no special laws regulating the operation of newspapers. Several laws, however, relate directly to the news-gathering activity of the press.

The Official Secrets Act of 1911 provides penalties for any unauthorized communication of official information by a servant of the Crown. The law contains no distinctions of any kind or degree. Consequently, all information learned by employees of the central government in the course of their duties is official as defined by the law. The definition of Crown employee, theoretically, reaches down to part-time gardeners at government-operated tourist centers. Prosecutions for offenses under the law may be instituted only with the consent of the attorney general.

Of particular importance to the press are laws covering contempt of court and libel. The number of contempt and libel cases is large and increasing, and they have involved attempts to force identification of sources and disclosure of privileged information.

Contempt of court falls under two broad categories: civil and criminal. Civil contempt involves willful disobedience of a court order or breach of a legal responsibility imposed by a court (e.g., disobedience of a subpoena). Examples of criminal contempt would be comments on judges, magistrates or court proceedings that are likely to impair public confidence in the administration of justice, interference with judicial proceedings (including refusal to reveal sources of information) and publication of any matter before or during a trial that may prejudice the outcome. The ruling in *Home Office* v. *Harman*, Queen's Bench Division, declared that where the court grants an order for discovery of documents in a legal proceeding, it is implied that the documents will be used only for the purposes of that legal action. This precludes use of such documents by reporters even if they have been read in open court. The intent is to prevent trial by the mass media. Contempt is not necessarily automatic; it depends on the circumstances of the case, including the intended use of the documents, the extent of disclosure, the granting of permission for use of the material and the date of the disclosure in relation to the trial.

In 1974 the *Report of the Committee on Contempt of Court* (Phillimore Committee) made proposals aimed at clarifying and liberalizing the contempt law, including a statutory definition of contempt in relation to the press and delineation of the period during which publication could bring contempt proceedings. Queen Elizabeth's message to Parliament in May 1979 indicated that amendments would be proposed to both contempt of court laws and the Official Secrets Act. Although by mid-1980 no amendments to the law had been proposed, in late November of that year the government published a bill that would go a long way toward unraveling the muddled and contentious areas of contempt statutes. Still, the relaxation of restrictions in the bill would not go as far as recommended by the Phillimore Committee. The proposed law would clarify the duration of strict liability in both criminal and civil proceedings. In criminal cases strict liability would begin at the time of arrest and continue until sentencing or acquittal. In civil cases strict liability would start at the date of trial or hearing and run to the time of sentencing or acquittal. A further protection provides that no liability exists if, after taking reasonable care, a reporter does not know or has no reason to suspect that proceedings have started. Comment in the press would be restricted during these periods of liability, which previously were not well-defined. The bill also contains provisions exempting fair and accurate reports of legal proceedings held in public and published contemporaneously, and provides for a new public interest defense for comments made in good-faith discussion of public affairs news items as long as the risk of prejudice to an identifiable proceeding is incidental to the discussion.

It is important to note that this proposed change in contempt of court law resulted from external pressure rather than from pressure within the United Kingdom. The bill was conceived to satisfy a burden imposed by the European Court of Human Rights as the result of a judgment given by the court on an appeal from *The Sunday Times.*

The Defamation Act of 1952 covers statements broadcast on radio and television as well as those published in the print media. Among the possible defenses to a charge of defamation are those of absolute privilege, which applies to speeches delivered in Parliament, statements made during judicial proceedings and certain state documents, and qualified privilege, which applies to the reporting of public inquiries, meetings, and proceedings of Parliament. In cases where qualified privilege is invoked, the defendant must show that the report was fair and accurate and published without malice. The defense of justification is available if the statement in question is substantially true. Fair comment can be used as a defense provided there are no errors of fact, no malice and the subject is public interest. Individuals in public life may not be attacked on the grounds of their fitness to hold office, but conduct in that office is not protected.

Libel suits are frequent and pose a problem in the exercise of journalistic responsibilities. It can be a particular problem for some magazines, such as *Private Eye,* which are satirical in content and, consequently, prone to statements bordering on the fine edge of libel. Of course, many libel suits charge that journalistic principles of veracity have given way to expediency. The Express Newspapers group was sued by a retired football player for an article in the *Daily Star* which suggested that he had refused to pose for a photograph with a visiting amateur football team because he would not receive compensation for doing so. Actually, the football player had been in Australia at the time the picture was taken. Express Newspapers paid damage and costs.

Some cases involve merely mistaken but unintentional attributions, quotes and references that are settled out of court. Nevertheless, these ordinary legal actions obscure the restrictions that libel law application has on the flow of information to the public through the press. For example, a report on an investigation into corruption among public officials would certainly be in the public interest. If, however, an official inquiry failed to produce any evidence of criminal acts by the public officials, the newspaper or broadcast operation could face a libel charge with little defense.

In defamation actions the owner, editor, printer and distributor of the news paper as well as author of the defamatory statement may all be held responsible and be required to pay damages.

The Public Bodies Act 1960 is a "sunshine" law guaranteeing admission of the press to local authority meetings. Access can be limited, however, because the act applies to committees and meetings where all local council members hold membership. The exclusion of a council person from the committee renders the act inapplicable. There are no laws governing access to documents comparable to the Freedom of Information Act in the United States.

Other laws that relate to the journalistic activity of the press include the Race Relations Act 1976, which imposes stringent liability on publishers of material that may incite racial hatred; the Obscene Publications Act 1959, which is rarely a problem for the ordinary press (a 1979 Committee on Obscenity and Film proposed modifications of the law but these do not directly affect the ordinary press); and prohibitions against the publication of certain details of divorce, domestic and rape case proceedings, legal proceedings involving juveniles, false and misleading advertising, advertising of remedies for certain diseases which are covered by public health law, and certain kinds of prize contests.

There is no comprehensive or general law to protect the privacy of nonofficial citizens of the United Kingdom. In 1972 a Committee on Privacy established by the Home Office, the Lord Chancellor's Office and the Scottish Office conducted a study on the possible need for protection of this sort. Legislation to establish a new tort seemed likely. Questions of invasion of privacy are dealt with by a Complaints Committee of the Press Council. The BBC established a Complaints Commission in 1972 and complaints can also be heard by the General Advisory Council of the BBC. The Independent Television Authority (ITA) established a Complaints Review Board in 1971. The BBC and ITA have more power to force retractions than does the Press Council.

The political system of the United Kingdom is characterized by an independent judiciary that is outside the control of the executive branch of government. This is a positive point for press freedom. Judges can only be removed from office by Parliament through the sovereign.

Censorship

The press has not been subjected to any censorship law for several centuries except during periods of national crisis, such as World War II. Restrictions on the press are roughly comparable to those in the United States, while differing in the specifics of enforcement and application.

Perhaps the most contentious issue related to government control of information is the practice of labeling national security and defense information with defense notices or "D-notices." These notices are formal letters outlining the information and requesting editors in the print and electronic media not to publish it. Compliance is expected but the notices are not binding. The labeling authority has no precise legal basis and is not directly authorized by the Official Secrets Act of 1911, although it is loosely based on it. The actual application of D-notices is accomplished by the D-Notice Committee, consisting of representatives from the press and broadcast industries and officials from the Ministry of Defence and the Home, Foreign and Commonwealth Offices. Consequently, this represents a form of media self-censorship on national security matters. Few would criticize the goal of protecting information in the interest of national security. The problem lies in the determination of which areas of information are important to that security and which are not.

The current list of 12 D-notices has been in effect since its adoption in 1971. The D-notices are Defense Plans, Classified Weapons, Royal Navy, Aircraft, Nuclear Weapons, Photography, Prisoners of War and Evaders, National and Civil Defense, Radio/Radar, British Intelligence Services, Cyphers and Communication and Whereabouts of Mr. and Mrs. Vladimir Petrov.

In May 1980 the Independent Broadcasting Authority canceled a scheduled program on the basis that it would have compromised national security. The program dealt with the alleged loss of secret documents and an attempt to cover up the loss and with foreign agent penetration of government communication services in the British colony of Hong Kong. Both the *Daily Mirror* and the *New Statesman* published the story.

The press and broadcasters have been critical of the D-notice system, which has no parallel in the world except in Australia. In mid-1980 the House of Commons Select Committee on Defence decided to investigate the entire process. Their report, published in August 1980, was highly critical of the system. It did, however, recommend that the D-notice practice continue until Parliament could replace Section 2 of the Official Secrets

Act 1911. When that might occur is unclear. Despite the intense criticism of D-notices, the testimony presented to the House of Commons committee was heavily in favor of retaining the system. The D-Notice Committee also favored continuing it with only one press member, the Press Association representative, dissenting.

According to Christopher Underwood, president of the Institute of Journalists and home affairs correspondent for the BBC, journalists are often asked to suppress other news items unrelated to national security. Official secrecy is often used to save the government from embarrassment. Information on a whole range of issues, including health, transportation, consumer affairs and food hygiene, can be controlled by citing the provisions of Section 2 of the Official Secrets Act of 1911.

The newspaper industry was affected by the serious disruptions in national life caused by World War II. During the years 1947-49, a Royal Commission on the Press was appointed to study and make recommendations on the future of the industry. The major impetus for the formation of the commission was the potential effect of ownership concentration on freedom of expression. Its final report provided very little justification for concern on that point, however.

Many newspapers failed in the years following the publication of the Royal Commission report, so a new, second Royal Commission on the Press was established in 1961-62, charged with examining economic factors affecting the press. A third commission was instituted in 1976-77 with a broad and far-ranging set of topics for consideration, including economic problems, union-management relations, journalist training, an enforceable charter on press freedom, and employment of women and racial minorities.

Government or industry action based on the recommendations of these various commissions has not been substantial, although the recommendations of the first commission did result in the formation of a Press Council in 1953. Currently the council includes an equal number of press and non-press persons and an independent chairman. The press representatives are both union and management personnel. In mid-1980 members of the National Union of Journalists withdrew from the Press Council because of "disaffection" with the way the council operated. Since a large majority of British journalists are NUJ members and the NUJ was influen-

tial in establishing the council, the union's action brings into question the future credibility of Press Council decisions.

The charge of the council is comprehensive, but it concentrates on preservation of press freedom, encouraging the highest professional standards and providing a method of accountability without government intervention. The council's Complaints Committee, which is also composed of an equal number of press and non-press members, hears a wide variety of complaints from individuals and organizations on matters such as news inaccuracy, sensationalism, harassment, trivialization, "check-book" journalism and invasion of privacy. Neither the council nor the Complaints Committee have enforcement powers beyond the sphere of public censure. Decisions are not legally binding and may be rejected by newspapers and individual journalists.

For example, in 1980 the council upheld complaints against the *New Statesman* for publishing statements attributed to a news source that the source had never made. (The statements concerned the murder of Communist leader Leon Trotsky in 1940.) The periodical, however, refused to recognize the judgment of the council.

In another case the *Daily Mail* reported that £1 coins from the Isle of Man on sale for £1 at the *Daily Mail* Ideal Home Exhibition in London would be worth £6 immediately after purchase. Actually, it would take some years for the coins to approach that value. When this was made known, the *Daily Mail* published a correction, but it was in the low visibility column "Money Mail." The council ruled that the original report had been misleading and the correction had not been adequate.

The council rejects appeals as well. In 1978 there was an outbreak of small pox apparently from a professor's laboratory at Birmingham University. The professor subsequently committed suicide. Birmingham magistrates eventually cleared the university of charges that the public health had been endangered. This incident and comment about it had received wide coverage and had undoubtedly placed a great deal of pressure on the professor of the laboratory. It was charged that the professor had suffered as a result of ceaseless inquiries, mainly from the press, which contributed to his state of mental exhaustion. The council rejected these charges and closed the case in February 1980.

In addition to handling complaints about press coverage, the council is responsible for addressing all matters that affect the freedom of the press. Wales Gas, a part of the nationalized British Gas Corporation, was chastised by the council in 1979 for attempting to exert economic pressure on the *North Wales Weekly News* by the withdrawal of its advertising. The paper had editorially criticized the Wales Gas liquid petroleum depot of Llandudno. The council ruled that the withdrawal of advertising was an unacceptable attempt to manipulate the press by applying commercial pressures.

There are other restrictions on access to certain information, such as the rules of parliamentary privilege. These rules prohibit the publication of information and reports from certain government committees prior to the introduction of the material in the House of Commons. All select committees of the House operate under the rules of parliamentary privilege. Further, any MP may request that the House go into secret session by calling out "Mr. Speaker, I spy strangers." A motion on that request is then voted upon without debate. If the motion is approved, the public and the press are required to leave the proceedings.

Anthony Smith summarized the status of censorship under the laws of the United Kingdom in his book *The British Press Since the War* (1974), stating:

> Newspapers have not lost any of the specific privileges won in previous generations ...but there is a series of specific issues which they cannot any longer deal with in the way they may want to and at the moment at which they may want to. Successive interpretations of specific laws, some of which have existed for centuries, are beginning to interfere with the intangible asset of Press freedom. Successive governments ...have not found it expedient or possible to alter those laws....

State-Press Relations

Britain has no ministry of information. Each of the major government departments has its own information staff, many of whom have worked in journalism. These staffs are charged with keeping newspapers and news-broadcasting services informed about the intentions and actions of their respective departments. They supply background material to reporters on statements made by the ministers in Parliament and give explanations of the reasoning behind various departmental decisions.

Another source of information on governmental affairs is the Central Office of Information, which is a nonministerial department with no policy-making responsibilities. The office handles government advertising, produces materials for use by the media and distributes the press notices of government departments. It also supplies press, radio and television material for British information posts overseas.

While some rules of Parliament may partially restrict the total free flow of information, e.g. parliamentary privilege, the parliamentary lobby allows newsmen access to members of Parliament, including government ministers. The lobby can be viewed as a tradition that encourages good state-press relations by affording journalists and politicians the opportunity for direct contact. Basically ministers and backbenchers utilize the system to give "background" (i.e., not for attribution) information to the approximately 130 journalists who cover Parliament. At the same time, the built-in anonymity restricts the usefulness of the lobby as a news source. It can be and is used by politicians as a device to test public opinion. Some argue that the lobby is merely a vehicle for managing or sanitizing the news; others point out that it provides an excellent source of information that would otherwise be difficult to obtain.

The large and growing proportion of libel cases against publishers is another friction point between the state and the press. Inaction by Parliament and the government, unlike with the contempt of court law, would indicate there is little possibility of relief from the stifling provisions of libel law.

The interpretation and use of the Official Secrets Act of 1911 by elected and nonelected governmental officals to control information and the application of D-Notices, as mentioned earlier, to defense and national security issues also generate frequent state-press conflicts and charges of political manipulation. One of the reasons for establishing the 1977 Royal Commission was clearly political: the Labour Party was concerned about what they considered to be a concentration of Conservative Party bias in newspapers.

One way to improve state-press relations that is being urged by many journalists and publishers is the passage of some sort of freedom of information law, perhaps along the lines of the one in the U.S. Proponents of such a law claim that it would reduce unnecessary government secrecy and increase the public's awareness of government activities. As the 1980s began, there was no indication that the government or the opposition was considering such legislation.

Some British writers and media critics recommend the acceptance of government intervention in the print media, citing the observations of the royal press commissions. They point out that there is already a trend in Western democracies toward government making crucial policy decisions affecting all the information industries of a nation. The government's role in the electronic media is singled out as an example of how the system would work. Essentially government would administer the media while the daily control of content would be left to the professional journalist and broadcaster. How complete editorial independence would be maintained is problematic. Nonetheless, there is pressure for a change in the basic relationship between government, the media and the audience in the United Kingdom.

Despite the problems the overall relationship between the government and the press is comfortable, permitting a high degree of press freedom. The right to criticize government policy and action has been a longstanding tradition. Yet, like in other democracies, the demands of journalists for free access to information and the timely right to use that information often conflicts with the government's need, or perceived need, to maintain secrecy or at least to regulate the disclosure of information for political or national security reasons.

Suspension or confiscation of newspapers by the government is unknown. There are no restrictions or punitive licensing procedures on newsprint availability (over three-fourths of the nation's newsprint is imported, a fact that certainly provides opportunities). The press receives no government subsidies directly and few tax concessions. The value-added tax, currently 15%, is added to the cost of most goods and services produced. Newspaper and periodical sales and advertising revenues are zero-rated for the purpose of this tax. Like all postal customers, newspaper and magazine publishers receive reduced postage rates for bulk mailing.

Attitude Toward Foreign Media

The British attitude toward foreign media is definitely friendly. The existence of an extensive national press and the parliamentary system of government, however, have a certain restrictive effect on news access. As a result of privileges afforded to the national press, and the protections governing release of government reports and other matters, much of the news is obtained through the journalists' parliamentary lobby. Thus, reporters from the national newspapers and other members of the lobby have an advantage over foreign correspondents.

Deportation of foreign correspondents is infrequent. One of the more celebrated cases occurred in 1977 when writer Philip Agee, a persistent critic of U.S. Central Intelligence Agency activities, was expelled by the government. The Home Office charged that Agee had maintained contact with foreign intelligence agents and had disseminated information harmful to national security. Concurrently, deportation proceedings were also carried out against another American journalist, Mark Hosenball. Both persons left Britain in the summer of 1977 after exhausting the appeal process. The principal issue of concern to the media in these cases was that both individuals had been deported through the authority of the Home Office without a formal listing of charges against them.

Import restrictions on foreign publications are nonexistent except for those that apply to obscene material, and a wide variety of foreign newspapers and periodicals are available in the United Kingdom, mostly in the metropolitan areas, where various immigrant communities and international business and diplomatic personnel reside.

Domestic contacts with international organizations are widespread and include both business and government media organizations. At the government level, the United Kingdom played a major part in drafting the *Declaration on the Media* prepared by the United Nations Educational, Scientific and Cultural Organization (UNESCO) in 1977-78. The last-minute intervention of the British Overseas Development minister with the director-general of UNESCO produced the compromise text that embodied most of the ideals of a free press. The key to that compromise was a promise from Western nations to assist in improving Third World communications.

Subsequently, UNESCO established the International Commission for the Study of Communications Problems to help Third World nations improve their media systems. The Commission's report, published in 1980 and known popularly as the MacBride

Report, endorsed the concept of government communication policies and the commitment of the media to the task of nation building. The United Kingdom, along with the European Economic Community, indicated preliminary approval of the report while the United States reacted negatively. A consensus of delegates to the UNESCO General Conference held in Belgrade, Yugoslavia in October, 1980 agreed to a resolution based on the MacBride Report. While expressing strong reservations, Western nations joined in the consensus. The United Kingdom was particularly disconcerted and threatened to refuse to take part in the consensus. Ultimately it did join but only after the British delegate read a statement expressing extreme displeasure with many of the resolution's provisions because they concentrated too much on the rights of governments and not enough on the rights of individuals.

News Agencies

London is the home of the world's first news agency, Reuters. Established in Aachen in 1851 by Paul Julius Reuter and transferred to London the following year, it is one of the most respected international news organizations. The agency has approximately 1,150 full-time and part-time correspondents in about 183 countries around the world. Connections are maintained with many other national and private agencies, resulting in a broad news network. Reuters is owned by the newspapers of the United Kingdom, New Zealand and Australia through The Newspaper Publishers Association, the Press Association Ltd., the Australian Associated Press and the New Zealand Press Association—under a trust agreement that guarantees the independence of the news service.

The Press Association Ltd., Britain's national news agency, is a cooperative, nonprofit agency owned by the principal British regional newspapers and those of the Irish Republic. National newspapers published in London may be members only if they also publish a Manchester edition. The Press Association Ltd. which owns a major portion of Reuters Ltd., provides Reuters and other international agencies with a full home news service, including general, parliamentary, legal, sports and financial news, and furnishes regional papers with world news items from Reuters and the Associated Press. The Exchange Telegraph Co. Ltd. (Extel), an

independent national agency founded in 1872, provided a home news service until 1965. It now supplies financial, commercial and sporting news to the media.

There are many specialized agencies, such as London Newspaper Services Ltd. (London news), Gemni News Service (Commonwealth affairs), Central Press Photos Ltd. (photography), Financial Information Co. Ltd. (financial news) and Features International (features). Feature syndication is less common in the United Kingdom than in some other nations.

The British press is also served by the Associated Press Ltd. and United Press International Ltd., both subsidiaries of the U.S. news agencies, and a multitude of foreign news bureaus from Commonwealth, European, Communist and Third World nations. Some of the prinicpal agencies are the Australian Associated Press Ltd., Deutsche Presse-Agentur (West Germany), Agence France-Presse, Magyar Tavirati Iroda (Hungary), Tass (Soviet Union) and the Ghana News Agency.

As might be expected, provincial daily newspapers depend heavily on news agencies for nonlocal content. National papers use the organizations for world news but rely on their own resources for domestic news. In recent years national newspapers have increased their dependence on news services to compensate for a reduction in international correspondents on their individual staffs.

Electronic News Media

The broacasting system of the United Kingdom has a dual character: commercial and noncommercial. In 1922 several radio manufacturers established the British Broadcasting Company. Its early success led to a revision in its structure and in 1926 it became a public corporation, the British Broadcasting Corporation, under a royal charter with a Board of Governors appointed by the Queen. In addition to its royal charter, the BBC operates under a license and agreement issued by the secretary of state for the Home Office. These agreements expire at different intervals and must be renewed by the government.

The BBC operates two national color television networks (BBC-1 and BBC-2), four national radio networks (Radio 1, 2, 3, and 4) and numerous local radio outlets. Radio 2 is the principal channel for sports news and Radio 4 is the primary news and information service.

BBC news and public affairs programming for radio and television is the responsibilty of the director of news and current affairs, who reports to the director-general of the BBC. The radio and television services have separate structures under the overall authority of the director. In the radio branch the editor controls all news and current affairs material. News and current affairs are separate functions in the television branch, although there is cooperation between the two. The director of news and current affairs meets weekly with radio and television editors and news executives to discuss editorial issues, standards for coverage and matters of general news policy that set the pattern for news and public affairs treatment and program content.

Domestically the BBC maintains a staff of regional correspondents to provide coverage of newsworthy items in Scotland, Wales and Northern Ireland. Outside London there are 11 BBC newsrooms that broadcast television and radio news bulletins and topical programs to regional audiences. The BBC also operates 20 local radio stations in England, each of which has its own news service. Every local radio station is connected with the appropriate TV newsroom in its area as well as with the main newsroom in London, giving the BBC's national network instant access to local news sources.

Correspondents with special expertise report on political affairs, national defense, industry, agriculture, economics, education, science and other topics. The network center in London operates a General News Service that functions somewhat like an internal news agency, collecting foreign and domestic news from many sources and distributing it to BBC radio and television outlets in London, the regions and/or to local radio stations.

The BBC draws international news from its own correspodents stationed in various countries as well as from the various news agencies based in London. In 1979 the BBC had 18 full-time foreign correspondents supplemented by an extensive network of stringers around the world. Additional international coverage is provided through the resources of the BBC Monitoring Service. This listening service, augmented by cooperative agreements with comparable U.S. and West German monitoring agencies, expands coverage possibilities to some 120 nations. The Monitoring Service gives the BBC newsrooms a 24-hour file of world news and a daily "Summary of World Broadcasts." Many times this service is the only source of news from nations where the flow of information is officially restricted or interrupted by political upheaval. At the same time, however, information obtained from the Monitoring Service must be treated cautiously because of the difficulty or impossibility of verification. Given the increasing cost of news operations, this service will probably be utilized more heavily in the future, since it is inexpensive relative to its usefulness.

The BBC has its own staff of TV camera crews throughout the United Kingdom and in the more important foreign nations. Videotape and film is also available from international agencies, the most prominent of which is Visnews, a nonprofit trust formed by the BBC, Reuters, the Australian Broadcasting Commission, the Canadian Broadcasting Corporation and the New Zealand Broadcasting Corporation. Headquartered in London, the service has over 170 subscribers in 95 countries and is the largest contributor to the daily Eurovision news exchange. The BBC participates in a three-times daily exchange of newsfilm with the Eurovision network, which is particularly valuable because of its contact with Eastern Europe as well as other parts of the world. Independent Television News Ltd. also utilizes the Eurovision network and communications satellites.

In October 1977 the BBC began a one-year experiment with electronic news-gathering (ENG) equipment, the use of which is fairly common in the United States and other developed nations. The full adoption of this service by the BBC was delayed pending final agreement with labor—specifically the Association of Broadcasting and Allied Staffs—a situation similar to union-management negotiations concerning the introduction of electronic technology in the newspaper industry.

Finally, in November 1980, ENG equipment was put into regular service. Prior to that time the BBC had been operating at a distinct disadvantge relative to broadcasting services in nations where the technology was already being utilized. ENG was used extensively during the royal wedding of Prince Charles and Lady Spencer in July 1981. The results of this first big test and its consequences have not yet been evaluated.

The BBC receives its financial support

from the public through an annual license fee on all television receivers. A large portion of these payments is diverted to the national treasury.

The advertising-supported part of the nation's broadcasting system is the responsibility of the Independent Broadcasting Authority (IBA), which was established by an act of Parliament in 1954 to administer commercial television and orginally called the Independent Television Authority (ITA). Parliament extended the IBA's purview to include local commercial radio stations in 1973. Under license authority from the secretary of state in the Home Office, the IBA controls the advertising, supervises the programming, and owns and operates the transmitters. Actual program production is handled on a contract basis by Independent Television (ITV) programming companies. In 1980 there were 15 independent television program companies, including Channel Television for the Channel Islands, and at the beginning of the year there were 19 Independent Local Radio (ILR) contractors.

Independent Tevelision News (ITN) is a nonprofit company that supplies national and international news to all ITV stations. It is jointly owned by all the ITV program contracting companies. Special events news programming is available as well as regular news programs, including the half-hour "News at Ten," noontime "News at One" and "News at 5:45." The newsrooms of the individual companies provide the news for their immediate area and feed regional stories of national significance to ITN, which also has a network of stringers throughout the United Kingdom and the world as well as its own news film staff. ITN has been using satellite transmissions since the mid-1970s to enhance its coverage of world affairs.

Like the BBC, ITN recently began experimenting with the use of ENG equipment. Grampian Television, serving northeast Scotland from studios in Aberdeen and Dundee, became the first of the independent commercial companies to win an accord with the unions allowing regular use of ENG. ITN reached similar agreements with the Association of Cinematograph, Television and Allied Technicans in July 1980 and with the National Union of Journalists in September 1980.

Independent Local Radio also has a national and international news network, Indpendent Radio News (IRN). The London Broadcasting Company (LBC), the all-news station in London, is the headquarters of IRN, distributing live news every hour around the clock and updated highlights every 15 minutes. Most ILR stations maintain direct daily contacts with various local authorities, such as the police and transport authority.

A popular kind of programming on local radio is the call-in or phone-in show. The BBC has similar programming on its local stations, but the independent stations use it more, some contend too much. Although the programs are often frivolous or innocuous they do enable audience participation and provide lengthy coverage on issues in the news, especially when the program features a guest.

The independent contracting companies of both ITV and ILR pay a fee to the IBA to cover the administrative and technical costs

Percentage Distribution of Television Programs	
BBC Network:	
Current Affairs, Features, Documentaries	17.6%
Sports	13.7
Children	8.2
Light Entertainment	6.4
Drama	5.2
Further Education	4.6
News	4.2
Schools	4.0
Music	1.5
Religion	1.5
Welsh Language	0.4
Continuity	5.2
Open University	13.6
Films and Imports	13.9
	100.0%
ITV:	
News	10.5%
Current Affairs, Documenatries, Arts	13.0
Religion	2.5
Adult Education	3.0
School	6.25
Pre-School	1.5
Children	10.0
Plays, Drama, Movies	30.75
Entertainment/Music	12.0
Sports	10.5
	100.0%

Percentage Distribution of Radio Programs	
BBC Network only:	
Music	58.4%
Current Affairs, Features, Documentaries	15.2
News	6.2
Drama	3.9
Sports	3.4
Light Entertainment	2.2
Religion	1.5
School	1.7
Further Education	1.2
Children	0.9
Continuity	1.5
Open University	3.9
	100.0%

ILR:

Independent Local Radio program distribution varies widely according to the station from all news and features to combinations of music, news, public affairs, education, sport, talk and children's programs.

of the system. Approximately five-sixths of ITV company profits are paid to the government in tax. Nevertheless, they are very profitable operations.

The broad outlook for radio and television in the United Kingdom, including the news operations, is positive. The Annan Committee (Committee on the Future of Broadcasting, 1977), established by the government to make recommendations on broadcasting policy for the 1980s, endorsed the dual system and a policy of controlled expansion. One of the most important issues considered by the committee was a plan for a fourth national television network. A bill authorizing the new network under the IBA was making its way through Parliament in 1980. The network's main transmitters are scheduled to be in place by the end of 1982 and it should be fully operable by 1984. Wales will have special priority on signal saturation from the inception of the service, with Welsh-language programming projected.

ILR is expanding too; a 50% increase in commercial local stations is planned for the early 1980s.

No changes are foreseen for BBC national network television or BBC national network radio beyond the eventual separation of Radio 1 and Radio 2 in areas where they share the same transmission facilities. BBC local radio is expanding at a rate comparable to that of ILR stations, straining the corporation's finances. As a result, some observers estimate, the BBC will have to ask for a substantial increase in the present license fee in the very near future.

Broadcast regulations governing news programming require impartiality, independence and balance in the treatment of controversial topics. Furthermore, the IBA and BBC are prohibited from editorializing. The IBA is charged with ensuring that news and news features get a sufficient amount of air time on the independent television network.

Government announcements of major importance are routinely included in newscasts. Other, less important announcements are aired according to arrangements worked out by the various government departments with the BBC and/or ITN. For example, material prepared by the Central Office of Information is broadcast on a regular, paid basis by the commercial broadcast companies. The BBC handles such material free as part of its normal news and public affairs programming.

The BBC is required to broadcast "an impartial account day by day prepared by professional reporters of the proceedings in both Houses of the United Kingdom Parliament." Since 1977 both the BBC and IBA have been permitted to broadcast the proceedings of Parliament directly. Although there is no continuous coverage, some debates and the "Prime Minister's Questions" are broadcast live. A bill authorizing TV coverage of parliamentary proceedings was proposed in the House of Commons in 1980.

Each year the BBC and IBA conclude arrangements with representatives of the leading political parties for balanced presentation of their respective positions. Broadcast time is allocated by a formula based on the number of votes cast by party in the previous election. Use of broadcast facilities by parliamentary candidates is regulated by the Representation of the People Act of 1969, which prohibits segments promoting a candidate's election unless rival candidates also take part in the segment or consent to it without taking part.

Government ministers have access to the public through the BBC by means of an aide memoire agreement in effect since 1969 (the original access agreement is decades older). In some instances a right of reply by the opposition is guaranteed.

A major innovation in the electronic media

has been the development of teletext and viewdata technologies. These systems permit the broadcasting of written information in multiple frames. Viewers may select different "pages" for display on their television screens by means of a special decoder. Ordinary TV picture and sound transmission is not impaired by such viewing.

The BBC introduced its teletext service in 1974. Called CEEFAX an anagram for "see facts," it presents general news items, travel information, weather forecasts, sport reports, market and financial developments and shopping guides. Updated for 18 hours each day on both BBC-1 and BBC-2 the broadcasts offer more than 300 "pages" of information. ITV has developed a competing news and information service called ORACLE, an acronym for "optional reception of announcements by coded line electronics." In 1979 the Post Office also entered the field with its Prestel system, a viewdata device that operates via the telephone network rather than broadcast transmissions.

These systems have their own staffs, but a large portion of news and information is provided by a new group of organizations known as Information Providers. Many newspapers, including the *Daily Telegraph* and those of Express Newspapers Ltd., are forging links with teletext and viewdata services like Information Providers.

The United Kingdom maintains one of the world's most extensive international broadcasting organizations. The authority for this system is contained in the BBC's royal charter and its operation is an integral part of the BBC. The commercial system plays no part in international broadcasting. The BBC independently determines the programming and exercises the same tradition of journalistic news judgment as in its domestic services. The government does, however, specify the languages to be broadcast and the length of time devoted to each language program. Financing is provided in the form of a special Treasury grant-in-aid approved by Parliament. Consequently the government is directly concerned and involved in the international broadcasting system, and in recent years budget cutters have consistently pressed for a reduction of the amounts appropriated to run the system.

The BBC External Services department has responsibility for international broadcasting. Within the department are various subunits, which oversee the operation of programs covering different parts of the world. The European Service conducts broadcasting through the French Language Services (including the European continent and Francophone Africa), the German Language Service, and the East European, Central European, Finnish (incorporated under Central European for administrative reasons) and South European Services. The Overseas Service comprises the African, Arabic, Eastern, Far Eastern and Latin American Services. The World Service, unmatched by any other nation, provides a complete range of entertainment and informational programming in English 24 hours a day around the world.

The objectives of the External Services are "to give unbiased news, to reflect British opinion and to project British life and culture and developments in science and industry." This is accomplished by the presentation of music, drama, light entertainment, sport, news and news interpretation, and talk programs on science, literature, the arts, religion, economics and politics. The scope of the subject matter is broad and attempts are made to develop programming relevant to the culture of the intended audience.

The news and editorial offices of the External Services are the largest in the BBC and among the largest of any broadcast agency in the world. Regularly scheduled newscasts are frequent (approximately 250 each day). News stories and editorial comments selected from a variety of British newspapers are also aired at regular intervals along with financial developements, supplied to the BBC World Service by the *Financial News*, and sports reports, an important part of each broadcast. Special radio newsreels provide closer analysis of important news events. All news programming is presented in a deliberate, factual and straightforward style. The pace, as is generally true of international broadcasting, is measured and relaxed.

Most of the External Services' broadcasting originates in London. In 1980 the BBC maintained 47 transmitters in Great Britain and another 32 relay transmitters overseas, such as a Caribbean relay station on Antigua, which is shared with Deutsche Welle, the West German service orginating out of Köln. Each week the External Services broadcast 711 hours of programming in 17 European languages and 21 non-European languages plus English. The BBC estimates that approximately 75 million adult listeners tune in at least once a week.

The size of the audience and the extent of

signal coverage, however, do not reflect the full impact of the BBC External Services. The domestic broadcasting systems of numerous small nations rebroadcast the BBC transmissions, and several countries utilize the BBC's Transcription Service, which records and markets part of the External Services output for delayed local broadcast. This service includes entertainment programs, where the time factor is of little relevance, as well as a topical service, airmailed weekly, covering world affairs, science, sports, economics, British affairs and other subjects.

The External Services department is also responsible for the BBC Monitoring Service, located in Reading, just west of London. This service, which was begun prior to World War II and subsequently shared with a monitoring unit in the United States, monitors and translates foreign radio transmissions. Monitoring reports are provided to appropriate government departments and represent a news source for the BBC's domestic and international newsrooms. Summaries are published at frequent intervals (some daily). Subscribers to these services include foreign governments, newspapers and periodcials and news agencies.

The attitude indicated in the declarations and commission reports on the mass media issued by UNESCO could reduce the effectiveness of British international broadcasting in the future. Restrictions on the activity of foreign correspondents and the desire by many governments to direct the flow of information to their people through their own domestic media will affect the accuracy and timely reporting of news. Criticism of all international broadcasting, not just that of the BBC, is common among nations and is usually a no-win situation. In the latter part of 1979 the BBC External Services' broadcasts to Iran were criticized as aiding the collapse of the Shah's government. Subsequently the new regime of the Ayatollah Khomeini attacked the BBC for aiding its enemies.

Education & Training

There are two ways of becoming a journalist in the United Kingdom. Direct recruitment by a regional or local newspaper or selection for a one-year pre-entry program given by the National Council for the Training of Journalists (NCTJ), which represents the major press organizations. The first route has been fading, and currently almost all prospective candidates for a career in journalism receive some formal training. In addition journalism candidates generally take part in an apprenticeship that includes a period of on-the-job training.

The NCTJ provides short courses for journalists and conducts examinations culminating in the the award of a proficiency certificate. Courses for reporters are given at a number of centers. Further professional training is available periodically in the form of study programs organized by the newspapers belonging to the NCTJ. Postgraduate courses in journalism are offered at the Centre for Journalism Studies at Cardiff University in South Wales and at the City University in London. Cardiff University started a master's degree program in journalism in 1976. The City University is also planing to implement a master of arts degree program in media policy studies in 1981-82.

Each year several young Commonwealth journalists spend three months working and studying in Britain under the Commonwealth Press Union Harry Brittain Memorial Fellowship Scheme. The Thomson Foundation holds training courses for journalists from all parts of the world and provides consultants and tutors for courses in journalism held overseas.

The majority of journalists do not have a university degree or background, which has been cited as a possible reason for the lack of prestige afforded journalists in Britain compared, for example, with that given their counterparts in the United States. Those who do have a university background (approximately 40 percent) tend to strive for Fleet Street or radio/television employment early in their careers. Fleet Street newspapers do not recruit beginning journalists except on rare occasions for certain specialist positions. The BBC trains a small group each year for broadcast news; the independent companies ordinarily recruit from newspapers, although broadcast news training, financed by the IBA, was started at Cardiff University in 1980.

The major associations for the practicing journalist are the National Union of Journalists, the Institute of Journalists and the Guild of British Newspaper Editors. The national newspaper publishers are represented by the Newspaper Publishers Association and the provincial and London suburban press form the membership of the

Newspaper Society. Regional organizations include the Scottish Daily Newspaper Society, representing the daily and Sunday newspaper publishers of Scotland; the Scottish Newspaper Proprietors Association, representing the Scottish weekly publishers; and the Associated Northern Ireland Newspapers, an association of weekly publishers in Northern Ireland.

Summary

The British press is one of the world's most important and extensively developed news media. For years it has had one of the highest readerships in the world. However, during the last decade the traditional national and provincial newspapers have experienced a drop in readership and in sales, and the total number of newspapers continues to decline, a trend highlighted by the demise in 1980 of the nation's largest selling evening newspaper, the London *Evening News*.

The newspaper industry is beset by serious economic problems, including inefficient production techniques, overstaffing and increasing newsprint costs. The bleak financial situation is aggravated by high inflation and the resistance of the industry's labor unions to the introduction of cost-effective computerized technology. These problems threaten the survival of the nation's independent, private-enterprise press, and unless they are successfully addressed by management and the unions, the possibility of government intervention or even eventual administrative control is not an unrealistic scenario.

Another, less serious threat to the newspaper industry is increasing competition from the electronic media. The BBC, the commercial ITV and the Post Office have developed and introduced videotext systems for dissemination of news and other information, called CEEFAX, ORACLE and Prestel respectively. Competition from radio and TV has eaten and will continue to eat into newspaper advertising revenues, although it is felt that this competition can be met.

The electronic media are booming. A new fourth television channel is under construction and additional local commercial radio and BBC radio stations are going on the air. The commercial stations are very profitable and will continue to be. The BBC, however, is experiencing some economic problems. The service receives its funding from a television license fee, and budget projections suggest a hefty increase may be required.

Broadcasters are not faced with the same degree of union-management friction that exists in the newspaper field. There is, however, resistance to the introduction of new technology as demonstrated by the belated entry of both the commercial television stations and the BBC television networks into the area of electronic news gathering. On the positive side, the advances made in the teletext field evince a commitment to new electronic media technology, and the cost of electronic equipment continues to decrease. This is also true of the electronic technology used in newspaper printing plants, but the advantage is somewhat offset by the continuing increase in newsprint and delivery costs.

The overall outlook for the newspaper industry is not good, and there are some serious economic and industrial relations problems that must be addressed soon before the erosion becomes irreparable and affects the tradition of a free press that the United Kingdom has exported to so many nations. But if the national newspapers should ever get their house in order and adopt the technology that is (and has been for some time) readily available to them—i.e., cost-effective short print runs, facsimile transmissions and satellite printing—it all points in one direction: extensive regional editionizing and a consequent dramatic collapse in revenues for Britian's hitherto prosperous provinical press.

CHRONOLOGY

1976	Closed shop union dispute between government, publishers and journalists' unions begins to become a significant issue in newspaper industrial relations.
1977	Parliament approves live radio

broadcasts of its proceedings. Annan Committee issues it *Report on the Future of Broadcasting*.

Royal Commission on the Press issues its final *Report*.

1978	*The Times* and *The Sunday Times* suspend publication in union-management dispute.		Initial planning and development of fourth commercial TV network begins.
1979	Independent Local Radio and local BBC radio expand number of stations with government approval.		Parliament considers clarifications of contempt of court law.
	The Times and *The Sunday Times* resume publication.	**1981**	*The Times* and *The Sunday Times,* due for closure in March, bought by Rupert Murdoch from International Thomson Organisation Ltd. for £11 million ($27.3 million).
1980	*Evening News*, a London evening newspaper, ceases publication. No city in the United Kingdom now has more than one evening newspaper.	**1982**	Breakfast TV due to start, networked from London.

BIBLIOGRAPHY

Beharrell, Peter, and Philo, Greg. *Trade Unions and the Media.* London, 1977.

Benn's Press Directory. London, 1979.

Boyce, George, Curran, James, and Wingate, Pauline. *Newspaper History from the 17th Century to the Present Day.* London, 1978.

British Broadcasting Corporation. *BBC Handbook.* London, 1980.

Callender Smith, Robin. *Press Law.* London, 1978.

Chibnall, Steve. *Law-and Order News: An Analysis of Crime Reporting in the British Press.* London, 1977.

Cleverley, Graham. *The Fleet Street Disaster.* London, 1976.

Curran, James. *The British Press: A Manifesto.* London, 1978.

Grundy Bill. *The Press Inside Out.* London, 1976.

Havighurst, Alfred F. *Britain in Transition.* Chicago, 1979.

Independent Broadcasting Authority. *Television and Radio.* London, 1980.

Industrial Relations in the National Newspaper Industry. Cmnd. 6680, London, 1976.

Munro, Colin R. *Television, Censorship and the Law.* Westmead, 1979.

Murphy, David. *The Silent Watchdog: The Press in Local Politics.* London, 1976.

Murray, George. *The Press and the Public: The Story of the British Press Council.* Carbondale and Edwardsville, Ill., 1972.

Royal Commission on the Press. *Final Report.* Cmnd. 6810, London, 1977.

Royal Commission on the Press. *Interim Report: The National Newspaper Industry.* Cmnd. 6433, London, 1976.

Royal Commission on the Press. *Report.* Cmnd. 1811, London, 1962.

Royal Commission on the Press. *Report.* Cmnd. 7700, London, 1949.

Schlesinger, Philip. *Putting 'Reality' Together: BBC News.* London, 1978.

Simon, Jenkins. *Newspapers: The Power and the Money.* London, 1979.

Smith, Anthony. *The British Press Since the War.* Newton Abbot, 1974.

United Kingdom. *Report of the Committee on Contempt of Court.* Cmnd. 5794, London, 1974

————. *Report of the Committee on Defamation.* Cmnd. 5909, London, 1975.

————. *Report of the Committee on the Future of Broadcasting.* Cmnd. 6753, London, 1977.

————. *Report of the Committee on Obscenity and Film Censorship.* Cmnd.7772, London, 1979.

————.*Report of the Committee on Privacy.* Cmnd. 5012, London, 1972.

————. *Report of the Departmental Committee on Section 2 of the Official Secrets Act 1911.* Cmnd. 5104, London, 1972.

UNITED STATES

by George Kurian
(Press Laws & Censorship section by Aviam Soifer)

BASIC DATA

Population: 221,196,000
Area: 9,363,396 sq. km. (3,615,207 sq. mi.)
GNP: US$1.69 trillion (1978)
Literacy Rate: 99.9%
Language(s): English
Number of Dailies: 1,763 (1979)
  Aggregate Circulation: 62,223,040
  Circulation per 1,000: 282
Number of Nondailies: 7,954 (1979)
  Aggregate Circulation: 42,347,512
  Circulation per 1,000: 191
Number of Periodicals: 10,236
Number of Radio Stations: 8,532 (1979)

Number of Television Stations: 990 (1979)
Number of Radio Receivers: 444 million (1978)
  Radio Receivers per 1,000: 2,009
Number of Television Sets: 218.5 million (1978)
  Television Sets per 1,000: 988
Total Annual Newsprint Consumption: 11.24 million metric tons (1979)
  Per Capita Newsprint Consumption: 50.8 kg. (112 lb.)
Total Newspaper Ad Receipts: US$14.49 billion (1979)
  As % of All Ad Expenditures: 29.1

Background & General Characteristics

Historical Background

In 1990 the U.S. press will be 300 years old. It was born in Boston on September 25, 1690, with the publication of the *Publick Occurrences, Both Foreign and Domestick* by Benjamin Harris, author of the celebrated *New England Primer.* Harris' paper did not survive its first issue. The Colonial authorities suppressed it because it was published without official permission and because it contained offensive items on the alleged savagery of the Indians, then allies of the English.

During the next 30 years a number of short-lived papers appeared, such as the *Boston News Letter,* published by the local postmasters who, as in Europe, enjoyed franking privileges and access to news sources. But the first serious paper in the history of the American Colonies was the *New England Courant,* published in Boston by James Franklin. Published without a royal license, it survived for six years, until Franklin was jailed and ordered not to publish any newspapers in Massachusetts. Subsequently, he moved to Rhode Island, where, in Newport,

he brought out that colony's first newspaper.

It was James' younger brother, Benjamin Franklin, who could claim the title of the first successful publisher and journalist in North America. His paper, *The Pennsylvania Gazette,* was one of the best known publications of his day, carrying news and literary comment couched in Ben's wry and inimitable style. He was also involved in the development of other newspaper ventures, including foreign-language newspapers. A man of many talents and facets, Ben represented the ideal combination of a printer, journalist, publisher and scientist who was also a good businessman and a great statesman.

By 1730 the Colonial press had gained sufficient stature to be considered by the government as a nuisance. To provide an object lesson, the Colonial authorities turned on John Peter Zenger, publisher of the *New York Weekly Journal,* launching a prosecution against him for seditious libel. In a landmark case, Zenger was found guilty but freed because of public opinion. It was the first major judicial decision to shape the course of U.S. press history.

As the clouds of the Revolutionary War began to gather in the 1770s, the press, then 35 newspapers strong, was increasingly drawn into the struggle. All three sides, Tory, Whig and Radical, were represented in the press. Tory views were propounded in such newspapers as James Rivington's *Gazette* and Whig views in the *Boston Gazette, Country Journal* and *Pennsylvania Chronicle.* By the mid-1770s the press was covering its first war. Despite poor communications, difficulties in obtaining supplies and newsprint, and harrassment from British military authorities, the press did a remarkably good job of reporting the news. There were few correspondents and it took weeks for news of battles to reach one end of the country from the other, but every reader could follow the fortunes of war, even when they seemed to go against the Colonists. Some newspapers even brought out extras to carry fast-breaking news between their weekly editions.

The press that emerged from the war, like the nation itself, found itself engaged in new struggles. The first was to define the constitutional structure of the young republic. The press helped to publicize the constitution and to stimulate national debate. The principle of press freedom was enshrined in the First Amendment, which reads in part, "Congress shall make no laws...abridging the freedom of speech or of the press...." These 14 words serve as the bulwark of a free press and make it possible for American media to serve as a watchdog over governmental actions and individual rights. The Founding Fathers also enunciated the philosophical basis of press freedom as eloquently as the French libertarians. Thomas Jefferson said, "Were it left to me to decide whether we should have a government without newspapers, or newspaper with government, I should not hesitate a moment to prefer the latter." In defending Harry Croswell, publisher of *The Wasp,* in 1804, Alexander Hamilton presented a case for press freedom that is often quoted even today.

The first U.S. dailies were started in Philadelphia around the 1780s. By the 1820s there were about 25 dailies and more than 400 weeklies. Circulations were small, seldom exceeding 1,500 in the larger cities. Partisan politics dominated the news, but space was also devoted to literary miscellany and social news. A few were distinguished papers, conforming to Jefferson's definition of a responsible press: *The National Intelligencer,* the New York *Evening Post* and *The Journal of Commerce.* They were small in format, with few headlines and illustrations.

The U.S. press experienced what has been described as its first revolution in the 1830s. By this time, the press had passed into the hands of such veterans as Noah Webster, John Fenno, Philip Freneau, and William Cobbett; the Industrial Revolution had created new businesses and increased the demand for advertising; the urban population was growing and more people were acquiring a higher education; and above all, (Andrew) Jacksonian democracy demanded an informed electorate. Not partisan debate nor commercial information, but news became the primary product in newspapers. The new newspapers were called "penny papers" because they sold for a penny each. The first of such penny papers was founded by Benjamin Day in 1833. Called the *New York Sun* (with the slogan "It Shines For All"), it reached a circulation of 8,000 within six months, outselling its nearest rival by two to one. The *Sun*'s success encouraged James Gordon Bennett to start the *New York Herald* in 1834. His purpose was to outdo the *Sun* in every respect: "to record facts, on every public and proper subject, stripped of verbiage and coloring, with comments suitable, just, independent, fearless, and good-tempered...." Despite his unabashed sensationalism, Bennett pioneered in the development of the media, and many of his innovations survive to this day. The *Herald* was one of the first newspapers to have regular departments such as sports, finance and society. His major impact was in the field of news gathering. He introduced the system of "beat" reporters and employed correspondents in key cities in the United States and abroad. He had a nose for the dramatic, a flair for the outrageous. No one but Bennett would have sent a totally unknown reporter named Henry Morton Stanley on an assignment to find an English evangelist named David Livingstone in the heart of Africa.

If Bennett was the innovator, then Horace Greeley was the reformer. His *Tribune* was started in 1841 to give New Yorkers an inexpensive newspaper less brash than the *Sun* and the *Herald,* and to serve as a true Whig organ. The *Tribune*'s circulation of 200,000 in the 1850s never approached that of the *Herald,* but in influence it towered above all its contemporaries. When Greeley spoke, the nation listened. He not only discussed issues, he challenged the conscience of his readers, especially on such issues as slavery, protective tariff, the development of the West and the advancement of the rights of labor. His "Prayer of 20 Millions" editorial in August 1862 was believed to have inspired Lincoln's Emancipation Proclamation, issued in January 1863. Greeley is also thought to have played an important role in the Republican convention that chose Lincoln as the standard bearer. Greeley himself was the presidential nominee of the liberal Republicans in 1872.

The mid-1850s also witnessed the founding of some of the more familiar names in U.S. media today: *The New York Times, The Baltimore Sun* and *The Chicago Tribune. The New York Times* was founded by Henry J. Raymond in 1851 and soon gained a reputation for its interpretive articles, well-balanced coverage and objectivity. Another major event was the founding of the Associated Press in 1848.

As the Civil War engulfed the nation and the media, newspapers tried hard to maintain their objectivity. Few of them were extremists, even in the South. But as the war progressed, journalists joined in the general trend of fanning the flames of hatred. Censorship was employed for the first time, by both North and South, to stop reports that could retard the war efforts. Also for the first time, photographs were used to add a whole new dimension to news coverage. Mathew Brady's photographs captured the horrors of war in a way that set the standard for all later news photographers.

For a few decades after the end of the Civil War the press was in doldrums. It was not until the 1890s that it experienced a second revolution, this time heralded by massive technological breakthroughs. These included the linotype, half-tone engraving, the stereotype, web-fed rotary presses, color printing techniques, the typewriter and the telephone. New editors also appeared who had the vision to convert these innovations into a whole new kind of journalism. Among these was Joseph Pulitzer, a Hungarian immigrant who came to the United States as a mercenary in the Union cause. Virtually penniless at the end of the Civil War, he became a reporter in St. Louis, saving up enough money to buy the *St. Louis Dispatch* at a sheriff's sale. Later, he acquired the *Post* and merged the two into the *Post-Dispatch*. In the 1880s he acquired the *New York World*, making it, by 1892, the nation's largest newspaper, with a circulation of 374,000. Pulitzer is best remembered for his many

gimmicks and stunts, such as sending Nellie Bly, alias Elizabeth Cochran, on a trip around the world à la Jules Verne, and his many crusades, such as those against business monopolies. But his most significant contribution to the profession was his uncompromising emphasis on "accuracy, accuracy, accuracy," editorial integrity, clear and concise writing and extensive use of illustrations.

Very soon Pulitzer became embroiled in a circulation war with another media giant, William Randolph Hearst. Out of this struggle came the term Yellow Journalism, as papers lowered their standards of reportage in order to lure readers away from their competitors. The turn of the century was indeed the heyday of yellow journalism; it is estimated that at least one-third of the newspapers in the nation's 21 largest cities were distinctly yellow. In this struggle Hearst had the edge, if only because of his nearly unlimited financial resources and his ability to attract the best talents in the business. Yellow journalism peaked during the Spanish-American War, which Hearst appears to have personally promoted. At the height of the war, Hearst's New York *Journal* had a circulation of 1.5 million, with the *World* not too far behind. Hard pressed to maintain such inflated circulations after the end of the war, newspapers turned to lurid staples, such as sex, crime and violence. Public reaction to such extremes of sensationalism grew stronger after President McKinley's assassin confessed that he had been stirred up by something he had read in Hearst's newspapers.

If Hearst and Pulitzer hogged the media scene, there were a number of others who made quiet but positive contributions. Men like E. L. Godkin of the *New York Post,* Henry W. Grady of *The Atlanta Constitution,* Henry Watterson of the Louisville *Courier-Journal,* Charles Dana of the *New York Sun,* Joseph Medill of *The Chicago Tribune* and William R. Nelson of the *Kansas City Star* helped to build up a kind of journalism that stressed seriousness and a balance between news and opinion. Another development was the acquisition in 1896 of *The New York Times* by Adolph Ochs (rescuing it from impending bankruptcy) and its conversion into one of the world's finest newspapers of record.

The U.S. press emerged in the 20th century as a mature and financially strong institution. In the years before World War I, there were 2,600 dailies and 14,000 weeklies serving a population of some 91 million. Fierce competition and the natural laws of survival of the fittest forced many weak newspapers to fall by the wayside every year. During the four years of World War I, over 100 newspapers ceased publication or merged with their competitors. The period also witnessed a recrudescence of sensational journalism, this time called Jazz Journalism. Its leader was the New York *Daily News,* founded by Joseph M. Patterson in 1919. By 1924 it had the nation's largest circulation, a lead it held on to until 1980. Hearst's *Daily Mirror* and Bernarr MacFadden's *Daily Graphic* were equally jazzy. The *Daily Graphic* concentrated on sensational stories so heavily that it did not even subscribe to a wire service. A number of imitators, all tabloids, soon appeared in other cities, including Chicago, Los Angeles, Washington, and Denver. At the other end of the spectrum, the same period witnessed the founding of one of the best-known practitioners of serious journalism: *The Christian Science Monitor,* one newspaper that is perhaps better known abroad than in the United States. Founded by the Christian Science Church in 1908 at the suggestion of Mary Baker Eddy, its official purpose is "to injure no man, but to bless all mankind."

Chain newspapers under the same ownership, while not uncommon in the latter part of the 19th century, became a major characteristic of the U.S. press only in the first quarter of the 20th century. Hearst, the front-runner, had become the nation's largest newspaper chain by the end of World War I, and the Scripps-McRae League, founded in the late 19th century, had expanded to more than 30 papers in 15 states. Milton McRae dropped out by 1914 and was replaced by Roy Howard; the resulting organization became known as Scripps-Howard.

Meanwhile, under editor Frank I. Cobb, the *New York World* had returned to some measure of respectability as a champion of liberal ideas. Even Hearst had begun to curb his taste for sensationalism and to concentrate on building up his communications empire, which now included magazines and a wire service. William Lippard McLean had successfully transformed the small *Evening Bulletin* into Philadelphia's major daily (which, according to its matter-of-fact slogan, "Nearly Everyone Reads"), with a circulation of 220,000. A new media empire was being founded by Gardner Cowles, Sr., who moved from banking to newspapers by acquiring the Des Moines *Register & Leader,* the *Evening Tribune* and others.

Chastened and sobered by World War I and the Great Depression and confronted by a world no longer safe for democracy, the press began paying increasing attention to world events as well as economic crises. It was challenged not only to report events but to interpret them. A new breed of writers developed. Called syndicated columnists, they were typified by that pundit of all pundits, Walter Lippmann, whose writings had the sonorous ring and authority of a Delphic oracle. With one well-turned phrase he could deflate national reputations or build them up. While Lippmann was the best known, there were a number of others, equally influential, who pioneered in the development of the political column: David Lawrence (later to found *U.S. News & World Report*), Frank Kent of the Baltimore *Sun,* Mark Sullivan of the New York *Herald-Tribune,* and Dorothy Thompson, one of the figures associated with the legendary Algonquin Club. Later these were joined by Drew Pearson, Raymond Clapper, Marquis Childs, the Alsop brothers, Joseph and Stewart, Roscoe Drummond and George Sokolsky.

Generally conservative by tradition, most newspapers opposed the New Deal. The American Newspaper Publishers Association (ANPA) led the opposition, which was only partially successful. The government's right to regulate the business side of newspaper operations was firmly established. But government efforts to interfere with free expression through prior restraint or unjust taxation were rejected by the judiciary.

The press was even less successful in warding off the economic pressures caused primarily by competition from newsmagazines *Time* and *Newsweek,* the electronic media and motion pictures. The 1930s and 1940s were particularly hard, leading to a steady decline in the total number of newspapers. Between 1937 and 1944 alone there were 360 mergers and suspensions, bring the total down to 1,745. Among the names that vanished were the two New York dailies, the *World* and the *Tribune.* In a related development, newspaper chains were becoming more prominent. John S. Knight, editor and publisher of the *Akron Beacon Journal,* acquired the *Detroit Free Press* in 1940 and *The Miami Herald* and *Tribune* in 1937. John Cowles acquired *The Minneapolis Star* and *The Minneapolis Journal* in 1939. James M. Cox acquired *The Miami News* and *The Atlanta*

Journal in the 1930s. Frank E. Gannett had put together a chain of 16 newspapers, mostly in New York state. Samuel I. Newhouse was another name that became known nationally. Many non-chain newspapers were able to survive successfully despite changes in ownership. *The Washington Post* became the capital's top daily after Eugene Meyer purchased it from receivership in 1933. Similarly, *The Milwaukee Journal* did not lose its prestige or influence even after the death of its long-time editor, Lucius W. Neiman. The Louisville *Courier-Journal*, which had passed on to the Bingham family in 1917, and the *Atlanta Constitution*, which had passed from the Grady to the Howell family, continued to be the leaders in the South. The control of the Kansas City *Star* was acquired by its staff, which did not diminish its crusading spirit.

During World War II the press again voluntarily subjected itself to censorship. Under Byron Price, a former AP editor, the Office of Censorship developed a Code of Wartime Practices for the American Press, which was generally adhered to by newsmen. At the same time the Office of War Information, under Elmer Davis, was in charge of disseminating information designed to boost morale.

After every war the U.S. press has had to undergo a period of agonizing readjustment. The years after World War II were no different. The economic signals were contradictory and even confusing. On the one hand, the *Herald Tribune,* now owned by John Hay Whitney, lost between $15 and $20 million in 10 years. On the other hand, *Editor & Publisher,* the industry's voice, reported that some newspapers turned handsome profits, up to 23 percent before taxes. On the one hand, advertising revenues were increasing dramatically, despite competition from television; on the other hand, rising costs were forcing newspapers to cut back on services and increase prices. Rising postal rates, skyrocketing newsprint prices, and higher employee compensation were biting into profits. Technological developments were opening up opportunities to produce newspapers faster with fewer workers, while at the same time a rash of strikes gave the newspaper industry one of the worst records in industrial relations. There were extensive shutdowns in New York, Detroit, Boston, San Jose, Portland, St. Paul, Seattle, Cleveland and St. Louis. *The Detroit News* and the *Detroit Free Press* suffered one of the nation's longest newspaper strikes, from November 27, 1967 to August 20, 1968, a total of 267 days.

Newspapers continue to rely on technology to face the challenge of inflation. Typesetting was revolutionized in the 1960s by the use of photocomposition and electronic computers and in the 1970s by video display terminals (VDT), optical character readers (OCR) or scanners, floppy disks and computer storage. Many smaller newspapers have switched to offset, including over 400 dailies.

Rising costs and the heavy investments needed for this newer technology have reinforced the trend toward groups or chains. This phenomenon may turn out to be the most important development in the U.S. press in the last quarter of the 20th century. Of the nation's daily newspaper cities, only 2.5 percent have separately owned and competing general circulation dailies. Despite general alarm, these twin trends toward monopoly and concentration have continued unchecked. Efforts were begun in Congress in 1967 to help maintain competition among general circulation papers in 22 cities. The resulting Newspaper Preservation Act of 1970 offers limited exemption from antitrust prosecution to certain newspapers. The act was designed to permit competing newspapers to join production, circulation and advertising operations if one of them was in financial distress.

Because of their dual role as messenger and as gatekeeper,* newspapers have always been heavily involved in any national debate. It is not surprising therefore that in the stormy decade of the 1970s, in a society where the informant is becoming as important as the information and, in the late Marshall McLuhan's words, the medium is becoming as important as the message, the U.S. press found itself swirling in controversies, often on the defensive. Often there was a confusion between its purely business activities and its intellectual and social functions. In some cases the press has been blamed for the events it reported, and in others it has been blamed for describing problems without providing solutions. As national needs multiply and national resources shrink in the 1980s, the U.S. press may be required to redefine its functions and provide leadership and direction as well as information.

*See preface for a discussion of this term, which is gaining increasing currency.

Table 1
Number of Daily Newspapers
Total Number of U.S. Morning, Evening and Sunday Newspapers and Their Circulation 1920–1979

Year	Morning	Evening	Total M & E[1]	Sunday
1920	437	1,605	2,042	522
1925	427	1,581	2,008	548
1930	388	1,554	1,942	521
1935	390	1,560	1,950	518
1940	380	1,498	1,878	525
1945	330	1,419	1,749	485
1946	334	1,429	1,763	497
1950	322	1,450	1,772	549
1955	316	1,454	1,760	541
1960	312	1,459	1,763	563
1965	320	1,444	1,751	562
1970	334	1,429	1,748	586
1971	339	1,425	1,749	590
1972	337	1,441	1,761	605
1973	343	1,451	1,774	634
1974	340	1,449	1,768	641
1975	339	1,436	1,756	639
1976	346	1,435	1,762	650
1977	352	1,435	1,753	668
1978[2]	355	1,419	1,756	696
1979[3]	382	1,405	1,763	719

[1] There were 24 "all-day" newspapers in 1979. They are listed in both morning and evening columns but only once in the total.
[2] Revised figures.
[3] Preliminary figures.
Source: *Editor & Publisher.*

Table 2
Daily Newspaper Circulation
Growth of U.S. Morning, Evening and Sunday Circulation, 1946–1979

Year	Morning	Evening	Total M & E	Sunday
1946	20,545,908	30,381,597	50,927,505	43,665,364
1950	21,266,126	32,562,946	53,829,072	46,582,348
1955	22,183,408	33,963,951	56,147,359	46,447,658
1960	24,028,788	34,852,958	58,881,746	47,698,651
1965	24,106,776	36,250,787	60,357,563	48,600,090
1970	25,933,783	36,173,744	62,107,527	49,216,602
1971	26,116,131	36,155,127	62,231,258	49,664,643
1972	26,078,386	36,431,856	62,510,242	50,000,669
1973	26,524,140	36,623,140	63,147,280	51,717,465
1974	26,144,966	35,732,231	61,877,197	51,678,726
1975	25,490,186	35,165,245	60,655,431	51,096,393
1976	25,858,386	35,118,625	60,977,011	51,565,334
1977	26,742,318	34,752,822	61,495,140	52,429,234
1978[1]	27,656,739	34,333,258	61,989,997	53,990,033
1979[2]	28,574,879	33,648,161	62,223,040	54,367,487

[1] Revised figures.
[2] Preliminary figures.
Source: *Editor & Publisher.*

Size

The U.S. press is the largest in the world in terms of both number of newspapers and aggregate circulation. In 1979, 1,763 daily newspapers and 719 Sunday newspapers were published in the United States, with an aggregate circulation of 62,223,040 for the dailies and 54,367,487 for the Sunday papers. Per capita circulation is 282 per 1,000 inhabitants for the dailies and 246 per 1,000 for the Sunday papers; according to *The Book of World Rankings,* the United States ranks 20th in the world in this respect.

Chain newspapers are published by 163 newspaper groups, of which 49 publish two newspapers, 32 publish three, 14 publish four and 68 publish five or more. Dailies are published in 1,533 cities; 181 have two or more dailies.

Contrary to popular impression, the number of dailies has not declined substantially during the past two decades. Since 1944 the number has remained remarkably stable, rising to 1,786 in 1952 and falling to a low of 1,748 in 1970. During the same time, Sunday papers have been rising steadily in numbers.

Although afternoon newspapers have been declining both in number and circulation since their peak in the late 1960s, there are still more afternoon papers than morning papers—1,405 to 382—and p.m.'s have the majority of the sales—33.6 million daily compared to 28.5 million for a.m.'s. The shift to morning publication evident for a number of years has picked up momentum recently. According to *presstime,* the magazine of the American Newspaper Publishers Association, 39 afternoon papers switched to morning publication between 1979 and 1981.

Bucking the trend are a number of successful afternoon dailies, most of them in the suburbs, such as *Newsday* on Long Island, N.Y. and *The Record* in Bergen County, N.J. These papers prospered as the city papers chose to ignore the shift of readers to the suburbs because of higher delivery costs. Most successful afternoon papers are in small cities and towns with circulations of less than 50,000 and do not have daily competition from another newspaper. In some cases, such as the Oakland *Tribune* and *The Milwaukee Journal,* both afternoon and morning newspapers are published under the same ownership. Only a few big-city afternoon dailies, such as *The Detroit News,* the *Houston Chronicle* and *The Seattle Times,* are strong enough to withstand competition from a morning paper.

The most promising development for bolstering falling circulations is the so-called all-day paper, a basic package of features and advertising that routinely updates the major breaking stories, sports results and stock tables. Some afternoon papers, like the Dallas *Times-Herald,* use this format to break into the morning field, and certain morning papers adopted it to deter potential afternoon rivals. There are now 30 self-styled all-day papers, including the *New York Post, The Detroit News* and *The Times-Picayune* and *The States-Item* of New Orleans. The pattern of ads in these papers remains constant through the 24-hour cycle but the headlines vary. Many papers have achieved substantial reductions in production, editorial and distribution costs by employing the all-day format. Generally, only the morning edition is available by home delivery; the p.m. editions are found at newsstands and vending machines.

Almost all newspapers in the United States are strictly local papers. There is no truly national newspaper, as in the United Kingdom and Japan. *The National Observer,* published by Dow Jones, was probably the closest thing to a national newspaper that the United States ever had. Nor does the United States have a party press in the same sense as Continental countries. Most American dailies take an independent position on politics. The majority of them, however, tend to take conservative positions more often than liberal ones. The major exceptions are *The New York Times, The Washington Post* and the *St. Louis Post-Dispatch,* which have consistently followed the liberal road, especially at election times.

In 1979 U.S. daily newspapers averaged 70 pages for all morning editions, 59 pages for evening editions and 207 pages for Sunday editions—up from 64, 56 and 196 pages respectively in 1978. (This rise is in spite of steep increases in the price of newsprint.) The typical Sunday or weekend edition carries five or more separate sections. It has been estimated that it will take an adult, at least five hours at moderate reading speed, to read an average Sunday paper.

Types of Newspapers

As in every other free press system, U.S. newspapers are responsive to audience needs, and need to be for their survival. Each paper therefore tends to develop its own personality and to be associated with certain qualities in the minds of its readers. Nevertheless, there are certain broad categories that stand out and thereby merit discussion. These are the following: (a) suburban newspapers, (b) weeklies, (c) minority, especially black newspapers, (d) student newspapers, (e) ethnic and foreign language newspapers, (f) shoppers or free newspapers and (g) underground or counterculture newspapers.

Suburban Newspapers. Historically, the press has followed the people. When the great rush to the suburbs began in the 1950s, the press was not far behind. The Census Bureau estimated in 1980 that about 62 percent of the urban population lived in suburbs, as compared to 37.6 percent in 1970. The growth in the number and circulation of suburban dailies has been correspondingly dramatic. Between 1971 and 1975 the number of suburban newspapers is estimated to have increased by 10 percent and their circulation by 21 percent, to more than 37 million, compared to 6.2 million in 1950. The suburban share of total circulation is over 50 percent, as compared to 21.1 percent in 1950. The Suburban Newspapers of America organization currently has a membership of 850, a gain of 800 in the space of eight years. Nearly 60 of these are dailies. The Suburban Press, Inc. represents 1,100 suburban newspapers.

Suburban newspapers differ widely in quality. Some are little more than "community bulletin boards" or shopping sheets. On the other end of the spectrum is *Newsday*, considered the most successful suburban daily newspaper currently being published. Founded by the Guggenheim family in 1940, it was acquired by the Times Mirror Company in 1970, which has preserved the paper's unique suburban character as the voice of Nassau and Suffolk counties on Long Island, N.Y. With a 1980 circulation of 492,580, *Newsday* is one of the 10 largest newspapers in the United States.

During recent years, suburban newspaper groups have been established in a number of metropolitan areas. These include the Comcorp group of Cleveland and Harte-Hanks Newspapers of Texas. Metropolitan newspapers, such as *The New York Times, Los Angeles Times, Philadelphia Bulletin* and *Chicago Tribune*, have also moved into the suburban market with zoned editions, special supplements and editorial and advertising sections, as well as improved news coverage of local community events.

Weekly Newspapers. At the end of 1979, 7,954 weeklies were being published in the United States, an increase of 281 over 1978. This was the highest figure in 14 years. Total weekly newspaper circulation was 42.3 mil-

Table 3

Daily Newspapers By Circulation Groups: Growth (U.S.), 1946–1979

| | Number of Daily Newspapers | | | | | Dailies Over 50,000 | |
| | | Circulation | | | | | |
Year	Total	Under 50,000	50,000– 100,000	100,001– 250,000	Over 250,000	Number	Percentage
1946	1,763	1,564	91	70	38	199	11.3
1950	1,772	1,571	82	84	35	201	11.3
1955	1,760	1,548	94	82	36	212	12.1
1960	1,763	1,540	96	83	44	223	12.7
1965	1,751	1,510	111	88	42	241	13.8
1970	1,748	1,491	127	92	38	257	14.7
1971	1,749	1,497	123	91	38	252	14.4
1972	1,761	1,505	127	91	38	256	14.5
1973	1,774	1,519	129	86	40	255	14.4
1974	1,768	1,513	130	86	39	255	14.4
1975	1,756	1,504	135	81	36	252	14.3
1976	1,762	1,512	131	83	36	250	14.2
1977	1,753	1,494	137	85	37	259	14.8
1978	1,756	1,487	140	92	37	269	15.3
1979[1]	1,763	1,498	142	88	35	265	15.0

[1]Preliminary figures.
Sources: ANPA *Editor & Publisher.*

lion, more than 2 million over 1978. Average circulation also rose to its highest level ever, 5,324, and total estimated readership was a record 169.4 million.

These figures dumbfounded critics who had predicted a few years ago that the weekly newspaper was a dying institution. But both demographics and the new technology seem to favor their continued growth. Nicknamed the Grassroots Press, weekly newspapers provide services and perform functions tailored to the specific informational and economic needs of thousands of small communities. Gerald Stone and Chris Gulyas, using a random sample of 763 weeklies in the *National Directory of Weekly Newspapers* (1977), found that 54 percent of the nation's weeklies are published in agricultural-industrial communities, 35 percent in suburban areas and 11 percent in resort communities. About 58 percent are published on Thursdays. Nearly 81 percent have no competition. Another random national survey found that 54 percent of the weekly editors are conservative, 24 percent middle of the road and 22 percent liberal.

In a related but separate category are general interest weeklies addressed to national audiences. Two of the best known are the *National Enquirer*, published by Generoso (Gene) Pope, Jr., and the *Star*, published by Rupert Murdoch. Distributed mainly through supermarkets and convenience stores, these papers have achieved a multimillion circulation, purveying an endless mix of romance, health tips, psychic predictions and intimations of scandal.

Minority Newspapers. Almost every one of the hundreds of minority groups—each an ethnic island in itself—is served by its own press. The largest and most representative of these is the so-called black press. Described by Gunnar Myrdal as the greatest single force in the black community, it dates back to 1827 when the first black newspaper, *Freedom's Journal*, was founded. Since then over 3,000 black newspapers have appeared, of which only 165 were being published in 1979. This represents a decline of 22.5 percent since 1974, when 213 papers were active. Total circulation in 1979 stood at 2,901,162, down from 4,369,858 in 1974, a decline of 33.6 percent. The number of full-time staff members also dropped from 2,523 in 1971 to 1,880 in 1979, a decline of 25 percent. According to Henry G. La Brie III's *A Survey of Black Newspapers in America*, the principal reason for this decline is "legacy. When the publisher dies, the newspaper dies with him." A second is the inability of black newspapers to serve their basic constituency while depending on white advertising for

Table 4

Numbers of Suspended, Merged, Changed-Frequency and New U.S. Daily Newspapers, 1962–1978

Year	Outright Suspensions	Mergers	Conversions to Less Than Daily	Total Terminations	New Dailies	Net Gain (Loss)
1962	9	2	7	18	17	(1)
1963	11	1	8	20	21	1
1964	7	1	6	14	15	1
1965	8	4	3	15	13	(2)
1966	6	3	5	14	21	7
1967	7	4	4	15	10	(5)
1968	3	4	2	9	12	3
1969	13	5	4	22	26	4
1970	12	3	7	22	17	(5)
1971	8	4	5	17	16	(1)
1972	11	5	7	23	27	4
1973	6	4	4	14	35	21
1974	6	7	4	17	18	1
1975	7	6	2	15	13	(2)
1976	1	0	2	3	14	11
1978	8	3	3	14	27	13
Total	115	53	70	238	276	37

Sources: 1962-70: Ben H. Bagdikian, "Report of An Exaggerated Death"; 1971-78: *Editor & Publisher*.

					Table 5					
					Weekly Newspapers					
				U.S. Weekly Newspapers and Their Circulation, 1960–1979						

Year	Total Weekly Newspapers	Average Circulation	Total Weekly Circulation	Estimated Readership
1960	8,138	2,606	21,327,782	85,311,128
1965	8,003	3,260	26,088,230	104,352,920
1970	7,610	3,866	29,422,487	117,689,948
1971	7,567	4,030	30,495,921	121,983,648
1972	7,553	4,236	31,997,341	127,989,364
1973	7,641	4,572	34,938,800	139,935,200
1974	7,612	4,702	35,792,409	143,569,636
1975	7,486	4,698	35,176,130	140,704,520
1976	7,530	4,955	37,313,556	149,254,224
1977	7,466	5,075	37,892,883	151,571,532
1978	7,673	5,245	40,243,795	160,975,180
1979[1]	7,954	5,324	42,347,512	169,390,048

[1]Preliminary figures.
Source: ANPA.

survival. Other reasons cited include inadequate financing, poor news coverage, sensationalism, lack of editorial direction—some 37 percent of black newspapers do not even have an editorial page—and, above all, a shortage of skilled reporters and writers.

Black newspapers are published in 34 states and the District of Columbia, with the largest number in Florida (17) and California (14). About 46 percent are less than 20 years old. Most are members of the National Newspaper Association. The bellwether of the black press is New York's *Amsterdam News*, which converted to a tabloid format in 1979. Many of the more prosperous ones belong to groups or chains, of which there were half a dozen in the late 1970s. The largest is the John Sengstacke group, which published, among others, the Chicago *Daily Defender* and the *New Courier*. The others are the Afro-American group of Baltimore, the Post Newspapers of California, the New Leader group in Louisiana, and the World or Scott group in Atlanta, Birmingham and Memphis.

The Chicano movement of the 1960s led to the development of a Chicano press—as distinct from the Spanish-language press—with a strength of some 50 newspapers by 1979. Many of them, such as *El Malcriado*, are radical papers. Originally limited to California, they have spread to New Mexico, Arizona, Texas and Colorado.

Because of the general weakness and lack of influence of the minority press, minority pressure groups have often attempted to influence the general or white press through a number of tactics. These have included pickets, economic boycotts and letter and telephone campaigns. The NAACP (National Association for the Advancement of Colored People) has used the boycott method successfully a number of times against newspapers that allegedly report adversely on black issues or failed to provide adequate coverage. The Philadelphia *Evening Bulletin* is believed to have lost between 25,000 and 50,000 subscribers as a result of a campaign started by 400 black ministers alleging overemphasis on black crime in the *Bulletin*'s pages.

Student Newspapers. An estimated 1,800 student newspapers are being published in U.S. campuses, with a total circulation of six million. About 100 of these are published at least four times a week and are classified as dailies. Some have circulations up to 50,000, with full-time professional editors and hundreds of contributors and reporters. In some communities the campus newspaper is also the only local newspaper. Most campus newspapers have publication boards that include a cross section of students, faculty and outside journalists. In addition, there is invariably an adviser who is a cross between censor and liaison. Formerly advisers had the right to review all copy and change or eliminate stories before publication, but recent court decisions have restricted this right. The larger papers employ full-time professional journalists as publisher, business manager, advertising director, and editor. Others, like the Ivy League college newspapers, *The Daily Californian* at the University of California at Berkeley, the University of Kentucky *Kernel*, and the University of Florida *Alligator,* are independent corporations and members of the American Newspaper Publishers Association.

Many student newspapers gravitated toward the radical movement in the 1960s and 1970s and still exude a countercultural flavor. They are particularly concerned with four areas: civil rights, foreign affairs, student rights and politics. As a result, the campus newspapers are increasingly in conflict with administrators. The surface conflicts are specific, but beneath the apparent issues are basic disagreements regarding the purpose and function of a campus press as well as differing interpretations of First Amendment guarantees. The most common disagreements relate to the increasing use of obscenity and four-letter words, legalization of drugs, endorsement of political candidates, violence and even dress codes. Student editors resort to extreme tactics to make their publications "relevant," and administrators feel compelled to defend the institution's integrity. Some newspapers also had run-ins with the IRS over their tax-exempt status following their endorsement of political candidates.

Ethnic & Foreign Language Newspapers. An ethnic newspaper is defined as one published in a foreign language or in English but addressed to a specific national or racial group. There were 215 such newspapers in the United States in 1979, with a total circulation of 2.2 million. Most of them are members of the American Foreign Language Newspaper Association. Changing patterns of immigration, following more liberal national quotas since 1965, are expected to promote the growth of an ethnic press.

Shoppers or Free Newspapers. George Brandsberg in his *The Free Papers* has described shoppers, as free newspapers are called, as the major mass medium in hometown America. "Shoppers" are defined as papers that consist mostly of advertising, delivered free to households in a designated circulation area. Most are published weekly and distributed by carrier boys or third-class mail or both. They are also known as pennysavers. "Free community papers," on the other hand, are provided free to at least half of those who receive them and contain as much as 25 percent news of general interest. Some types of free newspapers are also called "controlled circulation papers." There were 6,000 free papers in publication in 1978, with a circulation of 34 million, or roughly half the circulation of the nation's dailies. They averaged 32 pages per issue, of which 74 percent was advertising. According to the National Association of Advertising Publishers, they carried $500 million in advertising in 1978. Large chains have also emerged in this field, such as Harte-Hanks Communications, which owns the largest shopper group in the United States.

Underground Newspapers. One of the newest phenomenon in U.S. press is what is called alternative (or underground or counterculture) newspapers. An offshoot of the anti-establishment tide of the 1960s, it was first thought of as an aberration that would soon disappear from the media scene. But like the man who came to dinner but remained to stay, the underground press refused to go away. It has now been accepted as a more or less permanent feature by media-watchers. It probably began in 1955 when Norman Mailer, Don Wolfe, John Wilcock and Ed Fancher started the *Village Voice* in Greenwich Village, New York City. Profane and iconoclastic in its approach to both language and news, it set the tone for many of its imitators and competitors. Its later history is a commentary on the decline of the counterculture. Acquired by Clay Felker, publisher of *New York* magazine, a magazine for the affluent, it finally became part of the

Table 6

Foreign Language Newspapers, 1979

Arabic	5	Italian	12
Armenian	10	Japanese	9
Bulgarian	2	Korean	1
Carpatho-Russian	2	Latvian	2
Chinese	11	Lithuanian	12
Czech	6	Norwegian	5
Danish	1	Polish	13
Dutch	1	Portuguese	3
Estonian	1	Rumanian	2
Finnish	4	Russian	4
French	6	Serbian	1
German	24	Slovak	8
Greek	10	Spanish	21
Hebrew	1	Swedish	6
Hungarian	10	Ukrainian	5
(East) Indian	1	Urdu	1
Iranian	1	Yiddish	4
Irish	4	Yugoslavian	7

Source: *Editor & Publisher International Yearbook*

establishment by passing into the control of Australian media baron Rupert Murdoch in 1976. On the West Coast the leading underground paper was the Los Angeles *Free Press*, a sex rag that expanded from a four-page giveaway to a 48-page weekly with a paid circulation of 95,000. It became a casualty of the graying of the Americas in the late 1970s and died in 1978. *Underground Press in America*, published in 1970, listed over 450 papers with a multimillion circulation and a high pass-along readership. The most successful among them were the *Berkeley Barb*, the San Francisco *Oracle* and *Rolling Stone*, which, despite its tabloid format, often passes off as a magazine. In its heyday the underground press had its own news services, the Underground Press Syndicate, founded in 1966, and the Liberation News Service, founded in 1967. Although the subculture that it served has withered, many underground newspapers still survive, faltering and unsteady.

Self-Regulation and Press Councils

In its desire to ward off government regulation, the U.S. press has made a number of efforts at self-regulation. However, these efforts have been intermittent, hesitant and half-hearted. It is clear that U.S. newspapers do not want anyone looking over their shoulders or second-guessing their actions. Some steps have been made in the direction of self-regulation in recent years. The most notable of these is the National News Council, perhaps the only such council in the world, an independent watchdog agency composed of journalists, lawyers, businessmen and others. Founded neither by the government nor by the press but by a philanthropic organization, it was set up in 1973 with a $100,000 grant from the Twentieth Century Fund. Its stated purpose was to "judge complaints concerning the accuracy and fairness of news reporting in the United States and to initiate studies and to report on issues involving the freedom of the press."

When the Council began its work it restricted itself to complaints to the national news media, but from 1974 it has accepted complaints about the print and electronic media from any citizen anywhere in the country. To avoid putting the media in double jeopardy, the Council requires all complainants to sign a waiver promising not to take their case to the Federal Communications Commission or the courts. This does not, of course, prevent the FCC from taking up the complaint on its own after seeing the Council's report. The Council also does not pass judgment on the merits of opinions expressed in the media so long as the distinction between news and opinions is clearly maintained. As with other press councils, NNC has no teeth—no formal enforcement powers. Some see this as a sign of weakness, while others see it as a source of strength. The Council's findings reach all practitioners of journalism, published periodically under the title *In the Public Interest* and also in the *Columbia Journalism Review.*

During the first five years of its operation, the NNC received over 600 complaints; 75 percent were settled without the necessity of a formal decision. Only 59 of the complaints were decided against the media. The Council has also issued ethical guidelines for the guidance of newsmen, commissioned a study on access to the press, and initiated a project toward making presidential press conferences more responsive to the public.

Despite these gains the Council remains, in the words of its chairman, Norman E. Isaacs, "unloved by the media." For example, *The New York Times*' A. O. Sulzberger has remained consistently hostile to the Council from its inception, alleging that even though it is nongovernmental, "we fear that it would encourage an atmosphere of regulation in which government intervention might gain public acceptance." Similarly, the American Broadcasting Company (ABC) views the Council as "redundant and dangerous." The media also resent the dominance of the Council by outsiders and nonnewsmen. Opposition also comes from those who feel that the Council is too weak. By siphoning off complaints from the FCC, the argument goes, the Council is in effect letting the networks off the hook. Against such resistance, the Council has been slow to make headway. It is also faced with a financial problem; the Twentieth Century Fund has discontinued its annual subsidy and the media have not yet opened up their pursestrings.

In addition to the NNC, there are a number of local news councils. The idea for local press councils was first mooted by Chilton Bush, director of Stanford's Department of Communications in the 1930s. It was not until 1946, however, that the first council was established, in Colorado. More than two dozen such councils were started when the Mellett (after Lowell Mellett) Fund for a Free and Responsible Press financed experimental local press councils in 1967. Some of them serve small communities—Littleton, Colorado; Bend, Oregon; Redwood City, California; and Sparta and Cairo, Illinois; others serve cities—Seattle, St. Louis and Honolulu. The largest and the most successful has been the Minnesota Council, the first statewide press council in the United States. Founded in 1971, it received 225 complaints during the first eight years of its operation, most of them involving allegations of inaccuracy or unfairness in reporting.

Another development in self-regulation is the appointment of in-house ombudsmen. The Louisville *Courier-Journal* has been credited with this innovation in the late 1960s. Other papers followed, and by 1979, over 20 newspapers had full-time ombudsmen on their staff. Ben Bagdikian, the former in-house watchdog of *The Washington Post*, defined his role as not that of an adversary representing the public against the management, but of a performance monitor, checking the quality of journalism against the paper's own standards.

Internal Organization

The management structure of the publishing organization is basically the same in both large and small newspapers. The typical daily has at least nine departments: Corporate Officers; General Management and Business; Advertising Department; Circulation Department; Promotion and Marketing; News Executives; Editors and Managers; Personnel Department, and Mechanical Department. The editorial staff is usually headed by an editor, followed by managing editors, executive editors, news editors, city editors, Sunday editors, and associate editors. The number of department managers is usually a good indication of the size of a newspaper. Most newspapers have departments dealing with auto, art, books, education, fashions, food, home furnishings, radio, religion, society, sports and travel. Some have a special Hot Line (sometimes called Action Line) editor providing a variety of services to the consumer.

Not all editors enjoy the same autonomy and authority within the organization. In general, U.S. editors today are a less-visible and less-known breed than their counterparts a century ago. Their niche in the journalistic world has been taken over by the columnists and commentators, whose growing influence is reflected in the fact that they are now known by the more potent name of "opinionmakers." In a survey conducted by the National Conference of Editorial Writers in the late 1970s, James J. Kilpatrick, William F. Buckley, Jr. and George Will emerged as the top conservative columnists, Tom Wicker and Joseph Kraft as the top liberals, Rowland Evans and Robert Novack, David Broder and Jack Anderson as top reporters, and Art Buchwald as the top humorist.

Almost as influential and certainly as well known are the political cartoonists. Most daily newspapers use cartoons on a regular basis (*The New York Times* is a notable exception), and those with larger circulations have full-time staff cartoonists. Two of the best all-around cartoonists are Pat Oliphant of the recently defunct *Washington Star* and Herbert Block (Herblock) of *The Washington Post*. Jeff MacNelly of *The Richmond News Leader* was counted among the top three prior to his retirement in 1981. Others cited as consistently good are Paul Conrad of the *Los Angeles Times*, Don Wright of *The Miami News*, John Fischetti of the defunct Chicago *Daily News*, Bill Sanders of the *Kansas City Star*, Charles Werner of *The Indianapolis Star*, Dick Yardley of the Baltimore *Sun*, Cliff Baldowski of *The Atlanta Constitution*, Ross Lewis of *The Milwaukee Journal*, Tom Little of the Nashville *Tennessean*, Joe Parrish of *The Chicago Tribune*, C. D. Batchelor of the New York *Daily News*, Don Hesse of the *St. Louis Globe-Democrat*, Tom Engelhardt of the *St. Louis Post-Dispatch*, Hugh Haynie of the Louisville *Courier-Journal*, Lou Grant of the Oakland *Tribune*, Jim Ivey of the *San Francisco Examiner*, Frank Miller of *The Des Moines Register* and Scott Long of *The Minneapolis Tribune*. Garry Trudeau's "Doonesbury" cartoons are in a class by themselves and are extremely popular with the young.

The editorial staff performs the most important function in a newspaper: they determine what goes into it and what does not. The caliber of U.S. editors is undoubtedly among the finest in the world. In 1979 a study commissioned by the National Conference of Editorial Writers found that most of them are men, although the proportion of women has increased from 2.4 percent in 1971 to 7 percent in 1979. The median age is 48.14, unchanged from 1971; only 7 percent were under 30, while 47.5 percent were over 50. Understandably, their educational levels were way over the national average: more than 83 percent had baccalaureate degrees. Their median salary was $24,000, up from $16,750 in 1971. Nearly 43 percent said they were Democrats, 35 percent said they were Republicans, and 22 percent claimed they were independents. The majority said that their political views were similar to those of their publishers, and that they were seldom or never compelled to write against their political beliefs.

Elite Newspapers

Over the years, U.S. newspapers have been ranked and re-ranked in an effort to determine the standards of excellence in journalism. The rankings that are most often cited are the 1974 Edward L. Bernays poll of newspaper publishers, the *Saturday Review* poll of journalism educators, *Time* magazine's selections of 1974 and *The Elite Press: Great Newspapers of the World,* by John Merrill and Harold Fisher. (For a more complete discussion of these rankings see The World's Elite Newspapers.)

The top 11 from the Bernays poll are listed according to the percentage of respondents who considered them to be the ideal newspapers.

The Edward L. Bernays Poll

	%
The New York Times	82
The Washington Post	76
Los Angeles Times	73
The Miami Herald	59
The (Louisville) Courier-Journal	52
The Chicago Tribune	40
The Milwaukee Journal	39
The Wall Street Journal	37
St. Louis Post-Dispatch	36
The Christian Science Monitor	33
The Boston Globe	33

The *Saturday Review* poll also used percentages to determine the most highly regarded newspapers in the country.

The *Saturday Review* Poll

	%
The New York Times	71
The Christian Science Monitor	46
The Wall Street Journal	42
St. Louis Post-Dispatch	39
The Milwaukee Journal	35
The Washington Post	34
The Louisville) Courier-Journal	22
The Chicago Tribune	16
(Chicago) Daily News (defunct)	12
The (Baltimore) Sun	11
The Atlanta Constitution	10
The Minneapolis Tribune	10
Kansas City Star	9
Los Angeles Times	9

Time's selections did not use percentages in its rankings but listed the top 10 alphabetically.

Time Selections

The Boston Globe
The Chicago Tribune
Los Angeles Times
The (Louisville) Courier-Journal
The Miami Herald
The Milwaukee Journal
Newsday
The New York Times
The Wall Street Journal
The Washington Post

John Merrill and Harold Fisher include a slightly different list in their *World's Great Dailies, 1979.* Using eliteness as a yardstick, they chose:

The Atlanta Constitution
The (Baltimore) Sun
The Christian Science Monitor
Los Angeles Times
The (Louisville) Courier-Journal
The Miami Herald
The New York Times
St. Louis Post-Dispatch
The Wall Street Journal
The Washington Post

The last-named list forms the basis for the following profiles of the most outstanding newspapers in the United States.

The Atlanta Constitution. Founded by Carey Wentworth Styles in 1868, *The Atlanta Constitution* was the voice of the New South after the Civil War. Its stature was in no small measure due to Henry W. Grady, who was among the last of the statesmen-journalists of the 19th century. After Grady, Ralph McGill and Eugene Patterson continued to guide the paper's growth into excellence. Currently owned by Cox Enterprises, it has a circulation of 218,807. Nearly 80 percent of this circulation goes to subscribers. Of the news hole, some 10 percent is assigned to international news, 20 percent for national news and 30 percent for local news. It considers itself a liberal paper, usually supporting Democrats for political office and displaying considerable social concern. According to Hal Gulliver, the editor, "A good newspaper should be guided by the old thesis of striving to afflict the comfortable and comfort the afflicted." The *Constitution* has some 125 editors and writers, of whom at least two are full-time investigative reporters. A typical issue consists of 52 pages, with four sections. There are weekly tabloid extras providing additional coverage for the four main suburban areas.

The (Baltimore) *Sun.* Founded in 1837 by Arunah S. Abell, *The Sun* (originally *The Baltimore Sun*) has been the epitome of respectability and aristocracy. Owned by the same family since its inception, it has been sustained by a sense of continuity and a sense of mission. Politically independent, it has sided with both Republicans and Democrats. Conservative on economic matters, it takes a liberal line on civil and human rights and often takes strong editorial stands on issues. The *Sun*'s major strengths lie in its comprehensive international and national coverage. It has full-time correspondents in eight foreign cities, and its roster includes such distinguished names as Paul Ward, Price Day, Philip Potter, Michael Parks and Henry Truitt. With 14 reporters in Washington, the paper is able to provide in-depth coverage of the Washington scene.

In 1910 A. S. Abell Company acquired the Baltimore *World* and renamed it the *Evening Sun.* The two now form a group known as Sunpapers. A. S. Abell also operates two TV stations, four radio stations, a publishing firm and an industrial park, with annual revenues of $50 million and a work force of 2,000. The combined daily circulation of the Sunpapers is 350,848 on weekdays and 374,989 on Sundays, more than double that of its competitor, the *News-American.*

The Sun places great stress on objectivity.

Reporters are actively discouraged from taking part in politics, community affairs or nonjournalistic enterprises and prohibited from accepting press junkets and other freebies. As a result it has won numerous awards, including nine Pulitzer Prizes. A typical issue is 40 to 44 pages in length, divided into three sections. The Sunday edition often runs to 200 or more pages, plus special magazine sections. Advertising takes up about 55 percent of the space; and of the news hole, national and international news make up 10 percent each, editorials 14 percent, local news 10 percent and analysis 1 percent.

The Christian Science Monitor. The Christian Science Monitor is unique in the sense that it is not merely a newspaper but also an institution and a moral force in its own right. Tightly organized and well edited, it stresses purpose, significance and permanence in the news. Reflective, dispassionate and noncontentious, it somehow manages to appear detached from all the news it reports so well. The *Monitor* is also unusual in the sense that it is one of the few papers owned by a church, officially the First Church of Christ. This explains some of its departures from conventional journalism. Christian Science believes in spiritual healing, so that the word "die" is avoided in favor of "pass on." Smoking and drinking are verboten, and the paper has airbrushed glasses and cigarettes out of news photographs—although Winston Churchill usually appeared with a cigar in hand. It never prints the words "damn" or "hell" except in direct quotes. The church influence extends to an advertising policy that rejects ads for tobacco, alcohol, pharmaceuticals, X-rated movies and racy books.

In the words of its editor emeritus, Erwin Canham, the *Monitor*'s strength stems from its "attitude of confidence in good. . . . Hence the *Monitor* has always been profoundly dedicated to a crusading, reformative approach to human affairs. . . . [It] tries to present the nature of reality. . . . to make a meaningful pattern out of a complex world." According to former editor John Hughes, the *Monitor*'s proper role is that of a problem solver. "We edit the paper so that the reader is not in a pit of despair. We describe solutions." But the *Monitor* does not pull punches and does not exclude hard reporting on social problems. Politically the paper is nonpartisan and does not endorse anyone for office. The last presidential candidate that received its endorsement was Dwight Eisenhower. In the late

1920s and 1930s the *Monitor* had a stable of writers who have become legends in the profession: Erwin Canham, Roscoe Drummond, Richard Strout, Harold Hobson, Cora Digby, Willis Abbott, Drew Pearson and Robert S. Allen. Today a corps of 50 seasoned correspondents provides the bulk of the reports. These include eight full-time correspondents in London, Bonn, Johannesburg, Hong Kong, Moscow, Athens, Tokyo and a Latin American correspondent based in Boston. Ten writer reporters and one photographer keep an eye on Washington, D.C.

The *Monitor* is an attractive, compact newspaper with a six-column makeup and generous use of photographs. A typical issue contains 24 to 28 pages. It has won the Edmund C. Arnold Typography Award three consecutive times, giving it permanent possession of the trophy. A weekly international edition is published outside London. The *Monitor* provides two syndication services, one bought by 159 U.S. newspapers and 30 foreign papers. Among the many awards that it has won are four Pulitzer Prizes, and five Overseas Press Club Awards in as many years.

As a national newspaper, the *Monitor* outsells *The New York Times* in 35 states. It also circulates in 120 countries of the world, making it one of the best-known international newspapers.

Los Angeles Times. Once described as the house organ of the Republican Party, the stodgy *Los Angeles Times* underwent a total facelift during the 1960s to become one of the nation's most admired dailies. The architect of this transformation was Publisher Otis Chandler, who not only demolished the paper's old image but in the process built a new media empire that includes three newspapers (*Newsday* of Long Island, the Dallas *Times Herald* and the Orange Coast *Daily Pilot*), a paper mill, seven book-publishing firms, seven magazines, six information services, two television stations and 19 cable systems. Founded in 1881 by Thomas Gardiner and Nathan Cole, the paper had been acquired by Harrison Gray Otis, later passing on to Otis's son-in-law, Harry Chandler. Within two years after Otis, grandson of Harry, took over the publisher's chair, the paper had begun to impress media watchers. In 1962 the *Times* had but one overseas correspondent; today it has 18, including such distinguished names as William Tuohy, Joe Morris, Jack Foisie and Robert Elegant. The *Times'* foreign correspondents also enjoy greater free-

dom than their co-professionals. The national coverage has also improved, with 24 correspondents in the nation's capital, and domestic bureaus in six major cities. At the local level, special editions were added for Orange County in 1968 and San Diego County in 1978.

The result was not merely a better newspaper but also increased circulation and advertising linage. By 1980 the *Los Angeles Times* had overtaken *The New York Times* and the *Chicago Tribune* to become the nation's third-largest selling newspaper (the first two being *The Wall Street Journal* and the New York *Daily News*). In 1978 the paper reported running 158 million lines of advertising, including 5.8 million classified ads, some 40 million more lines than the next U.S. paper and the most of any newspaper in the world.

An average weekday edition of the *Times* contains more than 200 pages, and its Sunday edition over 416 pages. It consumes more newsprint than any other U.S. daily. The typical daily consists of at least five parts, with the first 32-page section covering the major international and national news. To date, the *Times'* writers have garnered nine Pulitzer Prizes, 12 Society of Professional Journalists/Sigma Delta Chi Awards and nine Overseas Press Club Awards. The *Times* operates two syndication services; the one in association with *The Washington Post* is subscribed to by over 430 newspapers around the world.

The (Louisville) *Courier-Journal.* Called by its owners, the Bingham family, a public trust, *The Courier-Journal* (Louisville was dropped some time ago) is aimed at "solid citzens...with an appetite for news." Considered a liberal paper, it generally follows a Democratic line. It also considers itself primarily a regional newspaper serving Kentucky and southern Indiana. Its circulation has never been larger than 200,000, and the number of its editorial staff has also been small, around 135. But it excels in the accuracy and fairness of its presentation of news and its vigorous editorial page. Between 1918 and 1978 it won seven Pulitzer Prizes as well as a number of other awards.

The Miami Herald. Part of the Knight-Ridder Newspapers chain, *The Miami Herald* has tirelessly pursued the goal of being the best paper in the Deep South. In naming the *Herald* as one of the 10 best dailies in the United States, *Time* praised it for its "hell-for-leather legwork" and its international coverage. With a staff of 350, of whom 210 are writers, the *Herald* places emphasis on news; in fact, it ranks among the top five leaders in total news linage. It also publishes a Spanish-language daily section and an English-language international edition that is air-lifted to Latin American countries. Its daily circulation of 444,058 makes it one of the best-selling papers in the South. Between 1950 and 1975 the paper won three Pulitzer Prizes. The paper has also been a leader in protecting First Amendment press freedom rights.

The New York Times. To those who have read Gay Talese's *The Kingdom and the Power, The New York Times* might be aptly described as "the news as theater." Behind the clean, well-edited product that appears every morning is an ongoing drama, in which newsmen and editors themselves are the actors. But the paper itself seems to remain untouched by such human transactions. Its excellence has not been questioned; indeed, *Time* described it as the "platinum bar by which editors across the country measure their own papers." Exploring the secrets of its preeminence, Executive Editor A. M. Rosenthal found four of them: "The *Times* is a newspaper of continuity. The *Times* is a newspaper of relativity because it grades the importance of the news. The *Times* maintains a decent level of discourse. The *Times* is a newspaper of objectivity." If it were to be characterized in one word, that would be "thoroughness."

The *Times* claims a number of superlatives as well. Its total news staff of around 650 is the largest in the U.S. As of 1978, *Times*men had won 42 Pulitzer Prizes, more than any other newspaper. Its Sunday edition of over 400 pages in the largest in the world. From nearly two million words that flow into the 1.3-acre newsroom the staff culls 70 pages, or 152,000 words, of information, so large that Publisher Arthur Ochs Sulzberger one remarked, "Anyone who claims to have read the entire paper every day is either the world's fastest reader or the world's biggest liar."

Under the slogan, "More than Just the News," since 1976 the *Times* has introduced several special insert sections for different days of the week: "Weekend" on Fridays, "Home" on Thursdays, "Living" on Wednesdays, "Science, Education and Medicine" on Tuesdays and "Sports Monday." In 1976 the paper switched from an eight-column-per-page format to one of six columns for news and nine for advertisements. This has in-

creased the advertising space without adversely affecting the news hole/ad ratio, which stands at 30:70. The op-ed and editorial pages have been brightened and the Book Review renovated. As a result of these innovations, circulation is nudging a million copies daily, spread over every state and major town in the United States and most countries of the world. The *Times'* foreign coverage, already one of the best in the world, has improved in recent years as a result of eyewitness reports from its large foreign staff. Thirty-two full-time correspondents working out of 23 bureaus and 25 part-timers constitute the paper's worldwide information-gathering network. The *Times* may be also the only newspaper to subscribe to all the five major international news services: AP, Reuters, UPI, AFP and Tass.

St. Louis Post-Dispatch. The *St. Louis Post-Dispatch* is essentially Joseph Pulitzer's legacy to the American media. His journalistic commandments, chipped in granite in a plaque, still form the creed of the paper. It calls on the *Post-Dispatch* to:

> always fight for progress and reform, never tolerate injustice or corruption, always fight demagogues of all parties, never belong to any party, always oppose privileged classes and public plunderers, never lack sympathy with the poor, always remain devoted to the public welfare, never be satisfied with merely printing news, always be drastically independent, never be afraid to attack wrong, whether by predatory plutocracy or predatory poverty.

Still owned by the Pulitzer family, the *Post-Dispatch* has never wavered in its commitment to these seminal principles. John Merrill and Harold Fisher have compared it to the *Guardian* of England. "Both papers are highly literate, hard-hitting liberal dailies, which make it their business to puncture pomposity and suggest rational solutions to human problems. Both shun emotionalism, detest bigotry in any form, and lash out against extremists wherever they are found. Both prod and agitate their readers into grappling with important issues of their day." John Gunther called it the "most effective liberal newspaper in the United States," while Adlai Stevenson described it as "one of the best papers on earth." *Newsweek* once noted that the *Post-Dispatch* "has won more crusades, perhaps, than any other American daily." Appropriately, the paper has won the

Pulitzer Prize five times and its staff members have received an additional ten.

The *Post-Dispatch*'s main strengths are its international coverage, which was expanded under Joseph Pulitzer II, its interpretive articles, and vigorous and well-written editorials. The paper is made up of several sections. Weekday issues run from 44 to 60 pages and the Sunday edition from 120 to 160 pages plus three magazine sections. About two-thirds of the space is devoted to advertisements. On the whole, the *Post-Dispatch* presents an attractive appearance. Making all this possible are 175 editorial staff members, many of them with advanced graduate degrees.

The Wall Street Journal. The Wall Street *Journal* is an improbable paper for the title of the largest selling newspaper in the United States. Edited for the businessman and not for the masses, it is redolent of the dignified boardrooms and not the boardwalks. Yet, since its inception on July 8, 1889, it has managed to combine dignity in content with good journalism. Its staple is still financial news, but its national and international coverage is as broad as that of general papers. According to *Time*, it is also one of the most widely quoted conservative dailies.

The Journal has a daily circulation of 1,798, 516 (about 85 percent of which goes to subscribers) in four different regional editions across the country. The parent company also publishes the *Asian Wall Street Journal, Barron's, Book Digest* and 20 daily community papers, owns the AP-Dow Jones Wire, a number of book-publishing firms, and has a 49 percent interest in the *Far Eastern Economic Review.*

The paper has never departed from its gray format: line drawings are used instead of pictures; the makeup is vertical, with few headlines. One of the few innovations over the years was the addition of an op-ed page in 1978. The *Journal* has a staff of 4,100, about 200 of whom are writers and editors. There are 31 correspondents in Washington, D.C., and 32 abroad. The paper's accuracy and reliability inspire a confidence from its gray-flannel audience that is unmatched by any other paper in the United States.

The Washington Post. No newspaper is closer to the levers of power in the United States than *The Washington Post*, which appears on the breakfast tables of everyone who is someone in Washington, from the president down. No other paper is also as conscious of its power or flaunts it so tirelessly. Founded in 1877 as a humble three-

cent paper by Stilson Hutchins, the *Post* displayed early some of the characteristics by which it is known today: perseverance in pursuing stories and boldness in reporting them. It passed through two owners before it was acquired by Eugene Meyer, a New York banker who had no publishing experience. Determined to improve the paper's quality, Meyer drew up seven principles, the first of which summed it all: "The first mission of a newspaper is to tell the truth, as nearly as the truth can be ascertained." He attracted distinguished columnists, such as Walter Lippmann, Dorothy Thompson and Westbrook Pegler, and published Drew Pearson's "Washington Merry-Go-Round." By 1943 *Time* was calling it one of the world's 10 greatest newspapers. By the time he handed over reins to his son-in-law, Philip Graham, Meyer had given the paper "the three priceless ingredients of success; integrity, decency and powerful idealism."

Until his brilliant career ended in suicide, Philip Graham was a spark plug that pushed the *Post* to new heights. He was responsible for buying out the rival *Times-Herald* in 1954, for acquiring *Newsweek* in 1961, for establishing the joint *Washington Post–Los Angeles Times* national news service, and for setting up the *Post*'s first foreign news bureau in London. When Katherine Graham assumed control of the paper in 1963, she brought Benjamin Bradlee in as editor. The two have worked as a team in propelling the *Post* toward a unique combination of profitability and excellence; Bradlee believes the two terms are synonyms. Bradlee has added more and better horseflesh, as he calls his editorial writers. He has spruced up page one, added the style section, brought in Art Buchwald to enhance the op-ed page and introduced a livelier sports section.

The *Post*'s reputation is built on its unrivaled track record in investigative coups and exposes. The list is long, led by the uncovering of the Watergate burglary that led to the unmaking of President Nixon, one of the rare instances in which a newspaper made history. It was also in the pages of the *Post* that the nation first learned of Vice President Spiro Agnew's itchy hand, Representative Wayne Hays's use of federal funds to hire his mistress as secretary, the South Korean government's attempts to buy certain members of Congress and other political horror tales.

The *Post* employs more than 2,300 persons full time and another 500 part time. It has a total editorial staff of 416, including 11 full-time and 23 part-time foreign correspondents. The *Post* has won over 900 local and national awards, including 15 Pulitzer Prizes. It is also financially sound. Profits have increased each year since 1975 and are bound to grow with the death of its rival the *Star* in 1981 and the conversion of the nation's capital into a one-paper town. In total ad linage it ranks third in the nation, behind only *The New York Times* and the *Los Angeles Times*.

Magazines

The U.S. periodical press is a half century younger than the newspaper press. The first

U.S. magazine was published in Philadelphia on February 13, 1741 by Andrew Bradford, a London-born printer. Called *American Magazine, or a Monthly View of the Political State of the British Colonies*, it lasted only three months. (Benjamin Franklin's *General Magazine*, founded just three days later, lasted for six months.) Another 150 years passed before the first mass circulation magazine appeared. In October 1893 Frank A. Munsey, publisher of *Munsey's Magazine*, introduced the concept of achieving a large circulation by reducing his selling price to a dime, that is, less than his cost of production, and deriving his profits from a

Table 7
Number of U.S. Magazines, 1950–1980

Year	U.S. Periodicals[1]	A.B.C. General and Farm Magazines[2]	PIB Measured Magazines[3]
1950	6,960	250	84
1951	6,977	247	83
1952	7,050	252	84
1953	7,142	258	86
1954	7,382	259	93
1955	7,648	272	81
1956	7,907	282	88
1957	7,907	278	83
1958	8,074	270	81
1959	8,136	274	79
1960	8,422	273	79
1961	8,411	273	80
1962	8,616	278	79
1963	8,758	274	81
1964	8,900	282	85
1965	8,990	275	86
1966	9,102	276	91
1967	9,238	279	93
1968	9,400	287	92
1969	9,434	302	90
1970	9,573	300	89
1971	9,657	293	91
1972	9,062	302	83
1973	9,630	306	85
1974	9,755	316	93
1975	9,657	327	94
1976	9,872	336	93
1977	9,732	373	96
1978	9,582	369	102
1979	9,719	401	102
1980	10,236		100

Sources:
[1] *Ayer Directory of Publications,* Ayer Press (annual).
[2] MPA Circulation 1A, 2nd six months; A.B.C. Publisher's Statements.
[3] Publishers Information Bureau, Inc.

larger volume of advertising. Other publishers, such as Cyrus Curtis, Edward Bok and S. S. McClure, followed him; together they dominated the golden age of U.S. magazine publishing, which lasted well into the 1930s.

After the shakedown of the 1950s and 1960s, the U.S. magazine industry is settling down to a period of steady but unspectacular growth. The value of shipments, the Bureau of Census's principal indicator, was estimated in 1978 at $6.61 billion, up 210 percent

from 1960 and 107 percent from 1970. Its actual share of the GNP has dropped from 0.4215 percent in 1960 to 0.3138 percent in 1978, reflecting the fact that the magazine industry has not kept pace with the growth of the economy. As a segment of the print media, magazines account for only 25 percent of the value of shipments, a share that has held relatively steady over the years.

In 1977 the industry had 71,400 employees, an increase of 7 percent since 1972. The leading states in employment are New York,

Table 8
Circulation of All A.B.C. Magazines, General and Farm (Excluding Comics), 1950–1979

Second Six Months Averages
Combined Circulation Per Issue

Year	No. Magazines or Groups	Single Copy	Subscription	Total	U.S. Adult Population (Add 000)	Circulation per 100 Adults
1950	250	61,998,611	85,270,929	147,259,540	104,596	140.8
1951	247	64,157,748	87,345,788	151,503,536	105,159	144.1
1952	252	68,716,845	90,651,696	159,368,541	105,902	150.5
1953	258	68,109,367	94,925,139	163,034,506	106,830	152.6
1954	259	67,456,118	97,510,768	164,966,886	107,990	152.8
1955	272	71,073,877	108,891,354	179,965,231	109,342	164.6
1956	282	73,874,770	111,856,119	185,730,889	110,549	168.0
1957	278	68,305,833	113,104,515	181,410,348	111,725	162.4
1958	270	63,384,915	119,939,875	183,324,790	112,832	162.5
1959	274	62,609,711	112,979,455	185,589,166	114,091	162.7
1960	273	62,295,487	128,136,349	190,431,836	115,461	164.9
1961	273	60,696,623	134,966,829	195,663,452	117,207	166.9
1962	278	61,977,422	138,680,320	200,657,742	118,655	169.1
1963	274	62,578,172	140,645,067	203,223,239	120,072	169.3
1964	282	64,953,619	142,917,837	207,871,456	121,466	171.1
1965	275	66,538,850	148,947,898	215,486,748	123,804	174.1
1966	276	68,554,898	157,106,899	225,661,797	125,687	179.5
1967	279	71,275,957	160,848,702	232,124,659	127,536	182.0
1968	287	71,183,468	165,917,867	237,101,335	129,512	183.1
1969	302	71,587,283	170,205,937	241,793,220	131,623	183.7
1970	300	70,701,105	173,462,984	244,164,089	134,118	182.1
1971	293	73,296,562	169,157,331	242,453,893	136,659	177.4
1972	302	80,739,026	161,679,162	242,418,188	139,240	174.1
1973	306	83,947,248	161,954,594	245,901,842	141,683	173.6
1974	316	85,055,173	163,767,774	248,822,947	144,152	172.6
1975	327	85,580,704	165,250,505	250,831,209	146,800	170.9
1976	336	90,555,940	164,864,879	255,420,819	149,474	170.9
1977	373	92,757,602	171,190,950	263,948,552	152,089	173.5
1978	369	91,756,399	173,933,368	265,689,767	154,682	171.8
1979	401	89,717,939	176,936,774	266,654,713	157,529	169.3

Source:

Circulation: A.B.C. records covering the *second* six months of each year.

Population: U.S. Bureau of the Census midyear estimates of the resident population 18 year and older.

Illinois, California and the District of Columbia, accounting for approximately 62 percent of the employment. The same states were in the lead in 1972, when their relative share was 59 percent. The total wage bill was $1.045 billion, up from $708 million in 1972 and $461 million in 1963.

Tables 7 and 8 show the growth in the number and circulation of U.S. magazines. The total number of magazines went over the 10,000 figure for the first time in 1980, after remaining in the nine thousands since 1966.

Circulation also reached an all-time high of 266.654 million in 1979, despite the fact that circulation per 100 adults was down to 169 per 100, as compared to 183.7 per 100 in 1969. The share of subscription sales has also declined to 67 percent in 1979 from 73 percent in 1970. This trend may be the result of a deliberate shift in marketing policy, with publishers concentrating more on quality than on numbers. Rapidly increasing postal costs—up 413 percent between 1971 and 1979—have forced publishers to look more to

Table 9
The Cost of Magazines to the Reader, 1960–1979

Year	Average Single Copy Price[1]	Index 1960 = 100	Average Yearly Subscription Price[1]	Index 1960 = 100
1960	$ .39	100	$ 4.58	100
1961	.41	105	4.68	102
1962	.41	105	4.79	105
1963	.42	108	4.89	107
1964	.46	118	5.25	115
1965	.46	118	5.32	116
1966	.49	126	5.51	120
1967	.51	131	5.60	122
1968	.55	141	6.05	132
1969	.58	149	6.52	142
1970	.63	162	7.16	156
1971	.63	162	7.38	161
1972	.64	164	7.57	165
1973	.68	174	7.72	169
1974	.81	208	8.98	196
1975	.87	223	10.14	221
1976	.98	251	11.52	252
1977	1.09	280	12.70	277
1978	1.21	310	14.86	324
1979	1.33	341	16.30	356

[1]Base: The single-copy and one-year subscription prices reported to the Audit Bureau of Circulations, in effect on December 31 of each year, for 50 leading magazines in advertising revenue for that year.

Table 10
Number of Periodicals, by Frequency, 1950–1979

	1950	1960	1970	1979	Percent Change 1950–1979
Weekly	1,443	1,580	1,856	1,764	22.2%
Semimonthly	416	527	589	594	42.8
Monthly	3,694	4,113	4,314	3,850	4.2
Bimonthly	436	743	957	1,043	139.2
Quarterly	604	895	1,108	1,261	108.6
Other	367	564	749	1,207	228.9
Total	6,960	8,422	9,573	9,719	39.6

Source: *Ayer Directory of Periodicals.*

newsstands and supermarkets, where women's magazines already dominate.

Not surprisingly, magazine prices have advanced more rapidly than consumer prices in the 1970s, as Table 9 shows. Based on 1960=100, the index of single-copy magazine prices rose to 341 in 1979, and the index of subscription prices to an even higher 356. Academic journals and technical and business periodicals have risen in price even more steeply.

According to the Bureau of Census, 3,041 publishing companies were active in the magazine field in 1977. Their gross fixed assets were worth $810.5 million. Only 536 had more than 20 employees each. The over 9,700 magazines that they published can be roughly divided into three categories: consumer, farm, and business, their shares of the market being 60 percent, 2 percent, and 38 percent respectively. The most common frequency appears to be monthly, with 40 percent of all magazines published at that interval. But as Table 10 shows, the bimonthly format is becoming more popular, rising between 1950 and 1979 by 607 more titles, or 139 percent. Quarterlies are limited by and large to scholarly journals.

The advertising ratio has remained more or less constant over the years, as Table 11 shows. The editorial share still remains close to a healthy 50 percent. Traditionally magazines have derived the bulk of their revenues from advertisers, especially business magazines with limited or controlled circulations.

However, magazines have been hardest hit as a result of competition from the electronic media. The magazine's share of the advertising dollar has fallen from 20 percent in 1945 to 9.4 percent in 1978. Correspondingly, advertising revenues have fallen precipitously from 60 percent of total consumer magazine revenues to 45 percent, forcing magazines to raise their prices as well as ad rates, which have escalated between 1950 and 1978 from an average of $5,886 per page to $20,597 per page. Table 12 shows advertising expenditures in magazines between 1935 and 1978. It reveals that while the magazine share of total advertising has been weakening, it has continued to make modest gains in absolute terms.

The magazine industry shows relatively less concentration of ownership than other industrial sectors. It became even more fragmented between 1947 and 1972. The largest magazine, *TV Guide*, accounts for only 5.5 percent of the combined per-issue sales of 375 audited magazines. Time, Inc., the largest publisher in revenues, accounts for only 12.7 percent of all revenues. Table 13 shows that the top four publishers accounted in 1977 for 20 percent of industry receipts, the eight largest for 30 percent and the 12 largest for 37 percent. Standard Rate and Data Service identifies 285 multiple title publishers publishing 1,308 titles, or 13.5 percent of the total title count. Of these, 92 groups published two or more consumer and farm magazines, for a total of 383 titles. Tables 14 and 15 identify the largest of these groups by revenues and by circulation. Among the strictly business publishers, McGraw-Hill leads in circulation and Harcourt Brace Jovanovich in number of titles.

There is a natural life cycle in most magazines; the strength of the industry seems to lie in its ability to generate more and more new titles to replace those that fall by the wayside. This proliferation of titles and its ability to exploit fleeting social trends, hobbies, pursuits and cults have enabled the industry to confound its obituary writers. The same logic applies to group publishers who accumulate a stable of small but profitable titles, not simply for the economies of scale, but for diluting their risk among as many titles as possible. In fact the biggest moneymakers in the industry are not the big names but small specialized titles with a durable and loyal market, such as *Stereo Review, Modern Photography, Boating* or *Pickup*. Essentially, no magazine competes

Table 11
Relationship of Advertising to Editorial Linage in Magazines, 1947–1979

Year	% Advertising	% Editorial	Total
1947	53.1	46.9	100.0
1957	49.6	50.4	100.0
1961	44.6	55.4	100.0
1964	46.4	53.6	100.0
1966	46.6	53.4	100.0
1967	46.7	53.3	100.0
1969	47.3	52.7	100.0
1970	46.0	54.0	100.0
1971	46.8	53.2	100.0
1973	49.3	50.7	100.0
1975	46.5	53.5	100.0
1976	49.3	50.7	100.0
1977	51.1	48.9	100.0
1978	51.8	48.2	100.0
1979	52.4	47.6	100.0

Source: *Russell Hall Magazine Editorial Reports.*

Table 12
Advertising Expenditures in Magazines, 1935–1978

	Total	Magazines (millions)	Business Publications (millions)	Percent of All Advertising Expenditures
1935	187	$ 136	$ 51	11.1%
1945	569	365	204	19.8
1950	766	515	251	13.4
1955	1,175	729	446	12.8
1960	1,550	941	609	13.0
1965	1,870	1,199	671	12.3
1970	2,063	1,323	740	10.5
1975	2,458	1,539	919	8.7
1976	2,910	1,875	1,035	7.3
1977	3,473	2,252	1,221	9.1
1978	4,120	2,700	1,420	9.4

Sources: 1935–1970: *Historical Statistics of the U.S.*; 1970–1978: *Advertising Age*.

Table 13
Concentration in the Periodical Publishing Industry, 1947–1977

	1947	1958	1963	1967	1972	1977
Number of companies	2106	2246	2562	2430	2451	NA
Value of shipments (billions)	$1.1	1.7	2.3	3.1	3.5	4.8
Percentage accounted for by:						
4 largest	34	31	28	24	26	20
8 largest	43	41	42	37	38	30
20 largest	50	55	59	56	54	37
50 largest	NA	69	73	72	69	NA

Source: U.S. Bureau of the Census, Census of Manufacturers.

Table 14
Largest Magazine Publishers in the U.S., by Revenue, 1978

	Revenue from Magazine Publishing (millions)	Number of Domestic Magazines
1. Time Inc.	$572	6
2. Reader's Digest Assn. Inc.	312	1
3. Triangle Publications, Inc.	310	2
4. Washington Post Co.	242	1
5. McGraw-Hill, Inc.	232	29
6. Charter Co.	196	4
7. CBS Inc.	150	8
8. Hearst Corp.	145	14
9. Ziff-Davis Publishing Co.	140	15
10. New York Times Co.	131	4
11. Meredith Corp.	120	5
12. Playboy Enterprises	113	3

Source: Knowledge Industry Publications.

Table 15

Largest Consumer Magazine Publishers, by Total Annual Circulation, 1978

	Total Annual Circulation (thousands)	Total Combined Circulation per Issue	Number of Magazines Published
1. Triangle Publications, Inc.	1,051,360	21,299	2
2. Time Inc.	492,623	10,377	6
3. Reader's Digest Assn.	220,452	18,371	1
4. New York Times Co.	157,349	10,890	5
5. Washington Post Co. (Newsweek)	153,868	2,959	1
6. Hearst Corp.	145,016	12,085	12
7. Charter Co.	143,645	11,970	4
8. Meredith Corp.	121,788	10,618	5
9. CBS Inc.	112,261	13,392	8
10. Scholastic Magazines	94,846	6,066	10
11. McCall Publishing Co.	80,482	6,707	2
12. Times Mirror Co.	75,496	5,446	6
13. Playboy Enterprises	69,730	5,811	3
14. Ziff-Davis Publishing Co.	59,030	5,135	10
15. Macfadden Group, Inc.	50,626	4,219	8
16. Newhouse (Condé Nast)	49,747	4,303	9
17. Petersen Publishing Co.	49,628	4,136	11
Total	3,185,890	159,117	102

Source: Knowledge Industry Publications.

with another; it is a unique product, a monopoly by itself.

A discussion of the U.S. magazine industry will not be complete without a look at foreign publishers in the U.S. market. At least five foreign media conglomerates have obtained a foothold in the United States:
• Gruner & Jahr (itself 75 percent owned by Bertelsmann Gutersloh), Germany's largest magazine publisher, acquired Parents' Magazine Enterprises.
• Daniel Filipacchi, French publisher of *Paris-Match,* acquired Popular Publications, including *Argosy* and *Camera 35.*
• Australian Rupert Murdoch took over *New York, Village Voice* and other publications and started the *Star.*
• Harlequin Enterprises of Canada acquired Laufer Company, which publishes *Tiger Beat* and other periodicals for teenagers, and also the Rona Barrett gossip magazines.
• The British Reed group acquired Cahners, publisher of business magazines.

Organizations

The U.S. press is represented by hundreds of associations at the national and local levels.

• The American Newspaper Publishers Association is the principal industry spokesman. Founded in 1887, it was located for a time in Rochester, N.Y., and New York City before it moved to its permanent headquarters at Reston, Va. In 1980 the association had a membership of 1,372. Affiliated institutions include ANPA Foundation and its related Newspaper Education Program, ANPA Research Institute, a technical consulting and research division engaged in quality testing, ANPA Credit Bureau, ANPA News Research Center at Syracuse, N.Y., and the Newspaper Readership Council. Also located in ANPA offices at Reston are the International Circulation Managers Association, International Newspaper Promotion Association and the Newspaper Personnel Relations Association.
• The National Newspaper Association, composed of small dailies and weeklies, was founded in 1885. It has 4,100 active members.
• The National Newspaper Publishers Association, founded in 1940, is a group of black newspapers with 142 members.
• Suburban Newspapers of America, founded in 1971, is the only trade association representing suburban and urban community newspapers.

Table 16

50 Leading A.B.C. Magazines, 1979
(Based on average circulation per issue, 2nd six months of 1979)

Rank	Circulation	% Change vs. 1978	Rank	Circulation	% Change vs. 1978
1. TV Guide	19,043,358	– 2.3	25. V.F.W. Magazine	1,829,180	– 0.1
2. Reader's Digest	17,888,680	– 0.5	26. Smithsonian	1,812,084	+ 6.1
3. National Geographic	10,413,639	+ 2.8	27. Popular Science	1,800,319	– 1.2
4. Better Homes & Gardens	8,097,651	+ 0.8	28. Outdoor Life	1,709,872	– 2.4
5. Family Circle	7,753,604	– 7.5	29. Hustler	1,700,873	+12.8
6. Woman's Day	7,560,329	– 6.5	30. Today's Education	1,694,024	+ 0.5
7. McCall's	6,526,745	– 0.2	31. Mechanix Illustrated	1,680,245	+ 1.2
8. Ladies' Home Journal	5,502,149	– 8.8	32. Elks Magazine	1,644,618	+ 0.8
9. Good Housekeeping	5,271,172	– 1.7	33. Popular Mechanics	1,642,570	+ 1.1
10. Playboy	5,249,010	+ 0.0	34. True Story	1,604,178	– 2.5
11. National Enquirer	5,024,180	– 6.3	35. Workbasket	1,569,788	–14.9
12. Penthouse	4,711,849	+ 2.2	36. Midnight Globe	1,552,579	–13.8
13. Redbook	4,303,951	– 3.6	37. Boys' Life	1,516,405	+ 0.5
14. Time	4,272,888	+ 0.0	38. Parents Magazine	1,456,311	– 4.0
15. The Star	3,292,106	+ 1.7	39. Seventeen	1,450,625	+ 0.0
16. Newsweek	2,934,530	+ 0.3	40. Sunset	1,403,481	+ 2.3
17. Cosmopolitan	2,747,042	+ 1.7	41. Farm Journal	1,337,873	– 5.2
18. American Legion	2,592,065	– 0.3	42. Life	1,332,074	– 4.6
19. Sports Illustrated	2,274,819	+ 0.1	43. Ebony	1,262,619	+ 1.7
20. People Weekly	2,264,087	– 8.6	44. Nation's Business	1,256,270	+ 5.9
21. U.S. News & World Report	2,042,910	+ 0.3	45. Changing Times	1,233,718	– 6.3
22. Field & Stream	2,021,381	– 0.4	46. Sport	1,207,633	– 4.8
23. Glamour	1,879,402	– 2.0	47. New Woman	1,195,756	+16.9
24. Southern Living	1,862,667	+14.1	48. Psychology Today	1,177,988	– 0.0
			49. Bon Appetit	1,144,718	+ 6.2
			50. House & Garden	1,084,277	+ 1.0

Source: American Magazine Publishers Association.

• The Inland Daily Press Association, founded in 1885 to represent Midwest publishers, is the nation's oldest and largest regional association. It has over 500 members.
• The Southern Newspaper Publishers Association, founded in 1903, covers 14 Southern states, with its headquarters at Atlanta.
• The Society of Professional Journalists, Sigma Delta Chi, founded in 1909, is the nation's largest and oldest organization representing professional journalists. Women were first admitted in 1969. There are 35,000 members, of whom 80 percent are professionals and 20 percent students. Activities are also conducted by the society's 291 chapters—131 professional and 160 campus. The Society publishes *The Quill*, a monthly, from its headquarters in Chicago.
• The American Society of Newspaper Editors, founded in 1922, brings together over 900 editors of daily newspapers.
• The Magazine Publishers Association,

founded in 1919, is the principal spokesman for the magazine industry. Its 163 member companies publish 606 magazines.
• The American Society of Magazine Editors, founded in 1963, is a forum for magazine editors, with a membership of 233.
• The National Press Photographers Association, founded in 1946, represents photojournalists. It has a membership of 3,000 active, 2,000 associate and 1,000 student members.
• The Reporters Committee for Freedom of the Press, founded in 1970, is a legal research and defense fund for protecting the First Amendment rights of the media to gather and publish news.

Economic Framework

The Setting

The U.S. press rests on twin foundations: legally on the First Amendment and economically on the free enterprise system.

Table 17
Magazine Advertising Revenue, 1950–1979
General Magazines[1]

Year	Revenue	No. of Magazines
1950	$ 430,616,558	84
1951	480,065,294	83
1952	519,708,822	84
1953	566,440,991	86
1954	572,326,323	93
1955	622,005,729	81
1956	693,233,867	88
1957	710,785,633	83
1958	671,366,930	81
1959	760,630,046	79
1960	829,727,760	79
1961	815,015,746	80
1962	852,482,727	79
1963	906,779,205	81
1964	971,666,981	85
1965	1,048,765,191	86
1966	1,139,072,743	91
1967	1,135,334,589	93
1968	1,169,652,713	92
1969	1,221,370,544	90
1970	1,168,668,178	89
1971	1,235,175,433	91
1972	1,297,682,163	83
1973	1,309,161,028	85
1974	1,366,328,994	93
1975	1,336,313,425	94
1976	1,621,992,896	93
1977	1,965,410,809	96
1978	2,374,175,378	102
1979	2,671,052,606	102

[1]Sunday supplements are excluded.

Source: Publishers Information Bureau.

American newspapers are business enterprises as well as purveyors of information, and they can function well in one capacity only if they do well in the other.

The American newspaper business is very much a product of the free enterprise system. The term "free enterprise" does not mean that constraints are not applied at every level of economic activity to protect both the buyer and the seller. The complexities of any business require that the public authorities, representing the people, exercise some measure of oversight, if only to curb abuses. But what characterizes the U.S. free enterprise system are four distinctive traits that constitute the four ingredients of its success. These are, in descending order of importance, individualism, consumer choice, competition, and the profit motive. Applied to newspapers, this means that the dynamism of a newspaper is only the sum total of the dynamism of the individuals who write and produce it, that if publishers do not create a salable product, they will not be in the business very long, that competition provides principal stimulus to efficiency and progress, and that profits are perceived not only as a yardstick of performance but as a requisite for survival.

As they emerged into the 1980s U.S. newspapers seem to have overcome the problems of transition into the post-McLuhan age. The economic signals are all go. The newspaper business currently ranks 10th among all U.S. industries in the value of goods shipped and third in employment. Industry growth rates have generally equalled and sometimes exceeded those of the economy. Expenditures on newspaper advertising grew faster than the GNP, newsprint consumption has kept pace with the GNP, circulation advanced as fast as the population between the ages 21 and 65 and newspaper employment surpassed all other manufacturing sectors in growth rate expansion in employment. Confirming the continued prospects for robust growth in the 1980s, the 1978 *U.S. Industrial Outlook* of the U.S. Department of Commerce predicted that newspaper publishing will maintain a record of real growth just under 5 percent into the eighties. The new technology is expected to improve their outlook even further by enabling them to reach smaller targeted audiences at less cost.

There are two other indicators that attest to the continued vitality of the U.S. press. According to the 1977 Census of Manufacturers, newspapers spent an estimated $475.4 million on capital outlays, especially plant expansion and modernization, compared to $267.8 million in 1970. Another vote of confidence in the industry is the willingness of entrepreneurs to pay hefty sums for newspaper properties. In 1977 Newhouse acquired Booth Newspapers for $300 million, Capital Cities Communications acquired the Kansas City *Star* and *Times* for $125 million and Gannett acquired Speidel for more than $170 million.

Data released by the Bureau of Census in 1977 reveal that the newspaper industry leads other forms of media in all critical areas. The total value of receipts was reported at $12.996 billion, an increase of 57 percent over 1972. A significant portion of

Table 18
Value of All Newspaper Shipments Compared To Gross National Product, 1960–1978
(Index: 1970 = 100)

Year	GNP (current billions)	Growth Index	Year to Year % Increase	Value of Receipts (billions)	Growth Index	Year to Year % Increase
1960	$ 506.0	52	—	$ 4.1	59	—
1965	688.1	70	36.0%	5.2	74	26.8%
1970	982.4	100	42.7	7.0	100	34.6
1971	1,063.4	108	8.2	7.4	106	5.7
1972	1,171.1	119	10.1	8.3	119	12.2
1973	1,306.6	133	11.6	8.9	127	7.2
1974	1,412.9	144	8.2	9.6	137	7.9
1975	1,528.8	156	7.3	10.5	150	4.2
1976	1,706.5	174	11.6	11.7	167	12.0
1977	1,889.6	192	10.7	13.3	190	13.7
1978	2,107.0	214	11.5	14.8	211	10.4
Compound Annual % Increase	8.2%				7.4%	

Estimates of U.S. Bureau of Domestic Commerce.

Sources: GNP: U.S. Bureau of Economic Analysis; Newspaper Shipments: U.S. Dept. of Commerce, *U.S. Industrial Outlook*, annual.

this change was accounted for by Sunday newspapers, which increased by 54 percent, and other newspapers, which increased by 98 percent. Value added by manufacture was $9.403 billion, a gain of 51 percent. There were 8,815 establishments classified as newspapers, of which 2,131 had more than 20 employees. The gross value of fixed assets of these establishments was $4.992 billion.

As a percentage of the GNP, value of all newspaper shipments has declined from 0.810 percent in 1960 to 0.702 percent in 1978. Table 18 compares GNP growth rates with newspaper receipts growth rates.

Circulation

Circulation of daily newspapers reached 62 million in 1978, one million below the peak of 63 million reported in 1973. (See Table 2.) Sunday circulation reached 54 million, a new peak.

Daily circulations in the four geographical regions of the United States are shown in Table 19. The largest circulation growth took place in the South, where daily circulation rose by one million, or 6.3 percent, during a 10-year period. The West also gained, its circulation expanding by 700,000, or 6.8 percent, during the same period. On the other hand, circulation dropped in both the North-east and North Central regions. Sunday circulations increased in all regions, particularly in the South, where it grew by 16 percent, and in the West, where it grew by 13 percent.

Table 20 shows circulation by size of city. While aggregate circulation has expanded, all classes of towns and cities, except those of less than 100,000 inhabitants, have been losing readers and subscribers. The decline was related inversely to the size of the city: 19.8 percent in cities of over one million inhabitants, 16.7 percent in cities of between one-half and one million inhabitants, 7 percent in cities of between one-quarter and one-half million inhabitants and 1.7 percent in cities of between 100,000 and 250,000 inhabitants. On the other hand, daily newspaper circulation expanded by 17.2 percent in the smallest category of towns. Their 1978 circulation, totaling 24 million, was substantially greater than that of any other category of cities. The same pattern held true in the case of Sunday papers, with the circulations gaining by 4.4 percent in the case of smallest cities and declining by 10 percent in the case of the largest cities.

Several developments are responsible for these anomalies in circulation patterns. First, many small city newspapers have added Sunday editions during the past decade, resulting in larger Sunday circulations. Second, higher prices of metropolitan papers have affected their out-of-town circulations. Last, the tight supply of newsprint and rising production and distribution costs have prompted many metropolitan papers to eliminate unprofitable or marginally profitable circulation routes.

By groups, 11 newspaper companies enjoy over-one-million circulations as shown in Table 21. Together, they account for 49 percent of the total circulation in the United States.

Although per capita circulation has declined in the United States, it is believed that

Table 19
Regional Changes in Circulation of U.S. Daily Newspapers, 1968–1978
Daily Circulation

Region	1968	1978	Change	Percent Change
Northeast	16,791,222	15,290,763	−1,500,459	−8.9
North Central	17,747,486	16,321,632	−1,425,854	−8.0
South	16,070,067	17,090,182	1,020,115	6.3
West	9,568,466	10,223,762	655,296	6.8
Total U.S.	60,177,241	58,926,339	−1,250,902	−2.1

Sunday Circulation

Region	1968	1978	Change	Percent Change
Northeast	12,899,644	13,491,708	592,064	4.6
North Central	13,448,927	13,573,461	124,534	0.9
South	13,815,454	16,068,295	2,252,841	16.3
West	8,091,071	9,141,279	1,050,208	13.0
Total U.S.	48,255,096	52,274,743	4,019,647	8.3

Source: Standard Rate and Data Service, Inc.

Table 20
Changes in Circulation of Daily Newspapers in Cities of Various Sizes, 1968–1978
Daily Circulation

City Size	1968	1978	Change	Percent Change
Less than 100,000	20,483,232	24,002,613	3,519,381	17.2
100,000 to 250,000	9,801,523	9,635,016	−166,507	−1.7
250,000 to 500,000	7,785,378	7,239,206	−546,172	−7.0
500,000 to 1 million	10,472,316	8,719,020	−1,753,296	−16.7
1 millon and over	11,634,792	9,330,484	−2,304,308	−19.8
All U.S. Dailies	60,177,241	58,926,339	−1,250,902	−2.1

Sunday Circulation

City Size	1968	1978	Change	Percent Change
Less than 100,000	9,659,837	14,042,807	4,382,970	45.4
100,000 to 250,000	8,531,974	9,299,656	767,682	9.0
250,000 to 500,000	7,622,773	7,663,346	40,573	0.5
500,000 to 1 million	9,831,282	9,865,028	33,746	0.3
1 million and over	12,609,230	11,403,906	−1,205,324	−9.6
All U.S. Dailies	48,255,096	52,274,743	4,019,647	8.3

Source: Standard Rate and Data Service, Inc.

readership is close to saturation levels in many areas. Nearly four out of five people between the ages of 18 and 30 read a newspaper one or more times a week. Since each newspaper is read by 2.14 persons, actual newspaper readership could be close to 132 million, give or take a few million. Readership is more intensive among the over-50 group (79 to 90 percent), among the over $25,000 a year group (75 percent), among college graduates (74 percent), among whites (68 percent) and among males (70 percent). Young adults are the least reached group, with a penetration of only 18.6 percent.

Distribution

The weakest link in the newspaper chain is distribution. For over a hundred years the system has not changed from the kids tossing the paper onto the lawn each day. Called little merchants or independent news carriers, there are 1.2 million of them in the United States. They deliver 87 percent of all newspapers. But over the years critics have blamed them for the sluggish growth in circulation; newsboys are also expected to solicit new customers, and poor, improper or unreliable delivery leads to reader dissatisfaction. Carrier turnover is also high, up to 175 percent a year. In the inner cities the youngsters are often hassled and robbed.

As a result, there have been a number of efforts by newspapers to shift to newspaper-owned distribution systems. A Supreme Court ruling that newspaper firms could not arbitrarily fix prices or restrict sales territories once papers have been delivered to the little merchants has also prompted newspapers to seek alternatives. The *Los Angeles Times* has completely eliminated the independent carrier system and replaced it with a network of 200 full-time and 1,000 part-time employees. The Nashville *Tennessean* and *Banner* have similarly changed to a system of deliveries compensated on an hourly wage basis. Some papers have introduced paid-in-advance (PIA) subscriptions, freeing the carrier from having to make weekly or biweekly collections.

Some 13 percent of newspapers are distributed by means other than home delivery. These include newsstand, vendor and vending machine sales, particularly in cities of

Table 21
The 20 Largest U.S. Newspaper Companies
Ranked by Daily Circulation, 1980

	Daily Circulation	Number of Dailies	Sunday Circulation	Number of Sundays
1. Gannett Co., Inc.	3,548,242	82	3,412,975	53
2. Knight-Ridder Newspapers, Inc.	3,419,064	33	4,024,589	21
3. Newhouse Newspapers	3,215,694	29	3,510,298	21
4. The Tribune Co.	2,935,314	8	3,916,124	6
5. Dow Jones & Co., Inc.	2,096,290	21	329,827	9
6. Times Mirror Co.	2,064,575	7	2,487,042	5
7. Scripps-Howard Newspapers	1,825,634	17	1,561,806	7
8. Hearst Newspapers	1,390,643	13	2,142,531	9
9. Cox Enterprises, Inc.	1,148,381	16	1,193,293	11
10. Thomson Newspapers (U.S.)	1,088,908	67	647,805	30
11. The New York Times Co.	1,031,608	10	1,569,478	6
12. Cowles Newspapers	995,994	10	1,183,211	7
13. Capital Cities Communications, Inc.	955,282	5	776,321	4
14. News America Publishing, Inc. (Murdoch)	786,655	3	181,953	1
15. Central Newspapers, Inc. (Pulliam)	756,828	7	765,066	4
16. Freedom Newspapers, Inc. (Hoiles)	739,351	29	668,077	17
17. The Washington Post Co.	711,525	3	894,875	2
18. Field Enterprises, Inc. (Chicago)	675,995	1	710,633	1
19. Evening News Association (Detroit)	671,471	4	818,741	1
20. The Copley Press, Inc.	639,547	9	631,555	6

Source: John Morton Newspaper Research.

Table 22
Major Newspapers and Their Circulations, 1980
(Includes All Audit Bureau of Circulations Newspapers with Daily Circulation over 100,000)

Newspaper	Daily	Sunday	Newspaper	Daily	Sunday
Albany, N.Y. Times-Union (m)	82,207	149,516	Little Rock: Ark. Democrat (e)	66,275	119,052
Albany, N.Y. Knickerbocker			Little Rock: Ark. Gazette (m)	129,274	154,569
News (e)	51,780		Long Beach Independent (m)	64,709	135,811
Akron Beacon Journal (e)	161,835	218,969	Long Beach Press-Telegram (e)	70,704	
Allentown Call (m)	103,258	154,805	Long Island, N.Y.: Newsday (e)	492,580	557,933
Asbury Park Press (e)	105,368	139,787	Los Angeles Herald-Examiner (e)	283,710	302,525
Atlanta Constitution (m)	218,807		Los Angeles Times (m)	1,024,322	1,276,195
Atlanta Journal (e)	211,081	501,867	Louisville Courier-Journal (m)	190,942	331,103
			Louisville Times (e)	151,977	
Baltimore News-American (e)	150,502	229,777			
Baltimore Sun (m&e)	350,848	374,989	Madison, Wis. State Journal	76,348	127,830
Bergen Co. (N.J.) Record (e)	150,378	213,799	Memphis Commercial Appeal (m)	203,847	282,484
Birmingham News (e)	178,074	217,352	Memphis Press Scimitar (e)	94,731	
Birmingham Post-Herald (m)	68,349		Miami Herald (m)	444,058	576,261
Boston Globe (m&e)	491,682	710,731	Miami News (e)	61,910	
Boston Herald American (m)	241,021	306,484	Milwaukee Journal (e)	323,932	515,108
Buffalo Courier-Express (m)	126,197	254,482	Milwaukee Sentinel (m)	163,224	
Buffalo News (e)	269,474	170,410	Minneapolis Star (e)	206,700	
			Minneapolis Tribune (m)	230,815	597,180
Camden (N.J.) Courier-Post (e)	126,498				
Charlotte News (e)	51,809		Nashville Banner (e)	84,134	
Charlotte Observer (m)	169,400	241,194	Newark Star-Ledger (m)	407,844	574,966
Chicago Sun-Times (m)	657,275	700,315	New Haven Register (e)	100,093	140,979
Chicago Tribune (m&e)	789,767	1,146,474	New Haven Journal-Courier (m)	37,264	
Christian Science Monitor (m)	172,470		New Orleans Times-Picayune (m)	213,283	323,302
Cincinnati Enquirer (m)	186,732	293,826	New Orleans States-Item (e)	111,043	
Cincinnati Post (e)	168,227		New York Daily News (m)	1,554,604	2,202,601
Cleveland Plain Dealer (m)	392,688	454,922	New York Post (e)	654,314	
Cleveland Press (e)	300,889		New York Times (m)	914,938	1,477,499
Columbia, S.C. State (m)	106,180	126,300	Norfolk Ledger-Star (e)	94,332	
Columbia, S.C. Record (e)	32,882		Norfolk Virginia-Pilot (m)	125,787	200,680
Columbus, Ga. Enquirer (m)	34,590	70,841			
Columbus, Ga. Ledger (e)	30,904		Oakland Tribune (m&e)	190,189	180,628
Columbus, O. Citizen-Journal (m)	112,195		Oklahoma City Oklahoman (m)	181,994	287,371
Columbus, O. Dispatch (e)	202,949	341,568	Oklahoma City Times (e)	84,657	
			Omaha World-Herald (m&e)	235,313	278,520
Dallas News (m)	286,955	353,677	Orange Co. (Cal.) Register (m&e)	230,533	259,783
Dallas Times Herald (e)	249,890	345,736	Orlando Sentinel-Star (m&e)	201,383	243,704
Dayton Journal-Herald (m)	100,886				
Dayton News (e)	140,674	217,220	Palm Beach Post (m)	93,117	141,097
Denver Post (e)	260,331	351,149	Palm Beach Times (e)	31,019	
Denver: Rocky Mountain News (m)	271,153	293,004	Peoria Journal Star (m&e)	102,556	120,003
Des Moines Register (m)	210,577	390,537	Philadelphia Bulletin (e)	458,849	529,706
Des Moines Tribune (e)	82,201		Philadelphia Inquirer (m)	425,075	837,209
Detroit Free Press (m)	601,721	710,018	Philadelphia News (e)	231,310	
Detroit News (e)	630,573	827,168	Phoenix Gazette (e)	112,781	
Flint Journal (e)	106,777	106,045	Phoenix Republic (m)	260,090	399,819
Fort Lauderdale News (e)	102,065	201,543	Pittsburgh Post Gazette (m)	185,215	
Ft. Worth Star-Telegram (m&e)	240,579	256,664	Pittsburgh Press (e)	271,502	659,998
Fresno Bee (m)	130,279	151,766	Portland, Me. Press-Herald (m)	53,616	
			Portland, Me. Express (e) & Maine		
Grand Rapids Press (e)	125,222	147,360	Sunday Telegram	29,813	115,519
Hartford Courant (m)	212,244	289,124	Portland Oregonian (m)	248,229	420,938
Honolulu Advertiser (m)	85,640		Portland: Oregon Journal (e)	105,485	
Honolulu Star-Bulletin (e)	118,952	203,938	Providence Bulletin (e)	141,759	
Houston Chronicle (e)	348,601	436,940	Providence Journal (m)	75,435	228,306
Houston Post (m)	330,203	394,853			
Indianapolis News (e)	143,449		Raleigh News & Observer (m)	131,921	165,289
Indianapolis Star (m)	215,858	357,694	Raleigh Times (e)	35,194	
Jacksonville Journal (e)	47,177		Richmond News Leader (e)	114,295	
Jacksonville: Fla. Times Union (m)	153,508	199,315	Richmond Times Dispatch (m)	135,360	216,047
Kansas City Star (e)	273,758	406,467	Rochester Democrat-Chronicle (m)	125,316	232,367
Kansas City Times (m)	314,007		Rochester Times-Union (e)	121,897	
Knoxville News-Sentinel (e)	102,488	158,987			

Table 22 con't

Newspaper	Daily	Sunday	Newspaper	Daily	Sunday
Sacramento Bee (m)	203,779	233,034	Spokane Spokesman-Review (m)	76,648	124,185
Sacramento Union (m)	103,859	105,303	Springfield, Ill. State Journal-Register (m&e)	71,171	71,788
St. Louis Globe-Democrat (m)	264,609	264,603	Springfield, Mass Union (m)	72,195	
St. Louis Post-Dispatch (e)	247,237	241,904	Springfield, Mass. News (e) & Sunday Republican	75,729	142,380
St. Paul Dispatch (e)	114,858		Syracuse Herald-Journal (e)	113,678	231,470
St. Paul Pioneer Press (m)	100,672	241,904	Syracuse Post-Standard (m)	82,181	
St. Petersburg Independent (e)	43,593				
St. Petersburg Times (m)	230,143	288,775	Tacoma News Tribune (e)	107,860	111,071
Salt Lake City Tribune (m)	113,956	189,310	Toledo Blade (e)	167,590	209,154
Salt Lake City Deseret News (e)	75,865		Tucson Daily Star (m)	74,284	138,266
San Antonio Express (m)	82,371	185,413	Tulsa Tribune (e)	76,314	
San Antonio News (e)	76,594		Tulsa World (m)	122,385	211,152
San Antonio Light (e)	122,600	187,857			
San Diego Union (m)	201,798	321,792	Wall St. Journal (m) (total)	1,798,416	
San Diego Tribune (e)	125,756		Washington, D.C. Post (m)	601,417	827,938
San Francisco Examiner (e)	159,325		Washington, D.C. Star (e)	345,641	326,512
San Francisco Chronicle (m)	506,600	669,665	Wichita Eagle (m)	120,043	174,832
San Jose Mercury (m)	154,983	269,821	Wichita Beacon (e)	37,221	
San Jose News (e)	68,000		Winston-Salem Journal (m)	71,696	95,143
Seattle Post-Intelligencer (m)	197,123	222,998	Winston-Salem Sentinel (e)	37,731	
Seattle Times (e)	260,762	348,678	Youngstown Vindicator (e)	103,298	153,036
Shreveport Times (m)	87,822	126,255			
South Bend Tribune (e)	106,370	125,754			
Spokane Chronicle (e)	61,580				

larger size. In rural areas newspapers are distributed and paid for by mail, like magazines. In certain situations agency operators handle all area newspapers, frequently using one carrier to deliver competing newspapers. A typical newspaper receives 70 to 75 percent of the single-copy price as revenue, and slightly more in the case of hotels, stores and newsstands. Vending-box sales, however, yield up to 90 percent of the single-copy price, and mail subscriptions 100 percent.

Prices. Newspapers derive between 20 and 30 percent of their revenues from circulation sales. Single-copy and subscription prices must therefore be constantly reviewed and adjusted upward to ensure maximum sales and profitability. As late as 1972 most dailies charged only 10 cents a copy, and only 350 charged 15 cents. But by the end of 1978 only 80 newspapers were selling at 10 cents; 811 were selling at 15 cents, 711 for 20 cents and 144 for 25 cents. One solitary paper is still selling for five cents. Given the present inflationary rates, it is possible that some newspapers will be selling for a dollar a copy within this century.

According to the U.S. Department of Labor, newspaper prices, while steep, still trail consumer prices. While consumer prices soared by 13.3 percent in 1979, newspaper prices went up by only 9.3 percent. Even at 20 cents

a day, newspapers are cheaper than a pack of cigarettes. The average annual subscription of around $100 is equal to about 10 hours of earnings for a white collar worker in the late 1970s.

One study on the effect of price increases on circulation found that in 59.4 percent of the cases circulation continued to climb despite an increase in price. Smaller newspapers, especially those in one-newspaper communities and affluent suburbs, find it easier to pass along their increased costs to the readers than do bigger city papers. Some newspapers also charge higher rates for subscribers in outlying areas and for home-delivered copies. For example, *The New York Times* charges higher prices beyond a 50-mile radius of New York City. This is usually justified by the reasoning that a newspaper cannot charge a local advertiser for circulation in areas beyond their regular trading area.

Interestingly, a hike in prices can sometimes hurt a competitor more than it hurts the paper. For example, *The Milwaukee Journal* experienced a decline in out-of-town circulation when suburban newspapers raised their prices. Apparently, people who had subscribed to two newspapers found that they could no longer afford both and decided to retain only the local paper.

Table 23
Single-Copy Sales Price
U.S. Daily and Sunday Newspapers,[1] 1965–1979

Year	Daily 5¢	10¢	15¢	20¢	25¢	Sunday 5¢	10¢	15¢	20¢	25¢	30¢	35¢	40¢	45¢	50¢	55¢	60¢	65¢	70¢	75¢
1965	456	892	3	2	–	21	128	190	143	45	5	–	–	–	–	–	–	–	–	–
1966	328	1,140	4	2	–	17	140	170	166	57	5	1	–	–	–	–	–	–	–	–
1967	232	1,305	5	2	–	15	120	172	161	80	5	3	1	–	–	–	–	–	–	–
1968	134	1,493	9	3	–	8	104	158	161	100	17	11	–	–	1	–	–	–	–	–
1969	77	1,581	19	3	–	5	91	144	160	126	16	26	–	–	1	–	–	–	–	–
1970	46	1,507	139	5	1	2	89	115	140	161	30	35	3	–	4	–	–	–	–	–
1971	29	1,394	277	4	2	1	84	98	125	181	47	43	6	–	5	–	–	–	–	–
1972	23	1,350	319	3	2	1	77	90	126	193	46	42	8	–	5	–	–	–	–	–
1973	19	1,275	425	4	2	–	73	88	96	221	54	51	10	–	7	–	–	–	–	–
1974	20	817	855	35	4	2	64	68	64	200	47	111	27	3	23	–	1	–	–	1
1975	4	428	1,153	137	10	–	37	61	49	170	58	157	37	3	51	1	4	–	–	1
1976	2	297	1,185	240	16	–	27	64	43	158	51	178	38	7	77	–	4	–	1	2
1977	1	197	1,151	369	25	–	13	49	31	138	46	198	36	8	103	–	7	–	–	4
1978	1	140	1,030	520	56	–	9	68	25	126	39	200	37	6	148	–	14	1	–	6
1979	1	80	811	711	144	–	8	65	20	112	29	176	37	5	211	–	23	–	1	15

This table reflects only those daily and Sunday newspaper single copy sales prices of 5¢ increments to illustrate a trend. Newspapers selling for odd cents have been omitted, as have specialized newspapers.

Source: ANPA

Profits

A newspaper has a dual responsibility, toward its investors and its readers. The responsibility to its readers is an overriding one because the press enjoys special privileges under the First Amendment. Nevertheless, the responsibility to investors or owners can be ignored only at the peril of losing the newspaper's economic independence. As media critic Ben Bagdikian put it, "On the one hand, the daily newspaper in the United States is a product of professionals whose reporting is supposed to be the result of disciplined intelligence.... If this reportage is in any way influenced by concern for money-making it is regarded as corrupt journalism. On the other hand, the newspaper has to remain solvent and has to make a profit or else it will not survive. If it doesn't make money there will be no reporting of any kind, ethical or unethical. If the corporate end of the enterprise does not have an effective concern for making money, it will be regarded by everyone, including journalists, as incompetent, negligent, and a disservice to its community." A similar view was expressed by Otis Chandler: "You cannot have a good editorial product or provide community service unless you have good profits."

Economic independence also enables a paper, in the words of John Colburn, publisher of *The Californian,* "to resist pressures from politicians, bureaucrats, advertisers, and special interest groups." It is often the financially ailing paper that lowers it editorial standards. Most newspaper executives would tend to agree with Benjamin Bradlee of *The Washington Post* that "excellence is profitability."

Estimation of the profitability of U.S. newspapers is difficult for two reasons: First, some 1,500 newspapers are privately owned and are under no obligation to reveal their earnings. Second, many of the public companies also own radio and television stations; some publish magazines, and have other diverse interests, such as book publishing and newsprint production. It is not always possible to separate these interests and determine the share of newspaper profits.

Nevertheless, *Editor & Publisher* reported in 1977 that, among the companies whose stock is available to public, 23 newspaper groups earned as much as 25 percent of their gross revenue before taxes and between 4 percent and 18 percent of their operating revenues. Table 24 shows that the average return is closer to 9 percent, although the expatriate giant, Thomson of Canada, has a

Table 24
Revenue and Profit for Publicly Owned Newspaper-Owning Firms, 1978

	1978 Revenue (thousands)	Net Profit (thousands)	% Return on Sales
Affiliated	$ 159,801	$ 8,974	5.6%
Capital Cities	367,476	54,033	14.8
Dow Jones	363,601	44,248	12.1
Gannett	690,128	83,104	12.0
Harte-Hanks	184,560	15,737	8.5
Knight Ridder	878,875	76,756	8.7
Lee	104,690	15,914	15.2
Media General	243,699	17,972	7.4
Multimedia	110,630	15,601	14.1
New York Times	491,558	15,550	3.2
Thomson	306,476	56,559	18.5
Times Mirror	1,427,931	125,147	8.8
Washington Post	520,398	49,720	9.6
Median			9.6
Fortune 500 Median			4.8

Source: Knowledge Industry Publications.

Table 25
Chain Ownership, U.S. Daily
Newspapers, 1910–1976

Year	Number of Chains	Number[1] of Chain-owned Dailies	Total Number of Dailies	% Chain-owned	% of Daily Circulation of Chain-owned Dailies	Number[2] of Independent Voices
1910	13	62	2,202	2.8%	–	2,153
1930	55	311	1,942	16.0	43.4%	1,686
1940	60	319	1,878	17.0	–	1,619
1953	95	485	1,785	27.0	45.3	1,395
1960	109	560	1,763	31.8	46.1	1,312
1970	157	879	1,748	50.3	63.0	1,026
1976	167	1,047	1,762	59.4	71.0	882

[1]The totals reflect dailies, not separate establishments. Thus a single establishment publishing a morning and evening edition is counted as two dailies.

[2]This total reflects the number of different owners = number of chains plus the number of non-chain-owned dailies.

Sources: Editor & Publisher, July 9, 1977; Sterling and Haight, The Mass Media: Aspen Institute Guide to Communication Industry Trends.

18.5 percent return. (This is probably what Roy Thomson meant when he said that media ownership is like a license to print money.) This compares with a return of 6.9 percent for all printing and publishing and 5.4 percent for all companies in the Fortune 500 list.

Newsprint is by far the largest single item of expenditure in a newspaper, accounting for 28.9 percent (a share which has remained more or less constant despite sharp increases in newsprint prices), while editorial costs are among the lowest, at 9 percent. Smaller newspapers tend to spend more on editorial costs than metropolitan dailies if only because newsprint and ink costs are that much higher for the larger papers (average: 83 pages). The switch to cold type is expected to bring production costs down to a point where they will be less than editorial costs.

Competition & Monopoly

The ownership structure of the daily newspaper industry has undergone rather dramatic changes during the 20th century. Once dominated by local, family enterprises, newspapers are becoming subsidiaries of large corporations or part of chains. Table 25 documents this trend. In 1910 there were only 13 chains owning a total of 62 daily newspapers, accounting for less than three percent of all U.S. dailies. By 1930, 55 chains owned 311 dailies, whose combined circulations accounted for 43 percent of the total U.S. circulation. By 1960 nearly 30 percent of all dailies were chain-owned, by 1976, nearly 60 percent, accounting for 70 percent of U.S. daily circulation. The disappearance of the independent newspaper and the resulting stilling of editorial voices are among the principal concerns of the U.S. press watchers in the 1980s.

Of the 1,536 U.S. cities that had daily newspapers at the end of 1977, only 35, or 2.2 percent, had direct competition—that is, independently owned and operated firms separately producing daily newspapers that actively compete with one another for reader attention and advertising dollars. This has not always been true. While 90 percent of U.S. daily circulation originated in directly competitive cities in 1953, only 33 percent did so in the late 1970s. Only 12 percent of Americans live in multipaper cities in the early 1980s, compared to 26 percent in 1948, 21 percent in 1958 and 15 percent in 1968. Tables 26 and 27 illustrate the decline. Other data also establish the dimensions of this phenomenon. The 10 largest groups had annual revenues in the late 1970s estimated at one-

fourth of the industry total. Cross-media owners control more than a third of the daily newspapers, a fourth of the television stations, and almost a tenth of AM and FM radio stations. The combined holdings of groups, cross-media owners, conglomerates and other mass-media-related firms encompass almost three-fifths of daily newspapers, more than four-fifths of television stations and slightly more than one-fourth of AM and FM radio stations.

Another disturbing development is that most U.S. cities and towns do not have daily newspapers. Of the 7,000 urban settlements, only 1,760 have newspapers, about 25 percent. This also was not always so. In 1890 there were 1,348 urban places and 1,600 daily newspapers, a surplus of 19 percent. The 75 percent of U.S. urban communities without their own dailies have to depend on outside papers for their information and publicity needs. It is not unusual for one metropolitan newspaper to hog the market in all surrounding counties. *The Atlanta Constitution*, for example, sells in 55 counties, of which only 16 have their own daily.

Because the rate at which the big fish are swallowing the small ones in the U.S. media has been accelerating, it does not require a crystal ball to predict that the small, independent paper will soon become an endangered species or disappear entirely.

The attrition of competition and the expansion of chains are related, cause-and-effect phenomena. Of the 1,082 papers owned by chains, only 0.5 percent have local printed competition. Of these, only seven-tenths of one percent have face-to-face competition, or competition in the same time of day, including those with agency agreements that per-

	Table 26	
	Average Daily Circulation by	
	Number of Competing Firms, 1923–1978	
Year	**Mean Daily Circulation of Monopoly Papers**	**Mean Daily Circulation of Competing Papers**
1923	4,308	22,869
1933	8,077	48,123
1943	12,334	89,079
1953	18,278	134,977
1963	23,779	203,638
1973	28,033	235,313
1978	28,330	215,524

Sources: J. N. Rosse, B. M. Owen, J. Dertouzos, "Trends in the Daily Newspaper Industry 1923–1973"; *1978 Editor & Publisher International Yearbook.*

Table 27

Competition in the Newspaper Industry, 1923–1978

Year	No. of Firms in Multi-Paper Cities	% of Firms in Multi-Paper Cities	% of Daily Papers Sold by Firms in Multi-Paper Cities
1923	1,182	59.8	88.8
1933	562	32.2	73.9
1943	318	19.9	64.2
1948	253	16.5	62.0
1953	218	13.7	54.2
1958	168	10.9	51.7
1963	127	8.2	43.3
1968	97	6.3	36.1
1973	84	5.4	32.2
1978	78	4.9	28.3

Sources: J. N. Rosse, B. M. Owen, J. Dertouzos, "Trends in the Daily Newspaper Industry 1923–1973"; *1978 Editor & Publisher International Yearbook.*

mit them to legally fix prices and share profits.

The chains have also introduced a further distortion into the picture. Within the past 15 years leading newspaper corporations have become strong competitors in the stock market. This has introduced a third constituency for daily newspapers: stock market investors. News companies must constantly expand in size and rate of profits in order to maintain their stock-market attractiveness. The economic function of a chain newspaper has become that of an accumulator of capital for the parent corporation, capital that is to be used to acquire other properties elsewhere.

Monopolies in newspapers are opposed for a number of reasons, but primarily because they are monopolies: they violate the basic principle of competition on which the free enterprise system is founded. Further, concentrated control of news is different from control of other commodities, dog food, say. The potential for regimentation is there, even if it is never exercised.

A number of powerful economic forces have encouraged and continue to encourage the development of group ownership. First and foremost, current tax laws favor the investment of accumulated reserves. Under IRS regulations, undistributed earnings are not taxed as personal income if used in the acquisition of additional newspaper properties. Also, family-owned enterprises have become prime targets of merger activity as the result of the incidence of estate duties. Rapid changes in newspaper technology

have also favored the larger corporation, which is able to finance plant modernization and the introduction of new equipment more effectively. Traditionally, economics of scale have played a pivotal role in the dominance of one-newspaper towns. A larger firm is able to produce at a lower per-unit cost than smaller ones. In many instances, many small-town papers just cannot afford competition. Newspapers also continue to be profitable investments. They generate large amounts of cash not only from profits but also from depreciation and amortization of goodwill. They also carry low debt in relation to invested capital. Antitrust rulings have encouraged newspaper owners to spread their interests over a wider geographical area. For example, the *Los Angeles Times* was forced to sell its morning-evening-Sunday combination in nearby San Bernardino, but not prevented from acquiring *Newsday* of Long Island and the *Times Herald* of Dallas.

Studies in the editorial integrity of chains reveal that, contrary to their professions of independence, the vast majority of chains supported political candidates with the same political background as their owners. Some openly require their editors to endorse the candidates of their choice, as James M. Cox, publisher of *The Atlanta Constitution,* did in 1972. However, national chains tend to be more liberal in this respect than smaller or local ones.

Critics of newspaper concentration have their own critics, who contend that concen-

Table 28
Trends, 1923–1978

Year	No. Firms	Total Daily Circulations Millions	Mean Circulation	Median Circulation
1923	1,977	30.5	15,405	3,871
1933	1,745	36.6	20,974	4,731
1943	1,597	44.1	27,615	6,072
1948	1,536	51.3	33,416	7,322
1953	1,582	54.3	34,325	8,217
1958	1,545	57.2	37,028	9,104
1963	1,552	59.7	38,497	9,803
1968	1,547	60.8	39,313	10,521
1973	1,566	61.3	39,135	11,643
1978	1,580	59.4	37,571	11,967
% Change 1923–78	-20%	95%	144%	209%

Sources: J. N. Rosse, B. M. Owen, J. Dertouzos, "Trends in the Daily Newspaper Industry 1923–1973"; *1978 Editor & Publisher International Yearbook.*

tration in the U.S. press (1) is not as intense as it is made out to be, (2) is not as bad as it is made out to be and (3) is positively beneficial to the industry. In support of the first contention, it is claimed that the newspaper industry is less concentrated than not only allied publishing industries but also other manufacturing sectors. Whereas the four largest newspaper firms accounted for 17 percent of dollar shipments in 1972, the four largest aircraft manufacturers controlled 59 percent and the four largest radio and television set manufacturers 49 percent. They also point out that the average size of chain newspapers remains very small—45,000 in the case of Gannett and only 17,000 in the case of Thomson. Moreover, in comparison to other developed countries, newspaper ownership is relatively diverse in the United States. While the 20 largest firms controlled 43 percent of the circulation in the United States, the comparable percentages were 54.9 percent for Spain, 88.5 percent for Canada and 100 percent for Ireland. Lastly, as Table 29 illustrates, the largest 25 percent of newspaper firms accounted for a lower percentage of daily circulation in 1978 than they did in 1923.

The distribution of circulation among newspapers has remained remarkably stable over the past 55 years, as Tables 29 and 30 show. The smallest quartile produced 2.2 percent of all papers sold in 1923 and three percent of all papers sold in 1978, while the

Table 29
Percent of Total Daily Circulation by Quartiles, 1923–1978

Years	Smallest 25%	Second 25%	Third 25%	Largest 25%	Total
1923	2.2	4.8	10.4	82.5	100
1933	2.2	4.4	9.2	84.2	100
1943	2.2	4.2	9.3	84.3	100
1948	2.2	4.2	9.1	84.5	100
1953	2.3	4.4	9.7	83.6	100
1958	2.3	4.5	9.7	83.5	100
1963	2.4	4.6	10.0	83.0	100
1968	2.5	4.9	10.7	81.9	100
1973	2.8	5.4	11.4	80.4	100
1978	3.0	5.9	12.2	78.9	100

Table 30
Percent of Total Daily Circulation for Largest 10%, 5%, 1% Firms, 1923–1978

Years	10%	5%	1%
1923	64.9	50.3	22.6
1933	67.4	52.8	23.2
1943	66.6	51.3	22.4
1948	67.9	52.5	22.8
1953	66.6	50.8	21.0
1958	66.5	50.2	19.2
1963	65.7	52.3	22.1
1968	64.8	50.3	20.7
1973	66.3	49.3	20.6
1978	61.3	47.9	19.8

Sources: J. N. Rosse, B. M. Owen, J. Dertouzos, "Trends in the Daily Newspaper Industry 1923–1973"; *1978 Editor & Publisher International Yearbook.*

largest quartile sold 82.5 percent in 1923 and 78.9 percent in 1978. In 1978, 19.8 percent of all daily newspapers were sold by one percent of newspaper firms, 50 percent of the papers by the largest five percent of firms, and 60 percent of the papers by the largest 10 percent of firms. These percentages also have changed but slightly since 1923.

Pro-concentration critics also point out that despite the increased collective impor-tance of chains, they remain individually less significant. No chain today has the relative strength that the Hearst papers once had. Of course, Hearst's potential influence at that time was mitigated by the existence of direct newspaper competition in each city. In contrast, today's group-owned firms are usually the only newspaper in a town. For example, none of Gannett's papers face direct competition. It is also necessary to keep in

Table 31
Major Newspaper Groups, 1977

Group	No. of[1] Dailies	% of U.S. Total	Daily (000) Circulation	% of U.S. Total
Knight-Ridder	34	1.9%	3,681	6.0%
Newhouse	29	1.6	3,204	5.3
Tribune (Chicago)	6	.3	3,099	5.1
Gannett	73	4.1	2,772	4.5
Scripps-Howard	17	1.0	1,895	3.1
Times-Mirror	4	.2	1,880	3.1
Dow-Jones[2]	14	.8	1,783	2.9
Hearst	7	.4	1,436	2.4
Cox	17	1.0	1,179	1.9
New York Times	10	.6	975	1.6
Capital Cities	4	.2	950	1.6
Thompson	57	3.2	935	1.5
Total 12 Groups	272	15%	23.9 million	39%
155 Other Groups	775	44%	19.7 million	32%
All Groups	1,047	59%	43.6 million	71%

[1]Total reflects the number of editions, thus a firm selling both morning and evening editions is counted as two dailies.
[2]Includes the *Wall Street Journal,* which is not, strictly speaking, a general interest daily.
Source: *Editor & Publisher,* July 9, 1977.

Table 32
Decline in Multiple-Newspaper Cities
in the U.S.
1923–1978

Year	Total Cities With Newspapers	Cities Having More Than One Paper	
		Number	% of Total
1923	1297	502	38.7
1933	1426	243	17.0
1943	1416	137	19.7
1948	1392	109	7.8
1953	1453	91	6.3
1958	1447	70	4.8
1963	1476	51	3.5
1968	1493	43	2.9
1973	1519	37	2.4
1978	1536	35	2.3

Sources: Rosse, Owen, Dertouzos, "Trends in the Daily Newspaper Industry," Studies in Industry Economics #57, Stanford University, 1975; *1978 Editor & Publisher Yearbook*

mind the active rivalry among chains themselves, leading to the rise of new leaders and the decline of older ones. Hearst controlled 10 percent of the newspaper market in 1946 but only 2.2 percent in 1978. The Scripps-Howard group has also suffered a severe erosion in its market share. On the other hand, the names of Gannett, Newhouse and Thomson, unfamiliar names half a century ago, appear at the top of the list of leading chains.

A more persuasive line of reasoning is that although concentration seriously diminishes the readers' choice of newspapers, it does not by itself lead to control of news or regimentation of opinion. Americans still have access to a plethora of alternative print and non-print media sources with every conceivable slant and bias.

On balance, there is still no conclusive evidence that group ownership confers substantial monopoly power, given the localized structure of competition in the industry. Gannett's ownership of the Santa Fe *New Mexican* has little impact on the Battle Creek (Michigan) market, where the chain owns the *Enquirer* and *News*. On the other hand, there is little evidence that group ownership confers significant social benefit. Chains have some capital market advantages and better access to financial resources, and there may also be economies associated with centralized management. They may also be able to resist local pressures more easily, engage in investigative efforts and sustain public service programs and provide better training to

their employees. But these are marginal advantages if chains should serve to inhibit the generation of ideas and flow of news that is the ultimate purpose of a press.

Competition of sorts has been kept alive in more than 20 cities by the passage of the Newspaper Preservation Act of 1970. This act grants exemption from antitrust laws for joint operating agreements between two newspapers. It permits two newspapers, one of which is failing, to enter into a joint operating agreement that combines all commercial operations but retains separate and competing news and editorial departments. However, such arrangements require the permission of the attorney general, who will determine if one of the papers is, in fact, a failing newspaper.

As the only industry specifically protected by the constitution, the U.S. press has had few run-ins with the Justice Department, particularly its antitrust division. A notable exception was the landmark *Associated Press* v. *the United States* case in 1945, where the government charged the AP with restricting membership in cities where it already had members. In a classic interpretation of the First Amendment, the Supreme Court said, "Freedom to publish is guaranteed by the Constitution but freedom to combine to keep others from publishing is not. Freedom of the press from governmental interference under the First Amendment does not sanction repression of that freedom by private interests."

In another case, involving the New Orleans

Table 33
Share of Total Dollar Shipments by Largest Firms
1947–1972

Year	Newspapers
1947	
4 largest companies	21%
8 largest	26
50 largest	N.A.
1958	
4 largest companies	17
8 largest	24
50 largest	51
1963	
4 largest companies	15
8 largest	22
50 largest	52
1967	
4 largest companies	16
8 largest	25
50 largest	56
1972	
4 largest companies	17
8 largest	28
50 largest	60

Source: U.S. Bureau of Census, Census of Manufacturers.

Times-Picayune, the Supreme Court affirmed the legality of a morning-evening combined advertising rate offered by the owner of two papers under the same management. Another antitrust suit involved McClatchy Newspapers, owners of *The Sacramento Bee, The Fresno Bee, The Modesto Bee* and several radio and TV stations, charged with monopoly practices by the owner of *The Sacramento Union.*

No antitrust actions have been so far launched against newspaper groups, although a preliminary inquiry was announced into Rupert Murdoch's New York purchases. In 1978, however, the Federal Trade Commission held a symposium on concentration of ownership in all forms of mass media, and this was interpreted as a clear signal of the FTC's growing concern in this field.

Advertising

Newspaper advertising has grown slightly faster than the U.S. economy, expanding eightfold since World War II. As Table 34 shows, it reached $14.585 billion in 1979, of which 14.3 percent was for national advertising. According to the *World Advertising Ex-*

Table 34
National, Local and Total
Newspaper Advertising, 1946—1979

Year	National Newspaper Advertising (millions of dollars)	Local Newspaper Advertising (millions of dollars)	Total Newspaper Advertising[1] (millions of dollars)	Index	Gross National Product[1] (billions of dollars)	Index
1946	238	917	1,155	100.0	208.5	100.0
1950	518	1,552	2,070	179.2	284.8	136.6
1955	712	2,365	3,077	266.4	398.0	190.9
1960	778	2,903	3,681	318.7	503.7	241.6
1965	784	3,642	4,426	383.2	684.9	328.5
1970	891	4,813	5,704	493.9	977.1	468.6
1971	991	5,207	6,198	536.6	1,054.9	506.0
1972	1,103	5,905	7,008	606.8	1,158.0	555.4
1973	1,111	6,484	7,595	657.6	1,294.9	621.0
1974	1,194	6,807	8,001	692.7	1,406.9	674.8
1975	1,221	7,221	8,442	730.9	1,516.3	727.2
1976	1,502	8,408	9,910	858.0	1,700.1	815.4
1977	1,677	9,455	11,132	963.8	1,887.2	905.1
1978[1]	1,787	10,920	12,707	1,100.2	2,106.9	1,010.5
1979[2]	2,085	12,500	14,585	1,262.8	2,369.5	1,136.5

[1] Revised figures
[2] Preliminary figures
Source: U.S. Department of Commerce, McCann-Erickson Inc.; Newspaper Advertising Bureau

Table 35

Leading Newspapers in Advertising Linage, 1978

Newspaper	Full-Run Linage (000)	Part-Run Linage (000)	Total Linage (000)
1. Los Angeles Times (m)	104,975	48,630	153,605
2. Chicago Tribune (m/e)	71,956	47,130	119,086
3. Houston Chronicle (e)	101,515	10,092	111,607
4. Fort Lauderdale News (e)	85,102	6,183	91,285
5. Washington Post (m)	79,806	11,163	90,969
6. Miami Herald (m)	69,363	18,883	88,246
7. Houston Post (m)	75,103	8,008	83,111
8. Milwaukee Journal (e)	62,805	15,596	78,401
9. Dallas Times-Herald (e)	66,086	3,565	69,651
10. Detroit News (e)	58,039	11,604	69,643
11. St. Petersburg Times (m)	51,876	16,471	68,347
12. Atlanta Journal (e)	66,191	1,576	67,767
13. Cleveland Plain Dealer (m)	61,421	5,059	66,480
14. Chicago Sun-Times (m)	48,207	13,268	61,475
15. Tampa Tribune (m)	48,289	10,111	58,400

Source: *Editor & Publisher.*

penditures, 1979, the United States leads the world in both total advertising expenditures and newspaper advertising expenditures. Per-capita ad expenditures are $224.37, also the highest in the world. Its nearest competitor, Sweden, is $22.78 behind. The United States also leads in advertising as a percentage of GNP, with 2.02 percent as against 1.88 percent for its nearest rival, also Sweden. However, it must be noted that in this last respect U.S. advertising expenditures have remained unchanged since 1940 and have actually declined from an all-time high of 3.2 percent in 1920.

Table 36

Advertising Content

Ratio of Advertising to Total Content of U.S. Daily and Sunday Newspapers 1946–1978

Year	Mornings	Evenings	Sundays	Total
1946	52.9%	55.9%	53.1%	54.5%
1950	57.5	60.4	54.6	58.3
1955	60.9	61.8	58.2	60.7
1960	60.2	60.3	56.4	59.4
1961	59.7	59.6	55.3	58.7
1962	60.0	60.1	56.2	59.2
1963	60.2	59.9	56.4	59.3
1964	60.4	60.3	57.4	59.7
1965	60.9	61.0	59.1	60.5
1970	61.6	61.4	61.5	61.5
1971	62.9	62.2	63.1	62.6
1972	64.4	64.5	64.4	64.4
1973	65.7	64.9	66.2	65.5
1974	65.5	64.9	66.8	65.6
1975	63.2	63.0	65.7	63.7
1976	62.7	62.1	66.5	63.5
1977	62.4	61.3	66.6	63.1
1978	62.4	61.5	67.4	63.4
1979	NA	NA	NA	NA

Source: Media Records.

Newspaper ad revenues are the function of two components: linage (total agate lines) and the rate per line. Because rates tend to vary and rise steeply periodically, a more meaningful yardstick would be total linage. In 1978 *Media Records,* the industry's statistician, counted 4.87 billion lines in 203 papers, down from 5.25 billion lines in 247 papers the previous year. Table 35 shows the *Los Angeles Times* leading all with nearly 34 million lines over its nearest competitor, *The Chicago Tribune.* The list does not include *The New York Times,* which was strikebound for three months in 1978 but nevertheless ran 57,846,000 lines.

Table 37 shows the newspaper share of national advertising from 1939, a year in which it enjoyed a 39.5 percent share. With the introduction of television, this share began to drop precipitously until 1962, by which time it had yielded 10 percentage points. But it has held to this magic 29 percent ever since with remarkable tenacity. Even so, the newspaper share is equal to those of television, radio and magazines combined.

The advertising ratio in U.S. newspapers (the ratio of advertisement space to the news hole) has steadily risen since 1946, when it was 54.5 percent, to its present 63.4 percent. The highest ratio was reported in 1974, when it reached 65.6 percent. Because of the large size of most newspapers, this does not mean that news is being sacrificed to give more space to advertisers. Even so, the insertion of a vast amount of advertising is an impediment to smooth reading. Often the news stories appear as thin rivulets meandering through forests of double-page ad spreads.

Newspapers exercise considerable control over their ads through their acceptability standards. The U.S. Supreme Court upheld in 1971 the right of a newspaper to refuse advertising without assigning reasons. The Court held that a newspaper is not a common carrier and does not have to sell its space to everyone who requests it.

A fundamental issue that has troubled the U.S. press from its very beginnings is the subtle pressure that advertisers exert on the editorial content of newspapers. These pressures can take various forms: an ad boycott, or a "request" by an important advertiser to kill a story that could hurt his business, or to run a puff story in the news columns. John Fischer, a former editor of *Harper's,* admits that these pressures exist, but says they are miniscule. He said, "Only three times in 14 years of editing this magazine did I run into

Table 37 Newspapers' Share of Total Advertising Revenue, 1939–1977	% of Total Adv.
1939	39.5%
1940	38.6%
1941	37.5
1942	36.9
1943	32.8
1944	36.1
1945	32.4%
1946	34.6
1947	34.5
1948	35.8
1949	36.7
1950	36.3%
1951	35.1
1952	34.5
1953	34.0
1954	32.9
1955	33.6%
1956	32.5
1957	31.8
1958	30.8
1959	31.3
1960	30.8%
1961	30.4
1962	29.4
1963	28.9
1964	29.1
1965	29.0%
1966	29.3
1967	29.1
1968	28.9
1969	29.4
1970	29.2%
1971	29.9
1972	30.1
1973	30.2
1974	29.9
1975	29.9%
1976	29.4
1977	29.1

Source: Federal Trade Commission.

anything that could be called advertising pressure and in each case it was trivial." He, however, agreed that such things are sometimes done by "weaker" newspapers. Robert Lasch, editor of *St. Louis Post-Dispatch*, says, "Fischer says advertisers seldom attempt to dictate policy and virtually never succeed. I hope he is right in the latter generalization, but I know from experience that they try, they try."

The classic reasoning behind advertising pressures is that if something is bad for business, it is bad for the community. If the local paper does not promote the economic interests of business, then the only way to retaliate is through economic sanctions. According to Clay Felker, former publisher of *New York* magazine, there are circumstances under which an editor can afford to be tough with advertisers and other circumstances in which he will have to knuckle under. Felker says, "We can be tough with one or two of them, but not with all of them at the same time."

Over the years there have been numerous instances of subtle and not-so-subtle pressures from advertisers to which the press had to knuckle under:

• *Atlanta Constitution* columnist B. J. Phillips wrote an editorial-page column against a rate increase sought by the Georgia Power Company. Next morning Phillips and Editor Eugene Patterson were asked to resign.

• Two of the largest retail stores in Boston objected to an anti–Vietnam War ad in *The Boston Globe* and withdrew $55,000 worth of advertising in the Sunday edition.

• A column by Mike Royko that called car salesmen "deceitful liars" caused the Auto Dealers Association of Portland, Oregon to withdraw for 30 days all its classified ads in *The Oregonian* and the *Oregon Journal*.

• *The New York Times* was forced to sell off

Table 38
Newspapers' Share of Media Advertising Revenue, 1978–79

		1978[1]		1979[2]		%
		Million	**% of Total**	**Million**	**% of Total**	**Change**
Daily Newspapers	Total	$12,707	28.9	$14,585	29.3	+14.8
	National	1,787	4.1	2,085	4.2	16.6
	Local	10,920	24.8	12,500	25.1	14.5
Magazines		2,597	5.9	2,930	5.9	12.8
Television	Total	8,979	20.4	10,195	20.5	13.5
	Network	3,975	9.0	4,540	9.1	14.2
	Spot	2,581	5.9	2,890	5.8	12.0
	Local	2,423	5.5	2,765	5.6	14.0
Radio	Total	3,052	6.9	3,385	6.8	11.0
	Network	147	0.3	170	0.3	15.0
	Spot	620	1.4	680	1.4	9.8
	Local	2,285	5.2	2,535	5.1	11.0
Farm Publications		104	0.2	120	0.2	14.0
Direct Mail		5,987	13.6	6,650	13.3	11.1
Business Publications		1,400	3.2	1,595	3.2	14.0
Outdoor		466	1.1	535	1.1	14.8
		307	0.7	350	0.7	14.0
		159	0.4	185	0.4	16.4
Miscellaneous		8,678	19.8	9,835	19.7	13.4
		4,485	10.2	5,060	10.2	12.8
		4,193	9.6	4,775	9.5	13.9
GRAND TOTAL		23,990	54.6	27,070	54.3	12.8
GRAND TOTAL		19,980	45.4	22,760	45.7	13.9
TOTAL—ALL MEDIA		$43,970	100.0	$49,830	100.0	+13.3

[1] Revised figures
[2] Preliminary
Source: McCann-Erickson Inc.

its eight medical journals because of an ad boycott by pharmaceutical companies.

• Safeway Stores banned *The Atlantic Monthly* from being sold on their premises because of a cover article called "Rip-Off at the Supermaket."

Advertising pressures on the media will continue as long as newspapers are financially vulnerable and remain unconcerned by the ethical implications of such pressures.

Newsprint

Newsprint is the largest single variable in newspaper costs, and its consumption is one of the most reliable indexes of cost growth. Total U.S. newsprint consumption reached a record 10.87 million metric tons in 1978 and 11.24 million tons in 1979. The daily newspaper share of this total declined to a little over 76 percent in 1978. However a substantial proportion of the decline was due to the increased use of preprints, which properly should be considered a part of the newspaper. Total consumption of newsprint expanded by 23 percent from 1968 to 1978; newspaper consumption by 12 percent. From 1975 to 1979 newsprint consumption rose more rapidly than the real GNP.

U.S. producers supplied 37.3 percent of daily newspapers' newsprint requirements during 1978, up from 33.1 percent 10 years

Table 39
Newsprint Prices
General Newsprint Prices in the Eastern U.S.,[1] 1957–1979

Year	Price	Year	Price
1957	$135	1972	$165
1966	140	1973	200
1967	143	1974	235
1968	143	1975	260
1969	148	1976	285
1970	152	1977	305
1971	160	1978	320
		1979	375

[1]Prices through 1973 are for 32-pound newsprint; thereafter, 30-pound. Prices cited were in effect at end of year.
Sources: ANPA, U.S. Department of Commerce.

earlier. From 1968 to 1978 U.S. mills increased their tonnage 26.5 percent and Canadian mills 8.7 percent. As a result the Canadian share of the market declined from 64.4 percent to 62.5 percent. Overseas suppliers accounted for 2.5 percent of the U.S. market in 1968 but only 0.1 percent in 1978.

After decades of steady prices and even oversupply, newsprint prices took off in 1970 and jumped almost 147 percent between 1970 and 1980, as shown in Table 39. Rising prices have forced U.S. dailies to introduce conservation measures, such as trimming sizes.

Table 40
Newsprint Consumption
Comparison of U.S. Newsprint Consumption to National Economic Growth, 1966–79

Year	Newsprint Consumption (000's metric tons)	Growth Index	Real GNP ($ billion)	Growth Index
1966	8,582	100.0	981.0	100.0
1970	9,119	106.3	1,075.3	109.6
1971	9,250	107.8	1,107.5	112.9
1972	9,941	115.8	1,171.1	119.4
1973[1]	10,794	125.8	1,233.4	125.7
1974[1]	10,284	119.8	1,210.7	123.4
1975[1]	9,254	107.8	1,191.7	121.5
1976[1]	9,611	112.0	1,271.0	129.6
1977	10,230	119.2	1,332.7	135.8
1978[1]	10,874	126.7	1,385.3	141.2
1979[2]	11,240	131.0	1,431.7	145.9

[1]Revised figures
[2]Preliminary figures
Sources: ANPA, U.S. Department of Commerce.

Table 41

Comparison of Newspaper Employment to Total U.S. Employment, 1946–79

Year	Newspaper Employment (in 000's)	Male Total (in 000's)	Female Total (in 000's)	Growth Index	Total U.S. Employment (in 000's)	Growth Index
1946	248.5	NA	NA	100.0	57,039	100.0
1950	280.1	NA	NA	112.7	58,920	103.3
1955	302.1	NA	NA	121.6	62,171	109.0
1960	325.2	NA	NA	130.9	65,778	115.3
1965	345.4	NA	NA	139.1	71,088	124.6
1970	372.2	274.7	97.5	149.8	78,627	137.8
1971	371.0	272.0	99.0	149.3	79,120	138.7
1972	378.7	274.5	104.2	152.4	81,702	143.2
1973	385.5	273.9	111.6	155.1	84,409	148.0
1974	385.4	267.7	117.7	155.1	85,936	150.7
1975	378.5	258.3	120.2	152.3	84,783	148.6
1976	382.8	258.2	124.6	154.0	88,558	155.3
1977	395.2	262.7	132.5	159.0	90,546	158.8
1978	406.2	263.9	142.3	163.5	94,373	165.5
1979	420.7	268.2	152.5	169.3	96,945	170.0

Source: U.S. Department of Labor, Bureau of Labor Statistics.

Employment & Industrial Relations

The newspaper business is labor intensive: about 37 cents out of every revenue dollar goes for payroll, compared to 14 cents in the automobile industry, 22 cents in steel, 20 cents in textiles and six cents in petroleum.

Total employment in the industry reached 420,700 in 1979, after crossing the 400,000 mark in 1978. Newspaper employment has grown more slowly than the national employment; based on 1960=100, the newspaper employment index was 123 in 1978, compared to the civilian employment index of 142. The total wage bill in 1977 was approximately $4.291 billion, of which $1.80 billion represented wages paid to production workers.

Although the percentages vary, an average daily newspaper has about 15 percent of its staff in editorial, 10 percent in sales and advertising, 15 percent in business office and administration, 12 percent in circulation, sales and delivery, and about 48 percent in production.

Newspaper production workers had average wages of $6.67 per hour in 1977, making them the highest paid workers in nonagricultural industries. Unionized workers received higher wages, up to $8.17 per hour in some cities. In 1979 the mean mechanical union hourly wage was $8.64 for mailers, $9.41 for typographers and $9.62 for pressmen. Actual wages, however, varied, with Anchorage, Alaska, not surprisingly, leading the list. Salaries in the newsroom began around $10,000 and went up to $30,000 to $50,000. The U.S. Department of Labor rates prospects for new journalism graduates as good to excellent, predicting greater demand for copyeditors and photojournalists.

Women have always constituted a minority in newspaper publishing. Recently even venerable institutions such as *The New York Times* and *Reader's Digest* have been penalized under the Equal Employment Opportunities Act and the Affirmative Action Program for discrimination against women. In 1979 women constituted 36.2 percent of the newspaper personnel, compared with 26 percent in 1970. Despite a few names at the top of the mastheads, such as Katharine Graham of *The Washington Post* and Helen K. Copley of Copley Newspapers, there were few women at management levels or in board rooms. A 1977 Indiana University study showed that the daily newspaper industry lagged behind others in the promotion of women to executive positions.

The position of blacks and ethnics was even worse. An American Society of Newspaper Editors study in 1978 said that only 1,700 persons belonging to minorities were employed on the news staffs of daily newspapers. Of that number, 62 percent were blacks, 12 percent Orientals, 12 percent Chicanos, 10 percent Latinos, and 4 percent Amerindians. Although the total represented only four percent of newspaper personnel in the country, it was a significant improvement on the one percent reported a decade ago. The study noted that about two-thirds of the nation's newspapers had no minority employes, and close to 90 percent had no minority editors.

Production departments of newspapers had unions even before the Civil War, but editorial and business employes were organized only after Heywood Broun started the American Newspaper Guild in 1933. In 1979 newspaper workers were represented by four major unions: the Newspaper Guild, representing the white collar; the International Printing and Graphic Communications Union, created through the 1973 union of Pressmen and Stereotypers; the International Typographical Union, representing mailing room and composing room personnel, and the Graphic Arts International Union, formerly the Lithographers and Photoengravers. In addition, newspapers have to deal with other unions, such as Teamsters representing delivery truck drivers. The extent of unionization varies from newspaper to newspaper. *The New York Times*, for example, has to deal with as many as 14; but 75 percent of all newspapers, including large ones such as *The Miami Herald* and the *Los Angeles Times*, do not have any unions. The International Typographical Union, the largest union, has contracts with about 450 papers, and the Newspaper Guild with 135.

Not only are newspapers vulnerable to strikes and work stoppages, but such strikes can be often very destructive and even fatal. Unlike other industries, newspapers cannot stockpile or make up lost production after the strike is over. An edition that is not printed on a given day is lost forever. Lost advertising and circulation revenues are also permanently forfeit. A strike can be a crushing blow to a financially ailing newspaper. Labor problems have contributed to the demise of several newspapers, such as the New York *Herald Tribune*. Even when it survives a strike, a newspaper will lose much of its competitive edge for a number of years. The New York *Daily News* has not still regained circulation lost during the 1978 strike.

However, the introduction of new technology is bound to give management the advantage in the 1980s. It has been said that the crippling 1978 New York strike, which cost newspapers over $100 million, might be the last major strike because new technology

will have made unions irrelevant by the time the next contract is due. According to Benjamin Bradlee of *The Washington Post,* "The state of the art is such that a handful of people can now put out the paper." *The Washington Post,* in fact, did so during the 1975 strike, when the presses were manned by 35 persons, mostly executive personnel, replacing a normal complement of 205 pressmen! To offset this development the International Typographers Union and the Newspaper Guild have been exploring avenues for consolidation.

Table 42 shows that the number of strikes has declined in 1979. Whether this represents a permanent trend is a question neither the unions nor the management can really answer.

Table 42

Newspaper Strikes, 1951–1979

Year	No. of Strikes Started	Cities	Newspapers Involved
1951	3	3	3
1952	14	12	18
1953	13	13	22
1954	7	7	8
1955	11	9	17
1956	14	19	23
1957	31	29	48
1958	38	29	44
1959	40	25	42
1960	10	9	12
1961	10	8	8
1962	27	17	26
1963	25	15	24
1964	24	16	23
1965	12	11	14
1966	30	22	40
1967	35	25	32
1968	27	20	29
1969	23	14	22
1970	30	27	38
1971	26	18	24
1972	22	16	25
1973	34	23	32
1974	28	23	30
1975	25	19	21
1976	11	10	12
1977	18	13	17
1978	30	14	19
1979	10	7	10

Source: ANPA.

Press Laws & Censorship
by Aviam Soifer

In the United States, freedom of the press is much more than a legal concept. It is almost a religious tenet. The U.S. Constitution, as interpreted by the Supreme Court, is something of a secular religion; the First Amendment to that Constitution, which protects the freedom of the press, is a core element of the proclaimed beliefs of most Americans. American reverence for a free press is identified with the tradition of Milton and Mill; the writings of Thomas Jefferson and James Madison are unique American contributions to that freedom. As a legal matter, it is widely thought that the freedom of the press enjoys a special, favored position among constitutional values.

Litigation involving questions of freedom of the press in America is almost exclusively a 20th-century phenomenon, however. For every famous early victory for freedom of the press, such as the refusal of a New York jury in 1735 to convict printer John Peter Zenger of seditious libel for his attacks on the colonial governor, there were many instances of successful prosecutions of members of the press for "abuse" of the privileges of their position. Furthermore, recent historical evidence reveals that even someone as vigorously open-minded as Thomas Jefferson was prone to saying brave things about guaranteeing a free press but acting in what appears to have been quite a different manner. Jefferson's eloquence about free newspapers, including the claim that a free press is even more important than a free government, was perhaps the most famous of his brilliant libertarian arguments, made most powerfully in opposition to the Alien and Sedition Acts of 1798. For example, Jefferson wrote:

> The basis of our government being the opinion of the people, the very first object should be to keep that right; and were it left to me to decide whether we should have a government without newspapers or newspapers without government, I should not hesitate a moment to prefer the latter. But I mean that every man should receive these papers, and be capable of reading them.

But in *Legacy of Suppression* (1960), which includes a detailed study of Jefferson's deeds as president, Professor Leonard Levy demonstrates that even Jefferson was not above the use of federal law to suppress Federalist Party newspapers, which were particularly vitriolic in their opposition to President Jefferson and his political allies.

The history of America in the 19th century is full of examples of overt suppression of newspapers. Successful attempts to limit or punish the press generally occurred on the state level, but occasionally the federal government engaged in such conduct as well. For example, generals such as Andrew Jackson during the War of 1812 and Ambrose E. Burnside during the Civil War halted publication when they deemed it necessary for reasons of military advantage. One of the oft-repeated claims of the antislavery movement before the Civil War was that the southern "Slave Power" successfully excluded all antislavery arguments from the South through denial of postal service, destruction of pamphlets and papers, and worse.

President Abraham Lincoln had the editors arrested and ordered the military occupation of two New York newspapers that opposed his Administration when they printed bogus news of increased draft calls. Similarly, President Theodore Roosevelt charged, in a special message to Congress in 1908, that the publisher Joseph Pulitzer was guilty of criminal libel against the United States. Roosevelt tried to have Pulitzer prosecuted for his attacks on the construction of the Panama Canal.

The story of the war fever that gripped the country during World War I, told most vividly by Zechariah Chafee, Jr., is the sobering tale of frequent and successful suppression of the press. Famous judicial decisions of this period, written for the United States Supreme Court by the highly respected Justice Oliver Wendell Holmes, Jr., rejected freedom of the press claims with apparent ease. Paradoxically, the post–World War I period—and in part the influential writing of Professor Chafee—marked a turning point. Soon thereafter the Supreme Court in *Gitlow* v. *New York* (1925) made the First Amendment binding on the states. In a series of famous dissents and separate concurrences, Justice Holmes and Brandeis began to introduce into modern First Amendment doctrine the notion of a free marketplace of ideas. Soon the Court was declaring the press to have a particularly important function as a source of information in a democracy and as a check upon governmental abuse.

Justice Hugo Black summed up this vital theme in the American constitutional law of the 20th century. In his final, concurring opinion, when the Court decided in 1971 to reject the government's claim of sufficient power to enjoin publication of the Pentagon Papers, and at the end of a distinguished judicial career as the foremost proponent of absolute protection for freedom of the press, Justice Black wrote:

> The Government's power to censor the press was abolished so that the press would remain forever free to censure the Government. The press was protected so that it could bare the secrets of government and inform the people.

Constitutional Provisions & Guarantees Relating to Media

The basis for most discussion about freedom of the press in the United States is the First Amendment to the federal Constitution. That amendment, ratified in 1791, four years after the Constitution itself, provides: "Congress shall make no law ... abridging the freedom of speech, or of the press...." Several fundamental questions immediately arise concerning the interpretation of these famous words. These problems may be divided into four areas:

Congress Shall Make... Is the protection guaranteed by the First Amendment limited to protection against acts of Congress? In a federal system such as that of the United States, which has two distinct formal legal systems—the laws of the federal government and the laws of the states—this issue is of immense practical importance. Most of the law affecting individuals directly and daily is state law, yet the words of the First Amendment contain an explicit barrier only to laws made by Congress. Is the press therefore vulnerable to laws enacted by the legislatures and municipalities of the 50 states?

For more than a half century it has been clear that the protections of the First Amendment are not limited to protections against actions by Congress. The reach of the First Amendment was extended in 1925 to acts of state legislatures in the U.S. Supreme Court decision *Gitlow* v. *New York* (1925). Since 1925 the U.S. Supreme Court has expanded the scope of the amendment's coverage to include actions by municipal agencies, members of the executive branches of both federal and state governments, and all public officials and administrators. Even the actions of state courts were deemed covered in *New York Times Co.* v. *Sullivan* (1964).

The First Amendment protects freedom of the press from the action of any public officer, agency or governmental body. Its scope does not include protection from actions by private parties.

No Law. Is the command that Congress make "no law" abridging free speech or a free press limited to formal lawmaking? What of administrative actions, executive orders, judicial injunctions? Does the constitutional prohibition extend to restraints on the press imposed by private parties? What about laws that don't proclaim an attack on freedom of the press but nevertheless have that effect? It is obvious that in modern postindustrial states such as the United States any number of significant regulations and restraints arise that are not formal statutes passed by Congress. The extent to which the First Amendment provides a shield against them, and conceivably against private power as well, is a core issue for the law of freedom of the press in the United States.

The protection of the First Amendment certainly extends beyond formal lawmaking. The constitutional armor it provides the press includes protection against administrative rules and regulations, executive orders, and judicial injunctions and rulings. Generally the amendment's protection does not reach actions and restraints imposed by private parties.

There are two caveats that accompany this principle, however. First, the notion that constitutional rights in general are guaranteed only against official action, deemed "state action" in the term used by American lawyers, produced a great deal of pressure on courts to attempt to distinguish between public and private action. Over a decade ago Professor Charles Black referred to the state action doctrine as "a conceptual disaster area." If anything, the situation has worsened in the intervening years. Therefore, while it is clear that one person can tell another to stop handing out leaflets in his living room because of what they say, it is not clear that a private university receiving substantial governmental benefits may do the same thing in a college dormitory without implicating First Amendment rights. It is not even entirely clear that the owner of the private living room in the above example can involve public officials, such as the police, in his attempt to stop the leaflets without bringing First Amendment considerations into play. It is therefore a commonplace that the First Amendment protection of freedom of the press extends only to official or state action, and not to purely private restraints on the press. How the "essential dichotomy" between public and private is resolved, however, remains an intractable problem in American constitutional law.

Second, the U.S. Supreme Court has at times hinted that excessive concentration in news dissemination might itself constitute a violation of the First Amendment. In *Associated Press* v. *United States* (1945), the United States Supreme Court held that the First Amendment provided no immunity from antitrust laws for publishers. In his opinion for the majority, Justice Black wrote:

> Surely a command that the government itself shall not impede the free flow of ideas does not afford non-governmental combinations a refuge if they impose restraints upon that constitutionally guaranteed freedom. Freedom to publish means freedom for all and not for some. Freedom to publish is guaranteed by the Constitution, but freedom to combine to keep others from publishing is not. Freedom of the press from governmental interference under the First Amendment does not sanction repression of that freedom by private interests.

The issue of concentration has been a basic element of the American law governing television and radio, and has led to a variety of doctrines imposing responsibilities, the owners of station licenses to provide access and certain kinds of coverage. Concentration in the print media has not produced similar legally enforceable obligations to date, with the exception of a 1975 Federal Communications Commission restriction upon the common ownership of daily newspapers and broadcast stations in the same geographic area. In fact, newspapers enjoy exemption from the normal order of antitrust legislation by special congressional legislation, the Newspaper Preservation Act of 1970.

It should be noted, however, that concentration in the print media and scholarly commentary and criticism of this trend has increased markedly in recent years. Courts have not yet heeded the suggestions of scholarly critics, nor have they added practical teeth to the observation made in *Associated Press* v. *United States*. The difficulties posed by monopoly or massive and interlocking concetrations for a freedom premised upon the idea of a free marketplace are among legal issues that will undoubtedly be litigated and much discussed in the 1980s.

Abridging. What is meant by the constitutional term "abridging"? Does the protection extend only to actions intended to abridge the freedoms guaranteed in the First Amendment, or does it encompass actions, govern-mental or private, that have the indirect effect of limiting free speech or the freedom of the press? "Abridging" could be interpreted to imply that the thing—e.g., freedom of the press—that cannot be abridged must exist already. It is possible, for example, to argue that the constitutional protection should not extend to developments in the processes and technology of mass communications, such as radio and television, which were introduced after the framers and ratifiers adopted the First Amendment in 1791.

It is not necessary to prove that a governmental action was intended to abridge the freedom of the press to make a constitutional claim under the First Amendment. Proof of such motive, however, is always relevant to such a claim. Furthermore, a governmental motive to fetter or punish the press may be sufficient to support a claim of a First Amendment violation.

A good example of the way in which a "bad" motive on the part of a governmental official may be sufficient occurred in *Grosjean* v. *American Press* (1936). At the behest of Huey Long, the powerful governor of Louisiana, the Louisiana legislature enacted a statute providing that any newspaper with a circulation of over 20,000 copies would be required to pay a license tax of two percent of its gross receipts. General license taxes have customarily been upheld by American courts; further, judges traditionally allow legislatures broad discretion in tax schemes, and tend overwhelmingly to defer to legislative judgment when it comes to tax classifications. In *Grosjean*, however, it was clear to the U.S. Supreme Court that Governor Long had had the tax enacted in order to punish the New Orleans *Times-Picayune*, which had been critical of him and his policies. The Court unanimously held:

> The tax here is bad not because it takes money from the pockets of the appellees.... It is bad because, in the light of its history and of its present setting, it is seen to be a deliberate and calculated device in the guise of a tax to limit the circulation of information to which the public is entitled in virtue of the constitutional guarantees.

Even a restraint imposed with the best of motives, such as a judge's order prohibiting discussion of a pending criminal trial in order to assure the defendant a trial free of prejudicial publicity, was held to be an unconstitutional restraint. In *Nebraska Press Assoc.* v. *Stuart* (1976), this was the

Court's view of such a "gag order," at least in the absence of efforts by a judge to use other, less drastic alternatives prior to impostition of the restraint.

The U.S. Supreme Court has emphatically and repeatedly held that the protection accorded to the press by the First Amendment is not limited to established or generally recognized publications. As Justice Black summarized for the Court in *Mills* v. *Alabama* (1966), "The Constitution specifically selected the press, which includes not only newspapers, books, and magazines, but also humble leaflets and circulars, to play an important role in the discussion of public affairs." And although the vital role of the press is generally discussed primarily in terms of public affairs, the Court has made it clear that First Amendment protections extend to matters that merely entertain, in *Time, Inc.* v. *Hill* (1967), and constitute a vital element of the American system of freedom of expression. Commentators ranging from Alexander Meiklejohn to Herbert Marcuse and Robert Bork have attacked the concept of the free marketplace of all ideas, which is at the core of much of First Amendment law; they suggest various limitations: only political speech, for example, or particular emphases for protected expression. Yet the Supreme Court continues to hold that freedom of the press is not limited to the freedom to report or editorialize about political matters.

The constitutional rules and legal interpretations governing radio and television are quite different, however, based largely on the notion of the inherent technological limits of the available avenues of communication. Nonprint mass media have been heavily regulated in terms of ownership, public responsibility and providing access. Television and radio are not devoid of First Amendment protections; nevertheless, they are less fully protected that are the print media, and limitations and regulations are much easier for the government to justify. The argument in support of this differential treatment relies more on claims related to technology than on arguments that cite the intent of the framers of the Constitution, although such arguments are sometimes made.

Freedom of Speech... or of the Press. Is freedom of the press substantially different from freedom of speech? Should journalists or owners of mass media enjoy special protections not shared by their fellow citizens? Does the constitutional protection extend only to the "organized press"? Does it include the electronic as well as the print media? Debate is raging today among scholars and judges about whether the speech and press guarantees are coextensive. At issue is what, if any, legal consequences flow from the idea that the press plays a particular role in American life, as a check on government and a source of information to the public. In the past decade, no more significant concern for the law of freedom of the press arose than this controversy.

A related issue is the question of access. Does protection provided to the press by the First Amendment entail some affirmative guarantee of access? Is it unconstitutional to exclude the press from matters of public interest, such as legislative hearings, court trials, jails and mental hospitals? Even if some affirmative right of press access were recognized, the problems of allocating scarce resources—e.g., seats at a presidential press conference or a much publicized criminal trial—remain quite troublesome. Issues of an affirmative right of press access to governmental operations—and corresponding claims for press immunity or special treatment when governmental officials seek access to press operations—figured prominently in recent litigation. They remain in flux today.

The fact that there are two phrases in the First Amendment, one guaranteeing "freedom of speech" and another, separate phrase concerning "freedom of the press," produced a vigorous debate during the past decade concerning whether the press can legitimately claim additional First Amendment protections beyond those claimed by all citizens. The dispute was touched off by Justice Potter Stewart's speech at the Yale Law School in 1974 (reprinted the following year: Stewart, "Or of the Press," 26 Hastings L.J. 631 [1975]), in which he suggested that the press should enjoy special constitutional protections. Justice Stewart appeared to limit his claim to the rights of what he alternately called the "organized press," the "established news media" and the "established press." At least two law review symposia, one in the *Hofstra Law Review* and one in the *University of Miami Law Review*, have already been devoted to consideration of the implications of such an approach, and discussion of the question by virtually all the other leading legal experts on the First Amendment has appeared recently.

Those in favor of special protections for the press point to its vital role in providing a check on government, as well as being a source of information to the populace. This "checking function," it is maintained, warrants guaranteeing the press special privileges as a surrogate or fiduciary for the public. Those opposed to special privileges for the press point to the definitional problems that such an approach would entail. It would put government officials, courts or the press in the position of defining who was and who was not a bona fide beneficiary of the extra constitutional protection. They also suggest that with special privileges inevitably will come the argument that the press has special reciprocal responsibilities enforceable against it. Therefore, they argue, the press, by virtue of claiming special freedom, will ultimately find itself less free.

One commentator, Professor C. Edwin Baker, proposes a scheme differentiating between an absolute freedom of speech for individuals and an additional, institutional freedom of a more limited sort for the press. He would uphold a press claim to be free from newsroom searches, thereby rejecting the Supreme Court's holding in *Zurcher* v. *Stanford Daily* (1978). At the same time, Professor Baker suggests that the press should not be able to claim a particular right of access to public events, or special defenses against defamation suits. Finally, Professor Baker makes the point that it is important to distinguish among the interests of journalists, owners and the public.

In a series of decisions during the 1970s concerning First Amendment defenses against the obligation of journalists to give testimony to grand juries, and the power of the police to search a newsroom, the Supreme Court appeared to reject the idea that members of the press should be treated differently from other citizens. In cases arising out of the attempt of judges to exclude members of the press from courtrooms, a splintered Court determined that both the press and the public generally could be excluded from preliminary hearings and that both generally had a right of access to trials themselves. In the course of these two decisions, *Gannett Co., Inc.* v. *DePasquale* (1979) and *Richmond Newspapers, Inc.* v. *Virginia* (1980) respectively, the justices refused to reach the claim that the press had a unique, additional First Amendment right. In *Houchins* v. *KQED, Inc.* (1978), the Court appeared to hold that the press has no special right of access greater than the public generally enjoys. The decision was handed down without a majority opinion, however, and involved only seven of the nine justices of the U.S. Supreme Court.

The claim for special press protection remains a normative claim that has not commanded a Supreme Court majority; at the same time it is obvious that, as a practical matter, *The New York Times* or *The Washington Post* enjoy practical advantages and access to official governmental functions not enjoyed by the average woman- or man-in-the-street, or even the journalist working for a struggling "underground" paper.

State Constitutions. It is important to note that the federal Constitution is not the only constitution protecting the legal rights of Americans. Each of the 50 states has its own constitution, and these constitutions generally contain language protecting freedom of the press in terminology at least somewhat different from that used in the First Amendment to the U.S. Constitution. In the American federal system, the U.S. Constitution clearly enjoys supremacy. It is nevertheless open to a state court to interpret a *state* constitutional protection of freedom of the press, for example, more broadly than the federal Constitution's protections have been interpreted by the U.S. Supreme Court. This is the case so long as such broader guarantees are not actually in conflict with any provisions of the federal Constitution. For a variety of reasons—including, but not limited, to recent changes in the balance of federalism, decreased access to the federal courts and judge-shopping for the jurists most likely to be sympathetic to one's claims—there has been increased reliance upon state constitutional provisions for civil liberties claims.

For example, the California Supreme Court recently held that the right to distribute handbills within a privately owned shopping center was protected under the California constitution, although it was clear that such leafletting was not protected under the federal Constitution according to a series of recent decisions by the U.S. Supreme Court interpreting the First Amendment. The California case was appealed to the U.S. Supreme Court on a claim made by the owner of the shopping center that he was deprived of his private property rights, which he argued were protected by the other provisions of the U.S. Constitution; the shopping center owner claimed, in this instance, that the California Supreme Court had ruled in favor of freedom of expression in a way inconsistent with rights under the U.S. Constitution, and that its ruling could not stand. In an opinion written by Justice Rehnquist, the U.S. Supreme Court in *Prune Yard Shopping Center* v. *Robins* (1980) sustained the power of the California court to go further than the U.S. Supreme Court would have gone in guaranteeing freedom of communication, and held that the interpretation of the California constitution's protections was not inconsistent with the U.S. Constitution.

A state constitution, therefore, may be more protective of freedom of the press than the federal Constitution. In fact a number of distinguished justices, sitting on both federal and state supreme courts, have begun to advise lawyers to make use of this particular oddity of the American dual system. It remains a relatively rare occurrence, however.

Press Laws in Force

Due largely to the presence of the First Amendment to the U.S. Constitution and analogous provisions in the constitutions of the 50 states, there are not many press laws in force in the United States. Public opinion generally appears to value and to support freedom of the press, at least in the abstract. The legislative representatives of the people do not tend to enact laws that obviously restrict the press.

To the extent that press laws do exist, they tend to provide additional protections and legal rights for journalists in categories in which the rights provided were held not to be constitutionally required. Several recent examples include: the Privacy Protection Act of 1980, establishing protections from police searches of newsrooms; a variety of journalist shield laws; and both federal and state Freedom of Information and "sunshine" laws.

One exception is the definitional approach, which excludes some types of publication altogether from First Amendment protection. Until the 1970s, commercial speech frequently was held to be so excluded; obscenity still is entirely without constitutional protection. Additional exceptions include nuclear and military secrets, publication appropriating copyrighted materials, and defamation.

Registration & Licensing of Newspapers & Journalists

The First Amendment long has been thought to preclude any requirements that newspapers and journalists be registered or licensed. Even before the expansion of the rights of the press through judicial rulings following World War I, Americans had identified with the English tradition of opposition to any requirement of prior governmental approval or licensure. John Milton's *Areopagitica* may have been narrow in the actual protected religious freedom it proclaimed, but its message that the pursuit of truth required opposition to licensing was received and expanded from the early 18th century onward in America. Even before the Supreme Court began to expand the scope of the practical legal protections afforded by the First Amendment, the Court approved the notion, derived from Blackstone, that government could not impose any restraint prior to publication, although it could punish after it was published anything that violated the law (*Patterson* v. *State of Colorado ex. rel. Attorney General* [*1970*]).

Nevertheless, requirements that owners and executives of general newspapers and magazines file sworn statements listing owners, stockholders and editors in order to qualify for mailing privileges at lower costs have been upheld, in *Lewis Publishing Co.* v. *Morgan* (1913).

More recent decisions emphasized that the post office must be evenhanded in administering the second-class mailing privilege available to publications, in *Hannigan* v. *Esquire* (1946), and that postal authorities may not burden receipt of foreign mail by requiring a special request card, in *Lamont* v. *Postmaster General* (1965). The Court also protected the anonymous distribution of handbills, and invalidated a Los Angeles ordinance requiring identification of the sponsors or authors of such materials.

Talley v. California (1960). In a series of decisions in the late 1930s and early 1940s involving the distribution and sale of printed materials by members of the Jehovah's Witnesses, the U.S. Supreme Court emphasized that both licensing and discriminatory taxation are constitutionally invalid. Perhaps the most emphatic statement of this repeated theme was in the words of Chief Justice Hughes in *Lovell* v. *Griffin* (1938). He wrote:

> The struggle for the freedom of the press was primarily directed against the power of the licensor....The prevention of that restraint was a leading purpose in the adoption of the constitutional provision....The press in its historic connotation comprehends every sort

of publication which affords a vehicle of information and opinion.

The Court concluded its discussion, which invalidated a municipal requirement of written permission prior to distribution of handbills, with an approving quotation *Ex parte Jackson* (1877) that noted: "Liberty of circulation is as essential to that freedom [of the press] as liberty of publishing; indeed, without circulation, the publication would be of little value."

The Court recently rejected a broad right-of-circulation claim, however, and upheld a regulation of the U.S. Postal Service that absolutely bars placement of printed material in private mail boxes if it does not carry postal stamps in the requisite amount. In *U.S. Postal Service* v. *Council of Greenburgh Civic Association* (1981), the Court held that this rule does not violate the First Amendment rights either of potential recipients or of the public service organizations wishing to use this distribution method.

The decision invalidating licensing, taxation and distribution restrictions still stand. This indicates that the U.S. Supreme Court will scrutinize any attempt to regulate the distribution as well as the publication of printed material. Even if the government has a legitimate purpose in such laws, the Court will look closely to make certain that they are not aimed at the press, administered in a discriminatory fashion or used as a pretext for an unconstitutional licensing scheme.

Statutory Protections

A recent trend in press law has been for both Congress and state legislatures to respond to some U.S. Supreme Court decisions that reject First Amendment claims by extending statutory protections to journalists. It must be emphasized that when the Court denies a claim—that a journalist should enjoy a special privilege against newsroom searches, for example, or against being compelled to testify before a grand jury about confidential sources—the ruling generally says nothing that precludes legislative initiatives to extend such protection. At times the Court explicitly invites statutory responses. Such protections may be and often are granted as a matter of statutory entitlement rather than of constitutional law.

Specific examples include: protection of the press from newsroom searches, journalist

shield laws and Freedom of Information acts.

Protections of the Press from Newsroom Searches. The Privacy Protection Act of 1980 is a federal statute prohibiting police searches of newsrooms for evidence of criminal activity by nonjournalists, unless the police obtain a subpoena—rather than a search warrant—thereby giving news gatherers notice and the opportunity to challenge the authorities' right to the material in court. The statute establishes special protection for the press in the form of additional statutory protections from police searches for "any work product materials possessed by a person reasonably believed to have a purpose to disseminate to the public a newspaper, book, broadcast, or other similar form of public communication." The relevant congressional committee report specifically noted, "This legislation was prompted by *Zurcher* v. *Stanford Daily* (1978), which involved the search of a student newspaper for evidence of a crime." Because the *Zurcher* decision rejected claims for special protections available to the press under either the First or the Fourth Amendment, which protects all citizens "against unreasonable search and seizure" the Senate Judiciary Committee decided to enact statutory protections applicable to all federal, state and local governments for "those engaged in First Amendment activities." Congress also mandated the development by the Department of Justice of guidelines for federal officials to cover documentary evidence sought from nonsuspects who are not included in the special protections for the press contained in the 1980 act.

It is worth noting that the committee report mentioned that no witness testifying in favor of the bill, with the exception of the Department of Justice, advocated limiting such statutory protection to the press. Indeed, representatives of the press "were among the strongest proponents of expanding the legislation to protect all innocent third parties from arbitrary search and seizure, expressing concern about singling out the press for special treatment." As enacted, however, the Privacy Protection Act of 1980 is an unusual example of federal legislation that does specifically single out those engaged in First Amendment activities for special protection.

Journalist Shield Laws. Slightly over half the states have enacted some form of special statues to provide journalists with at least some legal shield against the inquires of law enforcement personnel or grand juries concerning confidential sources. While a sharply divided Supreme Court held in *Branzburg* v. *Hays* (1972) that the U.S. Constitution does not protect journalists from such disclosures, it said nothing to preclude legislatures from extending such protections to journalists by statute. Additionally the U.S. Department of Justice has promulgated internal guidelines that recognize the sensitive nature of inquiries aimed at journalists and attempt to limit overzealous law enforcement in this area.

The 26 state shield laws currently in effect differ greatly in the degree of protection they afford journalists. More than half of these state statutes are phrased in terms of nearly absolute protection against being compelled to disclose news sources. The other statutes provide only "qualified protection," by establishing a presumptive privilege that can be overcome if a substantial reason to do so is demonstrated.

The statutes, and the U.S. Department of Justice guidelines, differ greatly in terms of who is included in their protections; how strong, and in what form, a showing must be to overcome their protections; and what type of material is protected. Surveys and discussion of journalist shield laws may be found in Joel M. Gora's *The Rights of Reporters* (New York, 1974), and Willard Eckhardt, Jr. and Arthur Duncan McKey's, "Reporter's Privilege: An Update," 12 Conn. L. Rev. 435 (1980).

Even in the absence of a journalist shield law, it appears that "a majority of the U.S. Supreme Court recognizes at least some degree of constitutional protection for newsgatherers' confidences." So Justice Brennan recently stated when, in his capacity as a circuit justice, he stayed a civil contempt adjudication against a Massachusetts television journalist in *In re Roche* (1980). Invocation of such constitutional protection by journalists continues to be treated on a case-by-case basis. Factors weighed in such determinations include the type of proceeding involved; the availability of the information from alternative, albeit less convenient, sources; and the possibility that harassment of the press by government officials is an element of the inquiry. Therefore, for example, the Supreme Court refused to stay or to review contempt proceedings against Myron Farber, a reporter for *The New York Times* who was jailed when he refused to turn over documents the defendant in a murder trial sought and claimed were important to the defense case. In other situations, however, particularly in

the context of civil litigation, reporters have resisted disclosure of sources with success, even without statutory protection.

Freedom of Information Acts. In the 1960s and 1970s both the federal government and most state governments enacted Freedom of Information Acts and so-called sunshine laws. These provisions open up government records and meetings to public scrutiny. Such statutes are not constitutionally compelled, but the access they provide to public meetings and records is invaluable for journalists as well as other citizens. These statutory provisions differ in detail and tend to include exempted categories.

The federal Freedom of Information Act, first adopted in 1966 and since amended to broaden its coverage, is a good example of the possible access—and the broad exemptions from its coverage—contained in such statutes. Freedom of Information statutes tend to be limited to the records of the executive branch of the relevant government, while sunshine laws sometimes open a broader range of public meetings. Courtroom proceedings are generally not covered by either type of statute. A survey and discussion of some of the most recent provisions of these types may be found in Anthony S. Mathews, *The Darker Reaches of Government,* chapters 4 and 5 (University of California Press, Berkeley, 1978).

Defamation. Several categories of publication are restricted or forbidden despite the First Amendment. One such category, never held by a majority of the Supreme Court to be protected by the First Amendment, is defamation. Indeed, until the Court revolutionized the law of defamation by "constitutionalizing" some First Amendment limitations on defamation in *New York Times Co.* v. *Sullivan* (1964), the legal standards for defining and remedying defamation were left almost entirely to the states. There was often little concern for First Amendment values. The constitutional theory prior to the *Times* decision was that defamation—i.e., libel when the defamatory language was written; slander when it was spoken—was presumed to be false, and therefore not protected by the First Amendment. In the words of the great torts scholar Dean William L. Prosser:

Defamation is...that which tends to injure "reputation" in the popular sense; to diminish the esteem, respect, goodwill or confidence in which the plaintiff is held, or to excite adverse, derogatory or unpleasant feelings or opinions against him. It necessarily, however, involves the idea of disgrace.

While truth generally constituted a defense under the law in most states, the burden of proving truth was on the defendant newspaper in a libel action against it. Further, the common law permitted recovery for certain published statements viewed as automatically *per se* defamatory. These included erroneous statements, such as that a person had a "loathesome disease," accusations of serious criminal conduct, and charges against someone that were inconsistent with that person doing his or her job in a professional manner (e.g., "Public official A is a Communist"; "Dr. B. is a butcher").

The Supreme Court transformed the landscape of American defamation law with its *Times* decision in 1964. An Alabama jury had awarded damages of a half million dollars to a Birmingham police official in a state court suit against *The New York Times* and civil rights advocates for what appeared to be only a slight inaccuracy. An advertisement seeking support for the civil rights movement claimed that police had surrounded and blocked a black college campus; the plaintiff was not even mentioned by name. In an opinion written by Justice Brennan the Supreme Court invalidated the $500,000 award, on the basis of the First Amendment. Justice Brennan emphasized that the First Amendment contemplates a system of freedom of expression in which "debate on public issues should be uninhibited, robust and wide-open." Therefore, Brennan wrote, even some falsehood had to be allowed; obligating the press to warrant the truth of all that it prints would reduce its vigor and limit public debate.

The test enunciated in the *Times* decision made the press liable for defamatory falsehood against public officials only if such officials could prove "actual malice."

At first the Supreme Court extended application of the extremely hard-to-prove "actual malice" test to all "public figures" and to all matters "of public or general interest." In *Gertz* v. *Robert Welch, Inc.* (1974), however, the Burger Court cut back and held that the "actual malice" standard, which protected the press even when it published falsehoods, should apply only to alleged defamation concerning public officials and public figures, narrowly defined. The same decision did prohibit all presumed and punitive damages without "actual malice." Otherwise, both state and federal governments were free to

impose any particular libel test they chose upon any standard of journalistic "negligence." Since *Gertz* the Court has limited the category of "public figure" quite drastically.

The Court also rejected First Amendment claims in *Herbert* v. *Lando* (1979). The case involved a plaintiff who sought to prove that television coverage of his role in Vietnam amounted to defamation, even under the "actual malice" standard, which he conceded was applicable to him because he was a public figure. The Court held that he could inquire, in the preparation of his case, into the mental state and editorial decisions of defendants involved in putting together the news segment about him.

Obscenity. Obscenity is entirely excluded from First Amendment protection. Obscenity, however, remains quite difficult for a judge to define when she or he sees it, despite Justice Stewart's famous words to the contrary. Yet the Supreme Court has made it clear that it is constitutionally permissible for any governmental unit to legislate against obscenity. Under Chief Justice Burger the Court rejected the notion of a national standard, which had been adopted by the Court under Chief Justice Warren. The newer standard leaves the definition and regulation of obscenity up to local community standards. In *Miller* v. *California* (1973) and its companion case, *Paris Adult Theatre I* v. *Slaton* (1973), the Burger Court proclaimed the test for obscenity to be:

(a) whether the "average person, applying contemporary community standards" would find that the work, taken as a whole, appeals to the prurient interest,
(b) whether the work depicts or describes, in a patently offensive way, sexual conduct specifically defined by the applicable state law, and
(c) whether the work, taken as a whole, lacks serious literary, artistic, political, or scientific value.

Blasphemy. Laws against blasphemy, which were commonplace for decades after the adoption of the First Amendment, have long since been removed from the statutes of both state and federal jurisdictions, or held to be invalid.

Official Secrets and Contractual Restraints. Other categories of publication still held to be validly legislated against include military and atomic secrets. Nevertheless, if a journalist obtains such forbidden information, the government or anyone else faces a heavy burden in attempting to convince a court to restrain publication in advance. The United States has no Official Secrets Act. This fact, and its implications for a broad concept of freedom of the press, has been stressed repeatedly in judicial decisions and political and scholarly commentary.

One additional legal restriction upon freedom of the press recently challenged and upheld is the practice of including a prohibition against future disclosure in the employment contracts between the government and its employees. In *Snepp* v. *United States* (1980), the Supreme Court, without waiting for briefs or hearing oral argument, held that a former Central Intelligence Agency employee could constitutionally be required by judicial order to submit all his future writings to the CIA for prior approval. Further, Frank Snepp was ordered to pay to the government all profits that he had received or would receive from his book *Decent Interval* (1977). This was despite the government's concession, at least for purposes of the litigation, that the book, a critical account of the final days of U.S. forces in Vietnam, contained no classified information. In ordering a "constructive trust" on behalf of the government, the Court's brief *per curiam* opinion said simply that Snepp had signed an agreement obligating him to submit any publication for prior review, and that the government had "a compelling interest in protecting both the secrecy of information important to our national security and the appearance of confidentiality so essential to the effective operation of our foreign intelligence service."

Laws Protecting the Privacy of Nonofficial Citizens

The law of defamation has undergone a transformation since *New York Times Co.* v. *Sullivan* (1964), premised on the idea of an "uninhibited, wide-open and robust" system of freedom of expression. Nevertheless, the values of privacy and reputation remain protected, and individuals who are not public figures are still able to recover damages for either libel or slander on a showing of negligence and actual damage. In fact, privacy has been found to be a constitutionally protected right although it is nowhere mentioned explicitly in the text of the Constitution.

Additionally, remedies evolved in the private law of torts for privacy invasion remain in force today. Dean William L. Prosser distinguished four branches of torts, which may be overlapping in a particular case. These are:

1. Intrusion on the plaintiff's physical solitude
2. Publication of private matters violating the ordinary decencies
3. Putting plaintiff in a false position in the public eye, as by signing his name to a letter attributing to him views that he does not hold
4. Appropriation of some element of plaintiff's personality for commercial use.

A major distinction between invasion of privacy and defamation is that truth is not always a defense in an action claiming invasion of privacy; in contrast, truth is an adequate defense in a defamation suit. Generally but not always, finding a story "newsworthy" provides a complete defense to an invasion of privacy claim.

Issues of where to draw the line between privacy and freedom of the press have not been fully worked out yet. Dean Prosser summarized the difficulties when he wrote in his *Handbook of the Law of Torts* 844 (3rd ed., 1964), that the law of privacy comes "into head-on collision with the constitutional guaranty of freedom of the press."

Thus far the U.S. Supreme Court has been able to avoid full consideration of that collision course. For example, in cases involving the publication of the identity of the victim of a brutal rape-murder, *Cox Broadcasting Co.* v. *Cohn* (1975), and the identity of a juvenile offender, in the face of a state statute barring such identification, *Smith* v. *Daily Mail Publishing Co.* (1980), the Court held that because the identities at issue were already available to the public through open court records, it was not valid to prohibit the newspapers from publishing them.

In a separate but related area, however, the Supreme Court upheld the claim of one Zacchini, the Human Cannonball, against a television station that broadcast his entire 15-second act as part of its news coverage. Zacchini triumphed over the First Amendment defense on the grounds that he had a protected right of publicity, which the media could not appropriate.

An obvious analogy for the print media is the law of copyright. It is generally not possible to copyright news itself. A journalist's unique treatment of a news event may be protected by copyright law, however, so that it may not be appropriated by someone else.

Prepublication Censorship Procedures

There are no official prepublication censorship procedures applicable to the print media. However, it is possible for government agencies to compel that books and articles by their employees must be precleared by means of contractual agreements at the start of the employment relationship. Such preclearance demands by the Central Intelligence Agency have been upheld by the courts. A ruling similar to *Snepp* v. *United States* was handed down in the lower courts when the CIA successfully enjoined publication of a book by a former CIA official, Victor Marchetti, based on the secrecy agreement he signed as a condition of employment, in *United States* v. *Marchetti* (4th Cir.) 466 F. 2d 1309, *cert. denied* (1972) and *Knopf* v. *Colby*, 509 F.2d 1362 (4th Cir.), *cert. denied* (1975).

While there is a strong presumption against prior restraints in the American law of freedom of the press, there is no absolute rule against such court-ordered restraints. Government lawyers can and sometimes do go to court to seek to enjoin publication, as the federal government did on several notable ocasions during the 1970s.

Case Studies in Censorship

The best-known recent example of an attempt by government officials to censor the press by means of obtaining an injunction against publication was undoubtedly the attempt by the Nixon Administration to stop publication of the so-called Pentagon Papers by *The New York Times* and *The Washington Post*. Additionally, in a case that never reached a final resolution because the federal government dropped its efforts to enjoin publication, the U.S. Department of Energy was able to convince a lower federal court judge to stop publication of an article allegedly revealing secrets about the hydrogen bomb, in *United States* v. *Progressive, Inc.* 467 F. Supp, 990 (W.D. Wis. 1979). Another important example of a censorship attempt during the past decade was the unsuccessful effort by Nebraska courts to forestall publication of information touching upon a pending criminal trial, in *Nebraska Press Association* v. *Stuart* (1976).

In these decisions the presumption against prior restraint remains strong, but it appears to have been weakened somewhat in terms of the legal test the Court applied, even as it invalidated prior restraints. Furthermore, the continuation of the injunction against the *Progressive* magazine for seven months, only to have the case dropped after it was argued but before it could be decided on appeal, reveals that loopholes in the doctrine against prior restraint remain available to the government and may even have broadened during the past decade.

The Pentagon Papers. The Pentagon Papers was a set of highly classified materials concerning the history of U.S. involvement in Vietnam, prepared at the instigation of the Pentagon. It was made available to a number of major newspapers in *seriatim* fashion by a former government employee who had had a role in compiling it.

The government sought injunctions against publication, based on the claim that a prior restraint was justified because publication of articles based on the Pentagon Papers would cause grave and irreparable injury to the United States. Within two weeks of the government's first attempt in court to stop publication, the Supreme Court met in an extraordinary session to consider the issue.

In a very brief *per curiam* opinion, by a six to three vote the Supreme Court determined that the government failed to meet "the heavy burden of showing justification of such a restraint."

In addition, however, each of the nine justices wrote separately to explain a broad range of reasons for support or opposition to the outcome reached. The six justices in the majority divided as follows:

Justices Black and Douglas argued that the government did not, under any circumstances, have power to "make laws enjoining publication or current news and abridging freedom of the press in the name of 'national security.'"

Justice Brennan basically agreed, but with a caveat even more limited than the famous reservation expressed in *Near* v. *Minnesota* (1931), in which Chief Justice Hughes said that prior restraint could be allowed only in exceptional cases, such as publication which involved "actual obstruction to [government's] recruiting services or the publication of the sailing dates of transports or the number and location of troops."

Justices Stewart and White argued that a prior restraint could be justified if, and only if, the government could show "direct, immediate, and irreparable damage to our Nation or its people."

Justice Marshall did not discuss the basic

ment on the absence of authority for the executive branch to invoke the jurisdiction of the courts in an attempt to halt publication of national security information.

The three dissenters (Justices Harlan and Blackmun and Chief Justice Burger) believed that courts should give only limited review to a determination by the executive branch that disclosure would "irreparably impair" national security.

Several justices indicated that subsequent punishment of newspaper officials for violation of World War I Espionage Act would be acceptable. The mere fact of publishing classified information is not criminal, however, although the fact of its classified status may be quite relevant to showing criminal intent. Federal law clearly prohibits publication of a few specific kinds of information, such as photographs or drawings of vital military installations or crytographic systems. There is also a general prohibition, based on the old Espionage Acts, against "communication" that occurs with "intent or reason to believe that the information is to be used to the injury of the United States, or to the advantage of any foreign nation." There is serious doubt as to whether the term "communication" ever covers publication directed to a public audience.

The Progressive *Case.* These and additional knotty statutory issues arose in the context of government allegations of the publication of atomic secrets in *United States* v. *The Progressive, Inc.,* 467 F. Supp. 990 (W.D. Wis. 1979). These were never definitely resolved, however, because the government withdrew its suit for an injunction when the so-called secrets were widely published. It is significant, however, that the government was able to "temporarily restrain" publication of the article for seven months, even though it conceded that the article was based upon information already available to the public.

Nebraska Press Association *v.* Stuart *(1976).* In the *Nebraska Press Association* case, Nebraska state judges imposed and sustained an order to restrain the press from publishing any facts about a particularly gruesome murder of six members of a family in a small Nebraska town. The Supreme Court unanimously invalidated the "gag order." Chief Justice Burger's opinion, for five of the justices, noted that "prior restraints on speech and publication are the most serious and least tolerable infringement on First Admendment rights." Yet the legal test applied by the chief justice balanced a

number of factors, and only then invalidated the judicial prior restraint because alternative methods had been available and because the restraining order would not be entirely effective in any event. Chief Justice Burger appeared to rely on the weak form of the old "clear-and-present danger" test—invoked in *Dennis* v. *United States* (1951) to uphold the conviction of leaders of the Communist Party under the Smith Act—as the majority's basis for legal analysis of the prior restraint in the Nebraska "gag order" case.

In another case involving an effort to stop publication of information touching upon a state judiciary, *Landmark Communications, Inc.* v. *Virginia* (1978), the Supreme Court was again unanimous in its decision to invalidate restraint upon publication. In this case, however, it was a state statute rather than a judicial order at issue. Here it was punishment for an accurate report, based on information lawfully obtained by the newspaper, concerning a pending inquiry about the disability or misconduct of a state judge. The action taken against the newspaper was punishment after the fact of publication, rather than a prior restraint. Nevertheless, the Court sided with the newspaper, the Virginia *Pilot,* and invoked the First Amendment to invalidate the Virginia statute that made it a criminal offense to divulge information about proceedings before the Virginia Judicial Inquiry and Review Commission.

Summary. The past decade produced a number of instances in which censorship through the imposition of prior restraints failed. Neither allegations of national security nor of the need to guarantee the integrity of judicial proceedings sufficed in the face of strong First Amendment claims. Yet the doctrinal underpinning of these victories for the press appeared somewhat less vigorous than in earlier decades.

Media Self-Regulation

Press Councils and Clubs. In the United States the existence of press councils is entirely voluntary. Any enforcement of ethical rules or standards of reporting by such councils is rare. On a national level the only significant press council is the National News Council, established in 1973, and even its significance is still somewhat in doubt.

The National News Council is an unofficial body, suggested by a task force sponsored by the Twentieth Century Fund. Its function is to receive and review complaints of bias or inaccuracy by those organizations, wire services, newspapers, magazines and broadcast services that cover and supply national news. The council is composed of nine members from news organizations and five members from the public at large. During its short history the council has been applauded by scholars for its work in reviewing complaints. Its existence was cited repeatedly and approvingly by the Supreme Court in the course of its decision in *Miami Herald Publishing Co.* v. *Tornillo* (1974), in which the Court unanimously and emphatically rejected an attempt by the state of Florida to guarantee access to the print media by statute. Given the voluntary nature of participation in the council, however, and lingering doubts about the weight behind its resolution of complaints brought to it, it is still too early to tell how much influence the council will have. For an account of the handling of complaints by the National News Council in its first years, see its report *In The Public Interest* (New York, 1975).

Press clubs and similar voluntary and partially social organizations exist on national, state and local levels. These organizations do enjoy some practical power in terms of allocation of such scarce resources as press passes and seats at news conference held by government officials. Courts generally try to stay out of disputes covering the policies of such press clubs.

Press-Pass Denials. The leading example of judicial consideration of the authority of such organizations was the review of a decision by the Periodical Correspondents' Association to exclude a representative of *Consumer Reports* from the periodical press galleries of Congress. U.S. District Court Judge Gesell held that such power to exclude a journalist from access to the special congressional press galleries, delegated to the press association by Congress, violated the First Amendment. On appeal, however, the District of Columbia Court of Appeals reversed Judge Gesell, on the grounds that the decision by the press association to exclude a representative of *Consumer Reports,* premised on the idea that the publication was not independent but rather the voice of a group committed to consumer advocacy, was a decision reached under power delegated by Congress, and was therefore nonjusticiable, i.e., beyond the reach of the judicial branch since committed to the authority of the legislative branch of the federal government (*Consumers Union of United States, Inc.* v. *Periodical Correspondents' Association,* 515 F. 2d 1341 [D.C. Cir. 1975]).

An interesting contrast occurred in a case involving presidential press credentials. There the Secret Service denied Robert Sherrill, long the Washington correspondent of *The Nation,* a White House press pass even though he had credentials for the House and Senate press galleries. In deciding Sherrill's claim the District of Columbia Court of Appeals found that it did have authority to reach the merits. Circuit Judge McGowan held that "arbitrary or content-based criteria for press pass issuance are prohibited under the First Amendment," and that there is an additional public interest in assuring that "restrictions on newsgathering be no more arduous than necessary." The Secret Service was therefore ordered to institute a system of formal procedural protections, beyond its vague reference to "reasons of security," prior to denying any "bona fide journalist" the press facilities generally available to all, in *Sherrill* v. *Knight,* 569 F. 2d. 124 (D.C. Cir. 1977).

Similar rulings have invalidated the exclusion of particular journalists or these from various underground papers from mayoral press conferences and police records otherwise available to the press.

It is clear that questions of limiting access to public facilities remain somewhat unresolved. The general approach taken by the courts has been to invalidate exclusions of particular correspondents or particular publications if they appear to be arbitrary or based on personal animosity. However, both Congress and the executive branch have been given some leeway to demonstrate good reasons for exclusions—e.g., the exclusion of lobbyists who seek access under the guise of journalists, or to protect the safety of the chief executive. Furthermore, exclusions of particular persons by private press associations has not been litigated yet, and may be held to be unreachable by the courts as not sufficiently involving state action.

Internal Monitoring. A final check upon journalistic decisions and excesses, which grew markedly during the 1970s, is the phenomenon of internal monitoring. There were at least a dozen journalism reviews; the best known is probably the *Columbia Journalism Review.* A number of the largest newpapers instituted systems of "house critics" or "ombudsmen," who on occasion publish their findings and internal criticisms. A number of the major papers introduced "Op-Ed" pages, columns written by people from outside the staffs of the papers. Many publications also increased the visiblility of the "corrections" they run. Finally, numerous papers carry vigorous letters-to-the-editor columns and even, on occasion, editorials written by a reader.

Administrative Rules Restricting Officials from Giving Information to the Press; Freedom of Information Acts

There are approximately 100 federal statutes containing provisions that either prohibit disclosure or authorize some official or agency to withhold information. Additionally agencies nearly always develop their own internal rules and regulations prohibiting disclosure. It is impossible to discuss with any specificity here the scope or impact of all these restraints at the federal level, or to begin to analyze parallel provisions and their practical effect in the 50 state governments.

The federal Freedom of Information Act, passed in 1966 to become effective in 1967 and since amended several times, sought initially to retain many of the existing statutory federal nondisclosure provisions. In *Federal Aviation Administration* v. *Robertson* (1974), the U.S. Supreme Court determined that when the Freedom of Information Act was passed, Congress "intended to leave largely undisturbed existing statutes dealing with disclosure of information by specific agencies." In response, Congress passed the so-called Sunshine Act of 1976, which applied the Freedom of Information approach to some elements of the statutory restraints then in force.

The Supreme Court also construed the statute to continue to exempt an executive branch decision to classify information from judicial review, even when it was Congresswoman Patsy T. Mink of Hawaii who questioned the classification and sought the information, in *Environmental Protection Agency* v. *Mink* (1973).

In *Department of the Air Force* v. *Rose* (1976), however, the Supreme Court rejected the argument of the Air Force Academy that case summaries of honor code hearings were exempted from disclosure to student editors of a law review, even if the names of the individuals involved were removed. The Court described the statute's intention as being to create "a workable compromise between individual rights and the preservation of public rights to Government information."

For a discussion of the complicated issues of statutory construction involved in attempts to obtain information through federal statutes, see Elias Clark, "Holding Government Accountable: The Amended Freedom of Information Act," 84 Yale L.J. 741 (1975); Project "Government Information and the Rights of Citizens," 73 Mich. L. Rev. 971 (1975); and the surveys "Developments under the Freedom of Information Act," published annually by the Duke Law Journal. See also Anthony Mathews, *The Darker Reaches of Government* (University of California Press, Berkeley, 1978). For a detailed review of general legal issues under the Freedom of Information Act and related statutes, see Kenneth Culp Davis, *Administrative Law of the Seventies* (Lawyers Co-operative Publishing Co., Rochester, N.Y., 1976, and cumulative supplements).

Among the categories largely exempted from the reach of the Freedom of Information Act are foreign affairs and defense matters. The United States has an extensive federal classification system, generally left intact despite the new statutes providing access to governmental affairs and records. For a discussion of the structure of restraints in a defense context, see Harold Edgar and Benno Schmidt, Jr., "The Espionage Statutes and Publication of Defense Information," 73 Colum. L. Rev. 929 (1973).

The Right to Critize Government: Theory & Practice

There is no more basic element of freedom of the press in America than the idea that a free press is essential to serve the people as an active check upon and critic of government. While some people debate the appropriate scope of First Amendment protection for the press in other realms, there is virtual unanimity about the vital role of the press in performing this "checking function."

That the press should perform an active, critical part in the American democracy has been a major theme since the founding of the Republic. James Madison and Thomas Jefferson were among the most eloquent proponents of such a function for the press. Madison, for example, explained that the press in the United States had to enjoy greater freedom than in England because it was essential, in a government in which the people retained the ultimate responsibility, that the press aid the people in checking executive and legislative overreaching and incompetence. Jefferson similarly believed the press to be a "formidable censor of the public functionaries, by arraigning them at the tribunal of public opinion." This role for the press, he argued, "produces reform peaceably, which must otherwise be done by revolution."

These and similar remarks by Madison, Jefferson and other participants in the early political history of the United States may be found in Leonard Levy, ed., *Freedom of the Press from Zenger to Jefferson: Early American Libertarian Theories* (Bobbs-Merrill Co., Indianapolis, 1966), and Marvin Meyers, ed., *The Mind of the Founder: Sources of the Political Thought of James Madison,* 299, 330–31 (Bobbs-Merrill Co., Indianapolis, 1973). For a major recent scholarly contribution that treats the historical and philosophic sources and the current theory and reality of the role of the press as a check upon government, see Vincent Blasi, "The Checking Value in First Amendment Theory," 1977 Am. Bar Found. R. J. 521.

In recent years the Supreme Court has frequently echoed and expanded upon the theme developed by Madison and Jefferson. Justice Hugo Black summed up the idea that the press performs an essential function as a check upon governmental errors and abuses in a democracy. Writing for the majority in *Mills* v. *Alabama* (1966), he said:

> Whatever differences may exist about interpretations of the First Amendment, there is practically universal agreement that a major purpose of the Amendment was to protect the free discussion of governmental affairs.... Thus the press serves and was designed to serve as a powerful antidote to any abuses of power by governmental officials and as a constitutionally chosen means for keeping officials elected by the people responsible to all the people whom they were selected to serve.

The 1970s provided remarkable evidence of the power of the press to check government. Both the withdrawal of American troops from Vietnam and the withdrawal of Richard Nixon from the presidency serve as examples of the phenomenon. While it is impossible to claim a direct cause-and-effect relationship between critical press coverage and these events, there can be little doubt that both were occasioned at least in part by persistent, critical news coverage that altered American public opinion. Similar examples of the impact of the press, albeit less dramatic, may also be discovered throughout the recent history of state and local governments.

Increased concentration of major circulation newspapers in the hands of fewer and fewer owners and a greater role for newspaper chains and media conglomerates today, present practical difficulties in assuring a diversity of critical reportage and editorial opinion in the United States. Nevertheless, both theory and reality support the idea of a vigorous brand of critical journalism in the United States. The legal protections of the freedom of the press also extend beyond major newspapers with mass circulation to a large number of small, critical publications that serve as gadflies, critics and advocates.

There is widespread popular faith in the United States in the idea, expressed by Justice Black, that:

> Suppression of the right of the press to praise or criticize governmental agents and to clamor and content for or against changes ...muzzles one of the very agencies the Framers of our Constitution thoughtfully and deliberately selected to improve our society and keep it free.

Managed News

There is no official means for government to manage news in the United States. Nevertheless, government officials often attempt to control the flow of information. They do so in subtle ways, largely by exploiting the symbiotic relationship they enjoy with leading journalists. Exchanges of information, background briefings, grants of special access and the like become the weaponry for informal attempts to control or influence the flow of information. Both cocktail party exchanges and intentional news "leaks" are typical parts of the armament in the ongoing close, love-hate relationship of government officials and working press.

Government officials frequently supply secret information to members of the press for an almost infinite number and mixture of motives. A regular scenario in Washington, D.C., for example, involves renewed attempts by high Administration officials to discover and to plug "leaks." Simultaneously, "whistle-blowers," ambitious politicans and disgruntled civil servants vie with one another and with some high officials themselves in the recognition that knowledge is power; the information they possess and will sometimes share with journalists is a potent weapon in whatever particular battles they wish to fight or campaigns they hope to launch. Nearly every politician attempts to be an expert in press relations, and many boast privately of an ability to handle or manage the press. A presidential news conference is a prime example of the paradoxical combination of the attempts to control the flow of news in the very course of providing journalists with information and a chance to ask questions. The American tradition of journalism still boasts of countless examples of stories dug up despite subtle and ingenious attempts by high officials to manage the news.

Accordingly, it can be said that in the United States there is no official effort to manage the news. Through an endless variety of unofficial devices, however, government officials attempt both to control information and to provide journalists with leads and stories.

Editorial Influence on Government Policies. There can be no question that there is editorial influence on government policies. Both coverage and editorial commentary on the American involvement in Vietnam affords a dramatic example, although the exact impact is impossible to isolate or quantify. Similarly, editorial comment about abuses by and within the Nixon Administration clearly contributed to the change in the public perception of the president, and ultimately to his resignation. Editorial criticism clearly played a role in the resignation of Bert Lance in the Carter Administration and of Max Hugel in the Reagan Administration.

It is probably impossible to demonstrate a direct cause-and-effect correlation between critical editorial commentary and government policies. Nevertheless, some direct relationship between the two undoubtedly has been present throughout American history. A fundamental premise of First Amendment theory is that such editorial influence would and should occur freely.

For example, the Supreme Court invalidated a ban on election-day editorials about matters before the voters on the very day they were published, in *Mills* v. *Alabama* (1966). The High Court also rejected the claim that a newspaper should be obliged to allow access to persons who wish to respond to its coverage or editorial positions, in *Miami Herald Publishing Co.* v. *Tornillo* (1974). The Court unanimously voted to invalidate a

Florida statute requiring newspapers to give candidates for public office, whom they had attacked editorially, a right of access to equal space in which to reply. Chief Justice Burger's majority opinion stated, "A responsible press is an undoubtedly desirable goal, but press responsibility is not mandated by the Constitution and like many other virtues it cannot be legislated." To uphold an affirmative right of access, Burger wrote, "fails to clear the barriers of the First Amendment because of its intrusion into the function of editors." Burger concluded his opinion, in which the Court recognized the modern economic realities that "place in a few hands the power to inform the American people and shape public opinion," with the following argument about the practical and unconstitutional difficulties of any attempt to control that power:

> The choice of material to go into a newspaper, and the decisions made as to limitations on the size and content of the paper, and treatment of public issues and public officials—whether fair or unfair—constitute the exercise of editorial control and judgment. It has yet to be demonstrated how governmental regulation of this crucial process can be exercised consistent with First Amendment guarantees of a free press as they have evolved to this time.

It should be noted that the Supreme Court has adopted an entirely different approach to access to television and radio, and that it has allowed some governmental regulation of newspaper advertising as well.

Suspension and Confiscation of Newspapers

No newspapers have been suspended or confiscated since 1970. The only possible exception might be for obscure journals said to be obscene publications. If such instances have occurred since 1970, the publishers involved never sought to make great legal battles of the issue or to publicize such actions. Even with hard-core obscenity the government is required to provide a quick judicial hearing with full procedural protections. Furthermore, a government official is not allowed to confiscate all copies of a publication alleged to be obscene, pending the outcome of the judicial determination (*Roaden* v. *Kentucky* [1973] and *Heller* v. *New York* [1973]; see also *Freedman* v. *Maryland* [1965]).

Jailings of Newsmen

The jailing of newsmen is an extremely rare phenomenon in the United States. Even when judges have attempted to punish journalists for critical coverage of judicial conduct during trials, the Supreme Court generally has invalidated the contempt citations on the grounds of the First Amendment, as in *Bridges* v. *California* (1941) and *Wood* v. *Georgia* (1962).

In the 1970s, however, the Court appeared to determine, in *Branzburg* v. *Hayes* (1973) and its companion cases, that journalists enjoyed no special First Amendment defense when compelled to give testimony before grand juries. This analysis has been extended to testimony sought by law enforcement officials and by trial judges acting upon request of defense attorneys who claim a need for the information in order to prepare their defenses.

The best-known example of a journalist resisting, to the extent of going to jail rather than comply with a judicial order to disclose, involved Myron Farber, a reporter for *The New York Times*. Farber had investigated and reported on a series of mysterious deaths at a New Jersey hospital. After his articles appeared, New Jersey authorities investigated and indicted Dr. Mario Jascalevich for murder. His defense attorneys sought all notes, statements and other materials in the possession of Farber and *The New York Times* relevant to the case, for possible use in their defense effort. A New Jersey judge decided that he would himself examine such materials and then determine what should be turned over. Farber refused to comply. The judge then found the reporter and *The New York Times* in contempt of court. Since the criminal trial was proceeding, time was of the essence. Two Supreme Court Justices refused to grant a stay and appellate review was thereby made impossible (*New York Times Co.* v. *Jascalevich* [1978]). Farber spent 40 days in jail, and *The New York Times* spent over a million dollars in fines and legal fees. Farber's incarceration ended when Dr. Jascalevich was acquitted.

In a discussion of such cases as *Branzburg* and the Myron Farber case, Professor Thomas I. Emerson recently stated, "Instead of concern that the press remain 'uninhibited, robust and wide-open,' the Burger Court is satisfied if the press is not subjected to 'official harassment.'"

It is still the case, however, that law enforcement personnel and judges do not lightly seek to order journalists to disclose confidential sources or similar information. This is in part because they know that they are likely to become involved in time-consuming and expensive court fights, and that many judges will continue to require a strong showing of need for the information, and the absence of alternative sources.

There have been few journalists other than Farber held in contempt and incarcerated. The most notorious additional example occurred at the beginning of the decade. William Farr, a reporter for the *Los Angeles Herald-Examiner,* spent 46 days in jail for contempt because he refused to divulge how he obtained a copy of a deposition taken in connection with the Charles Manson murder trial. No other reporters have been incarcerated for nearly as long as the periods Farber and Farr served.

Cases in which reporters are ordered to produce information are reported in *News Media and the Law,* published periodically by The Reporters Committee for Freedom of the Press, Washington, D.C.

State Control over the Press

There is no direct or overt state control of the press through subsidies, allocation of newsprint, advertising, manipulation of labor unions, import licenses for printing equipment or licensing of journalists. To a great extent government policy lurks in the background of the free market generally; it similarly provides much of the context in economic matters directly affecting the press.

For example, American labor law is largely governed by statutory provisions enacted by Congress, and the relationship of newspapers and reporters are controlled in the same way as in any other industry. Payments for official legal notices do provide a minor subsidy to established newspapers, although in many jurisdictions regulations require that such notices be spread evenhandedly among all publications. There is no obvious policy of manipulation of advertising support by the government. Newsprint is allocated by the market; several of the largest newspapers have invested directly in newsprint supply companies and the tax laws indirectly encourage such investments. There are no unusual import licenses required for printing equipment.

There is no official licensing of journalists, beyond the admission of reporters to press galleries. In numerous cases involving underground or radical newspapers, the courts have held that it is unconstitutional for government officials to discriminate or differentiate among publications. For a collection of such lower court decisions, see Joel Gora, *The Right of Reporters: The Basic ACLU Guide to a Reporter's Rights* (Sunrise Books/E. P. Dutton & Co., New York, 1974).

State-Press Relations

Just as there is a separation of church and state in the United States, there is a separation of media and state that is as jealously guarded. State-press relations do not therefore loom large in any discussion of the press or in press history; the principal restraints on the press are not administrative but judicial. (These are dealt with in the section on Press Laws & Censorship.)

Nevertheless, over the years there has been on ongoing love-hate relationship between the press and the presidency that illustrates the strengths and weaknesses of both institutions. All U. S. presidents have made efforts to manipulate or manage the news. Party papers were used by the early presidents to boost their own image and tar and feather that of their opponents. Andrew Jackson is believed to have had 60 full-time journalists on the government payroll. But with the decline of the party press and the establishment of AP in the mid 1850s, the presidency found itself at the mercy of the press for sustaining a favorable public image.

Till the turn of the century there was no regular channel of communication between the White House and the press. The White House press corps dates back only to 1895, when William W. Price of the Washington *Evening Star* stationed himself at the Pennsylvania Avenue portico intently interviewing presidential callers. Within a few years there was a sizable group of reporters on White House doorstep every day. It was so large that Theodore Roosevelt ordered that a room next to his secretary's office in the new West Wing be set aside for the press. Roosevelt is believed to have been the first to use the term "partnership" to describe the relationship between the presidency and the press. The first formal presidential press conferences were introduced by Woodrow Wilson. He promised to meet with reporters twice a week, but discontinued the practice in 1915. The conferences, however, gave rise to the White House Correspondents' Association, founded in 1914 with 11 charter members.

The White House had become the nation's most prestigious beat. By the time FDR moved into the White House, press relations had become critical enough to warrant the appointment of a full-time press secretary. He brought into this post an intimate friend and supporter, Stephen Early, who claimed that he was the first person at the bedside of the president every morning. Later years saw the transformation of the office of press secretary into that of the presidential spokesman, one of the most visible personalities in an administration. With the institution of live televised press conferences by John F. Kennedy, the press corps swelled in number. New press facilities were built during the Nixon administration, on top of FDR's swimming pool. Today 60 or more reporters attend the daily briefings by the press secretary and 300 reporters can be expected for a presidential press conference. The White House Press Correspondents' Association has grown to 900 members and its offshoot, The White House News Photographers' Association, to 400. They typically describe themselves as "the White House press" instead of mentioning the paper they work for.

There are several well-defined stages in a president's relations with the media. "Honeymoon" is the term most often used to describe the first stage. During this phase of the relationship there is an identity of interests and a willingness on the part of the press to gloss over news unfavorable to the president. According to Ed Bradley, a CBS TV correspondent, the administration provides more briefings, more releases and more photo opportunities. Since the president is only settling down in his executive chair, the air is redolent of the sweet aroma of promises, not the arid smoke of burnt-out programs. There are also the unavoidable comparisons between the new, "open" administration and that of former presidents.

The honeymoon stage soon comes to an end when reporters become interested in news stories that emphasize the administration's involvement in controversies and conflicts over policies. Now begins the competitive stage, characterized by news manipulation and media massaging. There is a retreat from the open presidency; the White House specifies increasingly restrictive conditions under which officials may talk to reporters, and seeks to curb unauthorized disclosures of information. The administration typically alleges leaks while at the same time using leaks to manipulate news.

The third stage is described as the

estrangement stage: the president and his assistants denounce the media as irresponsible. In addition to such denunciations, the president may cancel subscriptions, as John F. Kennedy did to the *Herald Tribune,* or declare certain correspondents personae non gratae as Nixon did CBS correspondent Dan Rather.

The last stage, as the president approaches the end of his presidency (or reelection), is that of detachment. The door to the presidency is now closed and the press is given staged media events with restricted coverage. There is a marked decrease in the number of press conferences and press briefings. The president's contacts with reporters are more likely to be more carefully structured and limited to occasions and places that allow favorable coverage. Another aspect of this stage is the direct approach to special interest groups, allowing the president to bypass the White House corps.

Timothy Crouse, in *The Boys on the Bus,* summarized this cycle as follows: "Every president when he enters the White House promises an open administration. He swears he likes reporters. All the while the president is struggling to suppress an overwhelming conviction that the press is trying to undermine his administration, if not the Republic.... Every president from Washington on came to recognize the press as a natural enemy and eventually tried to manipulate it and muzzle it." It must be remembered that Crouse was writing during the Nixon days when the press corps resembled an infantry platoon advancing against an enemy stronghold. Nevertheless, the adversarial relationship holds true of all administrations. Noted political scientist Richard Hofstetter gave the following succinct description of the interdependence of the press and the presidency: "News media and politicians coexist in an environment perhaps best characterized as unstable and dynamic; both news persons and politicians are essential to each other in different ways and yet both operate within a context in which the causes and consequences of the other's behavior are frequently at odds. News personnel need access to newsworthy events that politicians control in large part, and politicians need channels of access to the public that news personnel control in large part."

Public scrutiny is the best guarantee of an open administration (or, as Justice Brandeis put it, sunlight is the best disinfectant). In this respect, the United States is perhaps the most sunlit country in the world. Neverthe-less, vast amounts of government information are legally denied to the public on the ground that they are classified. This classification system, which had its origins during World War II, extends to all levels of government. It has become so large that agencies exist to publish reports of declassified documents and to hear appeals. During the McCarthy era the executive acquired unqualified privilege to control the flow of information out of government channels. The president could withhold information by executive privilege, through top secret ("For Eyes Only") classification and through statutes specifically mandating secrecy. One problem, however, was that the classification system does not have a legal basis but is built up on a series of presidential orders. These orders also make it a crime to obtain, collect and transmit such classified information to unauthorized persons. According to Representative William S. Moorhead, there are hundreds of millions of classified documents, 75 to 99 percent of which do not contain information vital to national security. Both President Nixon and President Carter took some steps to reduce the number of documents that are classified unnecessarily. Nixon reduced the number of agencies and officials that could classify information and permitted more data to be made available to the public. President Carter reduced still further the number of agencies with classification authority, cut the number of years a document would be automatically classified, and established a new agency to review classification procedures. The revised guidelines provided that documents be classified section by section, which would eliminate the practice of classifying entire documents because of one of two key paragraphs.

One particularly undesirable side effect of overclassification was that it encouraged leaks. According to Senator Daniel P. Moynihan, sooner or later everyone in government is involved in leaks. He said that "such disclosures are now a part of the way we run our affairs." Just as there are "bad" leaks, which may embarrass the administration, there are "good" leaks, which may serve administration interests and are actually planted, sometimes with the knowledge of the reporter. A classic case is Alfred Atherton, one of Henry Kissinger's top assistants, leaking transcripts of secret discussions between his boss and Arab and Israeli leaders showing Kissinger to be "at the apogee of his genius."

Growing executive secrecy prompted Kent Cooper, executive director of the AP, to call for a constitutionally guaranteed right to know, complementing the right to publish. Without adequate access to news sources the press's freedom to publish is meaningless. Efforts to secure this right led to the passing in 1966 of the Freedom of Information Act, designed to open up the federal bureaucracy to public scrutiny. The law applies to all federal executive branch and administrative agencies, with certain exemptions. These exemptions covered national defense documents, trade secrets and financial data, such as income tax returns, given to the government as confidential, and personal and medical files. The law provides that documents can be classified only under specific executive orders. The law also gave every citizen the right of access to government information even if it did not concern him. The burden of responsibility was placed on the agency withholding information rather than on the individual who requested it. Weaknesses in the law led to the passage in 1974 of 17 amendments designed to close loopholes. These amendments authorized a federal judge to examine agency records privately to determine if they were properly withheld and to overturn the agency's classification if not satisfied, and also reduced the time given to an agency to respond to requests for documents.

The right to know gained a fresh boost when the Congress passed the Sunshine Law in 1976. The law opened the meetings of about 50 boards and agencies to the public, but provided for exceptions when meetings could be closed. Compliance varies with only about half of the 1,003 meetings held during the first six months after the law went into effect being open to the public.

The press has come under criticism for not using the Freedom of Information act remedies for non-disclosure as widely as they were expected to. During a 10-year period, only 90 requests were made by the media out of a total of 254,637 requests from the public. Nevertheless, the press has used the act effectively as a coercive tool to pry information from unwilling bureaucrats.

Attitude Toward Foreign Media

Foreign media enjoy the same rights and privileges as domestic media in the United States. They are not subject to any special restrictions in areas such as visas, transmission of cables, or imports. There are no special accreditation procedures for foreign correspondents. Washington, D.C. and New York are among not only the largest but also the most sought-after stations for foreign newsmen. In 1980 there were 2,973 foreign correspondents in Washington, D.C., the largest such concentration in the world. Almost all of them are members of the prestigious Overseas Press Club of America, Inc. or the Foreign Press Association of New York. The Foreign Press Center of Washington and New York assists resident and visiting foreign media representatives in their coverage of the U.S. scene.

Although there are no laws specifically prohibiting foreign participation in U.S. media (except in broadcasting where FCC bars all aliens, alien governments and alien corporations from holding more than 25 percent of the voting stock in a potential licensee, foreign presence has not been significant. A Bureau of Economic Analysis benchmark survey in 1974 listed 60 foreign-owned or -affiliated companies with 26,566 employes in the printing and publishing industry, which in the light of a total industry figure of 42,000 establishments indicates a miniscule penetration. But since 1974, as the value of the dollar plummeted in overseas markets, making U.S. investments more attractive, the foreign share of the media market has expanded. The U.S. Office of Foreign Investment recorded a total of 49 transactions in the media sector from 1974 to 1978. Even this number is still quite small compared to the total number of transactions recorded by the Office of Foreign Investment—approximately 1,700. Most of the foreign investors in the printing and publishing sector were from the United Kingdom (18) and Canada (17), accounting for 59 percent of the transactions. The Netherlands accounted for six, West Germany for five, Australia and France for three, and Argentina, South Korea, Saudi Arabia, Sweden, and Switzerland for one each. In dollar terms, the largest transaction was the acquisition of Bantam Books by the Agnelli interests of Italy for $70 million. Australia was second (reflecting Rupert Murdoch's forays) and Canada third. Within the printing and publishing sector, the newspaper industry was only the third most popular, recording 14 transactions, with Canadian investors, led by Thomson Newspapers, accounting or 50 percent. Australia and the United Kingdom recorded two transactions each. In geographical terms, New York led with 31 transactions, with the next leading state, California, accounting for only five.

In terms of corporate concentration, it is possible to identify several highly visible foreign investors. The most prominent of these is the Thomson interests of Canada, headed by Kenneth R. Thomson. (See Appendix on Media Multinationals for more details.) Another repeat investor from Canada is Torstar Corporation, publisher of the *Toronto Star,* but their acquisitions are limited to book and periodical publications. British investors include Sir Isaac Pitman & Sons (three transactions), S. Pearson & Sons, Ltd. (two transactions), Morgan-Grampian, Ltd. (two transactions) and Vere Harmsworth (also two transactions through his Daily Mail and General Trust). The Netherlands is represented by two publishers, Elsevier Publishing, a publishing conglomerate operating in 11 countries, and VNU NV, a Dutch publisher active in the book industry; West Germany by Gutersloh Bertelsmann, and France by Daniel Filipacchi. Rupert Murdoch, the Australian investor, is in a class by himself because, unlike Thomsons, he goes after better-known properties and is guided by an apparently insatiable acquisitive instinct.

Given the traditional U.S. open door policy toward foreign investors, it is surprising that foreign investors have not made a more serious and determined attempt to capture a slice of the U.S. market. Even at the present rate of acquisitions, foreign involvement in this sector will be statistically insignificant in the determinable future. What foreign interest exists is directed mostly toward book publishing and periodicals, making the newspaper industry one of the most American of all industrial sectors.

U.S. Press & UNESCO. From the end of World War II, the U.S. press has taken an active role in fostering international media cooperation. Beside participating in the International Press Institute (first at Zurich and later at London), it was one of the founders of the Inter-American Press Association (IAPA). (For some time IAPA was charged with being a CIA front organization, but this charge was later effectively refuted.) But it was not until 1978 that the U.S. press found itself assuming the role of the leader of the free press of the world pitted against the majority of the Third World countries, supported, if not led on, by the Soviet Union. It was in that year that the UNESCO issued its now controversial declaration calling for a new international information order. It is not the purpose of this section to go into the polemics of the issue, but only to define the U.S. response. The United States found itself unalterably opposed to the Declaration as well as the subsequent report of the Sean MacBride Commission, appointed by UNESCO to "achieve a freer and more balanced flow of information."

Stripped of the multiple layers of rhetoric in which they are smothered, the main complaints of the Communist and Third World nations that sponsored the declaration were as follows:
• Massive imbalance of news flowing from advanced countries to the developing ones.
• Control of most of the news coming to the Third World by Western agencies owned and operated by and from advanced countries.
• News reporting on the Third World focusing on sensational or negative aspects.
• Dominance of Western ideas, resulting in a kind of cultural imperialism.
• Near total dependence on information systems of developed countries, which does not permit developing countries sufficient opportunity to originate information.

These complaints, along with many others, form an overture for a series of demands. The main ones call for:
• Throwing off the dominance of transnational corporations as vestiges of colonialism and as threats to sovereign and cultural integrity.
• Establishing independence and equity in access to global communication resources.
• Expansion of assistance programs to speed communication development.
• Promotion of the Non-Aligned News Agencies Pool.
• Imposition of duties, encumbrances, and responsibilities upon the media.
• A mandated right of reply when inaccuracies in the media are alleged.
• Legitimization of limitation of access to news sources.
• The right to censor or restrict the flow of information across national borders.
• Establishment of a supranational tribunal to monitor media behavior.

Although the United States represents a minority of voices in UNESCO, it is recognized by Third World spokesmen that without its cooperation and involvement there can be no significant change in the present information order. The U.S. response is therefore significant not only because it is the predictable opposition of a free press to the old philosophy of statism, but also because it presents an American agenda for a better world communication order, one that incorporates diverse national values as well as modern technological capability. The U.S. response was based on the following premises:

• Media disparities between the developed and developing world constitute a long-range problem. The most effective way of overcoming them is not through restrictive covenants imposed upon those with highly developed facilities and competence in the mass media, but rather by helping other states improve their own communication capacities.

• Government control of the press is not a cure for the media ills of the Third World. Nor is fettering the freedom of foreign newsmen operating across national boundaries, nor the imposition of regulations that would limit dissemination of domestic news abroad to state-controlled agencies. These approaches are all negative, restrictive, suppressive and even oppressive. What are needed are measures that open up channels of communication rather than close them.

• It is putting the cart before the horse to speak of a truly worldwide communication system in the absence of concrete and costly steps at the national level to build the necessary infrastructure and to train the people who must operate it. This goal will take massive investments and a new set of priorities on the part of individual developing countries. Only a country with a strong domestic communication sytem can expect to make its voice heard and its weight felt around the world. The current prominence of the U.S. media did not happen overnight but took decades of growth on the home turf. A national communication system also cannot aspire to worldwide acceptance unless it is free—and perceived as free—of government domination. Who, for example, trusts Tass?

• Rather than generalities, the international media community must concern itself with concrete and practical measures on which there can be little disagreement: reduced international postal rates for newspapers, periodicals and books, preferential telecommunication tariffs, easier access to international satellite services, better training and cheaper equipment, and paper.

• A fair distribution of informational wealth is an acceptable goal of world communication policy, but it must be sought within a general framework of freedom. It must enhance, not diminish, the ability of people to receive and impart information within the country as well as without.

In a related response, a number of U.S. and foreign newspapers and press organizations founded the World Press Freedom Committee to coordinate a technical assistance program to the press of developing countries. The principal thrust of its programs is to train journalists and to provide equipment; in doing so it has made U.S. publishers more sensitive to the needs of the Third World press.

News Agencies

Two of the Big Five international news agencies are American: Associated Press (AP) and United Press International (UPI). AP, the older of the two, was founded in 1848, when it was known as the New York Associated Press (NYAP). NYAP went out of business in 1892 and a new AP, founded in the Middle West and incorporated in Illinois, took its place. It was reorganized again in 1900 and incorporated in New York. UPI, which describes itself as the only privately owned international news service (others being either cooperatives or state-owned), was founded in 1958 through a merger of the United Press and International News Service. United Press Association, the major partner, was founded in 1907 by E. W. Scripps, then publisher of Scripps-McRae (later Scripps-Howard) Newspapers, principally to counter AP's virtual monopoly in this field. Noted for its lively writing, UP pioneered in the transmission of feature stories by leased wire, the use of bylines, and supplying news to radio. INS was established in 1909 by William Randolph Hearst and entered the international field about 1930. Although often in the red financially, it had on its staff some of the nation's best reporters, including H. R. Knickerbocker, Richard Tregaskis, Frank Coniff and Bob Considine.

With 122 domestic and 65 foreign bureaus and a total of more than 2,500 full-time employees, AP is easily the world's largest newsgathering organization. It claims a number of firsts. It was the first to convert from Morse code to teleprinters, in 1914; first with wire transmission of pictures, in 1935; first to start a full-time sports wire, in 1946; first to transmit news via typesetter tape, in the early 1950s; first to use cathode ray terminals; first to use laser beams to transmit and receive pictures; first to beam news via satellite, and first to transmit stock tables at 50,000 words a minute. Cooperatively owned by 1,400 newspapers and over 5,000 radio and television stations—who are also required to contribute their news to it—AP has over 10,000 worldwide subscribers and an audience estimated at 1 billion in 115 countries. Over the years 15 AP reporters and photographers have been killed in the line of duty. It has won 31 Pulitzer Prizes. In recent years it has stepped up its interpretive and investigative reporting and added specialists in science, religion and urban affairs. In 1970 it set up a "mod squad" to report news of special interest to the under-30 set.

Still controlled by E.W. Scripps Company, UPI serves 9,000 subscribers in 92 countries. It operates 177 bureaus worldwide, 92 located in the United States and 81 abroad. It has a full-time staff of 1,823, of whom 1,245 work in the United States. UPI Newspictures serves more than 1,400 newspapers and television stations around the world. In addition, UPI provides an array of other services: the TV Newsfilm Service, launched in 1951, which provides footage to the ABC and NBC networks in the United States and 120 television stations and networks in 70 countries abroad; UPI Audio Service, which provides voice coverage to 900 radio and television stations; UPI Cable Newswire, serving CATV systems; UPI Unistox Service, a high-speed transmission system for delivery of stock market information; DataNews, which delivers news directly into computers; the Special Washington Wire; news bulletins for ships at sea; the UPI Compix, which undertakes photographic assignments for business and industrial firms; UPI International Features, and UNICOM News, a commodity and economic wire service, launched in 1977 and jointly owned by UPI and Commodity News Services, a subsidiary of Knight-Ridder Newspapers.

AP's 1981 annual budget of $151 million would place it on the Fortune 500 list. The UPI budget is about half of that of its rival. Because it is a cooperative in which members pay a pro-rata share of the total costs, AP was able to ride the inflationary 1970s better than UPI, which reportedly faced serious financial troubles by the end of the decade. UPI has not returned a dividend to its stockholders for over 20 years. Since 1961, its last profitable year, it has suffered a total loss of $17 million.

Both AP and UPI are in the forefront of the technological revolution that is reshaping the newspaper industry. Both pioneered in the introduction of video terminals. UPI developed the DataNews system, which delivers a copy at 1,200 words per minute directly into computers, and the DataStox services, which provides computer-to-computer delivery of financial tabular reports. AP developed DataStream and DataFeature, both high-speed transmission systems, and Laserphoto system, which delivers by laser beams dry glossy prints of photographic reproduction quality. In the 1980s both are expected to move into satellite transmissions and earth stations.

A more recent development is the growth of press services affiliated with major newspapers and available to any customer through leased wires. The largest of these are the New York Times News Service, the Los Angeles Times–Washington Post News Service, the Chicago Tribune Press Service, Dow Jones News Services, The Christian Science Monitor and Photo Service, Copley News Service, the Independent Newspaper Alliance and Gannett News Service.

Newspaper syndicates perform slightly different functions; they deal less with news than with features, such as cartoons, comic strips and columns. Their scope is also much broader; the *Syndicate Directory* lists over 50 different categories. There are over 300 newspaper syndicates, distributing over 10,000 features, with an estimated combined sales of $100 million. The five largest are the Newspaper Enterprises Association, owned by the Scripps-Howard interests; United Features Syndicate, also owned by Scripps-Howard; King Features, owned by Hearst; the Field Newspaper Syndicate, and the Chicago Tribune–New York News Syndicate. For many readers, the features and columns these syndicates supply help to offset what James Reston calls the "dailiness" of daily newspapers.

Electronic News Media

Unlike books and magazines, radio and television compete directly with newspapers both for advertising dollars and for audiences. The electronic media are also structured differently, presenting features unlike any in the newspaper industry. They are also more pervasive and engrossing, influencing social mores more directly and swaying minds more powerfully.

Regular commercially licensed sound broadcasting began in the United States in 1920. Approximately 93 percent of all radio stations are privately owned and financed entirely through advertising. In 1978 these stations numbered 8,532—4,526 AM and 4,006 FM. Most of these stations are affiliated with one of four national networks: 1,250 with four program networks of the American Broadcasting Companies, 246 with the Columbia Broadcasting System, 236 with the National Broadcasting Company and 581 with the Mutual Broadcasting System. In addition, the Keystone Broadcasting System, the transcription network for rural America, has 1,140 affiliated stations. There are also 135 regional radio networks or groups comprising three to 70 or more stations. Some 325 AM and 170 FM radio stations are owned by newspaper and magazine publishers. Noncommercial radio consists entirely of FM stations, most of them operated by colleges, universities and public authorities for educational purposes and financed by public and/or private funds, subscriptions and some advertising. Over 100 of these stations are linked nationally by the National Public Radio Agency, which receives funds from the Corporation for Public Broadcasting, set up under the Public Broadcasting Act of 1967. The corporation is financed by both federal and private funds.

International short-wave broadcasting is conducted mainly by the Voice of America, operated by the International Communication Agency. The VOA is heard in 35 regularly scheduled languages and is on the air for 805 hours a week. The Department of Defense's Armed Forces Radio and Television Network (AFRTV) broadcasts news and a variety of other programs in English to the local transmitters operated by the U.S. armed forces abroad via its short-wave transmitters on the Atlantic and Pacific coasts and a relay transmitter in the Philippines. International broadcasting is also conducted by private organizations, such as ABC International and Radio New York Worldwide, as well as a number of Christian evangelistic ministries, of which the most prominent is Radio Station KGEI, The Voice of Friendship, owned and operated by the Far East Broadcasting Company.

Television began on an experimental basis in the United States in the 1920s. In 1979 there were 990 licensed and operating sta-

tions, of which 76 percent were commercially owned. Almost all commercial stations are affiliated to a network; the three largest are the American Broadcasting Companies (ABC), with five owned stations, 200 primary network affiliates and 141 secondary affiliates; Columbia Broadcasting System (CBS), with five owned and operated and 215 affiliated stations, and the National Broadcasting Company (NBC), with five owned and operated stations and 219 affiliates. In a typical week about 66 percent of the affiliated stations' programming is supplied by the networks. Network affiliates are on the air for an average of 122 hours weekly and non-network stations for 79 hours weekly, carrying 10 percent and 18 percent respectively of local live programming. There are also 23 regional television networks.

The 220 noncommercial educational stations cover more than 80 percent of the nation's population. A growing number are run by Christian evangelistic ministries, such as the Christian Broadcasting Network, the PTL Club and Trinity Broadcasting. Many of the strictly educational stations are linked together by the Public Broadcasting Service. There are, in addition, a number of regional networks linked together by live-relay facilities. All stations use 525-line definition.

To overcome reception difficulties due to distance and terrain features and to accommodate restricted programs, such as sports events, the use of Community Antenna Television (CATV) systems has been greatly expanded in recent years. The industry today divides into two major segments: the larger and traditional cable industry, built on carriage of broadcast television signals, and the newer and faster-growing pay cable television. While subscribers pay for either system, pay cable is almost always one or more premium channels for which there is an additional cost over and above the monthly charge for the basic service. In 1978 there were 4,001 cable systems (compared to 70 in 1952, 640 in 1960, 2,490 in 1970 and 3,506 in 1975), with 13 million subscribers (compared to 14,000 in 1952, 650,000 in 1960, 4.5 million in 1970 and 9.8 million in 1975) and an average number of 3,242 subscribers per system (compared to 200 in 1952, 1,016 in 1960, 1,807 in 1970 and 2,795 in 1975). In 1978 17.7 percent of TV homes also had cable, compared to 0.1 percent in 1952, 1.4 percent in 1960, 7.6 percent in 1970 and 14.3 percent in 1975. Large systems, such as Mission

Cable of San Diego with over 100,000 subscriber homes, offer their subscribers a choice of 44 programs, but the vast majority of the systems offer an average of 15 programs. Systems with over 10,000 subscribers are required by the FCC to install feedback channels for audience participation. No system may relay more than three national networks and three independent stations in the 50 highest television density areas, or three networks and two independents in other areas. The three largest cable operators in 1978 were Teleprompter, with 1,161,000 subscribers, Time, Inc., with 750,000 and Warner Communications, with 600,000. Time, Inc.'s Home Box Office dominates the pay cable field, with 1,545,000 subscribers, or 66 percent of all subscribers. Newspapers account for a significant 10 percent of cable television ownership, with 308 systems, a decline from 14 percent and 486 systems in 1975.

Radical changes have taken place in broadcasting within the last 30 years. Sponsored programs have given way to programming in which different advertisers participate, buying time in much the same way as they buy space in the print media. While the average commercial has shrunk from 60 to 30 seconds, the ratio of commercial minutes to program minutes has risen to 1:3, and the number of commercials aired has doubled. Control of programming has also effectively passed into the hands of the networks. The so-called program production companies or package agencies are using the vast under-used production facilities of Hollywood to produce at least 80 percent of prime-time programming under contract to the networks. The number of network hours broadcast has also steadily increased over the past 15 years. Economics make it more favorable to the local stations to use syndicated material than to produce their own programs. Nearly 65 percent of affiliate programming time is devoted to network programs. The resulting economic picture is somewhat complex. The networks sell audiences to advertisers on behalf of stations, and purchase programs on behalf of stations. Thus they are in effect agents for stations (who are their clients), while advertisers are the ultimate customers. The product sold is the audience, and the programs are the bait used to attract it. Affiliates are, in effect, paid by the networks for airing the programs.

Broadcasting is the most intensively regulated of all media. The regulation is based not

Table 43
AM, FM and Television Stations, 1950-1977

	AM Radio				FM Radio				Television			
	1950	1960	1970	1977	1950	1960	1970	1977	1950	1960	1970	1977
Number commercial stations	2,061	3,431	4,267	4,472	733	688	2,184	2,837	97	515	677	728
Number educational stations	25	25	25	25	48	162	413	839	-	44	185	256
Total number of stations	2,086	3,456	4,292	4,497	781	850	2,597	3676	98	559	862	984
% network affiliates	56%	33%	50%	62%	-	-	-	-	98%	96%	84%	84%
Number employed	52,000	51,700	65,000	70,500	-	1,300	6,100	15,900	14,000	40,600	58,400	67,200
Total revenues (in millions)	$444.5	$597.7	$1,077.4	$1,845.9	$2.8	$9.4	$84.9	$428.7	$105.9	$1,268.6	$2,808.2	$5,889.0
Total pre-tax earnings (in millions)	$68.2	$45.9	$104.0	$204.4	-	-	($11.1)	$41.6	($9.2)	$244.1	$453.8	$1,401.0
% total advertising exp.	11%	6%	7%	7%[1]	-	-	-	-	3%	13%	18%	20%
% families with receivers	95%	96%	98%	99%	-	10%	74%	95%	9%	87%	95%	98%
FCC Budget (in millions)	$6.7	$10.5	$24.5	$46.7[1]	(See under AM)	(See under AM)			(See under AM)	(See under AM)		
FCC employees	1,285	1,396	1,537	2,136[1]	(See under AM)	(See under AM)			(See under AM)	(See under AM)		

[1]1976

Sources: Christopher H. Sterling and Timothy R. Haight, The Mass Media: Aspen Institute Guide to Communications Industry Trends.

on social or economic needs but on the technical limitations of the space spectrum—the allottable frequencies. A broadcast license is thus a limited privilege that entitles the licensee to use a specific frequency for a specified period (usually three years) and is renewable only if deemed in the public interest.

The oversight agency of the broadcasting industry is the Federal Communications Commission (FCC), set up under the Communications Act of 1934. Although enacted before television became a mass medium, the act has not been substantially amended since. The law vested in the commission not only watchdog functions but also licensing and rulemaking powers, subject only to "public interest, convenience and necessity," three criteria that have always guided the commission's decisions. The most comprehensive definition of the scope of these powers is Justice Felix Frankfurter's opinion for the majority in *National Broadcasting Company* v. *United States* in 1941. Upholding the commission's chain broadcasting regulations, the justice said, "The Act itself establishes that the commission's powers are not limited to the engineering and technical aspects of regulation of radio communication....[It] does not restrict the commission merely to supervision of the traffic. It puts upon the commission the burden of determining the composition of that traffic." Acting on this mandate, the commission has followed a policy of seeking to achieve diversity in both content and ownership, not only to

deal with monopolistic trends but because it felt that diversity was a legitimate end in itself. To achieve this goal, the commission has consistently sought structural regulation designed to prevent and remove imbalances in ownership. The 1934 law specifically applies antitrust laws to the field of broadcasting and calls for revocation of any station license from an owner accused of monopolistic activities, and for refusal of future applications from the offender. For more or less the same reasons, the FCC has always held that the best broadcast station is one that is locally owned and operated—a principle known as localism. Ironically, the present concentration is the result of this very policy, which limits the number of licenses in any one city to three. Since all the licenses have been taken up, there is only room for three networks. If the market were free to reshuffle the resources, there would probably be more networks.

The development of television as a dominant social force led the FCC in 1955 to conduct an inquiry into the structure and operation of network broadcasting. It resulted in an extensive study commonly known as the Barrow Report. The purpose of the report was to determine "whether the present operation of television and radio networks and their relationships with stations and other components of the industry tend to foster or impede the development of a nationwide, competitive broadcasting industry." In 1970, after extensive investigations, the FCC

Table 44
Group Ownership in Broadcasting, 1929–1976

Year	Total Number of Stations	Number of Group Owners	Number of Group-Owned Stations	Percent of Stations under Group Ownership
Radio				
1929	600	12	20	3.3%
1939	764	39	109	14.3
1951	2232	63	253	11.3
1960	3398	185	765	22.5
1976	4130	373	1297	31.4
Television				
1948	16	3	6	37.5%
1952	108	19	53	49.1
1956	441	60	173	39.2
1960	515	84	252	48.9
1966	585	111	324	55.4
1976	710	119	415	58.0

Source: Sterling and Haight.

Table 45

Television Group Ownership, 1977

	Number of Stations	Weekly Circulation		Daily Circulation	
		Total (millions)	Mean (thousands)	Total (millions)	Mean (thousands)
Group-owned	345	218.4	633.9	132.1	382.8
Independent	265	65.2	246.0	37.3	140.8
TOTAL	610	283.6	464.9	169.4	277.6

% Group-owned

Firms	Weekly Circulation	Daily Circulation
57%	77%	78%

Source: *Television Factbook 1978.*

adopted a rule designed to lessen the networks' oligopsony in the marketplace. The Prime-Time Access Rule (PTAR), as it is known, has two parts. The first reduces network bargaining power vis-à-vis program producers by prohibiting the network from acquiring subsidiary rights and off-network syndication rights in the programs they purchase. The second part prohibits network affiliated stations from broadcasting network programs or network reruns between 7 and 8 p.m., thus reducing prime-time network programming by half an hour. The purpose of the latter half of the rule was to permit local stations to air more independent programs in prime time.

In 1977 the FCC announced another inquiry, prompted by allegations contained in the Department of Justice antitrust complaints filed against the three major networks. Specifically, the study focused on the alleged dominance of the Big Three networks, the relationships between networks and their affiliated stations, and the anticompetitive effects of network programming on the development of alternative programming sources.

Multiple ownerships are as common in broadcasting as they are in the print media, as shown in Table 44. In radio there were 373 group owners, with 1,297 stations, and in television there were 119 group owners, with 415 stations. The percentage of group ownership was higher in television: 58 percent compared to radio's 31.4 percent. Group stations are, generally speaking, in the larger markets. One-third of the groups active in the top 100 markets had but two stations, while 25 groups had three stations, 27 had four, 14 had five, nine had six, and four the

full complement of seven television stations. (The maximum number of stations permitted by FCC under one owner is seven, of which only five may be VHF.) In mid-1977 Park Broadcasting became the first group owner to have 21 stations, seven in each service. In two major ownership changes in 1978, General Electric, owner of 17 stations, purchased Cox Broadcasting with 11 television and radio stations for $500 million, and Combined Communications, owner of 19 stations, merged with Gannett chain with its three stations for $370 million. As a result of such trading up, the cumulative proportion of television households reached by the top 15 groups has increased over the years. As they reach the maximum number of permissible stations, groups have also diversified into other fields, including program production.

Table 45 shows that 77 percent of U.S. households view group stations. The average audience for a group member is 2½ times that of an independent station. Table 46 presents data on the 14 groups that had the largest combined audiences in 1977. Leading the list is CBS, which reaches about six percent of the national audience, followed by NBC and ABC, each with 5.4 percent. In terms of market share, these numbers are of the same magnitude as the largest newspaper chains. Although not as large as the networks, numerous other groups own stations with impressive audience reach. Metromedia reaches nearly 13 million, or 4.5 percent of the national audience. Some of the leaders are newspaper publishers, such as *The Washington Post,* Scripps-Howard and Cox.

Concerned over group dominance in stations in the top 50 markets (serving 75 percent of television homes), the FCC banned

Table 46
Major Television Groups, 1977

Group	Number of Stations	Weekly Circulation (millions)	National Total	Daily Circulation (millions)	National Total
CBS	5	15.8	5.6%	10.1	6.0%
ABC	5	15.2	5.4	9.2	5.4
NBC	5	15.0	5.3	9.2	5.4
Metromedia	6	12.7	4.5	6.5	3.8
RKO General	4	8.8	3.1	3.8	2.2
Westinghouse	5	8.4	3.0	5.1	3.0
Storer	7	6.7	2.4	4.1	2.4
Field Communications	5	6.2	2.2	2.7	1.6
Capital Cities	6	5.6	2.0	3.6	2.1
Cox Broadcasting	5	4.9	1.7	2.7	1.6
Gaylord	7	4.9	1.7	2.7	1.6
Taft Broadcasting	6	4.5	1.6	2.5	1.5
Scripps-Howard	6	4.0	1.4	2.5	1.5
Post-Newsweek	4	3.8	1.4	2.3	1.4

Source: *Television Factbook, 1978,* Television Digest, Inc.

the acquisition of any further stations in these markets by an applicant with two VHF or three television stations of any kind. This policy was later abandoned in favor of a case-by-case consideration. A number of similar attempts followed: to limit ownership to no more than four stations within any one state, to limit ownership to no more than one station of any kind per market, and to ban newspaper-broadcast station cross-ownership.

One of the oldest regulatory concerns is the cross-ownership of newspaper and broadcast facilities, especially in the same market. Table 47 shows the extent of newspaper ownership of broadcast media in 1977. The

Table 47
Group Ownership of Daily Newspapers and Radio and TV Stations, 1977
Number of Local Establishments

	Total	Newspapers	Radios	TV Stations
Total Number of Local Establishments	10,280	1,580	7,982	718
Number of Establishments Owned by Conglomerates*	3,363	948	1,971	509
Number of Independent Establishments	6,917	632	6,011	209
% Independent	67%	40%	75%	29%
Share of Audience of Independent Establishments	—	27%	—	15%

Sources: *Broadcasting Yearbook,* 1978; *Television Factbook,* 1978; *Editor and Publisher International Yearbook,* 1978.

figures do not reveal the degree of media conglomeration within the local market. For example, Newhouse's 29 different media facilities have a penetration of over 25 percent of households in 11 markets. Although newspaper ownership is declining both in absolute and relative terms in the radio market, it has been increasing in the more lucrative television field. In 1975 the FCC issued a report banning new joint ownerships of television stations and newspapers located in the same town. The new rule also required divestiture where the only newspaper in a city owned either the only radio or the only television station. Existing cross-ownerships were exempted until sold, when they would have to be broken up as well. This question was finally laid to rest when the Supreme Court upheld the FCC, accepting the principle of "reasonable interchangeability" in the acquisition and ownership of media properties by groups.

Education & Training

Journalism education in the United States dates back to 1869, when General Robert E. Lee, then president of Washington College, now Washington and Lee University, recommended that 50 press scholarships be made available to young men interested in journalism and printing careers. Although the college did so, the project was discontinued following the death of Lee a year later. It was nearly 40 years later, in 1908, that the nation's first school of journalism was established by the University of Missouri of Columbia, Mo. The school and its curriculum were greeted with outright derision by the journalistic community; H. L. Mencken called them little better than those that teach barbering.

Today there are 80 accredited and 264 non-accredited schools and departments of journalism across the country, and their number is expected to grow. The past 20 years, particularly, have been marked by an explosion in college journalism enrollments—from 11,390 in 1960 to 71,594 in 1979. (The term "journalism major" is defined as a person concentrating in news-editorial, advertising, broadcast news, public relations, magazine journalism, community journalism, photojournalism, home economics journalism, agricultural journalism, or science and technical writing, or a person preparing for a career in journalism research or journalism education.) The steady climb in journalism baccalaureates—by 199 percent from 1970/71 to 1975/76—is in sharp contrast to the decline in the number of bachelor's degree awards in other fields, by 38.1 percent in English literature, 35.6 percent in mathematics, 22.4 percent in foreign languages and 18.4 percent in social sciences.

The most dramatic trend in journalism

Table 48
Top Journalism Schools in the U.S., 1978–1980

By Total Enrollment				By Graduate Students			
Schools	1980	1979	1978	Schools	1980	1979	1978
1. Texas at Austin	2,432	1,599	2,798	1. Missouri	282	238	223
2. Syracuse	1,942	2,033	2,057	2. Texas at Austin	238	97	229
3. Ohio U.	1,758	1,944	874	3. Syracuse	208	186	201
4. Cal. State, Fullerton	1,659	1,532	1,307	4. Minnesota	157	131	204
5. Alabama	1,579	1,397	1,214	5. Ball State	115	67	103
6. Michigan State	1,454	1,609	1,266	6. Indiana	107	100	106
7. Tennessee, Knoxville	1,372	1,232	1,123	7. Ohio State	101	84	86
8. Florida	1,235	1,178	1,200				
9. Texas Tech	1,220	1,139	1,003				
10. Middle Tennessee	1,170	1,008	608				
11. Glassboro State	1,169	987	960				
12. South Carolina	1,157	1,118	1,051				
13. Wisconsin-Madison	1,093	947	881				
14. Missouri	1,080	1,056	1,902				
15. Nebraska-Lincoln	1,043	1,096	1,112				
16. Oklahoma	1,036	1,011	958				

Source: *Journalism Educator.*

education is the increasing percentage of females, who now constitute the majority, with 56 percent. If this trend continues, the typical newsroom, now a male bastion, will no longer be so by the mid 1980s. There has also been a significant increase in minority enrollments, from 7 percent in 1978 to 12 percent in 1979 and from 4.7 percent to 7.1 percent for blacks. Even within the minority category, females outnumber males by 62 to 38 percent.

Journalism schools prepare students for careers other than newspapers as well as for newspapers. In addition to news-editorial, the traditional slot for newspaper journalists, the three other major sequences are advertising, broadcast journalism and public relations. Of the total enrollment, 26 percent were listed as news-editorial, 15 percent advertising, 18 percent broadcasting and 11 percent public relations. Interest in the news-editorial area has been declining while that in others has been gaining.

In addition, most newspapers offer internships, whether or not for academic credit. The *Student Guide to Mass Media Internships* lists 3,700 intern positions available, of which 1,334 were offered by dailies and 734 by weekly newspapers. There is also a growing emphasis on continuing education and mid-career training of professionals. In 1980 the Northwestern University's Medill School of Journalism inaugurated what Dean I. W. Cole believes is the first of its kind, a one-year graduate program in management for journalists with at least three years' experience.

The U.S. Department of Labor's Bureau of Statistics reports that the need for newspaper reporters will grow from the current 45,000 to 53,000 by 1990. The Bureau estimates that there will be an average of 2,400 job openings annually in the next 10 years.

Summary

Trends

The American Newspaper Publishers Association describes newspapers as "the medium of the future." The newspaper of the future may not be the traditional product, but the so-called electronic newspaper. According to Keith Fuller, general manager of the Associated Press, "The newspaper industry is being propelled into the era of electronic delivery of information to homes and businesses. No one knows how big the market will be, but the newspapers should not be left

at the post once the race gets under way.... There is no reason for a newspaper to abdicate its role as the traditional purveyor of information merely because the delivery might expand to include home terminals."

The newspaper of the future is already taking shape today. The first of the so-called home information retrieval systems went into operation in 1974 in Great Britain, introduced by the BBC. Called CEEFAX, it was broadcast on the otherwise unused sidebands of television wavelengths. Available to TV sets equipped with decoders, the system offers such material as program listings, price surveys and horserace tips. CEEFAX was a one-way system and did not permit user feedback. A two-way system called Viewdata was introduced in 1979 under the tradename Prestel. Operated by the Postal Service over telephone lines, it offers restaurant listings, timetables and even games. Subscribers can also use its two-way capability to buy goods on credit from participating merchants. In the United States, the system is being pioneered by Knight-Ridder under the trade name Viewtron. It includes a specially equipped television set, a hand-held remote control coder and a keyboard for communicating with the system. Participants can choose from four categories of information—labeled information, shopping, education and messages—with a total of 10,000 frames or full screens of information, each equivalent to a newspaper page. Information is indexed within each category to permit precise selection. The Associated Press is putting together a special newswire for Viewtron.

In the newsroom, the next advance will be pagination, or computerized page layouts. Pagination transfers to the editor most of the remaining functions of the now obsolete composing room. It will also eliminate paste-up processes and trimming. Fiber optics and magnetic bubble storage will increase enormously the speed and quantity of information that can be transmitted and processed. Fiber optics, for example, will be able to carry 10 million bits of information per second. This would allow the electronic transmission of a newspaper page with moving pictures. Satellites also could be used to transmit full pages to remote printing plants, as *The Wall Street Journal* is already doing. The introduction of video display terminals to newsrooms has, in the words of one expert, "killed off the dinosaurs on the front end of the system." Now the dinosaurs on the back end are being wiped out. This will mean significantly altered content and the capability to produce on-demand newspapers, with each reader or demographic unit receiving only the sections and types of news desired.

While many of these developments may have to wait until the 21st century for their full exploitation, the state of the art itself features several technological breakthroughs: laser scanners and laser plate engravers; computer-controlled ink jets that spray ink onto the newsprint, thus eliminating press plates altogether; electronic text processing and automated typesetting, and on-line display terminals for advertisers. New microwave transmitting technology is already enabling newspapers to transmit page images for printing at satellite plants. *The Minneapolis Star and Tribune* is one of the first newspapers in the world without a composing room. The ANPA Research Institute is perfecting a low-cost microwave receiver that can fit on the roof of a newspaper plant to receive information via a satellite instead of telephone lines. There is also an improved capacity to report news quickly. Portable remote terminals allow a reporter to prepare copy in the field and transmit it directly to a newsroom computer by telephone. Newspapers are also using lighter weight newsprint, a basis weight of 28 lb., as opposed to 32 lb. in 1965. New fibers obtained from sugarcane stalks and kenaf, a farm product grown in most parts of North America, are replacing trees as the source of newsprint.

Despite all these innovations, the Gutenberg legacies will survive. Newspapers will always remain a print medium. Even when the product changes, the function remains the same: to record, to inform, to comment.

CHRONOLOGY

1976   Don Bolles, award-winning investigative reporter for the *Arizona Republic,* slain while working on a story dealing with organized crime.
National Labor Relations Board rules that journalists are not professionals and therefore not exempt from its purview.
The 159-year-old *Hartford Times* ceases publication.
Congress passes "Government in the Sunshine" Law.

1977   Rupert Murdoch, Australian press magnate, buys New York *Post,* the Newhouse group buys Booth Newspapers and Gannett buys Speidel chain.
FCC bans cross-media ownership.

1978   Supreme Court holds that newsroom searches are valid and that the news media enjoys no special immunity from court-approved searches by police officers. Supreme Court also upholds cross-media ownership ban.
Time, Inc. buys *Washington Star* from Joe L. Allbritton.
Strike shuts down the three New York papers for three months.

Chicago *Daily News* folds.
New York Times reporter Myron Farber jailed for contempt of court for defying court order to reveal source of informaton.
New York Times settles sex bias suit.

1979   *Wall Street Journal* overtakes New York *Daily News* as the nation's largest selling paper.
Cincinnati papers *Post* and *Enquirer* conclude agreement on joint operations under the Newspaper Preservation Act.

1980   Congress passes bill protecting journalists' notes from police searches.
Fairness Doctrine is relaxed.
Times Mirror ordered to sell either its *Hartford Courant* or two cable TV stations.
Times Mirror Company acquires *Denver Post.*
Atlantic, Cue, Us, Saturday Review and *Harper's* change hands.
Nation's first cable TV news network launched by Ted Turner.
North American Newspaper Alliance disbanded and replaced by Independent Newspaper Alliance.

1981   *Washington Star* folds.

BIBLIOGRAPHY

Agee, Warren K. *Mass Media in a Free Society.* Lawrence, Kan., 1969.

Bagdikian, Ben H. *The Effete Conspiracy: And Other Crimes by the Press.* New York, 1972.

Balk, Alfred. *A Free & Responsive Press.* New York, 1973.

Barron, Jerome A. *A Freedom of the Press for Whom? The Right of Access to Mass Media.* Bloomington, Ind., 1973.

Blanchard, Robert O. *Congress & the News Media.* New York, 1974.

Bogart, Leo. *The Press & its Public.* Hillsdale, N.J., 1981.

Brandsberg, George. *The Free Papers: A Comprehensive Study of America's Shopping Guide and Free Circulation Newspaper Industry.* Ames, Iowa, 1969.

Cater, Douglass. *The Fourth Branch of Government.* Boston, 1959.

Compaine, Benjamin. *Who Owns the Media?* New York, 1979.

_____. *The Newspaper Industry in the 1980s.* White Plains, N.Y., 1980.

Crouse, Timothy. *The Boys on the Bus: Riding with the Campaign Press Corps.* New York, 1976.

Devol, Kenneth S. *Mass Media & the Supreme Court.* New York 1976.

Duscha, Julius, and Fischer, Thomas G. *The Campus Press.* Washington, D.C., 1973..

Edward, Gerald J. *The Social Responsibility of the Press.* Minneapolis, 1963.

Emery, Edwin, and Emery, Michael. *The Press and America.* Englewood Cliffs, N.J., 1978.

Gillmor, Donald M. *Free Press & Fair Trial.* Washington, D.C., 1966.

Glessing, Robert J. *The Underground Press in America.* Bloomington, Ind., 1970.

Gordon, George N. *The Communications Revolution: A History of Mass Media in the United States.* New York, 1977.

Hiebert, Ray Eldon. *The Press in Washington.* New York, 1966.

Hohlenberg, John. *The News Media: A Journalist Looks at His Profession.* New York, 1968.

Hulteng, John L. *The News Media: What Makes Them Tick.* Englewood Cliffs, N.J., 1979.

Hynds, Ernest C. *American Newspapers in the 1980s.* New York, 1980.

Keogh, James. *President Nixon and the Press.* New York, 1972.

La Brie, Henry G. *The Black Press in America.* Iowa City, Iowa, 1980.

Liebling, A. J. *The Press.* New York, 1961.

Lindstrom, Carl E. *The Fading American Newspaper.* New York, 1960.

Lister, Hal. *The Suburban Press: A Separate Journalism.* Columbia, Mo., 1975.

MacDougall, A. Kent. *The Press: A Critical Look from the Inside.* Princeton, N.J., 1972.

Marbut, F. B. *News from the Capitol: The Story of Washington Reporting.* Carbondale, Ill., 1971.

Marzolf, Marion. *Up From the Footnote: A History of Women Journalists.* New York, 1977.

Merrill, John C., and Fisher, Hal. *The World's Great Dailies: Profiles of 50 Newspapers.* New York, 1980.

Mott, Frank Luther. *American Journalism: A History, 1690–1960.* New York, 1962.

Owen, Bruce M. *Economics & Freedom of Expression: Media Structure and the First Amendment.* Cambridge, Mass., 1975.

Pember, Don. *Mass Media in America.* Chicago, 1981.

_____. *Mass Media Law.* Dubuque, Iowa, 1977.

Pollard, James E. *The Presidents & the Press.* New York, 1947.

Read, William H. *America's Mass Media Merchants.* Baltimore, 1977.

Reston, James B. *The Artillery of the Press.* New York, 1967.

Rivers, William L., et al. *Back Talk: Press Councils in America.* San Francisco, 1971.

Sim, Jim Cameron. *The Grass Roots Press: America's Community Newspapers.* Ames, Iowa, 1969.

Spragens, William C. *The Presidency & the Mass Media in the Age of Television.* Washington, D.C., 1978.

Sterling, Christopher, and Haight, T. *The Mass Media: Aspen Institute Guide to Communication Industry Trends.* New York, 1978.

Talese, Gay. *The Kingdom and the Power.* New York, 1969.

Tebbel, John. *The Compact History of the American Newspaper.* New York, 1969.

_____. *The Media in America.* New York, 1974.

Udell, Jon G. *Economic Trends in the Daily Newspaper Business, 1946 to 1970.* Madison, Wis., 1972.

_____. *The Economics of the American Newspaper.* New York, 1978.

Wicker, Tom. *On Press: A Top Reporter's Life in and Reflections on American Journalism.* New York, 1978.

Wynar, Lubomyr R., and Wynar, Anna T. *Encyclopedia Directory of Ethnic Newspapers & Periodicals in the United States.* Littleton, Colo., 1976.

VENEZUELA

by Luis Ortega and Robert N. Pierce

BASIC DATA

Population: 14.78 million
Area: 911,680 sq. km. (236,125 sq. mi.)
GNP: 171.68 billion bolivares (US$40 billion)
(1978)
Literacy Rate: 74.1%
Language(s): Spanish
Number of Dailies: 69 (1979)
  Aggregate Circulation: 2.5 million (1979)
  Circulation per 1,000: 169 (1979)
Number of Nondailies: 3
  Aggregate Circulation: 500,000
  Circulation per 1,000: 39
Number of Periodicals: 147

Number of Radio Stations: 168
Number of Television Stations: 8
Number of Radio Receivers: 503 million
  Radio Receivers per 1,000: 407
Number of Television Sets: 1.5 million
  Television Sets per 1,000: 116
Total Annual Newsprint Consumption: 99,900
metric tons
  Per Capita Newsprint Consumption: 7.7 kg.
  (16.94 lb.)
Total Newspaper Ad Receipts: 1.6 billion
bolivares (US$374 million) (1979)
  As % of All Ad Expenditures: 38.8

Background & General Characteristics

Economic vigor and political stability through the 1970s have helped Venezuela achieve the highest degree of press freedom in its 160-year history. At present, privately owned radio, television and press operate side by side with a government media system dedicated to the UNESCO ideal of media as a national resource. There are neither real censorship nor economic restraints limiting press, radio and TV, but a major issue has been shaping up since 1980 over the proper role for the media in a developing society. The issue pits the government, seeking to limit wild consumerism and promote national development through public channels against the privately owned media and media advertisers decrying any government control or limitation as an attack on press freedom and the free enterprise system. Continued prosperity and increasing social development are seen as the keys to national stability and plurality and freedom of the press during the 1980s.

Venezuela's first newspaper was the *Gaceta de Caracas*, founded in 1808, shortly after the arrival of the first printing press.

Spanish colonial neglect—Venezuela being considered a remote outpost of Bogotá—helped foster a more independent, democratic tradition in that country than in most of colonial Latin America. Still, Venezuela's history is one of a long line of authoritarian and dictatorial rulers. Venezuelan elites have long desired democracy, yet often found themselves suffering under dictatorships. With the overthrow of dictator Marcos Pérez Jiménez in 1958, Venezuela embarked on an up-to-now unbroken succession of democratically elected governments, but universal press freedom did not follow automatically.

The young democracy was internally unstable and ripe for the hemispheric socialistic proselytizing by Fidel Castro. During the early 1960s, the government fought communists and other subversive elements and moved to suppress their media organs. In 1963, Rómulo Betancourt, the first popularly elected president to complete a term in office, outlawed the communist parties and closed down their media. Since then, the governments through the late 1960s and into the early 1970s chiseled away at subversives and their media—and also at extremist and subversive material in the more moderate media—to the point that today there is rarely more than the loyal opposition commonly found in the press of democratic nations. The communist parties and their organs were allowed to resurface in the 1970s, but they have posed no real threat to the government. Since the communist crisis of the 1960s, incidents of government suppression of the media have been limited to denying terrorists and their sympathizers a public platform for their ideas and demands. Overly critical personal attacks on the president have also been regularly suppressed.

Political stability and freedom of the press have benefited greatly from Venezuela's economic prosperity. Even before the democratic governments, Venezuela's oil wealth enabled its rulers to carry out industrial and social development programs that helped create a growing middle class of more affluent and educated media users. In 1971, according to the census of that year, 77 percent of Venezuelans 10 years or older were literate. No more recent estimates are available, but the numbers have certainly increased during the decade. As economic prosperity led to greater political stability, the government relaxed its censorship of unfavorable news. In 1980 the press openly challenged government programs and pointed out policy failures. Government advertising in the private media—for a long time an influential tool used selectively to force media compliance with official policies—is losing some power to commercial advertisements as the private sector provides a more diverse financial base for the media, lessening their dependence on government ad money.

Demographic patterns in Venezuela help make the media available to a very large percentage of the population. Venezuela's population is concentrated along the Caribbean coast and the northern mountain range that also parallels the coastline. The large area south of the Orinoco River is sparsely populated and still undeveloped. Of the approximately 69 dailies in Venezuela in 1979, only four were published south of the Orinoco—an area slightly larger than the land north of the river. In 1970, 2.4 percent of the national territory (centered around the federal district and the small adjoining states of Aragua, Carabobo, and Miranda, all located on the Caribbean coast) accounted for 70 percent of the nation's industrial production. Three-quarters of the industrial employment and one-third of the population were to be found in that area. Venezuela surpassed Argentina

in 1976 as Latin America's most urbanized society; by 1978 over 80 percent of the country's population was living in cities.

This heavy urbanization, a product of Venezuela's rapid economic expansion, makes media delivery to most of the population easy, but it has also created some of Venezuela's most acute problems. Public and social services have been severely strained by the population migration to the cities, and a critical housing shortage has created stark pockets of misery among the affluence. Swarms of tin shacks girdle the major cities; by some estimates, nearly half of Caracas's 2.8 million people live in slums. The situation has helped spark a growing social awareness in both the print and broadcast media, where investigative and analytical journalism is on the rise.

The great majority of Venezuelans are an amalgam of white, Negro and Indian ancestry, but they share a common culture based on Hispanic traditions enriched by African and Indian contributions. Spanish is the official language, and 96 percent of the population is Roman Catholic. Indian dialects are spoken in remote areas of the interior by approximately 200,000 Amerinds. Economic and social classes exist, including a significant number of chronically poor, but there is a growing middle class and the people consider themselves members of essentially the same ethnic group. The media, as a whole, address this audience as a homogeneous, relatively affluent group, promoting similar consumer habits among all classes of readers and viewers. The leading print and broadcast outlets, all concentrated in Caracas, focus most of their coverage on events in the capital. Regional radio and press cover the interior, while the few leading dailies in other cities report both local and capital events.

The cultural effects of media have been an issue in Venezuela since the advent of television. As early as 1962, evidence indicated that television's most persistent message was that drinking and smoking were indispensable for social success. The government finally banned tobacco and alcohol commercials on television in 1980, as part of the new regulations surrounding the introduction of color broadcasting. The regulations say in effect that the nation's media, especially the electronic media, have a duty to cooperate with the government's plan for press, radio and TV as a national resource. Television programs must be rated for their levels of sex and violence, and programs that generally go against Venezuelan values are prohibited. The new regulations have drawn mixed reviews—but they have also been thoroughly analyzed and debated in the media.

The 1978 presidential campaign showed all the country's media at their best. Venezuela has two major parties, the COPEI party (Comité de Organización Político Electoral Independiente) of Christian Democrats, and the Acción Democratica (AD), both moderately liberal. Also in the 1978 campaign were, among others, the socialist MAS (Movimiento Al Socialismo) and Independent parties (the latter's candidate now directs a new popular daily newspaper). The Supreme Electoral Council monitored the campaign, enforcing political advertising limits and upholding laws against inaccurate or defamatory propaganda. Approximately $100 million was spent for campaign advertising, most of it on television.

All of the major and most of the minor media covered the campaign conscientiously and objectively, analyzing and reporting a broad spectrum of opinions on the issues. Economic resources, not ideologies, were the final arbiters of how much propaganda any party could disseminate. Only one incident of campaign censorship occurred—when an issue of a weekly newsmagazine was confiscated for carrying an editorial allegedly disrespectful to the president.

Television—which is the country's largest advertising medium—was intensively used. While this medium has a shorter history than the press in politics, the 1973 and 1978 presidential elections established TV as the decisive element in forming public opinion. The Independents, COPEI and AD all hired U.S. media experts to run their campaigns, whose overall tone was sophisticated and vigorous. Venezuelans are required by law to vote, and every element of the nation's mass communication—from wall posters and soundtrucks to television—was freely used, to the point of saturation to sway the electorate.

Critics argue that Venezuela is losing its identity in the glut of unrestrained media material—a sizable portion of it foreign, and most of it blatantly consumerist—now available to the public. However, the 1978 presidential campaign pointed out the degree to which Venezuela's media have become institutionalized in a very short time. As late as 1957 freedom of the press existed in Venezuela only at the whim (which was seldom) of dictator Pérez Jiménez. In 1980

Venezuela was embroiled in a tripartite power struggle among government, business and the media in which each depended on—and contended with—the others, all with the goal of ultimately retaining public support.

Print media in Venezuela are both lively and varied. In 1979, the country had approximately 69 daily newspapers. There were also about 20 general-interest magazines and some 127 trade and institutional periodicals.

In spite of the increasing popularity of the electronic media, press circulation has soared in the last 20 years, because of the improved literacy rate and the heightened political consciousness of the population since the end of the dictatorships. Newspaper circulation doubled in the year following the overthrow of Pérez Jiménez in 1958. Average circulations for the leading dailies increased from 10,000 in 1945 to over 100,000 in the 1970s.

The press is based mainly in Caracas, although about a dozen cities (including Caracas) publish more than one paper. All but one are in the provinces north of the Orinoco River and concentrated in the highly populated area along the Caribbean coast. Maracaibo's leading daily, *Panorama*, rivals the leading Caracas dailies in both circulation and national influence.

Caracas supported 10 daily papers in 1980, at least six of which had circulations above 100,000. These are made available nationally through a very efficient air distribution system. One of the leading Caracas dailies, *El Nacional*, puts out a facsimile edition in Maracaibo. Geographic concentration of the population makes distribution to a large percentage of readers easy, but delivery to all parts of the interior is hardly less efficient and dependable

While the provincial press is growing in importance and resources, it is much more limited in scope than the national press in Caracas and, more recently, Maracaibo. Provincial papers stress local coverage and depend more heavily on the government-operated news agency, Venpres. Outside Caracas and Maracaibo, the circulation figures for dailies range from 3,000 to 25,000, with an average of 10,000.

El Nacional and *El Universal* are Venezuela's elite newspapers. Both are owned by families. *El Nacional*, independent and liberal, runs a Sunday supplement, "Séptimo Dia," considered the country's best. *El Universal*, also independent, is conservative, basically a businessman's paper; it also owns the national news agency, INAC.

Major Venezuelan Dailies

Newspaper	Circ.	Format	Date Founded	Ave. pp.
El Nacional	135,000	Standard; a.m.; Sun.	1943	130
El Universal	130,000	Standard; a.m.; Sun.	1909	130
Ultimas Noticias	160,000	Tabloid; a.m.; Sun.	1941	100
El Diario de Caracas	33,000	Tabloid; a.m.; Sun.	1979	30
El Mundo	110,000	Standard; p.m.	1958	30
2001	100,000	Standard; p.m.; Sun.	1973	30
Meridiano	100,000	Tabloid; a.m.; Sun.	1969	35
Panorama	95,000	Standard; a.m.; (Maracaibo) Sun.	1914	70
La Religion	10,000	Standard; a.m.	1890	
Daily Journal	13,000	Tabloid; a.m.; (English language); Sun.	1945	30

*Circulation figures are unreliable. ABC moved into Venezuela in 1973 after serving only *Panorama* and *El Nacional* for years.

Ultimas Noticias has the highest circulation of any Venezuelan daily. *El Diario de Caracas* is the country's newest daily. Started in May 1979 by an ex-presidential candidate and ex-governor of Caracas, Diego Arria, it has quickly become a very sophisticated tabloid with elite readership—even considered by some to be the best daily in Venezuela. *El Diario* has done some good social reporting and is the only Spanish-language paper in the country that runs regular editorials. Unfortunately, *El Diario* is in financial trouble.

El Mundo, 2001 and *Meridiano* are all large-circulation, popular dailies that emphasize sports, sensational news and entertainment. *Meridiano* and *2001* feature much color photography, but all three carry little serious news. *El Mundo* is published by the Capriles group, and *2001* belongs to the DeArmas empire.

La Religion is Venezuela's oldest newspaper; the official paper of the Catholic Church in Venezuela, it was founded in 1890. In 1974 economic conditions forced the paper to stop publication for seven months. It reappeared in 1975 with updated machinery and new personnel.

The *Daily Journal* is Venezuela's only English-language newspaper. Operated by U.S. nationals residing in Caracas, it publishes editorials in English and Spanish —the only major paper besides *El Diario* to run editorials regularly. Its circulation is low and its quality suffers from lack of modern equipment and money. The country's only

other foreign-language publications are small weekly papers published in Caracas by the city's Jewish, Italian, French and German communities.

Maracaibo's daily, *Panorama*, is a leading prestige newspaper with national distribution and an elite readership. It is owned by the Pineda family. Maracaibo is the hub of the oil-rich northwestern part of Venezuela and the second largest city. Other newspapers in the interior worth noting are the daily *Critica*, also of Maracaibo; *El Impulso*, published in Barquisimeto; and *El Caraboveño* in Valencia. These dailies are all located in fast-growing urban areas. The communist parties publish two small papers in the capital, *Punto* and *Tribuna Popular*, and there are a few other minority-owned publications catering to specialized interests.

Magazines and periodicals are popular in Venezuela and range in quality and prestige from pulp print sensationalist publications to glossy, elite newsmagazines similar in style and format to *Time*. Most periodicals and magazines are published in Caracas, and their circulations are much smaller than those of the leading dailies.

The most influential of the magazines are the newsweeklies *Bohemia, Elite, Resumen, Momento, Auténtico* and *Zeta*, which are popular among a smaller, more political audience. *Momento* and *Bohemia* are DeArmas publications; Capriles publishes *Elite*. Circulation figures are unreliable and can vary widely, depending on the source. Estimates range from about 30,000 to 60,000 for

Bohemia to about 5,000–10,000 for *Resumen*. Quality varies from serious, analytical news coverage in *Bohemia, Resumen* and *Auténtico* to the more general-interest approach of *Elite, Momento* and *Zeta*, which include popular features such as horoscopes, personality gossip and a fair amount of cheesecake with their news. *Número*, a new economics magazine founded in 1980, has won ready acceptance from business and government leaders. *Venezuela Gráfica* is a popular Capriles chain publication. The DeArmas group also publishes Spanish-language versions of several popular foreign magazines including *Popular Mechanics, Cosmopolitan, Good Housekeeping* and *Harper's Bazaar*.

As a whole, the media in Venezuela can be said to be nonpartisan in their approach to presenting information. Television and radio, licensed in the public interest, have little leeway in this area. News programs are short and straightforward, although talk shows and public affairs programs take more opinionated positions and they include a wide range of opinion on each issue. The press restrains its editorial power through a curious policy that is the legacy of Venezuela's years of repressive governments. Print media were forced to stop their editorials under dictatorships and never got back into the habit after democracy was established. Although editors will express their opinions on extraordinary occasions, they prefer not to dilute the power of the editorial through overuse. The tradition may be on its way out. As mentioned above, the *Daily Journal* recently began running its editorials in English and Spanish, and *El Diario de Caracas*, which has risen to such quick prominence, is the only other paper to run editorials in Spanish. Nonpartisanship in the press also derives from the fact that during the years of dictatorships, and even into the first decade of democratic governments, the media that tended to survive were those that were not affiliated with any narrow group or ideology.

The press is able to remain nonpartisan and present a broad segment of opinion by turning over its editorial pages to guest columnists. Writing mostly signed articles, they are political leaders, journalists or government or business representatives—all usually partisan and identified with specific political parties. Pseudonymous writers are also popular. By presenting a balance of opinions in this manner, the press provides readers with a broad spectrum of information and commentary.

Moreover, certain journalistic devices have been developed to inject editorial opinion. Papers use opinion roundups, cartoons, slanted headlines, and opinions inserted into news stories to add their own points of view. A favorite method of editorializing is the *mancheta*, a boxed, one-sentence headline found in the opinion pages. This usually makes pointed remarks about some item in the news.

Unfortunately, news is not always accurate. Venezuelan media suffer from occasional careless reporting, especially in the popular dailies and magazines. Sometimes errors result from a desire to sensationalize the news. According to *2001*, the United States invaded Iran four times in 1980. *Resumen* magazine has a reputation for unreliable information—resulting from its director's political zeal.

The weekly magazines can be classified as nonpartisan, but their editorial tone is set by the opinions of their directors. *Zeta* magazine, directed by Rafael Poleo, is extremely anti-Castro. *Resumen*'s Jorge Olavarria has a long history of running afoul of officialdom for his hard-hitting coverage of alleged government corruption, although in 1980 the position of the magazine was pro-government.

The general tone of news reporting is dull. Venezuelan journalists are often called *cronistas*, or chroniclers, as a result of their stiff, mechanical reporting. Verbatim transcripts of speeches and events are very common, and the style is verbose. It is the newsweeklies, with their editorial flavor, that lead the way in analytical and interpretive reporting. Television—and to a lesser extent radio—is becoming a major source of information and a significant public forum. Enterprise reporting about poverty and other social problems is increasing in all media. Documentaries on television and investigative features in the print media are finding greater acceptance. Several of the more serious newsweeklies indicate on their mastheads awards received for journalism. *Momento* and *Resumen* have each received the national journalism prize.

Other elements of Venezuelan media that are used by both private and government operations are wall posters and sound trucks. Despite the rising popularity of the electronic media, wall posters are still a significant element of mass communication in Venezuela, especially during elections, when they literally cover nearly all exposed public surfaces.

Economic Framework

Venezuela provides a case study in the impact of oil wealth on the growth of the media. The Venezuelan press has experienced consistent growth both in number of newspapers and in circulation ever since the oil boom began transforming the economy in the mid-1960s. The number of dailies has grown from 33 in 1965 to 69 in 1979; circulation from 608,000 to almost 2.5 million in 1979. In both respects, Venezuela leads all its Latin American neighbors where in many cases the press actually declined in the same period.

Venezuela's press ownership is totally private. Families and corporate enterprises control the largest dailies and most business periodicals and general-interest magazines. The bulk of the provincial and smaller press, as well as a few newsweeklies, are owned by individuals. Political parties have always maintained party newspapers, most of them weeklies, but no party owns any major media.

The two largest corporate publishing enterprises in Venezuela are Cadena Capriles and Grupo DeArmas. The respective founders, Miguel Angel Capriles and Armando DeArmas, began as partners in a small distribution venture. Capriles is one of Venezuela's most colorful journalists, DeArmas a self-made businessman. They went their own way after a short time. Today the Capriles chain owns magazines and several dailies, including *Ultimas Noticias*, a popular Caracas-based tabloid. The DeArmas company has branched out internationally. It operates the largest publishing concern in the Latin American market, Editorial America, located in Miami. In 1978 it produced 10 magazines and 24 special publications. Its 1977 revenues reached 128.76 million bolivares ($30 million), with profits of 4,292,000 bolivares ($1 million).

DeArmas distributes many Spanish-language versions of popular foreign magazines, and plans to begin publication of a series of half-sized, half-priced periodicals aimed at the lower-income market. Also projected (for 1984) is an English-language version of a popular Spanish magazine for the U.S. market.

Individual and corporate ownership—as well as cross-ownership—of media are common in Venezuela, but monopolies are illegal.

Price hikes of up to 50 percent in October of 1980 drove the cost of the average weekday paper to 1.50 bolivares (37 cents) and the Sunday edition to 2–2.50 bolivares (50–67 cents). Average prices for weekly magazines reached six bolivares ($1.50).

Newspaper advertising revenues have risen pari passu with circulation. Between 1972 and 1979 they grew threefold from $113 million to $374 million, placing Venezuela second only to Brazil in overall contribution of advertising to newspaper revenues.

Government advertising still makes up a significant part of press revenues, especially among the smaller circulation and provincial publications. Consumer advertising, which traditionally supports private media, has been on the increase. Broadcast media accounts for the largest percentage of total ad revenues. In 1980 the government's television entertainment medium, Channel 8, began accepting commercial ads.

Newspaper ad-to-news ratios vary but the majority of the leading media maintain at least 70:30. One exception is the new *El Diario de Caracas*, which permits only 30 percent advertisements.

Newsprint availability has not been a problem in Venezuela since 1973, when it was feared widespread shortages might cause the collapse of 20 dailies and up to 200 weeklies.

Salaries in the media, as determined by union scales, are relatively high with respect to the national economy. The average reporter's wage at a leading daily starts at about 51,600 bolivares ($12,000). An experienced editor earns from 77,400–94,600 bolivares ($18–22,000). In the smaller press and the electronic media, wages are considerably lower.

Venezuelan media have had a few labor problems in modernizing their operations, although in 1980 *El Nacional* was experiencing difficulty trying to computerize its operations and lay off about 100 printers.

The major labor union in the newspaper industry is the National Syndicate of Press Workers, which is affiliated with the communist-dominated International Organization of Journalists. Nevertheless, communist influence in the rank and file of journalists is muted and strikes are infrequent. Employers are better organized, being represented by two groups: Asociacion Venezolana de Periodistas and Bloque de Prensa.

The leading dailies and periodicals benefit from the very latest computerized technology, with the provincial and smaller press less well equipped. The major problem with the new technological devices is that not enough Venezuelans are skilled in their use. This accounts for a significant number of foreign specialists in many sectors of the Venezuelan economy.

Press Laws

Economics, politics, social conditions and traditions are still shaping Venezuelan communications policy. Economic development is providing the media with a growing marketplace of advertisers and consumers. Competition is strong for the advertising dollar and an audience. Government (which in Venezuela is centrally structured, giving the executive branch the lead in setting policy) seeks to prevent abuse of the media. All the Venezuelan constitutions have endorsed freedom of the press, but it has only been in the last 20 years that the government has allowed a significant amount of press freedom, and less than 10 since the people have grown to expect such freedom as a national norm.

In 1979 the Venezuelan government assured the Inter-American Press Association that it had no intention of controlling or regulating the country's private media. It said it would, instead, program its own media as an example for the others. But the private media have always been regulated in Venezuela, not only by the constitution, which outlines responsibilities as well as rights, but by the newest regulations on television content that went into effect in 1980 (tied to the start of color broadcasting).

The reasons for the government's focus on the electronic media are manifold. The comparatively low penetration of print as compared with broadcast media may be a reason. The press is more traditionally an opinion leader, and essentially the latest government regulations are not directed against news operations but rather at commercialism, cultural invasion, sex, violence and general social corruption. The early democratic governments resorted to controlling the media to maintain national order. With a sense of that order having been institutionalized, the state now seeks to use the media as a tool for education. Radio and TV, with their greater penetration, are best suited for the job.

Venezuela's government-media relationship is based not on news censorship, of which there is none, but on an ideological struggle over the necessary role of press and broadcast outlets. The relationship is based on laws, guidelines and traditional attitudes that define the proper use of the media as a public forum for debate as much as a giver of information.

The Venezuelan Constitution states, in Article 66, that everyone "has the right to express his thoughts by the spoken word or in writing, and to make use of every means of dissemination without prior censorship"; but "statements that constitute criminal offenses are subject to punishment." The 1961 constitution also forbids propaganda that incites disobedience to laws. Within this legal framework, the governments since 1958 at times have curtailed freedom of expression in pursuit of the national interest. President Betancourt suspended constitutional guarantees for 14 months during the communist crisis in the early 1960s, outlawing the Communist Party media. Extremist elements in the press were systematically weeded out during the entire decade, with the surviving media acquiring a marked degree of self-control in the process.

The constitution provides other guidelines that affect the media. It sets standards for the practice of professions; forbids monopolies; prohibits anonymous communications, propaganda for war or offenses against public morals. It also charges the Ministry of Communications with upholding the FCC-style laws that regulate the broadcast media.

The law further provides for professional secrecy regarding sources, except in criminal cases, and delegates control of foreign journalists to the Ministry of Work, which authorizes all hirings.

Licensing provisions in the press laws can be used to control those who anger the authorities, either in the country's domestic or international media, but such actions are rarely used. Foreign media and journalists have no trouble getting the necessary permits.

The main body of law governing the press is the Law of Journalism, passed in 1972. This sets up professional requirements for all journalists except editorial writers and those writing for in-house and special-interest publications. It also outlines violations, sanctions and guarantees, and requires registration by all journalists in the Colegio (the National Academy of Journalists). The law applies to all public information functions including the public relations arms of nonjournalistic institutions. Management personnel are not considered journalists.

There are laws protecting citizen privacy and prohibiting deceptive advertising. Libel laws exist, especially for offenses against the Venezuelan president, and there are regulations on the amount of political advertising permitted during the different stages of the 14-month-long presidential campaigns.

The Colegio is the main council that intercedes with the government in the media's behalf. As a journalism guild, it acts as the self-regulator of the press. The Venezuelan Association of Newspapermen (AVP), a professional union, is another significant press council that helps with self-regulation. Some AVP members are also politicians, which gives the union added influence.

The Bloque de Prensa and the local members of the Inter-American Press Association (IAPA) are the two main press groups that concentrate on protecting the economic interests of the print media. Bloque de Prensa is a wholly Venezuelan organization, representing not only the leading dailies in Caracas but dailies and weeklies throughout the country. The Bloque has been accused of favoring economic stability over criticism. Venezuela's leading daily, *El Nacional*, was forced to retire from the Bloque in the mid-1970s for editorially criticizing child pornography in a magazine owned by the DeArmas group, also a Bloque member. The fact that *El Nacional* had public support in the face of the ostracism made no difference.

Television and radio have their own special-interest lobbies, La Camara de la Television and Camara de la Radio.

While all the laws applying to press journalism also cover the broadcast media, the additional state policies regarding electronic outlets are all geared to molding the content of radio and television in a positive, socially uplifting and educational direction. Since the Carlos Andrés Pérez presidency of 1973–78, Venezuela has moved to develop the electronic media constructively. Pérez, himself a former journalist—as are many Venezuelan politicians—was deeply committed to the UNESCO guidelines for a new world information order, as well as to establishing Venezuela as a regional economic and political leader. The new regulations concerning the broadcast media signify a basic change in government policy from a passive, reactionary force against dissent and disorder toward an active, guiding power in shaping media as a national resource.

Two major new regulations that affect the content of the broadcast media are the Law of Education and the 1980 Regulations for Color Television. The former makes private media more responsible for programming in the national interest. It has been received negatively by broadcasters and advertisers as a threat to press freedom and as government interference in free enterprise. The color-television regulations banned all alcohol and tobacco advertising (which accounted for approximately 40 percent of the ad revenues of one of the privately owned channels) and set new limits on total commercial time per hour. It also added new restrictions on content judged detrimental to viewers, setting up a rating system for programs and a family viewing period from 6 to 10 p.m. daily. This restriction most affected the soap operas (*telenovelas*), which feature controversial topics.

Censorship

Press censorship was extremely rare by 1980. *Resumen*'s director has managed to run afoul of the government on several occasions because of his extremely bitter attacks on the president; one entire issue in 1978 was confiscated for carrying an article accusing the president of lining his pockets through corruption. In 1980, interestingly, the new party in power censured that now-former president for specific allegations of corruption similar to the accusations in *Resumen*.

Economic stability, institutionalization of democratic ideals, and the media's acquired self-control make censorship unnecessary while public opinion makes it unacceptable. As already mentioned, the government has been successful in passing restrictions on the ads and program content in the broadcast media—but only because it has had the support of the public.

State-Press Relations

Traditionally, censorship as practiced by Venezuela's dictatorships and early democratic governments was designed to suppress dissent against the government or to avoid embarrassment, both considered threats to an unstable state. Methods of enforcement included jailings, confiscations, closings, fines and suspensions. While these methods have not changed the new government communication policies provide a different framework within which the authorities exercise control over the media. In the mid-1970s, Channel 2—one of the major privately owned TV stations—was suspended for a short time because it aired an interview with representatives of the kidnappers of an American businessman. In 1980 Channel 2 was again suspended for a short time for broadcasting an expose of conditions in a government mental clinic; it was charged that the station violated the family-hour standards of positive program content. At the same time, officialdom permits *El Nacional* to run a front-page headline reporting that 62 percent of the people are unhappy with the government because of the high cost of living and rampant crime.

Although magazines, due to their more partisan positions, have suffered the most government suppression in recent years, all the media experienced official intervention even to the end of the 1970s. In 1971 a television station charged that the government arrested and beat up four reporters and destroyed their film of student riots. In 1976 police entered the offices of *El Nacional* to discourage publication of a terrorist letter of demands in the kidnapping of a U.S. business executive. Several of Venezuela's best-known journalists have been charged, arrested or jailed for overstepping government limits on the broadcast or publication of sensitive information.

Special-interest lobbying by the business sector has at times been indirectly responsible for press censorship. In the early 1960s *El Nacional* was accused by elements in the business sector of having a pro-communist, anti-United States slant. Led by officials of several U.S.-owned firms, including Sears Roebuck, the business community started an advertising boycott of the paper. Faced with bankruptcy, *El Nacional* surrendered and fired several reporters. Its editor also resigned.

The government has been accused of using expropriation as a criminal sanction. Owens-Illinois's Venezuela holdings were expropriated in 1976 following the company's payment for the publication of a communique sent by kidnappers of one of the company's U.S. executives. The government denies punishment as a motive for its act.

Government advertising has long been a potent weapon with which to promote media compliance with state policies. Newspapers are more susceptible than magazines, and rural papers more so than the large urban dailies. Television and radio remained largely unaffected until 1980, when the government began accepting commercials on Channel 8, its state entertainment outlet, and also moved to limit both the total ad time on television and the products advertised, banning alchohol and tobacco commercials. How this will affect the economic vitality of private television remains to be seen, but it should work to make the networks less economically stable.

In a typical incident involving the press in the 1970s, a government official made a telephone call to the owner of *2001* because of dissatisfaction with the support the newspaper was giving to the opposition. The caller threatened the loss of government advertising, and soon after, the owner replaced several journalists with reporters more sympathetic toward the incumbent administration.

Attitude Toward Foreign Media

Foreign correspondents in Venezuela have no trouble getting visas but they may write only for foreign publications while in the country. The hiring of foreign journalists to work for Venezuelan media is under the control of the Ministry of Work. Journalists need valid credentials while under contract in Venezuela.

The policies relating to the operation of foreign media and foreign journalists include limits on ownership, accreditation requirements for journalists, and certain other restrictions designed to protect national interests.

In 1974 the government ordered all foreign investors to sell any interests in Venezuelan broadcast media amounting to more than 20 percent. This policy was in keeping with similar government moves in business, where efforts are being made to return control of Venezuela's economy to Venezuelans.

The Colegio laws apply to all foreign journalists working in the country. There are no import restrictions on foreign publications although the government limited the importation of large television sets in order to give the domestic industry a chance to get on its feet before the introduction of color broadcasting.

The American news agencies, AP and UPI, have complained of high government rates on transmission lines into the interior, ostensibly to favor the official Venpres.

Sensitive over what it considers a bias in

the international news flow, the government reacted strongly in 1976 when UPI erroneously reported—for a short time—the assassination of Colombian President Adolfo López Michelsen over its international wires. The UPI contract with the state television was cancelled. Foreign journalists also were detained, jailed and expelled for violating Venezuelan policy against embarrassing or destablizing news in the early democratic years. In 1976 three U.S. reporters were detained and expelled for covering terrorist activities to which the government was sensitive. The reporters maintained they were thrown out for discovering an embarrassing connection between the Venezuelan security police and a known Cuban CIA informant working as one of the country's top security officials.

The Venezuelan government actively supports the concepts of UNESCO's "new world information order." On an international level, Venezuelans are helping to organize a new OPEC news agency, to be based in Vienna. In 1979 the official Venezuelan domestic news agency, Venpres, joined with domestic agencies in Colombia, Ecuador, Peru, Bolivia, Panama, Costa Rica, the Dominican Republic, Jamaica and Suriname to form ASIN (Acción de Sistemas Informativos Nacionales: Action by National Information Systems) to provide for the regional exchange of news and offer a more balanced flow of Latin American news to the rest of the world.

The government also feeds Venpres and ministry information through its embassies and consulates to governments and media around the world. Foreign governments regularly disseminate propaganda and information materials inside Venezuela or beam in radio. The Voice of America alone places approximately 175 hours of packaged programs a month on 36 radio stations. Other countries also beam in short-wave transmissions.

Venezuela had no foreign reporters anywhere prior to 1973, but by 1980 the leading dailies maintained correspondents in Latin America, North America, and Europe.

News Agencies

Venpres the government-operated agency, provides a domestic news service by teletype, free to urban and provincial newspapers. Its coverage is naturally pro-government, but it is a useful news source for the major media. Provincial and smaller papers rely on it even more. Venpres uses its own journalists and limits Caracas service to its own coverage. In the interior, however, it also carries ANSA (Italian) and Reuters (British) news.

Venpres was incorporated in 1977 into the Ministry of Information and Tourism. The ministry has control of all the ways a democratic government can intervene in the mass-communications process. Its duties are to coordinate all the information, advertising, and promotional material of all the government agencies and manage all government revenues spent on advertising. The ministry also manages all official printing, audiovisual productions, and advertising campaigns; researches public opinion, and sets cinema and tourist rates.

All the major news agencies sell or give away their services in Venezuela. AP, UPI, Reuters, AFP, ANSA, EFE, dpa, NCNA, LATIN, Prensa Latina, Tass and Novosti are all represented in Caracas. Venezuelan papers also have Venpres and *El Universal*'s national news agency, INAC, as well as a variety of special services from *The New York Times, Newsweek, U.S. News & World Report, Time* and the *Christian Science Monitor* to serve them. INAC serves only ten clients due to personnel and equipment limitations. A new agency, Agencia Venezolana de Noticias (AVN), was started in 1980 by a U.S. citizen who formerly served as a press official for the Venezuelan government.

Electronic News Media

The government operates a radio and television network. Television began in Venezuela as a state-owned station in 1953. In 1979 there were over 1.5 million receivers including an estimated 90,000 color sets, this despite the fact that Venezuela had no color broadcasting until the end of that year. Television is found in many public places and there is much group viewing. Venezuelans have near-total exposure to TV, and are regular viewers.

The state network, Televisoras Nacionales, broadcasts an entertainment service, Channel 8, and an educational service on Channel 5. All Venezuelan television is based in Caracas but is made available throughout the country through a series of transmitter and repeater stations that numbered 44 in 1979. One government channel uses no relays. Its transmission tower is located on one of the mountains near Caracas and reaches the most heavily populated areas in the north—stretching from Maracaibo to Caracas. The government radio network transmits nationally through affiliates in the interior. Radio has over 92 percent penetration in Venezuela, and although primarily an entertainment medium, government uses it in its national development programs. In 1973 a small radio station was placed in the wild area south of the Orinoco to broadcast in Spanish, the official language, and four Indian dialects still spoken in that area. The government also plans to extend its radio to all of the Caribbean by 1983. The service would be a "Voice of Venezuela" type of propaganda program.

The official channels have significantly lower ratings than the commercial networks. Government broadcast media as a whole are comparatively small and low-budget in comparison with the commercial media. The state radio network has conducted "radio schools" to teach literacy and other basic subjects to adults, but it is only recently that the government has begun to pay serious attention to the potential of radio and television. In 1980 the government television network began accepting commercial advertisements.

Venezuela had no color transmission until December 1979, because the government considered it wasteful and frivolous. Part-time color transmission was permitted on only Channel 5 for six months before approval of full-time color broadcasting on all networks in June 1980. Venezuela chose the American NSIC system when it began color broadcasting.

In 1980 there were two Caracas-based commercial television networks, and license applications were in process for new stations in Maracaibo and Barquisimeto. Commercial telecasting originated shortly after government TV, and developed as an entertainment medium. Maracaibo had a television station for a short time in the early 1960s, but in 1980 all domestic programs were produced in Caracas.

The daily schedule of programming consists of imported entertainment series (mostly of U.S. origin) and old movies, locally produced game and variety shows, *telenovelas* (soap operas) and public affairs programs. News programs are short and straightforward, while talk shows depend more on the opinions of the host. Sports are popular.

The commercial networks produce *telenovelas*, which are marketed through a free-zone office in Miami to all Latin American countries except Cuba. Novela series can run up to 200 hours, and Venezuela's products are sophisticated and well made. Indeed, *telenovelas* and game programs are the most common local product. News shows and public affairs programming are improving in both quality and quantity after years of neglect.

Imported television shows, especially U.S. products, account for a significant portion of the programming. Seventy-five percent of all households had TV sets in 1980, and more than 90 percent of the population lived in areas reached by the medium. In 1971 Venezuela installed an earth satellite station.

Television stations are granted licenses by the government to operate in the public interest. In 1974 Venezuela restricted foreign ownership to 20 percent in electronic media. U.S. broadcasting networks owned interests in Venezuelan television, but their shares amounted to only 10 percent.

The commercial networks are owned by corporate enterprises. Radio Caracas Television, on Channel 2, has distinguished itself as a vigorous, hard-hitting station, a fact that has given it trouble with the government on some occasions. The owners, the Phelps family, also have interests in a radio chain and one of the leading Caracas dailies. Vene-Vision, Channel 4, is owned by the Cisneros family, with interests in radio stations, grocery stores and other businesses throughout the country.

Television received approximately 50 percent of total ad revenues in 1980, compared to 40 percent for newspapers and 10 percent for radio. Magazines did very poorly. Television ratings are performed by DATOS, a private marketing survey company. The ratings in early 1980 gave Channel 2 a 24 percent share, Channel 4 a 30 percent share, government Channel 5 a .5 percent share and government Channel 8 a five percent share.

Radio's historical tradition in Venezuela is as an entertainment medium. It became practically universal following the introduction of the transistor in the 1960s. Because of its penetration, radio is extremely important in Venezuela. In 1980, 92 percent of all homes had radios. (There were also approximately 500,000 car radios.) Nationwide, these radios picked up approximately 168 stations, including one FM station (in Caracas). There were three commercial networks—Radio Tropical, Radio Rumbos and Radio Continente—but most stations remained independent and network affiliates seldom carried the entire Caracas-based transmissions.

The networks and chains are owned by families or corporate enterprises, provincial stations mostly by families or individuals; some in the larger cities also are affiliated with a chain or network. A number of provincial stations are linked to the government network.

Stations are licensed to operate in the public interest. They may rent their licenses to other individuals. Unlike television stations, radio stations rent out air time for entertainment programming. The practice is common with small stations.

Most programming is locally oriented, a mixture of continual commercials, pop music, a "screaming headlines" style of newscasting, and sports.

Foreign governments beam broadcasts into Venezuela, and local embassies and foreign information services disseminate reams of information and propaganda material, but the most significant impact of foreign media material is in the consumerist advertising and entertainment programs that flood commercial television. This is one of the government's main areas of concern in the media.

Education & Training

Journalism training for print and broadcast media is offered at three state universities and one private school. Central University in Caracas has a fine physical plant, and the University of Zulia and the University of the Andes, both in the interior, also offer good programs based on theoretical and practical experience. Andrés Bello Catholic University in Caracas, a private school, also offers a four-year program. All state education is free in Venezuela, including universities, and there is not enough space yet to accommodate all applicants.

Summary

In Venezuela, the communication media have played a greater role since 1958 in teaching political and social values. They have joined public schools, unions and local political organizations in replacing the family and church as the primary molder of the individual.

It can be argued that the media issue in Venezuela has shifted from censorship to control, but it must also be recognized that the public—and its opinion—has grown in power during the two decades of freedom since 1958. The public supported the government when it curtailed a bombardment of political insults, but it would not support a limit to real freedom of expression.

In 1980 Venezuela still had that freedom, but the goverment had—and still has—more weapons of control than ever before. Colegio laws have been strengthened. Newspapers are being pressured by the Colegio to add clauses to labor contracts, to prevent owners from participating in news handling. Some media people see management losing control of news, leaving it in the hands of journalists. Reporter power will grow.

The president often criticizes television, but there has been no talk of nationalizing the broadcast industry. Private broadcasters fear the trend in the 1980s is toward total government engulfment of the commercial electronic media, or at least of television. A pan-media council was formed recently to point out and fight government incursions into press freedom.

The government takes regular criticism from press, radio and TV for its failures and unpopular moves, and it responds to public opinion as reflected in those media. In the mid-1970s an official memorandum was circulated to newspaper editors, instructing them to confirm all information about the executive branch with the secretary general of the presidency or with the Ministry of Information. The memorandum caused such an outcry in the press that the government backed away, claiming it had only tried to increase the accuracy of the information process.

In a speech in August 1980 the president oulined the government's communications policy, calling for the creation of strong Latin American and other regional news agencies, to counter bias in the international news flow controlled by U.S. and European wire services. The speech reaffirmed the administration's commitment to the need to orient the mass media within the social context to which Venezuela aspires. Media were described as a public service, and the right to be informed was given priority over the right to inform. The president pledged to guarantee freedom of expression as the only acceptable proof of the sincerity of the government's new information order.

In spite of its economic and political stability, Venezuela has undergone a restless period until very recently. As late as 1977 guerrillas in the remote interior provinces were still fighting government forces. Even in 1979 labor unrest led to student riots. In that same year the new government ushered in a degree of austerity to counter the wild expansion that came in the wake of the 1973 oil boom. Consolidation and diversification of the economy is the theme for the 1980s. Regional ambitions have cooled somewhat for lack of money, and also because Venezuela's neighbors balk at her ambition to become an economic and political leader in the region.

If the government can make progress toward its ambitious goals of economic and social development, it can maintain public support as it contends with the business sector and the media in pursuing its policies. Any major dissension among these three national powers may result in the polarization of the population, thus weakening the national stability that is the basis for continued freedom of expression. Tied as they are into the fabric of a working democracy, business, government and the media all have a reason for acting to maintain public support. This is the challenge of the 1980s for Venezuela.

CHRONOLOGY

1971   Police arrest and beat up four Venezuelan TV reporters, destroy their film of student riots. Station complains, police apologize.

1972   Law of Journalism passed.

1973   *Punto*, new communist party paper, begins publication.

1974   Government limits foreign investment in broadcast media to maximum total of 20 percent.

1976   Venezuela expels three U.S. reporters for vague reasons relating to their coverage of terrorist activities. Reporters claim it is because they recognized the number two man in Venezuelan security as former Cuban CIA informer.

Television Channel 2 temporarily suspended for airing interview with representatives of kidnappers of a U.S. business executive.

Police enter *El Nacional* to discourage publication of letter written by kidnappers of Owens-Illinois executive.

Owens-Illinois's Venezuela holdings expropriated soon after company pays for publica-

tion of communique sent by the executive's kidnappers.

UPI wire service contracts cancelled and service reduced to Venezuelan television after false alarm on assassination of Colombian president.

1978   *Resumen* magazine director Jorge Olavarría has two run-ins with government for libelous articles on president; is charged and seeks asylum in Nicaraguan embassy; later goes to Miami.

1979   Venpres forms regional news agency, ASIN, with nine Latin American nations.

Olmedo Lugo of *El Nacional* jailed in Caracas for writing article charging Ministry of Information official with taking kickbacks on government advertising.

1980   Color television regulations set new moral standards and advertising limits for television.

Channel 2 temporarily suspended for airing controversial program about government mental hospitals during family time.

BIBLIOGRAPHY

Anuario Estadistico. Caracas, annually.

Blank, David E. *Politics in Venezuela.* Boston, 1973.

Composición de Programas en las Teleemisoras Comerciales. Caracas, 1968.

Country Data Sheet. Caracas: U.S. Embassy, 1980.

Documentos Fundamentales Para Una Mejor Comprension de la Politica de Comunicación Social del Estado Venezolano. Caracas, 1980.

Inter-American Press Association. *Report of the Committee on Freedom of the Press and Information.* Miami, annually.

Mújica, Héctor. *Sociologia Venezolana de la Comunicación.* Caracas, 1974.

Ortíz, Gabriel. *La Prensa Entre la Lealtad y el Miedo.* Bogotá, 1976.

Pérez, Carlos Andrés. *Information for Freedom.* Caracas, 1976.

Pierce, Robert N. *Keeping the Flame.* New York, 1979.

Rivera, Marta Colomina de. *El Huesped Alienante.* Caracas, 1967.

The Media in Venezuela. Caracas: U.S. Embassy, 1973.

UNESCO. *World Communications.* Paris, 1975.

Venneman, Howard, ed. *Venezuela at the Polls.* Washington, D.C., 1980.

Weil, Thomas E., et al. *Area Handbook for Venezuela.* Washington, D.C., 1971.

YUGOSLAVIA

by Paul Underwood

BASIC DATA

Population: 22,274,000 (1980)
Area: 255,892 sq. km. (98,800 sq. mi.)
GNP: D981.667 billion (US$53.790 billion)
(1979)
Literacy Rate: 80.3%
Language(s): Serbo-Croatian, Slovene,
Macedonian
Number of Dailies: 27
  Aggregate Circulation: 2 million
  Circulation per 1,000: 89.8
Number of Nondailies: 2,512
  Aggregate Circulation: 13.47 million
  Circulation per 1,000: 619
Number of Periodicals: 1,500

Number of Radio Stations: 23 (including 14
local stations)
Number of Television Stations: 9
Number of Radio Receivers: 4,548,000
  Radio Receivers per 1,000: 209
Number of Television Sets: 3,701,000
  Television Sets per 1,000: 170
Total Annual Newsprint Consumption: 78,800
metric tons (1977)
  Per Capita Newsprint Consumption: 3.6 kg.
(7.92 lb.) 1977
Total Newspaper Ad Receipts: NA
  As % of All Ad Expenditures: NA

Background & General Characteristics

Yugoslavia, the largest country in the Balkans, is a Communist-ruled state that by Soviet standards operates in a very unorthodox fashion. It is a federation of six republics: Serbia, Croatia, Bosnia-Herzogovina, Slovenia, Macedonia and Montenegro. Two autonomous provinces—the Vojvodina and Kosovo-Metohija—are officially a part of Serbia. Despite rapid industrialization since World War II, the economy is still heavily agricultural. Industry tends to be concentrated in the north, with the south relatively underdeveloped despite considerable investment there in recent years.

The country is one of the most ethnically diverse in Europe, even though the majority of its more than 22 million people are Slavs. Its varied component peoples are marked by differences in tradition and outlook that have made their relationship since their union in 1918 an uneasy one. Many of these differences stem from the fact that Yugoslavia straddles one of the most persistent dividing lines in history. Here lay the frontier between the Eastern and Western Roman Empires;

between the Greek Orthodox and Roman Catholic Churches; between Islam, represented by the invading Turks, and Christendom; between the Latin and Cyrillic alphabets. These divisions forced the development of the people of the region along different paths. As a result, their descendants today are aware of their differences from one another despite their common ethnicity.

The Slavs have not always been in the Balkans. They slowly drifted down from their original homeland in what is now western Russia during the chaos that followed the breakup of the Old Roman Empire. By the end of the seventh century they had reached and overspread much of the Balkan Peninsula. Lingering Roman and, later, Venetian influences remained strong along the Adriatic littoral, but to the east the overwhelming attraction was the sumptuous civilization of the Byzantine Empire. The national characters of the various units making up the Yugoslav Federation are still marked by these and other similar influences.

The Slovenes, who live in the northwestern corner of the country—tucked in next to the Austrian and Italian frontiers—have never had a unified state of their own. They have their own separate language and are predominantly Roman Catholic, as are their neighbors immediately to the east, the Croats. The latter are much more numerous, however. There are about 4.5 million of them, compared to little more than 1.5 million Slovenes. Unlike the Slovenes, the Croats, after periods of Frankish and then Byzantine domination, were able to establish an independent kingdom, which lasted until 1102 A.D. when King Kaloman of Hungary also became king of Croatia. As in the case of Slovenia, this union was dissolved only with the collapse of the Austro-Hungarian Empire. However, the greater part of Dalmatia, along the Adriatic Coast, passed under Venetian control and was separate from Croatia for many centuries.

It is at the border between Croatia and Serbia, the next republic to the east, where the differences most strain the national fabric. While the Serbs and the Croats speak essentially the same language, the Croats use the Latin alphabet, the Serbs, the Cyrillic. The Croats are Roman Catholic, the Serbs are Orthodox. While the Croats constituted part of the West's military frontier against the Turkish sweep into Europe, the Serbs lived under the Turkish yoke for more than 400 years after their empire fell under the sweep. However, Serbia is the largest republic in the federation with more than eight million people.

South of Serbia lies Macedonia, which was ruled by the Byzantines, the Bulgarians and the Serbs before the Turkish invasion. The Macedonians are Orthodox, like the Serbs. They also use the Cyrillic alphabet but they speak a different, though related language. In their case, freedom from the Turks came only in 1912.

Bosnia-Herzogovina lies to the west of Serbia and south of Croatia. Its people are mainly Serbs or Croats, Orthodox and Roman Catholic, speaking the common language and using both alphabets. A complicating factor is a large Moslem population—40 percent of the total—who are descendants of medieval Bosnians who elected to embrace Islam after the Turks wiped out their independent kingdom in the aftermath of the Serbian defeat.

The last of the six constituent republics is Montenegro, which straddles the barren mountains just north of Albania, in an almost inaccessible natural fortress. Its people succeeded in staving off recurring invasions to remain a small island of liberty in

the Turkish sea that engulfed the Balkans. The Montenegrins are predominantly Orthodox; they speak Serbo-Croatian and use the Cyrillic alphabet.

Wedged in between Montenegro and Macedonia along the Albanian frontier is the autonomous province of Kosovo-Metohija. Its population is almost 75 percent Albanian and Moslem. The Albanian language is used, along with Serbo-Croatian, in administration and public activity, including the media. But the most ethnically diverse area of the country is the Vojvodina, which lies to the north, between Serbia proper and Hungary. Its population includes more than 30 different ethnic groups, the most important of which, in addition to Serbs and Croats, are Hungarians, Slovaks, Rumanians and Ruthenians.

Illiteracy is still a problem, particularly in the south. It is officially acknowledged that about 15 percent of the population is illiterate, despite concerted efforts. Yugoslavia has made considerable progress since the days before World War II when it was one of the poorest countries in Europe, but it still has not pulled up to the level of the richer Communist-ruled neighbors, such as East Germany or Czechoslovakia. Its per capita income of just over 119,410 dinar ($1,800) puts it in the ranks of the medium-developed nations.

Despite the fact that Yugoslavia is a Communist-ruled state, its newspapers and broadcast news operations resemble those of the West much more than those of their Soviet-bloc neighbors, both in appearance and content. The quality of reporting and comment is high, and while there are restrictions and controls, the degree of freedom enjoyed by news people is unsurpassed by any other Communist-ruled country.

Printing presses were set up in Montenegro and Croatia in the last part of the 15th century and later appeared in Bosnia, Serbia and Slovenia. These were limited to the production of religious works, however. Neither political nor economic conditions were conducive to the development of the press. In fact, the first periodicals in any of the South Slav languages were printed outside the borders of present-day Yugoslavia, beginning with the *Slaveno-Serbski Magazin,* which appeared in Venice in 1768. The first Serbian-language newspaper, the *Serbskija Novini,* was published in Vienna in 1791.

The first newspaper to be published within the territory of Yugoslavia, and also the first to be published in Slovenian, was the *Ljubl-*

janske Novice, which appeared in Ljubljana, the Slovenian capital, from 1797 to 1800. In the 1780s the Austrian Emperor Joseph II had permitted publication of a newspaper for Croats called the *Kroatischer Korrespondent,* but it had to be printed in German. Napoleon's administration in Dalmatia also allowed one called the *Kraljiski Dalmatin* to be published at Zadar, on the Adriatic, from 1806 to 1810. But the real beginning of the Croatian press dates from 1835, when Ljudevit Gaj founded the weekly *Narodna Novine* ("People's Paper") in Zagreb, the Croatian capital.

The first newspaper to be printed in Serbia was the *Novine Serbske,* which appeared at Kragujevac in 1834. *Vestnik* of Novi Sad was the first in the Vojvodina in 1848.

The Serbs rose in revolt in 1804, under the leadership of George Petrovic, better known as Karageorge. For nine years they held off the Turks before resistance collapsed in 1813. Two years later it was renewed under the leadership of Milos Obrenovich and this time the Serbs were more successful, winning a grant of autonomy that enabled them to go their own way even though unqualified independence did not come until 1878. This Serbian success encouraged Gaj, who was deeply imbued with the ideas of Panslavism. For his paper and his other writing, he chose from the various forms of spoken Croatian what is known as the "sto" dialect and gave it a Latin alphabet. This became the model for modern written Croatian. At almost the same time, a Serb named Vuk Karadzic compiled a Serbian dictionary and worked out a modernized spelling, also based on the "sto" dialect. The adoption of this dialect as a written language by the two peoples simultaneously became a determining factor in the development of the region.

After the wave of revolutions that swept Europe in 1848, the press led a precarious existence, harried by arbitrary governments. Even the areas under Austro-Hungarian rule suffered. By the end of the 1850s only eight papers survived in all the South Slav lands. One of these was the first Serbian language daily, the *Srbski Dvenik,* which first appeared in 1852 at Novi Sad, in the Vojvodina.

The climate soon began to change, however. Vienna relaxed its controls in Croatia and Slovenia. The first Croatian daily, *Obzor* ("Survey"), was established in 1860. In Serbia, Prince Milos had been succeeded by his son, Michael, who actually encouraged the press. By 1867, 24 Serbian, 20 Croatian and

11 Slovene newspapers and periodicals were on the market.

The second half of the 19th century witnessed the birth of newspapers in other sections of what was to become Yugoslavia. The first to be published in Bosnia-Herzegovina—the *Bosanski Vjestnik*—appeared in Sarajevo in 1866, the first in Montenegro—the *Crnogorac*—in 1871, and the first in Kosovo-Metohija—the *Prizren*—in the same year. By 1880 the number of newspapers and periodicals in the region had increased to almost 200.

In Serbia, this development was aided by the adoption of a constitution in 1889 that guaranteed freedom of the press. Although the constitution was set aside from 1893 to 1903, it provided the foundation for democratic development. But Serbia was the only part of the South Slav world to enjoy such freedoms. Vienna kept the press in Slovenia and Croatia on a tight rein and suppressed all papers in Bosnia when it annexed that area. In Montenegro the controls were almost as tight, while the Turks still barred the publication of any periodicals in the lands they ruled.

The restoration of the constitution in 1903 supplied a spark that led to a press explosion in Serbia. As early as 1905, 20 dailies were published in Belgrade, and by 1910, 775 new papers and journals had been founded. Most of them were mouthpieces of political parties or groups, highly partisan but not very informative. One notable exception was the Belgrade daily *Politika,* which had been founded in 1903 by the Ribnikar daily. It tried to present as complete and impartial news coverage as possible and soon became recognized as the best in the country.

World War I broke out in 1914 following the assassination of the Austrian Archduke Franz Ferdinand in the Bosnian city of Sarajevo. Despite initial triumphs, Serbia and Montenegro were occupied by German and Austrian forces. All newspapers were suppressed. Only authorized publications of the occupying armies were permitted. In Croatia and Slovenia severe censorship was imposed; even tighter controls were the rule in Bosnia-Herzogovina.

The surrender of Germany and Austro-Hungary in 1918 opened the way for the unification of the South Slav peoples. A Kingdom of the Serbs, Croats and Slovenes was proclaimed in December of that year. (It was renamed the Kingdom of Yugoslavia in 1929.) Most of the newspapers that had been suppressed were soon able to resume publication. New ones also appeared. Shortly after its formation the new state boasted 61 daily papers. Many of these were short-lived, however. Between 1921 and 1939, the number of newspapers and periodicals being published ranged at various times all the way from 648 up to 1,108.

The immediate postwar years also saw the establishment of the first Yugoslav news agency, called Avila, which began by issuing a daily news bulletin in French for the foreign press. Later it established links with foreign agencies and began supplying a service to the domestic press.

The new state ran into difficulties at the start. The Serbs who wanted a centralized regime with Belgrade in control clashed with the Croats and others who demanded a decentralized federal union. A new constitution providing for a centralized system was finally adopted in 1921, but opposition not only remained strong but actually increased as the decade wore on. For the press, too, this constitution was a step backwards. Freedoms were actually more restricted than under the 1889 document.

Internal divisions festered and were reflected in a press that was increasing in numbers but also increasingly partisan. Finally, in 1929, King Alexander suspended the constitution and established a royal dictatorship. All political parties were abolished and censorship imposed. Much of the party press simply disappeared or went underground. Among these were two Communist publications, *Borba* and *Kommunist*—names that would become prominent in the future.

Alexander was assassinated in 1934. His brother, Prince Paul, was named regent for Alexander's 12-year-old son, King Peter. Under Paul's administration controls were eased but not abandoned.

By 1937 Yugoslavia counted 50 dailies, printed in six different languages. Most of them were comparatively small. The largest was *Politika,* with 146,000 circulation. Two other Belgrade papers, *Vreme* and *Pravda,* followed with 65,000 and 45,000, respectively. Next came two Zagreb dailies, *Novesti* with 23,000 and *Jutarnji List* with 21,000.

When World War II broke out, the Yugoslav government succeeded in staying neutral despite strong Nazi pressure. But in 1941 it finally bowed to Berlin and signed a pact with the Axis. Public indignation ran high, and two days later the regime was overthrown and a new anti-Axis government installed. The Germans and Italians retaliated by invading the country and crushing the Yugoslav armies within two weeks. The country was divided up; the Germans, Italians, Bulgarians and Hungarians all staked out areas of occupation. They also set up a rump Croatian state under a Nazi-style regime. Newspapers and radio stations were seized and only official occupation organs were allowed to publish.

Resistance continued in the countryside, however. Guerrilla bands harried Axis communication lines. Underground newspapers appeared to keep the people informed and to further the fight for liberation. Two main groups of resistance fighters emerged: the Chetniks, who were anti-Communist and generally favored the Serbian royal house, and the Communist-led pro-federation Partisans. They fought each other while fighting the invaders, a struggle finally won by the Partisans under their leader, Josip Broz, better known as Tito.

According to official records, the Partisan side alone published 3,648 periodicals—newspapers, journals and bulletins—as well as 5,468 books and pamphlets during the war. The best known of their papers was *Borba,* the same one that had been forced underground back in the 1920s, which was now the organ of the Central Committee of the Yugoslav Communist Party.

Belgrade was liberated in October 1944, and within a week newspapers were on sale in its streets. *Politika* reappeared to take its place alongside *Borba* and other Partisan papers. The Ribnikars had aided Tito before the war and many of *Politika*'s staff had fought with the Partisans, so the papers was able to resume operations without difficulty.

By January 1945, 30 papers were being published throughout the country, most of them former Partisan publications. Rebirth of the pre-war party press was severely restricted by censorship. Later that year, with the war in Europe ended and Partisan control of the country assured, a special Constituent Assembly declared the monarchy ended and a Federal Peoples' Republic established. Laws were passed nationalizing all means of production, including press organizations, printing houses, paper mills and radio transmitters. All institutions of society were reorganized on the Soviet model.

The press's role was to serve as a mouthpiece of the Communist Party and to propagandize its plans and aims. Ministries of information were set up in each of the six constituent republics as well as on the federal level to supervise and monitor the press. Content was checked before publication. The

Tanjug news agency, which had been organized by the Partisans during the war, held a monopoly on the internal distribution of news.

A 1946 press law limited the right to publish to political parties, trade unions and official groups. Publications were subsidized by the government and administered by Party-approved directors. Newsprint, equipment and other materials were supplied by the government. The law guaranteed freedom of the press, but this was highly qualified. In addition to prohibiting the distribution of publications encouraging revolt, sabotage and the overthrow of the socialist system, it punished the spreading "of false information that threatened the national interest." One of Tito's top aides was quoted later as explaining that the law "gives almost unlimited freedom of expression, excluding from this liberty only quislings. It protects the benefits of democracy against those who, by abusing civil liberties, seek to violate the constitutional order with anti-democratic aims in view. Through its just distribution of newsprint and its nationalization of the large printing works, the state has given the press real material aid and the possibility of developing itself into a really free press."

In 1948 Yugoslavia was expelled from the Cominform and boycotted by all Soviet-bloc states. Tito and his aides were forced to rethink their system, and they devised a new structure less rigid than the Soviet model. A keystone was the concept of workers' self-management, which meant a dwindling away of state ownership and the decentralization of authority in many areas of society, including the media. In essence, workers' self-management means that the people who work in any particular enterprise run that enterprise with a minimum of interference from central authority. This has widened enormously the scope and effectiveness of the Yugoslav press. The Party is still there to see that bounds are not overstepped and controls are tightened or relaxed from time to time in response to both external and internal developments, but the Yugoslav media give their readers and listeners a more complete and more accurate picture of the world than is available in any other Communist-ruled country.

More than 2,500 newspapers, including 27 dailies, are now published in Yugoslavia, as well as just over 1,500 periodicals. In addition, there are 196 weeklies, as well as 10 papers that are published several times a week but not daily. Three of the dailies are specialist publications, two covering sports and the third economics and business. Sixteen of the general dailies are morning papers and seven are eveningers. The average total circulation of all 27 is over two million copies.

Since the decentralization policy pursued by the Tito regime included the press, each of the republics and the autonomous regions has its own newspapers and broadcast operations, including papers in both the majority and minority languages of the area. A total of 64 papers, including three of the dailies, are published in nine different languages: Albanian, Bulgarian, Czech, Hungarian, Italian, Rumanian, Ruthenian, Slovak and Turkish. The three minority-language dailies are *Magyar Szo* of Novi Sad (Hungarian), *La Voce del Populo* of Rijeka (Italian) and *Rilindja* of Pristina (Albanian). Three of the majority-language dailies are published in Slovene, two in Macedonian and the rest in Serbo-Croatian. Religious organization publish more than 127 periodicals, including newspapers as well as magazines and journals. The only political orientation permitted is Communist.

Another group of specialized publications has come into existence since the promulgation of the nation's most recent constitution in 1974. This established an elaborate pyramidal system of local, regional, and republic assemblies, each choosing delegates to the next highest, culminating in the national parliament, the Skupcina. The republics started issuing papers for the information of the delegates, and now even some of the larger towns and communes are doing the same. Some of these are independent publications, others are issued as bulletins or as supplements of standard newspapers.

Most Yugoslav newspapers are full size but several are tabloid, including *Politika* and *Vecernje Novosti,* the top two in the nation in terms of circulation. All of them print considerably more pages than is usual in Communist-ruled countries. For instance, *Politika* runs an average of 36 to 40 pages an issue on weekdays, including 10 to 15 pages of ads. The Saturday papers are generally larger, averaging more than 50 pages, about half of them devoted to ads. *Borba* usually prints about 18 pages but devotes far less space to ads. *Oslobodjenje* of Sarajevo, a paper that is important regionally but not nationally, averages 24 to 26 pages, with about a third of the total space given over to ads.

The official statistics for 1977 listed a total of 2,538 newspapers printed in 1,081,001,000 copies. The magazine total was 1,509, in 358,679,000 copies. There are Sunday editions but no magazine sections in the Western sense, although *Politika* publishes a slick-paper TV supplement in color as part of its expanded Saturday edition. Yugoslav publishing houses prefer to spin off what could be considered magazine sections as separate publications. Probably the outstanding example of this is *Politika*'s *Ilustrovana Politika,* which, in terms of circulation, is the fourth largest weekly in the country.

10 Largest Dailies by Circulation		
Newspaper	Place of Publication	Circulation
1. *Vecernje Novosti*	Belgrade	366,000
2. *Politika*	Belgrade	285,000 (daily) 320,000 (Sunday)
3. *Vecernji List*	Zagreb	267,000
4. *Politika ekspres*	Belgrade	260,000
5. *Sportske Novosti*	Zagreb	155,000
6. *Sport*	Belgrade	109,000
7. *Delo*	Ljubljana	93,740
8. *Vjesnik*	Zagreb	86,600
9. *Oslobodenje*	Sarajevo	83,380
10. *Slobodna Dalmatija*	Split	65,000

Borba, which must be listed among the three most important newspapers in the country simply because of its role as the national voice of the Socialist Alliance, publishes only 50,000 copies in two editions, one printed in Belgrade in Cyrillic letters and the other printed in Zagreb in Latin letters. Nevertheless, it is ranked with *Politika* and *Vjesnik* as one of the three most influential papers in the country. *Politika* and *Borba* are the two papers that are distributed nationally, although *Vjesnik* and *Vecernje Novosti* are widely available in various parts of the country.

There are three other dailies with circulations of more than 50,000. Four others have between 25,000 and 50,000. Six fall between 10,000 and 25,000, with three having less than 10,000.

Economic Framework

As indicated previously, Yugoslavia is a Communist-ruled country that is different in many ways from the Soviet-bloc states. Since 1948, the regime has steered a middle course between a centrally planned economy and a free-market system. Agriculture is predominately in private hands, although large socialized units are important market factors. The state is also involved in large-scale purchasing of farm products. Private enterprise is substantial in handicraft and service industries.

Under the workers' self-management system, society as a whole owns the means of production but ultimate control is vested in the workers of each enterprise, represented by their workers' councils. State authority over these councils is limited to certain net-revenue distribution rules and other indirect controls, although the Party has a further check because of its discipline over members sitting on councils. However, over the years the formal autonomy of the councils has tended to grow.

Much of the economy operates on a competitive market basis although state intervention exists, particularly in the form of subsidies, allocations and bank credits. The system is very complex, and it is often very difficult to determine the precise roles of the Party, the various government bodies from the local to the federal level, the workers' councils and the enterprise management in economic decision making. Many observers believe the balance of powers not only varies from time to time but from place to place; enterprises embodying more experience, demonstrated skills and market advantages operate under fewer constraints than those less fortunate.

As with all enterprises, the media are managed on a commercial basis by their workers' council and selected managements. Publishing houses are expected to make a profit from sales and advertising. This has led newspaper enterprises to expand into the periodical field with a variety of popular, even sensationalist publications designed to increase total income.

Commercial self-interest has revolutionized the Yugoslav newspaper scene, resulting in livelier copy, special supplements, color printing, better designed formats, cartoons, comics and other features. Newspapers are not supposed to compete with one another but certainly the people on their staffs, particularly those in Belgrade, feel a sense of competition, at least for reader interest.

Foreign newspapers and other publications are sold freely in the major cities and there is no attempt to prevent people from listening to foreign broadcasts. As a result, Yugoslav news people feel they must match the coverage provided by Western media if they are to be accepted by their own public, and their selection and treatment of news is much more like that of Western European papers than of Soviet-bloc media. Editorial and comment, however, follow the official line, which is usually much more critical of the West than of the Soviets and their allies.

Newspaper circulations appear to be growing somewhat again after a decline that became evident in the early 1970s, but the number of copies per person is still low compared to most other European countries. This is due in part to the relatively high illiteracy rate, although a survey in the late 1960s indicated that as many as 25 percent of the total population never looked at a newspaper. Furthermore, much of the increase that has been registered lately has favored papers that appear monthly or intermittently, such as the delegate-information periodicals.

Radio is generally considered the most widely used and most important information medium. Television has been growing steadily, but it has difficulty reaching people in more remote areas.

Obviously, there is no private ownership of newspapers in the Yugoslav system. Legally, papers may be published by any "organized activity" as long as the people involved are approved. As a result, there are many different sponsors, or "founders," as they are called. All the dailies, however, are tied in one way or another to the Socialist Alliance. Among the more important weeklies, *Kommunist,* which has a circulation of nearly 300,000, is published by the Yugoslav League of Communists; the Federation of Trade Unions publishes *Rad;* the Union of Youth publishes *Mladost,* and so on.

There are far fewer publishing houses than the number of papers would indicate because each of the larger enterprises issues several publications. For example, the Borba organization also publishes the big afternoon tabloid, *Vecernje Novosti,* as well as the daily *Sport* and a variety of magazines and journals. The Politika publishing house is also responsible for the afternoon *Politika ekspres,* the weekly *Ilustrovana Politika* and another group of journals and magazines. In fact, the only Belgrade daily not published by one of these two houses is *Privredni Pregled* ("Economic Review").

The concentration is complete in Zagreb, where the Vjesnik publishing house is responsible for all three dailies as well as the popular weekly *Vjesnik u Srijedu* ("Wednesday's Herald"). Ninety percent of the total national circulation, including all dailies, most of the weeklies and most of the magazines, are published by just 47 enterprises. The top 10 dailies account for 80 percent of all daily circulation.

Yugoslavia produces most of her own newsprint requirements. Publishing houses enjoy subsidized prices for supplies, as well as reduced transport and postage rates. The fact that the media have become commercial enterprises makes them more dependent on advertising, but it is highly doubtful that advertisers could have any direct editorial influence. The essential power is political and an advertiser would have to work through political channels to really affect media policy.

Most full-time Yugoslav journalists are members of republic or provincial professional organizations affiliated with the Yugoslav Federation of Journalists. Membership in these organizations is voluntary; applicants have to have been employed in journalism for at least two years to qualify. The Federation lists more than 6,000 members, but there is no indication of how many of these may have gone into other related types of work, nor is there any figure for the number of people working as journalists who are not members. Production workers belong to affiliates of the Yugoslav Federation of Trade Unions. Neither the journalist organizations nor the trade unions have played any effective role in obtaining greater press freedoms. Changes that have occurred have been decided on and put into effect by the Party and government leadership, almost without reference to these groups. Furthermore, the main complaint of the production people has been not press freedom but what they see as the failure of the trade unions to work for their interests.

Yugoslavia has been afflicted with serious inflation for a number of years, and prices of newspapers and periodicals have increased in response to the general rise in the price level.

Press Laws

Since the imposition of a tightly controlled Soviet-style system after World War II, the Yugoslav press system has been revamped several times, both as a result of constitutional changes and alterations in press laws. The most recent constitution, promulgated in 1974, guarantees freedom of the press, speech and assembly. It also provides that "citizens, organizations and citizens' associations may, under conditions specified by statute, publish newspapers and other publications and disseminate information through the media of information." A unique provision establishes the right of citizens to information. It requires the media to inform the public "truthfully and objectively" about developments at home and abroad "which are of concern for their life and work and of questions of concern to the community."

But this document also makes clear the limits. One provision notes that "the Socialist Alliance...the working people and citizens, the League of Communists of Yugoslavia, as the leading ideological and political force, and other socio-political organizations and all organized socialist forces...shall guide social development...."In practice this means that the press is free to report as long as its activity does not question the Communist one-party system or established policies of the Party and government. Practice has also made it clear that comment must be in step with the current Party line, particularly when it involves foreign policy matters. For example, criticism of the Soviet Union and other Soviet-bloc states is tolerated only when it fits with the regime's aims of the moment.

The criminal code includes laws against the incitement of criminal acts against the people and state, against the armed forces, or against the self-managing socialist order. It bars the publication of information considered a military secret or that might obstruct promotion of friendly relations with other states, that insults the honor of the (Yugoslav) nations and nationalities, that "degrades" the nation's parliament and presidency or insults foreign nations or heads of foreign states. In addition to military secrets, state and commercial secrets are also protected.

Three of the code's articles have been particularly significant in freedom-of-information cases: Article 118 makes it an offense to circulate "propaganda against the governmental or social order or against political, economic, military or other important measures of the people's authority"; Article 175 covers damaging the reputation of a foreign state, and Article 125 bars the distribution of any material, particularly abroad, that has been banned by the authorities.

Almost all the freedom-of-information cases that have gained international atten-

tion—for example, those involving Milovan Djilas and Mihajlo Mihajhov—have not been, strictly speaking, press freedom cases. Djilas had been removed as editor of *Borba* for some time before his arrest; Mihajhov was a university lecturer. Both men were convicted under one or more of the criminal code articles noted above.

However, the same laws have been used to punish newsmen for their writings. In 1969, the editor of the Belgrade fortnightly *Knjizevne Novine* ("Literary News") was sentenced to six months in prison for an article attacking the 1968 Soviet invasion of Czechoslovakia. The regime itself had been highly critical of the invasion earlier, but this particular article was a source of embarrassment because it appeared just before a visit of Brezhnev to Belgrade. There have been a number of cases in which specific issues of publications have been banned because they contained similar articles critical of one of the neighboring Communist regimes.

The various republics and provinces have separate but virtually identical laws governing public communications. All bar publication of material injurious to morals or harmful to the education of children. All also establish the right of organizations and people to reply to printed or broadcast material if the reply adds essentially to the already published information. Individual citizens, work organizations and "socio-political communities" also have the right to demand the correction of erroneous or misleading information if their "persons, prestige, rights or interests" have been violated. Editors are obliged to publish the correction unless it is false or it was not submitted within the specified time period (15 days for newspapers).

The federal constitution specifies that the work of state agencies and other organizations, both economic and administrative, in general, must be made public. However, it permits exceptions provided they are specified by law or rules of self-management bodies.

The judiciary in Yugoslavia is an arm of the government and verdicts normally reflect the government's view. However, in recent years, appeals courts have more often than not reversed the lower courts in freedom-of-information cases.

Censorship

There is no formal censorship in Yugoslavia but there are a variety of informal censorship mechanisms. Top editorial posts are generally held by Party members who are well acquainted with the official line and are subject to Party discipline. They come from the same social background as the politicians, whom they see often and with whom they confer on important issues.

Pressure also can be exerted through the so-called social or publisher's councils that are another feature of the Yugoslav press system. These councils are made up of representatives of the general public; each publishing house has one. Its duties include approving the appointment of a responsible editor and helping to plan the publication's programs. Following the Zagreb students riots in 1971 and the resulting "nationalities crisis," the party began pushing these councils to formulate and evaluate personnel policy and review the activities of editorial boards, particularly with regard to political questions.

The most effective control mechanism, however, is the Party organization within the publishing house itself. In 1972 the Party urged members in the media to "undertake energetic measures to put an end to all destructive writing, to remove from leadings positions all those who do not accept the political course of the LCY [the Party], to make impossible writings which are contrary to the LCY and factional activity through the press."

Since Communists are in a majority or near majority in most publishing houses, the self-management system gives them the means of doing just that. The most publicized examples of this sort of thing occurred during 1972, when the editors of a number of the most influential papers, including *Borba, Politika, Vjesnik* and *Vjesnik u Srijedu*, were removed. They all were publicly accused of supporting pro-Serbian or pro-Croatian policies, but the *Politika* man asserted later he had been told he was "too liberal."

What can happen to an offending editor was made clear in a resignation letter written by the *Knjizevne Novine* editor mentioned earlier. Noting that his article had "provoked unfavorable reactions within the competent state and political quarters," he charged that "the press has joined in the negative appraisal of my article and its brutal attack questions even my political and moral integrity. ... The disagreement with me has turned into a reckless campaign against me, public and anonymous," the letter continued. "Pressures from various sides have created a situation wherein I find it impossible to continue performing my duty as the head and responsible editor of this paper."

State-Press Relations

Official information offices exist in Yugoslavia on both the federal and republic levels. The Federal Committee for Information is charged with informing the public, through the media, on the general situation in the country and on the work of the federal ministries and other governmental organs. There are also Secretariats of Information in each of the republics and the provinces, whose job it is to furnish information about governmental matters and other official business in their particular areas. The Federal Committee, along with the Press Section of the Foreign Ministry, also deals with foreign correspondents working in the country.

The Yugoslav press is free to report as it wishes on a wide variety of subjects, including some that are taboo in other Communist-ruled countries. It can criticize government actions in certain fields as long as it does not question the essentials of the system. Anything that could be construed as exacerbating the nationalities issue is also dangerous.

Generally speaking, when it comes to important political questions or foreign policy issues, particularly relations with the Soviet bloc, Yugoslav journalists tend to fit in with the government rather than function as critics. The Party is still on record as insisting that the media "cannot be a mere mirror of everything that is happening and of all trends of thought in various sectors of our society, but must be active socialist forums of self-managers, forums which, with their clear-cut, ideological-political orientation, have a place in the forefront of the struggle for socialist progress of society." The situation exemplifies the inherent dilemma of the Yugoslav system: how to reconcile the freedoms inherent in the self-management, decentralized structure that has developed with the continuation of one-party rule.

A study of coverage of the 1978 Camp David accords indicates how things work. The first stories by Yugoslav correspondents based in Washington were favorable, almost indistinguishable in fact from the coverage in major Western European papers. The following day the general tone of the Yugoslav press was a bit more cautious, particularly when it became apparent that the Arab states were lining up in strong opposition, but it was still upbeat. The third day, a Yugoslav government statement declared that any settlement in the Middle East would require an Israeli withdrawal to within her pre-1967 borders and the establishment of a Palestine state under the leadership of the PLO. From that moment on, all comment agreed with those guidelines. No hint of any contrary views was to be found in any major Yugoslav daily.

Usually, unwary newspeople who fall afoul of the restrictions are forced to resign or are removed from their jobs but are not otherwise punished. Most of the editors who lost their positions in the purge that followed the 1971-72 nationalities crisis still work as journalists although at least two of them, Fran Barbieri of *NIN* and Aleksandr Nenadovic of *Politika,* were also expelled from the party. A few have been jailed, however. The editor of *Knjizevne Novine,* mentioned earlier, was lucky. On appeal, his sentence was suspended. But the editor of a paper called *Hrvatski Tjednik* (Croatian Weekly) was sentenced in 1972 to four years in jail and his publication abolished on charges of subversion. A woman journalist was sentenced to a year in jail in that same year.

Issues of newspapers and other periodicals that contain articles the regime does not like are banned. This happened fairly frequently during the period from 1971 to 1975. Most of the cases involved nondailies or journals, although at least one issue of *Politika* was banned in 1974. Some of the more frequent victims of these actions included: *Student,* the student publication of the University of Belgrade; *Glas Koncila,* a Roman Catholic fortnightly in Zagreb, and two philosophical journals, *Praxis* of Zagreb and *Filosofia* of Belgrade. These last two had long been a source of annoyance to the regime, largely because of their publication of "revisionist" Marxist views, and eventually were closed down completely.

Attitude Toward Foreign Media

Foreign correspondents in Yugoslavia must obtain special visas through the Ministry of Foreign Affairs. Applicants must show proof that they represent established publications. If approved, they receive two-year visas, which are their work permits. There is no censorship, and no prior permission is necessary to send material to their publications.

There have been relatively few cases of correspondents running into serious trouble in recent years. Hans Peter Rullman, a correspondent of the West German news magazine *Der Spiegel,* was arrested in 1970 on charges of espionage, along with two Yugoslavs. All were sentenced to prison but were pardoned by President Tito. Johann F. Balvany, a correspondent for a Swiss features agency and other journals, was expelled in 1972. Michael Bartelemy, a special correspondent for Radio-France International, was expelled in 1980 after he had spent two days in Zagreb.

Yugoslavs who voice unacceptable views to foreign newsmen may find themselves in more trouble than the correspondents themselves. A case in point occurred in 1981 when a dissident Croatian writer was sentenced to two years in prison for critical remarks made in interviews with Western reporters.

Under the 1974 press law, distribution of foreign newspapers and periodicals is free. However, specific issues may be banned if they contain something that constitutes a "criminal offense against the state, peoples or armed forces" or that "jeopardizes peace, advocates aggression, violates honor and respect for the peoples of Yugoslavia and its institutions," or "false and alarming reports that can cause unrest."

Such bannings are not uncommon although they, too, occurred most frequently in the 1971–75 period. During the first six months of 1974 alone, there were at least 52 cases involving Western European papers, including some of the most prestigious. The stories causing the bans all dealt with the internal situation in Yugoslavia and allegedly either questioned the solidity of the regime or suggested the rebirth of Stalinist tendencies. It was pointed out that it took about three weeks for the bans to be announced, so that the offending issues actually had been sold and read before the prohibition could become effective, a situation that still pertains.

Under the law, foreign ownership of the media is prohibited. In fact, it is against the law to issue any printed material or broadcast radio or TV programs if the resources for their publication or broadcast are obtained from foreign sources. Advertisement and subscription income, of course, are exempted.

Nevertheless, foreign media have had a profound impact on the shape of the Yugoslav news scene. A survey taken by Yugoslavs themselves in 1975 indicated that about every sixth person in the country listened occasionally or even frequently to "foreign radio propaganda." As a result of this and the relatively free circulation of Western periodicals, the Yugoslav media cannot ignore important issues as so often happens in Soviet-bloc countries.

Apparently in keeping with the non-aligned policy of the government, the Federation of Jugoslav journalists is not a member of either the Soviet bloc's International Organization of Journalists or the West's International Federation of Journalists. It does participate, however, in the European Congress of Journalists and has a representative on the standing committee of European Journalists.

Yugoslavia supports the 1978 UNESCO Declaration.

News Agencies

Tanjug is the only Yugoslav news agency. Founded by the Partisan military command in 1943, it took over the old Avila agency at the end of the war. Until 1952 it was an arm of the government, enjoying a monopoly on news distribution. Its directors were appointed by the government and its operations were financed out of the national budget.

From 1952 until the mid-1960s it operated with a greater measure of independence under its own workers' council, but the government retained a considerable measure of control. Even now, although it is officially autonomous, the government still has some say in the operations since its payments for services constitutes about a third of the agency's income and it has the right to name three members of the 34-person workers' council. Three other members represent the print media, three the broadcast media, and the Tanjug staff chooses the other 25.

Tanjug lost its monopoly over news collection and distribution step by step, beginning in the 1950s when individual newspapers began to send their own correspondents abroad. By the 1960s, the larger ones had their own networks of correspondents in various parts of Yugoslavia itself. Eventually they obtained the right to subscribe directly to foreign news services.

Today, Tanjug has six bureaus throughout the country—one in each of the republics and provincial capitals—as well as correspondents or stringers in every major town. It also has 40 correspondents abroad, many in Third World capitals not regularly covered either by the international news agencies or the big Yugoslav dailies. The agency supplies news to the media, to factories and to government agencies on four nationwide teletype circuits. It has exchange agreements with 90 countries and is the operating manager of the so-called Non-Aligned News Agencies Pool, in which a number of Asian, African, Latin American and Middle East countries participate.

A study made in the mid-1970s showed that about 60 percent of the news processed by Tanjug for relay to its customers came from the big Western agencies. The bulk of the agency's growth during that decade was in the supply of economic and trade information to the nation's industrial and commercial enterprises. Its income from this service amount to about a third of its annual revenues. Since the government pays another third, this means the Yugoslav media are the source for only a third of Tanjug's income.

Yugoslav statistics list more than 70 accredited correspondents representing news organizations of other countries stationed in Yugoslavia. All the major international news agencies as well as the national agencies of the Soviet-bloc countries maintain bureaus in Belgrade. Many of Europe's more important papers are also represented there, either by regular staff correspondents or stringers.

Electronic News Media

Decentralization is also a characteristic of Yugoslav broadcasting. Yugoslav Radio and Television (JRT) is a federation of organizations established on the republic and provincial level. Each of these political divisions has its own facilities, established by the state. These broadcast centers are independent, self-managing organizations, financing their activities largely from license fees and income from advertising. They also receive some subsidies from the budgets of the republics, provinces, cities and some larger economic enterprises.

The whole structure is administered on the federal level by a management board and a secretary-general. The holder of that office in the mid-1970s described his job as that of an umpire, rather than a boss. His problems stemmed from the fact that each of the centers produces its own programs for its specific region but also wants to get as much as possible on the national hookups.

Each of the larger radio centers broadcasts on several channels. Radio Belgrade operates a short-wave international service and four domestic programs. Radio Zagreb airs four different services, including one aimed at Yugoslavs working in Western European countries. Radio Sarajevo has four services and Ljubljana and Novi Sad, three each. Novi Sad transmits its main program in five languages: Serbo-Croat, Hungarian, Rumanian, Slovak and Ruthenian. Radio Pristina broadcasts in Serbo-Croatian and Albanian. Radio Skopje not only broadcasts in Macedonian but also in Bulgarian and Albanian. Even some local stations transmit in more than one language. For example, Radio Koper, on the Istrian peninsula next to the Italian border, transmits in Slovenian and Italian and the station in Nis, near the Bulgarian border, transmits in Serbo-Croat and Bulgarian.

All together, Yugoslavia had 188 radio transmitters operating in 1977, broadcasting a total of 317,000 hours of programs. License holders totaled 4,548,000, indicating an average of one radio to every 1.5 households.

Television operates in the same fashion. There are TV centers broadcasting in color in Belgrade, Zagreb, Ljubljana, Sarajevo, Skopje, Titograd, Novi Sad and Pristina. Belgrade, Zagreb and Ljubljana operate two channels each. In 1977 there were 3,701,000 TV license holders, or one for every 1.8 households.

Each of these centers produces programs for its own region and also participates in national network operation. For example, as far as news in concerned, a center is responsible for reporting events in its area. Stories of more than regional interest are offered to the Belgrade center for inclusion on the main evening news show. If the offering is accepted, the control will switch to the regional center for that particular segment.

Programming also is imported from the United States and European countries. A considerable amount is also relayed from the Eurovision and Intervision linkages in Western and Eastern Europe.

As with radio, a number of the centers broadcast in more than one language.

Education & Training

Journalism courses are offered in the Universities of Belgrade, Zagreb, Ljubljana, Novi Sad, Skopje and Pristina, and postgraduate studies in mass communication are available at Belgrade, Zagreb and Ljubljana. The Center for Research of Public Opinion and Mass Communication of the faculty of Sociology at Ljubljana has established an international reputation for mass communi-

cation research. Belgrade also has a separate Institute for Journalism. Its efforts are directed chiefly toward improvement in the skills of people already working for the media. It provides specialized three-month programs as well as correspondence courses. It also sponsors a variety of seminars on journalistic issues and problems as well as research on press questions.

The two principal journalistic organizations in the country are the Federation of Yugoslav Journalists and the Association of Newspaper Publishers, to which most of the newspaper publishing organizations belong. The publishers' association is concerned with business matters, such as the marketing and sale of papers, price policies, agency services, relations with printing facilities and self-managing agreements. It represents its members in dealing with the state and other organs and organizations. The Journalists Federation attempts to deal with such concerns as professional ethics, the living and working conditions of journalists, ideological and political questions, education and training, as well as the advancement of journalism as a profession.

Summary

The key questions facing the Yugoslav press today are the same as those facing the whole of Yugoslav society: Can the national fabric be maintained in the face of the divisive forces inherent in the nationalities issue and the possibilities this could offer for outside interference? Can a way be found to resolve the inherent contradictions between the self-management system and the Party's monopoly of political power?

There are reasons for optimism. After Tito's death Yugoslavia did not collapse into chaos as many expected. Except for some initial nervousness, the system continued to function normally. This does not mean the dangers have disappeared. Nationalistic forces are still strong. But economic development and the linking of the various peoples through mass communications have tended to diminish the degree of parochialism. Most still consider themselves Croats or Serbs or whatever, not Yugoslavs, but some new glue has been added to the structure.

On the second question, too, there is a basis for hope. The Yugoslavs have been experimenting, tinkering with the system, ever since they were expelled from the Soviet bloc;

there is no reason to suppose they will not continue to do so. There is a strong liberal element in the party, as in the nation as a whole. The idea of a legal political opposition has been discussed at high levels. Both the degree and the pace of evolution in this area depends, however, almost as much on the international political climate as on internal forces.

These two questions aside, the Yugoslav press worries about economic problems common to Western Europe: the price and supply of newsprint, the competition for advertising revenue from broadcasting, the declining rate of growth in circulations coupled with rising costs. None of these threaten the financial security of the publishing enterprises at this time, but they suggest a slowdown of growth and development in the immediate future.

CHRONOLOGY

1956 Ownership of press transferred to employee societies.
1958 National news agency, Tanjug, granted monopoly of news distribution within country.
1960 Government promulgates new press law.
1969 Editor of *Knjizevne Novine* sentenced to six months in prison.

1972 Following nationalities crisis and student riots, press purged of dissenting journalists. Editor of *Hrvatski Tjednik* sentenced to four years in prison.
1974 New constitution relaxes press controls.
Politika is banned temporarily.

BIBLIOGRAPHY

Boyd-Barrett, Oliver. *The International News Agencies.* Beverly Hills, Calif., 1980.

Bryan, Carter R. "The Press System of Yugoslavia." *Journalism Quarterly,* Summer, 1966.

Clissold, Stephen, ed. *A Short History of Yugoslavia.* Cambridge, 1966.

Doder, Dusko. "Yugoslavs Tune in on Foreign News." *Washington Post,* June 19, 1975, p. A23.

Dvornik, Francis. *The Slavs in European History and Civilization.* New Brunswick, N.J., 1962.

Federal Secretariat for Information. *Facts About Yugoslavia.* Belgrade, 1979.

Federal Statistical Office. *Statistical Handbook of Yugoslavia.* Belgrade, 1979.

Hanson, Philip. *Advertising and Socialism.* White Plains, N.Y., 1974.

International Press Institute. *The Press in Authoritarian Countries.* Zurich, 1959.

Kempers, F. "Freedom of Information and Criticism in Yugoslavia." *Gazette,* vol. 13, no. 1, p. 3, and vol. 13, no. 4, p. 317, 1967.

Lekovic, Zdravko and Bjelica, Mihalo. *Communication Policies in Yugoslavia,* Paris, 1976.

Merrill, John C., Bryan, Carter R., and Alisky, Martin. *The Foreign Press.* Baton Rouge, La. 1970.

Olson, Kenneth E. *The History Makers.* Baton Rouge, La., 1966.

Paulu, Burton. *Broadcasting in Eastern Europe.* Minneapolis, 1974.

Portal, Roger. *The Slavs, A Cultural and Historical Portrait of the Slavonic Peoples.* New York, 1969.

Radio Free Europe. "Circulation of West European Papers in Yugoslavia." *RFE Research Report,* July 16, 1974.

Radio Fee Europe. "Editor of Knjizevne Novine Resigns." *RFE Research Report,* September 19, 1969.

Radojkovic, Miroljub. "Political Participation and Mass Media in Yugoslavia." *Gazette,* vol. 21, no. 3, 1975, p. 136.

Robinson, Gertrude Joch. *Tito's Maverick Media.* Urbana, Ill. 1977.

Schopflin, George, ed. *The Soviet Union and Eastern Europe.* New York, 1970.

Stavrianos, L. S. *The Balkans Since 1453.* New York, 1966.

UNESCO. *World Communications.* New York and Paris, 1975.

ZAMBIA

By Harold A. Fisher

BASIC DATA

Population: 5.472 million (1978, est.)
Area: 752, 614 sq. km. (290, 586 sq. mi.)
GNP: NA
Literacy Rate: NA
Language(s): English, Chibemba, Chinyanja, Chitonga, Silozi, Kikaonde, Chilunda, Luvale
Number of Dailies: 2 (1979)
  Aggregate Circulation: 110,000 (1979)
  Circulation per 1,000: 20 (1979)
Number of Nondailies: 3 (1979)
  Aggregate Circulation: NA
  Circulation per 1,000: NA
Number of Periodicals: 25

Number of Radio Stations: 1
Number of Television Stations: 1
Number of Radio Receivers: 120,000 (1978, est.)
  Radio Receivers per 1,000: 22 (1978, est.)
Number of Television Sets: 50,000 (1978, est.)
  Television Sets per 1,000: 9 (1978, est.)
Total Annual Newsprint Consumption: 1,200 metric tons (1979)
  Per Capita Newsprint Consumption: 0.25 kg. lb. (0.55 lb.) (1979)
Total Newspaper Ad Receipts: NA
  As % of All Ad Expenditures: NA

Background & General Characteristics

Zambia's newspaper industry is small, underdeveloped and almost completely under government ownership and control. It also still reflects the strong expatriate influences on its early development.

The nation's two dailies, the *Times of Zambia* and the *Zambia Mail,* (both state owned or controlled), concentrate on Zambian events, particularly news relating to government and the ruling party's activities. Their contents are aimed primarily at the interests of the educated and elite urban Zambians. Since independence the Zambian government has developed a system of small provincial papers designed to serve the country's predominantly agricultural populace. Until recently, daily circulation had mostly extended along the "line of rail" and road system in the heavily populated areas between Livingstone in the south and the Copperbelt in the north. Despite mounting production costs and sale prices, dailies and periodicals have experienced steadily increasing circulations as the educational levels of the population have risen.

When Zambia became independent in 1964, its educational system was poorly developed and illiteracy ran high. Because the colonial British had not stressed education for the African populace, adult illiteracy was still estimated at over 52 percent in 1969. At independence, fewer than 100 university graduates (including two doctors, one lawyer and one engineer) and just over 1,000 holders of secondary school certificates were available to run the country.

Since independence, the government of President Kenneth Kaunda has been investing heavily in education. Between 1964 and 1973 enrollments in primary and secondary schools increased 214 percent. The University of Zambia opened in 1966 with 312 students; by 1975, 2,500 students were enrolled. Also by 1975, some 88 percent of all primary-age children were attending school. In that year, the budget for education reached about 100 million kwacha ($155.52 million).

Further, to overcome adult illiteracy the government has initiated night courses and has built Adult Education centers, especially in the rural areas where little education had been available before independence.

Although the country's low education and high illiteracy have helped to keep readership of dailies and periodicals down, the recent rise in newspaper circulation figures attests to the stress placed on education in Zambia. However, the majority of readers remain urban dwellers, partly because of distribution problems in areas where adequate roads and rail lines have only recently begun to penetrate.

Since the pre-independence years, the Zambians who have purchased newspapers have been those who can best afford them—government officials, professionals and the urban and mine workers with at least some education.

Zambia's heaviest concentration of population ranges along a line from Livingstone on the Zambezi River to the copper-mining belt in the north. To export the copper via South Africa, the British colonial government built a rail line linking these areas in the early 1900s. A parallel road system followed. The country's media distribution system developed along these transportation lines, since newspapers could be delivered easily and quickly in the towns connected by rail and/or road. Even radio transmitters, and later television, were designed to beam their signals primarily along this north-south axis. Today that heavy population and media-distribution relationship remains largely unchanged.

Since independence, however, the Zambian government has begun to concentrate on communications links other than those with South Africa. Thanks to Chinese aid, the Tan-Zam rail line now connects the Copperbelt with Tanzania, opening regular communication with Zambia's vast northeastern regions. Chinese aid has also helped Zambia build east-west, all-weather roads. More recently, Zambian Airways has opened airfields in the country's western and northern extremities. These improvements are making possible more efficient distribution of the media to the sparsely populated outer boundaries of the nation.

When the British came to Zambia, they established English as the "lingua franca" of the region. English was the medium taught in schools and the language employed in commerce. Today, it remains Zambia's official language. Some 30 tribal dialects are also spoken, but the seven principal African languages are Chibemba, Chinyanja, Chitonga, Silozi, Kikaonde, Chilunda and Luvale. Since Zambia's population totals only around 5.5 million, this profusion of languages splinters readership and makes distribution of news and information difficult and expensive. Lingual diversification has also led the Zambia Broadcasting Service to program its daily Home Services in the above mentioned seven languages—plus English—and the Zambian Information Service to publish rural newspapers in six of the vernaculars.

The quality of Zambian journalism reflects the lack of lengthy national press traditions, shortage of experienced and competent editors and reporters, pressures and interference—first by colonials and now by Zambian party and government officials—and inability to cover all the news adequately. The *Times of Zambia* has tried to present to its readers a broad spectrum of objective national and international news and commentary. But because it has seemed oriented more toward resident Europeans and has represented big business, the *Times* has come under government pressures not to publish or to exercise extreme care in its reporting. The government-owned *Zambia Daily Mail*, meantime, has virtually omitted foreign news while concentrating on government and party news and affairs. Both papers have been attuned to urban readers; neither has adequately covered the rural areas, particularly in the northeast and in the west. Both papers have had to operate in an atmosphere where both the government and most of the reading public either equate straight news with commentary or place loyalty to the nation above straightforward reporting of the truth.

Despite these shortcomings, the two papers are typographically attractive and their makeup is well balanced. Both have employed pictures well. Both are information oriented. The *Daily Mail* has presented numerous features about Zambians. Neither dwells on the sensational. Even the advertising in the *Times* has been reserved in content and quantity.

However, this serious approach has not been true of the Sunday *Zambia News*. It is generally filled with lightweight features, sensational photographs and syndicated British materials.

Until Zambia became independent, newspapers were monopolized by European expatriates, and the meager indigenous Zambian journalistic traditions proved a factor that made government takeover of the press easier.

For many years, the *Livingstone Mail*, founded in 1906 by pharmacist Leopold

Moore, served as Zambia's (then Northern Rhodesia's) only newspaper. Published primarily for the white colonials, it played a key role in providing news of the settler community and in shaping their opinions. It regularly attacked the British South Africa Company, which was devoted to exploiting the area's mineral resources, and instead gave its loyalty to the British Crown. The *Mail* has continued as an English-language weekly.

In 1947 Dr. Alexander Scott launched the *Central African Post,* the first newspaper in the capital city of Lusaka. A decade later, the Argus Group of South Africa bought the *Post.* This thrice-weekly publication failed in 1962 because of low circulation.

The earlier of Zambia's two dailies, the *Times of Zambia,* was started as a semi-weekly publication in 1944 by Sir Roy Welensky under the title *The Northern News.* The Argus syndicate purchased it in 1951 and made it a daily in 1953. By 1958 it claimed a circulation of 18,000. During the 1950s and early 1960s the *News* opposed British colonialism, promoted continuation of white rule in South Africa, supported federation (of the two Rhodesias and Nyasaland) and Welensky's United Federal Party—and even cooperated with African politicians when that was discreet. When it saw the inevitability of independence, it began to treat Africans, and especially members of the dominant United National Independence Party (UNIP), in a less condescending fashion. It showed special deference to Kaunda, UNIP's leader.

Lonrho, the London and Rhodesian Mining and Land Company conglomerate, purchased the *News* late in 1964, shortly after Zambia gained its independence. Richard Hall, a friend of Kaunda and a strong supporter of Africans, was named its editor in 1965, the same year the *News* was renamed the *Times of Zambia.* In the early 1970s, under the editorship of Dunston Kamana, the *Times* became critical of some UNIP politicians, and also of government inefficiency. In 1975 UNIP said it would take over the *Times,* but lacked the funds to do so. Late in 1980, however, this was done by UNIP, as Zambia's sole political party. Lonrho ceased to run the *Times,* and Zambia became a nation without an independently owned daily.

The roots of Zambia's other daily, the *Zambia Daily Mail,* are even more shallow. It started in 1960 in Lusaka as the weekly *African Mail* and became the *Central African Mail* in 1962. The government of Zambia bought a 51 percent controlling interest in it in 1965, named it the *Zambia Mail* in 1967 and later renamed it the *Zambia Daily Mail.* The government instructed its editors to explain and support government policies while also reflecting public opinion. It appeals primarily to the educated urban reader, but part of its content is also directed to rural readers in the provinces.

The only other tradition begun during Zambia's brief press history has again involved the government. Wisely, the Zambian Information Service saw the need, in the interests of unity and development, to provide for the vast rural areas of the west and northeast. Since shortly after independence, the Information Service has published and distributed six provincial papers in vernacular languages.

In contrast with many African pre-independence movements, none of the Zambian political parties had a press voice of its own. This lack of an indigenous pre-independence press stemmed from the fact that there were almost no competent, trained or experienced Zambian journalists under colonial and settler rule. What few Africans did work for papers in Northen Rhodesia usually came from Southern Rhodesia. In general, Northern Rhodesian Africans were even prevented from involvement in journalism that professed to be in their own interests. Neither the *Bantu Mirror* (founded 1936) nor the *African Weekly* (1943), both intended for African readers, employed any African reporters until 1953. Thus, Zambia entered statehood almost devoid of an indigenous press tradition, or even of journalistic experience.

Both Zambian dailies are in English. The six provincial papers published by the Zambian Information Service (ZIS) include *Tsopano* for readers of Chinyanja in the east; *Imbila* in Chibemba for the northeast; *Lukanga* for speakers of the Bemba and Lenje tongues; *Intanda* for Tonga readers; *Liseli* for Lozi-language readers; and the trilingual *Ngoma* for those who speak Lunda, Kaonde or Lenje. While most periodicals are English-language publications, a few are published in Chibemba or Chinyanja.

Lusaka is the nation's only city with competing newspapers. Both the *Times* and the *Daily Mail* are now published there, although in its earlier days the *Times* was published in Ndola.

As of 1979, the *Times of Zambia* claimed a

circulation of about 65,000, while the *Zambia Daily Mail* had approximately 45,000. The Sunday *Zambia News* claims to sell 30,000 copies.

Some of the periodicals published by the government report fairly high circulations. *Orbit,* a children's educational comic published by the Ministry of Education, circulates 65,000 copies. ZIS's fortnightly *Imbila* for Bemba-speaking rural readers distributes about 27,000 copies. The *Mining Mirror,* under government supervision since the mines were nationalized in 1971, sells 60,000 copies. One other publisher of periodicals operating under government auspices is the University of Zambia. It publishes *Adult Education,* the *Zambia Law Journal* and *Zango,* a social and cultural quarterly. None of these university publications has wide circulation, however.

Some periodicals represent private interests or blend official and private interests, and some of them also have fair-sized circulation figures. *Chonogololo,* published by the Wild Life Conservation Society, sells about 30,000 copies. *African Panorama,* a political and economic affairs journal, distributes about 15,000 copies. The *National Mirror,* an ecumenical religious publication with a circulation of about 40,000, is published by Multimedia Zambia, a cooperative church body that cooperates closely with the Ministry of Information, Broadcasting and Tourism. The Franciscan Fathers put out the 11,500-circulation Bembe monthly *Icengelo,* which concentrates on social, educational and religious matters. Almost without exception, all publications of significance voice the views of Zambia's lone ruling party, UNIP.

Economic Framework

Most of Zambia's economic wealth stems from mineral resources, especially copper; in the late 1960s, shortly after independence, copper exports accounted for half of the nation's income. The overall income from the country's underground wealth—copper, cobalt, lead, zinc and manganese—gave Zambia nearly 280-million-kwacha ($200 million) favorable export-import balance in 1968, making her the richest of Africa's new nations.

However, world demand for copper decreased sharply in the late 1960s and early 1970s. Whereas mining's contribution to Zambia's GDP had averaged 35 percent since 1964, by 1977 it had fallen to 21 percent. The drop brought hardship to the nation's economy and development plans. A declining GDP, devaluation of the currency and inflation all served to stagnate the Zambian economy between 1976 and 1978. Fortunately, a steep rise in the price of another mineral in which Zambia is rich—cobalt—plus some recovery in copper prices, has somewhat alleviated the country's economic problems. However, the government has still found it necessary to order stringent budget cuts and to increase taxes on some items this past year. The economic crises, coupled with increasing government controls, have also kept the media from developing as rapidly as they should to be of maximum benefit to development.

Private interests are represented by several periodicals; the government owns and operates all other publications. Private journals include three religious publications, *Icengolo* and the *Sun,* both owned by the Roman Catholic Church, and the *Mirror,* under cooperative Protestant ownership. One other publication, *Productive Farming,* is owned and published by the Commercial Farmers' Bureau.

As indicated earlier, distribution of print materials in Zambia has historically been along the north-south "line of rail" running between Livingstone through Lusaka to Ndola, Kitwe and Changola in the north. Recently, improved rail, road and air transportation systems are making dailies and periodicals more readily available to residents in the outlying provinces.

Zambia must import all its newsprint. The sharp price increases of this commodity since the early 1970s have seriously hurt the publishing industry. The price of a ton of newsprint in Zambia rose by 100 percent between January and September 1973. And a steep, continuing newsprint-price rise has caused the dailies to lose money, and has forced both the *Times* and the *Mail* to operate below a normal profitability level; by 1974, the *Times* was losing 2,000 kwacha ($4,975) per day, mostly because of newsprint expenses. Amid these spiraling costs, the only answers the two papers have found to remain financially viable have been to (1) double their prices and later increase them again, and (2) cut the size of their papers. The prices and the cuts dropped consumption of newsprint from 2,100 metric tons in 1970 to 1,200 tons in 1976. Even so, because of high transport costs the price of newsprint in Zambia is among the world's highest. When Zambia was feeling the worst pinch of the world mining recession and was faced with foreign exchange problems late in 1978, it was thought for a while the *Times* and the *Mail* might have to close down because of newsprint starvation.

The *Times of Zambia* has carried a respectable volume of advertising. Commercial ads are generally conservative in tone and modest in size. Newspapers also run a considerable amount of classified ads, and the government has used dailies, periodicals and the broadcasting media for its own advertising.

Press Laws

The Republic of Zambia is directed by Dr. Kenneth Kaunda, who, as president, is head of state and commander in chief of the armed forces. The country's sole authorized political party is the United National Independence Party (UNIP), led by the president. UNIP's 25-member Central Committee makes the nation's major policy decisions. Kaunda propagates a philosophy of humanism for the nation, stressing individual dignity, non-exploitation, equal opportunity, hard work, self-reliance, cooperation, loyalty and participatory democracy. The fundamental freedoms and rights of the individual are guaranteed in the Bill of Rights of the 1973 revised constitution.

Shortly after independence, President Kaunda expressed his government's attitude toward the press in his speech to the seventeenth assembly of the International Press Institute:

We will not challenge the freedom of the press and...it [is] not our intention...to take over completely the operation of the one commercial newspaper company. [We recognize] the importance of an independent press completely objective and free from the influence of Government....Africa requires complete understanding from other members of the international community. The cause which we are following is one not only for Africa but for the world as a whole and the press has a positive role to play and it must play it if man is to survive.

However, at independence and until 1980, the *Times of Zambia* was the nation's only independent daily. Since it was owned by a British conglomerate, it was subject to a number of government pressures to conform, and to support the development of the country. UNIP accused the *Times* of "fostering alien elements" when the paper defended the judiciary in 1967. The paper's editor was caught between pressures from UNIP on one hand and from whites opposed to his pro-African stand on the other.

As world demands for Zambia's mineral resources declined, government pressures increased. President Kaunda took over some business firms in 1968, and although his government denied it wanted to control Lonrho and the *Times,* it obviously did want a share of the profits and influence over the paper. Then negotiations for nationalization of the *Times* were begun and the president's press secretary, Dunston Kamana, was finally appointed editor.

In 1975, in a move to prop up Zambia's ailing economy and to halt land speculation by the country's growing capitalist class, Kaunda announced the nationalization of privately held land, private hospitals, movie theaters and the *Times of Zambia* and its sister Sunday paper, the *Zambia News.* The two papers and the movie theaters had all been owned and operated by Lonrho. In nationalizing the *Times* and *News,* the president accused them of "irresponsibility" and of running "unpatriotic and obscene" articles at a time when he wished them to reflect official party and government views. From that time forward, the *Times* was considered by many to be the official organ of UNIP. The effect of the nationalization was to bring all the Zambian media under state control.

But UNIP failed in 1975 to raise the finances necessary for the takeover, so the two papers continued to operate on the same policies and in a style similiar to the past. And the government continued its pressures on the *Times.* The final takeover by UNIP occurred late in 1980, at which time Lonrho ceased running the *Times* and the *News.* Many considered the expropriation the end of independent press freedom in Zambia.

Censorship

The Zambian press has never experienced outright censorship, but it has come under sufficient official pressures for editors to have elected self-censorship on sensitive issues. During the late 1960s, President Kaunda occasionally asked the *Times* not to publish stories that might have caused anti-white riots. The *Times* tried to be discreet, especially about the nation's potentially most explosive problem—tribalism. Early in 1980 editor Naphy Nyalugwe was forced to read an apology before Parliament for an article critical of government, a pressure designed to elicit self-censorship.

However, several years ago the government did draft a Press Council Bill, which is slated to become law in 1981. The bill contains six clauses that will restrict or censor all journalists. One clause calls for the chairmanship and membership of the new Press Council to be vested in nonjournalist members of UNIP's Central Committee. Another would make it an official offense for any journalist to write articles critical of UNIP or to report government misdeeds. A third stipulates the founding of a Press Association of Zambia, which would officially take care of the interests of all journalists. In the event of the bill's passage, the journalists' rights to criticize government would be revoked and pre-censorship would be in effect in Zambia.

State-Press Relations

Zambia has always kept a watchful eye on the media. While *Times* editors like Nyalugwe were pressured to comply with government wishes, the *Daily Mail,* as a state paper, was under compulsion to report party and government news, to feature certain Zambians and to distribute in remote areas. It had to learn to seek consensus and to avoid divisive issues or news.

Not all government management of news has been negative, however. The Zambian Information Service has been performing a valuable function through its publication of vernacular provincial papers, even though the contents of these papers have been slanted to favor govenment views. At present, the Ministry of Information, Broadcasting and Tourism controls and operates all the communications media.

Attitude Toward Foreign Media

In general, foreign journalists have been accorded considerable freedom in Zambia. The exception has been in reporting of military operations. Early in 1980 an Australian television journalist was killed and his New Zealand cameraman detained in a Lusaka jail for filming a bridge damaged by Rhodesian commandos. Foreign journalists have generally been provided free access to the country, but they have had difficulty obtaining information except through official sources.

Zambia has been receptive to the journalistic training program of the International Press Institute and the president has publicly thanked IPI for its training of Zambian journalists. Numerous Zambians have also received broadcast training from representatives of overseas corporations.

The Zambian government aligns itself with African and other developing countries in its desire for an all-African press agency and more balanced flow of information.

News Agencies

Zambia has just one national news service, the Zambia News Agency (ZANA). Until 1969 the Zambia Information Service functioned as a domestic news agency, with rural coverage coming from the provincial information officers in each of the country's eight provinces and from 37 district offices, who sent information to ZIS, which then distributed the news to the media. ZANA's late start may at least be partially attributed to the lack of trained Zambians to staff it. ZANA prepares all new copy for Zambian radio and television services, which then voice the news verbatim as the agency has prepared them.

A number of foreign agencies maintain bureaus in Lusaka. In 1979 there were seven: Agence France-Presse, EFE (Spain), Novosti and Tass (USSR), Tanjug (Yugoslavia), Reuters (United Kingdom) and Associated Press (United States).

Electronic News Media

All Zambian broadcasting services are government funded and controlled. The Zambia Broadcasting Service provides radio programming in English and seven Zambian languages via two powerful medium wave (426 kw) and three high-frequency transmitters to the nation's estimated 120,000 receivers. Television-Zambia operates VHF service from Kitwe, Lusaka and Broken Hill to the owners of some 50,000 sets. In addition, the Educational Broadcasting Unit provides radio and television programming for an educational in-schools service. In 1974, the government also opened an earth satellite station, which is providing contact with the world via the Intelsat system.

Since 1949, when the Federation's director of information, Harry Franklin, introduced a cheap "saucepan special" receiver, radio has played a key role in Zambia's mass media milieu, and the transistor increased its prominence in the 1960s and 1970s. Radio's importance stems partly from the fact that distribution of the print media failed to reach far beyond the Livingstone-Copperbelt "line of rail," partly from the nation's high illiteracy, partly from the low purchase cost for a set and partly because it is prestigious to own a radio. Television remains too expensive for the masses and does not reach far beyond the urban areas.

The government has sought to make broadcasting a tool for developing and unifying the country. High percentages of the radio's Home Service schedule are given to instructional talks, education, news and current affairs. The service has conducted a radio farm-forum project with some 600 participating farm groups. It has broadcast adult literacy programs in all seven major vernacular languages. It has carried out a heavy schedule of in-school broadcasts and even some adult education programs in English.

Most educational television programming has originated in Kitwe, where the Educational Television Service, operated by the Ministry of Education, is based. Like many developing nations, Zambia has been seeking to replace foreign programming with its own productions. A high percentage of Zambian-produced telecasts are informational in nature: news, public affairs and education.

News broadcasts are read in English and in all major vernaculars. Recently, the radio service was presenting about eight newscasts daily, but Television-Zambia was giving just one ten-minute nightly news bulletin. ZANA holds responsibility for the content and preparation of all newscasts; the broadcasting services merely provide the news readers who do not alter the scripts given them. Most newscasts begin with a story about President Kaunda. At least half of the items focus on the Zambian government; major world stories may go unreported to explain in greater detail some governmental action. Many of the problems in the broadcast news service have been largely attributable to Zambia's lack of skilled reporters, writers, editors and even news readers.

Education & Training

Until Zambia became independent, its press and broadcasting media were monopolized by expatriates. There was an almost complete lack of experienced or trained Zambian print journalists, and in broadcasting only one trained and nine trainee African technicians.

Since independence, Zambians have received journalistic and broadcast training from a variety of sources. The International Press Institute has conducted six-month institutes which some Zambians have attended. Others have received writing training at the Ecumenical Center in Kitwe. The BBC, CBC, German government, the British government—through its Center for Educational Development Overseas,—the Thomson Foundation Television College, UNESCO and the All-Africa Conference of Churches Training Center in Nairobi have all trained Zambian broadcasters in extended workshop or institute-type courses. But few Zambians have had the opportunity to receive either prolonged training or to gain broad liberal-arts university educational backgrounds as preparation for their service to the media.

Summary

Under the present one-party political structure, it appears that Zambian government domination of the media will continue until it is complete. Some of the moves to control may be justified by the government's need to concentrate on peaceful development, but the prospects of a free, independent press do not appear bright for the near future. "At the same time, continued high costs of newsprint, the competing demands of development and the growing thirst of an ever-better-educated public promise to place increasingly heavier demands on Zambia's small, inadequately trained and generally inexperienced media staff.

CHRONOLOGY

1974   Zambia's earth satellite station opened.

1975   Nationalization of private land, theaters and newspapers announced and takeover of papers owned by South African conglomerate begun.

1978 Periodical *Africa Panorama,* a political, economic, social and cultural affairs journal, founded.

1980 *Times of Zambia* editor forced to read apology before Parlia-ment for his article critical of government.

Final takeover of country's last independent daily, *Times of Zambia,* by ruling party, UNIP.

1981 Expected ratification of Press Council bill that would forbid journalists to criticize government or UNIP.

BIBLIOGRAPHY

"Africa Hard Hit by Newsprint Shortage." *IPI Report,* March 1974, 10.

Africa South of the Sahara, 1979–1980. London, 1979.

A Humanist Handbook. Lusaka, 1976.

"Bringing Newspapers to Africa's Villagers." *IPI Report,* August 1978, 7–8.

Grotpeter, John J. *Historical Dictionary of Zambia.* London, 1979.

Hachten, William A. *Muffled Drums: The News Media in Africa.* Ames, Iowa, 1971.

Head, Sydney W. *Broadcasting in Africa.* Philadelphia, 1974.

Merrill, John, Bryan, Carter, and Alisky, Marvin. *The Foreign Press.* Baton Rouge, LA., 1970.

"Press Freedom Report, 1975: Zambia." *IPI Report,* December 1975, 14.

"Press in Africa is Starved of Newsprint." *IPI Report,* December 1974, 12.

"Reporter Dies Three Months after Zambia Shooting Incident." *IPI Report,* January–February 1980, 4.

The Development Bank of Zambia: Annual Report 1979. Lusaka, 1980.

"The World Press Freedom Review of 1978." *IPI Report,* January 1979, 12.

"World Press Freedom Review, 1980: Zambia." *IPI Report,* December 1980, 16.

Zambia-in-Brief. Lusaka, 1979.

Zambia, 1964–1974. Lusaka, 1975.

"Zambia Tightens its Grip." *IPI Report,* November 1980, 3.

ZIMBABWE

by Harold A. Fisher

BASIC DATA

Population: 7.14 million (1979, est.)
Area: 390,308 sq. km. (150,658 sq. mi.)
GNP: Z$1.92 billion (US$3.37 billion) (1979)
Literacy Rate: NA
Language(s): English, Sindebele, Chischona, Que Que
Number of Dailies: 3
   Aggregate Circulation: 111,184 (1979)
   Circulation per 1,000: 15.5 (est.)
Number of Nondailies: 8
   Aggregate Circulation: NA
   Circulation per 1,000: NA
Number of Periodicals: 29 (1979)

Number of Radio Stations: 2
Number of Television Stations: 2
Number of Radio Receivers: 270,000 (1977)
   Radio Receivers per 1,000: 39 (est.)
Number of Television Sets: 80,000 (1977, est.)
   Television Sets per 1,000: 11 (est.)
Total Annual Newsprint Consumption: 13,100 metric tons
   Per Capita Newsprint Consumption: 2 kg. (4.4 lb) (1977)
Total Newspaper Ad Receipts: NA
   As % of All Ad Expenditures: NA

Background & General Characteristics

Zimbabwe's press reflects the period of colonial dominance, transition and early independence through which the nation has gone in recent years. The small but lively newspaper industry, first controlled—and sometimes attacked—by the white settler minority, now finds itself under pressures from the government of Robert Mugabe in independent Zimbabwe.

As is often typical of developing countries, Zimbabwe's media have been strongest in the few urban areas. Its newspapers have circulated primarily in cities—among the relatively elite and cosmopolitan readers—where delivery has been facilitated by good transportation. However, Zimbabwe has a higher literacy rate and a better media system than many newly independent African countries.

A number of active weeklies and periodicals supplement the somewhat limited coverage provided by the nation's dailies. However, the industry suffers from a number of serious problems, among them the effects of the recent guerrilla war, a multiplicity of languages, sparse population in some regions, a dearth of trained journalists and encroaching governmental domination.

Zimbabwe remains predominantly rural. Population is sparse, with only about 18 people per square kilometer. About 65 percent of the total labor force finds employment in agriculture. Except for mining, major industries are few, but a number of light industries have sprung up in recent years. Only eight percent of the potential labor force is engaged in manufacturing, construction and other industrial work.

Just two cities in Zimbabwe have populations of over 70,000: Salisbury, the capital, with approximately 625,000 residents, and Bulawayo, with slightly over 350,000. A system of all-weather roads, railways and air routes link the main cities, but vast rural areas still have limited access to the urban centers. The nation still suffers from 14 years of isolation when transportation links with neighboring Zambia and Mozambique were severed as a result of freedom-fighter harassment of the government.

Zimbabwe's official language is English. There are several African languages and dialects, the principal ones being Sindebele, Chishona and Que Que, but since most educated Zimbabweans have received their formal schooling in English, it remains the principal language, of both the country and the press.

Because of a strong insistence on primary education for all children between the ages of six and 11, the percentage of illiteracy has been dropping steadily. (However, a fairly low literacy rate persists among the adult rural populace.) In 1977 some 850,000 children were enrolled in primary schools, or about 12 percent of the entire population. In the past, many pupils have not had the opportunity of going beyond the primary level, but that condition is changing. Secondary school enrollments doubled between 1965 and 1975, but even then only nine percent of those aged 12 to 17 years were attending high school. In 1979 the University College of Zimbabwe, located in Salisbury and the nation's only university, reported an enrollment of 1,931 students. Much of the media audience reflects a low level of formal education.

Most African families in Zimbabwe subsist on rather low incomes. Farm and mining workers are not highly paid and few Africans own farms, businesses or industries. From 1965 the wage gap between Africans and Europeans widened until, in 1978, the latter were receiving, on average, eleven times as much wage income as the typical African. The Mugabe government is pledged to narrowing this gap, to redistributing land and to improving the African's economic plight. Meanwhile, however, the low purchasing power of African nationals depresses sales of newspapers, radios and television sets, thus lowering the total audience for all media.

In general, press and broadcasting content has been good and informational. But until independence in 1980, the information was targeted to the expatriate European audiences, with only limited consideration of African needs and interests. Broadcasting has always been controlled by the government. Controls of the print press were first exercised by European authorities, especially against any who opposed the white regime, but more recently those controls have been imposed by African authorities. Under rule of the British Colonial Office—and also of the breakaway white government that proclaimed its "independence" in 1965—the press was administered and operated by expatriates; few African journalists were trained or included on newspaper staffs.

While newspapers have largely circulated among the educated elite, television, too, has been restricted to the wealthy, although it has also been used effectively for educational purposes. Radio, in the meanwhile, has become the medium of the Zimbabwean masses, and its status as such promises to grow as programs more appropriate to the common people are developed by Zimbabwean writers and producers.

During the period of white rule, the Rhodesian press primarily focused on information and entertainment for the European minority; now it may be assumed that this same press, under the leadership of African nationals, will center more on information pertinent to black Zimbabweans and on the tasks of nation building. If the pattern set by other developing countries is followed, the press will have less of an adversary role and more of an educational function.

The roots of Zimbabwe's press extend back to the early 1890s when—in the country then called Southern Rhodesia—small papers sprang up in several British settlements after they had occupied Mashonaland. The most important of these, the *Rhodesia Herald,* was founded in 1891 as the *Mashonaland Herald and Zambesian Times,* a hand-written, crudely duplicated paper edited by one W. E. Fairbridge. Until independence for Zimbabwe became almost an assured fact, the *Herald* and its co-publication, the *Sunday Mail,* were the country's most influential papers, and consistently supported the European governments dominating Rhodesia.

Today, all three dailies in Zimbabwe (Salisbury's *Herald,* Bulawayo's *Chronicle* and Umtali's *Post*) are published in English, as well as both Sunday papers (Salisbury's *Sunday Mail* and Bulawayo's *Sunday News*). Only a few periodicals are published in African languages. Perhaps the most important of the latter publications have been the monthlies *Mashoko e Que Que* and *Der Rhodesier,* with circulations of just 2,000 and 1,500 respectively. (Strictly speaking, *Der Rhodesier* is not an African-language journal, being printed in Afrikaans, a low Dutch dialect spoken in South Africa.) There are also a number of agriculturally oriented weeklies and periodicals, among them *Cattle World* (circulation 16,178), *Country Times, The Farmer* (7,000), *Modern Farming* (6,400) and the *Rhodesia Agricultural Journal* (1,600). An industrial review monthly, a development magazine, a financial gazette, several regional weeklies and special interest magazines complete the offerings of the Zimbabwean press.

Zimbabwe's two important dailies are the *Herald,* published in Salisbury with a reported 1979 circulation of 77,617, and Bulawayo's *Chronicle,* with a 1979 circulation of 33,367. The Umtali *Post* is small, its circulation just over 3,500. Salisbury's *Sunday Mail* circulates over 93,000 copies, while Bulawayo's *Sunday News* claims just over 29,000.

Economic Framework

Four priorities awaited Prime Minister Robert Mugabe's attention when he was sworn into office on April 18, 1980: resettlement of over a million refugees and displaced persons from the earlier guerrilla fighting; rehabilitation of some 36,000 African revolutionary fighters; reconciliation of races, tribes and political parties; and, perhaps most important of all, reconstruction of the country's war-torn economy. Mugabe's administration faced wide disparities between a small, privileged elite and a large, poor and neglected majority. Almost no middle class existed. The entire economy was sagging. Per capita income totaled about $400 per person. Land had to be redistributed.

Several measures were taken immediately. People were given land and tools to begin again. Social services programs underwriting school and hospital fees were developed. Help was given to former guerrilla fighters. Assistance came from the European Economic Community. Diversification of agriculture and industry was immediately begun. This new economic reconstruction program was undertaken without threat to the whites remaining in the country or to foreign investors; it did not even fundamentally alter the capitalist economy that Mugabe had inherited. One indicator of the success of the new beginning could be seen in the real GDP growth rate for 1980: about seven percent. But there was still need for large injections of investment in mining and industry to make the economy not only viable but dynamic.

Zimbabwe's official policy, summed up as "Growth with Equity," was officially introduced about a year after independence. It calls for more equitable ownership of natural resources, including land. The plan envisions that individuals, corporations and the state owning land, minerals and other assets, with the state promoting ownership and partici-pation by Zimbabwe nationals. At the same time, the Mugabe government has appealed to the international community, and has received a $1.8 billion fund for the country's rural development program, for payment of guerrilla war damages, for rehabilitation of refugees and for a large-scale program to train nationals in needed skills. With this infusion of capital, the government hopes to achieve a real growth rate of eight percent per year. This promise of economic improvement should serve to boost more general consumer purchase and use of the mass media.

Under white rule, ownership of the Rhodesian press was predominantly in the hands of the South African Argus Group, which published the country's five major newspapers: (the *Herald* and the *Sunday Mail* in Salisbury, the *Chronicle* and the *Sunday News* in Bulawayo and the Umtali *Post*). The group's chief competitor during the years of Ian Smith's breakaway regime was the London-based conglomerate, the London and Rhodesia Company (Lonrho), which owned the *Zimbabwe Times* (basically a black newspaper) until it was banned for breaking regulations forbidding publication of activities of the guerrilla Patriotic Front. Lonrho also owned the *World,* a black daily that closed after only a few issues.

When Zimbabwe became independent, it inherited the media system already owned either by the British colonial government or the private corporations. Recently, the Mugabe government has formed the Zimbabwe Mass Media Trust, taking over controlling financial interest in the Argus Group's "big five." While the possible effects of new governmental controls are as yet unknown, it appears quite likely this expropriation will achieve its avowed purpose of placing Zimbabwe African nationals in media decision-making roles, and that it may also assure the economic strength of the papers during a period of transition from a predominantly white audience to an African readership.

Zimbabwe has a better road and transport system than many developing countries, so distribution, except for the sparsely settled western regions, has been both more even and easier than in many newly independent nations. However, Salisbury and Bulawayo continue to be the two important publication and broadcasting production centers.

Zimbabwe produces the bulk of its own newsprint. In 1977 it consumed about 13,100 thousand metric tons, of which some 12,000 tons came from national sources. As elsewhere in Africa, the cost of newsprint has been rising sharply.

Press Laws, Censorship & State-Press Relations

Throughout its history and development, the Rhodesia/Zimbabwe press has been harassed by government intervention and controls. This problem was exacerbated during the period of colonial rule because the press generally constituted a service only for the white settler minority and because Africans increasingly sought to use the press in their struggle for freedom. The development of controls can best be seen in the historical context.

African newspaper publication began with the *Bantu Mirror* in the 1930s. In 1943 the Paver brothers of South Africa formed African Newspapers, Ltd. (ANL). With the encouragement of the Southern Rhodesian government, ANL acquired control of the *Bantu Mirror* in Bulawayo and started the *African Weekly* in Salisbury. During the decade of 1950–60, ANL continued to flourish, initiating *The Harvester* for African farmers and *The Recorder* for teachers. In 1956 it founded the *African Daily News*. Although ANL cooperated closely with the white government to keep its publications politically innocuous, its African editorial and writing staffs were allowed considerable freedom. Throughout the 1950s Africans comprised no real threat to the ruling white minority.

In 1962 Lord Thomson, owner of London's *Sunday Times* and a chain of other newspapers, bought out ANL. Under Thomson's ownership, the *African Daily News* developed such a strongly pro-African nationalistic editorial policy that Ian Smith's Rhodesian Front government banned it and other ANL publications in 1964. In the same move, the few attempts at truly indigenous African newspaper publication, such as the *Zimbabwe Sun* and *Chapupu*, were also banned, and several African newsmen were jailed without cause. The government's Ministry of Information then replaced the suppressed African press in 1965 with a free propaganda paper of its own, the *African Times*. That led to the development of several African newspapers published irregularly by externally based African political organizations, such as the Zimbabwe African National Union and the Zimbabwe African People's Union.

ZAPU published the *Zimbabwe Review* and ZANU's official organ, the *Zimbabwe News*, was published in Maputo, Mozambique. At the same time, there was a proliferation of smaller African periodicals that occurred within Rhodesia itself.

During the 1960s, broadcasting also found itself under increasing governmental strictures. The Federation government (of Northern and Southern Rhodesia and Nyasaland) had taken over English-language broadcasts in the 1950s, establishing the Federation Broadcasting Corporation (patterned after the BBC) in 1958. After the Federation's breakup in 1963, the Southern Rhodesian government took control of all radio broadcasting under the Southern Rhodesian Broadcasting Corporation (later called the RBC). In 1964 the white Rhodesian Front government also bought the Rhodesian Television Company, which had been a private commercial operation, thus gaining a full monopoly over all broadcasting. All of the corporation's board members and news service personnel were replaced by Rhodesian Front supporters. Ian Smith openly declared he would use the broadcast media to offset criticism by the independent press. The BBC programming aired until that time was replaced with broadcasts more favorable to the Front, or with direct propaganda material produced by the South African Broadcasting Corporation and the Rhodesian Broadcasting Corporation. Government monopoly over broadcasting has continued to the present.

After 1964, tensions and struggles between the press and the Rhodesian Front government mounted. Shortly before Rhodesia's Unilateral Declaration of Independence (UDI) in 1965, the Smith government instituted emergency regulations that permitted open censorship of the press. In the turmoil a mere month after UDI, the Rhodesian Front justified this censorship on the grounds that a state of war existed. The move was intended primarily to control the Argus Group newspapers that had editorially opposed UDI. Subsequently, the Argus publications were pre-censored, to which editors responded by leaving blank columns rather than run the revised material, and by printing notices calling attention to the censorship. Although new regulations in 1966 forbade such editorial tactics, the papers ignored them and got away with it, because the government feared having UDI challenged in court.

Then the Smith government set up a permanent Board of Censorship to examine all films and publications. It dealt harshly with materials expressing political or moral ideas unacceptable to the regime. However, censorship restrictions and government criticisms of the press were eased somewhat in 1968. Some reports indicate the relaxation was due to a secret agreement that newspapers would thereafter exercise tighter self-censorship. It appears that most editors chose to "stay alive" by revealing little of the struggle for freedom and by reporting nothing in depth of a political nature.

But the Smith regime's grip on the communications media tightened again in 1970, when all postal, telephone and telegraph services were placed under the government-owned Telecommunications Corporation. After a period of neutrality, growing discontent among Europeans toward the Smith government emboldened the press in 1973 to charge the Rhodesian Front with political blundering in proclaiming its UDI, its adoption of the 1969 "republican" constitution and its closure of the Zambian border. In more frontal attacks, the press also maintained that restrictions begun in the name of security were now being broadened to cover incompetence within the regime and that government ministries were uncooperative in sharing vital information. The government countered by accusing the press of distortions, lying, misrepresentations and collaboration with the country's enemies. Once again it toughened its stance by ejecting several foreign correspondents, and also by arresting and sentencing a trusted Rhodesian journalist, Peter Niesewand, for reporting on terrorist attacks on the Beira-Tete railway line in neighboring Mozambique.

The government's vendetta continued in 1974 with the banning of the weekly *Moto,* a Roman Catholic publication with a predominantly black readership, for calling terrorists "liberators" and "freedom fighters." Earlier in the year, an edict had been issued governing the introduction of new journals and controlling the import of newsprint. And yet another step to dominate the press, authorities designated certain reporters who indicated they would be willing to submit their stories for censorship scrutiny as "war correspondents."

A year later, the government set up a special committee under the Ministry of Law and Order to advise which publications should be prohibited or banned "in the interests of public safety or public order." That

was followed in 1976 by still another form of censorship—to combat "terrorism and subversion" and to counter the "intense psychological pressures" on the country. Police were authorized to enter media offices and seize information. While the government asserted the new regulations were not designed to stifle criticism, it cited two examples of "false reporting," which clearly showed it was unhappy with press accounts.

The censorship net tightened once more in 1977 when newspapers were barred from publishing stories on the deportations of persons deemed harmful to the security of the state after a Roman Catholic nun had reported the miserable conditions in "protected" black villages. Also in 1977 foreign correspondents were placed under the same censorship laws as Rhodesian journalists.

The Smith government's anti-press campaign reached a climax in 1978 when the *Zimbabwe Times,* the country's only remaining daily newspaper serving black readers, was shut down; its editor, Herbert Munangatire, was charged with publishing false materials and war information harmful to national security without first seeking military approval, and with forbidden reporting on the black Patriotic Front. To avoid certain imprisonment, Munangatire was forced into exile in London. By the end of 1978, thanks to pressures from Great Britian, the United Nations and individual countries—and within Rhodesia itself from Mugabe's and Joshua Nkomo's guerrillas—it could be seen clearly that time was running out for the Rhodesian Front.

During 1979, Bishop Abel Muzorewa served as prime minister for interim Zimbabwe-Rhodesia arrangements, after which Britain's Lord Soames governed until April 18, 1980, when the Republic of Zimbabwe came into being under Mugabe's prime ministership. The interim government's Executive Council had agreed to toughen up on censorship, but it quickly lost credibility by postponement of the promised one-man, one-vote elections.

When Mugabe's ZANU party came to power, it first criticized the media for a biased approach to news coverage and for having served as a propaganda tool under the white government. One of the new administration's first steps was to assign loyal party members to key positions in the nation's radio and television newsrooms. But the minister of information, Dr. Nathan Shamuyarira, announced it was his government's clear intention to establish a "free and independent media and broadcasting system."

However, the honeymoon ended quickly. In October, the Mugabe government reimposed the requirement that all foreign correspondents must register with the Ministry of Information and also be properly accredited, so as to eliminate what it called "contentious and negative reporting" about the new nation. Foreign correspondents were issued 24-hour renewable temporary permits, allowing the government to deny facilities and residence to any journalists who proved to be irresponsible in their reporting or representations of the country. The government explained that the restrictions had been imposed because adverse coverage was preventing the foreign investments and tourism needed for the economy.

A month later, Finance Minister Enos Nkala was warning that the country's independent newspapers might be brought under control for being "out of step" with national needs. It was a stab at the white-owned-and-operated press. Nkala described the *Herald, Chronicle* and *Sunday Mail*, all owned by the Argus Group, as being "imperialist and racist" and indicated that black editors would replace Europeans on their staffs.

Early in 1981 the Mugabe government purchased a controlling interest (45 percent) in the above three publications, and also in the Umtali *Post* and Bulawayo *Sunday News*, and formed the Zimbabwe Mass Media Trust to control the papers. The trust—established with funds from Nigeria—was described as "non-government, non-party and non-profit-making." Officials declared that it would not impair press freedom and would eventually enable black editors to take over from whites. However, the newspapers' owners and editors, opposition leaders such as Joshua Nkomo, and the International Press Institute all expressed fears that total control of the flow of news by the Zimbabwe government would follow. As of this writing, those fears have not materialized.

The Zimbabwe Constitution, like that of Rhodesia before it, does guarantee individual rights and liberties and freedom of expression, but there are no explicit guarantees of press freedom. The judicial system, likewise, is not insulated from administrative pressures. For example, the president appoints an ombudsman for the Judicial Service Commission to investigate complaints against actions taken by federal or local authorities.

Attitude Toward Foreign Media

In Zimbabwe, regulation and control of the media fall under the jurisdiction of the Ministry of Information and Tourism. The present government is continuing the negative attitude toward foreign correspondents held by its predecessor. As under the Smith regime, correspondents must register with the government, are given 24-hour permits, are held as accountable for all they say or write as are local journalists, and come under the same regulations. Failure to obtain and renew the permits is punishable by a $1,500 fine and/or two years imprisonment. The action, taken in October 1980, was in response to unfavorable reporting by foreign journalists, especially from South Africa, who predicted chaos and civil war within the new nation. At the time, however, the minister of information reassured the press that censorship, per se, would not be renewed.

Zimbabwe aligns itself with other African nations on the question of a balanced flow of information. With them, it seeks establishment of an all-African news agency and better reporting of development news. It would favor the UNESCO-backed attempt to provide regulation to "protect" journalists.

News Agencies

At present, Zimbabwe has no national news agency, but plans for such an agency, run by the government, were announced in October 1980.

Foreign news bureaus with representatives in Salisbury include Agence France-Presse, AP, UPI, Reuters and the South African News Agency. A private subsidiary of the South African Press Association, the Inter-African News Agency, Ltd., functioned under colonial rule and has continued to operate in the newly independent state.

Electronic News Media

The government of Zimbabwe has continued the tradition of state ownership of radio and television broadcasting begun by its colonial forerunners. The Zimbabwe Broadcasting Corporation operates four radio services: general, commercial, African and foreign. The first two are intended primarily for news, information and entertainment in the English language. The African service broadcasts in three vernacular languages and in English, while the foreign service is directed to Mozambique in Portuguese and in three vernacular languages. All told, the corporation broadcasts 29 news services daily to the 250,000-plus radio receivers in the country.

The Zimbabwe Television Corporation, with studios in Salisbury and Bulawayo, also provides daily news services to the nation's 70,000 or more television receivers. Its schedule is supplemented by informational and educational programs prepared by the Ministry of Education.

Education & Training

In the colonial era, African journalists had little opportunity for formal training in the media. The few African journalists who were trained often served first as apprentices for whites. The legacy of this system is a dearth of African editors and reporters prepared to operate the press in their own newly independent nation.

However, as independence neared, positive if belated steps were taken to provide Zimbabwe journalists with more adequate career preparation. In 1979, the Zimbabwe nationalist movements, ZANU, ZAPU and the United African National Council (UANC) combined with the International Press Institute in a ten-month journalism training course for 25 Zimbabwean students. The course, held in City University, London, was run by IPI and included training in writing, reporting, editing, production, shorthand, modern African history, the media, politics and national development. Students were attached to the staffs of British and provincial papers for short periods.

A year later, Justin Nyoka, then director of Zimbabwe's Department of Information and a former BBC correspondent in Rhodesia, opened a six-month intensive course for 22 Zimbabwe journalists in Salisbury. This program was an all-Zimbabwean venture, with all staff, both black and white, coming from within the country. It was also the first project of the Media Training Programme in Zimbabwe, sponsored jointly by the African Educational Trust and IPI. The course director was C. C. Chimutengwende, a Zimbabwe journalist with many years of practical experience.

The Mugabe government has plans to establish a permanent mass communications training institute. At present, universities in the country do not have well-developed journalism and mass-media training programs.

Under the Rhodesian government, African broadcasters had better training opportunities than their print-media counterparts. Although relatively few were so favored, a number were trained in the BBC, Thomson Television Foundation College and similar institute programs.

Summary

Under white rule in Rhodesia, the media were operated by and for the white settler population. They contained little for the black majority, so few Africans used them. Only a few broadcasters and practically no print journalists were trained during this period.

As the Ian Smith government came under increasing pressures and criticism from restive African freedom movements seeking independence, and from negative world opinion about its stance on minority rule, it became increasingly restrictive toward the press. Papers were banned, journalists exiled or jailed and controls steadily tightened—until the regime itself was no longer viable.

When Zimbabwe gained its independence in 1980, the Mugabe government first guaranteed a "free and independent media system." But within a year moves had been made to restrict foreign journalists and to take over the controlling interests in the nation's five largest papers.

Thus, the country's press has roller-coastered under two governments from relative freedom to near-total government control to promised freedom—and again to government ownership and control at present.

One encouraging sign is the resolve of the Zimbabwean government to establish training programs that will create professionally skilled African journalists. Unfortunately, the increased governmental domination of the print media since independence does not bode well for a free press in Zimbabwe. The small handful of newspapers and the current shortage of trained African journalists—which will be felt for some time to come—together with rising costs and as-yet-low educational levels, forebode a long uphill struggle for Zimbabwe's press.

CHRONOLOGY

1976 Rhodesian police authorized to enter media offices and seize information.

1977 Newspapers barred by Smith regime from reporting deportation of persons harmful to security of state.
Foreign correspondents placed under same restrictions as Rhodesian journalists.
Zimbabwe Times, country's only black paper, banned.

1980 Mugabe government promises free and independent media.

Zimbabwe government restores permit requirement for foreign correspondents.

Government rebukes Argus Group, says it will replace European newspaper personnel with Africans.

1981 Zimbabwe Mass Media Trust formed to control nation's three leading dailies and two Sunday papers as government takes over ownership and operation of press.

BIBLIOGRAPHY

Africa South of the Sahara, 1979-1980. London, 1979.

"A New Deal for the Rural Population." *The Courier,* no. 66, March-April, 1981, pp. 22-25.

"Another Year of Lost Battles." *IPI Report* 22:1 (January 1973): 7.

"Banned Daily's Chief may Get Seven Years Jail." *IPI Report* 27:10 (November 1978): 3.

"Banned Paper Back after Hush Trip." *IPI Report* 28:3 (March 1979): 3.

"EEC-Zimbabwe Cooperation." *The Courier,* no. 66, March-April, 1981, p. 26.

"Family Pleads for Life of Missing Reporter." *IPI Report* 27:9 (October 1978): 2.

Hachten, William A. *Muffled Drums: The News Media in Africa.* Ames, Iowa, 1971.

Head, Sydney W. *Broadcasting in Africa.* Philadelphia, 1974.

"Media Training Programme in Zimbabwe." *IPI Newsletter,* July 1980, p. 9.

"Meet the Future Editors of the New Zimbabwe." *IPI Report* 28:3 (March 1979): 11.

Merrill, John, Bryan, Carter, and Alisky, Marvin. *The Foreign Press.* Baton Rouge, La., 1970.

"New Rhodesian Censorship Rule Remains Untested." *IPI Report* 25:8 (August 1976): 1-3.

"Paper, Paste, Scissors... and Gun, but Blacks Get a Daily." *IPI Report* 27:8 (September 1978): 4.

"Press Freedom Report, 1975: Rhodesia." *IPI Report* 24:12 (December 1975): 8, 14.

Rasmussen, R. Kent. *Historical Dictionary of Rhodesia/Zimbabwe.* London, 1979.

"Rhodesia—No Censors, But..." *IPI Report* 22:3 (March 1973): 1, 3, 4.

"Rhodesian Black Newspaper Banned." *IPI Report* 23:11 (November 1974): 12.

"The First Year of Independence: Walking a Tightrope." *The Courier,* no. 66, March-April, 1981, pp. 15-21.

"The World Press Freedom Review of 1978: Zimbabwe." *IPI Report* 28:1 (January 1979): 11.

"Training for the New Zimbabwe." *IPI Report* 29:1 (January/February 1980): 13.

UNESCO. *Statistical Yearbook, 1978-1979.* Paris, 1980.

"World Press Freedom Review, 1979: Zimbabwe." *IPI Report* 28:12 (December 1979): 5.

"Zimbabwe—A First Step." *IPI Report* 30:7 (January 1981): 14.

"Zimbabwe." *IPI Report* 29:6 (December 1980): 16.

"Zimbabwe Revives Permits." *IPI Report* 29:5 (November 1980): 3.

"Zimbabwe Takeover Criticized." *IPI Report* 30:7 (January 1981): 4.

"Zimbabwe: Turning Swords into Ploughshares." *The Courier,* no. 66, March-April, 1981, pp. 11-14.

"Zimbabwe's Press Takeover: 'National Interest?'" *Wall Street Journal,* March 12, 1981, p. 26.

SECTION III:
Smaller & Developing Press Systems

AFGHANISTAN

BASIC DATA

Population: 14,866,000
Area: 647,500 sq. km. (245,000 sq. mi.)
GNP: A129 billion (US$2.9 billion) (1978)
Literacy Rate: 10%
Language(s): Dari, Pushtu
Number of Dailies: 13
  Aggregate Circulation: 77,000
  Circulation per 1,000: 4
Number of Nondailies: 11
  Aggregate Circulation: 89,000
  Circulation per 1,000: 5
Number of Periodicals: 25
Number of Radio Stations: 1
Number of Television Stations: 1
Number of Radio Receivers: 1,000,000
  Radio Receivers per 1,000: 67
Number of Television Sets: 20,000
  Television Sets per 1,000: 1.3
Total Annual Newsprint Consumption: 1.2
metric tons
  Per Capita Newsprint Consumption: 0.06 kg.
(0.13 lb.)
Total Newspaper Ad Receipts: NA
  As % of All Ad Expenditures: NA

The first newspaper to appear regularly in Afghanistan was the *Seraj al-Akhbar* ("Lamp of the News"), founded in 1912 by Amir Habibullah. Published in Persian, it became too outspoken for the ruler, opposing the official policy of friendship with the British, and was replaced by another daily called *Aman-i-Afghan* ("Afghan Peace"), which was edited for several years by Mahmud Tarzi, a close associate of Habibullah.

Until about 1950 the number of publications and the level of production remained very limited. During the fifties and sixties, the press experienced steady growth under the direction of professional journalists, some of them trained abroad. With the fall of the monarchy and the establishment of a Communist republic, the daily press was taken over by the government and became virtually government organs.

Currently, the two most important dailies are *Anis,* an evening paper published in Dari and Pushtu, and *Haqiqat Enqelab Sawer* ("Truth of the April Revolution"), the official organ of the Communist Party and the government, also published in Dari and Pushtu. *Anis* is the larger of the two, with a circulation of around 24,000, while *Haqiqat Enqelab Sawer* claims a circulation of 20,000. Kabul has three other dailies, including the English-language *Kabul New Times* (formerly the *Kabul Times*). Ten papers, mostly with small circulations, are published in the provincial capitals of Faizabad, Mazar-i-Sharif, Baghlan, Herat, Bost, Sheberghan, Taloon Khar, Farah, Qandahar, and Gardiz. Four of them are published in Pushtu and the others in both Dari and Pushtu.

The periodical press consists of 25 titles, including four published by the Ministry of Information and Culture and two published by the Ministry of Education. The most influential of these is *Khalq,* the organ of the ruling People's Democratic Party, which resumed publication in 1979 after having been banned for a number of years. *Khalq* is published in five languages: Dari, Pushtu, English, Baluchi, and Urdu.

Afghan newspapers place little emphasis on human interest stories and rarely publish news about crime. A rather surprising amount of space is devoted to foreign news; reports from foreign capitals take up three-fourths of the front pages of each issue of these papers, and sometimes there are extensive translations from foreign papers and periodicals. News from Moscow is regularly played up. Most of the domestic news items are supplied by the Ministry of Information and are designed to create a favorable image of the Babrak Karmal regime. The few advertisements that appear in the papers are mostly official notices.

The national news agency is the Bakhtar News Agency, directed by the Ministry of Information and Culture. It is the main channel to the foreign press for all official statements and announcements. It also publishes the *Bakhtar News Bulletin,* a mimeographed sheet in English, directed at the foreign community in Kabul.

Partly as a result of official policy and partly as a result of widespread illiteracy, estimated at 90 percent, the majority of the Afghans remain generally unaware of happenings in the outside world. Foreign newspapers circulate only among the high officials of the government. Apart from the two Soviet news agencies, Tass and APN, only Tanjug maintains a permanent bureau in Kabul. The absence of modern news channels is made up by the rumor factories of the Kabul bazaars, where news, embellished with fiction, spreads with amazing rapidity. Shabnamas, or night letters, also circulate widely.

The principal medium of official propaganda is the National Radio-TV (formerly Radio Afghanistan), which is operated by the Ministry of Communications. With medium- and short-wave transmitters, National Radio-TV broadcasts its home service in Dari, Pushtu, Nuristani, Uzbeki, Turkmani, and Baluchi and its foreign service in Urdu, Arabic, English, Russian, German, Dari and Pushtu for 132 hours a week. Because radios are expensive, the government has installed loudspeakers in all the larger towns. Television broadcasting began in 1978 with a transmission range of 50 km.

ALGERIA

BASIC DATA

Population: 18,542,000
Area: 2,460,500 sq. km. (950,000 sq. mi.)
GNP: 102.5 billion dinars (US$24.6 billion) (1978)
Literacy Rate: 25%
Language(s): Arabic, French
Number of Dailies: 4
  Aggregate Circulation: 236,000
  Circulation per 1,000: 13
Number of Nondailies: 3
  Aggregate Circulation: 107,000
  Circulation per 1,000: 6
Number of Periodicals: 39
Number of Radio Stations: 13
Number of Television Stations: 6
Number of Radio Receivers: 3,000,000
  Radio Receivers per 1,000: 173
Number of Television Sets: 520,000
  Television Sets per 1,000: 29
Total Annual Newsprint Consumption: 8,300 metric tons
  Per Capita Newsprint Consumption: 0.5 kg. (1.1 lb.)
Total Newspaper Ad Receipts: NA
  As % of All Ad Expenditures: NA

In colonial Algeria all daily newspapers and most periodicals were French-owned and French-language. Except for occasional government and missionary pamphlets and a few short-lived periodicals, there was no Arabic-language press. The educated Algerians had access to newspapers from Paris, which reached Algiers on the same date of publication.

During the Civil War, the press faced enormous difficulties through censorship and seizure by French authorities on the one hand and threats and reprisals from extremist groups, both Arab and French, on the other. Most of the French-owned press supported, without qualifications, the demand of the colons (settlers) for a French Algeria; a few voices of moderation, such as the *Oran Republicain,* favored a French-Muslim rapprochement, but they were eventually forced into editorial silence by the terrorist tactics of extremists.

During this period the French government banned the publication and distribution of all nationalist publications, with the result that by 1956 not a single Arabic-language newspaper or periodical was being published in Algeria. However, many nationalistic pamphlets and newssheets, printed clandestinely in the country or smuggled in from abroad, were widely circulated. Among these was *El Moudjahid,* the official organ of the Front de Liberation Nationale (FLN, National Liberation Front), first published in French in Tunis in 1956.

For a few years after independence in 1962, the Algerian press enjoyed a relative freedom, which it possessed neither before nor after. Opposition papers were permitted to continue publication, although the government exercised control through intimidation and periodical threats of nationalization. The press, following an instinct for self-preservation, adopted a pro-regime policy on most controversial issues. Even so, the government began expressing irritation with press comments and rebuking editors for criticism of party and state policies. The government became particularly intolerant of French publications on the ground that they were "hostile to the independence of Algeria." The entry and sale of many French newspapers and periodicals were prohibited, and others were subjected to frequent seizures and delays in distribution.

Nevertheless, European-owned dailies, particularly *La Depeche d'Algerie,* survived the transition fairly well and even enjoyed high circulations. But at the same time, conscious of the dangers posed by a hostile regime, they exercised strict self-censorship, scrupulously refraining from any criticism or comments that could be construed as objectionable in official quarters. The sole open voice of opposition was the Communist *Alger Republicain,* which enjoyed the second highest circulation of any Algerian newspaper. It specialized in exposes of government failures. The weakest of the newspaper groups was the FLN-controlled press, which included *Al Shaab,* an Algiers Arabic-language daily, *Le Peuple,* an Algiers French-language daily, and *La Republique,* an Oran French-language daily. Although backed by government and party funds, FLN papers were poorly written and badly produced.

In September 1963, without prior warning, the offices of *La Depeche d'Algerie, l'Echo d'Oran* and *Le Depeche de Constantine* were occupied by police and army troops. The government broadcasts announcing the nationalization of the European-owned press did not accuse the affected newspapers of current offenses but merely denounced their colonialist past. Radio Algiers said that the takeover would "end attacks on our country," and praised it as a great victory "over hired pens, absurd tendentious propaganda and filthy psychological campaigns." The nationalizations were in line with Ben Bella's socialization program, under which all European-owned lands and businesses were brought under state ownership. By 1964 the government control over the press was total. The FLN appointed the editors of all newspapers and monitored their ideological conformity. The press was characterized as a channel of information between government and the people operating within the socialist system. The press's function was defined as transmitting and explaining official policies and educating citizens through the judicious selection of informational and ideological material.

After the 1965 coup that brought Houari Boumedienne to power, the Ministry of Information and Culture gradually asserted itself as the principal agent of control over the press. Under close government tutelage the press accomplished the transition from Ben Bella's orthodox Marxism to Boumedienne's pragmatic socialism smoothly and with no overt censorship measures. Through a 1968 ordinance journalists were admonished to perform their work in a spirit of militant fervor and to report on the achievements of the new socialist order. To affirm the principle of collegiality, directors and editors of newspapers were replaced by anonymous editorial boards staffed by party die-hards. During this period, some newspapers were suspended and others merged; the resulting structure remained unchanged throughout the Boumedienne years.

Today, the daily press consists of four newspapers. The leading daily is the *El Moudjahid,* published in French from Algiers. Formed from the merger of the Communist organ *Alger Republicain* and *Le Peuple, El Moudjahid* is the official mouthpiece of the government. While official speeches and documents make up the bulk of its columns, it is often critical of various state-run enterprises. Its social and cultural articles reflect the growing influence of Islamic fundamentalists. Another leading spokesman for Islamic revival is *Al Shaab,* an Arabic-language daily, also published from Algiers. The two other dailies, *an Nasr* and *al Joumhouriya,* both published in Arabic, are issued from Constantine and Oran respectively. *El Moudjahid* has a reported circulation of 130,000, up from 80,000 in 1969. The others, with a circulation of around 30,000 each, have made no gains in circulation during the 1970s.

The periodical press is also owned or controlled by the government. The weekly *Revolution et Travail* is the organ of the General Union of Algerian Workers, the influential monthly *El Djeich* is the organ of the army, and *El Djezair* is published by the Ministry of Tourism.

Because of the dominance of political considerations, the quality of journalism has suffered over the years. Didactic in tone, the newspapers play up officially approved material with little or no analysis or comment. Recently, culture and entertainment are being featured more prominently. Among the most popular features are comic strips lampooning the chronic housing shortage, bureaucratic bumbling, and other favorite topics. The language used in these cartoons is the pidgin Francarabe, widely used in coastal cities.

The Algerian press is an urban institution; it has virtually no impact on the rural areas where over 14 million illiterates live. Even among educated Algerians, the press has only a limited influence because newspapers function primarily as government gazettes.

As an FLN-owned institution, the Algerian press is not subject to the laws of the marketplace and its revenues and expenditures are buried in the party budget. Its finances are independent of circulation, and all editors are appointed by and are subject to the party hierarchy. Algerians maintain the fiction that the press speaks for the party and not for the state; the distinction is immaterial because party and state are one and the same.

Almost all Algerian journalists belong to the Union Algerienne des Journalistes, which is affiliated to the Union Generale des Travailleurs Algeriens.

While all of the printed and electronic media are controlled and monitored by the government, there are no specific agencies designated as censors. There are no constitutional sanctions for suppression of freedom of expression and none have been found necessary so long as the party/state own and direct the media. Because of the lack of specific guidelines, editors often bend over backwards to avoid incurring the displeasure of the powers that be. Even when government policies are criticized, no names are ever named.

Foreign newspapers and magazines are freely available, but certain issues containing offensive material are summarily seized. The French-language weekly *Jeune Afrique* is permanently proscribed. Special visas are required for foreign correspondents and prior approval for cables.

Algeria is one of the most vehement supporters of UNESCO attempts to legitimize state control over the media in the developing world.

The Algerian Press Service (Algerie Press Service, APS), founded in Tunisia during the independence struggle, has been the exclusive national news agency since 1963. Officially, its task is to "collect, verify, and comment on news worthy of interest." Its principal sources of information are AFP, the Maghrib Arab Press and the Tunisia Africa Press, but it maintains independent offices in Rabat, Tunis, Cairo, Paris, Prague, Moscow, Rome, Geneva, London and New York.

All broadcasting is the responsibility of Radiodiffusion-Television Algerienne (RTA), a state-owned and operated but financially autonomous public corporation. The radio service consists of three networks broadcasting in French, Arabic and Kabyle on both medium- and short-wave. News and information broadcasts account for 10 percent of the approximately 300 hours of weekly programming. The entire country is covered by radio broadcasts; television service is available only to the population living in the northern parts of the country through a network of seven main transmitters and six auxiliaries.

Journalists are trained at the Ecole Nationale Supreieure de Journalisme in Algiers.

ANGOLA

BASIC DATA

Population: 6,580,000
Area: 1,245,790 sq. km. (481,000 sq. mi.)
GNP: 140.79 billion kwanza (US$3.06 billion) (1979)
Literacy Rate: 10–15%
Language(s): Portuguese
Number of Dailies: 2
  Aggregate Circulation: 41,000
  Circulation per 1,000: 7.3
Number of Nondailies: 17
  Aggregate Circulation: NA
  Circulation per 1,000: NA
Number of Periodicals: 5
Number of Radio Stations: 1
Number of Television Stations: NA
Number of Radio Receivers: 118,000 (1977)
  Radio Receivers per 1,000: 18
Number of Television Sets: NA
  Television Sets per 1,000: NA
Total Annual Newsprint Consumption: 700 metric tons (1977)
  Per Capita Newsprint Consumption: 0.1 kg. (0.2 lb.) (1977)
Total Newspaper Ad Receipts: NA
  As % of All Ad Expenditures: NA

At the time of the MPLA takeover of Angola, the two most important newspapers were the evening *Diario de Luanda* and the morning *A Provincia de Angola,* both published from Luanda. The *Provincia de Angola,* the older of the two, founded in 1923, had a circulation of 41,000. One of the first acts of the MPLA regime was to close the evening *Diario* and to rename the morning daily *O Journal de Angola.* Six years later *O Journal de Angola* remains the country's sole daily, with the exception of the official gazette, *Boletim Oficial. O Journal's* circulation has not been reported since independence but it is believed to have declined slightly from the pre-civil war figure. Aggregate circulation is slightly higher than that of Mozambique, at 7.3 per 1,000.

In contrast to the daily press, the periodical press appears crowded. At least 22 periodicals were reported on the eve of independence, and although it is not certain how many have been weeded out, periodicals appear to be thriving in the new republic. Seven of the periodicals are published from Luanda, two from Melanje, two from Benguela, and one each from Huambo, Mocamedes, Lobito, Moxico, Lubango, Uige, Novo Redondo and Bie. Seventeen of the periodicals are published weekly.

As in Mozambique, the press suffers from a lack of trained journalists. In the years immediately following independence the daily *Journal* was edited by one of the few white journalists who had openly espoused the black nationalist cause. A national center for journalism opened in Luanda in 1976, but its syllabus has not been settled.

As in Mozambique, the practical difficulties in producing the distributing conventional newspapers have led to the proliferation of wall newspapers, often collages of materials cut out from an assortment of publications and pasted together. Most factories and schools have their own newpapers, which are changed weekly. Outside of the main towns, newspapers and periodicals are distributed by the army.

Censorship of political expression exists although the constitution guarantees freedom of expression. The circulation of Western journals is tightly restricted. The government is particularly sensitive to criticisms in the foreign press and has frequently expelled foreign correspondents who reported on its own failures or the succession of opposition guerrilla movements. Few Western correspondents have been granted visas in recent years.

The national news agency is the Angolan News Agency, developed by a British expatriate, Michael Wolfers, a friend of MPLA leaders and long-time correspondent for the London *Times*. The national radio station is Radio Nacional de Angola. There is no television service.

BAHRAIN

BASIC DATA

Population: 373,000
Area: 596 sq. km. (238.4 sq. mi.)
GNP: 804 million Bahrain dinars (US$2.08 billion) (1979)
Literacy Rate: 40%
Language(s): Arabic

Number of Dailies: 4
  Aggregate Circulation: NA
  Circulation per 1,000: NA
Number of Nondailies: NA
  Aggregate Circulation: NA
  Circulation per 1,000: NA
Number of Periodicals: 13
Number of Radio Stations: 2
Number of Television Stations: 1
Number of Radio Receivers: 93,500
  Radio Receivers per 1,000: 260
Number of Television Sets: 80,000
  Television Sets per 1,000: 225
Total Annual Newsprint Consumption: NA
  Per Capita Newsprint Consumption: NA
Total Newspaper Ad Receipts: NA
  As % of All Ad Expenditures: NA

The press in Bahrain dates from the 1930s. From then until 1957 it was a largely independent institution with few controls on its freedom. But then, because the press supported the riots and strikes of labor groups in the mid-1950s, the government suspended all independent publications. In 1965 the government issued a press law that permitted the development of newspapers according to specific guidelines that proscribed criticism of the royal family, the government or friendly foreign countries. After 1965 the press began to grow again, and in 1967 the country's first Arabic daily, *Akhbar al Khalij,* began publication under the ownership of Abdulla Mardi.

By 1980 four dailies and over a dozen periodicals had been established in the kingdom. Of the four dailies two are in Arabic, including *Akhbar al Bahrain,* published by the Ministry of Information, and two are in English: *Awali Daily News,* published by the Bahrain Petroleum Company, and *The Gulf Daily News.* For the most part the press remains in private hands. Circulation, limited to the affluent Arabs and the large expatriate community, has never been larger than the 10,000 copies claimed by *Akhbar al Khalij.* Because of the lack of trained native journalists, even Arabic papers are dependent on expatriate talent. *Akhbar al Khalij* is heavily staffed by Egyptians, while the English papers are edited by British journalists.

Some 13 periodicals are published in Arabic and English, addressed mostly to tourists. Among them the largest circulation is enjoyed by *Gulf Mirror* (15,000), which also circulates in Kuwait, Oman, Qatar, United Arab Emirates and parts of Saudi Arabia.

The Bahraini press is generally described as loyalist. Even in the absence of formal censorship, there is no media dissent or activism. By inclination as well as by a sound instinct for self-preservation, the press has shown no desire to assume the role of an opposition. There was a brief upsurge of press candor during the short-lived experiment with an elected parliament from 1973 to 1975, but when the government suspended the assembly the press relapsed into its neutral posture. Weeklies tend to be more politically oriented than dailies, with *Al Adhwaa* occupying the center, *Sada al Usbu* the left and *Mujtama al Jadid* the right of the political spectrum.

Bahrain has no national news agency. The electronic media are operated by two state-owned agencies: the Bahrain Broadcasting Station and Bahrain Television. There is also a commercial radio station broadcasting in English called Radio Bahrain. News and information account for 20 percent of radio programming.

BURMA

BASIC DATA

Population: 34,004,000 (1980)
Area: 678,600 sq. km. (262,000 sq. mi.)
GNP: 35.28 billion kyats (US$5.14 billion) (1979)
Literacy Rate: 70% (official claim)
Language(s): Burmese
Number of Dailies: 7
  Aggregate Circulation: 339,500
  Circulation per 1,000: 12
Number of Nondailies: 133
  Aggregate Circulation: 1,285,680
  Circulation per 1,000: 47
Number of Periodicals: 600
Number of Radio Stations: 1
Number of Television Stations: None
Number of Radio Receivers: 693,000
  Radio Receivers per 1,000: 22
Number of Television Sets: None
  Television Sets per 1,000: None
Total Annual Newsprint Consumption: 10,800 metric tons (1977)
  Per Capita Newsprint Consumption: 0.3 kg. (.66 lb.)
Total Newspaper Ad Receipts: NA
  As % of All Ad Expenditures: NA

Upon independence, Burma inherited a well-established press with both English and vernacular papers. The English-language papers, such as the *Guardian,* were British-owned and British-edited, and to all appearances were Burmese versions of Fleet Street dailies. The Burmese and other vernacular newspapers had smaller circulations and poorer printing facilities, but they effectively reached classes of readers the English-language newspapers could not.

Within a year of independence the government began to move against the press, closing *Thorryah,* which had been founded in 1911. In 1966 a decree was passed that newspapers could print only in English and Burmese, thus eliminating seven Indian and Pakistani and five Chinese newspapers. In the same year, Ne Win's Revolutionary Council, then in the midst of a concerted drive to eliminate foreign influences from the country, nationalized all foreign newspapers, including the influential *Guardian,* and in 1969 followed this move by taking over 13 printing presses. By the Printers and Publishers Registration Act, all publishers were required to apply for registration certificates each year. A 10-member body, headed by a Central Press Chief Controller, was created to manage the nationalized press.

These moves were designed to change the character of the press and to reduce its size and limit its influence, and they accomplished just that. The total number of dailies has dropped from 31 in 1962 to eight in 1980, all of them state-owned and run by the News and Periodicals Corporation, in which the state holds 100 percent of the shares.

Burmese Newspapers (1980)

Title	Date of Founding	Circulation
Botahtaung ("The Vanguard")	1958	75,000
The Guardian	1886	17,500
Kyehmon ("The Mirror")	1957	90,000
Loke Tha Phithu Nay Zin	1963	90,000
Myanma Alin ("The New Light of Burma")	1914	26,000
Rangoon Daily	1946	21,000
The Working People's Daily	1963	20,000

Six of the seven daily newspapers are published in English, all are morning papers, published in Rangoon, and generally cost 68 kyats. They enjoy a combined circulation of 58,500 out of an aggregate circulation of 339,500, or about 17 percent. This circulation also provides a much needed clue to the prevalence of English in this country that has tried hard to shed Western influences and to close doors of communication with all non-Burmese cultures. Per capita circulation is 12 per 1,000 inhabitants, which is close to the Asian average; Burma ranks 108th in the world in this respect.

The periodical press has also shrunk since independence but still contains a few notable journals: *Forward,* published by the Information and Broadcasting Department with a circulation of 36,000; *Shwe Thwe,* published by the Sarpay Beikman Management Board with a circulation of 90,000; and *Teza,* published by the Myawaddy Press with a circulation of 60,100.

The 1974 constitution enjoins censorship of the media. But discussions of national policy that do not praise the Burmese Way to Socialism are banned. Censorship is also a tool in Burma's ongoing "war against decadent alien cultures." In August 1976 the Central Press Registration Board issued a long list of dos and don'ts for printers and publishers. The document set out the principles under which the board would censor material for publication. "Everyone has the freedom of literary expression and publication," it said, "so long as the freedom is used subject to the provisions of the constitution and truly in the interests of the people." Among the dos was publication of literature "that would educate and inspire the people for active participation in socialist constuction." Among the don'ts was publication of literature lauding capitalism and "decadent literature incompatible with Burmese national culture." All new publications require state licenses, which are not always routinely granted. In 1978 13 applications were received by the Central Press Registration Board, of which only six were granted and only three finally appeared on the market. One reason for the reluctance to permit new publications may be the high cost of newsprint, all of which has to be imported from Bangladesh. In 1977 Bangladesh required part of the payment for newsprint imports in hard currency, resulting in a media crisis of sorts.

Foreign correspondents are made to feel unwelcome, and the government's sensitivities to foreign reports are notorious. In 1976 Jacques Lamoureaux of AFP was expelled for filing "false" reports on Burma's law and order situation and thereby harming the dignity of Burmese leaders. Lamoureaux was the second foreign correspondent to be expelled from Burma; a correspondent of Hsinhua was ordered out of the country in 1967. The BBC is often taken to task for reporting on Burmese insurgent groups. The state-owned press lashes out at BBC, accusing it of being a "spokesman of insurgent groups" and "stabbing Burma in the back."

The national news agency is the News Agency of Burma (NAB), which replaced the privately owned Burma Press Syndicate. NAB has no foreign correspondents, its international news being obtained from Tass, AP, Reuters, AFP and Hsinhua.

The state-owned Burma Broadcasting Service operates a radio service; there is no television as yet. News and information account for 20 percent of the radio programming.

Journalism education is confined to courses taught in the Burma Translation Society's School of Journalism in Rangoon. Although ill paid, journalism is considered a dignified profession among the Burmese, and as a result it has been able to attract a number of talented and intelligent people in recent decades.

CYPRUS

BASIC DATA

Population: 619,000
Area: 9,251 sq. km. (3,700 sq. mi.)
GNP: C£664 million (US$1.92 billion) (1979)
Literacy Rate: 89%
Language(s): Greek, Turkish
Number of Dailies: 17
  Aggregate Circulation: 72,000
  Circulation per 1,000: 107
Number of Nondailies: 18
  Aggregate Circulation: NA
  Circulation per 1,000: NA
Number of Periodicals: 19
Number of Radio Stations: 4
Number of Television Stations: 2
Number of Radio Receivers: 96,500 (Greek sector only, 1978)
  Radio Receivers per 1,000: 156

Number of Television Sets: 67,850 (Greek sector only, 1978)
Television Sets per 1,000: 110
Total Annual Newsprint Consumption: 1,600 metric tons (1977)
Per Capita Newsprint Consumption: 2.3 kg. (5.06 lb.)
Total Newspaper Ad Receipts: NA
As % of All Ad Expenditures: NA

Since 1974 Cyprus has been divided into two separate zones. The northern zone, consisting of 40 percent of the national territory, is inhabited predominantly by Turkish Cypriots and occupied by Turkish troops; and the southern zone, inhabited by Greek Cypriots, is under the jurisdiction of the government of Cyprus. The island's press is also divided into Greek and Turkish sectors, the former being published and distributed only in the south and the latter only in the north.

The press of the Greek sector comprises 11 dailies, all in Greek except for one, the *Cyprus Mail* in English. All are published in the morning except for *Apogevmatini.* The Greek press is also relatively young; only one newspaper currently being published predates 1950. Almost all shades of political opinion are represented in the press; the right wing by *Demokratiko Virna,* the nationalists by *Phileleftheros,* the socialist EDEK by *Ta Nea,* the progovernment interests by *Apogevmatini,* the Democrats by *Eleftheri Kypros* and the Communist AKEL by *Haravghi.* The five largest selling newspapers are *Phileleftheros* (20,000), *Haravghi* (13,500), *Agon* (12,000), *Makhi* (12,000) and *Cyprus Mail* (5,740).

The Turkish sector offers six dailies including the *News Bulletin* published five times a week by the Public Information Office of the "Turkish Federated State of Cyprus." All papers appear in the morning. The oldest, *Halkin Sesi,* founded in 1942, is an independent Turkish nationalist paper as is *Bozkurt,* founded in 1951. *Zaman,* founded in 1973, is the official organ of the National Unity Party of Raif Denktas. Both *Bozkurt* and *Halkin Sesi* enjoy circulations of 5,000. The aggregate circulation of all Cypriot newspapers is reported by UNESCO at 72,000, or 107 per 1,000 inhabitants. Cyprus ranks 40th in the world in per capita circulation of dailies.

In addition, 18 weeklies and 19 periodicals are published in the Greek and Turkish sectors combined. Of the weeklies, four are published in English. The weeklies have relatively larger circulations than the dailies. The *Cyprus Bulletin* is published by the Cyprus Public Information Office in eight languages and has a circulation of over 47,250; the liberal *Alithia* has a circulation of 14,500; the independent *Tharos* has a circulation of 9,200; the progovernment *Dimokratia,* organ of the AKEL Party, has a circulation of 8,000 and *Ergatiko Vima,* organ of the Pancyprian Federation of Labor, has a circulation of 8,300. Private ownership is the norm in both Greek and Turkish sectors, although a number of dailies and nondailies act as the mouthpieces of political parties.

There is no censorship in either zone, but publication permits are required in the Greek sector. Such a permit is granted only on the deposit of CY£500 ($1,500) or a bank guarantee for the amount. All journalists are issued press cards by the Press Information Office. The Press Law prohibits the proprietor or managing editor of a newspaper from receiving any subsidy from a foreign government. Newspapers are required to "publish free of charge, not later than in the second issue of the newspaper after receipt thereof, a correction without additions or omissions of any statement of fact published in such newspaper if so requested by the person referred to in such statement and any such correction shall be given the same prominence as the original statement." Eighteen provisions of the criminal code also refer to the legal responsibilities of publishers.

The Public Information Office, set up in 1965, is the central channel for the dissemination of information dealing with government policies and activities. It coordinates all government information programs and also functions as a press liaison. Foreign correspondents are expected to contact the office on arrival.

The national news agency is the Cyprus News Agency, founded in 1976. Its daily news bulletin is used by Reuters in their international service.

The Cypriot Broadcasting Corporation is a semigovernmental body originally modelled after the BBC, that operates both radio and television services. The radio programs are broadcast from the main station in Nicosia and two relay stations at Pamphos and Limassol and two transmitters on Mount Olympus. Turkish radio and television are operated by Radio Bayrak and Bayrak TV. There are no organized training facilities for journalists on Cyprus.

ICELAND

BASIC DATA

Population: 227,000 (1980)
Area: 102,952 sq. km. (41,181 sq. mi.)
GNP: 642.53 billion (US$2.37 billion) (1979)
Literacy Rate: 99.5%
Language(s): Icelandic
Number of Dailies: 6
  Aggregate Circulation: 120,000
  Circulation per 1,000: 524
Number of Nondailies: 49
  Aggregate Circulation: NA
  Circulation per 1,000: NA
Number of Periodicals: 302
Number of Radio Stations: 2
Number of Television Stations: 2
Number of Radio Receivers: 65,000
  Radio Receivers per 1,000: 293
Number of Television Sets: 61,812
  Television Sets per 1,000: 272
Total Annual Newsprint Consumption: 3,600
  metric tons (1977)
  Per Capita Newsprint Consumption: 17.9 kg.
  (39.4 lb.)
Total Newspaper Ad Receipts: NA
  As % of All Ad Expenditures: NA

Newspaper publishing started in Iceland in 1848 with the weekly *Thjooolfur*, which served the 1,100 residents of Reykjavik with reports of domestic and foreign affairs. Some 25 years later, the newspaper *Isafold* was founded. It has survived to this day as part of a weekly paper in Akureyri, *Islendingur-Isafold*.

The first daily newspaper to appear was *Visir* in 1910. It is now an afternoon daily, with a circulation of about 21,000 and an average size of 20 pages. It supports the Independence (or Conservative) Party. Of the five remaining dailies, the one with the largest circulation is *Morganbladid* (Morning News), a conservative paper with a circulation of 40,000. It is the oldest morning daily, founded in 1913, and has an average issue running to 36 pages. The second oldest morning daily is *Timinn*, organ of the Progressive Party. Founded in 1916, it has an average size of 26 pages and a circulation of 18,000 on weekdays and 20,000 on Sundays. Founded in the same year, *Althyubladid* (The Labor Journal) is the organ of the Social Democratic

Party. Selling only 5,000 copies per issue, *Althyubladid* has the smallest circulation of all dailies and is only published on weekdays. Slightly to its left is *Thjodviljinn* (Will of the People), organ of the left-wing Socialist People's Union. Founded in 1935, it normally runs 16 pages and has a circulation of 12,000. The youngest of the dailies is *Dagbladid* (The Daily News), founded in 1975. An independent paper, in five years it managed to become the nation's second largest selling daily with a press run of 25,000 copies.

In addition, most political parties publish weeklies in other regional centers. The Social Democratic Party publishes *Althyudumadurinn in Akureyri,* and the Progressive Party publishes *Dagur in Akureyri* and *Einherji in Siglufjordur.* The Independence (Conservative) Party publishes *Siglfirdingur* in Siglufjordur. Two of the morning papers, *Morganbladid* and *Timinn,* publish special Sunday supplements of 12 to 16 pages. All Icelandic dailies are tabloids. The total circulation of all dailies is 120,000, with a per capita circulation of 524 per 1,000 inhabitants. Iceland ranks fifth in the world in this respect.

All the dailies except *Morganbladid* share common printing facilities established in early 1972. Almost all the leading journalists are members of Bladamannafelag Islands (The Union of Icelandic Journalists).

The Icelandic media enjoy absolute freedom. There is no censorship of any kind nor any state-imposed restrictions on domestic or foreign reporters. Iceland has no national news agency.

The state-owned Rikisutvarpid (Icelandic State Broadcasting Service) is in charge of both radio and television. News and information accounts for 16 percent of radio programming and 25 percent of television programming. Nearly 70 percent of television programs are imported, mostly from the United States.

IRAN

BASIC DATA

Population: 38,146,000
Area: 1,647,240 sq. km. (658,896 sq. mi.)
GNP: NA
Literacy Rate: 37%
Language(s): Farsi (Persian)
Number of Dailies: NA

Aggregate Circulation: NA
  Circulation per 1,000: NA
Number of Nondailies: NA
  Aggregate Circulation: NA
  Circulation per 1,000: NA
Number of Periodicals: NA
Number of Radio Stations: 14
Number of Television Stations: 17
Number of Radio Receivers: 10 million
  Radio Receivers per 1,000: 263
Number of Television Sets: 2.1 million
  Television Sets per 1,000: 55
Total Annual Newsprint Consumption: 25,500 metric tons
  Per Capita Newsprint Consumption: 0.8 kg. (1.76 lb.)
Total Newspaper Ad Receipts: NA
  As % of All Ad Expenditures: NA

At the time of the Islamic Revolution of 1979, Iran had a vigorous press with 20 daily and 21 weekly newspapers and 27 weekly and 44 monthly magazines published in Teheran. Eighty-five registered newspapers appeared in the provinces. With the exception of a small number of political organs and official publications, all newspapers were owned by private individuals. Three major groups dominated the press: The Ettela'at Group owned by the Farhad Massoudi family, which included *Ettela'at,* two foreign-language dailies, two weeklies and four popular weekly magazines; the Kayhan Group owned by the Mesbazadeh family, including *Kayhan, Kayhan International,* a weekly sports paper, two popular weekly magazines, and a medical magazine; and the Echo of Iran Group owned by Jahangir Behrouz, including the daily, weekly and monthly *Echo of Iran,* the monthly *Iran Trade* and an annual almanac. In addition, there were newspapers in Armenian and French and a specialized business and financial daily, the *Bourse.*

Despite the multiplicity of newspapers and periodicals and their generally good financial health, the press was subject to severe restrictions by the imperial government. The Press Law of 1955 as modified in 1963 defined even the qualities of education and character required in newspaper publishers and declared as illegal newspapers with a circulation of less than 3,000 and magazines with a circulation of 5,000. In 1965 the cabinet approved the Reporters' Code of Journalism, which required reporters to be licensed by the Ministry of Information. The law also banned all communist publications in the country. Aggregate circulation of daily newspapers was nudging the half million mark when the Pahlavi regime fell in 1979.

The seizure of power by Ayatollah Khomeini was first marked by an enlargement of the freedoms of speech and the press. The new Islamic Republic seemed to offer much greater scope for freedom of expression and even for some dissent. But by August 1979 it was evident that the regime had other intentions and was fashioning new instruments of repression. The new press law of August 1979 established severe penalties for insulting political and religious leaders. During August and early September 41 newspapers and magazines were closed and 18 foreign correspondents were expelled. Relenting somewhat, the government permitted eight of the closed newspapers to reopen in October and licensed 28 new newspapers, mostly run by the Islamic hardliners.

In April 1980 the new regime launched a concerted attack on press freedom. The newly created Ministry of National Guidance began to take on the role of a national censor. The ministry began by purging itself of more than 90 percent of its employees who were charged with suffering from "Western hang-ups." In the beginning some journals managed to escape systematic censorship by playing one faction of the ruling group against another. By June 1980, however, even these possibilities came to an end as the mullahs, originally only one of the factions in the revolutionary front, succeeding in taking over virtually all branches of government and posing a threat even to the moderate group backing President Abolhasan Bani-Sadr.

The year 1980 will go down in Iranian press history as one of its darkest periods. Scores of newspapers were closed while hundreds of journalists were thrown into jail. According to the now illegal National Union of Iranian Journalists, more than 75 percent of Iranian journalists—an estimated 3,000—are in exile, in jail or unemployed.

The Iran–Iraq war offered the hardliners a fresh opportunity to destroy the remaining vestiges of a free press, leading President Bani-Sadr to lament in the columns of his own newspaper, *Enquelaab Eslami,* "that there is no trace of press freedom in Iran today." The moderate *Enquelaab Eslami* itself was under fire from the clerical organ, *Islamic Republic,* which was described by Foreign Minister Sadegh Ghotbzadeh as "one of the most corrupt in Iranian press history." A newspaper launched by Ghotbzadeh was closed down after he was arrested on charges of "insulting the republic." Ghotbzadeh was later released on Khomeini's orders but his newspaper ceased publication after its offices were raided and "sealed" by the zealots. Newspapers belonging to the Soviet-aligned Tudeh Party and the Islamic-Marxist party, The People's Combatants, have also been shut down despite both groups' key role in toppling the shah.

In November 1980 the regime lifted a ban on journalists working for American and British news organizations. All American journalists left Iran in July 1980 after their credentials were not renewed. An Iranian Jewish journalist, Simon Farzami, went on trial in Teheran on charges of spying for the United States on the strength of documents found in the American Embassy. Farzami was the editor of the French-language journal, *Journal de Teheran,* which ceased publication shortly after the revolution.

In April 1981 the opposition paper *Mizan* was closed by the authorities following the arrest of its editor. The newspaper was the mouthpiece of the former premier, Mehdi Bazargan. Its editor, the former commerce minister, Riza Sadr, was accused of slander, libel, disturbing national security and publishing false reports. *Mizan* had been outspoken in its criticism of the hardliners' handling of the American hostage crisis and had even questioned the legality of the seizure of the American Embassy. *Mizan* was permitted to resume publication after 19 days, and Riza Sadr was released from prison on bail pending his trial for libel.

In June 1981 the clergy mounted an attack on President Bani-Sadr. In an effort to silence all dissent, the prosecutor general banned the last opposition paper in the country, *Enquelaab Eslami,* along with three other moderate newspapers. Bani-Sadr's comment on this occasion provides an appropriate clue to the direction of the Islamic Republic: "Past experience shows that suppression of the press is a prelude to the establishment of a dictatorship."

Repression of the press at home has led to its expansion abroad. By November 1980 over 100 Iranian publications had appeared abroad, mostly in the United States and Western Europe, claiming a combined circulation of over 200,000. Many of them were published by anti-Khomeini groups dedicated to bringing down the rule of the mullahs.

The national news agency is Pars News Agency (PANA), founded in 1936 and operated by the Ministry of Information. Radio and television are run by the Voice and Vision of Islamic Republic of Iran, a semi-autonomous government authority, which replaced Radio Iran and National Iranian Television in 1979.

The Islamic government's relations with the foreign media have always been hostile. Drastic curbs imposed during the seizure of the American Embassy remain in force, including a ban on unsupervised interviews with government officials and a requirement that foreign correspondents renew their press cards and visas every three months. Iran's journalism schools and mass media faculties were closed in October 1980 for "Islamization and purification."

IRAQ

BASIC DATA

Population: 13,134,000 (1980)
Area: 445,480 sq. km. (172,000 sq. mi.)
GNP: 8.98 billion Iraqi dinars (US$30.43 billion) (1979)
Literacy Rate: 20%
Language(s): Arabic
Number of Dailies: 4
　Aggregate Circulation: 80,000
　Circulation per 1,000: 6.5
Number of Nondailies: 6
　Aggregate Circulation: NA
　Circulation per 1,000: NA
Number of Periodicals: 179
Number of Radio Stations: 2
Number of Television Stations: 8
Number of Radio Receivers: 2,000,000
　Radio Receivers per 1,000: 168
Number of Television Sets: 475,000
　Television Sets per 1,000: 40
Total Annual Newsprint Consumption: 4,900 metric tons (1977)
　Per Capita Newsprint Consumption: 0.4 kg. (0.88 lb.)
Total Newspaper Ad Receipts: NA
　As % of All Ad Expenditures: NA

The earliest Iraqi publications were official and semiofficial newspapers published during the latter half of the 19th century under

Turkish rule. Printed in Arabic and Turkish, they carried mostly official announcements and a few commercial notices. During the early 1900s more than 50 newspapers were published in Baghdad and other cities, but no dailies. By 1914 most of them had been banned by the Turkish authorities.

With the establishment of the British mandate came a rapid growth in nationalist papers. The attainment of nominal independence in 1930 gave rise to a new class of transient newspapers operating as the personal mouthpieces of politicians and probably funded by them. When they fell from office the newspapers fell with them, to be replaced by others founded by the new leaders. This personalized type of journalism and its highly political orientation remained characteristic of the Iraqi media until the fall of the monarchy in 1958.

During the British mandate the newspapers were subject to licensing, although freedom of the press was guaranteed by the Organic Law of 1925. Some newspapers, such as *Al-Istiqlal* ("Independence") and *Al-Furat* ("Euphrates"), were critical of the mandate and clamored for its end. Nationalist sentiments were again on the rise in the 1940s during the negotiations preceding the Treaty of Portsmouth (1948), which regulated matters of mutual defense between the two countries. The newspapers *Al-Jihad* ("Crusade") and *Al-Yaqda* ("Vigilance") led the campaign aganst it. This led to the promulgation of formal censorship in 1950, which, however, was rarely invoked until 1952. The number of newspapers was sharply reduced after the governmental crisis of 1952 and the Baghdad riots. A new censorship law prohibited "irresponsible criticism of the government," under threat of suspension. The return of Nuri as-Said as prime minister in 1954 brought about the dissolution of all political parties and the suspension of their party organs. Eighteen such newspapers were closed. Newspapers were forbidden to comment adversely on the Baghdad Pact or to attack powers with which Iraq had friendly relations.

For a year after the revolution of 1958 the press enjoyed a degree of freedom that it had not enjoyed before and that it was destined never to enjoy again. A number of leftist publications appeared on the scene and a few of them enjoyed substantial circulations: *Ittihad as-Sha'ab* ("The People's Unity"), *Sawt al-Ahrar* ("Voice of Freedom"), *Ar Ra'i*

al'amm ("Public Opinion"), *Al Insaniyah* ("Humanity") and *Al Thawrah* ("The Revolution"). But within a year Prime Minister Abdul Karim Qasim blamed the press for creating confusion and disrupting national unity. In 1959 the Press Association Law was promulgated requiring all qualified journalists to become members of the government-sponsored Press Association (also called Journalists Association). The law reaffirmed the freedom of the press but stipulated that "enemies of the country" would be denied press licenses and that only true news would be published.

Restrictions on the press grew in number and intensity until 1967 when the government abolished all private newspapers and took over the function of publishing under the direction of the newly established Press and Printing Organization and the Ministry of Culture and Guidance. The government defined the rationale of this move thus: "The current battle the Arab nation is waging against imperialism, Zionism and reaction requires that the Iraqi press be guided on sound national lines...to disseminate sound ideas, provide true guidelines, and carry out constructive criticism that would preserve the state."

As of 1980 four dailies were published in the country.

Iraqi Dailies (1980)

	Circulation	Date of Founding
Al Thawrah ("The Revolution")	35,000	1968
Al Jumhuriyah ("The Republic")	35,000	1958
The Baghdad Observer	3,500	1967
Al Iraq (formerly *Al Taakhi*)	6,500	1969

All Iraqi dailies are post-revolutionary institutions. The press is also exclusively Baghdadian; no daily newspapers are published outside the capital. The continued existence of the English-language *Baghdad Observer* is an interesting anomaly in a country that was among the first in the Arab world to turn its back on Western legacies.

The aggregate circulation of 80,000 (in a country with a population of 13 million) is low by any standard but may be explained by the fact that the circulation of the five dailies is limited to Baghdad and its environs. The other major cities, such as Mosul, Sulaymaniyah, Samarra, Hillah, Najaf, Nasiriyah, and Basra, depend on weeklies and periodicals. Per capita circulation in the late 1970s was 6.5 per 1,000 inhabitants, among the lowest in the Arab world and among the bottom 50 in the world.

Because newsprint is in short supply, most newspapers are limited to eight pages. Arab political news and editorial comments are prominently featured, usually on the first page. Translations from the foreign press fill the second page, while page three is often devoted to items of interest to women and youth. Approximately one-fourth to one-third of the space is used for advertisements, most of them official tenders and drab, colorless sales notices placed by government-owned firms.

Although suppression of national minorities, such as the Kurds, is part of official policy, a minor concession has been made to them by permitting a partly Kurdish daily called *Al Iraq* (formerly *Al Taakhi*). Its low circulation of around 6,500 and the fact that it is published from Baghdad rather than from northern Iraq, where the Kurds are concentrated, illustrate the government's general disinterest in this venture.

The Press and Printing Organization, which publishes all national dailies, is administered by a board of directors whose members are appointed by the government. They include the chief editors of all newspapers, a representative of the Ministry of Culture and Guidance, the head of the Department of Journalism in Baghdad University, and representatives from the Journalists and Printers Unions. The law also provides for appointment to the board of five part-time members representing "writers, thinkers, and experts." Decisions of the Board are subject to approval by the Ministry of Culture and Guidance.

Both *Al Jumhuriyah* and *Al Thawrah* enjoy equal circulations and influence, although the former is regarded as the government mouthpiece and the latter as the organ of the Baath Party. All papers share editorial and production facilities; since the whole economy is state-controlled they do not have to compete for the advertising dinars. The budget of the Press and Printing Organization is incorporated into the national budget.

Journalists are represented by General Union of Posts, Telegraph, Printing and Information Workers, which is affiliated to the Baathist-dominated General Federation of Trade Unions. Strikes are illegal.

The principal law relating to the media is Law 155 of 1967, which nationalized the press and placed it under the control of the General Establishment for Press and Printing (GEPP). GEPP produces all the newspapers although they are sponsored by other organizations: *Al Thawrah* by the Baath Party, *Al Jumhuriyah* and *The Baghdad Observer* by the Ministry of Information and *Al Iraq* by the Kurdish Democratic Party. Possibly the sponsors handle the editorial work, but the lines of authority are not clearly drawn. Despite its being a state-owned and state-run paper, *Tariq al Sha'ab* was suspended in April 1979 as a rebuff to the Communist Party. All editors are also senior officials of the Ministry of Culture and Guidance. Thus, the censors are also the editors.

The import and distribution of foreign publications are controlled through the issue of licenses. Foreign correspondents require special visas, and all cables must be submitted to the Ministry of Information for prior approval. The government backs the 1978 UNESCO Declaration on the media.

The national news agency is the Iraqi News Agency, founded in 1959. It is headed by a board of directors, including representatives from the Ministry of Culture and Guidance, the Ministry of Defense, the Ministry of Foreign Affairs and others. Much of the domestic reports originate from the government departments themselves; for international news coverage the agency depends on AP, Reuters, MENA, and dpa.

Electronic media are under the Iraqi Broadcasting and Television Establishment, which controls the Broadcasting Station of the Republic of Iraq (Idaa'h Baghdad and Idaa'h Sawt Al Jamahir) and eight television stations at Baghdad, Kirkuk, Mosul, Basrah, Missan, Muthanna, Um Qasr and also the Kurdish Television. Radio programming covers the entire national territory with both home and foreign programs. News and information account for 11 percent of radio programming and 18 percent of television programming.

Journalism training is provided at the Department of Journalism of the Baghdad University, although only a few journalists hold any professional qualifications or degrees. Most reporters and editors are graduates of secondary schools, while some at best have one or two years of university education.

The Iraqi press is described as a "mobilization press," that is, a press designed solely to promote the interests of the ruling group. It functions within an environment that is generally described as revolutionary but in many respects is reactionary. Although passive toward the regime in power, its tone is strident and contentious toward all others. Finally, because it reflects accurately a society in which there is no public dissent, debate or opposition, the Iraqi press is politically inert and dormant.

IVORY COAST

BASIC DATA

Population: 7,898,000
Area: 323,750 sq. km. (129,500 sq. mi.)
GNP: CFA francs 1.78 trillion (US$8.56 billion) (1979)
Literacy Rate: 65%
Language(s): French
Number of Dailies: 1
 Aggregate Circulation: 38,000
 Circulation per 1,000: 5
Number of Nondailies: 1
 Aggregate Circulation: NA
 Circulation per 1,000: NA
Number of Periodicals: 11
Number of Radio Stations: 6
Number of Television Stations: 11
Number of Radio Receivers: 206,000 (1978)
 Radio Receivers per 1,000: 26
Number of Television Sets: 154,000 (1978)
 Television Sets per 1,000: 20
Total Annual Newsprint Consumption: 800 metric tons (1977)
 Per Capita Newsprint Consumption: 0.1 kg. (0.22 lb.)
Total Newspaper Ad Receipts: NA
 As % of All Ad Expenditures: NA

The Ivorian press was entirely French in ownership and character until the first African-owned and -edited newspaper in the Ivory Coast was launched in the mid-1930s. The Breteuil family established *Abidjan-Matin,* as its second successful West African daily, modeled on its flagship paper, *Dakar-Matin,* in Dakar, Senegal. Between then and 1960 over 30 newspapers were established by Africans or French residents and survived for a short time before vanishing.

Financing was a major factor in the failure of new journalistic ventures since both newsprint and printing equipment had to be imported, mostly from France, and were taxed on entry, sometimes as high as 30 percent of the total value. Another factor contributing substantially to the lack of an indigenous, independent press was the sale of French metropolitan dailies, which reached Abidjan by air within 24 hours of publication. Both the French and the educated African elite preferred the French newspapers as a matter of course because of their broader and more sophisticated coverage of world affairs. Ivorians also had read *Afrique Nouvelle,* a weekly established by the Roman Catholic White Fathers in Dakar and considered the best source of news in French West Africa. *Afrique Nouvelle* had a large number of Africans on its staff but was nevertheless viewed as a European paper.

In 1964 the government took over *Abidjan-Matin* from the Breteuil family and converted it into *Fraternité-Matin,* which continues to serve as the nation's sole daily. In 1980, it had a circulation of 38,000. *Fraternité,* the former weekly organ of the ruling Parti Démocratique de Côte d'Ivoire (PDCI), became *Fraternité-Hebdo,* the weekly edition of *Fraternité-Matin.* Initially, the editorial address of *Fraternité* was President Houphouet-Boigny's residence, and it was printed in Paris. It has since established an editorial office in Treichville and is printed by the government printer. The mastheads of both *Fraternité-Matin* and *Fraternité-Hebdo* read like a who's who in Ivorian government: President Houphouet-Boigny is the political director; Philippe Yace, PDCI secretary general, is the director, and Minister of Education Laurent Dona Fologo is the assistant director.

In addition to party and government funds, *Fraternité-Matin* receives its principal revenues from advertising. Out of a regular issue of six pages two are devoted to advertising, mostly classified ads and schedules of local movie houses. Often the premiere of a new film receives a full-page advertisment. The daily has only limited circulation outside the Abidjan-Grand-Bassam complex. Only about 15 percent of the copies are sent by rail or plane to the interior towns. Many of the editors and journalists on the staff are still French, but the paper has never been noted for its news coverage, and its main appeal is to sport fans. Ivorians continue to prefer Parisian dailies, which circulate freely.

Ivory Coast has an extensive periodical press, which makes up for the lack of a more varied daily press. With few exceptions, the periodicals are aimed at the educated elite, both French and African. There is virtually no vernacular press and no publications addressed specifically to neoliterates. The largest periodical publisher is the government, which brings out the *Journal Officiel, Bulletin Quotidien*, the monthly *Eburnea* and *Bulletin Mensuel de Statistiques*. The Christian magazine *Djeliba* has a circulation of 6,000. Other publications serve the Abidjanians: *Abidjan 7 Jours* and *La Semaine d'Abidjan*. The Chamber of Commerce and the Inter-Afrique Presse also publish periodicals.

There are few Ivorian professional journalists. In the 1960s the government began a program of training young Ivorian journalists in France but not all of them were absorbed by the media on their return. When the Association Ivorienne des Journalistes Professionnels (AIJP) was founded in 1961, it had only 20 members, of whom four were Ivorians. AIJP meets with some regularity for "dinner debates" at which a prominent member of the government or a visiting foreign dignitary usually speaks and answers questions. These debates are an important source of contacts for the journalists in the capital since press conferences are seldom held.

The Information Service, established by the Ministry of Public Service and Information, serves as another contact between the government and the media. It has editorial as well as photographic sections. A number of Halls d'Information, or information centers, have been established in the major towns. The centers are headed by directors who also serve as press correspondents for the government. The Information Service also publishes a wall newspaper, which is posted at government offices throughout the country.

The constitution gives no specific guarantee of press freedom. Nevertheless this is embodied in the preamble to the French Declaration of the Rights of Man of 1789 and the Universal Declaration of 1948. Yet, because there are so few publications in the country and still fewer publications outside of the government-run press, it has not been necessary to define the limits of this freedom. The Ivorian press is certainly not free by Western standards, nor is it unfree by African standards. There are occasional bannings and confiscations, but they are so infrequent that they do not indicate an official determination to suppress the media. The media are supposed to play a positive role in promoting national unity and development. Criticism is permitted so long as it refers to shortcomings of policy execution rather than of the policies themselves. Restrictions on the Ivorian press are offset, however, by the access that all Ivorian readers have to foreign publications. These are not seized even when they criticize the government.

A 1959 law, "Strengthening the Protection of Public Order," made it a criminal offense to publish false news that brings into disregard the laws of the country, injures the morals of the population, or discredits political institutions, "whether done with mischievous intent or not." These acts are punishable by one to three years in prison and by a fine of CFAF 500,000 ($2400) to CFAF 2,500,000 ($12,000). The offending editors and journalists may be expelled from the country for up to five years.

As in the case of the other countries of former French West Africa, existing media facilities are concentrated in urban areas where the educated 10 percent of the population live. Relatively few papers reach the interior, and the penetration of the electronic media is negligible. The Ivorian media therefore, can be properly called the Abidjan-Grand-Bassam media; rural affairs seldom intrude on the cosmopolitan media, and the media rarely affect the lives of the rural inhabitants.

The national press agency is Agence Ivorienne de Presse (AIP), established in 1961. AIP has taken over all contracts with foreign news agencies, and only AIP may disseminate news in the country. The agency is under the direct control of the Ministry of Information. Although described as an independent organ, its stated policy is to ensure government control of the news. During its early years AIP was headed by French nationals and it continues to employ French workers on its staff. Besides the daily *Bulletin Quotidien*, AIP publishes the fortnightly English-language bulletin, *Ivory Coast*. Two small news agencies also operate in the country: Edipress and Société d'Information et de Diffusion Abidjanaise.

Radio and television are controlled by Radiodiffusion Ivoirienne and Télévision Ivoirienne. The principal medium-wave station is at Abidjan with a relay station at Bouake and VHF transmitters at Abidjan, Bouafle, Man and Koun-Abbrosso. Television was introduced in 1963 and color television in 1973. There are 11 stations.

Training for Ivorian journalists has been mainly in apprenticeships. The government sponsors journalism students for training in Paris. A course for journalists is offered by the University of Dakar, Senegal, where UNESCO makes available one scholarship a year for an Ivorian journalist.

KOREA, NORTH

BASIC DATA

Population: 19,014,000 (1980)
Area: 121,730 sq. km. (47,000 sq. mi.)
GNP: 35.3 billion won (US$19.72 billion) (1979)
Literacy Rate: 90%
Language(s): Korean
Number of Dailies: 12
  Aggregate Circulation: NA
  Circulation per 1,000: NA
Number of Nondailies: NA
  Aggregate Circulation: NA
  Circulation per 1,000: NA
Number of Periodicals: NA
Number of Radio Stations: 1
Number of Television Stations: NA
Number of Radio Receivers: 175,000
  Radio Receivers per 1,000: 9.2
Number of Television Sets: NA
  Television Sets per 1,000: NA
Total Annual Newsprint Consumption: 1,300 metric tons (1977)
  Per Capita Newsprint Consumption: 0.08 kg. (0.18 lb.)
Total Newspaper Ad Receipts: NA
  As % of All Ad Expenditures: NA

Patterned after the Chinese press, the North Korean press is a vast propaganda machine designed more to guide the people than to inform them. All papers are published by the government, the Worker's Party and its affiliated organization. In 1980 the *Korean Year Book* listed 12 dailies, all published in Pyongyang. Some are noted as affiliated with specific organizations.

- *Jokook Tongil,* Organ of the Committee for the Peaceful Reunification of Korea
- *Joson Inmingun,* Organ of the People's Army
- *Kyowen Shinmoon,* Organ of the Ministry of General Education
- *Minjoo Chosun,* Organ of the Government of the Democratic People's Republic
- *Nongup Keunroja,* Organ of the Central Committee of the Korean Agricultural Working People's Union
- *Pyongyang Shinmoon*
- *Rodong Chongyon,* Organ of the Central Committee of the Socialist Working Youth League of Korea
- *Nodong Sinmun,* Organ of the Central Committee of the Workers' Party of Korea
- *Rodongja Shinmoon,* Organ of the General Federation of Trade Unions
- *Saenal,* Organ of the League of Socialist Working Youth of Korea
- *Sonyon Sinmun,* Organ of the League of Socialist Working Youth
- *Tongil Sinbo*

Except for *Nodong Sinmun,* which enjoys, by unconfirmed reports, a circulation of 700,000, the circulation of other papers appears to be quite small, limited to Party and state cadres and managers with responsibility for implementing official policies. Newsstands are absent in North Korean cities, and it is doubtful if any of these papers are designed for popular consumption.

In addition, the party committee in each province publishes a four-page newspaper of varying frequency. These newspapers are designed to increase production and mobilize worker support for national programs.

The periodical press follows the same pattern. The most popular magazine is *Kunroja,* published by the Central Committee of the Workers' Party, with a circulation of over 300,000. Interestingly, more periodical publications appear in foreign languages than in Korean. Some of them, such as *Korea Today* (published in English, Chinese, French, Russian and Spanish), are richly illustrated and printed on glossy paper for the benefit of overseas readers.

The pacesetter of the North Korean press is *Nodong Sinmun,* published by the Central Committee of the Workers' Party. Its editor in chief also heads the Korean Journalists' Union, and is always a high-ranking Party member with access to its inner councils. About 28 percent of articles and news items in a sample issue of this paper concerned domestic politics and inspirational guide-lines to the masses. Another 25 percent attacked the United States and South Korea, and 20 percent discussed economics and edu-cation. If *Nodong Sinmun* is the country's *Pravda*, then its *Izvestia* is *Minju Choson*, organ of the government, which enjoys a cir-culation of 100,000.

Each edition of a newspaper is planned in detail far in advance of the date of publica-tion. Editors follow instructions from the Party regarding the placement of articles, choice of type, and length of feature stories. All newspapers have the same format and almost the same content. The first and second pages usually contain the Party lead-ers' speeches in full (even down to the pauses and applauses) or Party directives. The third page features provincial and departmental news; international news usually appears on the fourth page. A few themes run throughout the paper: the glorification of Kim il Sung, the national economic achievements, the unifica-tion of Korea, and denunciations of South Korea and the United States.

The majority of the news items are sup-plied by the Korean Central News Agency. Copies of articles selected by KCNA or writ-ten by staff members are usually submitted to the newspaper by noon of the day prior to publication. These are then reviewed by members of the editorial board and by the appropriate Party committee. Articles are expected to conform, in both language and form, to standards specified by the Party. Although they are written by journalists well trained in propaganda techniques and dedi-cated to the Communist ideology, the articles are screened on three levels: first internally, then by the appropriate bureau of the State Administration Council, and finally by the Propaganda and Agitation Department of the Workers' Party.

All journalists are required to belong to the Korean Journalists Union. The union is divided into four sections: propaganda and organization, international reporting, editor-ial and training. The union also operates a special institute offering both a two-year and a six-month course of study.

The national news agency is the Korean Central News Agency (KCNA), run directly by the State Administration Council. The agency publishes a daily news bulletin in Korean, periodical bulletins in English and Russian, and a national yearbook.

Broadcasting is the responsibility of the Central Broadcasting Committee of the State Administration Council, although actual administration is shared with the Workers' Party. With seven medium-wave and 12 short-wave stations, the home service's two programs are on the air for a total of 40 hours a day. Loudspeakers are installed in factories and in open spaces in all towns. A rudimen-tary television network is operating but no details are available.

KUWAIT

BASIC DATA

Population: 1,318,000 (1980)
Area: 16,058 sq. km. (6,200 sq. mi.)
GNP: KD 6.02 billion (US$12.87 billion) (1979)
Literacy Rate: 60%
Language(s): Arabic (official); English widely used
Number of Dailies: 7
  Aggregate Circulation: 65,000
  Circulation per 1,000: 77
Number of Nondailies: 19
  Aggregate Circulation: 145,000
  Circulation per 1,000: 128
Number of Periodicals: 49
Number of Radio Stations: 1
Number of Television Stations: 1
Number of Radio Receivers: 550,000
  Radio Receivers per 1,000: 489
Number of Television Sets: 540,000
  Television Sets per 1,000: 478
Total Annual Newsprint Consumption: 5,900 metric tons (1977)
  Per Capita Newsprint Consumption: 5.2 kg. (11.5 lb.)
Total Newspaper Ad Receipts: NA
  As % of All Ad Expenditures: NA

When Kuwait attained full independence in 1961, it had no print media worth the name. As a result of government policies and encouragement, a popular and respected press soon emerged. Until the early 1970s the government extended financial subsidies to new newspapers and periodicals started by Kuwaitis. The freedom offered to reporters and editors encouraged immigration of jour-nalists from throughout the Arab world. The salaries were good and the press regulations less stringent than those experienced by most Arab journalists at home. In a short while, Kuwait had a press that media observers compared to Lebanon in its diversity, political influence and economic strength.

Kuwait's oldest dailies are *al Ra'y al Amm* and *al Siyassah,* both of which were established in the 1960s. The former is a strong supporter of the royal family and friend of the West (although differing occasionally with certain U.S. positions) as well as an opponent of Baath-type Arab socialism and Soviet-type Communism. On the other hand, *al-Siyassah,* while supporting the royal family, is more outspoken and liberal and tends to take a more investigative approach to official programs and policies. Its chief editor, Ahmed Jarallah, specializes in interviews with Arab leaders. Occasionally it has shown a moderate Marxist slant and sympathy for the radical regimes in the Arabian Peninsula.

The most popular paper on the newsstands is *Al Qabas.* Founded only in 1972, it achieved the highest circulation within four years. Owned by a group of local businessmen, *Al Qabas* emphasizes business interests, uses translations from the foreign press, tries to be objective in its coverage of news and events and gives more space to Palestinian writers. A fourth daily, *al Watan,* while outspokenly critical of the Kuwaiti government, espouses democratic ideals, such as free speech, and provides in-depth coverage of foreign affairs. The most recent of the Arabic dailies, *al Anba,* has strong links with the Kuwaiti business community and is a staunch advocate of Arab social values as well as capitalism. Occupying the center of the political spectrum are the two English-language dailies, *The Kuwaiti Times* and *Arab Times,* the latter owned by the Siyassah group.

The strength of the Kuwaiti press may be partly explained by the fact that all these papers are owned by rich and powerful Kuwaiti families with excellent social connections. In a traditional society such ties lend weight to any undertaking and make it more easily accepted.

The six daily newspapers have an aggregate circulation of 65,000, or 77 per 1,000 inhabitants, the highest in the Arab world. Combined with the fact that Kuwait has also the second highest GNP per capita in the region, it is evident that Kuwaiti press has a strong economic base as well.

There is a clear division between the moderate and radical wings of the Kuwaiti press. The majority are moderates, but there is a highly vocal and visible minority of radical journalists of Palestinian origin.

Government actions against the press have been relatively mild; the most drastic measure has been a three-month crackdown. No press establishment has ever lost its license over a conflict with the government. At the same time, the government retains on paper the right to enforce strict controls over the media. The Kuwaiti press is forbidden by law from criticizing the emir, or quoting him without authorization. It may not publish information that would affect the value of the national currency or create misgivings about the Kuwaiti economy or advocate the overthrow of the government by force. Before the press law amendment of 1976 the government could not take direct action to suspend an offending newspaper but could only take it to court. Under the press regulations of 1976 any newspaper license may be suspended by the Council of Ministers for a period not exceeding two years and by the minister of information for a period not exceeding three months. Any newspaper or journal may also be permanently suspended at the discretion of the Council of Ministers. This power was limited in its exercise to newspapers that (a) served the interests of a foreign government or organization, (b) obtained any sort of assistance from a foreign state or (c) contradicted the national interests. The government explained that these restrictions became necessary because "negative aspects" of the press had to be corrected. The prime minister said, "With unlimited freedom, the press has become irresponsible.... Giving it freedom without controls has made some papers obedient instruments in the service of objectives alien to our country, which work to corrupt society, propagate self-interested rumors, and sow trivialities and sedition among our ranks."

Pre-censorship is not used except during a national emergency such as the 1967 war, and censorship of imported print materials is rare. The primary means of government influence over the press continues to be persuasion. *Ra'y al Am* provides an interesting case study of how this persuasion works. In 1978 the paper was banned for three days for carrying a cartoon of Egyptian vice president Mubarak. But within months the paper had swung behind official policy. Later, the paper even cancelled its newsprint and other printing contracts with Canada to protest the move of the Canadian embassy from Tel Aviv to Jerusalem.

But the Kuwaiti press has to face dangers from other sources. In 1980 *Ra'y al Am's* presses and offices were damaged by two explosions, which the government blamed on dissident (Palestinian) elements.

Kuwait maintains an open door to foreign correspondents. There are no special restrictions, such as special visas, and no prior approval for cables. As noted earlier, the import and distribution of foreign periodicals do not require restrictive licenses. In fact, Kuwait is one of the principal pipelines of Arab communications with the West. However, the government, in common with other Arab states, wholeheartedly supports the 1978 UNESCO Declaration on the Media.

The national news agency is the Kuwaiti News Agency (KUNA), founded in 1976. KUNA does not have a monopoly on the acquisition of foreign news, and the media are permitted to subscribe directly to AP, Tass or any other news service.

The electronic media are controlled by the Kuwait Broadcasting Service and Television of Kuwait, both operated by the state. The radio service has both medium-wave and short-wave transmitters, while the television service has five main, two auxiliary and one experimental transmitters, covering not only the small kingdom but also parts of southern Iraq, Saudi Arabia and other Gulf states. News and information account for 10 percent of radio programming and 22 percent of television programming.

Both the government and the public point with pride to the Kuwaiti press as among the freest and most vigorous and diverse (after Lebanon) in the Arab world. The press is owned by a varied group of influential people who are respected for wealth and public involvement. Moreover, the political system, while absolutist, makes diversity and competition possible, and even encourages them. The government's policies of cooperation with all major political movements in the region and of employing non-Kuwaitis in positions of authority make it more tolerant of a free press.

LIBERIA

BASIC DATA

Population: 1,818,000
Area: 111,370 sq. km. (43,000 sq. mi.)

GNP: $890 million (US$890 million) (1979)
Literacy Rate: 24%
Language(s): English; also 28 tribal dialects
Number of Dailies: 2
   Aggregate Circulation: 10,000
   Circulation per 1,000: 6
Number of Nondailies: 1
   Aggregate Circulation: 5,000
   Circulation per 1,000: 3
Number of Periodicals: 6
Number of Radio Stations: 4
Number of Television Stations: 1
Number of Radio Receivers: 260,000
   Radio Receivers per 1,000: 144
Number of Television Sets: 10,000
   Television Sets per 1,000: 5
Total Annual Newsprint Consumption: NA
   Per Capita Newsprint Consumption: NA
Total Newspaper Ad Receipts: NA
   As % of All Ad Expenditures: NA

As the oldest independent black state in West Africa, Liberia has also one of the continent's oldest presses. It began in 1826 when Charles Force began printing the *Liberia Herald* on a hand-operated press given to him by an American missionary. The paper did not survive its founder, who died within a few months. It was, however, revived four years later by another black American, John B. Russwurm, who had worked on the first black newspaper in the United States, *Freedom's Journal.* For the next 32 years Russwurm waged a tireless battle against slavery, which he excoriated with religious fury. The last of *Herald's* editors was a West Indian writer named Wilmot Blyden; when Blyden left to become a professor at Liberia College, the *Herald* folded in 1862.

Eight years earlier, Edward James Royce, the first pure Negro to become the president of Liberia, had founded the *Liberian Sentinel.* Numerous competitors followed: *The Liberian Advocate, Monrovia Observer, The Liberia Bulletin* and the *Whirlwind.* Although they were all affiliated to some political faction, few were independent of the True Whig Party, which by the end of the 19th century had established itself as the dominant factor in national life.

The only paper to survive World War II was the *Liberian Star,* founded in 1939 as a weekly. In 1946 it was joined by *The Daily Listener,* founded by Charles Cecil Dennis, a member of parliament. In the same year

President Tubman's ruling True Whig Party founded the *Liberian Age* as a biweekly. It started as a private venture but was subsidized by the Tubman Administration. For most of the Tubman and Tolbert years the *Star,* the *Age* and the *Sunday Express* (founded by John Fitzgerald Scotland in 1974) dominated the press. The *Star* was the first to fold. The British Thomson organization, which owned it, decided to jettison it along with many other African properties in 1968. *The Daily Listener,* although bolstered by state funds, entered the 1970s in dire financial straits. Its publisher Dennis had launched two more papers in 1970 and had so overstretched his resources that all three papers closed in 1973.

Of the 19 newspapers established in Liberia since 1826, only one—the *Age*—was being published at the time of the 1980 military coup. The reasons were not merely economic. The Tubman years emasculated the press to such a degree that one observer has called it the Sycophantic Press. Although Tubman used less blunt methods than other African autocrats, the result was the same: the press was bludgeoned into submission.

Although the administration was corrupt, criticism was taboo. Any journalist disagreeing with the president felt the weight of presidential displeasure almost immediately. Charles Frederick Taylor, publisher of the *African Nationalist* was convicted of libeling Tubman in 1947 and remained in jail for 25 years until President Tolbert released him. During the 1960s and 1970s many journalists were locked up for terms varying from 24 hours to several years. Incarceration was not the only means of dealing with offending newsmen. In 1951 Samuel Richards, editor of *The Friend,* organ of the opposition Independent True Whig Party, incurred the wrath of the president. He was locked up and a gang of toughs broke into his press and destroyed the printing equipment. *The Friend* never appeared again. When the *Independent Weekly* was started in 1954 as an opposition voice by a naturalized Liberian, Mrs. Bertha Corbin, she was jailed for contempt of legislature and forced to leave the country and her paper was closed. In fact, in dealing with the opposition Tubman was as ruthless as his peer and contemporary, Pap "Doc" Duvalier of Haiti.

Tubman's heavy arm fell not only on opposition journalists but also on editors of the *Age,* the official voice of the True Whig Party. Two of its editors, Henry B. Cole and Aston S. King, were dismissed for mild criticisms of the government, and their successor, Stanley B. Peabody, was jailed briefly. The message was not lost on the editors, who learned that good journalism is not always good survivalism. During most of the Tubman and Tolbert years the Liberian front pages were full of adulatory articles praising the genius and accomplishments of the men in power. While this was not unusual by the standards of its neighbors, it demonstrated that the ostensibly democratic character of the regime was only a facade.

The 1980 coup led by a group of noncommissioned troops (described by a former administration official as a "bunch of high school dropouts") brought a change in masters but not much else. With the suspension of the constitution, civil and political rights have no legal bases but are exercised at the suffrance of the regime. The press remains free of institutionalized censorship, but editors steer clear of all controversial and sensitive subjects out of a healthy instinct for self-preservation. Local news dealers refuse to distribute even international publications critical of the Doe regime.

The *Liberian Age* continues to be the country's sole daily, not counting *The New Liberian,* a newspaper published by the Ministry of Information. The *Age's* circulation of 10,000 has not changed significantly during the past decade. The *Sunday Express* continues to be published by a private organization. It claims a circulation of 5,000. Per capita circulation is six per 1,000, close to the African average.

The periodical press consists of some six titles, of which only *The Liberian Outlook,* a monthly, deserves mention. Liberia has no national news agency.

All forms of broadcasting are controlled by the Liberian Broadcasting Corporation, which also oversees the official radio station, ELBC, and the official television station, ELTV. Monrovia is the site of one of the best-known Christian Evangelistic radio stations in Africa, ELWA, run by the Sudan Interior Mission.

LIBYA

BASIC DATA

Population: 2.933 million
Area: 1,758,610 sq. km. (703,444 sq. mi.)
GNP: LD 692 billion (US$23.4 billion) (1979)

Literacy Rate: 35%
Language(s): Arabic
Number of Dailies: 1
   Aggregate Circulation: 64,000
   Circulation per 1,000: 26
Number of Nondailies: 8
   Aggregate Circulation: 192,000
   Circulation per 1,000: 65
Number of Periodicals: NA
Number of Radio Stations: 15
Number of Television Stations: 13
Number of Radio Receivers: 130,000
   Radio Receivers per 1,000: 45
Number of Television Sets: 155,000
   Television Sets per 1,000: 53
Total Annual Newsprint Consumption: 600
   metric tons
   Per Capita Newsprint Consumption: 0.2 kg.
   (0.44 lbs.)
Total Newspaper Ad Receipts: NA
   As % of All Ad Expenditures: NA

The People's Socialist Libyan Arab Republic lies on the north-central coast of Africa, just to the west of Egypt. Only about two percent of the country is arable, the rest consisting of barren rock-strewn plains and desert. This is the principal reason for the country's relatively small population, estimated at about 2.5 million. In addition, about one million foreigners live and work in the country.

Most of the population lives either in the narrow, relatively fertile coastal strip along the Mediterranean, or on oases scattered in the south. About 20 percent are concentrated in the two principal cities of Tripoli and Benghazi. The Libyans are primarily a mixture of Arab and Berber. Ninety-seven percent are Arabic-speaking Moslems. Illiteracy, estimated at about 60 percent, is a serious problem.

Libya has been an independent nation only since 1951. For centuries it had been subject to foreign rule. Italians wrested the country from the Turkish Empire in 1912 and ruled it until the defeat of Axis forces in North Africa in 1943. The British then administered the area until 1951 when a constitutional monarchy was installed, headed by King Idress al-Sanussi. He was deposed in a 1969 army coup lead by Colonel Muammar al-Qaddafi, who has controlled the government since then.

The only newspapers in the country before independence were owned by foreigners, mostly British; and these employed the only Libyan journalists then working. With independence the government and various private interests also entered the market. Within a few years, the country counted nine dailies, five printed in Arabic, three in English and one in Italian. There were also four biweeklies and seven weeklies printed in English as well as one weekly printed in Italian. Two of the Arabic-language dailies were government organs, one of which was published in Tripoli and the other in Benghazi.

Political parties were forbidden. Nevertheless, the papers represented views that ranged from conservative, religious and anti-communist on the one hand, to leftist and radical on the other. The government allowed independent, and even opposition, papers to publish, but these had to abide by strict press laws.

When Colonel Qaddafi and his Revolutionary Command Council (RCC) seized power, they moved immediately to establish their own party, now known as the Arab Socialist Union, and their own newspaper, *al-Thawrah* (The Revolution), to help explain their ideas. Meanwhile they continued the previous government's ban on competing organizations or party newspapers.

Qaddafi also quickly muzzled the private press, cutting back sharply on subsidies that the monarchy had given to those papers as well as to the government's own publications. Early in 1970 he proclaimed that government advertising could appear only in *al-Thawrah*. Then in January 1972 the RCC suspended all newspapers for "corruption of public opinion." All eventually had their publishing licenses revoked. Even *al-Thawrah* disappeared. However, its place was taken later that year by a new government daily called *al Fajr al Jadid* (The New Dawn), which is still the only daily in the country. It is published by the Ministry of Information and has a circulation of 28,000, with eight pages an issue.

There are two weeklies published in the country. *Al-Zahaf al-Akhdar* (The Green March), an ideological publication that reflects Colonel Qaddafi's ideas, is published by the Revolutionary Council and has a circulation of about 35,000. *Al-Jamahiriya* (The Land of the Masses), has a circulation of about 20,000 and is published by the women's revolutionary committees in Tripoli.

In addition, there are six bimonthlies. They are:

• *al-Shorti* (The Policeman), which has a circulation of about 45,000. It is the only publication in Libya that reports on crime and hence the most popular. However, it does not publish names or addresses of criminals.

•*al-Ard* (The Land), an agricultural publication with a circulation of 18,000.

•*al-Montigoon* (The Producers), published by the nation's workers' union with a circulation of 17,000.

•*al-Mua'alm* (The Teacher), published by the teachers' union with a circulation of 14,000.

•*al-Taleb* (The Student), published by the Libyan Students' Union, with a circulation of 21,000.

•*al-Mwaf* (The Employee), published by the white collar workers' union, with a circulation of 22,000.

All these papers have come into existence since 1974 when Colonel Qaddafi published his "Green Book," a compilation of reflections on how things should operate in Libya. The first chapter in the "Green Book" concerns the press and is, quite literally, the press law of the country. In January 1980 the government's company for publications issued additional guidelines that amount to censorship rules. These stipulate that only literature of the 1969 revolution is to be published; that priority is to be given to the political thought of the revolution; that young writers who truly express the ideology of the revolution are to be encouraged; that no private writing or expression of personal feeling is to be published unless it agrees with the revolution's thought; that nothing from earlier Libyan writers is to be published that does not serve the revolution's interest; that symbolic or nonfactual writing, or any light work of written art is not to be published; that writers are not to be paid for their intellectual work in order to discover which are true revolutionaries and which are writing only for money, and finally that a committee selected by the country's writers' union must evaluate any literary or artistic work before it can be published.

In addition, key sections of the "Green Book" assert:

The press is a means of expression of the society and cannot be the means of expression of a natural or corporate person. Logically and democratically, therefore, the press can not be owned by either of these.

Any newspaper owned by an individual is his own and expresses only his point of view. Any claim that a newspaper represents public opinion is groundless because it actually expresses the viewpoints of a natural person. Democratically, a natural person should not

be permitted to own any means of publication or information.

However, he [a natural person] has the natural right to express himself by any means.... Any journal issued by a trading association or by a chamber of commerce is only a means of expression for this particular social group. It represents its own point of view and not the viewpoint of public opinion. This applies to all corporate and natural persons in society.

The democratic press is that which is issued by a popular committee comprising all the various categories of society. In this case only, and not otherwise, will the press or any information medium be an expression of the whole society and a bearer of the viewpoint of its categories, and thereby the press or information medium will indeed be democratic.

If the Medical Association issues a journal, it must be purely medical. Similarly, this applies to other categories. The natural person has the right to express only himself and he is not entitled, from the democratic point of view, to express anybody else's. In this way what is called the problem of press freedom in the world will be solved radically and democratically. The continuing problem of press freedom in the world today is generally the product of the problem of democracy. It cannot be solved unless the entire crisis of democracy in the whole society is solved....

The union newspapers follow these rules literally. They deal only with issues of concern to their members, such as working or living conditions. They never comment on national or international events and, of course, never criticize any government rules or decisions. The unions sponsoring the bimonthlies, moreover, are not unions in the Western sense of the word but are units of government-picked national congresses. Their papers are financed by the government through its Secretariat of Information. They are also printed in government print shops and are distributed by the government.

Jamahiriya News Agency (JANA) is the successor of the former Libyan News Agency, which was established in 1964 before Qaddafi's coup. It is the only news agency in the country and the only organization permitted to subscribe to foreign wire services. All incoming foreign news must go through it. Not only does it select news, but it usually edits and makes its own interpretation of the items that are then passed on to the media. It operates under the Secretariat of Information and subscribes to all the world's major agencies. It also takes part in operations of the Non-Aligned News Agencies Pool, which is administered by the Yugoslav agency Tanjug.

All broadcasting is tightly controlled by the government. There are three radio and three TV stations in the cities of Tripoli, Benghazi and Sabha, but programming is centralized in Tripoli. There is almost no local input, even from the other two bigger cities. All operations and programming are under the supervision of the government's Secretariat of Information.

Many, if not most, Libyans depend on foreign broadcasts for their knowledge of world events. The most popular news source is the British Broadcasting Corporation, but many people also listen to Egyptian and Tunisian radio, as well as to the Arabic-language broadcasts from Radio Monte Carlo.

Those who can afford relatively expensive antennas can also watch TV broadcasts from Italy, Malta, Egypt and Tunisia, particularly during the summertime. In addition, many Libyans are buying videotapes and videodiscs for entertainment. Many videotapes, smuggled in from abroad, are now available on the black market.

LUXEMBOURG

BASIC DATA

Population: 358,000 (1980)
Area: 2,590 sq. km. (1,000 sq. mi.)
GNP: LF127.35 billion (US$4.54 billion) (1979)
Literacy Rate: 98%
Language(s): French, German, Luxembourgish
Number of Dailies: 5
   Aggregate Circulation: 156,100
   Circulation per 1,000: 443
Number of Nondailies: NA
   Aggregate Circulation: NA
   Circulation per 1,000: NA
Number of Periodicals: 16
Number of Radio Stations: 1
Number of Television Stations: 1
Number of Radio Receivers: 182,800 (1978)
   Radio Receivers per 1,000: 511
Number of Television Sets: 86,500 (1978)
   Television Sets per 1,000: 242
Total Annual Newsprint Consumption: NA
   Per Capita Newsprint Consumption: NA

Total Newspaper Ad Receipts: NA
   As % of All Ad Expenditures: NA

Luxembourg is a blend of France and Germany. The official language of the civil service, law and parliament is French but German is the primary language in other areas. This dichotomy is carried over into the media. Most dailies and periodicals are published in both French and German.

Luxembourg has two of the oldest dailies in Europe. The venerable *Luxembourger Vort/ La Voix du Luxembourg,* founded in 1848, is one of the most distinguished Christian Democratic and Catholic newspapers on the Continent. The liberal *Letzeberger Journal* is also over 100 years old, having been founded in 1880. Three other dailies are published in the country: *Le Republican Lorrain, Tageblatt/Le Journal d'Esch,* and *Zeitung vum Letzeburger Vollek.* With the exception of *Le Republican Lorrain,* the other dailies are affiliated to political parties: *Luxemburger Wort* to the Christian Social Party, *Tageblatt* to the Socialist Party, *Letzeburger Journal* to the Liberal Party, also known as Democratic Party, and *Zeitung vum Letzeburger Vollek* to the Communist Party. The most widely read dailies in the duchy are *Le Soir* and *Het Laatste Nieuws,* both published in Brussels. Among the domestic dailies, *Luxemburger Wort* has the highest circulation (77,600), followed by *Tageblatt* (32,500) and *Le Republican Lorrain* (24,000). The Communist daily has the lowest circulation of all, less than 8,000. Aggregate circulation of domestic dailies is 156,100, or 443 per 1,000. Luxembourg ranks fourth in the world in per capita daily newspaper circulation.

The periodical press consists of 16 titles; the majority are commercial and industrial journals. The largest circulation is reported by the illustrated weekly *Revue,* which sells over 29,700 copies. Luxembourg has no national news agency.

Luxembourg is one of the few countries in the world where radio and television services are operated by a private commercial company. French financial interests have a majority shareholding in this company, known as Compagnie Luxembourgeoise de Telediffusion, or Radio-Tele-Luxembourg, for short. Its finances are derived entirely from advertising revenues.

MADAGASCAR

BASIC DATA

Population: 8,461,000
Area: 595,700 sq. mi. (238,280 sq. mi.)
GNP: MGF562 billion ($2.49 billion) (1979)
Literacy Rate: 45%
Language(s): Malagasy
Number of Dailies: 12
   Aggregate Circulation: 65,000
   Circulation per 1,000: 7
Number of Nondailies: 31
   Aggregate Circulation: 291,000
   Circulation per 1,000: 34
Number of Periodicals: 44
Number of Radio Stations: 1
Number of Television Stations: 1
Number of Radio Receivers: 600,000
   Radio Receivers per 1,000: 75
Number of Television Sets: 6,000
   Television Sets per 1,000: 0.75
Total Annual Newsprint Consumption: 3,500 metric tons
   Per Capita Newsprint Consumption: 0.4 kg. (0.88 lb.)
Total Newspaper Ad Receipts: NA
   As % of All Ad Expenditures: NA

The first printing and publishing facilities were established on Madagascar by Protestant missionaries in the 1860s. The press of the London Missionary Society held the title of Official Printer to the Queen of Malagasy until the 1880s when the Merina government established its own press. The Roman Catholics who arrived soon after the Protestants also established their own printing presses.

The island's first newspaper, *Gazety Malagasy*, appeared in the 1870s. It was followed within the next decade by the *Madagascar Times* and *Le Progres de l'Imerina*. The influence of the British Protestants made English the predominant language during this period, and for a time three English-language newspapers flourished in Tananarive, now Antananarivo: *Madagascar Times, Madagascar News* and *Madagascar World*. The French press, with little or no official support, was limited to provincial centers, such as Tamatave and Diego-Suarez.

With the establishment of a French Protectorate in 1894, the fortunes of the two rival language presses were reversed. By the eve of World War I, privately owned French-language newspapers such as *L'Echo de Tananarive, L'Echo du Sud, Madecasse* and *Le Colon* dominated the island's press. The first official Malagasy-language newspapers, *Vaovao*, founded in 1894, marked the birth of the indigenous press.

Between the world wars the Malagasy newspapers became either increasingly literary on the one hand or nationalistic on the other. Nationalist sentiments were promoted in such publications as *L'Aurore* and *L'Opinion*. In the 1930s an expanded Malagasy-language press had four leading newspapers: *Takariva, Firenena Malagasy, Ny Pariny* and *Ny Gazetinsika*.

The press survived a brief period of repression following the 1947 revolt. The 1950s witnessed a relative relaxation of controls and the expansion of circulation and readership. By the 1960s there were 18 dailies, 48 weeklies and 90 other periodicals serving a potential audience of 5.5 million literates. Many of these publications were backed financially by political parties or religious groups.

In the early 1980s there are 12 daily newspapers, of which the most influential and the best selling is the *Madagascar-Matin*, published in French and Malagasy with a circulation of 30,300. There are three government publications: *Madagasikara Mahaleotena* (5,000), *Bulletin Quotidien*, published by the national news agency, ANTA, and *Atrika*. Despite a reduction in the political role of the press under the military regime, opposition voices are still heard through *Imongo Vaovao*, which supports the policy positions of the leftist Party of the Congress for the Independence of Madagascar. Basically independent positions are maintained by the dailies *Ny Gazetinsika* and *Maresaka* (5,500). The humorous newspaper, *Hehy*, is considered moderate but supports leftist positions occasionally. It has a relatively large circulation of 15,000. The aggregate circulation of all dailies is reported by UNESCO as 65,000, or 10 per 1,000 inhabitants. Madagascar ranks 113th in the world in this respect.

In addition, UNESCO reports 31 nondailies with an aggregate circulation of 291,000. About two-thirds are published in French and about half are printed weekly. All but four of the weeklies are published in Antananarivo. There is various government publications and research reports such as the *Journal Officiel de la République Malgache*, founded in 1883. The Catholic Church publishes two influential journals, *Fanilo* and *Lakroani Madagasikara*. The progovernment periodical press is led by *Vaovao* with a circulation of over 17,000.

Most of the dailies are limited to about eight pages. Editorials usually appear on the front page. The larger dailies have their own foreign correspondents, but most depend on the Agence Nationale d'Information "Taratra" (ANTA) for both domestic and foreign news. Some newspapers have featured columnists. Subscription rates are high, and because of poor distribution systems newspapers rarely circulate outside their place of publication.

Freedom of the press has been increasingly restricted by the military regime. There is prepublication censorship, and criticism of the government tends to be subtle and indirect. The Ministry of Information maintains close watch on the media, and journalists are required to "disregard information likely to be harmful to the government's socialist development policies." Western publications are not generally available in the country. Journalists are represented by the Press Syndicate of Madagascar.

The national news agency is the Agence Nationale d'Information "Taratra" (ANTA), which was founded in 1977 to replace Agence Madagascar Presse, founded in 1962. The agency, which functions under the Ministry of Information, publishes the daily *Bulletin Quotidien* with a circulation of 800. ANTA has six permanent offices and a staff of 40.

Radiodiffusion-Télévision Malagache operates 10 radio transmitters and four television transmitters. Radio Madagasikara operates two home service networks reaching 90 percent of the population. News and information make up 19 percent of the programming as compared to 47 percent in the daily press. About 10 percent of the population is reached by television. About 70 percent of the programs are imported.

A professional training center for journalists was established in 1965 at the University of Madagascar. It provides a three-year course in press, radio and television.

MALTA

BASIC DATA

Population: 331,000
Area: 313 sq. km. (125.2 sq. mi.)

GNP: Maltese £302.8 million (US$890 million) (1979)
Literacy Rate: 83%
Language(s): Maltese, English
Number of Dailies: 5
  Aggregate Circulation: 60,000
  Circulation per 1,000: 200
Number of Nondailies: NA
  Aggregate Circulation: NA
  Circulation per 1,000: NA
Number of Periodicals: 160
Number of Radio Stations: 1
Number of Television Stations: 1
Number of Radio Receivers: 70,800
  Radio Receivers per 1,000: 214
Number of Television Sets: 70,800
  Television Sets per 1,000: 214
Total Annual Newsprint Consumption: 200 metric tons (1977)
  Per Capita Newsprint Consumption: 0.6 kg. (1.32 lb.)
Total Newspaper Ad Receipts: NA
  As % of All Ad Expenditures: NA

For an island only 316 sq. km. in area with a population slightly over 300,000, Malta has one of the most developed press systems in the world. The daily press comprises five newspapers, two in English and three in Maltese. The oldest English daily is *The Times*, founded in 1935 and owned by Mabel Strickland, and the oldest Maltese daily is *L'Orizzont*, founded in 1962 and published by the General Workers' Union. Competing with *The Times* is the English-language *Daily News*, founded in 1964, while the other two Maltese dailies are *Il-Hajja* and *In-Taghna*, both founded in 1970. Only the circulations of three dailies are known: *The Times* (16,000), *Daily News* (12,000) and *L'Orizzont* (18,000). The best estimates of aggregate circulation place it at close to 60,000, or 200 per 1,000 inhabitants, close to UNESCO's saturation point.

Politics and organized labor play a major role in the press. *L'Orizzont* and *Daily News* are pro-Labor, while *In-Taghna* is affiliated to the opposition Nationalist Party. *The Times* supports the Progressive Constitutional Party. The periodical press is even more vigorous than the daily one. There are over 160 titles of all frequencies, of which 77 are in Maltese, 63 are in English and 20 are bilingual. Political weeklies dominate the periodical press. The Labor Party brings out *The Voice of Malta, Il-Hsieb, It-Torca, Ir-Repubblika, Sport* and other magazines, while the rival Nationalist Party publishes *The Democrat, Il-Mument, Il-Poplu* and others. Other major periodicals include the Catholic church's *Lehen is-Sewwa* and *Il-F'Ghawdex*, the Progressive Constitutional Party's *Forward/Il Quddiem*, and Malta University Press's *Journal of Maltese Studies* and *Lehen il-Malti* and the Department of Information's *Malta Today*.

The press is generally free of constitutional and administrative restraints. Malta has no national news agency. The privately owned Associated News (Malta) was founded in 1968 and maintains a permanent bureau in London.

Broadcasting services are subject to the provisions of the Broadcasting Ordinance and are under the overall supervision of the Malta Broadcasting Authority, an independent statutory body. Both radio and television services are provided by a private company, Xandir Malta, a division of Telemalta Corporation.

MAURITIUS

BASIC DATA

Population: 943,000
Area: 1,856 sq. km. (742.4 sq. mi.)
GNP: Mauritian Rs 5.95 billion (US$970 million) (1979)
Literacy Rate: 60%
Language(s): English, French, Hindi, Chinese
Number of Dailies: 12
  Aggregate Circulation: 90,000
  Circulation per 1,000: 94
Number of Nondailies: 9
  Aggregate Circulation: NA
  Circulation per 1,000: NA
Number of Periodicals: 9
Number of Radio Stations: 3
Number of Television Stations: 5
Number of Radio Receivers: 105,039
  Radio Receivers per 1,000: 117
Number of Television Sets: 75,704
  Television Sets per 1,000: 84
Total Annual Newsprint Consumption: 1,000 metric tons
  Per Capita Newsprint Consumption: 1.1 kg. (2.42 lb.)
Total Newspaper Ad Receipts: NA
  As % of All Ad Expenditures: NA

The Mauritian press, like Mauritius itself contains great ethnic and linguistic diversity. The island's four main communities—Hindus, Creoles, Chinese and Muslims—have managed for nearly a century to preserve their own distinct social identity and culture, and the press has been their principal means of maintaining their separate status and interests. There are 12 daily newspapers serving a population of less than a million—a ratio of one daily to every 80,000 people, one of the highest in the world.

Mauritius has the oldest newspaper currently being published in Africa—*Le Cerneen*—the organ of the sugar industry, founded in 1832. It predates South Africa's *Eastern Province Herald* by 13 years. The second oldest daily is *Le Mauricien,* representing Creole interests, founded in 1908. The growth of the Chinese and Indian communities during the first quarter of the 20th century led to the founding of the first Chinese daily, *Chinese Daily News,* in 1932 and the first Indian-owned daily, *Advance,* in 1939. Two more papers were founded in the 1950s, both Chinese: *New Chinese Commercial Paper* in 1956 and *China Times* in 1953. The spate of new dailies continued well into the 1960s and 1970s: *Star* in 1963, *L'Express* in 1963, *Le Militant* in 1969, *Liberation* and *The Nation* in 1971 and *Le Populaire* in 1973. The survival ratio of the new dailies was also high, and very few dailies folded despite the intense competition.

The largest-selling daily is *L'Express* with a circulation of over 18,000, followed by *Le Cerneen* (13,000), *Le Mauricien* (12,000), *Star* (10,000), *Advance* (9,500), *Le Militant* (8,000) and *The Nation* (7,000). Chinese papers are surprisingly able to survive with smaller circulations; one has a circulation of 1,000. Aggregate circulation is reported by UNESCO at 90,000 or 94 per 1,000 inhabitants. Mauritius ranks 51st in the world in per capita circulation of dailies. With the exception of the three Chinese dailies, all daily newspapers are published in both French and English, but for historical reasons French is preferred over English.

UNESCO also reports seven weeklies, two fortnightlies, five monthlies and four periodicals published at less frequent intervals. Two of the weeklies enjoy large circulations of nearly 25,000 copies each: *Week-End* and *Le Dimanche.* Periodicals include a Roman Catholic weekly with a circulation of over 9,000 and weeklies in Hindi and Chinese.

The constitutional guarantees of freedom of speech and press have been generally observed except for the period from 1971 to 1976 when censorship was imposed to put a lid on ethnic tensions.

There is no national news agency. Reuters and AFP maintain permanent bureaus in Port Louis and together have 258 subscribers. The Mauritius Broadcasting Corporation controls both radio and television. The domestic radio service reaches 100 percent of the population with one medium-wave transmitter and two short-wave transmitters. The television service operates five main and four auxiliary stations. About 90 percent of the radio programs and 35 percent of the television programs are nationally produced.

MONGOLIA

BASIC DATA

Population: 1,666,000
Area: 1,564,619 sq. km. (625,848 sq. mi.)
GNP: 3.68 billion tugrik ($1.270 billion) (1979)
Literacy Rate: 80%
Language(s): Khalkha Mongol
Number of Dailies: 1
  Aggregate Circulation: 120,000
  Circulation per 1,000: 80
Number of Nondailies: 27
  Aggregate Circulation: NA
  Circulation per 1,000: NA
Number of Periodicals: 32
Number of Radio Stations: 1
Number of Television Stations: 1
Number of Radio Receivers: 140,300
  Radio Receivers per 1,000: 87
Number of Television Sets: 40,800
  Television Sets per 1,000: 25
Total Annual Newsprint Consumption: 2,300
  metric tons (1977)
  Per Capita Newsprint Consumption: 1.5 kg.
  (3.3 lb.)
Total Newspaper Ad Receipts: NA
  As % of All Ad Expenditures: NA

All newspapers in Mongolia are published by the Mongolian People's Revolutionary Party and its affiliated organs. The oldest newspaper, *Unen* (Truth), the Mongolian equivalent of *Pravda,* was founded soon after

the establishment of the Mongolian Communist Party. The *Unen* was followed by *Dzaluuchuudyn Unen* (Young People's Truth), founded in 1924 by the Central Committee of the Revolutionary Youth League and *Ulaan Od* (Red Star), founded in 1930 by the Ministries of Defense and Public Security. Although described as dailies, both *Dzaluuchuudyn Unen* and *Ulaan Od* are published only 144 days a year or 12 times a month. *Hodolmor* (Labor), organ of the Central Council of Trade Unions, is similarly published 144 days a year.

There are also 18 provincial newspapers published biweekly by the aymag (provincial) party and executive committees. They include one published in Kazakh in Bayanolgiy Aymag. Several cities have their own newspapers, such as *Ulaanbaataryn Medee* (Ulan Bator News) founded in 1954 and issued 208 times a year.

The periodical press comprises six weeklies and bimonthlies and 40 titles issued less frequently. Of the weeklies the most influential are *Pionyeriyn Unen* (Pioneers' Truth) organ of the Central Committee of the Revolutionary Youth League, with a circulation of over 132,000, and *Ediyn Dzasag* (Economics), organ of the Central Committee of the Mongolian People's Revolutionary Party. The Ministry of Agriculture publishes two weeklies: *Sotsialist Hodoo Aj Ahuy* (Socialist Agriculture) and *Shine Hodoo* (New Countryside), while the Writers' Union and the Ministry of Culture publish *Utga Dzohiol Urlag* (Literature and Art). The oldest periodical is *Namyn Am'dral* (Party Life), founded in 1923 by the Central Committee of the Mongolian People's Revolutionary Party. The Central Committee also publishes *Uhuulagch* (Agitator) and *MAHN-yn Tov Horony Medee* (MRRP Central Committee News).

Circulation figures are available only for *Unen* (120,000) and a few other nondailies and periodicals. Per capita daily circulation is 80 per 1,000 inhabitants.

The Mongolian press is closely patterned after the Soviet press; even the titles of the major newspapers are the Mongolian equivalents of Soviet publications. While all papers are owned and published by the MRRP and its organs, specific control of the press is exercised by the State Committee for Information, Radio and Television. The Committee is responsible not only for editorial direction but also for finances, distribution and allocation of newsprint. The State Committee also brings out a number of foreign-language propaganda publications such as *News from Mongolia* in English, *Les Nouvelles de Mongolie* in French, *Novosti Mongoli* in Russian and *Monggu Xiaozibao* in Chinese. The national news agency is Montsame (Mongol Tsahilgaan Medeeniy Agentlag — Mongolian Telegraph Agency), founded in 1957.

All broadcasting comes under the authority of the State Committee for Information, Radio and Television. Ulan Bator radio is equipped with long-wave and short-wave transmitters. The television center at Ulan Bator, built with Soviet aid, transmits mostly Moscow-produced programs through Molniya satellite. Journalistic training is provided at the University of Ulan Bator.

MOZAMBIQUE

BASIC DATA

Population: 10,172,000
Area: 786,762 sq. km. (303,770 sq. mi.)
GNP: 129.43 billion escudos ($US2.6 billion) (1979)
Literacy Rate: 15%
Language(s): Portuguese
Number of Dailies: 2
  Aggregate Circulation: 19,000
  Circulation per 1,000: 2
Number of Nondailies: NA
  Aggregate Circulation: NA
  Circulation per 1,000: NA
Number of Periodicals: 4
Number of Radio Stations: 1
Number of Television Stations: NA
Number of Radio Receivers: 230,000 (1977)
  Radio Receivers per 1,000: 23
Number of Television Sets: NA
  Television Sets per 1,000: NA
Total Annual Newsprint Consumption: 1,300 metric tons (1977)
  Per Capita Newsprint Consumption: 0.1 kg (0.2 lb)
Total Newspaper Ad Receipts: NA
  As % of All Ad Expenditures: NA

Although smaller than Angola in size, Mozambique was the most important of Portugal's colonies in Africa. Like other colonial powers, the Portuguese were not anxious to establish a press in their colonies, fearing

that it might easily become a focus of dissent. The first daily in Mozambique was started by the English-speaking community of Lourenco Marques. In 1905 the daily *Lourenco Marques Guardian* made its appearance in the capital. Perhaps out of a deference to the colonial authorities, the *Guardian* completely ignored African news and published only news affecting England and Englishmen. It was not until 1956, when the Archbishop of Lourenco Marques bought the paper and changed its name to *Diario,* that it began publishing in Portuguese. Even then, the archbishop considered the paper primarily as a medium for his ultraconservative politics. Competing ideologically with the *Diario* was the *Diario de Moçambique,* founded in 1950 by the liberal bishop of Beira, who had entered publishing in 1932 with the weekly *A Voz Africana.* While the editor of *A Voz Africana* was an African, the bishop was believed to be the editorial writer. The constant friction between the ultraconservative archbishop and the liberal bishop enlivened the media politics of the colony until the 1960s.

To counter the liberal voice of *Diario de Mozambique,* the major Portuguese trading company, Companhia de Moçambique, sponsored *Noticias de Beira,* first as a biweekly and later as a daily. By the end of the 1960s, as the forces of conservatism became more powerful, *Noticias de Beira* took over *A Voz Africana.* In the capital itself the voice of right-wing conservatism was heard through the colony's biggest paper, *Noticias,* founded in 1926 by a retired army captain, Manuel Simoes Vaz. From the time of the Fascist takeover of the Lisbon government in 1933 *Noticias* was virtually the official government paper, with both morning and evening editions.

In addition to *Diario de Moçambique,* the liberal press included *Tribuna* and *A Voz de Moçambique. Tribuna* was founded in 1962 by Joao Reis and a group of progressive Moçambicanos of every color. Until it was taken over by Banco Nacional Ultramarino, *Tribuna* was the outstanding liberal organ of the colony. *A Voz de Moçambique* was founded in the 1950s by a group of political moderates known as Associação dos Naturais de Moçambique. Although only moderately pro-African, *A Voz de Moçambique* came into repeated conflict with the government censors and was eventually taken over by the Banco Nacional Ultramarino.

The non-European press was small and ill-financed. The most important publication in this sector was *O Brado Africano,* the weekly organ of the Associação Africana, a "coloreds" (i.e., mixed-race) organization. In its heyday during the 1930s it sold over 40,000 copies.

The Mozambican press was still struggling to establish itself as a credible and economically viable institution when the storm of African insurrection broke out in 1964. The FRELIMO, one of the most dedicated of African guerrilla groups, soon proved itself to be more than a "native rabble," as Lisbon described it. The effect on the press was almost lethal. All liberal and African editors and publishers were arrested by the hard-line generals who had been sent to take over the colonial administration in Lourenco Marques. Although the authorities did not formally nationalize the press, the official Banco Nacional Ultramarino did just that indirectly by foreclosing on newspapers that owed them money. Among the newspapers taken over by the bank were *Tribuna, Noticias,* and *A Voz de Moçambique.* The bank appointed a hard-line right-winger, Antonio Mario Zorro, as editor in chief of both *Tribuna* and *Noticias.* Zorro radically changed the tone of both papers by refusing to print any stories that he personally disliked. Zorro was at the helm for just four years when the Fascist government in Lisbon was overthrown and Marcello Caetano was replaced by General Antonio Spinola and later by General Costa Gomes and General Vasco Goncalves. With the white regime tottering and the FRELIMO sweeping down from the north, Zorro left for Lisbon, leaving the direction of his papers to Rui Knopfli, a liberal newspaperman. Protesting Knopfli's support of the FRELIMO, the white right-wingers bombed the presses of both *Noticias* and *Tribuna* about three months before the Lisbon coup of November 25, 1974, sounded the death knell of the Portuguese Empire.

The FRELIMO government that succeeded the Portuguese as rulers of the country in 1975 remains adamantly Marxist. Soon after it took power, the privately owned press ceased to exist. Only two newspapers were allowed to continue: *Noticias,* the morning daily in Maputo (formerly Lourenco Marques), and *Noticias de Beira,* the morning daily in Beira. The former claims a circulation of 13,000 and the latter of 6,000. Aggregate circulation is 19,000, or 2 per 1,000 inhabitants, one of the lowest in the world.

The periodical press has shrunk to four titles, three in Maputo and one in Beira. The only significant journal is the official gazette, *Boletim da Republica de Moçambique.*

All journalists are required to be members of the officially sponsored Organização Nacional das Journalistas, founded in 1978. This organization functions not so much as a trade union as an indoctrination school.

The government has frequently called for a network of national and local correspondents but it has not been reported whether it has succeeded in establishing such a network. It is probable that existing party faithfuls will be doubling as correspondents. Sometimes party cells are used as distribution points for newspapers.

As a Marxist government, the FRELIMO has not tried to keep up even the appearance of a free press. The term "freedom of the press" does not find a place in the constitution. The only clue to FRELIMO's communication policies is in the report of a seminar on national media held in Macomia soon after independence. In the absence of specific press laws, the report could be interpreted as the guiding philosophy of FRELIMO with respect to the media, and as the official definition of the role of the press in the new setup.

During the early part of the seminar many of the lower cadre wanted to scrap the conventional press altogether. "The journalistic technique," they noted, "is rooted in the bourgeois concept of journalism copied from the Western capitalistic model." Deemphasizing the role of the press, the seminar noted the 90 percent illiteracy in the country and declared that the press is not relevant in relation to other means of developmental communication. The importance of the press was primarily as an ideological tool. The seminar attacked journalists as persons "with a mentality rooted in bourgeois capitalism.... The deficiencies of the press tend to reflect the deficiencies of the professional classes who work in them, the majority of them of petit bourgeois origin who have no knowledge of the life of the masses." The seminar called for a remodeled press "placed at the service of the masses within the political direction of the FRELIMO." It recommended that the "journalistic technique should be strictly conditioned by the concrete realities of Mozambique and by the revolutionary political line directed toward national reconstruction.... Newspapers should portray a vision of the world corresponding to the dynamic class struggle.... The press should relate to the larger masses."

On a more practical level, the seminar

recommended the popularization of wall newspapers, called People's Newspapers, on the Chinese model. These newspapers were to have a maximum life of seven days, with completely new revisions every three days. They were to be displayed so that they could be read standing up in marketplaces, factories, schools, and near wells and taps, and protected from the rain with little roofs. If paper was not available, other materials like wood and scrap paper from old packaging were to be used. Even alternative writing materials, such as a charcoal, were not to be shunned. The contents of the papers were to be limited to local issues; international events were to be reported only when they relate to the class struggle. The wallpapers were to be designed to increase literacy and make the people "understand the revolutionary process."

Mozambique's relations with the foreign media have suffered from constant ideological strain. Western correspondents are generally unwelcome and their entry is rigidly restricted. Import of books and publications is permitted only from socialist countries with a few exceptions.

The national news agency is Agencie de Informação de Moçambique, whose office on Ho Chi Minh street is the hub of FRELIMO's media operations. The official radio station is Radio Moçambique, founded in 1975. There is no television service.

NEPAL

BASIC DATA

Population: 14,719,000 (1980)
Area: 141,000 sq. km. (54,595 sq. mi.)
GNP: NRs 21.48 billion (US$1.79 billion) (1979)
Literacy Rate: 12%
Language(s): Nepali, Hindi
Number of Dailies: 12
  Aggregate Circulation: 116,900
  Circulation per 1,000: 10.6
Number of Nondailies: 52
  Aggregate Circulation: 4,400
  Circulation per 1,000: 0.3
Number of Periodicals: 94
Number of Radio Stations: 2
Number of Television Stations: None
Number of Radio Receivers: 200,000
  Radio Receivers per 1,000: 15
Number of Television Sets: None
  Television Sets per 1,000: None

Total Annual Newsprint Consumption: NA
  Per Capita Newsprint Consumption: NA
Total Newspaper Ad Receipts: NRs 162,000 (US$600,000) (1979)
  As % of All Ad Expenditures: 58.9

The earliest Nepali newspaper was the *Gorkha Patra,* founded in 1953 by the ruling Rana family. On the fall of the Ranas, the paper was taken over by the government and continued to dominate the press. The decade following the fall of the Ranas witnessed the establishment of a number of dailies. The number reached 12 in 1960 and has remained unchanged since.

Daily Newspapers in Nepal (1980)

Newspaper	Circulation	Political Orientation
Commoner (English)	7,000	Pro-Indian
Dainik Nepal (Nepali)	1,000	Pro-Indian
Gorkha Patra (Nepali)	35,000	Official
The Motherland (English)	1,200	Independent
Naya Samaj (Nepali)	3,000	Anti-Indian
Nepal Bhasa Patrika (Newari)	1,200	Mildly anti-Government
Nepal Samachar (Nepali)	900	Independent
Nepali (Hindi)	12,500	Pro-Indian
The New Herald (English)	15,000	Independent
The Rising Nepal (English)	20,000	Official
Samaj (Nepali)	2,100	Pro-Chinese
Samaya (Nepali)	18,000	Independent

All newspapers are published at Katmandu, and their circulation is almost entirely confined to the Katmandu Valley. Circulation elsewhere is limited not only by illiteracy but by lack of distribution facilities, a traditional distrust of the written word among the rural people, and a general lack of interest in politics, to which the press devotes the major share of its attention.

The aggregate circulation of all dailies in 1980 was 116,900, or 10.6 copies per 1,000 inhabitants, which is lower than that of India but higher than that of Bangladesh.

But, significantly, the overall circulation has grown more than tenfold, from 11,800 to 116,900, in the past 20 years. Much of this gain is accounted for by the newer papers: *Samaya, The New Herald* and *The Rising Nepal.* The number of English-language newspapers has also doubled during the same period, while the number of Nepali papers has declined from eight to six. English-language papers account for 37 percent of the aggregate circulation.

However, the commanding position in Nepali press is held by *Gorkha Patra,* not only because of its circulation (which is close to one-third of total daily circulation) but also because it is the mouthpiece of the government and required reading for all officials. It carries all government announcements, public service notices, and news of government contracts. It is generally eight pages in size and, like other Nepali newspapers, is printed on newsprint that is as rough and spongy as bread. It uses few photographs because of the absence of adequate printing facilities and technically trained personnel. Cartoons are almost never used.

The national preoccupation with Indian policies and intentions is reflected in the press, which is and always has been divided into pro-Indian and anti-Indian. In Nepali lexicon, anti-Indian is almost invariably pro-government, and vice versa. The only exceptions are the leftist publications, which, following a different tack, are divided into pro-Moscow and pro-Peking.

All newspapers, in addition, have strong ethnic, caste and political biases that affect almost all news items. Objective reporting is the exception rather than the rule. Editors are not always consistent in their loyalties, resulting in rapid shifts of allegiance. Often a paper carries a vigorous denunciation of a leading personality one week, only to support him wholeheartedly next week. Some of these quirks may be due to the fact that almost all editors, writers and correspondents are without formal journalistic training and, further, are very poorly paid. Most of them also come from the Newar and Pahari Brahman communities, and reveal the caste prejudices of these communities as a matter of course.

In addition to dailies there are over 40 other publications of varying frequencies. Nepali readers also have access to the far superior coverage of world events provided by Indian newspapers and magazines. Many Indian morning papers are flown into Katmandu by midday, including *The Times of India, Statesman* and *Hindustan Times.* A few Chinese publications also circulate within the kingdom.

The constitution of Nepal guarantees freedom of speech and expression within limits. As in the case of many other countries, the limits are more stringent than the guarantees; they include the preservation of the security of Nepal, maintenance of law and order, friendly relations with foreign states, good relations among people of different classes, good conduct, health, comfort, decency, economic interests, morality of the people, protection of the interests of minors and women, prevention of internal disorder or external invasion, contempt of court or parliament, and subversion of the constitution or any law.

Nepal's first press law was promulgated in 1965. Called the Press and Publications Act, it stated among other things, that nothing can be printed that abets or incites to commit murder or any violent crime or praise any person charged or convicted of such a crime; that diverts government employees from their duty or loyalty; that foments hatred or disrespect of the king; that is obscene, immoral, or foments ill-will among various classes. Section 30-C of the act promised that the government would grant loans and facilities to newspapers that contributed to "healthy journalism, with full loyalty to the nation, the king and the Panchayat system and with the national viewpoint and the national interest in mind." Among the punitive actions available to the government under this act are the powers to fine, confiscate or cancel newspaper registrations, to confiscate security deposits of newspapers and require new ones and to ban news stories that might disturb the peace or friendly relations with other nations.

A second act, called the Press and Publications Act, was rushed through parliament in 1975. The act gives the government sweeping powers against offending journalists and papers and to ban criticisms about the king, the royal family, the government and its agencies and diplomatic representatives. It also prohibits attempts to weaken the "moral fiber of society through libellous, baseless and unwholesome comments and use of words, symbols or illustrations and materials likely to encourage racial prejudice." It also provides for prior censorship of reports of foreign correspondents. The government is authorized to close newspapers without giving reasons.

The act also altered the composition and functions of the press council. Originally a sort of ombudsman that dealt with complaints about the press, it was composed of four members of the Nepal Journalists Association, with the president of the association serving as secretary. By 1975 the council had already become a paraofficial body, with the director of information taking over the role of secretary. The 1975 act regularized the transformation of the council into an official body; the number of nominees from the press was reduced to two, while the number of official appointees was increased to seven. This nine-member council drew up a code of ethics that reflects the government's own media philosophy. Two weeks after the passing of the 1975 act, the government banned three dailies and four weeklies.

A change of government, however, brought some relief to the media. The new prime minister, Tulsi Giri, lifted the ban on all newspapers except two dailies and two weeklies. When Kirti Nidhi Bista returned to power in 1977 he removed the ban on the remaining four, saying, "You are all free."

State control over the press is exercised through other indirect means as well. These include the allocation of newsprint, channeling of subsidies and grants to pro-government newspapers, called "healthy" papers, and news management through the state-owned news agency, Rashtriya Samachar Samiti. Not only are advertisments denied to anti-government newspapers, but even private corporations are persuaded to boycott them.

Censorship of reports filed by foreign correspondents is legal, but is rarely exercised. No special visas are required for foreign correspondents, and there has been generally no confrontation between the state and foreign media. The government has supported in principle the UNESCO 1978 Declaration, which reflects its own attitudes.

The national news agency is the Rashtriya Samachar Samiti (RSS), which, under a 1962 decree, has the exclusive right to collect and distribute news within the country. At least six foreign news agencies are represented in Katmandu, almost all of them by local stringers.

Radio broadcasting is controlled exclusively by the state-owned Radio Nepal, whose two transmitters (one a gift of the Australian government) cover a wide range of territory in Nepal and parts of India. The country has no television.

PARAGUAY

BASIC DATA

Population: 3,206,000
Area: 406,630 sq. km. (162,652 sq. mi.)
GNP: 399 billion guaranies (US$3.17 billion)
Literacy Rate: 40%
Language(s): Spanish
Number of Dailies: 5
   Aggregate Circulation: 175,000
   Circulation per 1,000: 60
Number of Nondailies: NA
   Aggregate Circulation: NA
   Circulation per 1,000: NA
Number of Periodicals: 20
Number of Radio Stations: 29
Number of Television Stations: 2
Number of Radio Receivers: 185,000
   Radio Receivers per 1,000: 62
Number of Television Sets: 56,000
   Television Sets per 1,000: 19
Total Annual Newsprint Consumption: 3,100 metric tons
   Per Capita Newsprint Consumption: 1.1 kg. (2.42 lb.)
Total Newspaper Ad Receipts: NA
   As % of All Ad Expenditures: NA

Paraguay has one of the youngest and smallest presses in Latin America. The oldest current daily, *La Tribuna,* was founded only in 1925. The second oldest paper, *Patria,* was founded in 1946 and is the official organ of the National Republican Association, commonly known as the Colorado Party. The three other dailies were all founded after the accession of President Alfredo Stroessner: *ABC Color* in 1967, and *Ultima Hora* and *Hoy* in 1977. All dailies are published in the capital, Asunción. The only paper published outside the capital, *Sucesos* in Encarnación, folded in the 1970s.

In terms of circulation, *ABC Color* is the leader with 65,000 copies, followed by *Ultima Hora* with 40,000, *La Tribuna* and *Hoy* each with 30,000 and *Patria* trailing with 10,000. Aggregate circulation is 175,000, or 60 per 1,000 inhabitants, above average for Latin America and 87th in the world.

All papers describe themselves as indepent, although it is difficult to determine what their independence consists of. Paraguay has no strong journalistic traditions, and none of the five dailies can be considered distinctive in their editorial policies, reportage or format. *La Tribuna* is perhaps a cut above the others; its 16 daily pages carry a broad coverage of national and world news. *Patria,* the organ of the ruling party, is closely read by officials and diplomats because it prints government documents fully, and because its editorials reflect official opinion on national issues. It is a full-sized, eight-page publication, drab and colorless. *ABC Color* comes closest to a mass circulation daily. A tabloid, with as many as 30 pages in an average issue, it is heavily illustrated and usually carries a color supplement of comic strips of United States origin. Within four years of their founding *Ultima Hora* and *Hoy* have managed to gain substantial circulations; *Ultima Hora,* in fact, outsells *La Tribuna* by 10,000 copies.

Of the periodical press only the Christian weekly *Comunidad* is noteworthy. A number of scholarly and professional journals are published under government auspices.

Freedom of the press is guaranteed by Article 73 of the constitution. This freedom, however, is exercised with considerable restraint and within narrow limits. Editorial comments are couched in mild words lest they appear critical. Publishers and editors have every reason to be cautious because a provision in the criminal code makes it a crime to denigrate the state or one of its officials. Through a long process of trial and error the press has learned which subjects are taboo, which are permissible and which should be handled diplomatically without offending anyone.

High military officers and the president and his family are off limits to any kind of comment. Certain other topics, however, such as terrorism by landowners against tenants, abusive acts by the police and corruption in government services, may be reported and may or may not bring official retaliation depending on the circumstances. It is not unusual for a journalist to be jailed for no apparent reason, as happened twice to Alcibiades Gonzalez of *ABC Color*. In 1980 *El Pueblo*, organ of the "opposition" Febrerista Party, was closed permanently for criticizing government action in giving asylum to former Nicaraguan dictator Anastasio Somoza. One of the editors of the Liberal Party publication, *El Radical*, was jailed when his paper reprinted some articles that had already appeared in *La Opinion* of Buenos Aires and *O Estado de Parana* of Curitiba,

Brazil. *El Radical* itself was subsequently forced to close down. Significantly, Paraguay has always been at the bottom of the scale in press freedom according to K. Q. Hill and P. A. Hurley's *Thirty-Year Survey of Press Freedom in Latin America.*

In addition, the government periodically issues guidance to the directors and senior editorial staff of all leading newspapers regarding news items that it wishes to have published and the way in which they are to be presented. This guidance sometimes extends to foreign media as well. Six foreign news agencies are represented in Asuncion, including AP, UPI and dpa. There is no national news agency.

The National Telecommunications Administration (Administración Nacional de Telecomunicaciones, ANTELCO) exercises general supervision of radio and television. With the exception of Radio Nacional, all radio stations are privately owned and commercially operated. There are 29 radio stations (11 of them FM) and two television stations, one in Asunción and the other in Encarnación, both of them commercial. Journalism training is provided by the Catholic University of Asunción and the Journalism Institute of the National University.

Paraguay has been described as a nation of silence, and its press might be aptly described as a press on a leash. It has not known freedom in modern times. It is also among the least studied of Latin American press systems, a condition that seems to suit the interests of its rulers.

PUERTO RICO

BASIC DATA

Population: 3,215,000 (1977)
Area: 8,897 sq. km. (3,435 sq. mi.)
GNP: $10.14 billion (1979)
Literacy Rate: 88%
Language(s): Spanish, English
Number of Dailies: 5
    Aggregate Circulation: 430,000
    Circulation per 1,000: 134
Number of Nondailies: 10
    Aggregate Circulation: NA
    Circulation per 1,000: NA
Number of Periodicals: 14
Number of Radio Stations: 81
Number of Television Stations: 17

Number of Radio Receivers: 2,000,000
Radio Receivers per 1,000: 625
Number of Television Sets: 650,000
Television Sets per 1,000: 203
Total Annual Newsprint Consumption: NA
Per Capita Newsprint Consumption: NA
Total Newspaper Ad Receipts: NA
As % of All Ad Expenditures: NA

Puerto Rico occupies an unusual niche in the press of the Western Hemisphere. In language and the social traditions of the audience it serves it is part of the Latin American press; yet in terms of structure, economic framework and traditions of press freedom it is closer to the U.S. press. U.S. influence is also strong in printing technology and standards of journalism. Another significant factor is the access that U.S. newspapers and magazines have to the Puerto Rican market and that the island's newspapers have to the large and growing Puerto Rican community in New York and other Eastern Seaboard states. The large U.S. tourist population in Puerto Rico also stimulates the growth of the press in the island.

The five dailies of San Juan also share some common characteristics. Except for *The San Juan Star* all are published in Spanish. All appear in the morning. All have rather loose political ties; only one daily is officially affiliated to a political party—*Claridad*, the organ of the Socialist Party. All others describe themselves as independent.

The oldest of the five dailies is *El Nuevo Dia*, founded in 1909 and now published by Luis Ferre, who was active in the Statehood Movement for a long time. *El Mundo* was founded 10 years later, and *Claridad* and *The San Juan Star* 50 years later, in 1959. The youngest of the dailies is *El Vocero*, which also enjoys the largest circulation—close to 160,000. The runners-up are *El Mundo* and *El Nuevo Dia*, with circulations of 130,000 and 113,000 respectively. *The San Juan Star*, with a circulation of 42,000, is the favorite paper of English-speaking tourists.

Aggregate circulation of the daily press is estimated by UNESCO at 430,000, or 134 per 1,000 inhabitants. Puerto Rico ranks 38th in the world in per capita circulation.

Popular Puerto Rican magazines enjoy large circulations. *Vea TV Guide* sells 84,000 copies per issue, *Angela Luisa* 20,000, *Bohemia* 55,000 and *Avance* 40,000.

Puerto Rico, an active member of international press organizations, has never been cited for violations of press freedom in recent years. In addition to specific constitutional guarantees of press freedom and free speech, there is a strong tradition of a privately owned press free from administrative restraints.

Puerto Rico has no national news agency. AP, UPI and EFE maintain bureaus in San Juan. All radio and television stations are commercially run, except for the government-owned educational networks. there are 81 commerical radio and 17 commercial TV stations.

SENEGAL

BASIC DATA

Population: 5,591,000
Area: 196,840 sq. km. (76,000 sq. mi.)
GNP: 459.8 billion CFA francs (US$ 2.2 billion) (1979)
Literacy Rate: 5%
Language(s): French
Number of Dailies: 1
Aggregate Circulation: 25,000
Circulation per 1,000: 5
Number of Nondailies: NA
Aggregate Circulation: NA
Circulation per 1,000: NA
Number of Periodicals: 37
Number of Radio Stations: 5
Number of Television Stations: 2
Number of Radio Receivers: 295,000
Radio Receivers per 1,000: 57
Number of Television Sets: 2,000
Television Sets per 1,000: 0.4
Total Annual Newsprint Consumption: 700 metric tons (1977)
Per Capita Newsprint Consumption: 0.1 kg. (0.22 lb.)
Total Newspaper Ad Receipts: NA
As % of All Ad Expenditures: NA

The earliest Senegalese newspapers were French weeklies that appeared during the last two decades of the 19th century. The three more durable ones were *Le Reveil du Senegalais* (founded in 1885), *Le Petit Senegalaise* (founded in 1886) and *L'Union Africaine* (founded in 1896). Dakar was important enough for the French Socialist Party to found *L'Afrique Occidentale Francaise* in it in 1907. It was Senegal's first political paper.

Not much happened until 1933, when the Breteuil chain of Paris decided to found *Paris-Dakar*. It became a daily in 1935 and later changed its name to *Dakar-Matin*, under which name it became one of the best known papers in French West Africa. But perhaps the greatest paper in Senegalese history was *Afrique Nouvelle*, founded by the Roman Catholic White Fathers in 1947. During the 1960s *Afrique Nouvelle* was perhaps the most distinguished and respected publication in black Africa. Produced and edited mostly by Africans, although still controlled by the White Fathers, it espoused a moderate political position while championing African freedom and unity. At its zenith it sold over 20,000 copies, but by the early 1970s circulation had begun to drop, and it was suspended indefinitely in 1972. *Dakar-Matin* also ceased publication in 1970 and was replaced by a new daily called *Le Soleil du Senegal*. In 1980 it was the only daily published in the country, with a circulation of around 25,000.

Twenty-three periodicals are also published in the country. The largest circulations are claimed by *L'Unite Africaine* and *Le Moniteur Africain du Commerce et de l'Industrie*.

Control of the media rests with the Ministry of Information. Its importance is reflected in the fact that over 1 percent of the national budget is spent on its operations—more than the share allocated to industrial development. It is responsible for the accreditation of all journalists; both foreign and domestic correspondents have to secure press cards from the ministry in order to work in the country.

Senegal had a relatively open media system, without too many restrictions and without direct censorship, until 1979, when a new press law was passed. The law followed the resumption of a legal opposition press in 1976. While the circulations of opposition papers are small, their barbs are pointed, and few government ministers or officials have remained unscathed. The press law has 80 articles, including one requiring all publications to be submitted for approval to the minister of information, the minister of the interior, the minister of justice and the solicitor general. Another article created a quasi-governmental commission empowered to renew or revoke a journalist's press card on the basis of his reports during the preceding year. Public officials who are disparaged in any Senegalese publication are required by law to be informed and given equal space to rebut the charge in the same issue.

In its first year of operation the new press law did not seem to dampen the opposition press. While one editor was condemned in 1980 to 18 months in prison for "disseminating false information," charges against two other opposition papers were dismissed by the court. One opposition paper won a court case for defamation against the government-sponsored *Youth Journal*.

The Senegalese Press Agency (Agence de Presse Senegalaise, APS) is an arm of the Ministry of Information. It has a small staff at Dakar and virtually no regional reporters. It depends for overseas news on its three foreign bureaus in Paris, Washington and Addis Ababa, and on AFP.

Radio broadcasting is under the control of Office de Radiodiffusion Television du Senegal (ORTS), a state agency. With two medium-wave and five short-wave transmitters and four regional stations, ORTS reaches most of the country.

SIERRA LEONE

BASIC DATA

Population: 3,391,000 (1980)
Area: 72,261 sq. km. (27,900 sq. mi.)
GNP: Le 789.5 million (US$ 750.5 million) (1979)
Literacy Rate: 10%
Language(s): English
Number of Dailies: 1
  Aggregate Circulation: 12,000
  Circulation per 1,000: 4
Number of Nondailies: 9
  Aggregate Circulation: 90,000
  Circulation per 1,000: 32
Number of Periodicals: 26
Number of Radio Stations: 2
Number of Television Stations: 1
Number of Radio Receivers: 315,000
  Radio Receivers per 1,000: 91
Number of Television Sets: 15,000
  Television Sets per 1,000: 4.3
Total Annual Newsprint Consumption: 100 metric tons (1977)
  Per Capita Newsprint Consumption: 0.03 kg. (0.07 lb.)
Total Newspaper Ad Receipts: NA
  As % of All Ad Expenditures: NA

The Sierra Leone press is among the oldest in Africa. The first printing press was in operation within a decade of the founding of the colony, and the first newspaper, the official *Sierra Leone Gazette*, appeared in early 1801. It was probably the first newspaper published in sub-Saharan black Africa. It appeared intermittently until 1870, when the colonial government commenced publication on a regular basis, since then it has continued unbroken to this day.

The first private newspaper, the *Sierra Leone Watchman*, appeared in 1842 under the auspices of the Wesleyan Methodist Missionary Society. In the 1880s, a particularly prolific period for newspapers, a dozen publications were active. Only the *Sierra Leone Weekly News* survived the decade, remaining the country's most prominent newspaper until the years immediately preceding World War II, representing moderate Creole interests. The rise of political parties and increase in political activities in the 1950s favored the establishment of newspapers as party organs. These included three papers published by the Sierra Leone People's Party (SLPP)—the *Observer*, the *Vanguard* and *Unity*—the People's National Party's *Liberty*, the All People's Congress's (APC) *We Yone* and the United Progressive Party's *Shekpendeh*.

The first abridgment of press freedom in modern times began with SLPP, the party in power until 1967; these pressures continued under the short-lived military rule and the later APC regime. In 1971 President Siaka Stevens ordered the seizure of the privately published *Unity Independent* in Freetown. It then reopened almost immediately as *The Nation*, under government ownership. One by one the opposition papers folded until only two dailies, both government owned, were left: the *Daily Mail* and *The Nation*. Subsequently, even *The Nation* went under, leaving only the *Daily Mail* to serve the entire nation in the 1980s. With a circulation of around 12,000, the *Daily Mail* is a tabloid of usually four to eight pages published seven days a week.

In the absence of a competitive daily press, the periodical press has flourished. The most prominent is *We Yone*, the twice weekly APC party newspaper. It has not only more pages than the *Daily Mail*, but a better coverage of domestic and foreign news. Almost as popular is the privately owned *Sunday Flash*. The Ministry of Information and Broadcasting issues the monthly *Sierra Leone Newsletter*, intended mostly for circulation abroad. All the principal periodicals are in English, but the Provincial Literature Bureau publishes

two magazines, one in Mende and the other in Temne.

Sierra Leone has no national news agency, but President Stevens has announced that than an official agency would be soon established since "the image given to Third World countries by the press in developed countries is unfortunately always distorted."

The Sierra Leone Broadcasting Service, operated by the Department of Broadcasting, controls both radio and television. The radio home service, reaching 90 percent of the population, is broadcast on one medium-wave transmitter and two short-wave transmitters in English and four African languages. News and information account for 33 percent of radio programming and 30 percent of television programming.

SOMALIA

BASIC DATA

Population: 3,510,000
Area: 637,140 sq. km. (246,000 sq. mi.)
GNP: 3.24 billion shillings (US$ 514 million) (1979)
Literacy Rate: 5%
Language(s): Somali (official); Arabic and Italian widely understood
Number of Dailies: 1
  Aggregate Circulation: 12,000
  Circulation per 1,000: 3
Number of Nondailies: 2
  Aggregate Circulation: 2,500
  Circulation per 1,000: 0.8
Number of Periodicals: 5
Number of Radio Stations: 1
Number of Television Stations: None
Number of Radio Receivers: 75,000
  Radio Receivers per 1,000: 21
Number of Television Sets: None
  Television Sets per 1,000: None
Total Annual Newsprint Consumption: 600 metric tons (1977)
  Per Capita Newsprint Consumption: 0.2 kg. (0.44 lb.)
Total Newspaper Ad Receipts: NA
  As % of All Ad Expenditures: NA

At the time of independence Somalia had a rudimentary press, but one that was free. Because of the lack of a nationally accepted orthography for Somali, publications appeared in English, Italian or Arabic and one in Osmanya, a form of written Somali. Their readers combined probably constituted little more than three or four percent of the population. Of the 15 periodicals that appeared fairly regularly in 1968, only four had circulations over 1,000 copies; three of these were owned by the government and the fourth by the ruling party, Somali Youth League.

After the military takeover in 1969 the independent Somali press died. By the early 1970s all periodicals and newspapers were issued by the Ministry of Information and National Guidance or by other government bodies. The Somali press at this time consisted of the *October Star*, in English, its Italian version, *Stella d'Ottobre*, and its Arabic version, *Nagmat Uktibir*, the weekly *The Dawn*, in English, and the magazines *New Era,* in English (with its Italian version, *Nuova Era*), and the English-Arabic *Horseed* (*Al-Taliah* in Arabic).

In 1973 a major change was effected in the press when the new Somali national script was introduced. A new daily appeared under the title *Xiddigta Oktoobar*, replacing the three foreign-language editions. It was printed entirely in the new script. *The Dawn* was also discontinued. *Horseed*, however, continued, with Italian as the main language.

In late 1980 the country's only daily continued to be *Xiddigta Oktoobar*, with a circulation of around 12,000, yielding a national per capita circulation of 4 per 1,000 inhabitants. Published in tabloid form, it averages four pages per issue.

Horseed is published every Friday, also in tabloid form, eight pages to an issue. Usually half the paper is in Italian and the other half in Arabic, with occasional articles in English. The masthead describes the paper as "independent," but the Marxist-Leninist orientation is unmistakable. The Ministry of Information and National Guidance continues to publish the *New Era* in English, Italian and Arabic editions, primarily for distribution abroad, in addition to a Somali edition for domestic consumption. Total circulation is estimated at 8,000 copies.

Because the press is entirely state-owned, there is little need for formal censorship or other forms of control over news flow. Apart from ANSA, the Italian agency, no other foreign news agency is regularly represented in Mogadishu. This has saved the government the trouble of devising controls over the flow of news abroad.

The national news agency is the Somali National News Agency (SONNA), which is designated as the sole agency for the reception and distribution of foreign press agency services. It publishes a daily news bulletin in English.

Foreign news comes from AFP, Reuters, and Tass.

Broadcasting is operated by the Somali Broadcasting Service, which manages Radio Hargeisa in the northern region and Radio Mogadishu in the capital. News and information account for 36 percent of radio programming.

SUDAN

BASIC DATA

Population: 18,378,000 (1980)
Area: 2,504,530 sq. km. (167,000 sq. mi.)
GNP: Sudanese £2.4 billion (US$ 6 billion) (1979)
Literacy Rate: 5%
Language(s): Arabic
Number of Dailies: 2
  Aggregate Circulation: 26,000
  Circulation per 1,000: 2
Number of Nondailies: 2
  Aggregate Circulation: 30,000
  Circulation per 1,000: 2
Number of Periodicals: 20
Number of Radio Stations: 1
Number of Television Stations: 1
Number of Radio Receivers: 1,400,000
  Radio Receivers per 1,000: 83
Number of Television Sets: 100,000
  Television Sets per 1,000: 6
Total Annual Newsprint Consumption: 600 metric tons (1977)
  Per Capita Newsprint Consumption: 0.4 kg. (0.088 lb.)
Total Newspaper Ad Receipts: NA
  As % of All Ad Expenditures: NA

Sudan's first newspaper was an Arabic biweekly called *al Sudan,* founded by three Syrian journalists in 1903. Throughout the early years the Sudanese press was owned, published, edited and read by non-Sudanese. Two Greek merchants published an English weekly in the 1910s, to which they added an Arabic supplement. Only in 1919 did the first native Sudanese newspaper appear; called

Hadarat al Sudan ("Sudanese Culture"), it pleased the British because it opposed union with Egypt and supported the continuance of British rule. However, after the pro-union armed uprising of 1924, the colonial administration decided to limit the scope of both political and media activities. As a result the press turned its attention to literary matters, with which the British were less concerned. In 1930 the government promulgated its first press ordinance giving the state licensing authority, although there was no need to exercise this authority often. The year 1935 was a landmark: the country's first daily, *al Nil* ("The Nile") was founded. Four years later a second daily, *Sawt al Sudan,* followed. After World War II many political parties started their own newspapers.

In 1956 Sudan became independent. At the time, Sudan had 16 intensely partisan newspapers, including six dailies. The National Unionist Party, which controlled the government, was supported by two dailies, while the opposition Ummah Party was supported by one. By the time of the military-led coup of Gen. Ibrahim Abboud, the press had grown to seven dailies, four semi-weeklies, 15 weeklies and 15 publications that appeared at less frequent intervals. All party newspapers were effectively suppressed during the Abboud regime, but after his overthrow a degree of political competition was restored and with it came a second spring to the Sudanese press. New newspapers continued to be established, existing ones expanded, although many small ones closed within weeks of publishing their first issue. By 1968 there were 13 dailies, two semi-weeklies and 13 weeklies. All dailies were published in Khartoum, but some periodicals were published in Al Ubayyid, Wad Madani, Juba, and Malakal. Except for four in English and one in Greek, all publications were in Arabic.

This was the situation when censorship was reimposed in 1968. Further restrictions were imposed in the aftermath of the 1969 coup led by General Jafar Numeiry. Through the government-owned radio, the ruling Revolutionary Command Council (RCC) accused the press of distorting government statements, of practicing excessive commercialism, and of propagating foreign ideologies. In 1970 the RCC nationalized all privately owned Sudanese newspapers and news agencies and further suspended all publications except those of the government. Four Arabic-language dailies and one English-language daily were among those that initially survived the nationalization

decree. President Numeiry declared that his takeover was necessary because some "newspapers were mere tools serving the objectives and goals of British imperialism and certain newspapers have become trumpets for saboteurs, publishing fabricated reports of the imperialist newspapers that have launched a psychological war against the revolution."

The nationalized press was placed under the control of an agency designated as the Sudanese Press Corporation, which managed two publishing companies: the Al Rai Amm Printing Company and the Ayam Printing Company. Although the corporation was originally intended as a short-term arrangement to coordinate and integrate rather than directly control press operations, in the course of time it became a controlling authority. Its major functions included acting on all new newspaper and magazine requests for registration and certifying the membership of journalists in the press union. It was expected to act favorably only in cases where the applicant's ideological framework was sympathetic to the goals and philosophies of the regime. The corporation's other responsibilities included improvement of newspaper distribution, expansion and improvement of press facilities, the training of personnel and making recommendations to the RCC for improving the political regulation of the press. In 1971 the RCC indicated that the overall goals of the corporation had been met, and then proceeded to dissolve it, transferring its powers to the Ministry of Information and Culture. Actual management of each publishing house was vested in a managerial council, composed of the chief editor as chairman, management and printing directors and workers' representatives.

In late 1980 two dailies remained in circulation: *Al Ayam* ("The Days") and *Al Sahafa* ("The Press"). Their circulations are reported variously by different sources: in some *Al Ayam* has a circulation of 13,000 and *Al Sahafa* of 8,500, while in others the former has a circulation of 60,000 and the latter of 50,000. Because of this discrepancy, aggregate circulation is not ascertainable with any degree of accuracy; the *1976 UNESCO Statistical Yearbook* reported it at 26,000, which would yield a per capita circulation of less than two per 1,000. Low as it is, such a figure fits well with the reported literacy rate and other indicators.

Each of these newspapers consists of only eight pages. Editorials and major news items crowd the front page, while inside pages are devoted to social news, sports, entertainment and letters to the editor. A daily column featuring commentaries by foreign correspondents appears on the last page. Advertisements are not numerous. Newspaper circulation is limited to the larger towns and has not penetrated rural areas. Delivery of Khartoum newspapers to southern towns was initiated during the 1960s, but they are usually received several days after publication.

Most of the periodicals are also published by the two state-owned publishing houses. These include the *Nile Mirror* and *Sudanow,* published by the Ministry of Culture and Information; *El Kibar,* published by the Ministry of Education; and *El Guwat El Musallaha,* the armed forces weekly.

The media philosophy of the Sudan government is not noticeably different from that of other Arab regimes of the same mold. According to an official source, the role of the media is to "play an important role in the...revolution...by clarifying the path before the masses." The decree that nationalized the newspapers stated: "Newspapers shall be the property of the people in whose name and on whose behalf they shall be run by the Sudanese Socialist Union. [They shall be run] in harmony with the general political plan of the Sudanese Socialist Union." President Numeiry shares the contempt most Arab leaders express for the private press. One year after seizing power, he said: "Most papers have gone to great lengths to appraise the course of the revolution, giving arbitrary interpretations.... Certain newspapers have broken up speeches and statements by members of the RCC and ministers,...distorted those speeches and published fragments to convey the opposite sense from the original statements....Certain newspapers have been concentrating on cleverly destroying the positive achievements of the revolution." As in other Arab countries, the regime is not satisfied with partial support from the press; it requires total and unqualified support such as could be provided only by a servile, nationalized press serving as an arm of the government.

Nevertheless, the attitude of the Numeiry regime is less restrictive toward foreign correspondents, and there have been few confrontations with the Western media over published reports. No special visas are required for foreign correspondents and cables are not subject to prior approval. The government subscribes to the UNESCO Declaration on the Media, which accurately reflects its own internal position.

The national news agency is the Sudan News Agency (SUNA), founded in 1946 and, thus, the oldest national news agency in the Arab world, predating even MENA. It receives overseas news from AP, Tass, MENA, AFP and SANA (Syria).

The Sudan Broadcasting Service (SBS), a government department within the Ministry of Information and Culture, operates three medium-wave transmitters and five short-wave transmitters but reaches only a small portion of the vast territory. The Sudan Television Service, with stations at Omdurman, Gezirah, Atbarah and Port Sudan, depends mainly on a microwave network to extend its coverage. News and information account for 19 percent of radio programming and 23 percent of television programming.

SYRIA

BASIC DATA

Population: 8,534,000 (1980)
Area: 186,480 sq. km. (72,000 sq. mi.)
GNP: Syrian £2.25 billion (US$8.920 billion) (1979)
Literacy Rate: 40%
Language(s): Arabic
Number of Dailies: 7
  Aggregate Circulation: 129,400
  Circulation per 1,000: 18
Number of Nondailies: 6
  Aggregate Circulation: NA
  Circulation per 1,000: NA
Number of Periodicals: 35
Number of Radio Stations: 6
Number of Television Stations: 5
Number of Radio Receivers: 1,370,000
  Radio Receivers per 1,000: 173
Number of Television Sets: 250,000
  Television Sets per 1,000: 32
Total Annual Newsprint Consumption: 800 metric tons (1977)
  Per Capita Newsprint Consumption: 0.1 kg. (0.22 lb.)
Total Newspaper Ad Receipts: US$14 million (1979)
  As % of All Ad Expenditures: 20.4

The Syrian press dates from the early 1900s, when the Young Turks forced the Ottoman government to relax restrictions on freedom of expression. Newspapers were started in Damascus and Aleppo by budding journalists, mostly Christian, and by nationalist politicians educated in the American University of Beirut or the Istanbul College. These newspapers were suppressed during World War I and resumed again under the rule of Prince Faysal in 1919 and 1920. The press continued to grow under the French, although licenses to publish were extended only to Francophile publishers.

During the first decade of independence the country went through considerable political instability, which was reflected in the growth of the press. The press was reorganized under every new regime. All newspapers were run by interest groups with strong ties to one party or another; a few were linked to foreign interests.

All this was changed when the Baathists took over in the 1960s. Syrian parties were banned in 1958, and the former party press never reappeared. The Baath regime did not have to suppress an opposition press; it simply withered away in the climate of regimentation that the Baathists introduced. The press, like the nation, speaks with one voice.

Seven newspapers are listed in the official press directory.

Syrian Daily Newspapers

	Circulation	Place of Publication	Date of Founding
Al Thawrah	50,000	Damascus	1964
Al Ba'ath	-50,000	Damascus	1964
Tishrin	4,500	Damascus	1974
Al Jamahir al Arabiyah	10,000	Aleppo	1966
Al Shahab	9,000	Aleppo	1977
Barq al-Shimal	6,400	Aleppo	1978
Al Fida	4,000	Hama	1963

No existing daily is older than the Baath coup of 1963. The aggregate circulation of all dailies, 129,400 in 1980, actually declined during the late 1970s from 133,500 in 1976. The per capita circulation is 18 per 1,000 inhabitants, the sixth highest in the Arab world. The two leading newspapers, *Al Thawrah,* published by the Ministry of Information, and *Al Ba'ath,* published by the Baath Party, account for over 78 percent of the national circulation, and serve as the country's *Izvestia* and *Pravda.* Both are

published from Damascus and share editorial and production facilities. Aleppo's three newspapers have a combined circulation of only 25,400. Syria's oldest paper in publication, *Al Fida* of Hama, has also the smallest circulation, which has shrunk by half during the past four years.

Unlike the Lebanese press, Syrian newspapers display few French influences. Editorials, generally placed on the first page, are signed by the editor and are composed in a different style and print from news stories. In content, however, news items are often indistinguishable from editorials because of their poetic style, interlarded with quotations from the Koran in true Arab fashion. Most news stories are rewrites of official press releases.

In quality and variety the periodical press surpasses the daily press because of the greater official latitude toward nondailies and the greater participation of private interests. In addition to publications by learned societies and government ministries, there are numerous magazines brought out by religious and literary groups, some of them in French, such as the influential *Syrie et Monde Arabe.*

The Syrian press has experienced brief periods of freedom, but tight control has been the rule. Control is exercised primarily through licensing individual publications and through the allocation of newsprint. Direct censorship has been in force since 1956, but its intensity has varied according to the severity of the successive national and foreign crises to which the country has been subject since independence. Since the beginning of the Lebanese civil war, the government has unleashed a campaign of terror against the media. In 1978 10 journalists, including Adnan Baghajati, editor of *Al-Ba'ath,* were barred from writing, bringing to 120 the number of journalists reportedly purged since 1976.

Numerous official agencies participate in the control of the communications media. The principal organization is the Ministry of Information, which censors domestic and foreign press, controls the radio and television networks, supervises the Agence Arabe Syrienne d'Information and the Al-Baath Publishing House. The Press Organization for Printing, Publishing and Distribution is also under the jurisdiction of this ministry.

The Lebanese crisis has also brought the government into conflict with foreign correspondents. Foreign correspondents were not allowed to enter Syria during the height of the disturbances. Correspondents living in Lebanon who reported adversely on Syrian moves were threatened by the government with assassination. The only U.S. news organization represented in Damascus is AP with a resident stringer.

The national news agency is the government-owned Syrian Arab News Agency (SANA). The agency is operated by an administrative council headed by the minister of information. Few foreign correspondents are stationed in Damascus; most cover Syria from representatives stationed in Beirut.

The country's radio and television network is operated by the state-owned Syrian Broadcasting and Television Corporation. The television station transmits from seven to eight hours a day; the radio station is on the air for 19 hours a day. News and information account for 25 percent of radio programming and 23 percent of television programming. Baathist propaganda and Islamic readings dominate the programming.

The Communications Institute, founded in 1970 in Damascus, offers two-year certificate courses to aspiring journalists. The Ministry of Information conducts short courses for practicing journalists.

While Syria has not yet taken the final step of nationalizing the press (as the Baathist regime in Iraq did), a de facto state-mobilized press exists, and the Assad government has shown in recent years that it can be heavy-handed in dealing with its critics. Through constant intimidation, the press has been reduced to the status of an agent of the regime.

TUNISIA

BASIC DATA
Population: 6,392,000
Area: 164,206 sq. km. (65,682 sq. mi.)
GNP: 2.75 billion dinars (US$6.95 billion) (1979)
Literacy Rate: 50%
Language(s): Arabic, French
Number of Dailies: 5
    Aggregate Circulation: 232,000
    Circulation per 1,000: 39
Number of Nondailies: 107
    Aggregate Circulation: 732,000
    Circulation per 1,000: 121
Number of Periodicals: 104
Number of Radio Stations: 4

Number of Television Stations: 2
Number of Radio Receivers: 800,000 (1979)
    Radio Receivers per 1,000: 127
Number of Television Sets: 229,918 (1979)
    Television Sets per 1,000: 36
Total Annual Newsprint Consumption: 5,000 metric tons
    Per Capita Newsprint Consumption: 0.8 kg. (1.76 lb.)
Total Newspaper Ad Receipts: NA
    As % of All Ad Expenditures: NA

The Tunisian press has a history extending back to 1861 when *al Raid al Tunisi* was founded as an official government publication. During the early years of the French Protectorate (1881–1956), French newspapers dominated the press because of the large French population and because of official encouragement. The leading French newspaper was *La Depeche Tunisienne,* successor to *Le Petit Tunisien,* founded in 1889. *La Depeche* had the largest circulation among all newspapers until it closed in 1961 for financial reasons. Its place was later taken by *La Presse,* founded in 1956. Owned by a Tunisian named Henry Smadja, it was politically noncommitted and slightly pro-French. Smadja was detained by the police in 1967, fined, and forced to leave the country. *La Presse* subsequently passed into government hands and lost much of its influence and readership. Of the nationalist newspapers the most influential was *La Voix du Tunisien,* the organ of the Old Destour Party. Until he founded his own newspaper, *L'Action Tunisienne* in 1932, Habib Bourguiba was a contributor to *La Voix du Tunisien.* In 1933 the French closed down all nationalist papers, but *L'Action Tunisienne* was permitted to reopen in 1938. From 1948 to 1952 the newspaper *Mission* was Bourguiba's ideological mouthpiece.

Following independence in 1956, the Parti Socialiste Destourien (PSD) founded the daily *L'Action* as its organ, along with its Arabic edition, *Al Amal.* Competing with them was the Arabic daily *Assabah* (or *Al Sabah*), which was pro-Youssefist prior to 1965.

Five dailies are published today in Tunisia, all of them in the capital. The state-owned press consists of three dailies: *L'Action* and *La Presse,* both in French, and *Al Amal* in Arabic. The private press consists of the Arabic *Assabah* and the most recent of the French-language newspapers, *Le Temps,* founded in 1975 by the owners of *Assabah.* *L'Action, Al Amal* and *Assabah* enjoy a circulation of around 50,000 each, while the other two dailies sell around 40,000 copies. Aggregate circulation is reported by UNESCO to be 232,000, or 39 per 1,000 inhabitants. Tunisia ranks 82nd in the world in per capita circulation.

UNESCO also reports 107 nondailies, of which 16 are published one to three times a week, and 104 periodicals. The aggregate circulation figures are 732,000 for nondailies and 870,000 for periodicals, yielding a circulation of 121 per 1,000 for the former and 144 per 1,000 for the latter. One periodical is published in English and one in Italian. A number of them are published by government agencies or PSD organs. The only opposition publication is *Ar-Rai,* published by the Social Democrat Group. A pro-communist monthly called *Tribune de Progrès* was published from 1958 to 1962, but it was suppressed in 1962 along with the official Communist monthly, *Al Talia.*

The best known Tunisian periodical, *Jeune Afrique,* is published outside the country—in Paris. Founded in 1955 by a group of Tunisian intellectuals, including Ben Yahmed, Bourguiba's first minister of information, and Mohammed Masmoudi, member of the PSD political bureau, it was suspended a number of times for its candid editorials before it moved to Paris. *Jeune Afrique* circulates widely in Francophone Africa and claims to be the best-selling magazine in over 10 African countries.

Tunisian dailies exhibit many of the features associated with the French press. Most have a six- to eight-page format; the front pages carry the editorials and international news; national events and local columnists are on page four; page five carries light features; sports occupy page six and seven with more international news and comic strips on the back page. The pages have a staid look with few photographs or large headlines. An occasional headline is red, and there is extensive use of boxes on the first page. The standard of language, both Arabic and French, is considered good.

Although Tunisia is an authoritarian state, neither the state nor the ruling PSD party has tried to monopolize the press. Privately owned newspapers and periodicals have survived. Even the PSD papers were not created after independence as a matter of deliberate policy but are carryovers from the years of nationalist struggle when Bourguiba, a journalist himself, needed an organ for his ideol-

ogy. The weaknesses of the Tunisian press have their roots in the colonial period. The French controlled, censored and restricted it to the extent that a vigorous press did not develop. It also suffered from financial and staffing problems which weakened its ability to withstand government pressures.

The Tunisian Press Code affirms freedom of the press but limits that freedom where necessary "to protect society from anything injurious to tranquillity, security and public order," and to "protect the state and the constituted agencies of government against anything liable to cause foreign or domestic disorders." Government control of the media is pervasive. The news media are dominated by information provided by government agencies. There is very little difference in content between the PSD-owned newspapers and the private ones. Presidential speeches and press conferences and official statements are given the same kind of preferential treatment. On politically important subjects and issues of national policy the basic approach tends to be the same in all papers. The non-PSD papers may add a few details and slightly different interpretations, and some may occasionally show a slightly more aggressive style without departing from the official guidelines.

Specific press policies are formulated by the Ministry of Information and Culture and implemented through at least three semiofficial agencies. The official news agency Tunis-Afrique Press (TAP) receives and edits domestic and international news supplied to the print and electronic media. Société Nationale d'Édition et de Diffusion issues "visas" for books, periodicals and newspapers coming into the country. The Société Nationale de Publicité supervises the format, content and placing of advertisements and also influences media content through subsidized advertising. The ministry has also the power to close down or suspend newspapers. In practice, controls over the press are not strictly applied and the press is rarely censored if only because the editors tacitly recognize their limits and generally hew the government line. The leadership can more effectively discipline a straying editor by a phone call asking him not to repeat the offense. The government also maintains its control over the press through the PSD-dominated Union of Tunisian Journalists and through the issue of press cards without which no journalist may legally function.

The national news agency, Tunis-Afrique Presse, is a public corporation, founded in

1961. With a permanent staff of nearly 200, it provides a full coverage of domestic news but depends on AFP and UPI for 75 percent of its foreign news.

Radio and television broadcasting are operated by the government-owned Radiodiffusion Télévision Tunisienne under the Ministry of Information and Culture. Radio is the most important communications medium both in frequency of impact and size of audiences. The programs include about 11 to 14 news bulletins each day and at least one ideological program called "Presidential Directives." French radio and television programs are also popular in the country.

The Tunis University's Institute of Press and Information Sciences has offered a four-year course in journalism since 1967. State aid is available for the training of journalists and broadcasting personnel.

UNITED ARAB EMIRATES

BASIC DATA

Population: 862,000 (1980)
Area: 82,880 sq. km. (32,000 sq. mi.)
GNP: DH51.96 billion (US$12.99 billion) (1979)
Literacy Rate: 25%
Language(s): Arabic
Number of Dailies: 3
  Aggregate Circulation: NA
  Circulation per 1,000: NA
Number of Nondailies: 3
  Aggregate Circulation: 2,000
  Circulation per 1,000: 8
Number of Periodicals: 8
Number of Radio Stations: 4
Number of Television Stations: 2
Number of Radio Receivers: 50,000
  Radio Receivers per 1,000: 167
Number of Television Sets: 80,000
  Television Sets per 1,000: 339
Total Annual Newsprint Consumption: NA
  Per Capita Newsprint Consumption: NA
Total Newspaper Ad Receipts: NA
  As % of All Ad Expenditures: NA

In 1972 *Al Ittihad* became the first daily newspaper published in the United Arab Emirates—known as the Trucial Shaykhdoms

before independence in 1971, because they were bound by truces or treaties with the United Kingdom. A number of weeklies and monthlies had sprouted up in the late 1960s, including *Akhbar Dubai, Ras al Khaymah, al Shuruq, al Khalij* and the *Abu Dhabi News. Al Ittihad* had been published by the Ministry of Information and Culture of Abu Dhabi and remained in government hands after independence and the formal establishment of the UAE Federation in 1972. The next milestone was the launching of the *Emirate News*, directed at the growing number of non-Arab workers in the federation, among whom English was the lingua franca. In order to promote the development of the print media, the federal government provided substantial subsidies to publishing enterprises. These subsidies were often diverted by the recipients to other schemes and ventures, with the result that the media remained weak and stunted. The only exception, perhaps, was the new daily *al Wahdah,* founded in 1973 by an Egyptian editor.

In 1976 the government removed *Al Ittihad* and *Emirate News* from direct state control and placed them under an autonomous but state-controlled corporation called the Al Ittihad Press and Publishing Corporation. The Minister of Information and Culture is its chairman of the board.

Currently the press is overwhelmingly in private hands, although it continues to receive state subsidies. Three dailies were being published in 1981: *Al Ittihad/Emirates News,* designated as the official newspaper of UAE, with a circulation of 24,000 (16,000 for the Arabic edition and 8,000 for the English edition), *al Wahdah* and *al-Khalij Times.* The last is published from Dubai and the other two from Abu Dhabi. No information is available on the aggregate circulation of the dailies. In addition, two news bulletins are issued daily: the *UAE Press Service Daily News* and the *Recorder.*

The periodical press is varied and healthy, reflecting an affluent readership. Among the more popular journals are *al-Dhafra, Gulf News, Gulf Mirror* and *al Tijarah.*

Despite the absence of strong government controls, all newspapers follow the government line. Press law focuses not so much on newspapers as on journalists, giving the government authority to issue or revoke licenses without giving reasons. This power is rarely used, but the law's existence lends weight to comments, usually conveyed informally, the Information Ministry passes to the editors from time to time.

The national news agency is the Emirates News Agency, founded in 1976.

The United Arab Emirates Radio, as the national broadcasting service is called, broadcasts over a wide area, with stations in Abu Dhabi, Dubai, Ras al-Khaima and Sharjah. The United Arab Emirates Television Service operates stations at Abu Dhabi, Dubai and Ras al-Khaima.

URUGUAY

BASIC DATA

Population: 2,919,000
Area: 186,998 sq. km. (74,799 sq. mi.)
GNP: 43.07 billion pesos (US$6.11 billion) (1979)
Literacy Rate: 90.5%
Language(s): Spanish
Number of Dailies: 11
　Aggregate Circulation: 700,000
　Circulation per 1,000: 250
Number of Nondailies: 48
　Aggregate Circulation: NA
　Circulation per 1,000: NA
Number of Periodicals: 335
Number of Radio Stations: 89
Number of Television Stations: 19
Number of Radio Receivers: 1.63 million (1978)
　Radio Receivers per 1,000: 603
Number of Television Sets: 361,000 (1978)
　Television Sets per 1,000: 134
Total Annual Newsprint Consumption: 11,600 metric tons (1977)
　Per Capita Newsprint Consumption: 4.1 kg. (9.02 lb.)
Total Newspaper Ad Receipts: NA
　As % of All Ad Expenditures: NA

Uruguay has been described as a nation of newspaper readers. The oldest paper, *Bien Publico,* was founded in 1878, and for many decades it was the voice of the Christian Democrats and Catholic reformers. It became the tabloid *BP Color* in 1962. The second oldest, *El Dia,* was founded in 1886 by Batlle y Ordonez, the most important figure in Uruguayan political history. The newspaper served as a sharp and powerful weapon in his campaigns against authoritarianism and in the promotion of liberal ideas and social reforms. *El Diario Español,* the newspaper of the majority Spanish community, was founded in 1905, the same year in which *Diario Oficial,* the government gazette, was established. The period of World War I witnessed the founding of four more newspapers: the Blanco papers—the morning *El Pais,* founded in 1918, and the afternoon *La Plata,* founded in 1914; *La Gaceta Comercial,* founded in 1916 and *La Manana,* the morning Colorado daily, founded in 1917. *La Manana* added an evening affiliate, *El Diario,* in 1923. Two more evening newspapers, *Vida Maritima,* and the government-sponsored *Mundo Color,* complete the list of Montevideo dailies.

A number of dailies have fallen by the wayside. These include *Accion,* the organ of the Colorado liberals, *El Debate,* founded in 1931 by the late Luis Alberto de Herrera, the leader of the Blancos, and *El Popular,* the Communist Party daily, which was proscribed by the military along with the leftist intellectual weekly, *Marcha.*

Montevideo is the media center of the country; the capital's dailies account for 90 percent of total national circulation. Because of the size of the country, morning editions of Montevideo newspapers can reach any provincial town on the day of publication. Nevertheless, there is a flourishing provincial press. *Editor & Publisher* lists 15 papers published in eight towns: Canelones, Florida, Mercedes, Minas, Paysandu, Rocha, Salto and San Jose. Almost all provincial papers have very small circulations, usually under 5,000, with the exception of *El Telegrafo* of Paysandu with sales of 8,600 copies.

The largest selling daily is the evening tabloid *El Diario,* with a circulation of 170,000. The two other Conservative dailies, *El Pais* and *El Dia,* also enjoy large circulations with 120,000 and 84,000 copies respectively. *La Plata* is next in circulation among the evening tabloids with 90,000 copies, followed by *Mundo Color* with sales of 60,000. Among morning newspapers *La Manana* with 40,000 copies, and *El Diario Español* with 20,000 copies have the smallest circulations. The financial and business daily *La Gaceta Comercial,* which is published every morning except Saturday and Sunday, has a circulation of 8,500. Aggregate circulation of all Uruguayan papers is reported by UNESCO as 700,000, or 250 per 1,000 inhabitants. Uruguay ranks 26th in the world in this respect.

In addition, UNESCO reports 48 nondailies, 36 of them published one to three times a week, and 335 periodicals. One Montevideo weekly is published in English.

The closure of the leftist weekly *Marcha,* noted for its well-written literary and performing arts reviews, has left a gap that has not yet been filled.

Despite the setbacks and buffetings of recent years, the Uruguayan press remains overwhelmingly in private hands. The major dailies are owned by or affiliated to the principal political parties, the Colorado and the Blanco. *El Pais* is the major Blanco daily. *El Dia, El Diario* and *La Manana* are linked to different factions of the Colorado Party. The restrictions imposed by the military regime have severely tested party loyalties.

The principal labor union in the newspaper industry is the Association of the Uruguayan Press, affiliated to the International Organization of Journalists. Like other labor unions, it does not have effective rights to organize, negotiate or strike. Publishers and owners belong to the Press Association of Uruguay and the Newspaper Association of Uruguay.

Until the military coup in 1973, Uruguay enjoyed one of the freest press systems in Latin America. K.Q. Hill and P.A. Hurley in their *Thirty-Year Survey of Press Freedom in Latin America* ranked Uruguay's press freedom as excellent under civilian rule. In contrast, IAPA in 1977 stated flatly that there is no freedom of the press in Uruguay. Government moves against the press began within four months of the military intervention. The official decree of June 1973 established severe restrictions on the media, including full censorship. Newspapers could publish only at their peril anything that undermined the prestige of the armed forces or encouraged "the enemies of the republic," such as the left-wing Tupamaros. The very word "Tupamaros" could not be printed unless it was contained in an official statement being reported. The IAPA called the decree, a "cause for mourning." The pressures against the press continued unrelentingly through the years that followed.

In 1974 the government placed all national and international communications under the direct control of a National Telecommunications Administration. When two Montevideo newspapers published a letter signed by 100 prominent Uruguayans and urging a return to democracy, the junta prohibited all political comments in the press. The government also told the editors to ignore stories about rape, bigamy, abortions and corruption of minors in order to protect public morals. The Communist daily *El Popular* and weekly *Marcha* were suspended.

In 1977 a foreign journalist working for *El Dia* was expelled after the newspaper published a phrase in its classified ad section that was considered insulting to the military. The paper itself was closed for 10 days. Afterwards, *El Dia* was denied certain tax benefits and its editor, Leonardo Guzman, was exiled to Argentina. The Rio Negro paper *El Heraldo* was also closed.

In 1978 the UPI correspondent in Montevideo was detained and questioned about an alleged business impropriety. When *El Dia* wrote an editorial lauding press freedom as "a principal tool of the cultural process and of all economic, social and political freedoms as well," it was denied further official advertising.

In 1979 one editor was jailed twice for criticizing the government, and two newspapers had their government advertising suspended. The newspapers were required not to go beyond official communiques in reporting subversive or antiterrorist activities, military promotions, demotions and troop movements. Foreign news agencies were required to submit daily copies of their dispatches to the interior ministry. Some editors called publicly for a relaxation of press restrictions when General Luis Queirolo invited criticism of the regime after taking over as army commander. A few days later, General Queirolo, trying to project a stern image, ordered editors not to publish photographs of him smiling.

There was a notable increase in media freedom during 1980 with extensive public discussion of the military-sponsored new constitution both in print and on the radio and television. Journalists became increasingly bold in questioning government officials and in expressing opposition to government policy. At the same time, government pressures continued to mount. The editor of a leading monthly was held for eight days, a radio news commentator was detained and harassed for critical comments on a nonpolitical subject, and several of Uruguay's foremost journalists resigned under pressure after disputes concerning publication of controversial material. Reporting on all political party activities was banned. While foreign publications from noncommunist countries were freely available, there were two reported instances of a foreign weekly newsmagazine being taken off the newsstands.

Confronted with such hostility, the press has learned to operate under a system of self-censorship. Uruguayan editors have become masters in the art of using words with double meanings, and readers have mastered the art of reading between the lines. Such self-censorship is not due entirely to the survival instincts of the media; it is closely watched and monitored by the National Office of Public Relations (DINARP). Its most commonly used weapon is summary suspension, and its second most common one is the withdrawal of state advertising support.

Since the closure of Agencia Nacional de Informaciones in 1967 there has been no national news agency. Foreign news agencies represented in Montevideo include AP, UPI, AFP, Reuters, ANSA, Prela and Tass.

Broadcasting is under the control of the Administración Nacional de Telecomunicaciones. There are 29 medium- and short-wave stations and three FM stations in the Montevideo area and 57 radio stations outside the capital. The government radio service, Servicio Oficial Difusion Radio Electrica (SODRE) has three medium-wave and four short-wave transmitters. Television began transmitting in 1956 and now covers the entire country and across the Plata estuary with four television stations in the capital and 15 in the provinces. Channel 10 is owned and operated by the Raul Fontaina family, which also owns Radio Carve. Between 40 and 60 percent of the programs are imported. The nation's only school of journalism is at the Universidad de la Republica del Uruguay.

VIETNAM

BASIC DATA

Population: 52,719,000
Area: 329,707 sq. km. (131,883 sq. mi.)
GNP: NA
Literacy Rate: 65%
Language(s): Vietnamese
Number of Dailies: 6
  Aggregate Circulation: 700,000
  Circulation per 1,000: 14
Number of Nondailies: NA
  Aggregate Circulation: NA
  Circulación per 1,000: NA
Number of Periodicals: 17
Number of Radio Stations: 2
Number of Television Stations: 7
Number of Radio Receivers: 5.5 million (1975)
  Radio Receivers per 1,000: 105

Number of Television Sets: 2 million (1976)
  Television Sets per 1,000: 40
Total Annual Newsprint Consumption: 2,000 metric tons (1977)
  Per Capita Newsprint Consumption: 0.03 kg. (0.07 lb.)
Total Newspaper Ad Receipts: NA
  As % of All Ad Expenditures: NA

The Vietnamese press is an entirely Communist creation. No newspaper of the French colonial period (1867–1945) survives in the North or in the South. Another major characteristic is that the daily press is limited to the two main cities of Hanoi and Ho Chi Minh City and the periodical press almost exclusively to Hanoi.

Of the six dailies published in the country, four are less than six years old, founded only after the unification of North and South in 1975. The principal daily is *Nhan Dhan,* the official organ of the Communist Party founded by Ho Chi Minh in 1946. Its circulation of over 300,000 reflects its standing as the voice of the nation and as mandatory reading for all government officials and party workers. The armed forces, with a strength estimated at over one million, publishes its own newspaper, *Quan Doi Nhan Dhan,* with a circulation of 200,000. Hanoi's most recent daily, *Hanoi Moi* (New Hanoi), was founded in 1976. It is a general paper not directed toward any specific audience.

The southern newspapers, all published from Ho Chi Minh City, have much smaller circulations compared to the northern ones. The two largest selling newspapers, *Giai Phong* (Liberation) and *Tin Sang* (Morning News), were both founded in 1975 and have circulations of around 45,000 each. *Dai Doan Ket,* the Vietnam Fatherland Front's official paper founded in 1977, is the ideological organ, but its circulation has not been reported. Aggregate circulation of Vietnamese newspapers has not been available to UNESCO for a number of years but is estimated at around 700,000, or 14 per 1,000 inhabitants, one of the lowest among countries of comparable size.

The Communist Party is the largest periodical publisher. Its principal publication is *Tap Chi Cong San,* founded in 1955 as *Hoc Tap.* The Vietnamese Socialist Party publishes *To Quoc,* a monthly, and the Federation of Trade Unions puts out the weekly *Lao Dong.* The Catholic Church is perhaps the only major publisher outside of the party and the government. It publishes the weekly *Chinh Nghia* in Hanoi and *Cong Giao va Dan Toc* in Ho Chi Minh City. The Committee for Cultural Relations with Foreign Countries brings out a number of illustrated and relatively well-produced magazines for foreign consumption. These include *Viet-Nam Courier*, *Vietnamese Studies*, *Viet-Nam* and *Women of Viet-Nam* in English, French, Spanish, Russian and Chinese.

The national news agency is the Vietnam News Agency based in Hanoi. The only non-Communist news agency represented in Hanoi is AFP.

Radio and television are operated by the Vietnam Radio and Television Commission. The Voice of Vietnam has two separate program networks in Hanoi and Ho Chi Minh City. There are seven television stations at Hanoi, Hue, Qui Nhon, Da Nang, Nha Trang, Ho Chi Minh City and Can Tho.

Training courses in journalism are organized periodically by the Vietnam Journalists' Association, which claims a membership of 5,200.

ZAIRE

BASIC DATA

Population: 28,504,000
Area: 2,343,950 sq. km. (937,580 sq. mi.)
GNP: Zaire 14.21 billion ($7.02 billion) (1979)
Literacy Rate: 5%
Language(s): French; also Lingala, Kikongo, Chiluba
Number of Dailies: 4
  Aggregate Circulation: NA
  Circulation per 1,000: NA
Number of Nondailies: NA
  Aggregate Circulation: NA
  Circulation per 1,000: NA
Number of Periodicals: 100
Number of Radio Stations: 7
Number of Television Stations: 1
Number of Radio Receivers: 130,000
  Radio Receivers per 1,000: 4.5
Number of Television Sets: 7,500
  Television Sets per 1,000: 0.2
Total Annual Newsprint Consumption: 1,100 metric tons (1977)
  Per Capita Newsprint Consumption: 0.04 kg. (.09 lb.)

Total Newspaper Ad Receipts: NA
As % of All Ad Expenditures: NA

For a country of its size and resources Zaire has a small and underdeveloped press. Only four dailies are published in the country: the morning *Salongo* and the evening *Elima* in Kinshasa, *Mjumbe* in Lubumbashi and *Boyoma* in Kisangani. Zaire was also one of the earliest African countries to nationalize its press and one of the 14 African countries in which a nongovernmental press does not exist. During the authenticity campaign launched by President Mobutu Sese Seko in the mid-1970s, the names of the newspapers were Africanized even though they were being published in French. The circulations of none of the four dailies are reported but it is believed that aggregate circulation has declined considerably from the 200,000 copies reported by UNESCO in 1976.

In addition to total ownership of the press, the Mobutu regime exercises a whole range of statutory controls over all forms of communication. Journalists may be imprisoned for showing "disrespect" to the government, and criticism of the president is considered a criminal offense. No journalist may practice his profession unless certified and licensed by the government. All articles and opinion pieces have to be reviewed by a government review commission before and after publication, even though journalists are not generally harassed if a piece is rejected by the board before publication. Zaire has also highly restrictive libel and sedition laws and preventive detention acts without the possibility of judicial remedies because the judiciary is subject to executive control.

Not only do these laws exist in the statute book, but they are invoked fairly often in order to intimidate journalists. During 1980 there were a number of journalists arrested for criticisms directed against even local and regional officials. Because of the severity of these restrictions and the frequency of their application, Dennis L. Wilcox ranks Zaire's press at the bottom of the scale in press freedom, and describes it as being subject to more controls than any African country with the exception of Guinea and Congo.

Relations with the foreign media reflect a similar intolerance. From time to time certain issues of foreign magazines are banned by the government. An AFP correspondent was expelled from the country in 1980 for writing articles critical of the government.

Although cables do not require special clearance, foreign journalists require prior permission to enter the country and are subject to summary expulsion.

According to the UNESCO, the periodical press consists of over 100 titles, but most of them are specialized journals issued by learned bodies and the Université Nationale. Kinshasa has two weeklies, and three more are published in the provinces.

The smallness of the press notwithstanding, Zaire has two of the finest news agencies in Africa. The official news agency is the Agence Zaire Presse (AZAP), founded as Agence Congolaise de Presse in 1960. The agency has an editorial staff of 30 at its headquarters in Kinshasa in addition to 19 reporters, 15 staff correspondents in the provinces and two permanent staff correspondents at its European office in Brussels. The second agency is Documentation et Informations Africaines (DIP), founded in 1956 by the Catholic Bishops of Congo, Rwanda and Burundi. Since 1965 it has been an independent private company but still maintains links with its founders.

The government-owned national broadcasting service, La Voix du Zaire, is now one of the most powerfully equipped in Africa with 16 transmitters. Besides the national station at Kinshasa, there are six regional stations at Lubumbashi, Mbandaka, Bukavu, Kasai, Kisangani and Mbuji-Mayi. Zaire Television is a government-owned commercial station, which is on the air for 40 hours each week.

Training in journalism is provided at the Department of Information Sciences of Lubumbashi campus of the Université Nationale and at the Centre d'Enseignement Superieur de Journalisme at Kinshasa. More intensive courses are organized by the Maison de la Presse in the capital.

SECTION IV:
Minimal & Underdeveloped Press Systems

NATIONS WITH MINIMAL MEDIA

The media systems of 65 countries are described in this section. They are grouped together for one of three reasons: they have a very rudimentary or underdeveloped press; they are ministates because of the smallness of their territory or population; or current information about their press ranges from sparse to nonexistent. Together, these 65 countries have only 67 daily newspapers (out of a world total of 8,210); 28 of them have no dailies of any kind, not even mimeographed sheets, such as those in many African countries; and 43 have no news agencies. Twenty-six of these countries are in Africa, 18 in Asia and Oceania, 15 in Latin America and six in Europe. Although lumped together, some of these countries show greater signs of development than others. Yet the press in these nations suffers from one constraint or another making growth beyond a certain level difficult or even improbable. The growth of the press is predicated on a certain critical mass in terms of literacy, economics, population, technology and political freedoms; it requires the synergistic action of all these factors to sustain a viable press system. Each of these 65 countries lacks one or more of these factors even when it has an otherwise healthy press.

	Dailies	**Nondailies**
ANDORRA	No dailies.	One weekly *Poble Andorra* (4,000). Six other periodicals.
ANTIGUA	No dailies.	Three nondailies: *The Leader*, official organ of the Progressive Labor Movement, *The Workers's Voice* (3,000), official organ of the Antigua Labor Party, and *The Outlet*, organ of the Antigua Caribbean Liberation Movement.
BAHAMAS	Four dailies: *The Nassau Guardian* (9,650), *The Tribune* (17,500), and *The Herald*, all from Nassau, and *The Freeport News* from Freeport.	Mostly tourist magazines.
BARBADOS	One daily: *Advocate-News*, founded in 1895 (27,200 on weekdays and 36,900 on Sundays), owned by Thomson Holdings, Ltd.	Two nondailies: the twice-weekly *The Nation* (23,821 on Wednesdays and 32,810 on weekends) and the *Sunday Sun* (20,500). The periodical press numbers 130 titles.
BELIZE	One daily, *The Belize Times*, owned by the ruling People's United Party (4,000).	Five periodicals, two of them published by the government: *Government Gazette* and the monthly *New Belize* (9,000). Both *The Beacon* and *The Reporter* have circulations over 5,000.
BENIN	The Office National d'Édition, de Presse et d'Imprimerie runs the nation's two dailies: *Ehuzu* and *Bulletin d'Agence Beninoise de Presse*. The former has a reported circulation of 10,000.	Half a dozen periodicals, of which the most popular is the Catholic *La Croix du Benin*.
BERMUDA	One daily: the *Royal Gazette*, founded in 1828 (13,450).	The weekly *Bermuda Sun* (12,686), the weekly *The Mid-Ocean News* (14,500) and the monthly *The Bermudian* (10,000).
BHUTAN	No daily.	The weekly government bulletin *Kuensel* has editions in three languages: English, Dzonkha and Nepalese.
BOTSWANA	One daily: *Botswana Daily News* (15,000 in English, 7,500 in Tswana).	Two weeklies published by the government: *Kutlwano* (10,000) and *Mafeking Mail and Botswana Guardian*, published outside the kingdom at Mafeking in South Africa. Of some 50 periodicals three are published by the three major political parties.

News Agencies	Electronic News Media	Other Comments
No news agency.	Two privately owned radio stations: Radio Andorra and Sud-Radio.	
No news agency.	Antigua & Barbuda Broadcasting Service operates ABS Radio and Television. Privately owned Radio ZDK operated by Grenville Radio.	
No news agency.	ZNS Broadcasting Corporation operates radio and TV.	*The Nassau Guardian* is one of the oldest newspapers in the Caribbean, founded in 1844.
No national news agency.	Radio Barbados and CBS TV administered by the Caribbean Broadcasting Corporation. There is also a commercial service called Barbados Rediffusion.	British influences are very strong in the island's media.
No national news agency.	Radio Belize is a semicommercial government-operated service.	Although Spanish is the most widely spoken language, the press is entirely English.
Agence Benin-Presse is a department of the Ministry of Information.	The state-owned La Voix de la Révolution has stations at Cotonou and Parakou.	Benin has a Marxist-Leninist regime, and the media are under total state control.
No national news agency.	Two broadcasting organizations: The Bermuda Broadcasting Company, which operates ZBM Radio and ZBM TV, and the Capital Broadcasting Company which operates ZFB Radio and ZFB TV. The former is a quasi-public organization.	
No national news agency.	27 radio stations of which eight are for transmitting flood warning data.	
No national news agency.	Radio Botswana at Gaborone.	

	Dailies	Nondailies
BRUNEI	No dailies.	Four weeklies: *Borneo Bulletin* (30,000), an independent English weekly, *Pelita Brunei*, published by the Information Section of the State Secretariat (31,500), and two employee newspapers published by the Brunei Shell Petroleum Company.
BURUNDI	One daily: *Le Renouveau du Burundi*, published by the Ministry of Information.	Two weeklies; *Burundi Chrétien* published by the archdiocese of Gitega and *Ubumwe* (20,000). Four other periodicals include *Le Burundi en Images*.
CAMBODIA	One daily: *Sapordamean Kangtoap Padivoat*, published by the Vietnamese-controlled army.	No information available.
CAMEROON	One daily: *Cameroon Tribune* (20,000) published by SOPECAM.	Except for Christian journals, the periodical press is also state-owned. Of the 18 major periodicals, the largest selling are the English-language ones: *Cameroon Outlook* (13,000), *Cameroon Times* (12,000) and *Cameroon Tribune* (8,000). Most of the others are in French.
CAPE VERDE	No dailies.	Six nondailies of which three are published by the government: *Boletim Informativo* (1,500), *Boletim Oficial da Républica de Cabo Verde* and *Voz di Povo*, and one by PAIGC, *Unidade e Luta*.
CENTRAL AFRICAN REPUBLIC	One daily: *Centrafric Press*, organ of the Mesan Party.	Three periodicals: the monthly *Bangui-Match* and *Ta Tene* and the fortnightly *Journal Officiel de la République Centrafricaine*.
CHAD	Only daily, *Info-Chad*, a mimeographed bulletin published by Chad Press Agency.	One weekly, *Informations Economiques*, published by the chamber of commerce, and two monthlies, including the *Journal Officiel de la République du Tchad*.
COMOROS	No dailies.	No nondailies; three periodicals with an aggregate circulation of 1,100.
CONGO	Five dailies: *Le Courrier d'Afrique* (45,000), *L'Eveil de Point Noire*, *Le Journal de Brazzaville*, *Le Petit Journal de Brazzaville* and *Journal Officiel*.	Periodicals include the well-known *La Semaine Africaine*, published by the archdiocese of Brazzaville, and *Etumba*, the weekly journal of the Parti Congolaise du Travail.

News Agencies	Electronic News Media	Other Comments
No national news agency.	Radio & Television Brunei broadcasts daily; color television was introduced in 1975.	
Agence Burundaise de Presse.	The only radio station is the government-owned Voix de la Révolution at Bujumbura.	The state controls all media other than Catholic; Mild criticism is permitted. There is no interference with the distribution of foreign publications.
Saporamean Kampuchea is the information service of the ruling KNUFNS (Kampuchean National United Front for National Salvation).	Samleng Pracheachon Kampuchea (Voice of the Kampuchean People) is the broadcasting arm of KNUFNS.	
SOPECAM (Société Publicité Edition du Cameroun).	Radiodiffusion du Cameroun with four stations at Yaounde, Douala, Garoua and Buea.	Political criticism is discouraged through occasional intimidation and harassment of journalists. Some foreign publications have been seized by the government.
No national news agency.	Two government stations: Emissora Oficial de Républica de Cabo Verde and Voz de São Vicente.	
Agence Centrafricaine de Presse (ACAP), formerly, the Bangui branch of AFP.	Radio: one station, La Voix de la République Centrafricaine.	
Agence Tchadienne de Presse (ATP).	One radio station, Radiodiffusion Nationale Tchadienne.	Changes in the media following the civil war in the country are not reported. All printing facilities are owned by the government.
No news agency.	One radio station, Radio Comoros at Moroni.	
Agence Congolaise d'Information (ACI), owned by the government.	La Voix de la Révolution Congolaise operated by Radiodiffusion Télévision Nationale Congolaise with a main station at Brazzaville.	A Marxist-Leninist state, Congo exercises, owns and controls the media except for one newspaper. In 1980 the government lifted the import ban on 30 foreign publications and began permitting foreign journalists to visit the country.

	Dailies	**Nondailies**
DJIBOUTI	No daily.	Three periodicals: bimonthly *Carrefour Africain*, published by a Roman Catholic mission, monthly *Djibouti Aujourd'hui* and the weekly *Le Reveil de Djibouti*, published by the official Information Service.
DOMINICA	No daily.	Four nondailies: the weekly *Official Gazette* (500), *New Chronicle* (3,000) and *The Star* (2,000); and the fortnightly *The Dominica Link* (3,000).
EQUATORIAL GUINEA	No daily.	One irregularly published periodical, *Unidad de la Guinea Ecuatorial.* A semiweekly, *Ebano,* began publication in 1980.
FIJI	Two dailies: *Fiji Times* (25,650) and *Fiji Sun* (28,500).	Nondailies include the weeklies *Nai Laiakai* in Fijian and *Shanti Dut* in Hindi, published by *Fiji Times & Herald,* and *Sun Sport Weekly* and *Sunday Sun,* published by the Fiji Sun group, the Ministry of Information's *Fiji* and a number of tourist magazines.
FRENCH GUIANA	One daily: *La Presse de la Guyane* (16,000).	One biweekly: *France-Guyane* (3,500) and three monthlies: *Ça ou Ça, La Guyane Agricole,* and *Le Jeune Garde.*
GABON	Two dailies: *L'Union* (15,000), published by Société Nationale de Presse et d'Édition, and *Gabon-Matin* (18,000), published by the Agence Gabonaise de Presse.	Periodicals include *Dialogue,* organ of the Parti Démocratique Gabonais, *Gabon d'Aujourd'hui,* published by the Ministry of Information, the semimonthly *Journal Officiel* and *Ngondo,* published by the Agence Gabonaise de Presse.
GAMBIA, THE	No daily.	Five nondailies: *Gambia News Bulletin,* the government newspaper issued three times weekly, *Gambia Outlook, The Gambian, The Sun* and *The Worker,* the organ of the Gambia Labor Congress; a fortnightly, *The Nation.*
GIBRALTAR	One daily: *Gibraltar Chronicle* (2,300), founded in 1801.	Six nondailies: *Calpe News* in English and Spanish (550), *Gibraltar Evening Post,* an independent weekly (1,500), the official *Gibraltar Gazette* (370), *Panorama,* an independent weekly (1,800), *Vox,* an English weekly with Spanish sections (1,000), and *Gibraltar Libre* in English and Spanish (500).

News Agencies	Electronic News Media	Other Comments
No national news agency.	One station, Radiodiffusion-Télévision de Djibouti.	
No national news agency.	One radio station, run by the Dominican Broadcasting Corporation.	
No national news agency.	Two radio stations, both government-run: Radio Ecuatorial at Bata, Rio Muni and Radio Malabo.	
No national news agency.	The Fiji Broadcasting Commission runs 10 AM and two FM stations in two national networks, Radio Fiji One and and Radio Fiji Two.	
No national news agency.	Radio service forms France Regions 3: Region Antilles-Guyane with two stations: Radio Guyane-Inter and and Téléguyane.	
Agence Gabonaise de Presse.	Radiodiffusion-Télévision Gabonaise operates La Voix de la Rénovation and Radio 2 with main station at Libreville and relays at Franceville and Oyem; two TV stations at Libreville and Port-Gentil.	
No national news agency.	Two radio stations: Radio Gambia, a noncommercial government service and Radio Syd, a commercial station serving Swedish and German tourists.	
No national news agency.	The Gibraltar Broadcasting Corporation (GBC) runs Radio Gibraltar and GBC-TV.	

	Dailies	Nondailies
GRENADA	No daily.	Three nondailies: *The Free West Indian* (1,500), founded in 1915, the official *Government Gazette* and *The New Jewel Movement Weekly*.
GUADELOUPE	One daily: *France-Antilles* (20,000).	Four nondailies: *Le Progrès Social, L'Etincelle, Match* and *Combat Ouvrier.*
GUINEA	One daily: *Horoya* (c. 10,000), organ of the ruling Parti Démocratique de Guinee.	Three nondailies: *Fonikee,* organ of the Jeunesse Démocratique Africaine, *Le Travailleur de Guinee,* organ of the Confédération Nationale des Travailleurs Guineens, and *Journal Officiel.*
GUINEA-BISSAU	No daily.	The country's only publication, the official *No Pintcha,* appears three times a week.
KIRIBATI	No daily.	Three nondailies: the weekly *Atoll Pioneer,* published by the Broadcasting & Publications Authority, the monthly *Te Uekera,* also published by the same authority, *Te Itoi ni Kiribati,* published by the Catholic Church, and *Te Kaotan te Ota,* published by the Protestant Church.
LAOS	Three dailies: *Vientiane May,* organ of the Party Committee of Vientiane, *Siang Pasason,* organ of the Central Committee of the Lao People's Revolutionary Party, and *Khao San Pathet Lao,* army organ.	Fortnightly Noum Lao (Lao Youth), organ of the Lao People's Revolutionary Youth Union; several provinces publish newsletters.
LESOTHO	No daily.	Five nondailies, including three weeklies: *The Lesotho Weekly* and *Mochochonono* (3,000), published by the Department of Information, *Moeletsi oa Basotho* (12,000), published by the Catholic Church, and two fortnightlies: *Leselinyana la Lesotho,* published by the Lesotho Evangelical Church (25,000), and *Mohlabani.*
LIECHTENSTEIN	One daily: *Liechtensteiner Vaterland,* organ of the Fatherland Union (5,400).	One five-times weekly, *Liechtensteiner Volksblatt* (7,000), organ of the Progressive Citizens Party.

News Agencies	Electronic News Media	Other Comments
No national news agency.	Radio Free Grenada and Television Free Grenada, both government owned.	The island's only independent daily, *The Torchlight* was suspended by the New Jewel government in 1980. People's Law No. 18 makes it a criminal offense punishable by a fine of up to $10,000 and/or three years in prison to be even remotely involved in the publication or distribution of any newspaper not directly under government control. A national media code is being drawn up.
No national news agency.	Guadeloupe is served by French radio and television Region #3— Region Antilles-Guyane.	
Agence Guineenne de Presse.	Radio station at Conakry run by Radiodiffusion Nationale de Guinee.	
No national news agency.	One radio station at Bissau operated by Radiodifusão da Républica da Guine-Bissau.	
No national news agency.	One station, Radio Kiribati, at Bairiki on Tarawa atoll.	
Khao San Pathet Lao, division of the Ministry of Information.	National Radio of Laos at Vientiane; seven provincial radio stations.	
No national news agency.	One radio station, Radio Lesotho, at Maseru. There are plans to establish television service.	
Presse- und Informationsstelle der Furstlichen Regierung.	No radio or television facilities.	

	Dailies	**Nondailies**
MACAO	No daily.	Two weeklies: *Boletim Oficial,* and *Luso Chines;* a twice-weekly, *O Clarim;* a twice-monthly, *Confluência;* and two irregular publications: *Democracia em Marcha* and *Diário de Macau,* all in Portuguese; in addition, five Chinese language nondailies.
MALDIVES	Three dailies: *Aafathis* in Divehi and English and *Haveer* and *Sunlight* in Divehi.	Two weeklies: *Hafta* in Divehi and *Outlook* in English; three monthlies: *Aabaaru, Amaaz* and *Faiythoora,* and in Divehi.
MALI	One daily: *L'Essor-La Voix du Peuple,* organ of the Military Committee for National Liberation.	One weekly, *Podium;* and three monthlies: *Bulletin de Statistiques, Kibaru* and *Sunjata.*
MARTINIQUE	One daily: *France-Antilles* (25,000).	Six nondailies: *Aujourd'hui Dimanche, Carib Hebdo, Le Courrier* (3,000), *Justice* (8,000), *Le Naif* and *Le Progressiste* (13,000).
MAURITANIA	No daily.	Nondailies include *Al-Akhbar* in Arabic; and *Journal Officiel, Nouakchott Information* and *Le Peuple* in French.
MONACO	Special Monaco editions of French newspapers published at Nice, France: *Nice-Matin* and *L'Espoir de Nice.*	*Tribune de Monaco* and one official weekly journal, *Journal de Monaco.*
NAURU	No daily.	A fortnightly *Bulletin* is distributed free. A new independent weekly, *Nauru Post,* launched in 1980.
NETHERLANDS ANTILLES	Six dailies: *Amigoe di Aruba* in Dutch (3,500), *Amigoe di Curaçao* (10,000), Catholic daily in Dutch, *Beurs-en Nieuwsberichten,* Dutch daily of Curaçao (8,000), *The News* in English of Aruba (3,500), *Nobo* (17,000), Dutch daily of Curaçao and *La Prensa* (10,750), Dutch daily of Curaçao. Aggregate circulation is 52,750 or 214 per 1,000 inhabitants.	Three weeklies: *La Cruz* and *Curacaosche Courant* of Curaçao and *The Local* of Aruba; and one fortnightly: *NosIsla* of Curaçao.
NIGER	*Le Sahel,* a mimeographed daily news bulletin of the Service de l'Information (3,000).	The weekly *Sahel Hebdo,* the monthly *Journal Officiel* and the quarterly *Nigerama.*

News Agencies	Electronic News Media	Other Comments
No national news agency.	One government radio station, Emissora de Radiodifusão de Macau and one private commercial radio station, Emissora Vila Verde.	
No national news agency.	Radio Maldives is a department of the Ministry of Information and Broadcasting.	
Agence Malienne de Presse et Promotion (AMPA).	One government station, Radio Mali at Bamako.	
No national news agency.	Martinique is served by French radio and television Region 3— Region Antilles-Guyane.	
Agence Mauritanienne de Presse (AMP).	Radio is controlled by Radiodiffusion Nationale de Mauritanie with one station at Nouakchott; and television by Agence Mauritanienne de Télévision et de Cinéma.	
Agence Télégraphique operated by AFP.	Radio and TV are government-operated, but time is sold to commercial sponsors. The French government has a controlling interest in Radio Monte Carlo. Trans World Radio is a Christian evangelical station broadcasting in 35 languages.	
No national news agency.	Government-owned Radio Nauru.	
No national news agency.	Four radio stations in Aruba, three in Curaçao, one in Saba and one in St. Maarten. Transworld Radio has a station in Bonaire broadcasting Christian evangelistic programs in 15 languages.	
No national news agency.	One radio station: La Voix du Sahel.	

	Dailies	Nondailies
OMAN	One daily: *Al Watan.*	One twice-weekly: *Oman;* two weeklies: *Akhbar Oman* and *Times of Oman* in English; five periodicals including *Al-Akidah* (18,000), a weekly illustrated magazine, and the fortnightly *Al Nahda.*
QATAR	Two dailies: the English-language *Daily News Bulletin* (with an Arabic edition) and the Arabic-language *Dar Al-Ouroba* (10,000).	Four weeklies: *Gulf Times* (9,500), *Al-Ahad, Al-Fajr* and *Arrayah;* six monthlies: *Al-Doha,* published by the Ministry of Information (40,000), *Al-Jawhara,* magazine for women, *Al-Khalij al-Jadeed, Al-Sakr,* sports magazine, *Al-Mashal,* published by the Qatar Petroleum Producing Authority, and *Diaruna Wal Alam,* published by the Ministry of Finance and Petroleum.
RÉUNION	Three dailies: *Journal de l'Île la Réunion* (26,000), *Quotidien de la Réunion et de l'Ocean Indien* (20,000) and the Communist Party organ, *Termoignages* (6,000).	Seven periodicals, including the weekly *La Gazette* (4,700), and publications by the Réunion University, Chamber of Agriculture, Chamber of Commerce and Industry and the CFDT trade union.
RWANDA	No daily.	14 nondailies, including *Hobe* (60,000), *Imahvo* (40,000), *Kinya Mateka* (10,000), *Journal Officiel,* issued by the president's office, *Diapason, L'Informateur* and *Nouvelles du Rwanda,* published by the Université Nationale du Rwanda.
ST. CHRISTOPHER-NEVIS-ANGUILLA	No daily.	Two nondailies: *Democrat* and *The Labour Spokesman* (1,200); both published at Basseterre; the monthly *Government Information Service Bulletin* and *Official Gazette* of Anguilla.
ST. LUCIA	No daily.	*The Voice of St. Lucia,* founded 1885, still appears thrice weekly (5,000). Other nondailies include *The Castries Catholic Chronicle* (1,200), the weekly *The Crusader* (2,000), the fortnightly *The Vanguard* and *The Star.*
ST. VINCENT	No daily.	Two weeklies: *The Star,* organ of the St. Vincent Labour Party, and *The Vincentian* (3,500); also *Government Bulletin* (300) and *Government Gazette* (370).

News Agencies	Electronic News Media	Other Comments
No national news agency.	Two radio stations: Radio Oman and Radio Salalah, and two television systems at Muscat and Dhofar.	
Qatar News Agency.	Radio Qatar and Qatar Television, both government-owned.	
No national news agency.	Réunion is served by French radio and television Region 3.	
Agence Rwandaise de Presse.	One radio station at Kigali run by Radio diffusion de la République Rwandaise. Kigali is also the location of a relay station of Deutsche Welle, the German network.	
No national news agency.	ZIZ Radio & Television of Basseterre and Radio Anguilla.	
No national news agency.	The government-owned Radio St. Lucia and the private Radio Caribbean International. Television conducted by the commercial station, St. Lucia Television Service.	
No national news agency.	Radio St. Vincent.	

	Dailies	Nondailies
SAN MARINO	No daily.	The main periodicals are political party organs: the Socialist *Il Nuovo Titano*, the Christian Democratic *San Marino* and the Communist *La Scintilia*. The *Bollettino Ufficiale* appears irregularly.
SÃO TOMÉ & PRINCIPE	No daily.	Two weeklies; *Diário da República*, published by the Imprensa Nacional, and *Revolução*, published by the Ministry of Information.
SEYCHELLES	Two dailies: *The Nation* (3,600), published by the Information Department, and *Le Seychellois* (500), published by the Farmers' Association.	One weekly: the Catholic *L'Écho des Îles*. Another weekly, *Weekend Life*, was suspended in 1979.
SOLOMON ISLANDS	No daily.	Two weeklies: *Solomons News Drum* (3,000), published by the Government Information Service, and *Solomons Toktok* (2,000), an independent newspaper.
SURINAME	Five dailies in Dutch: *Aktueel* (5,000), *Suriname, De Vrije Stem* (5,000), *De Ware Tijd* (15,000) and *De West* (9,000); three Chinese language papers: *De Vrijheid, Fa Sien Paw* and *Lam Foeng*.	One twice-weekly: *Koeriers;* six weeklies: *C.L.O. Bulletin*, organ of Central Organization for Civil Servants, Catholic *Omhoog, Onze Tijd, Pipel, De Volksbode*, and *Volkskrant;* one biweekly: *Advertentieblad van de Republiek Suriname* and one monthly: *Mini World*, in Spanish and English.
SWAZILAND	One daily: *The Times of Swaziland* (6,000), founded in 1897.	Two nondailies: the weeklies *Ummbiki* and *News from Swaziland*, published by the Government Information Services.
TOGO	Two dailies: *Togo en Marche* and *Journal Officiel*, both published by the government.	One weekly: *Bulletin d'Information de l'Agence Togolaise de Presse*, published by the Ministry of Information; one fortnightly: *Présence Chretienne*, and seven monthlies, including six official publications: *Togo Dialogue, Le Lien, Image du Togo, Gamesu, Espoir de la Nation* and *Bulletin de Statistiques*.

News Agencies	Electronic News Media	Other Comments
No national news agency.	No radio or television broadcasting agency.	
No national news agency.	One radio station, Radio Nacional de São Tomé e Príncipe.	
No national news agency.	One national radio service, Radio Seychelles. The Far East Broadcasting Association has a station on Mahe broadcasting Christian evangelical programs.	
No national news agency.	The Solomon Islands Broadcasting Corporation operates one radio station at Honiara.	
Four press agencies: Surinaams Nieuws Agentschap (SNA); Informa, the Suriname News Service; IPS; and Prinfo.	Six radio stations: Stichting Radio-omroep Suriname, a government-run commercial station, Radio A.B.C., Radio Apintie, Radio Paramaribo, Radika and Radio Nickerie. The last two stations serve East Indian listeners exclusively. The only television station is the government-owned Surinaamse Televisie Stichting (STVS).	While there is no formal censorship, the press has received sharp reprimands from the new military regime. The army has advised the press not to say anything that will "harm the revolution." A five man communications policy board has been set up to direct government policies toward the media.
No national news agency.	Three radio services: the official Swaziland Broadcasting Service, the commercial Swaziland Commercial Radio or Radio Swazi and Trans World Radio, the Christian evangelical radio ministry. Television is operated by the Swaziland Television Broadcasting Corporation.	
Agence Togolaise de Presse.	Radio is operated by Radiodiffusion du Togo and television by Télévision Togolaise.	

	Dailies	Nondailies
TONGA	No daily.	One weekly: *Tonga Chronicle*, published by the government with a circulation of 4,300 in Tongan and 1,200 in English; a biannual: *Faikava* and a quarterly: *Tokanga*.
TUVALU	No daily.	One fortnightly: *Tuvalu Newsheet* (300), published by the Broadcasting and Information Division.
UPPER VOLTA	Three dailies: *L'Observateur, Notre Combat* and *Bulletin Quotidien d'Information.*	All nondailies are officially sponsored, including the *Journal Officiel* and *Bulletin Mensuel de Statistique.* The *Carrefour Africaine* is the most popular periodical.
VANUATU	No daily.	One weekly tabloid: *Nabanga;* and one quarterly: *Vanuatu Viewpoints.*
VATICAN	The semiofficial *L'Osservatore Romano,* founded in 1861. Weekly editions are published in English, Spanish, Portuguese, German and English.	The official monthly *Acta Apostolicae Sedis,* a record of the encyclicals, acts of the Sacred Congregations, etc.
WESTERN SAMOA	No daily.	One fortnightly government publication: *Savali* Samoan (7,000) and English (2,000); six weeklies: *The Observer, The Samoa Times* (5,000), *Samoa Weekly* (4,500), *South Seas Star* (5,000), *Sunrise Journal* and *Tusitala Samoa.*
YEMEN ARAB REPUBLIC	Two government-owned dailies: *Al Thawra* (The Revolution) and *Al Gumhuryyah* (The Republic), the former published in Sanaa and the latter in Taiz.	Two fortnightlies: *Sanaa* and *Al Yemen,* and six weeklies: *Al Bilad, Mareb, As-Sabah, As-Salaam, Al Shaab* and *Al Tawn.* Politically, *Al Bilad* and *Al-Yemen* are to the right of center, and *Sanaa* and *Al Shaab* to the left.
YEMEN, People's Democratic Republic of	One daily: *14 October* (20,000), published by the government.	The weekly *Al-Thawra,* organ of the Central Committee of the Yemen Socialist Party, and the monthly *Al-Thaqafa-al-Jadia* (3,000), issued by the Ministry of Culture and Tourism.

News Agencies	Electronic News Media	Other Comments
No national news agency.	Only radio services are operated by the Tonga Broadcasting Commission, an independent statutory body.	
No national news agency.	Radio Tuvalu.	
Agence Voltaique de Presse, founded in 1963 under UNESCO auspices.	The national radio station is La Voix du Renouveau and the national television station Volta-vision.	
No national news agency.	The government-owned radio station, Radio Vanuatu.	
Agenzia Internationale Fides (AIF).	Radio Vatican, founded in 1931 and located within the Vatican City.	
No national news agency.	One radio station operated by the Western Samoa Broadcasting Service.	
Saba News Agency, founded in 1970.	Three radio stations at Sanaa, Taiz and Hodeida. A television station opened in 1975.	In 1976 all media were placed under the control of the Saba General Organization for Press and News.
Aden News Agency. The Agency issues *The Aden News Bulletin* in English and Arabic.	The state-owned Democratic Yemen Broadcasting Service runs the national radio and television service.	All media are controlled by the Ministry of Information. The ministry also controls the sole printing house in the country, the 14 October Corporation for Printing and Publishing.

SECTION V:
APPENDICES

I
THE WORLD'S FIFTY GREAT DAILIES

(From: *The World's Great Dailies: Profiles of Fifty Newspapers*
by John C. Merrill and Harold A. Fisher. New York, 1980)

ABC (Spain)
Aftenposten (Norway)
The Age (Australia)
Al Ahram (Egypt)
Asahi Shimbun (Japan)
The Atlanta Constitution (U.S.)
The (Baltimore) *Sun* (U.S.)
Berlingske Tidende (Denmark)
Borba (Yugoslavia)
The Christian Science Monitor (U.S.)
Il Corriere della Sera (Italy)
The Daily Telegraph (U.K.)
O Estado de S. Paulo) (Brazil)
Le Figaro (France)
Frankfurter Allgemeine (West Germany)
The Globe and Mail (Canada)
The Guardian (U.K.)
Ha'aretz (Israel)
Helsingin Sanomat (Finland)
The Hindu (India)
Izvestia (Soviet Union)
Jornal do Brazil (Brazil)
Los Angeles Times (U.S.)
The (Louisville) *Courier-Journal* (U.S.)
The Miami Herald (U.S.)

Le Monde (France)
Neue Zürcher Zeitung (Switzerland)
The New York Times (U.S.)
Osservatore Romano (Vatican City)
El País (Spain)
Pravda (Soviet Union)
Die Presse (Austria)
Rand Daily Mail (South Africa)
Renmin Ribao (China)
The Scotsman (U.K.)
La Stampa (Italy)
St. Louis Post-Dispatch (U.S.)
The Statesman (India)
Süddeutsche Zeitung (West Germany)
The Straits Times (Singapore)
Svenska Dagbladet (Sweden)
Sydney Morning Herald (Australia)
The Times (U.K.)
The Times of India (India)
La Vanguardia Española (Spain)
The Wall Street Journal (U.S.)
The Washington Post (U.S.)
Die Welt (West Germany)
Winnipeg Free Press (Canada)
The Yorkshire Post (U.K.)

II
NEWS AGENCIES OF THE WORLD
By Names
By Abbreviations and Bylines

By Names				
Name of News Agency	Abbreviation	Founding Date	Place	Rating ABCDE
Aden News Agency	ANA	1970	Aden	E
Agence Arabe Syrienne d'Information	AASA	1966	Damascus	D
Agence Belga (Agence Télégraphique Belge de Presse)	BELGA	1920	Brussels	B
Agence Benin-Presse	ABP	1961	Cotonou	E
Agence Burundaise de Presse	ABP	-	Bujumbura	E
Agence Centrafricaine de Presse	ACP	1974	Banjui	E
Agence Congolaise d'Information	ACI	1961	Brazzaville	E
Agence Day	AD	1897	Brussels	C
Agence France-Presse	AFP	1944	Paris	A
Agence Gabonaise de Presse	AGP	1961	Libreville	E
Agence Guinéenne de Presse	AGP	1960	Conakry	E
Agence Ivoirienne de Press	AIP	1961	Abidjan	E
Agence Malienne de Press et Promotion	AMPP	1977	Bamako	E
Agence Mauritanienne de Presse	AMP	-	Nouakcott	E
Agence Nationale d'Information "Taratra"	ANTA	1962	Antananarivo	E
Agence Parisienne de Presse	APP	1949	Paris	C
Agence de Presse Senegalaise	APS	1959	Dakar	E
Agence Républicaine d'Information	ARI	-	Paris	D
Agence Rwandaise de Presse	ARP	-	Kigali	E
Agence Tchadienne de Presse	ATP	1964	N'djamena	E
Agence Télégraphique	AT	-	Monte Carlo	D
Agence Togolaise de Presse	ATP	1975	Lomé	E
Agence Voltaique de Presse	AVP	1963	Ouagadougou	E
Agence Zaire-Presse	AZAP	1957	Kinshasa	E
Agencia EFE	EFE	1939	Madrid	B
Agência Europeia de Imprensa	AEI	-	Lisbon	D
Agência de Informação de Moçambique	AIM	-	Maputo	E
Agencia de Información Nacional	AIN	-	Havana	E
Agencia Informativa Orbe de Chile	AIO	1952	Santiago de Chile	C
Agência Literária Imprensa e Promocoes	ALIP	-	Lisbon	E
Agencia Los Diarios	ALD	1910	Buenos Aires	C
Agência Meridional	AM	1931	Rio de Janeiro	C
Agencia Mexicana de Noticias	AMEX	1968	Mexico City	C

[1]Explanation of ratings: A = major international news agency; B = major national agency with some international news-gathering facilities and bureaus; C = national news agency of a developed or large nation; D = national news agency of an underdeveloped or small nation; E = minor news agency.

Name of News Agency	Abbreviation	Founding Date	Place	Rating ABCDE
Agência Nacional	AN	1946	Brasilia	C
Agência Noticiosa Brastele	ANB	1970	Rio de Janeiro	D
Agência Noticiosa Portuguesa	ANOP	-	Lisbon	C
Agência Noticiosa Terceiro Mundo	ANTM	-	Lisbon	E
Agência Universal de Imprensa	UNIPRESS	-	Lisbon	D
Agentstvo Pechati Novosti	NOVOSTI	1961	Moscow	B
Agenzia Internazionle Fides	FIDES	1926	Vatican City	B
Agenzia Nazionale Stampa Associate	ANSA	1945	Rome	A
Agentia Romana de Presa	AGERPRESS	1949	Bucharest	C
Akajans	AKAJANS	-	Ankara	D
Albanian Telegraphic Agency	ATA	1945	Tirana	D
Algemeen Nederalnds Persbureau	ANP	1934	The Hague	B
Allgemeiner Deutscher Nachrichtendienst	ADN	1946	Berlin	B
Algérie Presse Service	APS	1961	Algiers	E
Anatolian News Agency	ANATOLIA	1920	Ankara & Istanbul	E
Angola Press	ANGOP	-	Luandu	E
ANKA Ajansi	ANKA	1973	Ankara	D
Asian News Service	ANS	-	Hong Kong	E
Associated Press	AP	1848	New York	A
Associated Press of Pakistan	APP	1948	Islamabad	D
Athens News Agency	ATHENAGENCE	1896	Athens	B
Austria Presse-Agentur	APA	1946	Vienna	B
Australian Associated Press	AAP	1935	Sydney	B
Australian United Press	AUP	1928	Melbourne	C
Bakhtar News Agency	BNA	1939	Kabul	E
Bangladesh Sangbad Sangasta	BSS	1972	Dacca	D
Bulgarska Telegrafitscheka Agentzia	BTA	1898	Sofia	B
Canadian Press	CP	1917	Toronto	B
Carribbean News Agency	CANA	-	Bridgetown, Barbados	B
Centralna Angecja Fotograficzna	CAF	1951	Warsaw	D
Central News Agency	CNA	1924	Taipei	C
Central Press	CP	-	Madrid	B
Centre d'Information de Presse	CIP	1946	Brussels	C
Ceskoslovenska Tiskova Kancelar	CTK	1918	Prague	B
Chiao Kwang News Photo Service	CK	-	Taipei	D
China News Service	CNS	1952	Beijing	B
China Youth News Agency	CYNA	-	Taipei	D
Colombia Press	CP	-	Calle, Colombia	C
Colpisa	Colpisa	-	Madrid	D
Cyprus News Agency	CNA	1976	Nicosia	D
Deutsche Presse-Agentur	dpa	1949	Hamburg	A
Dow Jones News Service	DJ	-	New York	C
Eastern News Agency	ENA	1972	Dacca	E
Emirates News Agency	WAM	1977	Abu Dhabi	E
Ethiopian News Agency	ENA	1941	Addis Ababa	E
Europa Press	EUROPA	-	Madrid	D
Euskadi Press	EP	-	Madrid	D
Exchange & Telegraph Company	EXTEL	1872	London	C
Gemini News Service	GEMINI	-	London	E
Ghana News Agency	GNA	1957	Accra	E
Hapdong News Agency	HNA	1945	Seoul	D
Hindustan Samachar	HS	1948	New Delhi	C
Hurriyet Haber Ajansi	HHA	1963	Istanbul	D
Iberia Press	IP	-	Madrid	D
IKA Haber Ajansi	IKA	1954	Ankara	D

Name of News Agency	Abbreviation	Founding Date	Place	Rating A B C D E
Independent Newspaper Alliance (formerly North American Newspaper Alliance)	INA	1922	New York	D
Informaciónes Mexicanas	INFORMEX	1960	Mexico City	C
Inter-African News Agency	IANA	1964	Salisbury, Zimbabwe	E
International News Service	INS	-	Hong Kong	E
Iraqi News Agency	INA	1959	Baghdad	E
Itonut Israel Meougnedet	ITIM	1950	Tel Aviv	C
Jamahirya News Agency	JANA	-	Tripoli	E
Jewish Telegraphic Agency	JTA	1919	Jerusalem	C
Jiji Tsushin-Sha	Jiji	1945	Tokyo	B
Jordan News Agency	JNA	1965	Amman	E
Kenya News Agency	KNA	1964	Nairobi	E
Khao san Pathet Lao	KPL	-	Vientiane	E
Korean Central News Agency (Chung Yang Tong Shin)	KCNA	1949	Pyongyang	E
Kuwait News Agency	KUNA	1976	Kuwait	E
Kyodo Tsushin	Kyodo	1945	Tokyo	B
Lembaga Kantoberita Nacional Antara	ANTARA	1937	Jakarta	C
Logos Agência de Informacão	LAI	1928	Madrid	C
Maghreb Arabe Presse	MAP	1959	Rabat	D
Magyar Tavirati Iroda	MTI	1880	Budapest	C
Malawi News Agency	MANA	1966	Lilongwe	E
Mencheta Agência	MECHETA	1882	Madrid	D
Middle East News Agency	MENA	1955	Cairo	B
Mongol Tsahilgaan Medeeniy Agentlag	MONTSAME	1957	Ulan Bator	E
Multipress	MULTIPRESS	-	Madrid	E
News Agency of Burma	NAB	1963	Rangoon	E
News Agency of Nigeria	NAN	1978	Lagos	D
Newspaper Enterprise Association	NEA	1902	New York	D
New Zealand Press Association	NZPA	1879	Wellington	C
Norsk Presse Service	NPS	1960	Oslo	C
Norsk Telegrambyra	NTB	1867	Oslo	C
Noticias Argentinas	NA	1973	Buenos Aires	D
Noticias Mexicanas	NOTIMEX	1968	Mexico City	C
Novinska Agencija Tanjug	TANJUG	1943	Belgrade	B
Orbis Press Agency	OPA	1977	Prague	D
Orient Press	OP	1952	Seoul	D
Oy Suomen Tietotoimisto Finsko Notisbyren	STT-FNB	1887	Helsinki	C
Pakistan Press International	PPI	1959	Karachi	D
Pars News Agency	PANA	1936	Teheran	D
Pertubohan Berita Nacional Malaysia	BERNAMA	1967	Kuala Lumpur	D
Philippines News Agency	PNA	1973	Manila	D
Polska Agencja Interpress	PAI	1966	Warsaw	D
Polska Agencja Prasowa	PAP	1944	Warsaw	C
Prensa Latina (Agencia Informativa Latinoamericana)	PRELA	1959	Havana	C
Presse Services	PS	1929	Paris	C
Presse- und Informationsstelle der Fürstlichen Regierung	PIFR	1963	Vaduz	D
Press Trust of India	PTI	1949	Bombay	B
Press Trust of Sri Lanka	PTSL	1951	Colombo	D
Qatar News Agency	QNA	-	Doha	E
Rapid News Agency	RNA	-	Hong Kong	E
Rastriya Samachar Samiti	RSS	1962	Katmandu	E

World Press ENCYCLOPEDIA
V.2

Name of News Agency	Abbreviation	Founding Date	Place	Rating ABCDE
Reuters	Reuters	1851	London	A
Ritzaus Bureau	RB	1866	Copenhagen	C
Saba News Agency	SNA	1970	Sanaa	E
Samachar Bharati	SB	1966	New Delhi	D
Saudi Press Agency	SPA	1970	Riyadh	D
Schweizerische Depeschenagentur	SDA	1894	Berne	C
Science Service-Agence Barnier	SS-AB	-	Paris	D
Shihata	SHIHATA	1976	Dar-es-Salaam	E
Sierra Leone News Agency	SLNA	1979	Freetown	E
Sisa News Agency	SNA	1951	Seoul	E
Société Publicité Édition du Cameroun	SOPECAM	1977	Yaounde	E
Sofia Press Agency	Sofiapres	1967	Sofia	C
Somalia National News Agency	SONNA	-	Mogadishu	E
South African Press Association	SAPA	1938	Johannesburg	C
South Pacific News Service	SPNS	1948	Wellington	E
Sudan News Agency	SUNA	1955	Khartoum	E
Surinaams Nieuws Agentschap	SNA	-	Paramaribo	E
Svensk-Internationella Pressbyran	SIP	1927	Stockholm	C
Svenska Nyhetsbyran	SN	-	Stockholm	C
Telegrafnoye Agenstvo Sovietskovo Soyuza	Tass	1925	Moscow	A
Telenoticiosa Americana	TELAM	1945	Buenos Aires	B
Telepress International	TI	1964	Buenos Aires	D
Tidningarnas Telegrambyra	TT	1921	Stockholm	C
Tunis-Afrique-Presse	TAP	1961	Tunis	E
Turk Haberler Ajansi	THA	1950	Istanbul	C
Uganda News Agency	UNA	-	Kampala	E
United News of India	UNI	1961	New Delhi	E
United Press of Canada	UPC	-	Toronto	C
United Press International	UPI	1958	New York	A
United Press of Pakistan	UPP	1949	Karachi	D
Vietnam News Agency (Vietnam Thong Tin Xa)	VNA	1945	Hanoi	D
Wakalat Al-Anbaa Al-Wataniyah	WAW	1964	Beirut	E
World News Service	WNS	-	Hong Kong	E
Xinhua (formerly Hsinhua)	XINHUA	1937	Beijing	A
Yurt Haberler Ajansi	YHA	1950	Ankara	D
Zambia News Agency	ZANA	-	Lusaka	E

BY ABBREVIATIONS/BYLINES

ABBREVIATION/BYLINE	Full Name	Place
AAP	Australian Associated Press	Sydney
AASI	Agence Arabe Syrienne d'Information	Damascus
ABP	Agence Benin-Presse	Cotonou
ABP	Agence Burundaise de Presse	Bujumbura
ACAP	Agence Centrafricaine de Presse	Bangui
ACI	Agence Congolaise d'Information	Brazzaville
AD	Agence Day	Brussels
ADN	Allgemeiner Deutscher Nachrichtendienst	Berlin
AEI	Agência Europeia Imprensa	Lisbon
AFP	Agence France-Presse	Paris
Agerpress	Agentia Romana de Presa	Bucharest
AGP	Agence Gabonaise de Presse	Libreville
AGP	Agence Guinéenne de Presse	Conakry
Akajans	Akajans	Ankara
AIM	Agência de Informacã o de Mocambique	Maputo
AIN	Agencia de Información Nacional	Havana
AIOC	Agencia Informativa Orbe de Chile	Santiago
AIP	Agence Invoirienne de Presse	Abidjan
ALD	Agencia Los Diarios	Buenos Aires
ALIP	Agência Litéraria Imprensa e Promocões	Lisbon
AM	Agencia Meridional	Rio de Janiero
AMEX	Agencia Mexicana de Noticias	Mexico City
AMP	Agence Mauritanienne de Presse	Nouakchott
AMPA	Agence Malienne de Presse et Promotion	Bamako
AN	Agência Nacional	Brasilia
ANA	Aden News Agency	Aden
ANA	Anatolian News Agency	Ankara
ANB	Agência Noticiosa Brastele	Rio de Janeiro
ANGOP	Angop	Luanda
ANKA	ANKA Ajansi	Ankara
ANOP	Agência Noticiosa Portuguesa	Lisbon
ANP	Algemeen Nederlands Persbureau	The Hague
ANS	Asian News Service	Hong Kong
ANSA	Agenzia Nazionale Stampa Associata	Rome
ANTA	Agence Nationale d'Information "Taratra"	Antananarivo
ANTARA	Lembaga Kantoberita Nasional Antara	Jakarta
ANTM	Agência Noticiosa Terceiro Mundo	Lisbon
AP	Associated Press	New York
APA	Austria Presse-Agentur	Vienna
APP	Agence Parisienne de Presse	Paris
APP	Associated Press of Pakistan	Islamabad

ABBREVIATION/BYLINE	Full Name	Place
APS	Agence de Presse Senegalaise	Dakar
APS	Algérie Presse Service	Algiers
ARI	Agence Républicaine d'Information	Paris
ARP	Agence Rwandaise de Presse	Kigali
AT	Agence Télégraphique	Monte Carlo
ATA	Albanian Telegraphic Agency	Tirana
ATHENAGENCE	Athens News Agency	Athens
ATP	Agence Tchadienne de Presse	N'djamena
ATP	Agence Togolaise de Presse	Lomé
AUP	Australian United Press	Melbourne
AVP	Agence Voltaique de Presse	Ouagadougou
AZAP	Agence Zaire-Presse	Kinshasa
BELGA	Agence Belga	Brussels
BERNAMA	Pertubohan Berita Nasional Malaysia	Kuala Lumpur
BNA	Baktar News Agency	Kabul
BNA	Bangladesh News Agency	Dacca
BTA	Bulgarska Telegrafitscheka Agentzia	Sofia
CAF	Centralna Agencja Fotograficzna	Warsaw
CANA	Caribbean News Agency	Bridgetown
CIP	Centre d'Information de Presse	Brussels
CKNPS	Chiao Kwang News Photo Service	Taipei
CNA	Central News Agency	Taipei
CNA	Cyprus News Agency	Nicosia
CNS	China News Service	Beijing
Colpisa	Colpisa	Madrid
CP	Canadian Press	Toronto
CP	Central Press	Madrid
CP	Colombia Press	Calle
CTK	Ceskoslovenska Tiskova Kancelar	Prague
CYNA	China Youth News Agency	Taipei
DJ	Dow Jones News Service	New York
dpa	Deutsch Presse-Agentur	Hamburg
EFE	Agencia EFE	Madrid
ENA	Eastern News Agency	Dacca
ENA	Ethiopia News Agency	Addis Ababa
EP	Euskadi Press	Madrid
Europa	Europa Press	Madrid
Extel	Exhange & Telegraph Company	London
FIDES	Agenzia Internationale Fides	Vatican City
GEMINI	Gemini News Service	London
GNA	Ghana News Agency	Accra
HHA	Hurriyet Haber Ajansi	Istanbul
HNA	Hapdong News Agency	Seoul

ABBREVIATION/BYLINE	Full Name	Place
HS	Hindustan Samachar	New Delhi
IANA	Inter-African News Agency	Salisbury
IKA	IKA Haber Ajansi	Ankara
INA	Independent Newspaper Alliance	New York
INS	International News Service	Hong Kong
INA	Iraqi News Agency	Baghdad
INFORMEX	Informaciones Mexicanas	Mexico City
IP	Iberia Press	Madrid
ITIM	Itonut Israel Meougnedet	Tel Aviv
JANA	Jamahiriya News Agency	Tripoli
Jiji	Jiji Tsushin-sha	Tokyo
JNA	Jordan News Agency	Amman
JTA	Jewish Telegraphic Agency	Jerusalem
KCNA	Korean Central News Agency	Pyongyang
KNA	Kenya News Agency	Nairobi
KPL	Khao San Pathet Lao	Vientiane
KUNA	Kuwait News Agency	Kuwait
Kyodo	Kyodo Tsushin	Tokoyo
LAI	Logos Agência de Informação	Madrid
MANA	Malawi News Agency	Lilongwe
MAP	Maghreb Arabe Presse	Rabat
MENA	Middle East News Agency	Cairo
Mencheta	Agéncia Mencheta	Madrid
MONTSAME	Mongol Tsahilgaan Medeeniy Agentlag	Ulan Bator
MTI	Magyar Tavirati Iroda	Budapest
Multipress	Multipress	Madrid
NA	Noticias Argentinas	Buenos Aires
NAB	News Agency of Burma	Rangoon
NAN	News Agency of Nigeria	Lagos
NEA	Newspaper Enterprise Association	New York
Notimex	Noticias Mexicanas	Mexico City
NOVOSTI	Agentstvo Pechati Novosti	Moscow
NPS	Norsk Presse Service	Oslo
NTB	Norsk Telegrambyra	Oslo
NZPA	New Zealand Press Association	Wellington
OP	Orient Press	Seoul
OPA	Orbis Press Agency	Prague
PAI	Polska Agencja Interpress	Warsaw
PANA	Pars News Agency	Teheran
PAP	Polska Agencja Prasowa	Warsaw
PIFR	Presse- und Informationsstelle der Fürstlichen Regierung	Vaduz
PNS	Phillippines News Service	Manila

ABBREVIATION/BYLINE	Full Name	Place
PPI	Pakistan Press International	Karachi
PRELA	Prensa Latina Agencia Informativa Latino-Americana	Havana
PS	Presse Services	Paris
PTI	Press Trust of India	Bombay
PTSL	Press Trust of Sri Lanka	Colombo
QNA	Qatar News Agency	Doha
RB	Ritzaus Bureau	Copenhagen
Reuters	Reuters	London
RNA	Rapid News Agency	Hong Kong
RSS	Rastriya Samachar Samiti	Katmandu
SAPA	South African Press Association	Johannesburg
SB	Samachar Bharati	New Delhi
SDA	Schweizerische Depeschenagentur	Berne
SHIHATA	Shihata	Dar-es-Salaam
SIP	Svensk Internationella Pressbyran	Stockholm
SLNA	Sierra Leone News Agency	Freetown
SN	Svenska Nyhetsbyran	Stockholm
SNA	Saba News Agency	Sanaa
SNA	Sisa News Agency	Seoul
SNA	Surinaams Nieuws Agentschap	Paramaribo
SONNA	Somali National News Agency	Mogadishu
SOPECAM	Société Publicité Édition du Cameroun	Yaounde
SPA	Saudi Press Agency	Riyadh
SPA	Sofia Press Agency	Sofia
SPNS	South Pacific News Service	Wellington
SS-AB	Science Service-Agence Barnier	Paris
STT-FNB	Oy Suomen Tietotoimisto Finska Notisbyran	Helsinki
SUNA	Sudan News Agency	Khartoum
TANJUG	Telegrafska Agencija Nova Jugoslavija	Belgrade
TAP	Tunis-Afrique-Presse	Tunis
Tass	Telegrafnoye Agentzvo Sovietskovo Soyuza	Moscow
TELAM	Telenoticiosa Americana	Buenos Aires
THA	Turk Haberler Ajansi	Istanbul
TPI	Telepress International	Buenos Aires
TT	Tidningarnas Telegrambyra	Stockholm
UNA	Uganda News Agency	Kampala
UNI	United News of India	New Delhi
UNIPRESS	Agência Universal de Imprensa	Lisbon
UPC	United Press of Canada	Toronto
UPI	United Press International	New York
UPP	United Press of Pakistan	Karachi

ABBREVIATION/BYLINE	Full Name	Place
VNA	Vietnamese News Agency	Hanoi
WAM	Emirates News Agency	Abu Dhabi
WAW	Wakalat Al-Anbaa Al-Wataniyah	Beirut
WNS	World News Service	Hong Kong
XINHUA	Xinhua	Beijing
YHA	Yurt Haberler Ajansi	Ankara
ZANA	Zambia News Agency	Lusaka

III
SELECTED PERIODICALS DEALING WITH THE PRESS

Black Journalism Review   Bimonthly
  644 N. Michigan Avenue
  Suite 1010, Chicago IL 60611

CPU Quarterly   Quarterly
  Commonwealth Press Union
  Studio House, 184 Fleet Street
  London EC4A 2DU, England

Cadernos de Jornalismo e Comunicacão
  Jornal do Brasil   Bimonthly
  Av. Brasil 500 ZC-00
  Rio de Janeiro, Brazil

Cahiers de la Presse Française   10 issues/year
  Fédération Nationale de la Presse Francaise
  6 Bis rue Gabriel-Laumain
  Paris (10e), France

Catholic Journalist   Monthly
  Catholic Press Association
  119 North Park Avenue
  Rockville Center, NY 11570

Columbia Journalism Review   Bimonthly
  Columbia University
  Graduate School of Journalism
  700 Journalism Building
  New York, NY 10027

Content   11 issues/year
  Barry Zwicker
  91 Raglan Avenue
  Toronto, Ontario M6C 2K7, Canada

Correspondence de la Presse   Daily
  Société Générale de Presse
  13 Avenue de l'Opera
  75001 Paris, France

Dagspressen   Monthly
  Norwegian Newspapers Association
  Rosenkrantzgate 3
  Oslo 1, Norway

Dansk Fagpresse   Quarterly
  Dansk Fagpresseforening Borgergade
  32 Street
  DK-1300 Copenhagen K, Denmark

Dansk Presse   10 issues/year
  Danish Newspapers Association
  Pressens Hus, Skindergade 7
  1159 Copenhagen K, Denmark

Democratic Journalist (also French, Russian,
Spanish editions)   Monthly
  International Organization of Journalists
  Parizska 9 110 01
  Prague 1, Czechoslovakia

Écho de la Presse et de la Publicité   Weekly
  Editions Jacquemart
  19 rue des Prêtres-Saint-Germain-
  l'Auxerrois
  Paris (1er) France

Editor & Publisher: The Fourth Estate   Weekly
  575 Lexington Avenue
  New York, NY 10022

Eleftherotypia   Monthly
  Socratous 59 Street
  Athens, Greece

F.I.E.J. Bulletin   Quarterly
  Fédération Internationale des Éditeurs de
  Journaux et Publications
  6 rue du Faubourg Poissonniere
  75010 Paris, France

Fourth Estate   Monthly
  Box 3184 Station C
  Ottawa, Ontario K1Y 4J4
  Canada

Gazette   Quarterly
  Kluwer, B.V. Box 23
  Deventer, Netherlands

Giornalismo Europeo   Bimonthly
  Comunità Europea dei Giornalisti
  Via Venti Settembre 26
  00187 Rome, Italy

Grassroots Editor   Quarterly
  International Society of Weekly
  Newspaper Editors
  Department of Journalism
  Northern Illinois University
  De Kalb, IL 60115

IAPA News   Semi-Monthly
  Inter-American Press Association
  2911 N.W. 39th Street
  Miami, FL 33142

IPI Report   Monthly
  International Press Institute
  City University
  280 St. John Street
  London ECIV 4PB, England

Index on Censorship   Quarterly
  Writers & Scholars International Ltd.,
  21 Russell Street
  London WC2B 5HP, England

Indian Press   Monthly
  Indian & Eastern Newspaper Society
  IENS Building, Rafi Marg
  New Delhi 11001, India

Information und Meinung   Quarterly
   Niederoesterreichisches Presshaus
   Gutenbergstr. 12
   A-1300 St Poelten, Austria

International Press Journal   Bimonthly
   Box 758 Station F
   Toronto, Ontario, Canada

Interstages   8 issues/year
   Institut Belge d'Information et de
   Documentation
   3 rue Montoyer
   B-1040 Brussels, Belgium

Journalism Educator   Quarterly
   Association for Education in Journalism
   Department of Journalism
   University of Minnesota
   Minneapolis, MN 55455

Journalism History   Quarterly
   Department of Journalism, California State
   University
   Darby Annex 103
   Northridge, CA 91330

Journalism Monographs   4 issues/year
   Association for Education in Journalism
   School of Journalism
   University of Kentucky
   Lexington, KY 40506

Journalism Quarterly   Quarterly
   Association for Education in Journalism
   Department of Journalism
   University of Minnesota
   Minneapolis, MN 55455

Journalism Studies Review   Monthly
   Center for Journalism Studies
   University College
   Cardiff, England

Journalist   Monthly
   Australian Journalists Association
   93 Clarence Street
   Sydney 2000, Australia

Journalist   Monthly
   National Union of Journalists
   314-320 Grays Inn Road
   London WC1X 8DP, England

Der Journalist   Monthly
   Deutscher Journalisten-Verband
   Verlag Rommerskirchen und Co.,
   Bonner Str. 47
   5486 Remagen-Rolandseck, West Germany

Journalisten   11 issues/year
   Norsk Journalistlag Rosenkrantzgate 3,
   Oslo 1, Norway

Journalisten   Monthly
   Svenska Journalistfoerbundet
   Vegagatan 4
   113 29 Stockholm, Sweden

Journalistes Français   Monthly
   Syndicat des Journalistes Français
   Paul Parisot, 5 rue Geoffrey Márie
   Paris 9e, France

Matrix   Quarterly
   Women in Communications
   Box 9561
   Austin, TX 78766

Media   Monthly
   Syme Media Enterprises Ltd.
   Room 1303
   World Trade Center, Hong Kong

Media Development   Quarterly
   World Association for Christian
   Communication
   122 King's Road
   London SW3 4TR, England

Medien-Journal   Quarterly
   Oesterreichische Gesellschaft fuer
   Kommunikationsfragen Schippergasse 70
   A-1210 Vienna, Austria

Nasa Stampa   Monthly
   Savez Novinara Jugoslavije
   Trg Republike 5
   Belgrade, Yugoslavia

Neue Deutsche Presse   Semi-Monthly
   Verband der Journalisten der DDR
   Friedrichstr. 101
   108 Berlin, East Germany

New Journalist   Bimonthly
   Box K750
   Haymarket, New South Wales 2000
   Australia

Novinar/Journalist   Monthly
   Novinar, Norodni tr 17
   Prague 1, Czechoslovakia

Overseas Press Bulletin   Semi-Monthly
   Overseas Press Club of America
   55 East 43rd Street
   New York, NY 10017

P.C.I. Review   Quarterly
   Press Council of India
   10 Janpath
   New Delhi 11001, India

Periodista   Bimonthly
   Colegio Nacional de Periodistas
   Casa Nacional de Periodista
   Avenida Andres Bello
   Caracas, Venezuela

Presstime   Monthly
   American Newspaper Publishers'
   Association
   P.O. Box 17407
   Dulles International Airport
   Washington, D.C. 20041

Press/Pers   Quarterly
   Association Belge des Éditeurs de Journaux
   rue Belliard 20
   B-1040 Brussels, Belgium

Presse Actualité   9 issues/year
   Bayard Presse
   5 rue Bayard
   75380 Paris Cedex 08, France

Pressens Tidning   10 issues/year
   Svenska Tidningsutgivarefoereningen
   S. Foerlags AB, Box 45136
   104 30 Stockholm 45, Sweden

Pubblicista   Monthly
   Via Monte Cervialto
   00139 Rome, Italy

Quill   Monthly
   Society of Professional Journalists
   Sigma Delta Chi
   35 East Wacker Drive
   Chicage, IL 60601

Shimbun Kenkyu   Monthly
Shimbun Kyokai Ho   Weekly
   Nihon Shinbun Kyokai
   Nipon Press Center Building
   2-1 Uchisaiwai-cho
   2 Chome, Chi-yoda-ku Tokyo 100, Japan

SZV Aktualitaten   Bimonthly
   Swiss Newspaper Publishers' Association
   Morgartenstrasse 29 Postfach 1465
   8036 Zurich, Switzerland

Suomen Lehdisto/Finland's Press   Monthly
   Finnish Newspaper Publishers' Association
   Kalevankatu 4 V Floor 00100
   Helsinki 10, Finland

Tidnings Nytt   Monthly
   AB Svenska Pressbyraan Fach 104
   24 Stockholm 30, Sweden

Trabajador del Perodismo   Bimonthly
   Casa del Periodista
   Apdo 2096
   Panama City, Panama

UK Press Gazette   Weekly
   Bouverie Publishing Company, Ltd.
   Cliffords Inn, Fetter Lane
   London EC4 1PJ, England

Unsere Zeitung   Monthly
   Eilers und Schuenemann
   Verlagsgesellschaft
   Schuenemannhaus
   2800 Bremen 1, West Germany

Washington Journalism Review   Monthly
   3122 M Street NW
   Washington, D.C. 20007

Zhurnalist   Monthly
   Izdatel'stvo Pravda
   U1 Pravdy 24
   Moscow 125047, USSR

IV
MEDIA MULTINATIONALS

The media are among the most jealously guarded national resources. Almost all countries in the world have legal and administrative restrictions on the purchase, ownership and operation of the media by foreign interests. In many Third World countries foreign participation in a news medium is considered almost an infringement of national sovereignty, and even in developed countries such as Canada, it invariably causes a furor in nationalist circles. Thus the media have not witnessed the rise of multinationals in the same way as banking, mining or industry.

Nevertheless, it is possible to identify at least two media multinationals. Significantly, both are restricted to Australia, the United Kingdom and the English-speaking countries of North America. The older of the two is the Thomson group. Founded by Roy (later Lord) Thomson, a legendary media baron, Thomson group has newspaper and nonnewspaper interests in Canada, its home base, the United Kingdom, the United States and the Caribbean. The Canadian and North American operations are separate from the United Kingdom holdings, and the only thing common between them is the secrecy that shrouds them.

The Canadian operation, headed by Kenneth R. Thomson, is based in Toronto and controls 40 daily newspapers, with a total circulation of 1,190,000, and 12 weeklies with a total circulation of 75,000. Thomson Newspapers is also active in U.S. newspaper publishing. It has more than 20 subsidiaries and publishes about 92 daily and 19 weekly newspapers with an aggregate daily circulation of about 1.5 million. Although the circulation of the entire group is not large by mass-media standards, Thomson Newspapers is characterized by an extremely efficient organization resulting in one of the largest returns on investment (ROI) in the industry, close to 25 percent annually.

Since the sale of *The Times* and *The Sunday Times* to Rupert Murdoch, the Thomson Organization no longer has a flagship in London of the same class. The Thomson group has also been reducing its visibility in the Caribbean where it had a number of papers in the 1950s and 1960s. The largest newspaper of Thomson West Indian Holdings is *Advocate-News* of Barbados.

If Thomson is becoming less of a multinational than it was before, Rupert Murdoch's organization is becoming more so. An Oxford graduate who learned journalism on the *Daily Express* and *News Chronicle,* Murdoch has gained strength from his keen awareness of markets. However, he has been accused of buying newspapers and then taking them "down market" to build up circulation by using sleazy photos and sensational stories.

His purchase of the prestigious *Times* and *Sunday Times* of London has made Murdoch one of the most powerful publishers on both sides of the Atlantic and in Australia. His empire includes the *Daily Sun,* the largest selling London daily, *News of the World*, the largest selling newspaper in the world, several British magazines and regional newspapers and a 12 percent interest in an independent television channel.

In the United States he owns the *New York Post*—which he bought from Dorothy Schiff for $30 million and which he soon doubled in circulation—*New York* magazine, *The Village Voice* and two newspapers in Texas. In Australia he owns the *Australian* a serious Syndey newspaper, and other properties in Perth and Adelaide.

In recent years German and French media barons have expanded their interests in book and magazine publishing abroad but have not as yet ventured into newspaper publishing.

V
PRESS-RELATED ASSOCIATIONS, UNIONS & ORGANIZATIONS

International

Association for the Promotion of the International Circulation of the Press (DISTRIPRESS), Zurich. Founded in 1955 to promote freedom of the press and free flow of printed matter across national borders. 360 members. Publishes *Distripress News.*

Commonwealth Press Union, London. Founded in 1909 to promote the welfare of the Commonwealth press and oppose measures likely to affect its freedom. Over 800 newspapers, news agencies and periodicals in 32 countries. Publishes *The CPU Quarterly.*

Fédération Internationale des Editeurs de Journaux et Publications/International Federation of Newspaper Publishers, Paris. Founded in 1948 to safeguard the ethical and economic interests of newspapers and to represent the interests of the industry at the international level. Membership: national organizations in 27 countries. Publishes *FIEJ Bulletin, FIEJ-DOC* and *FIEJ-NOTES,* all in French and English.

INCA-FIEJ Research Association (IFRA), Darmstadt, West Germany. Founded in 1961 to develop methods, machines and techniques for the newspaper industry, to set standards and specifications, and to investigate economy and quality problems in newspaper printing and publishing. 429 newspaper members and 44 trade associate members. Publishes *Newspaper Techniques.*

International Catholic Union of the Press/Union Catholique Internationale de la Presse, Geneva. Founded in 1927 to link Catholic print publications and to represent the interests of the Catholic press at international organizations. Members include the Federation of Catholic Press Agencies, International Federation of Catholic Journalists, International Federation of Catholic Dailies and International Federation of Church Press Associations. Publishes *UCIP Informations.*

International Federation of Audit Bureaux of Circulations, Madrid. Founded in 1963 to encourage and facilitate the exchange of information and experience between member organizations, to work toward greater standardization and uniformity in the reporting of circulations, to encourage the establishment of audit bureaus of circulations where they do not exist, and to cooperate with national and international advertising agencies. 23 member organizations. Publishes *Circulating Auditing Around the World.*

International Federation of Journalists (IFJ), Belgium. Founded in 1952 as a breakaway from the Communist-dominated International Organization of Journalists. IFJ is dedicated to freedom of the press and freedom of journalists according to Article 19 of the Universal Declaration of Human Rights. In pursuit of this goal it provides factual information for use in collective bargaining, conducts professional surveys, assists exchange programs for journalists, and organizes seminars and training programs. IFJ has sent fact-finding missions to countries where press freedom is under threat and conducted studies of the needs of journalists in developing countries. It has spearheaded protests against harassment, persecution and detention without trial of journalists. It also actively opposes the 1978 UNESCO Declaration on the Media, which it believes could lead to government control of the press. Although not officially affiliated with the International Confederation of Free Trade Unions, it has an associate status in that organization.

IFJ has 81,877 members worldwide in 27 affiliated unions:

Argentina	Federación Argentina de Periodistas
Austria	Österreichische Journalistengewerkshaft

Belgium	Union Professionnelle de la Presse Belge
Canada	Newspaper Guild
Denmark	Dansk Journalistforbund
Finland	Suomen Sanomalehtimiesten Liitto
France	Syndicat National des Journalistes
	Syndicat National des Journalistes (FO)
	Syndicat des Journalistes Francais (CFDT)
Germany, West	Deutscher Journalisten-Verband
	Deutsche Journalisten-Union
Greece	Union des Redacteurs des Journaux Quotidiens d'Athenes
Iceland	Association of Icelandic Journalists
Israel	National Federation of Israeli Journalists
Korea, South	Journalists Association of Korea
Lesotho	Lesotho Union of Journalists
Liberia	Press Union of Liberia
Luxembourg	Association Luxembourgeoise des Journalistes
Netherlands, The	Nederlandse Vereniging van Journalisten
Norway	Norsk Journalistlag
Sweden	Svenska Jouranlistforbundet
Switzerland	Association de la Presse Suisse
Tunisia	Association des Journalistes Tunisiens
Turkey	Turkiye Gazeteciler Sendikasi
United Kingdom	National Union of Journalists
United States	Newspaper Guild
Zaire	Union Nationale de la Presse du Zaire

IFJ publishes *Direct Line,* a monthly newsletter, and *IFJ Information,* an annual.

International Federation of the Periodical Press/Fédération Internationale de la Presse Périodique, London. Founded in 1925 to represent and promote the periodical press and to facilitate contacts among periodical publishers. 104 members in 31 countries.

International Organization of Journalists (IOJ)/Organisation Internationale des Journalistes, Prague. Founded in 1946 as the successor to the Federation of Journalists founded in 1926 with headquarters in Paris and the International Federation of Journalists founded in London after the fall of Paris to the Nazis in World War II. Within a few years of its founding the IOJ was taken over by the Communists, leading some affiliated organizations to break off and form the International Federation of Journalists. Its Communist orientation is evident in its charter, which calls for a "struggle against fascist progaganda of any sort, the protection of freedom of…journalists against the influence of monopolist and financial groups and the…rights of colonial peoples and national minorities" and "…a struggle against…every form of journalistic activity in the service of individuals or particular groups of society which are contrary to those of the working masses." The 1976 IOJ congress called upon its members to "support the efforts of socialist countries to develop mass media in socialist society…to denounce the imperialist system of information which tries to influence public opinion in the developing countries…[to] support the just fight of progressive journalists of capitalist countries for democracy, particularly to support their fight against the process of concentration in mass media by the press monopolies and to continue to fight for the right of peoples to live in peace and in freedom."

IOJ membership comprises national unions of journalists, national IOJ groups and individual members. National affiliates include:

Algeria	Union of Algerian Journalists
Argentina	Press Syndicate of Córdoba
	Association of Journalists of Buenos Aires
Bolivia	Democratic Union of Workers of the Bolivian Press
Cameroon	National Union of Journalists
Colombia	National Collegium of Journalists
Congo	National Union of Congolese Journalists
Czechoslovakia	Czechoslovak Union of Journalists
Dominican Republic	National Syndicate of Professional Journalists

El Salvador	National Union of Journalists
Gambia, The	Gambia Journalists Association
Guyana	Union of Guyanese Journalists
Japan	Japan Congress of Journalists
	Association of Japanese Journalists
Madagascar	Press Syndicate of Madagascar
Nicaragua	National Union of Journalists
Peru	Federation of Journalists of Peru
Rumania	Council of Rumanian Journalists
South Africa	South African Journalists Union
Syria	Syrian Journalists Union
Uruguay	Association of the Uruguayan Press
Yemen (PDR)	Democratic Yemeni Journalists Organization
Zimbabwe	Association of Journalists of Zimbabwe

IOJ publishes a number of journals, including *Democratic Journalist* (monthly in English, French, Russian and Spanish); *Interpressgrafik;* (quarterly); *Information Bulletin* (bimonthly); and *Afrique Mass Media.*

International Press Institute (IPI), London. Founded in 1951 as a nongovernmental association of editors, publishers and broadcasters who support the principles of a free and responsible press. Membership, exceeding 2,000, is drawn from 62 countries. An executive board of 24 national representatives is elected annually. National committees are established in every country where there are five full members. The institute is active in promoting the free flow of news and in journalism training in developing countries. More than 300 of Africa's leading journalists are IPI-trained. Actions in defense of press freedom range from formal protests to representation at trials of journalists. The institute's principal publication is the *IPI Report.*

World Association for Christian Communication (WACC)/Association Mondiale pour la Communication Chrétienne, London. Founded in 1975 in combination with the Agency for Christian Literature Development. WACC's program include training of Christian journalists, research and exchange of information. Membership in 61 countries includes both church-related and secular organizations. There are six regional associations. WACC publishes the quarterly *Media Development* (formerly *WACC Journal).*

World Press Freedom Committee, c/o *The Herald,* Miami. Founded in 1972 as a coordinating agency for 32 journalism organizations on five continents to (1) act in unison against major threats to the media; (2) monitor global forums, such as UNESCO, in which the media have come under attack; (3) conduct programs of assistance to the media of developing countries; and (4) serve as a clearinghouse for equipment for Third World media.

Regional

Africa	**Union of African News Agencies,** Algiers. Founded in 1963. **Union Internationale des Journalistes Africains** (UIJA), Paris.
Asia	**Asian Mass Communication Research & Information Center,** Singapore. Jointly sponsored by the Government of Singapore and the Friedrich-Ebert Stiftung, an independent foundation in West Germany, it is one of the regional documentation centers coordinated by UNESCO. Publications include *Media Asia* and *Asian Mass Communication Bulletin.* **Organization of Asian News Agencies** (OANA), Jakarta. Founded in 1961 under UNESCO auspices to promote technical and professional cooperation among Asian national news agencies. **Press Foundation of Asia,** Manila. Founded in 1967 as an independent nonprofit organization and as a professional forum for Asian

journalists. Its efforts are directed toward reduction of newspaper costs and improvement of editorial and management techniques within the Asian setting. Membership includes 300 newspapers. Publishes the weekly *Data Asia* and the annual *Asian Press & Media Directory*.

Europe **Association of European Journalists/Association des Journalistes Européens,** Rome. Founded in 1963 to facilitate access to sources of European information. 1,000 members and national associations in 10 countries.
European Alliance of Press Agencies/Alliance Européene des Agences de Presse, Brussels. Founded in 1957. 23 member nations.

Latin America **Centro Internacional de Estudios Superiores para America Latina (CIESPAL),** Quito, Ecuador. Founded in 1958 with UNESCO assistance as a regional training center for journalists.
Inter-American Federation of Working Newspapermen's Organizations, Panama City. Founded in 1960 to promote the establishment of trade unions for journalists in the Western Hemisphere. 29 organizations in 24 countries.
Inter-American Press Association, Miami. Founded in 1942 to guard the freedom of the press in the Americas. IAPA maintains a scholarship fund and the Technical Center, which

publishes seminars and serves as a consulting agency. It also issues annually a highly regarded survey of press freedom in the Western Hemisphere. 900 active and 60 associate members. IAPA's principal organ is the bimonthly *IAPA News.*
Union Latinamericana de Prensa Católica/Latin American Catholic Press Union, Montevideo, Uruguay. Founded in 1959 to coordinate and improve the Catholic press in Latin America. Membership includes national groups and local associations.

National

Afghanistan **Journalists Association,** Kabul.
Albania **Union of Albanian Journalists,** Tirana. Publishes *Hosteni, Tribuna e Gazetarit.*
Algeria **Union Algereine des Journalistes,** Algiers.
Argentina **Asociación de Entidades Periodisticas Argentinas,** Buenos Aires.
Federación Argentina de Periodistas, Buenos Aires.
Press Syndicate of Cordoba, Cordoba.
Australia **Australian Journalists Association,** Sydney.
Australian Newspapers Council, Melbourne. Membership: 6 metropolitan dailies.
Australian Provincial Press Association, Sydney.
Country Press Association of South Australia, Adelaide.
Regional Dailies of Australia, Melbourne. 32 members.
Austria **Österreichische Jour-**

nalistenwerkschaft, Vienna.

Verband Österreichischer Zeitungherausgeber und Zeitungsverleger / Austrian Newspaper Publishers Association, Vienna. Publishes *Handbuch Österreichs Presse, Werbung, Graphik.*

Österreichischer Zeitschriftenverband /Association of Periodical Publishers, Vienna. 162 members.

Bangladesh

Bangladesh Federal Union of Journalists, Dacca.

Bangladesh Sangbadpatra Karmachari Federation, Dacca.

Bangladesh Sangbadpatra Press Sramik Federation, Dacca.

Belgium

Association Belge des Editeurs de Journaux /Belgische Vereniging van de Dagbladuitgevers, Brussels. 38 members. Publishes *La Presse/De Pers.*

Association Générale de la Presse Belge/ Algemene Belgische Persbond, Brussels. 1,000 members.

Fédération de la Presse Periodique de Belgique, Brussels.

Syndicat des Journalistes, Brussels. 157 members.

Union Professionnelle de la Presse Belge, Brussels.

De Vlaamse Journalistenclub, Brussels.

Bolivia

Asociación Nacional de Periodistas, La Paz.

Asociación Nacional de Prensa, La Paz.

Democratic Union of Workers of the Bolivian Press, La Paz.

Brazil

Associação Brasileira de Imprensa, Rio de Janeiro. 4,000 members.

Federação Nacional dos Journalistas Profissionais, Brasilia.

Bulgaria

Union of Bulgarian Journalists, Sofia. 3,157 members. Publishes *Bulgarski Zhurnalist, Pogled.*

Cameroon

National Union of Journalists, Yaounde.

Canada

Canadian Community Newspapers Association, Toronto. 668 members.

Canadian Daily Newspaper Publishers Association, Toronto. 89 members.

Canadian Periodical Publishers Association, Toronto.

Canadian Section of the Commonwealth Press Union, Hamilton, Ontario.

National Press Club of Canada, Ottawa.

Periodical Press Association, Toronto.

Chile

Asociación Nacional de Prensa, Santiago.

Colombia

Asociación Colombiana de Periodistas, Bogotá.

Asociación de Diarios Colombianos, Bogotá. 32 members.

Asociación Nacional de Trabajadores de la Prensa, Bogotá.

Asociación de Periodistas de Bolivar, Cartagena.

Circulo Colombiano de Reporteros Graficos, Bogotá.

Circulo de Periodistas de Bogotá, Bogotá.

Colegio Nacional de Periodistas, Bogotá.

Federación Nacional de Trabajadores de la Prensa, Bogotá.

Reporteros Sindicalizados de Antioquia, Medellin.

Congo	**National Union of Congolese Journalists.**
Costa Rica	**Colegio de Periodisas de Costa Rica,** San José.
Cuba	**Union de Periodistas de Cuba,** Havana.
Czechoslovakia	**Czech Union of Journalists,** Prague. 3,100 members. Publishes *Svet v Obrazech*.
	Czechoslovak Union of Journalists, Prague. 4,900 members. Publishes *Novinar, Sesity Novinare*.
	Slovak Union of Journalists, Bratislava. 1,800 members. Publishes *Vyber*.
Denmark	**Dansk Journalistforbund,** Copenhagen.
	Danske Dagblades Forening/Danish Newspapers Association, Copenhagen
	Federation of Danish Newspapers, Copenhagen.
	Illustrated Press Publishers Association, Copenhagen.
	Kobenhavnske Dagblades Samraad/Copenhagen Newspaper Publishers Association, Copenhagen.
Dominican Republic	**National Syndicate of Professional Journalists,** Santo Domingo.
Egypt	**Syndicate of Egyptian Journalists,** Cairo.
El Salvador	**Asociación de Periodistas de El Salvador,** San Salvador.
	National Union of Journalists, San Salvador.
Finland	**Aikakauslehtien Liitto/Finnish Periodical Publishers Association,** Helsinki.
	General Union of Journalists, Helsinki.
	Sanomalehtien Liitto-Tidningarnas Forbund/Finnish News-
	paper **Publishers Association,** Helsinki. 79 members. Publishes *Suomen Lehdisto*.
	Suomen Sanomalehtimiesten Liitto/Union of Journalists in Finland, Helsinki. 4,200 members. Publishes *Sanomalihtimies Journalisten*.
France	**Comité de Liaison Professionnel de la Presse,** Paris.
	Confédération de la Presse Française, Paris.
	Fédération Française des Agences de Presse, Paris.
	Fédération Nationale de la Presse Française, Paris.
	Fédération Nationale de la Presse d'Information Spécialisée, Paris.
	Fédération Nationale des Syndicats et Associations Professionnelles de Journalistes Français, Paris. 7,000 members.
	Institut Francais de Presse et des Sciences de l'Information, Paris.
	Syndicat des Journalistes Français, Paris.
	Syndicat National des Journalistes, Paris.
	Syndicat National de la Presse Quotidienne Regionale, Paris.
	Union Nationale de la Presse Périodique d'Information, Paris.
	Union de la Presse Française à Diffusion Nationale et Internationale, Paris.
	Union Syndicale de la Presse Culturelle et d'Informations Spécialisées, Paris. 2,000 members.
Gambia, The	**Gambia Journalists Association,** Banjul.
Germany, East	**Verband der Journa-**

	listen der DDR, Berlin. 8,000 members. Publishes *Neue Deutsche Presse.*
Germany, West	**Bundesverband Deutscher Zeitungsverleger/Association of Newspaper Publishers,** Bonn.
	Deutsche Journalisten-Union, Bonn.
	Deutscher Journalisten-Verband/German Journalists Union, Bonn. Membership: 12 Land Associations. Publishes *The Journalist.*
	Deutscher Presserat/ German Press Council, Bonn. 20 members.
	Verband Deutscher Zeitschriftenverleger /Association of German Periodical Publishers, Bonn.
	Verein der Auslandischen Presse in Deutschland/Foreign Press Association, Bonn.
Greece	**Enossis Syntakton Imerission Ephimeridon Athinon/Journalists Union of the Athens Daily Newspapers,** Athens. 860 members.
	Enossis Syntakton Periodikou Typou/ Journalists Union of the Periodical Press, Athens. 160 members.
	Union des Editeurs de Journaux Quotidiens d'Athenes, Athens.
Guatemala	**Asociación de Periodistas de Guatemala,** Guatemala City.
Guyana	**Union of Guyanese Journalists,** Georgetown.
Honduras	**Asociación de Prensa Hondurena,** Tegucigalpa.
Hong Kong	**Chinese Language Press Institute,** Hong Kong. Membership: 100 Chinese-language news-

	papers worldwide (outside People's Republic of China).
	Hong Kong Chinese Press Association, Hong Kong.
	Hong Kong Journalists Association, Hong Kong. 600 members.
	Hong Kong Press Club, Hong Kong.
	Newspaper Society of Hong Kong, Hong Kong.
Hungary	**Magyar Ujsagirok Orszagos Szovetsege /National Association of Hungarian Journalists,** Budapest. 4,700 members. Publishes *Magyar Sajto.*
Iceland	**Bladamannafelag Islands/Union of Icelandic Journalists,** Reykjavik.
India	**All-India Newspaper Editors Conference,** New Delhi. 273 members.
	All-India Small and Medium Newspapers Association, Delhi.
	All-India Small and Medium Newspapers Federation, Kanpur.
	Commonwealth Press Union (Indian Section), Calcutta.
	Indian and Eastern Newspaper Society, New Delhi. 360 members. Publishes *IENS Annual Press Handbook.*
	Indian Federation of Working Journalists, New Delhi. Publishes *The Working Journalist.*
	Indian Journalists Association, Calcutta.
	Indian Language Newspapers Association, Bombay. 315 members. Publishes *Language Press Bulletin.*
	National Union of Journalists, New Delhi. Membership: 14

affiliated unions. Publishes *Inkworld*.

Press Club of India, New Delhi.

Press Guild of India, Bombay.

Press Institute of India, New Delhi. Publishes *Vidura, Data India*.

Specialized Publications Association, Bombay.

Indonesia   **Persantuan Wartawan Indonesia/Indonesian Journalists Association,** Jakarta. 3,000 members.

Press Council of Indonesia, Jakarta.

Serikat Penerbit Suratkabar/The Newspaper Publishers Association, Jakarta.

Yayasan Pembina Pers Indonesia/The Press Foundation of Indonesia, Jakarta.

Ireland   **Provincial Newspapers Association of Ireland,** Dublin.

Israel   **Daily Newspaper Publishers Association of Israel,** Tel Aviv.

National Federation of Israeli Journalists, Tel Aviv.

Italy   **Associazione della Stampa Estera in Italia,** Rome.

Federazione Italiana Editori Giornali, Rome. 276 members.

Federazione Nazionale della Stampa Italiana, Rome. 16,000 members; 14 affiliated unions.

Unione Stampa Periodica Italiana, Rome. 4,000 members.

Jamaica   **Press Association of Jamaica,** Kingston. 150 members. Publishes *PAJ News*.

Japan   **Association of Japanese Journalists,** Tokyo.

Foreign Correspondents Club of Japan, Tokyo. 325 members.

Foreign Press Center, Tokyo.

Japan Congress of Journalists, Tokyo.

Japanese Magazine Publishers Association, Tokyo. 59 members.

Nihon Shinbun Kyokai/Japan Newspaper Publishers and Editors Association, Tokyo. Membership includes 162 companies, 113 newspapers, 4 news agencies, and 47 radio and television companies. Publishes *The Japanese Press* (annual), *Shimbun Kenkyu* (monthly), *Shimbun Kyokai Ho* (weekly), *Nihon Shimbun Nenkan* (annual), *Shimbun Insatsu Gijutsu* (quarterly), *Shimbun Keiei* (quarterly), *NSK News Bulletin* (quarterly) and *Shimbun Kokaku Ho* (monthly).

Kenya   **National Union of Journalists,** Nairobi.

Korea, South   **Journalists Association of Korea,** Seoul.

Korea Journalists Fund, Seoul.

Korean Newspaper Editors Association, Seoul.

Korean Newspaper Publishers Association, Seoul. 42 members.

The Korean Newspapers Association, Seoul. 32 members.

The Korean Press Ethics Commission, Seoul.

Korean Press Institute, Seoul.

Kwan-Hun Club, Seoul. Publishes *Shinmun Yuon-koo*.

The Press Center of Korea, Seoul.

Lebanon   **Lebanese Press Syn-**

dicate, Beirut. 18 members.

Lesotho **Lesotho Union of Journalists,** Maseru.

Liberia **Press Union of Liberia,** Monrovia.

Liechtenstein **Presse- und Informatiosamt der Fürstlichen Regierung,** Vaduz. Publishes *Press Folder.*

Luxembourg **Association Luxembourgeoise des Editeurs de Journaux,** Luxembourg.

Republic **Press Syndicate of Madagascar,** Antananarivo.

Madagascar **Malaysian Press Institute** (formerly, The Southeast Asia Press Center), Kuala Lumpur.
National Union of Journalists, Kuala Lumpur.
Persatuan Perchetakan Akhbar Malaysia /Malaysian Newspaper Publishers Association, Kuala Lumpur.

Mali **Syndicat National de l'Information de la Presse et de l'Industrie du Livre,** Bamako.

Mexico **Agrupación Nacional Periodistica,** Mexico City.
Asociación de Diarios Independientes, Mexico City.
Asociación Nacional de Periodistas, Mexico City.
Union of Democratic Journalists, Mexico City.

Mongolia **Union of Mongolian Journalists,** Ulan Bator.

Mozambique **Organização Nacional das Journalistas,** Maputo.

Nepal **Nepal Journalists Association,** Katmandu. 900 members.
Press Council, Katmandu.

Netherlands, The **Buitenlandse Pers-** vereniging in Nederland/Foreign Press Association in the Netherlands, Amsterdam. 70 members.
Centraal Bureau voor Courantenpubliciteit van de Ned. Dagbladpers/Central Advertising Bureau of the Netherlands Daily Press, Amsterdam.
Fédération des Associations d'Editeurs de Périodiques de la CEE/Federation of Associations of Editors of Periodicals of EEC, Amsterdam.
De Nederlandse Dagbladpers/The Dutch Association of Daily Newspaper Publishers, Amsterdam. 48 members.
De Nederlandse Nieuwsbladpers/The Netherlands Newspaper Press, The Hague. 120 members. Publishes *N.N.P. de Nederlandse Nieuwsbladpers.*
Nederlandse Organisatie van Tijdschrift-Uitgevers/Netherlands Association of Periodical Publishers, Amsterdam. 100 members. Publishes *NOTU-Schrift.*
Nederlandse Vereniging van Journalisten/Netherlands Union of Journalists, Amsterdam. 4,000 members. Publishes *De Journalist.*

New Zealand **Commonwealth Press Union (New Zealand Section),** New Plymouth.
National Press Club, Wellington.
New Zealand Community Newspapers Association, Putaruru.
New Zealand Journalists Union, Welling-

ton. 1,000 members.
New Zealand Press Association, Wellington.
New Zealand Press Council, Wellington.
Newspaper Proprietors Association of New Zealand, Wellington.
Newspaper Publishers Association of New Zealand, Wellington. 45 members.
Northern Journalists Union, Auckland.

Nicaragua **National Union of Journalists,** Managua.
Union de Periodistas de Nicaragua, Managua.

Nigeria **Newspaper Proprietors Association of Nigeria,** Lagos.
Nigerian Guild of Editors, Lagos.
Nigerian Institute of Journalism Lagos.
Nigerian Press Council, Lagos.
Nigerian Union of Journalists, Lagos.

Norway **Norsk Journalistlag,** Oslo. 3,400 members. Publishes *Journalisten*.
Norsk Presseforbund, Oslo.
Norske Avisers Landsforbund, Oslo.
Norwegian Newspaper Publishers Association, Oslo.

Pakistan **All-Pakistan Newspaper Employees Confederation,** Karachi.
All-Pakistan Newspapers Society, Karachi.
Council of Pakistan Newspaper Editors, Karachi.
Pakistan Federal Union of Journalists, Lahore.

Panama **Sindicato de Periodistas de Panama,** Panama.

Peru **Asociación Nacional de Periodistas del Peru,** Lima. 3,500 members.
Federación de Periodistas del Peru, Lima.

Philippines **Catholic Press Association of the Philippines,** Manila.
Manila Overseas Press Club, Manila.
National Press Club of the Philippines, Manila. 540 members.
Print Media Organization, Manila.
Publishers Association of the Philippines, Manila.

Poland **Polish Journalists Association,** Warsaw.

Portugal **Associação da Imprensa Diária,** Lisbon.
Associação da Imprensa Não-Diária, Lisbon.

Rumania **Consiliul Ziaristilor/ Journalists Council,** Bucharest. Publishes *Presa Noastra*.

Singapore **Foreign Correspondents Association of Southeast Asia,** Singapore.
Singapore National Union of Journalists, Singapore.
Singapore Press Club, Singapore.

South Africa **Newspaper Press Union of South Africa,** Johannesburg. 172 members.
South African Journalists Union, Johannesburg.
South African Society of Journalists, Johannesburg.

Spain **Asociación de Editores de Diarios Espanoles,** Madrid. Membership 49 daily newspapers.
Asociación de la Prensa de Barcelona, Barcelona. 587 members.
Asociación de la

Prensa de Bilbao, Bilbao. 100 members.
Asociación de la Prensa de Madrid, Madrid. 1,500 members. Publishes *Hoja del Lunes, Memoria.*
Asociación de la Prensa de Sevilla, Seville.
Asociación de la Prensa de Valencia, Valencia.
Federación de Asociaciones de la Prensa de España, Madrid. 4,000 members in 49 associations.

Sri Lanka   **Press Association of Sri Lanka,** Colombo.
Sri Lanka Foreign Correspondents Association, Colombo.
Sri Lanka Press Council, Colombo.

Sweden   **Centerpressen/Center Party's Press Organization,** Stockholm.
Svenska Journalistforbundet/Swedish Union of Journalists, Stockholm. 11,337 members. Publishes *Journalisten.*
Svenska Tidingsutgivareforeningen/ Swedish Newspaper Publishers Association, Stockholm. 240 members. Publishes *Pressens Tidning, Tidnings Teknik.*
Sveriges Vansterpressforening/The Liberal Party Press Association, Stockholm. 145 members.
Tidningarnas Arbetsgivareforening/ Newspaper Employers Association, Stockholm. 156 members.
VECTU/The Swedish Magazine Publishers Association, Stockholm.

Switzerland   **Association Suisse des Editeurs de Journaux/Schweizerischer Zeitungsverleger-Verband/Swiss Newspaper Publishers Association,** Zurich. 260 members.
Verein der Schweizer Presse/Association de la Presse Suisse/ Swiss Press Association, Berne.

Taiwan   **Taipei Journalists Association,** Taipei. 2,799 members. Publishes *Chinese Journalism Yearbook.*

Thailand   **Foreign Correspondents Club of Thailand,** Bangkok.
Journalists Association of Thailand, Bangkok.
Press Association of Thailand, Bangkok.
Provincial Journalist Association of Thailand, Sara Buri.
Provincial Press Association of Thailand, Bangkok.
Reporters Association of Thailand, Bangkok.

Tunisia   **Association des Journalistes Tunisiens,** Tunis.

Turkey   **Gazeteciler Cemiyeti,** Istanbul.
Turkish Journalists Union, Istanbul.
Turkiye Gazette Sahipleri Sendikasi, Istanbul.

USSR   **USSR Union of Journalists,** Moscow. 60,000 members.

United Kingdom   **Institute of Journalists,** London.
National Union of Journalists, London. 28,520 members. Publishes *The Journalist.*
Newspaper Press Fund, London. 4,650 members.
Newspaper Publishers Association,

London. Membership: 9 member groups; 19 newspapers.

Newspaper Society, London.

Periodical Publishers Association, London. 150 members.

The Press Council, London.

Scottish Daily Newspaper Society, Glasgow.

Scottish Newspaper Proprietors' Association, Edinburgh.

United States **Accuracy in Media,** Washington, D.C. Watchdog organization for promoting accuracy and fairness in reporting. 12,000 members. Publishes *AIM Report.*

Agricultural Publishers Association, Chicago, Ill.

American Association of Schools and Departments of Journalism, DeKalb, Ill. 73 member schools.

American Business Press, New York, N.Y. 110 member companies producing 550 publications.

American Jewish Press Association, Philadelphia, Pa. 46 full and 11 associate members.

American Newspaper Publishers Association (ANPA), Reston, Va. Membership: 1,365 daily newspapers. Publishes *presstime, Facts About Newspapers.* Affiliated organizations include ANPA Research Institute at Easton, Pa. and ANPA Foundation at Reston, Va.

American Press Institute, Reston, Va. Nonprofit training organization holding seminars for journalists. Publishes

The API Roundtable.

American Society of Journalism School Administrators, DeKalb, Ill. 120 members.

American Society of Magazine Editors, New York, N.Y. 233 members.

American Society of Newspaper Editors, Easton, Pa. 900 members. Publishes *The Bulletin.*

Associated Church Press, Geneva, Ill. Founded in 1919 as the Editorial Council of the Religious Press. 125 active and 13 associate members. Publishes *Newslog.*

Associated Press Managing Editors Association, New York, N.Y. 600 members. Publishes *APME News.*

Association of American Editorial Cartoonists, Wilmington, Del.

Association for Education in Journalism (AEJ), DeKalb, Ill. Founded as the American Association of Teachers of Journalism. 1,700 members. Publishes *Journalism Quarterly, Journalism Educator, Journalism Abstracts, Journalism Monographs.*

Catholic Press Association, Rockville Center, N.Y. 260 active and 100 associate members. Publishes *Catholic Journalist.*

Center for Investigative Reporting, Oakland, Calif. Nonprofit independent organization promoting investigative reporting on the West Coast. Publishes *"Raising Hell."*

Foreign Press Asso-

ciation, New York, N.Y.

Freedom of Information Center, Columbia, Mo. Clearinghouse on freedom and flow of information. Publishes *Center Report.*

Gridiron Club, Washington, D.C. 130 members.

Inland Daily Press Association, Chicago, Ill. The oldest and largest regional association of daily newspapers. 500 members. Publishes *Personnel Bulletin.*

International Circulation Managers Association, Reston, Va.

International Labor Press Association, Washington, D.C. Affiliated with AFL-CIO.

International Newspaper Advertising Executives, Danville, Ill.

International Newspaper Promotion Association, Reston, Va.

International Society of Weekly Newspaper Editors, DeKalb, Ill.

Journalism Education Association, Independence, Mo. Organization of journalism directors in senior and junior high schools. 1,200 active, 20 associate and 5 student members. Publishes *Communication: Journalism Education Today.*

Magazine Publishers Association, New York, N.Y. 163 member companies publishing 606 magazines and 6 associate (foreign) member companies. Publishes monthly *Newsletter.*

National Association of Advertising Publishers, Madison, Wis.

National Conference of Editorial Writers, Washington, D.C. 370 members. Publishes *The Masthead.*

National Federation of Press Women, Blue Springs, Mo. 4,300 members in 44 local chapters. Publishes *Press Woman.*

National News Council, New York, N.Y. Media ombudsman. Publishes *Newsletter.*

National Newspaper Association, Washington, D.C. Membership: 4,100 comprising mostly small and weekly publications. Publishes *Publishers Auxiliary.*

National Newspaper Publishers Association, Washington, D.C. Membership: 142 black newspapers. Publishes *NNPA Black Press Handbook.*

National Press Club, Washington, D.C.

National Press Photographers Association, Durham, N.C. 3,000 members in 30 professional and student chapters. Publishes *News Photographer.*

Newspaper Advertising Bureau, New York, N.Y.

The Newspaper Guild, Washington, D.C. The largest and oldest labor union of journalists in the print media. Affiliated with the AFL-CIO, the Canadian Labor Congress and the International Federation of Journalists, which it helped found in 1952. The Guild has 200 contracts with newspapers, news services and magazines. 34,000 members. Publishes *The Guild Reporter.*

Overseas Press Club,

New York, N.Y.
Reporters Committee for Freedom of the Press, Washington, D.C. Legal research and defense fund for protecting the First Amendment rights of the media to gather and publish news. 6,000 members. Publishes *The News Media and the Law.*

The Society of Professional Journalists, Chicago, Ill. The largest and oldest professional society of journalists. Founded in 1909 as Sigma Delta Chi, a journalism fraternity. The present name was adopted in 1973. 35,000 members (80 percent professional and 20 percent student) in 291 chapters (131 professional and 160 campus). Publishes *The Quill.*

Southern Newspaper Publishers Association, Atlanta, Ga. 440 members. The affiliated SNPA Foundation conducts seminars for news-editorial personnel of member newspapers. Publishes *SNPA Bulletin.*

Suburban Newspapers of America, Chicago, Ill. 173 member companies representing 800 newspapers in urban and suburban communities. Publishes *Suburban Publishers.*

United Nations Correspondents Association, New York, N.Y.

Washington Journalism Center, Washington, D.C. Founded by the late W. M. Kiplinger to foster a better understanding of national issues through a better reporting of public affairs.

Women in Communications, Austin, Tex. Founded in 1909 as Theta Sigma Phi; present name adopted in 1972. 9,000 members in 78 professional and 83 campus chapters. Publishes *The Matrix.*

Women's Institute for Freedom of the Press, Washington, D.C. Organization monitoring news coverage of women, discrimination against women in the media and the media services for meeting women's needs. Publishes *Media Report To Women, Women & Media: A Documentary Sourcebook.*

Uruguay	**Asociación de Diarios del Uruguay,** Montevideo.
	Asociación de la Prensa Uruguaya, Montevideo.
Venezuela	**Asociación Venezolana de Periodistas,** Caracas.
	Bloque de Prensa, Caracas.
	Colegio Nacional de Periodistas, Caracas.
	National Syndicate of Press Workers, Caracas.
Vietnam	**Vietnam Journalists Association,** Hanoi. 6,000 members.
Yemen (PDR)	**Democratic Yemeni Journalists Organization.**
Yugoslavia	**Savez Novinara Jugoslavije/Federation of Yugoslav Journalists,** Belgrade. 6,000 members. Publishes *Nasa Stampa.*
Zaire	**Union Nationale de la Presse Zaire,** Kinshasa.
Zimbabwe	**Association of Journalists of Zimbabwe.**

VI
MEDIA RANKINGS

(From: *The Book of World Rankings* by George Thomas Kurian.
Facts on File, Inc., New York, 1979.)

Daily Newspapers

A daily general-interest newspaper is defined as a publication devoted primarily to recording events of current public affairs, international affairs, politics, etc., and one that is published at least four times a week. National statistics on daily newspapers (unlike those relating to periodicals) are fairly accurate. In the mid-1970s, 7,900 newspapers were being published in the world. The regional distribution is as follows:

Asia	2,230	(excluding China, Vietnam and North Korea)
North America	1,935	
Europe	1,660	
Latin America	1,075	
Africa	190	
Oceania	120	
Soviet Union	690	

Number of Countries: 156
Midpoint: 7
Period Covered: Mid-1970s
Type of Ranking: Number of Daily General Interest Newspapers; Highest to Lowest

Highlights & Findings: Nearly 23% of all newspapers in the world are published in the United States. The top 10 nations account for 65% of the total. The number of daily newspapers is related to a number of factors, such as the extent of freedom of the press, literacy, the number of languages spoken in the country and historical traditions of free communications.

Regions	Africa	Asia & Oceania	Europe	Western Hemisphere
Most	Mauritius (61)	India (2)	Soviet Union (3)	United States (1)
Least	Upper Volta (155)	Papua New Guinea (151)	Vatican (156)	St. Kitts-Nevis-Anguilla (153)

Rank	Country	Number of Daily Newspapers	Rank	Country	Number of Daily Newspapers	Rank	Country	Number of Daily Newspapers
	TOP 10		53	Cambodia	16	106	Rhodesia (Zimbabwe)	3
1	United States	1,815	54	Cuba	15	107	Trinidad & Tobago	3
2	India	835	55	Philippines	15	108	Tanzania	3
3	Soviet Union	691	56	Bolivia	14	109	South Yemen	3
4	Turkey	437	57	Egypt	14	110	Albania	2
5	West Germany	334	58	Bulgaria	13	111	Bahamas	2
6	Brazil	280	59	Cyprus	12	112	Burundi	2
7	Mexico	256	60	El Salvador	12	113	Cameroon	2
8	Japan	180	61	Mauritius	12	114	Guadeloupe	2
9	Indonesia	172	62	Nigeria	12	115	Libya	2
10	Argentina	164	63	Guatemala	11	116	Malawi	2
			64	Saudi Arabia	11	117	Martinique	2
	UPPER MIDDLE		65	Zaire	11	118	Namibia	2
11	Sweden	135	66	Dominican Republic	10	119	New Caledonia	2
12	Canada	121	67	Singapore	10	120	Niger	2
13	Spain	115	68	Madagascar	9	121	Reunion	2
14	United Kingdom	111	69	Morocco	9	122	Senegal	2
15	Greece	106	70	Ethiopia	8	123	Seychelles	2
16	Pakistan	102	71	Honduras	8	124	Sierra Leone	2
17	France	98	72	Laos	8	125	Somalia	2
18	Netherlands	95	73	Paraguay	8	126	United Arab Emirates	2
19	Switzerland	95	74	Burma	7	127	Zambia	2
20	Hong Kong	82	75	Haiti	7			
21	Norway	80	76	Iraq	7			
22	Italy	78	77	Ireland	7		**BOTTOM 29**	
23	Australia	70	78	Luxembourg	7	128	Angola	1
24	Finland	60	79	Nicaragua	7	129	Antigua	1
25	Thailand	56	80	Surinam	7	130	Barbados	1
26	Denmark	49				131	Belize	1
27	Venezuela	49		**LOWER MIDDLE**		132	Benin	1
28	Chile	47	81	Costa Rica	6	133	Bermuda	1
29	Poland	44	82	Kuwait	6	134	Botswana	1
30	Columbia	40	83	Macao	6	135	Cook Islands	1
31	East Germany	40	84	Malta	6	136	Faroe Islands	1
32	New Zealand	39	85	Panama	6	137	Fiji	1
33	South Korea	36	86	Syria	6	138	French Guyana	1
34	Peru	35	87	Yemen Arab Republic	6	139	Gabon	1
35	Lebanon	33	88	Iceland	5	140	Gibraltar	1
36	Malaysia	31	89	Mozambique	5	141	Grenada	1
37	Australia	30	90	Netherlands Antilles	5	142	Guam	1
38	Bangladesh	30	91	Puerto Rico	5	143	Guinea	1
39	Belgium	30	92	Algeria	4	144	Guinea-Bissau	1
40	Portugal	30	93	Chad	4	145	Lesotho	1
41	Uruguay	30	94	French Polynesia	4	146	Liechtenstein	1
42	Czechoslovakia	29	95	Ghana	4	147	Maldives	1
43	Ecuador	29	96	Jordan	4	148	Mali	1
44	Nepal	29	97	Sudan	4	149	Mauritania	1
45	Hungary	27	98	Tunisia	4	150	Mongolia	1
46	Yugoslavia	26	99	Uganda	4	151	Papua New Guinea	1
47	South Africa	24	100	Congo	3	152	Rwanda	1
48	Israel	23	101	Guyana	3	153	St. Kitts-Nevis-Anguilla	1
49	Iran	20	102	Ivory Coast	3	154	Togo	1
50	Rumania	20	103	Jamaica	3	155	Upper Volta	1
51	Sri Lanka	18	104	Kenya	3	156	Vatican	1
52	Afghanistan	17	105	Liberia	3			

Source: *Editor & Publisher International Yearbook.*

Daily Newspaper Circulation

Because the circulation of daily newspapers is in most countries certified by audit bureaus, statistics relating to the circulation of dailies are fairly reliable. (For the definition of a daily newspaper see the ranking of countries by number of daily newspapers published). The total circulation of daily newspapers worldwide in the mid-1970s was 408 million, equal to 130 per 1,000 inhabitants and 175 per 1,000 inhabitants aged 10 years and older. The regional distribution is as follows:

Region	Total (million)	Per 1,000 Inhabitants	Per 1,000 Inhabitants 10 Years and Older
Africa	6	14	21
North America	66	281	334
Latin America	23	70	100
Asia	90	64	90
Europe	115	243	289
Oceania	7	305	389
Soviet Union	101	396	473

(The figure for Asia does not include China, North Korea and Vietnam.)

Number of Countries: 142
Midpoint: 51 per 1,000
Period Covered: Mid-1970s
Type of Ranking: Circulation of Daily Newspapers per 1,000 Inhabitants; Total Circulation of Daily Newspapers; Highest to Lowest

Highlights & Findings: Since newspaper readership is directly related to rates of literacy, circulation of daily newspapers is highest in countries with near total literacy. Of the top 10, eight are in Europe. Of the bottom 10 countries, eight are in Africa. However, in poorer countries each copy of a daily tends to be read by more people as it is passed around. The ratio of readership to circulation may be therefore higher in countries lower down this scale.

Regions	Africa	Asia & Oceania	Europe	Western Hemisphere
Most	Mauritius (51)	Japan (2)	Sweden (1)	United States (20)
Least	Rwanda (142)	South Yemen (134)	Faroe Islands (141)	Cuba (121)

Rank	Country	Daily Newspapers Circulation per 1,000	Total Circulation (000)
	TOP 11		
1	Sweden	572	4,678
2	Japan	526	57,820
3	East Germany	472	7,946
4	Luxembourg	447	161
5	Iceland	431	94
6	Finland	425	1,970
7	Norway	412	1,657
8	Switzerland	402	2,573
9	Soviet Union	397	100,928
10	Israel	394	1,337
11	Australia	394	5,320
	UPER MIDDLE		
12	United Kingdom	388	21,700
13	New Zealand	376	1,058
14	Hong Kong	349	1,325
15	Denmark	341	1,723
16	Austria	320	2,405
17	Netherlands	315	4,100
18	West Germany	312	19,298
19	Czechoslovakia	300	4,436
20	United States	287	61,222
21	Liechtenstein	277	61
22	Poland	248	8,429
23	Belgium	239	2,340
24	Hungary	233	2,454
25	Bulgaria	232	2,023
26	Uruguay	229	637
27	Netherlands Antilles	223	54
28	Ireland	222	693
29	France	214	11,341
30	Canada	213	4,872
31	Singapore	201	412
32	Bermuda	196	11
33	Guam	173	18
34	South Korea	173	6,010
35	Guyana	155	120
36	Bahamas	152	31
37	New Caledonia	144	18
38	Puerto Rico	132	405
39	Rumania	129	2,716
40	Cyprus	121	78
41	Mexico	116	4,763
42	Italy	113	6,296
43	Gibraltar	111	3
44	Argentina	108	2,773
45	Greece	107	162
46	Lebanon	98.6	283
47	Barbados	98	24

Rank	Country	Daily Newspapers Circulation per 1,000	Total Circulation (000)
48	Spain	98	3,491
49	Trinidad & Tobago	92.6	100
50	Peru	91.9	1,436
51	Mauritius	91	82
52	Venezuela	89	1,067
53	Yugoslavia	89	1,896
54	Costa Rica	88	174
55	Malaysia	87	1,038
56	French Polynesia	86	11
57	Kuwait	86	80
58	Panama	79	131
59	Surinam	78.5	33
60	Mongolia	78	112
61	Martinique	74	27
62	Portugal	70	612
63	South Africa	70	1,776
64	Guadeloupe	68	24
65	Jamaica	64.2	131
66	Seychelles	60	3.5
67	El Salvador	58.5	234
68	Antigua	57	4
69	Reunion	54	27
70	Colombia	52.8	1,248
71	Ghana	51	500
	LOWER MIDDLE		
72	Ecuador	49	331
73	Sri Lanka	49	612
74	Albania	46	115
75	Bangladesh	46	356
76	Nicaragua	42.1	91
77	Dominican Republic	42	197
78	Brazil	39	4,050
79	Honduras	36	99
80	Bolivia	35	199
81	Fiji	35	20
82	Tunisia	33	190
83	Cook Islands	32	8
84	Togo	32	7
85	Macao	30	171
86	Belize	29	4
87	Paraquay	27.5	73
88	Guatemala	27.1	165
89	French Guyana	25	1.5
90	Thailand	24	849
91	St. Kitts-Nevis-Anguilla	23	1.5
92	Zambia	22	106
93	Egypt	21	773
94	Morocco	21	360
95	Botswana	20	14

Rank	Country	Daily Newspapers Circulation per 1,000	Total Circulation (000)
96	Haiti	20	93
97	Jordan	18	49
98	Rhodesia (Zimbabwe)	18	116
99	Iraq	17.2	192
100	Algeria	17	285
101	Libya	17	41
102	Philippines	16.1	686
103	India	16	9,383
104	Indonesia	15.9	2,171
105	Iran	15	484
106	Guinea-Bissau	11	6
107	Saudi Arabia	11	96
108	Burma	10	319
109	Kenya	10	134
110	Sierra Leone	10	30
111	Yemen Arab Republic	10	56
112	Nigeria	9.7	613
113	Madagascar	9	59
114	Mozambique	9	79
115	United Arab Emirates	9	2
116	Syria	8.7	64
117	Liberia	7.6	13
118	Ivory Coast	7.2	35
119	Papua New Guinea	7	18
120	Senegal	6	25
121	Cuba	5.6	53
122	Pakistan	5	358
123	Uganda	5	58
124	Tanzania	4.5	70
125	Cameroon	3.9	25
126	Ethiopia	2.5	70
127	Angola	2	14
128	Malawi	1.8	9
129	Zaire	1.8	45
130	Laos	1.5	5
131	Lesotho	1.2	1
	BOTTOM 11		
132	Guinea	1	5
133	Somalia	1	4
134	South Yemen	1	2
135	Mali	0.5	3
136	Chad	0.4	1.5
137	Niger	0.4	1.3
138	Benin	0.3	1
139	Upper Volta	0.3	2
140	Mauritania	0.2	3
141	Faroe Islands	0.1	3.7
142	Rwanda	0.04	0.2

Source: *UNESCO Statistical Yearbook; World Communications.*

Advertising Expenditures

Advertising performs several critical functions in a free-enterprise economy: it creates and sustains demand for consumer and industrial goods; it virtually finances the media, both print and electronic; and it serves as the link between the industrial and communications sectors. Advertising expeditures

may be therefore accepted as one reliable index of the state of the economy. Because of the element of risk in advertising, it reflects the business community's confidence in the future and in its own ability to control that future.

Number of Countries: 86
Midpoint: $7.47
Period Covered: 1976
Type of Ranking: Advertising Expenditures per Capita in Dollars; Advertising Expenditures as Percentage of GNP; Total Advertising Expenditures in Dollars; Highest to Lowest

Highlights & Findings: Total advertising expenditures in the non-Communist world exceeded $59 billion in 1976. This amount exceeds the GNP of all but 15 countries in the world. Nearly 57% of the total was spent in the United States. The top 10 countries—the United States, Australia, Brazil, Canada, France, Japan, the Netherlands, Spain, the United Kingdom and West Germany—account for 88% of the total. Print continues to be the most important media category in all regions of the world except Latin America, where television is the principal medium.

Regions	Africa	Asia & Oceania	Europe	Western Hemisphere
Most	South Africa (33)	Australia (8)	Switzerland (3)	United States (1)
Least	Ethiopia (86)	Nepal (85)	Cyprus (54)	Honduras (73)

Rank	Country	Per Capita $	Advertising Expenditures as Percentage of GNP	Total ($million)
	TOP 10			
1	United States	156.69	1.98	33,720.0
2	Bermuda	110.00	1.65	6.6
3	Switzerland	109.59	1.23	701.4
4	Canada	103.40	1.20	2,378.1
5	Denmark	99.41	1.30	507.0
6	Sweden	91.81	1.03	752.8
7	Finland	82.19	1.38	386.3
8	Australia	82.06	1.07	1,116.0
9	Netherlands	81.28	1.30	1,121.7
10	Norway	72.73	0.95	290.9
	UPPER MIDDLE			
11	Austria	56.13	1.18	421.0
12	West Germany	48.56	0.68	2,986.3
13	France	47.31	0.72	2,502.5
14	Netherlands Antilles	44.50	0.69	8.9
15	Japan	43.05	0.88	4,856.0
16	Bahrain	41.00	0.65	12.3
17	United Kingdom	40.25	1.04	2,249.9
18	New Zealand	39.52	1.02	122.5
19	Spain	36.73	1.25	1,322.3
20	Iceland	35.50	0.39	7.1
21	Puerto Rico	30.09	0.99	96.3
22	Belgium	29.73	0.47	294.3
23	Luxembourg	28.25	0.47	11.3
24	Singapore	22.04	0.85	50.7
25	Hong Kong	20.00	0.92	88.0
26	Venezuela	19.36	0.77	240.1
27	Ireland	18.69	0.92	59.8
28	Kuwait	17.70	0.13	17.7

Rank	Country	Per Capita $	Advertising Expenditures as Percentage of GNP	Total ($ million)
29	Jamaica	17.24	1.03	36.2
30	Bahamas	17.00	0.68	3.4
31	Argentina	16.80	1.40	431.8
32	Israel	16.74	0.42	58.6
33	South Africa	13.11	1.09	342.1
34	Lebanon	11.63	0.94	34.9
35	Brazil	11.54	1.40	1,260.0
36	Italy	10.69	0.42	601.0
37	Taiwan	10.36	1.00	168.9
38	Costa Rica	9.95	0.83	19.9
39	Trinidad & Tobago	9.91	0.44	10.9
40	Saudi Arabia	9.63	0.16	88.6
41	Malta	8.00	0.48	2.4
42	Mexico	7.71	0.46	480.6
43	Panama	7.47	0.64	12.7
	LOWER MIDDLE			
44	Portugal	7.24	0.52	68.8
45	Greece	6.70	0.26	61.6
46	Dominican Republic	6.38	0.77	30.6
47	Turkey	6.32	0.62	254.0
48	Peru	5.89	0.65	94.8
49	Chile	5.44	0.46	57.1
50	South Korea	5.21	0.69	187.0
51	Uruguay	5.07	0.39	15.7
52	Ecuador	4.78	0.68	34.9
53	Libya	4.36	0.06	10.9
54	Cyprus	4.00	0.24	2.4
55	Colombia	3.79	0.69	92.5
56	Surinam	3.75	0.25	1.5
57	Malaysia	3.42	0.57	42.1

Rank	Country	Per Capita $	Advertising Expenditures as Percentage of GNP	Total ($ million)
58	Thailand	3.04	0.82	130.8
59	Rhodesia (Zimbabwe)	2.79	0.52	18.1
60	Syria	2.72	0.32	20.7
61	Nicaragua	2.50	0.31	5.5
62	Jordan	2.46	0.53	6.9
63	Zambia	2.24	0.41	11.4
64	Guatemala	1.95	0.28	12.3
65	Mauritius	1.89	0.28	1.7
66	Bolivia	1.79	0.36	10.4
67	Iraq	1.70	0.11	19.6
68	Iran	1.58	0.08	53.7
69	Egypt	1.52	0.44	57.9
70	Philippines	1.35	0.32	59.0
71	Paraguay	1.30	0.21	3.5
72	El Salvador	1.20	0.22	4.9
73	Honduras	1.03	0.27	3.2
74	Sudan	0.95	0.24	15.3
75	Kenya	0.93	0.59	12.9
76	Nigeria	0.82	0.21	52.8
	BOTTOM 10			
77	Morocco	0.71	0.15	12.6
78	Indonesia	0.45	0.20	63.4
79	Liberia	0.39	0.18	0.7
80	Sri Lanka	0.33	0.15	4.7
81	Ghana	0.25	0.08	2.6
82	India	0.23	0.15	138.3
83	Pakistan	0.20	0.10	14.5
84	Bangladesh	0.13	0.12	10.8
85	Nepal	0.05	0.05	0.6
86	Ethiopia	0.03	0.03	0.9

Source: *World Advertising Expenditures*, 1978, © Starch INRA Hooper by permission

Radio Transmitters

The number of radio transmitters operating worldwide on a regular basis is 25,510 distributed as follows:

Africa	700
North America	8,470
Latin America	4,270
Asia	2,730
Europe	5,980
Soviet Union	3,030
Oceania	330

In all countries radio is either operated by the government or is subject to government licensing. These figures are therefore extremely reliable.

Number of Countries: 148
Midpoint: 11
Period Covered: 1976
Type of Ranking: Total Number of Radio Transmitters and Total Transmitting Power in Kw; Highest to Lowest

Highlights & Findings: The degree of concentration in the top 10 bracket is less than that for TV; the 10 leading countries account for 68% of the world total. The top three nations operate half of all radio transmitters. It is interesting to note that many of the more industrially advanced countries such as Japan, France and West Germany have fewer radio transmitters than television transmitters.

Regions	Africa	Asia & Oceania	Europe	Western Hemisphere
Most	Mozambique (44)	Japan (5)	Soviet Union (2)	United States (1)
Least	Seychelles (138)	Western Samoa (148)	Malta (135)	Turks & Caicos (147)

Rank	Country	Total Number of Radio Transmitters	Total Transmitting Power (kw)	Rank	Country	Total Number of Radio Transmitters	Total Transmitting Power (kw)	Rank	Country	Total Number of Radio Transmitters	Total Transmitting Power (kw)
	TOP 10			50	Hungary	37	1,689.0	100	Burma	5	250.0
1	United States	7,785	N.A.	51	Morocco	33	1,779.5	101	French Polynesia	5	68.0
2	Soviet Union	3,034	N.A.	52	Bulgaria	32	2,095.0	102	Maldives	5	73.0
3	Italy	1,964	2,939.09	53	Netherlands	30	1,125.5	103	Nepal	5	120.25
4	Brazil	999	2,640.99	54	Iceland	29	132.8	104	Somalia	5	71.0
5	Japan	944	3,996.9	55	Sri Lanka	24	335.6	105	Togo	5	126.0
6	Mexico	668	4,218.1	56	Pakistan	22	1,256.0	106	Benin	4	35.1
7	Indonesia	586	N.A.	57	Zaire	22	1,044.0	107	Botswana	4	21.05
8	Canada	531	N.A.	58	Jamaica	21	47.57	108	Cameroon	4	22.0
9	Yugoslavia	487	6,879.0	59	Turkey	21	4,834.25	109	Cape Verde	4	...
10	Spain	406	4,870.0	60	Angola	19	N.A.	110	Cyprus	4	42.5
				61	Denmark	19	752.41	111	Djibouti	4	12.05
	UPPER MIDDLE			62	Ireland	18	975.0	112	Faroe Islands	4	12.0
11	Austria	399	3,507.7	63	Algeria	17	4,000.0	113	Gambia	4	4.56
12	United Kingdom	364	6,903.3	64	Ivory Coast	17	N.A.	114	Macao	4	...
13	West Germany	346	21,079.0	65	Vatican	17	1,105.25	115	Martinique	4	62.0
14	Norway	343	2,006.0	66	Madagascar	16	203	116	Mauritania	4	55.0
15	Philippines	333	11,408.55	67	Singapore	16	1,140.0	117	New Caledonia	4	64.0
16	France	290	5,911.40	68	Liberia	15	123.3	118	New Hebrides	4	6.0
17	Sweden	282	1,120.0	69	Malawi	15	149.0	119	Reunion	4	20.0
18	Peru	279	875.32	70	Senegal	14	321.1	120	Rwanda	4	58.05
19	Colombia	244	1,925.0	71	Greenland	13	62.35	121	Sao Tome & Principe	4	N.A.
20	Venezuela	235	1,686.25	72	Niger	13	40.75	122	Yemen Arab Republic	4	170.0
21	Ecuador	232	371.0	73	Iraq	12	910.0	123	South Yemen	4	63.5
22	Chile	229	873.1					124	Barbados	3	11.02
23	Australia	219	2,646.0		*LOWER MIDDLE*			125	Comoros	3	N.A.
24	Thailand	217	3,211.15	74	Hong Kong	11	90.0	126	Gibraltar	3	3.0
25	Switzerland	211	3,011.0	75	Fiji	11	40.5	127	Mauritius	3	30.0
26	Portugal	180	4,736.34	76	Syria	11	1,340.0	128	St. Helena	3	N.A.
27	Argentina	163	2,716.98	77	Brunei	10	74.0	129	Antigua	2	6.0
28	Dominican Republic	146	262.7	78	Congo	10	65.10	130	British Virgin Islands	2	10.0
29	India	146	5,739.90	79	Gabon	10	157.1	131	Falkland Islands	2	6.5
30	Czechoslovakia	123	N.A.	80	Ghana	10	108.0	132	Guadeloupe	2	24.0
31	Panama	117	172.6	81	Pacific Islands	10	29.5	133	Guam	2	12.5
32	Uruguay	101	N.A.	82	Trinidad & Tobago	9	32.45	134	Guinea-Bissau	2	N.A.
33	Finland	96	2,458.0	83	Ethiopia	8	651	135	Malta	2	6.0
34	Guatemala	95	355	84	Kuwait	8	2,476.0	136	St. Lucia	2	10.25
35	Puerto Rico	95	218	85	Tunisia	8	1,053.0	137	St. Pierre & Miquelon	2	5.0
36	South Korea	94	2,488.0	86	Guyana	7	44.1	138	Seychelles	2	11.0
37	Malaysia	92	3,557.5	87	Sudan	7	490.0	139	Tonga	2	20.0
38	East Germany	66	3,260.5	88	Swaziland	7	130.49				
39	El Salvador	65	N.A.	89	Afghanistan	6	305.05		*BOTTOM 9*		
40	Rumania	62	N.A.	90	Bahamas	6	21.35	140	Cayman Islands	1	0.1
41	New Zealand	61	484.0	91	Burundi	6	38.75	141	Cook Islands	1	10.0
42	Iran	53	6,460.0	92	Belize	6	24.0	142	Gilbert Islands	1	10.0
43	Greece	51	762.0	93	Central African Empire	6	135.56	143	Nauru	1	0.13
44	Mozambique	49	N.A.	94	French Guyana	6	9.1	144	Niue Island	1	0.25
45	Belgium	48	1,574.5	95	Lebanon	6	237.0	145	Norfolk Island	1	0.05
46	Nigeria	46	1,190.75	96	Monaco	6	1,035.0	146	St. Vincent	1	0.25
47	Egypt	43	4,886.0	97	Qatar	6	161.05	147	Turks & Caicos	1	1.5
48	Bolivia	39	N.A.	98	Bahrain	5	23.01	148	Western Samoa	1	10.0
49	Israel	39	2,667.3	99	Bermuda	5	5.25				

Source: *UNESCO Statistical Yearbook.*

Radio Receivers

David Lerner in *The Passing of Traditional Society: Modernizing the Middle East* has described the radio as the principal instrument of political and economic modernization in developing societies.

Other scholars have drawn attention to the relation between radios per capita and mass participation and competitiveness.

Number of Countries: 182
Midpoint: 144 per 1,000
Period Covered: 1975
Type of Ranking: Number of Radios per 1,000 and Total Number of Radios; Highest to Lowest

Highlights & Findings: In 1975, 938.2 million radio receivers were in use around the world. Of this figure, the United States alone accounted for 401.6 million or 42.8%. The United States is also among the few countries that does not require licenses or charge license fees for radios. The top 10 nations account for 60% of the total number of radios and the bottom 10 nations for 0.2%. South Yemen's extraordinarily high ranking for a poor country is apparently due to the fact that Aden, its capital, is a center for smugglers of electronic goods.

Regions	Asia & Oceania	Africa	Europe	Western Hemisphere
Most	New Zealand (4)	Algeria (76)	United Kingdom (7)	United States (1)
Least	Nepal (182)	Ethiopia (180)	Albania (123)	Dominican Republic (142)

Rank	Country	Radios per 1,000	Total Number of Radios (000)
	TOP 10		
1	United States	1,895	401,600
2	Bermuda	909	50
3	Canada	894	20,252
4	New Zealand	892	2,700
5	Argentina	838	21,000
6	British Virgin Islands	750	9
7	United Kingdom	750	42,000
8	St. Lucia	748	81
9	Japan	658	70,794
10	Pacific Islands	632	72
	UPPER MIDDLE		
11	Belize	588	80
12	St. Pierre & Miquelon	583	3.5
13	Puerto Rico	572	1,755
14	French Polynesia	565	70
15	Faroe Islands	563	23
16	Netherlands Antilles	550	131
17	Norfolk Island	550	1.1
18	Fiji	532	300
19	Luxembourg	515	176
20	Nauru	514	3.6
21	Turks & Caicos	500	3
22	Uruguay	495	1,500
23	Barbados	477	116
24	Lebanon	474	1,321
25	Falkland Islands	467	0.9
26	Soviet Union	461	116,110
27	Bahamas	457	14
28	Finland	427	1,997
29	Bahrain	412	100
30	South Yemen	407	600
31	Malta	401	129
32	Belgium	384	3,769
33	Sweden	378	3,086
34	Syria	374	2,500
35	East Germany	356	6,114
36	Guyana	346	268
37	West Germany	337	20,909
38	Denmark	336	1,693
39	Western Samoa	329	50
40	France	324	17,000
41	Cayman Islands	321	3.5
42	Cyprus	321	206
43	Jamaica	320	633
44	Norway	320	1,277
45	Switzerland	314	2,036
46	Monaco	313	7.5
47	New Caledonia	303	36
48	Mexico	301	17,514
49	St. Vincent	300	30
50	Chile	298	3,100
51	Andorra	295	6.5
52	Iceland	295	64
53	Austria	288	2,170
54	Ireland	287	886
55	Netherlands	284	3,846
56	Ecuador	279	1,700
57	Greece	279	2,500
58	Czechoslovakia	266	3,910
59	Surinam	264	109
60	Bulgaria	262	2,273

Rank	Country	Radios per 1,000	Total Number of Radios (000)
61	Iran	249	8,000
62	Hungary	243	2,541
63	Poland	237	7,988
64	United Arab Emirates	237	51
65	Hong Kong	235	1,000
66	Trinidad & Tobago	235	250
67	Kuwait	231	215
68	Spain	229	8,050
69	Italy	228	12,641
70	Greenland	224	11
71	Israel	221	680
72	Grenada	219	21
73	Gilbert Islands	214	12
74	Australia	214	2,815
75	Cuba	199	1,805
76	Algeria	198	3,220
77	Jordan	198	529
78	Antigua	193	14
79	Yugoslavia	193	4,081
80	Reunion	185	91
81	San Marino	181	3.4
82	St. Helena	180	0.9
83	Niue Island	175	0.7
84	Portugal	174	1,516
85	Gabon	173	90
86	Seychelles	161	9.0
87	Panama	159	260
88	Liberia	156	261
89	Venezuela	147	1,709
90	Rumania	146	3,066
91	South Korea	144	4,812
92	Singapore	142	320
93	Egypt	140	5,115
94	Brunei	133	20
95	Peru	131	2,010
96	Mongolia	129	166
97	Gibraltar	126	3.4
98	Mauritius	125	107
99	Thailand	125	5,111
100	Comoros	121	36
101	Gambia	118	60
102	Colombia	117	2,805
103	Iraq	116	1,250
104	Djibouti	115	12
	LOWER MIDDLE		
105	Madagascar	112	855
106	Ghana	110	1,060
107	Swaziland	110	53
108	New Hebrides	108	10
109	Turkey	107	4,096
110	Tonga	102	10
111	Zaire	101	2,448
112	Cameroon	96	603
113	Sao Tome & Principe	95	7.5
114	South Africa	94	2,335
115	Martinique	90	31
116	El Salvador	85	300
117	Botswana	83	55
118	Cook Islands	83	2.0
119	Sudan	80	1,310
120	Bolivia	78	425
121	Morocco	77	1,300

Rank	Country	Radios per 1,000	Total Number of Radios (000)
122	Costa Rica	74	142
123	Albania	72	173
124	Nigeria	69	5,000
125	Paraguay	68	176
126	Senegal	66	286
127	Mauritania	64	82
128	Congo	61	80
129	Brazil	60	6,275
130	Guadeloupe	60	21
131	Nicaragua	60	126
132	Vietnam	60	2,550
133	Honduras	54	158
134	Benin	52	150
135	Tunisia	49	277
136	French Guyana	48	2.8
137	Guatemala	47	261
138	Libya	45	105
139	Philippines	43	1,825
140	Solomon Islands	42	7.7
141	Central African Empire	41	70
142	Dominican Republic	41	185
143	Kenya	40	510
144	Indonesia	39	5,000
145	Laos	38	125
146	Rhodesia (Zimbabwe)	37	225
147	Sri Lanka	37	505
148	Niger	36	145
149	Rwanda	32	133
150	Malaysia	31	365
151	Macao	29	9
152	Burundi	27	100
153	Equatorial Guinea	26	7.5
154	Malawi	26	125
155	India	25	14,848
156	Guinea	24	105
157	Togo	23	50
158	Burma	22	659
159	Sierra Leone	22	61
160	Somalia	22	67
161	Uganda	22	250
162	Maldives	21	2.4
163	Zambia	21	100
164	Angola	20	116
165	Haiti	20	91
166	Cape Verde	19	5.2
167	Mozambique	19	176
168	Chad	18	70
169	Guinea-Bissau	17	9
170	Ivory Coast	17	75
171	Upper Volta	17	100
	BOTTOM 11		
172	China	16	12,000
173	Tanzania	16	231
174	Pakistan	15	1,015
175	Cambodia	14	112
176	Mali	13	75
177	Yemen Arab Republic	13	86
178	Lesotho	11	11
179	Saudi Arabia	11	85
180	Ethiopia	7	200
181	Afghanistan	6	111
182	Nepal	6	76

Source: *UNESCO Statistical Yearbook.*

Television Transmitters

The number of television transmitters operating worldwide on a regular basis is 24,980 distributed as follows:

Africa	200
North America	4,360
Asia (excluding China, Vietnam and North Korea)	6,610
Europe	11,250
Latin America	450
Soviet Union	1,750
Oceania	360

Because television in all countries is either operated by the government or is subject to government licensing, these figures are extremely reliable.

Number of Countries: 99
Midpoint: 17
Period Covered: 1976
Type of Ranking: Total Number of Television Transmitters; Highest to Lowest

Highlights & Findings: The degree of concentration in the top 10 bracket is unusually high; the 10 leading countries account for 79.1% of all transmitters. More than half of all transmitters are operated by the top three nations: Japan, the United States and France.

Regions	Africa	Asia & Oceania	Europe	Western Hemisphere
Most	Algeria (25)	Japan (1)	France (3)	United States (2)
Least	Djibouti (97)	Singapore (99)	Malta (98)	St. Vincent (93)

Rank	Country	Number of Transmitters	Rank	Country	Number of Transmitters	Rank	Country	Number of Transmitters
	TOP 10		34	Venezuela	39	67	Cyprus	5
1	Japan	6,117	35	Malaysia	38	68	India	5
2	United States	3,695	36	Turkey	38	69	Madagascar	5
3	France	3,001	37	Denmark	30	70	South Yemen	5
4	Soviet Union	1,749	38	Belgium	28	71	Ghana	4
5	Italy	1,199	39	Egypt	28	72	Liberia	4
6	West Germany	1,153	40	Ireland	28	73	Mauritius	4
7	Czechoslovakia	788	41	Israel	28	74	Antigua	3
8	Spain	741	42	Chile	27	75	Colombia	3
9	Norway	665	43	Hong Kong	26	76	El Salvador	3
10	Canada	661	44	Morocco	23	77	French Guyana	3
			45	Hungary	22	78	Gabon	3
	UPPER MIDDLE		46	Philippines	22	79	Guadeloupe	3
11	United Kingdom	596	47	Netherlands	21	80	Qatar	3
12	Switzerland	583	48	Ecuador	19	81	Monaco	3
13	Austria	461	49	French Guyana	19	82	Pacific Islands	3
14	East Germany	461	50	Puerto Rico	17	83	St. Pierre & Miquelon	3
15	Yugoslavia	430	51	Jamaica	13	84	Sudan	3
16	Sweden	358	52	Reunion	13	85	Trinidad & Tobago	3
17	Australia	198				86	Zaire	3
18	Rumania	194		*LOWER MIDDLE*				
19	Iran	157	53	Guatemala	12		*BOTTOM 13*	
20	Bulgaria	154	54	Nigeria	10	87	Barbados	2
21	New Zealand	144	55	Panama	10	88	Bermuda	2
22	Finland	83	56	Saudi Arabia	10	89	Bolivia	2
23	Argentina	82	57	Tunisia	10	90	Gibraltar	2
24	Iceland	80	58	Ethiopia	8	91	Guam	2
25	Algeria	75	59	Lebanon	8	92	Jordan	2
26	Mexico	71	60	Dominican Republic	7	93	St. Vincent	2
27	Poland	69	61	Kuwait	7	94	Senegal	2
28	Brazil	66	62	New Caledonia	7	95	Bahrain	1
29	South Korea	59	63	Pakistan	7	96	Congo	1
30	Greece	54	64	Syria	7	97	Djibouti	1
31	Peru	52	65	Iraq	6	98	Malta	1
32	Thailand	48	66	Martinque	6	99	Singapore	1
33	Portugal	41						

Source: *UNESCO Statistical Yearbook.*

Television Sets

In the mid-1970s there were 357 million television sets in use in 123 countries around the world. Compared to radio, television has made only modest gains in recent years in the developing countries, where a television set is still a luxury. However, the growth of satellite communications augurs a breakthrough in making television a truly universal medium. Another area in which there has been considerable progress is color television. Although no separate statistics are available for color television sets, the proportion of black-and-white sets has been steadily decreasing in all industrially advanced countries.

Number of Countries: 124
Midpoint: 61 per 1,000
Period Covered: 1974
Type of Ranking: Per Capita Television Sets and Total; Highest to Lowest

Highlights & Findings: The United States accounts for nearly 34% of the world total; the United States and the Soviet Union together account for nearly 49%. Fifty-six countries require licenses for the use of television sets, while others, including the United States, impose no fees.

Regions	Africa	Asia & Oceania	Europe	Western Hemisphere
Most	Reunion (62)	New Zealand (13)	Monaco (1)	United States (2)
Least	Mozambique (124)	India (122)	Albania (115)	Haiti (110)

Rank	Country	Television Sets per 1,000	Total (000)	Rank	Country	Television Sets per 1,000	Total (000)	Rank	Country	Television Sets per 1,000	Total (000)
	TOP 10			42	Israel	134	441	83	Vietnam	26	500
1	Monaco	667	16	43	Cyprus	133	85	84	Algeria	25	410
2	United States	571	121,100	44	Yugoslavia	132	2,784	85	Djibouti	23	2.3
3	Canada	366	8,232	45	Bahrain	123	30	86	Morocco	23	382
4	Bermuda	354	20	46	Uruguay	116	350	87	Paraguay	21	53
5	Sweden	348	2,841	47	Rumania	114	2,405	88	Guatemala	19	106
6	St. Pierre & Miquelon	340	1.7	48	Singapore	114	252	89	South Yemen	18	30
7	United Kingdom	315	17,641	49	Panama	112	183	90	Egypt	17	610
8	Denmark	308	1,556	50	Greece	106	950	91	Philippines	17	711
9	West Germany	305	18,920	51	New Caledonia	106	14	92	Thailand	17	715
10	East Germany	297	5,096	52	French Polynesia	105	13	93	Honduras	16	46
				53	Venezuela	103	1,200	94	St. Lucia	16	1.7
	UPPER MIDDLE			54	Trinidad & Tobago	94	100	95	Saudi Arabia	14	122
11	Finland	269	1,261	55	Mexico	84	4,885	96	Turkey	12	458
12	Switzerland	264	1,714	56	Brazil	83	8,650	97	Rhodesia (Zimbabwe)	10	57
13	New Zealand	261	791	57	Surinam	80	33	98	Gabon	10	5.1
14	Netherlands	259	3,510	58	Costa Rica	78	150	99	Ivory Coast	9	40
15	Luxembourg	257	88	59	Chile	72	750	100	Senegal	8	35
16	Norway	256	1,021	60	Portugal	66	572	101	St. Vincent	7	0.6
17	Belgium	252	2,464	61	Cuba	65	595	102	Sudan	6	100
18	Austria	247	1,856	62	Reunion	61	30	103	Liberia	5	8.5
19	Czechoslovakia	245	3,602					104	Zambia	5	22
20	France	235	12,335		*LOWER MIDDLE*			105	Congo	3.8	3.8
21	Japan	233	25,564	63	Greenland	55	2.7	106	Cambodia	3.3	26
22	Malta	232	75	64	French Guyana	52	3.0	107	Libya	3	6
23	Gibraltar	230	6.2	65	Iraq	50	520	108	Kenya	3	37
24	Iceland	230	50	66	Jamaica	49	97	109	Ghana	3	33
25	Australia	226	3,013	67	South Korea	48	1,619	110	Haiti	2.9	13
26	Hungary	219	2,296	68	Iran	47	1,500	111	Sierra Leone	2.2	6
27	Italy	213	11,817	69	Martinique	45	16	112	Mongolia	2.1	3
28	Soviet Union	208	52,500	70	Mauritius	44	38	113	Nigeria	1.8	110
29	Puerto Rico	206	625	71	Colombia	43	971	114	Pakistan	1.8	125
30	Barbados	203	40	72	Guadeloupe	37	13				
31	Kuwait	196	182	73	Ecuador	36	250		*BOTTOM 10*		
32	Hong Kong	185	785	74	Nicaragua	36	75	115	Albania	1.7	4
33	Poland	181	6,100	75	Dominican Republic	34	156	116	Uganda	1.4	15
34	Argentina	180	4,500	76	Brunei	33	5	117	Madagascar	1.0	7.5
35	Ireland	178	550	77	Malaysia	33	390	118	Upper Volta	1.0	5.5
36	San Marino	174	3.3	78	Jordan	32	85	119	Ethiopia	0.8	20
37	Spain	174	6,125	79	Syria	31	224	120	Indonesia	0.7	275
38	Antigua	171	12	80	El Salvador	28	111	121	China	0.6	500
39	Bulgaria	168	1,457	81	Peru	28	425	122	India	0.5	275
40	Netherlands Antilles	143	34	82	Tunisia	27	147	123	Zaire	0.3	7
41	Lebanon	135	375					124	Mozambique	0.1	1

Source: *World Communications.*

INDEX

INDEX

100, 101, 117, 128, 146, 164, 165, 177, 187, 194, 215, 226, 240, 241, 253, 266, 293, 297, 300, 305, 314, 322, 328, 356, 370, 386, 392, 405, 416, 426, 444, 465, 480, 488, 489, 504, 515, 522, 548, 567, 576, 588, 602, 636, 637, 655, 683, 704, 713, 721, 727, 729, 731, 738, 748, 749, 762, 770, 783, 790, 803, 825, 847, 856, 887, 914, 915, 917, 936, 947, 949, 961, 992, 1008, 1011, 1012, 1019, 1031, 1032, 1056, 1064, 1068, 1094, 1095, 1102, 1107, 1135, 1138

Associated Press Ltd. (U.K.)—936

Associated Press Managing Editors Association (U.S.)—1158

Associated Press of Pakistan (APP) (Pakistan)—1135,1138

Associated Press v. United States—992

Association—See key words for organizations not listed below

Association Belge des Editeurs de Journaux (Belgische Vereniging van de Dagbladuitgevers) (Belgium)—1151

Association de la Presse Suisse **(Switzerland)**—845, 1148

Association des Journalistes Professionnels de Belgique (AJPB)—143, 147

Association des Journalistes Tunisiens (Tunisia)—1148,1157

Association for the Promotion of the International Circulation of the Press (DISTRIPRESS) (Switzerland)—1147

Association Generale de al Presse Belge (Algemene Belische Persbond) (Belgium)—147, 1151

Association Luxembourgeoise des Editeurs de Journaux (Luxembourg)—1155

Association Luxembourgeoise des Journalistes (Luxembourg)—1148

Association Suisse des Editeurs de Journaux (Schweizerischer Zeitungsverleger-Verband) (Swiss Newspaper Publishers Association) (Switzerland)—1157

Associazione della Stampa Estera in Italia (Italy)—1154

Asturias Semanal **(Spain)**—814

AT—See Agence Telegraphique

ATA (Albanian Telegraphic Agency)—See Albanian Telegraphic Agency

ATA (Asociation de Teleradiodifusoras Argentinas)—See Asociacion de Teleradiodifusoras Argentinas

Ataturk, Kemal—886, 883

Ateitis **(U.S.S.R.)**—911

Athanasiadis, G.—402

ATHENAGENCE—See Athens News Agency

Athens Daily Post **(Greece)**—400

Athens Newspaper Distribution Agency (Greece)—402

Athens News Agency (ATHENAGENCE) (Greece)—405, 1135, 1139

Athens Newspaper Vendors, Union of (Greece)—401

Athipat **(Thailand)**—870

Aththa **(Sri Lanka)**—822

Atlanta (Ga.) Constitution, The **(U.S.)**—56, 947-949, 957-959, 974, 978, 979, 986, 1133

Atlanta (Ga.) Journal **(U.S.)**—974, 984

Atlantic Monthly, The **(U.S.)**—987

Atoll Pioneer **(Kiribati)**—1120

ATP (Agence Tchadienne de Presse)—See Agence Tchadienne

de Presse

ATP (Agence Togolaise de Presse)—See Agence Togolaise de Presse

Atrika **(Malagasy)**—1085

Au Boon-haw—449, 871

Auby, Jean Marie—350, 351

Auckland Star **(New Zealand)**—662, 664, 665

Audet—649; see also newspaper names

Augstein, Rudolf—385

Aujourd'hui Dimanche **(Martinique)**—1122

AUP—See Australian United Press

Ausra **(U.S.S.R.)**—911

AUSTRALIA—107-119; see also specific subjects

Australian, The **(Australia)**—54, 110, 113

Australian Associated Press (AAP)—117, 727, 729, 731, 936, 1138, 1135

Australian Broadcasting Commission (ABC) (Australia)—452, 731, 790, 937

Australian Financial Review **(Australia)**—113

Australian Journalists Association (Australia)—112, 115, 1150

Australian Newspapers Council (Australia)—1150

Australian Provincial Press Association (Australia)—1150

Australian United Press (AUP) (Australia)—1135, 1139

AUSTRIA—121-132; see also specific subjects

Austria Press-Agentur (Austria)—123, 1135, 1138

Austrian Press Council (Austria)—32-35, 37, 127

Autentico **(Venezuela)**—1026

Auto-Journal **(France)**—344

Auto-Touring **(Austria)**—128

Avance **(Nicaragua)**—678

Avanti **(Italy)**—529

Avisa Relation oder Zeitung **(Germany)**—3

A Voz Africana **(Mazambique)**—1089

AVP—See Agence Voltaique de Presse

Avriani **(Greece)**—400

AVRO (Netherlands)—655

Awali Daily News **(Bahrain)**—1066

Awolowo, Obafemi—689

Aydinlik **(Turkey)**—886

Ayer NW ABH International—64

Ayk **(Lebanon)**—597

Azad **(Bangladesh)**—134

Azad **(India)**—708

Azad **(Pakistan)**—709

AZAP—See Agence Zaire-Presse

Azikiwe, Nnamdi—688

Aztag **(Lebanon)**—597

B

Backgrounder **(Malawi)**—607

Baer, Douglas—184

Bagdikian, Ben—957

Baghdad Observer, The **(Iraq)**—1073, 1974

BAHAMAS—1114-1115; see also specific subjects

Bahasa Malaysia **(Malaysia)**—616

BAHRAIN—1066-1067; see also specific subjects

Bailby, Edouard—214

Bakhtar News Agency (BNA) (Afghanistan)—1135, 1139

Bakhtar News Bulletin **(Afghanistan)**—1062

Baldowski, Cliff—957

Baltimore (Md.) News-American **(U.S.)**—974

Baltimore (Md.) Sun **(U.S.)**—40, 50, 947, 974

Balvany, Johann F.—1046

Banda, Dr. Hastings Kamuze—605, 607-609

Bandaranaike, Sirimavo—825

Bandaranaike, W. R. D.—821, 824

Bangkok Post **(Thailand)**—449, 787, 871, 873

Bangkok World **(Thailand)**—871

BANGLADESH—133-136; see also specific subjects

Bangladesh Federal Union of Journalists (Bangladesh)—1151

Bangladesh Sangbadpatra Karmachari Federation (Bangladesh)—1151

Bangladesh Sangbadpatra Press Sramik Federation (Bangladesh)—1151

Bangladesh Sangbad Sangasta (BSS) (Bangladesh)—136, 1135, 1139

Bangladesh Television Corporation—136

Bangladesh Times **(Bangladesh)**—471-473

Bangui-Match **(Central African Republic)**—1116

Ban Muang—870, 871

Banner (Nashville, Tenn.) **(U.S.)**—973, 974

Bantu Mirror **(Zambia)**—1053

Bantu Mirror **(Zimbabwe)**—1062

Baraza **(Kenya)**—570, 571

BARBADOS—1114-1115; see also specific subjects

Barbados Rediffusion **(Barbados)**—1115

Barbieri, Fran—1046

Barid Al-Charikat **(Egypt)**—309

Barid Paris **(Lebanon)**—596

Barios de Chamorro, Violeta—681

Barita Harian **(Malaysia)**—621

Barq al-Shimal **(Syria)**—1101

Barras, Yevgeny—913

Barre, Raymond—344

Barrett, Edward W.—661

Barricada **(Nicaragua)**—677, 678, 680, 684

Barron's Book Digest **(U.S.)**—962

Baruah, U. L.—488

Bashiruddin, S.—490

Bashkimi **(Albania)**—81, 82

Basler Zeitung **(Switzerland)**—841, 843

Bataviasche Courant **(Indonesia)**—496

Bataviasche Koloniale Courant **(Indonesia)**—495

Bataviasche Nieuwsblad **(Indonesia)**—496

Bataviasche Nouvelles **(Indonesia)**—495

Batavia Shimbun **(Japan)**—551

Batchelor, C. D.—957

Bates & Co., Ted—62, 873

Batista, Fulgencio—258

Bauer Group—380; see also newspaper names

Bauern-Echo **(East Germany)**—364, 365

Bayern-Kurier **(West Germany)**—377

BBC—See British Broadcasting Company

BBDO International Inc.—62

Beacon **(Jamaica)**—542

Beacon, The **(Belize)**—1114

Bedoya, Juan G.—815

Beeld **(South Africa)**—795, 796, 798

Behrouz, Jahangir—1071

Beirut **(Lebanon)**—601

Belasco, Balisario—213

BELGA—See Agence Belga

Belgian Information and Documentation Institute (INBEL)—144

Belgische Radio et Televisie (BRT) (Belgium)—146, 147

BELGIUM—137-148; see also specific subjects

Believer, The **(Ghana)**—390, 393

BELIZE—1114-1115; see also specific subjects

Belize Times, The **(Belize)**—1114

Ben Bella, Ilakut—479

Bengal Gazette **(India)**—330

Benih Mardika **(Indonesia)**—496

BENIN—1114-1115; see also specific subjects

Bennett, James Gordon—946

Bennett, Thomas—475

Bennett Coleman and Company—478; see also newspaper names

Bennouna, Mehdi—644

Benton & Bowles Inc.—62

Bergens Tidende **(Norway)**—702

Berg Group—291; see also newspaper names

Bergman, Earl—480

Berita Buana **(Indonesia)**—498, 500

Berita Harian **(Malaysia)**—615

Berita Harian **(Singapore)**—786, 787, 789

Berita Minggu **(Malaysia)**—615

Berita Minggu **(Singapore)**—786

Berita Petang Sarawak **(Malaysia)**—616

Berita Publishing—616, 617; see also newspaper names

Berkeley (Calif.) Barb **(U.S.)**—956

Berliner am Abend **(East Germany)**—365

Berliner Morgenpost **(East Germany)**—363

Berliner Morgenpost **(West Germany)**—50, 377

Berliner Rundfunk **(East Germany)**—371

Berliner Tageblatt **(West Germany)**—375

Berliner Zeitung **(East Germany)**—363, 365-367

Berlingske **(Denmark)**—39, 40, 50-52, 56, 287-290

Berlingske Tidende **(Denmark)**—1133

BERMUDA—1114-1115; see also specific subjects

Bermuda Broadcasting Company (Bermuda)—1115

Bermuda Sun **(Bermuda)**—1114

Bermudian, The **(Bermuda)**—1114

BERNAMA—See Pertubohan Berita Nasional Malaysia

Bernays, Edward L.—49, 958

Berner Zeitung **(Switzerland)**—843

Bernstein, Lester—269

Bertelsmann, Gutersloh—1010

Bertelsmann A.G.—380

Better Business Bureau **(U.S.)**—72

Better Homes & Gardens **(U.S.)**—969

Beurs-en Nieuwsberichten **(Netherlands Antilles)**—1122

Beutler, Warwick—502

Beuve-Mery, Hubert—343, 352

Bhattacharjea, Ajit—483

Bhoomiputra **(India)**—478

Bhupal, K.—490

BHUTAN—1114-1115; see also specific subjects

Bidault, Georges—654

Bien Publico **(Uruguay)**—1105

Bilad al Sa'udiyah **(Saudi Arabia)**—781

Bild am Sonntag **(West Germany)**—376, 648